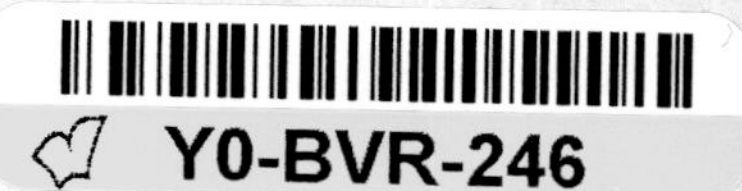

Praise for *Novel & Short Story Writer's Market*

"Still one of the best and most thorough—if not the most comprehensive—guides to writers' markets available."

—*American Reference Books Annual*

"This is your bible . . . very highly recommended." —*Amelia*

"A thorough and complete resource with plenty of information and fiction markets for both beginning and established fiction writers."

—*Writer's Write*

1999 NOVEL & SHORT STORY WRITER'S MARKET

2,000 PLACES TO SELL YOUR FICTION

EDITED BY

BARBARA KUROFF

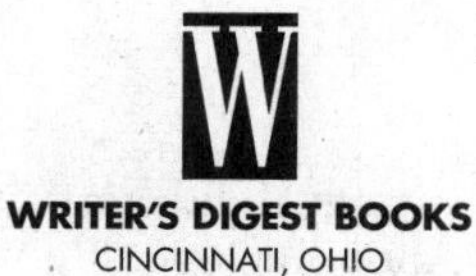

WRITER'S DIGEST BOOKS

CINCINNATI, OHIO

If you are a publisher of fiction and would like to be considered for a listing in the next edition of ***Novel & Short Story Writer's Market***, send a SASE (or SAE and IRC) with your request for a questionnaire to ***Novel & Short Story Writer's Market***—QR, 1507 Dana Ave., Cincinnati OH 45207. Questionnaires received after July 15, 1999, will be held for the 2001 edition.

Managing Editor, Annuals Department: Cindy Laufenberg
Production Editor: Anne Bowling

Writer's Digest Books website: http://www.writersdigest.com

International Standard Serial Number 0897-9812
International Standard Book Number 0-89879-876-0

Cover designed by Clare Finney
Cover illustration by David Danz

Attention Booksellers: This is an annual directory of F&W Publications.
Return deadline for this edition is April 30, 2000.

contents at a glance

Contents

Writing Fiction

Craft & Technique

Personal Views

For Mystery Writers

Resources

From the Editor

Bonnie's story . . .

Three years ago, Bonnie quit her job as a secretary to write fiction. A few of her stories have been published by a local university journal and in local newspapers. Lately, Bonnie has been concentrating her efforts on writing mysteries, and a few of her stories have "almost" been published by several of today's top mystery magazines. Bonnie is accustomed to the rejections that arrive in the mail but heartened by the occasional personal note from an editor saying nice things about her writing. Several editors have even confessed how close they came to publishing one of Bonnie's stories—"but. . . ." As disappointing as rejection can be, even rejection with a nice note, Bonnie keeps writing. For, although she sometimes thinks she should give up on writing her stories, she doesn't. "Writing," says Bonnie, "is my exasperating, frustrating best friend."

Bonnie came to my attention recently when she was a participant in one of the focus groups we regularly hold here at F&W headquarters in Cincinnati. At these focus groups we ask writers what they like and don't like about our books in a continuing effort to make sure we are meeting writers' needs. When Bonnie left with the other focus group attendees that night, she left behind a lot for me to think about as I completed this book. And so, for writers out there like Bonnie who consider fiction writing "their exasperating, frustrating best friend," this is what we've included in this edition of *Novel & Short Story Writer's Market*:

Markets and more markets . . .

This book lists over 2,000 markets for your fiction. New to this edition, symbols before most markets tell you at a glance if a market pays, offers greater opportunities to beginning writers, and more. (Check the inside front and back covers for a complete list of symbols used here.)

Agents, agents, agents . . .

Our new Literary Agents section (page 131) contains information on more than 60 agents who represent beginning as well as established writers, and the Literary Agents Category Index (page 154) lists agents according to the categories of fiction they represent. For tips on finding the right agent for you, read Agent Targeting (page 118).

Markets for your screenplays . . .

In talking with fiction writers at our focus groups and at conferences, many say they are also interested in writing screenplays. That's why we've included our new Screenwriting section (page 516) where you'll find markets for your television and movie scripts. Rob Thomas (page 526) talks about making the switch from writing novels for young adults to his debut as a screenwriter for *Dawson's Creek* and then his success as the creator of the ABC-TV series *Cupid*.

Bonnie, you're going to love this!

For the first time, this year we've included an entire section of information *just for mystery writers*. Called simply For Mystery Writers, this section includes an overview of today's mystery market; interviews with mystery writers, including "Queen of Suspense" Mary Higgins Clark (page 62); a step-by-step guide to Plotting the Mystery Novel by Judith Greber (page 74); an alphabetical listing of all the mystery markets in this book; and a list of valuable resources specifically for mystery writers. And for you other genre writers we've included For Romance Writers (page 77) and For Science Fiction & Fantasy Writers (page 95).

The inspiration to keep writing . . .

Given the talent, persistence seems to be *the* single element leading to success as a writer. This edition of *Novel & Short Story Writer's Market* contains interviews with a number of writers who persevered to achieve success. Olivia Goldsmith (page 24) survived a failed marriage, a job she disliked and 27 rejections from publishers before her first novel, *The First Wives Club* became a bestseller and hit movie. Ron Franscell (page 472) worked ten hours a day at his daily newspaper in Gillette, Wyoming, and went home each night to work on *Angel Fire*, his powerful, award-winning first novel. Following his all-consuming desire to write fiction, Rick Bass (page 40) left a career as a petroleum geologist and moved with his wife and two dogs to Yaak, Montana. Twelve years later, his award-winning short fiction has positioned him among today's top writers. In 1998, Bass's first novel, *Where the Sea Used to Be*, received rave critical reviews. Pearl Cleage (page 432), a nationally known playwright whose first novel, *What Looks Like Crazy on an Ordinary Day*, was chosen as an Oprah's Book Club™ selection, advises writers to be persistent and have the confidence to stand behind their own work.

Lorella's story . . .

On those days when Bonnie or any of you reading this feel like giving up on writing, I recommend you read what Lorella Mascot (page 51) says. Lorella and I have been talking on the phone since 1995 and communicating more recently by e-mail. When I first heard from her, she had completed a correspondence school in writing, was getting a divorce, taking care of a son and working full-time in a Las Vegas hotel. Like Bonnie with her mystery stories, Lorella wanted desperately to get her horror stories published. She kept sending out stories and the rejections kept coming back. She even gave up for a while until she decided, "If I was going to try writing again, I was going to do it all the way." Then in mid 1998, Lorella had a story published in *Black Petals*. She was ecstatic when she called to let me know, and I am delighted to include her among this year's First Bylines writers. (By the time we went to press, Lorella had three more stories accepted for publication.)

Tips on the craft of writing fiction . . .

Writers who succeed usually have done so after a great deal of developing their writing skills. Arthur Golden (page 28) set a goal at age 25 to become a fiction writer, then honed his craft for 15 years before his first novel, *Memoirs of a Geisha*, hit the bestseller lists. Ann Beattie (page 33) talks about her evolution as a writer since the early '70s through the publication of *Park City*, her most recent collection of short stories. In our Craft & Technique section, award-winning author Josip Novakovich (page 9) shows step-by-step how he created his story "Sheepskin."

How to write the query and synopsis . . .

Do you, as many writers do, find yourself staring at a blank page when trying to write a *query* or *synopsis*? Even if you've written them before, Queries That Made It Happen (page 107) and Producing a Knockout Novel Synopsis (page 117) will provide the information and confidence you need to produce either like a pro.

And there's lots more . . .

Read through the Table of Contents and you'll locate more information sure to help you get writing, keep writing, and, most importantly, get published. And do let us know how we're doing and how *you're* doing. Write us or e-mail us. Just as Bonnie, Lorella and all the other writers we talked with this year helped make this a better book, your comments are welcome as we begin the next edition of *Novel & Short Story Writer's Market.*

Barbara Kuroff

Editor
nsswm@fwpubs.com

How to Use This Book to Publish Your Fiction

Like most of the people who use *Novel & Short Story Writer's Market*, chances are you've already put a great deal of time and effort into your writing. Many of you write regularly and are well-read, especially in the area in which you write. Some of you are formally studying writing while some are receiving feedback on your work by sharing it with a writers' group. You've been spending lots of time on writing and rewriting your work, making it the best it can be, and now you feel it's time to share your work with others.

If we could open this book with just one piece of advice it would be this: Take as much care searching for potential markets for your work as you have in crafting it. With this in mind, this book is designed as a tool to help you in your search, and we hope you will use it as a starting place for your overall marketing plan. The temptation when using any book like this is to go straight to the listings and start sending out your work. Perhaps this is the fastest, but it's not the most efficient route to publication.

While we do offer listings of over 2,000 markets and other opportunities for fiction writers, the listings contain only a portion of the information available to you in *Novel & Short Story Writer's Market*. In addition to the listings, we offer interviews with published authors and editors and a wide range of articles on the craft of writing, and information on all aspects of marketing and publishing your work. Reading the material covered here, as well as other books on writing and publishing, will help you make informed decisions that will further your writing career.

WHAT YOU'LL FIND HERE

Novel & Short Story Writer's Market is divided into three parts, each presenting a different type of information. The first part is Writing Fiction. Here we provide articles on the craft of writing, in-depth interviews with established authors, and informational pieces on the business of publishing. **New this year are three sections specifically for genre writers:** For Mystery Writers, For Romance Writers, and For Science Fiction & Fantasy Writers. Each of these sections contains information specific to that genre: articles on the craft, interviews with editors and authors, resources for writers of that genre, and an alphabetical listing of markets in this book which publish that genre.

Following Writing Fiction is The Markets, the heart of the book. This part is divided into nine sections. Our **new Literary Agents section** lists over 60 agents, most of whom work with beginning as well as established writers. The Literary Magazines section includes literary journals of all sizes. Next comes the Small Circulation Magazines section, featuring publications (most paying) with circulations of under 10,000. Our Zines section follows and includes a number of exciting formats that welcome the voices of new writers. The Consumer Magazines section features popular magazines with circulations of more than 10,000. After this is the Small Press section, which includes small presses publishing three or less titles each year. Book Publishers, the next section, features listings of small and mid-size independent presses publishing more than three titles each year, university presses and other nonprofit presses, and publishers of commercial hardcover, trade paperback and mass market books. Our **new Screenwriting section** offers tips and markets for writers wanting to sell their TV and movie film scripts.

Finally, the Contests and Awards section offers listings for contests, awards and grants available to fiction writers.

Most of the listings in these market sections are from North America. There are also Canadian listings noted with a maple leaf symbol ( ) and some international markets denoted by a ( ) symbol. Many of these international markets are open to writers of English from all over the world.

Throughout The Markets, you'll find features called Insider Reports. These are short interviews with editors, publishers and writers designed to give you an inside look at specific writing areas and a behind-the-scenes look at particular publications or publishers. These pieces offer valuable tips on breaking into markets in their areas of expertise.

Resources, the last section of the book, is included for the support and information those listed there provide to writers, including places to make contact with other writers. Here you will find Conferences & Workshops, Organizations, Publications of Interest to Fiction Writers and Websites of Interest.

DEVELOPING YOUR MARKETING PLAN

After reading the articles and interviews that interest you, the next step in developing your marketing plan is to use the book to come up with a preliminary list of potential markets. If you are not sure what categories your work falls into or if you just want to explore the possibilities, start by reading the section introductions and browsing through the sections to find markets that interest you. This approach will familiarize you with the many different types of markets for your writing and may lead you to a market you haven't thought of before.

To help you with your market search, we include a Literary Agents Category Index, beginning on page 154. Magazine and book publishers are included in the Category Index beginning on page 632. The Category Index is divided into sections corresponding to the major fiction categories. You'll find fiction types such as adventure, mainstream, religious, regional, etc. Subject headings are then followed by the names of magazines and book publishers expressing an interest in that specific type of fiction.

You may notice that not all the listings in the magazine and book publisher sections appear in the Category Index. Some said they were only interested in very specific topics such as fiction about hiking or hot air ballooning or about the Civil War. Whether your writing subjects are general or specific, we recommend a combination of the browsing method and the Category Index method.

RANKING CODES

To further help you narrow your list of potential markets, we include ranking codes that identify the level of openness of each listing. These codes, Roman numerals **I** through **V**, appear just after each listing's name. In the agents, magazine and book sections, codes indicate whether editors are open to work from writers on all levels, are only open to work by established writers, only accept work by writers from a certain region or who write on a specific subject, or are closed to unsolicited submissions. In the Contest section, ranking codes let you know if entries should be published or unpublished or should be work from certain groups of writers or about certain regions. The ranking codes and explanations for each are given after each section introduction.

READING THE LISTINGS

Once you've come up with a list of potential markets, read each listing carefully. You will find you can further streamline your list based on the market's editorial statement, advice, specific needs, terms, payment and reputation. While different sections contain slightly different listings, there are some things all listings have in common.

Many listings begin with one or more symbols. (Refer to the inside covers of this book for quick reference.) Here's what each icon stands for:

- listing is new to this edition.
- listing is Canadian.
- listing is outside the U.S. and Canada.
- listing offers greater opportunities by buying a larger amount of freelance/unagented manuscripts or otherwise being more open to work from new writers.
- change in contact information from last year's edition.
- publisher only accepts submissions through agents.
- company's publications have received awards recently.
- $ listing pays money.
- listing is an online market.
- listing is a cable TV market (in Screenwriting section).
- listing does not accept queries or freelance submissions.

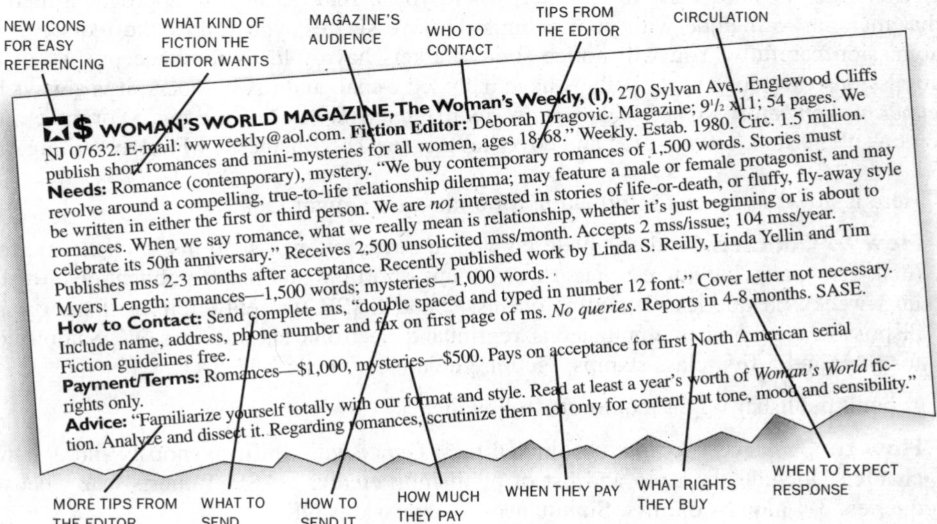

$ WOMAN'S WORLD MAGAZINE, The Woman's Weekly, (I), 270 Sylvan Ave., Englewood Cliffs NJ 07632. E-mail: wwweekly@aol.com. **Fiction Editor:** Deborah Dragovic. Magazine; 9½ x11; 54 pages. We publish short romances and mini-mysteries for all women, ages 18-68." Weekly. Estab. 1980. Circ. 1.5 million.
Needs: Romance (contemporary), mystery. "We buy contemporary romances of 1,500 words. Stories must revolve around a compelling, true-to-life relationship dilemma; may feature a male or female protagonist, and may be written in either the first or third person. We are *not* interested in stories of life-or-death, or fluffy, fly-away style romances. When we say romance, what we really mean is relationship, whether it's just beginning or is about to celebrate its 50th anniversary." Receives 2,500 unsolicited mss/month. Accepts 2 mss/issue; 104 mss/year. Publishes mss 2-3 months after acceptance. Recently published work by Linda S. Reilly, Linda Yellin and Tim Myers. Length: romances—1,500 words; mysteries—1,000 words.
How to Contact: Send complete ms, "double spaced and typed in number 12 font." Cover letter not necessary. Include name, address, phone number and fax on first page of ms. *No queries*. Reports in 4-8 months. SASE. Fiction guidelines free.
Payment/Terms: Romances—$1,000, mysteries—$500. Pays on acceptance for first North American serial rights only.
Advice: "Familiarize yourself totally with our format and style. Read at least a year's worth of *Woman's World* fiction. Analyze and dissect it. Regarding romances, scrutinize them not only for content but tone, mood and sensibility."

After the name and contact information for each listing, you'll find a brief description of the market's publishing philosophy and intended audience. Following this is often a physical description of the magazine or books published. Physical descriptions can tell you a lot about the market's budget and give you hints about its quality and prestige. There is a brief explanation of printing terms to help you get a better picture of the publications as they are described in the listings. This information is included in Printing and Production Terms Defined on page 627. Also check the establishment date, circulation or number of books published.

In some listings, following the profile, we've added our own editorial comment, set off by a bullet. This feature allows us to pass on additional information we've learned about the listing. Included here is information about the market's honors or awards or its treatment of writers.

For example, here is the editorial comment for *Ploughshares*:

• Work published in *Ploughshares* has been selected continuously for inclusion in the *Best American Short Stories* and *O. Henry Prize* anthologies. In fact, the magazine has the honor of having the most stories selected from a single issue (three) to be included in *B.A.S.S.* Recent guest editors have included Richard Ford, Tim O'Brien and Ann Beattie.

Next comes the **Needs** section of the listing. In addition to a list or description of the type of work the market is seeking, you'll also find how much work the market receives from writers in a given time, how much it publishes and what percentage of its writing is acquired through agents. This will help you determine your competition. Also included are specifics on length and other requirements.

The **Needs** section of *Ellery Queen's Mystery Magazine* offers the following information:

Needs: "We accept only mystery, crime, suspense and detective fiction." Receives approximately 400 unsolicited fiction mss each month. Accepts 10-15 mss/issue. Publishes ms 6-12 months after acceptance. Agented fiction 50%. Published work by Peter Lovesey, Anne Perry, Marcia Muller and Ruth Rendell. Publishes 11 new writers/year. Length: up to 7,000 words, occasionally longer. Publishes 1-2 short novels of up to 17,000 words/year by established authors; minute mysteries of 250 words; short, humorous mystery verse. Critiques rejected mss "only when a story might be a possibility for us if revised." Sometimes recommends other markets.

After **Needs** comes **How to Contact**, where you'll find out how to approach a market and what material to include with your submission. We suggest you follow the requirements for submission carefully. You will notice some markets have told us they accept disk or e-mail submissions. Although some listings have included e-mail and fax numbers, it is always best to *get permission before submitting a manuscript to a publisher by fax or e-mail*. For more information on submission, presentation and cover letters, see The Business of Fiction Writing on page 121.

Here is how the contact information for a magazine might look:

How to Contact: Send complete ms with a cover letter or send ms in electronic form (disk or e-mail). Include estimated word count, short bio and list of publications. Reports in 3 weeks on queries; 2 months on mss. Send SASE for reply, return of ms or send disposable copy of ms. Simultaneous, reprint and electronic submissions OK. Sample copy for SAE and 5 first-class stamps. Fiction guidelines for 8½×11 SAE.

A book publisher might require the following:

How to Contact: Accepts unsolicited mss. Query with outline/synopsis and 3 sample chapters. Include short bio and list of publishing credits. SASE. Reports in 2 weeks on queries; 3-4 months on mss. Simultaneous submissions OK.

Next is the **Payment/Terms** section. When possible, we've provided a range of payment, but note that many publications in the Literary and Zine sections pay only in copies or subscriptions. We also indicate when you will be paid and for what rights. For more on rights and what to look for concerning terms, see the Business of Fiction Writing.

The **Payment/Terms** information for *Asimov's Science Fiction* magazine is:

Payment/Terms: Pays 6-8¢/word for stories up to 7,500 words; 5¢/word for stories over 12,500; $450 for stories between those limits. Pays on acceptance for first North American serial rights plus specified foreign rights, as explained in contract. Very rarely buys reprints. Sends galleys to author.

When an editor provided additional information that might be of benefit, we include that in the **Advice** section at the end of listings. Editor C. Michael Curtis tells writers the following in the **Advice** section of *The Atlantic Monthly* listing:

Advice: When making first contact, "cover letters are sometimes helpful, particularly if they cite prior publications or involvement in writing programs. Common mistakes: melodrama, inconclusiveness, lack of development, unpersuasive characters and/or dialogue."

LEARNING MORE ABOUT A MARKET

Your marketing research should begin with a careful study of the listings, but it should not end there. Whenever possible obtain a sample copy or catalog. Editors and successful writers agree there is no substitution for reading copies of magazines that interest you. Likewise, you should familiarize yourself with the books of publishers to whom you'd like to submit.

To find out more about a potential market, send a self-addressed, stamped envelope (SASE) for submission guidelines. Most magazines have sample copies available for a modest price. For book publishers, check *Books in Print* at the library to find the publishers of books you admire or feel are similar to the one you are writing. The library also has publishing industry magazines such as *Publishers Weekly* as well as magazines for writers. Some of these magazines are listed in Publications of Interest to Fiction Writers beginning on page 617. These can help keep you informed of new publishers and changes in the field.

THE FOLLOW THROUGH

After carefully studying and narrowing your list of potential markets to those who represent the most suitable places for your work, the next step, of course, is to mail out your work. If you have any questions on how to present your work, see The Business of Fiction Writing. When in doubt, remember to make it as easy as possible for editors to read and respond to your work. They're a busy lot and will not waste time with submissions that are messy and difficult to read. It may be good writing, but the editor may never read a poorly presented manuscript to find that out. If you show you care about your work, the editor will too.

Also keep accurate records. We've asked our listings to indicate how long it will take them to report on a submission, but at times throughout the year the market may get behind. Note that with small magazines and literary journals (especially those published by universities) response time tends to be slower in the summer months. Keeping track of when you send your manuscript will help you decide when it is time to check on the status of your submission.

Writing Fiction

Putting It All Together

BY JOSIP NOVAKOVICH

In my experience and that of many other writers, it seems clear that writing a piece of fiction is a series of concrete tasks: introducing a character, describing a setting, creating a scene, writing a provocative dialogue, and so on. Some writers resist the notion of exercises, but they do exercises all the time by setting themselves such concrete assignments.

Some stories may arise from a scene, or a dialogue, or a character sketch, and the other supporting scenes can be created along the way as you need them. Other stories may come from a general notion of what the setup should be, and then you gradually assemble the pieces you need, such as persons, places, and the escalation of action.

Now that we've looked at each element in turn, let's look at how they all unite to form a finished piece. I will show you how a story came together for me—how I assembled various elements created in exercise-like sketches I assigned to myself. Showing how my story came into being may appear selfish, and perhaps it is, but I cannot truly know or explain the creative process that any other writer underwent to complete a story. I know only how my own imagination made the connections necessary to bring a story to life. And even in my own story, I cannot explain everything. But I will try. So read the following story. Then we can discuss how it was developed, one step at a time.

SHEEPSKIN

Since I can't tell this to anybody, I'm writing it, not just to sort it out for myself, but for someone nosy who'll rummage through my papers one day. In a way I want to be caught. But I won't call this story a confession. I should pretend that it's somebody else's story, that it is fiction. I wish I could set it in a different country—outside Croatia and outside the former Yugoslavia—and that it was about somebody else, a former self, a formerly uniformed me. I don't mean that I want a complete break with my past—nothing as dramatic as suicide, although, of course, I've entertained thoughts of it, but the thoughts have not entertained me. I have survived knives and bombs: I should be able to survive thoughts and memories.

I'll start with a scene on a train in western Slavonia. Though it was hot, I closed the window. Not that I am superstitious against drafts as many of our people are. Dandelion seeds floated in, like dry snowflakes, and all sorts of pollens and other emissaries of the wild fields filled the air with smells of chamomile, menthol, and other teas. It would have been pleasant if I hadn't had a cold that made me sneeze and squint. The countryside

---

JOSIP NOVAKOVICH *is the author of* Apricots From Chernobyl, *a collection of essays, and the short story collections* Yolk *and* Salvation and Other Disasters. *He has won a Whiting Award, a Richard Margolis Prize for Socially Important Writing, three Pushcart Prizes, an O. Henry award and an NEA fellowship. His* Fiction Writer's Workshop, *published by Story Press in February 1995, was released in paperback in January 1998. His work has appeared in* The New York Times Magazine, DoubleTake, STORY, Ploughshares, Paris Review, *and* The Best American Poetry '97. *He teaches writing at the University of Cincinnati. This article was excerpted from* Writing Fiction Step by Step *copyright © 1998 by Josip Novakovich. Used with permission of Writer's Digest, a division of F&W Publications, Inc. For credit card orders phone toll free 1-800-289-0963.* *(See the interview with Novakovich on page 460.)*

seemed mostly abandoned. Croats from Serbian Kosovo had moved into the villages where Serbs used to live, but they did not plant, sow, or harvest, because they had no legal rights to do so until formal land deeds were signed. Only a few could track down the Serbs who had run away.

I had never seen vegetation so free and jubilant. The war had loosened the earth, shaken the farmers off its back. Strewn mines kept them from venturing into the fields, but did not bother the flowers. The color intensity of grasses and beeches in the background gave me dizziness I could not attribute to my cold. I saw a fox leap out of orange bushes of tea. Of course, it was not tea, but many of these wildflowers would be teas, curing asthma, improving memory, and filling you with tenderness. If we had stuck to drinking tea, maybe the war would have never happened.

I leaned against the wooden side of the train, but gave up, since the magnum I had strapped on my side pressed into my arm painfully. I would have probably fallen asleep, intoxicated with the fields and the musty oil, which doused the wood beneath the tracks. As a child I had loved the oily smell of rails; it had transformed for me the iron clanking of the gaps in the tracks into a transcontinental guitar with two hammered strings and thousands of sorrowful frets that fell into diminished distances. I'd have dozed off if every time I leaned against the vibrating wall of the train the gun hadn't pinched a nerve and shaken me awake. And just when I was beginning to slumber, the door screeched.

A gaunt man entered. I was startled, recognizing my old tormentor from the Vukovar hospital. He took off his hat and revealed unruly cowlicked hair, grayer than I remembered it. His thick eyebrows that almost met above his nose were black. I wondered whether he colored them.

The man did not not look toward me, although he stiffened. I was sure he was aware of me. I had dreamed of this moment many times, imagining the first thing I'd do if given the opportunity would be to jump at the man, grab his throat, and strangle him with the sheer power of rage. My heart leaped, but I didn't. I gazed at him from the corner of my eye. He looked a little thinner and taller than I remembered. I did not know his name, but in my mind I had always called him Milos. I ceased to believe we coexisted in the same world—imagined that he was in Serbia, off the map as far as I was concerned.

I looked out the window, and the sunlit fields glowed even more, with the dark undersides, shadows, enhancing the light in the foreground. The train was pulling into Djulevci. The Catholic church gaped open, its tower missing, its front wall and gate in rubble, the pews crushed, overturned, and the side wall had several big howitzer holes; only here and there pale mortar remained, reflecting the sun so violently that my eyes hurt. At the train station there was a pile of oak logs, probably a decade old, but still not rotten. And past the train station stood the Serb Orthodox church, pockmarked. It probably wouldn't be standing if there hadn't been guards around it, night and day. The Croatian government wanted to demonstrate to the world—although journalists never bothered to come to this village—how much better Croats were than Serbs, but that was just a show. The Croat policemen sat on chairs, one wiggled a semi-automatic rifle, and the other tossed a crushed can of Coke over his shoulder.

There was a time when I would have thrown grenades into the church, owing to my traveling companion and other Serb soldiers who had surrounded and choked the city of Vukovar for months. Fearing that I would starve to death, I had minced my sheepskin jacket and made a soup out of it. The day before the soldiers invaded the city, I'd seen a cat struck in the neck with schrapnel. I picked her up and skinned her. I overgrilled her because I was squeamish to eat a cat, and once I had eaten most of her, I grew feverish. I wasn't sure whether the cat had gotten some disease from rats—I would not have been surprised if I had caught the plague this way—or whether it was sheer guilt and disgust with myself, that I had eaten a cat, that made me ill. My body, unused to food, just could not take it; I was delirious in the hospital, but there was no doubt, what I saw was not a dream: soldiers laughing, crashing wine bottles on the chairs, dragging old men in torn pajamas out of their hospital beds. A man with black eyebrows and a gray cowlick that shot out trembling strands of hair above his forehead came to my side and spat at me. He pulled the sheet off my bed and stabbed my thigh with a broken wine bottle. I coiled and shrieked, and he uncoiled me, pulling my arms, and another man pulled my legs, while the third one pissed over my wound and said, "This is the best disinfectant around, absolutely the best. *Na zdravlye!*"

"There, pig, you'll thank me one day, you'll see," said Milos, and stabbed my leg again.

Other soldiers came and dragged a wailing old woman down the stairs.

"How about this guy?" one of the soldiers asked about me.

"No, he's bleeding too much," said Milos. "I don't want to get contaminated by his shitty blood."

A tall French journalist came in and took pictures of me, and muttered in English.

"What are you staring at?" I asked. "There are worse sights around."

"Yes, but they are not alive," he said. He carried me out, while my blood soaked his clothes. He pushed me into the jeep, and we drove out and passed several checkpoints without any inspection. He took me to the Vinkovci hospital, which was often bombed. Two nurses pulled glass from my leg, tied rubber above and below the wound, stitched me up, wrapped the wound—all without painkillers. I wished I could swoon from the pain. I ground my teeth so hard that a molar cracked.

Thanks a lot for the pleasure, I thought now and looked at my silent companion on the train. At Virovitica, we'd have to change trains. Mine was going to Zagreb, and I did not know whether he was going there, or east, to Osijek.

He got out of the compartment first, and I did not want to be obvious about following him. Many peasants with loud white chickens in their pleated baskets filled the corridor between us.

When I jumped off the train into the gravel, his head covered with a hat slid behind a wall. His shadow moved jerkily on the gray cement of the platform, but I could not see the shadow's owner. Milos must have been behind the corner. Maybe he was aware of being followed.

I thought he could be waiting for me in ambush. People walked and stepped on his shadow, but they could not trample it, because as they stepped on it, it climbed on them, and I was no longer sure whether it was Milos' shadow or whether they were casting shadows over each other. Not that it mattered one way or another, but I suppose that's part of my professional photographer's distortion and disorientation that I look at light and shadow wherever I turn, and I frame what I see in rectangular snatches; I keep squaring that world, in my head, to some early and primitive cosmology of a flat earth, where nothing comes around.

I rushed past the corner. There was a kiosk stocked with cigarettes and many magazines featuring pictures of naked blondes. I stopped and pretended to be reading the train schedule posted at the station entrance so I could observe Milos' reflection on the glass over the orange departures schedule. He rolled the magazine he had bought into a flute, and entered a restaurant. I followed. There was an outdoor section under a tin roof, with large wooden tables and benches. A TV set was blaring out a sequence of Croatian President Tudjman kissing the flag at the Knin fort, after his forces captured Knin. The President lifted his clenched fist to the sky. What kind of kiss was it, from thin bloodless lips sinking through the concave mouth of an elderly stiffneck? I detest flags. Anyhow, I was not in a loving mood right then, toward anybody. In Vukovar we thought that Tudjman had abandoned us. Maybe he was partly responsible for my wantonly following a stranger down the stairs, to the lower level of the country dive. Milos sat below a window with fake crystal glass that refracted light into purple rays. I did not sit right away, but walked past him, following arrows to the bathroom across a yard with a fenced family of sheep with muddy feet, who eyed me calmly. I walked back and sat at a round table about two yards away from his.

He ordered lamb and a carafe of red wine in a perfect Zagreb accent. In Vukovar I remembered him using long Serb vowels, ironically stretching them. Maybe he was now afraid to be taken for a Serb. I couldn't blame him for that. Still, a man who could dissemble so well was dangerous, I thought.

I ordered the same thing. When I pronounced my order, I used the same wording as Milos, in my eastern Slavonian leisurely way, which to many people outside my region sounded similar to Serbian.

Milos looked at me for the first time and, hearing my voice, gave a start. The waiter, slumping in his greasy black jacket with a napkin hanging out of his pocket, eyed me contemptuously. His mouth was curled to one side, and one silver tooth gleamed, over his shiny fat lower lip.

He brought one carafe to Milos and one to me along with empty glasses. Milos drank, I drank. He opened his magazine to the centerfold of a blonde with black pubic hair, and then he stared at me. What was the point? Did he pretend that he thought I was a homosexual stalking him and about to proposition him, so this was his way of telling me, No I'm not interested? If he imagined he could confuse me this way so I would not be positive I had recognized him, he was dead wrong.

I had a postcard in my pocket; I pulled it out and began to write—I did not know to whom. To my ex-wife, who'd left me at the beginning of the war to visit her relatives in Belgrade? They had filled her head with nonsense about how Croats were going to kill her, and how even I might be a rabid Croat who would cut her throat. The nonsense actually served Miriana well; she got out right before the city was encircled by Serb troops and bombed. From what I heard she now lived with a widowed cardiologist whose Croatian wife had died of a heart attack. Miriana used to visit Belgrade frequently even before the war; she had probably had an affair with the cardiologist. Her running away from the fighting may have been simply a pretext for leaving me. Anyway, I didn't have her address, so I couldn't write to her—no big loss.

I wrote to my dead father instead, although this made no sense either. He had died of stomach cancer last year in Osijek, perhaps because of the war. Without the anxiety he could have lived with the latent stomach cancer for years.

"Hi, my old man. I wish you were here. Not that there'd be much to see—in fact, Virovitica has to be one of the dreariest towns in Slavonia. But the wine is good. . . ."

My meal arrived. I folded the postcard and put it in my pocket. The meat was lukewarm. Who knows when it was cooked—maybe days ago, and it stayed in the refrigerator. I grumbled as I cut.

Milos swore too, as he struggled. He asked for a sharper knife.

"This is awful! They charge so much and give you only the bone!" he said to me.

If he thought he could engage me in a conversation and thus appease me, he was wrong, although I did answer. "Yes, they figure only travelers would eat here anyway, and once they get our money and we're gone, they can laugh at us."

He gulped wine.

I navigated my blade through the stringy meat.

"Where are you from?" he asked me.

I called the waiter. "You forgot the salad."

"You haven't asked for it."

He was probably right, but I still said, "Yes, I did."

He soon brought me a plate of sliced tomatoes and onions, with oily vinegar. That helped subdue the heavy and rotten lamb taste. Funny how finicky I'd become in a hurry—not long before, I had chewed my leather shoes, certain I'd starve to death, and now I behaved like a jaded gourmet.

Milos bent down to search through his luggage. Maybe he's going to draw a gun? I thought. I slid my hand into my jacket.

Milos took out three dolls, the Lion King hyenas. What, is this possible? My torturer is buying toys for kids? He put the magazine and the hyenas into his traveling bag. Maybe that was his way of saying, I am not a guy who'd stab anybody, I'm a kind family man.

He looked toward me, and I felt self-conscious with my hand in my jacket. So it wouldn't look as though I was pulling a gun, I fumbled in the pocket and took out my pigskin wallet. The waiter eagerly came to my table. I gave him 50 kunas, certainly more than the meal was worth. "I need no change," I said.

"Excuse me, four and a half more kunas, please," asked the waiter. I gave him five coins.

"Preposterous, isn't it?" Milos said. "How can they charge that much for this? If I had known, I'd have controlled my appetite, could have bought another toy for my kids."

Was he appealing to me again? I had no sympathy for family men. My marriage failed perhaps because I had no kids. My business failed because the likes of Milos bombed my town, and here, I sat as a twitching mass of resentment. I took another gulp of wine. I first used a toothpick and then whistled through my teeth to clean out bits of meat that got stuck there.

Milos looked at me with annoyance. He clearly didn't like my whistling. So what, I thought. If it bothers you, I'll do more of it. And who was he to complain? He slurped wine as though it were hot soup. And with his sharp knife, sharper than mine, he cut through more lamb, and I couldn't escape remembering again how he'd cut into my leg.

I scratched the swollen scar through the woolen fabric of my pants. It itched to the point of my wanting to tear it.

"Do you think there are fleas here?" I asked loudly, as if to excuse my scratching, but looked at nobody.

The waiter strutted and dumped tiny coins on my table ostentatiously, probably to make a statement that it was beneath him to take my tip. The rattle of change scared two turquoise flies off my plate.

"Flies are all right," I said. Not much had changed since communism. I used to think that rudeness was a matter of fixed salaries, no incentive. But here, I was pretty sure the waiter was part-owner of this free enterprise establishment, and he was still rude, and did his best to disgust his customers. And of course customers hadn't changed either. They used to be rude, and I would continue to be rude. But before I could think of another insulting question, Milos asked one. "Hey, my friend, do you think I could buy a sheepskin jacket anywhere around here?"

This may have been a jab at me. But how could he have known I'd eaten a sheepskin jacket in Vukovar?

The waiter answered: "Maybe in a couple of hours. We are just getting some ready."

"Could I see them?" Milos was standing and picking up a thick cloth napkin that looked like a towel from his lap.

The waiter grabbed a large hair dryer from among plum brandy bottles on the shelf and waved to Milos to come along. Although I was not invited, I followed. They had identical bald spots on the pates of their heads.

Behind the sheep stall, in a shed filled with hay, on thick clothes wires hung two sheepskins, dripping blood into aluminum pots on the dusty dirt floor.

I wondered why the waiter collected the blood, why not simply let it soak the ground.

Maybe he made blood sausages; maybe he drank it, like an ancient Mongolian horseman.

The waiter aimed the blow dryer at a sheepskin, filling it with air. Rounded like a sail full of wind, the skin gave me a spooky impression that an invisible sheep was beginning to inhabit it.

"This'll be a terrific jacket," the waiter said. "Give it an hour, if you can spare."

"But what about the pattern?" Milos said. "What about the buttons?"

"Fuck buttons. You can get those anyplace. But fine sheepskin like this, nowhere. Two hundred kunas, is that a deal?"

Milos stroked the sheepskin's tight yellow curls.

"The winter's going to be a harsh one," said the waiter.

"Yes, but sheep won't save us from it," I said.

Milos quit stroking, and as he turned around, he stepped on the edge of a bowl, and blood spilled over his jeans and white socks and leather shoes.

"Seeing this is enough to make one become a vegetarian," I said to the waiter. I was beginning to feel nauseous.

"I'll be passing through town in two days again," said Milos. "Could I pick it up then?"

"No problem." The waiter walked back, Milos followed. The waiter pushed in a silvery CD, and Croatian pop came on, tambourines with electric organs that shook the speakers. The music was cranked beyond the point of clarity—blasted. No conversation was possible.

Milos walked into the backyard. I thought that his Serb soul wouldn't let him listen to Croat music. He gave me a look and winked. I wondered what he meant. The waiter smirked, perhaps thinking there was a gay connection established between Milos and me. Milos went into the toilet, an outhouse next to the sheep stall.

I went behind the outhouse. There was a hole in the gray wood through which I could see his back. I put the gun in the hole and shot through his spine. His body jolted forward and then fell back, right against the wall. I shot again. Blood flowed through the spacing between the dry planks. Because of the music, I was sure the waiter couldn't hear the shots.

I rushed away from the tavern yard through the rear gate. A train was whistling into the station. I jumped on the train even before it stopped. I wondered why I was running away. I should have been able to explain my deed—revenge against a war criminal. I went straight into the train toilet and shaved off my droopy mustache that made me look melancholy and forsaken. Now in the mirror I looked much younger, despite my receding hairline and the isolated widow's peak.

I thought I'd feel triumphant after my revenge. And I did feel proud as I looked at my cleared lip. Great, I am free from my sorrow, from the humiliation. I won.

But as I sat in the first-class coach and looked at round holes burnt into the velvet seat by cigarette butts, my heart pounded and I could barely draw a breath. The smell of stale tobacco and spilled beer irritated me. I turned the ashtray over, cleaned it with a paper towel and threw it out the window. The awful mutton seemed to be coming up to my throat. I was afraid.

If I was caught, and there was a trial, public sympathy would be with me. Many people want personal revenge. Forget institutional revenge, forget the International War Crimes Tribunal in Den Haage.

When I got off in Zagreb policemen in blue uniforms with German shepherds strolled on the platform but they did not stop me. They probably did not look for me. The war was going on in Krajina; one more civilian dead in the North made no difference.

Drunken people frolicked all over town, beeping their car horns, the way they did when their soccer clubs won. As I walked I expected a hand on my shoulder, from somewhere, perhaps the sky. It did not happen. But what happened was worse. At the tram stop, I saw a man exactly like Milos. I thought it was him. Were my bullets blanks? But where had the blood come from? How could Milos have made it to the train? When he saw me, I thought I noticed a fleeting recognition, the cowlick on his head shook, but that was too little reaction for what had happened in Virovitica. It was not Milos from the restaurant. This man was a little shorter and plumper. He looked genuinely like the man from Vukovar who had stabbed me, more than my Milos from Virovitica did. What if I had killed the wrong man? We rode in the same tram car. I forgot to buy my ticket, I was so stunned. He had his punched in the orange box near the entrance and stood, with one arm holding on to a pole. What to do? I wondered, as the tram jangled us around curves, and slim young ladies with tranquil made-up faces stood between us. I could not just kill the man, although this was probably the one that I should have killed in the first place. He got off at Kvaternik Square. Now I could blame him not only for my injury but for the death of an innocent man, his double. But I could have been wrong, again. I couldn't trust my "recognitions" anymore. I hadn't felt particularly ecstatic after my first murder, not for long anyway, and I was not looking for ectasy. So I did not follow this man. I was crazed enough that I could have killed him too, but I wanted to be alone. Enough stuffy trams, oily tracks, expressionless people.

I walked home, near the zoo, just south of the stadium. In the streets I saw another Milos look-alike. Was I hallucinating? It was getting dark, true, but I looked at this third Milos keenly. They all had the same gait, same graying and trembling cowlick, same heavy black brow. I was glad I hadn't killed the man on the tram. How many men would I have to shoot to get the right one? It was absurd, and I was afraid that I was going insane.

I watched TV in my messy efficiency. Crime, if this was crime, was no news. Only Serb mass exodus from Krajina and Croat mass exodus from Banja Luka and Vojvodina made the news along with Mitterand's prostate. I drank three bottles of warm red wine and still couldn't fall asleep.

Next morning, sleepless and hungover, on my way to buy a daily, I thought I saw a Milos look-alike, leaning against the window of an espresso café, staring vacantly, as though he were the corpse of my traveling companion from Virovitica.

In the papers I saw the picture of my man, "Murdered by an Unidentified Traveler": Mario Toplak, teacher of mathematics at the Zagreb Classical Gymnasium, survived by his wife Tanya, son Kruno, and daughter Irena. Clearly, I got the wrong man. This one was a Croat, judging by his name. But then, even the man in the Vukovar hospital could have been a Croat. He could have been drafted. The fact that he did not kill me and did not drag me out onto a bus to be shot in a cornfield now gave me the idea that wounding me may have saved me. I could not walk, and since I gushed blood it would have been too disgusting for anybody to carry me onto the bus, so I was left alone. He may have been a Serb, and he saved me nevertheless. Why hadn't I thought of that possibility before? Maybe I should have sought out the man to thank him. But thirst for revenge makes you blind. Is this a real thought? I'm probably just paraphrasing "Love makes you blind." I'm filling in the dots in prefab thoughts. Can I think?

At Toplak's funeral there were almost a hundred people, so I felt I was inconspicuous in the chapel. His wife wept, and his son, about four, and daughter, about five, did not seem to understand what was going on. "Where is Daddy? I want my daddy!" shouted Kruno.

"He's going to visit the angels in heaven, so he could tell us what it's like there. He'll bring back some tiny clouds who can sing in foreign tongues, you'll see." The widow whispered loudly. Maybe she was proud of how well she was shielding her kids from the truth.

"How can Daddy fly to heaven from here?" asked Irena.

I could see why she worried about that. The chapel was small, stuffy with perfume—I detest perfume, as though breathing wasn't hard enough without it!—and too cramped for an Ascension to take place. Tanya looked pathetic, tragic, dignified with her dark auburn hair, pale skin, and vermilion lips. Her skirt was slightly above the knee; she had thin ankles, a shapely waist with round, sexily tilted hip. She was in her mid-30s. After the funeral, I gave her a white carnation, which had fallen in front of me from a precariously laid bouquet during the prayer. (I wondered, could you make tea from carnations, at least for funerals?) "I knew your husband," I said. "I'm so sorry."

She took the flower mechanically and put it in her purse.

"Could I give you a call, to share memories of him with you?" I said.

"Not for a while. What would be the point anyway?" She gave me a look through her eyelashes, grasped her children's hands, and walked toward the chapel door. Kruno turned around, looked at the varnished casket, and asked, "How come the box has no wings? How will it fly?"

Toplak was in the phone book. I called her a month later but when she answered I put the receiver down. I was too excited, I couldn't talk. I feared that I wanted to confess to her. On several occasions I waited for hours not far from her house and followed her. Every Saturday morning she went to the neighborhood playground with her kids.

In the meanwhile, I had grown crazed and lucky in everything I did. I can't say that I was a shy man—I used to be, but photography, shoving my eyes into everybody's business and intimacy, freed me from that affliction. At the end of August 1995 I took on loans, sold a small house in Djakovo I had inherited from my father, rented a shop, and photographed a lot of weddings, funerals, births. I accosted couples in the park who seemed to be on the verge of getting married, got their phone numbers; I put up ads in all the funeral parlors, crashed funeral parties with my camera. I hired an assistant, made a lot of money. The country seemed to follow the same mood swings as I did. After Krajina was conquered and all the transportation lines in Croatia were opened again, and there were no more threats of bombing in Zagreb, everybody was on the make. Optimism, investment, spending—many people seemed to have money, while months before hardly anybody did. If I had talked to Tanya a couple of days after the funeral, I would have had nothing to show for myself, but just two months later, when I approached her at the playground while her kids were jumping up and down the slides, I could boast. It was a superb day, with leaves turning color and fluttering in the slanted rays of the afternoon sun.

I came up to her bench, camera slung around my neck, and said, "Hello, you look beautiful. Would you mind if I took several pictures of you?"

"Oh come on, that's an old line. Thanks for the compliment, but I don't think so." She did not even look at me, but laughed.

"I'm serious. I don't mean nudes, though I'm sure they would be wonderful too, but just your face, your figure, dressed. Your expression, your mood, that's art."

Here, she was taken aback by my speech, and she looked up at me, raising one of her pencil-defined eyebrows. I was standing against the sun, casting a shadow over her left shoulder but letting the sun blaze into her eyes—her hazel irises glowed with emerald undertones, like moss in a forest in the fall. Her eye colors composed well with the turning leaves, as the soul of raving colors. I wasn't lying—I did want to take her picture, and it would have been terrific.

"Do I know you?" she asked.

"Slightly, I came up to you at your husband's funeral and gave you a carnation."

"Oh yes. And even then you were about to offer something. What did you want to talk about then?"

"I was on the train with your husband that day," I said—actually, blurted out.

"Yes?" she said, and then looked over to the playground to see whether her kids were safe.

I waited and didn't say anything for several seconds. I did not want to give away any clues, but her husband was the only ostensible link I had with her—I wanted to use it, so she would not evade me and leave as a stranger. My desire for her was stronger than my impulse toward safety.

"We chatted briefly," I told her. "He told me how much he loved his family, you and the kids, particularly how crazy he was about you, how lucky to have such a beautiful wife. But that's not why I came to the funeral, to see how voluptuous you are." She grinned as though she understood that I was lying and waited for me to go on. "He went off to the restaurant, he was hungry. I was surprised when I did not see him come back to the train station, but I figured the meal must have been great if he'd miss the train out of that God-forsaken station for it. I hope, for his sake, that it was."

"Really, he talked to you about how much he loved me? I wish he'd told me he loved me. Anyway, I don't believe that he said it."

"Maybe he was shy with you."

"And not with you?" she said. "Maybe you're right. He was a moody self-obsessed mathematician. Anyhow, he was a homosexual. We hadn't slept together in two years. I don't know why I'm telling you all this, maybe just to let you know that I have reasons not to believe you."

"You seem to resent him." I was amazed. I had thought Milos was defending himself from a possible gay stalker in the restaurant, but he was actually trying to pick me up. The waiter may have been partly right to smirk and think there was a lewd connection being established.

"I know, it's irrational, but in a way I blame him for leaving us like this. Now I have to work full time, support the family, the kids are a mess, as though we didn't have enough problems."

"Did he serve in the army during the war? I've heard that in post-traumatic stress, many straight men go through a gay phase." I was bullshitting, just to appear natural, and also, to find out whether her husband was in Vukovar as a soldier, after all.

"That's interesting. Yes, he was in the army, in Zadar, and was wounded." She was studying me, and nibbling on a pencil eraser.

"What army?"

"Funny question."

"What work do you do?" I asked.

"Curious, aren't we? I teach English, mostly private lessons, and I teach at a school."

"Could I sign up for an intensive program?" I asked.

"That depends," she said.

"Don't you want to make money?"

"Sure, but there's something strange about you . . . I didn't mean it to come out like that. What I mean, I don't know you."

"Do you have to be intimate with people before you give them lessons?" I joked. It was not a good joke, but she laughed, perhaps because we were both tense.

She let me take pictures of her kids, I took several lessons, and paid well. She allowed me to take pictures of her, in her funeral dress, with the red lipstick. She could not be as pale as she'd been during the funeral, so we touched up her face with white powder to intensify the contrast with her hair. I don't know why I hadn't taken pictures at the funeral; it hadn't occurred to me then.

That was three weeks ago. I've taken her and the kids to the movies, to the zoo, and now that the first snow has fallen, I'll take them skiing. Tonight I've paid for a baby-sitter and Tanya and I took a walk in the old town, past the lanterns, in narrow cobbled streets.

A cold wind chapped my lips, and they hurt, until I kissed her in a dark corridor, a moist, tingling kiss. We trembled from excitement.

When I got home, I saw that I had vermilion lips. I had forgotten to wipe them. I am still filled with tenderness, and I'm drinking red wine. I'm looking forward to another date, tomorrow night, hoping to make love to her.

I don't know why I'm having success with her—perhaps too many men are in the army, many have been killed, and there's a shortage that may be working to my advantage. Maybe she's stringing me along, maybe she's suspecting me and investigating the case. I think my guilt gives me extraordinary confidence—I have nothing to lose. I am tempted to expose myself to her, and this temptation thrills me just as much as the erotic seduction does. I am dizzy from her images—and his—swarming in my head. I should go back to the western Slavonian fields, and gather wild flowers, bury myself in their scents and colors. Then I would not need to remember and rave on the page from a strange desire to be caught. I would live like a fox in a bush of red tea.

STORY IDEA

When I got the idea for "Sheepskin," I was not looking for a piece of fiction. In fact, I was trying to get interviews in a refugee camp near Vukovar in Croatia. Because I had no press credentials, the camp director was reluctant to help me. After we talked about it for a while, he did allow me to walk around the camp and talk with people, but without the credentials I was encountering too much skepticism. I ended up talking mostly with the camp director. He told me he was a Croatian soldier when Serb forces invaded Vukovar. When he was bedridden in the city hospital, soldiers came in and dragged many people out to nearby cornfields, where they were shot to death. A soldier whom he knew in childhood came to his bed and spat at him and insulted him. "I wonder what I'd do if I saw the guy again," said the director. "I can't vouch for my actions."

As I left the camp, the question of what he'd do lingered in my head. It would have been a great subject for a piece of nonfiction to get these two soldiers together, interview them, and see what happened. But who could find the Serb soldier? Without getting together with these soldiers, of course, I could only imagine their "relationship." Since I didn't actually know the camp director, and I didn't know the soldier at all, anything I wrote about them—if I did it in enough detail—would be fiction.

I decided to write a story based on the camp director's experience. This decision became, for me, like an assignment: Write a story of revenge involving two soldiers. But the idea wasn't fully developed enough in my mind for me to simply sit down and write.

POINT OF VIEW AND VOICE

Without much preparation, I tried to write the story in the third person, and I wasn't getting anywhere. The story was too abstract—still only an idea. *I* was not in the story. I needed to bring it closer to me. I thought that by using the first person point of view, I might make this happen, bringing the characters and events into clearer focus. However, I didn't want this voice to sound like me. I needed something different.

What kind of first-person voice would work? I wondered. The man, not knowing what he would do, would probably be contemplating, making decisions, retracting them, and so on. This kind of dialectical back-and-forth thinking brought to my mind the first-person narrators of Fyodor Dostoyevsky, particularly the one in his classic *Notes From Underground*. In earlier stories and sketches, I had already played with that kind of paradoxist voice, and I was pretty sure I could do something similar.

To give you a clearer idea of the source of the story's voice, here are brief excerpts from *Notes From Underground*.

> At the time I was only 24. My life was even then gloomy, ill-regulated, and as solitary as that of a savage. I made friends with no one and positively avoided talking, and buried myself more and more in my hole. At work in the office I never looked at any one, and I was perfectly well aware that my companions looked upon me, not only as a queer fellow, but even looked upon me—I always fancied this—with a sort of loathing. I was a spiteful official. I was rude and took pleasure in being so. I did not take bribes, you see, so I was bound to find a recompense in that, at least.

Here's my attempt at a similar voice, prompted by reading *Notes*.

> I'm perfectly well aware that I'm not entertaining anybody by the way I'm telling this: to entertain, one must make scenes, create the illusion that the events are really happening, like on a stage. Well, forget the stage; I have stage fright. Forget entertainment; I don't laugh at jokes.

I even deliberately adapted Dostoyevsky's phrase "I was perfectly well aware" to get myself in the right mode. And I used the same psychology: Dostoyevsky's unnamed narrator is highly self-conscious. I created my narrator to be the same way, suffering from stage fright. And I did not give him a name, to emphasize his paranoid tendency to hide, evade, and so on—which I thought could intensify his problem of attempting revenge.

This voice from a classic piece of literature, with the mental framework that comprises and evinces it, got my story moving. But still, though I could rave in the voice, I couldn't begin to see the action, to set it as if on a stage. Well, I didn't have the stage yet.

VISUALIZING THE STORY

I needed to determine where exactly the two soldiers should meet. From experience, I know that if I can visualize a setting, I can begin to see the story in scenes. In Croatia I had spent a lot of time on trains, and I missed them. I decided I could create the sensation of travel on a train, and that this would be a way to bring the two guys together.

But I was still getting stuck. I needed to visualize the protagonist and the antagonist, particularly the antagonist. If you've seen news footage of the war in Bosnia, you've probably noticed that many people in the Balkans look as though they are having a "bad hair day." It's a common feature among people from that part of the world. I must admit that I, too, have unruly hair, and I don't do much to subdue it. So I took this image of hair and developed it. I added strains of gray and a cowlick. At last, I began to see this character. I added thick, closely-set eyebrows and imagined him talking in a slow way. Although that was not much of a character yet, the visual prop got me through. So now I could begin seeing him and letting him move around on the stage.

For the second setting, I again needed something that would convince me that I was in the story—to help me see the fictional events. To fill this need, I found a real-life source. During my last trip to the Balkans, I had eaten at a restaurant with a strange atmosphere that seemed perfect for this story. The restaurant's specialty was lamb, but the meat was lukewarm and tasted old and lardy. Behind the restaurant there were many sheep bleating in stalls, and you had to pass by them on the way to the restroom. The atmosphere nauseated me slightly as I wondered if I was eating the parents or the kids of these sheep. My salad consisted of onion and tomatoes, but mostly onion. I can easily recall the taste of this meal and the smell of the place. I was sure that bringing my characters to this odd place would intensify the story.

The setting worked, or rather, convinced me to work. I think I doubted the possibility of executing the story until I got the characters eating at adjacent tables, eyeing each other, attempting to talk.

THE NARRATOR'S CHARACTER

As I began writing, I couldn't see what the narrator looked like, but this did not seem to be a big problem. His voice and way of thinking carried me through. Later, I gave him some features (receding hairline, a widow's peak, a possessed look). From his doubting-Thomas attitude to his self-conscious, hunted-and-hunter paranoia, the character evolved for me, or devolved, into a twisted, unreliable narrator who would not be the most pleasant person. He ends up stalking the murdered man's wife. He's obsessed with her. From his angle of vision it may not even appear that he's stalking, but he is, waiting behind the corners for her walks.

I made him into a photographer, partly out of a whim. I know quite a few photographers, and it seems to me there is some professional distortion that occurs in some of them: They hunt for images, and when they are interested in taking pictures of women, there is a predatory aura about them. I can't say that I was trying to ridicule photographers of nudes, but the idea certainly came to me easily from knowing some photographers like that. Once, in Paris, my photographer friend approached a pretty woman to flatter her on her good looks and to ask her to pose for him. She laughed, and when he asked, "What's funny?" she said, "You are the fourth guy in one hour who has used these lines on me. Can't you come up with something better?"

"Oh, no, these are not lines, this is my job," he said. So I made my nameless protagonist use this approach with the widow.

SUPPORTING MATERIALS

In Poland I stayed once with a family who put up foreign tourists for a small sum. Half of their house was a sty with sheep. The host had a nice sheepskin jacket, and I asked him whether he sold these jackets. He said he had none ready, but if I was willing to wait, he'd have one in a couple of hours. Then he pointed toward the live sheep. I declined. But I did use the anecdote in my story. I gave it to the antagonist, Milos, the supposed tormentor from the hospital. Why not let him try to buy the jacket? He's a wolf looking for sheep's clothing; at the same time, he's a sacrificial lamb, since he will be killed by mistake. To create a bit of eerie anticipation, I wrote:

> The waiter aimed the blow dryer at a sheepskin, filling it with air. Rounded like a sail full of wind, the skin gave me a spooky impression that an invisible sheep was beginning to inhabit it.

I played with the image of the jacket and a ghost inhabiting it. Who is going to be sacrificed? This image seemed so central that I decided to use it for the title. I also decided that it should be developed into a motif.

ACTION

I imagined that since my story was set in the context of war, in which a lot of murder had already taken place, it would make sense to include the murder rather than avoid it. Moreover, I had written too many stories in which not enough happened, in which temptations were not triumphant. Yes, I thought, I want as much event out of this as I can get. Let it happen.

However, this struck me as a bit too linear. A guy wants revenge and gets it. Not much of a story. So revenge should be only the first climax, the deceptive one, after which a bigger one should take place. I needed a twist.

Since my protagonist doesn't trust his own perceptions, I could make him doubt that he even killed the right guy. Once I did that, it struck me that I could externalize the possibility rather than limit this doubt to the narrator's perspective. Maybe he did kill the wrong guy. This approach seemed more interesting than his simply killing the right guy, so I went with it, introducing other Milos look-alikes.

THOUGHTS, PARAPHRASES, AND OTHER MIND-WIGGLES

Naturally, since I was writing in the first-person point of view, I had an open invitation to be thoroughly subjective. I could play with the theme of subjectivity, attempting to re-create another ego with his subjectivities and vicissitudes. I could focus on the character's thoughts. The character thinks about communism and post-communism (as I describe under the subheading "Politics" later in this chapter). Then he becomes self-conscious about his thinking, since he is self-conscious about everything. He has a thought, which he can deconstruct, to show himself that it actually isn't a real thought.

To execute this strategy, I went back to an exercise I'd created in *Fiction Writer's Workshop*, my first book of writing instruction. In that exercise I ask the reader to compile a list of proverbs, then substitute the subjects with opposites and near-opposites, as Oscar Wilde often did to create his humorous observations. ("Divorces are made in heaven.") I chose the old saying "Love makes you blind," changing it to "Revenge makes you blind." It didn't strike me as a successful paraphrase, but all the better; I could use it as a source of dissatisfaction for the narrator, for he will always be dissatisfied with something. Now he could expose himself to himself by over-analyzing his way of thinking. He could, with disgust, conclude that his thinking boils down to lame paraphrasing. Although this conclusion fills him with self-loathing, it is in itself a provocative thought. Perhaps all thought is merely variation on old themes with noun or verb substitutes.

MORE SETTINGS

The soil sustains. When I am stuck, I tell myself to add more soil, more setting. For the location of the funeral, where Milos goes to establish whether or not he has killed the right guy, I wanted to use an image of a morgue chapel in Père Lachaise, a cemetery in Paris where I went once to visit the graves of Balzac, Proust, and Chopin. During my visit there was a funeral service in progress, and outside a pale woman in black and red leaned against the wall and cried. Inside there were many wreaths, and the scent of perfume and incense was so intense that as it wafted out, I got a sickening sensation in my stomach. Still I looked in, amazed at the quantity of flowers.

I was seeing and smelling this morgue as I wrote the funeral scene; I simply transported the morgue from Paris to Zagreb, the setting of the second half of my story. "The chapel was small, stuffy with perfume—I detest perfume, as though breathing wasn't hard enough without it!—and too cramped for any Ascension to take place."

IMAGES

For me, images are the most pleasant aspect of story making. They help me stick with the story; they help me see it, experience it, and their power of association suggests many things I could add.

But even more than that, I simply like details. Once I have established a story line, I enjoy coming back to various paragraphs, to extend my way of seeing what's in them; new images work for me as beacons as I try to find my way out of the dark into a clear story.

I make up some details from associations on the spot, and I import others from my previous sketches, failed poems, journal notes, anywhere I can find them. In "Sheepskin," I focused on using visual images, which seemed especially appropriate for a story about a photographer.

Months before beginning the story, while writing a poem I came up with the comparison of train rails to a guitar neck. The poem failed, but as I worked on "Sheepskin," the metaphor came back to me. I added it to the story:

> As a child I had loved the oily smell of rails; it had transformed for me the iron clanking of the gaps in the tracks into a transcontinental guitar with two hammered strings and thousands of sorrowful frets that fell into diminished distances.

The metaphor became part of the narrator's musings as he sits on the train. I thought there would be no harm in bringing the iron clank to the reader's sensory sphere of associations. Furthermore, the image of thousands of sorrowful frets falling into diminished distances fits the theme of recurrence that emerges later as one antagonist gives way to another look-alike.

As I've said many times in this book, these connections and associations are the keys to writing fiction. They are what make the process so exciting—and so difficult to discuss in books or workshops. We can examine each element in turn, each step as it arises, but when we're deeply into the creation of a story or novel, the lines blur. One element folds into another, one image leads to many others.

ECHOING IMAGES

I have often been amazed at the variety of fruits, flowers, and plants that can be used to make tea. When I was growing up, we used several types of wildflowers, but today it seems that almost anything can be used. With this idea in mind, I decided to have the narrator view the fields of vegetation as not only flammable but drinkable. Like a red fox, like fire, in a bush of red tea. During a break from writing the story, I took a hike, and I saw a fox, struck with sunlight in a dark forest, that mesmerized me like an epiphany of wild freedom. I immediately wanted the fox to stay with me somehow, to inhabit my world, and so without hesitation I put this animal into the story. At first, I used it simply as a brief image.

> The color intensity of grasses and beeches in the background gave me a dizziness I could not attribute to my cold. I saw a fox leap out of orange bushes of tea. Of course, it was not tea, but many of these wildflowers would be teas if broken by human hands and dried in the sun. . . .

I used this description in the beginning of the story. Later, while grasping for an image with which to end the story, I kept coming back to the fox, visually, in my mind. I told myself, "You've used that already." But then I thought, "Is that a problem?" No, all the better, I concluded. To use the fox as a recurring image could round off the story. I didn't mean to preach in the end, to bring meanings together so overtly, but I did want to deliver an image with the power to express yearning for freedom and escape.

> I should go back to the western Slavonian fields, and gather wild flowers, bury myself in their scents and colors. Then I would not need to remember and rave on the page from a strange desire to be caught. I would live like a fox in a bush of red tea.

There are many ways of using images. Pairing them up, from one end of the story to the other, can create an echo that spans the distance of a canyon and tells you how far you've come.

POLITICS

Though I made up the events that occur in "Sheepskin," they occur within the context of real-life events, such as the war in Bosnia and the end of communist rule in Eastern Europe. This context gave me a platform for sneaking in general comments and observations about political realities, such as in the following excerpt.

> Not much had changed since communism. I used to think that rudeness was a matter of fixed salaries, no incentive. But here, I was pretty sure the waiter was part-owner of this free enterprise establishment, and he was still rude, and did his best to disgust his customers. And of course customers hadn't changed either. They used to be rude, and I would continue to be rude.

This comment reflects my own opinion (perhaps an overly simplistic one) about the new free-market systems in the former communist countries. At other times in the story, the narrator expresses general opinions that I do not share but that can work for him and the voice. These comments enlarge the scope of the story, adding a public, real-life quality to it.

While I was writing the story, the International War Crimes Tribunal in Den Haage was beginning its judgments on war criminals. I wondered how satisfying the mild sentences from such a distant place would be for the victims of the war. Surely these victims would want a stronger sense of retribution. This feeling helped me to explore the theme of personal revenge. It struck me that if there are five million people injured by the war, and if all of them took revenge into their hands, the real war would begin after the old one was settled. What impossible chaos this would cause! So although I had no political agenda, I did want to comment on the suspect nature of revenge after war. How would you know who was responsible? Could you always identify the soldiers? How would you know that the soldiers were free agents? Perhaps they were forced, perhaps they even practiced restraint and saved the victims to some extent. Each case is different, and conducting a full investigation for every case is impossible.

Writing the story helped me sort out some of my thoughts on the subject, almost like an experiment, so I could see for myself what revenge could look like, and what possible implications there could be in revenge that is highly individualized rather than sociologically abstract.

Fiction allows us to conduct such experiments, to jump into something that passionately concerns us and to live it through the playfulness of imagination rather than through the folly of uncontemplated action. Without fiction, I could be a warrior or a paranoid schizophrenic; instead, I'm someone who plays with words when work and family and forests don't claim me.

Olivia Goldsmith: Putting Women on Top

BY DEE PORTER

Author of seven novels, including *The First Wives Club*, Olivia Goldsmith is credited with creating a new genre W.O.T. (Women On Top). Goldsmith's stories encourage and empower women in an entertaining manner. "The world seems set up so women can't win. But no one acknowledges that. I write about the lies we have been told: if we just dress right, meet the right guy, be 'super woman' or 'super mom' we'll be happy forever. Nonsense! I write to comfort women, to tell them sequentially, perhaps you can 'have it all' but don't kill yourself trying to be that image." In all of Goldsmith's stories, her message comes through clearly: believe in who you are inside as an individual "with all the accompanying defects and dreams" and don't worry that you don't look like Cameron Diaz.

© 1996 Sigrid Estrada

Goldsmith is a bouncy, vivacious woman with soulful dark eyes, a great laugh and an air of comic self-deprecation. She is also a complex, interesting person who loves four-hour hikes, gardening, museums and reading. Her interest in interior design has led her to renovate a 1793 home in Vermont. She hates cooking but is great at "take out." Born in the Bronx, she is the eldest of three sisters. Goldsmith had a conventional New York childhood, went to public school and then attended NYU. After college, she became a marketing consultant for computer companies where she formed an acute distaste for the American corporate culture, a distaste that runs through all her work.

Using what she knew about marketing, Goldsmith says she did everything she could to market herself and her first book, *The First Wives Club*. When the publishers wished she could be "more glitzy" for the "women's market" she donned a blond wig and spiked heels for media interviews. "I always thought I wrote social satire," she says. "But they tried to sell my novels as sex and shopping novels."

A large part of Goldsmith's success is that she treats writing as a business with all its disciplines. As a former marketing consultant, she knows that one must fill the needs and desires of the audience—the readers—before her own as a writer. She covers important issues for women,

---

DEE PORTER *has been involved in a variety of creative interests which include writing nonfiction, fiction and screenplays. She is the co-author of* Gangs, A Handbook for Community Awareness *(Facts On File). She interviewed Jack Canfield for the* 1999 Writer's Market.

balancing serious topics with humor. "The themes of my stories are often very bitter pills. I have to coat these pills with as much humor as I can, to make them easy to swallow. I write about heart-breaking subjects; I couldn't bear it if I couldn't add humor to my stories."

When asked about her writing background, she replies, "I was always good at essays in school but didn't even consider fiction writing until I was in my thirties. At that point, I was deeply dissatisfied with my life. My marriage had failed, and though I was very successful in business I was very unhappy with my work. I just could not find any meaning. I loved reading and I thought about chucking it all and trying to write a novel. But then I had to get over the 'who do I think I am to assume I could be a writer?' scenario. I gave myself three years to write a book." She lived on her savings and stayed at her sister's unheated guest house in East Hampton, because her former husband had control of their summer home. "I was the only woman I knew who lost the house, the apartment and the car. Adversity had worn me down, yet at the same time made me stronger."

Goldsmith says reading and observing people prepared her for writing. "I've always been interested in what people do and why they do it. I try to balance internal conflict against the action. I know I'm not a lyrical writer. I never even attempted poetry. What I do have is the ability to be a fairly good storyteller. I know how to push the story forward . . . to plot. But it's never easy. I work at it. I am a good craftsperson."

Her book reviews consistently state that "Goldsmith is right on target . . . clearly an insider." She insists she's not an insider but that her research skills are excellent. "One of the things I try to do is to describe or get into a very particular world. Obviously I've never been a New York socialite, as the characters in *The First Wives Club* are. And I never worked on Seventh Avenue as the designer in *Fashionably Late* did. I just do a lot of research. I'm also a good observer and very good listener. Some reviewers give me this mysterious woman image, like I'm really some low-key celebrity writing under a pseudonym."

For *Fashionably Late,* Goldsmith not only interviewed the assistants of many designers, she also watched designing in studios. She watched and then wrote about the creation of fashion as fabric is pinned and fitted onto models. "I'm really proud of my research," she says. To round out her understanding of a particular field, Goldsmith sniffs out what might seem unlikely sources of information. "You get the best dirt by talking to secretaries and gophers. There's a saying, 'no man is a hero to his valet,' and believe me, no one is a saint to his secretary. This fashion idea of women versus their actual perception of themselves, along with the way they are manipulated, absolutely fascinates me."

Goldsmith's characters are so well developed and sympathetic they seem drawn from real people, but that is not usually the case. Occasionally, though, Goldsmith does model a character after a real person. "I was doing a book signing in the Bookstall in Winnetka. It was pouring rain and nobody came. So the store owner [Roberta Rubin] and I sat there and talked about books. I looked at her and thought, 'Yeah, people like her make the book business a worthy place to be.' She became a model for a character in *Bestseller.*"

Before creating her characters, Goldsmith looks for a theme, "a central visual image. Once I understand the theme, then I create characters who are archetypal of the issue I'm describing and exploring. For example, in *The First Wives Club* the theme was discarded wives, women who were good enough to support their husbands through school and raise the family. Once they were 'used' [no longer needed], they were traded in for younger 'trophy wives.' As I envisioned them, my three heroines first coped with the problem [of being traded for younger women] through excesses: one drank too much, one ate too much and the other loved too much. Then I created the archetypal husbands: one who'd always cheated, one who'd stolen, and one who thought he was perfect."

Goldsmith writes to please her audience. "I started off writing a historical novel, but after the first 250 pages I knew there was a problem when I didn't even want to read it! I noticed it wasn't effective to write for myself, but for the imagined pleasure of the reader. I work at jokes and surprises and plot twists. These aren't fun to write. My point is that it can be dangerous to become self absorbed in one's writing. It's difficult to edit and cut out all that 'beautiful prose.' But you can't let yourself be self-indulgent. When you're thinking of writing for the audience, the unnecessary stuff goes. I try to structure 'gifts of surprise' balanced with humor. In *Bestseller* I deliberately did not mention the gender of Alex until the reader really got to know and like this person. Where Alex is at last in bed with Emma there's a surprise for the reader, not for the characters. It wasn't easy; try writing without pronouns for 200 pages."

Goldsmith also uses her marketing skills in creating her books. She studied the existing market and found a special niche. "I always know the ending before I start and then I develop the characters to fit the scenario. A lot of writers say they let their characters explore and create the story. I looked at commercial fiction and noted that while women had changed their roles in society, in the family and in the workplace, the novels hadn't reflected that. Ten years ago, women's fiction was not about the real problems today's women deal with. I thought I could do commercial fiction about real women that both entertained and presented a point of view. But what was it? It certainly did not fit into the established genre lines such as romance, mystery or suspense. In London they wanted to come up with a name for this niche. They even ran a contest to name the type of book I write. They finally came up with the term W.O.T. (Women on Top)."

Goldsmith's writing process is very structured. "I am a merciless editor. I work on a manuscript from 8 a.m. until 12 noon daily, 7 days a week. Then after lunch I spend about an hour editing the work I've done the day before. My office is very neat, but while working I often have piles of chapters, research and notes organized on the floor. I love the end of writing a book, because I get to throw away all the notes and old drafts. Filled trash bags signal the finish to a project."

While Goldsmith is very successful today, it wasn't always that way. She has had a lot of obstacles to overcome. *The First Wives Club* was created out of a combination of factors: her horror at her own bad marriage; the fact that many of the corporate CEOs she'd met confided in her—to her disgust—about their affairs. "I developed a real understanding of these lonely guys who are raping the earth." But the book was seen as too harsh. Editors hated it. *The First Wives Club* was rejected 27 times.

But, perseverance paid off—big time. Goldsmith had just returned from New England and was about to quit writing when Hollywood called to tell her that three producers, all women, were bidding over her manuscript. "These three powerful women producers fighting over my manuscript and it wasn't even published!" The three were Dawn Steel, Sherry Lansing and Paula Weinstein. The agent asked her, "Which one do you think shares your vision most closely?" Goldsmith replied: "The one whose check clears first." It was Sherry Lansing, then an independent producer at Paramount, who offered an extra $50,000. "I think she realized how strapped I was," says Goldsmith. Suddenly with a movie deal in the works, publishers were eager to see her manuscript. The book made *The New York Times* bestseller list and has been translated into 31 languages. Six years after the publication of *The First Wives Club*, the movie finally came out. The rest is history.

Each subsequent Goldsmith book has its own unique theme, but with the same basic message:

- In *Fashionably Late*, Goldsmith skewers the fashion industry and its marketing wiles, which prey on the insecurities of women (while exploiting female design talent).
- *Flavor of the Month* came from a remark made by a 60-year-old, heavy-set lady who told Goldsmith she "just wished she looked like Julia Roberts. I felt so sorry for her, for all of us." The book is all about female images and non-existent perfection. *Flavor of the Month* examines the cult of beauty in Hollywood, with the central character as a gifted but unattractive actress who completely remodels herself through plastic surgery to become a movie star.
- *Bestseller* came from Goldsmith's own experience with the publishing world. In *Bestseller*, she wanted to get across the anxiety of a struggling writer, "the worry about how to pay the damn bills." Goldsmith tweaks the world of publishing with an insider's story about five would-

be bestselling novelists who are in what she calls "a horse race for the bestseller list." In conjunction with the book, HarperCollins sponsored a contest for unpublished authors. Out of the top five manuscripts submitted to the competition, one was picked for publication.

- *Marrying Mom* is a novel about a family's efforts to marry off the busybody septuagenarian heroine of the tale so she will be too preoccupied to interfere in her children's lives. "When my mother was thinking of moving to New York, I thought, 'what if?' and expanded it. I wanted to do something about how aging takes women off the dating market. These desperate children decide to have their mother meet Mr. Perfect and get married."
- In *Switcheroo*, Goldsmith explores what she calls " 'the John Derek Syndrome': you notice how each one of his wives was a younger 'lookalike' version of the former one?" In *Switcheroo*, when wife number one finds out there's a mistress, she's not only hurt and angry but astounded when she meets her younger double; it's like looking in the mirror ten years earlier. She talks the mistress into changing places for a while so both women can experience what they're not getting. "All wives want romance; all girlfriends want security. Women are crazy, too."

That most of Goldsmith's books have been optioned for movies is no accident. One reason her novels work so well as films is the way she writes them. "I like to write the story almost as a screenplay format first, because that format focuses on the character, dialogue and action. It makes a great outline."

Goldsmith's advice for new writers with their sights on Hollywood is practical. "Take the money, be grateful, and have a good lawyer. Most of the rest isn't up to you." There's a great difference between screenplays and novels. In the novel the writer has complete control; with the screenplay the writer has very little. "I look at the screenplay as an adoptive child: make sure it has a good home and get on with your next project."

Goldsmith's advice for novel writers is to persevere. "At first it was hard for me to sit in an office chair staring at a blank page for even 20 minutes—there was always something else that needed doing. I had to work my way up to the four hours. It wasn't easy." To be more productive, Goldsmith advises to "Edit as you go. Split the day between creating and analyzing, two different skills. Edit something from the previous day. That way you don't have to do such a heavy edit at the end of 200 pages."

Just as she does, Goldsmith advises writers to keep reading. "Some people refuse to read another author's material for fear of picking up their style. I found my own style wasn't influenced by this factor. Reading feeds me."

What does Goldsmith consider to be her greatest success? "Seeing my book on a store bookshelf; seeing the advertising for my books on the walls of the London subway and being reviewed in *The New York Times*." As for personal achievements, she says, "I'm proud I've been able to present a more balanced image of women. And I consider it a personal triumph to have 50- to 70-year-old heroines."

It's important to note, too, that even when Goldsmith finally succeeded in her own career, she was surprised to find that other hurdles lay ahead. She likens this part of herself to Susann Baker Edmonds, the aging women's fiction writer in *Bestseller*, who feels the pressure of being unable to live up to each of her previous successes. "I know what the pressure is like now, and I went to see a psychiatrist—really. After about three sessions he laughed and said, 'Oh, I see. You thought when you were successful, things got better, instead of more complicated with harder problems.' The guy was right. I don't have one less problem than I had before—they're just different. Success has its own demons. Its hard to keep things simple. Sometimes I think I'd really like to be a grocery store bagger, where you can think and observe whatever you want as long as you remember to put the bread on the top."

Although Goldsmith truly loves being a writer, if she had to do it all over again, there are a few things she'd do differently. "I'd make sure all of my original titles were used. *Fashionably Late* was originally *Designer Genes*. And let's see . . . I'd also be taller, thinner, more glamorous." She laughs. "Of course, I'm joking about the last part."

Learning by Doing: Arthur Golden's *Memoirs of a Geisha*

BY JOANNE MILLER

Arthur Golden taught himself to write. At the age of 25, he set a goal to become a fiction writer, and in the 15 years since, has researched and practiced the art of writing. Much of this time, he concentrated almost entirely on one project, a novel about the life of a Japanese geisha. After meticulous research and two complete revisions of his original manuscript, *Memoirs of a Geisha* was published by Alfred A. Knopf. It became an international sensation within weeks. The story spans 60 years in the life of Sayuri, who is sold as a child by her impoverished father, becomes a celebrated geisha, then chooses to spend her final years in America. *Memoirs of a Geisha* remained on *The New York Times* Bestseller List for more than six months. *Kirkus Reviews* called it ". . . an auspicious, unusual debut." Golden, a Boston-based father of two, accomplished a tour-de-force using the first person voice. *The Washington Post* commented, "Sayuri's voice never falters—it is, to the end, utterly consistent. *Memoirs of a Geisha* is a breathtaking performance twice over, once by its bewitching central figure, and once by the masterful puppeteer who has given her life."

Credit: © Jerry Bauer

Learning to write

Though Arthur Golden studied creative writing in graduate school, he says, "My true learning began much earlier when I set out to become a really good writer. That meant understanding what writing was about." Golden, who describes himself as being "of an analytical turn of mind," broke the study of writing into separate components and began haunting the library, reading every book on writing he could find. He instinctively dismissed advice that didn't work for him, such as learning about dialogue by eavesdropping on real-life conversations. "Dialogue between people talking and dialogue on the page have nothing to do with each other," he says.

JOANNE MILLER *interviewed Isabel Allende and Ron Carlson for the* 1998 Novel & Short Story Writer's Market, *and is the author of* Pennsylvania Handbook, *a comprehensive guide to the beauty, history and attractions of the Keystone State.*

Four or five years passed before Golden felt he understood some of the elements he studied. The concept of structure proved difficult: "Structure is much more than plot. *Remains of the Day*, which was narrated by the butler, could have been told chronologically, from his earliest days in service to the end. Though still an interesting tale, it wasn't the story the author wanted to tell. By structuring the story in a non-chronological way—by having the butler choose what he would and wouldn't tell—and the way it's told, the reader is able to understand the narrator's sensibilities. The book is about the butler's denial, not only of his employer's Nazi sympathies, but of what he himself has missed in life. The author structured the book to show a man in denial."

Golden feels that any writer can make great headway by reading and analyzing: "Quite a number of books influenced me: *Great Expectations*, *Lolita*, *Pride and Prejudice*, *Henderson the Rain King*. The significant thing is that I read every book twice. The first time for enjoyment, as a reader, and the second time, as a writer. The second time, you can see the writer's hand, where and how you're being set up." Above all, Golden considers the constant practice of writing the truest and best way to become a good writer.

During the past ten years, Golden has also taught creative writing to adults. "Through teaching, I've learned that writing is seldom about words; it's about what you're trying to create with words. A good story depends as much upon its parts—characters, setting, structure—as upon words. Story gives momentum and meaning to events. If you went to a dinner party and the host did several unusual things throughout the evening—made a toast by smashing a bottle of wine on the radiator, for instance—it might seem like good material for a story. But out of context, this isolated event has no meaning. By contrast, an event that is seemingly less memorable can have bone-chilling significance if you put a story behind it. Suppose the host of the dinner party lets his gaze linger on you a moment longer than it should. Meaningless? Not if you're having an affair with the host's wife."

Though he didn't use an outline for his own work, Golden says, "I always knew where I was headed. I wanted to reveal the world of the geisha, and I had a reasonably good idea of the turns the story would take."

Research

Golden's first version of the book was based on his background (he has a Master's Degree in Japanese history and spent a year editing an English-language magazine in Japan), and considerable research in both Japanese and English printed materials. "I have piles of books—on Japanese food, clothing design, tea ceremony—which I used to spark my imagination. I never just describe something trait by trait; on the page, time has to move: a plate of food is brought to life, say, when someone pokes at it with chopsticks."

After years of work, Golden scrapped his 750-page first draft when he met a geisha, Mineko, who was willing to show him her private world. "The printed material failed me because a novelist needs highly specific information. Where do geishas eat their meals? When do they put on their elaborate make-up? Books give only general information, but a novel lives and dies by the specificity of its detail. That may be why people say, 'Write what you know.' I'd change that to 'Know what you write'."

Pacing

A review in *Newsweek* claimed that *Memoirs* . . . is "full of cliffhangers great and small . . . a novel that refuses to stay shut." Golden says, "Pacing is one of the things I find hardest to teach and to explain. It has to do with keeping the story flowing. In some moments the story flows forward; in others the writer may dwell for a time on material that enriches or deepens the novel's meaning. The reader must always have the feeling of movement."

Creating characters

Birthing a character is a kind of negotiation, Golden says. "A writer must draw on a certain knowledge of people, gathered by observation; but creating a character on the page is more a matter of finding material that works. Initially, you may write something true to the character you have in mind, but when you read it the next day, it's flat. Your second pass may be more compelling, but perhaps it isn't the person you meant to create. Finally, you find a compromise—material that suggests a complex, believable human being while still being close enough to what you set out to achieve. If you want to write vividly, you can't have any way of knowing beforehand exactly what you'll end up with."

For Golden, details create the character, and the challenge for the writer is to find details that are sharp and strongly suggestive. "In the real world, most people wake up pretty much the same way—that won't work on the page. When your character wakes up, what precisely does he or she do—throw the alarm clock across the room, or sleep until the sun falls across his or her face? Try to make certain it isn't something predictable."

Character creation was sometimes challenging for the author. "I struggled with one of my characters, the Chairman. I felt he was something of a father figure for Sayuri. My parents divorced when I was young, and my father died when I was 13. It seemed that when the Chairman was on the page, my imagination died. It was extremely difficult; I fought against it. Each time he appeared on the page, I worked hard to add a little something more, to round him out."

Hatsumomo, the beautiful, arrogant, mean-spirited geisha who makes Sayuri's life difficult, is a finely detailed antagonist. About her, Golden says, "Conflict is fundamental to storytelling, and Hatsumomo serves the function of an obstacle that shows us Sayuri's mettle and how much she's willing to go through to get what she wants. Hatsumomo isn't based on anyone I know, but in my research on Asian culture, there were plenty of examples of older women making younger women's lives miserable. I needed Hatsumomo not just to show certain aspects of the world of geisha, but also to structure the book."

Point of view

For six years, Golden doubted his own ability to cross the "cultural divides" of sex and nationality in order to write *Memoirs* in the first person. What changed his mind? "After the second draft, I realized that I'd produced a dry book; it suddenly dawned on me that using a third-person narrator had kept too great an emotional distance between the reader and the character. I knew the geisha world well enough to assume the voice of the narrator. I love to write dialogue, and a first person narrative is nothing but dialogue. I wanted Sayuri's voice to reflect aspects of her character, chiefly her cleverness. Her cleverness would bring trouble upon her—for example, by bringing her to the attention of Mr. Tanaka, who arranged for her sale as a child, and later to the attention of Hatsumomo, who perceived her as a rival for supremacy in the okiya (geisha house). Once I felt I had created a believable female Japanese voice with an aspect of cleverness, I knew I had it. I'm not sure how I kept the voice consistent; there were certain ways the character would naturally express things and when something felt inconsistent, I cut it."

Some readers were astonished that Golden, a white, American male, successfully portrays a Japanese woman from childhood to middle age. "But that's what writers do—put themselves into other people's lives." He points out the importance of dramatization as a method for "entering" characters, eliciting emotions from the reader, and helping the reader identify with the character. "Describing a feeling in the abstract doesn't work, but creating a situation in which the reader can recall an emotion does work, and emotion is universal. Even though sexes and cultures are different, many experiences are similar enough to create the effect. For instance, I could say, 'Have you ever felt impending failure?' Or I could say, 'Have you ever been up all night, working on an important project that's due at 8 a.m., and you look up, bleary-eyed at the clock, see it's 4 a.m., and realize there's no way you're going to finish in time?' Then you experience the feeling."

Problem solving

Golden has two primary problem-solving methods: "One, I close my eyes and run the scene in my mind, and two, I brainstorm. I use a tape recorder and talk into it, making different suggestions for the solution."

He was continually challenged to find new ways to describe the world of the geisha. "I learned a while back that a scene that takes place in one room is forever associated with that room. So I created many different settings." In one scene, Golden invented a ritual to introduce the reader to geisha make-up. Since he didn't want to give the impression that the ritual was authentic, he limited it to one geisha house.

When working on the structure of *Memoirs*, Golden was faced with finding a new focus for the narrative after it became clear that Sayuri could no longer fulfill her desire to return home. "At times, I felt like a surgeon taking a heart out and trying to transplant it into another patient across the hall," he says. Part of his solution was to bring in a character that fascinated Sayuri, but who would only be accessible to her if she were a top-level geisha.

Golden has a distinctive method for coming up with descriptive metaphors such as this passage, in which Sayuri thinks about the loss of her parents: "Grief is like a window that will open of its own accord. The room goes cold and we can do nothing but shiver. Each time it opens a little less, and a little less. . . ." He says, "I eliminate the universe of things that are not applicable to the way the character would see the problem. In Sayuri's case, she wouldn't use a television-based metaphor; something to do with nature might be more likely. If I don't come up with anything I like that day, I save what I've written and look at it the next day. Something usually sparks my imagination. I do it until I'm sure it's right."

Using a "frame"

Framing Sayuri's story with a translator's introduction solved a lot of technical problems in the story line, Golden says. "When I wrote the book in the third person, the narrator was free to step away and offer interpretation, including bits on cultural background. But how could a geisha who has lived in Kyoto all her life interpret her world for us? So I decided Sayuri would spend the last years of her life in New York, so she would be familiar with American cultural mores, and, as she's being interviewed by a Westerner, she can interpret her story for us."

Golden had another reason for using a translator's preface: "My friend, mystery writer Camilla Crespi, saw the third draft of the manuscript without the translator's introduction. It started with Sayuri talking about her childhood. She asked 'who is this woman?'. She was right; the reader had no context in which to imagine and understand Sayuri. The preface provides that context."

On writing

"My goal is 2,000 words a day, which usually takes about six hours. Of course, starting a new book, chapter, or scene goes more slowly, but I keep hammering away, paragraph after paragraph. With all that material, I'm not afraid to cut. The words are not so precious. Though I don't discard anything, I almost never reuse it; it never fits in anywhere. I only have one ritual, and that's to procrastinate as long as possible. But I'm at work by 10 a.m. every day."

Golden managed to stick with the book during the ten-year gestation because he believed in himself as a writer, and in the material. "I knew I was learning. Over time, I'd developed confidence in my own judgment, and I'd come to regard problems as opportunities."

Arthur Golden's next book is in the planning stages. "I have ideas, a story in mind, but I'm not sure where—or when—to set it. Writing a first novel on speculation is very different from having had a novel published, especially when it has garnered some acclaim. I want to keep in mind what it was like to write *Memoirs* . . . and to shut out the voices of critics so I don't write to them. I'd rather write my next novel addressing my faults as I see them. I'm trying very hard to block all expectations, and write from what I believe."

Does Arthur Golden think anyone can learn to write? "I think there probably is such a thing as literary talent, though I resisted the idea for many years. I had to confess that some of my students just seemed to get it. It made me look at myself. I went back in my files and looked at the early things I had written. I was surprised to see that, though there was a lot for me to learn, the material was basically pretty good. How and why some people develop into good writers is very mysterious. But here's something to keep in mind: there are many different kinds of literary talent, and you don't know what you've got, or how much, until you work very hard to develop it."

Eluding Labels: Ann Beattie on the Evolution of Craft

BY ANNE BOWLING

Credit: © Jimm Roberts

Few authors offer their audiences as detailed a look at the evolution of their writing as has Ann Beattie. With her first publication in *The Atlantic Monthly* and *The New Yorker* in the mid-1970s, Beattie became known as a minimalist wonderchild who, at age 25, found her work published alongside such acknowledged short story masters as John Updike and Donald Barthelme. Since that auspicious beginning, Beattie has gone on to publish six collections of short stories and six novels which show a steady and progressive maturation of her craft.

"The constant evolution of technique and empathic humanity of these new stories make clear that the mature Beattie is even better than the famous Beattie," wrote Andy Solomon in *The Washington Post* of Beattie's most recent collection of short stories, *Park City* (Alfred A. Knopf, 1998). Comprised of eight new stories and many previously published works, *Park City* was hailed by *Publishers Weekly* as "a generous, very welcome volume of stories from one of the most influential masters of the form."

The Beattie myth began in the early '70s when she was working toward a Ph.D. in literature at the University of Connecticut. Her short stories came to the attention of Professor J.D. O'Hara, who "taught me more about writing than I could have imagined learning elsewhere," Beattie says in an interview in *Ploughshares*. "He did it all by writing comments in the margins of my manuscripts . . . I would put a story in his mailbox, and he would return it, usually the next day, in my student teaching assistant mailbox."

O'Hara began shipping Beattie's work off to literary quarterlies, and a couple of short story publications later, he suggested she try *The New Yorker*. An encouraging letter from an editor fortified her through 22 rejections before Beattie's first short story was accepted there, and at age 25 she signed a first-read contract and began a relationship of fairly steady publication. Interestingly, many of her early stories were literally written in a few hours. "I'm kind of amazed, in retrospect, myself," Beattie says.

In 1976, Doubleday simultaneously released her short story collection *Distortions* and her first novel *Chilly Scenes of Winter*. Her spare, unsentimental, almost photographic prose earned

---

ANNE BOWLING *is production editor for* Novel & Short Story Writer's Market *and a Cincinnati-based freelance writer.*

her comparisons with John Cheever, J.D. Salinger and Joseph Heller as a chronicler of a generation—in her case, baby boomers moving aimlessly through the directionless 1970s. Of Beattie's second novel, *Falling in Place*, Richard Locke wrote in *The New York Times Book Review*: "the most impressive American novel this season establishes Ann Beattie not merely as the object of a cult or as an 'interesting' young novelist, but as a prodigiously gifted and developing young writer who has started to come of age."

Despite her early acceptance among literary circles, and the subsequent telling and retelling of her quick rise to recognition, Beattie works hard to separate "Beattie the writer" from "Beattie the myth." While the story is not quite apocryphal, it is close enough to trouble her with its repetition. Of her early stories, which she concedes were written cleanly in rough draft form, she says: "There was absolutely nothing that I pulled out of the typewriter and said 'and now, off to *The New Yorker*.' Interviewers always present it the other way, because it sounds so much more glamorous, like some crazed genius is pulling pages out of her typewriter . . . nothing wasn't revised." Many of her early short stories were rejected, she points out, and of the first novel she wrote, she says: "If someone read me a paragraph from it, I wouldn't recognize it as mine. It never got published, so if I did a lot of things wrong, I don't remember them, mercifully."

Beattie's writing today shows a complexity unknown in her earlier work—she bridges her once-characteristic aloof distances to bring the reader in closer to her characters, and shows her growing mastery of formal and technical concerns. Writes Solomon: "Her later (work) displays a constant growth frustrating to those who want to arrest Beattie in time." Here Beattie discusses her work, her myth, and the way her writing has evolved over the past 25 years.

Andy Solomon's review of *Park City* in *The Washington Post*, in which he calls "the mature Beattie even better than the famous Beattie," must have been gratifying, particularly in light of the fact that you may feel haunted by readers of your early fiction and their expectations of you. How has the process of writing changed for you?

In terms of the actual physical process, the novels are more complex. I don't think it's debatable, whatever its virtues or lack thereof, that *Another You* is a radically different novel than *Chilly Scenes of Winter* in terms of what goes on formally. Obviously that's going to take more doing, more thinking, and a different kind of brain power than writing a novel that is largely dialogue, revealing itself in the minute, present tense. I don't think those things are necessarily liabilities, but it wouldn't be of continuing interest to me to be doing *Chilly Scenes* redux, so I think that one thing is setting yourself different standards.

I think another thing is that when I started publishing I had read for 20 years, and now I've read for 25 years longer. While I'm not reading other people really trying to think what I can appropriate, in number I've read so many different things that in a way it does make you feel like a deer in the headlights—"why go on?" There's so much already that's extremely good. But in another way I think that if I feel as I do that there's so much good stuff going on, that in itself is a very encouraging thing. So while physical energy may have diminished somewhat, intellectually there's a different kind of energy. I plain work less hours than I used to work, but I think it was easier to work a number of hours doing something simpler like *Chilly Scenes*, without the inevitable self-consciousness that comes with a lot of years of writing that you have to try to get rid of. To some extent I think it's just a function of age; in another way I think it's a function of being a better reader, and a more various reader, than I used to be.

And I'm kind of feeling too—and I don't know if it's related to age or not—that things are really wide open. That the test of something is whether you can pull it off. I think probably without meaning to I would have been inhibited by the you-should-nots when I started writing, and I don't think there's anything I should not do now. I understand that some things are going to be problematic going into them, but I wouldn't say categorically any longer that I would think just to avoid them.

You began your writing career as a very distinctive stylist, and as you developed you seem to have broadened your style to incorporate more traditional elements of fiction, such as interior monologue and exploring your characters' pasts. This would seem almost to be the reverse of the usual arc of a writer's development—do you agree, and if so, how do you account for it?

I think it's an interesting point you raise—I hadn't really thought about it quite in those terms, but I guess I would have to grant the point that it would be more conventional to have begun where I've ended, in the present day. I would think that partly I assumed when I was writing those early stories that I was catching a moment in time, but as an older person, and as society has changed, too—I wouldn't call it hubris, I don't think it was ego that made me assume I could catch a moment in time—but I was almost writing the stories as though they were music, as though they were background music to something, and I don't think there's any musical score anymore. It no longer occurs to me that I could or that it would be valid to try to catch a moment in time.

I really think society has changed and I've evolved too, and those very quick kind of close-up shots are no more interesting to me now than they would be to a beginning photographer. When you first have your telephoto lens, you can't resist zooming in on the bird that's all the way across the field. Those things are inherently interesting because you believe in that technique. But then you realize that it's kind of a cheap shot, you know, that's not the only way to get a bird, or even the most revealing way to get a bird. It's just that technology and your proclivity have led you to the telephoto lens. And if you're going to use only the telephoto lens, you're going to be very constrained.

Park City wouldn't have interested me enough to try in rough draft if I had thought "this is something that if I get the telephoto I can get right into focus." Whereas in earlier stories—I would say all the stories in *Distortions*—that's what I was given to do in those days. That's the person I was. It seemed appropriate to the times, but it just doesn't anymore. It seems not the only method, and probably a pretty expedient one. Believe me I don't think I'm the telephoto lens any longer.

Was it a relatively short period of time from when you began writing fiction until you were first published in *The Atlantic Monthly* and *The New Yorker*?

Some people might look at it as a fairly short period, but I wrote only two or three stories a year for a couple of years. And, except for possibly showing one or two of those to personal friends, I didn't really have any kind of an audience, nor was I thinking in terms of submitting. I was thinking in terms of getting better at what I was doing, but I wasn't thinking at all "is this in shape to send to a magazine?" That was the farthest thing from my mind. So over a period of several years, the stories began to come quicker. Say, in the last year or year and a half. And it is true that in number *The New Yorker* accepted either number 21 or 22, I can't remember. But they had been writing to me for more than a year rejecting stories.

Where did you find the tenacity to continue submitting after some 20 rejections from *The New Yorker*?

I was tenacious, but I don't want to say I would just grit my teeth every time I got a rejection, and said "I will prevail." It's hard to really explain the whole atmosphere, but it was something I was doing for fun. If you're playing softball for fun, and you don't hit a home run, the stakes are different than if you're playing for the Red Sox. So if I didn't get a home run, in effect, it really wasn't that devastating. There were individual notes of rejection that, although they may not have meant to be unkind, sort of disillusioned me as to how careful a reading someone had given something. And I was actually published in *The Atlantic Monthly* before I was published in *The New Yorker*, although both of them pretty much recognized my work at the same time—I was sending it at the same time and they were pulling it out of the slush pile at the same time.

Generally, I would say I was not feeling that I was tenacious in terms of pursuing my life's work, because why would you call something that is in effect your hobby something you were tenacious about? That's supposed to not even apply to hobbies, and I really did in the beginning just think of it as my hobby.

How did Professor J.D. O'Hara's mentorship affect your writing? Did he guide and inspire you?

At a loss for a better word, I have to say what we had was a business relationship, not a personal relationship. As I understand the term "mentor," the personal is very much a part of it. It was personal to the extent that he was tremendously kind in extending himself, even though I wasn't his student. It was incredibly generous of him to go out of his way to be nice to a graduate student who was rumored to have talent. It's always inspirational to have someone take you seriously, and when I saw that he was going out of his way—because by implication he took me seriously, he had nothing invested in my succeeding or failing, I wasn't even his student—then I suppose I couldn't say he didn't inspire me in that way. But it was never as though I had a coach saying "come on, you can do it." It was "if you're going to do this, I'm going to take it seriously, and by editorial comments call things to your awareness that you might not think about from an intelligent outside perspective." And that's tremendously helpful.

Whose writing did you admire at the time and why?

I can tell you some of the contemporary writers I read just because I picked up their books—Joyce Carol Oates's book *Them*, which I thought was fabulous, and I was very interested in Reynolds Price's writing, and John Updike, and also Joy Williams and Raymond Carver. In those days Gordon Lish was the fiction editor of *Esquire*, the one magazine that I did subscribe to. And that's where I first saw Carver. I guess what I saw was that these people, in some ways that would be hard to articulate, were just really expressing their own sensibility, and I felt like I could imagine—maybe wrongly—what their personalities were. It seemed like very personal work. Updike's work seemed to be very personal, whether I was right or wrong to this day I don't really know, even though I know Updike now, but it seemed as though you might as well just put your cards on the table. That's the one common denominator I learned from the rather random but enthusiastic reading I did of a small number of people.

Your first novel *Chilly Scenes of Winter* was published simultaneously with your short story collection *Distortions* in 1976. You called this "an extremely unusual marketing technique and probably one that was very smart." How did you pull off that coup?

What happened really was that *The Atlantic Monthly* pulled me out of the slush pile. Subsequently I had lunch with an editor, and when I mentioned to him that I was finishing the manuscript of the novel, he said "why don't you send it to me, and if I like it I'll send it to Atlantic Little Brown." I did that, and he did pass it on to ALB, and in fact they were quite nice. They wrote back and said something to the effect that I was clearly quite talented, although this book wasn't for them, and they actually suggested to me that I get an agent. So that came right from the press, saying "you're very talented and you probably shouldn't just be out there on your own, kid, get yourself an agent." And they sent me a list of names, and I did get an agent.

The first person I approached was willing to represent me. Of course, I wasn't that much of a liability at that point. I probably had a dozen stories out in *The New Yorker*. I didn't know that then, but looking back I know already being published didn't exactly put me in the world's most humble position. So I actually signed with this agent before I met the agent, and subsequently went to New York. That first agent sent the book to several places that expressed interest, but not so much interest that they made an offer. Then she sent it to Doubleday, and I believe Doubleday said "and wouldn't she also have a collection of short stories at this point?," whereupon the agent said "well, wouldn't she?" And I did sign with Doubleday for those first two books.

Some writers regard short stories at least in part as a training ground for novel writing, but you've said you much prefer writing the former to the latter. What is it about short story writing that appeals to you, and do you consider it a more demanding form?

I feel like anything I say would be trying to explain something that is unexplainable, in that I think I have a gift for short story writing. I think my specific gifts, which may be the writing of dialogue, the acute observation of the natural world, etc., are certainly things that are part of all writing. But it seems to me the things that are my strong suit are more easily drawn upon in the short story than in the novel. That's not to say a novel couldn't possibly be as much of an achievement—it's just that in the actual physical writing of a short story, I can play with only my strong suits, whereas in a novel I have to play with other things as well.

Your work has earned you a great deal of high praise, but also a number of detractors. Do you pay attention to critics, and how did you learn to handle them constructively?

That's a really difficult question because it covers so much territory. So much has been written about me I can't categorically say yes or no, I do. Up until the point when *Dara Falcon* was published, I did read whatever was written about me. At some point, either through the publisher or even from my mother seeing something in the newspaper and clipping it out and saying, "Look, dear, this is about you," I used to look at things. But I realized that it was too debilitating for me when I read the reviews of *Dara Falcon*.

It's not that I can't take criticism; it's that so many critics had not realized *Dara Falcon* was written from the point of view of an unreliable narrator—*The Great Gatsby* being the classic example of this. What is Nick Carraway doing there? This is not an omniscient book about somebody named Jay Gatsby. This is really a book about what Nick Carraway, who is representative of a lot of things, thinks about Gatsby. He has a particular personality, and a particular bias. If you were to see Gatsby as Nick sees him it would be a very foolish book, and if you were to see *My Life Starring Dara Falcon*, with the angry, repressed, ironically Dara-esque herself narrator as being a straightforward guide, it would be nonsense. At some point I don't excuse people for being bad readers. If I was too subtle I was my own worst enemy in being so subtle that they were totally hoodwinked. But I don't understand that with *Dara Falcon* any more than I understand thinking there's one universal perspective in *The Great Gatsby* and that Nick Carraway is an extraneous figure. That simply is bad reading. And I think I had kidded myself to some extent that I was getting much more objective readings in the past than I had been. It seems so disheartening to think about who it was out there commenting on books that I just thought this isn't helpful. There came a point after which I couldn't imagine ever again reading anything that was written about me—it stung, not the criticism but its lack of understanding—just because it was written about me. I look at them the same way I look at movie reviews, which is to find out if they liked it or didn't like it without it spoiling the plot.

In writing *Another You*, it seems you faced every writer's nightmare, when you came to the realization 350 pages (and on deadline) into the novel that it wasn't right, and you needed major revisions to 90 percent of the book. How did you come to that realization, and how long did it take to reconcile yourself to that idea and begin anew?

I went on much too long. My intuition is not bad, but here's what happens: at a certain point, you can write prose well. And I was writing prose well. But that doesn't really count for anything.

I've often said that I finally had to admit that the novel was stillborn. There's no absolute gauge of that the way there is in real life. I mean, if a child physically is stillborn, this is measurable. It's not ever really measurable about a stack of paper. But I don't think you can kid yourself. If it looks right, and it's formed right, and it just isn't exceeding itself, if it doesn't seem to have more life rather than less life, I'm sure many writers would say, well, can I revise this? And in my case I thought I'm just going to pull the plug on this and start from scratch. I wasn't pleased, but I didn't think it was the end of the world.

The first draft was radically different from the *Another You* that emerged—it was really just a different book. But 150 pages into the revision, when I was still wondering "how am I going to let the reader know more than the characters know?", I came up with the idea of the device of the letters, which had been two-way letters in the initial book. I suddenly realized they could be one-way letters; they could define some character, rather than my doing it point-blank. And as the recipient of these letters, you could come to understand another character in terms of what sensibility would create these letters. Since the letters are going to be read by the reader, not by the characters, I don't need to use things that are hard to deal with and have them be convincing—like flashbacks, or filling in the past in some cumbersome and more intrusive way. I certainly could have—it's exposition. But it seemed to me the idea of letting something seem to stand on its own and have a kind of life that superseded what the writer was manipulating (although that's manipulated too), you can have the little sort of false facade that those things are real and are interrupting this narrative. And all of them ultimately are artificial, but they can seem to have an immediacy that the larger narrative doesn't have. So as a device to fill in the past, the letters were the one thing that did occur to me to carry over.

I don't think these things are brainstorms, but when you're just completely lost in how to do something, the simplest things can seem an epiphany. I remember writing *Falling in Place*, and much to my surprise having the brother shoot his sister. And I was so distraught about this not for the obvious reasons, but because I just lost a very interesting character. I spent hours—literally hours—wracking my brain, "is this the right action? Yes, it was. Where do we go from here? I can't imagine." And then realizing, just because he shot her doesn't mean she's dead. But really, three hours just to come up with that? I shouldn't be on anybody's emergency rescue team. The intensity of this sometimes stops you from seeing the obvious.

To what extent does what the market will bear affect the choices you make regarding experimentation with style and structure?

The honest answer is that, in effect, the market will bear nothing now. So I might as well do absolutely anything that I want. More even than when I began. For me personally, I consider things so closed down, and I consider the business so bad, that I'd be a fool not to do the most radical thing I could think of. Perversely, it's kind of liberating. I could do without this perspective, but I'm pretty convinced that from where I am, this is a pretty necessary perspective to have.

In what way would you say publishing is closed down?

Personally, I'd say there are fewer markets than when I started writing. Even places like *The New Yorker*, and we don't know anything about the new *New Yorker*, but even the Tina Brown *New Yorker*, didn't necessarily publish fiction in every single issue. I just think in terms of the slots open to all writers, me included, there are less. And a lot of places have turned to what I see as a kind of tokenism. For instance *Esquire*, when Gordon Lish was the fiction editor, I think was finding and publishing some wonderful people. I don't think those people have to be searched for so hard anymore, because I think there are more of them. But what *Esquire* is doing is printing short shorts. The last page of the magazine is a one-page short story, which is a difficult form and so on and so forth, but I think *Esquire* is considering it as a token acknowledgment of fiction. Well, if I write anything longer than what's going to print to a page, there goes *Esquire* (as a market for it). At the same time I think they are better distributed, which is a factor because what you want is an audience. But I think *Ploughshares* is terrific, I think *Salmagundi* is terrific—that's where *Park City* the title story was published. Then there's *Double Take*, which is relatively new and which does publish fiction. But there are not enough of these magazines to pick up the number of people who are good now, who I would really like to see in print.

I've read that you're considering moving out of short stories altogether. Why?
In point of fact, I don't write 'em anymore.

Do you plan to pick it up again in the future?
I don't know—that's why it's a hard thing to say. What I don't like is the feeling that I'm doing something as a private protest—I don't think that's courageous, I think that's asinine. I don't really know psychologically how much my lack of being drawn to writing short stories is because I have assimilated the fact that this is all but impossible in terms of publishing them, or whether it's just a change. I certainly do have a lot more novels under my belt at this point, and they interest me more than they did years ago, because I am more interested by formal concerns. I am more interested in the 11th way of moving through time, and those things are better grappled with in the longer form. So it's hard for me to say. I wish I could answer the question for my own piece of mind, as to whether I just felt personally defeated or whether this is maybe something that's perfectly fine, and I'm telling myself I should be dealing with another form. I don't know the answer. I don't think it should have happened, I can tell you that. And I don't speak for myself, but to writers: I don't feel this should have happened.

Is there a piece of advice you could share with beginning authors, something you know now that you wish you had known then?
Just between you and me, I would think that anything I do know now, I'm glad I didn't know then. But I really do think that, as a writer, nothing is to be gained by justifying yourself or explaining yourself to other people. I wouldn't want that to be misconstrued to mean that I don't think young writers should listen to criticism. I think they should listen a lot to criticism. But I think also that young writers need to know this: there are a lot of people out there who would like to be doing what you're doing, or who delude themselves that they could be doing what you're doing. It's very important for them to think that you're just like them. Well, you're really not, if you've taken the whole year to (write), and they haven't taken the whole year to sit there and write. You're not better or worse, but you're not just like them. You're only alleviating their anxiety, which doesn't help you at all. Why should you care about their anxiety or anyone else's? You're only giving your own resources of energy away if you spend time pointlessly agreeing that you're like nonwriters. You're not.

Rick Bass: Natural Influences, Natural Talent

BY JEFFREY HILLARD

Photo © Graham Baker

As strange as it may sound, Rich Bass's work as a petroleum geologist on Mississippi oil rigs and quarries prepared him for the life of a fiction writer. "I had a gift for smelling out oil. It took a tremendous amount of time—long, late days and nights, but I succeeded here and there," Bass says. The same can be said for the writing career that eventually flourished—Bass's instincts, dedication and talent have certainly brought him several literary lucky strikes.

Bass's discovery of the world of fiction was initially daunting—he wondered if he could write stories of the sort he loved to read. He was, however, no stranger to publishing. He had witnessed, in the mid-1980s, the publication of two slim collections of personal essays on his Texas youth: *The Deer Pasture* and *Wild to the Heart*. Yet he hesitated to jump into fiction—especially with no formal training in the craft itself. "At first I thought it might be foolish to even try," he says. He soon realized, though, that penning early drafts of short stories provided an adventure he'd never before imagined could exist.

In the late 1980s, after nearly four years on oil fields, Bass accepted a recommendation by a clerk at Lemuria Bookstore in Jackson to read a novel that would unexpectedly transpose his life as full-time geologist to full-time writer. The book was Jim Harrison's classic *Legends of the Fall*. "It changed my life forever," Bass says. "I was no longer hesitant." He had devoured books during those years, but, he says, "It was that title novella's huge landscape, span of time, and embattled family that captivated me. I read it straight through twice in a row. Then I picked up my pen and couldn't stop writing."

Nearly 12 years later, Bass's steady output has resulted in a collection of short stories (*The Watch & Other Stories*, W.W. Norton & Co.); two collections of novellas (*Platte River*, Ballantine; and *The Sky, The Stars, The Wilderness*, Houghton Mifflin); and his first full-length novel, *Where the Sea Used to Be* (Houghton Mifflin), published last year. His award-winning work has positioned Bass among writers "who can bring the wilderness back alive and pin it to the page," wrote a reviewer for *The New York Times*. In a starred review of the new novel, *Publishers Weekly* noted Bass "employs lyrical prose that conveys both the beauty of nature and how its complex, unpredictable ecosystems can be easily destroyed by humans."

JEFFREY HILLARD *has published a volume of poetry,* Pieces of Fernald, *and teaches writing at the College of Mount St. Joseph in Cincinnati, Ohio.*

Bass's first few stories appeared in magazines such as *The Paris Review* and *Mississippi Review*, and soon after, he and his wife packed their belongings and two dogs in a pick-up truck and headed west. They had no agenda but to stop when a place and landscape suited them. He knew the northern Rockies from his undergraduate years as a student in wildlife science at Utah State University. Bass cruised all the way to Yaak, Montana, a remote valley near the Montana-Idaho-Canadian border. There he found work caretaking a ranch in a region where telephones and electricity were sparse. "I knew I could write here," he says of the Yaak Valley, where he still lives today. "It went right with my rather anti-city-life temperament. We were after remoteness, and there was hardly anything here except wildlife." The single wood stove that heated a drafty one-bedroom house appealed to Bass and his wife, and the fact that the house, built in 1903, was the oldest in the valley thrilled them. After all, they could look out a plate glass window and see bald eagles, deer, moose, and in winter, otters at play on pond ice.

And Bass could write every day, all day. The pace, in fact, was so slow in Yaak that he "practiced looking around at things—constantly," he says. To this day, when he isn't writing, he hikes, camps, or hunts during season. Observing, he says, lets him collect imaginative fodder for his stories. Bass's compulsion for writing inspired him to experiment with different genres: fiction, journalism, memoir writing. After his memoir, *Oil Notes*, was published in 1989, his first short story collection, *The Watch*, soon appeared. The pace of living in Yaak may have been slow, but Bass's artistic pace surged. He landed a highly respectable agent; his output was prodigious. By 1991, his stories landed in several anthologies, and he published regularly in two of the most widely-respected literary magazines, *The Paris Review* and the now-defunct *The Quarterly*. His books garnered reviews in *Time* and *Outside* magazines, and he contributed articles to major magazines. His skills as a fiction writer, according to some magazines, were comparable to those of Harrison, Barry Hannah, Joy Williams and Eudora Welty—writers, ironically, whose books he fell in love with while living in Mississippi.

But Bass proved he had great range, too. In 1993, he published *The Ninemile Wolves*, a journalistic account of his time spent researching wolf behavior with wolf biologists. The book helped influence a grassroots campaign to relocate wolves in the western U.S. It thrust Bass into a national spotlight and compelled his nonfiction readers to seek out his fiction. But to Bass, fiction has always been most important. "The fiction is where I can always let loose and let a story unwind. I never have a plan for a story. I just start with a moment, an instance in my mind. I don't worry about where it will take me. That's why I don't view many of my stories as having plots per se," he says. "Although my stories frame specific moments or characters, several strands of action tend to weave through a story. I look forward to getting lost in a story. Being lost is OK. It just takes your imagination deeper into a place it really wants to go. If you're a writer, you'll know when it's time to resurface."

It wasn't until writing *Platte River*—his first of two published volumes of novellas—that certain stylistic and narrative flourishes became recognizable to both Bass and his reading public. His characters, for instance, possess a stunning ability to survive outdoors (often in the wildest places in the country), have tremendous athletic prowess, or have larger-than-life appetites for living. Yet these zealous, flamboyant traits are suffused with tenderness and compassion as the story progresses. Bass's short stories and novellas often feature characters as desperate outsiders, who either embrace or battle wanderlust, and eventually to encounter a moment so human and evocative that it shakes their belief systems. *The Chicago Tribune* has described his stories as having "every hallmark of the natural writer—that lucid, free-flowing, particularly American talent whose voice we can hear in Twain, Fitzgerald, and Hemingway."

As one may not expect with stories that depict wilderness, Bass is often more at home rendering larger-than-life female characters. "I don't really find it a challenge," he says. "I find it natural. Male or female, we all crave similar things. My imagination just takes a turn to imbue female characters with as much life as my male characters might have."

Bass never predetermines the length of a short story. It all depends upon where the characters and narrative take him. He explains that this is part of his struggle in creating a story, and a methodology he won't try to change. "If the story insists upon a lot of length, I'm happy with the novella. If not, then it's a short story," he says. He can also fathom when his subject matter beckons to be shaped into a personal essay and when it becomes fiction. Like his fiction, he doesn't impose any narrative conditions on his essays, because to him both forms tell a story. "Except with the essay it's more the case that I might be asking the reader to affect some change, to consider what I'm writing about, although I'm also painting a picture," he says. "With the fiction, I don't expect anything. I just discover the story myself."

Bass's readers know it is difficult to predict what he'll publish next. Between 1991 and 1998, he published eight books, four of which were fiction, including his second collection of novellas, *The Sky, the Stars, the Wilderness.* One nonfiction book, *The Lost Grizzlies*, chronicled Bass's search for evidence of the last remaining grizzly bears in Colorado's San Juan Mountains. All of the books were written in Yaak, although he was on the road "a tremendous amount of time" researching *The Lost Grizzlies* and covering environmental issues for magazines such as *Audubon*, *Sierra*, *Men's Journal*, *Condé Nast Traveler*, *Outside*, and *Sports Afield*.

In those years, too, his wife Elizabeth gave birth to their two daughters. After years of struggling as a writer, residuals from book sales and major journalism assignments allowed them to build a home in the Yaak Valley in 1995. That year, Bass also received the James Jones Society First Novel Fellowship Award for his then work-in-progress, *Where the Sea Used to Be*, a novel he in fact started back in Mississippi and labored on for nearly 15 years, before it was finally published in 1998.

Where the Sea Used to Be is the novel that Bass planned to finish long before 1998. It's the novel, he says, that tore at his psyche week after week for years, plaguing him through "thousands of pages and endless drafts" before it became the story that it most wanted to be. This novel, for Bass, is the pinnacle of his career thus far, because it proved to him that he could write a novel. It was a complicated, decade-consuming project that saw many characters and events come and go. It also proved that his prevalent themes—the natural world, survival and love—could be interwoven. When the short stories were firing up in his imagination and pouring out with little difficulty, his novel stymied him to an extent that he questioned his skills as a storyteller. "I kept thinking, 'I'm writing miserably on this novel; I'm a wash-out as a novelist. What should I do?' " But, as his characters typically do in his stories, Bass persevered. He battled the expanse of a seemingly endless project, and won. He got several deadlines postponed in order to write the novel "the way it wanted to be told."

Bass regards his concentration toward his work as unflagging, which is the attitude he has carried out into his recent life as environmental activist for the preservation of the valley in which he lives. Since 1993, he and others in Yaak have waged a major effort to prevent vast timber industry clear-cutting in the Yaak. The reason for so much cutting, Bass says, is because the Yaak region is not protected nationally. He's produced "many, many hundreds of letters and memos" to people around the country—to congressmen, the vice president, and president—culminating in a tireless campaign which has certainly cut into his time for fiction, he says.

But the effort has been marginally successful. Bass says it must continue; there is much of the natural world to save. "If it weren't for all the supporters here and around the country, I might not be living here now," he says. "The letter-writing is rigid, of course, but strangely I try to tell the story about the Yaak even in an attempt to ask people for support." He rarely signs books or guest lectures without mentioning the now-widespread effort to save the Yaak Valley. If his readers or audience are willing, they can write a two-sentence letter pleading, "Please protect the last roadless cores in Yaak Valley, Montana, as wilderness," he says. "That's verbatim, too."

Bass plans to live in Yaak for the rest of his life. He plans to write there, as he's done so successfully the last ten years, for a long time to come. Since he's learned to listen to the woods and the landscape around him, and articulate stories to us of a strange natural world he knows very intimately, Bass is hungry to launch a new novel, to "lose himself once again,'' he says, in a story that will lead him to some other discovery, to something he knows is waiting for him deep in his imagination.

ADVICE FOR WRITERS FROM RICK BASS

What do you know now that you wish you'd known when you first started writing fiction while searching for oil?

I wish I had the time to furiously study the crafting process of the novel: how a novel is shaped, how to give a balance of attention toward characters, narrative, and perhaps pacing. It took me 15 years to learn how to write a novel. I'm not sorry about the way I learned to write stories, although my early apprenticeship might have been more interesting if I'd had a course or two in novel writing as a whole. At Utah State, I never had the opportunity to take a creative writing class per se. Also, I knew the importance of reading, but I would say I wish I'd known how to ''study'' stories back then, what made them tick, why the writer did this or that to get the story to work. The notion of ''studying writing'' is so important to the serious student of writing.

What advice would you share with a good friend trying to break into publishing today?

Never compromise your ideals, desires, or vision for your own personal fiction. Never reduce it to a lower common denominator. That doesn't mean you don't make necessary editorial adjustments in the work; it means you stick with your true desire and to the question of why you want to write that particular story in the first place. Strive very high, which means it may take a very long time to get a piece of fiction right. And the more reading you do, the more it will positively impact your own writing.

Editor & Ally: A Conversation with Simon & Schuster's Chuck Adams

BY KELLY MILNER HALLS

As an editor of works by Mary Higgins Clark and a whole stable of equally prestigious authors, Chuck Adams, Simon & Schuster vice president, undoubtedly spends many a book party night knee deep in glitz and glamour.

His day job is an entirely different story.

"Most of my days begin with meetings," Adams says. "Editorial meetings. Marketing meetings. Book jacket meetings. Sales meetings. I meet with authors. I meet with agents. I meet with people from movie studios. I meet with other editors. I meet with the press. I meet with colleagues in my office. I meet with them on the phone. In fact we're on the phone all the time."

As the first round of schmoozing winds down and the phone receiver lands warm in its cradle, Adams tackles an ominous load of internal paperwork. "For every book I buy," he says, "I write a tip sheet—an explanation of what the book is, and why it's so great, four or five key sales points, a synopsis of the book, catalog copy, and flap copy. I don't write the press releases for each book, but I do read them. I have to be sure the person that wrote the release actually read the book."

With one or two breaks for coffee and a working lunch thrown in for good measure, Adams at last turns to what every editor loves and fears most—the latest batch of editorial submissions. "After all," he says, "it's our responsibility as editors to bring in the next big book." Adams approaches every submission hopefully. "Whenever I pick up a manuscript, I want to say yes," he says. "I'm always optimistic. But it's easier to say no."

Why? "Simple," he says. "There are many, many people who want to write, but few who really have something to say. You've got to have something to say, if you hope to find an audience. You've got to find a way to reach them. And you've got to find a hook."

Finding a manuscript with a distinctive voice and that hypnotic hook isn't easy. Adams's assistant first reviews the slush pile, then passes those works with promise on to her boss. Of the few he actually sees, maybe ten percent will receive serious consideration. "Remember,"

KELLY MILNER HALLS *has been a full-time professional writer for almost a decade. Her work has been featured in the* Atlanta Journal Constitution, Chicago Tribune, Denver Post, Fort Worth Star-Telegram, Writer's Digest *magazine and numerous children's magazines. She has been a contributing editor at* Dinosaurus Magazine, the Dino Times. *Her first book* Dino Trekking *was a 1996 American Booksellers 'Pick of the List' science book.*

Adams says, "the way this business works, the editors are the ones on the firing line. I've got to convince my publisher your book will be read."

Adams and most editors are pulling for the writer. But he's borne witness to a disturbing trend. "I get a sense that there is an antagonism between the editor and writer," he says. "I recently went to a conference and stumbled on a 'hate editors' session. I felt like I was going to get stoned before I got out of there. But we need you, and you need us. To succeed, we have to work together.

"There is no science to this," Adams admits. "We're just hoping we bring in the right things. But we're always willing to take chances on projects if they strike us emotionally. So that's what you should be trying to do. You should be trying to strike a chord with an editor, trying to make them respond." Because, he says, if the editor responds, it's very likely the reader will too.

"And that," Adams says, "is what it's all about."

Novel & Short Story Writer's Market caught up with Chuck Adams at the Writer's Roundtable Conference in Richardson, Texas, where he was a keynote speaker. Who is Chuck Adams? And what makes him one of the best? Read on to find out.

Is there a common error you see in submissions that cross your desk?

Most common is the writer not being clear himself about what he's going to write. Too many writers feel they should want to write "the bestseller." They're so intent on reaching the greatest number of people, they think they're going to write for everybody. So their book becomes something we can't sell to anybody.

What everybody forgets, and what we sometimes forget in New York, is that Danielle Steel is Danielle Steel. She sells to one group of people. Mary Higgins Clark is another bestseller, and she sells to another group of people. Jackie Collins is also a bestseller, and she sells to yet another group of people. There is some overlap in all of them, but each has a different kind of audience. There are many different audiences out there for bestselling authors.

Do bestselling authors write for their audiences, or for themselves?

Well, it's the same thing actually. The good ones are writing books they really believe in, books they really want to write, and it finds the audience. That's a real success.

How can struggling writers avoid that pitfall?

The most important thing is to be honest, write from the heart, write with passion, write with integrity. Writers who read Danielle Steel and say, "I can write that crap" are going to write crap. They're going to write down to the reader, because they're not writing with any integrity. They've got to be honest. The reader will know.

I was talking with a lady who was writing a children's book, which unfortunately I have no expertise in. But my sense of her writing and my sense of kids is that kids don't like to be treated like kids. And she was writing to kids. You have to write simply to adults if you want to reach kids.

And the fact is, you can't write down to anybody. They know when you do. I see writers who feel superior to their material, superior to their readers. They figure, "I'll make money," and some of them do. But it's short lived, if they do. Readers know.

How do you and co-editor Michael Korda help writers like Mary Higgins Clark stay fresh?

Mary's ideas are her own. We work with her more on a technical level. We talk through plot points and her characters. She knows her audience. She knows what her audience wants. I fine tune, help put the polish in the writing.

Is that your goal with all new writers you edit? To eventually work them up to the same standard Mary Higgins Clark sets?

Usually, there are two distinct talents. Being able to write well and being able to tell a story are not the same talent. Being able to tell a story is more important in terms of commercial fiction. I can usually look at somebody's writing, and if they have energy and they're telling a story—whether it's wonderful prose or not—that's somebody I'm going to be interested in. Because you cannot edit energy into someone's work and you cannot teach storytelling. You can help teach people how to structure things, but they have to come up with the ideas.

Do you think writers are born, rather than made?

I believe so, really. Same thing with editors. God knows, there is no school for editors out there. We learn by the seat of our pants. I think I have a talent for editing certain things. There are other things I'd be terrible at, certain kinds of books I couldn't begin to touch. So there are different kinds of editors, different talents involved. But it's all talent of one kind or another.

Is a new writer's darkest sin not doing his homework? Spending too little time on research?

Probably so, yeah, although I also have a complaint with people who do too much research. It's like how an actor works. He may try to prepare for a part by going back and creating a history for that character. He may want to know what his character's childhood was like, what he did in school, how he got where he is. And all that background comes through in the performance. But it's never said. It's not portrayed on the screen.

Writers need to do research, build a character's history, but the reader doesn't need or want to read it all. If you write the book well enough, all your research will show . . . it'll come through, the same way it does for the actor, whether you're writing fiction or nonfiction.

Do you approach editing fiction and nonfiction differently?

Well, that's one thing that's somewhat unique about me. I approach everything as if it were fiction, which can be a problem–which is why I'm not good at editing certain kinds of books.

I'm always looking for the story. I'm looking for the story line. To me, when you hand a reader the opening page of your book or manuscript, you're handing them the end of a rope. They're going to move, step by step, following this rope, all the way through the book. If you break the rope, the reader is lost. That applies to fiction or nonfiction.

Can you give us an example of a nonfiction book that's followed that format?

Well, I can give you an example where we did a really bad job. It was a book called *No Regrets*, a biography of Marietta Tree. I did not buy this book— I inherited it because the original editor had a conflict. It was reassigned to me and that was probably a mistake, because my instinct is always to bring out the story.

I encouraged the author to treat it like a novel, and she did. But she was criticized by book reviewers for putting words into the characters' mouths. This was a biography, but I still wanted to entertain; it was a great story. We wound up with some great scenes, but the critics were right. The approach was a mistake.

Can you tell us about a nonfiction success story?

Kitty Dukakis. I edited her autobiography years ago. Jane V. Scovall, the co-writer, did a good job because her ego didn't come through. She became the person she was talking to. But it wasn't an easy job. Kitty tended to ramble, so I got a *very* thick manuscript. She had written paragraphs about every hairdresser she'd ever had. So I had to find the story, I had to carve out whole sections and say, "Kitty, I know you want to talk about your aunt and how great she is, but it's your story, not your aunt's story."

Do you consider editing an art form in itself?

Yes, I do. I think it's a distinct talent.

How did you get your editorial start?

I have always been a pretty good writer. I got good grades on things I knew nothing about just because I could express myself well—I was able to b.s. my way through things. In college, because I had taken a typing course in high school rather than a study hall, I knew how to type, and that was rare.

So some of the guys in the dorm would ask, "Will you type my paper for me?" I charged them 50 cents a page to type it. If they wanted me to correct the spelling, punctuation and grammar, I would charge 75 cents a page. And if they wanted me to rewrite it so it actually made sense, it would be $1 a page. I began to realize I had a talent for it, because they started getting better grades. But I didn't plan to go into publishing. I had a law degree, so I was going to go into law.

It was the Vietnam era, and I was going to go into officers' candidate school. I had already committed to four years. But I didn't pass the physical examination, which was surprising. It was like somebody had given me back four years. I had already started working on Wall Street as a lawyer and I was really unhappy with it. I realized I could make a living at it, but I wasn't cut out for it, so I was going to be a lousy lawyer and miserable. So I just decided to start all over again.

Has your background in law been helpful?

The law training has actually been good, yes. They don't teach you law, they teach you how to think a certain way—how to analyze, how to tear things apart and put them back together again. So yes, it's been very helpful. It's taught me to never take anything at face value—to always take things apart and put them back together again.

For you, what background and qualities would the perfect author have?

It's hard to say with background. But it helps if someone has a sense of humor and a sense of fun. That doesn't mean they should be writing funny, but they can see the absurdity of life, the quirks people have and how to use them and adapt them into their work. Mary Higgins Clark is a good example. She does that well. Barbara Hall, author of *Close to Home*, is the same, except she looks on the dark side.

Is entertainment the bottom line?

For me, as an editor, I guess it is. I think the most important thing is to get people to pick up a book and read. I mean, Harlequin romances are great. They're not art, but they're great because people are reading them. I'm not trying to inform, so I guess entertainment is what I'm really geared to.

What's next for you?

I'd like to do some writing myself. I'm actually co-ghosting a novel with an editor at Random House. Our names will not be on it, but we're writing it together for another company because they had someone under contract who couldn't write it.

How does it feel to be on the other side of the editorial process?

Well, it's interesting because I will write something that I think is perfectly fine, then the person I'm ghosting for will say, "I don't like what the character does here." So I go back and rewrite it. I don't always agree, but she's right. I'm not writing for myself, I'm writing for her. She's got to be happy with it.

Would you like to do it for yourself someday?

I'd like to, yes. But I haven't figured out what I want to write yet. I've got lots of ideas. If I were going to write anything now, I'd probably try to write about New York in the '60s and early '70s when I first came here. I've always been fascinated with what draws people to a place like New York, with how some people survive and some don't. It's the old "best of everything, boys and girls together" kind of book. They are wonderful books and nobody's writing them anymore, so I'd like to try to fill that niche.

First Bylines

BY CHANTELLE BENTLEY

How does a writer become a published author? Does it require the perfect cover letter, an exquisitely written synopsis, knowing the right people, attending the right schools or workshops? Each of these elements can help further you down the path toward publication, but only one thing will get you published—a well-written, interesting story.

Following are four very interesting stories about four very different writers and how they each achieved what seems to be the most difficult task a writer can face—getting a first novel or short story published.

MARISA KANTOR STARK
Bring Us the Old People, *Coffee House Press*

Photo credit: Michael Patten

Since the age of ten, Marisa Kantor Stark has kept a diary. Now in her twenties, Stark chronicles life through her imaginative detailing of the lives of others. "People and experiences in my life trigger my imagination. I find myself working my way into my character's head and emotions—almost melding with the character—until it's hard for me to distinguish between the real life person and the person I have created. Then, I write from there."

Stark's use of corporeal images to coax her musings have served her well—especially as she began volunteering at a Jewish nursing home near Princeton University where she studied creative writing. "There I met one of the most remarkable people I have ever known. A tiny vibrant woman . . . a fighter in every sense of the word, who possessed a great inner strength that I came to admire more and more as I got to know her better." This woman told Stark of her life in Europe, of her experiences during World War II, of relocating to America, and of living her final days in a nursing home. "It was clear to me she had a story to tell, and I wanted to hear it. I used to rush home from our meetings to jot down notes about things she had said. Her voice and her story slowly took over my mind. I knew I had to write this novel."

This fictionalized version of the woman's story became Stark's thesis for her creative writing program at Princeton. Working one-on-one with her mentor Russell Banks (whose works include *Cloudsplitter*, *The Sweet Hereafter: A Novel* and *Continental Drift*, all published by HarperCollins), Stark developed the thesis into the novel *Bring Us the Old People*.

Banks was so taken with Stark's novel that he gave it to his agent, Diana Finch of the Ellen Levine Literary Agency, after Stark's graduation in fall 1995. Although the Ellen Levine Agency does not take a large percentage of new writers, Finch agreed to represent Stark on Banks's recommendation. Together, Finch and Stark made changes to the manuscript. Then, Finch began the process of getting Stark's name and work out to various publishing houses.

Bring Us the Old People attracted the attention of Coffee House Press, a small nonprofit publisher based in Minneapolis, Minnesota. In July of 1997, Coffee House accepted Stark's manuscript. She says, "I had no idea what to expect, if there would be huge cuts or big changes.

CHANTELLE BENTLEY *is the editor of* Poet's Market.

But, in my case, it wasn't like that at all—only a few suggestions to change a word here and there." A little over a year after acceptance, *Bring Us the Old People* was published.

Coffee House handled most of the promotion for *Bring Us the Old People*, which was the top book for its Fall 1998 season. The publisher scheduled readings for Stark in New York City (where she resides), Boston, Minneapolis and Chicago. With all this personal attention, Stark is pleased by her book's placement at a smaller house. "I think, for a first novel, going with a small press was really good. I received a lot of publicity which I don't think I would have received at a larger house."

During the time between her book's acceptance and publication, Stark began attending the graduate program for creative writing at Boston University and, while there, completed a second novel. Her mentor at Boston University was novelist Leslie Epstein (*Pandaemonium*, St. Martin's Press; and *King of the Jews*, W.W. Norton & Company). Epstein gave Stark the encouragement she needed to stay focused and keep writing even when she doubted her work's worth. "All of a sudden I'd fall into modes of self-hating where I'd decided all my writing was junk and I'd wasted the last seven months. Those are the times when he [Epstein] would be standing there saying, 'This is great.' Sometimes you need that, if the person really believes in your work. I mean, I don't want someone telling me my work's great if it's junk. But, assuming it's a person whose opinion you can trust, it's good to have someone who can keep you on your feet."

However, Stark doesn't think that particular someone can be found only in a writing program. In fact, she doesn't believe taking writing classes at a university or attending workshops can create writers. "If you don't have it in you, a thousand writing programs cannot teach you how to write. I knew how to write a novel from years and years of reading. Personally, I don't believe in learning to write a novel. I don't believe you can go down to the local Barnes & Noble bookstore and buy the $9.95 book on how to write a mystery novel and sit down and write one. Although I know people do it, and maybe it works for them, but maybe those aren't the best novels.

"To me, the best books are written by people who have it in them to write and who are just writing from within themselves. This doesn't mean they will sit down and write the perfect novel on the first try. They'll sit down and write what comes from them, and then they'll have to figure out how to refine it. The most useful thing, outside yourself, is finding one person you can really trust to help you. It's good to have an outsider look at your work just to get another perspective on things. Because, sometimes, you become completely immersed in what you're doing and are too close to see all the nuances."

With one novel in print, another completed and under consideration with her agent, Stark has moved on to other projects. Recently, she has written two plays (one which was produced at a summer theater in Vermont), two children's books and, currently, is working on a poetry collection. Stark says, "I do plan to write another novel, but I don't have any specific plans right now. At some point, I would also like to teach creative writing at a university—one or two classes, nothing heavy. I don't want a career in teaching; I want my career to be writing."

Stark admits that without her connections, publishing *Bring Us the Old People* would have been a lot harder. "Not because I believe the quality of my book would be any different, but just because it's a lot harder to get people to sit up and pay attention when you are a new writer. So, for people who have no contacts or no idea where to start, the small presses who accept unagented submissions are the best places to begin. These presses are often looking for the hidden talent in the undiscovered writer.

"My main advice in terms of writing is to just hang in there. That's the hard thing, and I don't have a formula for how to do it. I just know you have to believe in yourself and believe your writing is good and keep writing. I write because it's something in myself that I need others to see. There is something very upsetting about writing and then putting it in a drawer."

LORELLA MASCOT
"Night Drive," *Black Petals*

Author Lorella Mascot's interests have always crept along the edge of darkness. "As a kid, I wanted to be an actress. I used to dress as the grim reaper with a black velvet robe and white skeleton makeup. I really got into that."

Now, with a teenage son and a full-time job at a hotel in Las Vegas, Mascot acts out her imagination on the page. "To me, everyday life is pretty humdrum. I get bored with the same routine—going to work, coming home, having dinner, washing dishes. Writing horror stories is exciting. It enables me to go into another world."

Playing on fears and phobias is another exciting aspect of the horror genre for Mascot. In fact, she says, the more things you are afraid of the better for your writing. "I've been scared of many things since childhood. You know the old saying 'Write what you know.' Well, I believe in writing what most disturbs me. If I can get into something that really scares me then the story should deeply affect the reader."

Drawn to horror fiction by stories from authors like Ray Bradbury, Mascot began, in 1993, to explore the writing process through reference books on fiction writing. One of her first purchases was the book *How to Create Short Fiction* by Damon Knight. "I've always been attracted to short stories and that book really made me want to write. So, I just started writing. But after a year, I felt I was missing something. I thought, 'If I really want to do this, maybe I should take a class.' " Unable to physically attend a college or community writing class, Mascot began looking into correspondence writing schools. She selected the Washington D.C.-based NRI School of Writing.

In late 1995, with her NRI coursework completed, Mascot began submitting her work. "I was steadily sending out stories but nobody took anything. I think my heart wasn't 100 percent into publishing my work at the time. I had all this negative stuff going on—getting divorced, living in a place where there wasn't privacy or quiet. Although I know you aren't supposed to take rejection personally, I became overwhelmed." Mascot took a break from writing while she put her life back in order.

After working through her negative karma, Mascot and her son moved into their own apartment in February of 1998. By April, she again started to feel the writing bug's bite. "I was on my way to work one morning and I had this thought in my head, 'Why are you sitting around not doing anything? You really should be writing.' " Mascot began thinking about all the story ideas she still had tucked away. "I decided if I was going to try writing again, I was going to do it all the way."

Mascot unpacked her reference books, set up her computer and settled back into her role as writer. While preparing her writing space, Mascot became angry over all the time she had wasted. But instead of being debilitated by the anger, she used it to motivate herself. "I said to myself, 'Well, I'm a little bit behind now so I better get going.' "

To brush up her writing skills, Mascot began reworking the stories that had been rejected nearly two years earlier. Then, on June 24, she sent the revised story "Night Drive" to the Wisconsin-based horror/fantasy zine *Black Petals*. "On Friday, July 3, I went to the mailbox and saw the SASE I'd sent with the submission. I knew it was a yes or no. I walked around the mailroom shaking and sweating and saying, "Please, God, let this be a yes. Finally, I opened it up and it was a yes!"

Along with the acceptance, the editor of *Black Petals*, D.M. Yorton, suggested a number of changes for the manuscript. Mascot says, "Even though there were ten pages of corrections, I was thrilled they were interested. I sat right down that evening to work on them, finishing in two nights. I learned so much from those suggestions. I really needed the instruction." Mascot even took notes so she wouldn't repeat the errors on her next story. Then, with corrections in place, Mascot returned the manuscript. "Night Drive" was scheduled for publication in the April 1999 issue of *Black Petals*.

Having ironed out some of the wrinkles in her writing style, Mascot submitted her second story to *Black Petals*, a short fiction piece titled "The Halloween Man." This time the piece was accepted without any suggested revisions. Since then, Mascot has had two more stories accepted for publication. "Crawl by Night" will appear in the March 1999 issue of *Dark Starr*, a horror/sci-fi/mystery/occult zine published in California, and "Candlelight" is scheduled for publication in the new horror zine *Monster Mush*.

Always up for a challenge, Mascot plans on completing a short story collection manuscript within the next three years. "All I can do right now is take one day at a time, using each day to further my writing. I want every story to be better than the last—more gripping, more emotional. It's a challenge against yourself and a focus I really believe you need. It's like walking on a tightrope. Don't let anyone push you off. If you want to be on that tightrope bad enough, you're going to hold on."

JUNE SPENCE
Missing Women and Others, *Riverhead Books*

Photo credit: © 1997 Robin Foster

Through richly detailed, absorbing stories, June Spence relates the lives of ordinary men and women in such a way that you wish to place your own life story in her hands to see what beauty becomes of it. This ability to evoke an emotional connection with her readers has brought Spence publication in such notable magazines as *The Crescent Review*, *The Oxford American*, *Puerto Del Sol*, *Seventeen* and *The Southern Review*.

Success did not happen overnight or without hard work, however. In 1994, while completing the MFA program at Bowling Green State University, Spence's first publication came when the short story *Isabelle & Violet* was included in the July issue of *Seventeen*. After graduation, Spence continued to write, submit, and publish short stories as she worked for a publishing house in northwest Ohio producing industry newsletters and PR publications. "I learned very quickly, however, that was not what I wanted to do," says Spence. "Because, when you come home after generating copy all day, you don't have anything left for your own work." Spence quit and returned to her hometown of Raleigh, North Carolina. She then used her technical writing experience to secure freelance work in writing and editing.

While still working at the Ohio-based publishing house, Spence had amassed enough short stories to collect into a book-length manuscript. But rather than compete with all the other would-be authors and published writers for the attention of agents and editors through regular submission channels, she decided to submit the manuscript to first-book competitions. "These contests are a forum for unknown writers because they are looking to discover new talent. Where else are you going to be read with that in mind?"

The manuscript constantly underwent changes—exchanging old stories for new ones—as Spence submitted it to approximately 12 different first-book competitions. All the competitions were sponsored by reputable, long-standing small presses with reasonable entry fees and prizes that included publication. One version of the manuscript caught the eye of Leonard Michaels, judge for the 1995 Willa Cather Fiction Award offered by Helicon Nine Editions.

With her winning manuscript scheduled to be published by Helicon Nine the following summer, Michaels offered Spence an even greater opportunity—the possibility of being read by a larger house. "Leonard Michaels was very good about taking me under his wing and getting my manuscript read. Getting published seems to require that," says Spence. "I don't think moving and shaking and knowing all the right people is the way. First, I don't know how to do that and, second, I think you would spend all your time finagling and no time writing. However, I do think it helps to have a writer who knows a lot of editors and a lot of other writers, people to whom you can say, 'Hey, I want you to take a look at this manuscript.' Just to get read by an agent or editor, you have to have something that distinguishes your work from the rest of the slush pile."

Helicon Nine was also very supportive of Michaels's suggestion. "If they had wanted to, they could have said, 'The grounds are you submitted to us. You won the contest. We get first dibs on the manuscript.' But instead they said, 'That's the kind of thing we hope will happen as a result of our competition. It's a way to get new writers out there. If Leonard Michaels scores a larger press, that would be a wonderful thing for you and a good thing for us, too.' "

With Michaels's direction, Spence began sending sample stories to editors and agents. Almost immediately, Cindy Spiegel at Riverhead Books, a member of Penguin Putnam Inc., showed an interest and began speaking with Spence in earnest about publishing the collection. Besides Michaels's recommendation, Spiegel was impressed with the publication credits Spence had collected on her own. "The credits confirmed for Spiegel that others, in addition to Michaels, had thought my work was good enough to take a chance on. It all bolsters the effort."

But before a deal could be secured, Spiegel suggested Spence obtain an agent. She was referred to Nicole Aragi at Watkins Loomis Agency, Inc. (Junot Diaz's agent for the instantly successful short story collection *Drown*, also published by Riverhead Books.) By early 1996, a contract was signed.

But with no specific date as to when the manuscript would be placed on the production calendar, Spence viewed her collection with an eye toward possible improvements. "I wanted to include some new material and cut a couple of the older, weaker stories. Then, Cindy and I rethought the order of the stories and their connections to each other and how they would appear. Cindy was wonderful about flagging problem areas and asking questions. I ended up feeling that nothing underwent any major change, but that it was all better for having been carefully rethought."

Spence and Spiegel casually edited the short story collection over the course of a year and a half. Then, in the fall of 1997, Riverhead placed the book on the production schedule. With this, Spence needed to select a name for the collection. She says, "By the time that fall rolled around, the story 'Missing Women,' which first appeared in *The Southern Review*, had been selected for inclusion in the 1997 volume of *The Best American Short Stories*. So, partly for that reason and because I liked what it suggested about the rest of the book, the title became *Missing Women and Others*."

With a press run of 17,500 copies, *Missing Women and Others* hit the desks of reviewers and the shelves of bookstores in July 1998. Right away, the book received some very fortunate attention. First, it was selected for Barnes & Noble's Discover New Writers Series, placing it in a special display in Barnes & Noble stores nationwide. Then, the collection was favorably reviewed by both *Publishers Weekly* and *The New York Times*.

Nevertheless, Spence and Riverhead were both realistic about the potential success for *Missing Women and Others*. "I don't have giant expectations for how well a short story collection can do, because I think a collection can do well and still not end up on a bestseller list or rake in the royalties." Spence says Riverhead's expectations were reassuring. "They seemed to be willing to make an investment on what I could accomplish beyond the first book."

With that in mind, Spence has begun tackling a new form. She says, "Riverhead has optioned my next book and we've sort of agreed it would be a novel. In about a year, they want to see what I have done. So I hope to have a nice chunk of manuscript, at least part of a good draft, to hand over to my editor."

Both Spence's agent and editor agree there is no formula for how long it's supposed to take to write a novel. "Some people crank out a novel a year, some take seven years. I don't know what it's going to take for me. Frankly, I'm a slow producer. Also, it's my first attempt at a novel so I don't know exactly what I'm doing. I have a strong feeling, however, that you just have to write one to learn how to do it, to find out if it's going to be worth a damn. Then, if it isn't, you can throw that manuscript away and go back and write another."

JOHN EARLY
Flesh and Metal, *Carroll & Graf Publishers, Inc.*

Anne Lennox Photography

While driving the deserted roads of his home state of South Dakota, author John Early cultivated the seed of a story. "I remember very clearly being at the intersection of two highways; one of those South Dakota places where there just isn't anybody around. While sitting at the stop sign I thought, 'If an accident occurred at this intersection there likely wouldn't be any witnesses or survivors. The people coming to investigate could really make anything they wanted out of it, create any kind of accident.' "

The image of that accident bounced around Early's head for 20 years while he worked as an insurance adjuster then shifted to a profession more closely related to his college education—teaching freshman composition at North Dakota State and, later, Moorhead State University in Minnesota.

Toward the end of Early's time as an adjuster, he began writing short stories as a way to work through his negative feelings about the insurance business. Early continued and intensified his writing after he moved to teaching. "I really started writing in earnest then. I started producing quite a few short stories, quite a bit of poetry, and even succeeded in publishing some of them regionally." After a number of years of writing and publishing short fiction and poetry, Early set his sights on writing a novel.

Over the next three years, the seed of the story planted in Early's brain at the deserted South Dakota intersection blossomed into a full-length novel. "Before I wrote this novel, I had written a lot of stories that were more literary in nature. They weren't strongly plot driven. There wasn't tension. There wasn't some central event that caused repercussions." But that changed with *Flesh and Metal*, a crime novel driven by grief, fraud and revenge.

After completing the manuscript, Early searched for an agent to represent the book. "I bought a reference book listing literary agents and went through the whole list. I selected agents that seemed to deal with my kind of book. Then, I sent out packets, ten at a time, with a cover letter, query and synopsis." Early's toughest task in creating the packet was getting the synopsis to match the book stylistically. "You need to identify something unique about your story. For me, it was the book's style. Then, the synopsis needed to reflect that style. I found the synopsis terribly difficult to write."

In total, Early mailed the submission packets to 30 agents. He received a request to see the entire manuscript from Jane Dystel of Jane Dystel Literary Management who, ultimately, agreed to represent Early.

Dystel submitted the manuscript for *Flesh and Metal* to more than 15 publishing houses. The first to show interest in the book was Carroll & Graf Publishers, an independent trade publisher located in New York City. "After Jane called to tell me of their interest in the book, Carroll & Graf's publisher and executive editor, Kent Carroll, called me himself. We spent over an hour talking about the book. During that time, he didn't say one good thing about it. I thought, 'Oh boy, this guy hates my book. There is no way in hell I am ever going to be able to revise it to satisfy him.' "

The conversation continued with Carroll offering observations on the book and asking for Early's opinions on those observations. Early says, "It finally dawned on me that he knew every character in the book. Then I thought, 'Why would this guy take so much time talking to me about my book if he wasn't interested?' I think he wanted to determine if I was somebody they could work with. Perhaps the call was more of a personality check than anything." Early must have passed the personality test because, in March of 1997, Carroll & Graf agreed to publish the book.

The next step for Early was to tackle a list of suggested revisions. The primary suggestion dealt with the novel's beginning. "I started the novel with the main character, Jake Warner, having already experienced the bad things that happen to him in the story. From the first, you see him in a state where he doesn't care about anything. Carroll & Graf objected to that, saying they thought there should be something at the beginning to indicate what Jake had lost, because [without it] the reader won't be interested in what he wants to get back." Early agreed and added almost 30 pages to the beginning. "I had some short stories about Jake that fit right into the story line. So I didn't have any trouble altering the book to fit what they wanted."

From the book's spring acceptance until late summer, Early revised the manuscript. Then, he did another round of revisions from early fall until early winter. He returned the manuscript, with the completed final revisions, to Carroll & Graf just before Christmas of 1997.

Flesh and Metal was published in July of 1998 with a print run of 4,500 copies. Carroll & Graf distributed the book nationally through Barnes & Noble, Crown, Ingram and Waldenbooks; and mailed over 300 review copies. Early spent most of his time that summer producing mailings and trying to schedule as many readings, reviews and book signings as he could.

With the publication of *Flesh and Metal*, Early has learned a lesson about the type of fiction he should be writing. "My aspirations have traditionally been more literary, but maybe that's why my short stories weren't as engaging as they could have been. Plot and tension are my weak areas." Early plans to revisit some of his earlier stories and revise and strengthen them with the style he has developed as a result of writing *Flesh and Metal*.

For new novelists, Early suggests reading the work of others to improve their writing and develop their own voices. "I think reading can teach you a lot about writing. But, ultimately, it's assimilating what you've been taught by other writers and allowing their voices to work on you, to feel them. Then once you feel those voices, your own emerges."

Special Markets

Mystery Editors Speak Out

BY BARBARA KUROFF

The mystery genre remains strong, and even seems to be enjoying a significant resurgence in popularity. In 1997, Houghton Mifflin, publisher of the prestigious annual series *Best American Short Stories*, published its first *The Best American Mystery Stories* and followed up with a 1998 edition. In his Forward to the first edition, series editor Otto Penzler, proprietor of New York's famous Mysterious Bookshop and a former mystery publisher, points out that, along with its popularity, mystery fiction has changed:

> Nowadays, much more is expected of the mystery novel, and even of the short story. We have come to expect the same depth of characterization that we do from general fiction, the same sort of intelligent and/or amusing dialogue, the same door opening to let us into a previously unknown or unexplored world. But we also expect a carefully constructed story line that rewards our close attention with a realistic conclusion that answers all the questions posed along the way. No loose ends in these stories; no unexplained activities.

The sources of stories included in the first *Best American Mystery Stories* support Penzler's assessment that today's good mystery fiction is fine fiction as well. The anthology includes stories first printed in *Alfred Hitchock Mystery Magazine* and *Ellery Queen's Mystery Magazine*. But also appearing is a story written by Joyce Carol Oates and first published in the prestigious "literary" journal STORY, two-time winner of the National Magazine Award for Fiction. Penzler goes on to say that most non-mystery magazines he solicited for stories said they didn't publish mysteries—until he provided his broad definition of a mystery as any story "in which a crime, or the threat of a crime, is central to the theme." And Penzler's definition of crime extends from those threats against an individual to those directed against governments.

The 1998 resurrection of the classic mystery magazine *The Strand* also supports the opinion that the well-written mystery is gaining in popularity. First launched in 1891, *The Strand* published the works of some of the greatest writers of the 20th century: Agatha Christie, Dorothy Sayers, Margery Allingham, W. Somerset Maugham, Graham Greene, P.G. Wodehouse, H.G. Wells, Aldous Huxley and many others. In 1950, economic difficulties in England caused a drop in circulation which forced *The Strand* to cease publication. As with the writers originally published in the magazine, A.F. Gullie, editor of the new *Strand*, wants "mysteries and short stories written in the classic tradition of this century's greatest authors." (See page 332 for the complete listing for *The Strand*).

To get a straight-from-the-editor perspective on what is happening with the mystery genre today, I contacted the following editors for their comments, including tips on how to get your mystery short story or novel published:

- Sara Ann Freed, executive editor, Mysterious Press
- Janet Hutchings, editor, *Ellery Queen's Mystery Magazine*
- Margo Power, editor, *Murderous Intent Mystery Magazine*
- Frederick A. Raborg, Jr., editor, *Amelia Magazine*
- Natalee Rosenstein, vice president/senior executive editor, Berkeley Publishing Group
- Melissa Ann Singer, senior editor, Forge/Tor Books
- David Workman, senior editor, *Cozy Detective Mystery Magazine*
- Carolyn Zagury, RN, president, Vista Publishing, Inc.

How has the market for mystery changed? Or has it?

Singer: It seems to me there are a lot of people interested in reading mysteries, but whether we are still in the middle of a boom or heading for the end of the boom is hard to say. Forge/Tor Books does not have a mystery line as such and tends to judge titles and authors on their individual merits and performance, rather than as part of a larger category list.

Power: It appears [the mystery market] is more open to short stories than it was in the past. As far as short fiction goes, beginning writers have the same chance as established writers of getting published in *Murderous Intent*. A good story is the key. As for novelists, a real advantage I see for the beginner is that he or she doesn't have a "poor" sell-through history, so it's possible someone might take a chance on the new writer. But established writers have name recognition and a following of readers. They will usually continue to publish as long as the sell-through remains positive.

Rosenstein: Mysteries are more popular than ever and there is more competition than ever, with more new titles being published each month. But beginning writers who are willing to take smaller advances have the opportunity to be published. And established writers have name recognition and word-of-mouth working for them.

Workman: The mystery market is larger and growing rapidly, especially in the small press marketplace. Mystery writers today also have the advantages of more small presses, the stability of mystery newsletters, and better communication of information to and among writers.

Freed: The market has changed. Too many books are published and readers are daunted by the number of choices. But beginning writers with no sales history do have an edge. Writers with no sales history are easier to sell to chains than established writers whose recent books did not sell well. Chains buy books based on sales history, not buyers' enthusiasm for a writer.

Zagury: Readers seem to be looking for plots that reflect real life, something they can relate to. We specialize in nurse and allied health professional authors. Today's public has a fascination for mysteries set in health care.

What are the biggest disadvantages for today's beginning and established mystery writers?

Rosenstein: Beginners face stiff competition. They may not be able to stand out in the crowd. Established writers' sales may not justify larger advances, and a poor track record (sales wise) can be difficult to overcome.

Freed: Publishing houses have less patience for "growing" an author. If a series hasn't grown by the third book, its days are numbered.

Singer: Today there is less time than there used to be for an author to establish herself. I remember when it was relatively easy for a publisher to publish six or more novels by a particular writer before expecting that author to break through to a higher level of success or possibly break out of the genre. Now it seems many publishers expect writers to make that jump with only two or three books under their belts. Of course, this is true in many categories, not just mystery.

Power: Beginning writers are having a rough time, as they always have. They need to learn the craft and once they have, they need an agent to get through to the larger publishers. But agents are as difficult to acquire as publishers. And established writers, unless they are really big names, are constantly having to take time from writing to do their own marketing or else stand the risk of being dropped due to low sales.

What are your criteria for deciding to publish a mystery manuscript?

Raborg: We consider plot, conflict, foreshadowing, motif, denouement, professionalism, and, sadly, length. We use up to 5,000 words. Longer, only if the story truly sparkles.

Rosenstein: We look at a manuscript for original voice, a good plot and well-developed characters. We especially look for some kind of "hook" to make a manuscript stand out.

Hutchings: We look for good writing with an interesting, original plot.

Freed: The writing style and subject matter has to hook us from page one. Sometimes, we look for a mystery with a specific theme: food, for example.

Workman: We would accept a manuscript that adheres to our guidelines, is clever, and has a strong story with characters that have heart and soul.

Singer: First of all, a manuscript has to be a good, entertaining book. It should keep a reader guessing right up to the end . . . but if it's the sort of novel where the reader knows right away whodunit (and even why) then the actions of the characters should be compelling enough to keep the reader interested all the way. However, the author should play fair with the reader and make sure all necessary clues are present within the text—the investigator or problem-solver can't possess facts unknown to the reader. The investigator or problem-solver has to have a fair amount of intelligence, and not ignore clues that are incredibly obvious to the reader.

I do tend to look for series potential in the investigating character. I don't like scenes where the villain explains the dastardly plot to the hero(ine). An interesting setting helps make a book appealing—or a new perspective on a familiar setting (the U.S. Senate from the view of the janitor, for instance).

Power: Since I work basically with short stories, I'm looking for good writing, spelling and punctuation, as well as stories that offer something slightly different. I love humor, exotic settings, unforgettable characters and realistic plots along the cozy/soft-boiled lines. And writers should show the story, not tell it.

Where do most mystery manuscripts submitted to you fall short of meeting your criteria for publication?

Raborg: They are too pat or simplistic; too quickly written with little direction. They simply are not interesting, even boring in many cases. Too many are shopworn and dated.

Rosenstein: They lack originality and have weak plotting.

Hutchings: Tired plot, poor writing!

Freed: When characters aren't drawn well, we never get to know them or care about them. We're also let down when an exciting beginning collapses midway through the book because the writer hasn't thought through the crime.

Workman: The writer's lack of formal training: they tell, don't show, or they hurry their endings or leave unanswered questions.

Zagury: Poor plot development and poor character development. Often too many sub-plots do not connect.

Singer: Most of the time, the problem is that within a chapter or two I have figured out the villain and the motive. Usually by the time all the characters are introduced I know where the book is going. To some extent this is because I have read so many mysteries in my personal and professional life, and I've learned to discount this. But I really prefer to get at least halfway through a book before figuring out the puzzle at its core.

The second most common problem occurs in books featuring amateur crime solvers, particularly in their first appearances. Too often they are so naive that they cannot see clues or treachery when it is right in front of them, no matter how obvious these things may be to the reader. Some innocence is nice, of course, when one is first investigating a crime of some kind, but stupidity wears thin very quickly, and the main character should learn from his errors.

Thirdly, many writers seem to have trouble creating a good supporting cast. They have spent so much time and energy inventing their investigator and villain that they forget about things like supporting characters and red herrings. The difficulty here is that in these manuscripts the identity of the villain is made all the more apparent because he is the only well-developed character other then the investigator.

Power: Manuscripts fall short for us when they don't have something slightly different to offer. Or the plots don't work, or the characters just don't come to life. And too often the stories are told rather than shown.

What kinds of mystery are you especially looking for now?

Raborg: We love the Gothic and romantic, but there's nothing wrong with a good "gat and moll" tale either.

Freed: We are looking for intelligent "cozies" with female sleuths.

Hutchings: We look for strong stories *without* graphic violence.

Zagury: Mysteries for us must be healthcare-related.

Singer: This is a difficult question to answer, because at Forge/Tor Books there are several editors buying mysteries, but all in a limited way. We do not have a mystery line, nor do we have a strict requirement of a specific number of mystery titles per month, and we have several ongoing series. In general, we are not looking for cozies or for much in the way of hard-boiled. Other than that, we are open to just about anything—look at writers we are already publishing for a guide. We would rather see proposals than query letters and will accept queries by telephone if you are not sure it's our sort of thing.

What are your best tips for mystery writers wanting to get published today?

Raborg: Read the masters—Christie, Wolfe, Gardner, MacDonald. We have such a wealth of past titles to choose from as examples. But don't copy; try to be unique in clue and denouement. Persist. Develop your narrative and dialogue skills. Read the work you have written to test the dialogue. Act out your plot line to be sure it flows and seems realistic enough that the reader will willingly suspend disbelief. Be professional and neat in presentation. Send fresh copy. Study the stories in several issues of magazines you would like to be published in. Know the machinery of fine fiction, like foreshadowing and motifs.

Rosenstein: Develop a series concept. Work on plotting and characters. Keep writing.

Freed: Write from your heart and never send a book to an agent or editor that you don't think is the best you can write. Study the competition at mystery bookshops and websites.

Workman: Submit, write! Then submit and write some more. Only by writing can you improve your craft.

Hutchings: Write a good story and be original.

Zagury: Grab the readers in the first pages—make them want more. Be persistent and learn from rejection letters in order to improve your manuscript.

Power: Everyone says this, but it's so true: keep on writing and honing your craft. Come up with something different, not bizarre, just a different slant on an old theme. Keep on keeping on. It's tough out there, but never impossible. If the big markets aren't ready for you yet, try the smaller presses.

"First, Be a Storyteller": An Interview with Mary Higgins Clark

BY DEE PORTER

Few writers command the instant name recognition of Mary Higgins Clark. Not unlike Alfred Hitchcock and Agatha Christie, her name has become synonymous with mystery for those who read the genre, and for many of those who don't. But Higgins Clark has traveled a 30-year road to become "America's Queen of Suspense" as the bestselling woman suspense writer in the U.S.

Born and raised in New York, Higgins Clark grew up in an Irish family ("The Irish are, by nature, storytellers," she says). Despite working at an advertising agency and as a flight attendant, getting married and eventually having five children, Higgins Clark says she knew from the time she was a child she wanted to write. "The first thing I wrote was a poem, when I was seven," she says. "It was pretty bad, but my mother thought it was beautiful and made me recite it for everyone who came in. I'm sure the captive audience was ready to shoot me, but that kind of encouragement really nurtures a budding talent.

"Also from the time I was seven, I kept diaries," she says. "I can read them now and look back at what I was like at different ages. I still keep diaries; they are a great help to my novels. No one has seen them—they are locked in a trunk."

Photo credit: Bernard Vidal

Shortly after her marriage, Higgins Clark began writing short stories. Six years and 40 rejection slips later, she sold her first piece in 1956 to *Extension* magazine for $100. "I framed that first letter of acceptance," she recalls. She followed that publication with her first book, a biography of George Washington, *Aspire to the Heavens*, which Higgins Clark recalls "was a commercial disaster and remaindered as it came off the press. But it showed that I could write a book and get it published."

Commercial success waited until after publication of her second novel, *Where Are The Children?* (Simon & Schuster, 1975), the first of a string of 17 bestselling novels, many of which have been made into film for cable and network television. Her books are published in translation

---

DEE PORTER *has been involved in a variety of creative interests which include writing nonfiction, fiction and screenplays. She is the co-author of* Gangs, A Handbook for Community Awareness *(Facts on File). She interviewed Jack Canfield for the 1999 edition of* Writer's Market.

around the world, and in the U.S. alone she has 45 million books in print. Her most recent novels, *You Belong To Me* and *All Through the Night*, were published by Simon & Schuster in 1998. Here Higgins Clark talks about her life and what makes her writing work.

You are known as "America's Queen of Suspense." What do you consider the essence of your talent?

Being a storyteller. Isaac Bashevis Singer, who was a dedicated suspense reader, made a simple but profound observation on receiving the Mystery Writers of America award as Mystery Reader of the Year. He said a writer must think of himself or herself primarily as a storyteller. Every book or story should figuratively begin with the words "once upon a time." It is true now as it was in the long ago days of wandering minstrels, that when these words are uttered, the room becomes quiet, everyone draws close to the fire and the magic begins.

Your books are worldwide bestsellers. Why do your novels have such broad appeal?

Readers identify with my characters. I write about people going about their daily lives, not looking for trouble, who are suddenly plunged into menacing situations.

In one of your 1998 thrillers, *You Belong To Me*, prominent investment banker Regina Clausen falls prey to a serial killer on a luxury cruise. How realistic is this premise?

Women traveling alone are receptive to romance, hoping they'll meet a "special someone." Even successful, sophisticated women can be lured into dangerous, sometimes fatal, relationships.

Also in *You Belong To Me*, a married woman calls a radio call-in program under an alias, saying she had a shipboard romance which might shed light on the case of Regina Clausen. Why did you use a call-in show as a major plot element?

People reveal their most intimate feelings and experiences on TV and radio shows and, as in this novel, their revelations sometimes lead to frightening consequences.

When did you start your writing career?

After I was married, I signed up for a writing course at New York University. There, I got advice from a professor which has always served me well. He said: "Write about what you know. Take a dramatic incident with which you are familiar and go with it." I thought of my experience as a stewardess on the last flight to Czechoslovakia before the Iron Curtain went down, and gave my imagination free rein. "Suppose," I reflected, "the stewardess finds an 18-year-old member of the Czech underground hiding on the plane as it is about to leave?" This, my first story and my first sale, was called "Stowaway."

What early experiences influenced you?

I grew up in the Bronx, where my father was the owner of Higgins Bar and Grille. When I was ten years old, I had a terrible shock. Coming home from early Mass one morning, I found a crowd of neighbors outside the house. My father had died in his sleep. My mother went on to raise me and my two brothers alone. When I had said goodnight to my father, I didn't know it was for the last time. His sudden death jolted me into awareness of the fragility of life. My mother's example taught me resilience. The characters in my books are resilient and resourceful. When calamity strikes, they carry on.

When my father died, our whole existence changed. My mother tried to get a job, but at that time it was practically impossible for women in late middle-age to return to the job market. She took babysitting jobs and, while I was in high school, I worked as a babysitter and switchboard operator. After graduating from high school, I went to secretarial school so I could get a job and help with the family finances.

How did you find time to write books while raising your own five children and holding a job?

When my children were young, I used to get up at 5 a.m. and write at the kitchen table until 7 a.m., when I had to get them ready for school. For me, writing is a need. It's the degree of yearning that separates the real writer from the "would-be's." Those who say, "I'll write when I have time, when the kids are grown up or when I have a quiet place to work," will probably never do it.

After publication of your first book, a biography, what made you turn to the field of mystery and suspense?

I decided to write a book that would, hopefully, outsell *Aspire to the Heavens*. One of the best clues about what to write is what one likes to read. I decided to see if I could write a suspense novel. It was like a prospector stumbling on a vein of gold. I wrote *Where Are The Children?*, my first bestseller and a turning point in my life and career.

What got you started on that book?

In New York, there was a sensational court case in which a beautiful young mother was on trial for murdering her two small children. I didn't write about that case, but asked myself the question: "Suppose your children disappear and you are accused of killing them—and then it happens again?" *Where Are the Children?* is about a woman whose past holds a terrible secret. Nancy Harmon had been found guilty of murdering her two children and only released from prison on a legal technicality. She abandons her old life, changes her appearance and leaves San Francisco to seek tranquility on Cape Cod. Now she has married again, has two more lovely children and a life filled with happiness . . .Until the morning when she looks for her children, finds only a tattered mitten, and knows that the nightmare is beginning again.

How did you sell your first manuscript to Simon & Schuster?

After my first short story sold, a friend showed it to her agent. The agent, Patricia Myrer, phoned and said she wanted to represent me; we were together for the next 30 years. Pat submitted *Where are the Children?* to publishers. Two of them, Doubleday and Harper, turned it down on the basis that women in jeopardy might upset their women readers. Phyllis Grann, now president of Penguin Putnam, Inc., was then an editor at Simon & Schuster. She bought it, and I have been with Simon & Schuster ever since.

Is the suspense market healthy now for new writers trying to break in?

Yes, if they naturally enjoy it, read it and understand it.

Where do you get the ideas for your books?

In *A Stranger Is Watching*, I use the issue of capital punishment from the viewpoints of a victim and an objective observer. It also shows how life and death can hinge on a tiny twist of fate.

***The Cradle Will Fall* deals with women victimized by a ruthless doctor. Is medicine a subject of particular interest to you?**

Yes,, particularly the subject covered in this book, which is medical research in fertility. The so-called "test-tube" baby had just been born. One article predicted that there would soon be surrogate mothers and host mothers. I thought, "suppose a brilliant doctor is experimenting with his patients' lives in his desire to make a breakthrough?" And I was on my way with the book. At the time I wrote this novel, one of my daughters was an assistant prosecutor. She was the source of in-house advice about the legal aspects of this novel.

Stillwatch is set in Washington. What drew you to this milieu?

The 1984 election was coming up. I anticipated the Democrats tapping a woman vice-president and decided to beat them to it. You can imagine my glee when, just as the book was coming out, Walter Mondale chose Geraldine Ferraro as his running mate.

In that book, I deal with two women's relationships to their past—one determined to learn the truth at all costs, and another for whom emergence of the truth will mean the end of her dreams. In creating the setting, I was aided in part by my friend, Francis Humphrey Howard, sister of the late Senator Hubert Humphrey, who introduced me to Washington life.

Weep No More, My Lady takes place in a luxurious spa. Why did you choose this setting for a suspense novel?

It used to be only the rich could afford to go to spas. Today, with the wide-spread interest in health and beauty, there are affordable spas all over the country. An intriguing thought crossed my mind—"suppose a killer in a wet suit is stalking the grounds of one of these spas?"

Incidentally, two people who become ongoing characters for me made their debut in this novel—Alvirah Meehan, the cleaning woman who won the $40 million lottery, and her husband Willy, a plumber. They are central characters in my latest novel *All Through the Night*.

When you first introduced these characters, did you intend that they would appear in later works?

On the contrary—I intended to kill them off in *Weep No More, My Lady*. My daughter, suspense writer Carol Higgins Clark, prevailed on me to keep her alive. Alvirah and Willy are now the protagonists of a series, the first of which was *The Lottery Winner*.

Alvirah and Willy had worked all their lives—she as a cleaning woman and he as a plumber. Winning $40 million in the New York State lottery released Alvirah's sense of adventure to pursue a new career as a *New York Globe* columnist and amateur sleuth, often to the dismay of not only criminals, but also the police. But it never changed Alvirah and Willy's innate wisdom about what really matters in life.

Having reached the pinnacle of success, could you visualize a life of leisure?

No—never. Somebody once said, if you want to be happy for a year, win the lottery. If you want to be happy for a lifetime, love what you do. That's the way it is for me. I love to spin yarns.

What advice would you offer new writers trying to break into fiction writing?

The basic advice is to write. Next, look at your book shelves and see what kinds of books you most enjoy reading—is it romance, science fiction, suspense, historical, biographical? The odds are your talents lie in that direction.

Why Writing the Mystery Appeals to Elizabeth Gunn

BY JEFF CRUMP

Elizabeth Gunn has always considered herself a writer-in-training. Before her first novel, *Triple Play* (Walker & Co.), she spent five years publishing travel and adventure stories in venues from *The New York Times* to the *Anchorage Daily News*, and, being an experienced diver, several boating magazines. Her hard work paid off—she now has a second novel, *Par Four* (Walker & Co.). Set in Minnesota, both mysteries center around Jake Hines, a detective called on to decode bizarre murders. The novels combine baseball and golf, respectively, with midwestern police procedural. *Triple Play* received impressive reviews, yet despite its success, Gunn sees *Par Four* as reaching beyond its predecessor—it's more developed and complicated, funnier, says Gunn.

Gunn's early short stories are still valuable to her. "The experience of seeing a published story, flaws and all, with your name on it for everyone to see, makes you work harder to improve your writing," she says. When she decided to try a novel, she wasn't confident she would find an agent, much less a publisher. Nevertheless, she wrote *Triple Play* in its entirety, wanting to prove to prospective agents that she could finish what she started. She wrote the best novel she could and "hoped it would be enough."

Gunn cites mystery/detective writers Thomas Harris and Agatha Christie as influences, as well as more "literary" figures such as Henry James, Edith Wharton and Joseph Conrad. "They all wrote things that stay in the mind," she says. "I'm interested in all kinds of writing." She reads historical novels, current events and scientific works. She's fascinated by how things work, from world wars and sailboats to fiction and the machinations of mysteries. The appeal of the mystery, as Gunn sees it, is the "romantic, comforting conceit, to pretend that evil is a 'problem' that can be 'solved.' " But there is another reason her first novel is a mystery. "It's obvious that almost all publishers are looking for mysteries." Gunn points to the many houses specializing in her genre: "I felt sure a mystery would be easier to sell than a mainstream novel." The Jake Hines series was clear in her mind, and she considered a mystery to be the "feasible next step" in her development as a writer. *Triple Play* would be a challenge she could only benefit from, whether it got published or not. At the very least, Gunn knew she'd learn a great deal about finding an agent.

Not interested in self-publishing, everything she read told her an agent was a necessity. Gunn attended several writers' workshops, listening to and meeting different agents. Turned down in person by one of them, she opened the *Guide to Literary Agents* (Writer's Digest Books) and began "churning out queries." At one workshop, an agent from New York told her that to be taken seriously, a writer must have a New York agent. Of the 24 queries, the first half were sent to New York. "They sent my stuff right back," she says, "and in the meantime I read about several first-time novelists who had agents from all around the country." Loosening up on geographical requirements, she concentrated on agents who read new writers.

When writing her queries, Gunn remembered another agent who said his goal was a clear desk at the end of each day. Fortunately, selling stories and articles had taught her to keep queries

---

JEFF CRUMP *is an assistant production editor for Betterway, North Light and Writer's Digest Books.*

short. Such precision can be a tall order, but for Gunn, that was the easy part. She simply, and scrupulously, followed the instructions in *Guide to Literary Agents*. She sent only what was asked for: the requisite number of chapters, usually accompanied by an outline or synopsis. According to Gunn, too many writers "flail around and fight the problem too much," while the process is basically, and perhaps deceptively, "paint-by-numbers." Nevertheless, she refers to the submission process as "hell." Within four months from the first mailing, Gunn was engaged in discussions with several agents about *Triple Play.* Kristin Lindstrom of the Lindstrom Literary Group in Arlington, Virginia, was one of them. First, she called to request the rest of the manuscript, then called a few weeks later to say she wanted to represent it. "She was the most positive, organized and together of the people I was talking to," Gunn says. "So I chose her."

Lindstrom didn't ask for any changes to the manuscript, which was fine for Gunn, who was already midway through *Par Four.* On top of preoccupation with her new book, her writing life has always been characterized by movement. Her dual addiction to travel and writing dictates that she is rarely in one place, often writing in boats and RVs—a schedule nonconducive to business dealings. Her fondest wish was to not get involved in the negotiations for *Triple Play*—that was Lindstrom's job. "I trust her to do what's best for us both," says Gunn. "Really, we haven't bothered each other much. I write books; she sells them; we both seem to stay happy." As Gunn reached "critical mass" with *Par Four* (her term for the obsessive stage of novel writing during which she works relentlessly until it's finished), Lindstrom scrutinized the "mercilessly opaque" contracts for *Triple Play*, selling it to Michael Seidman at Walker & Co. Lindstrom also made Seidman aware of the forthcoming sequel. *Triple Play* was sold on its own, but when *Par Four* was finished, Walker & Co. snatched it up. Seidman didn't ask for changes to either one.

During negotiations for *Triple Play*, Lindstrom kept Gunn periodically informed of her progress. For the most part, as Gunn had hoped, the writing and selling of the book were divided enterprises. Promotion, however, was a different story, particularly with *Par Four.* Walker & Co. sent out galleys and review copies for both novels, but for *Par Four*, book signings were scheduled. And now Gunn herself seeks out occasions for reading and signing her work. "I'll go to book clubs or any meeting that wants a speaker," she says. "I had a hard time with this at first; it felt like self-aggrandizement. But I'm learning."

And Gunn never stops learning. For now, she says, "I think exploring the problems confronting heartland police forces is interesting, so I hope to keep the series going," and she thanks friends in Minnesota law enforcement for sharing their knowledge of police work. But most of what goes into her work is lived experience—whether running a business, a family or staying alive on blue-water boats. She is not limiting her literary forecast exclusively to Jake Hines. She wants to publish more travel and nature articles, and "if I eat my vegetables and work hard, eventually a mainstream novel."

What Gunn loves about writing is that nothing goes to waste: "The most demeaning relationships, the most frustrating failures, even the rages and crashes and overdrafts, all end up as grist for the mill. The world becomes an endless line of credit to draw on, and sometimes the worst stuff is the most useful of all." Thanks to Lindstrom's handling, selling her novels won't provide much material. But due to the success of *Triple Play*, Gunn can now write full time, and there is a lot more material to come.

Plotting the Mystery Novel, or Learning to Think Backward

BY JUDITH GREBER

It's said that Whistler, the artist of "Mother" fame, spent a great deal of time pre-envisioning his paintings in such detail that when he mentally "saw" the completed work, he blended his paints into their ultimate hues on his palette. Applying the colors was swiftly done.

Other artists begin with a hazier image from which they draw one or more preliminary sketches, followed by layers of paint, brush stroke by brush stroke, a day's work often scraped off and begun again, changing and adding to the original idea until they get as close as they can to what they now know they want.

The same spectrum of possibilities applies to writing a novel, even one as crafted as a mystery. Plotting, or pre-envisioning, creates a roadmap for the trip ahead. You can either plan your entire route in advance, or proceed knowing only a general direction. Either way, you'll get there.

Some people are Whistlers who prepare outlines that can be hundreds of pages long and are actually first drafts. Others begin with a scrap, and off they go. Their first drafts are exploratory, and they ultimately became long outlines. Some writers can pre-vision to a point, and then, the only way through the murk ahead is by living the story—i.e., writing it and finding a way through. Here are the various approaches of just a few of today's writers:

- **Elizabeth George**'s intricately plotted novels are pre-planned only to about 50 pages of the manuscript. Then she writes and discovers what else is ahead. But before that, she devotes a great deal of preparation time to the characters, and in so doing, sees possibilities in how they might behave.
- **Janet LaPierre** gets as far as she can go on her initial idea and she composes a midpoint outline, a look back at what has happened so far. Then she projects what still has to happen.
- **Shelley Singer** starts her books wherever she has an idea for a scene and continues in every which way and direction until she figures out what connects those scenes.
- **Michael Connelly** knows what the case is going to be and who did it, but from then on, he "wings" it. "I find it's actually the best way to create," he says. "It gives you the most freedom and you enjoy it the most."
- **Tony Hillerman** "gropes" through, able to see "the details that make a plot come to life" only while writing the scene, in the mind of the viewpoint character. But he needs to be familiar with the location of the story, the nature of the crime, and a theme, plus have some idea of one or two characters in addition to the sleuth. Once finished, now knowing where the story has taken him, Hillerman rewrites the first or first few chapters. He says ". . . you don't have to be able to outline a plot if you have a reasonably long life expectancy."
- **P. D. James** spends more than a year planning each book she writes.

JUDITH GREBER *is the author of 13 novels, including 9 mysteries. As Gillian Roberts she writes the Amanda Pepper series, published by Ballantine. She was awarded an Anthony by World Con for her first book in the series; a more recent book was nominated for an Agatha. She teaches creative writing as an adjunct at the University of San Francisco and at the College of Marin. This article is excerpted from* You Can Write a Mystery *copyright © 1999 by Judith Greber. Used with permission of Writer's Digest Books, a division of F&W Publications, Inc. For credit card orders phone toll free 1-800-289-0963.*

- **James Lee Burke** doesn't know what's happening beyond a scene or two.
- **Lia Matera**, author of 13 mystery and suspense novels, says: "If, going in, I know too much of what's going to happen, I lose interest. I need to be in suspense as much as the reader does. As you might imagine, this means a tremendous amount of rewriting. Once I figure everything out . . . many scenes no longer work, my clues aren't in place, the moods and tone are likely to be wrong. It would be far less work to outline, and it would certainly mean less hand wringing and breast beating. But I would lose my juice for the story, so I guess I'm stuck . . . I have to be trapped in a corner, unable to write one more word, before I'll continue the painful process of plotting. I'd like to be an outliner, but I resent them for being so smug about something that's probably genetic."

PRESENTING THE PROBLEM

Beneath all the spins you'll put on it, your basic story is either how the protagonist/sleuth finds/vanquishes the killer or how the proposed victim and/or sleuth prevents the ultimate disaster from happening. So somewhere near the beginning you have to present the problem.

For example's sake, say you're intrigued by a news story about an embezzler. You were awed by his cleverness, appalled by his chutzpa or tempted that somebody in your office is doing the same thing. Doesn't matter. You were emotionally affected. You decided to use his crime as the basis of your mystery. Let your mind wander around possibilities. Where does the murder fit in? Why? How? Who?

Begin with who was killed and why. This "why," the motive, leads you into the backstory—what happened leading up to the murder, the reason for it, which is a great deal of what your sleuth is going to have to uncover.

Now—who? The corpse might be the embezzler, the embezzler's boss, the mailroom clerk who happened upon an incriminating bit of evidence, or somebody who was there to deliver a warrant or flowers or . . .

Or maybe there's no dead body—yet. There need not be one immediately, just a sense of impending danger. But the crime should happen relatively early in the book since it generates much of the action. If you're aiming for suspense—the bad thing that's going to happen—you may think about the crime in a different way. Maybe the embezzler is actually the hapless pawn of someone using his cleverness to destroy the company or wreak revenge on someone. Maybe the embezzler has become our protagonist—trying to break free, go straight, come clean before he's killed—but the noose keeps tightening.

The contemporary puzzle-mystery has by and large adopted the traditional suspense finale and no longer pretends that all the suspects would passively gather in the library to be told which of them committed the crime. The contemporary climactic end-scene will be a direct, generally physical confrontation with the killer.

GETTING FROM A TO Z

Now, to figure out how to get from A to Z—what happens in between the crime and the confrontation with the killer. Alas, that space looms as wide as the Grand Canyon, and worse, you've got to build a bridge across it to where you've planted your conclusion on the other side. Nobody ever said it was easy, just possible. It's also possible that the original spelling of "plotting" was "plodding."

What to do? Consider that crime novels are actually three stories. First, what physically happened. In this case, a dead person in the conference room had a bullet wound. Second, the theory of what happened. The police decide that poor X was the victim of an interrupted robbery. And third, what really happened. That's the story your sleuth will glimpse in bits and pieces, a.k.a. "clues" that shine through the surface veil, those facts that don't neatly dovetail with what supposedly happened.

So that your detective has a serious job ahead of him, think of four other people who, for different reasons, would also appreciate the victim's demise. (His ex-wife who's fatally ill and has come to realize how much money was hidden from her during the divorce. A corrupt off-hours cop who was providing security and also, it appears, a bit of special aid and comfort to the dead man's current wife. A woman who, with good cause, sued him for sexual harassment—and lost. A man hired to ghostwrite his autobiography who gets next to nothing—unless the book's a bestseller, which it might be if its subject died violently.)

Write down these reasons and draw lines to the dead person, connecting them. You've got five suspects now, counting the one you know is guilty. Five ways the crime might have happened. You've also got five aspects of the dead man's life, paths for your sleuth to follow into blind alleys and finally, home. Write bios of those people explaining who they are, why they hated the dead person, why they don't have a clear alibi, or why they behave oddly when informed of the news or questioned by the sleuth. Think about what else in their life they're protecting or hiding that will make them suspicious. I like to have every suspect lie. Most are hiding minor embarrassments, some, real, but non-related offenses, but they all twist the truth to serve their own purposes, and that makes the sleuth's job harder by generating wrong theories and misdirection.

Why isn't this an open and shut case? Or if it seems as if it is—why does your sleuth disagree with that opinion? What's odd about the murder to the sleuth? What is the initial and erroneous theory of what happened and why? Why does the sleuth think this isn't right?

If you aren't writing a police procedural, how does your sleuth come to be involved in this crime and why aren't the police functioning adequately? (This is when you'll envy those who are writing historical mysteries set in the days before there were official police forces.) This is often where what Alfred Hitchcock called "the MacGuffin" comes in. This is an element that gets the story going, often a gimmick that seems to be the issue—missing papers, a Maltese Falcon—but isn't the actual problem that will drive the novel or film. A MacGuffin, a side or secondary issue may pull your amateur sleuth—or PI who isn't allowed to investigate an open homicide—into action. Or it may set the police off in the wrong direction, but all the same, pull them into the actual story. If you use a MacGuffin, be sure its question is also answered, ideally before we get to the solution of the central question.

Is there a way to link the crime into the amateur's job? By virtue of her profession or personal life, does your sleuth know something seemingly unrelated to the crime and only she sees the connection?

Sometimes the amateur is driven to action because she's the prime suspect, but obviously, this can't be used too often if you're planning a series. Which of the suspects might she know or have access to so as to sleuth in some sane fashion? Did something she did or said make it worse for her buddy so that she feels obliged to do penance via sleuthing? Does she work for the embezzler? Date the biographer? Have her hair done at the same salon as the ex-wife?

Or, she might be linked to a bit player who'll provide one significant piece of the puzzle, or a lead toward it—witnesses, friends of friends, informants, gossips who unwittingly know something valuable, e.g., the dead man's fiancée or cleaning woman. ("And Lord knows what a mess his closet was with that shredder in there. No wonder he kept it locked—must have been ashamed of its looking like a big packing crate in there. Had to beg him to clean the place out every three months, and he took off from work so he could stand there watching me the whole time. Peculiar man, rest his soul.")

Figure out how your detective will reach some of the players. Could she possibly be a client of the same cleaning woman as the now-dead embezzler? If so—set it up early. Coincidence is fine to start events rolling, but never to solve the crime. So before you need it, establish that the cleaning lady exists, is late, is switching days with another client—something to make her later appearance feel natural. In fact, everything in your book that will eventually provide a surprise needs to be set up so the reader feels you played fair. Even if he's forgotten what you set up by the time it resurfaces, he'll then remember that you did establish that fact.

Are there links to any of the other suspects that need a preliminary establishing scene or mention? If you have a PI, and local law says PIs cannot investigate open homicide cases, then what permissible work is he doing that leads into this murder? Often his assigned case is something of a MacGuffin—not the real problem at all, but his involvement in it pulls him into something darker and more dangerous.

If it's a police case, what makes it more than run of the mill, of personal meaning to the detective? Next, ask yourself what has to happen in order to set up the above. Can you begin with the sleuth walking in on the dead man in the conference room or are there things we need to know beforehand? Sometimes you need to plant clues before the crime is committed—action or dialogue by the impending victim—something the sleuth doesn't particularly notice at the time, but in context, later, will recall. You might need to set up where your sleuth is before and during the crime so that his arrival at the inauspicious time and his weak alibi makes sense.

You want to introduce all your significant characters fairly early in the book, so think of ways to bring them on stage. This may be obvious, but worth saying: You never want to spring the hitherto unseen villain on the reader at the end. Let your mind float. See what follows 'what ifs.' Ask questions—how did this happen? Why would she be there? What would she do if she were there? Free associate. Don't strain to organize it at this point.

You can make anything happen if you make us believe this person would do that. Think about the character and why he'd behave a certain way. As always, check your reflex actions. If your first thought is that your character would run away from the situation—take a moment to consider whether a different course of action might be equally true but less predictable and more interesting.

What makes certain people suspects? Where were they at the time of the crime? Your sleuth will track down these false leads. For example: Ethel, the sexual harassment plaintiff, now works in another town. In order to time the killing so precisely, she had to know the details of the victim's erratic schedule. How did she know? How'd she get into the office before it was open? How did Ethel, who does not drive and has only one leg, get to the scene of the crime? How will your sleuth find these things out in order to formulate a theory?

A chapter might be built around discovering that Ethel was not where she should be at the time of the crime. (You can arrange these discoveries and scenes beginning with the least revealing and most confusing in order to keep the puzzle spinning.) Or around finding out that Ethel had hired an airport limo that a.m. (How'd the sleuth find that out? Picking through Ethel's trash—another scene? Wait—what made her do that?) However you set it up, we find out that Ethel went to the airport that morning at dawn. We've reached a seeming dead end—Ethel was in the air when the murder happened. Perhaps the sleuth takes a new tack, looks at somebody else with more interest.

Then, elsewhere, another scene built around the discovery that Ethel wasn't carrying luggage when she got into that limo and, from that, discovering that she immediately took a second shuttle from the airport to downtown, one block from the scene of the crime. Motive and opportunity. The sleuth revises the theory again, starts tracking Ethel but guess what? Just as she's about to be declared the murderer, Ethel herself is found dead. The logic of the puzzle changes one more time. And becomes more urgent because it's now obvious that the actual killer is willing to kill again rather than be caught.

Maybe. Or maybe Ethel's death had nothing to do with the other crime and when that's realized, the theory will again be in need of revision.

Eventually, you'll have a list of things that have to happen, each of which will become a scene that provides either a real or imagined clue or frustration as the sleuth hits another brick wall. Each plot point changes the status quo, and as in physics, each action produces a reaction. Something else now needs to be figured out and done.

AVOIDING PLOT CLICHÉS

Throughout, remember that character is destiny and your character is not an idiot. You want drama, but not because of behavior that makes the reader want to shake your sleuth silly. Avoid such plot machinations as having your protagonist agree to meet a suspect on a lonely pier late at night.

While on the subject of plot clichés—avoid the scene where someone tells the sleuth they possess vital information they'll share later. Of course, they'll be dead before a word of it is uttered.

Or the idiotic police force or D.A. Instead, make the officials' inability to solve this based on inadequate methodology or incorrect assumptions, but not plot-convenient denseness or orneriness.

Or the villain who postpones killing the protagonist because he needs to brag about how clever he's been. He hasn't been clever enough to read mysteries and see that during his monologue, our hero's going to figure a way out of this.

Or anything else that you've read and seen too often for it ever to feel new again.

Tell yourself your story often. You'll probably see more details each time. At each juncture, ask "what's the worst thing that could happen here?" and go for it. You'll increase the tension and advance the plot.

SUBPLOTS

You may have been told you need subplots, and indeed, they can enrich your story. But rather than think of them as extra plots you need to create, simply consider what else is going on in the protagonist's life beside foiling an evil-doer. Is he also facing a love, health, family, professional or financial impasse? How might that impact, reflect, enrich or further complicate the main story? What about the other characters? Remember—your story is what happens at the intersection of many people's individual stories. These other issues will come out of your characters and enrich the mix. Resolve these minor, secondary issues before you resolve the main one of guilt and apprehension.

SCENE BY SCENE

Transfer your jumble of doodles, lines, names and ideas to a more manageable medium. Screenwriters use 3×5 cards, putting one scene—one thing that has to happen—per card. Phrase your sentences as actions—"She visits the limo company but they refuse to open their records." If you can, also make note of the purpose of the scene. "She's so mad now, she's not worrying about protecting Ethel anymore, and she decides to go to the police." Such cues will generate action and remind you of motive and cause and effect more than, say, "checks out limo company."

Try to put characters into as many of your scenes as possible, so that you don't always have your solitary sleuth ruminating. Interaction with others is dramatic and provides tension—the sleuth wants information, the person being interviewed doesn't want to or can't provide it. Dialogue is action.

Eventually you'll have a tabletop of cards that will reveal where holes are. Don't worry if it seems scrappy; it's good and necessary to leave room for surprises. But the cards might show that you have your sleuth in two places at once, or arriving at a conclusion that has nothing supporting it or that nothing much happens for a long spell. That last plot problem was supposedly solved by Raymond Chandler by bringing in "a man with a gun." It's not a bad plan. Create action. Up the tension by introducing a new threat—always think in terms of "what's the worst that could happen now?"—or some dramatic change of behavior on the part of your characters.

Play with the order of scenes—take one away, combine the points of two of them into one solid scene, and so forth. If you hit a wall now—or in the writing process—when your character seemingly has become paralyzed and can't function usefully, look back and see if you can change the "given" that's called halt to present action. Does your sleuth really, truly, have to be half of Siamese Twins?

It can be useful to think in terms of stage and screen. Your drama, too, will have three acts. Your first act is roughly the first third of the book. It sets up and presents the crime, establishing the conflict. It also introduces your cast of characters, their relationships, and your setting.

The second "act" is devoted to complications and crises—the great middle-muddle, the sleuthing in a mystery, or further threats and escalating dangers in suspense. Protagonists try and fail and try, try again. In fact, there is almost a "rule of three"—the initial attempt establishes the problem and its difficulty, and nobody succeeds "if at first." If they did, there'd be no story. The second attempt and failure shows that it's a really big problem and not at all easily solved, and the third becomes the real test that breaks the pattern. (A fourth try seems excessive—give your sleuth a break!)

This is true in almost all quest stories and fairy tales. It's a pattern that works.

So theories prove wrong, often by the introduction of a second corpse, most often, the former prime suspect, and we try again. The tension is now sky high. This portion usually comprises the bulk of the book.

The third act eliminates more theories, thereby tying up subplots while it builds to "The Big Scene"—that do-or-die point of no return, the crisis, when the sleuth finally figures it out and confronts the villain, or the suspense protagonist finally meets his demon face-to-face.

And then, a brief coda for closure. This isn't an explanation of what you've already shown, but you can have a page or two giving the reader an idea of what's ahead, or what the events meant to the protagonist. And that's it.

When you write the first draft, no matter how much time and effort you lavished on your outline, parts of it are probably not going to work. New ideas will occur to you as you live the story, and you'll be wise to go with them and say "adios" to your best laid plans. The outline was a roadmap. The writing is the trip and real adventure.

Mystery Markets Appearing in This Book

Below is a list of mystery markets appearing in this edition of *Novel & Short Story Writer's Market*. To find page numbers of particular magazines or book publishing markets, go first to the General Index beginning on page 661 of this book. Then turn to the pages those listings appear on for complete information, including who to contact and how to submit your mystery short story or novel manuscript.

Magazines

Advocate, PKA's Publication
Aguilar Expression, The
Altair
Amelia
Anthology
Armchair Aesthete, The
Art:Mag
Bangtale International
Belletrist Review, The
Black Lily, The
Blast@explode.com
Blue Skunk Companion, The
BookLovers
Boys' Life
Breakfast All Day
Brownstone Review, The
Capers Aweigh
Chat
Chrysalis Reader
Climbing Art, The
Cochran's Corner
Compleat Nurse, The
Cosmopolitan Magazine
Cozy Detective, The
CZ's Magazine
Dagger of the Mind
Dan River Anthology
Dark Starr
Dogwood Tales Magazine
Downstate Story
Dream International/Quarterly
Drinkin' Buddy Magazine, The
Eclectica Magazine
Edge Tales of Suspense, The
Elf: Eclectic Literary Forum
Eureka Literary Magazine
Evansville Review
Expressions
Flying Island, The
Forbidden Donut
Free Focus/Ostentatious Mind
Fugue
Grasslands Review
Green's Magazine
Grit
Hardboiled
Hitchcock Mystery Magazine, Alfred
Indigenous Fiction
Japanophile
Lamplight, The
Lesbian Short Fiction
Lines in the Sand
Lite
Lynx Eye
Medicinal Purposes
Merlyn's Pen
Monthly Independent Tribune Times Journal Post Gazette News Chronicle Bulletin, The
Moose Bound Press
Murderous Intent
Musing Place, The
My Legacy
Mystery Time
New England Writers' Network
New Mystery
New Spy
Northeast Arts Magazine
Northwoods Journal
Oracle Story
Outer Darkness
Palo Alto Review
Pirate Writings
Play the Odds
Poetry Forum Short Stories
Post, The
Potpourri
Prisoners of the Night
PSI
Queen's Mystery Magazine, Ellery
Reader's Break
Rejected Quarterly, The
Screaming Toad Press
Se La Vie Writer's Journal
Seattle Review, The
Short Stuff Magazine for Grown-ups
Skylark
Spring Fantasy
SPSM&H
Storyteller, The
Strand Magazine, The
Street Beat Quarterly

Sunflower Dream, The
"Teak" Roundup
Texas Young Writers' Newsletter
Thema
32 Pages
Threshold, The
Timber Creek Review
Tucumcari Literary Review
Vincent Brothers Review, The
Vintage Northwest
Volcano Quarterly
Vox A
West Wind Review
Woman's World Magazine
Words of Wisdom
Writers' Intl. Forum
Yarns and Such

Book Publishers

Ageless Press
Alexander Books
Arcade Publishing
Artemis Creations Publishing
Avalon Books
Avon Books
Avon Flare Books
Bantam Books
Beggar's Press
Berkley Publishing Group, The
Bookcraft, Inc.
Books In Motion
Camelot Books
Carroll & Graf Publishers, Inc.
Cartwheel Books
Centennial Publications
Chinook Press
Clarion Books
Cumberland House Publishing
Dell Publishing Island
Doubleday Adult Trade
Duckworth Press
Dunne Books, Thomas
Fawcett
Fjord Press
Forge Books
Greycliff Publishing Co.
Gryphon Publications
Harcourt Brace & Company
Harlequin Enterprises, Ltd.
HarperCollins Publishers
HarperPaperbacks
Harvest House Publishers
Holt & Company, Henry
Houghton Mifflin Books for Children
Kaeden Books
Kensington Publishing Corp.
Knopf, Alfred A.
Morrow and Company, Inc., William
Nelson Publishers, Thomas
Peachtree Publishers, Ltd.
Philomel Books
Pocket Books
Presidio Press
Press Gang Publishers
Pride Publications and Imprints
Publishers Syndication, International
Putnam's Sons, G.P.
Random House Children's Publishing
Random House, Inc.
Random House, Inc. Juvenile Books
Russian Hill Press
St. Martin's Press
Seniors Market, The
Severn House Publishers
Soho Press
Stonewall Inn
Story Line Press
Tor Books
Turnstone Press
University of Neveda Press
Van Neste Books
Vista Publishing, Inc.
Walker and Company
Write Way Publishing

LOOKING FOR AN AGENT?

For a list of agents who represent mystery writers, see the Literary Agents Category Index, beginning on page 154.

Resources for Mystery Writers

Below is a list of invaluable resources specifically for mystery writers. For more information on the magazines and organizations listed below, check the General Index and the Publications of Interest and Organizations sections of this book. To order any of the Writer's Digest Books titles or to get a consumer book catalog, call 1-800-289-0963. You may also order Writer's Digest Books selections through Amazon.com or barnesandnoble.com.

MAGAZINES:

- *The Armchair Detective*, P.O. Box 929, Bound Brook NJ 08805-0929
- *Fiction Writer*, 1507 Dana Ave., Cincinnati OH 45207
- *Mystery Readers Journal*, Mystery Readers International, P.O. Box 8116, Berkeley CA 94707
- *Mystery Scene*, Box 669, Cedar Rapids IA 52406-0669
- *Writer's Digest*, 1507 Dana Ave., Cincinnati OH 45207

BOOKS:

Howdunit series (Writer's Digest Books):

- *Missing Persons: A Writer's Guide to Finding the Lost, the Abducted and the Escaped*
- *Murder One: A Writer's Guide to Homicide*
- *Armed and Dangerous: A Writer's Guide to Weapons*
- *Deadly Doses: A Writer's Guide to Poisons*
- *Cause of Death: A Writer's Guide to Death, Murder & Forensic Medicine*
- *Scene of the Crime: A Writer's Guide to Crime Scene Investigation*
- *Private Eyes: A Writer's Guide to Private Investigators*
- *Police Procedural: A Writer's Guide to the Police and How They Work*
- *Modus Operandi: A Writer's Guide to How Criminals Work*
- *Malicious Intent: A Writer's Guide to How Criminals Think*
- *Body Trauma: A Writer's Guide to Wounds and Injuries*
- *Amateur Detectives: A Writer's Guide to How Private Citizens Solve Criminal Cases*
- *Just the Facts, Ma'am: A Writer's Guide to Investigators and Investigation Techniques*
- *Rip-off: A Writer's Guide to Crimes of Deception*

Other Writer's Digest books for mystery writers:

- *How to Write Mysteries*
- *The Writer's Complete Crime Reference Book*
- *Writing the Modern Mystery*
- *Writing Mysteries: A Handbook by the Mystery Writers of America*
- *Writing the Private Eye Novel: A Handbook by the Private Eye Writers of America*

ORGANIZATIONS & ONLINE:

- The Mystery Writers' Forum: http://www.zott.com/mysforum/default.html (See complete listing in the Websites of Interest section of this book.)
- Mystery Writers of America, 17 E. 47th St., 6th Floor, New York NY 10017
- The Private Eye Writers of America, 407 W. Third St., Moorestown NJ 08057
- Sisters in Crime, P.O. Box 442124, Lawrence KS 66044-8933

The Romance Market Today

BY BARBARA KUROFF

The romance market is on the rise, according to the annual market study conducted by the Romance Writers of America (RWA) and reported in the June 1998 *Romance Writers' Report (RWR)*. Compiling information taken from book distributor Ingram's catalog, the *Romance Writers' Report, Romantic Times* magazine and publishers' catalogs, the RWA study announced that 737 more romance fiction titles were released than in their previous year's study (an increase of over 36%). Of the 2,757 romance novel releases, there were 1,466 contemporary, 660 historical, 193 Regency, 186 paranormal, 152 young adult and 101 inspirational. Companies publishing the most romance titles were Harlequin Enterprises (1,122 between Harlequin and Silhouette); Kensington Zebra (242 titles); Bantam (156 titles); Avon (138 titles); and Berkley/Jove (126 titles).

Reporting on the state of romance sub-genres for the July 1998 *Romance Writers' Report*, RITA-winning, bestselling **contemporary category romances** author Alison Hart notes, "Category publishing has steadily increased and continues to be vibrant in 24 languages in over 100 countries around the world." She also points out, "Unlike ten years ago, category titles now regularly appear on *The New York Times* and *USA Today* bestseller lists—another measure of our solid and growing popularity with readers." Hart advises aspiring contemporary category romance writers to read both older and current categories to better understand today's marketplace. That is because, she says, the readership of categories today includes both those who have been reading this mainstay of the genre for years, as well as new, younger readers.

Discussing the state of the **historical romance** in the July 1998 *RWR*, Kasey Michaels, RITA recipient and *New York Times* bestselling author of over 50 books, says, "Scotland sells, England sells, the American West sells, and everything else doesn't." She goes on to say that when the market for these historical romance locations becomes saturated, something new will sell. Also selling well, according to Michaels, are "One-on-one stories, those that concentrate quite firmly on the hero and heroine." She also says shorter books, rather than long, filled-with-description historical sagas are what readers want today. And she advises writers to guard against writing in the same era and location for so many books that readers will accept nothing else from you: " . . . unless you write different eras and countries from Book One on, be wary of changing eras and country 30 books into the game—and be doubly wary of changing the tone of your stories at the same time."

Regency writer Gail Eastwood says although the **Regency** sub-genre is suffering from shrinking print runs and lack of distribution, it is currently the strongest and most popular for historicals. As with contemporary romances, the readership is getting older. Unlike contemporaries, Regency is not attracting new young readers. Still Eastwood quotes agent Robin Rue as saying, "Regency is a field for fun, talented authors. . . . it's a real point of entry. I would be surprised to see it disappear anytime soon."

The **paranormal romance** sub-genre may be the most difficult for aspiring writers to break into today. Award-winning romance writer Deb Stover says "historical time travel seems to be a somewhat more stable market now than contemporary paranormal." But, she says, "Writers have to be brilliant to break in right now, and established authors must continue to grow." Stover suggests that those who love the sub-genre continue to write it but also "Diversify!" into other sub-genres. She also cautions writers that today's paranormal romance must be based in reality and quotes Jill Barnett, author of *Wild* and *Bewitching*: "The days when you can have your heroine stub her toe and land in Regency England are gone. Today's readers are too sophisticated."

Writing Romance on a Dare: An Interview with Amanda Scott

BY daSKARLES

Regency romance author Amanda Scott began her writing career on a dare. She had been reading a new Regency novel that hit the market after the popular romance author Georgette Heyer died, and "I got truly frustrated," she recalls. "It was probably the second or third one I had read where I thought the research was really terrible. What the author had done seemed to be taken from the Heyer books rather than from any other resources. I got so annoyed, I flung the book across the room and yelled, 'I can do better than this!' My husband heard me and challenged, 'Why don't you?' "

Since that challenge, Scott has written 35 books, and sold every one of them. The best-selling author has won numerous awards in her genre, among them the Romance Writers of America's RITA/Golden Medallion (for *Lord Abberley's Nemesis*) and *Romantic Times* awards for Best Regency Author and Best Sensual Regency (for *Ravenswood's Lady*). While her titles include 25 Regency romances (set in the strict social confines of Regency England from 1811 to 1820), 7 historical romances, and 3 contemporary romances, critics agree she excels at Regency. "Ms. Scott is a master of the Regency time frame, with impeccable characterizations that reflect the mores of the times but still appeal to the modern reader," wrote a reviewer in *Romantic Times*. Of her work a *Rendezvous* reviewer wrote: "There is no finer craftsman in the Regency genre today than the always impressive Amanda Scott."

The oldest of 4 children and an extended family of 18 cousins, Scott became the babysitter and storyteller. Because of all the stories in her head, she says, committing them to paper has always been a habit. In school, Scott recalls, she made up every book report she ever wrote—including the title, author and subject—and consistently got As. But her talent went unrecognized because she was never caught.

It was in college that Scott combined her interest in history with her love of storytelling. A history major who even then read Heyer's novels for pleasure, Scott found herself focusing her studies more and more on Regency England. She was inspired to try her hand at writing after finding herself drawn to two characters from two different Heyer novels, and wondering what

---

daSKARLES *has been a newspaper journalist/columnist and lecturer on how to turn personal experiences into books. She's published both short stories and magazine articles and presently writes a cooking column,* Handed-Down Recipes, *for a California regional magazine. She is also the author of* 201 Hot Cooking Tips *and* Writing for Fun, Posterity, and Money.

would happen if they met. Then she sat down and wrote a scene of what would happen. Over time, she played with it here and there, and when her husband later confronted her with the challenge, she pulled the piece out to see if she could develop it into a book.

Scott's first novel, *The Fugitive Heiress*, was 477 manuscript pages long. But Scott didn't realize at the time was that it was nearly 200 pages over the maximum allowed in Signet's Regency line. As it turns out, it didn't matter. "I just wrote the story until I was finished," she says. To find an agent, Scott checked listings in *Writer's Market* to find agents specializing in romance. She picked the one agent who would accept telephone queries, and when she phoned from home at 9 a.m. California time, a woman answered saying all the secretaries were at lunch, but perhaps she could answer her questions? Scott said she had written a book and wanted to know if the agent would represent her. The agent asked, "What kind of a book is it?" Scott answered, "A Regency." "Oh my God," said the agent. "Those things are selling like hotcakes. Can you write?" Scott said yes, and when the agent asked her if she had written anything else, the answer was also yes. Her first effort, as a Junior League project, was writing a coffee-table photo-essay book titled *Omaha City Architecture*. Scott had researched the book and written the text on an old Smith-Corona portable electric. It was the push the agent needed, Scott says. The agent asked Scott to send along her manuscript, and followed with a letter shortly after its receipt that stated, "Don't panic. I love it."

The agent also asked that the manuscript be cut 100 pages and gave Scott 5 suggestions for trimming. "Any one of them would have worked," Scott says, "and all of them showed me she had read the book, understood it, and knew what I wanted. She even suggested I use a single point of view because that would help eliminate a lot of stuff that was there." The first thing Scott did with the money from that book was throw out the portable electric and buy a word processor.

Since that first book sale, Scott has established a regular writing routine. During a slow period, Scott tries to write at least 3 pages a day and averages 15 pages a week. She says other than the occasional day off, she works anywhere from 6 to 8 hours per day, at peak times hitting 16 hours each day. Once she gets going, Scott estimates she writes close to 20 pages a day with very little revision. When she first begins a book, she pins down a year, such as 1803 or 1804. From there, she begins her research by scanning newspapers of the period for interesting articles, historical mysteries or anything on murder. Once an eight-line blurb in the *London Times* caught her interest. It was about a child who was approached by a witch and was afraid to go to the store for her mother. She used this information in *The Dauntless Miss Wingrave*.

Although Scott always outlines her books completely, she writes only a basic bio for each character, which includes the color of the characters' hair and eyes, and a timeline including the year the characters were born. The timeline enables Scott to know before writing whether, for example, the Battle of Waterloo happened when a particular character was 16. Despite her outlines, Scott did have a child character created in *Dangerous Illusions* surprise her in a later novel. At nine years old, Scott recalls, the character of Charlotte wanted her own book. Even many readers had written to find out what happened to the character. Then Scott wrote *Dangerous Games*, and up popped Charlotte in the middle of the story. It wasn't until Scott wrote *Dangerous Angels* that Charlotte finally became the main heroine in her own novel. "Sometimes minor characters try very hard to take over, but you just have to rein yourself in and finish the project you started," she says.

The first rule in writing nonfiction or fiction, Scott feels, is to write what you know. The second rule is to do your research and ask questions. Knowledge is power, she explains, and knowledge comes through research. It is how a person who has never lived in another time or geographical area writes with authority about the people who did.

"It's research that guides the writer who wants to hone her skills," says Scott. "It is what makes characters come alive." Many new writers think research is only for those who write historical novels, but to Scott every book requires research, because part of an author's purpose is to impel the reader into hearing the sounds, smelling the smells, and making her say, "I can tell the author has been here."

Once, when reading a contemporary novel about a hero who taught a small, frail 75-year-old woman to fly a helicopter, Scott became suspicious. By making a few phone calls, she found out that it was pure fantasy for the old lady to have learned to fly that particular aircraft. It required great strength, and unless she was very strong for her size it would be a problem for anyone who didn't know anything about helicopters. She also discovered other impossibilities in the author's story line: the helicopter the author had named would not hold an entire college class of 20 or 30 people, or enough gas required to fly from Hawaii to Oahu. Finding these glitches didn't make Scott throw the book across the room, but it did diminish her confidence that the author knew his subject, and it also kept her from seeking out a second book. "Research," Scott says, "is no more than recognizing that a question exists and then finding an answer."

Among all her books, Scott really doesn't have a favorite. She has enjoyed writing them all and says it is too hard to pick only one. To her it is like asking to name a favorite child. "If I must answer," she says with a smile in her voice, "it's the book I'm writing now." Her current project is writing a thriller, for a complete change of pace.

Scott recommends that new writers get their books out there. Promotion is the key to name recognition. It is important for new writers to get known locally. Once authors become regional bestsellers, other areas will start noticing their names. To writers who want to write and sell, Scott says: "Go for it! You'll never do it if you don't try."

Toni Blair: One of Romance's Precious Gems

BY DAVID BORCHERDING

Unlike many successful romance writers you ask, Toni Blair doesn't claim to have been writing or even reading romance novels all her life. In fact, she freely admits that up until two and a half years ago, she hadn't read them at all. "I was writing literary novels and started feeling like I could do this the rest of my life and nothing would ever come of it. When my friend Joni suggested I try writing romance, I scoffed and told her I hadn't read a romance since I was 15 years old. So she gave me a stack and told me to give them a chance, and after reading two of Jenny Crusie's books, I was hooked."

After learning the history of her writing career, some might think Blair gave up on her literary work too soon. After all, she'd had a short story, "Hands," nominated for the 1996 Pushcart Prize, and she had won the Kentucky Women Writer's Fellowship that same year. Blair herself had similar reservations: "At first, I thought it was a sacrifice I was making to further my chances of having a career in writing, but what I have discovered is that romance fits very well with my writing style and my sense of humor. I'm now totally committed to writing romance. I find it very challenging and completely fulfilling."

And completely successful, one might add. Blair has published three romance novels with Kensington's Precious Gems line. *The Cinderella Scheme* appeared on the shelves in June of 1998, and *Baby Love* was released the following month. Her third, *October Moon*, was released in October of that same year.

What is it like to write for Precious Gems?

Precious Gems has made this a very exciting year for me. They bought three books in five months, all of which are already on the shelf. It's a very quick process and gives me a lot to keep up with, but the quick turnaround time is wonderful. Most new writers won't see their books hit the shelves for at least a year or two after they deliver the finished manuscript to the publisher, and some of them are envious that my books are coming out so quickly. It's almost instant gratification—you don't have to have the big build-up of writing the book and then have it dissipate into nothing for two years.

I think that Precious Gems came along at a good time. The romance market is as tight as any other right now, and Precious Gems gives a lot more new writers the chance to be published.

DAVID BORCHERDING *is a writer and editor. He lives in Cincinnati, Ohio.*

Was *The Cinderella Scheme* the first romance novel you wrote?

Actually, I wrote 12 romance novels before that one.

Wait. You said you hadn't even started reading romance until two and a half years ago. Are you saying you wrote 12 novel length manuscripts in 2½ years?

Well, I write fast.

You can say that again! What's your writing day like?

I write every day, unless there's some reason that I can't. I'm usually at the computer by nine, I write until two, take a lunch break and get back to writing by three. Then I usually write until seven at night. If I'm really on a roll, I'll write until 11 or 12 p.m. I'm kind of a psychotic, addicted writer.

How did you develop such discipline?

To me, being a successful writer is all about drive and determination. There's nothing I can do to ensure I sell books since I have no control over editors or publishers, but the one thing I can do to help myself is make sure I get my butt in the chair to write. I've heard many writers say they treat their writing like a job—well, I do more than that. I treat my writing like a job where I'm the *boss*, where my actions can make or break everything, where the success of my business depends solely upon what I do each day to make it happen. I simply don't know any other way to do it. In the current publishing environment it takes giving 150%, so that's what I give. You have to want it that bad.

Some might say you can pound romance novels out so quickly because they all follow the same formula. Have you found them as formulaic as they are reputed to be?

Romance is like competitive figure skating. There are certain elements each skater has to complete or their score will go down, but how they complete those elements and what they do in addition to completing those elements is up to them. The fact that certain elements have to be included in a successful romance novel is what makes the writing truly challenging. I think it's much more challenging to write a romance novel than it is to write a literary novel, for instance. In a literary novel, you can skate all over the rink and do whatever you want. There are no rules. In romance, you have to learn to work these elements in while at the same time coming up with something new and different that will catch an editor's eye. It can be somewhat limiting, and the trick is to learn to not let them limit you.

Can you give us some idea what a few of these certain elements are?

The list is long and varies to some degree depending upon the kind of romance you're writing. Necessary in every romance, though, is a strong, likable heroine and a strong, successful hero who is attractive both physically and for what's on the inside. The heroine cannot seem slutty; if she's slept with many men, it has to have been before the story began and for the right reasons. The hero should seem like an experienced, capable lover. Essentially, the reader is looking for a heroine she can identify with and a hero she can fall in love with. Generally speaking, both characters should be goal-oriented people, and once they meet, it is important to keep them together as much as possible. If they are apart, they should certainly be thinking about each other. Neither character can be in a relationship with anyone else, and once they meet, they should have eyes for no one else but each other. Both characters have to learn and grow as a direct result of the relationship and the problems encountered through it.

Obviously, then, there is a lot of focus on the characters and their relationship. Any other elements that are "musts"?

There also has to be a conflict that puts them at great odds, be it differing lifestyles or directly opposing goals. And of course you have to have sexual tension and a happy ending. Oh, and you can never let your characters do something that the reader might not be able to forgive them for. There are probably many other things I'm forgetting, but those are some key elements.

What about taboos? Are there things you absolutely cannot do in a romance?

There are probably just as many taboos as there are "musts." Again, I couldn't possibly list them all, and some of them depend on what line you're writing for or your editor's personal preferences. But I can tell you that your main characters should not be musicians, writers or any other type of artist. Sports figures are also taboo. Other things you might not suspect to be taboo are land development stories, boats, mafia tie-ins and any mention of drugs. Some lines don't like exotic locales or the tropics. But again, what is or is not taboo depends on the line and the editor. Probably the biggest universal taboo is that you can't write about any controversial situation that may offend a reader.

Of course, this only applies to the new writer. Once you're established, you can start to get away with some of these things, and the bigger your name gets, the more you may be able to get away with it. Or you may be able to get away with it if it doesn't relate too closely to the plot; the more the taboo relates directly to the story or conflict, the bigger a no-no it becomes.

What advice would you give to a writer who is struggling with their work?

Go to conferences or find other ways to associate with writers. Even when I think my writing is fine, I'll go to a conference or a workshop and one thing the speaker mentions will leap out at me, and it ends up transforming the way I write. So be open to the fact that no matter how good you might think you write, you can always write better. There are plenty of people out there willing to share what they know, and you need to be receptive to that. At a good conference you can really find valuable tidbits of information. You can also discover new favorite authors and friends.

What advice would you give your best friend if she told you she wanted to write a romance?

I would tell her to learn the market, because it's much more complex than it seems. I would tell her to surround herself with other writers that she respects and be receptive to criticism, because it's the only way you can find the flaws in your craft and fix them.

What's the most important thing you would tell her?

It sounds trite, but I would tell her to believe in herself and never give up, and to be aware that you have to want to write more than anything. You must be willing to work very hard and make your writing one of the top priorities in your life.

How to Make Your Romance Characters Come to Life

BY PHYLLIS TAYLOR PIANKA

The secret to writing a salable romance novel lies in creating strong, believable, likable and sympathetic characters. Think about it. The romance novels you reread and refuse to part with are the books with the most memorable characters. It's the people who make up 70 percent of the story. The other 30 percent is plot. This rule holds true for most fiction. Even if the novel revolves around a mystery or a problem, there must be characters who ultimately will be affected by the outcome of the critical situation and the conflict.

One of the most common reasons for rejection is the author's failure to bring the characters to life. Irma Ruth Walker said, "I create my characters—I'd rather call them 'people'—from the inside out. Only when they come alive to me, when I know how they think and where they are coming from, do I worry about their physical appearance. To me, they all exist somewhere in this world—or in another."

I read once that no one can know a person better than the person himself, because it's what he does in private, when no one is watching, that determines his true character. Think about that when you are defining your characters.

BEYOND EXTERNAL QUALITIES

To build a character, you must go far beyond the visual, external qualities an individual possesses. Mixing together all the material attributes in a human system—hair color and eye color and body shape—does not make a person. If we limit the descriptions of our characters to the visual, we fail to bring our characters to life.

When an editor tells you your people are too slight or too shallow or lack depth, she means you have failed to delve deeply into their *psychological* makeup to give them *cause* for their behavior.

We cannot create believable, sympathetic characters without giving the reader a clue as to their backgrounds. Only in science fiction does a character appear on earth out of thin air. We all are multifaceted personalities—products of genetic evolution, past and present environments, and the fates that shape our individuality.

Character is created through a *layering process* that develops over a period of years, rather than through a single set of circumstances. To create believable characters, we must establish a past history for them. These layers consist of a multitude of influences such as race, nationality, economic status, religious background, family life, health, and many more.

Take, for example, two women. Each was reared as an only child in a wealthy home. Both grew up in California during the late 1960s. Both are attractive and intelligent. Now consider how their lives would evolve if one of the women, Katy, was reared by nurturing parents who

---

PHYLLIS TAYLOR PIANKA, *a bestselling author writing in both contemporary and historical romance categories, has sold 20 novels. Her publishers include Dell, Jove and Harlequin. This article is excerpted from* How to Write Romances (Revised and Updated) *copyright © 1998 Phyllis Taylor Pianka. Used with permission of Writer's Digest Books, a division of F&W Publications, Inc. For credit card orders phone toll free 1-800-289-0963.*

wanted nothing but the best for her, whereas the other woman, Stella, was brought up by parents who were cold and uncaring. To take it even farther, Katy's mother may have been a nursery school teacher who adored children, but Stella's mother was an actress who didn't want the world to know she was old enough to have a grown daughter.

Remember that you can make your people do anything as long as you properly motivate them. By digging through the layers of their personalities, you can discover how they would act or react to a situation. These details compose the fundamental traits of a character's identity and reveal his or her motivation.

Katy may rebel against her upbringing and become a permissive parent because she felt she was smothered by family affection, or she might be true to her upbringing and become the perfect parent.

Stella also has the choice of turning away from her family and making a decent life for herself because she learned from their mistakes. Or, she could follow her parents' example and end up as a cold person. The choice depends on the roles they play within the context of the plot. These twists and turns in the players' development keep a story from being predictable. This also explains how 20 different people can take the same basic characters and write a thousand different plots.

Debbie Macomber, a multipublished author, said "It's impossible to create a vibrant, excited character unless you know what motivates that person. To do that, I've constructed a profile in reverse. Instead of collecting background information on a character, I decide how that particular character will react in any given situation, keeping the plot in mind.

"An example of this would be the spider on the kitchen floor. My heroine sees the spider. How will she react? She can ignore the silly thing and pray it will be gone when she returns. She can squish it with her shoe and hurriedly kick it out of sight. Or she could squish it, get it into the sink, turn on the faucet and garbage disposal, and grind it up for five minutes until she is absolutely certain it's dead. Or she can phone the hero, tell him she's in grave danger and insist he come and rescue her.

"Once I have an idea how my character will react to a variety of everyday incidents, I walk him or her through the plot scene by scene and decide on the appropriate reaction."

Another device many writers use to better see their cast of players is to cut pictures out of catalogs or magazines of people who resemble those players. If you hang the pictures in front of your typewriter or computer so you can see them while you work, you will imprint those characters in your mind, and they will be less difficult to describe.

So, how does one create characters who will remain in the reader's thoughts long after the book is finished? There are many ways to show strong characterization. Here are seven suggestions.

1. SHOW CHARACTERIZATION THROUGH DIRECT NARRATIVE DESCRIPTION

Be careful of this one. It is easy to get carried away with telling what is happening, rather than showing. The problem is that you lose immediacy and remove the reader a step away from the action. If used with discretion, narration can be an asset to characterization, as in the following excerpt from *The Honeymoon Deal* by Kate Hoffman (Harlequin Temptation Romance #627):

> The white-haired matron was dressed as she always was—in cabbage roses. From the fabric of her dress to the decorations on her shoes, even springing from the ever-present hat perched on her head, cabbage roses of all shapes, sizes and colors seemed to envelop her. If that didn't constitute floral overload, Eunice's office was bedecked with the same fussy flowers, always leaving Lianne craving an elegant stripe or a simple check—or a bottle of aphid killer.

Note that the unusually long sentences in themselves may be considered a device. Shorter, tighter description would not have achieved the same effect. If a writer is describing a lean, athletic type, the tone and length of each sentence would instead be lean and strong.

In *Bride of the Sheikh* (Silhouette Intimate Moments #771), author Alexandra Sellers describes how the heroine, Alinor, is kidnapped during her wedding by Kavian, who claims she is still married to him. In this scene he has picked her up and faces the assembled guests:

> Everything stopped while that moment was recorded in time: the image of the white-robed prince, his skin tanned by the desert sun, his deep green eyes hard, his teeth bared in a smile of triumph and daring; in his arms a woman of pale, delicate beauty, a circlet of flowers on her brow, her ash-coloured hair tangled but flowing over the dark strong fingers that held her, her white silk skirt and the flowers she held falling in a mingled swathe to the floor, her eyes icy with fury. Behind them the rose window glowed with complementary colours of white, rose and blue. To the assembled, touched by wonder, they seemed a work of art.

Light, color, mood, setting—all these elements are tools the author uses to set this very visual scene through the use of narration.

2. SHOW CHARACTERIZATION THROUGH DIALOGUE

Dialogue is perhaps the most powerful tool for defining character to be found in the author's box of illusions. Rejections are often based on the author's inability to write believable and appropriate dialogue. For this reason, an entire chapter in my book *How to Write Romances* is devoted to writing dialogue.

3. SHOW CHARACTERIZATION THROUGH INTROSPECTION

Used judiciously, *introspection* (the character's unspoken thoughts) can enhance characterization by letting us see into the viewpoint person's mind. Example:

> Diane knew that Jason and Holly had never met but she detected a flicker of recognition in their eyes when she introduced them. She knew instantly that they were kindred souls. Takers.
>
> They were on their way up; clever, bright, and shallow as a saucer half filled with cream. And like the predators they were, they didn't give a damn about who the cream belonged to. It was theirs for the taking.
>
> There was no doubt in Diane's mind that this meeting would mark "finished" between her and Jason. She envied them their self-assurance, yet another part of her was glad that she had been brought up to respect the feelings of others. There was no way she could live with herself if she tried to play the game by their rules.

Through introspection we can understand how characters relate to others and we can begin to understand why the person feels as she does about those characters. In short, motivation. Knowing the private workings of a person's mind is like finding a key to the soul.

Flashes of introspection can also provide descriptions of others, thereby avoiding the cliché scene where the heroine sees herself in a mirror or shop window and thinks: *God, I'm beautiful, with my red hair streaming down my back, and my eyes shining clear and blue as a summer sky. My figure is great enough to . . .* Well, you get the picture.

One of my favorite reasons for using introspection is to have the ability to assess the heroine through the hero's eyes. It can strengthen the heroine by letting us know how much he cares for her, but it can also make a hero sympathetic, a hero who otherwise has negative traits that the author has yet to explain away or justify.

Editors do warn us not to "rehash scenes" that have been adequately covered through dialogue or action. Those redundant scenes usually take place while the heroine is in the shower or just falling asleep. They go something like this:

> Diane rolled over on her back and studied the patch of light on the ceiling as she thought about what Paul had said. Did he really love her? Would it be right for her to give up everything she had worked for just to be with him? She turned on her side, punching the pillow into a ball. He said there was no reason to put it in writing but she wondered.

Instead, if you feel you must establish her uncertainty, you can use direct dialogue with Paul instead of rehashed introspection.

> "I've thought about it, Paul, so much that it kept me awake most of the night. . . ."

Or simply allude to her problem with a line or two of transition:

> The conversation with Paul and her uncertainty over what to do kept Diane awake most of the night. When the alarm clock finally rang . . .

Introspection must serve a purpose beyond the passing of time. She may, for example, recall a word or phrase spoken earlier. That bit of dialogue may prove to be a clue that solves the crime. Even so, keep the introspection short and intersperse action within it.

4. SHOW CHARACTERIZATION THROUGH ACTIONS AND REACTIONS

The course of action we take is a direct result of how our personalities have been programmed. In delineating our characters we must always make certain that they stay within character. Everything they do and everything they think must be compatible with the way they have lived their lives. Their attitudes may adjust as they grow and mature but their basic philosophy of life will probably remain the same.

By showing a character in action, we let the reader see another side of that character's personality. The same holds true for reaction, which is similar to action but is usually more sudden, following a specific stimulus.

In the book *Family Ties* by Joanna Wayne (Harlequin Intrigue #444), Ashley and her son, Petey, have been on the run since her brother was killed while involved in a holdup. The robber assumes she has a large share of the money. Ashley's husband, Dillon, was shot and wounded just moments after their wedding ceremony. Shortly after that, he walked out on the marriage, unaware that she was pregnant with his child.

Now, two years later, the killer is out to find the money—even if it means Ashley must pay with her life.

> The storm had knocked out the phone, too. Thunder clapped again, and the whole apartment seemed to shake. She sucked in a calming breath. It was probably the storm that was spooking her. Still, Petey was in the next room. She had to protect him at any cost.
>
> She stood quietly and tried to think. The rain was all she could hear now, beating against the windows. No. There was something else, quieter. Like hushed breathing, low but distinct. She held her breath as the sudden smell of liquor and sweat accosted her senses.

The opening chapters help the reader understand the dichotomy of Ashley's back-street roots as opposed to Dillon's background of wealth and position. Here is an action scene that shows Ashley's love for her son and her courage in protecting him. With her son asleep in the back room, Ashley is being kidnapped:

> He pushed again, this time sending her careening against the edge of the kitchen table. "Out the back way. Real quiet. So I don't have to shoot a brave husband."
>
> "No, Please. Just leave and come back in the morning. I'll meet you here and we can look for the money together. I promise." She was grasping for any delay she could find.

Remember that you are in control. If it is essential to the story that your character suddenly behave outrageously, you can justify it. Give the character the proper motivation to make his or her actions believable. In this novel, the character's love for her son serves as the catalyst, but the chemistry between Ashley and Dillon is equally compelling.

5. SHOW CHARACTERIZATION THROUGH NAMES

The names we bestow upon our characters create pictures in the minds of our readers. They may know someone who has a similar name or they may associate the name with something or someone about whom they have heard. We can control these images up to a point.

It is wise to choose carefully before you become too involved in the book. I'm not good at changing names once my characters begin to breathe. If I'm forced to change a name, the character never seems quite real to me after that.

The names you select can establish your characters in a period of history, a geographic location, and, within reason, a profession. When was the last time you heard of a newborn child named Homer or Clyde or Maude? Those names were very common in the early 1900s, and it is unlikely that they will return to popularity in the near future.

Conversely, the rule of returning cycles is readily apparent when you think about the names people give to their children today. Jason, Sarah, Joshua and Amanda were very popular names at one time. They've come back. In 1986, Michael and Jessica were the most common names given to babies in California. If you wanted to set your novel in the 1940s, you would find that Linda and Paul were popular names at that time. A name-the-baby book that gives the origin and meanings of names can be helpful. Information is also available from state and federal birth statistics.

If your book is set in the South, you might consider using a double name such as Lucy Mae or Billy Bob. The names Jean Paul and Andre immediately signal French to the reader. These are handy tags that contribute to a character without the writer having to overwrite the book.

Certain surnames are more common in areas settled by large groups of immigrants. Norwegian and Swedish names are very widespread in Wisconsin where large numbers of Scandinavians made their homes. A glance through U.S. and foreign telephone directories at the public library will tell you in an instant what names are currently popular in most large cities.

Some people say names also reflect careers or lifestyles. Think of Dixie, Stella, Wanda and Mabel, and you think: waitress. Think of Roy, Elmo or Jake, and you think: manual labor. Think Michelle, Daphne, Winthrop or Trent, and you think: country club. Of course this is both oversimplification and stereotyping, but it is important to see characters in relationship to their names. While a name can't take the place of characterization, it's an important part of developing believable characters.

I recently discovered how awkward it is to use a given name that ends in *s* (James) or *ce* (Janice). In the singular there is no problem, but when you need the plural or possessive form, the name does not read well. I used the name Constance in *The Tart Shoppe* (Harlequin Regency) and began to regret it before I reached the third chapter. Some names are considered strong names and some are considered weak. Not all people agree on which are which, so you must train your ear to select names that clearly define the role you want your characters to play.

Several rules apply in naming characters

Don't use two or more given names beginning with the same letter. It is too difficult for the reader to keep the characters separate. (Don't remind me. I know. I was guilty of using Debra, David and Doug in *Midsummer Madness*. Even *I* got confused before the book was finished.)

Don't use peculiar or phony-sounding names unless you're writing science fiction—the reader can suspect you're making fun of her (according to a popular editor).

Don't use long complicated names for the main characters because it becomes tiresome to see them frequently repeated. Save long or foreign-sounding names for functional characters.

Don't, unless it's necessary to the plot, use unisex names spelled the same for both sexes—names such as Chris, Mickey, Nicky, Andy, Tony, Bobby, Terry, Jan, Lee, etc. It is confusing when you read it in the blurb on the back of the book, and it becomes confusing within the context of the story. Above all, avoid the plot ploy where the heroine goes to apply for a job and the male boss is furious because he thought she was a man when he read her unisex name. It has been used in romance novels more times than you can count.

6. SHOW CHARACTERIZATION THROUGH SIMILES AND METAPHORS

A simile is a comparison of two unlike objects using the introductory *like* or *as*: *His face was as wrinkled as a prune that had lain too long in the sun.* Another example: *His face was like a prune.*

A metaphor is a comparison of one object to another by transference of meaning: *His face was a prune that had lain too long in the sun.* Another example: *She was fire, he was ice. When they came together—meltdown.* Well, you get the idea.

Be careful not to use figures of speech that are anachronistic. In a historical novel, you would not write "her hair crackled with static electricity" if electricity had not been discovered. You should not use arctic comparisons if your novel takes place in the tropics.

Similes and metaphors add texture to a novel providing they are not clichés and providing they are appropriate to the story and not too abundant. It's like adding spices to the stew. A little adds zest, a little more is too much. Some editors like similes and metaphors in a romance novel, but other editors consider them purple prose. "He sought the honey that only she could offer as he plunged through the gates of paradise" is an example of a metaphor that might be considered excessive by some editors. Study the books in the line for which you want to write to see what's being done.

From *For the Love of Pete* by Rosalyn Alsobrook (St. Martin's Paperbacks contemporary romance) here are two examples of a simile: *Pete's jaw dropped like a metal bat on homeplate after a bunt.* And: *His mother had been acting a lot like Tweety bird in a room filled with Sylvesters.*

And a metaphor: *(She) . . . stared so many angry daggers through her water glass, Pete was surprised it didn't pop a half-dozen leaks.*

7. SHOW CHARACTERIZATION THROUGH LABELS OR TAGS

A label or tag is a device used to set one character apart from all others in the novel. The device can be an action or a possession or a catchphrase used only by that character. Again, we must carefully avoid clichés, such as the man running his fingers through his hair to show frustration and the woman going shopping for clothing when she is unhappy.

If you find creating a tag difficult, use television as a tool. Most series utilize tags for characters who appear frequently. What would *The Nanny* be without her nasal twang and tight micro-mini skirts? What would Kramer be without his fast slide when he enters Seinfeld's apartment? What would Tim, the tool man from *Home Improvement*, be without his tool belt and his ineptness? And what would Jim Carrey be without his rubber face?

In my novel *The Thackery Jewels*, a Regency trilogy from Harlequin, Emerald was studious. She was rarely seen without a book tucked in the pocket of her skirt. Amethyst was the nurturer who was psychologically unable to resist saving an injured creature, animal or human. Topaz was the adventurous one who would try anything once.

Dialogue tags associated with a single character can make the character visual if the tag is carefully chosen and not used too frequently. It could be a favorite expletive, a word that's mispronounced or misused, a tendency to drop the *g* on words ending in *ing*, or an often repeated phrase like "You catch my drift?" or "So?"

How do you make your characters sympathetic? In romance novels, because the hero and heroine are idealized characters, this element can be of particular importance. There are some simple solutions.

A "Pollyanna" type of character, who sees nothing but the good in everyone, is boring, unlikable and unbelievable. It would be impossible to involve her in any reasonable conflict. So how do we make our heroine exciting, sympathetic and realistic? The answer is to give her character flaws or a universal problem to which most people can relate.

A one-dimensional person has tunnel vision and straight-line emotions. Such a character in a short story or a novel is flat, cardboardlike, and lifeless. Remember that the balance of qualities should fall on the positive side for the hero and heroine. The less heroic the role, the more the balance can shift to the negative. Even the most villainous people should have at least one good point to make them believable.

When you search for negative traits for your hero and heroine, be careful to avoid those that are too negative, too unacceptable for the heroic role. Remember also that any positive trait, when carried to the extreme, can become a negative one. Example: mother love/smother love.

A few character traits

Positive: likes people; is charitable; honest; attractive; dependable; good sense of humor; sensitive; generous.

Negative: Tendency to be late; lack of drive (hero, in particular, must have a good reason); too much drive (must learn to slow down or redirect that drive); antisocial (must show strong justification and grow in character); too inflexible (must learn to compromise); limited sense of humor (must learn to laugh); too curious.

Here are some questions you might ask about your characters:

1. What things are important to this character, emotionally as well as physically: career, creature comforts, companionship, etc.?
2. Who or what has had the greatest influence on this character's life? Consider both negative and positive influences.
3. What does this character have to gain from the outcome of the critical situation and conflict? Remember that the protagonist, or viewpoint character, must have the most at stake.
4. What worries or depresses this character?
5. In whom does he or she confide? Who does he trust/distrust?
6. How does this character handle or react to disappointment, defeat, happiness, being alone (does he cherish solitude or does he constantly need to be surrounded by people)?
7. In a few words, tell your character's outlook on life. Does he feel that if you live by the book, life will be good to you? Or does he believe you only live once and you'll miss something if you don't learn to break a few rules?

Once you've created the characters, they are in your hands to manipulate as you please. But if you want the reader to accept them, you must know your characters well enough to predict how they will act or react in any given situation. Once you've achieved this, you'll discover what writers mean when they say their characters took over the book.

A CHECKLIST FOR CREATING COMPELLING CHARACTERS

1. Establish reader identification with your characters as close to the opening as possible.
2. Avoid the confusion of having too many characters. Instead, combine the roles and functions of two characters and let one do the work of two.
3. For maximum conflict and drama, look for characters who sharply contrast each other.
4. Give your reader someone to love, someone to hate.
5. Think visually. Give your characters visible traits or tags.
6. Make your characters perform instead of just letting them sit there. Don't *tell* about your characters. *Show*, through the use of action scenes, who your characters are.
7. Use dialogue wisely and in balance with narration and body language.
8. Avoid overuse of metaphors and similes. Be original in your descriptions. Leave some description to the imagination.
9. Write a case history of your main characters. Don't let them appear on earth the day the book opens. Give them backgrounds.
10. Keep your characters in character, but allow them to grow as individuals.
11. Be certain your characters are true to their time period and environment.
12. When choosing names for your characters, avoid using similar sounds and avoid using the same first letter. Save longer or foreign-sounding names for functional characters. Make certain the name is appropriate for the time period and the geographical location.
13. Always give your characters a sense of purpose in life, even if it is simply to survive.
14. In order to make your characters believable, give them the proper balance between positive and negative personality traits.
15. To make them sympathetic, give them a problem to which the reader can relate.
16. Avoid cliché characters by giving them some personal trait that sets them apart from similar characters.
17. When you have writer's block, try writing everything you know about your major characters.

Romance Markets Appearing in This Book

Below is a list of romance markets appearing in this edition of *Novel & Short Story Writer's Market*. To find page numbers of particular magazines or book publishing markets, go first to the General Index beginning on page 661 of this book. Then turn to the pages those listings appear on for complete information, including who to contact and how to submit your romance short story or novel manuscript.

Magazines

About Such Things
Advocate, PKA's Publication
Affable Neighbor
Aguilar Expression, The
Bangtale International
Blue Skunk Companion, The
BookLovers
Brilliant Corners
Brobdingnagian Times, The
Chat
Cochran's Corner
Cosmopolitan Magazine
CZ's Magazine
Dan River Anthology
Dogwood Tales Magazine
Downstate Story
Dream International/Quarterly
Drinkin' Buddy Magazine, The
Eternity Magazine
Eureka Literary Magazine
Evansville Review
Expressions
Eyes
Fugue
Gathering of the Tribes, A
Gay Chicago Magazine
Girlfriends Magazine
Gotta Write Network Litmag
Grit
Hayden's Ferry Review
Heretic Hollow
Home Times
Indigenous Fiction
Jeopardy
Jive, Black Confessions, Black Romance, Bronze Thrills, Black Secrets
Lamplight, The
Lutheran Journal, The
Lynx Eye
Matriarch's Way; Journal of Female Supremacy
Medicinal Purposes
Merlyn's Pen
Moose Bound Press
Musing Place, The
My Legacy
New England Writers' Network
New Writing
Northwoods Journal
Ohio Teachers Write
Outer Darkness
Palo Alto Review
PeopleNet DisAbility DateNet Home Page
Poetry Forum Short Stories
Poskisnolt Press
Post, The
Potpourri
PSI
Reader's Break
Rejected Quarterly, The
Romantic Hearts
Rosebud™
St. Anthony Messenger
Shades of December
Short Stuff Magazine for Grown-ups
Skylark
Spring Fantasy
SPSM&H
Storyteller, The
Sunflower Dream, The
"Teak" Roundup
Texas Young Writers' Newsletter
Threshold, The
Virginia Quarterly Review
Volcano Quarterly
Vox A
West Wind Review
Woman's World Magazine
Writers' Intl. Forum

Book Publishers

Avalon Books
Avon Books
Avon Flare Books
Bantam Books
Beggar's Press
Berkley Publishing Group, The
Bookcraft, Inc.
Books In Motion
Bouregy & Company, Inc., Thomas
Dell Publishing Island
Doubleday Adult Trade

Duckworth Press
Dutton
Harlequin Enterprises, Ltd.
HarperPaperbacks
Harvest House Publishers
Humanitas
Kaeden Books
Kensington Publishing Corp.
Laughing Owl Publishing, Inc.
Leisure Books
Lemeac Editeur Inc.
Love Spell
Masquerade Books
Nicetown
Orpheus Romance
Pocket Books
Prep Publishing
St. Martin's Press
Seniors Market, The
Severn House Publishers
Vista Publishing, Inc.
Zebra Books

LOOKING FOR AN AGENT?

For a list of agents who represent romance writers, see the Literary Agents Category Index, beginning on page 154.

Resources for Romance Writers

Below is a list of invaluable resources specifically for romance writers. For more information on the magazines and organizations listed below, check the General Index and the Publications of Interest and Organizations sections of this book. To order any of the Writer's Digest Books titles or to get a consumer book catalog, call 1-800-289-0963. You may also order Writer's Digest Books selections through writersdigest.com, Amazon.com or barnesandnoble.com.

MAGAZINES:

- *Fiction Writer*, 1507 Dana Ave., Cincinnati OH 45207
- *Romance Writers Report*, Romance Writers of America, 13700 Veterans Memorial, Suite 315, Houston TX 77014. (281)440-6885. Fax: (281)440-7510. E-mail: infobox@rwanational.com
- *Romantic Times Magazine*, 55 Bergen St., Brooklyn NY 11201. (718)237-1097
- *Writer's Digest*, 1507 Dana Ave., Cincinnati OH 45207

BOOKS:

- *How To Write Romances (Revised and Updated)*, Writer's Digest Books
- *Keys to Success: A Professional Writer's Career Handbook*, Attention: Handbook, Romance Writers of America, 13700 Veterans Memorial, Suite 315, Houston TX 77014-1023. (281)440-6885, ext. 21. Fax: (281)440-7510. E-mail: infobox@rwanational.com
- *Romance Writer's Sourcebook: Where to Sell Your Manuscripts*, Writer's Digest Books
- *The Writer's Guide to Everyday Life in Regency and Victorian England*, Writer's Digest Books
- *Writing Romances: A Handbook by the Romance Writers of America*, Writer's Digest Books

ORGANIZATIONS & ONLINE

- Romance Writers of America, Inc. (RWA), 3703 FM 1960 West, Suite 555, Houston TX 77068. (281)440-6885, ext. 21. Fax: (281)440-7510. E-mail: infobox@rwanational.com
- Romance Writers of America regional chapters. Contact National Office (address above) for information on the chapter nearest you.
- Romance Central: http://romance-central.com. Offers workshops and forum where romance writers share ideas and exchange advice about romance writing. (See complete listing in the Websites of Interest section of this book.)

The Science Fiction & Fantasy Market Today

BY BARBARA KUROFF

A recap of some publishing dynamics surrounding science fiction indicate that the genre is strong and should remain alive and vital into the next millenium:

- Science fiction titles included in the 1998 Modern Library's Top 100 list of the century's greatest novels included 5 science fiction selections with Aldous Huxley's *Brave New World* placing #5. And in at least one online survey launched in response to Modern Library's selections, the top eight novels picked by readers were all science fiction.
- Avon Books is publishing an original science fiction anthology series to be edited by Avon publisher Lou Aronica and senior editor Jennifer Brehl. Still untitled as we went to press, Brehl says they want any length, including novellas, and will pay 10¢ per word. The only requirement is that the fiction be excellent.
- Tor licensed electronic versions of new and reprint science fiction titles as a test deal to digital publisher Peanut Press. These "e-books" can be downloaded from the Internet, via the 3Com Palm Computing platform. Books will sell for approximately $12 per download and Tor will get a 25% royalty to split with writers.
- A four-part PBS documentary will chronicle the history of science fiction as "the 20th Century's most dynamic literary genre" and will pay "special attention to how it has shaped and reflected the consciousness of modern times," says Eric Solstein, head of the video crew shooting the series.
- Science fiction magazines *Amazing Stories* and *Weird Tales* have both been resurrected—*Amazing Stories* by Wizards of the Coast and *Weird Tales* by Warren Lapine (see the interview with Warren Lapine on page 98).

Today's editors seem to be fostering a return to classic science fiction. Gary Lavisi, owner of Gryphon Publications, is looking for "classic science fiction or science fiction in the classic mode." Lavisi credits small presses as the ones who "can publish classic material and material in the classic mode better than before to a wider and more appreciative audience."

Lavisi echoes the sentiments of most all today's science fiction editors when he says he is looking for "fascinating storytelling, a strong plot and well-developed characters, meaningful or insightful ideas—or, at least, most of these ingredients." As with other genres of fiction struggling for recognition in today's tight publishing market, science fiction must be excellent to be accepted for publication.

The fantasy end of the science fiction and fantasy fusion also remains strong. As with science fiction, this specialized genre requires an immersion in the genre; an understanding of the marketplace (read sample copies of magazines and book catalogs, and check out what's available in libraries and bookstores); excellence in writing, especially creative, well-crafted plots; and careful attention to mechanics. In Writing the World of Fantasy, beginning on page 96, Terry Brooks says of fantasy, "The magic must work in a consistent and balanced manner. The book must leave us with a feeling of comprehension and satisfaction at having spent time turning its pages to discover its end."

Writing the World of Fantasy

BY TERRY BROOKS

I remember vividly, 20 years later, what Lester del Rey repeatedly used to tell me about writing fantasy. Lester was a longtime writer, critic and editor in the fantasy/science fiction field, and I was fortunate enough to be able to work with him during the first 15 years of my professional career. Most of what I learned about being a commercial fiction writer, for better or worse, I learned from Lester. Lester used to say that it was harder to write good fantasy than any other form of fiction. Why? Because a writer of fantasy is free to invent anything, unfettered by the laws and dictates of this world and limited only by the depth of imagination and willingness to dream. The temptation to free-fall through a story chock full of incredible images and wondrous beings can be irresistible—but, when not resisted, almost invariably disastrous.

What he was telling me was that in creating a world populated by monsters and other strange life forms, reliant on uses of magic, and shimmering with images of childhood tales, legends and myths, a writer runs the risk of losing touch with reality entirely. Given the parameters of the world and characters that the writer has created, something of that world and those characters must speak to what we, as readers, know to be true about the human condition. If nothing corresponds to what we know about our own lives, then everything becomes unbelievable. Even the most ridiculous farce must resonate in some identifiable way with truths we have discovered about ourselves. Even the darkest sword and sorcery epic must speak to us of our own harsh experience.

Achieving this end as a fantasy writer demands mastery of a certain skill, one not uncommon with that required of a ship's captain charting a course at sea. When putting together a fantasy tale, a writer must navigate a treacherous passage that bears neither too hard to starboard nor too far to port in order to avoid arriving at an unforseen destination or, worse, ending up on the rocks. Fantasy writing must be grounded in both truth and life experience if it is to work. It can be as inventive and creative as the writer can make it, a whirlwind of images and plot twists, but it cannot be built on a foundation of air. The world must be identifiable with our own, must offer us a frame of reference we can recognize. The characters must behave in ways that we believe reasonable and expected. The magic must work in a consistent and balanced manner. The book must leave us with a feeling of comprehension and satisfaction at having spent time turning its pages to discover its end.

How does a writer accomplish this? Fantasy stories work because the writer has interwoven bits and pieces of reality with imagination to form a personal vision. Understanding the possibilities is a requirement to making choices. Those choices might include various forms of magic, types of weapons and armor, fantasy races and creatures, and ancient societies on which speculative fictional worlds and characters can be based. Each writer must choose the ones that work and make them the building blocks of a story's foundation.

TERRY BROOKS *has more than 15 million books in print worldwide. He published his first novel,* The Sword of Shannara, *in 1977. It became the first work of fiction ever to appear on* The New York Times *Paperback Bestseller List, where it remained over five months. His most recent novel is* A Knight of the Word. *This article is excerpted from* The Writer's Complete Fantasy Reference *© 1998 by the editors of Writer's Digest Books. Used with permission of Writer's Digest Books, a division of F&W Publications, Inc. For credit card orders phone toll free 1-800-289-0963.*

Description lends weight and substance to ideas, and nowhere is that more important than in a world that doesn't exist—at least outside the pages of the writer's story. So giving the reader an understanding of how a world looks, tastes, smells, sounds and feels is crucial. In fantasy, more than in any other form of fiction, the reader must feel transported to the world being created, while at the same time readily comprehending what it is he or she is experiencing. When an otherworldly character is introduced, the reader must be made to see the differences, but must recognize the similarities as well. Details ground the story's larger images and keep the reader engaged.

I happen to favor rather strongly the practice of outlining a book before trying to write it, and I would recommend it to beginning writers, in particular, for two reasons. First, it requires thinking the story through, which eliminates a lot of wasted time chasing bad ideas. Second, it provides a blueprint to which the writer can refer while working on a story over the course of months or even years. Use of an outline is not a popular practice because it is hard work. It isn't easy thinking a story through from start to finish. But writing a hundred pages that have to be discarded because they don't lead anywhere is a whole lot more unpleasant. Moreover, outlining gives a writer a chance to add to the details of the book, to pen notes in the margins, to decide how all those bits and pieces of reality I mentioned earlier will fit with those grand landscapes of imagination.

This seems a good place to stress the importance of "dream time" in the creative process. All good fantasy requires a certain amount of gestation, a period before pen is set to paper, or fingers to keyboard, in which a writer simply gives free rein to imagination and waits to see where it will go. After a path reveals itself, a writer should start to map that path, carefully noting which side roads are offered, what travelers await, where dangers might lurk, and how lessons could be learned. If the writer is patient enough, eventually a story will present itself. If it is the right story, it will demand to be written. It simply won't stand to be cooped up. But this is a process that is difficult to rush and one in which the writer must trust. It sounds a bit mystical, but it really isn't. It's puzzle building without a box cover. It's outlining in your mind.

There is one final lesson Lester taught me that I want to pass on before I end this. Some years back I was fussing to him about finding an idea for a story that hadn't been used before. I wanted something new and original. He gave me one of his patented smiles—the ones that always made him look like a cross between your kindly uncle and Jack Nicholson in *The Shining*—and told me in no uncertain terms that new ideas did not come along that often and that when they did, they came in disguise. It was better to take old, established ideas and just turn them over and over in your mind until you found a new way to look at them. Then write about what you saw.

It was good advice then. It's good advice now. Go forth, and write something magical.

Warren Lapine: Spinning in the DNA Helix

BY DAVID BORCHERDING

In 1993, with relatively little fanfare, Warren Lapine and two partners launched a science fiction magazine called *Harsh Mistress.* They took the title from Robert Heinlein's science fiction novel, *The Moon is a Harsh Mistress*, but it soon became clear from the adult submissions they started receiving that people weren't quite making the connection. After struggling under that title for two issues, Lapine bought out his partners, changed the title to *Absolute Magnitude*, and formed DNA Publications.

The bondage stories he'd been receiving under the old title quickly gave way to hard science fiction adventure stories by recognizable authors—Harlan Ellison, Alan Dean Foster, Allen Steele and others. New writers also found publication in *Absolute Magnitude*, and Lapine quickly struck a balance in each issue between well-known authors and undiscovered talent. (This format worked so well that in 1997, Tor Books collected 16 stories that appeared in the magazine from 1993 to 1997 into an anthology, eponymously titled *Absolute Magnitude.*)

With the success of the magazine, Lapine felt it was time for DNA Publications to branch out, and it did so in 1995 with *Dreams of Decadence*, a magazine of vampire fantasy fiction. Then in 1997, he bought the venerable *Weird Tales* and saved it from going out of print. Most recently, in early 1998, DNA Publications signed a publishing contract with *Aboriginal SF* magazine, and then a licensing agreement with *Altair* to publish an American edition of that Australian science fiction magazine.

Although they now fall under the same umbrella, each magazine has maintained its original editor. Charles Ryan still buys the stories for *Aborignal SF*; George Scithers handles all the submissions for *Weird Tales*; Angela Kessler edits *Dreams of Decadence*; and Robert Stephenson runs *Altair.* Lapine still edits *Absolute Magnitude*, even though the rapid growth of DNA Publications has left him with precious little free time. Despite this busy schedule, Lapine took time to speak with me over the phone.

Obviously, there's a drastic difference between the science fiction adventure of *Absolute Magnitude* and the vampire fantasy of *Dreams of Decadence*, but what are the differences between the science fiction you publish in *Absolute Magnitude* and the science fiction you publish in *Aboriginal* and *Weird Tales?*

DAVID BORCHERDING *is a writer and editor. He lives in Cincinnati, Ohio.*

Absolute Magnitude publishes more adventure-oriented science fiction than *Aboriginal. Aboriginal* still does a fair amount of adventure, but they tend to publish softer, more sociological science fiction. In many ways, it's like the difference between *Analog* and *Asimov's*—with the exception that Charlie would buy a good hard science fiction story if he got one. Although I'm sure Gardner Dozois at *Asimov's* says the same thing.

As for *Weird Tales,* that's primarily a dark fantasy magazine. They're interested in strange and bizarre stories about unusual settings. Their primary focus is Lovecraftian fiction and stories in the vein of Robert E. Howard's Conan tales. They take a few horrific science fiction stories, too.

Are there specific things these magazines are looking for?

I think we're all looking for good stories, ultimately. We're all looking for stories that take readers to different places, show them things they've never thought of, and in some way change them by the time they're done. We want to transform the readers. On a technical level, we look for as little exposition as possible to tell the story; we want to be shown the story, not told it.

What would be your definition of the ideal science fiction story?

The ideal story explores—within the confines of an adventurous setting—how some technological breakthrough will change what it means to be human.

Have you seen any stories lately that would fit that description?

I try to buy stories that are all like that. There was a story by a brand new writer in Issue #9 of *Absolute Magnitude* that fit that description very well. The author's name is Jim Greco, and the story is called "The Road to Wealth." Jim set the story in the near future and showed how different it would be to be a person in that time period and how that could affect relationships, and he had it all in the middle of an adventure story.

Besides Jim Greco, are there other writers who consistently write the kind of thing you're looking for?

Allen Steele is someone I'd look at if you were trying to sell me a story. He writes almost exactly what I'm looking for every time out. Read anything Allen's published anywhere. And the Shariann Lewitt novel I serialized is another good example.

What tips can you give writers hoping to publish in one of your magazines?

I always suggest that writers read the magazines and get a feel for what's being purchased. If you don't read the magazines, you can't ask what I think is an essential question, and that is, "What is it about this story that grabbed the editor and kept him reading past the first page?" And as you get to the middle, ask yourself, "Why is this story still holding the editor's interest?" Then look at the endings of each story and ask, "What is it about this story that, after the editor got all the way here, he still decided to buy the story?" I think if you read magazines with those questions in mind, you can start to see what will sell to a certain editor. That's the way to read, so your reading helps you as a writer. Reading is an important part of writing.

Are there one or two DNA Publications magazines that are especially open to new writers?

There are a lot of new writers in *Altair.* Because Robert is a new editor, he's more open to new writers. He might not notice some of the unevenness in the writing that someone like Charlie or myself or George Scithers—editors who have seen a lot of manuscripts—would notice immediately. Anytime someone's just started editing, that's a good time to hit them with a story from a new writer, because they're more forgiving than an established editor.

That said, *Dreams of Decadence* and *Absolute Magnitude* are both still trying to publish one new writer every issue. With the other DNA magazines, that's not a mission statement. Charlie Ryan is always trying to bring in new writers, though. And that's one of the things I'm proud of, that all the magazines here have discovered a number of new writers. George Scithers is responsible for the careers of people like S.P. Somtow, John M. Ford and even Barry B. Longyear.

We all understand that we have to find new writers, because established short story writers become new novelists, who then become established novelists who don't have time to write short stories. They move up the ranks and they're gone. When was the last time you saw a new short story by someone like Bruce Sterling or William Gibson? Those guys are novelists now, but they started out as short story writers. It happens with most writers, so we constantly have to find new writers to take their place.

What do you think is healthier right now in science fiction—the short story market or the novel market?

The short story field has more credible markets to be published in right now than it's had in a very long time. The last time there were this many credible markets was probably the Golden Age of Science Fiction. But it's also easier today to publish a first novel than it's ever been. I don't know if that makes the book publishing part of it more healthy, because it's harder to publish a second or third novel than it's ever been.

That sounds like the reverse of the way it's been. Usually if you publish your first novel, it gets easier to publish the second one. Why has that changed?

It's changed because of the way the chain stores do business, by ordering to sales. They look at a writer's previous book and say, "Well, we only sold this many copies, which isn't enough, so we don't want any of his next book." There's no time now for writers to get established; what their career will be is pretty much established on their first novel. Authors like Heinlein or Asimov or Anderson would not have book contracts today. They would not have made it to the point where they became huge science fiction writers, because publishers can't afford to develop midlist writers; there is no midlist today. So despite the fact that it's easier to publish a first novel than ever before, I'd have to say the short story market is a better place to be. But you can't make enough money to live in it.

It sounds almost like a Catch-22: it's easier to publish your first novel, but it's difficult to make a career as a science fiction novelist; and it's easier to establish a career as a science fiction short fiction writer, but you can't make a living with it.

Exactly.

What do you think of the field in general? Science fiction seems to go through these boom-and-bust cycles. Are we in a boom now?

I think we're just coming out of a bust and heading into a boom. That's been my feel for the magazines here. I discussed this with Gordon Van Gelder at this last year's Worldcon, and he said I probably have a rosier view than the rest of the field because DNA has been doing so damn well.

So for you, the science fiction field has been doing very well. That's not what you're hearing from other editors?

No. The major, established magazines—*Analog*, *Asimov's* and *The Magazine of Fantasy & Science Fiction*—are still losing circulation. The majors are all 5×8, digest-sized magazines that get buried on the big magazine racks in the chain stores, which is where most newsstand sales come from these days. And their subscriptions are down, mostly because places like Publisher's Clearinghouse cut all the science fiction magazines. Plus, they've been sold so many times and moved from this publisher to that publisher that they haven't done the subscription drives I've done, trying to get new subscribers.

In a lot of ways, it's also the "Dilberting" of science fiction. All these corporate people who don't understand publishing have their hands in it, and for three or four years, nobody's done the things for *Analog* and *Asimov's* that need to be done. The fact that they're still around is just a testament to the strength of science fiction.

It seems like science fiction is getting more literary, with authors like Jonathan Lethem and Jeff Noon and others of that stripe. Do you see that continuing?

Actually, I think we're on the way out of that, because the magazines that are starting to make it are the ones that almost defiantly say "We're not literary." I think that's why *Absolute Magnitude* out-sold *Century* and *Crank*—both of which were very much in that Lethem mold—five to one on the newsstand. I think the editors were trying very much to become more literary and more respected, and the readers really didn't care. *Absolute Magnitude* is geared toward the readers, not my college professors or editors from outside the field. I'm not looking for accolades from peers, I'm looking to make the readers happy. And I think the death of *Century* and *Crank*, and the fact that literary novels aren't selling all that well, is casting the field back towards the center.

And what is that center?

Hard science fiction. Adventure fiction. The kind of stories Heinlein, Clark, Asimov and Clement were writing. The kind of stuff that started the Golden Age of Science Fiction.

Hard science fiction and adventure fiction almost sound like opposites to me.

I don't see it that way. I'm always looking for adventure and movement in my hard science fiction. You can have both. Alan Steele is a great example of that. His fiction tends to be about adventures and yet there are tons of rivets, it's real hard science fiction. And Asimov used to do that, too. I think adventure fiction and hard science fiction appeals to the same group of readers. Publishing both hard science fiction and adventure fiction, I find that readers who like one tend to like the other.

I've been seeing a lot of e-zines lately. *Tomorrow SF* went completely electronic not too long ago, for example. Is that a coming trend?

I know that *Omni* couldn't make it happen, they couldn't make any money at all. However, Ellen Datlow believes in it and she's doing *Event Horizon* as an e-zine. I haven't heard from Algis Budrys, the editor of *Tomorrow*, whether or not he's making any money. Perhaps they'll make it because they're editors who have had a career outside of web publishing. But my own feeling is that it's just not going to happen. Nobody reads fiction online. The last thing I want to do after spending all day on my computer corresponding and laying out the magazine and doing other things on the computer is read fiction there too.

That's a different case for you than it is for the average reader. Most people don't spend as much time on the computer as you do.

True, but even people who don't use as much computer time as I do aren't willing to read 100 pages on the Internet. In my opinion, it's an inferior way to deliver the material, compared to a book. If you're well into the story and want to check something back in chapter one, it's a lot easier to get there in a book than it is to scroll backwards on your computer screen. And unless you're reading it on a laptop, it's also a lot easier to read a book underneath a tree, or in the tub or on the bus. So books and magazines are really superior to the Web for what it delivers.

Another problem is that nobody's figured out a good way to charge people for fiction on the Web. Maybe it's just a matter of educating Internet users so they stop thinking everything should be free. Because that's the way everyone feels on the Internet—"I'm not paying for anything. This is the Internet." So that could be the case, but at this point we have no way to know whether it's going to work or not. The jury's still way out.

Are there any other other trends you see happening in the science fiction field?

I don't know if you can call it a trend. I think the way magazines are published is changing. That is, single magazines are finding it tough to make it in today's publishing climate. One of the reasons I've done so well is because I have the support of a group of magazines. It's kind of a return to the way the magazine business used to be run. You see it with Sovereign Media's five magazines and my five magazines, and it's one of the reasons the Dell magazines—*Analog* and *Asimov's*—have done better than *The Magazine of Fantasy & Science Fiction*, which has no one to support it but Mercury Press. My hope is that if there is a return to this kind of group publishing, perhaps it will signal a return to the Golden Age, where we had a hundred genre magazines all publishing at the same time and all of them were making money.

EDITOR'S NOTE: At press time, DNA Publications acquired *Pirate Writings* magazine. Address and submission information will remain the same.

Science Fiction & Fantasy Markets Appearing in This Book

Below is a list of science fiction and fantasy markets appearing in this edition of *Novel & Short Story Writer's Market*. To find page numbers of particular magazines or book publishing markets, go first to the General Index beginning on page 661 of this book. Then turn to the pages those listings appear on for complete information, including who to contact and how to submit your science fiction or fantasy short story or novel manuscript.

Magazines

About Such Things
Absolute Magnitude
Adventures of Sword & Sorcery
Advocate, PKA's Publication
Affable Neighbor
Altair
Amazing Stories
Amelia
Analog Science Fiction & Fact
Anthology
Armchair Aesthete, The
Art Times
Art:Mag
Asimov's Science Fiction
Barbaric Yawp
Bardic Runes
Bear Essential Deluxe, The
Black Hammock Review, The
Black Lily, The
Black Petals
Blast@explore.com
Blue Skunk Companion, The
BookLovers
Boys' Life
Bradley's Fantasy Magazine, Marion Zimmer
Breakfast All Day
Brobdingnagian Times, The
Brownstone Review, The
Cafe Irreal, The
Callaloo
Capers Aweigh
Cat's Eye, The
Challenging Destiny
Chat
Chiricú
Chrysalis Reader
Climbing Art, The
Cochran's Corner
Communities Magazine
Companion in Zeor, A
Compleat Nurse, The
Compost Newsletter
Contact Advertising
Corona
Cozy Detective, The
CZ's Magazine
Dagger of the Mind
Dan River Anthology
Dark Matter
Dark Starr
Deadly Nightshade
Downstate Story
Dream International/Quarterly
Dreams & Visions
Drinkin' Buddy Magazine, The
Eclectica Magazine
Edge Tales of Suspense, The
Elf: Eclectic Literary Forum
Eternity Magazine
Eureka Literary Magazine
Evansville Review
Expressions
Fifth Di, The
5th Wall, The
Fish Drum Magazine
Flying Island, The
Forbidden Donut
Fugue
Gathering of the Tribes, A
Georgetown Review
Glass Cherry, The
Gotta Write Network Litmag
Grasslands Review
Green's Magazine
Grit
Gryphon Science Fiction and Fantasy Reader, The
Happy
Hayden's Ferry Review
Heaven Bone
Heretic Hollow
Home Planet News
Hurricane Alice
Iconoclast, The
Implosion
In the Spirit of the Buffalo
Indigenous Fiction
Inditer, The
Intertext
Jackhammer Magazine
Jeopardy
Lamp-Post, The

Left Curve
Lesbian Short Fiction
Lines in the Sand
Lite
Literal Latté
Lost Worlds
Lynx Eye
MacGuffin, The
Magazine of Fantasy and Science Fiction
Matriarch's Way; Journal of Female Supremacy
Medicinal Purposes
Mediphors
Merlyn's Pen
Minas Tirith Evening-Star
Mind in Motion
Mindsparks
Mississippi Review
Mobius
Moose Bound Press
Murderous Intent
Musing Place, The
My Legacy
Nebula, The
Neologisms
Nimrod
Northwoods Journal
Nyx Obscura Magazine
Oak, The
Of Unicorns and Space Stations
Ohio Teachers Write
Omnivore Magazine
On Spec
Outer Darkness
Outpost, The
Pablo Lennis
Pacific Coast Journal
Palo Alto Review
Parsec
Pegasus Online
Penny Dreadful
Pirate Writings
Play the Odds
Playboy Magazine
Poetry Forum Short Stories
Poet's Fantasy
Portable Wall, The
Poskisnolt Press
Potpourri
Prisoners of the Night
Purple Mist
Queen's Quarterly
Rag Mag
Ralph's Review
Reader's Break
RE:AL
Rejected Quarterly, The
Rockford Review, The
Rosebud™
Samsara
Screaming Toad Press
Seattle Review, The
Seductive Torture
Sepulchre
Shades of December
Shiver Magazine
Silver Web, The
Skylark
Slate and Style
Sorcerous Magazine
Southern Humanities Review
Space and Time
Spaceways Weekly
Spirit (Of Woman in the Moon), The
Spring Fantasy
SPSM&H
Starship Earth
Storyteller, The
Street Beat Quarterly
Struggle
Sunflower Dream, The
Talebones
Tampa Review
Texas Young Writers' Newsletter
Thema
32 Pages
Threshold, The
Thresholds Quarterly
Tomorrow
Urbanite, The
Verve
Vincent Brothers Review, The
Vintage Northwest
Volcano Quarterly
Weird Tales
West Wind Review
Works
Writers' Intl. Forum
Zothique

Book Publishers

Ace Science Fiction
Ageless Press
Alexander Books
Artemis Creations Publishing
Avon Books
Avon Eos
Baen Books
Bantam Books
Berkley Publishing Group, The
Black Heron Press
Blue Star Productions
Books In Motion
Brownout Laboratories
Carroll & Graf Publishers, Inc.
Cartwheel Books
Chinook Press
Circlet Press
Daw Books, Inc.
Del Rey Books
Delecorte/Dell Books for Young Readers
Dutton
FC2/Black Ice Books
Feminist Press at the City University of New York, The
Geringer Books, Laura
Gryphon Publications
HarperCollins Publishers
Hollow Earth Publishing
Humanitas
Kaeden Books
Masquerade Books

Morrow and Company, Inc., William
Nicetown
Our Child Press
Philomel Books
Pig Iron Press
Pocket Books
Pride Publications and Imprints
Putnam's Sons, G.P.
Random House, Inc.
Random House, Inc. Juvenile Books
Red Dragon Press
ROC
St. Martin's Press
Severn House Publishers
Smith, Publisher/Peregrine Smith, Gibbs
Spectra Books
Tor Books
TSR, Inc.
Ultramarine Publishing Co., Inc.
W.W. Publications
Warner Aspect
Whispering Coyote Press, Inc.
Woman in the Moon Publications
Write Way Publishing

LOOKING FOR AN AGENT?

For a list of agents who represent science fiction & fantasy writers, see the Literary Agents Category Index, beginning on page 154.

Resources for Science Fiction & Fantasy Writers

Below is a list of invaluable resources specifically for science fiction and fantasy writers. For more information on the magazines and organizations listed below, check the General Index and the Publications of Interest and Organizations sections of this book. To order any of the Writer's Digest Books titles or to get a consumer book catalog, call 1-800-289-0963. You may also order Writer's Digest Books selections through writersdigest.com, Amazon.com or barnesandnoble.com.

MAGAZINES:

- *Fiction Writer*, 1507 Dana Ave., Cincinnati OH 45207
- *Locus*, P.O. Box 13305, Oakland CA 94661
- *Science Fiction Chronicle*, P.O. Box 022730, Brooklyn NY 11202-0056. (718)643-9011. Fax: (718)522-3308. E-mail: sf_chronicle@compuserve.com
- *Writer's Digest*, 1507 Dana Ave., Cincinnati OH 45207

BOOKS:

Science Fiction Writing series (Writer's Digest Books)

- *Aliens and Alien Societies: A Writer's Guide to Creating Extraterrestrial Life-forms*
- *Space Travel: A Writer's Guide to the Science of Interplanetary and Interstellar Travel*
- *Time Travel: A Writer's Guide to the Real Science of Plausible Time Travel*
- *World-Building: A Writer's Guide to Constructing Star Systems and Life-supporting Planets*

Other Writer's Digest books for science fiction & fantasy writers:

- *The Craft of Writing Science Fiction That Sells*
- *How to Write Science Fiction and Fantasy*
- *How to Write Tales of Horror, Fantasy & Science Fiction*
- *Science Fiction and Fantasy Writer's Sourcebook, 2nd Edition*
- *The Writer's Complete Fantasy Reference*
- *The Writer's Guide to Creating a Science Fiction Universe*

ORGANIZATIONS & ONLINE:

- Science Fiction & Fantasy Writers of America, Inc., P.O. Box 171, Unity ME 04988-0171. E-mail: execdir@sfwa.org. Website: http://www.sfwa.org/
- Con-Tour: http://www.con-tour.com (See complete listing in the Websites of Interest section of this book.)

Queries That Made It Happen

BY TARA A. HORTON

It's an open cattle call at the literary agent's office and your query letter is auditioning. About ten other queries have shown up today, and this competition looks tough. But your query letter is confident. Luckily, the audition is not a cold read; rehearsed and prepared materials are required instead. The audition lasts two minutes—only two minutes to convince the agent your manuscript is perfect for the part of "Published Book."

How can you make those two minutes work to your advantage? Let's first talk about what you shouldn't do. Don't be wordy, vague or extreme. Agents don't have time to read a five-page thesis on how you and your book could make them money. They would hate to read the whole letter and not have a clue about your book's plot. They cringe at letters with arrogant closings like, "To learn more about my book, you'll just have to read it yourself"; and scoff at cheesy lines like, "You'd be crazy not to take this opportunity." And don't even consider writing a letter by hand, especially on flowery, purple stationery.

Conversely, agents crave a short letter (one page preferred, two pages max.) briefly summarizing your book and why you're the perfect person to write it. They need a letter professional in both content and appearance, one that's focused, and even a little creative. If you have previous writing experience, they'd love for you to briefly state that. And some agents would want to know if you've never published a book—they'd rather represent an unpublished client with no track record than a published author with an unsuccessful past. Show you are easy to work with and the best person for the job. You're not the only one who wants your query letter to convey, "This book could make money." The agent, believe it or not, wants that, too.

The following pages showcase actual queries submitted by writers who went on to find representation and publication. Two views are presented: the agent's reaction to the query and the author's explanation of how the query was put together. The authors even talk about what comes after writing the query: finding agents to send the letter to, and sorting and narrowing the positive replies.

Reading through these letters with the agents' notes and the authors' stories will help you discover where to get inspiration, what to include in your query and what to leave out. It's also therapy: you will find comfort knowing you are not alone in your agony, not the only one who spends days preparing for such a short, but oh-so-important "audition."

ELEMENTS OF A GOOD QUERY

- Correct name and address of agent.
- Typed on clean, conservative paper.
- Short, professional and to the point.
- Possibly creative, but never "cute," "clever" or "in your face."
- Previous publishing credits listed.

TARA A. HORTON *is the editor of* Songwriter's Market. *She lives in Cincinnati, Ohio with her husband.*

WHAT NOT TO WRITE IN A QUERY LETTER

In preparing to send me a query, a prudent author recently asked: "What are the worst things someone sending you a query can do?" In response, I've prepared a list of the biggest blunders and guaranteed turn-offs a writer can make in a submission. All of the following are taken from actual letters I've received over the years. Hopefully, by recognizing and avoiding these errors, you can make a good first impression on a potential agent.

Don't make mistakes

"I am sending you the first chapter of a completed manuscript I will further revise."

If YOU think it can be improved, then do it! Don't show it to me until you think it's in very good shape.

One writer sent me an e-mail full of errors, which I couldn't resist correcting. She replied with the following:

"Thanks for the comments. That is why editors are there—I am a brilliant storyteller, and have written numerous scripts for film and TV so I guess I'm doing well in that department—as for my punctuation—no biggie <huge grin> what spell check won't catch, my agent and my editor will."

I don't think so!

My least favorite:

"Dear Sirs"

Nobody here by that name. This one goes right in the trash.

Don't blow your own horn

"If you are looking for quality writing and very fine literature, I am the writer for you."

Let me make that decision. If your work is that good, I'll be able to tell.

"It is a one of a kind book whose time has come. That time is now."

This sentence manages to combine three clichés into total overkill.

And you wanna be an author?

"I've got a book that might need some help from a ghost writer to turn it into a real book . . . I'm an idea person, not a writer."

So why are you writing to me?

"This is one of those manuscripts you can't pass on because the story has great potential to go beyond bookhood. In fact, it may make a better film than a book."

If you think it's a film, don't send it to a literary agent. By the way—"bookhood"?

Make the lead compelling—but don't go too far

These examples speak for themselves:

"Enclosed please find a sample chapter from TITLE, the story of my mental breakdown while traveling around the world. Other people have traveled around the world, but I am the first person to have traveled around the world while being paranoid."

"We realize that your agency probably receives several disappointing submissions per year from writers who believe they have discovered the meaning of life."

Well, we haven't found the meaning of life yet, but we do get a lot of very good submissions. I hope these tips help you make your submissions one of the good ones!

By Lynn Rosen, Leap First Agency in New York

6534 Science Fiction Rd.
Chilliwack, British Columbia
Canada A1B 2C3

Richard Curtis
Richard Curtis Associates, Inc.
171 E. 74th St.
New York, NY 10021, USA

March 1, 1998

Dear Mr. Curtis:

I have recently completed a science fiction/fantasy novel entitled *Shiva 3000* and I hope you might consider taking me on as a client, with the goal of selling it to a major American publisher.

Since obtaining my BA in Writing from the University of Victoria, I have sold fiction to several professional magazines (such as *Fantasy and Science Fiction, Interzone, Aboriginal SF*) and anthologies (*Tesseracts 5* and *6, Synergy 5*). My novel blends literary aesthetics with the razzle-dazzle of contemporary science fiction, and I believe it would appeal to the same audience that has made bestsellers of works by William Gibson, Neal Stephenson, Jeff Noon, Dan Simmons and Nicola Griffith.

19th Century missionaries returning from India reported seeing Hindus throwing themselves under the wheels of a towering temple cart that carried a representation of the Hindu god, ''Jagannath;'' from these tales, we derived the English word, ''juggernaut.'' *Shiva 3000* is set in a far flung future India, where the million-plus gods of Hinduism have become real, where the god Jagannath does roll through the cities on an unstoppable chariot, massive, inexorable, crushing.

Another god, Kali, confronts the protagonist, Rakesh, with a task. Kali says a famous celebrity known as the Baboon Warrior must die. He must be killed by Rakesh.

Rakesh accepts. People are appalled to hear his goal, incredulous of his claim that it is his holy duty. Among the doubters he meets is a government Engineer, with his own problems. The Engineer has been expelled from the Palace, the victim of political skullduggery which soon comes to undermine stability of the government and the country. The Engineer vows to expose the young Prince who framed him, and joins Rakesh. Sex, violence, and human computers figure into the unfolding of events. In the end, Rakesh uncovers the true nature of the gods which guide their lives, and seizes control of the Jagannath—piloting it into the capital, to force the truth from the anomaly calling himself the Baboon Warrior.

The mythology and culture of India proved to be an inspiring milieu for a speculative novel. You are the first agent I have queried, and I hope you will take the time to consider *Shiva 3000*.

Yours truly,

An interesting, stimulating, inviting query letter.

Jan Lars Jensen

Validates himself as one worthy of serious consideration.

If he did his homework he would have easily learned Simmons is a client. If Jensen's notion was to subtly flatter me—well, he did.

This synopsis is irresistibly exotic. I said to myself, "This story is so bizarre, I have to read it to see if he has pulled it off."

He nailed me with this line. Now I absolutely had to see the manuscript to determine if the author was a master or a madman.

This flattered me again. I had to send for the manuscript before he decided to query his 2nd and 3rd picks. I contacted him moments after finishing the letter.

Comments provided by Richard Curtis of Richard Curtis Associates, Inc. in New York

JAN LARS JENSEN

Photo by Derek Fairbridge

Even with sales to magazines like *Aboriginal SF*, Jan Lars Jensen felt it might be difficult to find an agent for his science fiction novel *Shiva 3000*. "I realized the initial payoff for an agent would be small. A good strategy, I thought, might be to first interest an editor with a query and then use his or her response to land an agent. I quickly realized how few publishers consider unsolicited work."

The next step was finding an agent. Using the Internet and *Science Fiction Writer's Marketplace and Sourcebook* (Writer's Digest Books), Jensen compiled a list of potential agents. He ordered the agents according to his criteria: 1) a proven track record getting science fiction/fantasy writers published; 2) associated with authors he is familiar with; and 3) based in New York. A resident of British Columbia, Jensen sought an agent in New York, where the major publishers of science fiction and fantasy are based. His ideal agent would specialize in this genre and have what Jensen did not: "a lot of experience and a lifetime of publishing contacts."

By taking advantage of other available resources, Jensen pared down the list. A member of the Science Fiction and Fantasy Writers of America (SFWA), he perused this organization's directory to learn who agented some of his peers. "Richard Curtis caught my attention because he represented several authors I admired," says Jensen. "From another source, I learned that Richard had actually been the SFWA's agent for a period, which suggested to me he was respected within the field. I discovered that Richard had himself written some novels, and I liked that; he was a writer too, and if he did represent me, he might better understand writers' issues." Curtis went to the top of Jensen's list.

While putting together the query letter, Jensen tried to imagine the situation of the person who would read it. "I kept the letter short, assuming 1) agencies receive many queries; and 2) the more succinct, the more attention the contents of mine would receive. I also thought it important to establish my 'qualifications' quickly, so the reader would know I took my writing seriously. That's why I mentioned my degree and short story sales in the second line."

Describing the novel took more thought. Working against Jensen was a recent shrinking in the science fiction market. In addition, there were no comparable novels to his on the shelves. "I wasn't going to tell a potential agent I thought my novel would be a tough sell! So even though I thought originality was one of the novel's strengths, I didn't emphasize this. I would let Richard draw his own conclusions from the description, and when I compared my work to that of other writers, I chose authors whose success lay in offering something fresh and new."

Jensen sent off his carefully crafted query to Curtis, and soon after a positive reply came from his number one pick. Curtis had several publishers in mind for the book and received from Harcourt Brace a response that Curtis says, "agents only dream of." Harcourt Brace's commitment to publish the book in hardcover and to give it a high profile was exactly what Jensen had hoped for his novel. As a result, *Shiva 3000* will be published in the Spring of 1999.

Reflecting on his experience, the only thing Jensen might have done differently was to go directly to the agents. "I would not bother querying editors until you've exhausted possibilities with agents," he says. "In addition, writing short fiction and taking courses in writing have not only improved my skills but also—in situations like querying an agent—given me some valuable credibility. I have also benefited in unexpected ways from my membership in the SFWA, so I suggest writers join organizations appropriate to their goals.

"I didn't become a writer so I could spend my time struggling to put together the right query letter," Jensen says. "But the rewards are worth the effort, because, with luck, it can lead to a situation where the author never needs to write another."

123 Short Stories Blvd.
Alhambra, CA 98765
emailaddress@email.com
(818)555-2468

21 February, 1997

Ms. Charlotte Gusay
The Charlotte Gusay Literary Agency
10532 Blythe Avenue
Los Angeles, CA 90064

Dear Ms. Gusay:

Thank you for your response to my e-mail. As I indicated, I was offered a deal to publish a book of short stories. This is my first offer, and I am unfamiliar with the industry. I am therefore seeking agency representation and/or advisory service to deal with contract negotiation issues for this deal. I am also seeking agent representation in general for future work.

It's not unusual to be approached by a writer with a deal already in hand. This tells me, "Maybe I should have a look at this."

I located your agency first with *Yahoo!*, and then in the *Guide to Literary Agents*, which indicates that you might be interested in representing work similar to mine. I am seeking an agent in California. Your response was one of the warmer and more personal responses I received, so I am sending you a completed copy of my self-published short story collection. Also included are copies of the contract I was offered and a counter-offer I drew up. I realize the counter-offer is probably inappropriate in both content and format, but it gives you an idea of the things I wish to negotiate.

As a Chicano writer and reader, I think this book would appeal to Chicano and other Latino readers like myself. My work is a very conscious effort to straddle the two cultures—Latin American and U.S.—which have formed my life and literary sensibilities; I am just as indebted to Latin American authors like García Márquez, Vargas Llosa, and Borges, as I am to U.S. authors like Vonnegut, Hemingway, and Barth. In addition to this completed collection of stories, I am also currently at work on an experimental crime detective novel with film potential. I have included a one-page synopsis and a page of sample text from the novel.

Very helpful. He knows his market and knows where he fits in and where he departs.

I am 25 and have been writing fiction seriously for two years. In 1994, I earned a degree in American Literature from U.S.C. I was born and raised in San Jose, California, and now live in the Los Angeles area (Alhambra).

I would appreciate the opportunity to meet with you to further discuss the possibility of establishing a professional relationship. I can be reached at (818)555-2468. Thank you for your time. I look forward to hearing from you soon.

Best regards,

Rubén Mendoza
Enclosures

Overall, this query has a very positive and professional tone. It stands out because I represent his type of writing—it's a good match. Happily, his book was published within a year of this query and sold out its first printing.

Comments provided by Charlotte Gusay of the Charlotte Gusay Literary Agency in Los Angeles

RUBÉN MENDOZA

Photo by Youngblood Photography

The last thing Rubén Mendoza expected when he made his collection of stories into Christmas presents was to end up with a publishing deal. "At the time, I was not at all interested in being published or attracting sales," says Mendoza. "I figured I had another five, ten years at least before anyone cared enough for me to start seeking publication."

The ball began rolling for Mendoza after "much pushing and prodding" from his girlfriend. "I asked a local author friend of mine what she thought I should do with the book. I was really just seeking editing advice and trying to get a feel for how this kind of thing worked, expecting tips on how to improve my writing. She recommended I send a copy to her publisher, and I did; about a month later, the publisher sent me a contract offer."

Acting on advice from *Writer's Digest* magazine not to sign a contract on his own, Mendoza decided to get an agent. "I didn't know anything about getting an agent or why one would need an agent or how any of this worked at all. I conduct most of my business online, so my first step was to look up a few agents on the Internet. I was looking first for someone who was not afraid of communicating this way. I told them my situation through e-mail—that I had an offer in hand and needed help on it, as well as what I was working on at the time. Obviously it helped that I had an offer—I'm not sure how much response I would have received without it." (See this e-mail query below.)

Dear Ms. Gusay:

I was recently offered a deal to publish a book of short stories. This is my first offer and I am unfamiliar with the publishing industry; I am therefore seeking agency representation to deal with contract negotiation issues.

The book is finished and is provisionally titled *Lotería*. The stories range in length from about 700 to about 8,000 words, and would probably be best classified as serious literary experimental fiction.

I am 25 and have been writing fiction as long as I can remember. In 1994, I earned a degree in American Literature from the University of Southern California. Born and raised in East San Jose, California, I now live in the Los Angeles area.

If you are interested, I would very much appreciate the opportunity to send my work and/or meet with you to further discuss the possibility of establishing a professional relationship. Thank you for your time. I look forward to hearing from you soon.

Best regards,
Rubén Mendoza

Charlotte Gusay of The Charlotte Gusay Literary Agency was one of the first to respond to the e-mail query. ''She was local, and that was a plus for me,'' says Mendoza. ''While I like doing business online, I also need eventually to be able to meet with people face to face. Later, I got hold of a copy of the 1997 *Guide to Literary Agents* and looked her up there. I liked what her listing said about her, even though she was emphatic about not representing short stories (I was naively optimistic enough to figure I could change her mind—I think I was partly right). I received responses to my other e-mail queries as well, but Charlotte's was the warmest.''

It is typically Gusay's rule to request further information upon receiving an e-mail query. In response to this request, Mendoza sent a second query letter (see this query on page 111), a copy of the book and the contract he was offered.

Mendoza kept the queries basic, honest and to the point. ''I tried to maintain a very professional tone and imagined I was sending a formal résumé cover letter to apply for a job.'' The letters took about 15 to 20 minutes each to compose. ''They were not difficult to put together quickly because I was very clear from the beginning on what I needed, and perhaps because I had no pre-conceived notions or fears of how one should approach an agent.'' Professionalism and confidence were apparent—Mendoza received several positive replies.

During his communication with these interested agents, Mendoza got the feeling he was the one who should be happy about getting an agent's attention and not the other way around. The exception was Gusay. ''I found we were able to establish an equal footing and respect for one another in terms of the value of what each of us contribute to this partnership and how we treat one another,'' says Mendoza. ''I don't know that I would work with an agent otherwise—even if it meant not getting published.

''Gusay's response was immediate and very positive,'' says Mendoza. ''She was aggressive and showed an understanding not only of the work's commercial potential, but of its value as literature as well. That was most important to me considering how I'd stumbled into this whole situation from an almost purely non-commercial perspective. She also seemed to know the business, and that was the perfect combination of what I was looking for: good business sense coupled with good literary sense.''

Gusay assured Mendoza the offer he received was quite acceptable, but she wanted to shop *Lotería* around to other publishers just to test the waters. Not long after, St. Martin's Press made an offer for publication under their Buzz Books imprint. Mendoza says, ''I liked the idea that Buzz Books, which claimed to be promoting Los Angeles writing, was actually interested in publishing such an explicitly Latino work.'' This focus, along with Buzz's satisfaction with the book's title and concept (the other publisher wanted changes), convinced Mendoza he had found a home for his stories.

Mendoza advises aspiring authors to adopt his attitude of not being afraid of the rules. ''As long as the writing is good, as long as you continue to focus on writing for the sake of the writing . . . the rest will tend to 'fall into place,' as they say.''

Producing a Knockout Novel Synopsis

BY EVAN MARSHALL

Your novel is finished and ready to mail to an agent or editor. You shoot off a query letter (covered in step sixteen). The agent or editor asks to see your manuscript, *or* she asks to see a proposal: three chapters and a synopsis, or one chapter and a synopsis, or just a synopsis.

A *what*? A synopsis, a brief narrative summary of your novel. It's a vital marketing tool for a novelist, because it often has to do the entire job of enticing an agent or editor enough to want to read your novel. Think of the synopsis as a sales pitch for your book.

A synopsis has other uses, too. Later, when you sell your novel, your editor may ask you for a synopsis to be used as the basis for jacket or cover copy for your book. Other departments in the publishing house, such as Art or Sales or Publicity, may want to read your synopsis to get a quick idea of your story.

Even later, when it's time to sell your next novel, you'll be able to secure a contract solely on the basis of a synopsis and a few chapters, or just a synopsis. (The only time you should have to finish a book before selling it is the first time.) As you can see, the synopsis performs a number of important functions. It therefore deserves as careful attention as you've given the novel itself.

SYNOPSIS MECHANICS

The synopsis is formatted much like your manuscript. Use courier type; double-space all text; set your left, right and bottom margins at 1¼″ (3.2cm), your top margin at ½″ (1.3cm). Justify the left margin only.

On every page except the first, type against the top and left margins a slugline consisting of your last name, a slash, your novel's title in capital letters, another slash and the word *Synopsis*, like this: Price/UNDER SUSPICION/Synopsis. Number the pages consecutively in the upper right-hand corner of the page, against the top and right margins. The first line of text on each page should be about ¾″ (1.9cm) below the slugline and page number.

On the first page of your synopsis, against the top and left margins, type single-spaced your name, address and telephone number. Against the top and right margins, type single-spaced your novel's genre, its word count and the word *Synopsis*. (The first page of the synopsis is not numbered, though it is page 1.)

Double-space twice, center your novel's title in capital letters, double-space twice again, and begin the text of your synopsis.

See next page for how the synopsis of Sara Bradford's story would begin.

EVAN MARSHALL *is the president of The Evan Marshall Agency, a leading literary agency that specializes in representing fiction writers. A former book editor and packager, he has contributed articles on writing and publishing to* Writer's Digest *and other magazines. He is the author of* Eye Language *and a forthcoming series of mystery novels. This article is excerpted from* The Marshall Plan for Novel Writing *copyright © 1998 Evan Marshall. Used with permission of Writer's Digest Books, a division of F&W Publications, Inc. For credit card orders phone toll free 1-800-289-0963.*

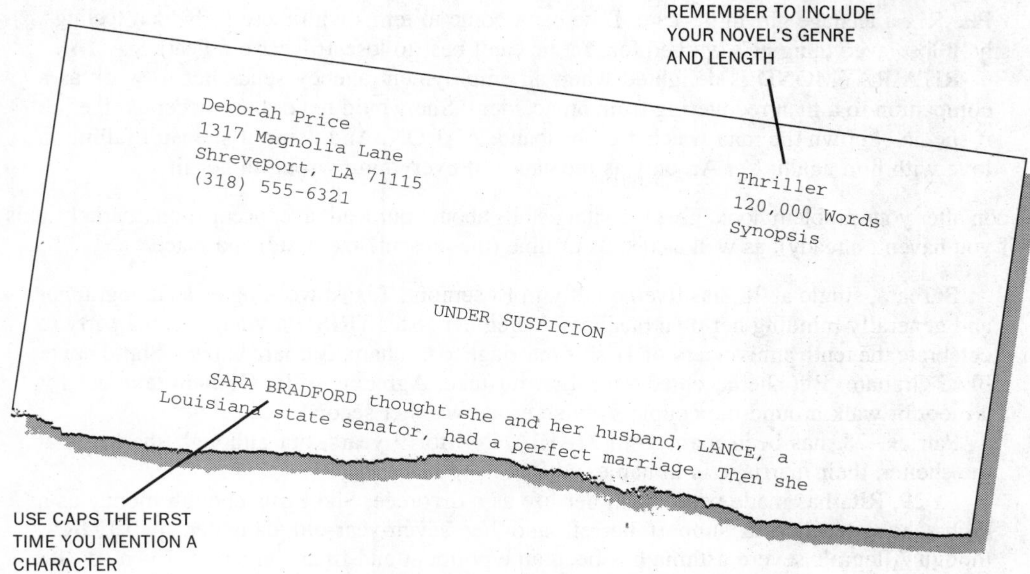

SYNOPSIS BASICS

Before we get to the subtleties of writing the synopsis, be aware of a few basic rules.

1. The synopsis is always written in the present tense (called the historical present tense).
2. The synopsis tells your novel's *entire* story. It doesn't leave out what's covered by the sample chapters submitted with it. Nor does it withhold the end of the story—for example, "who done it" in a murder mystery—in order to entice an agent or editor to want to see more. The synopsis is a miniature representation of your novel; to leave anything out is to defeat the purpose of the synopsis.
3. The synopsis should not run too long. An overlong synopsis also defeats its purpose. My rule is to aim for one page of synopsis for every 25 pages of manuscript. Thus a 400-page manuscript calls for a 16-page synopsis. If you run a page or two over or under, don't worry.
4. To achieve this conciseness, write as clean and tight as you can. Cut extra adverbs and adjectives. Focus on your story's essential details. Let's say, for example, you have a section in which your lead meets another character for dinner at a chic French bistro to try to convince her to lend him some money. We don't need to know where they had dinner or what they ate or even exactly what was said. We need something on the order of "Ray meets Lenore for dinner and tries to convince her to lend him the money. Lenore refuses." Actual dialogue is rarely, if ever, needed in the synopsis.
5. Don't divide your synopsis by chapters; write one unified account of your story. You can use paragraphing to indicate a chapter or section break.

HOW TO MAKE YOUR SYNOPSIS SIZZLE

Now, keeping all of the above in mind, translate your manuscript into synopsis. Begin with your lead and her crisis as the hook of your synopsis. Then tell how your lead intends to solve the crisis (what is her story goal?). For example:

> BARBARA DANFORTH has never been especially fond of her brother-in-law, GRAHAM, but she would never have murdered him. Yet all the clues point to her as Graham's killer. She'll have to prove her innocence if she doesn't want to end up as dead as Graham.
>
> PATRICK WARMAN, founder and director of Philadelphia's Friendship Street Shelter for runaway children, has always been careful to maintain a professional distance from the young people he helps. That's why he is especially horrified to realize he has fallen in love with

PEARL, a teenage girl in his care. If he can't come to terms with these forbidden feelings, he'll lose everything he's worked for. Yet he can't bear to lose 16-year-old Pearl.

RITA RAYMOND is delighted when an employment agency sends her to work as a companion to a man recovering from an accident. She would never have accepted the job if she had known the man was her ex-husband, AARON. And damn if she isn't falling in love with him again. Yet Aaron was the cause of everything wrong in her life.

Soon after your problem hook, give the vital details about your lead: age, occupation, marital status (if you haven't already), as well as details of time (the present? the past?) and place.

Barbara, single at 38, has lived quietly in Rosemont, Texas, working as a stenographer and generally minding her own business. When her sister TRISH invited her to a party to celebrate the tenth anniversary of Trish's marriage to Graham, Barbara balked. She'd never liked Graham. But she accepted—her first mistake. Agreeing to let Graham take her for a moonlit walk around the couple's lavish estate was her second. . . .

Patrick, 28, has been married to MARIANNE for 9 years, but although she helps at the shelter, their marriage is in name only. . . .

At 29, Rita has made peace with her life as a divorcée. She earns enough money as a high-school teacher to support herself and her seven-year-old daughter, ALLEGRA, though Allegra's severe asthma has been an emotional and financial strain. Even so, life these past five years without Aaron has been better than life was *with* him. . . .

Now continue telling your story, keeping to the main story points. Remember that the synopsis is not necessarily meant to convey the circumstances of *how* something happens; the happenings themselves are the concern here.

Most important, remember that *motivation and emotion are things that happen*; they are plot points, as important as any physical action a character might perform. Some of the worst synopses I've seen from would-be clients are dry and lifeless because these aspects have been left out.

Don't just tell us that Brandon tells Carla he's accepted the job in Sydney and that the next morning Carla has coffee at her friend Tanya's house and tells her the news. Tell us that when Brandon tells Carla he's accepted the job in Sydney, Carla sees her happy life collapsing around her. Devastated, the next morning over coffee she pours her heart out to Tanya.

Don't just tell us that Jake Hammond stomps into the bank and dumps a sack of money on the president's desk, announcing he's repaying his loan. Tell us that Jake, full of angry self-righteousness at how the bank has treated his sister, stomps into the bank and dumps the money on the president's desk.

The agents and editors who will read and evaluate your synopsis are looking for the same things as your eventual readers: emotion and human drama. Bear down on these life-breathing aspects of your story and you can't go wrong.

Indicate other characters' story lines in your synopsis by beginning a new paragraph and describing the character's actions. Sometimes transitions such as "Meanwhile" or "Simultaneously" or "At the hotel" can help ground the reader in time and place.

As you write the synopsis, think of it as your novel in condensed form, and present events in the same order that they occur in the novel itself. Also, reveal information at the same points you do so in your novel.

Stay "invisible" in your synopsis; by this I mean several things. First, don't use devices that emphasize the mechanics of storytelling. One of these is the use of such headings as "Background," "Setting" and "Time" at the beginning of your synopsis. All of these elements should be smoothly woven into the narrative. Another such device is the use of character sketches or descriptions at the beginning or end of the synopsis. For one thing, they go into more detail than is appropriate for a synopsis. Second, they make it difficult for the agent or editor to follow your story: If he reads the synopsis first, it's meaningless because he has no information about the characters. If he reads the character sketches first, they are equally meaningless because the characters are not presented in the context of the story. Characters and story do not exist independently of each other. Give any important facts or background when you introduce a character.

In the text, type a character's name in capital letters the first time you use it—a technique borrowed from film treatments. Also, to avoid confusion, always refer to a character the same way throughout the synopsis (not "Dr. Martin" in one place, "the doctor" somewhere else and "Martin" somewhere else).

Another way to stay invisible is to avoid referring to the structural underpinnings of your story. When I was a kid, we used to go to an amusement park with a scary jungle ride which went through a dark tunnel where a native jumped out and scared us silly. One day as we floated through the tunnel and the native jumped out, I noticed that the figure of the native had come loose from its metal support. I could see ugly gray metal and a tangle of electrical wires. The ride was never the same after that.

That's how I feel when I can see the scaffolding of a synopsis—for example, "In a flashback, Myron. . . ." Better to simply say "Myron remembers. . . ." Don't write "At the darkest moment of her Point of Hopelessness . . ."; just tell what happens. Avoid "As the story begins . . ." or "As the story ends . . ."; just tell the story.

As you near the end of the synopsis and your story's resolution, quicken the pace by using shorter paragraphs and shorter sentences. A staccato effect increases the suspense.

Above all, never in your synopsis review your story, as "In a nerve-jangling confrontation . . ." or "In a heart-wrenching confession. . . ." This kind of self-praise is amateurish and inappropriate in a synopsis, which presents "just the (story) facts, ma'am"; let your story's attributes speak for themselves.

Once your synopsis is finished, polish, polish, polish! In many cases your synopsis will be your foot in the door, and many agents and editors will judge your storytelling and writing style from this selling piece alone. When I receive a synopsis containing misspellings, poor grammar and sloppy presentation, I do not ask to see the manuscript. I assume it will contain the same kinds of errors.

One final word of advice: Don't try to write your synopsis from your section sheets. It's not impossible, but you'll make your life more difficult than necessary. The section sheets contain too great a level of detail; if you translate them, you're likely to find your synopsis running too long. Work from your manuscript, reading each section or chapter and then retelling it briefly, as you might if you were telling your story to a friend.

Writing the synopsis is an art you should become proficient in. A masterful synopsis starts selling your novel to an agent or editor before she even looks at your manuscript. In fact, a few times during my career I have read a synopsis so well-crafted that later I felt I had read the book! That's real magic.

KEYS TO A KNOCKOUT SYNOPSIS

- A well-written synopsis is a vital marketing tool for your novel, both before and after it's sold.
- Follow correct manuscript format.
- Write the synopsis in the present tense.
- Tell the entire story, with events in the same order as in the novel.
- Aim for a length of one synopsis page for every 25 manuscript pages.
- Focus on story essentials.
- Start with a problem-and-story-goal hook.
- Include characters' motivations and emotions.
- Don't let story mechanics show.

Agent Targeting: How to Find the Right Agent for Your Novel

BY JOHN MORGAN WILSON

Do you have to have an agent to get your book published? No. You can always self-publish (a daunting but doable task). Or you might submit to one or more of the many fine small presses that accept unsolicited material (but may pay no advances and have limited distribution and promotion).

But if your goal is to sell your book to a major publisher, you'll probably want an agent on your side. Why? Because more and more of the big houses only look at submissions that come in through established agents, letting the agents screen out much of the unsuitable material for them.

Now, the most challenging question: How do you find and land the right agent for you? The secret is to *aim carefully.* Instead of going blindly into your agent search, try "agent targeting." By that, I mean narrowing your list of prospective agents to those most likely to respond to your particular project and who have demonstrated the ability to sell similar or related material. After that comes the approach—contacting the agent to pitch your manuscript—in a manner that further enhances your chances of success (more tips on that later).

Here's how "agent targeting" works:

STEP 1: DO THE WORK

If you're an aspiring novelist, write your novel. This may sound obvious, but you'd be surprised how many would-be authors try to sell a novel they have yet to write. *Do not bother to pitch a novel to an agent that is not yet written; it is a waste of their time and yours.* Contracts for "ideas" and "concepts" only happen after you've established yourself as a fiction writer, because publishers know it's the *complete execution* of the story that counts.

With your novel completed, you move on to:

STEP TWO: DEFINE YOUR PROJECT

Identify as clearly as possible the type or genre of the book you have written or envision writing. If it's fiction, does it fit into the romance category? Horror, fantasy, science fiction, historical, thriller, mystery? If possible, further define it. If it's a mystery, for example, does it fit into a sub-genre, such as cozy, hard-boiled, gay male, lesbian, etc.? Does it qualify as "erotic," an expanding sub-genre in itself? Or is it less easily definable, falling into the more mainstream, midlist or literary areas of publishing?

Know what it is you are writing and hope to sell, and where it might fit into an agent's area

---

JOHN MORGAN WILSON *is a widely published freelance journalist and the author of* Inside Hollywood: A Writer's Guide to Researching the World of Movies and TV *and* The Complete Guide to Magazine Article Writing, *both from Writer's Digest Books. In 1996, he broke into fiction with* Simple Justice, *which won an Edgar Award from the Mystery Writers of America as the year's Best First Novel.* Simple Justice *was followed by* Revision of Justice *(1997) and* Justice at Risk *(1999), with the fourth Benjamin Justice mystery to be published in 2000. All were written under a contract with Doubleday that was initiated and negotiated by his New York agent, Alice Martell, of the Martell Agency.*

of interest, a publisher's crowded list, a bookstore's precious shelf space, and the overall trends of the book publishing marketplace.

STEP 3: PRIORITIZE YOUR POTENTIAL AGENTS

Your goal now is to compile a list of those literary agents who are most likely to respond to your particular novel manuscript, whether it's niche or more general interest, while eliminating or temporarily setting aside less appropriate choices. Where do you find agents, and how do you learn what they might be looking for, or already selling successfully?

- You're probably already reading and keeping a library of novels similar to your own in type and genre that you particularly value or admire, and regularly browsing bookstores for the same. Check the acknowledgments sections in those books to see if the authors mention their agents by name; then use the phone book or other resources to find those agents. (The rights departments of many publishing houses will provide agent information on specific authors if you call and request it.)
- Take note of agents and the types of books they sell when they are mentioned in trade publications such as *Publishers Weekly.* (Although my agent sells many nonfiction books, I became aware of her success with novels when her name turned up repeatedly in *PW* in connection with fiction sales. It was through her that I moved successfully from nonfiction to fiction writing.) Special issues of *PW*—such as those focusing on mysteries, romances, religious books, gay and lesbian titles and children's literature—are especially valuable for identifying agents who are successful in certain genres.
- Study the listings of agents beginning on page 131 of this edition of *Novel & Short Story Writer's Market*. Additional listings for agents can be found in the *1999 Guide to Literary Agents* (Writer's Digest Books) and the *Literary Marketplace (LMP)*. Other resources for information on individual agents are available in many public libraries and bookstores.
- The Society of Authors' Representatives (10 Astor Place, New York NY 10003) and the Independent Literary Agents Association (432 Park Ave. S., New York NY 10016) will send free lists of their members if you enclose SASE with your request.
- Meet agents in writing classes and conferences, or make contacts through established writers you meet. *A personal reference from a successful writer is probably the single best way to gain access to an agent, and get a faster, more attentive reading of your manuscript.* If you do "buttonhole" an agent at such an event, however, be prepared to discuss your book project clearly, thoroughly but succinctly. Nothing turns an agent off faster than an aspiring writer who hems and haws about a vague, poorly conceived "idea." Agents represent *writers*—not *would-be writers*.
- Become active in national writers' organizations. Many of these are open to unpublished writers, have regional groups, are excellent for networking and often sponsor events attended by agents. Many local writers' organizations do the same. The Council of Writers Organizations (1501 Broadway, Suite 1907, New York NY 10036) is a consortium of writers' groups with a membership approaching 25,000 individual members. Other notable organizations include the Author's Guild (234 W. 44th St., New York NY 10036), The National Writers Club (1450 S. Havana, Suite 620, Aurora CO 80012), the American Society of Journalists and Authors (1501 Broadway, Suite 1907, New York NY 10036), Mystery Writers of America (17 E. 47th St., 6th Floor, New York NY 10017) and Sisters in Crime (P.O. Box 442124, Lawrence KS 66044-8933), to name but a few. (For a more complete listing, see the Organizations section of this book.)
- Study published interviews with successful writers to see if their agents are quoted or named. If they sound right for you and your book, add their name to your growing list.

Warning: Do not look at agents so narrowly or literally that you overlook possibilities. An agent who has never sold a novel, but represents a number of sports journalists, might take a look at fiction with a strong sports theme. And so on. Use both your common sense and your imagination, looking for opportunities to break in that might not seem to be there at first glance.

Now that you've got your list of agents compiled, narrowed and prioritized, we come to:

STEP 4: MAKE YOUR APPROACH

In general, the best way to approach an agent is to query first. Some guidelines:

- Limit your pitch to one page.
- Capture the agent's attention quickly, from the first line.
- Identify your book by genre.
- Describe your main characters, setting and plot. (Suggestion: Study the promotional copy on the jackets of bestselling books in your genre to get an idea of the style and flavor needed to write an appealing description of your story.)
- Give the agent some background about you, including your credits, if you have any. Let her know briefly if there is anything in your background that will make your novel special (you are a nurse writing a mystery centered around a hospital).
- Include important details—for instance, if your fictional protagonist is intended as a series character—but refrain from *overselling* yourself. Be sincere, even enthusiastic, but avoid hyperbole.
- Do not apologize for yourself or your work in any way, or send up red flags signaling your lack of experience ("I realize I have no writing experience, but . . ."). Present yourself confidently and professionally. Above all, be sure your query letter is well crafted and carefully proofread—it is your calling card, the only thing the agent will have by which to judge you as a writer, a person, and a potential client. (For more information on query letters, see Queries That Made It Happen beginning on page 107 of this book.)
- With your query, include a self-addressed, stamped envelope (SASE), as well as your phone and fax numbers (and e-mail address if you are online). Multiple queries to agents are acceptable, and probably best done by mail or e-mail, rather than fax. If an agent is interested in you as a client, she will probably call or write, asking to see a completed or partial manuscript or outline and sample chapters, and perhaps a résumé. (At the very least, have voice mail or an answering machine to take calls when you are away; few agents will keep calling back.)

Be patient; an agent may take weeks or even months to get back to you, and a few never bother to reply at all. If too many weeks go by, and you are keen on a particular agent, you may want to query again, with a reminder note, or call the agent's assistant to see if he or she might check on your query. In the publishing world, a lot of paper gets lost in the shuffle.

Caution: Beware of agents who charge reading or consultation fees; very few are legitimate, successful agents. (Ditto for agents who try to steer you toward a vanity publisher that charges you money to edit or print your book.) If you have doubts about the legitimacy or track record of an agent, diplomatically ask to see a select client list with published titles, and make further inquiries to verify that the agent was actually involved in the sales.

Some authors grouse and grumble at having to depend on agents for access to the major publishing houses (and a few manage successful careers without them). Yet a good agent does much more than just play messenger for your manuscript. A good agent has a keen sense of publishing trends, and knows which publishers are in need of your kind of book (or already overstocked with same). A worthy agent will know which individual editors are most likely to respond positively to your material and support it down the line, crucial to almost any book these days. She will negotiate a better contract for you, maneuvering around legal and financial pitfalls, and be able to coordinate the sale of ancillary rights in other markets. In the best of situations, your agent will also become your editor, advisor and friend.

Whichever way you choose to go—with an agent or submitting on your own—never just "target" your manuscript out into the mail. Narrow and prioritize your list of targets, taking careful aim, and increase your chances of hitting the publishing bullseye—that *right* agent for you.

The Business of Fiction Writing

It's true there are no substitutes for talent and hard work. A writer's first concern must always be attention to craft. No matter how well presented, a poorly written story or novel has little chance of being published. On the other hand, a well-written piece may be equally hard to sell in today's competitive publishing market. Talent alone is just not enough.

To be successful, writers need to study the field and pay careful attention to finding the right market. While the hours spent perfecting your writing are usually hours spent alone, you're not alone when it comes to developing your marketing plan. *Novel & Short Story Writer's Market* provides you with detailed listings containing the essential information you'll need to locate and contact the markets most suitable for your work.

Once you've determined where to send your work, you must turn your attention to presentation. We can help here, too. We've included the basics of manuscript preparation, along with a compilation of information on submission procedures and approaching markets. In addition we provide information on setting up and giving readings. We also include tips on promoting your work. No matter where you're from or what level of experience you have, you'll find useful information here on everything from presentation to mailing to selling rights to promoting your work—the "business" of fiction.

Approaching magazine markets

While it is essential for nonfiction markets, a query letter by itself is usually not needed by most magazine fiction editors. If you are approaching a magazine to find out if fiction is accepted, a query is fine, but editors looking for short fiction want to see *how* you write. A cover letter can be useful as a letter of introduction, but it must be accompanied by the actual piece. Include basic information in your cover letter—name, address, a brief list of previous publications—if you have any—and two or three sentences about the piece (why you are sending it to *this* magazine or how your experience influenced your story). Keep it to one page and remember to include a self-addressed, stamped envelope (SASE) for reply. See the Sample Short Story Cover Letter on page 123.

Agents: Agents are not usually needed for short fiction and most do not handle it unless they already have a working relationship with you. For novels, you may want to consider working with an agent, especially if marketing to publishers who do not look at unsolicited submissions. For more on approaching agents and listings of agents willing to work with beginning and established writers, see our new Literary Agents section beginning on page 131. Also see Queries That Made It Happen, beginning on page 107. For information on over 500 agents, see *The Guide to Literary Agents* (Writer's Digest Books).

Approaching book publishers

Some book publishers do ask for queries first, but most want a query plus sample chapters or an outline or, occasionally, the complete manuscript. Again, make your letter brief. Include the essentials about yourself—name, address, phone number and publishing experience. Include only the personal information related to your story. Show that you have researched the market with a few sentences about why you chose this publisher. See the Sample Book Query Cover Letter on page 124.

The sample cover letter

A successful cover letter is no more than one page (20 lb. bond paper), single spaced with a double space between paragraphs, proofread carefully, and neatly typed in a standard typeface (not script or italic). The writer's name, address and phone number appear at the top, and it is addressed, ideally, to a specific editor. (If the editor's name is unavailable, address to "Fiction Editor.")

The body of a successful cover letter contains the name and word count of the story, the reason you are submitting to this particular publication, a short overview of the story, and some brief biographical information, especially when relevant to your story. Mention that you have enclosed a self-addressed, stamped envelope or postcard for reply. Also let the editor know if you are sending a disposable manuscript that doesn't need to be returned. (More and more editors prefer disposable manuscripts that save them time and save you postage.) When sending a computer disk, identify the program you are using. Remember, however, that even editors who appreciate receiving your story on a disk usually also want a printed copy. Finally, don't forget to thank the editor for considering your story. See the sample cover letters on pages 123 and 124.

Book proposals

A book proposal is a package sent to a publisher that includes a cover letter and one or more of the following: sample chapters, outline, synopsis, author bio, publications list. When asked to send sample chapters, send up to three *consecutive* chapters. An **outline** covers the highlights of your book chapter by chapter. Be sure to include details on main characters, the plot and subplots. Outlines can run up to 30 pages, depending on the length of your novel. The object is to tell what happens in a concise, but clear, manner. A **synopsis** is a very brief description of what happens in the story. Keep it to two or three pages. The terms synopsis and outline are sometimes used interchangeably, so be sure to find out exactly what each publisher wants. For detailed information on writing a synopsis, see Producing a Knockout Novel Synopsis, by Evan Marshall, beginning on page 114.

Manuscript mechanics

A professionally presented manuscript will not guarantee publication. But a sloppy, hard-to-read manuscript will not be read—publishers simply do not have the time. Here's a list of suggested submission techniques for polished manuscript presentation:

- **Use white, 8½ × 11 bond paper,** preferably 16 or 20 lb. weight. The paper should be heavy enough so it will not show pages underneath it and strong enough to take handling by several people.
- **Type your manuscript** on a computer using a laser or ink jet printer, or on a typewriter using a new ribbon.
- **Proofread carefully.** An occasional white-out is okay, but don't send a marked-up manuscript with many typos. Keep a dictionary, thesaurus and stylebook handy and use the spellcheck function of your computer.
- **Always double space and leave a 1¼ inch margin** on all sides of the page.
- **For a short story manuscript,** your first page should include your name, address and phone number (single-spaced) in the upper left corner. In the upper right, indicate an approximate word count. Center the name of your story about one-third of the way down, skip two or three lines and center your byline (byline is optional). Skip three lines and begin your story. On subsequent pages, put last name and page number in the upper right hand corner.
- **For book manuscripts,** use a separate cover sheet. Put your name, address and phone number in the upper left corner and word count in the upper right. Some writers list their agent's name and address in the upper right (word count is then placed at the bottom of the page). Center your title and byline about halfway down the page. Start your first chapter on the next page.

SAMPLE SHORT STORY COVER LETTER

Jennifer Williamson
8822 Rose Petal Ct.
Norwood OH 45212

January 15, 1999

Rebecca Rossdale
Young Woman Magazine
4234 Market St.
Chicago IL 60606

Dear Ms. Rossdale,

As a teacher and former assistant camp director I have witnessed many a summer romance between teens working at camp. One romance in particular touched me because the young people involved helped each other through a very difficult summer. It inspired me to write the enclosed 8,000-word short story, "Summer Love," a love story about two teens, both from troubled families, who find love and support while working at a camp in upstate New York.

I think the story will fit nicely into your Summer Reading issue. My publishing credits include stories in *Youth Today* and *Sparkle* magazines as well as publications for adults. I am also working on a historical romance.

I look forward to hearing from you.

Sincerely,

Jennifer Williamson
(513)555-5555

Encl.: Manuscript
SASE

SAMPLE BOOK QUERY COVER LETTER

Bonnie Booth
1453 Nuance Blvd.
Norwood OH 45212

April 12, 1999

Ms. Thelma Collins
Bradford House Publishing
187 72nd St., Fifth Floor
New York NY 10101

Dear Ms. Collins:

I am a published mystery writer whose short stories have appeared in *Modern Mystery* and *Doyle's Mystery Magazine*. I am also a law student and professional hair designer and have brought these interests together in *Only Skin Deep*, my 60,000-word novel set in the glamorous world of beauty care, featuring hair designer to the stars and amateur Norma Haines.

In *Only Skin Deep*, Haines is helping to put together the state's largest hair design show when she gets a call from a friend at the local police station. The body of famed designer Lynette LaSalle has been found in an Indianapolis motel room. She's been strangled and her legendary blonde mane has been shaved off. Later, when the bodies of two other designers are discovered also with shaven heads, it's clear their shared occupation is more than a coincidence.

Your successful series by Ann Smythe and the bestseller *The Gas Pump Murders*, by Marc Crawford, point to the continued popularity of amateur detectives. *Only Skin Deep* would make a strong addition to your line.

I look forward to hearing from you.

Sincerely,

Bonnie Booth
(513)555-5555

Encl.: three sample chapters
synopsis
SASE

Center the chapter number and title (if there is one) one-third of the way down the page. Include your last name and page number in the upper right of this page and each page to follow. Start each chapter with a new page.

- **Include a word count.** If you work on a computer, chances are your word processing program can give you a word count. If you are using a typewriter, there are a number of ways to count the number of words in your piece. One way is to count the words in five lines and divide that number by five to find an average. Then count the number of lines and multiply to find the total words. For long pieces, you may want to count the words in the first three pages, divide by three and multiply by the number of pages you have.
- **Always keep a copy.** Manuscripts do get lost. To avoid expensive mailing costs, send only what is required. If you are including artwork or photos, but you are not positive they will be used, send photocopies. Artwork is hard to replace.
- **Suggest art where applicable.** Most publishers do not expect you to provide artwork and some insist on selecting their own illustrators, but if you have suggestions, please let them know. Magazine publishers work in a very visual field and are usually open to ideas.
- **Enclose a self-addressed, stamped envelope (SASE)** if you want a reply or if you want your manuscript returned. For most letters, a business-size (#10) envelope will do. Avoid using any envelope too small for an 8½×11 sheet of paper. For manuscripts, be sure to include enough postage and an envelope large enough to contain it.
- **Consider sending a disposable manuscript** that saves editors time and saves you money. If you are requesting a sample copy of a magazine or a book publisher's catalog, send an envelope big enough to fit.
- **When sending electronic (disk or modem) submissions,** *contact the publisher first for specific information and follow the directions carefully.* Always include a printed copy with any disk submission. *Fax or e-mail your submissions only with prior approval of the publisher.*
- **Keep accurate records.** This can be done in a number of ways, but be sure to keep track of where your stories are and how long they have been "out." Write down submission dates. If you do not hear about your submission for a long time—about three weeks to one month longer than the reporting time stated in the listing—you may want to contact the publisher. When you do, you will need an accurate record for reference.

Mailing tips

When mailing short correspondence or short manuscripts:

- Fold manuscripts under five pages into thirds and send in a business-size (#10) envelope.
- Mail manuscripts five pages or more unfolded in a 9×12 or 10×13 envelope.
- Mark envelopes in all caps, FIRST CLASS MAIL or SPECIAL FOURTH CLASS MANUSCRIPT RATE.
- For return envelope, fold it in half, address it to yourself and add a stamp or, if going to a foreign country, International Reply Coupons (available for $1.05 each at the main branch of your local post office).
- Don't send by certified mail. This is a sign of a paranoid amateur and publishers do not appreciate receiving unsolicited manuscripts this way.

When mailing book-length manuscripts:

FIRST CLASS MAIL over 11 ounces (@ 65 8½× 11 20 lb.-weight pages) automatically becomes **PRIORITY MAIL. Stamped priority mail over 11 ounces must be handled by a postal employee.** You can see that, unless a postal employee comes to the publisher's office to pick up mail (and many large publishers do have in-house postal pickup), that publisher would need to take a manuscript weighing over 11 ounces to a post office to return it to a writer—even if that writer attached sufficient postage.

METERED MAIL, however, may be dropped in any post office box without being seen by a postal employee. But meter strips on SASEs should not be dated.

The Postal Service provides, free of charge, tape, boxes and envelopes to hold up to two pounds for those using PRIORITY and EXPRESS MAIL.

Requirements for mailing FOURTH CLASS and PARCEL POST have not changed.

CURRENT MAILING COSTS FOR FIRST CLASS POSTAGE VERSUS PRIORITY

FIRST CLASS MAIL:	PRIORITY MAIL:
1 ounce = 32 cents	12 oz.-2 lbs. = $3
2 ounces = 55 cents	2 lbs.-3 lbs. = $4
each additional ounce up to 16 ounces = 23 cents	3 lbs.-4 lbs. = $5
	4 lbs.-5 lbs. = $6

Main branches of local banks will cash foreign checks, but keep in mind payment quoted in our listings by publishers in other countries is usually payment in their currency. Also note reporting time is longer in most overseas markets. To save time and money, you may want to include a return postcard (and IRC) with your submission and forgo asking for a manuscript to be returned. If you live in Canada, see Canadian Writers Take Note on page 626.

Rights

Know what rights you are selling. The Copyright Law states that writers are selling one-time rights (in almost all cases) unless they and the publisher have agreed otherwise. A list of various rights follows. Be sure you know exactly what rights you are selling before you agree to the sale.

• **Copyright** is the legal right to exclusive publication, sale or distribution of a literary work. As the writer or creator of a written work, you need simply to include your name, date and the copyright symbol © on your piece in order to copyright it. Be aware, however, that most editors today consider placing the copyright symbol on your work the sign of an amateur and many are even offended by it. You can also register your copyright with the Copyright Office for additional protection. Request information and forms from the Copyright Office, Library of Congress, Washington DC 20559. To get specific answers to questions about copyright (but not legal advice), you can call the Copyright Public Information Office at (202)707-3000 weekdays between 8:30 a.m. and 5 p.m. EST. Publications listed in *Novel & Short Story Writer's Market* are copyrighted *unless* otherwise stated. In the case of magazines that are not copyrighted, be sure to keep a copy of your manuscript with your notice printed on it. For more information on copyrighting your work see *The Copyright Handbook: How to Protect and Use Written Works* by Stephen Fishman (Nolo Press, 1992).

• **First Serial Rights**—This means the writer offers a newspaper or magazine the right to publish the article, story or poem for the first time in any periodical. All other rights to the material remain with the writer. The qualifier "North American" is often added to this phrase to specify a geographical limit to the license.

When material is excerpted from a book scheduled to be published and it appears in a magazine or newspaper prior to book publication, this is also called first serial rights.

• **One-time Rights**—A periodical that licenses one-time rights to a work (also known as simultaneous rights) buys the *nonexclusive* right to publish the work once. That is, there is nothing to stop the author from selling the work to other publications at the same time. Simultaneous sales would typically be to periodicals without overlapping audiences.

• **Second Serial (Reprint) Rights**—This gives a newspaper or magazine the opportunity to print an article, poem or story after it has already appeared in another newspaper or magazine.

Second serial rights are nonexclusive—that is, they can be licensed to more than one market.

- **All Rights**—This is just what it sounds like. All Rights means a publisher may use the manuscript anywhere and in any form, including movie and book club sales, without further payment to the writer (although such a transfer, or *assignment*, of rights will terminate after 35 years). If you think you'll want to use the material later, you must avoid submitting to such markets or refuse payment and withdraw your material. Ask the editor whether he is willing to buy first rights instead of all rights before you agree to an assignment or sale. Some editors will reassign rights to a writer after a given period, such as one year. It's worth an inquiry in writing.
- **Subsidiary Rights**—These are the rights, other than book publication rights, that should be covered in a book contract. These may include various serial rights; movie, television, audiotape and other electronic rights; translation rights, etc. The book contract should specify who controls these rights (author or publisher) and what percentage of sales from the licensing of these sub rights goes to the author. For more information, see Selling Subsidiary Rights.
- **Dramatic, Television and Motion Picture Rights**—This means the writer is selling his material for use on the stage, in television or in the movies. Often a one-year option to buy such rights is offered (generally for 10% of the total price). The interested party then tries to sell the idea to other people—actors, directors, studios or television networks, etc. Some properties are optioned over and over again, but most fail to become dramatic productions. In such cases, the writer can sell his rights again and again—as long as there is interest in the material. Though dramatic, TV and motion picture rights are more important to the fiction writer than the nonfiction writer, producers today are increasingly interested in nonfiction material; many biographies, topical books and true stories are being dramatized.
- **Electronic Rights**—The marketing of electronic rights to a work, in this era of rapidly expanding capabilities and markets for electronic material, can be tricky. With the proliferation of electronic and multimedia formats, publishers, agents and authors are going to great pains these days to make sure contracts specify exactly *which* electronic rights are being conveyed (or retained).

Compensation for these rights is a major source of conflict between writers and publishers, as many book publishers seek control of them and many magazines routinely include electronic rights in the purchase of all rights, often with no additional payment. Alternative ways of handling this issue include an additional 15% added to the amount to purchase first rights to a royalty system based on the number of times an article is accessed from an electronic database.

Promotion tips

Everyone agrees writing is hard work whether you are published or not. Yet, once you arrive at the published side of the equation the work changes. Most published authors will tell you the work is still hard but it is different. Now, not only do you continue working on your next project, you must also concern yourself with getting your book into the hands of readers. It becomes time to switch hats from artist to salesperson.

While even bestselling authors whose publishers have committed big bucks to promotion are asked to help in promoting their books, new authors may have to take it upon themselves to plan and initiate some of their own promotion, sometimes dipping into their own pockets. While this does not mean that every author is expected to go on tour, sometimes at their own expense, it does mean authors should be prepared to offer suggestions for promoting their books.

Depending on the time, money and the personal preferences of the author and publisher, a promotional campaign could mean anything from mailing out press releases to setting up book signings to hitting the talk-show circuit. Most writers can contribute to their own promotion by providing contact names—reviewers, home-town newspapers, civic groups, organizations—that might have a special interest in the book or the writer.

Above all, when it comes to promotion, be creative. What is your book about? Try to capitalize on it. For example, if you've written a mystery whose protagonist is a wine connoisseur, you might give a reading at a local wine-tasting or try to set something up at one of the national wine events. For more suggestions on promoting your work see *The Writer's Guide to Promotion & Publicity*, by Elane Feldman (Writer's Digest Books).

ABOUT OUR POLICIES

We occasionally receive letters asking why a certain magazine, publisher or contest is not in the book. Sometimes when we contact a listing, the editor does not want to be listed because they: do not use very much fiction; are overwhelmed with submissions; are having financial difficulty or have been recently sold; use only solicited material; accept work from a select group of writers only; do not have the staff or time for the many unsolicited submissions a listing may bring.

Some of the listings do not appear because we have chosen not to list them. We investigate complaints of unprofessional conduct in editors' dealings with writers and misrepresentation of information provided to us by editors and publishers. If we find these reports to be true, after a thorough investigation, we will delete the listing from future editions. See Important Listing Information on page 130 for more about our listing policies.

If a listing appeared in our book last year but is no longer listed, we list it in the General Index, beginning on page 661, with a code explaining why it is not listed. The key to those codes is given in the introduction to the General Index. Sometimes the listing does not appear because the editor did not respond in time for our press deadline, or it may not appear for any of the reasons previously mentioned above.

There is no charge to the companies that list in this book. Listings appearing in *Novel & Short Story Writer's Market* are compiled from detailed questionnaires, phone interviews and information provided by editors, publishers and awards directors. The publishing industry is volatile and changes of address, editor, policies and needs happen frequently. To keep up with the changes between editions of the book, we suggest you check the monthly Markets columns in *Writer's Digest* and *Fiction Writer* magazines (both by Writer's Digest). Also check the market information on the Writer's Digest website at: http://www.writersdigest.com.

Club newsletters and small magazines devoted to helping writers also list market information. For those writers with access to online services, several offer writers' bulletin boards, message centers and chat lines with up-to-the-minute changes and happenings in the writing community. Some of these resources are listed in our Websites of Interest (page 621). Many magazine and book publishers offer updated information for writers on their websites. Check individual listings for those website addresses.

We rely on our readers as well, for new markets and information about market conditions. Write us if you have any new information or if you have suggestions on how to improve our listings to better suit your writing needs.

The Markets

IMPORTANT LISTING INFORMATION

● Listings are not advertisements. Although the information here is as accurate as possible, the listings are not endorsed or guaranteed by the editor of *Novel & Short Story Writer's Market*.
● *Novel & Short Story Writer's Market* reserves the right to exclude any listing that does not meet its requirements.

KEY TO SYMBOLS AND ABBREVIATIONS

N New listing in all sections
Canadian listing
International listing
A Agented material only
✓ Listing includes change in contact name, address or phone
Online publication
Award-winning publication
$ Market pays money
⊘ Accepts no submissions
★ Market buys large amount of unagented/freelance material
Cable TV market (in Screenwriting section)
● Comment by editor of *Novel & Short Story Writer's Market*
ms—manuscript; **mss**-manuscripts
b&w—black and white
SASE—self-addressed, stamped envelope
SAE—self-addressed envelope
IRC—International Reply Coupon, for use on reply mail from other countries

(See Glossary for definitions of words and expressions used in writing and publishing.)

COMPLAINT PROCEDURE

If you feel you have not been treated fairly by a listing in *Novel & Short Story Writer's Market*, we advise you to take the following steps:
• First try to contact the listing. Sometimes one phone call or a letter can quickly clear up the matter.
• Document all your correspondence with the listing. When you write to us with a complaint, provide the details of your submission, the date of your first contact with the listing and the nature of your subsequent correspondence.
• We will enter your letter into our files and attempt to contact the listing.
• The number and severity of complaints will be considered in our decision whether or not to delete the listing from the next edition.

The Markets

Literary Agents

Many publishers are willing to look at unsolicited submissions, but most feel having an agent is to the writer's best advantage. That's why this year for the first time we have included this section of 60+ agents who specialize in fiction, or publish a significant amount of fiction. These agents were also selected because of their openness to submissions from writers.

The commercial fiction field has become increasingly competitive. Many publishers have smaller staffs and less time. For that reason, more book publishers are relying on agents for new talent. Some publishers are even relying on agents as "first readers" who must wade through the deluge of submissions from writers to find the very best. For writers, a good agent can be a foot in the door—someone willing to do the necessary work to put your manuscript in the right editor's hands.

Agents' growing role not only includes discovering new writers who might otherwise get lost in the burgeoning slush piles of publishing houses. Along with smaller presses, agents are taking on midlist and otherwise "known," but not big-selling, authors who have been dropped by recent mergers of large publishing houses into even bigger publishing conglomerates.

It would seem today that finding a good agent is as hard as finding a good publisher. Many writers see agents as just one more roadblock to publication. Yet those writers who have agents say they are invaluable. Not only can a good agent help you make your work more marketable, an agent acts as your business manager and adviser, keeping your interests up front during and even after contract negotiations.

Still, finding an agent can be very difficult for a new writer. If you are already published in magazines, you have a better chance than someone with no publishing credits. (Many agents routinely read periodicals searching for new writers.) Although many agents do read queries and manuscripts from unpublished authors without introduction, referrals from their writer clients can be a big help. If you don't know any published authors with agents, you may want to attend a conference as a way of meeting agents. Some agents even set aside time at conferences to meet new writers.

All the agents listed here have said they are open to working with new, previously unpublished writers as well as published writers. None charge a fee to cover the time and effort involved in reviewing a manuscript or a synopsis and chapters. (Some legitimate agents do charge a "reading fee," but we encourage writers to first contact nonfee-charging agents.)

USING THE LISTINGS

It is especially important when contacting these busy agents that you read individual listings carefully before submitting anything. The first information after the company name includes the address and phone, fax and e-mail address (when available). **Member Agents** gives the names of individual agents working at that company (specific types of fiction an agent handles are indicated in parenthesis after that agent's name). The **Handles** section lists the types of fiction the agency works with. **Needs** includes any specific types of fiction the agency is currently looking for, as well as what they do not want to see. Reading the **Recent Sales** gives you the names of writers an agent is currently working with and, very importantly, publishers the agent has placed manuscripts with. **Writers' Conferences** identifies conferences an agent attends (and where you might possibly meet that agent). **Tips** presents advice directly from the agent to authors.

For information on how to find the right agent, read Agent Targeting, by Edgar-winning novelist John Morgan Wilson, beginning on page 118, and the Insider Report with Mark Walters, whose first novel was placed by agent Michael Carlisle, beginning on page 136. For a step-by-step guide to writing query letters to agents, see Queries That Made It Happen, beginning on page 107. Also, *The Guide to Literary Agents* (Writer's Digest Books) offers 500 agent listings and a wealth of informational articles on the author/agent relationship and other related topics.

We've assigned the agencies listed in this section a number according to their openness to submissions. Below are explanations of the codes that appear just after agent company names:

I Newer agency actively seeking clients.
II Agency seeking both new and established writers.
III Agency prefers to work with established writers, mostly obtains new clients through referrals.
IV Agency handling only certain types of work or work by writers under certain circumstances.

N **A.L.P. LITERARY AGENCY (I)**, Authors Launching Pad, P.O. Box 5069, Redwood City CA 94063. Phone/fax: (415)326-6918. Contact: Devorah B. Harris. Estab. 1997. Represents 8-12 clients. 40% of clients are new/unpublished writers. "We love books that have regional flavors. All serious book proposals with SASE will be answered with handwritten comments from folks who write and who care." Currently handles: 55% nonfiction; 15% scholarly books; 30% novels.

• Prior to opening her agency, Ms. Harris spent 9 years at Harper & Row, Scott Foresman, Little Brown and was a longtime board member of The LOFT, "the place for literature and arts in the Midwest."

Represents: Novels and nonfiction books. Considers these fiction areas: feminist; humor/satire; literary; regional; religious/inspirational; romance.
How to Contact: Send outline and 1-2 sample chapters. Reports in 2-4 weeks on queries and mss.
Needs: Actively seeking "fresh, juicy new titles from previously published authors." Does not want to receive children's books and science fiction. Obtains new clients through recommendations from others.
Recent Sales: New agency with pending sales.
Terms: Offers written contract, binding for life of book or until termination. One month notice must be given to terminate contract. Charges for photocopying, phone calls and mailing expenses "only if incurred and not to exceed $300."
Tips: "Let your cover letter be brief—that it may be an irresistable invitation to the rest of your writing."

N **AGENCY ONE, (I)**, 87 Hamilton St., S. Portland ME 04106. (207)799-5689. E-mail: mmccutc642@aol.com. Contact: Marc McCutcheon. Estab. 1997. Member of Authors Guild. Specializes in popular nonfiction and reference titles with long shelf lives, and science fiction. Currently handles: 50% nonfiction books; 50% novels.

• Prior to opening his agency, Mr. McCutcheon authored numerous books, including *Building Believable Characters*, *Writer's Guide to Everyday Life in the 1800s*, *Writer's Guide to Everyday Life From Prohibition through World War II*, *Roget's Super Thesaurus* (all published by Writer's Digest Books) and *Descriptionary*.

Represents: Novels and nonfiction books. Considers these fiction areas: action/adventure; science fiction.
How to Contact: Query or send synopsis/proposal. Reports in 2 weeks on queries; 3 weeks on mss.
Needs: Actively seeking popular science fiction. "Would love to see more medical and self-help books from professionals." Obtains new clients through recommendations from others and solicitation.
Recent Sales: New agency with no reported sales.
Terms: Agent receives 15% commission on domestic sales; 20% on foreign sales. Written contract. "Also, I'll bend over backwards to accommodate science fiction writers." May sometimes charge for photocopies.
Tips: "Always go the extra mile in your writing, in your research, and in your query and proposal presentation."

AGENTS RANKED I AND II are most open to both established and new writers. Agents ranked **III** are open to established writers with publishing-industry references.

AIKEN-JONES LITERARY, (I, II), P.O. Box 189, Depoe Bay OR 97341-0189. (541)765-7412. Contacts: Chris Jones, Ted Aiken. Estab. 1998. Represents 4 clients. 75% of clients are new/unpublished writers. Currently handles: 100% novels.

- Prior to opening their agency, Mr. Aiken published *Northwest Lives* magazine, worked for talent agency in Burbank, and served as a creative writing instructor. Mr. Jones was a professional reader/editor for *The Mountaineers* and a PR consultant.

Member Agents: Chris Jones (horror/supernatural); Ted Aiken (science fiction/fantasy).
Represents: Novels. Considers these fiction areas: fantasy; horror; psychic/supernatural; old gothic; science fiction; thriller/espionage.
How to Contact: Send outline and 3 sample chapters and SASE for response. *No phone calls*. Reports in 2 weeks on queries; 6-8 weeks on mss.
Needs: Actively seeking horror/supernatural with fresh voices and story lines that come together, taking the reader to new places.
Recent Sales: Prefers not to share information on specific sales.
Terms: Agent receives 15% commission on domestic sales; 20% on foreign sales. Offers written contract, binding for 1 year. 60 days notice must be given to terminate contract. Charges for postage and photocopying.
Tips: Obtains new clients through recommendations and solicitations.

LINDA ALLEN LITERARY AGENCY, (II), 1949 Green St., Suite 5, San Francisco CA 94123-4829. (415)921-6437. Contact: Linda Allen or Amy Kossow. Estab. 1982. Member of AAR. Represents 35-40 clients. Specializes in "good books and nice people."
Represents: Novels (adult) and nonfiction. Considers these fiction areas: action/adventure; contemporary issues; detective/police/crime; ethnic; feminist; gay; glitz; horror; lesbian; literary; mainstream; mystery/suspense; psychic/supernatural; regional; thriller/espionage.
How to Contact: Query with SASE. Reports in 2-3 weeks on queries.
Needs: Obtains new clients "by referral mostly."
Recent Sales: Prefers not to share information on specific sales.
Terms: Agent receives 15% commission. Charges for photocopying.

BETSY AMSTER LITERARY ENTERPRISES, (II), P.O. Box 27788, Los Angeles CA 90027-0788. Contact: Betsy Amster. Estab. 1992. Member of AAR. Represents over 50 clients. 40% of clients are new/unpublished writers. Currently handles: 75% nonfiction books; 25% novels.

- Prior to opening her agency, Ms. Amster was an editor at Pantheon and Vintage for 10 years and served as editorial director for the Globe Pequot Press for 2 years. "This experience gives me a wider perspective on the business and the ability to give focused editorial feedback to my clients."

Represents: Novels and nonfiction books. Considers these fiction areas: detective/police/crime; ethnic; literary; mystery/suspense.
How to Contact: For fiction, send query and first page. "Include SASE or no response." Reports in 2-4 weeks on queries; 4-8 weeks on mss.
Needs: Actively seeking "outstanding literary fiction (the next Jane Smiley or Wally Lamb) and high profile self-help/psychology." Does not want to receive poetry, children's books, romances, westerns, science fiction. Obtains new clients through recommendations from others, solicitation, conferences.
Recent Sales: *Esperanza's Box of Saints* (Scribner); *Chicana Falsa and Other Stories of Death, Identity, and Oxnard*, by Michele M. Serros (Riverhead); *Darkest Desire: The Wolf's Own Tale* (Ecco); *Baby Minds: Recognizing and Fostering Your Infant's Intellectual Development in the Critical First Years* (Bantam); *The Highly Sensitive Person in Love* (Broadway).
Terms: Agent receives 15% commission on domestic sales. Offers written contract, binding for 1-2 years. 60 days notice must be given to terminate contract. Charges for photocopying, postage, long distance phone calls, messengers and galleys and books used in submissions to foreign and film agents and to magazines for first serial rights.
Writers' Conferences: Maui Writers Conference; Pacific Northwest Conference; San Diego Writers Conference; UCLA Writers Conference.

MARCIA AMSTERDAM AGENCY, (II), 41 W. 82nd St., New York NY 10024-5613. (212)873-4945. Contact: Marcia Amsterdam. Estab. 1970. Signatory of WGA. Currently handles: 15% nonfiction books; 70% novels; 10% movie scripts; 5% TV scripts.

- Prior to opening her agency, Ms. Amsterdam was an editor.

Represents: Novels and nonfiction. Considers these fiction areas: action/adventure; detective; horror; humor; mainstream; mystery/suspense; romance (contemporary, historical); science fiction; thriller/espionage; westerns/frontier; young adult.
How to Contact: Send outline plus first 3 sample chapters and SASE. Reports in 1 month on queries.
Recent Sales: *Rosey In the Present Tense*, by Louise Hawes (Walker); *Flash Factor*, by William H. Lovejoy (Kensington); *Moses Goes to School*, by Isaac Millman (Farrar, Straus & Giroux). ***TV scripts optional/sold:*** ***Mad About You***, by Jenna Bruce (Columbia Tristar TV).
Terms: Agent receives 15% commission on domestic sales; 20% on foreign sales, 10% on scripts. Offers written

contract, binding for 1 year, "renewable." Charges for extra office expenses, foreign postage, copying, legal fees (when agreed upon).
Also Handles: Movie scripts (feature film), TV scripts (TV MOW, sitcom). Considers these script subject areas: comedy, mainstream, mystery/suspense, romance (comedy, drama).
Tips: "We are always looking for interesting literary voices."

N MALAGA BALDI LITERARY AGENCY, (II), 2112 Broadway, Suite 403, New York NY 10023. (212)579-5075. Contact: Malaga Baldi. Estab. 1985. Represents 40-50 clients. 80% of clients are new/previously unpublished writers. Specializes in quality literary fiction and nonfiction. Currently handles: 60% nonfiction books; 40% novels.

- Prior to opening the agency, Malaga Baldi worked in a bookstore.

Represents: Novels and nonfiction books. Considers these fiction areas: action/adventure; contemporary issues; detective; erotica; ethnic; experimental; feminist; gay; historical; lesbian; literary; mainstream; mystery/suspense; regional; thriller.
How to Contact: Query first, but prefers entire ms for fiction. Reports after a minimum of 10 weeks. "Please enclose self-addressed stamped jiffy bag or padded envelope with submission. For acknowledgement of manuscript receipt send via certified mail or UPS."
Needs: Actively seeking well-written fiction, New Age/metaphysics, family saga, fantasy, glitz, juvenile fiction, picture book, psychic/supernatural, religious/inspirational, romance, science fiction, western or young adult.
Recent Sales: Sold 13 titles in the last year. Prefers not to share information on specific sales.
Terms: Agent receives 15% commission on domestic sales; 20% on foreign sales. Offers written contract. Charges "initial $50 fee to cover photocopying expenses. If the manuscript is lengthy, I prefer the author to cover expense of photocopying."
Tips: "From the day I agree to represent an author, my role is to serve as his or her advocate in contract negotiations and publicity efforts. Along the way, I wear many different hats. To one author I may serve as a nudge, to another a confidante, and to many simply as a supportive friend. I am also a critic, researcher, legal expert, messenger, diplomat, listener, counselor and source of publishing information and gossip. I work with writers on developing a presentable submission and make myself available during all aspects of a book's publication."

N LORETTA BARRETT BOOKS INC., (II), 101 Fifth Ave., New York NY 10003. (212)242-3420. Fax: (212)691-9418. E-mail: lbarbooks@aol.com. President: Loretta A. Barrett. Contact: Kirsten Lundell or Loretta A. Barrett. Estab. 1990. Member of AAR. Represents 70 clients. Specializes in general interest books. Currently handles: 25% fiction; 75% nonfiction.

- Prior to opening her agency, Ms. Barrett was vice president and executive editor at Doubleday for 25 years.

Represents: Considers these fiction areas: action/adventure; cartoon/comic; confessional; contemporary issues; detective/police/crime; ethnic; experimental; family saga; fantasy; feminist; gay; glitz; historical; humor/satire; lesbian; literary; mainstream; mystery/suspense; psychic/supernatural; religious/inspirational; romance; sports; thriller/espionage.
How to Contact: Query first with SASE. Reports in 4-6 weeks on queries.
Recent Sales: Sold about 20 titles in the last year. Prefers not to share info. on specific sales.
Terms: Agent receives 15% commission on domestic sales; 20% on foreign sales. Offers written contract. Charges for shipping and photocopying.
Writers' Conferences: San Diego State University Writer's Conference; Maui Writer's Conference.

N JENNY BENT, LITERARY AGENT, GRAYBILL & ENGLISH, L.C.C., (I, II), 1920 N. St. NW, #620, Washington DC 20036. (202)861-0106. Fax: (202)457-0662. E-mail: jenlbent@aol.com. Contact: Jenny Bent. Estab. 1997. Represents 40 clients. 50% of clients are new/unpublished writers. "Since Graybill & English is both a literary agency and a law firm, we can offer our clients essential legal services." Currently handles: 75% nonfiction books; 25% novels.

- Prior to joining her agency Ms. Bent worked as an editor in book publishing and magazines.

Represents: Novels and nonfiction books. Considers these fiction areas: contemporary issues; detective/crime/police (hard-boiled detective); ethnic; family saga; gay/lesbian; literary; mainstream; mystery (malice domestic); romance; suspense.
How to Contact: Query. Send outline/proposal and SASE. "Please always include a bio or résumé with submissions or queries." *No calls please.* E-mail queries are OK. Reports in 2 weeks on queries; 1 month on mss.
Needs: Actively seeking quality fiction from well-credentialed authors. Does not want to receive science fiction, children's, self-help from non-credentialed writers. Otains new clients through recommendations, solicitations, conferences.
Recent Sales: Sold 13 titles in the last year. *Healing A.D.D.*, by Marcia Zimmerman (Holt); *The E Factor*, by Andreas Papas (HarperCollins); *A Stranger in the House*, by Neil Bernstein (Workman); *A Treasury of Royal Scandals*, by Michael Farquhar (Penguin).
Terms: Agent receives 15% commission on domestic sales; 25% on foreign sales. Offers written contract. 30

days notice must be given to terminate contract. Charges for office expenses, postage, photocopying, long distance.
Writer's Conferences: Hurston-Wright (Richmond, VA, summer); Washington Independent Writers Spring Writers Conference (Washington DC, May); Washington Romance Writers Spring Retreat; Virginia Romance Writers Conference (Williamsburg, VA, March).

N **PAM BERNSTEIN & ASSOCIATES, INC., (II)**, 790 Madison Ave., Suite 310, New York NY 10021. (212)288-1700. Fax: (212)288-3054. Contact: Pam Bernstein or Donna Downing. Estab. 1992. Member of AAR. Represents 50 clients. 20% of clients are new/previously unpublished writers. Specializes in commercial adult fiction and nonfiction. Currently handles: 60% nonfiction books; 40% fiction.

- Prior to becoming agents, Ms. Bernstein served as vice president with the William Morris Agency; Ms. Downing was in public relations.

Represents: Considers these fiction areas: contemporary issues; detective/police/crime; ethnic; historical; mainstream; mystery/suspense; romance (contemporary); thriller/espionage.
How to Contact: Query. Reports in 2 weeks on queries; 1 month on mss. Include postage for return of ms.
Needs: Obtains new clients through referrals from published authors.
Recent Sales: Sold 25 titles in the last year. *Tempest Rising*, by Diane McKinney-Whetstone (William Morrow).
Terms: Agent receives 15% commission on domestic sales; 20% on foreign sales. Offers written contract, binding for 3 years, with 30 day cancellation clause. 100% of business is derived from commissions on sales. Charges for postage and photocopying.

N **BOOK DEALS, INC., (I)**, Civic Opera Bldg., 20 N. Wacker Dr., Suite 1928, Chicago IL 60606. (312)372-0227. Contact: Caroline Carney. Estab. 1996. Represents 40 clients. 25% of clients are new/previously unpublished writers. Specializes in highly commercial and literary fiction and nonfiction. Currently handles: 75% nonfiction books, 25% fiction.

- Prior to opening her agency, Ms. Carney was editorial director for a consumer book imprint within Times Mirror and held senior editorial positions in McGraw-Hill and Simon & Schuster.

Represents: Novels and narrative nonfiction, how-to. Considers these fiction areas: contemporary issues; ethnic; feminist; humor/satire; literary; mainstream; sports; white collar crime stories; urban literature.
How to Contact: Fiction by referral only. Send synopsis, outline/proposal with SASE. Reports in 2-4 weeks on queries.
Needs: Actively seeking well-crafted fiction and nonfiction. Does not want to receive fantasy, science fiction or westerns.
Recent Sales: *How to Raise a Smarter Kid*, Roger Schank (HarperCollins); *The Most Important Thing I Know About the Spirit of Sport*, by Lorne Adrain (William Morrow); *Whose Body Is It Anyway?*, by Dr. Joan Kenley (Newmarket Press); *Usher: He Makes You Wanna . . .*, by Marc Malkin (Andrews McMeel); and *The Internal Frontier*, by Morris Shechtman (NewStar).
Terms: Agent receives 15% commission on domestic sales; 20% on foreign sales. Offers a written contract. Charges for photocopying and postage.

N **CURTIS BROWN LTD., (II)**, 10 Astor Place, New York NY 10003-6935. (212)473-5400. Member of AAR; signatory of WGA. Perry Knowlton, chairman & CEO. Peter L. Ginsberg, president.
Member Agents: Laura Blake Peterson; Ellen Geiger; Emilie Jacobson, vice president; Maureen Walters, vice president; Virginia Knowlton; Jennifer MacDonald; Andrew Pope; Clyde Taylor; Mitchell Waters; Dave Barber (translation rights).
Represents: Novels, novellas, short story collections, nonfiction books, juvenile books and poetry books. All categories of fiction considered.
How to Contact: No unsolicited mss. Query first with SASE. Reports in 3 weeks on queries; 3-5 weeks on mss (only if requested).
Needs: Obtains new clients through recommendations from others, solicitation, at conferences and query letters.
Recent Sales: Prefers not to share information on specific sales.
Terms: Offers written contract. Charges for photocopying, some postage.

N **CARLISLE & COMPANY, (II)**, 24 E 64th St., New York NY 10021. (212)813-1888. Fax: (212)813-9567. E-mail: mvc@carlisleco.com. Contact: Michael Carlisle. Estab. 1998. Represents 70 clients. "Few" clients are new/unpublished writers. "Expertise in nonfiction. We have a strong focus on editorial input on fiction before submission." Currently handles: 70% nonfiction books; 5% short story collections; 25% novels.

- Prior to opening his agency, Mr. Carlisle was the vice president of William Morris for 18 years. Ms. Fletcher was an agent and rights manager at the Carol Mann Agency. Mr. Bascomb was an editor at St. Martin's Press.

Member Agents: Michael Carlisle; Christy Fletcher (literary, fiction); Neal Bascomb (mainstream fiction, thriller/suspense, genre fiction).
Represents: Novels, short story collections and nonfiction books. Considers these fiction areas: literary; mainstream; mystery; romance; suspense; thriller/espionage.
How to Contact: Query with SASE. E-mail queries OK. Reports in 10 days on queries, 3 weeks on mss.
Needs: Does not want to receive science fiction or fantasy. Obtains new clients through referrals.

INSIDER REPORT

Mark Walters: on writing a novel and finding an agent

Credit: Barb Walters

Mark Walters

By any writer's standards, Mark Walters seems to be living a charmed existence. And the tale of how his first book, *Realizing Hannah*, came to be published is a novelist's dream come true. Prominent New York agent Michael Carlisle agreed to represent him just two weeks after receiving Walters' manuscript. Two weeks after that, Carlisle, who had started his own agency after working with the William Morris Agency for 18 years, sold the literary work to William Morrow and Co.

"I was surprised by how quickly he was able to do what he did," Walters says of Carlisle. "Had I been trying to shop the novel on my own, I couldn't have gotten anyone to read it." But getting Carlisle to consider his manuscript meant having the right connections, and Walters had the good fortune of knowing two professionals in the publishing community. For starters, his friend Carolyn Doty, a novelist who teaches at Kansas University, has a network which includes a number of prominent agents. Plus, Walters had been corresponding with Doris Cooper, an editor at William Morrow, since a section of *Realizing Hannah* was published in the *Atlantic Monthly.*

"As I was working on the novel, occasionally I would send out a chapter," says Walters. Soon after its publication, he received a call from Cooper. "She liked the piece in the *Atlantic* and wanted to know if I was doing anything else. I was on the verge of finishing the novel, so I sent her a draft."

But Cooper didn't think the manuscript was salable. Moreover, Walters was having difficulties finding an agent. "Carolyn gave me the name of two agents. I sent a copy to one who said it was hard to place literary fiction unless an agent really believed in the work, and she didn't take on my manuscript."

In the meantime, Cooper suggested Walters do a substantial revision of his novel. "I trusted her judgment and, in fact, added another subplot. I worked on it for another eight or nine months." With an increased confidence in his work, Walters once again contacted Doty. "I asked her if she knew an agent who would be a good fit for me and my manuscript. She suggested I call Carlisle."

Walters was surprised when Carlisle returned his initial call. "He laid down the ground rules, saying that if no other agent was reading my manuscript, he would read it in two weeks. He agreed to do this on the strength of Carolyn's referral. Less than two weeks later, he offered to take me on as a client."

A solid recommendation from a respected writer is often the best way writers can initiate the most important relationship of their career. "The referral from Carolyn and having a portion of the writing legitimized by publication in the *Atlantic* helped me get

INSIDER REPORT, *Walters*

my foot in the door," says Walters. Beyond luck, arriving at that point takes patience and diligent work. "If you take your time, cultivate a track record, and show your manuscript to people who are in positions to critique it, then you may begin to have doors open up for you."

But even Walters acknowledges, "It's been a long process for me." First, he spent time studying fiction in the Masters of Fine Arts program at Wichita State. After graduating in 1986, he started his Ph.D. in American Literature at the University of Kansas in Lawrence. At the same time, Walters says, "I was writing short fiction, which I was getting published regularly in *National Lampoon*. I was experimenting with different voices and trying to develop and perfect my craft before I attempted a novel."

Patiently cultivating his talent, Walters waited until he knew his writing was mature enough for a novel-length work. After beginning a full-time teaching job at William Jewell College, he would rise at 4 a.m. to write. After four years, he had a complete novel manuscript.

Realizing Hannah, which alternates between present and past tense, is "the nine months of a woman's pregnancy told from the point of view of her husband, Joe Shoe," says Walters. " 'Hannah' is Hebrew for grace, and one of the conflicts is Joe's coming to terms with grace. He is struggling with a lot of things: reconciling his need for control with his loss of it; his unhappiness with his marriage and the sudden demand for commitment; and his own sexual desires along with his sense of God and sin."

Walter's dedication to his craft paid off in the quality of the writing, which Carlisle calls graceful, beautiful and engaging. "The story-telling vehicle Walters uses is very original and smooth," says Carlisle. "*Realizing Hannah* is an original story. His strong voice gets you into a whole world pretty quickly. He is a real novelist." Walters regards his relationship with Carlisle as long-lasting. "His faith in me convinced me he was absolutely the right person. He's delightful—smart, funny and wonderfully eloquent. Carolyn had told me he was powerful and honest, and he is. He's always been upfront with me and was quite frank about the possibility of not being able to sell my novel." Carlisle kept Walters informed through the entire process. "He sent it to about eight places," says Walters. Any fears of not selling the manuscript were unfounded—William Morrow acquired the novel almost immediately. "Doris Cooper had already invested so much in it, and Carlisle was impressed with her."

Surprised by Carlisle's openness, Walters says, "I didn't know very much about agents. I thought an agent would occasionally talk to you and only when you had a manuscript to sell. The relationship seems more significant than I'd imagined. He and his assistant Mary Beth Brown have my best interests in mind and are always willing to answer my questions. He expects me to trust him, and I do, absolutely."

"In terms of my writing, he expects me to take my time and write the best fiction I can," Walters adds. Achieving this goal means being open to changes in his work. "I admit I've always been a snob about popular fiction and dismissed page turners as being insubstantial. I wanted to write a novel that someone would read slowly and linger over. By working with Doris, I'm learning that a strong narrative line does not have to compromise the character drive and complexity of the novel."

Walters hopes the marketplace doesn't influence his writing but admits, "it probably does, though teaching the canonical texts, which were rarely best sellers, keeps me honest and helps me maintain integrity in my writing. I have black and white photos of Vladimir Nabokov and William Faulkner above my desk. They both have menacing expressions on

INSIDER REPORT, *continued*

their faces—I look at them when I'm writing to remind me not to descend into shmaltz or predictability."

Maintaining high standards can be difficult, especially when many readers easily lose patience with literary novels. "There are fine writers who have such small audiences that agents won't take them on. The bottom line for most publishers is sales, and the general reading public drives the market. Unless somebody hooks up with an agent who believes in good character-driven fiction and can find a publisher who shares those beliefs, he or she is not going to have much luck."

Fortunately, Walters found such an agent. In fact, Carlisle was impressed enough with Walters' ability that he asked him to come along when he left William Morris to start his own agency. "I said yes. I didn't even think about it," says Walters. "I have a relationship with him, not the agency. I felt excited for him but also relieved and flattered. Being asked to join him reaffirmed my confidence."

Walters feels lucky to have an agent like Carlisle, an editor like Cooper and friends like Doty, as well as the support of his wife, Barb, and two young sons, Landon and Reid. Their encouragement, combined with Walters' talent and determination, is the perfect mix for a successful writing career. For writers without close connections, Walters offers this advice: "Select your agent as carefully as you do the venues for your short fiction. Do some reading and find out who an agent's clients are and the kinds of things they are publishing. I really believe that if you have genuine talent and if you're persistent and disciplined, and not wearied by the inevitable rejections along the way, eventually you'll make it."

—Donya Dickerson

Recent Sales: 15 projects sold in the last year. *Longitude*, by David Sobel (Walker & Co.); *Chaos*, by James Gleick (Viking); *The Half Life of Happiness*, by John Casey (Knopf); *Realizing Hannah*, by Mark Walters (William Morrow & Co.).

Terms: Agent receives 15% commission on domestic sales; 20% on foreign sales. Offers written contract, binding "for book only."

Writers' Conferences: Squaw Valley Community Conference (California).

Tips: "Be sure to write as original a story as possible. Remember, you're asking the public to pay $25 for your book."

N MARIA CARVAINIS AGENCY, INC., (II), 235 West End Ave., New York NY 10023. (212)580-1559. Fax: (212)877-3486. Contact: Maria Carvainis. Estab. 1977. Member of AAR, Authors Guild, American Booksellers Association, Mystery Writers of America, Romance Writers of America, signatory of WGA. Represents 30 clients. 10% of clients are new/previously unpublished writers. Currently handles: 29% nonfiction books; 15% juvenile books; 55% novels; 1% poetry books.

- Prior to opening her agency, Ms. Carvainis spent more than 10 years in the publishing industry as a senior editor with Macmillan Publishing, Basic Books, Avon Books, where she worked closely with Peter Mayer and Crown Publishers. Maria Carvainis is also a member of the AAR Board of Directors and AAR Treasurer.

Represents: Novels and nonfiction books. Considers these fiction areas: fantasy; historical; literary; mainstream; mystery/suspense; romance; thriller; children's; young adult. Query first with SASE. Reports within 2-3 weeks on queries; within 3 months on solicited mss.

Needs: Does not want to receive science fiction. "60% of new clients derived from recommendations or conferences. 40% of new clients derived from letters of query."

Recent Sales: *Silent Melody*, by Mary Balogh (Berkley); *The Guru Guide*, by Joseph H. Boyett and Jimmie T. Boyett (John Wiley and Sons); *Fat Tuesday*, by Sandra Brown (Warner Books); *Sheer Gall*, by Michael Kahn (Dutton/Signet). Other clients include Candace Camp, Pam Conrad, Catherine Hart, Samantha James, Gerrit Verschaur and Jose Yglesias.

Terms: Agent receives 15% commission on domestic sales; 20% on foreign sales. Offers written contract, binding for 2 years "on a book-by-book basis." Charges for foreign postage and bulk copying.
Writers' Conferences: BEA; Romance Writers of America; Frankfurt Book Fair; Novelists, Inc.

N **CASTIGLIA LITERARY AGENCY, (II)**, 1155 Camino Del Mar, Suite 510, Del Mar CA 92014. (619)755-8761. Fax: (619)755-7063. Contact: Julie Castiglia. Estab. 1993. Member of AAR, PEN. Represents 50 clients. Currently handles: 65% nonfiction books; 35% novels.

- Prior to opening her agency, Ms. Castiglia served as an agent with Waterside Productions, as well as working as a freelance editor and published writer of 3 books.

Represents: Novels and nonfiction books. Considers these fiction areas: contemporary issues; ethnic; glitz; literary; mainstream; mystery/suspense; women's fiction especially.
How to Contact: Send outline/proposal plus 2 sample chapters; send synopsis with 2 chapters for fiction. Reports in 6-8 weeks on mss.
Needs: Does not want to receive horror, science fiction or Holocaust novels. Obtains new clients through solicitations, conferences, referrals.
Recent Sales: *Remember the Time*, by Annette A. Reynolds (Bantam); *Managing Martians*, by Donna Shirley and Danelle Morton (Broadway Books); *Wild Turkey Moon*, by April Cristofferson (Tor/Forge).
Terms: Agent receives 15% commission on domestic sales; 20% on foreign sales. Offers written contract, 6 week termination. Charges for excessive postage and copying.
Writers' Conferences: Southwestern Writers Conference (Albuquerque NM August). National Writers Conference; Willamette Writers Conference (OR); San Diego State University (CA); Writers At Work (Utah).
Tips: "Be professional with submissions. Attend workshops and conferences before you approach an agent."

N **RUTH COHEN, INC. LITERARY AGENCY, (II)**, P.O. Box 7626, Menlo Park CA 94025. (650)854-2054. Contact: Ruth Cohen or associates. Estab. 1982. Member of AAR, Authors Guild, Sisters in Crime, Romance Writers of America, SCBWI. Represents 75 clients. 20% of clients are new/previously unpublished writers. Specializes in "quality writing in mysteries; juvenile fiction; adult women's fiction." Currently handles: 15% nonfiction books; 40% juvenile books; 45% novels.

- Prior to opening her agency, Ms. Cohen served as directing editor at Scott Foresman & Company (now HarperCollins).

Represents: Adult novels and juvenile books. Considers these fiction areas: detective/police; ethnic; historical; juvenile; literary; mainstream; mystery/suspense; picture books; romance (historical, long contemporary); young adult.
How to Contact: *No unsolicited mss.* Send outline plus 2 sample chapters. Must include SASE. Reports in 1 month on queries.
Needs: Obtains new clients through recommendations from others.
Recent Sales: Prefers not to share info on specific sales.
Terms: Agent receives 15% commission on domestic sales; 20% on foreign sales, "if a foreign agent is involved." Offers written contract, binding for 1 year "continuing to next." Charges for foreign postage and photocopying for submissions.
Tips: "A good writer cares about the words he/she uses—so do I. Also, if no SASE is included, material will not be read."

N **COLUMBIA LITERARY ASSOCIATES, INC., (II, IV)**, 7902 Nottingham Way, Ellicott City MD 21043-6721. (410)465-1595. Fax: Call for number. Contact: Linda Hayes. Estab. 1980. Member of AAR, IACP, RWA, WRW. Represents 30 clients. 10% of clients are new/previously unpublished writers. Specializes in women's commercial contemporary fiction (mainstream/genre), commercial nonfiction, especially cookbooks. Currently handles: 40% nonfiction books; 60% novels.
Represents: Novels and nonfiction books. Considers these fiction areas: mainstream; commercial women's fiction; suspense; contemporary romance; psychological/medical thrillers.
How to Contact: Reports in 2-4 weeks on queries; 6-8 weeks on mss; "rejections faster."
Recent Sales: Sold 20-30 titles in the last year. *Second Sight*, by Beth Amos (HarperPaperbacks); *Legend MacKinnon*, by Donna Kauffman (Bantam).
Terms: Agent receives 15% commission on domestic sales. Offers single- or multiple-book written contract, binding for 6-month terms. "Standard expenses are billed against book income (e.g., books for subrights exploitation, toll calls, UPS)."
Writers' Conferences: Romance Writers of America; International Association of Culinary Professionals; Novelists, Inc.
Tips: "CLA's list is very full; we're able to accept only a rare few top-notch projects." Submission requirements: "For fiction, send a query letter with author credits, narrative synopsis, first chapter or two, manuscript word count and submission history (publishers/agents); self-addressed, stamped mailer mandatory for response/ms return. (When submitting romances, note whether manuscript is mainstream or category—if category, say which line(s) manuscript is targeted to.) Please note that we do *not* handle: historical or literary fiction, westerns, science fiction/fantasy, military books, poetry, short stories or screenplays."

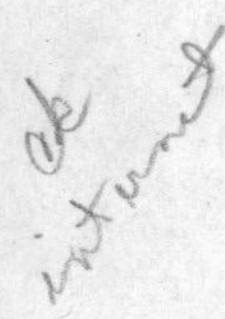

JAMES R. CYPHER, AUTHOR'S REPRESENTATIVE, (II), 616 Wolcott Ave., Beacon NY 12508-4247. (914)831-5677. E-mail: jimcypher@aol.com. Website: http://pages.prodigy.net/jimcypher/. Contact: James R. Cypher. Estab. 1993. Member of Horror Writers Association. Represents 57 clients. 46% of clients are new/previously unpublished writers. Currently handles: 64% nonfiction book; 36% novels.

- Mr. Cypher is a special contributor to Prodigy Service Books and Writing Bulletin Board. Prior to opening his agency, Mr. Cypher worked as a corporate public relations manager for a Fortune 500 multinational computer company for 28 years.

Represents: Novels and nonfiction books. Considers these fiction areas: literary; mainstream; crime fiction.
How to Contact: For fiction, send synopsis, 3 sample chapters and SASE. Reports in 2 weeks on queries; 6 weeks on mss.
Needs: Obtains new clients through referrals from others and networking on online computer services.
Recent Sales: *Hoare and the Portsmouth Atrocities* (historical crime fiction), by Wilder Perkins (St. Martin's Press); *Storyteller* (horror fiction), by Julie Anne Parks (Design Image Group).
Terms: Agent receives 15% commission on domestic sales; 20% on foreign sales. Offers written contract, with 30 day cancellation clause. Charges for postage, photocopying, overseas phone calls and faxes. 100% of business is derived from commissions on sales.
Tips: " 'Debut fiction' is very difficult to place in today's tight market, so a novel has to be truly outstanding to make the cut."

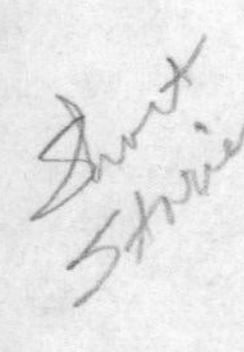

DARHANSOFF & VERRILL LITERARY AGENTS, (II), 179 Franklin St., 4th Floor, New York NY 10013. (212)334-5980. Estab. 1975. Member of AAR. Represents 100 clients. 10% of clients are new/previously unpublished writers. Specializes in literary fiction. Currently handles: 25% nonfiction books; 60% novels; 15% short story collections.
Member Agents: Liz Darhansoff, Charles Verrill, Leigh Feldman.
Represents: Novels, short story collections and nonfiction books. Considers literary and thriller fiction.
How to Contact: Query letter only. Reports in 2 weeks on queries.
Needs: Obtains new clients through recommendations from others.
Recent Sales: *Cold Mountain*, by Charles Frazier (Atlantic Monthly Press); *At Home in Mitford*, by Jan Karon (Viking).

THE DICKENS GROUP, (II), 3024 Madelle Ave., Louisville KY 40206. (502)894-6740. Fax: (502)894-9815. E-mail: sami@thedickens.win.net. Website: http://www.dickensliteraryagency.com. Contact: Alex Hughes. Estab. 1991. Represents 37 clients. 30% of clients are new/unpublished writers. "What sets the Dickens Group apart is a willingness to guide new writers." Currently handles: 50% nonfiction books; 50% novels.

- Prior to becoming agents, Dr. Solinger (president of Dickens) was a professor of pediatric cardiology; Ms. Hughes (vice president) was a professional screenwriter and editor. Ted Solinger (computer/electronic, fiction and nonfiction, sports, physical fitness).

Member Agents: Bob Solinger (literary and contemporary American fiction; westerns); (Ms.) Sam Hughes (top-list nonfiction, commercial and literary fiction).
Represents: Novels and nonfiction books. Considers these fiction areas: action/adventure; contemporary issues; detective/police/crime; ethnic; literary; mainstream; mystery/suspense; science fiction; thriller/espionage; westerns/frontier.
How to Contact: Query with SASE. Reports in 2 weeks on queries; 1 month on mss.
Needs: Actively seeking biographers, journalists, investigative reporters—"professionals writing fiction and nonfiction in their specialties." Does not want to receive unsolicited mss, poetry, essays, short stories. Obtains new clients through recommendations from others.
Recent Sales: *Nowhere to Hide*, by Gustave Carlson (Amacom); *Stars that Shine*, by Julie Clay (Simon & Schuster). Other clients include Mark Spencer (1996 Faulkner Award winner), *Love and Reruns in Adams County*; David Holland, Raymond Dix, Brenda Lee.
Terms: Agent receives 15% commission on domestic sales; 20% on foreign sales. Offers written contract "only if requested by author."
Tips: "Write a good concise, non-hyped query letter; include a paragraph about yourself."

SANDRA DIJKSTRA LITERARY AGENCY, (II), 1155 Camino del Mar, #515, Del Mar CA 92014. (619)755-3115. Contact: Sandra Zane. Estab. 1981. Member of AAR, Authors Guild, PEN West, Poets and Editors, MWA. Represents 100 clients. 30% of clients are new/previously unpublished writers. "We specialize in a number of fields." Currently handles: 60% nonfiction books; 5% juvenile books; 35% novels.
Member Agents: Sandra Dijkstra.

AGENTS WHO SPECIALIZE in a specific subject area such as computer books or in handling the work of certain writers such as gay or lesbian writers are ranked **IV**.

Represents: Novels and nonfiction books. Considers these fiction areas: contemporary issues; detective/police/crime; ethnic; family saga; feminist; literary; mainstream; mystery/suspense; thriller/espionage.
How to Contact: Send "synopsis and first 50 pages for fiction and SASE." Reports in 4-6 weeks on queries and mss.
Needs: Obtains new clients primarily through referrals/recommendations, but also through queries and conferences and often by solicitation.
Recent Sales: *The Mistress of Spices*, by Chitra Divakaruni (Anchor Books); *The Flower Net*, by Lisa See (HarperCollins); *Outsmarting the Menopausal Fat Cell*, by Debra Waterhouse (Hyperion); *Verdi*, by Janell Cannon (children's, Harcourt Brace); *The Nine Secrets of Women Who Get Everything They Want*, by Kate White (Harmony).
Terms: Agent receives 15% commission on domestic sales; 20% on foreign sales. Offers written contract, binding for 1 year. Charges for expenses from years we are *active* on author's behalf to cover domestic costs so that we can spend time selling books instead of accounting expenses. We also charge for the photocopying of the full manuscript or nonfiction proposal and for foreign postage."
Writers' Conferences: "Have attended Squaw Valley, Santa Barbara, Asilomar, Southern California Writers Conference, Rocky Mountain Fiction Writers, to name a few. We also speak regularly for writers groups such as PEN West and the Independent Writers Association."
Tips: "Be professional and learn the standard procedures for submitting your work. Give full biographical information on yourself, especially for a nonfiction project. Always include SASE with correct return postage for your own protection of your work. Query with a 1 or 2 page letter first and always include postage. Nine page letters telling us your life story, or your book's, are unprofessional and usually not read. Tell us about your book and write your query well. It's our first introduction to who you are and what you can do! Call if you don't hear within a reasonable period of time. Be a regular patron of bookstores and study what kind of books are being published. READ. Check out your local library and bookstores—you'll find lots of books on writing and the publishing industry that will help you! At conferences, ask published writers about their agents. Don't believe the myth that an agent has to be in New York to be successful—we've already disproved it!"

DONADIO AND ASHWORTH, INC., (II), 121 W. 27th St., Suite 704, New York NY 10001. (212)691-8077. Fax: (212)633-2837. Contact: Neil Olson. Estab. 1970. Member of AAR. Represents approximately 100 clients. Specializes in literary fiction and nonfiction. Currently handles: 40% nonfiction; 50% novels; 10% short story collections.
Member Agents: Edward Hibbert (literary fiction); Neil Olson; Ira Silverberg; Peter Steinberg.
Represents: Novels, short story collections and nonfiction books.
How to Contact: Query with 50 pages and SASE.
Recent Sales: Sold over 15 titles in the last year. Prefers not to share information on specific sales.
Terms: Agent receives 15% commission on domestic sales; 20% on foreign sales.

JANE DYSTEL LITERARY MANAGEMENT, (I, II), One Union Square West, New York NY 10003. (212)627-9100. Fax: (212)627-9313. Website: http://www.dystel.com. Contact: Miriam Goderich, Todd Keithley. Estab. 1994. Member of AAR. Presently represents 200 clients. 50% of clients are new/previously unpublished writers. Specializes in commercial and literary fiction and nonfiction plus cookbooks. Currently handles: 65% nonfiction books; 25% novels; 10% cookbooks.

- Prior to opening her agency, Ms. Dystel was a principal agent in Acton, Dystel, Leone and Jaffe.

Represents: Novels and nonfiction books. Considers these fiction areas: action/adventure; contemporary issues; detective/police/crime; ethnic; family saga; gay; lesbian; literary; mainstream; thriller/espionage.
How to Contact: Query. Reports in 3 weeks on queries; 6 weeks on mss.
Needs: Obtains new clients through recommendations from others, solicitation, at conferences.
Recent Sales: *No Physical Evidence*, by Gus Lee (Knopf); *The Sparrow*, by Mary Russell (Villard); *Lidia's Italian Table*, by Lidia Bastianich (William Morrow); *The World I Made for Her*, by Thomas Moran (Riverhead).
Terms: Agent receives 15% commission on domestic sales; 19% of foreign sales. Offers written contract on a book to book basis. Charges for photocopying. Galley charges and book charges from the publisher are passed on to the author.
Writers' Conferences: West Coast Writers Conference (Whidbey Island WA, Columbus Day weekend); University of Iowa Writer's Conference; Pacific Northwest Writer's Conference; Pike's Peak Writer's Conference; Santa Barbara Writer's Conference.

SANFORD J. GREENBURGER ASSOCIATES, INC., (II), 55 Fifth Ave., New York NY 10003. (212)206-5600. Fax: (212)463-8718. Contact: Heide Lange. Estab. 1945. Member of AAR. Represents 500 clients.
Member Agents: Heide Lange, Faith Hamlin, Beth Vesel, Theresa Park, Elyse Cheney, Dan Mandel.
Represents: Novels and nonfiction books. Considers these fiction areas: action/adventure; contemporary issues, detective/police/crime; ethnic; family saga; feminist; gay; glitz; historical; humor/satire; lesbian; literary; mainstream; mystery/suspense; psychic/supernatural; regional; sports; thriller/espionage.
How to Contact: Query first. Reports in 3 weeks on queries; 2 months on mss.
Needs: Does not want to receive romances or westerns.

Recent Sales: Sold 200 titles in the last year. Prefers not to share info. on specific sales. Clients include Andrew Ross, Margaret Cuthbert, Nicholas Sparks, Mary Kurcinka, Edy Clarke and Peggy Claude Pierre.
Terms: Agent receives 15% commission on domestic sales; 20% on foreign sales. Charges for photocopying, books for foreign and subsidiary rights submissions.

N REECE HALSEY AGENCY, (II, III), 8733 Sunset Blvd., Suite 101, Los Angeles CA 90069. (310)652-2409. Fax: (310)652-7595. Contact: Dorris Halsey. Also: Reece Halsey North, 98 Main St., #704, Tiburon CA 94920. (415)789-9191. Fax: (415)789-9177. Contact: Kimberley Cameron. Estab. 1957. Signatory of WGA. Represents 40 clients. 30% of clients are new/previously unpublished writers. Specializes mostly in books/excellent writing. Currently handles: 30% nonfiction books; 60% novels; 10% movie scripts.

- The Reese Halsey Agency has an illustrious client list largely of established writers, including the estate of Aldous Huxley and has represented Upton Sinclair, William Faulkner and Henry Miller. Ms. Cameron has recently opened a Northern California office and all queries should be addressed to her at the Tiburon office.

Member Agents: Dorris Halsey; Kimberley Cameron.
Represents: Novels and nonfiction books. Considers these fiction areas: action/adventure; contemporary issues; detective/police/crime; ethnic; family saga; historical; literary; mainstream; mystery/suspense; science fiction; thriller/espionage; women's fiction.
How to Contact: Query with SASE. Reports in 3 weeks on queries; 3 months on mss.
Terms: Agent receives 15% commission on domestic sales of books, 10% commission on script sales. Offers written contract, binding for 1 year. Requests 6 copies of ms if representing an author.
Writers' Conferences: ABA and various writer conferences, Maui Writers Conference.
Tips: Obtains new clients through recommendations from others and solicitation. "Always send a well-written query and include a SASE with it!"
Member Agents: Dorris Halsey; Kimberley Cameron. No reading fee.

N THE HARDY AGENCY, (II), 3020 Bridgeway, Suite 204, Sausalito CA 94965. (415)380-9985. Contact: Anne Sheldon, Michael Vidor. Estab. 1990. Represents 30 clients. 75% of clients are new/previously unpublished writers. Specializes in contemporary fiction and nonfiction. "We are accomplished in all areas of book publishing, including marketing and publicity." Currently handles: 30% nonfiction books; 70% novels.

- Prior to becoming agents, Ms. Sheldon was a publisher at a small press and Mr. Vidor was an advertising executive.

Member Agents: Anne Sheldon (fiction); Michael Vidor (nonfiction, commercial fiction).
Represents: Novels and nonfiction books. Considers these fiction areas: contemporary; literary; commercial.
How to Contact: Send query and/or 2 sample chapters. Reports in 1 month on queries and mss.
Needs: Actively seeking contemporary and commercial fiction, contemporary affairs, self-help, memoirs, alternative health, New Age, spirituality. Does not want to receive children's, romance or science fiction. Obtains new clients from recommendations.
Recent Sales: *The Book of Secrets*, by Robert Petro (HarperCollins); *Whiskey's Children*, by Jack Erdmann and Larry Kearney (Kensington); *Funerals for Horses*, by Catherine Ryan Hyde (Russian Hill Press); *Pay It Forward*, by Catherine Ryan Hyde (Simon & Schuster).
Terms: Agent receives 15% commission on domestic sales; 20% on foreign sales. Offers written contract, binding for 6 months. Charges for postage, copying. 100% of business is derived from commissions on sales.
Tips: Welcomes serious writers.

N JABBERWOCKY LITERARY AGENCY, (II), P.O. Box 4558, Sunnyside NY 11104-0558. (718)392-5985. Contact: Joshua Bilmes. Estab. 1994. Member of SFWA. Represents 40 clients. 25% of clients are new/previously unpublished writers. "Agency represents quite a lot of genre fiction and is actively seeking to increase amount of nonfiction projects." Currently handles: 25% nonfiction books; 5% scholarly books; 65% novel; 5% other.
Represents: Novels, nonfiction books and scholarly books. Considers these fiction areas: action/adventure; cartoon/comic; contemporary issues; detective/police/crime; ethnic; family saga; fantasy; gay; glitz; historical; horror; humor/satire; lesbian; literary; mainstream; psychic/supernatural; regional; romance; science fiction; sports; thriller/espionage.
How to Contact: Query. Reports in 2 weeks on queries.
Needs: Obtains new clients through recommendation by current clients, solicitation, "and through intriguing queries by new authors."
Recent Sales: Sold 20 titles in the last year. *Shakespeare's Champion*, by Charlaine Harris (Dell); *Deathstalker Honor*, by Simon Green (Roc); *Hot Blood X*, ed. by Jeff Gelb and Michael Garrett (Pocket); *Sex And Violence*, by Michael Ghiglieri (Perseus). Other clients include Tanya Huff, Elizabeth Moon, Brenda English, Scott Mackay and Marjore Kellogg.
Terms: Agent receives 12.5% commission on domestic sales; 20% on foreign sales. Offers written contract, binding for 1 year. Charges for book purchases, ms photocopying, international book/ms mailing, international long distance.
Writers' Conferences: Malice Domestic (Washington DC, April 1); World SF Convention (Australia, August);

Icon (Stony Brook NY, April).
Tips: "In approaching with a query, the most important things to me are your credits and your biographical background to the extent its relevant to your work. I (and most agents I believe) will ignore the adjectives you may choose to describe your own work. Please send query letter only; no manuscript material unless requested."

N JOY S. LITERARY AGENCY, (II), 3 Golf Center, Suite 141, Hoffman Estates IL 60195-3710. (847)310-0003. Fax: (847)310-0893. E-mail: joyco2@juno.com. Contact: Carol Joy Lippman. Represents 15 clients. 95% of clients are new/unpublished writers. "We are willing to look at a new writer's material and often give personal brief critiques for no extra change." Currently handles: 30% nonfiction books; 10% juvenile books; 10% scholarly books; 50% novels.

- Prior to becoming an agent, Ms. Joy was a bookstore owner for eight years.

Represents: Novels, nonfiction books, juvenile books and scholarly books. Considers these fiction areas: action/adventure; contemporary issues; literary; mainstream; religious/inspirational; suspense; thriller/espionage; westerns/frontier; young adult.
How to Contact: Query with outline/proposal and SASE. Reports in 2 weeks on queries; 1 month on mss.
Needs: Obtains new clients through queries by mail only.
Recent Sales: Prefers not to share information on specific sales.
Terms: Agent receives 15% commission on domestic sales. Offers written contract, binding for 2 years. 30 days notice must be given to terminate contract.
Writers' Conferences: Write-to-Publish (Wheaton IL, June); Christian Writers (Chicago IL, July); Bloomingdale Writers (Bloomingdale IL, September).
Tips: Proofread carefully. Always include SASE.

N ELAINE KOSTER LITERARY AGENCY, LLC, (I), 55 Central Park West, Suite 6, New York NY 10023. (212)362-9488. Fax: (212)712-0164. Contact: Elaine Koster. Member of Women's Media Group and Publishers' Lunch Club. Represents 30 clients. 25% of clients are new/unpublished writers. Specializes in quality fiction and nonfiction. Currently handles: 30% nonfiction books; 70% novels.

- Prior to opening her agency, Ms. Koster was president and publisher of Dutton NAL.

Represents: Novels and nonfiction books. Considers these fiction areas: action/adventure; confessional; contemporary issues; detective/police/crime; ethnic; family saga; feminist; gay/lesbian; glitz; historical; literary; mainstream; mystery (amateur sleuth, cozy, culinary, malice domestic); regional; suspense; thriller/espionage.
How to Contact: Query with outline, 3 sample chapters and SASE. No e-mail or fax queries. Reports in 3 weeks on queries; 1 month on mss.
Needs: Does not want to receive juvenile. Obtains new clients through recommendations from others.
Recent Sales: *The Danish Girl*, by David Ebershoff (Viking); *The Dress and Other Stories*, by David Ebershoff (Viking); *The Lithium Murder*, by Camille Minichino (Morrow); *So Much for Dreams*, by Sherri Devon (Dell).
Terms: Agent receives 15% commission on domestic sales; 20% on foreign sales. Offers written contract, 60 days notice must be given to terminate contract. Charges for photocopying, messengers, FedEx, books and book galley, ordered from publisher to exploit other rights, overseas shipment of mss and books, overseas phone and fax charges.
Tips: Obtains new clients through recommendation from others.

N BARBARA S. KOUTS, LITERARY AGENT, (II), P.O. Box 560, Bellport NY 11713. (516)286-1278. Contact: Barbara Kouts. Estab. 1980. Member of AAR. Represent 50 clients. 10% of clients are new/previously unpublished writers. Specializes in adult fiction and nonfiction and children's books. Currently handles: 20% nonfiction books; 60% juvenile books; 20% novels.
Represents: Novels, nonfiction books and juvenile books. Considers these fiction areas: contemporary issues; family saga; feminist; historical; juvenile; literary; mainstream; mystery/suspense; picture book; young adult.
How to Contact: Query. Reports in 2-3 days on queries; 4-6 weeks on mss.
Needs: Obtains new clients through recommendations from others, solicitation, at conferences, etc.
Recent Sales: *Dancing on the Edge*, by Han Nolan (Harcourt Brace); *Cendrillon*, by Robert San Souci (Simon & Schuster).
Terms: Agent receives 10% commission on domestic sales; 20% on foreign sales. Charges for photocopying.
Tips: "Write, do not call. Be professional in your writing."

N SABRA ELLIOTT LARKIN, (I), Bly Hollow Rd., Cherry Plain NY 12040-0055. Phone/fax: (518)658-3065. E-mail: becontree@taconic.net. Contact: Sabra Larkin. Estab. 1996. Represents 10 clients. 90% of clients are new/unpublished writers. Currently handles: 70% nonfiction books; 10% juvenile books; 20% novels.

- Prior to opening her agency, Ms. Larkin worked for over 30 years in publishing: 5 years in editorial at Dutton; 7 years at Ballantine Books in publicity and advertising; 10 years at Avon Books; and 10 years at Putnam Berkley as vice president of Publicity, Promotion, Advertising and Public Relations

Represents: Novels, nonfiction books, scholarly books, illustrated books/(adult) art and photography. Considers these fiction areas: action/adventure; contemporary issues; detective/police/crime; ethnic; experimental; family saga; glitz; historical; humor/satire; literary; mainstream; mystery/suspense; regional; romance (contemporary, historical); thriller/espionage.

How to Contact: Query. Send outline and 2-3 sample chapters with return postage. Reports in 1 month on queries; 2 months on mss.
Needs: Obtains new clients through recommendations from others.
Recent Sales: Sold 2 titles in the last year. *Water Rat*, by Marnie Laird (Winslow Press); *Winter Soups*, by Lisa Fosburgh (Country Roads Press). Other clients include Dorsey Fiske, Steve Stargen, Gretchen McKenzie, Ernest Barker.
Terms: Agent receives 15% commission on domestic sales; 20% on foreign sales. Offers written contract, binding for 5 years. 60 days notice must be given to terminate contract. Charges for postage and photocopying of mss. "Copies of receipts for dollar amounts are supplied to clients. Not applicable to contracted clients."

N **MICHAEL LARSEN/ELIZABETH POMADA LITERARY AGENTS, (II)**, 1029 Jones St., San Francisco CA 94109-5023. (415)673-0939. E-mail: larsonpoma@aol.com. Website: http://www.Larsen-Pomada.com. Contact: Mike Larsen or Elizabeth Pomada. Estab. 1972. Members of AAR, Authors Guild, ASJA, NWA, PEN, WNBA, California Writers Club. Represents 100 clients. 40-45% of clients are new/unpublished writers. Eager to work with new/unpublished writers. "We have very diverse tastes. We look for fresh voices and new ideas. We handle literary, commercial and genre fiction, and the full range of nonfiction books." Currently handles: 70% nonfiction books; 30% novels.

- Prior to opening their agency, both Mr. Larsen and Ms. Pomada were promotion executives for major publishing houses. Mr. Larsen worked for Morrow, Bantam and Pyramid (now part of Berkley), Ms. Pomada worked at Holt, David McKay, and The Dial Press.

Member Agents: Michael Larsen (nonfiction), Elizabeth Pomada (fiction, books of interest to women).
Represents: Novels and adult nonfiction books. Considers these fiction areas: action/adventure; contemporary issues; detective/police/crime; ethnic; experimental; family saga; fantasy; feminist; gay; glitz; historical; horror; humor/satire; lesbian; literary; mainstream; mystery/suspense; psychic/supernatural; religious/inspirational; romance (contemporary, gothic, historical, regency).
How to Contact: Query with synopsis and first 10 pages of completed novel. Reports in 6-8 weeks on queries. Always include SASE. Send SASE for brochure and title list.
Needs: Actively seeking commercial and literary fiction. "Fresh voices with new ideas of interest to major publishers." Does not want to receive children's books, plays, short stories, pornography.
Recent Sales: *Black Raven* (10th book in the Deverry Series), by Katharine Kerr (Bantam/Spectra); *A Crack In Forever*, by Jeannie Brewer (Simon & Schuster/Avon); *The Emerald Tablet: Message for the Millenium*, by Dennis William Hauck (Penguin).
Terms: Agent receives 15% commission on domestic sales; 15% on dramatic sales; 30% on foreign sales. May charge writer for printing, postage for multiple submissions, foreign mail, foreign phone calls, galleys, books, and legal fees.
Writers' Conferences: BEA; Santa Barbara Writers Conference (Santa Barbara); Maui Writers Conference (Maui); ASJA.

N **LEE COMMUNICATIONS, (II)**, 5060 N. 19th Ave., Suite 211, Phoenix AZ 85015. (602)246-9141. Fax: (602)242-9449. Contact: Cy Ellison. Represents 20 clients. 85% of clients are new/unpublished writers. Agent specializes in working with clients. Currently handles: 10% nonfiction books; 10% juvenile books; 5% movie scripts; 75% novels; 3% poetry.

- Prior to opening his agency, Mr. Ellison worked for over 50 years managing and creating conventions, publishing magazines, periodicals, books and marketing, working in sales promotion, and advertising over a 50 year period.

Represents: Novels, nonfiction books and juvenile books. Considers these fiction areas: action/adventure; detective/police crime; family saga; fantasy; historical; horror; mainstream; mystery (amateur sleuth, malice domestic); picture book; romance (contemporary, historical, regency); science fiction; suspense; thriller/espionage; westerns/frontier.
How to Contact: Send outline/proposal, 3 sample chapters and SASE. Reports immediately on queries; in 10 days on mss.
Needs: Actively seeking a condensed version of the ms, synopsis, story treatment, table of contents, bio of author. Does not want to receive unfinished or partially completed ms. Obtains new clients through referrals.
Recent Sales: Sold 2 titles in the last year. *From Hiroshima with Love*, by Raymond Higgins (P.C.I. Research); *Cats in Fact and Folklore*, by Virginia Holmgren (Macmillan).
Terms: Agent receives 15% commission on domestic sales; 15% on foreign sales. Offers written contract to the specific book. 30 days notice must be given to terminate contract.

LEVANT & WALES, LITERARY AGENCY, INC., (II, IV), 108 Hayes St., Seattle WA 98109-2808. (206)284-7114. Fax: (206)284-0190. E-mail: bizziew@aol.com. Contact: Elizabeth Wales or Adrienne Reed. Estab. 1988. Member of AAR, Pacific Northwest Writers' Conference, Book Publishers' Northwest. Represents 65 clients. We are interested in published and not-yet-published writers. Especially encourages writers living in the Pacific Northwest, West Coast, Alaska and Pacific Rim countries. Specializes in mainstream nonfiction and fiction, as well as narrative nonfiction and literary fiction. Currently handles: 60% nonfiction books; 40% novels.

- Prior to becoming an agent, Ms. Wales worked at Oxford University Press and Viking Penguin.

Represents: Novels and nonfiction books. Considers these fiction areas: cartoon/comic/women's; ethnic; experimental; feminist; gay; lesbian; literary; mainstream (no genre fiction).
How to Contact: Query first. "To Query: Please send cover letter, writing sample (no more than 30 pp.) and SASE." Reports in 3 weeks on queries; 6 weeks on mss.
Recent Sales: Sold 15 titles in the last year. *How Close We Come: A Novel*, by Susan S. Kelly (Warner Books); *Can I Get A Witness?: For Sister When The Blues Is More Than A Song*, by Julia A. Boyd (Dutton); *Savage Love*, by Dan Savage (Dutton); *Animals As Guides For The Soul*, by Susan Chernak McElroy (Ballantine).
Terms: Agent receives 15% commission on domestic sales. "We make all our income from commissions. We offer editorial help for some of our clients and help some clients with the development of a proposal, but we do not charge for these services. We do charge, after a sale, for express mail, manuscript photocopying costs, foreign postage and outside USA telephone costs."
Writers' Conferences: Pacific NW Writers Conference (Seattle, July).

ELLEN LEVINE LITERARY AGENCY, INC., (II, III), 15 E. 26th St., Suite 1801, New York NY 10010. (212)889-0620. Fax: (212)725-4501. Contact: Ellen Levine, Elizabeth Kaplan, Diana Finch, Louise Quayle Estab. 1980. Member of AAR. Represents over 100 clients. 20% of clients are new/previously unpublished writers. "My three younger colleagues at the agency (Louise Quayle, Diana Finch and Elizabeth Kaplan) are seeking both new and established writers. I prefer to work with established writers, mostly through referrals." Currently handles: 55% nonfiction books; 5% juvenile books; 40% fiction.
Represents: Novels, short story collections, nonfiction books and juvenile books. Considers these fiction areas: literary; mystery; women's fiction, thrillers.
How to Contact: Query. Reports in 3 weeks on queries, if SASE provided; 6 weeks on mss, if submission requested.
Needs: Obtains new clients through recommendations from others.
Recent Sales: *The Day Diana Died*, by Christopher Anderson (William Morrow); *Maxing Out: Why Women Sabotage Their Financial Security*, by Colette Dowling (Little, Brown).
Terms: Agent receives 15% commission on domestic sales; 20% on foreign sales. Charges for overseas postage, photocopying, messenger fees, overseas telephone and fax, books ordered for use in rights submissions.

LINDSTROM LITERARY GROUP, (I), 871 N. Greenbrier St., Arlington VA 22205-1220. (703)522-4730. Fax: (703)527-7624. E-mail: lindlitgrp@aol.com. Contact: Kristin Lindstrom. Estab. 1994. Represents 13 clients. 40% of clients are new/previously unpublished writers. Currently handles: 20% nonfiction books; 80% novels.
Represents: Novels and nonfiction books. Considers these fiction areas: action/adventure; contemporary issues; detective/police/crime; ethnic; family saga; fantasy; historical; mainstream; science fiction; thriller/espionage.
How to Contact: For fiction, send 3 chapters and outline with SASE to cover return of ms if desired. Reports in 6 weeks on queries; 2 months on mss.
Needs: Obtains new clients through references, guide listing.
Recent Sales: *The Crime Czar*, by Tony Dunbar (Dell Publishing); *Par Four*, by Elizabeth Gunn (Walker & Co.).
Terms: Agent receives 15% commission on domestic sales; 20% on foreign sales; 20% on performance rights sales. Offers written contract. Charges for marketing and mailing expense, express mail, UPS, etc.
Tips: "Include biography of writer. Send enough material for an overall review of project scope."

A LITERARY AGENCY FOR CHILDREN'S BOOKS, (II), 307 S. Carolina Ave., S.E., Washington DC 20003. (202)543-1043. Contact: Ann Tobias. Estab. 1988. Member of Children's Book Guild of Washington, Women's National Book Association, SCBWI. Represents 25 clients. 50% of clients are new/unpublished writers. "As a former children's book editor I believe I am of special help to my clients, as I understand the practices of the children's book publishing field." Currently handles 100% juvenile books.

- Prior to opening her agency, Ms. Tobias worked as a children's book editor at Harper, William Morrow and Scholastic.

Represents: Juvenile books. Considers these fiction areas: picture book texts; mid-level and young adult novels; poetry; illustrated mss.
How to Contact: Send entire ms with SASE. Reports immediately on queries; in 2 months on mss.
Needs: Actively seeking material for children. Obtains new clients through recommendations from editors. "Read a few books out of the library on how literary agents do business before approaching one."
Recent Sales: Sold 12 titles in the last year. Prefers not to share information on specific sales.
Terms: Agent receives 15% commission on domestic sales; 20% on foreign sales. No written contract. Charges

for photocopying, overnight mail, foreign postage, foreign telephone.

LOWENSTEIN ASSOCIATES, INC., (II), 121 W. 27th St., Suite 601, New York NY 10001. (212)206-1630. Fax: (212)727-0280. President: Barbara Lowenstein. Estab. 1976. Member of AAR. Represents 150 clients. 20% of clients are new/unpublished writers. Specializes in multicultural books (fiction and nonfiction), medical experts, commercial fiction, especially suspense, crime and women's issues. "We are a full-service agency, handling domestic and foreign rights, film rights, and audio rights to all of our books." Currently handles: 60% nonfiction books; 40% novels.

Member Agents: Barbara Lowenstein (president/agent); Nancy Yost (president/agent); Eileen Cope (agent); Norman Kurz (business affairs); Deborah Cateiro (associate agent).

Represents: Novels and nonfiction books. Considers these fiction areas: contemporary issues; detective/police/crime; erotica; ethnic; feminist; gay; historical; humor/satire; lesbian; literary mainstream; mystery/suspense; romance (contemporary, historical, regency); medical thrillers.

How to Contact: Send query with SASE, "otherwise will not respond." For fiction, send outline and 1st chapter. No unsolicited mss. "Please do not send manuscripts." Reports in 6 weeks on queries.

Needs: Obtains new clients through "referrals, journals and magazines, media, solicitations and a very few conferences."

Recent Sales: Sold approximately 75 titles in the last year. *Awakening the Buddha Within*, by Lama Surya Das (Broadway); *The Mozart Effect*, by Don Campbell (Avon); *Invasion of Privacy*, by Perri O'Shaughnessy (Dell). Other clients include Gina Barkhordar Nahai, Ishmael Reed, Lee Upton, Kevin Young, Michael Waldholz and Myrlie Evers Williams.

Terms: Agent receives 15% commission on domestic sales; 20% on foreign sales; 20% on dramatic sales. Offers written contract on a book-by-book basis. Charges for large photocopy batches and international postage.

Writers' Conference: Malice Domestic; Bouchercon.

Tips: "Know the genre you are working in and READ!"

DONALD MAASS LITERARY AGENCY, (III), 157 West 57th St., Suite 703, New York NY 10019. (212)757-7755. Contact: Donald Maass or Jennifer Jackson. Estab. 1980. Member of AAR, SFWA, MWA, RWA. Represents over 100 clients. 5% of clients are new/previously unpublished writers. Specializes in commercial fiction, especially science fiction, fantasy, mystery, romance, suspense. "We are fiction specialists; also noted for our innovative approach to career planning." Currently handles: 100% novels.

- Prior to opening his agency, Mr. Maass served as an editor at Dell Publishing (NY) and as a reader at Gollancz (London).

Member Agents: Donald Maass (mainstream, literary, mystery/suspense, science fiction); Jennifer Jackson (commercial fiction: especially romance, science fiction, fantasy, mystery/suspense).

Represents: Novels. Considers these fiction areas: detective/police/crime; fantasy; historical; horror; literary; mainstream; mystery/suspense; psychic/supernatural; romance (historical, paranormal, time travel); science fiction; thriller/espionage.

How to Contact: Query with SASE. Reports in 2 weeks on queries, 3 months on mss (if requested following query).

Needs: Actively seeking "to expand the literary portion of our list and expand in romance and women's fiction." Does not want to receive nonfiction, children's or poetry.

Recent Sales: Sold over 100 titles in the last year. *A Breach of Promise*, by Anne Perry (Fawcett Columbine); *Patriarch's Hope*, by David Feintuch (Warner Aspect); *Heir to the Shadows*, by Anne Bishop (Penguin USA/ROC); *Touch Not the Cat*, by Tracy Fobes (Pocket); *Flanders*, by Patricia Anthony (Berkley).

Terms: Agent receives 15% commission on domestic sales; 20% on foreign sales. Charges for large photocopying orders and book samples, "after consultation with author."

Writers' Conferences: Donald Maass: World Science Fiction Convention, Frankfurt Book Fair, Pacific Northwest Writers Conference, Craft of Writing/Greater Dallas Writers Association, and others. Jennifer Jackson: World Science Fiction and Fantasy Convention, RWA National, and others.

Tips: "We are fiction specialists. Few new clients are accepted, but interested authors should query with SASE. Subagents in all principle foreign countries and Hollywood. No nonfiction or juvenile works considered."

CAROL MANN AGENCY, (II, III), 55 Fifth Ave., New York NY 10003. (212)206-5635. Fax: (212)675-4809. Contact: Carol Mann. Estab. 1977. Member of AAR. Represents over 100 clients. 25% of clients are new/previously unpublished writers. Specializes in current affairs; self-help; psychology; parenting; history. Currently handles: 70% nonfiction books; 30% novels.

Member Agents: Gareth Esersky (contemporary nonfiction).

Represents: Considers literary fiction.

How to Contact: Query with outline/proposal and SASE. Reports in 3 weeks on queries.

Needs: Actively seeking "literary fiction." Does not want to receive "genre fiction (romance, mystery, etc.)."

Recent Sales: *The Making of a Classic: Hitchcock's Vertigo*, by Dan Aviler (St. Martin's); *Radical Healing*, by Rudolph Ballentine, M.D. (Harmony); *Hand to Mouth*, by Paul Auster (Holt); *Stopping Cancer Before It Starts*, by American Institute for Cancer Research (Golden). Other clients include Dr. William Julius Wilson, Barry Sears (*Mastering The Zone*), Dr. Judith Wallerstein, Lorraine Johnson-Coleman (*Just Plain Folks*), Pulitzer Prize

Winner Fox Butterfield and James Tobin, NBCC Award Winner for *Ernie Pyle* (Free Press).
Terms: Agent receives 15% commission on domestic sales; 20% on foreign sales. Offers written contract.
Tips: No phone queries. Must include SASE for reply.

N THE DENISE MARCIL LITERARY AGENCY, INC., (II), 685 West End Ave., New York NY 10025. (212)932-3110. Contact: Denise Marcil. Estab. 1977. Member of AAR. Represents 70 clients. 40% of clients are new/previously unpublished authors. Specializes in women's commercial fiction, business books, popular reference, how-to and self-help. Currently handles: primarily nonfiction.

- Prior to opening her agency, Ms. Marcil served as an editorial assistant with Avon Books and as an editor with Simon & Schuster.

Represents: Novels and nonfiction books. Considers these fiction areas: mystery/suspense; romance (contemporary).
How to Contact: Query with SASE *only*! Reports in 3 weeks on queries. "Does not read unsolicited mss."
Needs: Actively seeking "big, commercial books with solid plotting, in-depth characters, and suspense. Cyberthrillers may be the next hot topic." Does not want to receive "cozies or British-style mysteries." Obtains new clients through recommendations from other authors. "35% of my list is from query letters!"
Recent Sales: Sold 67 titles in the last year. *Good News For Bad Days*, by Father Paul Keenan (Warner Book); *Stepping Out With Attitude: Sister Sell Your Dream*, by Anita Bunkley (HarperCollins); *His Flame*, by Arnette Lamb (Pocket Books); *Getting Rich in America*, by Dr. Richard McKenzie and Dr. Dwight Lee (HarperCollins).
Terms: Agent receives 15% commission on domestic sales; 20% on foreign sales. Offers written contract, binding for 2 years. Charges $100/year for postage, photocopying, long-distance calls, etc. 100% of business is derived from commissions on ms sales.
Writers' Conferences: Maui Writers Conference (August); Pacific Northwest Writers Conference; RWA.
Tips: "Only send a one-page query letter. I read them all and ask for plenty of material; I find many of my clients this way. *Always* send a SASE."

N ELAINE MARKSON LITERARY AGENCY, (II), 44 Greenwich Ave., New York NY 10011. (212)243-8480. Fax: (212)691-9014. Contact: Yael Adler. Estab. 1972. Member of AAR and WGA. Represents 200 clients. 10% of clients are new/unpublished writers. Specializes in literary fiction, commercial fiction, trade nonfiction. Currently handles: 35% nonfiction books; 55% novels; 10% juvenile books.
Member Agents: Geri Thoma, Sally Wofford-Girand, Elizabeth Sheinkman, Elaine Markson.
Represents: Quality fiction and nonfiction.
How to Contact: Query with outline (must include SASE). SASE is required for the return of any material.
Recent Sales: *The First Horseman*, by John Case (Ballantine); *Life, the Movie*, by Neal Gabler (Knopf); *The Hidden Jesus*, by Donald Spoto (St. Martins).
Terms: Agent receives 15% commission on domestic sales; 20% on foreign sales. Charges for postage, photocopying, foreign mailing, faxing, long-distance telephone and other special expenses. "Please make sure manuscript weighs no more than one pound."

N THE EVAN MARSHALL AGENCY, (III), 6 Tristam Place, Pine Brook NJ 07058-9445. (973)882-1122. Fax: (973)882-3099. E-mail: evanmarshall@erols.com. Website: http://www.thenovelist.com. Contact: Evan Marshall. Estab. 1987. Currently handles: 50% nonfiction books; 50% novels.

- Prior to opening his agency, Mr. Marshall served as an editor with New American Library, Everest House, and Dodd, Mead & Co., and then worked as a literary agent at The Sterling Lord Agency.

Represents: Novels and nonfiction books. Considers these fiction areas: action/adventure; contemporary issues; detective/police/crime; erotica; ethnic; family saga; glitz; historical; horror; humor/satire; literary; mainstream; mystery/suspense; psychic/supernatural; religious/inspirational; romance; (contemporary, gothic, historical, regency); science fiction; thriller/espionage; westerns/frontier.
How to Contact: Query. Reports in 1 week on queries; 2 months on mss.
Needs: Obtains many new clients through referrals from clients and editors.
Recent Sales: *Cause for Alarm*, by Erica Spindler (Mira); *Maybe Tomorrow*, by Joan Hohl (Kensington); *A Gift of Sanctuary*, by Candace Robb (St. Martin's); *Sympathy for the Devil*, by Jerrilyn Farmer (Avon); *Going Out in Style*, by Joyce Christmas (Fawcett).
Terms: Agent receives 15% on domestic sales; 20% on foreign sales. Offers written contract.

N MARGRET MCBRIDE LITERARY AGENCY, (II), 7744 Fay Ave., Suite 201, La Jolla CA 92037. (619)454-1550. Fax: (619)454-2156. Estab. 1980. Member of AAR, Authors Guild. Represents 50 clients. 15% of clients are new/unpublished writers. Specializes in mainstream fiction and nonfiction.

- Prior to opening her agency, Ms. McBride served in the marketing departments of Random House and Ballantine Books and the publicity departments of Warner Books and Pinnacle Books.

Represents: Novels, nonfiction books and audio. Considers these fiction areas: action/adventure; detective/police/crime; ethnic; historical; humor; literary; mainstream; mystery/suspense; thriller/espionage; westerns/frontier.
How to Contact: Query with synopsis or outline. No unsolicited mss. Reports in 6 weeks on queries.
Needs: No screenplays.

Recent Sales: *Freeing Fauziya*, by Fauziya Kasinga with Layli Miller Bashir; *The Unimaginable Life*, by Kenny and Julia Loggins; *The Golden Door Cookbook*, by Michele Stroot; *Ain't Gonna Be The Same Fool Twice*, by April Sinclair; *Weddings*, by Collin Cowel.
Terms: Agent receives 15% commission on domestic sales; 10% on dramatic sales; 25% on foreign sales charges for overnight delivery and photocopying.

DORIS S. MICHAELS LITERARY AGENCY, INC., (II), 1841 Broadway, Suite #903, New York NY 10023-7137. (212)265-9474. Fax: (212)265-9480. Contact: Doris S. Michaels. Estab. 1994. Member of WNBA, AAR. Represents 30 clients. 50% of clients are new/previously unpublished writers. Currently handles: 40% nonfiction books; 60% novels.

- Prior to opening her agency, Ms. Michaels was an editor for Prentice-Hall, consultant for Prudential-Bache, and an international consultant for the Union Bank of Switzerland.

Represents: Novels and nonfiction books. Considers these fiction areas: action/adventure; contemporary issues; family saga; feminist; historical; literary; mainstream.
How to Contact: Query with SASE. No phone calls or unsolicited mss. Reports ASAP on queries with SASE; no answer without SASE.
Needs: Obtains new clients through recommendations from others, solicitation and at conferences.
Recent Sales: Sold 25 titles in the last year. *How to Become CEO*, by Jeffrey J. Fox (Hyperion); *The Neatest Little Guide to Personal Finance*, by Jason Kelly (Plume). Other clients include Maury Allen, Wendy Rue, Karin Abarbanel and Eva Shaw.
Terms: Agent receives 15% commission on domestic sales; 20% on foreign sales. Offers written contract, binding for 1 year, with 30 day cancellation clause. Charges for office expenses including deliveries, postage, photocopying and fax. 100% of business is derived from commissions on sales.
Writers' Conferences: BEA (Chicago, June); Frankfurt Book Fair (Germany, October); London Book Fair; Society of Southwestern Authors; San Diego State University Writers' Conference; Willamette Writers' Conference; International Women's Writing Guild; American Society of Journalists and Authors.

THE CRAIG NELSON COMPANY, (II), 77 Seventh Ave., Suite 8F, New York NY 10011-6621. (212)929-0163. Fax: (212)929-0168. E-mail: litagnt@aol.com. Website: http://members.aol.com/litagnt. Contact: Craig Nelson. Estab. 1997. Member of AAR, signatory of WGA. Represents 50 clients. 50% of clients are new/unpublished writers. Currently handles: 75% nonfiction books; 25% novels.

- Prior to becoming an agent, Mr. Nelson was the executive editor for two decades at Random House and HarperCollins.

Represents: Novels and nonfiction books. Considers these fiction areas: contemporary issues; ethnic; gay/lesbian; horror; humor/satire; literary; mainstream; suspense; thriller/espionage.
How to Contact: Query with SASE. "Prefer e-mail queries." Reports in 3-4 weeks on queries; 4-6 weeks on mss.
Needs: Actively seeking "page-turning thrillers, eye-opening journalism, original literary fiction."
Recent Sales: Sold 15 titles in the last year. *Untitled Memoirs*, by Steve Wozniak (Pocket); *The Deal*, by Joe Hutsko (Forge); *Tossed in My Salad*, by Martine Colette (HarperCollins); *How to Win Friends*, by Lynne Russell (St. Martin's).
Terms: Agent receives 15% commission on domestic sales; 20% on foreign sales. Offers written contract, binding for 30 days. 30 days notice must be given to terminate contract.

ALICE ORR AGENCY, INC., (II), 305 Madison Ave., Suite 1166, New York NY 10165. (718)204-6673. Fax: (718)204-6023. E-mail: orragency@aol.com. Website: http://www.romanceweb.com/aorr/aorr.html. Contact: Alice Orr. Estab. 1988. Member of AAR. Represents over 20 clients. Specializes in commercial ("as in nonliterary") fiction and nonfiction. Currently handles: 5% nonfiction books; 5% juvenile books; 90% novels.

- Prior to opening her agency, Ms. Orr was editor of mystery-suspense and romance fiction; national lecturer on how to write and get that writing published; and is a published popular fiction novelist.

Represents: Considers these fiction areas: mainstream; romance (contemporary, historical); mystery/suspense.
How to Contact: Send SASE for synopsis/proposal guidelines. "Send nonfiction proposal prepared according to this agency's guidelines only." For fiction, send synopsis and first 3 chapters. Reports in 2 months.
Needs: Actively seeking "absolutely extraordinary, astounding, astonishing work." Does not want to receive "science fiction and fantasy, horror fiction, literary nonfiction, literary fiction, poetry, short stories, children's or juvenile fiction and nonfiction." Obtains new clients through recommendations from others, writer's conferences, meetings with authors and submissions.
Terms: Agent receives 15% commission on domestic sales; 20% on foreign and film sales. No written contract.
Recent Sales: Sold over 20 titles in the last year. Prefers not to share info on specific sales.
Writers' Conferences: Edgar Allen Poe Awards Week; Novelists Ink Conference; International Women's Writing Guild Skidmore College Conference & Retreat; Romance Writers of America National Convention; Romantic Times Booklovers Convention.

PERKINS, RUBIE & ASSOCIATES, (IV), (formerly Perkins, Rabiner, Rubie & Associates), 240 W. 35th St., New York NY 10001. (212)279-1776. Fax: (212)279-0937. Contact: Lori Perkins, Peter Rubie. Estab.

1997. Member of AAR, HWA. Represents 130 clients. 15% of clients are new/previously unpublished writers. Perkins specializes in horror, dark thrillers, literary fiction, pop culture, Latino and gay issues (fiction and nonfiction). Rubie specializes in crime, science fiction, fantasy, off-beat mysteries, history, literary fiction, dark thrillers, narrative nonfiction. Currently handles: 60% nonfiction books; 40% novels.

- Lori Perkins is the author of *The Cheapskate's Guide to Entertaining; How to Throw Fabulous Parties on a Budget* (Carol Publishing) and *How to Get and Keep the Right Agent for You* (Writer's Digest Books). Prior to becoming an agent, she taught journalism at NYU. Mr. Rubie is the author of *The Elements of Storytelling* (John Wiley) and *Story Sense* (Writer's Digest Books). Prior to becoming an agent, Ms. Rabiner was recently editorial director of Basic Books at HarperCollins. She also taught nonfiction at Yale and authored *Thinking Like Your Editor: A Guide to Writing Serious Nonfiction*.

Represents: Novels and nonfiction books. Considers these fiction areas: detective/police/crime; ethnic; fact-based historical fiction; fantasy; horror; literary; mainstream; mystery/suspense; psychic/supernatural; science fiction; dark thriller.
How to Contact: Query with SASE. Reports in 3-6 weeks on queries with SASE; 10 weeks on mss.
Needs: Obtains new clients through recommendations from others, solicitation, at conferences, etc.
Recent Sales: *Big Rock Beat*, by Greg Kihn (Forge); *Piercing the Darkness: Uncovering the Vampires in America Today*, by K. Ramsland (Harper); *The Science of the X-files*, by Jeanne Cavelos (Berkley); *Keeper*, by Gregory Rucka (Bantam); *Witchunter*, by C. Lyons (Avon); *How the Tiger Lost Its Stripes*, by C. Meacham (Harcourt Brace).
Terms: Agent receives 15% commission on domestic sales; 20% on foreign sales. Offers written contract, only "if requested." Charges for photocopying.
Tips: "Sometimes I come up with book ideas and find authors (*Coupon Queen*, for example). Be professional. Read *Publishers Weekly* and genre-related magazines. Join writers' organizations. Go to conferences. Know your market and learn your craft."

PINDER LANE & GARON-BROOKE ASSOCIATES, LTD. (II), (formerly Jay Garon-Brooke Assoc. Inc.), 159 W. 53rd St., Suite 14E, New York NY 10019-6005. (212)489-0880. Vice President: Jean Free. Member of AAR, signatory of WGA. Represents 80 clients. 20% of clients are new/previously unpublished writers. Specializes in mainstream fiction and nonfiction. "With our literary and media experience, our agency is uniquely positioned for the current and future direction publishing is taking." Currently handles: 25% nonfiction books; 75% novels.
Member Agents: Nancy Coffey, Dick Duane, Robert Thixton.
Represents: Novels and nonfiction books. Considers these fiction areas: contemporary issues; detective/police/crime; family saga; fantasy; gay; literary; mainstream; mystery/suspense; romance; science fiction.
How to Contact: Query with SASE. Reports in 3 weeks on queries; 2 months on mss.
Needs: Obtains new clients through referrals and from queries.
Recent Sales: Sold 15 titles in the last year. *Nobody's Safe*, by Richard Steinberg (Doubleday); *The Kill Box*, by Chris Stewart (M. Evans); *Return to Christmas*, by Chris Heimerdinger (Ballantine); *All I Desire*, by Rosemary Rogers (Avon).
Terms: Agent receives 15% on domestic sales; 30% on foreign sales. Offers written contract, binding for 3-5 years.
Tips: "Send query letter first giving the essence of the manuscript and a personal or career bio with SASE."

AARON M. PRIEST LITERARY AGENCY, (II), 708 Third Ave., 23rd Floor, New York NY 10017. (212)818-0344. Contact: Aaron Priest or Molly Friedrich. Member of AAR. Currently handles: 25% nonfiction books; 75% fiction.
Member Agents: Lisa Erbach Vance, Paul Cirone.
Represents: Fiction and nonfiction books.
How to Contact: Query only (must be accompanied by SASE). Unsolicited mss will be returned unread.
Recent Sales: *Absolute Power*, by David Baldacci (Warner); *Three to get Deadly*, by Janet Evanovich (Scribner); *How Stella Got Her Groove Back*, by Terry McMillan (Viking); *Day After Tomorrow*, by Allan Folsom (Little, Brown); *Angela's Ashes*, by Frank McCourt (Scribner); *M as in Malice*, by Sue Grafton (Henry Holt).
Terms: Agent receives 15% commission on domestic sales. Charges for photocopying, foreign postage expenses.

SUSAN ANN PROTTER LITERARY AGENT, (II), 110 W. 40th St., Suite 1408, New York NY 10018. (212)840-0480. Contact: Susan Protter. Estab. 1971. Member of AAR. Represents 40 clients. 10% of clients are new/unpublished writers. Writer must have book-length project or ms that is ready to be sold. Works with a very small number of new/unpublished authors. Currently handles: 40% nonfiction books; 60% novels; occasional magazine article or short story (for established clients only).

- Prior to opening her agency, Ms. Protter was associate director of subsidiary rights at Harper & Row Publishers.

Represents: Novels and nonfiction books. Considers these fiction areas: detective/police/crime; mystery; science fiction, thrillers. Send short query with brief description of project/novel, publishing history and SASE. Reports in 3 weeks on queries; 2 months on solicited mss. "Please do not call; mail queries only."
Needs: Actively seeking thrillers, mysteries, science fiction. Does not want to receive westerns, romance, fantasy,

children's books, young adult novels, Star Wars or Star Trek.
Recent Sales: *Dreams and Nightmares*, by Ernest Hartman (Plenum); *New Teenage Body Book, rev. ed.*, by K. McCoy, Ph.D. and C. Wibhelsman, MD.
Terms: Agent receives 15% commission on domestic sales; 15% on TV, film and dramatic sales; 25% on foreign sales. "There is a $10 handling fee requested with submission to cover cost of returning materials should they not be suitable." Charges for long distance, photocopying, messenger, express mail, airmail expenses.
Tips: "Please send neat and professionally organized queries. Make sure to include an SASE or we cannot reply. We receive up to 200 queries a week and read them in the order they arrive. We usually reply within two weeks to any query. Please, do not call. If you are sending a multiple query, make sure to note that in your letter."

N HELEN REES LITERARY AGENCY, (II, III), 308 Commonwealth Ave., Boston MA 02115-2415. (617)262-2401. Fax: (617)236-0133. Contact: Joan Mazmanian. Estab. 1981. Member of AAR. Represents 50 clients. 50% of clients are new/previously unpublished writers. Specializes in general nonfiction, health, business, world politics, autobiographies, psychology, women's issues. Currently handles: 60% nonfiction books; 40% novels.
Represents: Novels and nonfiction books. Considers these fiction areas: contemporary issues; detective/police/crime; glitz; historical; literary; mainstream; mystery/suspense; thriller/espionage.
How to Contact: Query with outline plus 2 sample chapters. Reports in 2 weeks on queries; 3 weeks on mss.
Needs: Obtains new clients through recommendations from others, solicitation, at conferences, etc.
Recent Sales: *The Mentor*, by Sebastian Stuart (Bantam); *Managing the Human Animal*, by Nigel Nicholson (Times Books); *Breaking the Silence*, by William Beardslee (Little, Brown); *Stalin*, by Richard Louie (Counterpoint Press).
Terms: Agent receives 15% commission on domestic sales; 20% on foreign sales.

N LINDA ROGHAAR LITERARY AGENCY, INC., (II), 1106 Glenwood Ave., P.O. Box 41647, Nashville TN 37204. (615)269-5039. Fax: (615)297-3012. E-mail: lroghaar@aol.com. Contact: Linda L. Roghaar. Estab. 1996. Represents 31 clients. 70% of clients are new/unpublished writers. Specializes in women's issues, spirituality, history, self-help and mystery. Currently handles: 60% nonfiction books; 40% novels.

- Prior to opening her agency, Ms. Roghaar worked in retail bookselling for 5 years and as a publisher's sales rep for 15 years.

Represents: Novels and nonfiction books. Considers these fiction areas: humor/satire; literary; mystery (amateur sleuth, cozy, culinary, malice domestic); religious/inspirational.
How to Contact: Query with SASE. Reports in 2-4 weeks on queries; 6-12 weeks on mss.
Needs: Actively seeking spirituality; women's; mystery. Does not want to receive horror; romance; science fiction; cookbooks. Obtains new clients through recommendations from others, workshops.
Recent Sales: Sold 11 titles in the last year. *Conscious Collage*, by Beth Sirull and Kathy McDonald (Crown/Harmony); *The Courage to Start*, by John Bingham (Simon & Schuster); *Dark Night of Recovery*, by E. Bear (Health Communications); *Come What May, The Splice Girls Guide to Breast Cancer*, by the Splice Girls (Conari Press).
Terms: Agent receives 15% commission on domestic sales; negotiable on foreign sales. Offers written contract, binding for negotiable time.
Tips: "The process of finding the right agent is like eating an elephant—you do it one bite at a time. Stay the course. Write what you love. Join a writers group. Toughen up to criticism—get a helmet. Keep your day job."

N THE DAMARIS ROWLAND AGENCY, (I), 510 E. 23rd St., #8-G, New York NY 10010-5020. (212)475-8942. Fax: (212)358-9411. Contact: Damaris Rowland or Steve Axelrod. Estab. 1994. Member of AAR. Represents 40 clients. 10% of clients are new/previously unpublished writers. Specializes in women's fiction. Currently handles: 75% novels, 25% nonfiction.
Represents: Novels and nonfiction books. Considers these fiction areas: detective/police/crime; historical; literary; mainstream; psychic/supernatural; romance (contemporary, gothic, historical, regency).
How to Contact: Send outline/proposal. Reports in 6 weeks.
Needs: Obtains new clients through recommendations from others, at conferences.
Recent Sales: *The Perfect Husband*, by Lisa Gardner (Bantam); *My Dearest Enemy*, by Connie Brockway (Dell).
Terms: Agent receives 15% commission on domestic sales; 20% on foreign sales. Offers written contract, with 30 day cancellation clause. Charges only if extraordinary expenses have been incurred, e.g., photocopying and mailing 15 ms to Europe for a foreign sale. 100% of business is derived from commissions on sales.
Writers' Conferences: Novelists Inc.; RWA National; Pacific Northwest Writers Conference.

A BULLET INTRODUCES COMMENTS by the editor of *Novel & Short Story Writer's Market* indicating special information about the listing.

RUSSELL & VOLKENING, (II), 50 W. 29th St., #7E, New York NY 10001. (212)684-6050. Fax: (212)889-3026. Contact: Joseph Regal or Jennie Dunham. Estab. 1940. Member of AAR. Represents 140 clients. 10% of clients are new/previously unpublished writers. Specializes in literary fiction and narrative nonfiction. Currently handles: 40% nonfiction books; 15% juvenile books; 2% short story collections; 40% novels; 2% novellas; 1% poetry.
Member Agents: Timothy Seldes (nonfiction, literary fiction); Joseph Regal (literary fiction, thrillers, nonfiction); Jennie Dunham (literary fiction, nonfiction, children's books).
Represents: Novels, novellas, short story collections, nonfiction books and juvenile books. Considers these fiction areas: action/adventure; detective/police/crime; ethnic; juvenile; literary; mainstream; mystery/suspense; picture book; sports; thriller/espionage; young adult.
How to Contact: Query. Reports in 1 week on queries; 1 month on mss.
Needs: Obtains new clients through "recommendations of writers we already represent.
Recent Sales: *A Patchwork Planet*, by Anne Tylor (Knopf); *The House Gun*, by Nadine Gordimer (Farrar, Strauss & Giroux); *Truman Capote*, by George Plimpton (Doubleday); *Cookie Count*, by Robert Sabuda (Little Simon).
Terms: Agent receives 10% commission on domestic sales; 20% on foreign sales. Charges for "standard office expenses relating to the submission of materials of an author we represent, e.g., photocopying, postage."
Tips: "If the query is cogent, well-written, well-presented and is the type of book we'd represent, we'll ask to see the manuscript. From there, it depends purely on the quality of the work."

VICTORIA SANDERS LITERARY AGENCY, (II), 241 Avenue of the Americas, New York NY 10014-4822. (212)633-8811. Fax: (212)633-0525. Contact: Victoria Sanders and/or Diane Dickensheid. Estab. 1993. Member of AAR, signatory of WGA. Represents 75 clients. 25% of clients are new/previously unpublished writers. Currently handles: 50% nonfiction books; 50% novels.
Represents: Novels and nonfiction. Considers these fiction areas: action/adventure; contemporary issues; ethnic, family saga; feminist; gay; lesbian; literary; thriller/espionage.
How to Contact: Query and SASE. Reports in 1 week on queries; 1 month on mss.
Needs: Obtains new clients through recommendations, "or I find them through my reading and pursue."
Recent Sales: *Bebe's by Golly Wow*, by Yolanda Joe (Doubleday); *Santa & Pete*, by Christopher Moore and Pamela Johnson (Simon & Schuster); and *The Forbidden Zone*, by Michael Harker (Simon & Schuster).
Terms: Agent receives 15% commission on domestic sales; 20% on foreign sales. Offers written contract binding at will. Charges for photocopying, ms, messenger, express mail and extraordinary fees. If in excess of $100, client approval is required.
Tips: "Limit query to letter, no calls and give it your best shot. A good query is going to get a good response."

THE MARY SUE SEYMOUR AGENCY, (II, III), 475 Miner Street Rd., Canton NY 13617. (315)386-1831. Fax: (315)386-1037. E-mail: marysue@slic.com. Website: http://www.slic.com/marysue. Contact: Mary Sue Seymour. Estab. 1992. Member of AAR. Represents 50 clients. 20% of clients are new/unpublished writers. Specializes in nonfiction and fiction. Currently handles: 60% nonfiction books; 5% scholarly books; 30% novels; 5% textbooks.

- Prior to becoming an agent, Ms. Seymour taught in the pubic school system over 10 years.

Represents: Novels, textbooks, nonfiction books and scholarly books. Considers these fiction areas: action/adventure; contemporary issues; ethnic; family saga; glitz; historical; horror; humor/satire; literary; mainstream; mystery; psychic/supernatural; religious/inspirational; romance (contemporary, gothic, historical, regency); science fiction; sports; suspense; thriller/espionage; westerns/frontier; young adult.
How to Contact: Send outline/proposal with SASE. Reports in 1 week on queries; 1 month on mss.
Needs: Actively seeking well-written fiction. Does not want to receive poetry, short stories or plays. No fax queries or submissions without SASE. Obtains new clients through conferences, mail and recommendations from clients.
Recent Sales: *Love Talk*, by Wendy Wax (Kensington Publications); *Lady of the Knight*, by Tori Phillilps (Harlequin Historicals); *Millenium Project*, by Joe Massucci (Leisure Books).
Terms: Agent receives 12½% commission for published writers; 15% on domestic sales; 20% on foreign sales. Offers written contract, binding for 1 year. Contract may be terminated by letter at any time as long as no sales are pending.
Writers' Conferences: Virginia Romance Writers Conference (Williamsburg, March 1999); Romance Writers of America/Toronto (July 1999).

IRENE SKOLNICK, (II), 22 W. 23rd St., 5th Floor, New York NY 10010. (212)727-3648. Fax: (212)727-1024. E-mail: sirene35@aol.com. Contact: Irene Skolnick. Estab. 1993. Member of AAR. Represents 45 clients. 75% of clients are new/previously unpublished writers.
Represents: Adult fiction. Considers these fiction areas: contemporary issues; historical; literary.
How to Contact: Query with SASE, outline and sample chapter. No unsolicited mss. Reports in 1 month on queries.

Recent Sales: *An Equal Music*, by Seth Vikram; *Keaterskill Falls*, by Allegra Goodman; *Taking Lives*, by Pye.
Terms: Agent receives 15% commission on domestic sales; 20% on foreign sales. Sometimes offers criticism service. Charges for international postage, photocopying over 40 pages.

N SOUTHEAST LITERARY AGENCY, (II), P.O. Box 910, Sharpes FL 32959-0910. (407)632-5019. Contact: Debbie Fine. Estab. 1996. Member of IWWG. 75% of clients are new/unpublished writers. Currently represents: 40% novels; 50% nonfiction books; 8% stage plays; 2% multimedia.

- Prior to becoming an agent, Ms. Fine was a supervisor at a major bookstore chain and an editor in New York.

Represents: Novels, nonfiction, textbooks and juvenile. Considers these fiction areas: action/adventure; detective/police/crime; ethnic; family saga; fantasy; feminist; glitz; historical; humor/satire; juvenile; mainstream; mystery; psychic/supernatural; religious/inspirational; science fiction; sports; thiller/espionage; westerns/frontier; young adult.
Also Handles: Dream interpretation work.
How to Contact: Send entire ms with SASE, synopsis or outline and marketing letter. Reports in 1 week on queries; 2-4 on mss.
Needs: Actively seeking most categories. Does not want to receive anyone's first draft. Obtains new clients through conferences, referrals and queries.
Recent Sales: Sold 2 titles in the last year. *FL: The War Years*, by Thomas Benton (Wind Canyon Publishing, Inc.); *Secrets of the Lost City*, by Rossana Rossi and Ron Tracey (Book World Inc./Blue Star Productions).
Terms: Agent receives 10% commission on domestic sales; 20% on foreign sales. Offers written contract, binding for 6 months. Written notice of termination is effective on receipt. Charges for out-of-pocket expenses on behalf of authors.
Writers' Conferences: International Book Fair (Miami, November); Southeast Book Sellers Association (North Carolina, 1999).

N ROBIN STRAUS AGENCY, INC., (II), 229 E. 79th St., New York NY 10021. (212)472-3282. Fax: (212)472-3833. E-mail: springbird@aol.com. Contact: Robin Straus. Estab. 1983. Member of AAR. Specializes in high-quality fiction and nonfiction for adults. Currently handles: 65% nonfiction books; 35% novels.

- Prior to becoming an agent, Robin Straus served as a subsidiary rights manager at Random House and Doubleday and worked in editorial at Little, Brown.

Represents: Novels and nonfiction. Considers these fiction areas: contemporary issues; family saga; historical; literary; mainstream; thriller/espionage.
How to Contact: Query with sample pages. "Will not download e-mail inquiries." SASE ("stamps, not metered postage") required. Reports in 1 month on queries and mss.
Needs: Most new clients obtained through recommendations from others.
Recent Sales: Prefers not to share info.
Terms: Agent receives 15% commission on domestic sales; 20% on foreign sales. Offers written contract when requested. Charges for "photocopying, UPS, messenger and foreign postage, etc. as incurred."

N SUSAN TRAVIS LITERARY AGENCY, (I), 1317 N. San Fernando Blvd., #175, Burbank CA 91504-4236. (818)557-6538. Fax: (818)557-6549. Contact: Susan Travis. Estab. 1995. Represents 10 clients. 60% of clients are new/previously unpublished writers. Specializes in mainstream fiction and nonfiction. Currently handles: 70% nonfiction books; 30% novels.

- Prior to opening her agency, Ms. Travis served as an agent with the McBride Agency and prior to that worked in the Managing Editors Department of Ballantine Books.

Represents: Novels and nonfiction books. Considers these fiction areas: contemporary issues; ethnic; historical; literary; mainstream; mystery/suspense; romance (historical).
How to Contact: Query. Reports in 3 weeks on queries; 4-6 weeks on mss.
Needs: Does not want to receive science fiction, poetry or children's books. Obtains new clients through referrals from existing clients, and mss requested from query letters.
Terms: Agent receives 15% commission on domestic sales; 20% on foreign sales. Offers written contract, binding for 1 year, with 60 day cancellation clause. Charges for photocopying of mss and proposals if copies not provided by author. 100% of business is derived from commissions on sales.

N SCOTT WAXMAN AGENCY, INC., (II), 1650 Broadway, Suite 1011, New York NY 10019. (212)262-2388. Fax: (212)262-0119. E-mail: giles@interport.net. Contact: Giles Anderson. Estab. 1997. Represents 60 clients. 50% of clients are new/unpublished writers. Specializes in "both commercial fiction and nonfiction. We are particularly strong in the areas of crime fiction, sports and religion. Will look at literary fiction." Currently handles: 60% nonfiction books; 40% novels.

- Prior to opening his agency, Mr. Waxman was editor for five years at HarperCollins.

Member Agents: Scott Waxman (commercial fiction, sports, religion); Giles Anderson (literary fiction, commercial fiction).
Represents: Novels and nonfiction books. Considers these fiction areas: action/adventure; ethnic; historical; literary; hard-boiled detective; religious/inspirational; romance (contemporary, historical); sports; suspense.

How to Contact: Query. Reports in 2 weeks on queries; 4-6 weeks on mss. Discards unwanted or unsolicited mss.
Needs: Actively seeking strong, high-concept commercial fiction. Obtains new clients through recommendations, writers conferences, Internet, magazines.
Recent Sales: Sold 35 titles in the last year. *How Sweet the Sound*, by Cissy Houston (Doubleday); *The Ripken Way*, by Cal Ripkin, Sr. (Pocket); *Black Mountain*, by Les Standiford (Putnam); *Santa & Pete*, by Chris Moore and Pamala Johnson (Simon & Schuster).
Terms: Agent receives 15% commission on domestic sales; 20% on foreign sales. Offers written contract. 60 days notice must be given to terminate contract. Charges for photocopying, express mail, fax, international postage, book orders. Refers to editing services for clients only. 0% of business is derived from editing service.
Writers' Conferences: Celebration of Writing in the Low Country (Beaufort SC, August 6-9, 1999); Golden Triangle Writers Guild Conference (Beaumont TX, October 1999); FIU/Seaside Writers Conference (FL, October).
Reading Lists: Reads *Witness*, *Boulevard*, *Literal Latté*, *Mississippi Review*, *Zoetrope*, many others to find new clients.

N ANN WRIGHT REPRESENTATIVES, (II), 165 W. 46th St., Suite 1105, New York NY 10036-2501. (212)764-6770. Fax: (212)764-5125. Contact: Dan Wright. Estab. 1961. Signatory of WGA. Represents 23 clients. 30% of clients are new/unpublished writers. Prefers to work with published/established authors; works with a small number of new/unpublished authors. "Eager to work with any author with material that we can effectively market in the motion picture business worldwide." Specializes in "book or screenplays with strong motion picture potential." Currently handles: 50% novels; 40% movie scripts; 10% TV scripts.

- Prior to becoming an agent, Mr. Wright was a writer, producer and production manager for film and television (alumni of CBS Television).

Represents: Novels. Considers these fiction areas: action/adventure; detective/police/crime; feminist; gay; humor/satire; lesbian; literary; mainstream; mystery/suspense; romance (contemporary, historical, regency); sports; thriller/espionage; westerns/frontier.
How to Contact: Query with outline and SASE. Does not read unsolicited mss. Reports in 3 weeks on queries; 4 months on mss. "All work must be sent with a SASE to ensure its return."
Needs: Actively seeking "strong competitive novelists." Does not want to receive "fantasy or science fiction projects at this time."
Terms: Agent receives 10% commission on domestic sales; 10% on dramatic sales; 15-20% on foreign sales; 20% on packaging. Offers written contract, binding for 2 years. Critiques only works of signed clients. Charges for photocopying expenses.
Tips: "Send a letter with SASE. Something about the work, something about the writer."

N SUSAN ZECKENDORF ASSOC. INC., (II), 171 W. 57th St., New York NY 10019. (212)245-2928. Contact: Susan Zeckendorf. Estab. 1979. Member of AAR. Represents 35 clients. 25% of clients are new/previously unpublished writers. "We are a small agency giving lots of individual attention. We respond quickly to submissions." Currently handles: 50% nonfiction books; 50% fiction.

- Prior to opening her agency, Ms. Zeckendorf was a counseling psychologist.

Represents: Novels and nonfiction books. Considers these fiction areas: action/adventure; contemporary issues; detective/police/crime; ethnic; family saga; glitz; historical; literary; mainstream; mystery/suspense; thriller/espionage.
How to Contact: Query. Reports in 10 days on queries; 3 weeks mss. Obtains new clients through recommendations, listings in writer's manuals.
Needs: Actively seeking mysteries, literary fiction, mainstream fiction, thrillers. Does not want to receive science fiction, romance.
Recent Sales: *Scents of the Wight*, by Una-Mary Parker (Headline); *Fifth Avenue: The Best Address*, by Jerry Patterson (Rizzoli).
Terms: Agent receives 15% commission on domestic sales; 20% on foreign sales. Charges for photocopying, messenger services.
Writers' Conferences: Central Valley Writers Conference; the Tucson Publishers Association Conference; Writer's Connection; Frontiers in Writing Conference (Amarillo, TX); Golden Triangle Writers Conference (Beaumont TX); Oklahoma Festival of Books (Claremont OK); Mary Mount Writers Conference.

Literary Agents Category Index

Agents listed in the preceeding section are indexed below according to the categories of fiction they represent. Use it to find agents who handle the specific kind of fiction you write. Then turn to those listings in the alphabetized Literary Agents section for complete contact and submission information.

Erotica

Ethnic

Experimental

Family Saga

Fantasy

Feminist

Gay

Glitz

Koster Literary Agency, Elaine, LLC
Larken, Sabra Elliott
Larsen/Elizabeth Pomada Literary Agents, Michael
Marshall Agency, The Evan
Rees Literary Agency, Helen
Seymour Agency, The Mary Sue
Southeast Literary Agency
Zeckendorf Assoc. Inc., Susan

Historical
Baldi Literary Agency, Malaga
Barrett Books Inc., Loretta
Bernstein & Associates, Inc., Pam
Carvainis Agency, Inc., Maria
Cohen, Inc. Literary Agency, Ruth
Greenburger Associates, Inc., Sanford J.
Halsey Agency, Reece
Jabberwocky Literary Agency
Koster Literary Agency, Elaine, LLC
Kouts, Literary Agent, Barbara S.
Larken, Sabra Elliott
Larsen/Elizabeth Pomada Literary Agents, Michael
Lee Communications
Lindstrom Literary Group
Lowenstein Associates, Inc.
Maass Literary Agency, Donald
Marshall Agency, The Evan
McBride Literary Agency, Margret
Michaels Literary Agency, Inc., Doris S.
Perkins, Rubie & Associates
Rees Literary Agency, Helen
Rowland Agency, The Damaris
Skolnick, Irene
Southeast Literary Agency
Straus Agency, Inc., Robin
Travis Literary Agency, Susan
Waxman Agency, Inc., Scott
Zeckendorf Assoc. Inc., Susan

Horror
Aiken-Jones Literary
Allen Literary Agency, Linda
Amsterdam Agency, Marcia
Jabberwocky Literary Agency
Larsen/Elizabeth Pomada Literary Agents, Michael
Lee Communications
Maass Literary Agency, Donald
Marshall Agency, The Evan
Nelson Company, The Craig
Perkins, Rubie & Associates
Seymour Agency, The Mary Sue
Southeast Literary Agency

Humor/Satire
A.L.P. Literary Agency
Amsterdam Agency, Marcia
Barrett Books Inc., Loretta
Book Deals, Inc.
Greenburger Associates, Inc., Sanford J.
Jabberwocky Literary Agency
Larken, Sabra Elliott
Larsen/Elizabeth Pomada Literary Agents, Michael
Lowenstein Associates, Inc.
Marshall Agency, The Evan
McBride Literary Agency, Margret
Nelson Company, The Craig
Roghaar Literary Agency, Inc., Linda
Seymour Agency, The Mary Sue
Southeast Literary Agency

Juvenile
Cohen, Inc. Literary Agency, Ruth
Kouts, Literary Agent, Barbara S.
Literary Agency for Children's Books, A
Russell & Volkening

Lesbian
Allen Literary Agency, Linda
Baldi Literary Agency, Malaga
Barrett Books Inc., Loretta
Dystel Literary Management, Jane
Greenburger Associates, Inc., Sanford J.
Jabberwocky Literary Agency
Koster Literary Agency, Elaine, LLC
Larsen/Elizabeth Pomada Literary Agents, Michael
Levant & Wales, Literary Agency, Inc.
Lowenstein Associates, Inc.
Perkins, Rubie & Associates
Sanders Literary Agency, Victoria

Literary
A.L.P. Literary Agency
Allen Literary Agency, Linda
Amster Literary Enterprises, Betsy
Baldi Literary Agency, Malaga
Barrett Books Inc., Loretta
Bent, Literary Agent, Jenny, Graybill & English, L.L.C.
Book Deals, Inc.
Carlisle & Company
Carvainis Agency, Inc., Maria
Castiglia Literary Agency
Cohen, Inc. Literary Agency, Ruth
Cypher, Author's Representative, James R.
Darhansoff & Verrill Literary Agents
Dickens Group, The
Dijkstra Literary Agency, Sandra
Dystel Literary Management, Jane
Greenburger Associates, Inc., Sanford J.
Halsey Agency, Reece
Hardy Agency, The
Jabberwocky Literary Agency
Joy S. Literary Agency
Koster Literary Agency, Elaine, LLC
Kouts, Literary Agent, Barbara S.
Larken, Sabra Elliott
Larsen/Elizabeth Pomada Literary Agents, Michael
Levant & Wales, Literary Agency, Inc.
Levine Literary Agency, Inc., Ellen
Lowenstein Associates, Inc.
Maass Literary Agency, Donald
Mann Agency, Carol
Markson Literary Agency, Elaine
Marshall Agency, The Evan
McBride Literary Agency, Margret
Michaels Literary Agency, Inc., Doris S.
Nelson Company, The Craig
Perkins, Rubie & Associates
Pinder Lane & Garon-Brooke Associates, Ltd.
Rees Literary Agency, Helen

Mainstream

Mystery/Suspense

Picture Book

Psychic/Supernatural

Regional

Southeast Literary Agency

Religious/Inspiration

A.L.P. Literary Agency
Barrett Books Inc., Loretta
Joy S. Literary Agency
Larsen/Elizabeth Pomada Literary Agents, Michael
Marshall Agency, The Evan
Roghaar Literary Agency, Inc., Linda
Seymour Agency, The Mary Sue
Waxman Agency, Inc., Scott

Romance

A.L.P. Literary Agency
Amsterdam Agency, Marcia
Barrett Books Inc., Loretta
Bernstein & Associates, Inc., Pam
Carlisle & Company
Carvainis Agency, Inc., Maria
Cohen, Inc. Literary Agency, Ruth
Columbia Literary Associates, Inc.
Jabberwocky Literary Agency
Larken, Sabra Elliott
Larsen/Elizabeth Pomada Literary Agents, Michael
Lee Communications
Lowenstein Associates, Inc.
Maass Literary Agency, Donald
Marcil Literary Agency, Inc., The Denise
Marshall Agency, The Evan
Orr Agency, Inc., Alice
Pinder Lane & Garon-Brooke Associates, Ltd.
Rowland Agency, The Damaris
Seymour Agency, The Mary Sue
Travis Literary Agency, Susan
Waxman Agency, Inc., Scott
Lee Communications

Science Fiction

Agency One
Aiken-Jones Literary
Amsterdam Agency, Marcia
Dickens Group, The
Halsey Agency, Reece
Jabberwocky Literary Agency
Lee Communications
Lindstrom Literary Group
Maass Literary Agency, Donald
Marshall Agency, The Evan
Perkins, Rubie & Associates
Pinder Lane & Garon-Brooke Associates, Ltd.
Protter Literary Agent, Susan Ann
Seymour Agency, The Mary Sue
Southeast Literary Agency

Sports

Barrett Books Inc., Loretta
Book Deals, Inc.
Greenburger Associates, Inc., Sanford J.
Jabberwocky Literary Agency
Russell & Volkening
Seymour Agency, The Mary Sue
Southeast Literary Agency
Waxman Agency, Inc., Scott

Thriller/Espionage

Aiken-Jones Literary
Allen Literary Agency, Linda
Amsterdam Agency, Marcia
Baldi Literary Agency, Malaga
Barrett Books Inc., Loretta
Bernstein & Associates, Inc., Pam
Carlisle & Company
Carvainis Agency, Inc., Maria
Columbia Literary Associates, Inc.
Darhansoff & Verrill Literary Agents
Dickens Group, The
Dijkstra Literary Agency, Sandra
Dystel Literary Management, Jane
Greenburger Associates, Inc., Sanford J.
Halsey Agency, Reece
Jabberwocky Literary Agency
Koster Literary Agency, Elaine, LLC
Larken, Sabra Elliott
Lee Communications
Levine Literary Agency, Inc., Ellen
Lindstrom Literary Group
Lowenstein Associates, Inc.
Maass Literary Agency, Donald
Marshall Agency, The Evan
McBride Literary Agency, Margret
Nelson Company, The Craig
Perkins, Rubie & Associates
Protter Literary Agent, Susan Ann
Rees Literary Agency, Helen
Russell & Volkening
Sanders Literary Agency, Victoria
Seymour Agency, The Mary Sue
Southeast Literary Agency
Straus Agency, Inc., Robin
Zeckendorf Assoc. Inc., Susan

Westerns/Frontier

Amsterdam Agency, Marcia
Dickens Group, The
Joy S. Literary Agency
Lee Communications
Marshall Agency, The Evan
McBride Literary Agency, Margret
Seymour Agency, The Mary Sue

Young Adult

Amsterdam Agency, Marcia
Carvainis Agency, Inc., Maria
Cohen, Inc. Literary Agency, Ruth
Joy S. Literary Agency
Kouts, Literary Agent, Barbara S.
Literary Agency for Children's Books, A
Russell & Volkening
Seymour Agency, The Mary Sue
Southeast Literary Agency

Literary Magazines

This section contains markets for your literary short fiction. While many are university-affiliated and some independently owned, the editors at each have told us they are actively seeking fiction for their respective publications.

Although definitions of what constitutes "literary" writing vary, editors of literary journals agree they want to publish the "best" fiction available today. Qualities they look for in stories include creativity, style, flawless mechanics, and careful attention to detail in content and manuscript preparation. Most of the authors writing such fiction are well-read and well-educated, and many are students and graduates of university creative writing programs.

In this marketplace, however, fine writing will always take precedence over formal training. On page 170, *B&A: New Fiction* editor Michelle Alfano echoes the philosophy of most literary journal editors to say she does not care if a writer has been published previously. "I only care about the originality of the piece. I think excellence in writing should rule." On page 182, Marcia Preston, editor of *ByLine*, stands by that publication's mission statement "to encourage, motivate and give practical help to aspiring writers." Preston even says: "If we got a short story from a new writer and a short story from Stephen King, and we loved both stories, we would rather have the new writer's than Stephen King's."

STEPPING STONES TO RECOGNITION

Some well-established literary journals pay several hundred dollars for a short story. Those paying more include STORY which pays $1,000 per story and $750 per short short story. *Zoetrope* also pays $1,000 per story and $5,000 for stories commissioned by Coppola. Most, though, can only pay with contributor's copies or a subscription to their publication. However, being published in literary journals offers the important benefits of experience, exposure and prestige. Agents and major book publishers regularly read literary magazines in search of new writers. Work from among these journals is also selected for inclusion in annual prize anthologies such as *The Best American Short Stories*, *Prize Stories: The O. Henry Awards*, *Pushcart Prize: Best of the Small Presses*, and *New Stories from the South: The Year's Best*.

You'll find most of the well-known prestigious literary journals listed here. Many, including *Carolina Quarterly* and *Ploughshares*, are associated with universities, while others such as *The Paris Review* are independently published. STORY, published by the publisher of *Novel & Short Story Writer's Market*, won the coveted National Magazine Award for fiction in 1992 and 1995 and was a finalist for that award in 1994, 1996 and 1997.

Among the listings in this section you will find electronic literary magazines, an increasingly common trend at a time when paper and publishing costs rise while funding to university presses continues to be cut back or eliminated altogether. These electronic outlets for literary fiction also benefit writers by eliminating copying and postage costs and providing the opportunity for much quicker responses to submissions. *Also notice that some magazines with websites give specific information about what they offer on their websites, including updated writers guidelines and sample fiction from their publications.*

SELECTING THE RIGHT LITERARY JOURNAL

Once you have browsed through this section and have a list of journals you might like to submit to, read those listings again, carefully. Remember that this is information editors present to help you in submitting work that fits their needs. How to Use This Book to Publish Your

Fiction, starting on page 3, describes in detail the listing information common to all markets in our book, including information that pertains especially to literary publications.

This is the only section in which you will find magazines that do not read submissions all year long. Whether limited reading periods are tied to a university schedule or meant to accommodate the capabilities of a very small staff, those periods are noted within listings. The staffs of university journals are usually made up of student editors and a managing editor who is also a faculty member. These staffs often change every year. Whenever possible, we indicate this in listings and give the name of the current editor and the length of that editor's term. Also be aware that the schedule of a university journal usually coincides with that university's academic year, meaning that the editors of most university publications are difficult or impossible to reach during the summer.

FURTHERING YOUR SEARCH

It cannot be stressed enough that reading the listings for literary journals is only the first part of developing your marketing plan. The second part, equally important, is to obtain fiction guidelines and read the actual magazine. Reading copies of a magazine helps you determine the fine points of the magazine's publishing style and philosophy. There is no substitute for this type of hands-on research.

Unlike commercial periodicals available at most newsstands and bookstores, it requires a little more effort to obtain some of the magazines listed here. The new super chain bookstores are doing a better job these days of stocking literaries and you can find some in independent and college bookstores, especially those published in your area. You may, however, need to send for a sample copy. We include sample copy prices in the listings whenever possible.

Another way to find out more about literary magazines is to check out the various prize anthologies and take note of journals whose fiction is being selected for publication there. Studying prize anthologies not only lets you know which magazines are publishing award-winning work, but it also provides a valuable overview of what is considered to be the best fiction published today.

In addition to the N indicating new listings, we include other symbols to help you in narrowing your search. English-speaking foreign markets are denoted by a symbol. The maple leaf symbol identifies Canadian presses. If you are not a Canadian writer, but are interested in a Canadian press, check the listing carefully. Many small presses in Canada receive grants and other funds from their provincial or national government and are, therefore, restricted to publishing Canadian authors.

Information we feel will help you determine if a listing is the right market for you is noted in editorial comments identified with a bullet (●). The comments section also allows us to explain more about the special interests or requirements of a publication and any information we've learned from our readers that we feel will help you choose potential markets wisely. The symbol identifies publishers who have recently received honors or awards for their books.

Among the awards and honors we note are inclusion of work in:

- *Best American Short Stories*, published by Houghton Mifflin, 222 Berkeley St., Boston MA 02116.
- *New Stories from the South: The Year's Best*, published by Algonquin Books of Chapel Hill, P.O. Box 2225, Chapel Hill NC 27515.
- *Prize Stories: The O. Henry Awards*, published by Doubleday/Anchor, 1540 Broadway, New York NY 10036.
- *Pushcart Prize: Best of the Small Presses*, published by Pushcart Press, Box 380, Wainscott NY 11975.

The well-respected *Poet* magazine (published by Cooper House Publishing Inc., P.O. Box 54947, Oklahoma City OK 73154) annually honors the best literary magazines (those publishing both fiction and poetry). The program is titled The American Literary Magazine Awards and most recipients of editorial content awards have listings in this section. To find out more about the awards, see the *Poet*'s fall issue.

FOR MORE INFORMATION

See The Business of Fiction Writing for the specific mechanics of manuscript submission. Above all, editors appreciate a professional presentation. Include a brief cover letter and send a self-addressed envelope for a reply or a self-addressed envelope in a size large enough to accommodate your manuscript, if you would like it returned. Be sure to include enough stamps or International Reply Coupons (for replies from countries other than your own) to cover your manuscript's return.

If you're interested in learning more about literary and small magazines, you may want to look at *The International Directory of Little Magazines and Small Presses* (Dustbooks, Box 100, Paradise CA 95967); the *Directory of Literary Magazines*, published by the Council of Literary Magazines and Presses (3-C, 154 Christopher St., New York NY 10014-2839); or *The Association of American University Presses Directory* (584 Broadway, New York NY 10012).

The following is the ranking system we have used to categorize the listings in this section.

I Publication encourages beginning or unpublished writers to submit work for consideration and publishes new writers regularly.
II Publication accepts outstanding work by beginning and established writers.
III Publication does not encourage beginning writers; prints mostly writers with previous publication credits; very few new writers.
IV Special-interest or regional publication, open only to writers in certain genres or on certain subjects or from certain geographical areas.
V Closed to unsolicited submissions.

☑ **ABOUT SUCH THINGS, Literary Magazine, (I),** 1701 Delancey St., Philadelphia PA 19103. (215)842-3563. E-mail: aboutsuch@juno.com. Website: http://world.std.com/~pduggan/ast/astroot.html (includes writer's guidelines, samples of writing and art, subscription information, contact information). Editor: Laurel Webster Garver. **Fiction Editor:** E. Louise Lindinger. Magazine: 8⅜×10¾; 28-32 pages; 24 lb. paper; 80 lb. cover stock; illustrations. "We seek to provide a forum for Christian authors to publish work. We receive editorial guidance from a Presbyterian church in Philadelphia. Our audience is primarily educated, professional, church-going intellectuals who live in or have a connection with Philadelphia." Semiannually. Estab. 1996. Circ. 400.
Needs: Ethnic/multicultural, fantasy, historical, humor/satire (particularly with religious/inspirational elements), literary, regional, religious/inspirational, romance, science fiction (soft/sociological), allegory. No erotica, horror, occult, feminist, gay. Receives 8 unsolicited mss/month. Accepts 1-3 mss/issue; 2-6 mss/year. Does not read February-April and August-October. Publishes ms 3 months after acceptance. Recently published work by Charles Chaim Wax, James Sullivan, E. Louise Lindinger, Gary Everson. Length: 2,000 words average; 300 words minimum; 3,000 words maximum. Publishes short shorts. Also publishes literary essays, literary criticism and poetry. Always critiques or comments on rejected mss.
How to Contact: Send complete ms with a cover letter. Include estimated word count, SASE, address, phone number, e-mail and submission on diskette in ASCII text. Reports on mss in 12 months. Send SASE for return of ms or send a disposable copy. Simultaneous submissions and reprints OK. Sample copy for $3 and 9×12 SAE with $1.01 postage. Fiction guidelines for #10 SASE.
Payment/Terms: Pays 2 contributor's copies for one-time rights; additional copies for $3. Sends galleys to author. Not copyrighted.
Advice: "We look for high quality in content, clarity, tone and characterization; also for impact, snappy dialogue, many-faceted and growing characters. Let any moral or spiritual lesson be an outgrowth of a solid plot and real characters. Be willing to let the story have resonance and tension by not tying up every loose end too tightly. Avoid making 'good' characters stereotypically 'churchy.' "

☑ **ACORN WHISTLE, (II),** 907 Brewster Ave., Beloit WI 53511-5621. E-mail: burwellf@lib.beloit.edu. **Editor:** Fred Burwell. Magazine: 8½×11; 75-100 pages; uncoated paper; light card cover; illustrations; photos. "*Acorn Whistle* seeks accessible and personal writing, art and photography that appeals to readers on both emotional and intellectual levels. Our intended audience is the educated non-academic. Connecting writers with readers is our foremost goal. We also encourage a friendly working relationship between editors and writers. We seek accessible and humane literary fiction for an audience that reads for pleasure and edification." Semiannually. Estab. 1995. Circ. 500.

Needs: Ethnic/multicultural, feminist, historical (general), humor/satire, literary, mainstream/contemporary, regional. No erotica, experimental, fantasy, horror, religious or science fiction. Would like to see more "stories with vivid characterization, compassion for its characters, vivid sense of place. Writing with a commitment to readership." Accepts 5-7 mss/issue; 10-15 mss/year. Publishes ms within a year after acceptance. Recently published work by Mary Waters, Tim Poland, Sylvia Reed and Ad Hudler. Publishes 2-6 new writers/year. Length: open. Publishes short shorts. Also publishes memoir and poetry. Often critiques or comments on rejected ms.

How to Contact: Send complete ms. Reports in 2 weeks on queries; 1-12 weeks on mss. Send SASE for reply, return of ms or send a disposable copy of ms. Simultaneous submissions OK. Sample copy for $7. Fiction guidelines for #10 SASE.

Payment/Terms: Pays 2 contributor's copies. Acquires first North American serial rights. Features expanded contributor's notes with personal comments from each author.

Advice: "We look for writing that is direct and human and makes the reader care—writing that communicates and illuminates the shared human experience, yet includes a variety of voices and backgrounds. Write what matters to you, rather than trying to impress an imaginary audience. Writing fueled by an author's passion *will* reach readers. Don't let rejections discourage you. And, if an editor says, "try again," try again . . . and again!"

☑ $ **ADVENTURES OF SWORD & SORCERY, (I, II)**, Double Star Press, P.O. Box 807, Xenia OH 45385. E-mail: double_star@yahoo.com. **Editor:** Randy Dannenfelser. Magazine: 8½×11; 80 pages; slick cover stock; illustrations. "We publish sword and sorcery, heroic and high fantasy fiction." Quarterly. Estab. 1995. Circ. 7,000.

Needs: Sword and sorcery, heroic and high fantasy fiction. "We want fiction with an emphasis on action and adventure, but still cognizant of the struggles within as they play against the struggles without. Include sexual content only as required by the story, but not excessive/porn." Receives approximately 250 unsolicited mss/month. Accepts 9 mss/issue; 36 mss/year. Publishes ms 1 year after acceptance. Agented fiction 5%. Recently published work by Mike Resnick, Stephen Baxter and Darrell Schweitzer. Publishes 8 new writers/year. Length: 5,000 words average; 1,000 words minimum; 20,000 words maximum. Also publishes literary criticism and book reviews (only solicited). Always critiques or comments on rejected mss.

How to Contact: Send complete ms with a cover letter. Include estimated word count, Social Security number, list of publications, phone number and e-mail address. Reports in 1 month on queries; 2 months on mss. Send SASE for reply, return of ms. No simultaneous submissions. Electronic submissions (e-mail, disk or modem) OK. Sample copy $6. Fiction guidelines for #10 SASE. Reviews novels and short story collections.

Payment/Terms: Pays 3-6¢/word on acceptance and 3 contributor's copies; additional copies 40% discount plus shipping. Acquires first North American serial rights. Sends galleys to author.

Advice: "Recently we are looking for more adventuresome work with settings other than generic medieval Europe. We look for real emotion in the prose. Think about the audience we are targeted at, and send us appropriate stories."

ADVOCATE, PKA'S PUBLICATION, (I, II), PKA Publications, 301A Rolling Hills Park, Prattsville NY 12468. (518)299-3103. Tabloid: 9⅜×12¼; 32 pages; newsprint paper; line drawings; b&w photographs. "Eclectic for a general audience." Bimonthly. Estab. 1987. Publishes 12,000 copies.

• *PKA's Advocate* editors tend to like positive, upbeat, entertaining material.

Needs: Adventure, contemporary, ethnic, experimental, fantasy, feminist, historical, humor/satire, juvenile (5-9 years), literary, mainstream, mystery/suspense, prose poem, regional, romance, science fiction, senior citizen/retirement, sports, western, young adult/teen (10-18 years). "Currently looking for equine (horses) stories, poetry, art, photos and cartoons." Nothing religious, pornographic, violent, erotic, pro-drug or anti-environment. Receives 60 unsolicited mss/month. Accepts 6-8 mss/issue; 36-48 mss/year. Publishes ms 4 months to 1 year after acceptance. Length: 1,000 words preferred; 1,500 words maximum. Sometimes critiques rejected mss.

How to Contact: Send complete ms with cover letter. Reports in 2 weeks on queries; 2 months on mss. SASE. No simultaneous submissions. Sample copy for $4 (US currency for inside US; $5.25 US currency for Canada). Writers guidelines for SASE.

Payment/Terms: Pays contributor's copies. Acquires first rights.

Advice: "The highest criterion in selecting a work is its entertainment value. It must first be enjoyable reading. It must, of course, be original. To stand out, it must be thought provoking or strongly emotive, or very cleverly

 **A BULLET INTRODUCES COMMENTS** by the editor of *Novel & Short Story Writer's Market* indicating special information about the listing.

plotted. Will consider only previously unpublished works by writers who do not earn their living principally through writing."

☑ **AETHLON, (I,II,IV)**, East Tennessee State University, Box 70, 683, Johnson City TN 37614-0683. (423)439-5994. E-mail: morefiel@access.etsu.edu. **Fiction Editor:** John Morefield. Magazine: 6×9; 180-240 pages; illustrations and photographs. "Theme: Literary treatment of sport. We publish articles on that theme, critical studies of author's treatment of sport and original fiction and poetry with sport themes. Most of our readers are academics." Semiannually. Estab. 1983. Circ. 800.

Needs: Sport. No fantasy, science fiction or horror. "Stories must have a sport-related theme and subject; otherwise, we're wide open." No personal memoirs. Receives 15-20 fiction mss/month. Accepts 6-10 fiction mss/issue; 12-20 fiction mss/year. Publishes ms "about 1 year" after acceptance. Recently published work by W.P. Kinsella, Jay Atkinson, Thomas Shane, Mell Morris, Ruth Tarson and Joseph Hullett. Publishes 2-3 new writers/year. Length: 2,500-5,000 words average; 500 words minimum; 7,500 words maximum. Also publishes literary essays, literary criticism, poetry. Sometimes critiques rejected mss.

How to Contact: Send complete ms and brief cover letter with 1-2 lines for a contributor's note. Reports in 6-12 months. SASE in size to fit ms. No simultaneous submissions. Electronic disk submissions OK. Final copy must be submitted on disk (WordPerfect). Sample copy for $12.50. Reviews novels and short story collections. Send books to Prof. Joe Dewey, Dept. of English, University of Pittsburgh-Johnstown, Johnstown PA 15601.

Payment/Terms: Pays 1 contributor's copy and 5 offprints.

Advice: "We are looking for well-written, insightful stories. The only criterion is literary excellence. A story should begin immediately to develop tension or conflict. It should have strong characters and a well-drawn setting. Don't be afraid to be experimental. Take more care with your manuscript. Please send a legible manuscript free of grammatical errors. Be willing to revise."

$ AFRICAN AMERICAN REVIEW, (II), Indiana State University, Department of English, Root Hall A218, Terre Haute IN 47809. (812)237-2968. Fax: (812)237-3156. E-mail: aschoal@amber.indstate.edu. Editor: Joe Weixlmann. **Fiction Editor:** Reginald McKnight. Magazine: 7×10; 176 pages; 60#, acid-free paper; 100# skid stock cover; illustrations and photos. "*African American Review* publishes stories and poetry by African American writers, and essays about African American literature and culture." Quarterly. Estab. 1967. Circ. 4,200.

- *African American Review* is the official publication of the Division of Black American Literature and Culture of the Modern Language Association. The magazine received American Literary Magazine Awards in 1994 and 1995.

Needs: Ethnic/Multicultural: experimental, feminist, gay, lesbian, literary, mainstream/contemporary. "No children's/juvenile/young adult/teen." Receives 50 unsolicited mss/month. Accepts 40 mss/year. Publishes ms 1 year after acceptance. Agented fiction 10%. Published work by Clarence Major, Ann Allen Shockley, Ishmael Reed. Length: 3,000 words average. Also publishes literary essays, literary criticism, poetry. Sometimes critiques or comments on rejected mss.

How to Contact: Send complete ms with a cover letter. Reports in 2 weeks on queries; 3 months on mss. Send SASE for reply, return of ms or send a disposable copy of ms. Sample copy for $6. Fiction guidelines for #10 SASE. Reviews novels and short story collections. Send books to Keneth Kinnamon, Dept. of English, Univ. of Arkansas, Fayetteville, AR 72701.

Payment/Terms: Pays $25-100 and 10 contributor's copies on publication for first North American serial rights. Sends galleys to author.

$ AGNI, (III), Creative Writing Program, Boston University, 236 Bay State Rd., Boston MA 02215. (617)353-5389. Fax: (617)353-7136. E-mail: agni@bu.edu. Website: www.webdelsol.com/AGNI (includes names of editors, short fiction, poetry and interviews with authors). **Editor-in-Chief:** Askold Melnyczuk. Magazine: 5½×8½; 320 pages; 55 lb. booktext paper; recycled cover stock; occasional art portfolios. "Eclectic literary magazine publishing first-rate poems and stories." Biannually. Estab. 1972.

- Work from *Agni* has been selected regularly for inclusion in both *Pushcart Prize* and *Best American Short Stories* anthologies. "We tend to be backlogged with fiction."

Needs: Stories, excerpted novels, prose poems and translations. No science fiction. Receives more than 250 unsolicited fiction mss/month. Accepts 4-7 mss/issue, 8-12 mss/year. Reading period October 1 through April 30 only. Recently published work by Alice Hoffman, Ha Jin, Jill McCorkle and Percival Everett. Publishes 1-10 new writers/year. Rarely critiques rejected mss.

How to Contact: Send complete ms with SASE and cover letter listing previous publications. Simultaneous and electronic (disk) submissions OK. Reports in up to 5 months. Sample copy for $9.

Payment/Terms: Pays $10/page up to $150; 2 contributor's copies; one-year subscription. Pays on publication for first North American serial rights. Sends galleys to author. Copyright reverts to author upon publication.

Advice: "Read *Agni* carefully to understand the kinds of stories we publish. Read—everything, classics, literary journals, bestsellers. People need to read and subscribe to the magazines before sending their work. It's important for artists to support the arts."

$ THE AGUILAR EXPRESSION, (II), 1329 Gilmore Ave., Donora PA 15033. (724)379-8019. **Editor:** Xavier F. Aguilar. Magazine: 8½×11; 10-16 pages; 20 lb. bond paper; illustrations. "We are open to all writers of a general theme—something that may appeal to everyone." Semiannually. Estab. 1989. Circ. 150.

- The editor is particularly interested in stories about the homeless in the U.S. but publishes fiction on other topics as well.

Needs: Adventure, ethnic/multicultural, experimental, horror, mainstream/contemporary, mystery/suspense (romantic suspense), romance (contemporary). No religious or first-person stories. Will publish annual special fiction issue or anthology in the future. Receives 10 unsolicited mss/month. Accepts 1-2 mss/issue; 2-4 mss/year. Recently publishes ms 1 month to 1 year after acceptance. Recently published work by Michael D. Cohen, R.G. Cantalupo and Kent Braithwaite. Length: 1,000 words average; 750 words minimum; 1,500 words maximum. Also publishes poetry.

How to Contact: Send complete ms with cover letter. Reports on queries in 1 week; mss in 1 month. Send SASE for reply to a query or send a disposable copy of ms. No simultaneous submissions. Sample copy for $6. Fiction guidelines for #10 SASE.

Payment/Terms: Pays $10 and 1 contributor's copy for lead story; additional copies at a reduced rate of $3. Acquires one-time rights. Not copyrighted. Write to publication for details on contests, awards or grants.

Advice: "Clean, clear copy makes a manuscript stand out."

✓ 🏆 **$ ALASKA QUARTERLY REVIEW, (II)**, University of Alaska—Anchorage, 3211 Providence Dr., Anchorage AK 99508. (907)786-6916. **Fiction Editor:** Ronald Spatz. Magazine: 6×9; 260 pages; 60 lb. Glatfelter paper; 10 pt. C15 black ink varnish cover stock; photos on cover only. *AQR* "publishes fiction, poetry, literary nonfiction and short plays in traditional and experimental styles." Semiannually. Estab. 1982. Circ. 2,200.

- Work appearing in the *Alaska Quarterly Review* has been selected for the *Prize Stories: The O. Henry Awards*, *Best American Essays*, *Best American Poetry* and *Pushcart Prize* anthologies. *The Washington Post* calls the *Alaska Quarterly Review*, "one of the nation's best literary magazines."

Needs: Contemporary, experimental, literary, prose poem, translations. Receives 200 unsolicited fiction mss/month. Accepts 7-13 mss/issue, 15-24 mss/year. Does not read mss May 15 through August 15. Length: not exceeding 90 pages. Recently published work by Richard Ford, William H. Gass, Patricia Hampl, Stuart Dybek, Alan Lightman and Hayden Carruth. Published new writers within the last year. Publishes short shorts.

How to Contact: Send complete mss with SASE. Simultaneous submissions "undesirable, but will accept if indicated." Reports in 2-3 months "but during peak periods a reply may take up to 6 months." Publishes ms 6 months to 1 year after acceptance. Sample copy for $5.

Payment/Terms: Pays 1 contributor's copy and a year's subscription. Pays $50-200 honorarium when grant funding permits. Acquires first rights.

Advice: "We have made a significant investment in fiction. The reason is quality; serious fiction *needs* a market. Try to have everything build to a singleness of effect."

N **ALL AMNESIA, (II)**, P.O. Box 661441, Los Angeles CA 90066. **Editor:** Monica Rex. Magazine: 8×11; 50 pages; illustrations and photos. "*Amnesia* is an experimental arts magazine: literary, visual, performance, mail art." Published "as possible." Estab. 1989. Circ. 500.

Needs: All themes/categories considered; short fiction. Legible mss in 8×11 format (for duplication in b&w or color); presented as received. Submissions cannot be returned. Length: 5,000 words maximum. Accepts 2 mss/year. Publishes 20 new writers/year. Recently published work by Jack Skelley, Michelle T. Clinton, Robin Carr, Elfenware, Natasha Bengal, Zoot, W4K7. Length: 5,000 words maximum. Publishes short shorts. Also publishes literary essays, literary criticism, poetry.

How to Contact: Send complete ms with a cover letter. Include bio (100 words maximum). Send disposable copy of ms. Simultaneous and reprint submissions OK. Sample copy for $5, 9×12 SASE. Reviews novels, short story collections and nonfiction books of interest to writers. Send books to editor.

Payment/Terms: Pays 2 contributor's copies. Acquires rights per issue and additional printing of same issue.

Advice: "*All Amnesia* approaches each issue as a collage of the best available work and is unique each time it comes together. It is approached as an art object itself, for careful presentation of artists."

ALPHA BEAT PRESS, (I, IV), 31 Waterloo St., New Hope PA 18938. (215)862-0299. **Editor:** Dave Christy. Magazine: 7½×9; 95-125 pages; illustrations. "Beat and modern literature—prose, reviews and poetry." Semiannually. Estab. 1987. Circ. 600.

- Work from *Alpha Beat Press* has appeared in *Pushcart Prize* anthologies. Alpha Beat Press also publishes poetry chapbooks and supplements. The magazine is known for writings associated with modern and beat culture.

MARKET CATEGORIES: (I) Open to new writers; **(II)** Open to both new and established writers; **(III)** Interested mostly in established writers; **(IV)** Open to writers whose work is specialized; **(V)** Closed to unsolicited submissions.

Needs: Erotica, experimental, literary and prose poem. No religious. Recently published work by Elliott, Joseph Verrilli, Chris Diamant, t.k. splake and Ed Galing. Published approximately 100 new writers within the last year. Length: 600 words minimum; 1,000 words maximum. Also publishes literary essays, literary criticism, poetry.
How to Contact: Query first. Reports on queries within 2 weeks. SASE. Simultaneous and reprint submissions OK. Sample copy for $10. Reviews novels and short story collections.
Payment/Terms: Pays in contributor's copies. Rights remain with author.
Advice: "*ABP* is the finest journal of its kind available today, having, with 20 issues, published the widest range of published and unpublished writers you'll find in the small press scene."

N **$ AMBIT, Poetry/Art/Short Fiction, (I, II)**, 17 Priory Gardens, London, N6 5QY, United Kingdom. Phone: 0181 3403566. Website: http://www.AMBIT.CO.UK. Editor: Martin Bax. **Fiction Editors:** Geoff Nicholson, J.G. Ballard. Magazine: 240cm×170cm; 100 pages; removable cover; illustrations and photos. Publishes "avant-garde material; short stories only, no novels." Quarterly. Estab. 1959. Circ. 3,000.
Needs: Erotica, ethnic/multicultural, experimental, gay, contemporary, translations. No fantasy/horror/science fiction. Receives 80 unsolicited mss/month. Accepts 5 mss/issue; 20 mss/year. Publishes ms up to 1 year after acceptance. Agented fiction under 1%. Publishes 10 new fiction writers/year. Length: 3,000 words average; 1,000 words minimum, 5,000 words maximum. Also publishes poetry.
How to Contact: Send 1-2 stories. Reports in 1 month. Send SASE with UK stamps or IRCs for reply, return of ms. Sample copy for $16. Fiction guidelines free.
Payment/Terms: Pays approx. £5/printed page and 2 contributor's copies on publication; additional copies $12. Acknowledgment if reprinted. Not copyrighted.

$ AMELIA, (II), 329 E St., Bakersfield CA 93304. (805)323-4064. **Editor-in-Chief:** Frederick A. Raborg, Jr. Magazine: 5½×8½; 124-136 pages; perfect-bound; 60 lb. high-quality moistrite matte paper; kromekote cover; four-color covers; original illustrations; b&w photos. "A general review using fine fiction, poetry, criticism, belles lettres, one-act plays, fine pen-and-ink sketches and line drawings, sophisticated cartoons, book reviews and translations of both fiction and poetry for general readers with eclectic tastes for quality writing." Quarterly. Plans special fiction issue each July. Estab. 1984. Circ. 1,750.

- *Amelia* sponsors a long list of fiction awards. It ranked #23 on *Writer's Digest*'s Fiction 50 list of top markets for fiction writers.

Needs: Adventure, contemporary, erotica, ethnic, experimental, fantasy, feminist, gay, historical, humor/satire, lesbian, literary, mainstream, mystery/suspense, prose poem, regional, science fiction, senior citizen/retirement, sports, translations, western. Nothing "obviously pornographic or patently religious." Receives 160-180 unsolicited mss/month. Accepts up to 9 mss/issue; 25-36 mss/year. Recently published work by Michael Bugeja, Jack Curtis, Thomas F. Wilson, Maxine Kumin, Eugene Dubnov, Matt Mulhern and Merrill Joan Gerber. Published new writers within the last year. Length: 3,000 words average; 1,000 words minimum; 5,000 words maximum. Usually critiques rejected mss.
How to Contact: Send complete ms with cover letter with previous credits if applicable to *Amelia* and perhaps a brief personal comment to show personality and experience. Reports in 1 week on queries; 2 weeks to 3 months on mss. SASE. Sample copy for $9.95. Fiction guidelines for #10 SASE. Sends galleys to author "when deadline permits."
Payment/Terms: Pays $35-50 on acceptance for first North American serial rights plus 2 contributor's copies; extras with 20% discount.
Advice: "Write carefully and well, but have a strong story to relate. I look for depth of plot and uniqueness, and strong characterization. Study manuscript mechanics and submission procedures. Neatness does count. There is a sameness—a cloning process—among most magazines today that tends to dull the senses. Magazines like *Amelia* will awaken those senses while offering stories and poems of lasting value."

✔ **AMERICAN LITERARY REVIEW, (II)**, University of North Texas, P.O. Box 311307, Denton TX 76203-1307. (940)565-2755. Website: http://www.engl.unt.edu/alr/ (includes short fiction, essays, poetry, subscription information, writer's guidelines, contest details). **Editor:** Lee Martin. Magazine: 7×10; 128 pages; 70 lb. Mohawk paper; 67 lb. Wausau Vellum cover. "Publishes quality, contemporary poems and stories." Semiannually. Estab. 1990. Circ. 900.
Needs: Mainstream and literary only. No genre works. Receives 50-75 unsolicited fiction mss/month. Accepts 4-8 mss/issue; 8-16 mss/year. Publishes ms within 2 years after acceptance. Published work by Jason Brown, Lex Williford, Lucy Ferriss and Mark Jacobs. Length: less than 7,500 words. Critiques or comments on rejected mss when possible. Also accepts poetry and essays.
How to Contact: Send complete ms with cover letter. Accepts queries/mss by fax. Reports in 2-3 months. SASE. Simultaneous submissions OK. Sample copy for $8. Fiction guidelines free.
Payment/Terms: Pays in contributor's copies. Acquires one-time rights.
Advice: "We like to see stories that illuminate the various layers of characters and their situations with great artistry. Give us distinctive character-driven stories that explore the complexities of human existance." Looks for "the small moments that contain more than at first appears possible, that surprise us with more truth than we thought we had a right to expect."

AMERICAN VOICE, (II), 332 W. Broadway, #1215, Louisville KY 40202. (502)562-0045. **Editor:** Frederick Smock. Magazine: 6×9; 150 pages; photos. Triannually. Estab. 1985. Circ. 2,000.

Needs: Literary. No children's or romance. Receives 150 unsolicited mss/month. Accepts 5-6 mss/issue. Recently published Isabel Allende, Kyle Potok, Kate Braverman and Leon Rooke. Length: "the shorter the better."

How to Contact: Send complete ms with a cover letter. Include bio. Reports in 6 weeks on mss. Sample copy for $7.

Payment/Terms: Payment varies.

AMERICAN WRITING; A Magazine, (I, II), Nierika Editions, 4343 Manayunk Ave., Philadelphia PA 19128. **Editor:** Alexandra Grilikhes. Magazine: 8½×5½; 96 pages; matte paper and cover stock; photos. "We publish new writing that takes risks with form, point of view, language, ways of perceiving. We are interested in the voice of the loner, the artist as shaman, the powers of intuition, exceptional work of all kinds." Semiannually. Estab. 1990. Circ. 2,500.

Needs: Contemporary, excerpted novel, ethnic/multicultural, experimental, feminist, gay, lesbian, literary, translations. "We're looking for more literary, experimental, contemporary writing—writing that drives you to write it." No mainstream, romance. Receives 100-200 unsolicited mss/month. Accepts 4-5 mss/issue; 10-11 mss/year. Does not read mss June, December, January. Publishes ms 6-12 months after acceptance. Agented fiction less than 1%. Recently published work by Cris Mazza, Deborah Elliott Deutschman, William Van Wert, Peter Constantine, Emil Draitser and Jim Janko. Publishes 6-8 new writers/year. Length: 3,500 words average; 5,000 words maximum. Publishes short shorts. Also publishes literary essays, personal essays, literary criticism, poetry. Critiques or comments on rejected mss "when there is time."

How to Contact: Send complete ms with a brief cover letter. Include brief bio and list of publications if applicable. Reports in 1 month on queries; 6-24 weeks on mss. Send SASE for reply, return of ms or send a disposable copy of ms. Simultaneous submissions OK. Sample copy for $6; fiction guidelines for #10 SASE.

Payment/Terms: Pays 2 contributor's copies; additional copies at half price. Acquires first rights or one-time rights.

Advice: "We look for intensity, vision, imaginative use of language, freshness, craft, sophistication; stories that delve. Read not just current stuff, but the old masters—Dostoyevsky, Chekhov and Hesse. Learn about subtlty and depth. Reading helps you to know who you are as a writer, writing makes you more that person, if you're lucky. Read one or two issues of the magazine *carefully.*"

THE AMETHYST REVIEW, (I, II), Marcasite Press, 23 Riverside Ave., Truro, Nova Scotia B2N 4G2 Canada. (902)895-1345. E-mail: amethyst@col.auracom.com. Website: http://www.col.auracom.com/~amethyst (includes writer's guidelines, names of editors, fiction excerpts, subscription info, contest guidelines, Editor's Picks and suggested reading). **Editors:** Penny Ferguson and Lenora Steele. Magazine: 8¼×6¾; 84 pages; book weight paper; card stock cover; illustrations. "We publish quality contemporary fiction and poetry of interest to the literary reader." Semiannually. Estab. 1993. Circ. 150-200.

Needs: Literary. Receives 25 unsolicited mss/month. Accepts 2-3 mss/issue; 4-6 mss/year. Publishes ms maximum 6 months after acceptance, "usually much sooner." Recently published work by Anjana Basu, Penny L. Ferguson, Craig Loomis, Joan Tovenati, Christian Jensen and Denise Kelly LeBlanc. Length: 5,000 words maximum. Publishes short shorts. Also publishes poetry. Sponsors contest; send SASE for information.

How to Contact: Send complete ms with cover letter. Include estimated word count, a 50-word bio and list of publications. Reports in 2-28 weeks on mss. Send SASE or SAE and IRCs for reply, return of mss or send a disposable copy of ms. Sample copy for $6 (current) or $4 (back issues). Fiction guidelines for SASE or SAE and IRCs. "Please do not send American stamps! We are no longer replying to submissions without adequate return postage." Reviews novels and short story collections "only by people we have published."

Payment/Terms: Pays 1 contributor's copy; additional copies $6. Pays on publication. Acquires first North American serial rights.

Advice: "For us, a story must be memorable because it touches the reader's heart or imagination. Quality is our criterion. Try to delight us with originality and craft. Send for guidelines and sample. We don't look for a specific type of story. We publish the *best* of what we receive. We are seeking literary quality and accessibility. A story that stands out gives the reader a 'tingle' and stays in your mind for days to come. Pay attention to detail, don't be sloppy. Care about your subjects because if you don't neither will the reader. Dazzle us with quality instead of trying to shock us!"

$ ANTIETAM REVIEW, (I, II, IV), Washington County Arts Council, 41 S. Potomac St., Hagerstown MD 21740. Phone/fax: (301)791-3132. Editor: Susanne Kass. **Fiction Editors:** Susanne Kass and Ann Knox. Magazine: 8½×11; 54-68 pages; glossy paper; light card cover; photos. A literary journal of short fiction, poetry and black-and-white photographs. "Our audience is primarily in the six state region. Urban, suburban and rural writers and readers, but copies are purchased nationwide, both by libraries as well as individuals. Sales and submissions increase yearly, and we have just celebrated our fifteenth year of continual publication." Annually. Estab. 1982. Circ. 1,800.

• *Antietam Review* has received several awards including First-runner Up (1993-94) for Editorial Content from the American Literary Magazine Awards. Work published in the magazine has been included in the

Pushcart Prize anthology and *Best American Short Stories*. The magazine also received a grant from the Maryland State Arts Council.

Needs: Condensed/excerpted novel, contemporary, ethnic, experimental, feminist, literary and prose poem. Wants more contemporary, ethnic, experimental. "We read manuscripts from our region—Delaware, Maryland, Pennsylvania, Virginia, West Virginia and Washington D.C. only. We read from September 1 through February 1." No horror, romance, inspirational, pornography. Receives about 100 unsolicited mss/month. Buys 8-10 stories/year. Publishes ms 2-3 months after acceptance. Recently published work by Leslie Carper, Becky Hagerston, Mario Rossilli, Stephen Murabita, Lee Fennell, David Conway and Louise Farmer Smith. Publishes 2-3 new writers/year. Length: 3,000 words average. Also publishes poetry.

How to Contact: "Send ms and SASE with a cover letter. Let us know if you have published before and where." Include estimated word count, 1-paragraph bio and list of publications. Reports in 2-4 months. "If we hold a story, we let the writer know. Occasionally we critique returned ms or ask for rewrites." Sample copy for $5.25. Back issue $3.15. Guidelines for legal SAE.

Payment/Terms: "We believe it is a matter of dignity that writers and poets be paid. We have been able to give $50-100 a story and $25 a poem, but this depends on funding. Also 2 copies." Buys first North American serial rights. Sends galleys to author if requested.

Advice: "We seek high quality, well-crafted work with significant character development and shift. We seek no specific theme, our look for work that is interesting involves the reader, and teaches us a new way to views the world. A manuscript stands out because of its energy and flow. Most of our submissions reflect the times (i.e. the news, current events) more than industry trends. We now require *accepted* stories to be put on disk by the author to cut down on printing costs. We are seeing an increase of first person narrative stories."

THE ANTIGONISH REVIEW, (I, II), St. Francis Xavier University, P.O. Box 5000, Antigonish, Nova Scotia B2G 2W5 Canada. (902)867-3962. Fax: (902)867-5563. E-mail: tar@stfx.ca. **Editor:** George Sanderson. Literary magazine for educated and creative readers. Quarterly. Estab. 1970. Circ. 800.

Needs: Literary, contemporary, prose poem, translations. No erotic or political material. Accepts 6 mss/issue. Receives 50 unsolicited fiction mss each month. Published work by Arnold Bloch, Richard Butts and Helen Barolini. Published new writers within the last year. Length: 3,000-5,000 words. Sometimes comments briefly on rejected mss.

How to Contact: Send complete ms with cover letter. SASE ("U.S. postage not acceptable"). No simultaneous submissions. Electronic (disk compatible with WordPerfect/IBM and Windows or e-mail) submissions OK. Prefers hard copy with disk submission. Reports in 6 months. Publishes ms 3 months to 1 year after acceptance.

Payment/Terms: Pays 2 contributor's copies. Authors retain copyright.

Advice: "Learn the fundamentals and do not deluge an editor."

$ ANTIOCH REVIEW, (II), Box 148, Yellow Springs OH 45387-0148. (937)767-6389. **Editor:** Robert S. Fogarty. Associate Editor: Nolan Miller. Magazine: 6×9; 128 pages; 50 lb. book offset paper; coated cover stock; illustrations "seldom." "Literary and cultural review of contemporary issues in politics, American and international studies, and literature for general readership." Quarterly. Published special fiction issue last year; plans another. Estab. 1941. Circ. 5,100.

Needs: Literary, contemporary, experimental, translations. No children's, science fiction or popular market. Accepts 5-6 mss/issue, 20-24 mss/year. Receives approximately 275 unsolicited fiction mss each month. Approximately 1-2% of fiction agented. Recently published work by Ed Falco, Ha Jin, Edith Pearlman and Rick De Mariuis. Published 1-2 new writers/year. Length: generally under 8,000 words.

How to Contact: Send complete ms with SASE, preferably mailed flat. Reports in 2 months. Publishes ms 6-9 months after acceptance. Sample copy for $6. Guidelines for SASE.

Payment/Terms: Pays $10/page; 2 contributor's copies. $3.90 for extras. Pays on publication for first and one-time rights (rights returned to author on request).

Advice: "Our best advice, always, is to *read* the *Antioch Review* to see what type of material we publish. Quality fiction requires an engagement of the reader's intellectual interest supported by mature emotional relevance, written in a style that is rich and rewarding without being freaky. The great number of stories submitted to us indicates that fiction still has great appeal. We assume that if so many are writing fiction, many must be reading it."

APHRODITE GONE BERSERK, (IV), A journal of erotic art, Red Wine Press, 233 Guyon Ave., Staten Island NY 10306. **Editors:** C. Esposito, E. Eccleston. Magazine: 5½×8½; 48 pages; illustrations and photos. "*AGB* publishes fiction, poetry, essays, photography, etc. that deal with the erotic or sexuality in all styles and from any perspective or orientation." Semiannually. Estab. 1996.

Needs: Erotica: condensed/excerpted novel, experimental, feminist, gay, lesbian, literary, translations. List of upcoming themes available for SASE. Receives 10 unsolicited mss/month. Accepts 3 mss/issue; 6 mss/year. Publishes ms 6-12 months after acceptance. Recently published work by Gerard Malanga, Lyn Lifshin and Arlene Mandell. Publishes short shorts. Also publishes literary essays, literary criticism, poetry.

How to Contact: Send complete ms with a cover letter. Reports in 2 weeks on queries; 1 month on mss. Send SASE for reply, return of ms or send a disposable copy of ms. Simultaneous and reprint submissions OK. Reviews novels or short story collections.

Payment/Terms: Pays 1 contributor's copy. Acquires one-time rights.
Advice: "Stay away from the cliché and tired, and write honestly from the heart. We do not allow industry trends to affect the type of fiction we accept for publication."

APPALACHIAN HERITAGE, (I, II), Hutchins Library, Berea College, Berea KY 40404. (606)986-9341. Fax: (606)986-9494. E-mail: sidney-farr@berea.edu. **Editor:** Sidney Saylor Farr. Magazine: 6×9; 80 pages; 60 lb. stock; 10 pt. Warrenflo cover; drawings and b&w photos. "*Appalachian Heritage* is a southern Appalachian literary magazine. We try to keep a balance of fiction, poetry, essays, scholarly works, etc., for a general audience and/or those interested in the Appalachian mountains." Quarterly. Estab. 1973. Circ. approximately 600.
Needs: Regional, literary, historical. "We do not want to see fiction that has no ties to Southern Appalachia." Receives 6-8 unsolicited mss/month. Accepts 2-3 mss/issue; 12-15 mss/year. Publishes ms 1-2 years after acceptance. Published work by Bettie Sellers, Robert Morgan, James Still and Wilma Dykeman. Published new writers within the last year. Length: 3,000 words maximum. Publishes short shorts. Length: 500 words. Occasionally critiques rejected mss.
How to Contact: Send complete ms with cover letter. Include estimated word count, 2-3-sentence bio and list of publications. Reports in 3-4 weeks on queries; 4-6 weeks on mss. Send SASE for reply, return of ms or send a disposable copy of ms. Simultaneous and electronic submissions OK. Sample copy for $6. Guidelines free.
Payment/Terms: Pays 3 contributor's copies; $6 charge for extras. Acquires first North American serial rights.
Advice: "Get acquainted with *Appalachian Heritage*, as you should with any publication before submitting your work."

ARACHNE, INC., In Praise of America's Grassroots Writers, (I, II, IV), 2363 Page Rd., Kennedy NY 14747-9717. **Editor:** Susan L. Leach. Magazine: 8½×5½; 30 pages; 20 lb. cover stock; illustrations and photos. "Rural theme. Sedate, conservative tone." Semiannually. Estab. 1981. Circ. 500.
Needs: Literary, regional, religious/inspirational. No erotica. Publishes special fiction issues or anthologies. Receives 20 unsolicited mss/month. Accepts 1-2 mss/issue; 4-5 mss/year. "Does not read after January and July publications." Publishes ms 3 weeks after acceptance. Recently published work by Anne Thore Beecham. Length: 1,500 words. Publishes short shorts. Also publishes literary essays, literary criticism and poetry. Often critiques or comments on rejected mss.
How to Contact: Query or send complete ms with a cover letter. Include estimated word count and 250 word bio. Reports in 2 weeks on queries. Send SASE for reply, return of ms or send disposable copy of ms. No simultaneous submissions. Sample copy for $5 and 8½×5½ SAE with 3 first-class stamps. Fiction guidelines for #10 SASE.
Payment/Terms: Pays 2 contributor's copies for first rights; additional copies $2.50. Sends galleys to author. Not copyrighted.
Advice: "Be willing to work with us to perfect your material. Don't try to do it all in one poem or short story."

✔ $ **ARARAT QUARTERLY, (IV)**, Ararat Press, AGBU., 55 E. 59th St., New York NY 10022. (212)319-6383. **Editor:** Dr. Leo Hamalian. Magazine: 8½×11; 72 pages; illustrations and b&w photographs. "*Ararat* is a forum for the literary and historical works of Armenian intellectuals or non-Armenian writers writing about Armenian subjects."
Needs: Condensed/excerpted novel, contemporary, historical, humor/satire, literary, religious/inspirational, translations. Publishes special fiction issue. Receives 25 unsolicited mss/month. Accepts 5 mss/issue; 20 mss/year. Length: 1,000 words average. Publishes short shorts. Length: 500 words. Also publishes literary essays, literary criticism, poetry. Sometimes critiques rejected mss and recommends other markets.
How to Contact: Send complete ms with cover letter. Reports in 1 month on queries; 3 weeks on mss. SASE. Simultaneous and reprint submissions OK. Sample copy for $7 and $1 postage. Free fiction guidelines. Reviews novels and short story collections.
Payment/Terms: Pays $40-75 plus 2 contributor's copies on publication for one-time rights. Sends galleys to author.

N ▣ **ARCHIPELAGO, (II, III), An International Journal On-Line of Literature, Art and Opinion**, Box 2485, Charlottesville VA 22902-2485. (804)979-5292. E-mail: editor@archipelago.org. Website: http://www.archipelago.org. **Editor:** Katherine McNamara. Magazine: 50-60 pages in download (print) edition, available from website. "Literary (print-based, in spirit) work, meaning well-formed, fine writing, on diverse subjects and in various genres with an international tone. Readership is educated, well-read, international." Quarterly. Estab. 1997. Circ. 23 countries, 6,000 hits/month.
Needs: Literary. "No academic, self-involved, 'hip' fiction." Receives several unsolicited mss/month. Accepts 1 ms/issue. Does not read mss in the month before publication. Usually publishes ms in next issue after acceptance. Recently published work by Victoria Slavuski and David Castleman. Publishes short shorts. Also publishes literary essays, literary criticism, poetry. Sometimes critiques or comments on rejected ms if requested.
How to Contact: Query first. Accepts queries by e-mail. Include brief bio. Reports in 1 month on queries; 2 months on mss. Send SASE for reply, return of ms. Simultaneous and reprint submissions OK. Reviews novels, short story collections and nonfiction books of interest to writers.
Payment/Terms: No payment. Acquires first rights and first electronic rights. Sends galleys to author. Copyright

reverts to author on publication.
Advice: "We look for superb writing; engaged, adult imagination."

✔ **ARKANSAS REVIEW, A Journal of Delta Studies, (II)**, Department of English and Philosophy, P.O. Box 1890, Arkansas State University, State University AR 72467-1890. (501)972-3043. Fax: (501)972-2795. E-mail: delta@toltec.astate.com. Website: http://www.clt.astate.edu/arkreview (includes guidelines, names of editors, ordering information, tables of contents). Editor: William C. Clements. **Fiction Editor:** Norman Lavers. Magazine: 8¼×11; 64-100 pages; coated, matte paper; matte, 4-color cover stock; illustrations and photos. Publishes articles, fiction, poetry, essays, interviews, reviews, visual art evocative of or responsive to the Mississippi River Delta. Triannually. Estab. 1996. Circ. 700.
Needs: Regional short stories, literary essays, literary criticism. "No genre fiction." Receives 30-50 unsolicited mss/month. Accepts 2-3 mss/issue; 5-7 mss/year. Publishes ms 6-12 months after acceptance. Agented fiction 1%. Recently published work by George Chambers, Raymond Federman, Carole Glickfeld, Michael Mooney, D.E. Steward, Leslie Edgerton, Marianne Luban, Edra Ziesk, Steve Yates and Lloyd Zimpel. Publishes 3-6 new writers/year. Also publishes literary essays and poetry. Always critiques or comments on rejected mss.
How to Contact: Send complete ms with cover letter. Accepts queries/mss by e-mail and fax. Include bio. Reports in 1 week on queries; 4 months on mss. Send SASE for reply, return of ms or send a disposable copy of ms. Sample copy for $6. Fiction guidelines free for #10 SASE.
Payment/Terms: Pays 5 contributor's copies; additional copies for $5. Acquires first North American serial rights.
Advice: "We publish new writers in every issue. We look for distinguished, mature writing, surprises, a perfect ending and a story that means more than merely what went on in it. We don't like recognizable imitations of currently fashionable writers. Writers with an Arkansas connection who are accepted for publication are automatically in the running for the $1,000 Seaton award for best work by an Arkansas-connected author (born there, lived there, went to school there). No application. Upon having your work accepted, state your Arkansas connection."

THE ARMCHAIR AESTHETE, (I, II), Pickle Gas Press, 59 Vinal Ave., Rochester NY 14609. (716)342-6331. E-mail: bypaul@netacc.net. Website: http://www.geocities.com/Sotto/Museum/1499/ (includes guidelines, editors, fiction and poetry). **Editor:** Paul Agosto. Magazine: 5½×8½; 30-40 pages; 20 lb. paper; 60 lb. color cover; illustrations. The Armchair Aesthete is a new publication providing an outlet for the creative writer while offering our audience (ages 9-90) a "good read." Quarterly. Estab. 1996. Circ. 100.
Needs: Adventure, fantasy (science fantasy, sword and sorcery), historical (general), horror, humor/satire, mainstream/contemporary, mystery/suspense (amateur sleuth, cozy, police procedural, private eye/hardboiled, romantic suspense), science fiction (soft/sociological), westerns (frontier, traditional). No racist, pornographic, avert gore or material intended for children. Plans to publish special fiction issue. Accepts 8-15 mss/issue; 32-60 mss/year. Publishes ms 3-9 months after acceptance. Agented fiction less than 5%. Recently published work by Alan Reynolds, Tom Pacheco, Joe Ducato, Paula Howard Palter and Doug Holder. Publishes 10-13 new writers/year. Length: 1,200 words average; 2,000 words maximum. Publishes short shorts. Also publishes poetry. Sometimes critiques or comments on rejected mss.
How to Contact: Send complete ms with a cover letter. Include estimated word count, 50-100 word bio and list of publications. Reports in 2-3 weeks on queries; 1-3 months on mss. Send SASE for reply, return of ms or send a disposable copy of ms. Simultaneous submissions, reprints and electronic submissions OK. Sample copy for $3 and 2 first-class stamps. Fiction guidelines free for #10 SASE. Reviews novels and short story collections.
Payment/Terms: Pays 1 contributor's copy on publication; additional copies for $3. Acquires one-time rights. Not copyrighted. Accepted works are automatically eligible for an annual contest.
Advice: "We look for a clever plot, thought-out characters, something that surprises or catches us off guard. Also, something that causes us to think after the stories end. Write on innovative subjects and situations. Submissions should be professionally presented and technically sound."

✔ **$ ARTFUL DODGE, (II)**, Dept. of English, College of Wooster, Wooster OH 44691. (330)263-2577. Website: http://www.wooster.edu/Artful_Dodge (includes writer's guidelines, editor's bios, interviews with authors, subscription information, history of the magazine). **Editor-in-Chief:** Daniel Bourne. Magazine: 150-200 pages; illustrations; photos. "There is no theme in this magazine, except literary power. We also have an ongoing interest in translations from Eastern Europe and elsewhere." Annually. Estab. 1979. Circ. 1,000.
Needs: Experimental, literary, prose poem, translations. "We judge by literary quality, not by genre. We are especially interested in fine English translations of significant contemporary prose writers. Translations should be submitted with original texts." Receives 40 unsolicited fiction mss/month. Accepts 5 mss/year. Published fiction by Edward Kleinschmidt, Terese Svoboda, David Surface, Leslie Pietrzyk and Zbigniew Herbert; and

READ THE BUSINESS OF FICTION WRITING section to learn the correct way to prepare and submit a manuscript.

INSIDER REPORT

B&A: New Fiction—break-in market for talented new writers

Michelle Alfano knows what it feels like to be an unpublished writer trying to break in. Her big break came in 1991 when *B&A: New Fiction* was the first to publish one of her stories. Later Alfano became an associate editor at *B&A* and, in 1997, was named fiction editor.

Now in a position to give other writers their first break, Alfano says, "We tend to focus on publishing new, emerging writers." And many writers published in *B&A* go on to publish with major publishing houses: Larry Hill with HarperCollins, Dennis Bock with Doubleday and Ken Sparling and Oakland Ross with Knopf, to name a few.

Alfano, 15 volunteers and 3 associate editors all work from their homes or their full-time work places. "We have no formal office," says Alfano, "unless you call the publisher's home an office." She and the associate editors share the task of reviewing 200-300 fiction submissions for each quarterly edition of *B&A*. "I ask them to forward the best submissions to me, and I in turn ask the other associates to read the work put forward." Alfano also asks her editors to do a preliminary edit or synopsis of why a story works. Then she decides if a story will be one of the six or seven included in the upcoming issue. When a story is finally selected for publication, she corresponds with the writer and does the final edits of one to three drafts of the proposed piece. She also secures the permission forms, bios and disk, and forwards them to the designer who puts the issue together.

Although unsolicited submissions of fiction are the norm at *B&A*, other features in the magazine are usually assigned. For the interviews with writers and book reviews that appear in each issue, Alfano says, "Our interviews editors stake out readings and approach writers for interviews, and the reviews editor will corral two or three writers to review mostly Canadian literary fiction and nonfiction."

The things that attract Alfano to an unsolicited fiction submission package may seem small and superficial, but, she says, "they are the things which tell me the writer cares about the work." She wants a clean, legible manuscript, double-spaced ("a single-spaced manuscript is a nightmare to get through when you have 20-30 submissions in front of you!") and a brief cover letter with the appropriate return postage if you've included a SASE ("Canadian stamps if you're in the U.S.—hey, we're a separate country, guys!"). Alfano also likes some indication that writers submitting stories have read *B&A*. "Don't for instance, send us vampire Gothic fiction; we never publish work of that type."

The things that compel Alfano to publish a story are "honesty, the moral ambiguity of complex characters, freshness, originality, poetic sensibility and sensuality." She advises writers to avoid clichés and to write with passion and honesty, "even if what comes out is disturbing or politically incorrect." She does, however, have "a problem with a juvenile fixation on bodily functions and emissions. Generally speaking, if the character is throwing up, urinating or defecating on the first page, I feel like the writer is trying to shock me into

INSIDER REPORT, *Alfano*

being interested in the piece. And I am decidedly not interested in this sort of presentation."

Other topics Alfano suggests writers avoid include "drunken nights in the college dorm; instead, give me a reason to care about your character." Alfano also advises that sexual and physical abuse as a plot device is starting to be a turnoff for her, "because it's now common in so many stories. That's not to say I would discount the story, but it does give me pause because it's become almost a cliché."

The most common mistake Alfano sees among new writers is their over-reliance on personal anecdote and memories for source material. "It's true that we are encouraged to write what we know, but I feel there should be an underlying theme or message that would pertain universally. How does a fight with your father when you were 14 pertain to the reader? Is it about the struggle for independence against an oppressive force? Is it about the loss of innocence as a child? Is it the classical Oedipal struggle of the son's need to overpower and dominate the father? We can and should think about the larger issues or themes at hand."

At a time when many lament the difficulty of getting published, especially for the first time, Alfano identifies one advantage for today's writers: "Virtually every topic is open territory for new writers. There are few taboos. You are free to explore areas that one generation ago writers were forbidden to talk about."

However, when not handled skillfully, this advantage can prove detrimental to writers. "Today, there is less of an attempt at subtlety, at creating a subtext," says Alfano. "Much of the new writing I receive is explicit, in your face, nothing held back. It's wide open: incest, child abuse, fetishist sex, necrophilia. Unfortunately, most of us are unable to broach these topics with subtlety and confidence. We plunge ahead with all the lurid details thinking that shocking information can or should pass for art."

Alfano also notes that *B&A*'s new publisher has opted for theme issues. "I am divided about this. On the one hand, it discourages good stories that don't fit into a category. On the other hand, it's interesting finding broad interpretations of stories that do fit our themes."

As for the perception by some that *B&A* only publishes or gives preference to Canadian writers, Alfano says, "We don't discount writers who are non-Canadian. Some former staff members have objected to publishing American writers. Sometimes the publisher who is trying to access federal and provincial grants to fund a magazine may encounter opposition to public funds going to American writers. But I personally don't care about the country of origin."

Alfano stresses again that at *B&A* it does not matter if a writer has been published previously. "I only care about the originality of the piece. I think excellence in writing should rule."

—*Barbara Kuroff*

interviews with Tim O'Brien, Lee Smith, Michael Dorris and Stuart Dybek. Published 1 new writer within the last year. Length: 10,000 words maximum; 2,500 words average. Also publishes literary essays, literary criticism, poetry. Occasionally critiques rejected mss.

How to Contact: Send complete ms with SASE. Do not send more than 30 pages at a time. Reports in 1 week to 6 months. No simultaneous or reprint submissions. Sample copies are $5 for older issues; $7 for current issues. Fiction guidelines for #10 SASE.

Payment/Terms: Pays 2 contributor's copies and honorarium of $5/page. Acquires first North American serial rights.

Advice: "If we take time to offer criticism, do not subsequently flood us with other stories no better than the first. If starting out, get as many *good* readers as possible. Above all, read contemporary fiction and the magazine you are trying to publish in."

ARTISAN, a journal of craft, (I, II), P.O. Box 157, Wilmette IL 60091. (847)673-7246. E-mail: artisanjnl@aol.com. **Editor:** Joan Daugherty. Tabloid: 8½×11; 36 pages. "The philosophy behind *artisan* is that anyone who strives to express themselves through their craft is an artist and artists of all genres can learn from each other." For artists and the general public. Quarterly. Estab. 1995. Circ. 200.

Needs: "We love to see 'literary' stories that can still appeal to a general audience—stories that are well-written and sophisticated without being stuffy. Nothing sexually or violently graphic with foul language unless it clearly contributes to the story." Receives 50 unsolicited mss/month. Accepts 6-8 mss/issue; 40 mss/year. Publishes ms 4-8 months after acceptance. Recently published work by Karl Harshbarger, Ed Dougherty and Paul McComas. Length: 2,000 words average; 4,000 words maximum. Publishes short shorts. Also publishes literary essays, literary criticism, poetry. Sometimes critiques or comments on rejected mss.

How to Contact: Send complete ms with cover letter. Include estimated word count. Reports in 1 month on queries; up to 6 months on mss. SASE for reply and send a disposable copy of ms. Electronic submissions (e-mail or ASCII) OK. Sample copy for $4.50. Fiction guidelines for #10 SASE. Guidelines also posted on the Internet at http://members.aol.com/artisanjnl. Will sponsor annual short fiction competition: $200 1st prize; $100 2nd prize. Send SASE for guidelines. Contest deadline is May 31.

Payment/Terms: Pays 2 contributor's copies; additional copies $3.50. Acquires first rights.

Advice: "Innovative phrasing and subject matter stand out. Strive to use fresh language and situations, but don't disregard the basics of good writing and storytelling."

ASIAN PACIFIC AMERICAN JOURNAL, (I, II, IV), The Asian American Writers' Workshop, 37 St. Marks Place, New York NY 10003-7801. (212)228-6718. Fax: (212)228-7718. E-mail: aaww@panix.com. Website: http://www.panix.com/~AAWW. **Editor:** Eileen Tabios. Magazine: 5½×8½; 150 pages; illustrations. "We are interested in publishing works by writers from all segments of the Asian Pacific American community. The journal appeals to all interested in Asian-American literature and culture." Semiannually. Estab. 1992. Circ. 1,500.

• *Asian Pacific American Journal* received a NEA grant in 1995.

Needs: Adventure, condensed/excerpted novel, erotica, ethnic/multicultural, experimental, feminist, gay, historical (general), humor/satire, lesbian, literary, mainstream/contemporary, regional, serialized novel, translations, Asian-American themes. "We are interested in anything related to the Asian American community." Receives 75 unsolicited mss/month. Accepts 15 mss/issue; 30 mss/year. Does not read September-October, March-April. Publishes ms 3-4 months after acceptance. Agented fiction 5%. Recently published work by Karen Hua, Shawn Wong, Diana Chang and Hun Ohm. Length: 3,000 words average. Publishes short shorts. Also publishes literary essays, poetry. Sometimes critiques or comments on rejected ms.

How to Contact: Send SASE for guidelines. Should include estimated word count, 3-5 sentence bio, list of publications. Reports in 1 month on queries; 4 months on mss. SASE for reply or send a disposable copy of ms. Simultaneous, reprint, electronic (disk, Macintosh or IBM, preferably Microsoft Word 5 for Mac) submissions OK. Sample copy for $12. Fiction guidelines for SASE. Reviews novels and short story collections.

Payment/Terms: Pays 2 contributor's copies; additional copies at 40% discount. Acquires one-time rights. Sends galleys to author. Sponsors contests, awards or grants for fiction writers. "Send query with SASE."

THE AZOREAN EXPRESS, (I, IV), Seven Buffaloes Press, Box 249, Big Timber MT 59011. **Editor:** Art Cuelho. Magazine: 6¾×8¼; 32 pages; 60 lb. book paper; 3-6 illustrations/issue; photos rarely. "My overall theme is rural; I also focus on working people (the sweating professions); the American Indian and Hobo; the Dustbowl era; and I am also trying to expand with non-rural material. For rural and library and professor/student, blue collar workers, etc." Semiannually. Estab. 1985. Circ. 600.

Needs: Contemporary, ethnic, experimental, humor/satire, literary, regional, western, rural, working people. Receives 10-20 unsolicited mss/month. Accepts 2-3 mss/issue; 4-6 mss/year. Publishes ms 1-6 months after acceptance. Length: 1,000-3,000 words. Also publishes short shorts, 500-1,000 words. "I take what I like; length sometimes does not matter, even when longer than usual. I'm flexible."

How to Contact: "Send cover letter with ms; general information, but it can be personal, more in line with the submitted story. Not long rambling letters." Reports in 1-4 weeks. SASE. Sample copy for $6.75. Fiction guidelines for SASE.

Payment/Terms: Pays in contributor's copies. "Depends on the amount of support author gives my press." Acquires first North American serial rights. "If I decide to use material in anthology form later, I have that right." Sends galleys to the author upon request.

Advice: "There would not be magazines like mine if I was not optimistic. But literary optimism is a two-way street. Without young fiction writers supporting fiction magazines the future is bleak because the commercial magazines allow only formula or name writers within their pages. My own publications receive no grants. Sole support is from writers, libraries and individuals."

BACKWATER REVIEW, (I, II), P.O. Box 222, Stn. B, Ottawa, Ontario K1P 6C4 Canada. E-mail: backwaters@sympatico.ca/backwaters. Website: http://www3.sympatico.ca/backwaters. **Editor:** L. Brent Robillard. Assistant Editor: Leslie Holt. Electronic magazine. "We are looking for poetry and prose that interpret the world in new and interesting ways. Our audience is of a literary bend."

• *The Backwater Review* sponsors the Hinterland Award for Prose. Send 1 unpublished short story or play.

Entry fee is $9 (includes subscription). Stories cannot exceed 5,000 words. Winning piece will receive $100 plus publication. Deadline is July 31. See website for more details.
Needs: "We publish poetry, short fiction, drama, essays, photography and small press book reviews." No science-fiction, fantasy or formula fiction of any kind. Recently published work by Dan Doyle, Matt Holland and Claire Mulligan. Publishes 24-30 new writers/year.
How to Contact: "We accept electronic submissions; however, we prefer snail mail."
Advice: "Write the truth, the whole truth, and nothing but the truth."

THE BALTIMORE REVIEW, (II), Baltimore Writers' Alliance, P.O. Box 410, Riderwood MD 21139. (410)377-5265. Fax: (410)377-4325. E-mail: hdiehl@bcpl.net. **Editor:** Barbara Diehl. Magazine: 6×9; 128 pages; 60 lb. paper; 10 pt. CS1 gloss film cover. Showcase for the best short stories and poetry by writers in the Baltimore area and beyond. Semiannually. Estab. 1996.
Needs: Ethnic/multicultural, experimental, literary, mainstream/contemporary. "Would like to see more well-written literary and somewhat traditional stories." No science fiction, westerns, children's, romance, etc. Accepts 8-12 mss/issue; 16-24 mss/year. Publishes ms 1-9 months after acceptance. Recently published work by Judith Slater, Lucinda Ebersole and Ann B. Knox. Publishes "at least a few" new writers/year. Length: 3,000 words average; 1,000 words minimum; 6,000 words maximum. Also publishes poetry. Sometimes critiques or comments on rejected mss.
How to Contact: Send complete ms with a cover letter. Include estimated word count, brief bio and list of publications. Reports in 1-3 months. Send SASE for reply, return of ms or send a disposable copy of ms. Simultaneous submissions OK. Sample copy for $8. Fiction guidelines free for #10 SASE.
Payment/Terms: Pays 2 contributor's copies on publication. Acquires first North American serial rights.
Advice: "We look for compelling stories and a masterful use of the English language. We want to feel that we have never heard this story, or this voice, before. Read the kinds of publications you want your work to appear in. Make your reader believe, and care."

$ B&A: NEW FICTION, (I, II), P.O. Box 702, Station P, Toronto, Ontario M5S 2Y4 Canada. (416)822-8708. E-mail: fiction@interlog.com. Website: http://www.interlog.com/~fiction. Publisher: Sam Hiyate. **Fiction Editor:** Michelle Alfano. Managing Editor: Shirley Moore. Magazine: 8½×11; 48 pages; bond paper; illustrations. "We publish new and emerging writers whose work is fresh and revealing, and impacts on a literary readership." Quarterly. Estab. 1990. Circ. 2,500.
Needs: Experimental, literary. No gratuitous violence, pornography or exploitive fiction. Publishes anthology every 2 years. Receives 100 unsolicited mss/month. Accepts 6-10 mss/issue; 24-40 mss/year. Publishes ms 3-6 months after acceptance. Recently published work by Timothy Findley and Ariel Dorfman. Length: 2,500 words average; 150 words minimum; 7,000 words maximum. Often critiques rejected mss. Sponsors fiction contest: $5,000 in prizes; up to 2,500 words; $18 entry fee includes subscription. SASE for information. Deadline March 11, 1999.
How to Contact: Send complete ms with a cover letter. Should include estimated word count, short bio, list of publications with submission. Reports in 1 month on queries; 3-6 months on mss. SASE for reply to a query or return of ms. Simultaneous (please advise) and electronic (e-mail and disk with hard copy) submissions OK. Sample copy for $6. Fiction guidelines for SASE. Reviews novels and short story collections.
Payment/Terms: Pays subscription to the magazine plus $35/printed page. Additional copies $6. Acquires first North American serial rights, electronic distribution for current issue sampling on Home Page, and the right to use work in anthology.
Advice: "Read *B&A* first. Know what kind of literary magazine you are submitting to. If it is consistent with your work, send us your best."

BARBARIC YAWP, (I, II), Bone World Publishing, 3700 County Rt. 24, Russell NY 13684. (315)347-2609. Editor: John Berbrich. **Fiction Editor:** Nancy Berbrich. Magazine: digest-size; 40-50 pages; 24 lb. paper; matte cover stock. "We are not preachers of any particular poetic or literary school. We publish any type of quality material appropriate for our intelligent and wide-awake audience." Quarterly. Estab. 1997. Circ. 100.
Needs: Adventure, experimental, fantasy (science, sword and sorcery), historical, horror, humor/satire, literary, mainstream/contemporary, psychic/supernatural/occult, regional, religious/inspirational, science fiction (hard, soft/sociological). Wants more humor, satire and adventure. "We don't want any pornography, gratuitous violence or whining." Receives 10-15 unsolicited mss/month. Accepts 10-12 mss/issue; 40-48 mss/year. Publishes ms within 6 months after acceptance. Recently published work by Mark Spitzer, Errol Miller and Jim Sullivan. Length: 600 words average; 1,000 words maximum. Publishes short shorts. Also publishes literary essays, literary criticism, poetry. Often critiques or comments on rejected mss.
How to Contact: Send complete ms with a cover letter. Include estimated word count, brief bio and list of publications. Reports in 2 weeks on queries; 1-4 months on mss. Send SASE for reply, return of ms or send a disposable copy of ms. Simultaneous submissions and reprints OK. Sample copy for $3. Fiction guidelines for #10 SASE.
Payment and Terms: Pays 1 contributor's copy; additional copies $3. Acquires one-time rights.
Advice: "We are primarily concerned with work that means something to the author, but which is able to transcend the personal into the larger world. Send whatever is important to you. We will use Yin and Yang. Work

must hold my interest and be well-crafted. Read, read, read; write, write, write—then send us your best. Don't get discouraged. Believe in yourself. Take risks."

THE BARCELONA REVIEW, (I, II), Correu Vell 12 - 2, 08002 Barcelona, Spain. Phone/fax: (00) 34 93 319 15 96. E-mail: barcelonareview@compuserve.com. Website: http://www.webshow.com/Barcelona/Review. **Editor:** Jill Adams. "The *BR* is an international review of contemporary, cutting-edge fiction published in English and Spanish with some Catalan. Our aim is to bring both new and established writers to the attention of a larger audience."

Needs: Short fiction and drama. Length: 4,000 words maximum (but will make exceptions in some rare cases). Also publishes articles and essays, book and film reviews and author interviews. "Most, but not all of our fiction lies somewhere out of the mainstream. Our bias is towards potent and powerful cutting-edge material; given that general criteria we are open to all styles and techniques and all genres. No slice-of-life stories, vignettes, raw autobiography posing as fiction. Anything sentimental or moralistic or didactic is immediately rejected." Published 8 new writers in first year; "we would like to quadruple that figure for 1999." Recently published work by Irvine Welsh, Alan Warner, A.M. Homes, Douglas Coupland and Poppy Z. Brite.

How to Contact: Send submissions by e-mail as an attached file. Hard copies accepted via mail but cannot be returned.

Payment/Terms: "In lieu of pay we offer a highly professional Spanish translation to English-language writers and vice versa to Spanish writers."

Advice: "We're after original, potent and powerful writing with a '90s feel that is literarily sound. We'd like to see more risks being taken, more writing with imaginative distinction."

BATHTUB GIN, (I), Pathways Press, P.O. Box 5154, Bloomington IN 47407. (812)323-2985. E-mail: charter@bluemarble.net. Website: http://www.bluemarble.net/~charter/btgin.htm. **Editors:** Chris Harter, Tom Maxedon. Magazine: 8½×5½; 48-52 pages; recycled 20-lb. paper; 60-lb. card cover; illustrations and photos. "*Bathtub Gin* is looking for work that has some kick to it. We are very eclectic and publish a wide range of styles. Audience is anyone interested in new writing and art that is not being presented in larger magazines." Semiannually. Estab. 1997. Circ. 150.

Needs: Condensed/excerpted novel, experimental, gay, humor/satire, lesbian, literary, mainstream/contemporary. "No horror, science fiction, historical unless they go beyond the usual formula." Receives 5 unsolicited mss/month. Accepts 2-3 mss/issue. Does not read mss September 15-November 1 and March 15-May 1; "we publish in mid-October and mid-April." Recently published work by Anjana Basu, J.L. Richesson and H.C. Aubrey. Length: 10 double-spaced pages maximum. Publishes short shorts. Also publishes literary essays, literary criticism, poetry. Often critiques or comments on rejected ms.

How to Contact: Send complete ms with a cover letter. Include estimated word count, 3-5 line bio. Reports in 1-2 months. Send SASE for reply, return of ms or send a disposable copy of ms. Simultaneous, reprint and electronic submissions (disk or modem) OK. Sample copy for $6 with 6×9 SAE and 4 first-class stamps. Fiction guidelines for #10 SASE. Reviews novels and short story collections.

Payment/Terms: Pays 1 contributor's copy; additional copies $6. Rights revert to author upon publication.

Advice: "We are looking for writing that contains strong imagery, is complex, and is willing to take a chance with form and structure."

BAYBURY REVIEW, (II), P.O. Box 462, Ephraim WI 54211. **Editor:** Janet St. John. Magazine: 5½×8½; 80-120 pages; glossy card cover, perfect-bound; b&w line art. "*Baybury Review* publishes quality fiction, poetry and nonfiction by emerging and established writers." Annually. Estab. 1997. Circ. 400.

Needs: Literary fiction. Receives 800 mss/year. Accepts 3-4 mss/year. Length: 5,000 words maximum. Publishes short shorts. Also publishes prose poetry and book reviews.

How to Contact: Open to unsolicited mss from June 1 through December 1 only. Send complete ms with SASE and optional cover letter. Reports in 3 months. Simultaneous submissions OK (please notify of acceptance elsewhere). Publishes ms up to 1 year after acceptance. Sample copy for $7.25.

Payment/Terms: Pays 2 contributor's copies. Acquires first North American serial rights.

Advice: "We are particularly interested in writers who explore the boundaries of conventional form."

BBR MAGAZINE, P.O. Box 625, Sheffield, S1 3GY, United Kingdom. E-mail: magazine@bbr-online.com. Website: http://www.bbr-online.com/magazine (includes names of editors, writer's guidelines and more). **Editor:** Chris Reed. Annually. Circ. 3,000. Publishes 20,000-30,000 words/issue.

Needs: "*Back Brain Recluse*, the award-winning British fiction magazine, actively seeks new fiction that ignores genre pigeonholes. We tread the thin line between experimental speculative fiction and avant-garde literary fiction." No genre fiction, or science fiction, fantasy or horror.

How to Contact: Enclose a SASE for the return of your manuscript if it is not accepted. Accepts queries by e-mail. "We are unable to reply to writers who do not send return postage. We recommend two IRCs plus disposable ms for non-UK submissions. One US$ is an acceptable (and cheaper!) alternative to IRCs. Please send all submissions to Chris Reed, BBR, P.O. Box 625, Sheffield S1 3GY, UK. We aim to reply to all submissions within 2 months, but sometimes circumstances beyond our control may cause us to take longer. Please enclose SAE if enquiring about a manuscript's status. No responsibility can be accepted for loss or damage to unsolicited material, howsoever caused."
Payment/Terms: "We are currently reading for issue #24, for which we will pay £10 ($15) per 1,000 words on publication. Familiarity with the magazine is strongly advised." Sample copy available in US for $10 from BBR, % Anne Marsden, 31192 Paseo Amapola, San Juan Capistrano CA 92675-2227. (Checks payable to Anne Marsden).
Tips: "Guidelines are not there for the editor's amusement. If you're serious about being published, pay attention to what the guidelines say."

THE BELLETRIST REVIEW, (I, II), Marmarc Publications, P.O. Box 596, Plainville CT 06062-0596. (860)747-2058. E-mail: mrlene@aol.com. Editor: Marlene Dube. **Fiction Editor:** Marc Saegaert. Magazine: 8½×11; 80 pages. "Our mission is to provide a forum for both published and unpublished writers to showcase quality short fiction. We are interested in compelling, well-crafted short fiction in a variety of genres. Our title *Belletrist*, means 'lover of literature.' This magazine will appeal to an educated, adult audience that appreciates quality fiction." Semiannually.

- The editors would like to see more "light" and humorous fiction.

Needs: Adventure, contemporary, erotica, horror (psychological), humor/satire, literary, mainstream, mystery/suspense, regional. "Particularly needs humor/satire." No poetry, fantasy, juvenile, romance, science fiction, westerns, or overblown horror or confessional pieces. Accepts 10-12 mss/issue; approximately 25 mss/year. Publishes ms within 1 year after acceptance. Recently published work by Edward Wahl, Peter Selgin, Ben Wilensky, Norbert Petsch. Publishes 6-8 new writers/year. Length: 2,500-5,000 words preferred; 1,000 words minimum; 5,000 words maximum. Comments on or critiques rejected mss when time permits. Special fiction contest in September (deadline: July 15). The award is $200. Send SASE for contest rules.
How to Contact: Send complete ms with cover letter including brief biographical note and any previous publications. "Do not send more than one manuscript at a time. The first page of your story should include your name, address and phone number in the upper left hand corner. Center the title and byline one-third of the page down. Three lines after that, begin the body of your work." Reports in 1 month on queries; 2 months on mss. SASE. "We prefer an envelope large enough to accommodate your 8½×11 format without having to fold it. It is not necessary to send your story by certified mail." Simultaneous submissions OK.
Payment/Terms: Pays contributor's copies. Acquires one-time rights.
Advice: "We select fiction on basis of quality—manuscripts stand out when the plot grabs us, and we care about the characters and what happens to them. Read your story out loud and get feedback from others—don't waste time on unnecessary detail, and hook the reader from the very beginning."

THE BELLINGHAM REVIEW, (II), Western Washington University, MS9053, Bellingham WA 98225. Website: http://www.wwu.edu/~bhreview (includes guidelines, poetry, fiction, nonfiction). **Editors:** Robin Hemley and Suzanne Paola. Magazine: 5½×8; 120 pages; 60 lb. white paper; varied cover stock. "A literary magazine featuring original short stories, novel excerpts, essays, short plays and poetry of palpable quality." Semiannually. Estab. 1977. Circ. 1,500.

- The editors would like to see more humor and literary fiction.

Needs: All genres/subjects considered. Accepts 1-2 mss/issue. Does not read between May 2 and September 30. Publishes short shorts. Published work by Sharon Solwitz, Michael Mardone, Lee Upton and Dori Sanders. Publishes 8-10 new writers/year. Length: 10,000 words or less. Also publishes poetry.
How to Contact: Send complete ms. Reports in 2 weeks to 3 months. Publishes ms an average of 6 months after acceptance. Sample copy for $5. Reviews novels and short story collections.
Payment/Terms: Pays 1 contributor's copy plus 2-issue subscription and small honorarium when available. Charges $2.50 for extra copy. Acquires first North American serial and one-time rights.
Advice: "We look for work that is ambitious, vital, and challenging both to the spirit and the intellect. We hope to publish important works from around the world, works by older, neglected writers, and works by unheralded but talented new writers."

☑ **BELLOWING ARK, A Literary Tabloid, (II)**, P.O. Box 45637, Seattle WA 98145. (206)440-0791. **Editor:** R.R. Ward. Tabloid: 11½×17½; 28 pages; electro-brite paper and cover stock; illustrations; photos. "We publish material which we feel addresses the human situation in an affirmative way. We do not publish academic fiction." Bimonthly. Estab. 1984. Circ. 500.

- Work from *Bellowing Ark* appeared in the *Pushcart Prize* anthology. The editor says he's using much more short fiction and prefers positive, life-affirming work. Remember, he likes a traditional, narrative approach and "abhors" minimalist and post-modern work.

Needs: Contemporary, literary, mainstream, serialized/excerpted novel. "Anything we publish will be true." No science fiction or fantasy. Receives 600-800 unsolicited fiction mss/year. Accepts 2-3 mss/issue; 12-18 mss/year. Time varies, but publishes ms not longer than 6 months after acceptance. Recently published work by Dave Ross, James Bernhard, Ann Applegarth and Susan Montag. Published 10-50 new writers/year. Length: 3,000-5,000 words average ("but no length restriction"). Publishes short shorts. Also publishes literary essays, literary criticism, poetry. Sometimes critiques rejected mss.

How to Contact: No queries. Send complete ms with cover letter and short bio. "Prefer cover letters that tell something about the writer. Listing credits doesn't help." No simultaneous submissions. Reports in 6 weeks on mss. SASE. Sample copy for $3, 9×12 SAE and $1.21 postage.

Payment/Terms: Pays in contributor's copies. Acquires all rights, reverts on request.

Advice: "*Bellowing Ark* began as (and remains) an alternative to the despair and negativity of the Workshop/Academic literary scene; we believe that life has meaning and is worth living—the work we publish reflects that belief. Learn how to tell a story before submitting. Avoid 'trick' endings—they have all been done before and better. *Bellowing Ark* is interested in publishing writers who will develop with the magazine, as in an extended community. We find *good* writers and stick with them. This is why the magazine has grown from 12 to 28 pages."

BELOIT FICTION JOURNAL, (II), Box 11, Beloit College WI 53511. (608)363-2577. E-mail: darlingr@beloit.edu. **Editor:** Clint McCown. Magazine: 6×9; 150 pages; 60 lb. paper; 10 pt. C1S cover stock; illustrations and photos on cover. "We are interested in publishing the best contemporary fiction and are open to all themes except those involving pornographic, religiously dogmatic or politically propagandistic representations. Our magazine is for general readership, though most of our readers will probably have a specific interest in literary magazines." Semiannually. Estab. 1985.

- Work first appearing in *Beloit Fiction Journal* has been reprinted in award-winning collections, including the *Flannery O'Connor* and the *Milkweed Fiction Prize* collections.

Needs: Contemporary, literary, mainstream, prose poem, spiritual and sports. Wants more experimental and short shorts. No pornography, religious dogma, science fiction, horror, political propaganda. Receives 400 unsolicited fiction mss/month. Accepts 8-10 mss/issue; 16-20 mss/year. Replies take longer in summer. Publishes ms within 9 months after acceptance. Published work by Rita Ciresi, David Evanier and Marisa Silver. Publishes 3 new writers/year. Length: 5,000 words average; 250 words minimum; 10,000 words maximum. Sometimes critiques rejected mss and recommends other markets.

How to Contact: Send complete ms with cover letter. Reports in 1 week on queries; 2-8 weeks on mss. SASE for ms. Simultaneous submissions OK if identified as such. Sample copy for $6. Fiction guidelines for #10 SASE.

Advice: "We're looking for a whizz-bang opening paragraph, interesting narrative line, compelling voice and unusual subject matter. Many of our contributors are writers whose work we have previously rejected. Don't let one rejection slip turn you away from our—or any—magazine."

BERKELEY FICTION REVIEW, (II), 201 Heller-ASUC Publications Library, University of California, Berkeley CA 94720. (510)642-2892. E-mail: naners@uclink4.berkeley.edu. Website: http://www.OCF.Berkeley.EDU/~bfr/. **Editor:** Elaine Wong. Magazine: 5½×8½; 180 pages; perfect-bound; glossy cover; some b&w art; photographs. "The mission of *Berkeley Fiction Review* is to provide a forum for new and emerging writers as well as writers already established. We publish a wide variety of contemporary short fiction for a literary audience." Biannually. Estab. 1981. Circ. 1,000.

Needs: Contemporary/mainstream, literary, experimental. "Quality, inventive short fiction. No poetry or formula fiction." Receives 60 unsolicited mss/month. Accepts 10-20 mss/issue. Recently published work by Dewitt Henry, Michael Stockham and Caleb Smith. Publishes work by 5-10 new writers/year. Also publishes short shorts. Occasionally comments on rejected mss.

How to Contact: Send complete ms to "Editor" with very brief cover letter and SASE. Simultaneous submission OK. Usually reports in 3-4 months, longer in summer. Sample copy for $8. Guidelines for SASE.

Payment/Terms: Pays 1 contributor's copy. Acquires first rights. Sponsors short story contest with $100 first prize. Entry fee: $6. Send SASE for guidelines.

Advice: "Our criteria is fiction that resonates. Voices that are strong and move a reader. Clear, powerful prose (either voice or rendering of subject) with a point. Unique ways of telling stories—these capture the editors. Work hard, don't give up. Don't let your friends or family critique your work. Get someone honest to point out your writing weaknesses, and then work on them. Don't submit thinly veiled autobiographical stories—it's been done before—and better. With the proliferation of computers, everyone thinks they're a writer. Not true, unfortunately. The plus side though is ease of transmission and layout and the diversity and range of new work."

BIBLIOTECH MAGAZINE, (I, II), Crisp Website Network, E-mail: editorial@crispzine.com. Website: http://www.crispzine.com. **Editorial Director:** Anthony Tedesco. Electronic magazine. "Our award-winning Bibliotech magazine features established fiction and poetry editors volunteering their creative and connective assistance to new 'under 35' writers, as well as multi-genre excerpts, interviews, information and inspiration for—and from—writers of all ages."

Needs: "Although we publish fiction from established writers of all ages, we only publish new writers who are 18-34. No juvenile, young adult or fiction over 1,000 words." Recently published work by Ben Mezrich, Evan Zall and A. Jake Cooney. Publishes 12 new writers/year.

How to Contact: Electronic submissions only. "Save a text-only copy and paste it into an e-mail message—not as an email attachment."

Advice: "Fiction is more difficult to read online so it needs to be short and fast-paced. Make readers laugh, wail or shriek right from the beginning, and keep them careening to the end. First-person caters to the Net's grassroots and community feel. Include suggestions on where to subtly divvy your fiction into 3-or-4 paragraph sections for easier online reading."

BILINGUAL REVIEW, (II, IV), Hispanic Research Center, Arizona State University, Box 872702, Tempe AZ 85287-2702. (602)965-3867. E-mail: kvhbrp@asu.edu. **Editor-in-Chief:** Gary D. Keller. Scholarly/literary journal of US Hispanic life: poetry, short stories, other prose and short theater. Magazine: 7×10; 96 pages; 55 lb. acid-free paper; coated cover stock. Published 3 times/year. Estab. 1974. Circ. 2,000.

Needs: US Hispanic creative literature. "We accept material in English or Spanish. We publish original work only—no translations." US Hispanic themes only. Receives 50 unsolicited fiction mss/month. Accepts 3 mss/issue; 9 mss/year. Publishes ms an average of 1 year after acceptance. Published work by Ernestina N. Eger, Leo Romero, Connie Porter and Nash Candelaria. Published work of new writers within the last year. Also publishes literary criticism on US Hispanic themes, poetry. Often critiques rejected mss.

How to Contact: Send 2 copies of complete ms with SAE and loose stamps. Accepts queries by e-mail. Reports in 1-2 months. Simultaneous and high-quality photocopied submissions OK. Sample copy for $7. Reviews novels and short story collections.

Payment/Terms: Pays 2 contributor's copies. 30% discount for extras. Acquires all rights (50% of reprint permission fee given to author as matter of policy).

Advice: "We do not publish literature about tourists in Latin America and their perceptions of the 'native culture.' We do not publish fiction about Latin America unless there is a clear tie to the United States (characters, theme, etc.)."

N **BLACK DIRT, (II)**, Midwestern Farmer's Market, Inc., Elgin Community College, 1700 Spartan Dr., Elgin IL 60123-7193. (847)697-1000. **Fiction Editor:** Rachael Tecza. Poetry Editor: Joanne Lowery. Magazine: 6×9; 100-200 pages; 60 lb. offset paper; 65 lb. cover; b&w illustrations and photos. Magazine publishing "fiction, poetry and essays that are fresh and surprising in language and vision. Our readers are literate adults looking to be challenged as well as entertained." Semiannually. Estab. 1998. Circ. 500.

Needs: Contemporary, feminist, humor/satire, literary, regional and experimental. "Would like to see more risky, speculative, experimental fiction." No "romance, juvenile, teen." Reading periods: March-May, September-November. Accepts 10-20 mss/year. Recently published work by Michael Martone, Dale Barrigar, David Harris Ebenbach and Jan English Leary. Publishes "at least one" new writer/year. Also publishes literary essays, poetry. Occasionally critiques rejected mss or recommends other markets.

How to Contact: Send complete ms with SASE. Reports in 1-3 months. No simultaneous submissions. Publishes ms 4-8 months after acceptance. Sample copy for $5.50 and $1 postage and handling.

Payment/Terms: Pays 2 contributor's copies plus one-year subscription. Authors retain rights.

Advice: "We look for surprising and confident writing, whether it be a traditional story or a piece of experimental fiction. We consider ourselves a reader's magazine and look for work that is challenging as well as entertaining. Be confident in your work but critical as well; don't send out stories that aren't ready. Be professional in your approach to magazines—there are hundreds of stories floating around so don't give an editor a reason not to read yours."

✓ **THE BLACK HAMMOCK REVIEW, A Literary Quarterly, (I, II, IV)**, 4150 Windcross Lane, Orlando FL 32839. (407)649-7647. **Editor:** Edward A. Nagel. Magazine: 8½×11; 40 pages; 20 lb. paper; illustrations and photos. "*The Black Hammock Review* is published by Quantum Press, a Florida non-profit cooperative. It was established to publish works which reflect rural motifs, for example, such settings as Oviedo, Geneva, Chuluota and the Black Hammock area in east-central Florida; however, other 'motifs' will be considered." Quarterly. Estab. 1992.

- Note that *The Black Hammock Review* is published co-operatively with memberships required and members share publishing costs. Editor Edward A. Nagel has published two novels, *No Entry*, with Four Walls Eight Windows (1995) and *The Heat Merchants*, with Creative Arts Book 10 (1999).

Needs: Ethnic/multicultural, experimental, fantasy (artistic), humor/satire, literary, contemporary, psychic/supernatural, regional, "bucolic themes." Does not want to see horror, commercial fiction. Receives 10 unsolicited mss/month. Accepts 4 mss/issue; 16 mss/year. Publishes ms 3 months after acceptance. Recently published work by Tito Perdue, Laura Albritton, Linda L. Dunlap, Kenton S. White and James Ploss. Publishes 6 new writers/year. Length: 2,500 words preferred; 1,500 words minimum; 3,500 words maximum. Also publishes literary essays, literary criticism, poetry. Always critiques or comments on returned mss.

How to Contact: Send complete ms with a cover letter. Should include bio (short), list of publications and brief statement of writer's artistic "goals." Reports in 2 weeks. Send SASE for reply, return of ms or a disposable copy of the ms. No simultaneous submissions. Sample copy for $5 and 8½×11 SAE.
Payment/Terms: *Charges membership fee: $25 for individual; $50 for 3 writers.* Fee waivers available for first-rate, first-time writers. Each member of the cooperative is assured publication of at least one carefully edited piece each year, subject to editorial approval. Pays $50-75 *for selected works of established authors* on publication for one-time rights. Pays 4 contributor's copies (or membership contribution); additional copies for $2.
Advice: Looks for "work that evokes in the reader's mind a vivid and continuous dream, vivid in that it has density, enough detail and the right detail, fresh with the author, and shows concern for the characters and the eternal verities. And continuous in that there are no distractions such as poor grammar, purple prose, diction shifts, or change in point of view. Short fiction that has a beginning, middle and end, organically speaking. Immerse yourself in the requested genre, format; work the piece over and over until it is 'right' for you, does what you want it to do; read the masters in your genre on a stylistic and technical level. Transmute your emotions into the work—write about what fascinates you, how people think and act; suspend moral and ethical judgment; 'see' as artist and 'write short.' Use John Gardner's *Art of Fiction*. Also, research your market thoroughly—write to named editor with SASE. Follow directions for submissions exactly. Immerse yourself in the genre, take writing courses from published writer of fiction."

BLACK JACK, (IV), Seven Buffaloes Press, Box 249, Big Timber MT 59011. **Editor:** Art Cuelho. "Main theme: Rural. Publishes material on the American Indian, farm and ranch, American hobo, the common working man, folklore, the Southwest, Okies, Montana, humor, Central California, etc. for people who make their living off the land. The writers write about their roots, experiences and values they receive from the American soil." Annually. Estab. 1973. Circ. 750.
Needs: Literary, contemporary, western, adventure, humor, American Indian, American hobo, and parts of novels and long short stories. "Anything that strikes me as being amateurish, without depth, without craft, I refuse. Actually, I'm not opposed to any kind of writing if the author is genuine and has spent his lifetime dedicated to the written word." Receives approximately 10-15 unsolicited fiction mss/month. Accepts 5-10 mss/year. Length: 3,500-5,000 words (there can be exceptions).
How to Contact: Query for current theme with SASE. Reports in 1 month on queries and mss. Sample copy for $6.75.
Payment/Terms: Pays 1-2 contributor's copies. Acquires first North American serial rights and reserves the right to reprint material in an anthology or future *Black Jack* publications. Rights revert to author after publication.
Advice: "Enthusiasm should be matched with skill as a craftsman. That's not saying that we don't continue to learn, but every writer must have enough command of the language to compete with other proven writers. Save postage by writing first to find out the editor's needs. A small press magazine always has specific needs at any given time. I sometimes accept material from writers that aren't that good at punctuation and grammar but make up for it with life's experience. This is not a highbrow publication; it belongs to the salt-of-the-earth people."

BLACK LACE, (I, IV), BLK Publishing Co., P.O. Box 83912, Los Angeles CA 90083-0912. (310)410-0808. Fax: (310)410-9250. E-mail: newsroom@blk.com. Website: http://www.blk.com. **Editor:** Alycee Lane. Magazine: 8⅛×10⅞; 48 pages; book stock; color glossy cover; illustrations and photographs. "*Black Lace* is a lifestyle magazine for African-American lesbians. Published quarterly, its content ranges from erotic imagery to political commentary." Estab. 1991.

- Member of COSMEP. The editor would like to see more full-length erotic fiction, politically-focused articles on lesbians and the African-American community as a whole, and nostalgia and humor pieces.

Needs: Ethnic/multicultural, lesbian. "Avoid interracial stories or idealized pornography." Accepts 4 mss/year. Recently published work by Nicole King, Wanda Thompson, Lynn K. Pannell, Sheree Ann Slaughter, Lyn Lifshin, JoJo and Drew Alise Timmens. Publishes short shorts. Also publishes literary essays, literary criticism, poetry.
How to Contact: Query first with clips of published work or send complete ms with a cover letter. Should include bio (3 sentences). Send a disposable copy of ms. No simultaneous submissions. Electronic submissions OK. Sample copy for $7. Fiction guidelines free.
Payment/Terms: Pays 2 contributor's copies. Acquires first North American serial rights and right to anthologize.
Advice: *Black Lace* seeks erotic material of the highest quality. The most important thing is that the work be erotic and that it feature black lesbians or themes. Study the magazine to see what we do and how we do it. Some fiction is very romantic, other is highly sexual. Most articles in *Black Lace* cater to black lesbians between these two extremes."

$ BLACK WARRIOR REVIEW, (I, II), Box 862936, Tuscaloosa AL 35486-0027. (205)348-4518. Website: http://www.sa.ua.edu/osm/bwr (includes writer's guidelines, names of editors, short fiction). Editor-in-Chief: Christopher Chambers. **Fiction Editor:** Matt McDonald. Magazine: 6×9; 200 pages; illustrations and photos. "We publish contemporary fiction, poetry, reviews, essays, photography and interviews for a literary audience. We strive to publish the most compelling, best written work that we can find regardless of genre or type, for a literate audience." Semiannually. Estab. 1974. Circ. 2,000.

- Work that appeared in the *Black Warrior Review* has been included in the *Pushcart Prize* anthology,

Best American Short Stories, *Best American Poetry* and in *New Short Stories from the South*.
Needs: Contemporary, literary, short and short-short fiction. No genre fiction please. Receives 200 unsolicited fiction mss/month. Accepts 5 mss/issue, 10 mss/year. Approximately 5% of fiction is agented. Recently published work by Barry Hannah, William Tester and Janet Burroway. Publishes 5 new writers/year. Length: 7,500 words maximum; 2,000-5,000 words average. Also publishes essays, poetry. Occasionally critiques rejected mss. Unsolicited novel excerpts are not considered unless the novel is already contracted for publication.
How to Contact: Send complete ms with SASE (1 story per submission). Simultaneous submissions OK. Reports in 1-4 months. Publishes ms 2-5 months after acceptance. Sample copy for $8. Fiction guidelines for SASE. Reviews novels and short story collections.
Payment/Terms: Pays up to $100 per story and 2 contributor's copies. Pays on publication.
Advice: "We look for attention to the language, freshness, honesty. Also, send us a clean, well-printed, typo-free manuscript. Become familiar with the magazine prior to submission. We're increasingly interested in considering good experimental writing and in reading short-short fiction. We read year round."

BLUE MESA REVIEW, (I, IV), Creative Writing Program, University of New Mexico, Dept. of English, Albuquerque NM 87131. (505)277-6347. Fax: (505)277-5573. E-mail: bluemesa@unm.edu. Website: http://www.unm.edu/~english/bluemesa/BLUEMESA.HTM (includes writer's guidelines, names of editors, short fiction). Editor: David Johnson. Magazine: 6×9; 300 pages; 55 lb. paper; 10 pt CS1; photos. "*Blue Mesa Review* publishes the best/most current creative writing on the market." Annually. Estab. 1989. Circ. 1,200.
Needs: Adventure, ethnic/multicultural, experimental, feminist, gay, historical, humor/satire, lesbian, literary, mainstream/contemporary, regional, westerns. Contact for list of upcoming themes. Receives 300 unsolicited mss/year. Accepts 100 mss/year. Accepts mss May-September; reads mss November-December; responds in January. Publishes ms 5-6 months after acceptance. Published work by Kathleen Spivack, Roberta Swann and Tony Mares. Publishes short shorts. Also publishes literary essays, poetry.
How to Contact: Send 2 copies of complete ms with a cover letter. Send SASE for reply. Sample copy for $12. Reviews novels, short story collections, poetry and nonfiction.
Payment/Terms: Pays 2 contributor's copies for one-time rights.
Advice: "Get to the point—fast. A short story does not allow for lengthy intros and descriptions. Take a class and get the teacher to edit you! Now that we are using themes, we would like to see theme-related stories. Avoid thought pieces on 'vacations to our enchanting state.' "

THE BLUE MOON REVIEW, (II), P.O. Box 48, Ivy VA 22945-0045. E-mail: editor@thebluemoon.com; fiction@thebluemoon.com. Website: http://www.TheBlueMoon.com. **Editor:** Doug Lawson. Electronic magazine: Illustrations and photos. Quarterly. Estab. 1994. Circ. 16,000.

- *Blue Moon Review* ranked #28 on *Writer's Digest*'s Fiction 50 list of top markets for fiction writers.

Needs: Experimental, feminist, gay, lesbian, literary, mainstream/contemporary, regional, translations. No genre fiction or condensed novels. Receives 40-70 unsolicited mss/month. Accepts 7-10 mss/issue; 51-60 mss/year. Publishes ms up to 9 months after acceptance. Published work by Edward Falco, Deborah Eisenberg, Robert Sward and Eva Shaderowfsky. Length: 3,000 words maximum. Publishes short shorts. Also publishes literary essays, literary criticism, poetry. Sometimes critiques or comments on rejected mss.
How to Contact: Send complete ms with a cover letter. Include a brief bio, list of publications and e-mail address if available. Reports in 1-2 months on mss. Send SASE for reply, return of ms or send a disposable copy of ms. Simultaneous and electronic submissions OK. Sample copy and fiction guidelines available at above website. Reviews novels and short story collections.
Payment/Terms: Offers prizes for fiction and poetry. Acquires first North American serial rights. Rights revert to author upon request.
Advice: "We look for strong use of language or strong characterization. Manuscripts stand out by their ability to engage a reader on an intellectual or emotional level. Present characters with depth regardless of age and introduce intelligent concepts that have resonance and relevance. We recommend our writers be electronically connected to the Internet."

THE BLUE SKUNK COMPANION, (I, IV), The Blue Skunk Society Inc., P.O. Box 8400, MSU 59, Mankato MN 56002-8400. (507)625-7176. Editor: Scott Welvaert. **Fiction Editor:** Blake Hoena. Magazine: 8×11; 35-45 pages; illustrations and photographs. "We publish fiction, poetry, nonfiction and essays that are inspired by life, not by classic literature, periods or styles. We intend to reach readers that wish to be entertained and moved no matter their age, race or culture." Semiannually. Estab. 1997. Circ. 100-500.

- *The Blue Skunk Companion* only accepts mss from authors from the Midwest region with a concentration on Minnesota writers.

Needs: Adventure, condensed/excerpted novel, ethnic/multicultural, experimental, fantasy (contemporary), historical (general), horror, humor/satire, literary, mainstream/contemporary, mystery/suspense (contemporary), psychic/supernatural/occult, regional, romance (contemporary), science fiction (contemporary), translations. "We do not want fiction/prose that falls into clichés." Receives 1-2 unsolicited mss/month. Accepts 5-7 mss/issue; 10-14 mss/year. Publishes ms 4-6 months after acceptance. Recently published work by Roger Sheffer, Brian Batt, Samuel Dollar and Kevin Langton. Length: 1,000-4,000 words average; 1,000 words minimum; 7,000 words maximum. Also publishes literary essays, literary criticism, poetry. Often critiques or comments on rejected mss.

How to Contact: Send complete ms with a cover letter. Include estimated word count, ½-1-page bio and list of publications. Reports in 1 month on queries; 2-3 months on mss. SASE. Simultaneous submissions OK. Sample copy for $5 and 9×12 SAE with 6 first-class stamps. Fiction guidelines for 4×12 SASE. Reviews novels and short story collections.
Payment/Terms: Pays free subscription to the magazine; additional copies for $5. Pays on publication. Acquires first rights. Not copyrighted.
Advice: "We look for a voice that sounds like a 'person' and not like a 'writer.' Good use of language as function, taste and art; not a boastful vocabulary. Try to avoid genre until you have a good grasp of mainstream and contemporary prose. Once that has been achieved, then your genre fiction will be much better. Always be fresh with ideas and themes. We feel that good fiction/prose can be found on the back shelves of bookstores and not on the bestsellers list."

✔ **BLUELINE, (II, IV)**, English Dept., SUNY, Potsdam NY 13676. (315)267-2043. E-mail: blueline@potsdam.edu. Website: http://www.potsdam.edu/engl/blueline.html. **Editor:** Rick Henry. Magazine: 6×9; 112 pages; 70 lb. white stock paper; 65 lb. smooth cover stock; illustrations; photos. "*Blueline* is interested in quality writing about the Adirondacks or other places similar in geography and spirit. We publish fiction, poetry, personal essays, book reviews and oral history for those interested in the Adirondacks, nature in general, and well-crafted writing." Annually. Estab. 1979. Circ. 400.
Needs: Adventure, contemporary, humor/satire, literary, prose poem, regional, reminiscences, oral history, nature/outdoors. Receives 8-10 unsolicited fiction mss/month. Accepts 6-8 mss/issue. Does not read January through August. Publishes ms 3-6 months after acceptance. Published fiction by Jeffrey Clapp. Published new writers within the last year. Length: 500 words minimum; 3,000 words maximum; 2,500 words average. Also publishes literary essays, poetry. Occasionally critiques rejected mss.
How to Contact: Send complete ms with SASE, word count and brief bio. Submit mss August through November 30. Reports in 2-10 weeks. Sample copy for $3.50. Fiction guidelines for 5×10 SASE.
Payment/Terms: Pays 1 contributor's copy for first rights. Charges $3 each for 3 or more extra copies.
Advice: "We look for concise, clear, concrete prose that tells a story and touches upon a universal theme or situation. We prefer realism to romanticism but will consider nostalgia if well done. Pay attention to grammar and syntax. Avoid murky language, sentimentality, cuteness or folksiness. We would like to see more good fiction related to the Adirondacks. If manuscript has potential, we work with author to improve and reconsider for publication. Our readers prefer fiction to poetry (in general) or reviews. Write from your own experience, be specific and factual (within the bounds of your story) and if you write about universal features such as love, death, change, etc., write about them in a fresh way. Triteness and mediocrity are the hallmarks of the majority of stories seen today."

BOGG, A Magazine of British & North American Writing, (II), Bogg Publications, 422 N. Cleveland St., Arlington VA 22201. (703)243-6019. **U.S. Editor:** John Elsberg. Magazine: 6×9; 64-68 pages; 70 lb. white paper; 70 lb. cover stock; line illustrations. "American and British poetry, prose poems, experimental short 'fictions,' reviews, and essays on small press." Published "two or three times a year." Estab. 1968. Circ. 850.

- The editors at *Bogg* are most interested in short, wry or semi-surreal fiction.

Needs: Very short experimental fiction and prose poems. "We are always looking for work with British/Commonwealth themes and/or references." Receives 25 unsolicited fiction mss/month. Accepts 1-2 mss/issue; 3-6 mss/year. Publishes ms 3-18 months after acceptance. Recently published work by Nigel Hinshelwood. Published 50% new writers within the last year. Length: 300 words maximum. Also publishes literary essays, literary criticism, poetry. Occasionally critiques rejected mss.
How to Contact: Query first or send ms (2-6 pieces) with SASE. Reports in 1 week on queries; 2 weeks on mss. Sample copy for $3.50 or $4.50 (current issue). Reviews novels and short story collections.
Payment/Terms: Pays 2 contributor's copies; reduced charge for extras. Acquires one-time rights.
Advice: "Read magazine first. We are most interested in prose work of experimental or wry nature to supplement poetry, and are always looking for innovative/imaginative uses of British themes and references."

✔ **BOOKLOVERS, (I, II)**, Jammer Publications, P.O. Box 93485, Milwaukee WI 53203-0485. (414)384-2300. E-mail: booklove@execpc.com. Website: http://www.execpc.com/~booklove. **Editor:** Tracy Walczak. Magazine: 8½×11; 32 pages; high-grade newsprint paper; photos. "*BookLovers* is a literary magazine aimed at avid readers and writers. Includes book reviews, author interviews, book lists, features on unique book stores and profiles of book discussion groups." Quarterly. Estab. 1992. Circ. 800.
Needs: Adventure, ethnic/multicultural, fantasy (children's), historical, humor/satire, literary, mainstream/contemporary, mystery/suspense (amateursleuth, cozy, police procedural), regional, romance (gothic, historical),

CHECK THE CATEGORY INDEXES, located at the back of the book, for publishers interested in specific fiction subjects.

serialized novel, sports, young adult/teen (adventure, mystery, science fiction). No science fiction/fantasy or pornography/violence. List of upcoming themes available for SASE. Receives 10 unsolicited mss/month. Buys 3-4 mss/issue; 10-12 mss/year. Publishes ms 6 months after acceptance. Published work by Shirley Mudrick, Lois Schmidt and Jane Farrell. Publishes 28-29 new writers/year. Length: 800-1,000 words average; 500 words minimum; 1,500 words maximum. Also publishes literary essays, literary criticism, poetry.
How to Contact: Send complete ms with a cover letter. Should include estimated word count and bio (200 words maximum). Reports in 2-3 months. Send SASE for reply, return of ms or send a disposable copy of ms. Simultaneous, reprint, electronic (Macintosh only) submissions OK. Sample copy for 9×12 SAE and 5 first-class stamps. Fiction guidelines for #10 SASE.
Payment/Terms: Pays 2-5 contributor's copies. Acquires one-time rights.
Advice: Looking for "unique story line, good grammar, syntax (very important), interesting literature-related articles and book reviews, articles written in succinct manner. Don't omit important details from your work. Readers want to feel as if they are personally involved in the story. Take care not to over-detail, though, and bore readers."

BOTTOMFISH MAGAZINE, (II), De Anza College, 21250 Stevens Creek Blvd., Cupertino CA 95014. (408)864-8623. Website: http://laws.atc.fhda.edu/documents/bottomfish/bottomfish.html. **Editor-in-Chief:** David Denny. Magazine: 7×8½; 80-100 pages; White Bristol vellum cover; b&w high contrast illustrations and photos. "Contemporary poetry, fiction, creative nonfiction, b&w graphics and photos." Annually. Estab. 1976. Circ. 500.
Needs: "Literary excellence is our only criteria. We will consider all subjects." Receives 50-100 unsolicited fiction mss/month. Accepts 5-6 mss/issue. Published work by Keith Dawson, Steven Carter and Sarah Hendon. Length: 500 words minimum; 5,000 words maximum; 2,500 words average.
How to Contact: Reads mss September through February. Submission deadline: February 1; publication date: end of March. Submit 1 short story or up to 3 short shorts with cover letter, brief bio and SASE. No reprints. Reports in 3-4 months. Publishes mss an average of 6 months to 1 year after acceptance. Sample copy for $5.
Payment/Terms: Pays 2 contributor's copies. Acquires one-time rights.
Advice: "Strive for originality and high level of craft; avoid clichéd or stereotyped characters and plots."

BOUILLABAISSE, (I, IV), Alpha Beat Press, 31 Waterloo St., New Hope PA 18938. (215)862-0299. **Editor:** Dave Christy. Magazine: 11×17; 120 pages; bond paper; illustrations and photos. Publishes Beat Generation, post-Beat independent and other modern writings. Semiannually. Estab. 1986. Circ. 600.

- Work included in *Bouillabaisse* has been selected for inclusion in the *Pushcart Prize* anthology.

Needs: Beat generation and modern sub-cultures: adventure, condensed/excerpted novel, erotica, literary. Receives 15 unsolicited mss/month. Accepts 2 mss/issue; 4 mss/year. Publishes ms 6 months after acceptance. Recently published work by A.D. Winans, Richard Morris, George Dowden and Daniel Crocker. Length: no limit. Publishes short shorts. Also publishes literary essays, literary criticism, poetry. Sometimes critiques or comments on rejected mss.
How to Contact: Query first. Include bio with submission. Reports in 1 week. Send SASE for reply or return of ms. Simultaneous submissions OK. Sample copy for $10. Reviews novels and short story collections.
Payment/Terms: Pays 1 contributor's copy.
Advice: "Read a sample before submitting."

$ BOULEVARD, (II), Opojaz Inc., 4579 Laclede Ave. #332, St. Louis MO 63108-2103. (314)361-2986. **Editor:** Richard Burgin. Magazine: 5½×8½; 150-225 pages; excellent paper; high-quality cover stock; illustrations; photos. "*Boulevard* aspires to publish the best contemporary fiction, poetry and essays we can print. While we frequently publish writers with previous credits, we are very interested in publishing less experienced or unpublished writers with exceptional promise." Published 3 times/year. Estab. 1986. Circ. about 3,000.

- *Boulevard* ranked #18 on *Writer's Digest*'s Fiction 50 list of top markets for fiction writers.

Needs: Contemporary, experimental, literary. Does not want to see "anything whose first purpose is not literary." Receives over 400 mss/month. Accepts about 8 mss/issue. Does not accept manuscripts between April 1 and October 1. Publishes ms less than 1 year after acceptance. Agented fiction ⅓-¼. Length: 5,000 words average; 8,000 words maximum. Publishes short shorts. Recently published work by Joyce Carol Oates, Alice Adams and Kate Brauerman. Publishes 10 new writers/year. Also publishes literary essays, literary criticism, poetry. Sometimes critiques rejected mss and recommends other markets.
How to Contact: Send complete ms with cover letter. Reports in 2 weeks on queries; 3 months on mss. SASE for reply. Simultaneous submissions OK. Sample copy for $8 and SAE with 5 first-class stamps.
Payment/Terms: Pays $50-150; contributor's copies; charges for extras. Acquires first North American serial rights. Does not send galleys to author unless requested.
Advice: "Surprising, intelligent, eloquent work always makes an impression." We are open to different styles of imaginative and critical work and are mindful of Nabokov's dictum 'There is only one school, the school of talent.' Above all, when we consider the very diverse manuscripts submitted to us for publication, we value original sensibility, writing that causes the reader to experience a part of life in a new way. Originality, to us, has little to do with a writer intently trying to make each line or sentence odd, bizarre, or eccentric, merely for the sake of being 'different.' Rather, originality is the result of the character or vision of the writer; the writer's

INSIDER REPORT

ByLine: magazine with a mission

Marcia Preston

Two characteristics immediately distinguish *ByLine* from other small literary magazines: monetary payment for submissions and a reputation for quality while frequently publishing new writers. These qualities extend from *ByLine*'s mission statement: to encourage, motivate and give practical help to aspiring writers, incentives that probably do as much to encourage writers as the magazine's how-to features.

"If we get a short story from a new writer and a short story from Stephen King, and we love both stories, we would rather have the new writer's work than Stephen King's," says Marcia Preston, publisher and editor-in-chief of *ByLine*.

Preston is quick to point out that quality is first priority. A writer's status comes second. Nevertheless, new writers' stories account for 3 or 4 of the 11 manuscripts in as many issues each year. To be one of those three or four, and earn the $100 paid for each manuscript, writers must examine every facet of their writing and submitting. Presentation, etiquette, topic choice and, of course, the writing itself, all impact the chances of getting published.

Perhaps the gravest mistake writers can make is to choose subjects based on trends rather than their own tendencies. Taking cues from the news, fads or other writers only detracts from a story's originality. *ByLine* editors can set their watches to the influx of stories on AIDS, cancer, natural disasters and child abuse following media coverage on these topics.

"We encourage writers to find hope, at least something slightly uplifting, as opposed to making [their stories] totally depressing at the end," Preston says.

Aside from unrelenting sadness, Preston's major problem with many stories is a lack of conflict and shallow characterization. Flannery O'Connor once said not to get subtle until the fourth page, and that adage applies here. Readers cannot know everything a writer leaves unsaid in a story. Move the plot along quickly, and don't be afraid to put good material right up front. A reader's impressions will form in the first two pages.

Preston's suggestions also extend to the written page itself. Occasionally writers get excited about having a new computer and attempt to accent the story with decorative fonts and special graphics. "Allow the writing to speak for itself," says Preston. Not only are unusual typefaces the mark of an amateur, but they also can make a story difficult to read. As with other courtesies, use common sense. Include an SASE, a concise cover letter and a clean copy of the manuscript.

ByLine editors will accept almost any genre, but writers who use expletives casually or employ violence should refrain from submitting—*ByLine* is a family-oriented magazine. From September to May, it entices young writers, from first grade up, with a student page, contests and cash prizes. But the magazine doesn't limit its incentives to youths.

In accordance with its mission, it holds at least four contests every month that range

INSIDER REPORT, *Preston*

from short genre fiction to novel chapters to poetry. One issue covers both July and August, so the magazine comes out 11 times each year. First-place winners earn $50-70. In addition, the editors publish comments from the judge about the general quality of the manuscripts, including suggestions and commentary on the winning piece. *ByLine* publishes the results, but it never prints winners' stories, so writers retain first serial rights. But the contests do provide motivation through deadlines, professional analysis and recognition in print. Contest entries require an entry fee, but not an SASE or a cover letter.

The magazine's flagship contests, and the greatest service to its readers, are the annual *ByLine* Literary Awards. Open only to subscribers, the literary awards are the most prestigious of the monthly competitions *ByLine* offers. The winning entry receives a $250 cash prize along with publication in the February issue. The story deadline for the literary awards is November 1.

Preston gets *ByLine* columnists and guest judges to look at entries for certain contests, but the day-to-day staff has three people—Preston, managing editor Kathryn Fanning and poetry editor Sandra Soli. Preston's husband, Paul, fills in as business manager when needed.

Preston bought *ByLine* in 1987. She had a second child in college and was looking for a "real job" after years of freelancing and teaching. Instead, Preston created her own job by buying *ByLine*. Founder Mike McCarville had lost interest after six years of running the publication, which at that time more closely resembled a newsletter. Preston, a charter subscriber, soon found herself investing money in the magazine instead of drawing a salary. So, soon after the purchase, she found another job editing a magazine for the National Cowboy Hall of Fame. Preston became a cowboy by day and worked at *ByLine* at night and on the weekends. Today, when she's not freelancing, her energy goes into serving her readers.

What makes *ByLine* unique is its commitment not just to showcase good writing, but to assist inexperienced writers in developing their talent. The contests help, but so do the editors' optimism and availability. Preston describes *ByLine* as an extended family. "We're very sensitive to feedback from them, and we are more user-friendly to new writers and writers who just have a few publication credits," Preston says. "There's so much negative feedback that writers get. We try to be a support line that gives them encouragement. We try to demystify the process for writers and show them ways they can succeed."

Perhaps the most refreshing aspect of the magazine is its screening of advertising. *ByLine* has run articles in the past on writing scams (check out the July/August 1998 issue). Preston is also careful to eliminate what she calls "junk advertising"—advertising intended to mislead and exploit writers eager for publication. This reader service is all the more admirable considering *ByLine*'s limited sources of revenue. The magazine is not affiliated with any university or writing program, and Preston likes it that way. It allows *ByLine* to transcend bureaucracy and make independent editorial choices.

"If you're going to do small press, you have to accept it for what it is," Preston says. "We have done what most small presses never do—be profitable. The magazine makes money. It just doesn't make big money."

Preston's right. Considering the magazine's emphasis on service, it appears *ByLine*'s readers are the ones who win big.

—Brad Crawford

singular outlook and voice as it shines through in the totality of his or her work."

N 🌐 **BREAKFAST ALL DAY (aka BAD), (I, II)**, 43 Kingsdown House, Amhurst Rd., London E8 2AS England. Phone: 0033 (0)2 35 40 33 26. **Editor:** Philip Boxall. Magazine: A4, 40 pages, 90 gsm bond paper; 100 gsm matt coated; illustrations and photos. "*Breakfast All Day* publishes good quality writing in a wide range of subjects and styles and without regard to the previous publication credits of contributors. We draw contributions from Britain, mainland Europe and North America. The intended audience is intelligent, reflective and appreciative of dry humour." Quarterly. Estab. 1995. Circ. 300.

- Member National Small Press Centre.

Needs: Erotica, ethnic/multicultural, experimental, fantasy (science fantasy), feminist, gay, humor/satire, literary, mainstream/contemporary, mystery/suspense (amateur sleuth, private eye/hardboiled), science fiction (hard science, soft/sociological), sports. No romantic fiction, sword and sorcery. Receives 100 unsolicited mss/year. Accepts 10 mss/issue; 40 mss/year. Publishes ms 1-4 months after acceptance. Recently published work by Gregory Arena, Linda Barnhart, William Borden, Kevin Decky, O'Neil De Noux, S.P. Elledge and Joel Ensana. Length: 2,000-3,000 words average; 1,000 words minimum; 4,000 words maximum. Publishes short shorts. Also publishes literary essays, poetry.
How to Contact: Send complete ms with a cover letter. Include estimated word count, half-page bio. Reports in 3-4 months. Send disposable copy of ms and copy on 3½" disk (ASCII file). Simultaneous submissions OK. Sample copy for $3 and 4 IRCs. Fiction guidelines for 1 IRC.
Payment/Terms: Pays contributor's copies. Acquires first rights.
Advice: "What makes a manuscript stand out is a distinctive voice, an economy of style and the ring of truth, albeit fictional truth. The most welcome contributions are insightful, sharp and personal, with an element of humour or irony, and representing an original point of view."

THE BRIDGE, A Journal of Fiction & Poetry, (II), 14050 Vernon St., Oak Park MI 48237. (248)547-6823. Editor: Jack Zucker. **Fiction Editor:** Helen Zucker. Magazine: 160 pages; matte cover. Semiannually. Estab. 1990.

- *The Bridge* has received grants from CLMP and Michigan Council of the Arts.

Needs: Serious, realistic. Publishes ms 12-18 months after acceptance. Recently published David Slavitt, Lynn Coffin and H.R. Francis. Length: 5,000-10,000 words average. Publishes short shorts. Also publishes literary essays, literary criticism, poetry.
How to Contact: Send complete ms with a cover letter. Reports in 4-8 months. SASE for reply, return of ms or send a disposable copy of ms. Simultaneous submissions OK. Sample copy for $7. Fiction guidelines for #10 SASE. Reviews novels and short story collections.
Payment/Terms: Pays 2 contributor's copies; additional copies for $7. Acquires first rights.

$ BRILLIANT CORNERS, A Journal of Jazz & Literature, (II), Lycoming College, Williamsport PA 17701. (717)321-4279. Fax: (717)321-4090. E-mail: feinstei@lycoming.edu. Editor: Sascha Feinsten. Journal: 6×9; 100 pages; 70 lb. Cougar opaque, vellum, natural paper; photographs. "We publish jazz-related literature—fiction, poetry and nonfiction." Semiannually. Estab. 1996. Circ. 1,800.
Needs: Condensed/excerpted novel, ethnic/multicultural, experimental, literary, mainstream/contemporary, romance (contemporary). Receives 10-15 unsolicited mss/month. Accepts 1-2 mss/issue; 2-3 mss/year. Does not read mss May 15-September 1. Publishes ms 4-12 months after acceptance. Very little agented fiction. Publishes short shorts. Also publishes literary essays, literary criticism and poetry. Often critiques or comments on rejected mss.
How to Contact: Send complete ms with a cover letter. Include 1-paragraph bio and list of publications. Reports in 2 weeks on queries; 1-2 months on mss. SASE for return of ms or send a disposable copy of ms. "Rarely accepts previously published work, and only by very established writers." Sample copy for $7. Reviews novels and short story collections. Send books to editor.
Payment/Terms: Pays $10-25 (when possible) on publication and 2 contributor's copies. Acquires first North American serial rights. Sends galleys to author when possible.
Advice: "We look for clear, moving prose that demonstrates a love of both writing and jazz. We primarily publish established writers, but we read all submissions carefully and welcome work by outstanding young writers."

THE BROWNSTONE REVIEW, (II), 335 Court St., Suite 114, Brooklyn NY 11231. **Fiction Editor:** Laura Dawson. Magazine: 5½×8½; 60 pages. "We publish any and all types of fiction, so long as the work is of highest quality. Our audience is primarily literary and expects a regular supply of excellent fiction." Semiannually. Estab. 1995. Circ. 250.
Needs: Literary, mainstream/contemporary. No romance, religious, children's stories or occult/gothic horror. Planning future special fiction issue or anthology. Receives 70 unsolicited mss/month. Accepts 3-6 mss/issue; 6-12 mss/year. Publishes ms 3-6 months after acceptance. Recently published work by William Keller, Jean Hey and Joe Evanisko. Length: 1,000-2,000 words average; 250 words minimum; 10,000 words maximum. Publishes short shorts. Also publishes poetry. Sometimes critiques or comments on rejected ms.
How to Contact: Send complete ms with a cover letter. Should include list of publications. Reports within 3

months. Send SASE for reply, return of ms or send a disposable copy of ms. Simultaneous submissions OK.
Payment/Terms: Pays 2 contributor's copies. Acquires first North American serial rights.
Advice: "Strong characters, natural (not expository) dialogue, a non-didactic tone, and a plot that reveals human nature in a way that doesn't clobber the reader over the head—these are qualities we look for in submissions. Avoid workshops and writing by committee. Read voraciously. Revise, revise, revise. We appreciate the drive towards multiple submissions, so long as writers are courteous about letting us know when a piece has been accepted elsewhere."

BURNT ALUMINUM, (II), P.O. Box 3561, Mankato MN 56001. (507)386-0592. **Editors:** Ben Hiltner and Sam Dollar. Magazine: 8½×7; 60 pages. "*Burnt Aluminum* is a mainstream fiction magazine. We prefer realistic themes." Semiannually. Estab. 1995. Circ. 150.
Needs: Condensed/excerpted novel, literary, mainstream/contemporary. No horror, mystery or science fiction. Receives 10 unsolicited mss/month. Accepts 6-8 mss/issue; 12-16 mss/year. Publishes ms 6 months after acceptance. Published work by Mike Magnuson and R.T. Bledsoe. Publishes 10-15 new writers/year. No preferred length.
How to Contact: Send complete ms with a cover letter. Include one-paragraph bio and list of publications with submission. Send SASE for reply, return of ms or send a disposable copy of ms. Simultaneous submissions OK. Sample copy for $4 and $1.50 postage.
Payment/Terms: Pays 2 contributor's copies. Acquires first North American serial rights.
Advice: "We prefer stories with strong characters and strong character development. Plot is secondary. We also prefer realistic fiction—stories representative of life in today's world. We do not like anything related to fantasy or horror or trivial writing."

BUTTON, New England's Tiniest Magazine of Poetry, Fiction & Gracious Living, (II), P.O. Box 26, Lunenburg MA 01462. E-mail: buttonx26@aol.com. Editor: S. Cragin. **Fiction Editor:** Adena Dawes. Magazine: 4×5; 34 pages; bond paper; color cardstock cover; illustrations; photos. Semiannually. Estab. 1993. Circ. 1,500.
Needs: Literary. No genre fiction, science fiction, techno-thriller. Receives 20-40 unsolicited mss/month. Accepts 1-2 mss/issue; 3-5 mss/year. Publishes ms 3-9 months after acceptance. Published work by Sven Birkerts, Stephen McCauley, Wayne Wilson, Romayne Dawney, Brendan Galvin, They Might Be Giants and Lawrence Millman. Length: 500-2,500 words. Also publishes literary essays, poetry. Sometimes critiques or comments on rejected mss "if it shows promise."
How to Contact: Request guidelines. Send ms with bio, list of publications and advise how you found magazine. Reports in 1 month on queries; 2-4 months on mss. SASE. Sample copy for $2. Fiction guidelines for SASE. Reviews novels and short story collections. Send book to editor.
Payment/Terms: Pays honorarium and multiple free subscriptions to the magazine on publication. Acquires first North American serial rights. Sends galleys to author if there are editorial changes.
Advice: "What makes a manuscript stand out? Flannery O'Connor once said, 'Don't get subtle till the fourth page,' and I agree. We publish fiction in the 1,000-3,000 word category, and look for interesting, sympathetic, believable characters and careful setting. I'm really tired of stories that start strong and then devolve into dialogue uninterupted by further exposition. Also, no stories from a mad person's POV unless it's really tricky and skillful. Advice to prospective writers: continue to read at least ten times as much as you write. Read the best, and read intelligent criticism if you can find it. We welcome submissions, and are always glad to hear from people curious about *Button*. Please don't submit more than twice in a year—it's more important that you work on your craft rather than machine-gunning publications with samples, and don't submit more than 3 poems in a batch (this advice goes for other places, you'll find . . .)."

$ BYLINE, (I, II), Box 130596, Edmond OK 73013-0001. (405)348-5591. E-mail: fanning@ibm.net. Website: http://www.bylinemag.com (includes writer's guidelines, names of editors, contest list and rules, ad rates and sample article from magazine). **Editor-in-Chief:** Marcia Preston. Managing Editor: Kathryn Fanning. Monthly magazine "aimed at encouraging and motivating all writers toward success, with special information to help new writers. Articles center on how to write better, market smarter, sell your work." Estab. 1981.

- Byline ranked #29 on *Writer's Digest*'s Fiction 50 list of top markets for fiction writers.

Needs: Literary, genre, general fiction. Receives 100-200 unsolicited fiction mss/month. Does not want to see erotica or explicit graphic content; no profane language (we don't consider 'damn' profane—use good judgment). Accepts 1 ms/issue; 11 mss/year. Published work by Michelle Barnett and Sybil Smith. Published many new writers within the last year. Length: 4,000 words maximum; 2,000 words minimum. Also publishes poetry and articles.
How to Contact: Send complete ms with SASE. Simultaneous submissions OK, "if notified. For us, no cover letter is needed." Reports in 6-12 weeks. Publishes ms an average of 3 months after acceptance. Sample copy, guidelines and contest list for $4.
Payment/Terms: Pays $100 on acceptance and 3 contributor's copies for first North American rights.
Advice: "We look for good writing that draws the reader in; conflict and character movement by stories end. We're very open to new writers. Submit a well-written, professionally prepared ms with SASE. No erotica or senseless violence; otherwise, we'll consider most any theme. We also sponsor short story and poetry contests."

THE CAFE IRREAL, International Imagination, (I, II), 124 S. Carapan Pl., Tucson AZ 85745. (520)624-8099. E-mail: cafeirreal@iname.com. **Editors:** Alice Whittenburg, G.S. Evans. E-zine; illustrations. "*The Cafe Irreal* is a webzine focusing on short stories and short shorts of an irreal nature." Semiannually. Online in 1998.

Needs: Experimental, fantasy (literary), science fiction (literary), translations. "No horror or 'slice-of-life' stories; no genre or mainstream science fiction or fantasy." Accepts 10-15 mss/issue; 20-30 mss/year. Publishes mss 6 months after acceptance. Recently published translations of works by Karel Schulz and A. Cernik. Length: no minimum; 2,000 words maximum (excerpts from longer works accepted). Publishes short shorts. Also publishes literary essays, literary criticism. Often critiques or comments on rejected ms.

How to Contact: "We only accept electronic submissions. E-mail us with complete manuscript as enclosed text, HTML or ASCII file." Include estimated word count. Reports in 2 months on mss. Reprint submissions OK. See website for sample copy and fiction guidelines.

Payment/Terms: Pays 1¢/word, $2 minimum on publication for first rights, one-time rights. Sends galleys (the html document via e-mail) to author.

Advice: "Forget formulas. Write about what you *don't* know, take me places I couldn't *possibly* go, don't try to make me care about the characters."

CALLALOO, A Journal of African-American and African Arts and Letters, (I, II, IV), Dept. of English, 322 Bryan Hall, University of Virginia, Charlottesville VA 22903. (804)924-6637. Fax: (804)924-6472. E-mail: callaloo@virginia.edu. Website: http://muse.jhu.edu/journals/callaloo (includes sample issues, copyright information, editorial information, submission guidelines). **Editor:** Charles H. Rowell. Magazine: 7×10; 250 pages. Scholarly magazine. Quarterly. "Devoted to publishing fiction, poetry, drama of the African diaspora, including North, Central and South America, the Caribbean, Europe and Africa. Visually beautiful and well-edited, the journal publishes 3-5 short stories in all forms and styles in each issue." Plans special fiction issue in future. Estab. 1976. Circ. 1,500.

- One of the leading voices in African-American literature, *Callaloo* has received NEA literature grants. Work published in *Callaloo* received a 1994 *Pushcart Prize* anthology nomination and inclusion in *Best American Short Stories*.

Needs: Contemporary, ethnic (black culture), feminist, historical, humor/satire, literary, prose poem, regional, science fiction, serialized/excerpted novel, translations. Also publishes poetry and drama. "Would like to see more well-crafted, literary fiction particularly dealing with the black middle class, immigrant communities and/or the black South." No romance, confessional. Themes for 1997-98: Dutch Antillean literature and emerging black male writers. Also a Sterling Brown special issue. Accepts 3-5 mss/issue; 10-20 mss/year. Length: no restrictions. Published work by Chinua Achebe, Rita Dove, Reginald McKnight, Caryl Philips, Jewell Parker Rhodes and John Edgar Wideman. Publishes 5-10 new writers/year.

How to Contact: Submit complete ms in triplicate and cover letter with name, mailing address, e-mail address, if possible, and SASE. Accepts queries/mss by e-mail and fax. Reports on queries in 2 weeks; 3-4 months on mss. Previously published work accepted "occasionally." Sample copy for $10.

Payment/Terms: Pays in contributor's copies. Acquires all rights. Sends galleys to author.

Advice: "We strongly recommend looking at the journal before submitting."

CALYX, A Journal of Art & Literature by Women, (II), Calyx, Inc., P.O. Box B, Corvallis OR 97339. (541)753-9384. Fax: (541)753-0515. E-mail: calyx@proaxis.com. Director: Margarita Donnelly. Senior Editor: Beverly McFarland. **Editors:** Teri Mae Rutledge, Linda Varsell Smith, Micki Reaman, Lois Cranston, Luz Delgado and Yolanda Calvillo. Magazine: 6×8; 128 pages per single issue; 60 lb. coated matte stock paper; 10 pt. chrome coat cover; original art. Publishes prose, poetry, art, essays, interviews and critical and review articles. "*Calyx* exists to publish women's literary and artistic work and is committed to publishing the work of all women, including women of color, older women, working class women, and other voices that need to be heard. We are committed to nurturing beginning writers." Biannually. Estab. 1976. Circ. 6,000.

Needs: Receives approximately 1,000 unsolicited prose and poetry mss when open. Accepts 4-8 prose mss/issue, 9-15 mss/year. Reads mss March 1-April 15 and October 1-November 15; submit only during these periods. Recently published work by Margaret Willey, Chitrita Banerji, Torie Olsen, Deidre Duffy and Andrea Silva. Publishes 10-20 new writers/year. Length: 5,000 words maximum. Also publishes literary essays, literary criticism, poetry.

How to Contact: Send ms with SASE and bio. Accepts requests for guidelines by e-mail. Simultaneous submissions OK. Reports in up to 8 months on mss. Publishes ms an average of 8 months after acceptance. Sample copy for $9.50 plus $2 postage. Guidelines available for SASE. Reviews novels, short story collections, poetry and essays.

Payment/Terms: "Combination of payment, free issues and 1 volume subscription."

Advice: Most mss are rejected because "the writers are not familiar with *Calyx*—writers should read *Calyx* and be familiar with the publication."

CAMBRENSIS, 41 Heol Fach, Cornelly, Bridgend, Mid-Glamorgan, CF33 4LN Wales. **Editor:** Arthur Smith. Quarterly. Circ. 500.

Needs: "Devoted solely to the short story form, featuring short stories by writers born or resident in Wales or

with some Welsh connection; receives grants from the Welsh Arts' Council and the Welsh Writers' Trust; uses artwork—cartoons, line-drawings, sketches etc." Length: 2,500 words maximum.
How to Contact: Writer has to have some connection with Wales. SAE and IRCs or similar should be enclosed with "Air mail" postage to avoid long delay.
Payment/Terms: Writers receive 3 copies of magazine. Send IRCs for a sample copy. Subscriptions via Blackwell's Periodicals, P.O. Box 40, Hythe Bridge Street, Oxford, OX1 2EU, UK or Swets & Zeitlinger B V, P.O. Box 800, 2160 S Z Lisse, Holland.

CAPERS AWEIGH, (I, II, IV), Cape Breton Poetry & Fiction, Capers Aweigh Press, 39 Water St., Glace Bay, Sydney, Nova Scotia B1A 1R6 Canada. (902)849-0822. **Editor:** John MacNeil. Magazine: 5×8; 80 pages; bond paper; Cornwall-coated cover. "*Capers Aweigh* publishes poetry and fiction of, by and for Cape Bretoners." Publication frequency varies. Estab. 1992. Circ. 500.
Needs: Adventure, ethnic/multicultural, fantasy, feminist, historical, humor/satire, literary, mainstream, contemporary, mystery/suspense, psychic/supernatural/occult, regional, science fiction. List of upcoming themes available for SASE. Receives 2 unsolicited mss/month. Accepts 30 mss/issue. Publishes ms 9 months after acceptance. Published work by C. Fairn Kennedy and Shirley Kiju Kawi. Length: 2,500 words. Publishes short shorts. Also publishes literary criticism, poetry. Sponsors contests only to Cape Bretoners fiction writers.
How to Contact: Query first. Send SASE for reply or send a disposable copy of ms. Electronic submissions OK (IBM). Sample copy for $4.95 and 6×10 SAE.
Payment/Terms: Pays free subscription to the magazine and 1 contributor's copy; additional copies for $4.95. Acquires first North American serial rights. Sends galleys to author.

THE CARIBBEAN WRITER, (IV), The University of the Virgin Islands, RR 02, Box 10,000—Kingshill, St. Croix, Virgin Islands 00850. (809)692-4152. Fax: (809)692-4026. E-mail: qmars@uvi.edu. Website: http://www.uvi.edu/extension/writer/carwrihm.htm. **Editor:** Erika J. Waters. Magazine: 6×9; 272 pages; 60 lb. paper; glossy cover stock; illustrations and photos. "*The Caribbean Writer* is an international magazine with a Caribbean focus. The Caribbean should be central to the work, or the work should reflect a Caribbean heritage, experience or perspective." Annually. Estab. 1987. Circ. 1,500.
Needs Contemporary, historical (general), humor/satire, literary, mainstream and prose poem. Receives 200 unsolicited mss/year. Accepts 15 mss/issue. Length: 1,000 words minimum. Also accepts poetry.
How to Contact: Send complete ms with cover letter. "Blind submissions only. Send name, address and title of manuscript on separate sheet. Title only on manuscript. Manuscripts will not be considered unless this procedure is followed." Reports "once a year." SASE (or IRC). Simultaneous submissions OK. Sample copy for $5 and $2 postage.
Payment/Terms: Pays 2 contributor's copies. Annual prizes for best story ($400); for best poem ($300); $100 for first publication.
Terms: Acquires one-time rights.
Advice: Looks for "fiction which reflects a Caribbean heritage, experience or perspective."

CAROLINA QUARTERLY, (II), Greenlaw Hall CB #3520, University of North Carolina, Chapel Hill NC 27599-3520. (919)962-0244. Fax: (919)962-3520. E-mail: cquarter@unc.edu. Website: http://www.unc.edu/student/orgs/cquarter (includes writer's guidelines, current contents, index to past contributors). **Editor-in-Chief:** Robert West. Fiction Editor: Brian Carpenter. Literary journal: 70-90 pages; illustrations. Publishes fiction for a "general literary audience." Triannually. Estab. 1948. Circ. 1,400.

- Work published in *Carolina Quarterly* has been selected for inclusion in *Best American Short Stories*, in *New Stories from the South: The Year's Best*, and *Best of the South. Carolina Quarterly* received a North Carolina Arts Council grant for 1997-98.

Needs: Literary. Receives 150-200 unsolicited fiction mss/month. Accepts 4-5 mss/issue; 14-16 mss/year. Publishes ms an average of 4 months after acceptance. Published work by Clyde Edgeton, Ron Carlson and Doris Betts. Publishes 2-3 new writers/year. Length: 7,000 words maximum; no minimum. Also publishes short shorts, literary essays, poetry. Occasionally critiques rejected mss.
How to Contact: Send complete ms with cover letter and SASE to fiction editor. Accepts queries by phone and fax. No simultaneous submissions. Reports in 2-4 months. Sample copy for $5; writer's guidelines for SASE.
Payment/Terms: Pays in contributor's copies for first rights.
Tips: "Some of the best stories we've published this year aren't the least bit novel in terms of plot or characters.

FOR EXPLANATIONS OF THESE SYMBOLS,
SEE THE INSIDE FRONT AND BACK COVERS OF THIS BOOK.

What usually stands out is the cohesion of the piece. Dead-on characters. Language that makes you read every word. We have seen some good manuscripts from African-American writers that transcended their genre—in this case, a road story, and a coming-of-age story. The type of fiction matters more than the language or vision of the writer. Ask yourself, does this really need to be said? We'd like to see fewer Charles Bukowski-like barfly/wino stories, fewer stories about dead or dying mothers or dead bodies that no one knows what to do with, stoner/slacker stories punctuated by an overdose or act of violence, anything resembling 'Kids,' 'Pulp Fiction' or the novels of Elmore Leonard, anything with decapitation or excessive vomitting. We've had it all this year. Anyone can think yo a absurd plot line, a wise-guy narrative, a junkie story or bizarre sex fantasy. The more perverse or taboo the subject the less shocking the story these days. I suppose someone publishes these things, but I know we're very tired of it all here. If these are the only kinds of stories you can come up with, try harder."

✓ **CAYO, A Chronicle of Life in the Keys, (II, IV)**, P.O. Box 4516, Key West FL 33041. (305)296-4286. **Editor:** Alyson Matley. Magazine: 8½×11; 40-48 pages; glossy paper; 70 lb. cover stock; illustrations and photos. Magazine on Keys-related topics or by Keys authors. Quarterly. Estab. 1993. Circ. 1,000.
Needs: Condensed/excerpted novel, experimental, literary, regional. Receives 4-5 unsolicited mss/month. Accepts 2-3 mss/issue; 8-12 mss/year. Published work by Alma Bond, Robin Shanley and Lawrence Ferlinghetti. Length: 3,000 words average; 800 words minimum; 3,000 words maximum. Publishes short shorts. Also publishes literary essays, poetry. Often critiques or comments on rejected mss.
How to Contact: Send complete ms with a cover letter. Include bio and list of publications with submission. Reports in 6 weeks on queries; 3 months on mss. Send SASE for reply, return of ms or send a disposable copy of ms. Simultaneous, reprint and electronic (ASCII text on disk) submissions OK. Sample copy for $4. Fiction guidelines for #10 SASE.
Payment/Terms: Pays in contributor's copies. Acquires one-time rights.
Advice: "The story has to stand on its own and move the reader."

N **CHANTEH, The Iranian Cross-Cultural Quarterly, (I)**, P.O. Box 703, Falls Church VA 22046. (703)533-1727. Fax: (703)536-7853. **Editor:** Saïdeh Pakravan. Magazine: 8½×11; 80 pages; illustrations and photos. "A multicultural magazine for second-generation immigrants and exiles adapting to new environments." Quarterly. Estab. 1992. Circ. 1,200.
Needs: Ethnic/multicultural (general), historical (Middle East), humor/satire, literary, mainstream/contemporary. No romance, erotic, science fiction. Receives 100 unsolicited mss/month. Accepts 1-2 mss/issue; 10 mss/year. Publishes ms 3 months after acceptance. Publishes 50% new writers. Length: 3,000 words average; 2,000 words minimum; 7,500 words maximum. Publishes short shorts. Also publishes literary essays, literary criticism, poetry.
How to Contact: Send complete ms with a cover letter. Include 25-word bio. Reports in 6 weeks. Send disposable copy of ms. Simultaneous submissions OK. Reviews novels, short story collections and nonfiction books of interest to writers.
Payment/Terms: Pays 2 contributor's copies. Acquires first North American serial rights.
Advice: "The material should preferably, though not exclusively, relate to the cross-cultural experience. This is more a trend than a fast rule. An exceptional submission will always be considered on its own merit."

$ **CHAPMAN**, 4 Broughton Place, Edinburgh EH1 3RX Scotland. **Fiction Editor:** Joy Hendry. Phone: 0131 557 2207. Fax: 0131 556 9565. Website: http://www.compura/com.chapman (includes samples from current issues, guidelines, catalog). Quarterly. Circ. 2,000. Publishes 4-6 stories/issue. Estab. 1970.
Needs: "*Chapman*, Scotland's quality literary magazine, is a dynamic force in Scotland, publishing poetry, fiction, criticism, reviews; articles on theatre, politics, language and the arts." No horror, science fiction. Recently published Quim Monzo, Dilys Rose, Leslie Schenck. Publishes up to 10 new writers/year. Length: 1,000 words minimum; 6,000 words maximum.
How to Contact: Include SAE and return postage (or IRC) with submissions.
Payment/Terms: Pays £9-50/page. Sample copy available for £4 (includes postage).

$ **THE CHARITON REVIEW, (II)**, Truman State University, Kirksville MO 63552. (816)785-4499. Fax: (816)785-7486. **Editor:** Jim Barnes. Magazine: 6×9; approximately 100 pages; 60 lb. paper; 65 lb. cover stock; photographs on cover. "We demand only excellence in fiction and fiction translation for a general and college readership." Semiannually. Estab. 1975. Circ. 700.
Needs: Literary, contemporary, experimental, translations. Accepts 3-5 mss/issue; 6-10 mss/year. Published work by Ann Townsend, Glenn DelGrosso, Dennis Trudell and X.J. Kennedy. Published new writers within the last year. Length: 3,000-6,000 words. Also publishes literary essays, poetry. Critiques rejected mss when there is time.
How to Contact: Send complete ms with SASE. No book-length mss. No simultaneous submissions. Reports in less than 1 month on mss. Publishes ms an average of 6 months after acceptance. Sample copy for $5 with SASE. Reviews novels and short story collections.
Payment/Terms: Pays $5/page up to $50 maximum and contributor's copy on publication; additional copies for $5.50. Buys first North American serial rights; rights returned on request.
Advice: "Do not ask us for guidelines: the only guidelines are excellence in all matters. Write well and study the publication you are submitting to. We are interested only in the very best fiction and fiction translation. We

are not interested in slick material. We do not read photocopies, dot-matrix, or carbon copies. Know the simple mechanics of submission—SASE, no paper clips, no odd-sized SASE, etc. Know the genre (short story, novella, etc.). Know the unwritten laws. There is too much manufactured fiction; assembly-lined, ego-centered personal essays offered as fiction."

CHASM, A Journal of the Macabre, (II, IV), P.O. Box 2549, Jamaica Plain MA 02130. Website: http://www.shore.net/~texas (includes writer's guidelines, names of editors, short fiction, interviews with authors, purchase information and stores where *Chasm* is available). **Editor:** Nat Panek. Magazine: 5×8½; 50-60 pages; 70 lb. vellum; illustrations and photos. "*Chasm* is a forum for high-quality, dark-themed fiction, poetry, literary journalism and artwork. Aimed at literate horror enthusiasts who want more from the genre than the mass media provides." Estab. 1995. Circ. 300.
Needs: Experimental, horror, psychic/supernatural/occult. Wants more "tight, well thought-out, surreal nature-of-reality stories." No "sword and sorcery fantasy." Receives 40 unsolicited mss/month. Accepts 5-6 mss/issue; 10-12 mss/year. Recently published work by K.S. Hardy, Ben Miller and William Sheldon. Publishes 2-3 new writers/year. Length: 5,000 words average; 100 words minimum; 6,000 words maximum. Publishes short shorts. Also publishes literary essays and poetry. Sometimes comments on or critiques rejected manuscripts.
How to Contact: Send complete manuscript with cover letter. Include 50-75 word bio and estimated word count. Reports in 2-4 weeks on queries; 2-3 months on manuscripts. Send SASE for reply, return of ms or send disposable copy of ms. Simultaneous and electronic (disk only) submissions OK. Sample copy for $5. Fiction guidelines for #10 SASE.
Payment/Terms: Pays 1 contributor's copy; additional copies $3. Sends galleys to author.
Advice: "Restrain your prose but not your imagination. Arresting language, imagery, characterization on the first page are key. Grabbing attention is the hard part—sustaining it only slightly less so. Mass market horror a la King, Barker, Koontz, etc. is a niche that is obviously full to overflowing, and needs no help from a small journal like *Chasm*. Writers who are further out on the fringes in terms of style and content—Harlan Ellison, Angela Carter, Lucius Shepard, Lisa Tuttle—are harder to find. That's where *Chasm* steps in."

✔ 🏆 **$ THE CHATTAHOOCHEE REVIEW, (I, II)**, Georgia Perimeter College, 2101 Womack Rd., Dunwoody GA 30338. (770)551-3019. **Editor:** Lawrence Hetrick. Magazine: 6×9; 150 pages; 70 lb. paper; 80 lb. cover stock; illustrations; photographs. Quarterly. Estab. 1980. Circ. 1,250.

- Fiction from *The Chattahoochee Review* has been included in *Best New Stories of the South*. It ranked #38 on *Writer's Digest*'s Fiction 50 list of top markets for fiction writers.

Needs: Literary, mainstream. No juvenile, romance, science fiction. Receives 900 unsolicited mss/year. Accepts 5 mss/issue. Recently published work by Larry Brown, Terry Kay, Merrill Joan Gerber and Mary Ann Taylor-Hall. Published new writers within the last year. Length: 2,500 words average. Also publishes creative nonfiction, interviews with writers, poetry reviews, poetry. Sometimes critiques rejected mss.
How to Contact: Send complete ms with cover letter, which should include sufficient bio for notes on contributors' page. Reports in 2-4 months. SASE. May consider simultaneous submission "reluctantly." Sample copy for $5. Fiction and poetry guidelines available on request. Reviews novels and short story collections.
Payment/Terms: Pays $20/page fiction; $15/page nonfiction; $50/poem. Acquires first rights.
Advice: "Arrange to read magazine before you submit to it." Known for publishing Southern regional fiction.

$ CHELSEA, (II), Chelsea Associates, Inc., Box 773, Cooper Station, New York NY 10276-0773. E-mail: rafoerster@aol.com. **Editor:** Richard Foerster. Magazine: 6×9; 185-235 pages; 60 lb. white paper; glossy, full-color cover; artwork; occasional photos. "We have no consistent theme except for single special issues. Otherwise, we use general material of an eclectic nature: poetry, prose, artwork, etc., for a sophisticated, literate audience interested in avant-garde literature and current writing, both national and international." Annually. Estab. 1958. Circ. 1,800.

- *Chelsea* sponsors the Chelsea Awards. Entries to that contest will also be considered for the magazine, but writers may submit directly to the magazine as well. *Chelsea* was the recipient of a New York State Council for the Arts grant in 1998-1999.

Needs: Literary, contemporary short fiction, poetry and translations. "No science fiction, romance, divorce, racist, sexist material or I-hate-my-mother stories. We look for serious, sophisticated literature from writers willing to take risks with language and narrative structure." Receives approximately 200 unsolicited fiction mss each month. Approximately 1% of fiction is agented. Recently published work by Rita Welty Bourke, Paget Norton, Kenneth J. Emberly, Richard Burgin, Laura Ridiy and Kevin McIlvoy. Publishes 1-2 new writers/year. Length: not over 25 printed pages. Publishes short shorts of 6 pages or less. Sponsors annual Chelsea Award, $750 (send SASE for guidelines).
How to Contact: Send complete ms with SASE and succinct cover letter with previous credits. No simultaneous submissions. Reports in 3 months on mss. Publishes ms within a year after acceptance. Sample copy for $7.
Payment/Terms: Pays contributor's copies and $15 per printed page for first North American serial rights plus one-time non-exclusive reprint rights.
Advice: "Familiarize yourself with issues of the magazine for character of contributions. Manuscripts should be legible, clearly typed, with minimal number of typographical errors and cross-outs, sufficient return postage. Most manuscripts are rejected because they are conventional in theme and/or style, uninspired, contrived, etc.

We see far too much of the amateurish love story or romance. We would like to see more fiction that is sophisticated, with attention paid to theme, setting, language as well as plot. Writers should say something that has never been said before or at least say something in a unique way. There is too much focus on instant fame and not enough attention to craft. Our audience is sophisticated, international, and expects freshness and originality."

$ CHICAGO REVIEW, (II), 5801 S. Kenwood Ave., Chicago IL 60637. Phone/fax: (773)702-0887. E-mail: chicago_review@uchicago.edu. Website: http://humanities.uchicago.edu (includes guidelines, editors' names, subscription information). **Fiction Editor:** Neda Ulaby. Magazine for a highly literate general audience: 6×9; 128 pages; offset white 60 lb. paper; illustrations; photos. Quarterly. Estab. 1946. Circ. 3,500.

• The *Chicago Review* has won two *Pushcart* prizes and an Illinois Arts Council Award.

Needs: Literary, contemporary and experimental. Accepts up to 5 mss/issue; 20 mss/year. Receives 80-100 unsolicited fiction mss each week. Recently published work by Hollis Seamon, Tom House, Rachel Klein and Doris Dörrie. Publishes 2 new writers/year. No preferred length, except will not accept book-length mss. Also publishes literary essays, literary criticism, poetry. Sometimes recommends other markets.

How to Contact: Send complete ms with cover letter. Accepts queries/mss by e-mail. SASE. No simultaneous submissions. Reports in 4-5 months on mss. Sample copy for $8. Guidelines with SASE. Reviews novels and short story collections. Send books to Book Review Editor.

Payment/Terms: Pays 3 contributor's copies and subscription.

Advice: "We look with interest at fiction that addresses subjects inventively, work that steers clear of clichéd treatments of themes. We're always eager to read writing that experiments with language, whether it be with characters' viewpoints, tone or style. We like a strong voice capable of rejecting gimmicks in favor of subtleties. We are most impressed by writers who have read both deeply and broadly, but display their own inventiveness. However, we have been receiving more submissions and are becoming more selective."

N CHICXULUB PRESS, Monograph/One-Shot Booklets (II), 6 Washington Place #3, Troy NY 12180. E-mail: chicxulu@capital.net. Editor: Dave Kress. **Fiction Editors:** Ed Desautels, Dimitri Anastasopoulos. Monographs/fiction primarily: 8×11½; 15-25 pages devoted to one author; copy paper; card stockcover. "We look for submissions from writers with novels, short story collections being prepared for publication. Our one-shot monographs are intended as 'can't-miss-teasers' for prospective readers of forthcoming books. Of course, we do not require every submission be taken from a forthcoming 'published' novel." Bimonthly (1 monograph every 2 months). Estab. 1994. Circ. 500.

Needs: Condensed/excerpted novel, experimental, literary, translations. No mainstream/contemporary. Receives 50 unsolicited mss/month. Accepts 1 mss/issue; 6 mss/year (individual monographs). Publishes ms 2 months after acceptance. Recently published work by Paul West, Carole Maso and Eurydice. Length: 10-15 pages. Sometimes critiques or comments on rejected ms.

How to Contact: Send complete ms with a cover letter. Include 3-line bio. Reports in 1 month on queries; 2 months on mss. SASE for reply, return of ms or send a disposable copy of ms. Simultaneous and reprint submissions OK; electronic submissions (disk or modem) encouraged. Sample copy for $2.50 and 8½×11½ SAE.

Payment/Terms: Pays 5 contributor's copies; additional copies $2. Acquires one-time rights.

Advice: "We like a good story, but we're also interested in writers who take chances with prose, who do not shy away from maximal expression in their fiction."

✓ CHIRICÚ, (II, IV), Ballantine Hall 849, Indiana University, Bloomington IN 47405. (812)855-5257. **Managing Editor:** Barbara Santos. "We publish essays, translations, poetry, fiction, reviews, interviews and artwork (illustrations and photos) that are either by or about Latinos. We have no barriers on style, content or ideology, but would like to see well-written material. We accept manuscripts written in English, Spanish or Portuguese." Annually. Estab. 1976. Circ. 500.

Needs: Contemporary, ethnic, experimental, fantasy, feminist, humor/satire, literary, mainstream, prose poem, science fiction, serialized/excerpted novel, translations. Published new writers within the last year. Length: 7,000 words maximum; 3,000 words average. Occasionally critiques rejected mss.

How to Contact: Send complete ms with cover letter. "Include some personal information along with information about your story." SASE. No simultaneous submissions. Reports in 5 weeks. Publishes ms 6-12 months after acceptance. Sample copy for $5. Guidelines for #10 SASE.

Advice: "Realize that we are a Latino literary journal so, if you are not Latino, your work must reflect an interest in Latino issues or have a Latino focus." Mss rejected "because beginning writers force their language instead of writing from genuine sentiment, because of multiple grammatical errors."

✓ CHIRON REVIEW, (I, II), 702 N. Prairie, St. John KS 67576-1516. (316)549-6156. E-mail: chironreview@hotmail.com. **Editor:** Michael Hathaway. Tabloid: 10×13; minimum 24 pages; newsprint; illustrations; photos. Publishes "all types of material, no particular theme; traditional and off-beat, no taboos." Quarterly. Estab. 1982. Circ. 1,200.

• *Chiron Review* is known for publishing experimental and "sudden" fiction.

Needs: Contemporary, experimental, humor/satire, literary. No didactic, religious or overtly political writing. Receives 100 mss/month. Accepts 1-3 ms/issue; 4-12 mss/year. Publishes ms within 6-18 months of acceptance. Published work by Geezus Lee, Michael Vanderslice, Gary Every, Cheryl Adams and Kathy Karlson. Length:

3,500 words preferred. Publishes short shorts. Sometimes recommends other markets to writers of rejected mss.
How to Contact: Reports in 6-8 weeks. SASE. No simultaneous or reprint submissions. Deadlines: November 1 (Winter), February 1 (Spring), May 1 (Summer), August 1 (Autumn). Sample copy for $4 ($8 overseas). Fiction guidelines for #10 SASE.
Payment/Terms: Pays 1 contributor's copy; extra copies at 50% discount. Acquires first rights.
Advice: "Research markets thoroughly."

$ CHRYSALIS READER, Journal of the Swedenborg Foundation, (II), The Swedenborg Foundation, P.O. Box 549, West Chester PA 19381-0549. (610)430-3222. Send mss to: Rt. 1, Box 184, Dillwyn VA 23936. (804)983-3021. **Editor:** Carol S. Lawson. Book series: 7½×10; 192 pages; archival paper; coated cover stock; illustrations; photos. "A literary magazine centered around one theme per issue. Publishes fiction, essays and poetry for intellectually curious readers interested in spiritual topics." Biannually. Estab. 1985. Circ. 3,000.
Needs: Fiction (leading to insight), contemporary, experimental, historical, literary, mainstream, mystery/suspense, science fiction, spiritual, sports. No religious, juvenile, preschool. Upcoming themes: "Choices" (January 1998); "Education" (September 1999). Receives 100 mss/month. Accepts 15-20 mss/issue; 20-40 mss/year. Publishes ms within 2 years of acceptance. Published work by Robert Bly, Larry Dossey, John Hitchcock, Barbara Marx Hubbard and Linda Pastan. Length: 2,000 words minimum; 3,500 words maximum. Also publishes literary essays, literary criticism, chapters of novels, poetry. Sometimes critiques rejected mss and recommends other markets.
How to Contact: Query first and send SASE for guidelines. Reports in 2 months. SASE. No simultaneous, reprinted or in-press material. Sample copy for $10. Fiction guidelines for #10 SASE.
Payment/Terms: Pays $75-250 and 5 contributor's copies on publication for one-time rights. Sends galleys to author.
Advice: Looking for "1. *Quality*; 2. appeal for our audience; 3. relevance to/illumination of an issue's theme."

$ CICADA, (II, IV), 329 "E" St., Bakersfield CA 93304. (805)323-4064. **Editor:** Frederick A. Raborg, Jr. Magazine: 5½×8¼; 24 pages; matte cover stock; illustrations and photos. "Oriental poetry and fiction related to the Orient for general readership and haiku enthusiasts." Quarterly. Estab. 1985. Circ. 600.
Needs: *All with Oriental slant*: Adventure, contemporary, erotica, ethnic, experimental, fantasy, feminist, historical (general), horror, humor/satire, lesbian, literary, mainstream, mystery/suspense, psychic/supernatural/occult, regional, contemporary romance, historical romance, young adult romance, science fiction, senior citizen/retirement and translations. "We look for strong fiction with Oriental (especially Japanese) content or flavor. Stories need not have 'happy' endings, and we are open to the experimental and/or avant-garde. Erotica is fine; pornography, no." Receives 30 unsolicited mss/month. Accepts 1 ms/issue; 4 mss/year. Publishes ms 6 months to 1 year after acceptance. Agented fiction 5%. Published work by Gilbert Garand, Frank Holland and Jim Mastro. Length: 2,000 words average; 500 words minimum; 3,000 words maximum. Critiques rejected ms when appropriate. Also publishes poetry.
How to Contact: Send complete ms with cover letter. Include Social Security number and appropriate information about the writer in relationship to the Orient. Reports in 2 weeks on queries; 3 months on mss (if seriously considered). SASE. Sample copy for $4.95. Fiction guidelines for #10 SASE.
Payment/Terms: Pays $10-25 and contributor's copies on publication for first North American serial rights; charges for additional copies. $5 kill fee.
Advice: Looks for "excellence and appropriate storyline. Strong characterization and knowledge of the Orient are musts. Neatness counts high on my list for first impressions. A writer should demonstrate a high degree of professionalism."

☑ $ CIMARRON REVIEW, (II), Oklahoma State University, 205 Morrill, Stillwater OK 74074-0135. (405)744-9476. **Associate Editors:** Todd Fuller and Jennifer Schell. Magazine: 6×9; 100 pages. "Poetry and fiction on contemporary themes; personal essay on contemporary issues that cope with life in the 20th century, for educated literary readers. We work hard to reflect quality. We are eager to receive manuscripts from both established and less experienced writers that intrigue us by their unusual perspective, language, imagery and character." Quarterly. Estab. 1967. Circ. 500.
Needs: Literary and contemporary. "Would like to see more work by Native American, African and Hispanic writers." No collegiate reminiscences, science fiction or juvenilia. Accepts 6-7 mss/issue, 24-28 mss/year. Published works by John Yau, Gordon Lish, Lee Martin and Jane Bradley. Published "many" new writers within the last year. Also publishes literary essays, literary criticism, poetry.

MARKET CATEGORIES: (I) Open to new writers; **(II)** Open to both new and established writers; **(III)** Interested mostly in established writers; **(IV)** Open to writers whose work is specialized; **(V)** Closed to unsolicited submissions.

How to Contact: Send complete ms with SASE. "Short cover letters are appropriate but not essential, except for providing *CR* with the most recent mailing address available." No simultaneous submissions. Reports in 3 months on mss. Publishes ms within 1 year after acceptance. Sample copy with SASE and $3. Reviews novels, short story collections, and poetry collections.
Payment/Terms: Pays one-year subscription to author, plus $50 for each prose piece. Acquires all rights on publication. "Permission to reprint granted freely."
Advice: "Don't try to pass personal essays off as fiction. Short fiction is a genre uniquely suited to the modern world. *CR* seeks an individual, innovative style that focuses on contemporary themes."

THE CLAREMONT REVIEW, The Contemporary Magazine of Young Adult Writers, (I, IV), The Claremont Review Publishers, 4980 Wesley Rd., Victoria, British Columbia V8Y 1Y9 Canada. (604)658-5221. Fax: (604)658-5387. E-mail: review@be.ca.com. **Editors:** Terence Young and Bill Stenson. Magazine: 6×9; 110-120 pages; book paper; soft gloss cover; b&w illustrations. "We are dedicated to publishing emerging young writers aged 13-19 from anywhere in the English-speaking world, but primarily Canada and the U.S." Biannually. Estab. 1992. Circ. 700.
Needs: Young adult/teen ("their writing, not writing for them"). Plans special fiction issue or anthology. Receives 10-12 unsolicited mss/month. Accepts 10-12 mss/issue; 20-24 mss/year. Publishes ms 3 months after acceptance. Recently published work by Leah Baade, Keeley Teuber, Lori A. May, Jenn Thompson. Length: 1,500-3,000 words preferred; 5,000 words maximum. Publishes short shorts. Also publishes prose poetry. Always comments on rejected mss.
How to Contact: Send complete ms with cover letter. Include 2-line bio, list of publications and SASE. Reports in 6 weeks-3 months. Simultaneous and electronic (disk or modem) submissions OK. Sample copy for $6 with 6×9 SAE and $2 Canadian postage. Guidelines free with SAE.
Payment/Terms: Pays 1 contributor's copy on publication for first North American and one-time rights. Additional copies for $6.
Advice: Looking for "good concrete narratives with credible dialogue and solid use of original detail. It must be unique, honest and a glimpse of some truth. Send an error-free final draft with a short covering letter and bio; please, read us first to see what we publish."

THE CLIMBING ART, (I, II, IV), 6390 E. Floyd Dr., Denver CO 80222-7638. (303)757-0541. E-mail: rmorrow@dnvr.uswest.net. **Editor:** Ron Morrow. Magazine: 5½×8½; 150 pages; illustrations and photos. "*The Climbing Art* publishes literature, poetry and art for and about the spirit of climbing." Semiannually. Estab. 1986. Circ. 1,200.
Needs: Adventure, condensed/excerpted novel, ethnic/multicultural, experimental, fantasy, historical, literary, mainstream/contemporary, mystery/suspense, regional, science fiction, sports, translations. "No religious, rhyming, or non-climbing related." Receives 50 unsolicited mss/month. Accepts 4-6 mss/issue; 10-15 mss/year. Publishes ms up to 1 year after acceptance. Agented fiction 10%. Publishes 25-30 new writers/year. Length: 500 words minimum; 10,000 words maximum. Publishes short shorts. Also publishes literary essays, literary criticism, poetry. Sometimes critiques or comments on rejected mss. Sometimes sponsors contests.
How to Contact: Send complete ms with a cover letter. Include estimated word count, 1-paragraph bio and list of publications. Accepts queries/mss by fax or e-mail. Reports in 2 weeks on queries; 2-8 weeks on mss. SASE. Simultaneous and electronic submissions OK. Sample copy $7. Reviews novels and short story collections.
Payment/Terms: Pays free subscription and 2 contributor's copies; additional copies for $4. Acquires one-time rights.
Advice: "Read several issues first and make certain the material is related to climbing and the spirit of climbing. We have not seen enough literary excellence."

$ CLOCKWATCH REVIEW, A Journal of the Arts, (II), Dept. of English, Illinois Wesleyan University, Bloomington IL 61702. (309)556-3352. E-mail: jplath@titon.iwv.edu. Website: http://titan.iwv.edu/~jplath/clockwatch/html (includes writer's guidelines, excerpts and interviews). **Editors:** James Plath and Zarina Mullan Plath. Magazine: 5½×8½; 64-80 pages; glossy cover stock; illustrations; photos. "We publish stories which are *literary* as well as alive, colorful, enjoyable—stories which linger like shadows," for a general audience. Semiannually. Estab. 1983. Circ. 1,500.

• *Clockwatch Review* is included in *Writer's Digest's Fiction 50*.

Needs: Contemporary, experimental, humor/satire, literary, mainstream, prose poem, regional. Receives 300 unsolicited mss/month. Accepts 2 mss/issue; 4 mss/year. Published work by Ellen Hunnicutt, Beth Brandt, Charlotte Mandel; published new writers within the last year. Length: 2,500 words average; 1,200 words minimum; 4,000 words maximum. Occasionally critiques rejected mss if requested.
How to Contact: Send complete ms. Accepts queries by e-mail. Reports in 6 months. SASE. Publishes ms 3-12 months after acceptance. Sample copy for $4.
Payment/Terms: Pays 3 contributor's copies and small cash stipend (currently $25, but may vary) for first serial rights.
Advice: "*Clockwatch* has always tried to expand the audience for quality contemporary poetry and fiction by publishing a highly visual magazine that is thin enough to invite reading. We've included interviews with popular musicians and artists in order to further interest a general, as well as academic, public and show the interrelation-

ship of the arts. We're looking for high-quality literary fiction that brings something fresh to the page—whether in imagery, language, voice or character. Give us characters with meat on their bones, colorful but not clichéd; give us natural plots, not contrived or melodramatic. Above all, give us your *best* work."

✓ **COLLAGES AND BRICOLAGES, The Journal of International Writing, (II)**, P.O. Box 360, Shippenville PA 16254. (814)226-5799. E-mail: cb@penn.com. **Editor:** Marie-José Fortis. Magazine: 8½×11; 100-150 pages; illustrations. "The magazine includes essays, short stories, occasional interviews, short plays, poems that show innovative promise. It is often focus or issue oriented—themes can be either literary or socio-political." Annually. Estab. 1987.

Needs: Contemporary, ethnic, experimental, feminist, humor/satire, literary, philosophical works. "Also symbolist, surrealist b&w designs/illustrations are welcome." Receives about 60 unsolicited fiction mss/month. Publishes ms 6-9 months after acceptance. Recently published work by Rosette Lamont, Eric Basso, Anne Blonstein, Jo Santiago and Kenneth Bernard. Published new writers within the last year. Publishes short shorts. Also publishes literary essays, literary criticism, poetry. Critiques rejected ms "when great potential is manifest."

How to Contact: Send complete ms with cover letter that includes a short bio. Reports in 1-3 months. SASE. Sample copy for $10; older back issues $5. Reviews novels and short story collections. "How often and how many per issue depends on reviewers available."

Payment/Terms: Pays 2 contributor's copies. Acquires first rights. Rights revert to author after publication.

Advice: "Avoid following 'industry trends.' Do what you must do. Write what you must write. Write as if words were your bread, your water, a great vintage wine, salt, oxygen. Also, very few of us have a cornucopia budget, but it is a good idea to look at a publication before submitting."

$ **COLORADO REVIEW, (II)**, English Department, Colorado State University, Fort Collins CO 80523. (970)491-5449. E-mail: creview@vines.colostate.edu. **Editor:** David Milofsky. Literary journal: 200 pages; 70 lb. book weight paper. Semiannually. Estab. as *Colorado State Review* 1966. Circ. 2,000.

• *Colorado Review*'s circulation has increased from 500 to 2,000.

Needs: Contemporary, ethnic, experimental, literary, mainstream, translations. Receives 300 unsolicited fiction mss/month. Accepts 3-4 mss/issue. Recently published work by Robert Olen Butler, T. Alan Broughton, Susan Welch; published new writers within the last year. Length: under 6,000 words. Does not read mss May through August. Also publishes literary essays, book reviews, poetry. Occasionally critiques rejected mss.

How to Contact: Send complete ms with SASE (or IRC) and brief bio with previous publications. Reports in 3 months. Publishes ms 6-12 months after acceptance. Sample copy for $8. Reviews novels or short story collections.

Payment/Terms: Pays $5/printed page for fiction; 2 contributor's copies; extras for $5. Pays on publication for first North American serial rights. "We assign copyright to author on request." Sends galleys to author.

Advice: "We are interested in manuscripts which show craft, imagination and a convincing voice. If a story has reached a level of technical competence, we are receptive to the fiction working on its own terms. The oldest advice is still the best: persistence. Approach every aspect of the writing process with pride, conscientiousness—from word choice to manuscript appearance."

✓ **COLUMBIA: A JOURNAL OF LITERATURE & ART, (II)**, 415 Dodge Hall, Columbia University, New York NY 10027. (212)854-4216. E-mail: arts-litjournal@columbia.edu. **Editors:** Dave King and Nova Ren Suma. Prose Editor: Dara Botvinick. Editors change each year. Magazine: 5¼×8¼; approximately 200 pages; coated cover stock; illustrations, photos. "We accept short stories, novel excerpts, translations, interviews, nonfiction and poetry." Biannually.

Needs: Literary and translations. Accepts 3-10 mss/issue. Receives approximately 125 unsolicited fiction mss each month. Does not read mss May 1 to August 31. Recently published work by Doris Dörrie, Ha Jin, Mary Gordon, Therese Svoboda and Lorrie Moore. Published 5-8 unpublished writers within the year. Length: 20 pages maximum. Publishes short shorts. "Contact for upcoming theme sections."

How to Contact: Send complete ms with SASE. Accepts computer printout submissions. Reports in 2-3 months. Sample copy for $8.

Payment/Terms: Offers yearly contest with guest editors and cash awards. Send SASE for guidelines.

Advice: "We always look for story—too often, talented writers send nice prose filled with good observations but forget to tell a story. We like writing which is lively, honest, thoughtful, and entertaining. Because our staff changes each year, our specific tastes also change, so our best advice is to write what you want to write."

✓ **COMPOST NEWSLETTER, (I, II)**, 11306 Pearl St., #202, Los Angeles CA 90064. E-mail: cnlit@aol.com. Editor: Peter Mooney. **Fiction Editors:** Daniel Dalessio and Patrick Sauer. Magazine: 7×8½; 24 pages; 20 lb. paper; illustrations. "*Compost Newsletter* is a literary publication of quality writing and art. We primarily publish fiction, poetry and black and white illustrations but we do consider nonfiction: commentary, humor and articles on the craft of writing. *CNL* is intended for a literary/general audience." Quarterly. Estab. 1981. Circ. 100.

Needs: Adventure, ethnic/multicultural, experimental, feminist, gay, historical, humor/satire, lesbian, literary, mainstream/contemporary, psychic/supernatural/occult, science fiction, senior citizen/retirement. "No pornography, religious novel excerpts or children's." Receives 8-10 unsolicited mss/month. Accepts 3-4 mss/issue; 12-

16 mss/year. Publishes ms 3-6 months after acceptance. Recently published work by Richard Grayson and Shelly Lowenkopf. Publishes 8 new writers/year. Length: 2,000 words average; 3,000-4,000 words maximum. Publishes short shorts. Also publishes literary essays, literary criticism, poetry. Sometimes critiques or comments on rejected mss.

How to Contact: Send complete ms with a cover letter. Include estimated word count and 1-paragraph bio. Accepts queries/mss by e-mail. Reports in 3-5 months. Send SASE for reply, return of ms or send a disposable copy of ms. Simultaneous submissions, reprints and electronic submissions OK. Sample copy for $2.50. Fiction guidelines free.

Payment/Terms: Pays 2 contributor's copies on publication; additional copies for $2.50. Acquires one-time rights.

Advice: "Quality is our number one priority. We are primarily interested in mainstream/literary fiction but anything interesting and well-written will catch our attention. Much of the fiction we publish has a clear and distinct voice. Furthermore, it grasps our attention at least by the second paragraph, then sustains its effect. In your cover letter (not necessary), do not brag. That happens all too often and it turns off an editor even before a manuscript is read—not a good start. Always include a SASE if you expect anything in return. Send your most polished work; revise, revise, revise. All successful writers do. Always give a word count. Know our publication, not necessarily to know what we publish, but to know the level at which the work we publish stands. Don't try to catch us off guard with surprising endings. The whole story should surprise us."

$ CONFRONTATION, (I), English Dept., C.W. Post of Long Island University, Brookville NY 11548. (516)299-2391, (516)299-2720. Fax: (516)299-2735. **Editor:** Martin Tucker. Magazine: 6×9; 190-250 pages; 70 lb. paper; 80 lb. cover; illustrations; photos. "We like to have a 'range' of subjects, form and style in each issue and are open to all forms. Quality is our major concern. Our audience is made up of literate, thinking people; formally or self-educated." Semiannually. Estab. 1968. Circ. 2,000.

• *Confrontation* has garnered a long list of awards and honors, including the Editor's Award for Distinguished Achievement from CCLM (now the Council of Literary Magazines and Presses) and NEA grants. Work from the magazine has appeared in numerous anthologies including the *Pushcart Prize, Best Short Stories* and *O. Henry Prize Stories*.

Needs: Literary, contemporary, prose poem, regional and translations. No "proseletyzing" literature. Accepts 30 mss/issue; 60 mss/year. Receives 400 unsolicited fiction mss each month. Does not read June through September. Approximately 10-15% of fiction is agented. Published work by Irving Feldman, David Ray, Lynn Freed and William Styron. Published many new writers within the last year. Length: 500-4,000 words. Publishes short shorts. Also publishes literary essays, poetry. Critiques rejected mss when there is time. Sometimes recommends other markets.

How to Contact: Send complete ms with SASE. "Cover letters acceptable, not necessary. We accept simultaneous submissions but do not prefer them." Accepts diskettes if accompanied by computer printout submissions. Reports in 6-8 weeks on mss. Publishes ms 6-12 months after acceptance. Sample copy for $3. Reviews novels, short story collections, poetry and literary criticism.

Payment/Terms: Pays $20-250 on publication for all rights "with transfer on request to author"; 1 contributor's copy; half price for extras.

Advice: "Keep trying."

CORONA, Marking the Edges of Many Circles, (II), Dept. of History and Philosophy, Montana State University, Bozeman MT 59717. (406)994-5200. **Co-Editors:** Lynda Sexson, Michael Sexson. Managing Editor: Sarah Merrill. Magazine: 7×10; 130 pages; 60 lb. "mountre matte" paper; 65 lb. Hammermill cover stock; illustrations; photos. "Interdisciplinary magazine—essays, poetry, fiction, imagery, science, history, recipes, humor, etc., for those educated, curious, with a profound interest in the arts and contemporary thought." Published occasionally. Estab. 1980. Circ. 1,000.

Needs: Comics, contemporary, experimental, fantasy, feminist, humor/satire, literary, prose poem. "Our fiction ranges from the traditional Talmudic tale to fiction engendered by speculative science, from the extended joke to regional reflection—if it isn't accessible and original, please don't send it." Receives varying number of unsolicited fiction mss/month. Accepts 6 mss/issue. Published work by Rhoda Lerman and Stephen Dixon. Published new writers within the last year. Publishes short shorts. Also publishes literary essays, poetry. Occasionally critiques rejected mss.

How to Contact: Query. Reports in 6 months on mss. Sample copy for $7.

Payment/Terms: Pays 2 free contributor's copies; discounted charge for extras. Acquires first rights. Sends galleys to author upon request.

Advice: "Be knowledgeable of contents other than fiction in *Corona*; one must know the journal."

$ COUNTRY FOLK, (I, II) (formerly Writer's Guidelines), HC77, Box 608, Pittsburg MO 65724. Fax: (417)993-5944. **Editor:** Susan Salaki. Magazine: 8½×11; 16 pages; 60 lb. opaque; illustrations and photos. Bimonthly. Estab. 1988. Circ. 1,000.

Needs: "Folklore, humorous anecdotes, stories of hauntings from the past." Receives 20 unsolicited mss/month. Buys 1 ms/issue; 6 mss/year. Publishes ms-3 months after acceptance. Length: 1,000 words maximum. Also publishes literary essays and literary criticism. Critiques or comments on rejected mss.

How to Contact: Send complete ms. Include estimated word count and bio (100 words). Reports in 1 week. SASE for reply or send a disposable copy of ms. Sample copy for $4. Reviews novels or short story collections.
Payment/Terms: Pays $1-25 and 1 contributor's copy on acceptance for first rights.
Advice: "Don't try to write. Just tell a story."

CRAB CREEK REVIEW, (V), 7265 S. 128th, Seattle WA 98178. (206)772-8489. Editors: Kimberly Allison, Harris Levinson, Laura Sinai and Terri Stone. Magazine: 6×9 paperbound; 50-80 pgs., line drawings. "Magazine publishing poetry, short stories, art and essays for adult, college-educated audience interested in literary, visual and dramatic arts and in politics." Published twice yearly. Estab. 1983. Circ. 450.
Needs: Contemporary, humor/satire, literary and translations. No confession, erotica, horror, juvenile, preschool, religious/inspirational, romance or young adult. Receives 20-30 unsolicited mss/month. Recently published work by David Lee, Joan Fiset, Perle Besserman and Yehuda Amichai. Published new writers within the last year. Length: 3,000 words average; 1,200 words minimum; 5,000 words maximum. Publishes short shorts.
How to Contact: Send complete ms with short list of credits. Reports in 2-4 months. SASE. No simultaneous submissions. Sample copy for $5. *Anniversary Anthology* $5.
Payment/Terms: Pays 2 contributor's copies; $4 charge for extras. Acquires first rights. Rarely buys reprints.
Advice: "We appreciate 'sudden fictions.' Type name and address on each piece. Enclose SASE. Send no more than one story in a packet (except for short shorts—no more than three, ten pages total). Know what you want to say and say it in an honest, clear, confident voice."

$ CRAB ORCHARD REVIEW, A Journal of Creative Works, (II), Southern Illinois University at Carbondale, English Department, Faner Hall, Carbondale IL 62901. (618)453-6833. Fax: (618)453-3253. Website: http://www.siu.edu/~crborchd (includes contest information and guidelines). **Editor:** Richard Peterson. Prose Editor: Carolyn Alessio. Managing Editor: Jon Tribble. Magazine: 5½×8½; 250 pages; 55 lb. recycled paper, card cover; photo on cover. "This twice-yearly journal will feature the best in contemporary fiction, poetry, creative nonfiction, reviews and interviews. Estab. 1995. Circ. 800.

- Winner of a 1998 and a 1997 Illinois Arts Council Literary Award.

Needs: Condensed/excerpted novel, ethnic/multicultural, literary, translations. No science fiction, romance, western, horror or children's. List of upcoming themes available for SASE. Receives 50 unsolicited mss/month. Accepts 5-8 mss/issue, 10-16 mss/year. Does not read during the summer. Publishes ms 9-12 months after acceptance. Agented fiction 5%. Recently published work by A. Manette Ansay, Bill Smoot, Andrew Lam, Geoff Schmidt and Edward Minus. Publishes 2 new writers/year. Length: 2,500 words average; 1,000 word minimum; 6,500 words maximum. Also publishes literary essays and poetry. Rarely critiques or comments on rejected mss.
How to Contact: Send complete ms with a cover letter. Include brief bio and list of publications. Reports in 3 weeks on queries; 4 months on mss. Send SASE for reply, return of ms. Simultaneous submissions OK. Sample copy for $6. Fiction guidelines for #10 SASE. Reviews books, small press and university press novels and story collections only. Reviews done in house by staff. Send review copies to Managing Editor Jon Tribble.
Payment/Terms: Pays $75 minimum; $5/page maximum plus 2 contributor's copies for first North American serial rights, plus a year's subscription.
Advice: "We look for well-written, provocative, fully realized fiction that seeks to engage both the reader's senses and intellect. Don't sent too often to the same market, and don't send manuscripts that you haven't read over carefully. Writers can't rely on spell checkers to catch all errors."

CRANIA, A Literary/Arts Magazine, (II), 1072 Palms Blvd., Venice CA 90291. E-mail: crania@digitaldaze.com. Website: http://www.digitaldaze.com/crania. **Editor:** Dennis Hathaway. "To bring literary and visual works of art of the highest quality to an audience potentially much larger than the audience reached by print media."
Needs: Fiction, poetry, essays, reviews. No genre fiction. Recently published work by Alyson Hagy, Alex Keegan and Alvin Greenburg.
How to Contact: Electronic submissions only. Send ms by e-mail.
Advice: "*Crania* welcomes submissions from new writers, but the magazine is not a bulletin board site where anyone can post their work. We urge potential contributors to read the magazine carefully, and to submit work that shows a facility with craft and a commitment to the idea of writing as an art."

$ CRAZYHORSE, (II), Dept. of English, Univ. of Arkansas, Little Rock, AR 72204. (501)569-3161. Managing Editor: Zabelle Stodola. Fiction Editor: Judy Troy. Magazine: 6×9; 140 pages; cover illustration only. "Publishes original, quality literary fiction." Biannually. Estab. 1960. Circ. 1,000.

- Stories appearing in *Crazyhorse* regularly appear in the *Pushcart Prize* and *Best American Short Stories* anthologies.

Needs: Literary. No formula (science fiction, gothic, detective, etc.) fiction. Receives 100-150 unsolicited mss/month. Buys 3-5 mss/issue; 8-10 mss/year. Does not read mss in summer. Published work by Lee K. Abbott, Frederick Busch, Andre Dubus, Pam Durban, H.E. Francis, James Hannah, Gordon Lish, Bobbie Ann Mason and Maura Stanton; published new writers within the last year. Length: Open. Publishes short shorts. Also publishes literary essays, literary criticism, poetry. "Rarely" critiques rejected mss.
How to Contact: Send complete ms with cover letter. Reports in 1-4 months. SASE. No simultaneous submis-

sions. Sample copy for $5. Reviews novels and short story collections. Send books to fiction editor.
Payment/Terms: Pays $10/page and contributor's copies for first North American serial rights. *Crazyhorse* awards $500 to the author of the best work of fiction published in the magazine in a given year.
Advice: "Read a sample issue and submit work that you believe is as good as or better than the fiction we've published."

☑ **THE CREAM CITY REVIEW, (I, II)**, University of Wisconsin-Milwaukee, Box 413, Milwaukee WI 53201. (414)229-4708. Website: http://www.uwm.edu:80/Dept/English/CCR (includes writer's guidelines, names of editors, table of contents from past issues, cover art scanned and magazine's history). Editors-in-Chief: Staci Leigh O'Brien and Amy E. DeJarlais. Contact: Fiction Editor. Editors rotate. Magazine: 5½×8½; 200-300 pages; 70 lb. offset/perfect-bound paper; 80 lb. cover stock; illustrations; photos. "General literary publication—an eclectic and electric selection of the best we receive." Semiannually. Estab. 1975. Circ. 2,000.
Needs: Ethnic, experimental, literary, prose poem, regional, translations. Does not want to see horror, formulaic, racist, sexist, pornographic, homophobic, science fiction, romance. Receives approximately 300 unsolicited fiction mss each month. Accepts 6-10 mss/issue. Does not read fiction or poetry May 1 through August 31. Published work by Gordon Lish, Doris Dörrie, Norman Lock, Cliff Hudder and Ray Isle. Publishes 6-7 new writers/year. Length: 1,000-10,000 words. Publishes short shorts. Also publishes literary essays, literary criticism, poetry.
How to Contact: Send complete ms with SASE. Simultaneous submissions OK if notified. Reports in 6 months. Sample copy for $5 (back issue), $7 (current issue). Reviews novels and short story collections.
Payment/Terms: Pays 1 year subscription or in copies. Acquires first rights. Sends galleys to author. Rights revert to author after publication.
Advice: "Read as much as you write so that you can examine your own work in relation to where fiction has been and where fiction is going. We are looking for strong, consistent, fresh voices."

THE CRESCENT REVIEW, (II), The Crescent Review, Inc., P.O. Box 15069, Chevy Chase MD 20825. (301)986-8788. Website: http://www.thecrescentreview.com (includes essays, interviews, guidelines, and more). **Editor:** J.T. Holland. Magazine: 6×9; 160 pages. Triannually. Estab. 1982.

- Work appearing in *The Crescent Review* has been included in *O. Henry Prize Stories*, *Best American Short Stories, Pushcart Prize* and *Black Southern Writers* anthologies and in the *New Stories from the South*.

Needs: "Well-crafted stories." Wants shorter-length pieces (though regularly publishes stories in the 6,000-9,000 word range). Wants stories where choice has consequences. Conducts two annual writers contests: The Renwick-Sumerwell Award (exclusively for new unpublished writers) and the Chekhov Award for Fine Storytelling. Does not read submissions May-June and November-December.
How to Contact: Reports in 1-4 months. SASE. Sample issue for $9.40.
Payment/Terms: Pays 2 contributor's copies; discount for contributors. Acquires first North American serial rights.

☑ **CRIPES!, (II)**, 110 Bement Ave., Staten Island NY 10310. **Editors:** Jim Tolan and Aimee Recont. Magazine: 5½×8½; 60 pages; card cover stock; illustrations; photos. "We look for poetry, prose, art, cartoons and many things in between—as long as it maintains a strong balance between passion (impulse) and craft. Estab. 1994. Circ. 300.
Needs: Condensed/excerpted novel, humor, literary, mainstream/contemporary. Especially looking for short short fiction. No religious or westerns. Receives 20-30 unsolicited mss/month. Accepts 1-2 mss/issue; 4-6 mss/year. Publishes ms within 1 year after acceptance. Recently published work by Tom Whalen, Matthew Firth, Kendall Delacambre, John Fleming and Perry Parks. Length: 1,500-2,000 words maximum. Publishes short shorts. Also publishes poetry. Often critiques or comments on rejected mss.
How to Contact: Send complete ms with a cover letter. Include a 1-paragraph bio and "tell us how you learned about us." Send SASE for reply or return of ms. Simultaneous submissions OK. Sample copy for $5.
Payment/Terms: Pays 1 contributor copy on publication. Acquires one-time rights.
Advice: Looks for "originality, unpredictability, fresh language, a carefully prepared manuscript, focus and playfullness. Look at *Cripes!* to see what we publish."

CROSSCONNECT, (I, II), P.O. Box 2317, Philadelphia PA 19103. (215)898-5324. Fax: (215)898-9348. E-mail: xconnect@ccat.sas.upenn.edu. Website: http://ccat.sas.upenn.edu/xconnect. **Editor:** David Deifer. "*CrossConnect* publishes tri-annually on the World Wide Web and annually in print, with the best of our Web issues, plus nominated work from editors in the digital literary community. *xconnect: writers of the information age* is a nationally distributed, full color, journal sized book." 5½×8½; trade paper; 200 pages.

- *CrossConnect* ranked #45 on *Writer's Digest*'s Fiction 50 list of top markets for fiction writers.

Needs: Literary and experimental fiction. "Our mission—like our name—is one of connection. *CrossConnect* seeks to promote and document the emergent creative artists as well as established artists who have made the transition to the new technologies of the Information Age." Recently published work by Bob Perelman, Paul Hoover and Yusef Komunyakaa. Publishes 25 new writers/year.
How to Contact: Electronic and traditional submissions accepted. "We prefer your submissions be cut and pasted into your mail readers and sent to us. No attached files unless requested." Send complete ms (up to three

stories) with cover letter and short bio. Previously published and simultaneous submission OK. Rarely comments on rejections.
Payment/Terms: Pays 1 contributor's copy for use in print version. Author retains all rights. Regularly sends prepublication galleys.
Advice: "Persistence."

✓ **CRUCIBLE, (I, II)**, English Dept., Barton College, College Station, Wilson NC 27893. (252)399-6456. Editor: Terrence L. Grimes. Magazine of fiction and poetry for a general, literary audience. Annually. Estab. 1964. Circ. 500.
Needs: Contemporary, ethnic, experimental, feminist, gay, lesbian, literary, regional. Receives 20 unsolicited mss/month. Accepts 5-6 mss/year. Publishes ms 4-5 months after acceptance. Does not normally read mss from April 30 to December 1. Published work by Mark Jacobs, William Hutchins and Guy Nancekeville. Length: 8,000 words maximum. Publishes short shorts.
How to Contact: Send 3 complete copies of ms unsigned with cover letter which should include a brief biography, "in case we publish." Reports in 1 month on queries; 3-4 months on mss (by June 15). SASE. Sample copy for $6. Fiction guidelines free.
Payment/Terms: Pays contributor's copies. Acquires first rights.
Advice: "Write about what you know. Experimentation is fine as long as the experiences portrayed come across as authentic, that is to say, plausible."

✓ **$ CURIO, (I)**, 81 Pondfield Rd., Suite 264, Bronxville NY 10708. (914)961-8649. Fax: (914)779-4033. Publisher: M. Teresa Lawrence. Editor and **Fiction Editor:** Mickey Z. Magazine: $8\frac{3}{8} \times 10\frac{1}{2}$; 45 lb. glossy paper; 60 lb. cover; illustrations and photos. "Written for the young, fashionable and literate American trendsetters. Promotes new ideas, opinions, thoughts and interests through a variety of mixed media art and written words. Quarterly. Estab. 1996.
Needs: Ethnic/multicultural, experimental, gay, humor/satire, literary, psychic/supernatural/occult. List of upcoming themes available for SASE. Receives 300 unsolicited mss/month. Accepts 5-10 mss/issue; 20-40 mss/year. Does not read July 15 to August 31. Publishes ms 4 months after acceptance. Length: 100 words minimum; 3,000 words maximum. Publishes short shorts. Also publishes literary essays, literary criticism and poetry.
How to Contact: Send complete ms with a cover letter. Include estimated word count and Social Security number. Reports in 3 months. Send a disposable copy of ms. Simultaneous, reprint and electronic (disk) submissions OK. Reviews novels and short story collections. Send books to Mickey Z., P.O. Box 522, Bronxville NY 11103.
Payment/Terms: Pays $140/page on publication for first rights.
Advice: "It has to be something that I haven't read anywhere else and that moves me to laugh, cry or simply get outraged. I want people to think about social issues."

✓ **CUTBANK, (II)**, English Dept., University of Montana, Missoula MT 59812. (406)243-6156. E-mail: cordrey@selway.umt.edu. Website: http://www.umt.edu/cutbank. **Editors-in-Chief:** Nicole Cordrey and Josh Corey. Editors change each year. Magazine: $5\frac{1}{2} \times 8\frac{1}{2}$; 115-130 pages. "Publishes serious-minded and innovative fiction and poetry from both well known and up-and-coming authors." Semiannually. Estab. 1973. Circ. 600.
Needs: "Innovative, challenging, experimental material." No "science fiction, fantasy or unproofed manuscripts." Receives 200 unsolicited mss/month. Accepts 6-12 mss/year. Does not read mss from April 1-August 15. Publishes ms up to 6 months after acceptance. Published new writers within the last year. Length: 40 pages maximum. Also publishes literary essays, literary criticism, poetry. Occasionally critiques rejected mss.
How to Contact: Send complete ms with cover letter, which should include "name, address, publications." Reports in 1-4 months on mss. SASE. Simultaneous submissions OK. Sample copy for $4 (current issue $6.95). Fiction guidelines for SASE. Reviews novels and short story collections. Send books to fiction editor.
Payment/Terms: Pays 2 contributor's copies. Rights revert to author upon publication, with provision that *Cutbank* receives publication credit.
Advice: "Strongly suggest contributors read an issue. We have published stories by Kevin Canty, Chris Offutt and Pam Houston in recent issues, and like to feature new writers alongside more well-known names. Send only your best work."

**FOR EXPLANATIONS OF THESE SYMBOLS,
SEE THE INSIDE FRONT AND BACK COVERS OF THIS BOOK.**

THE DALHOUSIE REVIEW, (II), Room 114, 1456 Henry St., Halifax, Nova Scotia B3H 3J5 Canada. Editor: Dr. Ronald Huebert. Magazine: 15cm×23cm; approximately 140 pages; photographs sometimes. Publishes articles, book reviews, short stories and poetry. Published 3 times a year. Circ. 650.

Needs: Literary. Length: 5,000 words maximum. Also publishes essays on history, philosophy, etc., and poetry.

How to Contact: Send complete ms with cover letter. SASE (Canadian stamps). Sample copy for $8.50 (Canadian) plus postage. Occasionally reviews novels and short story collections.

$ DAN RIVER ANTHOLOGY, (I), P.O. Box 298, S. Thomaston ME 04861. (207)354-0998. Fax: (207)354-8953. E-mail: cal@ime.net. Website: http://wz.ime.net/~cal (includes writer's guidelines, catalogue). **Editor:** R. S. Danbury III. Book: 5½×8½; 156 pages; 60 lb. paper; gloss 65 lb. full-color cover; b&w illustrations. For general/adult audience. Annually. Estab. 1984. Circ. 800.

Needs: Adventure, contemporary, ethnic, experimental, fantasy, historical, horror, humor/satire, literary, mainstream, prose poem, psychic/supernatural, regional, romance (contemporary and historical), science fiction, senior citizen/retirement, suspense/mystery and western. "Would like to see more first-person adventure." No "evangelical Christian, pornography or sentimentality." Receives 150 unsolicited fiction mss each submission period (January 1 through March 31). "We generally publish 12-15 pieces of fiction." Reads "mostly in April." Length: 2,000-2,400 words average; 800 words minimum; 2,500 words maximum. Also publishes poetry.

How to Contact: *Charges reading fee: $1 for poetry; $3 for prose* (cash only, no checks). Send complete ms with SASE. Reports by May 15 each year. No simultaneous submissions. Sample copy for $13.95 paperback, $13.95 cloth, plus $2.95 shipping. Fiction guidelines for #10 SASE.

Payment/Terms: Pays $4/page, minimum *cash advance on acceptance* against royalties of 10% of all sales attributable to writer's influence: readings, mailings, autograph parties, etc., plus up to 50% discount on copies, plus other discounts to make total as high as 73%. Acquires first rights.

Advice: "Know your market. Don't submit without reading guidelines."

$ DENVER QUARTERLY, (II, III), University of Denver, Denver CO 80208. (303)871-2892. Editor: Bin Ramke. **Fiction Editor:** Beth Nugent. Magazine: 6×9; 144-160 pages; occasional illustrations. "We publish fiction, articles and poetry for a generally well-educated audience, primarily interested in literature and the literary experience. They read *DQ* to find something a little different from a strictly academic quarterly or a creative writing outlet." Quarterly. Estab. 1966. Circ. 1,500.

- *Denver Quarterly* received an Honorable Mention for Content from the American Literary Magazine Awards.

Needs: "We are now interested in experimental fiction (minimalism, magic realism, etc.) as well as in realistic fiction and in writing about fiction. No sentimental, science fiction, romance or spy thrillers. No stories longer than 15 pages!" Recently published work by Lucie Broch-Broido, Judith E. Johnson, Stephen Alter and Jorie Graham. Published 5 new writers within the last year. Also publishes poetry.

How to Contact: Send complete ms and brief cover letter with SASE. Does not read mss May-September 15. Do not query. Reports in 3 months on mss. Publishes ms within a year after acceptance. Electronic submissions (disk, Windows 6.0) OK. No simultaneous submissions. Sample copy for $7 (anniversary issue), $6 (all other issues) with SASE.

Payment/Terms: Pays $5/page for fiction and poetry and 2 contributor's copies for first North American serial rights.

Advice: "We look for serious, realistic and experimental fiction; stories which appeal to intelligent, demanding readers who are not themselves fiction writers. Nothing so quickly disqualifies a manuscript as sloppy proofreading and mechanics. Read the magazine before submitting to it. We try to remain eclectic, but the odds for beginners are bound to be small considering the fact that we receive nearly 10,000 mss per year and publish only about ten short stories."

$ DESCANT, Descant Arts & Letters Foundation, P.O. Box 314, Station P, Toronto, Ontario M5S 2S8. (416)593-2557. **Editor:** Karen Mulhallen. Managing Editor: Mary Myers. Quarterly literary journal. Estab. 1970. Circ. 1,200.

Needs: Litarary. Also publishes poetry and literary essays. Submit seasonal material 4 months in advance.

How to Contact: Send complete ms. Sample copy for $8. Writer's guidelines for SASE.

Payment/Terms: Pays $100. Pays on publication.

Advice: "Familiarize yourself with our magazine before submitting."

N DESPERATE ACT, (I, II), Box 1081, Pittsford NY 14534. E-mail: des@aol.com. **Editors:** Gary Wiener, Steve Engle. Magazine: 5½×8½; 76-100 pages; 20 lb. paper; 80 lb. cover stock; illustrations and photos. Annually. Estab. 1995. Circ. 200.

Needs: Humor/satire, literary, mainstream/contemporary. List of upcoming themes available for SASE. Receives 5-10 unsolicited mss/month. Accepts 2-3 mss/issue. Publishes ms 6-12 months after acceptance. Publishes several new writers/year. Recently published work by Wendy Low, William Heyer, Martin Prieto and Ruth Lunt. Length: 2,500 words maximum. Publishes short shorts. Also publishes literary essays, literary criticism, poetry. Sometimes critiques or comments on rejected ms.

How to Contact: Send complete ms with a cover letter. Accepts queries/mss by e-mail. Include estimated word

count, short bio. Reports in 2-3 weeks on queries; 3-6 months on mss. SASE for return of ms or send a disposable copy of ms. Simultaneous submissions OK. Sample copy for $5. Fiction guidelines free. Reviews novels, short story collections and nonfiction books of interest to writers.
Payment/Terms: Pays 1 contributor's copy; additional copies $5. Acquires first North American serial rights. Not copyrighted.
Advice: "We favor regional writers but will consider good work from anywhere."

✓ **DIRIGIBLE, Journal of Language Art, (II)**, Dirigible Press, 101 Cottage St., New Haven CT 06511. (203)776-8446. E-mail: dirigibl@javanet.com. **Editors:** David Todd and Cynthia Conrad. Magazine: 4¼×7; 40-48 pages; 20 lb. white paper; card stock cover; illustrations. "We seek language-centered poetry, controlled experiments, fiction that is postmodern, paraliterary, nonlinear or subjective, and work that breaks with genre, convention, or form. Hybrid forms of writing and essays on aesthetics, poetics, reader experience and writing processes are also of interest to us." Quarterly. Estab. 1994. Circ. 500-800.
Needs: Experimental, literary, translations, avant garde. No realism or other mainstream genres. Wants to see more "poetic prose, imaginative fiction that experiments with style, narrative technique, language." Accepts 2-3 mss/issue; 8-12 mss/year. Publishes ms 1 month after acceptance. Recently published work by Fernand Roqueplan, Peoria Melville, Matvei Yankelevich, Mark E. Cull, Barbara Lefcowitz and John Lowther. Publishes 4-6 new writers/year. Length: 1,750 words average; 1 word minimum; 3,600 words maximum. Publishes short shorts. Also publishes literary essays, literary criticism, poetry.
How to Contact: Send complete ms with a cover letter. Reports in 1 month on queries; 1-3 months on mss. Send SASE for reply, return of ms or send a disposable copy of ms. No simultaneous submissions. Sample copy for $2 postage paid. Reviews novels and short story collections.
Payment/Terms: Pays 2 contributor's copies on publication; additional copies for $2 ppd. Acquires first rights.
Advice: "We are grinding an aesthetic ax and acceptance is dependent on our personal vision."

✓ **THE DISTILLERY: ARTISTIC SPIRITS OF THE SOUTH, (I, II)**, Motlow St. Community College, P.O. Box 88100, Tullahoma TN 37388-8100. (931)393-1500. Fax: (931)393-1681. Website: http://mscc.cc.tn.us/www/distillery. **Editor:** Niles Reddick. Magazine: 88 pages; color cover; photographs. "The editors seek well-crafted, character-driven fiction. Several of us are writers, as well, so we want to see high-quality work that inspires us. In this postmodern-postmodern era, we think epiphanies are back in vogue." Semiannually. Estab. 1994. Circ. 500.
Needs: Literary. Receives 8-10 unsolicited mss/month. Accepts 3-4 mss/issue; 6-8 mss/year. Does not read mss June 1-August 1. Publishes ms 6-12 months after acceptance. Recently published work by Janice Daugharty, William Petrick and Sally Bennett. Publishes "50%" new writers. Length: 2,000-4,000 words average; 4,000 words maximum. Also publishes literary essays, literary criticism, poetry.
How to Contact: Send complete ms with a cover letter. Include estimated word count, brief bio, list of publications. "No third-person bio, please. What a strange thing . . ." Reports 2 weeks on queries; 2-3 months on mss. SASE for reply or send a disposable copy of ms. Sample copy for $7.50. Fiction guidelines for SASE. Occasionally reviews novels and short story collections. Send books to editor.
Payment/Terms: Pays 3 contributor's copies on publication; additional copies for $7.50. Acquires first North American serial rights.
Advice: "We want fiction that inspires us, that moves us to laugh or weep. Even though we are jaded old teachers and editors, we still want to feel a chill run down our spines when we read a perfect description or evocative line of dialogue. Revise, revise, revise. Also, do not write for a 'market,' whatever that means. Find your voice. If that voice has something to say, others will find it too, eventually."

DODOBOBO, A New Fiction Magazine of Washington D.C., (I), Dodobobo Publications, P.O. Box 57214, Washington DC 20037. **Editor:** Brian Greene. Magazine: 5½×8½; 20-35 pages; illustrations and photos. "We're a literary fiction magazine which intends to give voice to writers the more well-known literary magazines would not be open to." Quarterly. Estab. 1994. Circ. 500.
Needs: Experimental and literary. Receives 20 unsolicited mss/month. Accepts 2-4 mss/issue; 8-16 mss/year. Publishes ms 1-12 months after acceptance. Length: 3,000 words maximum. Sometimes critiques or comments on rejected ms.
How to Contact: "Send complete ms, with or without cover letter." Reports in 2 months on mss. Send SASE for reply, return of ms or send a disposable copy of ms. Simultaneous and reprint submissions OK. Sample copy for $2 (including postage). Fiction guidelines for SASE.
Payment/Terms: Pays 2 contributor's copies. Acquires one-time rights. Sends galleys to author if requested.
Advice: "We like stories which illustrate the reality of the human experience—people's existential crises, their experiences with other people, with their own psyches. Get a copy or two of the magazine and read the stories we've printed."

$ **DOGWOOD TALES MAGAZINE, For the Fiction Lover in All of Us, (I, II)**, Two Sisters Publications, P.O. Box 172068, Memphis TN 38187. E-mail: write2me@aol.com. Website: http://www.dogwoodtales.com (includes writer's guidelines, contest information, subscription information, discussion pages for writers and readers). Editor: Linda Ditty. **Fiction Editor:** Peggy Carman. Magazine: 5½×8½; 52 pages; 20 lb. paper; 60 lb.

cover stock; illustrations. "Interesting fiction that would appeal to all groups of people. Each issue will have a Special Feature Story about a Southern person, place or theme." Bimonthly. Estab. 1993.

Needs: Adventure, mainstream/contemporary, mystery/suspense, romance. "Would like to see more short shorts with a beginning, middle and end (preferably a surprise ending). No erotica, children and westerns. Strong offensive language or subject matter will be automatic rejection. Accepts 7-9 mss/issue; 42-54 mss/year. Publishes ms within 1 year after acceptance. Recently published work by June King, John M. Floyd and Judy S. Dodd. Publishes 30-40 new writers/year. Length: 1,350 words preferred; 200 words minimum; 4,500 words maximum. Publishes short shorts. Length: 200-500 words. Sometimes critiques or comments on rejected mss.

How to Contact: Send complete ms with a cover letter. Should include estimated word count and list of publications. Reports within 10 weeks on mss. Send SASE for reply, return of ms or send a disposable copy of ms. Simultaneous and electronic submissions (disk, ASCII only, or modem) OK. Sample copy for $3.50. Fiction guidelines for #10 SASE or from website.

Payment/Terms: Pays ¼¢ to ½¢ per word on acceptance plus 1 contributor copy; additional copies at reduced rate. Acquires first serial rights and reprint rights.

Advice: "Make sure your submission adheres to acceptable manuscript format (double spaced, large enough print to read). Send stories that have real characters. Also, research the magazine you're sending to before sending your manuscript. Learn proper ways to submit and don't forget SASE."

$ DOUBLE TAKE, 1317 W. Pettigrew St., Durham NC 27705. Contact: Fiction Editor.

Needs: "Realistic fiction in all of its variety; it's very unlikely we'd ever publish science fiction or gothic horror, for example." Buys 12 mss/year. Length: 3,000-8,000 words.

How to Contact: Send complete ms with cover letter. Accepts simultaneous submissions. Reports in 3 months on mss. Sample copy for $12. Writer's guidelines for #10 SASE. Simultaneous submissions OK.

Payment/Terms: Pays "competitively." Pays on acceptance. Buys first North American serial rights.

Advice: "Use a strong, developed narrative voice. Don't attempt too much or be overly melodramatic, lacking in subtlety, nuance and insight."

✔ $ DOWNSTATE STORY, (II, IV), 1825 Maple Ridge, Peoria IL 61614. (309)688-1409. E-mail: ehopkins@prairienet.org. Website: http://www.wiu.bgu.edu/users/mfgeh/dss. **Editor:** Elaine Hopkins. Magazine: illustrations. "Short fiction—some connection with Illinois or the Midwest." Annually. Estab. 1992. Circ. 500.

Needs: Adventure, ethnic/multicultural, experimental, historical, horror, humor/satire, literary, mainstream/contemporary, mystery/suspense, psychic/supernatural/occult, regional, romance, science fiction, westerns. Accepts 10 mss/issue. Publishes ms up to 1 year after acceptance. Length: 300 words minimum; 2,000 words maximum. Publishes short shorts. Also publishes literary essays.

How to Contact: Send complete ms with a cover letter. Reports "ASAP." SASE for return of ms. Simultaneous submissions OK. Sample copy for $8. Fiction guidelines for SASE.

Payment/Terms: Pays $50 maximum on acceptance for first rights.

✔ ECLECTICA MAGAZINE, (II), P.O. Box 82826, Fairbanks AK 99708. (907)474-3494. Fax: (907)474-6841. E-mail: editors@eclectica.org. Website: http://www.eclectica.org (includes our entire publication, all back issues and all editorial information). **Editor/Fiction Editor:** Chris Lott. Electronic magazine. "We publish the best writing on the World Wide Web. Although we are literary by nature, we publish exceptional work in almost every genre and strive to show the quality and viability of the electronic medium through our high editorial standards." Estab. 1996.

- Sponsors annual, multi-genre contest. See website for details.

Needs: Ethnic/multicultural, experimental, fantasy, humor/satire, literary, mystery/suspense, science fiction, serialized novel, translations. Wants to see more short-shorts, experimental, work that is well-written but not afraid to try something new. No pornography, predictable genre or workshop literature. Publishes special fiction issues or anthologies. Receives 300 unsolicited mss/month. Accepts 4-6 mss/issue, 72-84 mss/year. Publishes ms 2-3 months after acceptance. Recently published work by Stanley Jenkins, Li Min Hua, Alex Keegan and Richard Cumyn. Publishes 30 new writers/year. Length: 7,500 words average; 100 words minimum; 90,000 words maximum. Publishes short shorts. Also publishes literary essays, literary criticism, reviews and poetry. Sometimes critiques or comments on rejected mss.

How to Contact: Send complete ms with a cover letter. Include up to 250 word bio and list of publications. Send correspondence to editors at eclectica.org; submissions to submissions@eclectica.org. Reports in 1 week on queries; 4-6 weeks on mss. Send SASE for reply, return of ms or send disposable copy of ms. Simultaneous, reprint and electronic submissions OK. Reviews novels and short story collections. Send books to "Reviews Editor."

Advice: "We look for error-free work with high energy and attention to craft . . . but often subtlety and attention to the music of language will put a piece over the top. Read the magazine, talk with the editors, proofread your manuscripts before sending them. Pay attention to editorial notes and requests for specific kinds of work and be persistent!"

N THE EDGE CITY REVIEW, (II), Reston Review, Inc., 10912 Harpers Square Court, Reston VA 20191. Fax: (703)716-5752. E-mail: ponick@erols.com. **Editor:** T.L. Ponick. Magazine: 8½×11; 44-52 pages; 60 lb.

paper; 65 lb. color cover. "We publish Formalist poetry, well-plotted artistic or literary fiction, literary essays and book reviews. Our editorial philosophy is right of center." Triannually. Estab. 1994. Circ. 500.

Needs: Humor/satire, literary, regional, serialized novel. "We see too much fiction that's riddled with four-letter words and needless vulgarity." Receives 10 unsolicited mss/month. Accepts 1-2 mss/issue; 3-6 mss/year. Publishes ms 4 months after acceptance. Length: 2,000 words average, 1,500 words minimum; 3,000 words maximum. Also publishes literary essays, literary criticism, poetry. Sometimes critiques or comments on rejected ms.

How to Contact: Send complete ms with a cover letter. Include estimated word count, 25-50 word bio, list of publications. Reports in 1 month on queries; 3-5 months on mss. Send SASE for reply, return of ms or send a disposable copy of ms. Electronic submissions (disk or modem) OK. Sample copy for $5. Reviews novels and short story collections. "No 'chapbooks' or self-published, please."

Payment/Terms: Pays 2 contributor's copies; additional copies $4. Acquires first North American serial rights. Sponsors contest; watch for announcements in major publications.

Advice: "We are looking for character-based fiction. Most fiction we receive does not grow out of its characters—but finely wrought characters, fully realized, are what we want to see."

ELF: ECLECTIC LITERARY FORUM, (I, II), P.O. Box 392, Tonawanda NY 14150. Phone/fax: (716)693-7006. E-mail: neubauer@bukfnet.net. Website: http://www.pce.net/elf (includes selected, fiction, staff, editorial commentary, writer's guidelines). **Editor:** C.K. Erbes. Magazine: 8½×11; 56 pages; 60 lb. offset paper; coated cover; 2-3 illustrations; 2-3 photographs. "Well-crafted short stories, poetry, interviews, reviews, Native American folklore, literary essays for a sophisticated audience." Quarterly. Estab. 1991.

Needs: Adventure, contemporary, ethnic, fantasy, feminism, historical, humor/satire, literary, mainstream, mystery/suspense (private eye), prose poem, regional, science fiction (hard science, soft/sociological), sports, western. No violence and obscenity (horror/erotica). Accepts 4-6 mss/issue; 16-24 mss/year. Publishes ms up to 1 year after acceptance. Recently published work by Vonda McIntyre, Áine Greaney, Myla Goldberg, Gary Earl Ross and R.G. Riel. Publishes 3-4 new writers/year. Length: 3,500 words average. Publishes short shorts. Length: 500 words. Sometimes critiques rejected mss.

How to Contact: Send complete ms with optional cover letter. Reports in 4-6 weeks on mss. SASE. Simultaneous submissions OK (if so indicated). Sample copy for $5.50 ($8 foreign). Fiction guidelines for #10 SASE.

Payment/Terms: Pays contributor's copies. Acquires first North American serial rights.

Advice: "Short stories stand out when dialogue, plot, character, point of view and language usage work together to create a unified whole on a significant theme, one relevant to most of our readers. We also look for writers whose works demonstrate a knowledge of grammar and how to manipulate it effectively in a story. Each story is read by an Editorial Board comprised of English professors who teach creative writing and are published authors."

EMRYS JOURNAL, (II), The Emrys Foundation, P.O. Box 8813, Greenville SC 29604. (864)235-0084. Fax: (864)455-4111. E-mail: jhn@ghs.org. **Editor:** Jeanine Halva-Neubauer. Catalog: 9×9¾; 80 pages; 80 lb. paper (glossy). "We publish short fiction, poetry, and essays. We are particularly interested in hearing from women and other minorities. We are mindful of the southeast but not limited to it." Annually. Estab. 1984. Circ. 400.

Needs: Contemporary, feminist, literary, mainstream and regional. Reading period: August 1-December 1, 1998. Accepts 18 mss/issue. Publishes mss in April. Length: 3,500 words average; 6,000 words maximum. Publishes short shorts. Recently published work by Keller Cushing Freeman.

How To Contact: Send complete ms with cover letter. Reports in 6 weeks. SASE. Sample copy for $15 and 7×10 SAE with 4 first-class stamps. Fiction guidelines for #10 SASE.

Payment/Terms: Pays in contributor's copies. Acquires first rights. "Send to managing editor for guidelines."

Advice: Looks for "fiction by women and minorities, especially but not exclusively southeastern."

ENTRE NOUS, (II), Stoneflower Press, 1824 Nacogdoches, Suite 191, San Antonio TX 78209. E-mail: stonflower@aol.com. **Managing Editors:** Brenda Davidson-Shaddox and Manda Russell. Magazine: 4×5½; approximately 50 pages; 50 lb. white offset paper; 67 lb. Vellum cover; illustrations and photographs. "We try to help writers find a market for their works and build credentials to help expand exposure." Quarterly. Estab. 1997.

Needs: Ethnic/multicultural, experimental, feminist, literary, mainstream/contemporary. No pornography or religious. Upcoming themes: fences/walls, rooms/spaces, music/dance, hope/renewal. Guidelines and themes available for SASE. Receives 25 unsolicited mss/month. Publishes ms 3-12 months after acceptance. Length: 2,000 words maximum (fiction). Also publishes poetry (line limit 40).

How to Contact: Send complete ms. "Don't try to convince me how good the story is via letter. Let the story speak." Include estimated word count, short paragraph bio, list of publications and awards won or other writing accomplishments. Reports in 2-3 months on mss. Send disposable copy of ms, but send SASE for response.

SENDING TO A COUNTRY other than your own? Be sure to send International Reply Coupons instead of stamps for replies or return of your manuscript.

Simultaneous, reprint and electronic submissions OK. Sample copy for $3, 6×9 SAE and 4 first-class stamps. Fiction guidelines for SASE.
Payment/Terms: Pays 1 copy of issue in which work appears. Acquires one-time rights.
Advice: "We look for technically good writing with good use of language. Study 'how-to' books. Take courses. Read other writers. Learn your craft. You're up against a wall of competitors."

$ EPOCH MAGAZINE, (II), 251 Goldwin Smith Hall, Cornell University, Ithaca NY 14853. (607)255-3385. Fax: (607)255-6661. **Editor:** Michael Koch. Submissions should be sent to Michael Koch. Magazine: 6×9; 128 pages; good quality paper; good cover stock. "Top level fiction and poetry for people who are interested in good literature." Published 3 times a year. Estab. 1947. Circ. 1,000.

• *Epoch Magazine* won the premiere *O. Henry Magazine* Award for best magazine of 1997. Work originally appearing in this quality literary journal has appeared in numerous anthologies including *Best American Short Stories*, *Best American Poetry*, *Pushcart Prize*, *The O. Henry Prize Stories*, *Best of the West* and *New Stories from the South*.

Needs: Literary, contemporary and ethnic. Accepts 15-20 mss/issue. Receives 500 unsolicited fiction mss each month. Does not read in summer (April 15-September 15). Published work by Ron Hansen, Jessica Treat, Rick Bass, D.R. MacDonald and Victoria Radel. Published new writers in the last year. Length: no limit. Also publishes personal essays, poetry. Critiques rejected mss when there is time. Sometimes recommends other markets.
How to Contact: Send complete ms with SASE. No simultaneous submissions. Reports in 3-4 weeks on mss. Publishes ms an average of 6 months after acceptance. Sample copy for $5.
Payment/Terms: Pays $5-10/printed page and contributor copies on publication for first North American serial rights.
Advice: "Read the journals you're sending work to."

ETCETERA, A Journal of Art & Literature & Thought & Communication & Eclectic et cetera, (I, II), Etcetera Press, P.O. Box 8543, New Haven CT 06531. (203)752-1959. E-mail: iedit4you@aol.com. **Editor:** Mindi Englart. Magazine: 5½×8; 32 pages; sandstone cover stock; illustrations and photographs. Semiannually. Estab. 1996. Circ. 500.
Needs: Adventure, condensed/excerpted novel, experimental, feminist, humor/satire, literary, senior citizen/retirement, serialized novel, translation. Wants more experimental and memoir-style fiction. No religious or romance. Receives 25 unsolicited mss/month. Accepts 2-3 mss/issue; 4-6 mss/year. Publishes ms 2 months after acceptance. Recently published work by Jared Millar, Robert Perchan and Steven Hirsch. Publishes 6-8 unpublished writers/year. Length: 1,800 words maximum. Publishes short shorts. Also publishes literary essays, poetry. Often critiques or comments on rejected ms if asked.
How to Contact: Send complete ms with a cover letter. Include estimated word count and 30-word bio. Reports on acceptances/rejections after March 15 and September 15 deadlines. Send SASE for reply, return of ms or send a disposable copy of ms. Simultaneous, reprint and electronic submissions OK. Sample copy for $3. Fiction guidelines for #11 SASE. Reviews novels and short story collections.
Payment/Terms: Pays 1 contributor's copy and 1-year subscription on publication. Acquires one-time rights. Sometimes sends galleys to author.
Advice: "Experimental, avant-garde, conceptual, thought-provoking, beautiful, ugly, sensitive, strange and humorous works are encouraged. Show us innovative use of language with a deep, insightful treatment of the topic."

EUREKA LITERARY MAGAZINE, (I, II), P.O. Box 280, Eureka College, Eureka IL 61530. (309)467-6336. Editor: Loren Logsdon. **Fiction Editor:** Nancy Perkins. Magazine: 6×9; 100 pages; 70 lb. white offset paper; 80 lb. gloss cover; photographs (occasionally). "We seek to be open to the best stories that are submitted to us. We do not want to be narrow in a political sense of the word. Our audience is a combination of professors/writers and general readers." Semiannually. Estab. 1992. Circ. 400.
Needs: Adventure, ethnic/multicultural, experimental, fantasy (science), feminist, historical, humor/satire, literary, mainstream/contemporary, mystery/suspense (private eye/hardboiled, romantic), psychic/supernatural/occult, regional, romance (historical), science fiction (soft/sociological), translations. "We try to achieve a balance between the traditional and the experimental. We do favor the traditional, though. We look for the well-crafted story, but essentially any type of story that has depth and substance to it—any story that expands us as human beings and celebrates the mystery and miracle of the creation. Make sure you have a good beginning and ending, a strong voice, excellent use of language, good insight into the human condition, narrative skill, humor—if it is appropriate to the subject." No drug stories of any kind. Receives 25 unsolicited mss/month. Accepts 4 mss/issue; 8-9 mss/year. Does not read mss mainly in late summer (August). Published work by James A. Surges, Richard L. Wendt, Dave Jackman, Patrick J. Murphy, Carol North and Stacy Lynn Smith. Published new writers within the last year. Length: 4,500 words average; 7,000-8,000 words maximum. Publishes short shorts. Also publishes poetry.
How to Contact: Send complete ms with a cover letter. Should include estimated word count and bio (short paragraph). Reports in 1 week on queries; 4 months on mss. Send SASE for reply, return of ms or send a disposable copy of ms. Simultaneous submissions OK. Sample copy for $5.
Payment/Terms: Pays free subscription to the magazine and 2 contributor's copies. Acquires first rights or

one-time rights.
Advice: "Does the writer tell a good story—one that would interest a general reader? Is the story provocative? Is its subject important? Does the story contain good insight into life or the human condition? We don't want anything so abstract that it seems unrelated to anything human. We appreciate humor and effective use of language, stories that have powerful, effective endings. Take pains with the beginning and ending of the story; both must work. Be sure the voice is genuine. Be sure the manuscript is free from serious surface errors and is easy to read."

EVANSVILLE REVIEW, (I, II), University of Evansville, 1800 Lincoln Ave., Evansville IN 47722. (812)488-1114. Website: http://www.evansville.edu/~elrweb. **Editor:** Ingrid Jendrzejewski. Editors change every 1-2 years. Magazine: 6×9; 120-150 pages; 70 lb. white paper; heavy laminated 4-color cover. Annually. Estab. 1990. Circ. 2,500.
Needs: "We're open to all creativity. No discrimination. All fiction, screenplays, nonfiction, poetry, interviews, photo essays and anything in between." No children or young adult. List of upcoming themes available for SASE. Receives 300 unsolicited mss/year. Does not read mss February-August. Agented fiction 2%. Recently published work by John Updike, Lewis Turco, Felix Stefanile, Dana Gioia, Willis Barnstone, James Ragan, Rachel Hadas and Josephine Jacobsen. Also publishes literary essays, poetry.
How to Contact: Send complete ms with a cover letter, e-mail or fax. Include 150 word or less bio and list of publications. Reports in 2 weeks on queries; 3 months on mss. Send SASE for reply, return of ms or send a disposable copy of ms. Simultaneous and reprint submissions OK. Sample copy for $5. Fiction guidelines free; check website.
Payment/Terms: Pays 5 contributor's copies on publication. Acquires one-time rights. Sends galleys to author if requested. Not copyrighted.
Advice: "Because editorial staffs roll over every 1-2 years, the journal always has a new flavor."

$ EVENT, (II), Douglas College, Box 2503, New Westminster, British Columbia V3L 5B2 Canada. Fax: (604)527-5095. Editor: Calvin Wharton. **Fiction Editor:** Christine Dewar. Assistant Editor: Bonnie Bauder. Magazine: 6×9; 144 pages; quality paper and cover stock; illustrations; photos. "Primarily a literary magazine, publishing poetry, fiction, reviews; for creative writers, artists, anyone interested in contemporary literature." Triannually. Estab. 1971. Circ. 1,000.
Needs: Literary, contemporary, feminist, humor, regional. "No technically poor or unoriginal pieces." Receives approximately 100 unsolicited fiction mss/month. Accepts 6-8 mss/issue. Recently published work by Julie Keith, Andrew Pyper and Kenneth Harvey. Published new writers within the last year. Length: 5,000 words maximum. Also publishes poetry.
How to Contact: Send complete ms, bio and SAE with Canadian postage or IRC. Reports in 1-4 months on mss. Publishes ms 6-12 months after acceptance. Sample copy for $5.
Payment/Terms: Pays $22/page and 2 contributor's copies on publication for first North American serial rights.
Advice: "A good narrative arc is hard to find."

✓ $ THE EVERGREEN CHRONICLES, A Journal of Gay, Lesbian, Bisexual & Transgender Arts & Cultures, (II), P.O. Box 8939, Minneapolis MN 55408-0939. (612)823-6638. E-mail: evergchron@aol.com. **Managing Editor:** Cynthia Fogard. Magazine: 7×8½; 90-100 pages; b&w line drawings and photos. "We look for work that addresses the complexities and diversities of gay, lesbian, bisexual and transgendered experiences." Triannually. Estab. 1985. Circ. 1,000.

- The magazine sponsors an annual novella contest; deadline September 30. Send SASE for guidelines.

Needs: Gay or lesbian: adventure, confession, contemporary, ethnic, experimental, feminist, humor/satire, literary, serialized/excerpted novel, suspense/mystery. "We are interested in works by artists in a wide variety of genres. The subject matter need not be specifically lesbian, gay, bisexual or transgender-themed, but we do look for a deep sensitivity to that experience. No sentimental, romantic stuff, fantasy or science fiction." Accepts 10-25 mss/issue; 30-52 mss/year. Publishes ms approximately 2 months after acceptance. Recently published work by Eileen Myles, Edward Cohen, Jane Eastwood, Eugene Kraft, Craig McWhorter and Mary Ann McFadden. Publishes 10-15 new writers/year. Length: 3,500-4,500 words average; no minimum; 5,200 words maximum. 25 pages double-spaced maximum on prose. Publishes short shorts. Sometimes comments on rejected mss.
How to Contact: Send 4 copies of complete ms with cover letter. Accepts queries by e-mail. "It helps to have some biographical information included." Submission deadlines: January 1 and July 1. Reports on queries in 3 weeks; on mss in 3-4 months. SASE. Electronic submissions (fax, e-mail) OK. Sample copy for $8 and $2 postage. Fiction guidelines for #10 SASE.

Payment/Terms: Pays $50 honorarium for one-time rights.
Advice: "We've seen a great increase in the number of unsolicited manuscripts sent to us for consideration. More and more competition in our specific genre of gay and lesbian writing. This means that the quality of the writing we publish is getting better—more readers and writers out there. We're looking for originality in perspective and/or language. Share your writing with others! Join writing groups."

☑ **EXPLORATIONS '99, (I, II)**, UAS Explorations, University of Alaska Southeast, 11120 Glacier Highway, Juneau AK 99801. (907)465-6418. Fax: (907)465-6406. E-mail: jnamp@acad1.alaska.edu. **Editor:** Art Petersen. Magazine: 5½×8¼; 60 pages; heavy cover stock; b&w illustrations and photographs. "Poetry, prose and art—we strive for artistic excellence." Annually. Estab. 1981. Circ. 750.
Needs: Experimental, humor/satire, traditional quality fiction, poetry, and art. Receives about 1,200 mss/year. Recently published work by Charles Bukowski, William Everson, David Ray, Ania Savage and Nicchia P. Leamer. 75% of work is by new writers.
How to Contact: *Reading/entry fee $6/story required.* Send name, address and short bio on *back* of first page of each submission. All submissions entered in contest. Submission postmark deadline is March 21. Reports in July. Mss cannot be returned. Simultaneous and reprint submissions OK. Sample copy for $5.
Payment/Terms: Pays 2 contributor's copies. Acquires one-time rights (rights remain with the author). Also awards 7 annual prizes of $1,000 for best story or poem, $500 for best story or poem in genre other than 1st Place, and more.
Advice: "It is best to send for full guidelines. Concerning poetry and prose, standard form as well as innovation are encouraged; appropriate and fresh *imagery* (allusions, metaphors, similes, symbols . . .) as well as standard or experimental form draw editorial attention. 'Language really spoken by men' and women and authentically rendered experience are encouraged. Unfortunately, requests for criticism usually cannot be met. The prizes for 1998 will be awarded by the poet and critic John Haines."

☑ **EXPRESSIONS, Literature and Art by People with Ongoing Health Problems and Disabilities, (IV)**, Serendipity Press, P.O. Box 16294, St. Paul MN 55118-1840. (612)552-1208. Fax: (612)552-1209. E-mail: dmamom@worldnet.att.com. **Editor:** Sefra Kobrin Pitzele. Magazine: 5½×8½; 60-84 pages; 60 lb. biodegradable paper; 80 lb. semigloss cover; illustrations and photographs. "*Expressions* provides a quality journal in which to be published when health, mobility, access or illness make multiple submissions both unreachable and unaffordable." Semiannually. Estab. 1993. Circ. 750.
Needs: *Material from writers with disabilities or ongoing health problems only.* Adventure, ethnic/multicultural, experimental, fantasy, feminist, gay, historical, horror, humor/satire, lesbian, literary, mainstream/contemporary, mystery/suspense, psychic/supernatural/occult, regional, religious/inspirational, romance, science fiction, senior citizen/retirement, sports and westerns. "We have no young readers, so all fiction should be intended for adult readers." Does not read mss from December 15 to February 1. Publishes ms 3-5 months after acceptance. Publishes 10-20 new writers/year. Length: 1,500-2,000 words average. Publishes short shorts. Also publishes literary essays, literary criticism, poetry. Sometimes critiques or comments on rejected mss. Sponsors a fiction contest. Send #10 SASE for more information. "Eight to ten reader/scorers from across the nation help me rank each submission on its own merit." Awards are $50 (first place), $25 (second place) and a year's subscription (third place).
How to Contact: *Requires $5 reading fee* (waived by request). Write for fiction guidelines; include SASE. Submission deadlines: May 15 and November 15. Reports in 2-6 weeks on queries; 2-4 months on mss. SASE for reply to query or return of ms. Simultaneous, reprint and electronic submissions OK. Sample copy for $6, 6×9 SAE and 5 first-class stamps.
Payment/Terms: Pays 2 contributor's copies. Acquires one-time rights.
Advice: "Only send clean, new, dark print copy with 1″ margins all around, name and page number on each page. We ask for two copies. Always send a short bio letter and name your submission in that letter. Always send SASE. And be patient."

FAT TUESDAY, (I, II), 560 Manada Gap Rd., Grantville PA 17028. (717)469-7517. Editor-in-Chief: F.M. Cotolo. Editors: B. Lyle Tabor and Thom Savion. **Associate Editors:** Lionel Stevroid and Kristen vonOehrke. Journal: 8½×11 or 5×8; 27-36 pages; bond paper; heavy cover stock; saddle-stitched; b&w illustrations; photos. "Generally, we are an eclectic journal of fiction, poetry and visual treats. Our issues to date have featured artists like Patrick Kelly, Charles Bukowski, Gerald Locklin, Chuck Taylor and many more who have focused on an individualistic nature with fiery elements. We are a literary mardi gras—as the title indicates—and irreverancy is as acceptable to us as profundity as long as there is fire! Our audience is anyone who can praise literature and condemn it at the same time. Anyone too serious about it on either level will not like *Fat Tuesday*." Annually. Estab. 1981. Circ. 700.

- *Fat Tuesday* is best known for first-person "auto fiction." Their 1997-1998 edition was published in audio format. They may publish future issues in this format.

Needs: Comics, erotica, experimental, humor/satire, literary, prose poem, psychic/supernatural/occult, serialized/excerpted novel and dada. "Although we list categories, we are open to feeling out various fields if they are delivered with the mark of an individual and not just in the format of the particular field." Does not want to see sci-fi, romance, mystery, mainstream in general. Receives 20 unsolicited fiction mss/month. Accepts 4-5 mss/

issue. Published new writers within the last year. Length: 1,000 words maximum. Publishes short shorts. Occasionally critiques rejected mss and usually responds with a personal note or letter.
How to Contact: Send complete ms with SASE. "No previously published material considered." No simultaneous submissions. Reports in 1 month. Publishes ms 3-10 months after acceptance. Sample copy (in print or audio) for $5.
Payment/Terms: Pays 1 contributor's copy. Acquires one-time rights.
Advice: "As *Fat Tuesday* crawls through its second decade, we find publishing small press editions more difficult than ever. Money remains a problem, mostly because small press seems to play to the very people who wish to be published in it. In other words, the cast is the audience, and more people want to be in *Fat Tuesday* than want to buy it. It is through sales that our magazine supports itself. This is why we emphasize buying a sample issue ($5) before submitting. Please specify in-print or audio issue. As far as what we want to publish—send us shorter works that are 'crystals of thought and emotion which reflect your individual experiences—dig into your guts and pull out pieces of yourself. Your work is your signature; like time itself, it should emerge from the penetralia of your being and recede into the infinite region of the cosmos,' to coin a phrase, and remember *Fat Tuesday* is mardi gras—so fill up before you fast. Bon soir."

FEMINIST STUDIES, (II, IV), Department of Women's Studies, University of Maryland, College Park MD 20742. (301)405-7415. Fax: (301)314-9190. E-mail: femstud@umail.umd.edu. Website: http://www.inform.umd.edu/femstud. Editor: Claire G. Moses. **Fiction Editor:** Shirley Lim. Magazine: journal-sized; about 200 pages; photographs. "Scholarly manuscripts, fiction, book review essays for professors, graduate/doctoral students; scholarly interdisciplinary feminist journal." Triannually. Estab. 1974. Circ. 7,500.
Needs: Contemporary, ethnic, feminist, gay, lesbian. Receives about 15 poetry and short story mss/month. Accepts 2-3 mss/issue. "We review fiction twice a year. Deadline dates are May 1 and December 1. Authors will receive notice of the board's decision by June 30 and January 30, respectively." Published work by Bell Chevigny, Betsy Gould Gibson and Joan Jacobson. Sometimes comments on rejected mss.
How to Contact: Send complete ms with cover letter. No simultaneous submissions. Sample copy for $12. Fiction guidelines free.
Payment/Terms: Pays 2 contributor's copies and 10 tearsheets. Sends galleys to authors.

N **FEMINIST VOICES, A Free Madison Newsjournal by Women for Women, (I)**, P.O. Box 853, Madison WI 53701-0853. (608)251-9268. Editors change each year. Small tabloid newspaper: 12-16 pages; newsprint; illustrations and photos. "*Feminist Voices* is an open forum by and for women with a commitment to supporting women's choices and the freedom to shape our own lives." Published 10 times/year. Estab. 1987. Circ. 7,000.
Needs: All categories—by women only. Plans specific themes. Receives 1 unsolicited ms/month. Accepts 0-1 ms/issue; 6-7 mss/year. Mostly publishes new writers. Length: 1,500 words maximum. Publishes short shorts. Also publishes literary essays, literary criticism, poetry. Rarely critiques or comments on rejected ms.
How to Contact: Send complete ms with a cover letter. Include estimated word count, short bio. Send ms on PC-compatible diskette if possible. SASE for return of ms or send a disposable copy of ms. Simultaneous and reprint submissions OK. Sample copy for $1. Fiction guidelines free. Sometimes reviews novels, short story collections and nonfiction books of interest to writers.
Payment/Terms: Pays free subscription to magazine on publication. Rights revert to author. Not copyrighted.

FICTION, (II), % Dept. of English, City College, 138th St. & Convent Ave., New York NY 10031. (212)650-6319/650-6317. Editor: Mark J. Mirsky. Managing Editor: Michael W. Pollock. Magazine: 6×9; 150-250 pages; illustrations and occasionally photos. "As the name implies, we publish *only* fiction; we are looking for the best new writing available, leaning toward the unconventional. *Fiction* has traditionally attempted to make accessible the unaccessible, to bring the experimental to a broader audience." Biannually. Estab. 1972. Circ. 4,500.

- Stories first published in *Fiction* have been selected for inclusion in the *Pushcart Prize* and *Best of the Small Presses* anthologies.

Needs: Contemporary, experimental, humor/satire, literary and translations. No romance, science-fiction, etc. Receives 200 unsolicited mss/month. Accepts 12-20 mss/issue; 24-40 mss/year. Does not read mss May-October. Publishes ms 1-12 months after acceptance. Agented fiction 10-20%. Published work by Harold Brodkey, Joyce Carol Oates, Peter Handke, Max Frisch, Susan Minot and Adolfo Bioy-Casares. Length: 6,000 words maximum. Publishes short shorts. Sometimes critiques rejected mss and recommends other markets.
How to Contact: Send complete ms with cover letter. Reports in approximately 3 months on mss. SASE. Simultaneous submissions OK, but please advise. Sample copy for $5. Fiction guidelines for SASE.
Payment/Terms: Pays in contributor's copies. Acquires first rights.
Advice: "The guiding principle of *Fiction* has always been to go to terra incognita in the writing of the imagination and to ask that modern fiction set itself serious questions, if often in absurd and comic voices, interrogating the nature of the real and the fantastic. It represents no particular school of fiction, except the innovative. Its pages have often been a harbor for writers at odds with each other. As a result of its willingness to publish the difficult, experimental, unusual, while not excluding the well known, *Fiction* has a unique reputation in the U.S. and abroad as a journal of future directions."

$ THE FIDDLEHEAD, (I, II), University of New Brunswick, Campus House, Box 4400, Fredericton, New Brunswick E3B 5A3 Canada. (506)453-3501. Editor: Ross Leckie. **Fiction Editor:** Norman Ravvin. Magazine: 6×9; 104-128 pages; ink illustrations; photos. "No criteria for publication except quality. For a general audience, including many poets and writers." Quarterly. Estab. 1945. Circ. 1,000.
Needs: Literary. No non-literary fiction. Receives 100-150 unsolicited mss/month. Buys 4-5 mss/issue; 20-40 mss/year. Publishes ms up to 1 year after acceptance. Small percent agented fiction. Recently published work by Seamus Ceallaigh; published new writers within the last year. Length: 50-3,000 words average. Publishes short shorts. Occasionally critiques rejected mss.
How to Contact: Send complete ms with cover letter. Send SASE and *Canadian* stamps or IRCs for return of mss. Reprint submissions OK. No simultaneous submissions. Reports in 2-6 months. Sample copy for $7 (US). Reviews novels and short story collections—*Canadian only.*
Payment/Terms: Pays $10-12 (Canadian)/published page and 1 contributor's copy on publication for first or one-time rights.
Advice: "Less than 5% of the material received is published."

THE 5TH WALL, a literary gallery for the exhibition of written art, (II), P.O. Box 22161, San Diego CA 92192-2161. (415)831-1514. E-mail: tchad@sfsu.edu. Editor: Chad Mealey. **Fiction Editor:** Chris Kalidor. Magazine: 4¼×11; 20 pages (varies); paper and cover stock vary. "Artwork created with words has as much value as artwork created with paint or ink or clay. We publish 'artwork' that often evades poetry or prose in a gallery format for the curious." Semiannually. Estab. 1991. Circ. 200.
Needs: Children's/juvenile, condensed/excerpted novel, experimental, humor/satire, literary, mainstream/contemporary, regional, science fiction, translations, unusual. List of upcoming themes available for SASE. Publishes special fiction issues or anthologies. Receives 10-15 unsolicited mss/month. Accepts 10 mss/issue; 20 mss/year. Publishes ms 1-4 months after acceptance. Recently published work by David Hurwitz, Richard Kostelanetz and Igor Korneitchouk. Length: 2,000 words average; 1 word minimum; 4,000 words maximum. Publishes short shorts. Also publishes literary essays and poetry. Often critiques or comments on rejected mss.
How to Contact: Query first for long pieces, otherwise send complete ms. Include 1 paragraph bio and list date, medium and price of artwork. Reports in 1 month on queries; 2-4 months on mss. Send SASE for reply, return of ms or send disposable copy of ms. Simultaneous, reprint and electronic submissions OK. Sample copy for $2 and #14 envelope with 2 first-class stamps. Fiction guidelines for #10 SASE.
Payment/Terms: Pays 80% minimum; 90% maximum and 1-10 contributor's copies on publication for one-time rights; additional copies $1 or $2.
Advice: "We view every manuscript as a piece of art. Is it a beautiful landscape? A dynamic abstract? Expressive? Is the piece executed in a way appropriate to the concept or subject? Forget the rules."

FILLING STATION, (I, II), Filling Station Publications Society, Box 22135, Bankers Hall, Calgary, Alberta T2P 4J5 Canada. Phone/fax: (403)253-2980. **Fiction Editor:** Meaghan. Magazine: 8½×11; 56 pages; 70 lb. offset paper; 80 lb. cover; illustrations and photos. "We're looking for writing that challenges the preconceptions of readers and writers alike, that crosses conventional boundaries and seeks out its own territory. We're particularly interested in new voices." Triannually. Estab. 1993. Circ. 500.
Needs: Ethnic/multicultural, experimental, feminist, gay, lesbian, literary, mainstream/contemporary, regional and translations. Receives 10-15 unsolicited submissions/month. Accepts 3-4 mss/issue; 10 mss/year. Publishes ms within 1 year after acceptance. Recently published work by Thomas Wharton, Golda Fried, Richard Brown, G.R. Gustafson and Robert Majamaa. Publishes 5-6 new writers/year. Length: 2,000 words average; 5,000 words maximum. Publishes short shorts. Also publishes literary essays, literary criticism and poetry.
How to Contact: Send complete ms with cover letter. Should include bio (20-30 words). E-mail queries: sankoffn@cadvision.com. E-mail submissions/general inquiries: cfthomps@cadvision.com. Reports in 1 month on queries; 4 months on mss. Send SASE for reply, return of ms or send a disposable copy of ms. Simultaneous and electronic submissions OK. Sample copy for $6, 9×12 SAE and 2 IRCs. Fiction guidelines for #10 SASE. Reviews novels and short story collections.
Payment/Terms: One-year subscription, beginning with the issue in which the author is published. Acquires first North American serial rights.
Advice: "We do not want work by people who know how to write but have nothing to say. Style is important, but so is the narrative framework. Also, if someone tells you it's already been done, that person is partially right—the question is how has it been done? If you are writing, you need to do it differently and get away from the familiar ruts . . . beyond composition and fluid use of the language, you need to make connections between things that have already been thought of but have never been connected before. Don't try to impress editors with flashy cover letters, name-dropping or stacks of credentials. Publishing, especially for small-run magazines, is increasingly expensive and difficult in an era of rising production costs and shrinking funding. The demands on any publisher in any market to seek out higher-quality work are correspondingly greater."

FISH DRUM MAGAZINE, (II), Murray Hill Station, P.O. Box 966, New York NY 10156. **Editor:** Suzi Winson. Magazine: 5½×8½; 80-odd pages; glossy cover; illustrations and photographs. "Lively, emotional vernacular modern fiction, art and poetry." Annually. Estab. 1988 by Robert Winson (1959-1995). "*Fish Drum*

includes lively, vernacular, prose and poetry that follows the working novel. Themes include Zen practice, the South West, et.al." Circ. 1,000.
Needs: Contemporary, erotica, ethnic, experimental, fantasy, literary, prose poem, regional, science fiction. "Most of the fiction we've published is in the form of short, heightened prose-pieces." Receives 6-10 unsolicited mss/month. Accepts 1-2 mss/issue. Also publishes literary essays, literary criticism, poetry.
How to Contact: Send complete manuscript. No simultaneous submissions. Reports on mss in 2-3 months. SASE. Reviews novels and short story collections.
Payment/Terms: Pays in contributor's copies. Charges for extras. Acquires first North American serial rights. Sends galleys to author.

THE FLORIDA REVIEW, (II), Dept. of English, University of Central Florida, Orlando FL 32816. (407)823-2038. Fax: (407)823-6582. Website: http://www.pegasus.cc.ucf.edu/~english/floridareview/home.htm (includes writer's guidelines, contest information and covers and table of contents of the six most recent issues. **Contact:** Russell Kesler. Magazine: 5½×8½; 120 pages; semigloss full-color cover; perfect-bound. "We publish fiction of high 'literary' quality—stories that delight, instruct and aren't afraid to take risks. Our audience consists of avid readers of contemporary fiction, poetry and personal essay." Semiannually. Estab. 1972. Circ. 1,000.
Needs: Contemporary, experimental and literary. "We welcome experimental fiction, so long as it doesn't make us feel lost or stupid. We aren't especially interested in genre fiction (science fiction, romance, adventure, etc.), though a good story can transcend any genre." Receives 200 mss/month. Accepts 4-6 mss/issue; 16-20 mss/year. Publishes ms within 3-6 months of acceptance. Recently published work by Richard Wirick, Daniel Ort and Debbie Lee Wesselmann. Publishes 2-4 new writers/year. Also publishes literary criticism, poetry and essays.
How to Contact: Send complete ms with cover letter. Reports in 2-4 months. SASE required. Simultaneous submissions OK. Sample copy for $6; fiction guidelines for SASE. Reviews novels and short story collections.
Payment/Terms: Pays in contributor's copies. Small honorarium occasionally available. "Copyright held by U.C.F.; reverts to author after publication. (In cases of reprints, we ask that a credit line indicate that the work first appeared in the *F.R.*)"
Tips: "We're looking for writers with a fresh voice, engaging situations and are not afraid to take risks. Read contemporary writers/literary magazines."

$ FLYING HORSE, P.O. Box 445, Marblehead MA 01945. **Editor:** Dennis Must. Associate Editor: David Wagner. Magazine: 6×9; 100 pages; 50 lb. Finch Opaque paper; 70 lb. cover stock; illustrations; photographs. "*Flying Horse* is an alternative literary journal. Although we welcome contributions from all talented artists, we particularly hope to give voice to those often excluded from the dominant media. For example, we actively encourage submissions from inner city learning centers, community and public colleges, prisons, homeless shelters, social service agencies, unions, the military, hospitals, clinics or group homes, Indian reservations and minority studies programs." Semiannually. Estab. 1996. Circ. 1,000.
Needs: Condensed/excerpted novel, ethnic/multicultural, experimental, literary, mainstream/contemporary, translations. Receives 75-100 unsolicited mss/month. Accepts 20 mss/issue; 40 mss/year. Publishes ms generally in the next issue. Recently published work by Mark Wisniewski, Pat Reid, Dennis Brutus and Frank Van Zant. Publishes 20 new writers/year. Length: 2,500-5,000 words average; 7,500 words maximum. Publishes short shorts. Also publishes literary essays, literary criticism and poetry. Occasionally critiques or comments on rejected mss.
How to Contact: Send complete ms with a cover letter. Include estimated word count and short bio with submission. Reports in 3 months on mss. Send SASE for reply, return of ms or send a disposable copy of ms. Simultaneous submissions OK. Sample copy for $4. Fiction guidelines for #10 SASE.
Payment/Terms: Pays $10-25 and 2 contributor's copies on publication for one-time rights. Sends galleys to author.
Advice: "*Flying Horse* seeks heterogeneity of voice. Circumstance, class and formal education are not weighed. Nor do we count writing credits. What moves us to say *yes* is the authority of a submitted work, its conviction and originality of expression. The reader will encounter authors from starkly diverse corners of our society in our journal. What unites us, our common fuel, is the *written word*, and our firmly held conviction in its powers of transformation."

THE FLYING ISLAND, (II, IV), Writers' Center of Indianapolis, P.O. Box 88386, Indianapolis IN 46208. (317)955-6336. **Editor:** Jerome Donahue. Tabloid: 24 pages; illustrations and photos. "A magazine of fiction,

FOR EXPLANATIONS OF THESE SYMBOLS, SEE THE INSIDE FRONT AND BACK COVERS OF THIS BOOK.

essays, reviews and poetry by Indiana-connected writers." Semiannually. Estab. 1979. Circ. 700.
Needs: Ethnic/multicultural, experimental, fantasy, feminist, gay, lesbian, literary, mainstream/contemporary, mystery/suspense, psychic/supernatural/occult, science fiction. Receives 1,000 unsolicited mss/year. Accepts 4-5 mss/issue; 8-10 mss/year. Does not read mss March-May and September-November. Publishes ms 2 months after acceptance. Length: 3,000 words average. Publishes short shorts. Also publishes literary essays, literary criticism and poetry.
How to Contact: Send two copies of complete ms with a cover letter. Should include short bio explaining Indiana connection. Write for guidelines. Reports in 3-5 months on mss. SASE for return of ms. Simultaneous submissions OK. Fiction guidelines for #10 SASE.
Payment/Terms: Pays 2 contributor's copies plus honorarium. Pays on publication.
Advice: "We have published work by high school and college students as well as work by 1994 Pulitzer Prize winner Yusef Komunyakaa and Edgar nominee Terence Faherty. Our readers enjoy a wide variety of settings and situations. We're looking for quality and we tend to overlook gimmicky and sentimental writing."

☑ **FORBIDDEN DONUT, (I)**, 1538 Woodlawn Circle, Waconia MN 55387. (612)929-0352. E-mail: wwood@earthlink.net. **Editors:** Brian Wood and Jon Cazares. Magazine: 8×10; 50 pages; illustrations and photos. "Our continuing mission is to seek out new writers and new artists, to explore strange new ideas and to boldly go where no editors have gone before." Quarterly. Estab. 1995. Circ. 500.
Needs: Adventure, experimental, fantasy (science fantasy, sword and sorcery), horror, humor/satire, literary, mainstream/contemporary, mystery/suspense (amateur sleuth, cozy, police procedural, private eye/hardboiled), psychic/supernatural/occult, science fiction (hard science/soft sociological). No romance or westerns. Receives 10-25 unsolicited mss/month. Accepts 5-10 mss/issue; 20-30 mss year. Publishes ms 1-3 months after acceptance. Length: 3,000 words average; 10,000 words maximum. Publishes short shorts. Also publishes literary essays and literary criticism. Critiques or comments on rejected mss at author's request.
How to Contact: Send complete ms with a cover letter. Include bio. Accepts queries by e-mail. Reports in 1-3 weeks on queries; 2-8 weeks on mss. Send a disposable copy of ms. Simultaneous, reprint and electronic submissions OK. Sample copy for $2. Fiction guidelines free. Reviews novel and short story collections. Send books "Attention: Z.H."
Payment/Terms: Pays $1 and 1 contributor's copy for one-time rights; additional copies $1.
Advice: "The best advice we can give as to what kind of story we might accept is conflict and dialogue. Conflict and dialogue tend to keep the story moving and keep the reader interested, while drawn-out descriptions of everything in sight cause the reader to bog down and become bored. Many great stories don't follow this rule, but those are much more difficult to write. We prefer not to get lengthy submissions through e-mail. Please send recommendations for illustrations or photography to accompany your stories."

N 🌐 $ **FRANK, An International Journal of Contemporary Writing and Art**, 32 rue Edouard Vaillant, 93100 Montreuil, France. **Editor:** David Applefield. "Semiannual journal edited and published in Paris in English." Circ. 3,000. Publishes 20 stories/issue. "At *Frank*, we publish fiction, poetry, literary and art interviews, and translations. We like work that falls between existing genres and has social or political consciousness." Send IRC or $3 cash. Must be previously unpublished in English (world). Pays 2 copies and $10 (US)/printed page. "Send your most daring and original work. At *Frank*, we like work that is not too parochial or insular, however, don't try to write for a 'French' market." Sample copy $10 (US/air mail included), $38 for 4 issues; guidelines available upon request. Subscriptions, inquiries, and an online edition of *Frank* available at http://www.paris-anglo.com.

FRONTIERS: A Journal of Women Studies, (II), Washington State University, Frontiers, Women's Studies, Box 644007, Pullman WA 99164-4007. E-mail: frontier@wsu.edu. **Editor:** Sue Armitage. Magazine: 6×9; 200 pages; photos. "Women studies; academic articles in all disciplines; criticism; exceptional creative work (art, short fiction, photography, poetry)."
Needs: Feminist, lesbian. Receives 15 unsolicited mss/month. Accepts 7-12 mss/issue. Publishes ms 6-12 months after acceptance. Publishes 10 new writers/year.
How to Contact: Send 3 copies of complete ms with cover letter. Reports in 1 month on queries; 3-6 months on mss. SASE. Writer's guidelines for #10 SASE. Sample copy for $9.
Payment/Terms: Pays 2 contributor's copies. Acquires first North American serial rights.
Advice: "We are a *feminist* journal. *Frontiers* aims to make scholarship in women studies, and *exceptional* creative work, accessible to a cross-disciplinary audience inside and outside academia. Read short fiction in *Frontiers* before submitting."

☑ $ **FUGUE, Literary Digest of the University of Idaho, (I)**, English Dept., Rm. 200, Brink Hall, University of Idaho, Moscow ID 83844-1102. (208)885-6156. Fax: (208)885-5944. E-mail: witt931@novell.uidaho.edu. Website: http://www.uidaho.edu/LS/Eng/Fugue (includes writer's guidelines, names of editors, short fiction). Managing Editor: Ryan Witt. Editors change frequently. Send to Executive Editor. Magazine: 6×9; 60-100 pages; 20 lb. stock paper. "We are interested in all classifications of fiction—we are not interested in pretentious 'literary' stylizations. We expect stories to be written in a manner engaging for anyone, not just academics and literati. If we could put together an 'ideal' issue, we would probably have 6 or 7 pieces of fiction,

each of which would run no more than 10 pages (printed—probably 15 or 16 manuscript pages), a modest essay, and maybe 10 or a dozen poems. The fiction would include a couple of solid 'mainstream/literaty' stories, at least one 'regional/local' story (preferably by a writer from the inland Northwest), at least one story by an ethnic writer (Chicano, Native American, Asian-American, African-American), at least one story that had some sort of international or cosmopolitan angle (set, perhaps, in Hong Kong or Quito and written by someone who really knew what he or she was doing), and at least one story that would be 'experimental' (including postmodernism, fantasy, surrealism . . .). Wit and humor are always welcome." Semiannually. Estab. 1990. Circ. 300.
Needs: Adventure, ethnic/multicultural, experimental, fantasy, historical, humor/satire, literary, mainstream/contemporary, regional. "We're looking for good ethnic fiction by ethnic writers; work with a cosmopolitan/international flavor from writers who know what they're doing; and intelligent and sophisticated mainstream and postmodern work." Does not want to see Dungeons & Dragons, Sword & Sorcery, Harlequin, "Cowboy Adventure Stories," True Confessions, etc. Receives 80 unsolicited mss/month. Accepts 4-8 mss/issue; 8-16 mss/year. Publishes ms 1 year after acceptance. Recently published work by Ed McClanahan and Raymond Federman. Publishes 6-7 new writers/year. Length: 3,000 words average; 50 words minimum; 6,000 words maximum. Publishes short shorts. Also publishes literary essays and poetry. Sometimes critiques or comments on rejected mss.
How to Contact: Send complete ms with cover letter. "Obtain guidelines first." Include estimated word count and list of publications. Report in 2 weeks on queries; 2-3 months on mss. SASE for a reply to a query or return of ms. No simultaneous submissions. Sample copy for $5. Fiction guidelines for #10 SASE.
Payment/Terms: Pays $5-20 on publication for first North American serial rights. All contributors receive a copy; extra copies available at a discount.
Advice: Looks for "competent writing, clarity and consideration for the reader; also stylistic flair/energy. Here are what we consider the characteristics of a 'good' story: Distinct voice. The quality of strangeness; engaging, dynamic characters; engaging language, style, craftsmanship; emotional resonance ('snap'); and an un-put-down-ability. Be original and inventive. Take chances, but present your work as a professional. Proper manuscript format is essential."

A GATHERING OF THE TRIBES, (II), A Gathering of the Tribes, Inc., P.O. Box 20693, Tompkins Square Station, New York NY 10009. (212)674-3778. Fax: (212)674-5576. E-mail: info@tribes.org. Website: http://www.tribes.org (includes highlights from previous 7 issues, mission statement, events). **Editor:** Steve Cannon. Magazine: 8×10; 100-200 pages; glossy paper and cover; illustrations and photos. A "multicultural and multigenerational publication featuring poetry, fiction, interviews, essays, visual art, musical scores. Audience is anyone interested in the arts from a diverse perspective." Estab. 1992. Circ. 2,000-3,000.
Needs: Erotica, ethnic/multicultural, experimental, fantasy (science), feminist, gay, historical, horror, humor/satire, lesbian, literary, mainstream/contemporary, romance (futuristic/time travel, gothic), science fiction (soft/sociological), senior citizen/retirement, translations. "Would like to see more satire/humor. We are open to all; just no poor writing/grammar/syntax." List of upcoming themes available for SASE. Receives 300 unsolicited mss/month. Publishes ms 3-6 months after acceptance. Published work of Carl Watson and Hanif Kureishi. 60-70% of fiction by new writers. Length: 500 words average; 200 words minimum; 2,500 maximum. Publishes short shorts. Also publishes literary essays, literary criticism and poetry.
How to Contact: Send complete ms with a cover letter. Include estimated word count, half-page bio, list of publications, phone and fax numbers and address with submission. Send SASE for reply, return of ms or send a disposable copy of ms. Simultaneous and reprint submissions OK. Sample copy for $10. Reviews novels and short story collections.
Payment/Terms: Pays 1 contributor's copy; additional copies $12-50. Sponsors contests, awards or grants for fiction writers. "Watch for ads in *Poets & Writers* and *American Poetry Review.*"
Advice: Looks for "unique tone and style, offbeat plots and characters, and ethnic and regional work. Type manuscript well: readable font (serif) and no typos. Make characters and their dialogue interesting. Experiment with style, and don't be conventional. Do not send dragged-out, self-indulgent philosophizing of life and the universe. Get specific. Make your characters soar!"

🍁 ☑ **$ GEIST, The Canadian Magazine of Ideas and Culture, (II)**, The Geist Foundation, 103-1014 Homer St., Vancouver, British Columbia V6B 2W9 Canada. (604)681-9161. Fax: (604)669-8250. E-mail: geist@geist.com. Website: http://www.geist.com (includes guidelines, names of editors, short fiction, issue previews). **Editor:** Barbara Zatyko. Magazine: 8×10½; illustrations and photographs. "*Geist Magazine* is particularly interested in writing that blurs the boundary between fiction and nonfiction. Each issue and most of the writing in *Geist* explores the physical and mental landscape of Canada." Quarterly. Estab. 1990. Circ. 5,000.
Needs: Condensed/excerpted novel, literary. Receives 25 unsolicited mss/month. Accepts 10 mss/issue; 40 mss/year. Publishes ms 2-12 weeks after acceptance. Recently published work by Austin Clarke, Ronald Wright and Lisa Moore. Publishes 20 new writers/year. Length: 200 words minimum; 5,000 words maximum. Publishes short shorts.
How to Contact: Send complete ms with a cover letter. Accepts queries/mss by e-mail. Include estimated word count and 1-2 line bio. Reports in 1 week on queries; 1-2 months on mss. Send SASE for reply, return of ms or send a disposable copy of ms. Reprint submissions OK. Fiction guidelines for SASE. Reviews novels and short story collections. Send books to Shannon Emmerson.

Payment/Terms: Pays $50-250 on publication and 8 contributor's copies; additional copies for $2. Acquires first rights. Send a SASE requesting contest guidelines.
Advice: "Each issue of Geist is a meditation on the imaginary country that we inhabit. Often that imaginary country has something to do with some part of Canada."

☑ $ **GEORGE & MERTIE'S PLACE: ROOMS WITH A VIEW, (II, III)**, Dick Diver Enterprises, P.O. Box 10335, Spokane WA 99209. (509)325-3738. **Editors:** Thomas & Mertie Duncan. Magazine: 8½×11; 4-8 pages; heavy stock, colored paper; illustrations. "We want well-written fiction and poetry, political and philosophical debate, humor, satire and jeremiad. Our audience will be literate Americans who like to read and to be challenged to think. They will enjoy the use of language." Monthly. Estab. 1995. Circ. 50.
Needs: Anything well written. Receives 20-30 unsolicited mss/month. Accepts 1-2 mss/issue; 10-15 mss/year. "We work 3 months ahead." Recently published work by John Taylor and Jeff Grimshaw. Length: 1,000 words average; 1 word minimum; 2,500 words maximum. Publishes short shorts. Also publishes literary essays, literary criticism, poetry. Comments on most rejected mss.
How to Contact: Send complete ms with a cover letter. Include estimated word count, very brief bio and a comment on the work itself, its gestation. Reports in 1-2 months. Send SASE for reply, return of ms or send a disposable copy of ms. No simultaneous submissions. Sample copy for $2 and SASE. Fiction guidelines for SASE.
Payment/Terms: Pays 1¢/word, at publication and 1 contributor's copy; additional copies for $1.50. Acquires first North American serial rights and republication in GMP anthology. Not copyrighted. Each issue has a possible $25 "best of issue" prize. Published work automatically entered.
Advice: "We look for character in the work and in the writer's persona. Don't be a workshop writer. It stands out like a sore proboscis."

☑ **GEORGETOWN REVIEW, (II)**, P.O. Box 6309, Southern Station, Hattiesburg MS 39406-6309. Phone/fax: (601)582-8677. E-mail: gr@georgetownreview.com. Website: http://www.georgetownreview.com (includes masthead, short fiction, poetry, guidelines). Editor: Steve Conti. **Fiction Editor:** Victoria Lancelotta. Magazine: 5½×8½; 150-200 pages; smooth offset paper; 10 pt. CS1 cover. "We want to publish quality fiction and poetry." Published twice a year. Estab. 1993. Circ. 1,000.
Needs: Condensed/excerpted novel, ethnic/multicultural, experimental, feminist, gay, humor/satire, lesbian, literary, science fiction. Wants to see more character-driven fiction. No romance, juvenile, fantasy or genre. Receives 150 mss/month. Does not read mss May through August. Agented fiction 10%. Recently published work by Claudia Mon Pere McIsaac, Caroline Langston and John Wallace. Length: 3,000 words average; 300 words minimum; 6,500 words maximum. Publishes short shorts. Length: 300 words. Also publishes poetry.
How to Contact: Send complete ms with a cover letter. Reports in 2-4 months on mss. SASE. Simultaneous and electronic submissions OK. Sample copy for $8. Guidelines free for SAE and 1 first-class stamp.
Payment/Terms: Pays 2 contributor's copies. Acquires first rights. Sends galleys to author.
Advice: "We simply look for quality work, no matter what the subject or style. Don't follow trends. Write with honesty and heart."

🏆 $ **THE GEORGIA REVIEW, (I, II)**, The University of Georgia, Athens GA 30602-9009. (706)542-3481. Website: http://www.uga.edu/~garev. **Editor-in-Chief:** Stanley W. Lindberg. Associate Editor: Stephen Corey. Assistant Editor: Janet Wondra. Journal: 7×10; 208 pages (average); 50 lb. woven old-style paper; 80 lb. cover stock; illustrations; photos. "*The Georgia Review* is a journal of arts and letters, featuring a blend of the best in contemporary thought and literature—essays, fiction, poetry, visual art and book reviews for the intelligent nonspecialist as well as the specialist reader. We seek material that appeals across disciplinary lines by drawing from a wide range of interests." Quarterly. Estab. 1947. Circ. 6,000.

- This magazine has an excellent reputation for publishing and was a finalist for the 1998 National Magazine Award in Fiction. The Georgia Review won that award in 1985.

Needs: Experimental and literary. "We're looking for the highest quality fiction—work that is capable of sustaining subsequent readings, not throw-away pulp magazine entertainment. Nothing that fits too easily into a 'category.' " Receives about 400 unsolicited fiction mss/month. Accepts 3-4 mss/issue; 12-15 mss/year. Does not read unsolicited mss in June, July or August. Would prefer *not* to see novel excerpts. Published work by Louise Erdrich, Sonia Gernes, Marjorie Sander, A.B. Paulson and Gary Cildner. Published new writers within the last year. Length: Open. Also publishes literary essays, literary criticism, poetry. Occasionally critiques rejected mss.
How to Contact: Send complete ms (one story) with SASE. No multiple submissions. Usually reports in 2-3 months. Sample copy for $6; guidelines for #10 SASE. Reviews short story collections.
Payment/Terms: Pays minimum $35/printed page on publication for first North American serial rights, 1 year complimentary subscription and 1 contributor's copy; reduced charge for additional copies. Sends galleys to author.

🏆 $ **THE GETTYSBURG REVIEW, (II)**, Gettysburg College, Gettysburg PA 17325. (717)337-6770. **Editor:** Peter Stitt. Assistant Editor: Jeff Mock. Magazine: 6¾×10; 170 pages; acid free paper; full color illustrations.

"Quality of writing is our only criterion; we publish fiction, poetry, and essays." Quarterly. Estab. 1988. Circ. 4,500.

- Work appearing in *The Gettysburg Review* has also been included in *Prize Stories: The O. Henry Awards*, the *Pushcart Prize* anthology, *Best American Poetry, New Stories from the South, Harper's*, and elsewhere. It is also the recipient of a Lila Wallace-Reader's Digest grant and NEA grants.

Needs: Contemporary, experimental, historical, humor/satire, literary, mainstream, regional and serialized novel. "We require that fiction be intelligent, and aesthetically written." Receives 200 mss/month. Accepts 4-6 mss/issue; 16-24 mss/year. Publishes ms within 1 year of acceptance. Published work by Robert Olen Butler, Joyce Carol Oates, Naeem Murr, Tom Perrotta, Jacoba Hood and Tom House. Length: 3,000 words average; 1,000 words minimum; 20,000 words maximum. Occasionally publishes short shorts. Also publishes literary essays, some literary criticism, poetry. Sometimes critiques rejected mss.

How to Contact: Send complete ms with cover letter September through May. Reports in 3-6 months. SASE. No simultaneous submissions. Sample copy for $7 (postage paid). Does not review books per se. "We do essay-reviews, treating several books around a central theme." Send review copies to editor.

Payment/Terms: Pays $25/printed page, subscription to magazine and contributor's copy on publication for first North American serial rights. Charge for extra copies.

Advice: "Reporting time can take more than three months. It is helpful to look at a sample copy of *The Gettysburg Review* to see what kinds of fiction we publish before submitting."

GINOSKO, (II, IV), (formerly Kenosis), P.O. Box 246, Fairfax CA 94978. (415)460-8436. **Editor:** Robert Cesaretti. Magazine: 4×6; 50-60 pages; standard paper; card cover; illustrations and photographs. Published "when material permits."

Needs: Experimental, literary, existential. Receives 20 unsolicited mss/month. Length: 30,000 words maximum. Publishes short shorts. Also publishes literary essays, poetry.

How to Contact: Send complete ms with a cover letter. Reports in 3 months on mss. SASE for return of ms. Simultaneous and reprint submissions OK.

Payment/Terms: Pays 1 contributor's copy. Acquires one-time rights.

Advice: "I am looking for a style that conveys spiritual hunger and depth yet avoids religiousity and convention. Motto: Between literary vision and spiritual realities."

THE GLASS CHERRY, A poetry magazine, (II), The Glass Cherry Press, 901 Europe Bay Rd., Ellison Bay WI 54210-9643. **Editor:** Judith Hirschmiller. Magazine: 5×7; 60 pages; high-tech laser paper; cover stock varies; illustrations and photos. "Our goal is to combine diversity with quality to promote good literature by a variety of writers. New writers are encouraged to submit." Quarterly. Estab. 1994. Circ. 500.

Needs: Condensed/excerpted novel, gay, historical, horror, lesbian, literary, mainstream/contemporary, science fiction, serialized novel, translations. We would like more translations, book reviews, plays and short fiction of personal glimpses (individual, unusual events of a personal nature). No pornography." Publishes special fiction issues or anthologies. Receives 6-12 unsolicited mss/month. Accepts 1-2 mss/issue; 4-8 mss/year. Publishes ms 1 year after acceptance. Recently published work by William Woodruff and Bill Embly. Publishes 3 previously unpublished writers/year. Length: 1,000 words maximum. Publishes short shorts. Also publishes literary essays, literary criticism and poetry. Critiques or comments on rejected ms "only if requested to do so by author."

How to Contact: Query first. Include short bio and list of publications with submission. Reports in 3 weeks on queries; 3 months on mss. SASE for reply. No simultaneous submissions. Sample copy for $5; back issue, $6. Fiction guidelines for #10 SASE. Reviews novels and short story collections.

Payment/Terms: Pays 1 contributor's copy. Acquires one-time rights.

Advice: "Work with good imagery—comfortable to read. A good piece of fiction is like talking with a person who tells it like it is without putting on airs—something you can relate to. Purchase a copy of the publication prior to submitting so you can see what they publish and if you want to be published by them."

$ GLIMMER TRAIN STORIES, (II), Glimmer Train Press, 710 SW Madison St., Suite 504, Portland OR 97205. (503)221-0837. Website: http://www.glimmertrain.com (includes writer's guidelines and a Q&A section for writers). **Editors:** Susan Burmeister-Brown and Linda Burmeister Davies. Magazine: 6¾×9¼; 160 pages; recycled, acid-free paper; 20 illustrations; 12 photographs. Quarterly. Estab. 1991. Circ. 21,000.

- The magazine also sponsors an annual short story contest for new writers and a very short fiction contest.

Needs: Literary. Receives 3,000 unsolicited mss/month. Accepts 10 mss/issue; 40 mss/year. Reads in January, April, July, October. Publishes ms 6-12 months after acceptance. Agented fiction 20%. Recently published work by Monica Wood, Judy Budnitz, Steven Polansky, Andre Dubus III, Peter Lefcourt and Susan Engberg. Publishes "about 8" new writers/year. Length: 1,200 words minimum; 8,000 words maximum.

How to Contact: Send complete ms with a cover letter. Include estimated word count. Reports in 3 months. Send SASE for return or send a disposable copy of ms (with stamped postcard or envelope for notification). Simultaneous submissions OK. Sample copy for $10. Fiction guidelines for #10 SASE.

Payment/Terms: Pays $500 and 10 contributor's copies on acceptance for first rights.

Advice: "If you're excited about a story you've written, send it to us! If you're not very excited about it, wait and send one that you are excited about. It's usually a good idea to do a lot of reading. This will often improve the quality of your own writing."

$ GRAIN, (II), Saskatchewan Writers' Guild, Box 1154, Regina, Saskatchewan S4P 3B4 Canada. Fax: (306)244-0255. E-mail: grain.mag@sk.sympatico.ca. Website: http://www.sasknet.com/corporate/skwriter (includes history, news, subscription and contest information). **Editor:** Elizabeth Philips. Literary magazine: 6×9; 128 pages; Chinook offset printing; chrome-coated stock; illustrations; some photos. "Fiction and poetry for people who enjoy high quality writing." Quarterly. Estab. 1973. Circ. 1,500.

• *Grain* ranked #49 on *Writer's Digest*'s Fiction 50 list of top markets for fiction writers.

Needs: Contemporary, experimental, literary, mainstream and prose poem. "No propaganda—only artistic/literary writing." No mss "that stay *within* the limits of conventions such as women's magazine type stories, science fiction; none that push a message." Receives 80 unsolicited fiction mss/month. Accepts 8-12 mss/issue; 32-48 mss/year. Length: "No more than 30 pages." Also publishes poetry and creative nonfiction. Occasionally critiques rejected mss.

How to Contact: Send complete ms with SASE (or IRC) and brief letter. Queries by e-mail OK. No simultaneous submissions. Reports within 4 months on mss. Publishes ms an average of 4 months after acceptance. Sample copy for $6.95 plus postage.

Payment/Terms: Pays $30-100 and 2 contributor's copies on publication for first Canadian serial rights. "We expect acknowledgment if the piece is republished elsewhere."

Advice: "Submit a story to us that will deepen the imaginative experience of our readers. *Grain* has established itself as a first-class magazine of serious fiction. We receive submissions from around the world. If Canada is a foreign country to you, we ask that you *do not* use U.S. postage stamps on your return envelope. If you live outside Canada and neglect the International Reply Coupons, we *will not* read or reply to your submission."

N GRANTA, The Magazine of New Writing, (II), 2-3 Hanover Yard, Noel Rd., London N1 8BE England. Phone: 0171 704 9776. Fax: 0171 704 0474. E-mail: editorial@grantamag.co.uk. **Editor:** Ian Jack. Magazine: paperback, 270 pages approx.; photos. "*Granta* magazine publishes fiction, reportage, biography and autobiography, history, travel and documentary photography. It rarely publishes 'writing about writing.' The realistic narrative—the story—is its primary form." Quarterly. Estab. 1979. Circ. 90,000.

Needs: Literary. "No fantasy, science fiction, romance, historical, occult or other 'genre' fiction." Themes decided as deadline approaches. Receives 100 unsolicited mss/month. Accepts 0-1 ms/issue; 1-2 mss/year. Percentage of agented fiction varies. Publishes 1-2 new writers/year. Length: open. Rarely critiques or comments on rejected ms.

How to Contact: Query first. Reports in 1 month on queries; 3 months on mss. Send SAE and IRCs for reply, return of ms or send a disposable copy of ms. Simultaneous submissions OK. Sample copy £7.99.

Payment/Terms: Pays 3 contributor's copies. Acquires variable rights. Sends galleys to author.

Advice: "We are looking for the best in realistic stories; originality of voice; without jargon, connivance or self-conscious 'performance'—writing that endures."

GRASSLANDS REVIEW, (I, II), P.O. Box 626, Berea OH 44017. (440)243-4842. E-mail: lkennelly@aol.com. Website: http://members.aol.com/GLReview/index.html (includes guidelines, contest information, sample text, table of contents for latest issue). **Editor:** Laura B. Kennelly. Magazine: 6×9; 80 pages. *Grasslands Review* prints creative writing of all types; poetry, fiction, essays for a general audience. "Designed as a place for new writers to publish." Semiannually. Estab. 1989. Circ. 300.

Needs: Contemporary, ethnic, experimental, fantasy, horror, humor/satire, literary, mystery/suspense, prose poem, regional, science fiction and western. Nothing pornographic or overtly political or religious. Accepts 5-8 mss/issue. Reads only in October and March. Publishes ms 6 months after acceptance. Published work by Yvonne Jackson, Patricia Valdata, Sara Perkins and Kathleen Driscoll. Publishes 3-5 new writers/year. Length: 100-3,500 words; 1,500 words average. Publishes short shorts (100-150 words). Also publishes poetry. Sometimes critiques rejected mss and recommends other markets.

How to Contact: Send complete ms in October or March *only* with cover letter. No simultaneous submissions. Reports on mss in 3 months. SASE. Sample copy for $4.

Payment/Terms: Pays in contributor's copies. Acquires one-time rights. Publication not copyrighted.

Advice: "A fresh approach, imagined by a reader for other readers, pleases our audience. We are looking for fiction which leaves a strong feeling or impression—or a new perspective on life. The *Review* began as an in-class exercise to allow experienced creative writing students to learn how a little magazine is produced. It now serves as an independent publication, attracting authors from as far away as the Ivory Coast, but its primary mission is to give unknown writers a start."

THE GREEN HILLS LITERARY LANTERN, (I, II), Published at North Central Missouri College and co-published by The North Central Missouri Writer's Guild, P.O. Box 375, Trenton MO 64683. (660)359-

CHECK THE CATEGORY INDEXES, located at the back of the book, for publishers interested in specific fiction subjects.

3948, ext. 324. E-mail: jsmith@ncmc.cc.mo.us. **Editors:** Jack Smith and Ken Reger. Fiction Editor: Sara King. Magazine: 5½×8½; 180-190 pages; good quality paper with glossy 4-color cover. "The mission of *GHLL* is to provide a literary market for quality fiction writers, both established and beginners, and to provide quality literature for readers from diverse backgrounds. We also see ourselves as a cultural resource for North Central Missouri. Our publication works to publish the highest quality fiction—dense, layered, subtle, and, at the same time, fiction which grabs the ordinary reader. We tend to publish traditional short stories, but we are open to experimental forms." Annually. Estab. 1990. Circ. 600.

• *The Green Hills Literary Lantern* received a Missouri Arts Council grant in 1998.

Needs: Ethnic/multicultural, experimental, feminist, humor/satire, literary, mainstream/contemporary and regional. "Fairly traditional short stories but we are open to experimental. Our main requirement is literary merit. Wants more quality fiction about rural culture." No adventure, crime, erotica, horror, inspirational, mystery/suspense, romance. Receives 30 unsolicited mss/month. Accepts 6-7 mss/issue. Publishes ms 6-12 months after acceptance. Recently published work by James Longstaff, Seteney Shami, Bruce Tallerman and Dika Lam. Publishes 0-1 new writer/year. Length: 3,000 words average; 5,000 words maximum. Publishes short shorts. Also publishes poetry. Sometimes critiques or comments on rejected mss.

How to Contact: Send complete ms with a cover letter. Include bio (50-100 words) with list of publications. Accepts queries (only) by e-mail. Reports in 3-4 months on mss. SASE for return of ms. Simultaneous submissions OK. Sample copy for $7 (includes envelope and postage).

Payment/Terms: Pays two contributor's copies. Acquires one-time rights. Sends galleys to author.

Advice: "We look for strong character development, substantive plot and theme, visual and forceful language within a multilayered story. Make sure your work has the flavor of life—a sense of reality. A good story, well-crafted, will eventually get published. Find the right market for it, and above all, don't give up. The cost of funding a literary magazine prevents us from publishing longer pieces (over 5,000 words), and it also means we have to reject some publishable fiction due to space limitation."

☑ **$ GREEN MOUNTAINS REVIEW, (II)**, Johnson State College, Box A-58, Johnson VT 05656. (802)635-1350. Editor-in-Chief: Neil Shepard. **Fiction Editor:** Tony Whedon. Magazine: digest-sized; 140-200 pages. Semiannually. Estab. 1975 (new series, 1987). Circ. 1,700.

• *Green Mountain Review* has received a Pushcart Prize and Editors Choice Award.

Needs: Adventure, contemporary, experimental, humor/satire, literary, mainstream, serialized/excerpted novel, translations. Receives 80 unsolicited mss/month. Accepts 6 mss/issue; 12 mss/year. Publishes ms 6-12 months after acceptance. Reads mss September 1 through May 1. Recently published work by Michael Darcher and Norberto Luis Romero. Publishes 0-4 new writers/year. Length: 25 pages maximum. Publishes short shorts. Also publishes literary criticism, poetry. Sometimes critiques rejected mss.

How to Contact: Send complete ms with cover letter. "Manuscripts will not be read and will be returned between May 1 and September 1." Reports in 1 month on queries; 3-6 months on mss. SASE. Simultaneous submissions OK (if advised). Sample copy for $5.

Payment/Terms: Pays contributor's copies, 1-year subscription and small honorarium, depending on grants. Acquires first North American serial rights. Rights revert to author upon request. Sends galleys to author upon request.

Advice: "We're looking for more rich, textured, original fiction with cross-cultural themes. The editors are open to a wide spectrum of styles and subject matter as is apparent from a look at the list of fiction writers who have published in its pages. One issue was devoted to Vermont fiction, and another issue filled with new writing from the People's Republic of China. The Fall/Winter 1999 issue will be devoted to literary ethnography."

GREEN'S MAGAZINE, Fiction for the Family, (I, II), Green's Educational Publications, Box 3236, Regina, Saskatchewan S4P 3H1 Canada. **Editor:** David Green. Magazine: 5¼×8½; 96 pages; 20 lb. bond paper; matte cover stock; line illustrations. Publishes "solid short fiction suitable for family reading." Quarterly. Estab. 1972.

Needs: Adventure, fantasy, humor/satire, literary, mainstream, mystery/suspense and science fiction. No erotic or sexually explicit fiction. Receives 20-30 mss/month. Accepts 10-12 mss/issue; 40-50 mss/year. Publishes ms within 3-6 months of acceptance. Agented fiction 2%. Recently published work by Myron Stein, Eugene Levin and Robert Redding. Publishes 10 new writers/year. Length: 2,500 words preferred; 1,500 words minimum; 4,000 words maximum. Also publishes poetry. Sometimes critiques rejected mss.

How to Contact: Send complete ms. "Cover letters welcome but not necessary." Reports in 2 months. SASE (or IRC). No simultaneous submissions. Sample copy for $5. Fiction guidelines for #10 SASE (IRC). Reviews novels and short story collections.

Payment/Terms: Pays in contributor's copies. Acquires first North American serial rights.

Advice: "No topic is taboo, but we avoid sexuality for its own sake, and dislike material that is needlessly explicit or obscene. We look for strongly written stories that explore their characters through a subtle blending of conflicts. Plots should be appropriate, rather than overly ingenious or reliant on some *deus ex machina*. It must be a compression of experience or thoughts, in a form that is both challenging and rewarding to the reader. We have no form rejection slip. If we cannot use a submission, we try to offer constructive criticism in our personal reply. Often, such effort is rewarded with reports from our writers that following our suggestions has led to placement of the story or poem elsewhere."

GREENSBORO REVIEW, (I, II), English Dept., 134 McIver Bldg., UNC Greensboro, P.O. Box 26170, Greensboro NC 27402-6170. (336)334-5459. E-mail: clarkj@fagan.uncg.edu. Website: http://www.uncg.edu/eng/mfa (includes writer's guidelines, literary awards guidelines, address, deadlines, subscription information). Editor: Jim Clark. **Fiction Editor:** Jill Martyn. Fiction editor changes each year. Send mss to the editor. Magazine: 6×9; approximately 152 pages; 60 lb. paper; 65 lb. cover. Literary magazine featuring fiction and poetry for readers interested in contemporary literature. Semiannually. Circ. 800.

- *Greensboro Review* won Pushcart Prizes in 1997 and 1998.

Needs: Contemporary and experimental. Accepts 6-8 mss/issue, 12-16 mss/year. Recently published work by Robert Morgan, George Singleton, Robert Olmstead, Ron McFarland and Ivy Goodman. Length: 7,500 words maximum.

How to Contact: Send complete ms with SASE. No simultaneous submissions. Unsolicited manuscripts must arrive by September 15 to be considered for the winter issue and by February 15 to be considered for the summer issue. Manuscripts arriving after those dates may be held for the next consideration. Reports in 2 months. Sample copy for $5.

Payment/Terms: Pays in contributor's copies. Acquires first North American serial rights.

Advice: "We want to see the best being written regardless of theme, subject or style. Recent stories from *The Greensboro Review* have been included in *The Best American Short Stories*, *Prize Stories: The O. Henry Awards*, *New Stories from the South* and *Pushcart Prize*, anthologies recognizing the finest short stories being published."

$ GULF COAST, A Journal of Literature & Fine Arts, (II), Dept. of English, University of Houston, Houston TX 77204-3012. (713)743-3223. Fax: (713)743-3215. **Fiction Editor:** Chris Haven. Editors change each year. Magazine: 6×9; 144 pages; stock paper, gloss cover; illustrations and photographs. "Innovative fiction for the literary-minded." Estab. 1984. Circ. 1,500.

- Work published in *Gulf Coast* has been selected for inclusion in the *Pushcart Prize* anthology and *Best American Short Stories*.

Needs: Contemporary, ethnic, experimental, literary, regional, translations. Wants more "cutting-edge, experimental" fiction. No children's, genre, religious/inspirational. Receives 150 unsolicited mss/month. Accepts 8-10 mss/issue; 16-20 mss/year. Publishes ms 6 months-1 year after acceptance. Agented fiction 5%. Published work by Diana Joseph, Karen Mary Penn, J. David Stevens, Darren Defrain, Brian Leung and Karla Kuban. Length: no limit. Publishes short shorts. Sometimes critiques rejected mss.

How to Contact: Send complete ms with brief cover letter. "List previous publications; please notify us if the submission is being considered elsewhere." Reports in 3-6 months. Simultaneous submissions OK. Back issue for $6, 7×10 SAE and 4 first-class stamps. Fiction guidelines for #10 SASE.

Payment/Terms: Pays contributor's copies and *small* honorarium for one-time rights.

Advice: "Rotating editorship, so please be patient with replies. As always, please send one story at a time."

GULF STREAM MAGAZINE, (II), Florida International University, English Dept., North Miami Campus, N. Miami FL 33181. (305)919-5599. **Editor:** Polly Roberts. Editors change every 1-2 years. Magazine: 5½×8½; 96 pages; recycled paper; 80 lb. glossy cover; cover illustrations. "We publish *good quality*—fiction, nonfiction and poetry for a predominately literary market." Semiannually. Estab. 1989. Circ. 500.

Needs: Contemporary, literary, mainstream. Nothing "radically experimental." Plans special issues. Receives 100 unsolicited mss/month. Accepts 5 mss/issue; 10 mss/year. Does not read mss during the summer. Publishes ms 3-6 months after acceptance. Published work by Christine Liotta, David Conway and Bonnie Zobell. Length: 5,000 words average; 7,500 words maximum. "Usually longer stories do not get accepted. There are exceptions, however." Publishes short shorts. Also publishes poetry. Sometimes critiques rejected mss.

How to Contact: Send complete manuscript with cover letter including list of previous publications and a short bio. Reports in 3 months. SASE. Simultaneous submissions OK "if noted." Sample copy for $4. Free fiction guidelines.

Payment/Terms: Pays in gift subscriptions and contributor's copies. Acquires first North American serial rights.

Advice: "Looks for good concise writing—well plotted with interesting characters."

HABERSHAM REVIEW, (I, II), Piedmont College, P.O. Box 10, Demorest GA 30535. (706)778-3000. **Editor:** Frank Gannon. Magazine. "General literary magazine with a regional (Southeastern U.S.) focus for a literate audience." Semiannually. Estab. 1991.

Needs: Contemporary, experimental, literary, mainstream, regional. Receives 100 unsolicited mss/month. Acquires 6-10 mss/issue. Published work by Janice Daugharty, James Kilgo, C.R. Crackel, Linda Hartford, Dixie Salazar, George Strange, Marshall Boswell, Steven Carter, Cynthia Morgan Dale and Pat Spears. Publishes 6 new writers/year. Publishes short shorts. Sometimes critiques rejected mss.

How to Contact: Send complete ms with cover letter. Accepts queries/mss by e-mail. Reports in 6 months on mss. SASE. No simultaneous submissions. Sample copy for $6.

Payment/Terms: Pays in contributor's copies. Acquires first rights.

Tips: "We look for fresh writing and technical skill. Keep working until you find your voice."

HALF TONES TO JUBILEE, (II), English Dept., Pensacola Junior College, 1000 College Blvd., Pensacola FL 32504. (904)484-1416. **Editor:** Walter Spara. Magazine: 6×9; approx. 100 pages; 70 lb. laid stock; 80 lb. cover. "No theme, all types published." Annually. Estab. 1985. Circ. 500.
Needs: Open. Accepts approx. 6 mss/issue. "We publish in September." Published work by Mark Spencer. Length: 1,500 words average. Publishes short shorts. Also publishes poetry.
How to Contact: Send complete ms with cover letter. SASE. Sample copy for $4. Free fiction guidelines.
Payment/Terms: Pays 1 contributor's copy. Acquires one-time rights.
Advice: "We are moving away from linear development; we are noted for innovation in style."

$ HAPPY, (I, II), The Happy Organization, 240 E. 35th St., 11A, New York NY 10016. (212)689-3142. Fax: (212)683-1169. E-mail: bayardx@aol.com. **Editor:** Bayard. Magazine: 5½×8; 100 pages; 60 lb. text paper; 150 lb. cover; perfect-bound; illustrations and photos. Quarterly. Estab. 1995. Circ. 500.

• *Happy* was ranked #16 in *Writer's Digest*'s Fiction 50 list of top markets for fiction writers.

Needs: Erotica, ethnic/multicultural, experimental, fantasy, feminist, gay, horror, humor/satire, lesbian, literary, psychic/supernatural/occult, science fiction. Receives 300-500 unsolicited mss/month. Accepts 25-30 mss/issue; 100-120 mss/year. 30-50% of work published is by new writers. Publishes ms 6-12 months after acceptance. Length: 1,000-3,500 words average; 6,000 words maximum. Publishes short shorts. Often critiques or comments on rejected mss.
How to Contact: Send complete ms with a cover letter. Include estimated word count. Accepts queries/mss by e-mail. Reports in 1 week on mss. Send SASE for reply, return of ms or send a disposable copy of ms. Simultaneous submissions OK. Sample copy for $9.
Payment/Terms: Pays $5/1,000 words, minimum $5 on publication and 1 contributor's copy for one-time rights.
Advice: "No more grumbling about what you should be—become what you intended!"

HAWAII REVIEW, (II), University of Hawaii English Dept., 1755 Pope Rd., Bldg. 31-D, Honolulu HI 96822. (808)956-3030. Fax: (808)956-9962. **Editor:** Jason Minami. Magazine: 6½×9½; 150-170 pages; illustrations; photos. "We publish short stories as well as poetry and reviews by new and experienced writers. As an international literary journal, we hope to reflect the idea that cultural diversity is of universal interest." For residents of Hawaii and non-residents from the continental US and abroad. Twice per year. Estab. 1972. Circ. 5,000.
Needs: Contemporary, ethnic, humor/satire, literary, prose poem, regional and translations. No genre fiction. Receives 50-75 mss/month. No more than 40 mss/issue; 130 mss/year. Recently published work by Mathew Cashion, Lee A. Tonouchi, Ron Carlson and Andrea Coruachio. Publishes 4 new writers/year. Length: 4,000 words average; no minimum; 8,000 words maximum. Occasionally critiques mss. Also publishes poetry.
How to Contact: Send complete ms with SASE. Reports in 3-4 months on mss. Sample copy for $10. Fiction guidelines for SASE.
Payment/Terms: Pays 4 contributor's copies.
Advice: "We select fiction based on excellent story, good sentence level writing, attention to detail, no overused story lines, no self-conscious narratives. We like story character development—characters the reader feels for—and a strong voice. Also well-crafted language that propels the eye forward."

HAYDEN'S FERRY REVIEW, (II), Box 871502, Arizona State University, Tempe AZ 85287-1502. (602)965-1243. Fax: (602)965-6704. E-mail: hfr@asu.edu. Website: http://news.vpsa.asu.edu/HFR/HFR.html. **Managing Editor:** Salima Keegan. Editors change every 1-2 years. Magazine: 6×9; 128 pages; fine paper; illustrations and photographs. "Contemporary material by new and established writers for a varied audience." Semiannually. Estab. 1986. Circ. 1,300.

• Work from *Hayden's Ferry Review* has been selected for inclusion in *Pushcart Prize* anthologies.

Needs: Contemporary, experimental, literary, prose poem, regional. Possible special fiction issue. Receives 250 unsolicited mss/month. Accepts 5 mss/issue; 10 mss/year. Publishes mss 3-4 months after acceptance. Published work by T.C. Boyle, Raymond Carver, Ken Kesey, Rita Dove, Chuck Rosenthal and Rick Bass. Length: No preference. Publishes short shorts. Also publishes literary essays.
How to Contact: Send complete ms with cover letter. Reports in 3-5 months from deadline on mss. SASE. Sample copy for $6. Fiction guidelines for SAE.
Payment/Terms: Pays 2 contributor's copies. Acquires first North American serial rights. Sends page proofs to author.

HEAVEN BONE, (II, IV), Heaven Bone Press, Box 486, Chester NY 10918. (914)469-9018. **Editors:** Steven Hirsch and Kirpal Gordon. Magazine: 8½×11; 96-116 pages; 60 lb. recycled offset paper; full color cover;

A BULLET INTRODUCES COMMENTS by the editor of *Novel & Short Story Writer's Market* indicating special information about the listing.

computer clip art, graphics, line art, cartoons, halftones and photos scanned in tiff format. "Expansive, fine surrealist and experimental literary, earth and nature, spiritual path. We use current reviews, essays on spiritual and esoteric topics, creative stories. Also: reviews of current poetry releases and expansive literature." Readers are "scholars, surrealists, poets, artists, musicians, students." Annually. Estab. 1987. Circ. 2,500.
Needs: Esoteric/scholarly, experimental, fantasy, psychic/supernatural/occult, regional, religious/inspirational, spiritual. "No violent, thoughtless or exploitive fiction." Receives 45-110 unsolicited mss/month. Accepts 5-15 mss/issue; 12-30 mss/year. Publishes ms 2 weeks-10 months after acceptance. Published work by Fielding Dawson, Janine Pommy Vega, Charles Bukowski and Marge Piercy. Published new writers within the last year. Length: 3,500 words average; 1,200 words minimum; 5,000 words maximum. Publishes short shorts. Also publishes literary essays, literary criticism, poetry. Sometimes critiques rejected mss.
How to Contact: Query first; send complete ms with cover letter. Include short bio of recent activities. Reports in 3 weeks on queries; 3-40 weeks on mss. Send SASE for reply or return of ms. Reprint submissions OK. Accepts electronic submissions via "Apple Mac versions of Macwrite, Microsoft Word or Writenow 3.0." Sample copy for $7. Fiction guidelines free. Reviews novels and short story collections.
Payment/Terms: Pays in contributor's copies; charges for extras. Acquires first North American serial rights. Sends galleys to author, if requested.
Advice: "Read a sample issue first. Our fiction needs are temperamental, so please query first before submitting. We prefer shorter fiction. Do not send first drafts to test them on us. Please refine and polish your work before sending. Always include SASE. We are looking for the unique, unusual and excellent."

$ HIGH PLAINS LITERARY REVIEW, (II), 180 Adams St., Suite 250, Denver CO 80206. (303)320-6828. Fax: (303)320-6828. **Editor-in-Chief:** Robert O. Greer, Jr. Magazine: 6×9; 135 pages; 70 lb. paper; heavy cover stock. "The *High Plains Literary Review* publishes poetry, fiction, essays, book reviews and interviews. The publication is designed to bridge the gap between high-caliber academic quarterlies and successful commercial reviews." Triannually. Estab. 1986. Circ. 1,100.
Needs: Most pressing need: outstanding essays, serious fiction, contemporary, humor/satire, literary, mainstream, regional. No true confessions, romance, pornographic, excessive violence. Receives approximately 400 unsolicited mss/month. Accepts 4-6 mss/issue; 12-18 mss/year. Publishes ms usually 6 months after acceptance. Recently published work by Michael Martone, Naton Leslie, Tony Ardizzone and Paula L. Woods. Published new writers within the last year. Length: 4,200 words average; 1,500 words minimum; 8,000 words maximum; prefers 3,000-6,000 words. Also publishes literary essays, literary criticism, poetry. Occasionally critiques rejected mss.
How to Contact: Send complete ms with cover letter. Include brief publishing history. Reports in 4 months. Send SASE for reply or return of ms. Simultaneous submissions OK. Sample copy for $4.
Payment/Terms: Pays $5/page for prose and 2 contributor's copies on publication for first North American serial rights. "Copyright reverts to author upon publication." Sends copy-edited proofs to the author.
Advice: "*HPLR* publishes *quality* writing. Send us your very best material. We will read it carefully and either accept it promptly, recommend changes or return it promptly. Do not start submitting your work until you learn the basic tenets of the game including some general knowledge about how to develop characters and plot and how to submit a manuscript. I think the most important thing for any new writer interested in the short story form is to have a voracious appetite for short fiction, to see who and what is being published, and to develop a personal style."

HILL AND HOLLER: Southern Appalachian Mountains, (II, IV), Seven Buffaloes Press, P.O. Box 249, Big Timber MT 59011. **Editor:** Art Cuelho. Magazine: 5½×8½; 80 pages; 70 lb. offset paper; 80 lb. cover stock; illustrations; photos rarely. "I use mostly rural Appalachian material: poems and stories, and some folklore and humor. I am interested in heritage, especially in connection with the farm." Annually. Published special fiction issue. Estab. 1983. Circ. 750.
Needs: Contemporary, ethnic, humor/satire, literary, regional, rural America farm. "I don't have any prejudices in style, but I don't like sentimental slant. Deep feelings in literature are fine, but they should be portrayed with tact and skill." Receives 10 unsolicited mss/month. Accepts 4-6 mss/issue. Publishes ms 6 months-1 year after acceptance. Length: 2,000-3,000 words average. Also publishes short shorts of 500-1,000 words.
How to Contact: Query first. Reports in 1 month on queries. SASE. Sample copy for $6.75.
Payment/Terms: Pays in contributor's copies. Acquires first North American serial rights "and permission to reprint if my press publishes a special anthology." Sometimes sends galleys to author.
Advice: "In this Southern Appalachian rural series I can be optimistic about fiction. Appalachians are very responsive to their region's literature. I have taken work by beginners that had not been previously published. Be sure to send a double-spaced clean manuscript and SASE. I have the only rural press in North America; maybe even in the world. So perhaps we have a bond in common if your roots are rural."

HOME PLANET NEWS, (II), Home Planet Publications, P. O. Box 415, New York NY 10009. (718)769-2854. **Co-editors:** Enid Dame and Donald Lev. Tabloid: 11½×16; 24 pages; newsprint; illustrations; photos. "*Home Planet News* publishes mainly poetry along with some fiction, as well as reviews (books, theater and art), and articles of literary interest. We see *HPN* as a quality literary journal in an eminently readable format and with content that is urban, urbane and politically aware." Triannually. Estab. 1979. Circ. 1,000.

- *HPN* has received a small grant from the Puffin Foundation for its focus on AIDS issues.

Needs: Ethnic/multicultural, experimental, feminist, gay, historical, lesbian, literary, mainstream/contemporary, science fiction (soft/sociological). No "children's or genre stories (except rarely some science fiction)." Upcoming themes: "Midrash." Publishes special fiction issue or anthology. Receives 12 mss/month. Accepts 1 ms/issue; 3 mss/year. Reads fiction mss only from February to May. Publishes 1 year after acceptance. Published work by Maureen McNeil, Eugene Stein, B.Z. Niditch and Layle Silbert. Length: 2,000 words average; 500 words minimum; 2,500 words maximum. Publishes short shorts. Also publishes literary criticism, poetry.
How to Contact: Send complete ms with a cover letter. Reports in 3-6 months on mss. Send SASE for reply, return of ms or send a disposable copy of the ms. Sample copy for $3. Fiction guidelines for SASE.
Payment/Terms: Pays 3 contributor's copies; additional copies $1. Acquires one-time rights.
Advice: "We use very little fiction, and a story we accept just has to grab us. We need short pieces of some complexity, stories about complex people facing situations which resist simple resolutions."

🌐 **HORIZON**, Stationsstraat 232A, 1770 Liedekerke Belgium. **Fiction Editor:** Johnny Haelterman. Annually. Circ. 720. Publishes several stories/issue.
Needs: "*Horizon* is a cultural magazine for a general public, therefore fiction should be suitable for a general public." Recently published Louis Friedman, Marco Knauff, Geoff Jackson and Jim Miller. Length: 300 words minimum; 7,500 words maximum. "A realistic treatment is preferred but a touch of fantasy is sometimes acceptable. No extreme violence or sex."
How to Contact: Enclose money or IRCs if you want your work back. "Submitting outside your country is mainly the same as in your own country, except that the postage costs are higher."
Payment/Terms: Payment in Belgian funds for original fiction in Dutch only. No payment for fiction in other languages but the writers receive two copies in that case. English fiction can be translated into Dutch without payment (two copies). Sample copy available for $10 (US).
Advice: "Puns are usually not translatable, so avoid writing stories with an essential part based on puns if you want your work to be translated."

🌐 **$ HU (THE HONEST ULSTERMAN)**, 49 Main St., Greyabbey BT22 2NF, Northern Ireland. **Fiction Editor:** Tom Clyde. 3 times/year. Circ. 1,000. Publishes 1-4 stories/issue. "Northern Ireland's premier literary magazine. Prime focus is poetry, but continues to publish prose (story, novel extract). 3,000 words maximum. "Must include sufficient means of return (IRCs, etc.). If we decide to publish, an IBM-type floppy disk version would be very helpful." Writers receive small payment and two contributor's copies. For 4 issues send UK £14 airmail or sample issue US $7. "Contributors are strongly advised to read the magazine before submitting anything."

HUCKLEBERRY PRESS, (II), Huckleberry Press Publishers, 2625 Alcatraz Ave., Suite 268, Berkeley CA 94705-2702. (510)268-9252. **Editor:** Melanie Booth. Magazine: 5½×8½; 90 pages; 40 lb. bond paper; card stock cover; illustrations and photographs. "*Huckleberry Press* strives to promote creative individual talents that have not yet been discovered, silenced, mass-marketed who speak with a distinctly literate and contemporary voice." Semiannually. Estab. 1996. Circ. 500.
Needs: Humor/satire, literary, mainstream/contemporary, regional. Wants to see more linear fiction—take us somewhere physically, ideologically or otherwise. No science fiction, horror, erotica, juvenile. Receives over 200 unsolicited mss/month. Accepts 4-6 mss/issue; 8-12 mss/year. Publishes ms 2-8 months after acceptance. Agented fiction 5%. Recently published work by Tom Hazuka, Leonard Cuang and Gwendollen Gross. Publishes 10 new writers/year. Length: 3,500 words average; 1,000 words minimum; 6,000 words maximum. Also publishes literary essays, poetry. Sometimes critiques or comments on rejected mss.
How to Contact: Send complete ms with a cover letter. Send SASE for guidelines. Include estimated word count and 50-word bio. Reports 2 weeks on queries; 2 months on mss. SASE. Simultaneous submissions OK. Sample copy for $4 and 9×6 SAE with 5 first-class stamps. Fiction guidelines for #10 SASE.
Payment/Terms: Pays 2 contributor's copies on publication; additional copies for $3. Acquires first North American serial rights.
Advice: "Don't try to distract the reader with concerts and techniques. Write with purpose. We want direct and uncompromising, literate writing."

☑ **THE HUDSON REVIEW, (II)**, 684 Park Ave., New York NY 10021. (212)650-0020. Fax: (212)774-1911. **Editor:** Paula Deitz. Magazine: 4½×7½; 176 pages; 50 Basis Miami book vellum paper; 65 Basis Torchglow cover. "*The Hudson Review* is a sourcebook of American culture that explores the current trends in literature and the arts. Each issue features poetry and fiction, essays on literary and cultural topics, book reviews, reports from abroad, and chronicles covering recent developments in film, theater, dance, music and art. We encourage and publish new writing in order to bring the creative imagination of today to a varied, responsive audience." Quarterly. Estab. 1948. Circ. 4,500. "Writers who wish to send unsolicited mss outside the normal reading period (June 1 to November 30) must have a subscription."
Needs: Literary. Receives 375 unsolicited mss/month. Accepts 1-2 mss/issue; 4-8 mss/year. Does not read from December 1 through May 31 (except for subscribers). Recently published work by Gary Krist, Barbara Haas and Joseph Epstein. Length: 8,000 words average; 10,000 words maximum. Also publishes literary essays, literary criticism and poetry.

How to Contact: Send complete ms with a cover letter. Include estimated word count. Reports in 6 weeks on queries; 12 weeks on mss. Send SASE for reply, return of ms or send disposable copy of ms. No simultaneous submissions. Sample copy for $8. Fiction guidelines free. Reviews novels and short story collections. Send book to editor.
Payment/Terms: Pays 2 contributor's copies; additional copies $3.50. Sends galleys to author.
Advice: "We do not specialize in publishing any particular 'type' of writing; our sole criterion for accepting unsolicited work is literary quality. The best way for you to get an idea of the range of work we publish is to read a current issue."

THE HUNTED NEWS, (I, II), The Subourban Press, P.O. Box 9101, Warwick RI 02889. (401)826-7307. **Editor:** Mike Wood. Magazine: 8½×11; 30-35 pages; photocopied paper. "I am looking for good writers in the hope that I can help their voices be heard. Like most in the small press scene, I just wanted to create another option for writers who otherwise might not be heard." Annually. Estab. 1991. Circ. 200.
Needs: Experimental, historical, horror, literary, mainstream/contemporary, regional, religious/inspirational, translations. "No self-impressed work, shock or experimentation for its own sake." Would like to see more religious/spiritual fiction. Receives 50-60 unsolicited mss/month. Acquires 3 mss/issue. Publishes ms within 3-4 months after acceptance. Published work by Alfred Schwaid, Steve Richmond, Darryl Smyers and Charles Bukowski. Publishes 10 new writers/year. Length: 700 words maximum. Publishes short shorts. Also publishes literary essays, literary criticism and poetry. Often critiques or comments on rejected mss.
How to Contact: Send complete ms with cover letter. Reports in 1 month. Send SASE for return of ms. Simultaneous and reprint submissions OK. Sample copy for 8½×11 SAE and 3 first-class stamps. Fiction guidelines free. Reviews novels or short story collections.
Payment/Terms: Pays 3-5 contributor's copies. Acquires one-time rights.
Advice: "I look for an obvious love of language and a sense that there is something at stake in the story, a story that somehow needs to be told. Write what you need to write, say what you think you need to say, no matter the subject, and take a chance and send it to me. A writer will always find an audience if the work is true."

☑ **THE ICONOCLAST, (II)**, 1675 Amazon Rd., Mohegan Lake NY 10547-1804. **Editor:** Phil Wagner. Journal. 8½×5½; 32-40 pages; 20 lb. white paper; 50 lb. cover stock; illustrations. "*The Iconoclast* is a self-supporting, independent, unaffiliated general interest magazine with an appreciation of the profound, absurd and joyful in life. Material is limited only by *its* quality and *our* space. We want readers and writers who are open-minded, unafraid to think, and actively engaged with the world." Published 8 times/year. Estab. 1992. Circ. 500-2,000 (special issues).

- *The Iconoclast* has grown from a 16-page newsletter to a 32-40-page journal and is, subsequently, buying more fiction.

Needs: Adventure, ethnic/multicultural, humor/satire, literary, mainstream/contemporary, science fiction. Wants to see more "literary fiction with plots." "Nothing militant, solipsistic, or silly." Receives 100 unsolicited mss/month. Accepts 3-6 mss/issue; 25-30 mss/year. Publishes ms 6-9 months after acceptance. Recently published work by Michael McIrvin, Bayard and Anthony W. Deannuntis. Publishes 8-10 new writers/year. Length: 2,000-2,500 words preferred; 100 words minimum; occasionally longer. Publishes short shorts. Also publishes essays, poetry. Sometimes critiques or comments on rejected mss.
How to Contact: Send complete ms. Reports in 1 month. Send SASE for reply, return of ms or send a disposable copy of the ms labeled as such. Sample copy for $2. Reviews novels and short story collections.
Payment/Terms: Pays 1-2 contributor's copies; additional copies $1.20 (40% discount). Acquires one-time rights.
Advice: "We like fiction that has something to say (and not about its author). We hope for work that is observant, intense and multi-leveled. Follow Pound's advice—'make it new.' Write what you want in whatever style you want without being gross, sensational, or needlessly explicit—then pray there's someone who can appreciate your sensibility. Read good fiction. It's as fundamental as learning how to hit, throw and catch is to baseball. With the increasing American disinclination towards literature, stories must insist on being heard. Read what is being published—then write something better—and different. Do all rewrites before sending a story out. Few editors have time to work with writers on promising stories; only polished."

THE IDIOT, (II), Anarchaos Press, 1706 S. Bedford St., Los Angeles CA 90035. **Editor:** Sam Hayes. Magazine: 5½×8½; 48 pages; 20 lb. white paper; glossy cardboard cover; illustrations. "For people who enjoy TV shows such as 'The Simpsons' and 'Mystery Science Theater 3000' as well as those who like Woody Allen and S.J. Perelman. We're looking for black comedy to make our audience (mostly bitter misanthropes) laugh. I've had letters from engineers to teenagers saying they loved it, so you have to be both funny and weird and sophisticated all at once." Annually. Estab. 1993. Circ. 250-300.
Needs: Humor/satire. Publishes ms 4-8 months after acceptance. Recently published work by Joe Deasy, Mark Lafferty, John Kearns and Margaret Magee. Publishes 6-10 new writers/year. Length: 1,500 words average; 2,500 words maximum. Publishes short shorts. Also publishes poetry. Sometimes critiques or comments on rejected mss.
How to Contact: Send complete ms with a cover letter. Include estimated word count and bio (30-50 words). Reports in 1 month on queries; 3 months on mss. Send SASE for reply, return of ms or send a disposable copy

of ms. Simultaneous, reprint and electronic submissions OK. Sample copy for $5.
Payment/Terms: Pays 1-2 contributor's copies. Acquires one-time rights. Sometimes sends galleys to author.
Advice: "Do not send anything if it isn't hilarious. If I don't laugh out loud by the second page I stop reading. It must be consistently funny—most submissions are merely 'cute.' Also, read the magazine to see what we're doing."

☑ **$ IMAGE, A Journal of the Arts & Religion, (II)**, The Center for Religious Humanism, 323 S. Broad St., P.O. Box 674, Kennett Square PA 19348. Phone/fax: (302)652-8279. E-mail: gwolfe@compuserve.com. Website: http://www.imagejournal.com. **Editor:** Greg Wolfe. Magazine: 7×10; 140 pages; glossy cover stock; illustrations and photos. "*Image* is a showcase for the encounter between religious faith and world-class contemporary art. Each issue features fiction, poetry, essays, memoirs, an in-depth interview and articles about visual artists, film, music, etc. and glossy 4-color plates of contemporary visual art." Quarterly. Estab. 1989. Circ. 3,000. Member CLMP.
Needs: Literary, humor/satire, regional, religious, translations. Receives 60 unsolicited mss/month. Accepts 2 mss/issue; 8 mss/year. Publishes ms within 1 year after acceptance. Agented fiction 5%. Recently published work by Madison Smartt Bell, Tim Winton, Wally Lamb, Jon Hassler, Ron Hansen, Denise Giardina and Doris Betts. Length: 5,000 words average; 2,000 words minimum; 8,000 words maximum. Also publishes literary essays and poetry.
How to Contact: Send complete ms with a cover letter. Include bio. Reports in 1 month on queries; 3 months on mss. Send SASE for reply, return of ms or send a disposable copy of ms. No electronic submissions OK. Sample copy for $10. Reviews novels and short story collections.
Payment/Terms: Pays $100 maximum and 4 contributor's copies on publication; additional copies for $5. Sends galleys to author.
Advice: "Fiction must grapple with religious faith, though the settings and subjects need not be overtly religious."

N 🌐 **$ IMAGO**, School of Media & Journalism, QUT, GPO Box 2434, Brisbane 4001 Australia. **Contact:** Dr. Philip Neilsen or Helen Horton. Published 3 times/year. Circ. 750. 30-50% fiction. *Imago* is a literary magazine publishing short stories, poetry, articles, interviews and book reviews.
Needs: "While content of articles and interviews should have some relevance either to Queensland or to writing, stories and poems may be on any subject. The main requirement is good writing." Length: 1,000 words minimum; 3,000 words maximum; 2,000 words preferred.
How to Contact: "Contributions should be typed double-spaced on one side of the paper, each page bearing the title, page number and author's name. Name and address of the writer should appear on a cover page of longer mss, or on the back, or bottom, of single page submissions. A SAE and IRCs with sufficient postage to cover the contents should be sent for the return of ms or for notification of acceptance or rejection. No responsibility is assumed for the loss of or damage to unsolicited manuscripts." Sample copy available for $A9. Guidelines, as above, available on request.
Payment/Terms: Pays on publication in accordance with Australia Council rates: short stories, $A90 minimum; articles, $A90 minimum; poems $A40; reviews, $A60. Also provides contributor's copy.

IN THE SPIRIT OF THE BUFFALO, A Literary Magazine (I), In the Spirit of the Buffalo, 1540 S.W. 14th St., Lincoln NE 68522. (402)476-0656. Fax: (402)464-1604. E-mail: buffalo369@aol.com. Website: http://www.opportunityassistance.com/mediamenagerie (includes guidelines, name of editor, poetry and short fiction). **Editor:** Mark A. Reece. Newsletter: 5½×8½; saddle stapled; photocopied; illustrations and photos. "*ITSOTB* is designed to be a positive influence for social awareness and change through creative personal expression. We publish poetry, short fiction, essays, cartoons, puzzles and artwork targeted toward adults who enjoy self-expression." Quarterly. Estab. 1996. Circ. 100-200.
Needs: Adventure, fantasy, historical, horror, humor/satire, literary, regional, science fiction (soft/sociological), westerns. "Would like to see more science fiction, westerns. "No erotica or sword and sorcery." Receives 4-5 unsolicited mss/month. Accepts 2-3 mss/issue; 8 mss/year. Publishes ms within 6 months after acceptance. Recently published work by Ralph H. Allen, Jr., O.M. Dicas and Lu Motley. Publishes 4-6 new writers/year. Length: 800 words average; no minimum; 1,000 words maximum. Publishes short shorts. Also publishes literary essays and poetry. Sometimes comments on rejected mss.
How to Contact: Send complete ms with a short cover letter or send e-mail. Reports in 3 months on mss. SASE for return of ms. Reprints and electronic submissions (e-mail) preferred. Sample copy and guidelines $3. Guidelines for #10 SASE.
Payment/Terms: Pays 1 contributor's copy on publication; additional copies for $1. Acquires one-time rights.
Advice: "Have a subtle lesson or moral that makes the story worth reading. Keep the work under 1,000 words and proofread. The story should have a purpose. I haven't seen enough short shorts. We prefer e-mail submissions because of the ease of typesetting. Use standard fonts so the document can be read by OCR software."

$ INDIANA REVIEW, (I, II), 465 Ballantine, Bloomington IN 47405. (812)855-3439. **Fiction Editor:** Laura McCoid. Editors change every 2 years. Magazine: 6×9; 200 pages; 50 lb. paper; Glatfelter cover stock. *Indiana Review* looks for daring stories which integrate theme, language, character and form. We like polished writing, humor, and fiction which has consequence beyond the world of its narrator. Semiannually. Estab. 1976. Circ. 3,000.

- *Indiana Review* won the 1996 American Literary Magazine Award. Work published in *Indiana Review* was selected for inclusion in the *O. Henry Prize Stories* anthology. This publication ranked #35 on *Writer's Digest*'s Fiction 50 list of top markets for fiction writers.

Needs: Ethnic, literary, regional, translations. Also considers novel excerpts. Receives 300 unsolicited mss each month. Accepts 7-9 prose mss/issue. Published work by Jason Brown, Dan Chaon and Lisa Glatt. Length: 1-35 magazine pages. Also publishes literary essays, poetry and reviews.

How to Contact: Send complete ms with cover letter. Cover letters should be *brief* and demonstrate specific familiarity with the content of a recent issue of *Indiana Review.* SASE. Simultaneous submissions OK (if notified *immediately* of other publication). Reports in 3 months. Publishes ms an average of 3-6 months after acceptance. Does not read mid-December through mid-January. Sample copy for $7.

Payment/Terms: Pays $5/page when funds available and 2 contributor's copies for North American serial rights.

Advice: "Because our editors change each year, so do our literary preferences. It's important that potential contributors are familiar with the most recent issue of *Indiana Review* via library, sample copy or subscription. Beyond that, we look for prose that is well crafted and socially relevant. We are interested in innovation, unity and social context. All genres that meet these criteria are welcome."

N $ INDIGENOUS FICTION, (II), I.F. Publishing, P.O. Box 2078, Redmond WA 98073-2078. Fax:(425)836-4298. E-mail: deckr@earthlink.net. **Editor:** Sherry Decker. Associate Editor: Evelyn Gratrix. Magazine: 5½×8½; 56 pages; 20 lb. white paper; 4-color glossy cover; illustrations. "*I.F.* wants literary stories from all areas: fantasy, dark fantasy, science fiction, horror, mystery and mainstream." Biannually. Estab. 1998. Circ. 250 estimated.

Needs: Adventure, erotica, ethnic/multicultural, experimental, fantasy (science fantasy, sword and sorcery, contemporary), feminist, horror, humor/satire, literary, mainstream/contemporary, mystery/suspense (amateur sleuth, romantic suspense), psychic/supernatural/occult, romance (futuristic/time travel, gothic), science fiction (soft/sociological, cross-genre). "No porn; children-physical/sexual abuse; hard-tech science fiction; gore; vignettes; it-was-all-a-dream; evil cats, unicorns; sweet nostalgia." Receives 30-40 unsolicited mss/month. Accepts 8-10 mss/issue; 16-20 mss/year. Publishes ms 6 months maximum after acceptance. Length: 4,500 words average; 500 words minimum; 8,000 words maximum. Rarely publishes short shorts. Also publishes poetry. Sometimes critiques or comments on rejected ms.

How to Contact: Send complete ms with a cover letter. Include estimated word count, brief bio and list of publications. Reports in 2 weeks on queries; 1 month on mss. Send SASE for reply, return of ms or send a disposable copy of ms. "We prefer a disposable manuscript." Accepts only queries by e-mail. Simultaneous submissions OK. Fiction guidelines for #10 SASE.

Payment/Terms: Pays $5-20 and 1 contributor's copy on publication for submission over 2,500 words; submission under 2,500 words receives contributor's copy only; additional copies $4.50. Acquires first North American serial rights and reprint rights. Sends galleys to author if ms edited.

Advice: "We want literary stories. By 'literary' we don't mean a long rambling piece of beautiful writing for the sake of beauty—we mean characters and situation should be fully developed, beautifully. We enjoy tales containing elements of the supernatural or the unexplained, dark moody stories, bizarre, odd, 'real' life; believable characters."

ink magazine, (II), P.O. Box 52558, 264 Bloor St. West, Toronto Ontario M5S 1V0 Canada. **Editor:** John Degen. Magazine: 8×6; 44 pages; card cover; illustrations and photos. "*ink* surveys the mess of creativity. Anything that can be reproduced in ink—poetry, fiction, art, interviews, recipes, postcards, maps, both real and imagined—we reproduce in *ink*." Quarterly. Estab. 1993. Circ. 500.

- Member of the Canadian Magazine Publisher's Association.

Needs: Literary, translations. Publishes only original, previously unpublished fiction, poetry and essays. Receives 100 unsolicited mss/month. Accepts 10 mss/issue; 40 mss/year. Recently published work by Al Purdy, Derek McCormack, Alexandra Leggat, Peter McCallum, Chris Chambers and Heidi Greco. Length: 2,000 words average; 3,000 words maximum. Often critiques or comments on rejected mss.

How to Contact: Query by mail. Include estimated word count and 2-3 sentence bio. Reports in 1-2 months on queries. Send SASE for reply. No simultaneous submissions. Electronic (disk) submissions OK. Sample copy for $3.50. Fiction guidelines available with SASE. Reviews novels and short story collections. Send books to editor.

Payment/Terms: Pays free subscription to magazine for first North American serial rights.

INTERIM, (II), Dept. of English, University of Nevada, Las Vegas NV 89154. (702)895-3458. **Editor:** James Hazen. Magazine: 6×9; 48-64 pages; heavy paper; semigloss cover with illustration. Publishes "poetry and short fiction for a serious, educated audience." However, they focus more on poetry than fiction. Semiannually. Estab. 1944; revived 1986. Circ. 600-800.

Needs: Contemporary, experimental, literary. No science fiction, outdoor adventure. Accepts 1-2 mss/issue.

Publishes ms 6 months to 1 year of acceptance. Recently published work by G.K. Wuori and Mark Wisniewski. Length: 7,500 words maximum.

How to Contact: Send 1 complete ms with cover letter. Reports on mss in 4-6 weeks. SASE. Sample copy for $5.

Payment/Terms: Pays in contributor's copies and two-year subscription to magazine.

Advice: "Don't send excerpts from novels or longer works. We like completed stories, written as such, with the ordinary virtues of the form: strong, interesting characters, movement, resolution, economy, intensity, or wholeness, harmony, radiance. *No simultaneous submissions in either poetry or fiction.* These are unfair to our volunteer, unpaid staff. We cannot study and debate your work only to find at the end that it's been accepted for publication somewhere else. We try to keep our end of the bargain by holding submissions no longer than 60 days."

THE INTERNATIONAL FICTION REVIEW, (II), Dept. of German & Russian, UNB, Fredericton, New Brunswick E3B 5A3 Canada. (506)453-4636. Fax: (506)453-4659. E-mail: lorey@unb.ca. Website: http://www.unb.ca/web/German_Russian/IFRmain.htm (includes writer's guidelines, names of editors, index vols. 24, 25). **Editor:** Chris Lorey. Magazine: 6×9; 144 pages. "A scholarly journal dedicated to world fiction." Annually. Estab. 1972. Circ. 500 worldwide.

Needs: Open to all categories. Publishes ms 12-18 months after acceptance. Length: 5-10 pages. Publishes short shorts. Also publishes literary essays, literary criticism. Always critiques or comments on rejected ms.

How to Contact: Query first. Accepts queries/mss by e-mail and fax. Include short bio, list of publications. Reports in 1 week on queries; 3 months on mss. Send SAE/IRC for reply, return of ms or send a disposable copy of ms. Sample copy $12. Fiction guidelines free. Reviews novels, short story collections and nonfiction books of interest to writers.

Payment/Terms: Pays contributor's copy. Acquires first rights. Sends galleys to author.

INTROVERT ALIVE, (I), (919)319-1913. E-mail: intromag@hotmail.com. Website: http://www.introalive.com. **Editors:** Brian Wilson and Jeremy Sarine. Electronic magazine. "We are looking for poetry, short stories, journal entries, random thoughts and writings about whatever happens to be in your head or your heart."

Needs: Literary. "We'd prefer not to have anything overly graphic. We want this magazine to be open to all ages." Would like to see more Christian writings. "While this is not a Christian magazine, we would like to have a wide variety of beliefs and religions represented." Recently published work by Richard Krol, Cris Inscoe, Michael Wilson, Adrian Penn, Nick Grimaldi, Anjana Basu and Amanda Pruitt. "We are dedicated to publishing unknown authors."

How to Contact: Electronic and traditional submissions. Send ms by e-mail at intromag@hotmail.com or postal mail to *Introvert*, 1220-F Hamilton Court, Cary NC 27511.

Advice: "Our best advice to writers? Be honest with yourself and with others. Be free in your heart and your mind. Don't be afraid to make a mistake or to offend someone. We often get offended by things that we haven't dealt with in ourselves, so offending someone is often only bringing to their attention something that they need to deal with. So next time something offends you, think about why it offends you. Then write about it and send it to us."

$ THE IOWA REVIEW, (I, II), University of Iowa, 308 EPB, Iowa City IA 52242. (319)335-0462. E-mail: iowa-review@uiowa.edu. **Editors:** David Hamilton and Mary Hussmann. Magazine: 6×9; 200 pages; first-grade offset paper; Carolina CS1 10-pt. cover stock. "Stories, essays, poems for a general readership interested in contemporary literature." Triannually. Estab. 1970. Circ. 1,500.

- Work published in *Iowa Review* regularly has been selected for inclusion in the *Pushcart Prize* and *Best American Short Stories* anthologies.

Needs: "We are always hoping to be surprised by work we then think we need. We feel we are quite open to a range of styles and voices. We seek either really good, mature, well developed stories with character, humanity, depth, insight and all that, distinguished literature would be, or really surprising off-the-wall stuff that does not seem sophomoric." Receives 300-400 unsolicited fiction mss/month. Agented fiction less than 2%. Accepts 4-6 mss/issue, 12-18 mss/year. Does not read mss April-August. Recently published work by Lee Montgomery, Barbara Bedway, Christine Japely, Marilyn Kryol, Ron Tanner, Susan Suchman Simone, Christian Hansen and Susanne Grabowski. Published new writers within the last year. Also publishes literary essays, literary criticism, poetry.

How to Contact: Send complete ms with cover letter. "Don't bother with queries." SASE for return of ms. Simultaneous submissions OK. Reports in 2-4 months on mss. Publishes ms an average of 6-12 months after acceptance. Sample copy for $6. Fiction guidelines for SASE. Reviews novels and short story collections (3-6 books/year).

Payment/Terms: Pays $10/page ($25 minimum) on publication and 2 contributor's copies; additional copies 30% off cover price. Acquires first North American serial rights.

Advice: "Spend a lot of quiet time thinking about what you do, and do it over and over, and care. Don't try to read my mind—show me yours. We have no set guidelines as to content or length; we look for what we consider to be the best writing available to us. We believe we select and publish some of the best new works written today. In fact, we especially encourage new writers and are pleased when writers we believe we have discovered, from their unsolicited manuscripts, catch on with a wider range of readers. It is never a bad idea either to look through an issue or two of the magazine prior to a submission."

$ JACKHAMMER MAGAZINE, (I, II), Introspect Publications, P.O. Box 782047, Wichita KS 67278. (316)681-3195. **Editor:** Ethan Benda. Magazine: 5½×8½; 36 pages; 30 lb. bond cover stock; illustrations and photos. "Freedom of emotion through written word and art." Semiannually. Estab. 1994. Circ. 200.

Needs: Erotica, ethnic/multicultural, historical, humor/satire, literary, psychic/supernatural/occult, science fiction (hard science), translations, young adult/teen. No "drug and alcohol glorification or racism." Publishes special fiction issues or anthologies. Recently published work by R. Erik Ott, J. Harvey and T. Hibbard. Length: 100 words average; 1,000 words maximum. Publishes short shorts. Also publishes literary essays, literary criticism and poetry.

How to Contact: Query first. Include half-page bio and sample of work. Reports in 3 weeks on queries. Sample copy for $1 and 2 first-class stamps. Fiction guidelines for #10 SASE.

Payment/Terms: Payment varies for first-rights. Sends galleys to author.

Advice: "The only thing you have to fear is rejection."

☑ $ JAPANOPHILE, (I, II, IV), Box 7977, Ann Arbor MI 48107. (734)930-1553. Fax: (734)930-9968. E-mail: jpnhand@japanophile.com. Website: http://www.japanophile.com (includes writer's guidelines, sample fiction). **Editor-in-Chief:** Susan Lapp. Magazine: 5¼×8½; 58 pages; illustrations; photos. Magazine of "articles, photos, poetry, humor, short stories about Japanese culture, not necessarily set in Japan, for an adult audience, most with a college background and who like to travel." Quarterly. Estab. 1974. Circ. 800.

- Most of the work included in *Japanophile* is set in recent times, but the magazine will accept material set back as far as pre-WWII.

Needs: Adventure, historical, humor/satire, literary, mainstream, and mystery/suspense. No erotica, science fiction or horror. Published special fiction issue last year; plans another. Receives 40-100 unsolicited fiction mss/month. Accepts 12 ms/issue, 20-30 mss/year. Recently published work by Suzanne Kamata, Amy Chavez and Matt Malcomson. Publishes 12 previously unpublished writers/year. Length: 3,200 words average; 2,000 words minimum; 6,000 words maximum. Also publishes essays, book reviews, literary criticism and poetry.

How to Contact: Send complete ms with SASE, cover letter, bio and information about story. Accepts queries/mss by e-mail and fax. Simultaneous and reprint submissions OK. Reports in 2 months on mss. Sample copy for $4; guidelines for #10 SASE.

Payment/Terms: Pays $20 on publication for all rights, first North American serial rights or one-time rights (depends on situation). Stories submitted to the magazine may be entered in the annual contest. *A $5 entry fee must accompany each submission* to enter contest. Prizes include $100 plus publication for the best short story. Deadline: December 31.

Advice: "We look for originality and sensitivity to cultural detail. Clarity and directness of expression make manuscripts stand out. Short stories usually involve Japanese and 'foreign' (non-Japanese) characters in a way that contributes to understanding of Japanese culture and the Japanese people. However, a *good* story dealing with Japan or Japanese cultural aspects anywhere in the world will be considered, even if it does not involve this encounter or meeting of Japanese and foreign characters. Some stories may also be published in an anthology with approval of the author and additional payment."

N JEOPARDY, Literary Arts Magazine, (II), CH 132, Western Washington University, Bellingham WA 98225. (360)650-3118. (360)650-7775. E-mail: jeopardy@cc.wwu.edu. Website: http://www.wwu.edu/~jeopardy (includes writer's guidelines, names of editors, short fiction, artwork, poetry, links to other online mags). **Editor:** James Houle. Editors change every year. Magazine: 6×9; 192 pages; 70 lb. paper; glossy cover stock; illustrations and photographs. "*Jeopardy Magazine*'s intended audience is an intelligent readership which enjoys risks, surprises and subtlety. Our philosophy is that reputation is nothing and words/images are everything." Annually. Estab. 1965. Circ. 1,000.

Needs: Adventure, contemporary, erotica, ethnic, experimental, feminist, gay, historical, humor/satire, lesbian, literary. No long stories. Receives 50-100 unsolicited mss/month. Accepts 4-8 mss/year. Does not read mss January 15-September 1. Publishes ms 3 months after acceptance. Length: 1,500 words average; 250 words minimum; 5,000 words maximum. Also publishes literary essays, poetry.

How to Contact: Send complete ms with cover letter and 50-word bio. SASE and disposable copy of the ms. Does not return mss. Simultaneous submissions OK. Reports in 1-6 months. Sample copy for $5. Fiction guidelines for #10 SASE.

Payment/Terms: Pays 1 contributor's copy. Acquires one-time rights.

Advice: "A clear, insightful voice and style are major considerations. Things that will get your manuscript recycled: tired representations of sex and/or death and/or angst. We like writers who take risks! Know your characters thoroughly—know why someone else would want to read about what they think or do. Then, submit your work and don't give up at initial failures. Don't send us stories about being a writer/artist and/or a college student/professor. We would like to see more fiction pieces which involve unique or unexpected situations and characters."

THE JOLLY ROGER, (I, II), P.O. Box 1087, Chapel Hill NC 27514. (919)406-7068. E-mail: drake@jollyroger.com. Website: http://www.jollyroger.com. **Editor:** Drake Raft. Electronic magazine. "Literature composed in the context of the Western Canon."

Needs: "Conservative and traditional fiction, epic poetry, prose and short stories. Looking for rhyme, meter, words that mean things, plot and character. Publishes an occasional novel or collection of poetry." Recently published work by Drake Raft, Becket Knottingham, Elliot McGucken and Bootsy McClusky. Publishes 10-20 new writers/year.

How to Contact: Electronic and traditional submissions accepted.

THE JOURNAL, (I, II), Poetry Forum, 5713 Larchmont Dr., Erie PA 16509. Phone/fax: (814)866-2543. (Faxing hours: 8-10 a.m. and 5-8 p.m.) E-mail: 75562.670@compuserve.com. **Editor:** Gunvor Skogsholm. Journal: 5½×8½; 18-20 pages; light card cover. Looks for "good writing—for late teens to full adulthood." Quarterly. Estab. 1989. Circ. 200.

- *The Journal* is edited by Gunvor Skogsholm, the editor of *Poetry Forum Short Stories* and *Short Stories Bimonthly*. This magazine is not strictly a pay-for-publication, "subscribers come first.'

Needs: Mainstream. Plans annual special fiction issue. No extreme horror. Receives 25-30 unsolicited mss/month. Accepts 1 ms/issue; 7-10 mss/year. Publishes mss 2 weeks to 7 months after acceptance. Agented fiction 1%. 80% of work published is by new writers. Length: 500 words preferred; 300 words average; 150 words minimum. Publishes short shorts. Length: 400 words. Sponsors contest. Send SASE for details.

How to Contact: Send complete ms. Accepts queries/mss by e-mail. Reports in 2 weeks to 7 months on mss. SASE. Simultaneous submissions OK. Accepts electronic disk submissions. Sample copy for $3. Fiction guidelines for SASE.

Payment/Terms: No payment. Acquires one-time rights. Not copyrighted.

Advice: "Subscribers come first!" Looks for "a good lead stating a theme, support of the theme throughout and an ending that rounds out the story or article. Make it believable, please don't preach, avoid propaganda, and don't say, 'This is a story about a retarded person'; instead, prove it by your writing. Show, don't tell."

☑ **THE JOURNAL OF AFRICAN TRAVEL-WRITING, (IV)**, P.O. Box 346, Chapel Hill NC 27514-0346. (919)929-0419. E-mail: ottotwo@email.unc.edu. Website: http://www.unc.edu/~ottotwo/ (includes guidelines, selected texts, table of contents). **Editor:** Amber Vogel. Magazine: 7×10; 96 pages; 50 lb. paper; illustrations. "*The Journal of African Travel-Writing* presents materials in a variety of genres that explore Africa as a site of narrative." Semiannually. Estab. 1996. Circ. 600.

- Sponsors annual award for best piece published in the journal.

Needs: Adventure, condensed/excerpted novel, ethnic/multicultural, historical, literary, translations. Accepts 1-4 mss/issue. Publishes ms 4-6 months after acceptance. Recently published work by Eileen Drew, Lisa Fugard and Sandra Jackson-Opoku. Also publishes literary essays, literary criticism and poetry. Sometimes critiques or comments on rejected mss.

How to Contact: Send complete ms with a cover letter. Sample copy for $6. Reviews novels and short story collections. Send books to editor.

Payment/Terms: Pays 5 contributor's copies for first rights. Sends galleys to author.

$ KALEIDOSCOPE: International Magazine of Literature, Fine Arts, and Disability, (II, IV), 701 S. Main St., Akron OH 44311-1019. (330)762-9755. Fax: (330)762-0912. **Editor-in-Chief:** Darshan Perusek, Ph.D. Senior Editor: Gail Willmott. Magazine: 8½×11; 56-64 pages; non-coated paper; coated cover stock; illustrations (all media); photos. "*Kaleidoscope* Magazine has a creative focus that examines the experiences of disability through literature and the fine arts. Unique to the field of disability studies, this award-winning publication is not an advocacy or rehabilitation journal. *Kaleidoscope* expresses the experiences of disability from the perspective of individuals, families, healthcare professionals, and society as a whole. Each issue explores a specific theme which deals with disability. Readers include people with and without disabilities." Semiannually. Estab. 1979. Circ. 1,000.

- *Kaleidoscope* has received awards from the American Heart Association, the Great Lakes Awards Competition and Ohio Public Images. The editors are looking for more fiction .

Needs: Personal experience, drama, fiction, essay, artwork. "Would like to see more fiction with emphasis on character study instead of action." Upcoming theme: "For Our Parents With Disabilities" (deadline March 1999); "The Created Environment" (deadline August 1999). No fiction that is sentimental, erotic, romantic or maudlin. Receives 20-25 unsolicited fiction mss/month. Accepts 10 mss/year. Approximately 1% of fiction is agented. Recently published work by Andre Dubus and Margaret Robison. Published new writers within the last year. Length: 5,000 words maximum. Also publishes poetry.

How to Contact: Query first or send complete ms and cover letter. Queries by fax are OK. Include author's educational and writing background and if author has a disability, how it has influenced the writing. Simultaneous submissions OK. Reports in 1 month on queries; 6 months on mss. Sample copy for $4. Guidelines for #10 SASE.

Payment/Terms: Pays $10-125 and 2 contributor's copies on publication; additional copies $5. Acquires first rights. Reprints permitted with credit given to original publication.

Advice: "Read the magazine and get submission guidelines. We prefer that writers with a disability offer original

INSIDER REPORT

David Lynn: striking a "dynamic balance" of fiction at *Kenyon Review*

Photo by Larry Hamill

David Lynn

As a writer, editor and teacher, David Lynn has only one rule for quality fiction: "Does it work?"

Lynn, editor since 1994 of the distinguished literary journal *The Kenyon Review*, says that's the only way to distinguish among the 5,000 submissions of fiction and poetry that come through the mailbox each year.

"I try to be as eclectic as possible," he says. "I'm not drawn to experiment for experiment's sake. I'm drawn to innovation to the extent that it advances a story."

As Lynn responds favorably to stories with that elusive "hook, something strong that captures the reader's attention one way or the other," he tends to respond negatively to material that is shopworn in plot, technique or language.

"I'm actually a real stickler for diction," he says. "If I see that a writer is not careful about word choice—a chosen word simply isn't right, it's out of place, it's a cliché, it's predictable—that sours me pretty quickly. It shows a kind of sloppiness for the craft for which I have very little patience.

"I'm very tired of stories about a loved one dying of cancer because it's done so often in fiction. It doesn't work well as art. I'm saying that, but later today I may open a manuscript about a loved one dying of cancer and it's surprising, it breaks all the rules. But that's very rare."

It's actually even more difficult to be accepted at *The Kenyon Review* than the 5,000 annual submissions might indicate, because a significant portion in each issue is solicited, Lynn says. "If you try to publish a truly distinguished magazine, it has to be a mix of the solicited and unsolicited. It's like seeding clouds. You work with writers and editors you admire and hope they send you material."

Despite this, Lynn emphasizes that a central mission of the magazine is to "discover exciting new talents, exciting new voices who are creating the best writing of the next generations. Big names don't always write great stuff. We're selective from among people we admire as well as unknowns."

Lynn tries to set "a dynamic, changing balance" of fiction, poetry and essays in each issue of *The Kenyon Review*. "Each issue is a little different," he says. In striking a balance, he contributes to a long and distinguished editorial legacy; *The Kenyon Review* has been one of the most influential magazines in 20th-century literature. Founded in the 1930s by John Crowe Ransom, it quickly became a home for the major writers of the mid-century. The magazine went out of business in 1970 and was revived in 1979.

The publication nearly died a second time, though, as Lynn assumed the editorship in 1994. The leadership of Kenyon College, where the magazine is based, considered eliminating the magazine because of budgetary concerns—concerns that overrode the con-

INSIDER REPORT, *Lynn*

tribution the magazine has made to American writing.

"Not all trustees are concerned with art and culture, and things external to the college. Their job is to maintain the stability of the institution," Lynn says. The trustees "felt the magazine had become very divorced from the life of the college."

Eventually, the trustees were persuaded to continue funding for the magazine, but made it clear they expected significant changes under Lynn's editorship. The magazine tightened its budget, and began sponsoring a number of programs, such as a summer writing institute, that make it a "flagship for writing at Kenyon College," Lynn says. Now, *The Kenyon Review* is incorporated separately from Kenyon College, with a board of trustees that is responsible for building an endowment and developing new funding sources.

Lynn feels putting some distance between the magazine and its academic setting is healthy. "I think it's critical," he says. "I'm very worried about all of the arts being academically based. It creates a very rigid relationship. One of my aspirations with *The Kenyon Review* is that is aspires to cross some of the boundaries that have come up. Creative writing must be read by people who are not academics."

Creative writing in general has become entwined with the university over the past several decades—and that's not good for literature, Lynn feels. Writers who spend too much time in the classroom can develop a false sense of what it takes to develop as writers.

"I'm very skeptical of MFA writing programs," he says. "They create homogeneity, and create false expectations about one's future. They provide a narrow education into what art and literature are. The best writers are people who are broadly educated."

Although Lynn is himself a writing teacher—he is on the faculty at Kenyon and published his first volume of short stories, *Fortune Telling* (Carnegie Mellon University Press), in 1998—he actively discourages his students from pursuing graduate study in writing, at least right away.

"The value of an MFA is for someone who's older, who's lived, has educated himself or herself as broadly as possible and now wants to spend the time pulling back from the world to push their craft to the next level," he says.

If the study of creative writing may not be of much benefit to young writers, the actual study of literature—a reader's education—can be of enormous benefit, Lynn says. A writer who doesn't gain such experience lacks "richness of perspective that good writers have. Aspiring writers need to read voraciously. And they need to live."

Lynn's own work shows the value of his advice. The stories gathered in *Fortune Telling* date back to the late 1980s, a period in which Lynn spent several years working outside higher education, in publishing. His stories showcase a subtle touch that engages characters from many walks of life—Jewish, Indian, Southern, Midwestern. They do not reflect the perspective of one who has never left the classroom.

Going out into the world to gain experience will likely mean writers do not earn a living as writers, at least as creative writers. "In Western civilization, most writers didn't support themselves by the pen, at least initially. Writing was something they did in the evenings and weekends. The writing was nurtured by the other living they were doing."

But just because literary writing can't provide a means to earn one's bread, that does not mean it does not provide some benefit. "Robert Penn Warren was once asked why he wrote," Lynn says, "With a big southern grin and drawl, he said, 'For the glory.' Writers write to be read."

—Kevin Walzer

perspectives about their experiences; writers without disabilities should limit themselves to our focus in order to solidify a connection to our magazine's purpose. Do not use stereotypical, patronizing and sentimental attitudes about disability."

KALLIOPE, A Journal of Women's Art, (II), Florida Community College at Jacksonville, 3939 Roosevelt Blvd., Jacksonville FL 32205. (904)381-3511. Website: http://www.fccj.org/Kalliope/Kalliope.htm. **Editor:** Mary Sue Koeppel. Magazine: 7¼×8¼; 76-88 pages; 70 lb. coated matte paper; Bristol cover; 16-18 halftones per issue. "A literary and visual arts journal for women, *Kalliope* celebrates women in the arts by publishing their work and by providing a forum for their ideas and opinions." Short stories, poems, plays, essays, reviews and visual art. Triannually. Estab. 1978. Circ. 1,550.

- Kalliope has received the Frances Buck Sherman Award from the local branch of the National League of Pen Women. The magazine has also received awards and grants for its poetry, grants from the Florida Department of Cultural Affairs and the Jacksonville Club Gallery of Superb Printing Award.

Needs: "Quality short fiction by women writers." Accepts 2-4 mss/issue. Receives approximately 100 unsolicited fiction mss each month. Recently published work by Glynis Kinnan, Rolaine Hoch Stein, Kathleen Spivack and Connie Mary Fowler. Publishes 3 new writers/year. Published new writers within the last year. Preferred length: 750-2,000 words, but occasionally publishes longer (and shorter) pieces. Also publishes poetry. Critiques rejected mss "when there is time and if requested."
How to Contact: Send complete ms with SASE and short contributor's note. No simultaneous submissions. Reports in 2-3 months on ms. Publishes ms an average of 1-3 months after acceptance. Sample copy: $7 for current issue; $4 for issues from '78-'88. Reviews short story collections.
Payment/Terms: Pays 3 contributor's copies or 1-years subscription for first rights. Discount for extras. "We accept only unpublished work. Copyright returned to author upon request."
Advice: "Read our magazine. The work we consider for publication will be well written and the characters and dialogue will be convincing. We like a fresh approach and are interested in new or unusual forms. Make us believe your characters; give readers an insight which they might not have had if they had not read you. We would like to publish more work by minority writers." Manuscripts are rejected because "1) nothing *happens*!, 2) it is thinly disguised autobiography (richly disguised autobiography is OK), 3) ending is either too pat or else just trails off, 4) characterization is no developed, and 5) point of view falters."

KELSEY REVIEW, (I, II, IV), Mercer County College, P.O. Box B, Trenton NJ 08690. (609)586-4800. E-mail: kelsey.review@mccc.edu. Website: http://www.mccc.edu (includes deadlines, date of publication). **Editor:** Robin Schore. Magazine: 7×14; 80 pages; glossy paper; soft cover. "Must live or work in Mercer County, NJ." Annually. Estab. 1988. Circ. 1,750.
Needs: Open. Regional (Mercer County only). Receives 120 unsolicited mss/year. Accepts 24 mss/issue. Reads mss only in May. Publishes ms 1-2 months after acceptance. Recently published work by Bruce Petronio, Mary Mallery, Janet Kirk and D.E. Steward. Publishes 6-7 new writers/year. Length: 2,000 words maximum. Publishes short shorts. Also publishes literary essays, literary criticism and poetry. Always critiques or comments on rejected mss.
How to Contact: Send complete ms with cover letter. SASE for return of ms. Accepts queries/mss by e-mail. No simultaneous submissions. Reports in 1-2 months. Sample copy free.
Payment/Terms: Pays 5 contributor's copies. Rights revert to author on publication.
Advice: Looks for "quality, intellect, grace and guts. Avoid sentimentality, overwriting and self-indulgence. Work on clarity, depth and originality."

KENNESAW REVIEW, (II), Kennesaw State University, Dept of English, 1000 Chastain Rd., Kennesaw GA 30144-5591. (770)423-6346. **Editor:** Dr. Robert W. Hill. Managing and Assistant Editor: Craig Watson. Magazine. "Just good fiction, all themes, for a general audience." Semiannually. Estab. 1987.
Needs: Excerpted novel, contemporary, ethnic, experimental, feminist, gay, humor/satire, literary, mainstream, regional. No romance. Receives 25-60 mss/month. Accepts 2-4 mss/issue. Publishes ms 12-18 months after acceptance. Published work by Julie Brown, Stephen Dixon, Robert Morgan, Carolyn Thorman. Length: 9-30 pages. Length: 500 words. Rarely comments on or critiques rejected mss.
How to Contact: Send complete ms with cover letter. Include previous publications. Reports 2 months on mss. SASE. Simultaneous submissions OK. Sample copy and fiction guidelines free.
Payment/Terms: Pays in contributor's copies. Acquires first publication rights only. Acknowledgment required for subsequent publication.
Advice: "Use the language well and tell an interesting story. Send it on. Be open to suggestions."

INTERESTED IN A PARTICULAR GENRE? Check our new sections for: **Mystery/Suspense**, page 57; **Romance**, page 77; **Science Fiction & Fantasy**, page 95.

☑ $ **THE KENYON REVIEW, (II)**, Kenyon College, Gambier OH 43022. (740)427-5208. Fax: (740)427-5417. E-mail: kenyonreview@kenyon.edu. **Editor:** David H. Lynn. "Fiction, poetry, essays, book reviews." Triannually. Estab. 1939. Circ. 5,000.

• Work published in the *Kenyon Review* has been selected for inclusion in *Pushcart Prize* anthologies.

Needs: Condensed/excerpted novel, contemporary, ethnic, experimental, feminist, gay, historical, humor/satire, lesbian, literary, mainstream, translations. Receives 400 unsolicited fiction mss/month. Unsolicited mss read only from September 1 through March 31. Publishes ms 12-18 months after acceptance. Recently published work by Joyce Carol Oates, Lewis Hyde, Reginald McKnight and Nancy Zafris. Length: 3-15 typeset pages preferred.

How to Contact: Send complete ms with cover letter. Reports on mss in 2-3 months. SASE. No simultaneous submissions. Sample copy for $8.

Payment/Terms: Pays $10/page on publication for first-time rights. Sends copyedited version to author for approval.

Advice: "Read several issues of our publication. We remain invested in encouraging/reading/publishing work by writers of color, writers expanding the boundaries of their genre, and writers with unpredictable voices and points of view."

KEREM, Creative Explorations in Judaism, (IV), Jewish Study Center Press, Inc., 3035 Porter St. NW, Washington DC 20008. (202)364-3006. Fax: (202)364-3806. **Editors:** Sara Horowitz and Gilah Langner. Magazine: 6×9; 128 pages; 60 lb. offset paper; glossy cover; illustrations and photos. "*Kerem* publishes Jewish religious, creative, literary material—short stories, poetry, personal reflections, text study, prayers, rituals, etc." Annually. Estab. 1992. Circ. 2,000

Needs: Jewish: feminist, humor/satire, literary, religious/inspirational. Receives 10-12 unsolicited mss/month. Accepts 1-2 mss/issue. Publishes ms 2-10 months after acceptance. Recently published work by Mark Mirsky and Anita Diamant. Length: 6,000 words maximum. Also publishes literary essays, poetry.

How to Contact: Send complete ms with a cover letter. Should include 1-2 line bio. Reports in 2 months on queries; 4-5 months on mss. Send SASE for reply, return of ms or send a disposable copy of ms. Simultaneous submissions OK. Sample copy for $8.50.

Payment/Terms: Pays free subscription and 2-10 contributor's copies. Acquires one-time rights.

Advice: "Should have a strong Jewish content. We want to be moved by reading the manuscript!"

N **KESTREL, A Journal of Literature and Art**, Division of Language and Literature, Fairmont State College, 1201 Locust Ave., Fairmont WV 26554-2470. (304)367-4815. **Editors:** Mary Stewart, John King, John Hoppenthaler. Magazine: 6×9; 100 pages; 60 lb. paper; glossy cover; photographs. "An eclectic journal publishing the best fiction, poetry, creative nonfiction and artwork for a literate audience. We strive to present contributors' work in depth." Semiannually. Estab. 1993. Circ. 500.

• *Kestrel* has received funding grants from the NEA and the West Virginia Commission of the Arts.

Needs: Condensed/excerpted novel, literary, translations. "No pornography, children's literature, romance fiction, pulp science fiction—formula fiction in general." Receives 10-20 unsolicited mss/month. Acquires 2-3 mss/issue; 4-6 mss/year. Publishes ms 3-12 months after acceptance. Recently published work by Colleen Anderson, Peter De Swart, Dinty Moore, Joan Connor, John Sullivan. Length: 1,500 words minimum; 6,000 words maximum. Publishes short shorts. Also publishes literary essays and poetry. Sometimes critiques or comments on rejected mss.

How To Contact: Send complete ms with "short but specific" cover letter. Include list of publications. Reports in 3-6 months on mss. SASE for return of ms or disposable copy of ms. No simultaneous submissions. Electronic (disk) submissions OK. Sample copy for $5.

Payment/Terms: Pays 5 contributor's copies. Rights revert to contributor on publication.

Advice: Looks for "maturity, grace and verve . . . whether you're 21 or 81 years old. Live with a story for a year or more before you send it anywhere, not just *Kestrel*."

LACTUCA, (I, II), % Mike Selender, 159 Jewett Ave., Jersey City NJ 07304-2003. (201)451-5411. E-mail: lactuca@mindspring.com. **Editor:** Mike Selender. Magazine: Folded 8½×14; 72 pages; 24 lb. bond; soft cover; saddle-stapled; illustrations. Plans to change format in 1999. Publishes "poetry, short fiction and b&w art, for a general literary audience." Published annually. Estab. 1986.

• *Lactuca* will change format in 1999. Please query for updated guidelines before submitting.

Needs: Adventure, condensed/excerpted novel, confession, contemporary, erotica, literary, mainstream, prose poem and regional. No "self-indulgent writing or fiction about writing fiction." Receives 30 or more mss/month. Accepts 10-12 mss/year. Publishes ms within 12-18 months of acceptance. Published work by Douglas Mendini, Tom Gidwitz and Ruthann Robson. Length: around 12-14 typewritten double-spaced pages. Publishes short shorts. Often critiques rejected mss and recommends other markets.

How to Contact: "Query first to see if we're reading before sending manuscripts." Cover letter should include "just a few brief notes about yourself. Please no long 'literary' résumés or bios. The work will speak for itself." No simultaneous or previously published work. Sample copy for $4. Fiction guidelines for #10 SASE.

Payment/Terms: Pays contributor's copies, depending on the length of the work published. Acquires first North American serial rights. Sends galleys to author. Copyrights revert to authors.

Advice: "We want fiction coming from a strong sense of place and/or experience. Work with an honest emotional depth. We steer clear of self-indulgent material. We particularly like work that tackles complex issues and the impact of such on people's lives. We are open to work that is dark and/or disturbing."

THE LAMPLIGHT, (II), Beggar's Press, 8110 N. 38 St., Omaha NE 68112. (402)455-2615. Editor: Richard R. Carey. **Fiction Editor:** Sandy Johnsen. Magazine: 8½×11; 60 pages; 20 lb. bond paper; 65 lb. stock cover; some illustrations; a few photographs. "Our purpose is to establish a new literature drawn from the past. We relish foreign settings in the 19th century when human passions transcended computers and fax machines. We are literary but appeal to the common intellect and the mass soul of humanity." Semiannually.

Needs: Historical (general), humor/satire, literary, mystery/suspense (literary), romance (gothic, historical). "Settings in the past. Psychological stories." Plans special fiction issue or anthology in the future. Receives 120-140 unsolicited mss/month. Accepts 2 mss/issue; 4 mss/year. Publishes ms 4-12 months after acceptance. Published work by James Scoffield and Philip Sparacino. Length: 2,000 words preferred; 500 words minimum; 3,500 words maximum. Publishes short shorts. Length: 300 words. Also publishes literary criticism and poetry. Critiques or comments on rejected mss.

How to Contact: Send complete ms with cover letter. Include estimated word count, bio (a paragraph or two) and list of publications. Reports in 1 month on queries; 2½ months on mss. SASE. Simultaneous and reprint submission OK. Sample copy for $10.95, 9×12 SAE. Fiction guidelines for #10 SASE. Reviews novels and short story collections.

Payment/Terms: Pays 1 contributor's copy. Acquires first North American serial rights.

Advice: "We deal in classical masterpieces. Every piece must be timeless. It must live for five centuries or more. We judge on this basis. These are not easy to come by. But we want to stretch authors to their fullest capacity. They will have to dig deeper for us, and develop a style that is different from what is commonly read in today's market."

THE LAMP-POST, of the Southern California C.S. Lewis Society, (II, IV), 29562 Westmont Ct., San Juan Capistrano CA 92675. (949)347-1255. E-mail: lamppost@ix.netcom.com. **Senior Editor:** James Prothero. Magazine: 5½×8½; 34 pages; 7 lb. paper; 8 lb. cover; illustrations. "We are a literary review focused on C.S. Lewis and like writers." Quarterly. Estab. 1977. Circ. 200.

- C.S. Lewis was an English novelist and essayist known for his science fiction and fantasy featuring Christian themes. He is especially well-known for his children's fantasy, *The Chronicles of Narnia*. So far, the magazine has found little fiction suitable to its focus, although they remain open.

Needs: "Literary fantasy and science fiction for children to adults." Publishes ms 9 months after acceptance. Recently published work by Rita Quinton and DJ Kolacki. Publishes 3-5 new writers/year. Length: 2,500 words average; 1,000 words minimum; 5,000 words maximum. Also publishes literary essays, literary criticism and poetry. Sometimes critiques or comments on rejected mss.

How to Contact: Query first or send complete ms with a cover letter. Accepts queries/mss by e-mail. Include 50-word bio. Reports in 6-8 weeks. Send SASE for reply, return of ms or send a disposable copy of ms. No simultaneous submissions. Reprints and electronic (disk) submissions OK. Sample copy for $3. Fiction guidelines for #10 SASE. Reviews fiction or criticism having to do with Lewis or in his vein. Send books to: Dr. David W. Landrum, book review editor, Cornerstone College, 1001 E. Beltline, NE, Grand Rapids MI 49525.

Payment/Terms: Pays 3 contributor's copies; additional copies $3. Acquires first North American serial rights or one-time rights.

Advice: "We look for fiction with the supernatural, mythic feel of the fiction of C.S. Lewis and Charles Williams. Our slant is Christian but we want work of literary quality. No inspirational. Is it the sort of thing Lewis, Tolkien and Williams would like—subtle, crafted fiction? If so, send it. Don't be too obvious or facile. Our readers aren't stupid."

✔ 🏆 **THE LAUREL REVIEW, (III)**, Northwest Missouri State University, Dept. of English, Maryville MO 64468. (660)562-1265. **Co-editors:** William Trowbridge, David Slater and Beth Richards. Associate Editors: Nancy Vieira Couto, Randall R. Freisinger, Steve Heller. Reviewer: Peter Makuck. Magazine: 6×9; 124-128 pages; good quality paper. "We publish poetry and fiction of high quality, from the traditional to the avant-garde. We are eclectic, open and flexible. Good writing is all we seek." Biannually. Estab. 1960. Circ. 900.

- A story published in *The Laurel Review* in 1996 was selected for inclusion in the annual *Pushcart Prize* anthology. Two others received special mention.

Needs: Literary and contemporary. No genre or politically polemical fiction. Accepts 3-5 mss/issue, 6-10 mss/year. Receives approximately 120 unsolicited fiction mss each month. Approximately 1% of fiction is agented. Recently published work by Karla J. Kuban, Ian MacMillan, Richard Duggin and Becky Bradway. Length: 2,000-10,000 words. Sometimes publishes literary essays; also publishes poetry. Reads September to May.

How to Contact: Send complete ms with SASE. No simultaneous submissions. Reports in 1-4 months on mss. Publishes ms an average of 1-12 months after acceptance. Sample copy for $3.50.

Payment/Terms: Pays 2 contributor's copies and 1 year subscription. Acquires first rights. Copyright reverts to author upon request.

Advice: Send $3.50 for a back copy of the magazine.

☑ $ **LE FORUM, Supplement Littéraire, (II, IV)** (formerly Rafale), Franco-American Research Organization Group, University of Maine, Franco American Center, 164 College Ave., Orono ME 04473-1578. (207)581-3764. Fax: (207)581-1455. E-mail: lisa_michaud@unit.maine.edu. **Editor:** Lisa Michaud. Tabloid size, magazine format: 4 pages; illustrations and photos. Publication was founded to stimulate and recognize creative expression among Franco-Americans, all types of readers, including literary and working class. This publication is used in university classrooms. Circulated internationally. Quarterly. Estab. 1986. Circ. 5,000.
Needs: "We will consider any type of short fiction, poetry and critical essays having to do with Franco-American experience. They must be of good quality in French as well as English. We are also looking for Canadian writers with French-North American experiences." Receives about 10 unsolicited mss/month. Accepts 2-4 mss/issue. Published work by Robert Cormier; published new writers within the last year. Length: 1,000 words average; 750 words minimum; 2,500 words maximum. Occasionally critiques rejected mss.
How to Contact: Send complete ms with cover letter. Include a short bio and list of previous publications. Reports in 3 weeks on queries; 1 month on mss. SASE. Simultaneous, reprint and electronic submissions (e-mail, fax) OK.
Payment/Terms: Pays $10 and 3 copies for one-time rights.
Advice: "Write honestly. Start with a strongly felt personal Franco-American experience. If you make us feel what you have felt, we will publish it. We stress that this publication deals specifically with the Franco-American experience."

N $ **LESBIAN SHORT FICTION**, 6507 Franrivers Ave., West Hills CA 91307-2814. (818)704-7825. E-mail: jinxbeers@aol.com. **Editor:** Jinx Beers. Magazine: 6×9; 160 pages; illustrations; photos. Quarterly. Estab. 1996. Circ. 500.

- *Lesbian Short Fiction* ranked #30 on *Writer's Digest*'s Fiction 50 list of top markets for fiction writers.

Needs: Adventure, erotica, ethnic/multicultural, lesbian, fantasy (space fantasy, sword and sorcery, lesbian), horror (dark fantasy, futuristic, psychological, supernatural), mystery/suspense (amateur sleuth, cozy, police procedural, private eye/hardboiled), romance (contemporary, gothic), science fiction (hard science/technological, soft/sociological), western (frontier saga, traditional), vignettes of lesbian life. No children's, juvenile, young adult or religious/inspirational. Receives 10-15 mss/month. Publishes 15-18 mss/issue; 60-70 mss/year. Does not read mss September 1-15. Publishes ms 18 months after acceptance. Publishes 4-6 new writers/year. Length: 4,000-5,000 words average; 500 words minimum; 10,000 words maximum. Also publishes literary criticism. Always comments on rejected mss.
How to Contact: Send complete ms with cover letter. Accepts queries/mss by e-mail. Include estimated word count. Reports on queries in 2 weeks; mss in 8 weeks. SASE for reply to query or return of ms. Simultaneous submissions OK. Sample copy for $5. Guidelines free for 9×4 SAE and 1 first-class stamp or IRC.
Payment/Terms: Pays 1¢/word and 2 contributor's copies on publication for first North American serial rights; additional copies for $6.50. Sends galleys to author. Sponsors contest. Guidelines for SASE.
Advice: "Submissions must have significant lesbian content; be a complete story rather than a scene; show strong characterization; and use a different/new approach. Rewrite until every word is perfect, then expect an editor to want changes."

☑ $ **LIBIDO, The Journal of Sex and Sensibility, (I, II, IV)**, Libido, Inc., P.O. Box 146721, Chicago IL 60614. (773)275-0842. E-mail: rune@mcs.com. **Editors:** Jack Hafferkamp and Marianna Beck. Magazine: 6½×9¼; 72-88 pages; 70 lb. coated; b&w illustrations and photographs. "*Libido*, to paraphrase Oscar Wilde, is the literary answer to a horizontal urge. Libido is about sex and sensibility—eroticism with reflection. Our audience is educated and liberated." fiarterly. Estab. 1988. Circ. 10,000.

- Specializing in "literary" erotica, this journal has attracted a number of top-name writers and was given a Venus Award from Good Vibrations, San Francisco.

Needs: Condensed/excerpted novel, confession, erotica, gay, lesbian. "We'd like more well-written eroticism—orientation doesn't matter; writing quality does." No "dirty words for their own sake, violence or sexual exploitation." Receives 25-50 unsolicited mss/month. Accepts about 5 mss/issue; about 20 mss/year. Publishes ms up to 1 year after acceptance. Recently published work by Carol Queen and William Levy. Publishes 5-10 new writers/year. Length: 1,000-3,000 words; 300 words minimum; 5,000 words maximum. Also publishes literary essays, literary criticism. Sometimes critiques rejected mss and recommends other markets.
How to Contact: Send complete ms with cover letter including Social Security number and brief bio for contributor's page. Reports in 6 months on mss. SASE. No simultaneous submissions. Reprint submissions OK. Sample copy for $8. Fiction guidelines for SASE. Reviews novels and short story collections.
Payment/Terms: Pays $25-100 and 1 contributor's copy on publication for one-time or anthology rights.
Advice: "Humor is a strong plus. There must be a strong erotic element, and it should celebrate the joy of sex. Also, stories should be well written, insightful and arousing. Bonus points given for accuracy of characterization and style."

☑ **THE LICKING RIVER REVIEW, (II)**, University Center, Northern Kentucky University, Highland Heights KY 41076. (606)572-5416. E-mail: underwoodh@nku.edu. **Editor:** Helen Underwood. Magazine: 7×11; 104 pages; photos. Annually. Estab. 1991. Circ. 1,500.
Needs: Experimental, literary, mainstream/contemporary. Receives 40 unsolicited mss/month. Accepts 7-9 mss/

year. Does not read mss February through July. Publishes ms 6 months after acceptance. Recently published work by Dallas Wiebe, Alfred Schwaid, Laurie Jones Neighbor, Brian Howard, Pax Riddle and dayna marie. Length: 5,000 words maximum. Publishes short shorts. Also publishes poetry.
How to Contact: Send complete ms with a cover letter. Include list of publications. Reports in 3-6 months on mss. SASE for return of manuscript or send disposable copy of ms. No simultaneous submissions. Sample copy for $5.
Payment/Terms: Pays 2 contributor's copies on publication.
Advice: Looks for "good writing and an interesting and well-told story. Read a sample copy first."

LIGHT MAGAZINE, (II), P.O. Box 7500, Chicago IL 60680. **Editor:** John Mella. Magazine: 6×9; 64 pages; Finch opaque (60 lb.) paper; 65 lb. color cover; illustrations. "Light and satiric verse and prose, witty but not sentimental. Audience: intelligent, educated, usually 'professional.' " Biannually. Estab. 1992. Circ. 1,000.
Needs: Humor/satire, literary. Upcoming theme: Ogden Nash parody issue. Receives 10-40 unsolicited fiction mss/month. Accepts 2-4 mss/issue. Publishes ms 6-24 months after acceptance. Published work by X.J. Kennedy, J.F. Nims and John Updike. Length: 1,200 words preferred; 600 words minimum; 2,000 words maximum. Publishes short shorts. Also publishes literary essays, literary criticism and poetry. Sometimes critiques or comments on rejected mss.
How to Contact: Query first. Include estimated word count and list of publications. Reports in 1 month on queries; 2-4 months on mss. Send SASE for reply, return of ms or send a disposable copy of ms. No simultaneous submissions. Electronic submissions (disk only) OK. Sample copy for $6 (plus $2 for 1st class). Fiction guidelines for #10 SASE. Reviews novels and short story collections. Send review copies to review editor.
Payment/Terms: Pays contributor's copies (2 for domestic; 1 for foreign). Acquires first North American serial rights. Sends galleys of longer pieces to author.
Advice: Looks for "high literary quality; wit, allusiveness, a distinct (and distinctive) style. Read guidelines first."

✓ **LINES IN THE SAND, (I, II)**, LeSand Publications, 890 Southgate Ave., Daly City CA 94015. (650)992-4770. E-mail: nsand415@aol.com. Editor: Nina Z. Sanders. **Fiction Editors:** Nina Z. Sanders and Barbara J. Less. Magazine: 5½×8½; 32 pages; 20 lb. bond; King James cost-coated cover. "Stories should be well-written, entertaining and suitable for all ages. Our readers range in age from 7 to 90. No particular slant or philosophy." Bimonthly. Estab. 1992. Circ. 100.

- *Lines In The Sand* is known for quirky fiction with surprise endings. Humorous and slice-of-life fiction has a good chance here.

Needs: Adventure, experimental, fantasy, horror, humor/satire, literary, mainstream/contemporary, mystery/suspense (private eye/hard-boiled, amateur sleuth, cozy, romantic), science fiction (soft/sociological), senior citizen/retirement, westerns (traditional, frontier, young adult), young adult/teen (10-18 years). "Would like to see more humorous, surprise endings." "No erotica, horror or pornography." Receives 70-80 unsolicited mss/month. Accepts 8-10 mss/issue; 50-60 mss/year. Publishes ms 2-4 months after acceptance. Recently published work by Carlos Brown, Wally Kennicutt and Wright Wolcott Salisbury. Publishes 10 new writers/year. Length: 1,200 words preferred; 250 words minimum; 2,000 words maximum. Publishes short shorts. Length: 250 words. Also publishes poetry. Often critiques or comments on rejected mss. Sponsors contests. To enter contest submit 2 copies of story, 2,000 words maximum, double-spaced, typed and $5 reading fee for each story submitted.
How to Contact: Send complete ms with cover letter containing estimated word count and bio (3-4 sentences). Reports in 2-6 months on mss. Send SASE for reply, return of ms or send disposable copy of themes. Simultaneous submissions OK. Sample copy for $3.50. Fiction guidelines for #10 SASE.
Payment/Terms: Pays one contributor's copy. Acquires first North American serial rights.
Advice: "Use fresh, original approach; 'show, don't tell'; use dialogue to move story along; and be grammatically correct. Stories should have some type of conflict. Read a sample copy (or two). Follow guidelines carefully. Use plain language; avoid flowery, 'big' words unless appropriate in dialogue."

N **LITE, Baltimore's Literary Newspaper, (I, II)**, P.O. Box 26162, Baltimore MD 21210. (410)719-7792. E-mail: pkinlock@bcpl.net. Website: http://LiteCircle.dragonfire.net (includes guidelines, current and back issues, literary news, staff contact information). **Editor:** David W. Kriebel. Tabloid: 11×14; 8 pages; 30 lb. newsprint paper; 2-4 illustrations; some photographs. "Poetry, short fiction, occasional nonfiction pieces, satire. Our audience is intelligent, literate, and imaginative. They have the ability to step back and look at the world from a different perspective." Bimonthly. Estab. 1989. Circ. 10,000.
Needs: Experimental, fantasy, historical (general), horror, humor/satire, literary, mystery/suspense (private eye), psychic/supernatural/occult, science fiction (hard science, soft/sociological). "No erotica, gay, lesbian. Nothing demeaning to any ethnic or religious group. No stories with an obvious or trite 'message.' No violence for its own sake." Receives 20-30 unsolicited mss/month. Accepts 1-2 mss/issue; 12-18 mss/year. Publishes mss 1-3 months after acceptance. Published work by Vonnie Crist, Barry Patrick Fitzsimmons and Elizabeth Ames. Publishes more than 30 new writers/year. Length: 1,500 words preferred; 3,000 words maximum (however, will consider serializing longer pieces). Publishes short shorts. Also publishes poetry. Comments on or critiques rejected mss if requested with SASE.
How to Contact: Request guidelines, then send ms and cover letter. Accepts queries/mss by e-mail. Include

"information on the writer, focusing on what led him to write or create visual art. We want to know the person, both for our contributors guide 'Names in Lite' and to help build a network of creative people." Reports in 6-12 months. SASE. Simultaneous submissions OK, but prefer them not to be sent to other Baltimore publications. Sample copy for 9×12 SAE and 3 first-class stamps. Fiction guidelines for #10 SASE.
Payment/Terms: Pays 5 contributor's copies; 5 extras for 9×12 SASE with 4 first-class stamps. Acquires one-time rights.
Advice: "We first look for quality writing, then we look at content and theme. It's not hard to tell a dedicated writer from someone who only works for money or recognition. Fiction that resonates in the heart makes us take notice. It's a joy to read such a story." Known for "offbeat, creative, but not overtly sexual or violent. We like characterization and the play of ideas. We don't like contrived plots or political propaganda masquerading as literature."

$ LITERAL LATTÉ, Stimulating Prose, Poetry & Art, (II), 61 E. Eighth St., Suite 240, New York NY 10003. (212)260-5532. E-mail: litlatte@aol.com. Website: http://www.literal-latte.com (includes guidelines, staff, samples from past issues, contest info, subscription info, online only specials). Accepts outstanding work by beginning and established writers. Editor: Jenine Gordon Bockman. **Fiction Editor:** Jeffrey Michael Gordon Bockman. Tabloid: 11×17; 24 pages; 35 lb. Jet paper; 50 lb. cover; illustrations and photos. "*LL* is a high-quality journal of prose, poetry and art distributed free in cafés and bookstores in New York, by subscription ($11/year) and by Ingram Periodicals." Bimonthly. Estab. 1994. Circ. 25,000.

- *Literal Latté* recently received a *Pushcart Prize*.

Needs: Experimental, fantasy (science), humor/satire, literary, science fiction. Receives 4,000 mss/year. Accepts 30-60 mss/year. Publishes ms within 1 year after acceptance. Published work by Ray Bradbury, Stephen Dixon and Robert Olen Butler. Publishes 4 new writers/year. Length: 6,000 words maximum. Publishes short shorts. Also publishes literary essays, poetry. Sometimes critiques or comments on rejected mss.
How to Contact: Send complete ms with a cover letter. Include estimated word count, bio, list of publications. Reports in 2-3 months on mss. SASE for reply. Simultaneous submissions OK. Sample copy for $5. Fiction guidelines for #10 SASE.
Payment/Terms: Pays free subscription, 5 contributor's copies and a minimum of $25. Acquires first rights. Sponsors contests and awards for fiction writers; send #10 SASE marked "Fiction Contest" or "Poetry Contest."
Advice: "Reading our paper is the best way to determine our preferences. We judge work on quality alone and accept a broad range of extraordinary stories, personal essays, poems and graphics. Include a SASE large enough to house our comments (if any), and news on contests, readings or revised guidelines. Don't send a postcard. Include a phone number, in case we have questions like 'Is this still available?' "

THE LITERARY REVIEW, An International Journal of Contemporary Writing, (II), Fairleigh Dickinson University, 285 Madison Ave., Madison NJ 07940. Phone/fax: (973)443-8564. E-mail: tlr@fdu.edu. Website: http://www.webdelsol.com/tlr/ (includes subscription information, chapbooks and selections from printed issues). **Editor-in-Chief:** Walter Cummins. Magazine: 6×9; 130 pages; professionally printed on textpaper; semigloss card cover; perfect-bound. "Literary magazine specializing in fiction, poetry, and essays with an international focus." Quarterly. Estab. 1957. Circ. 2,500.

- This magazine has received grants from a wide variety of international sources including the Spanish Consulate General in New York, the Program for Cultural Cooperation between Spain's Ministry of Culture and U.S. Universities, Pro Helvetia, the Swiss Center Foundation, The Luso-American Foundation, Japan-U.S. Friendship Commission. Work published in *The Literary Review* has been included in *Editor's Choice*, *Best American Short Stories* and *Pushcart Prize* anthologies. The editor would like to see more fiction with an international theme.

Needs: Works of high literary quality only. Upcoming theme: "Sources and Stories" (Fall 1998). Receives 50-60 unsolicited fiction mss/month. Approximately 1-2% of fiction is agented. Recently published work by Maureen O'Neill, Patricia Ward and Todd Pierce. Published 75% new writers within the last year. Acquires 10-12 mss/year. Also publishes literary essays, literary criticism, poetry. Occasionally critiques rejected mss.
How to Contact: Send 1 complete ms with SASE. "Cover letter should include publication credits." Reports in 3 months on mss. Publishes ms an average of 1½-2 years after acceptance. Sample copy for $5; guidelines for SASE. Reviews novels and short story collections.
Payment/Terms: Pays 2 contributor's copies; 25% discount for extras. Acquires first rights.
Advice: "We want original dramatic situations with complex moral and intellectual resonance and vivid prose.

FOR EXPLANATIONS OF THESE SYMBOLS, SEE THE INSIDE FRONT AND BACK COVERS OF THIS BOOK.

We don't want versions of familiar plots and relationships. Too much of what we are seeing today is openly derivative in subject, plot and prose style. We pride ourselves on spotting new writers with fresh insight and approach."

✔ ▣ **THE LITTLE MAGAZINE, (III)**, State University of New York at Albany, English Department, Albany NY 12222. E-mail: litmag@csc.albany.edu. Website: http://www.albany.edu/~litmag. **Editors:** Dimitri Anastasopoulos, Christina Milletti, Manny Savopoulos. "Web-based journal; publishes CD-ROM issue every 2 years. Includes fiction and poetry for a literary audience; also illustrations, photography, artwork. Fiction and poetry for a literary audience." Annually. Estab. 1965.

- *The Little Magazine* has published entirely on the Web since 1995.

Needs: Literary, multi-media, hypertext, experimental, feminist, humor/satire. No genre fiction. Receives "roughly" 600 mss/issue over a 3-month reading period. Accepts 20 mss/issue. Does not read June through August. Submissions accepted on a rolling basis September through May. Publishes ms 6 months after acceptance. Recently published work by Charles Bernstein and Anne Waldeman. Length: no limit. Publishes short shorts.
How to Contact: Send complete ms with SASE (or IRC) *on disk* (IBM or Mac) or by e-mail. Hard copy submissions also accepted. Reports in 2 months on queries; in 4 months on mss. Simultaneous and reprint submissions OK. Sample copy for $15.
Payment/Terms: Pays 2 contributor's copies (when published on CD-ROM).
Terms: Acquires first North American serial rights.
Advice: "We're looking for high-quality fiction and poetry that has been conceived as, or lends itself to, multi-media or hypertext production."

THE LONG STORY, (II), 18 Eaton St., Lawrence MA 01843. (508)686-7638. E-mail: rpbtls@aol.com. Website: http://www.litline.org/html/thelongstory.html (includes writer's guidelines, cumulative index, editorials and a description of the magazine). **Editor:** R.P. Burnham. Magazine: 5½×8½; 150-200 pages; 60 lb. paper; 65 lb. cover stock; illustrations (b&w graphics). For serious, educated, literary people. No science fiction, adventure, romance, etc. "We publish high literary quality of any kind, but especially look for stories that have difficulty getting published elsewhere—committed fiction, working class settings, left-wing themes, etc." Annually. Estab. 1983. Circ. 1,200.
Needs: Contemporary, ethnic, feminist and literary. Receives 30-40 unsolicited mss/month. Accepts 6-7 mss/issue. 50% of writers published are new. Length: 8,000 words minimum; 20,000 words maximum.
How to Contact: Send complete ms with a brief cover letter. Reports in 2 months. Publishes ms an average of 3 months to 1 year after acceptance. SASE. May accept simultaneous submissions ("but not wild about it"). Sample copy for $6.
Payment/Terms: Pays 2 contributor's copies; $5 charge for extras. Acquires first rights.
Advice: "Read us first and make sure submitted material is the kind we're interested in. Send clear, legible manuscripts. We're not interested in commercial success; rather we want to provide a place for long stories, the most difficult literary form to publish in our country."

LOONFEATHER, (II), P.O. Box 1212, Bemidji MN 56619. (218)751-4869. **Editor:** Betty Rossi. Magazine: 6×9; 48 pages; 60 lb. Hammermill Cream woven paper; 65 lb. vellum cover stock; illustrations; occasional photos. A literary journal of short prose, poetry and graphics. Mostly a market for Northern Minnesota, Minnesota and Midwest writers. Semiannually. Estab. 1979. Circ. 300.
Needs: Literary, contemporary, prose and regional. Accepts 2-3 mss/issue, 4-6 mss/year. Reads mss from September 1 through May 31. Published new writers within the last year. Length: 600-1,500 words (prefers 1,500). Accepting queries for novel length fiction submissions in the 1999 book year.
How to Contact: Send complete query, and short autobiographical sketch. Reports within 4 months. Sample copy for $2 back issue; $5 current issue.
Payment/Terms: Free author's copies. Acquires one-time rights.
Advice: "Send carefully crafted and literary fiction. The writer should familiarize himself/herself with the type of fiction published in literary magazines as opposed to family magazines, religious magazines, etc."

LOST AND FOUND TIMES, (II, IV), Luna Bisonte Prods, 137 Leland Ave., Columbus OH 43214. (614)846-4126. **Editor:** John M. Bennett. Magazine: 5½×8½; 56 pages; good quality paper; good cover stock; illustrations; photos. Theme: experimental, avant-garde and folk literature, art. Published irregularly (twice yearly). Estab. 1975. Circ. 375.
Needs: Contemporary, experimental, literary, prose poem. Prefers short pieces. The editor would like to see more short, experimental pieces. Also publishes poetry. Accepts approximately 2 mss/issue. Published work by Spryszak, Steve McComas, Willie Smith, Rupert Wondolowski, Al Ackerman. Published new writers within the last year.
How to Contact: Query with clips of published work. SASE. No simultaneous submissions. Reports in 1 week on queries, 2 weeks on mss. Sample copy for $6.
Payment/Terms: Pays 1 contributor's copy. Rights revert to authors.

☑ **LOUISIANA LITERATURE, A Review of Literature and Humanities, (I, II, IV)**, Southeastern Louisiana University, SLU 792, Hammond LA 70402. (504)549-5022. E-mail: jbedell@selu.edu. **Editor:** Jack Bedell. Magazine: 6¾×9¾; 150 pages; 70 lb. paper; card cover; illustrations. "Essays should be about Louisiana material; preference is given to fiction and poetry with Louisiana and Southern themes, but creative work can be set anywhere." Semiannually. Estab. 1984. Circ. 400 paid; 500-700 printed.

- The editor would like to see more stories with firm closure.

Needs: Literary, mainstream, regional. "No sloppy, ungrammatical manuscripts." Upcoming themes: Louisiana detective fiction, Tennessee Williams, music (jazz, Cajun, blues, etc.), and dog stories (planned for Fall 1997 through Spring 1999). Receives 100 unsolicited fiction mss/month. Accepts mss related to special topics issues. May not read mss June through July. Publishes ms 6-12 months maximum after acceptance. Recently published work by Robert Olen Butler, Patty Friedmann, Albert Davis and Robin Beeman. Published new writers within the last year. Length: 3,500 words preferred; 1,000 words minimum; 6,000 words maximum. Also publishes literary essays (Louisiana themes), literary criticism, poetry. Sometimes comments on rejected mss.
How to Contact: Send complete ms. Reports in 1-3 months on mss. SASE. Sample copy for $6. Reviews novels and short story collections (mainly those by Louisiana authors).
Payment/Terms: Pays usually in contributor's copies. Acquires one-time rights.
Advice: "Cut out everything that is not a functioning part of the story. Make sure your manuscript is professionally presented. Use relevant specific detail in every scene."

[N] **THE LOWELL REVIEW, (II)**, Instant Karma Press, 3075 Harness Dr., Florissant MO 63033. E-mail: rita@etext.org. **Editor:** Judith Dickerman-Nelson. Magazine: 5½×8½; 70-100 pages; offset paper; laminated card stock cover. "We are independently published and try to appeal to the nonacademic writer and reader. Thematically, we gravitate toward work that reflects the middle class/working class experience." Annually. Estab. 1994. Circ. 250.
Needs: Condensed/excerpted novel, ethnic/multicultural, feminist, gay, historical, humor/satire, lesbian, literary, mainstream/contemporary, regional. Receives 50 unsolicited mss during reading period. Accepts 1-3 mss/issue. Does not read between June and December. Publishes ms 6 months after acceptance. Recently published work by Jay Atkinson, Charles Larson, Terry Farish and Renard Farrell. Length: open. Publishes short shorts. Also publishes literary essays, poetry. Sometimes critiques or comments on rejected ms.
How to Contact: Send complete ms with a cover letter. Include 1-paragraph bio, short list of publications. Send SASE for reply, return of ms or send a disposable copy of ms. Simultaneous submissions OK. Electronic submissions (disk or modem) OK. Sample copy for $5. Fiction guidelines for #10 SASE.
Payment/Terms: Pays 1 contributor's copy; additional copies $5. Acquires first North American serial rights. Sometimes sends galleys to author.

☑ **LULLWATER REVIEW, (II)**, Emory University, P.O. Box 22036, Atlanta GA 30322. Editor-in-Chief: Becky Brooks. Associate Editor: Sharyn Eply. **Fiction Editor:** Marcelo Guerra. Magazine: 6×9; 100 pages; 60 lb. paper; photos. "We look for fiction that reflects the issues and lifestyles of today, in whatever form it might arrive, whether as a story, short story or a novel excerpt. We hope to reach the average person, someone who might not ordinarily read a publication like ours, but might be attracted by our philosophy." Semiannually. Circ. 2,000. Member of the Council of Literary Magazines and Presses.
Needs: Condensed/excerpted novel, ethnic/multicultural, experimental, feminist, gay, humor/satire, lesbian, literary, mainstream/contemporary, regional. "No romance, please." Receives 75-115 unsolicited mss/month. Accepts 3-7 mss/issue; 6-14 mss/year. "Response time is slower in the summer, but we are always reading." Publishes ms within 2 months after acceptance. Published work by Lynne Burris Butler, Meghan Keith-Hynes and Patricia Flinn. Length: 10 pages average; 25 pages maximum. Publishes short shorts. Length: 300-500 words. Also publishes poetry. Sometimes critiques or comments on rejected mss. Sponsors contest; send SASE for information in early Fall.
How to Contact: Send complete ms with cover letter. Include bio and list of publications. Reports in 1-2 weeks on queries; 2-3 months on mss. Send SASE for reply, return of ms or send a disposable copy of ms. Simultaneous submissions OK. Sample copy for $5. Back copy $4. Fiction guidelines for SASE.
Payment/Terms: Pays 3 contributor's copies; additional copies for $5. Acquires first North American serial rights.
Advice: "We at the *Lullwater Review* look for clear cogent writing, strong character development and an engaging approach to the story in our fiction submissions. Stories with particularly strong voices and well-developed central themes are especially encouraged. Be sure that your manuscript is ready before mailing it off to us. Revise, revise, revise!"

☑ **LUMMOX JOURNAL, (IV)**, Lummox Press/Productions, P.O. Box 5301, San Pedro CA 90733-5301. (562)439-9858. E-mail: lumoxraindog@earthlink.net. **Editor:** Raindog. Magazine: digest size; 20 pages; photocopy paper; illustrations and photos. "*The Lummox Journal* focuses on the process of creativity using interviews, reviews, articles and essays as exploratory tools. Lummox Press plans a yearly anthology of fiction and poetry entitled *Dufus* since the journal doesn't (as a rule) print unsolicited poetry and short fiction. There are always exceptions. . . . Audience: the curious literary literary bohemian." Estab. 1996. Circ. 200.
Needs: Experimental, historical, literary, regional, serialized novel. "Would like to see more 'micro' fiction that

focuses on creativity." Publishes special fiction and poetry anthology. Receives 1-2 unsolicited mss/month. Accepts 2-3 mss/year. Recently published work by Jay Alamares and Scott Wannberg. Length: 750 words average; 900 words maximum. Publishes short shorts. Also publishes literary essays, literary criticism and poetry.
How to Contact: Query first. Accepts queries/mss by e-mail. Include brief bio and estimated word count. Reports in 1-2 weeks on queries. Send SASE for reply, return of ms or send disposable copy of ms. Simultaneous and electronic (disk only) submissions OK. Sample copy for $2 and a 6×9 SAE with 2 first-class stamps. Fiction guidelines for #10 SASE. Reviews poetry and short story collections. Send books to editor.
Payment/Terms: Pays 1 contributor's copy for one-time rights; additional copies $2. Not copyrighted.
Advice: Looks for "well-written, reality based emotion (not buzzword rants), strength and genuine believability. Make sure it's something you want to see in print."

✔ $ **LYNX EYE, (I, II)**, ScribbleFest Literary Group, 1880 Hill Dr., Los Angeles CA 90041-1244. (213)550-8522. **Editors:** Pam McCully and Kathryn Morrison. Magazine: 5½×8½; 120 pages; 60 lb. book paper; varied cover stock. "*Lynx Eye* is dedicated to showcasing visionary writers and artists, particularly new voices." Quarterly. Estab. 1994. Circ. 500.
Needs: Adventure, condensed/excerpted novel, erotica, ethnic/multicultural, experimental, fantasy (science), feminist, gay, historical, horror, humor/satire, lesbian, literary, mainstream/contemporary, mystery/suspense, romance, science fiction, serialized novel, translations, westerns. Receives 500 unsolicited mss/month. Accepts 30 mss/issue; 120 mss/year. Publishes ms approximately 3 months after acceptance (contract guarantees publication within 12 months or rights revert and payment is kept by author). Published work by Anjali Banerjee, William J. Cobb, Kel Munger and Gustav Richar. Publishes 30 new writers/year. Length: 2,500 words average; 500 words minimum; 5,000 words maximum. Also publishes artwork, literary essays, poetry. Often critiques or comments on rejected mss.
How to Contact: Send complete ms with a cover letter. Include name and address on page one; name on *all* other pages. Reports in 2-3 months. Send SASE for reply, return of ms or send a disposable copy of ms. Simultaneous submissions OK. Sample copy for $7.95. Fiction guidelines for #10 SASE.
Payment/Terms: Pays $10 on acceptance and 3 contributor's copies for first North American serial rights; additional copies $3.95.
Advice: "We consider any well-written manuscript. Characters who speak naturally and who act or are acted upon are greatly appreciated. Your high school English teacher was correct. Basics matter. Imaginative, interesting ideas are sabotaged by lack of good grammar, spelling and punctuation skills. Most submissions are contemporary/mainstream. We could use some variety. Please do not confuse confessional autobiographies with fiction."

✔ **THE MACGUFFIN, (II)**, Schoolcraft College, Department of English, 18600 Haggerty Rd., Livonia MI 48152. (734)462-4400, ext. 5292 or 5327. Fax: (734)462-4558. E-mail: alindenb@schoolcraft.cc.mi.us. Website: http://www.schoolcraft.cc.mi.us (includes samples, guidelines, editorial contacts and subscription information). Editor: Arthur J. Lindenberg. **Fiction Editors:** Gary Erwin and Anne Hutchinson. Magazine: 6×9; 160 pages; 60 lb. paper; 110 lb. cover; b&w illustrations and photos. "*The MacGuffin* is a literary magazine which publishes a range of material including poetry, nonfiction and fiction. Material ranges from traditional to experimental. We hope our periodical attracts a variety of people with many different interests." Triannual. Quality fiction a special need. Estab. 1984. Circ. 600.
Needs: Adventure, contemporary, ethnic, experimental, fantasy, historical (general), humor/satire, literary, mainstream, prose poem, psychic/supernatural/occult, science fiction, translations. No religious, inspirational, confession, romance, horror, pornography. Receives 25-40 unsolicited mss/month. Accepts 5-10 mss/issue; 10-30 mss/year. Does not read mss between July 1 and August 15. Publishes ms 6 months to 2 years after acceptance. Agented fiction: 10-15%. Recently published work by Annaliese Hood, Jay Atkinson, Gary Eberle and Stuart Dybek. Published 30 new writers within the last year. Length: 2,000-2,500 words average; 100 words minimum; 5,000 words maximum. Publishes short shorts. Also publishes literary essays. Occasionally critiques rejected mss and recommends other markets.
How to Contact: Send complete ms with cover letter, which should include: "1. *brief* biographical information; 2. note that this *is not* a simultaneous submission." Reports in 2-3 months. SASE. Reprint and electronic (disk) submissions OK. Sample copy for $4; current issue for $4.50. Fiction guidelines free.
Payment/Terms: Pays 2 contributor's copies. Acquires one-time rights.
Advice: "We want to give promising new fiction writers the opportunity to publish alongside recognized writers. Be persistent. If a story is rejected, try to send it somewhere else. When we reject a story, we may accept the next one you send us. When we make suggestions for a rewrite, we may accept the revision. There seems to be a great number of good authors of fiction, but there are far too few places for publication. However, I think this is changing. Make your characters come to life. Even the most ordinary people become fascinating if they live for your readers."

✔ **THE MADISON REVIEW, (II)**, Department of English, Helen C. White Hall, 600 N. Park St., University of Wisconsin, Madison WI 53706. (608)263-0566. **Managing Editors:** Dan Fitzsimons and Emily Benz. Poetry Editors: Erin Hanusa and Trevor Schaid. Magazine: 6×9; 180 pages. "Magazine of fiction and poetry with special emphasis on literary stories and some emphasis on Midwestern writers." Semiannually. Estab. 1978. Circ. 1,000.

Needs: Experimental and literary stories, prose poems, novel excerpts and stories in translation. No historical fiction. Receives 10-50 unsolicited fiction mss/month. Acquires approximately 6 mss/issue. Does not read mss May through September. Recently published work by Leslie Pietrzyk, Stephen Shugart and Ira Gold. Published new writers within the last year. Length: 4,000 words average. Also publishes poetry.
How to Contact: Send complete ms with cover letter and SASE. Include estimated word count, 1-page bio and list of publications. "The letters should give one or two sentences of relevant information about the writer—just enough to provide a context for the work." Reports in 6 months on mss. Publishes ms an average of 4 months after acceptance. Sample copy for $2.50.
Payment/Terms: Pays 3 contributor's copies; $2.50 charge for extras.
Terms: Acquires first North American serial rights.

$ MALAHAT REVIEW, University of Victoria, P.O. Box 1700, STN CSC, Victoria, British Columbia V8W 2Y2 Canada. (250)721-8524. **Acting Editor:** Marlene Cookshaw. Quarterly. Circ. 1,800.

- *The Malahat Review* ranked #46 on *Writer's Digest*'s Fiction 50 list of top markets for fiction writers.

Needs: "General fiction and poetry, book reviews." Reports in 3 months. Publishes 3-4 stories/issue. Recently published work by Robert Sherrin, Natasha Waxman, Leon Rooke and Russell Smith. Length: 10,000 words maximum.
How to Contact: "Enclose proper postage on the SASE." Sample copy: $8 available through the mail; guidelines available upon request. No simultaneous submissions.
Payment/Terms: Pays $30/printed page and contributor's copies.
Advice: "We do encourage new writers to submit. Read the magazines you want to be published in, ask for their guidelines and follow them. Write for information on *Malahat*'s novella competitions."

manna, The Literary-Professional Quarterly of manna forty, inc., (I, IV), manna forty, inc., Route 1, Box 548, Sharon OK 73857-9761. (405)254-2660 (evenings). Fax: (405)256-2416. **Editor:** Richard D. Kahoe. Newsletter: 8½×11; 8 pages; 72 lb. recycled paper and cover; illustrations. "*manna* is interested only in nature/religion/psychology, and especially in interfaces of two or three of these subjects." Quarterly. Estab. 1987. Circ. 300-350.

- *manna* will not be published after December 1999.

Needs: Ethnic/multicultural, feminist, religious/inspirational, senior citizen/retirement. "We have room for only short-short fiction: parables, personal experience, etc." List of upcoming themes available for SASE. Receives 1 unsolicited mss/month. Accepts 1 mss/issue; 4-8 mss/year. Publishes ms 1-11 months after acceptance. Recently published work by Richard D. Kahoe and Charles Stephens. Publishes 2-5 new writers/year. Length: 500 words average; 150 words minimum; 750 words maximum. Also publishes literary essays, poetry. Always critiques or comments on rejected ms.
How to Contact: Send complete ms with a cover letter "telling who you are," estimated word count and 100-word bio. Reports in 1 month on mss. SASE for return of ms or send a disposable copy of the ms. Simultaneous and reprint submissions OK. Sample copy for SASE.
Payment/Terms: Pays 2 contributor's copies; additional copies for 25¢ plus postage. Acquires one-time rights.
Advice: Looking for "human interest, touching on two or more of our subject areas (nature, religion, psychology) and presuming good literary quality, grammar, word selection, etc. Don't send anything that is not relevant to at least one of our basic subjects. Submit to the periodicals that reflect your style, level of experience/publication record, and content—read guidelines and samples before submitting."

$ MANOA, A Pacific Journal of International Writing, (II), English Dept., University of Hawaii, Honolulu HI 96822. (808)956-3070. Fax: (808)956-7808. E-mail: mjournal-l@hawaii.edu. Website: http://www2.hawaii.edu/mjournal (includes writer's guidelines, names of editors, short fiction and poetry). Editor: Frank Stewart. **Fiction Editor:** Ian MacMillan. Magazine: 7×10; 240 pages. "An American literary magazine, emphasis on top US fiction and poetry, but each issue has a major guest-edited translated feature of recent writings from an Asian/Pacific country." Semiannually. Estab. 1989.

- *Manoa* has received numerous awards, and work published in the magazine has been selected for prize anthologies.

Needs: Contemporary, excerpted novel, literary, mainstream and translation (from US and nations in or bordering on the Pacific). "Part of our purpose is to present top U.S. fiction from throughout the U.S., not only to U.S. readers, but to readers in Asian and Pacific countries. Thus we are not limited to stories related to or set in the Pacific—in fact, we do not want exotic or adventure stories set in the Pacific, but good US literary fiction of any locale." Accepts 8-10 mss/issue; 16-20/year. Publishes ms 6 months-2 years after acceptance. Agented fiction 10%. Recently published work by Robert Olen Butler, Monica Wood and Barry Lopez. Publishes 1-2 new writers/year. Publishes short fiction. Also publishes essays, book reviews, poetry.
How to Contact: Send complete ms with cover letter or through agent. Reports in 4-6 months. SASE. Simultaneous submissions OK; query before sending e-mail. Sample copy for $10. Reviews novels and short story collections. Send books or reviews to Reviews Editor.
Payment/Terms: Pays "highly competitive rates so far," plus contributor's copies for first North American serial rights and one-time reprint rights. Sends galleys to author.
Advice: "*Manoa*'s readership is (and is intended to be) mostly national, not local. It also wants to represent top

US writing to a new international market, in Asia and the Pacific. Altogether we hope our view is a fresh one; that is, not facing east toward Europe but west toward 'the other half of the world.' Your own writing style and perspective or experience are as individual as fingerprints. Don't con yourself into imitation."

☑ **MANY MOUNTAINS MOVING, (II), a literary journal of diverse contemporary voices**, 420 22nd St., Boulder CO 80302-7909. (303)545-9942. Fax: (303)444-6510. E-mail: mmmine@concentric.net. Editor: Naomi Horii. **Fiction Editor:** Beth Nugent. Magazine: 6×8¾; 200 pages; recycled paper; color/heavy cover; illustrations and photos. "We publish fiction, poetry, general-interest essays and art. We try to seek contributors from all cultures." Triannually. Estab. 1994. Circ. 2,000.

• The editor would like to see more experimental, avant garde fiction.

Needs: Ethnic/multicultural, experimental, feminist, gay, historical, humor/satire, lesbian, literary, mainstream/contemporary, translations. No genre fiction. Plans special fiction issue or anthology. Receives 300 unsolicited mss/month. Accepts 4-6 mss/issue; 12-18 mss/year. Publishes ms 2-8 months after acceptance. Agented fiction 5%. Recently published work by Michael Dorsey, Daniela Kuper, Julie Shigekuni and Michael Ramos. "We try to publish at least one new writer per issue; more when possible." Length: 3,000-5,000 words average. Publishes short shorts. Also publishes literary essays, poetry. Sometimes critiques or comments on rejected mss.

How to Contact: Send complete ms with a cover letter. Include estimated word count, list of publications. Reports in 2 weeks on queries; 1-3 months on mss. Send SASE for reply, return of ms or send a disposable copy of ms. Simultaneous submissions OK. Sample copy for $6.50 and enough IRCs for 1 pound of airmail/printed matter. Fiction guidelines for #10 SASE.

Payment/Terms: Pays 3 contributor's copies; additional copies for $3. Acquires first North American serial rights. Sends galleys to author "if requested." Sponsors a contest, $200 prize. Send SASE for guidelines. Deadline: December 31.

Advice: "We look for top-quality fiction with fresh voices and verve. Read at least one issue of our journal to get a feel for what kind of fiction we generally publish."

MARYLAND REVIEW, (I, II), Department of English and Modern Languages, University of Maryland Eastern Shore, Princess Anne MD 21853-1299. (410)651-6552. E-mail: mandersn@umes-bird.umd.edu. **Editor:** Mignon H. Anderson. Literary journal: 6×9; 100-150 pages; quality paper stock; heavy cover; illustrations. "We have a special interest in African American and other literature of African orgin, but we welcome all sorts of submissions. Our audience is literary, educated, well-read." Annually. Estab. 1986. Circ. 500.

Needs: Contemporary, humor/satire, literary, mainstream, Black literature. No genre stories; no religious, political or juvenile material. Accepts approximately 12-15 mss/issue. Publishes ms "within 1 year" after acceptance. Recently published work by Sandra Hart Christian, Joel Roache and Skai Shadow. Publishes 4-10 new writers/year. Publishes short shorts. "Length is open, but we do like to include mostly pieces 1,500 words and under." Also publishes poetry.

How to Contact: Send complete ms with cover letter. Include a brief autobiography of approximately 75 words. Reports "as soon as possible." SASE, *but does not return mss*. No simultaneous submissions. "No fax copies, please. No submissions by e-mail." Sample copy for $10.

Payment/Terms: Pays in 2 contributor's copies. Acquires first serial rights only.

Advice: "Think primarily about your *characters* in fiction, about their beliefs and how they may change. Create characters and situations that are utterly new. We will give your material a careful and considerate reading. Any fiction that is flawed by grammatical errors, misspellings, etc. will not have a chance. We're seeing a lot of fine fiction these days, and we approach each story with fresh and eager eyes. Ezra Pound's battle-cry about poetry refers to fiction as well: 'Make it New!' "

☑ **$ THE MASSACHUSETTS REVIEW, (II)**, South College, University of Massachusetts, Amherst MA 01003. (413)545-2689. Fax: (413)577-0740. E-mail: massrev@external.umass.edu. Website: http://www.litline.org/html/massreview.html (includes general overview, information on editors, excerpts, guidelines). **Editors:** Mary Heath, Jules Chametzky, Paul Jenkins. Magazine: 6×9; 172 pages; 52 lb. paper; 65 lb. vellum cover; illustrations and photos. Quarterly. Estab. 1959. Circ. 1,200.

Needs: Short stories. Wants more prose less than 30 pages. No mystery or science fiction. Does not read fiction mss June 1-October 1. Published new writers within the last year. Recently published work by Stephen Dobyns, Chris Haven, Kim Bridgeford and Martha Conway. Approximately 5% of fiction is agented. Also accepts poetry. Critiques rejected mss when time permits.

How to Contact: Send complete ms. No ms returned without SASE. Simultaneous submissions OK, if noted. Reports in 2 months. Publishes ms an average of 9-12 months after acceptance. Sample copy for $7. Guidelines available for SASE.

CHECK THE CATEGORY INDEXES, located at the back of the book, for publishers interested in specific fiction subjects.

Payment/Terms: Pays $50 maximum on publication for first North American serial rights.
Advice: "Shorter rather than longer stories preferred (up to 28-30 pages)."

MATRIARCH'S WAY; JOURNAL OF FEMALE SUPREMACY, (I, II), Artemis Creations, 3395 Nostrand Ave., 2J, Brooklyn NY 11229-4053. Phone/fax: (718)648-8215. **Editor:** Shirley Oliveira. Magazine: 5½×8½; illustrations and photos. *Matriarch's Way* is a "matriarchal feminist" publication. Quarterly. Estab. 1996.
Needs: Condensed/excerpted novel, erotica (quality), ethnic/multicultural, experimental, fantasy (science, sword and sorcery), feminist (radical), horror, humor/satire, literary, psychic/supernatural/occult, religious/inspirational, romance (futuristic/time travel, gothic, historical), science fiction (soft/sociological), serialized novel. Receives 10 unsolicited mss/week. Often critiques or comments on rejected mss. 90% of work published is by new writers.
How to Contact: Query first, query with clips of published work or query with synopsis plus 1-3 chapters of novel. Accepts queries/mss by fax. Include estimated word count, bio and list of publications with submission. Reports in 1 week on queries; 6 weeks on mss. SASE for reply or send a disposable copy of ms. Sample copy for $4.50. Reviews novels and short story collections and excerpts "We need book reviewers desperately, original or reprints. We supply books."
Payment/Terms: Pays 1 copy of published issue. Acquires one-time rights.
Advice: Looks for "a knowledge of subject, originality and good writing style. If you can best Camille Paglia, you're on your way!"

$ MERLYN'S PEN: The National Magazine of Student Writing, Grades 6-12, (I, II, IV), Box 1058, East Greenwich RI 02818. (401)885-5175. Fax: (401)885-5222. E-mail: merlynspen@aol.com. Website: http://www.merlynspen.com (includes writer's guidelines, the first page of most stories that appear in our anthology collection: *The American Teen Writer Series*). **Editor:** R. Jim Stahl. Magazine: 8⅜×10⅞; 100 pages; 70 lb. paper; 12 pt. gloss cover; illustrations; photos. Student writing only (grades 6 through 12) for libraries, homes and English classrooms. Annual (each October). Estab. 1985. Circ. 6,000.

- Winner of the Paul A. Witty Short Story Award and Selection on the New York Public Library's Book List of Recommended Reading.

Needs: Adventure, fantasy, historical, horror, humor/satire, literary, mainstream, mystery/suspense, romance, science fiction, western, young adult/teen. "Would like to see more humor." Also publishes editorial reviews, poetry. Must be written by students in grades 6-12. Receives 1,200 unsolicited fiction mss/month. Accepts 50 mss/issue; 50 mss/year. Publishes ms 3 months to 1 year after acceptance. Publishes 50 new writers/year. Length: 1,500 words average; 25 words minimum; no maximum. Publishes short shorts. Responds to rejected mss.
How to Contact: Send for cover-sheet template. Accepts queries/mss by fax. *Charges submission fee: $1/title. For an additional $4, authors receive an extended editorial critique (100 or more words) of their submission in addition to the standard yes/no response.* Reports in 10 weeks.
Payment/Terms: Three copies of *Merlyn's Pen* plus up to 1,000 words $10; over 1,000 words $75; over 3,000 words $175; over 5,000 words $250. Published works become the property of Merlyn's Pen, Inc.
Advice: "Write what you *know*; write where you are. We look for the authentic voice and experience of young adults."

N MESSAGES FROM THE HEART, (I, II), P.O. Box 64840, Tucson AZ 85728. (520)577-0588. Fax: (520)529-9657. E-mail: lbsmith@theriver.com. **Editor:** Lauren B. Smith. Magazine: 4¼×10½; 20 pages; text weight, various papers; illustrations and photos. "A publication of writings, specifically letters, which nurture understanding between people. Intended audience: mainstream public interested in letter writing." Quarterly. Estab. 1993. Circ. 500.
Needs: Short stories about or containing letters. "We welcome submissions from children and have a student page." No erotica, science fiction, psychic. Receives 150-250 mss/month. Accepts 100 mss/year. Publishes ms 9-12 months after acceptance. Publishes 80 new writers/year. Length: 800 words maximum. Publishes short shorts. Also publishes literary essays, literary criticism, poetry.
How to Contact: Send complete ms with a cover letter. Accepts mss by e-mail. Reports in 3 weeks. Send SASE for return of ms or send a disposable copy of ms. Simultaneous submissions OK. Sample copy $5. Fiction guidelines free. Reviews novels, short story collections and nonfiction books about letter writing.
Payment/Terms: Pays 3 issues of magazine and 3 contributor's copies; additional copies $2.75. Acquires one-time rights.
Advice: "Speak from the heart, honestly, no gimmicks."

N THE METROPOLITAN REVIEW, (II), P.O. Box 32128, Washington DC 20007. Editor: Mary Claire Ray. **Fiction Editor:** William Beverly. Magazine: 8½×11; 32-64 pages; illustrations and photos. Literary/visual arts print journal. Semiannually. Estab. 1998.
Needs: Condensed/excerpted novel, humor/satire, literary, regional, translations. Receives 10 unsolicited mss/month. Accepts 2-3 mss/issue; 5-6 mss/year. Publishes ms 2-6 months after acceptance. Agented fiction 10%. Recently published work by Stuart Dybek and William J. Cobb (Issue 2). Length: 250 words minimum; 10,000 words maximum. Publishes short shorts. Also publishes literary essays, literary criticism, poetry. Often critiques or comments on rejected ms.
How to Contact: Send complete ms with a cover letter. Include 10-100 word bio. Reports in 2 weeks-3 months.

SASE. Simultaneous submissions OK if notified. Sample copy $6. Reviews novels and short story collections. Send books to fiction editor.
Payment/Terms: Pays 2 contributor's copies; additional copies $4. Acquires first rights.
Advice: "We look for efficient narration, surprising and resourceful characters, maturity, conviction, and a poet's ear."

$ MICHIGAN QUARTERLY REVIEW, University of Michigan, 3032 Rackham, Ann Arbor MI 48109-1070. (734)764-9265. E-mail: mqr@umich.edu. Website: http://www.umich.edu/~mqr (includes history and description of magazine; of current and forthcoming issues, subscription information). **Editor:** Laurence Goldstein. "An interdisciplinary journal which publishes mainly essays and reviews, with some high-quality fiction and poetry, for an intellectual, widely read audience." Quarterly. Estab. 1962. Circ. 1,800.

- Stories from *Michigan Quarterly Review* have been selected for inclusion in *The Best American Short Stories*.

Needs: Literary. No "genre" fiction written for a "market." "Would like to see more fiction about social, political, cultural matters, not just centered on a love relationship or dysfunctional family." Receives 200 unsolicited fiction mss/month. Accepts 2 mss/issue; 8 mss/year. Published work by Jonis Agee, Reginald Gibbons, George V. Higgins and Jennifer Moses. Length: 1,500 words minimum; 7,000 words maximum; 5,000 words average. Also publishes poetry, literary essays.
How to Contact: Send complete ms with cover letter. "I like to know if a writer is at the beginning, or further along, in his or her career. Don't offer plot summaries of the story, though a background comment is welcome." Reports in 6-8 weeks. SASE. No simultaneous submissions. Sample copy for $2.50 and 2 first-class stamps.
Payment/Terms: Pays $8-10/printed page on publication for first rights. Awards the Lawrence Foundation Prize of $1,000 for best story in *MQR* previous year.
Advice: "There's no beating a good plot and interesting characters, and a fresh use of the English language. (Most stories fail because they're written in such a bland manner, or in TV-speak.) Be ambitious, try to involve the social world in the personal one, be aware of what the best writing of today is doing, don't be satisfied with a small slice of life narrative but think how to go beyond the ordinary."

$ MID-AMERICAN REVIEW, (II), Department of English, Bowling Green State University, Bowling Green OH 43403. (419)372-2725. **Fiction Editor:** Michael Czyzniejewski. Magazine: 5½×8½; 100-150 pages; 60 lb. bond paper; coated cover stock. "We publish serious fiction and poetry, as well as critical studies in contemporary literature, translations and book reviews." Biannually. Estab. 1981.

- A story published in the magazine was reprinted in *Best American Short Stories of 1996* and *New Stories From the South* 1997.

Needs: Experimental, literary, memoir, prose poem, traditional and translations. Receives about 120 unsolicited fiction mss/month. Accepts 5-6 mss/issue. Does not read June-August. Approximately 5% of fiction is agented. Recently published work by Stuart Dybek, François Camoin, Alberto Ríos, David Foster Wallace, Nancy Roberts, Dab Chaon and Petertto Davis. Published 2-5 new writers within the last year. Also publishes literary essays and poetry. Occasionally critiques rejected mss. Sponsors the Sherwood Anderson Short Fiction Prize.
How to Contact: Send 1 10-20 page ms with SASE. No simultaneous submissions. Reports in about 3 months. Publishes ms an average of 6 months after acceptance. Sample copy for $5. Reviews novels and short story collections. Send books to editor-in-chief.
Payment/Terms: Payment offered pending funding; usually pays $10-50 on publication and 2 contributor's copies for one-time rights; charges for additional copies.
Advice: "We look for well-written stories that make the reader want to read on past the first page. Clichéd themes and sloppy writing turn us off immediately. Read literary journals to see what's being published in today's market. Also, find authors you like and read as much of their work as you can. Of course, don't give up on a story you believe in. We continue to see quality fiction no matter what is going on, as well as fiction from writers who seem uninformed. We recently published 2 shorts by Stuart Dybeck and would like to see more short submissions."

MINAS TIRITH EVENING-STAR, (IV), W.W. Publications, Box 373, Highland MI 48357-0373. (813)585-0985. **Editor:** Philip Helms. Magazine: 8½×11; 40 pages; typewriter paper; black ink illustrations; photos. Magazine of J.R.R. Tolkien and fantasy—fiction, poetry, reviews, etc. for general audience. Quarterly. Published special fiction issue; plans another. Estab. 1967. Circ. 500.
Needs: "Fantasy and Tolkien." Receives 5 unsolicited mss/month. Accepts 1 ms/issue; 5 mss/year. Published new writers within the last year. Length: 1,000-1,200 words preferred; 5,000 words maximum. Publishes short shorts. Also publishes literary essays, literary criticism, poetry. Occasionally critiques rejected mss.
How to Contact: Send complete ms and bio. Reports in 1-2 months. SASE. No simultaneous submissions. Reprint submissions OK. Sample copy for $1. Reviews novels and short story collections.
Terms: Acquires first rights.
Advice: Goal is "to expand knowledge and enjoyment of J.R.R. Tolkien's and his son Christopher Tolkien's works and their worlds."

MIND IN MOTION, A Magazine of Poetry and Short Prose, (II), Box 7070, Big Bear Lake CA 92315. **Editor:** Céleste Goyer. Magazine: 5½×8½; 64 pages; 20 lb. paper; 50 lb. cover. "We prefer to publish works of substantial brilliance that engage and encourage the reader's mind." Quarterly. Estab. 1985. Circ. 350.

- This magazine is known for surrealism and poetic language.

Needs: Experimental, fantasy, humor/satire, literary, prose poem, science fiction. No "mainstream, romance, nostalgia, un-poetic prose; anything with a slow pace or that won't stand up to re-reading." Receives 50 unsolicited mss/month. Acquires 10 mss/issue; 40 mss/year. Reads mss October through July. Publishes ms 2-12 weeks after acceptance. Recently published work by Elizabeth Howkins, Coral Hull, Bent Lorentzen and Mike Standish. Length: 2,000 words preferred; 250 words minimum; 3,500 words maximum. Also publishes poetry. Sometimes critiques rejected mss.
How to Contact: Send complete ms. "Cover letter or bio not necessary." SASE. Simultaneous (if notified) submissions OK. Sample copy for $3.50. Fiction guidelines for #10 SASE.
Payment/Terms: Pays 1 contributor's copy; charge for additional copies. Acquires first North American serial rights.
Advice: "We're now taking more stories per issue, and they may be a bit longer, due to a format modification. *Mind in Motion* is noted for introspective, philosophical fiction with a great deal of energy and originality."

☑ **THE MINNESOTA REVIEW, A Journal of Committed Writing, (I, II)**, Dept. of English, University of Missouri, Columbia MO 65211. (919)328-6388. Fax: (919)328-4889. **Editor:** Jeffrey Williams. Magazine: 5¼×7½; approximately 200 pages; some illustrations; occasional photos. "We emphasize socially and politically engaged work." Semiannually. Estab. 1960. Circ. 1,500.
Needs: Experimental, feminist, gay, historical, lesbian, literary. Receives 50-75 mss/month. Accepts 3-4 mss/issue; 6-8 mss/year. Publishes ms within 6 months-1 year after acceptance. Published work by Laura Nixon Dawson, Jameson Currier, Jiqi Kajane and Stephen Guiterrez. Length: 1,500-6,000 words preferred. Publishes short shorts. Also publishes literary essays, literary criticism, poetry. Occasionally critiques rejected mss and recommends other markets.
How to Contact: Send complete ms with optional cover letter. Reports in 2-3 weeks on queries; 2-3 months on mss. SASE. Simultaneous submissions OK. Reviews novels and short story collections. Send books to book review editor.
Payment/Terms: Pays in contributor's copies. Charge for additional copies. Acquires first rights.
Advice: "We look for socially and politically engaged work, particularly short, striking work that stretches boundaries."

☑ $ **MISSISSIPPI MUD, (I, II)**, 7119 Santa Fe Ave., Dallas TX 75223. (214)321-8955. **Editor:** Joel Weinstein. Magazine: 7¾×10; 96 pages; coated and uncoated paper; coated cover; illustrations; photographs. "*Mississippi Mud* publishes fiction, poetry and artworks reflecting life in America at the end of the 20th century. Good writing is its focus." Published irregularly. Estab. 1973. Circ. 1,600.

- Editor would like to see more non-didactic political fiction.

Needs: Excerpted novel, ethnic/multicultural, experimental, literary, mainstream/contemporary, translations. "No religious or romance." Receives 40-50 unsolicited mss/month. Accepts 8-10 mss/year. Publishes ms 8-18 months after acceptance. Recently published work by Kevin Phelan, Bill U'ren, Willie Smith, Ursula K. Leguin, Matt Sharpe and Toni Graham. Length: 5,000 words average; 100 words minimum; 25,000 words maximum. Publishes short shorts. Also publishes poetry. Sometimes critiques or comments on rejected mss.
How to Contact: Send complete ms with a cover letter. Include list of publications. Reports in 6-8 weeks on queries; 4-6 months on mss. Send SASE for reply, return of ms or send a disposable copy of ms. Simultaneous and electronic (disk) submissions OK. Sample copy for $6.
Payment/Terms: $50-100 and 2 contributor's copies on publication for first North American serial rights.
Advice: "We want good writing, a good story, originality. Look for the right markets: magazines where your writing fits."

MISSISSIPPI REVIEW, (III), University of Southern Mississippi, Box 5144, Hattiesburg MS 39406-5144. (601)266-4321. E-mail: fb@netdoor.com. Website: http://www.sushi.st.usm.edu/mrw/. **Managing Editor:** Rie Fortenberry. "Literary publication for those interested in contemporary literature—writers, editors who read to be in touch with current modes." Semiannually. Estab. 1972. Circ. 1,500.
Needs: Literary, contemporary, fantasy, humor, translations, experimental, avant-garde and "art" fiction. Quality writing. No juvenile or genre fiction. Buys varied amount of mss/issue. Does not read mss in summer. Recently published work by Jason Brown, Terese Svoboda and Barry Hannah. Length: 30 pages maximum.
How to Contact: Not currently reading unsolicited work. Sample copy for $8.
Payment/Terms: Pays in contributor's copies. Acquires first North American serial rights.
Advice: "May I suggest that you enter our annual *Mississippi Review* Prize competition (see Contests section in this book) or submit the work via e-mail to our World Wide Web publication, which is a monthly (except August) and publishes more new work than we are able to in the print version. Send submissions to fb@netdoor.com as ASCII files in the text of your e-mail message, or as Microsoft Word of WordPerfect attachments to your message."

$ THE MISSOURI REVIEW, (II), 1507 Hillcrest Hall, University of Missouri—Columbia, Columbia MO 65211. (573)882-4474. Fax: (573)884-4671. Website: http://www.missouri.edu/~moreview (includes guidelines, contest information, short fiction, poetry, essays, interviews, features and book reviews). **Editor:** Speer Morgan. Magazine: 6×9; 212 pages. Theme: fiction, poetry, essays, reviews, interviews, cartoons, "all with a distinctly contemporary orientation. For writers, and the general reader with broad literary interests. We present nonestablished as well as established writers of excellence. The *Review* frequently runs feature sections or special issues dedicated to particular topics frequently related to fiction." Published 3 times/academic year. Estab. 1977. Circ. 6,800.

- *The Missouri Review* ranked #37 on *Writer's Digest*'s Fiction 50 list of top markets for fiction writers. The editor would like to see more good comic fiction.

Needs: Condensed/excerpted novel, ethnic/multicultural, humor/satire, literary, contemporary. "No genre or flash fictions; no children's." Receives approximately 400 unsolicited fiction mss each month. Accepts 5-6 mss/issue; 15-20 mss/year. Recently published work by Daniel Akst, Jesse Lee Kercheval, Michael Byers, Talvikki Ansel and Steve Yarbrough. Publishes 6-10 new writers/year. No preferred length. Also publishes personal essays, poetry. Often critiques rejected mss.
How to Contact: Send complete ms with SASE. Include brief bio and list of publications. Reports in 10 weeks. Send SASE for reply, return of ms or send disposable copy of ms. Sample copy for $7.
Payment/Terms: Pays $20/page minimum on signed contract for all rights.
Advice: Awards William Peden Prize in fiction; $1,000 to best story published in *Missouri Review* in a given year. Also sponsors Editors' Prize Contest with a prize of $1,500 for fiction, $1,000 for essays and the Larry Levis Editors' Prize for poetry, with a prize of $1,500; and the Tom McAfee Discovery Prize in poetry for poets who have not yet published a book.

MOBIUS, The Journal of Social Change, (II), 1250 E. Dayton #3, Madison WI 53703. (608)255-4224. E-mail: smfred@aol.com. **Editor:** Fred Schepartz. Magazine: 8½×11; 32-64 pages; 60 lb. paper; 60 lb. cover. "Looking for fiction which uses social change as either a primary or secondary theme. This is broader than most people think. Need social relevance in one way or another. For an artistically and politically aware and curious audience." Quarterly. Estab. 1989. Circ. 1,500.
Needs: Contemporary, ethnic, experimental, fantasy, feminist, gay, historical, horror, humor/satire, lesbian, literary, mainstream, prose poem, science fiction. "No porn, no racist, sexist or any other kind of ist. No Christian or spiritually proselytizing fiction." Receives 15 unsolicited mss/month. Accepts 3-5 mss/issue. Publishes ms 3-9 months after acceptance. Published work by JoAnn Yolanda Hernández, Patricia Stevens and Rochelle Schwab. Length: 3,500 words preferred; 500 words minimum; 5,000 words maximum. Publishes short shorts. Length: 500 words. Always critiques rejected mss.
How to Contact: Send complete ms with cover letter. Reports in 2-4 months. SASE. Simultaneous and reprint submissions OK. Sample copy for $2, 9×12 SAE and 3 first-class stamps. Fiction guidelines for 9×12 SAE and 4-5 first-class stamps. "Please include return postage, not IRCs, in overseas submissions."
Payment/Terms: Pays contributor's copies. Acquires one-time rights and electronic rights for www version.
Advice: "We like high impact, we like plot and character-driven stories that function like theater of the mind." Looks for "first and foremost, good writing. Prose must be crisp and polished; the story must pique my interest and make me care due to a certain intellectual, emotional aspect. Second, *Mobius* is about social change. We want stories that make some statement about the society we live in, either on a macro or micro level. Not that your story needs to preach from a soapbox (actually, we prefer that it doesn't), but your story needs to have *something* to say."

N MOOSE BOUND PRESS, (I, II), Moose Bound Press Journals and Newsletters, P.O. Box 111781, Anchorage AK 99511-1781. Phone/fax: (907)333-1465. E-mail: mbpress@alaska.net. Website: http://www.alaska.net/~mbpress (includes writer's guidelines, philosophy, pictures and names of publisher and editor). Publisher: Robert L. Walker. **Editor:** Sonia Walker. Magazine: 8½×11; 100 pages; 20 lb. bond paper; card stock cover; illustrations and photos. "We cater to a general reading audience—something the entire family can enjoy." Quarterly. Estab. 1995. Circ. 500.
Needs: Adventure, children's/juvenile (adventure, animal, mystery), ethnic/multicultural, family saga, historical, humor/satire, literary, mainstream/contemporary, mystery/suspense (amateur sleuth, cozy), religious (inspirational), romance (historical, romantic suspense), science fiction, short story collections, western (frontier saga, traditional), young adult/teen (adventure, easy-to-read, historical, mystery/suspense, romance, series, sports, western). Alaska theme is not required. "No erotica or x-rated writing. We are a family-oriented press." List of upcoming themes available for SASE. Receives 50-75 unsolicited mss/month. Accepts 10 mss/issue; 85 mss/year. Publishes ms 6-12 months after acceptance. Publishes 80% new writers. Recently published work by Henry Marksburg, Lillian Withey, William Paxson, Suzanne M. Nye, Nancy L'enz Hogan and Ronale Anjun. Length: 1,500 words average; 500 words minimum; 2,000 words maximum. Publishes short shorts. Also publishes literary essays, poetry. Often critiques or comments on rejected ms.
How to Contact: Send complete ms with a cover letter. Accepts queries by e-mail. Include estimated word count, bio. Reports in 3 weeks on queries; 6 months on mss. Send SASE for reply, return of ms or send a disposable copy of ms. Simultaneous submissions OK. Sample copy $8 and $3 for postage and handling. Fiction guidelines for legal-sized SASE.

Payment/Terms: Acquires one-time rights. "We have an Editor's Choice Award which is mentioned within each journal and listed in newsletters. We do not give monetary awards."
Advice: "We like to see wholesome, energetic and uplifting writing from contributors. Stories do not have to have a happy ending." Alaska theme is not required.

N $ MUSHROOM DREAMS, (I, II), 14537 Longworth Ave., Norwalk CA 90650-4724. **Editor:** Jim Reagan. Magazine: 8½×5½; 32 pages; 20 lb. paper; heavy cover stock; illustrations. "Eclectic content with emphasis on literary quality." Semiannually. Estab. 1997. Circ. 100.
Needs: Literary. No gay, lesbian. Receives 10-15 unsolicited mss/month. Accepts 3 mss/issue; 6 mss/year. Publishes ms 6-12 months after acceptance. Recently published work by John M. Daniel, Cheri Gillis and Jo-Ann Godfrey. Length: 1,500 words average; 250 words minimum; 1,800 words maximum. Publishes short shorts. Length: 250 words. Also publishes poetry. Often critiques or comments on rejected ms.
How to Contact: Send complete ms with a cover letter. Include estimated word count, short paragraph bio. Reports in 1 week on queries; 6 weeks on mss. Send SASE for reply or return of ms. Simultaneous and reprint submissions OK. Sample copy $1. Fiction guidelines free.
Payment/Terms: Pays $2-20 and 2 contributor's copies on publication for first rights; additional copies $1.

✓ THE MUSING PLACE, The Literary & Arts Magazine of Chicago's Mental Health Community, (IV), The Thresholds, 2700 N. Lakeview, Chicago IL 60614. (773)281-3800, ext. 2465. Fax: (773)281-8790. E-mail: lkrinsky@thn.thresholds.org. **Editor:** Linda Krinsky. Magazine: 8½×11; 36 pages; 60 lb. paper; glossy cover; illustrations. "We are mostly a poetry magazine by and for mental health consumers. We want to give a voice to those who are often not heard. All material is composed by mental health consumers. The only requirement for consideration of publication is having a history of mental illness." Semiannually. Estab. 1986. Circ. 1,000.
Needs: Adventure, condensed/excerpted novel, ethnic/multicultural, experimental, fantasy (science fantasy, sword and sorcery), feminist, gay, historical (general), horror, humor/satire, lesbian, literary, mainstream/contemporary, mystery/suspense, regional, romance, science fiction and serialized novel. Publishes ms up to 6 months after acceptance. Published work by Allen McNair, Donna Willey and Mark Gonciarz. Length: 500 words average; 700 words maximum. Publishes short shorts. Length: 500 words. Also publishes poetry.
How to Contact: Send complete ms with a cover letter. Include bio (paragraph) and statement of having a history of mental illness. Reports in 6 months. Send a disposable copy of ms. Simultaneous and reprint submissions OK. Sample copy free.
Payment/Terms: Pays contributor's copies. Acquires one-time rights.

✓ THE NEBRASKA REVIEW, (II), University of Nebraska at Omaha, Omaha NE 68182-0324. (402)554-3159. E-mail: jreed@fa-cpacs.unomaha.edu. **Fiction Editor:** James Reed. Magazine: 5½×8½; 104 pages; 60 lb. text paper; chrome coat cover stock. "*TNR* attempts to publish the finest available contemporary fiction and poetry for college and literary audiences." Publishes 2 issues/year. Estab. 1973. Circ. 1,000.
Needs: Contemporary, humor/satire, literary and mainstream. No genre fiction. Receives 40 unsolicited fiction mss/month. Accepts 4-5 mss/issue, 8-10 mss/year. Reads for the *Nebraska Review* Awards in Fiction and Poetry September 1 through November 30. Open to submissions January 1-April 30; does not read May 1-August 31. Published work by Cris Mazza, Mark Wisniewski, Stewart O'Nan, Gerda Saunders and Tom Franklin. Published new writers within the last year. Length: 5,000-6,000 words average. Also publishes poetry.
How to Contact: Send complete ms with SASE. Reports in 1-4 months. Publishes ms an average of 6-12 months after acceptance. Sample copy for $2.50.
Payment/Terms: Pays 2 contributor's copies plus 1 year subscription; $2 charge for extras. Acquires first North American serial rights.
Advice: "Write stories in which the lives of your characters are the primary reason for writing and techniques of craft serve to illuminate, not overshadow, the textures of those lives. Sponsors a $500 award/year—write for rules."

NEOLOGISMS, A Journal of the Written Word, (I, II), Big Snapper Publishing, 1102 Pleasant St., #869, Worcester MA 01602. **Editor:** Jim Fay. Magazine: 8½×11; 50-80 pages; 60 lb. paper; 80 lb. cover stock; photos. "*Neologisms* is dedicated to the written word in all forms and shapes." Tri-quarterly. Estab. 1996. Circ. 150.
Needs: Experimental, fantasy, literary, science fiction (sociological). "No overly erotic, gay/lesbian, or children-oriented work." List of upcoming themes available for SASE. Receives 20 unsolicited mss/month. Accepts 5-8 mss/issue; 20-40 mss/year. Recently published work by Leslie Schenk, Greg St. Thomasino, Cheryl Townsend, Robert Ready, Jenny Curtis and Peter McGinn. Publishes 10 new writers/year. Length: 1,100 words average; 50

READ THE BUSINESS OF FICTION WRITING section to learn the correct way to prepare and submit a manuscript.

words minimum; 5,000 words maximum. Publishes short shorts. Also publishes literary essays, literary criticism and poetry.
How to Contact: Send complete ms with a cover letter. Include estimated word count, bio and list of publications. Reports in 2 months on queries; 4 months on mss. Send SASE for reply, return of ms or send a disposble copy of ms. Simultaneous submissions OK. Sample copy for $5. Free fiction guidelines. Reviews novels and short story collections.
Payment/Terms: Pays 1 contributor's copy; additional copies for $4. Acquires first rights "and option to use a second time if I ever do a 'Best of' issue." Sends galleys to author only if requested. Not copyrighted.
Advice: "Fiction must have originality and be able to catch my eye. Send stuff that mainstream America would probably not publish."

N **NEOTROPE, [experimental fiction], (II, IV)**, Broken Boulder Press, 834 Kentucky #3, Lawrence KS 66044. E-mail: apowell10@hotmail.com. **Editors:** Adam Powell, Paul Silvia. Magazine: 8½×11; 50 pages; card stock cover; illustrations and photos. "We view *Neotrope* as a deprogramming tool for refugees from MPW programs and fiction workshops. We are seeking highly original and aggressively experimental fiction." Semiannually. Estab. 1998. Circ. 100.
Needs: Experimental. "No genre fiction, nothing traditional." Receives 20-25 unsolicited mss/month. Accepts 7-10 mss/issue; 15-20 mss/year. Publishes ms 1-6 months after acceptance. Length: open. Publishes short shorts. Always critiques or comments on rejected ms.
How to Contact: Send complete ms with a cover letter. Reports in 2 weeks. Send SASE for return of ms. Simultaneous submissions OK, "but if we accept it we will use it, regardless of any other magazine's decision." Sample copy for $3, 9×12 SAE and 5 first-class stamps. "Prospective contributors can e-mail for a free sample copy." Fiction guidelines free.
Payment/Terms: Pays 1 contributor's copy; additional copies $2. Acquires one-time rights. Sometimes sends galleys to author.

NERVE COWBOY, (II, III), Liquid Paper Press, P.O. Box 4973, Austin TX 78765. **Editors:** Joseph Shields and Jerry Hagins. Magazine: 7×8½; 52-60 pages; 20 lb. paper; card stock cover; illustrations. "*Nerve Cowboy* publishes adventurous, comical, disturbing, thought-provoking, accessible poetry and fiction. We like to see work sensitive enough to make the hardest hard-ass cry, funny enough to make the most hopeless brooder laugh and disturbing enough to make us all glad we're not the author of the piece." Semiannually. Estab. 1996. Circ. 250.

- Sponsors an annual chapbook contest for fiction or poetry. Deadline January 31. Send SASE for details.

Needs: Literary. Receives 10 unsolicited mss/month. Accepts 2-3 mss/issue; 4-6 mss/year. Publishes ms 6-12 months after acceptance. Recently published work by Albert Huffstickler, Mark Smith, Catfish McDaris, Laurel Speer, Brian Prioleau, Marcy Shapiro, Susanne R. Bowers and Adam Gurvitch. Length: 750-1,000 words average; 1,500 words maximum. Publishes short shorts. Also publishes poetry.
How to Contact: Send complete ms with a cover letter. Include bio and list of publications. Reports in 2 weeks on queries; 4-6 weeks on mss. Send SASE for reply, return of ms or send disposable copy of ms. No simultaneous submissions. Reprints OK. Sample copy for $4. Fiction guidelines for #10 SASE.
Payment/Terms: Pays 1 contributor's copy for one-time rights.
Advice: "We look for writing which is very direct and elicits a visceral reaction in the reader. Read magazines you submit to in order to get a feel for what the editors are looking for. Write simply and from the gut."

N **NEW CONTRAST**, P.O. Box 44844, Claremont 7735 South Africa. **Contact:** Fiction Editor. Quarterly. Circ. 400. Publishes 2-3 stories/issue. "We publish short fiction, film scripts (extracts), plays (extracts), reviews and occasional pieces of nonfiction. The bulk of our journal is poetry, however." Length: no limit; "subject to the editor's discretion." Pays a book voucher worth R50 (50 rands) if writer already subscribes and a year's gift subscription if writer is not already subscriber. Prefers disk submissions with hard copy and any special features or instructions clearly marked. "If you are submitting on disk, the first line of each new paragraph should have a 5mm indent (please do not use spaces or the Tab key). If you want to submit your material via e-mail, please be sure to explain any special layout features which get lost in the process." Writer's guidelines available for SAE and IRCs.

NEW DELTA REVIEW, (II), Creative Writing Programs, English Dept./Louisiana State University, Baton Rouge LA 70803-5001. (504)388-4079. E-mail: wwwndr@unix1.snce.lsu.edu. **Editor-in-Chief:** Andrew Spear. Fiction Editor: Tray Stone. Editors change every year. Magazine: 6×9; 75-125 pages; high quality paper; glossy card cover; b&w illustrations and artwork. "No theme or style biases. Poetry, fiction primarily; also literary interviews and reviews." Semi-annual. Estab. 1984. Circ. 500.

- The magazine recently won a *Pushcart* Prize. *New Delta Review* also sponsors the Eyster Prizes for fiction and poetry. See the listing in the Contest and Awards Section of this book. Work from the magazine has been included in the *Pushcart Prize* anthology. This publication ranked #43 on *Writer's Digest*'s Fiction 50 list of top markets for fiction writers.

Needs: Contemporary, humor/satire, literary, mainstream, prose poem, translations. No novel excerpts, adventu re, sci-fi, juvenile. Receives 200 unsolicited mss/ month. Accepts 3-4 mss/issue, 6-8 mss/year. Recently published work by George Berridge, Jr., Ted Graf, Hayley R. Mitchell and Rebecah Edwards. Published new writers within

the last year. Length: 20 ms pages average; 250 words minimum. Publishes short shorts. Also publishes poetry. Rarely critiques rejected mss.
How to Contact: Send complete ms with cover letter. Cover letter should include estimated word count, bio, Social Security number and "credits, if any; no synopses, please." Accepts queries/mss by fax. No simultaneous submissions. Reports on queries in 3 weeks; 3 months on mss. SASE (or IRC). Mss deadlines September 1 for fall; February 15 for spring. Sample copy for $5. Reviews novels and short story collections.
Payment/Terms: Pays in contributor's copies. Charge for extras.
Terms: Acquires first North American serial rights. Sponsors award for fiction writers in each issue. Eyster Prize-$50 plus notice in magazine. Mss selected for publication are automatically considered.
Advice: "We want fiction that compells the reader to continue reading until the end. Keep reading what is being published in the small journals and 'Best of' anthologies, and write, and then rewrite."

$ NEW ENGLAND REVIEW, (II), Middlebury College, Middlebury VT 05753. (802)443-5075. E-mail: nereview@mail.middlebury.edu. **Editor:** Stephen Donadio. Magazine: 7×10; 180 pages; 50 lb paper; coated cover stock. A literary quarterly publishing fiction, poetry and essays with special emphasis on contemporary cultural issues, both in the US and abroad. For general readers and professional writers. Quarterly. Estab. 1977. Circ. 2,000.

- *New England Review* has long been associated with Breadloaf Writer's Conference, held at Middlebury College.

Needs: Literary. Receives 250 unsolicited fiction mss/month. Accepts 5 mss/issue; 20 mss/year. Does not read ms June-August. Published work by Sigrid Nunez, Carolyn Cooke, Padgett Powell, Chaim Potok and Robert Cohen. Published new writers within the last year. Publishes ms 3-9 months after acceptance. Agented fiction: less than 5%. Publishes short shorts occasionally. Sometimes critiques rejected mss.
How to Contact: Send complete ms with cover letter. "Cover letters that demonstrate that the writer knows the magazine are the ones we want to read. We don't want hype, or hard-sell, or summaries of the author's intentions. Will consider simultaneous submissions, but must be stated as such." Reports in 12-15 weeks on mss. SASE.
Payment/Terms: Pays $10/page, $20 minimum and 2 contributor's copies on publication; charge for extras. Acquires first rights and reprint rights. Sends galleys to author.
Advice: "It's best to send one story at a time, and wait until you hear back from us to try again."

NEW LAUREL REVIEW, (II), New Orleans Poetry Forum/New Laurel Review, P.O.. Box 770257, New Orleans LA 70112. (504)947-6001. **Editor:** Lee Meitzen Grue. Magazine: 6½×8; 125 pages; 60 lb. white paper; illustrations and photos. Journal of poetry, fiction, critical articles and reviews. "We have published such internationally known writers as James Nolan, Tomris Uyar and Yevgeny Yevtushenko." Readership: "Literate, adult audiences as well as anyone interested in writing with significance, human interest, vitality, subtlety, etc." Published irregularly. Estab. 1970. Circ. 500. Member of Council of Editors of Learned Journals.
Needs: Literary, ethnic/multicultural, excerpted novel, translations, "cutting edge." No "dogmatic, excessively inspirational or political" material. Acquires 1-2 fiction mss/issue. Receives approximately 25 unsolicited fiction mss each month. Does not read mss during summer months and December. Agented fiction 10%. Length: about 10 printed pages. Publishes short shorts. Also publishes literary essays and poetry. Critiques rejected mss when there is time.
How to Contact: Send complete ms with a cover letter. Include bio and list of publications. Reports in 3 months. Send SASE for reply or return of ms. No simultaneous submissions. Sample copy for $10. "Authors need to look at sample copy before submitting."
Payment/Terms: Pays 1 contributor's copy; additional copies $10, discounted. Acquires first rights.
Advice: "We are interested in fresh, original work that keeps a reader reading. Send a finished manuscript: clean."

$ NEW LETTERS MAGAZINE, (I, II), University of Missouri-Kansas City, University House, 5101 Rockhill Rd., Kansas City MO 64110. (816)235-1168. Fax: (816)235-2611. **Editor:** James McKinley. Magazine: 14 lb. cream paper; illustrations. Quarterly. Estab. 1971 (continuation of *University Review*, founded 1935). Circ. 2,500.
Needs: Contemporary, ethnic, experimental, humor/satire, literary, mainstream, translations. No "bad fiction in any genre." Published work by Tess Gallagher, Jimmy Carter and Amiri Baraka; published work by new writers within the last year. Agented fiction: 10%. Also publishes short shorts. Rarely critiques rejected mss.
How to Contact: Send complete ms with cover letter. Does not read mss May 15-October 15. Reports in 3 weeks on queries; 2-3 months on mss. SASE for ms. No simultaneous or multiple submissions. Sample copy: $8.50 for issues older than 5 years; $5.50 for 5 years or less.
Payment/Terms: Pays honorarium—depends on grant/award money; 2 contributor's copies. Sends galleys to author.
Advice: "Seek publication of representative chapters in high-quality magazines as a way to the book contract. Try literary magazines first."

NEW ORLEANS REVIEW, (I, II), Box 195, Loyola University, New Orleans LA 70118. (504)865-2295. Fax: (504)865-2294. E-mail: noreview@beta.loyno.edu. **Editor:** Ralph Adamo. Magazine: 8½×11; 160 pages; 60 lb. Scott offset paper; 12+ King James C1S cover stock; photos. "Publishes poetry, fiction, translations, photographs, nonfiction on literature and film. Readership: those interested in current culture, literature." Quarterly. Estab. 1968. Circ. 1,300.

Needs: "Storytelling between traditional and experimental." Recently published work by Gordon Lish, Alfred Schwaid, C. Semansky, Trudy Lewis, Ellen Gandt, Rodney Jones, William Matthews and Steve Stern. Publishes many new writers/year.

How to Contact: Send complete ms with SASE. Does not accept simultaneous submissions. Accepts disk submissions; inquire about system compatibility. Prefers hard copy with disk submission. Reports in 2-12 weeks. Sample copy for $9.

Payment/Terms: "Inquire." Most payment in copies. Pays on publication for first North American serial rights.

$ NEW WELSH REVIEW, Chapter Arts Centre, Market Rd., Cardiff Wales CF5 1QE United Kingdom. Phone: 01222 665529. Fax: 01222 665529. E-mail: robin@nwrc.demon.co.uk. **Editor:** Robin Reeves. "*NWR*, a literary quarterly ranked in the top five of British Literary magazines, publishes stories, poems and critical essays. The best of Welsh writing in English, past and present, is celebrated, discussed and debated. We seek poems, short stories, reviews, special features/articles and commentary." Accepts 16-20 mss/year.

Needs: Short fiction. Length: 2,000-3,000 words. Recently published work by Sian James, Ron Berry, Alun Richard, Lloyd Rees, Roger Granelli and Herbert Williams. Approximately 20% of fiction published each year from new writers.

Terms: Pays "cheque on publication and one free copy."

NEW WRITING, A Literary Magazine for New Writers, (I), P.O. Box 1812, Amherst NY 14226-7812. (716)834-1067. E-mail: newwriting@aol.com. Website: http://1812.simplenet.com. **Editor:** Sam Meade. Electronic magazine; illustrations and photographs. "We publish work that is deserving." Annually. Estab. 1994.

Needs: Work by new writers: action, experimental, horror, humor/satire, literary, mainstream/contemporary, romance, translations, westerns. Recently published work by Rob Doberge and Dom Leone. Publishes 20 new writers/year. Length: open. Publishes short shorts. Often critiques or comments on rejected mss. Sponsors an annual award.

How to Contact: Send complete ms with a cover letter. "Please send in e-mail, not as attached files." Include *brief* list of publications and *short* cover letter. Reports in 1-2 months. Send SASE for return of ms. Simultaneous submissions OK. Reviews novels and short story collections.

Payment/Terms: Acquires one-time rights.

Advice: "Don't send first copies of *any* story. Always read over, and rewrite!" Avoid "stories with characters who are writers, stories that start with the character waking, and death and dying stories—we get too many of them."

$ NEW YORK STORIES, (I, II), Laguardia Community College, English Department, E-103, 31-10 Thomson Ave., Long Island City NY 11101. (718)482-5677. Editor: Michael Blaine. Fiction Editor: Mark Wisnieski. Magazine: 9×11; 64-96 pages; photos. Quarterly. Estab. 1998.

Needs: Condensed/excerpted novel, erotica, ethnic/multicultural, experimental, feminist, gay, humor/satire, lesbian, literary, mainstream/contemporary, regional, senior citizen/retirement. Receives 300 unsolicited mss/month. Accepts 5-10 mss/issue; 20-40 mss/year. Does not read June through August. Publishes ms 6 months after acceptance. Agented fiction 5%. Length: 2,500-3,000 words average; 100 words minimum. Publishes short shorts. Also publishes literary essays. Sometimes critiques or comments on rejected mss.

How to Contact: Send complete ms with a cover letter. Include 1-paragraph bio and Social Security number. Reports in 2 months on queries; 2-3 months on mss. Send SASE for return of ms or send disposable copy of ms. Simultaneous submissions and reprints OK. Fiction guidelines for #10 SASE.

Payment/Terms: Pays $100 minimum; $1,000 maximum on publication.

Advice: "Fresh angles of vision, dark humor and psychological complexity are hallmarks of our short stories. Present characters who are 'alive.' Let them breath. To achieve this, revise, revise, revise. Lately, the industry of publishing fiction seems to be playing it safe. We want your best—no matter what."

$ NeWEST REVIEW, (II, IV), Box 394, R.P.O. University, Saskatoon, Saskatchewan S7N 4J8 Canada. (306)934-1444. Fax: (306)343-8579. E-mail: verne.clemence@sk.sympatico.ca. Editor: Verne Clemence. **Fiction Editor:** Allison Muri. Magazine: 40 pages; book stock; illustrations; photos. Magazine devoted to western Canada cultural and regional issues; "fiction, reviews, poetry for middle- to high-brow audience." Bimonthly (6 issues per year). Estab. 1975. Circ. 1,000.

Needs: "We want fiction of high literary quality, whatever its form and content. But we do have a heavy regional emphasis." No adventure or animal stories. Receives 15-20 unsolicited mss/month. Accepts 1 ms/issue; 10 mss/year. Recently published work by Jill Robinson, Richard Hetherton, Thomas Trofimuk and Don Grayton. Publishes 12 new writers/year. Length: 2,500 words average; 1,500 words minimum; 5,000 words maximum. Sometimes recommends other markets.

How to Contact: "We like *brief* cover letters." Accepts queries/mss by e-mail. Reports very promptly in a short letter. SAE, IRCs or Canadian postage. No multiple submissions. Electronic submissions (disk or e-mail) OK. Sample copy for $5.
Payment/Terms: Pays $100 maximum on publication for one-time rights.
Advice: "We don't want unpolished, careless submissions. We do want to be intrigued, entertained and stimulated. Polish your writing. Develop your story line. Give your characters presence. If we, the readers, are to care about the people you create, you too must take them seriously. Be bold and venturesome."

☑ $ **NIMROD, International Journal of Prose and Poetry, (II)**, University of Tulsa, 600 S. College Ave., Tulsa OK 74104. (918)631-3080. E-mail: ringoldfl@centum.utulsa.edu. Website: http://www.utulsa.edu/nimrod/nimrod.html (includes writer's guidelines, excerpts from published work, contest rules). **Fiction Editor:** Gerry McLoud. Magazine: 6×9; 160 pages; 60 lb. white paper; illustrations; photos. "We publish one thematic issue and one awards issue each year. A recent theme was "The City," a compilation of poetry and prose from all over the world. We seek vigorous, imaginative, quality writing. Our mission is to discover new writers and publish experimental writers who have not yet found a 'home' for their work." Semiannually. Estab. 1956. Circ. 3,000.
Needs: "We accept contemporary poetry and/or prose. May submit adventure, ethnic, experimental, prose poem, science fiction or translations." Upcoming theme: "Y2K.Connecting" (1999). Receives 120 unsolicited fiction mss/month. Published work by Linda Watanabe McFerris, Rea Nolan Martin, Lisa Harris, Rochelle Distelheim and Sheila Thorne. Published 5-10 new writers within the last year. Length: 7,500 words maximum. Also publishes poetry.
How to Contact: SASE for return of ms. Accepts queries by e-mail. Reports in 3-5 months. Sample copy: "to see what *Nimrod* is all about, send $10 for a back issue. To receive a recent awards issue, send $10 (includes postage).
Payment/Terms: Pays 2 contributor's copies, plus $5/page up to $25 total per author per issue for one-time rights, budget permitting.
Advice: "We have not changed our fiction needs: quality, vigor, distinctive voice. We have, however, increased the number of stories we print. See current issues. We look for fiction that is fresh, vigorous, distinctive, serious and humorous, seriously-humorous, unflinchingly serious, ironic—whatever. Just so it is quality. Strongly encourage writers to send #10 SASE for brochure for annual literary contest with prizes of $1,000 and $2,000."

96 Inc., (I, II), P.O. Box 15559, Boston MA 02215. (617)267-0543. Fax: (617)262-3568. **Fiction Editors:** Julie Anderson and Nancy Mehegan. Magazine: 8½×11; 50 pages; 20 lb. paper; matte cover; illustrations and photos. "*96 Inc.* promotes the process; integrates beginning/young with established writers; reaches out to audiences of all ages and backgrounds." Annual. Estab. 1992. Circ. 3,000.
Needs: All types, styles and subjects. Receives 200 unsolicited mss/month. Accepts 12-15 mss/issue; 30 mss/year. Agented fiction 10%. Recently published work by Kat Meads, Anesa Miller and Joe Lunevicz. Publishes 8-10 new writers/year. Length: 1,000 words minimum; 7,000 words maximum. Publishes short shorts. Also publishes literary essays, literary criticism and poetry. Sometimes critiques or comments on rejected mss.
How to Contact: Query first. Include estimated word count, bio (100 words) and list of publications. Reports in 3 weeks on queries; 6-12 months on mss. Send SASE for reply, return of ms or send a disposable copy of ms. Simultaneous and electronic submissions OK. Sample copy for $7.50. Fiction guidelines for #10 SASE. Reviews novels and short story collections on occasion.
Payment/Terms: Pays modest sum if funds are available, not depending on length or merit, free subscription and 4 contributor's copies on publication for one-time rights.
Advice: Looks for "good writing in any style. Pays attention to the process. Read at least one issue. Be patient—it takes a very long time for readers to go through the thousands of manuscripts."

N **NO EXPERIENCE REQUIRED, (I, II)**, D J Creations, P.O. Box 7573, The Woodlands TX 77387-7573. (281)367-3603. Fax: (281)367-7292. E-mail: dmbeason@aol.com or delray 77@aol.com. **Contact:** Editor. Editor changes each issue. Magazine: 5½×8½; 40-48 pages; marble text 24 lb. paper; 80 lb. cover stock; illustrations and photos. "We have no specific theme. Our philosophy is simple: we want to help new writers break into publication." Triannually. Estab. 1997. Circ. 350.
Needs: "We will consider most categories. No pornographic, erotica, racial/religious denegration." Receives 4 mss/month. Accepts 12-15 mss/issue; 35-50 mss/year. Recently published work by Michael McFarland, Doré

FOR EXPLANATIONS OF THESE SYMBOLS,
SEE THE INSIDE FRONT AND BACK COVERS OF THIS BOOK.

Hevenor, Martha James, Joseph Burns and Helen Ciancimino. Length: 1,200 words average; 1,300 words maximum. Publishes short shorts. Also publishes poetry. Always critiques or comments on rejected ms.
How to Contact: Send complete ms with cover letter. Include estimated word count, phone, net/e-mail address if applicable. Reports in 3-4 weeks on queries; 6-8 weeks on mss. Send SASE for reply, return of ms or send a disposable copy of ms. Simultaneous, reprint and electronic (disk or modem) submissions OK. Sample copy $3 and $1 postage. Fiction guidelines for #10 SASE.
Payment/Terms: Pays 2 contributor's copies; additional copies $3. Acquires one-time rights; rights revert to author.

N NORTH ATLANTIC REVIEW, (II), North Eagle Corp. of NY, 15 Arbutus Lane, Stony Brook NY 11790. (516)751-7886. **Editor:** John Gill. Magazine: 7×9; 320 pages; glossy cover. "General interest." Estab. 1989. Circ. 1,000.

- *North Atlantic Review* tends to accept traditional fiction.

Needs: General fiction. Has published special fiction issue. Accepts 40 mss/year. Publishes ms 6-10 months after acceptance. Length: 3,000-7,000 words average. Publishes short shorts. Sometimes critiques rejected mss.
How to Contact: Send complete ms with cover letter. Reports in 5-6 months on queries. SASE. Simultaneous and photocopied submissions OK. Sample copy for $10.

NORTH DAKOTA QUARTERLY, (II), University of North Dakota, Box 7209, University Station, Grand Forks ND 58202. (701)777-3322. Fax: (701)777-3650. E-mail: ndq@sage.und.nodak.edu. Website: http://www.192.41.6.160/ndq. Editor: Robert W. Lewis. **Fiction Editor:** William Borden. Poetry Editor: Jay Meek. Magazine: 6×9; 200 pages; bond paper; illustrations; photos. Magazine publishing "essays in humanities; some short stories; some poetry." University audience. Quarterly. Estab. 1911. Circ. 700.

- Work published in *North Dakota Quarterly* was selected for inclusion in *The O. Henry Awards* anthology. The editors are especially interested in work by Native American writers.

Needs: Contemporary, ethnic, experimental, feminist, historical, humor/satire, literary. Receives 20-30 unsolicited mss/month. Accepts 4 mss/issue; 16 mss/year. Published work by Naguib Mahfouz, Jerry Bumpus, Carol Shields, Rilla Askew and Chris Mazza. Published new writers within the last year. Length: 3,000-4,000 words average. Also publishes literary essays, literary criticism, poetry. Sometimes comments on or critiques rejected ms.
How to Contact: Send complete ms with cover letter. Include one-paragraph bio. "But it need not be much more than hello; please read this story; I've published (if so, best examples) . . ." SASE. Reports in 3 months. Publishes ms an average of 1 year after acceptance. Sample copy for $8. Reviews novels and short story collections.
Payment/Terms: Pays 2-4 contributor's copies; 30% discount for extras. Acquires one-time rights. Sends galleys to author.

NORTHEAST ARTS MAGAZINE, (II), P.O. Box 94, Kittery ME 03904. **Editor:** Mr. Leigh Donaldson. Magazine: 6½×9½; 32-40 pages; matte finish paper; card stock cover; illustrations and photographs. Bimonthly. Estab. 1990. Circ. 750.
Needs: Ethnic, gay, historical, literary, mystery/suspense (private eye), prose poem (under 2,000 words). No obscenity, racism, sexism, etc. Receives 50 unsolicited mss/month. Accepts 1-2 mss/issue; 5-7 mss/year. Publishes ms 2-4 months after acceptance. Agented fiction 20%. Length: 750 words preferred. Publishes short shorts. Sometimes critiques rejected mss.
How to Contact: Send complete ms with cover letter. Include short bio. Reports in 1 month on queries; 2-4 months on mss. SASE. Simultaneous submissions OK. Sample copy for $4.50, SAE and 75¢ postage. Fiction guidelines free.
Payment/Terms: Pays 2 contributor's copies. Acquires first North American serial rights. Sometimes sends galleys to author.
Advice: Looks for "creative/innovative use of language and style. Unusual themes and topics."

$ NORTHEAST CORRIDOR, (II), Beaver College, 450 S. Easton Rd., Glenside PA 19038. (215)572-2870. E-mail: balee@beaver.edu. Editor: Susan Balée. **Fiction Editor:** Deborah Goldschmidt. Magazine: 6¾×10; 120-220 pages; 60 lb. white paper; glossy, perfect-bound cover; illustrations and photos. "Interested in writers and themes treating the Northeast Corridor region of America. Literary fiction, poetry, drama, essays, interviews with writers." Annually. Estab. 1993. Circ. 1,000.

- *Northeast Corridor* has received grants from the Daphne Foundation, the Ruth and Robert Satter Foundation, the Cottonwood Foundation and the Nicholas Roerich Museum. An essay it published was listed in *Best American Essays*.

Needs: Literary: excerpted novel, ethnic/multicultural, feminist, humor/satire, literary, regional, translations. No religious, western, young adult, science fiction, juvenile, horror. "Needs literary stories with humor." List of upcoming themes available for SASE. Planning future special memoir issue or anthology. Receives 100 unsolicited mss/month. Accepts 2-6 mss/issue; 4-12 mss/year. Reads mss infrequently during June, July and August. Publishes ms 6 months after acceptance. Recently published work by Jessica Brilliant, Kermit Moyer, Rita Ciresi, Mark Winegardner and Jim Quinn and Lisa Borders. Publishes 5-6 new writers/year. Length: 2,500 words average;

1,000 words minimum; 4,500 words maximum. Publishes literary essays, interviews and poetry. Often critiques or comments on rejected mss.

How to Contact: Send complete ms with a cover letter. Include word count, 1-2 line bio and publications list. Reports in 2-4 months on mss. SASE for reply, return of ms or send a disposable copy of ms. Simultaneous submissions OK if indicated. Sample copy for $7, 9×12 SAE and $1.21 postage. Fiction guidelines for #10 SASE.

Payment/Terms: Pays $10-100 and 2 contributor's copies on publication for first North American serial rights; additional copies for $5/copy.

Advice: "In selecting fiction we look for love of language, developed characters, believable conflict, metaphorical prose, satisfying resolution. Read everything from Chekov to Alice Munro and write at least 10-20 stories before you start trying to send them out. We would like to see more humor. Writers should avoid sending work that is 'therapy' rather than 'art.' The best fiction is still to be found in small journals. The small tale well told appears here where it can be appreciated if not remunerated."

NORTHWEST REVIEW, (II), 369 PLC, University of Oregon, Eugene OR 97403. (503)346-3957. Editor: John Witte. **Fiction Editor:** Janice MacCrae. Magazine: 6×9; 140-160 pages; high quality cover stock; illustrations; photos. "A general literary review featuring poems, stories, essays and reviews, circulated nationally and internationally. For a literate audience in avant-garde as well as traditional literary forms; interested in the important writers who have not yet achieved their readership." Triannually. Estab. 1957. Circ. 1,200.

- *Northwest Review* has received the Oregon Governor's Award for the Arts. The work included in *Northwest Review* tends to be literary, heavy on character and theme. *Northwest Review* ranked #39 on *Writer's Digest*'s Fiction 50 list of top markets for fiction writers.

Needs: Contemporary, experimental, feminist, literary and translations. Accepts 4-5 mss/issue, 12-15 mss/year. Receives approximately 100 unsolicited fiction mss each month. Published work by Diana Abu-Jaber, Madison Smartt Bell, Maria Flook and Charles Marvin. Published new writers within the last year. Length: "Mss longer than 40 pages are at a disadvantage." Also publishes literary essays, literary criticism, poetry. Critiques rejected mss when there is time. Sometimes recommends other markets.

How to Contact: Send complete ms with SASE. "No simultaneous submissions are considered." Reports in 3-4 months. Sample copy for $4. Reviews novels and short story collections. Send books to John Witte.

Payment/Terms: Pays 3 contributor's copies and one-year subscription; 40% discount on extras. Acquires first rights.

$ NORTHWOODS JOURNAL, A Magazine for Writers, (I, II), Conservatory of American Letters, P.O. Box 298, Thomaston ME 04861. (207)354-0998. Fax: (207)354-8953. E-mail: cal@ime.net. Website: http://w3.ime.net/~cal (includes guidelines and catalogue). Editor: R.W. Olmsted. **Fiction Editor:** Ken Sieben. Magazine: 5½×8½; 32-64 pages; white paper; 65 lb. card cover; offset printing; perfect binding; some illustrations and photographs. "No theme, no philosophy—for people who read for entertainment." Quarterly. Estab. 1993. Circ. 500.

Needs: Adventure, erotica, experimental, fantasy (science fantasy, sword and sorcery), literary, mainstream/contemporary, mystery/suspense (amateur sleuth, police procedural, private eye/hard-boiled, romantic suspense), psychic/supernatural/occult, regional, romance (gothic, historical), science fiction (hard science, soft/sociological), sports, westerns (frontier, traditional). Publishes special fiction issue or anthology. "Would like to see more first-person adventure." No porn or evangelical. Receives 50 unsolicited mss/month. Accepts 12-15 mss/year. Recently published work by Paul A. Jurvie, Richard Vaughn, Bryn C. Gray and Sandra Thompson. Publishes 15 new writers/years. Length: 2,500 words maximum. Also publishes literary essays, literary criticism and poetry.

How to Contact: *Charges $3 reading fee per 2,500 words.* Read guidelines *before* submitting. Send complete ms with a cover letter. Include word count and list of publications. There is a $3 fee per story. Reports in 1-2 days on queries; by next deadline plus 5 days on mss. Send SASE for reply, return of ms or send a disposable copy of ms. No simultaneous submissions. Sample copies: $5 next issue, $7.95 current issue, $10 back issue (if available), all postage paid. Fiction guidelines for #10 SASE. Reviews novels, short story collections and poetry.

Payment/Terms: Varies, "minimum $4/published page on acceptance for first North American serial rights."

Advice: "Read guidelines, read the things we've published. Know your market."

✓ $ NOTRE DAME REVIEW, (II), University of Notre Dame, English Department, Creative Writing, Notre Dame IN 46556. (219)631-6952. Fax: (219)631-4268. E-mail: english.ndreview.1@nd.edu. **Editors:** William O'Rourke and John Matthias. Literary magazine: 6×9; 115 pages; 50 lb. smooth paper; illustrations and photographs. "The *Notre Dame Review* is an independent, non-commercial magazine of contemporary American and international fiction, poetry, criticism and art. We are especially interested in work that takes on big issues by making the invisible seen, that gives voice to the voiceless. In addition to showcasing celebrated authors like Seamus Heaney and Czelaw Milosz, the *Notre Dame Review* introduces readers to authors they may have never encountered before, but who are doing innovative and important work. In conjunction with the *Notre Dame Re-View,* the on-line companion to the printed magazine, the *Notre Dame Review* engages readers as a community centered in literary rather than commercial concerns, a community we reach out to through critique and commentary as well as aesthetic experience." Semiannually. Estab. 1995. Circ. 2,000.

Needs: Experimental, feminist, historical (literary), translations. "We're eclectic." Upcoming theme issues

planned. List of upcoming themes or editorial calendar available for SASE. Receives 15 unsolicited fiction mss/month. Accepts 4-5 mss/issue; 10 mss/year. Does not read mss May through August. Publishes ms 6 months after acceptance. Recently published work by Seamus Heaney, Denise Levertov and Czeslaw Milosz. Length: 3,000 words maximum. Publishes short shorts. Also publishes literary criticism and poetry. Sometimes comments on rejected ms.
How to Contact: Send complete ms with cover letter. Include 4-sentence bio. Reports in 3-4 months. Send SASE for response, return of ms, or send a disposable copy of ms. Simultaneous submissions OK. Sample copy for $6.
Payment/Terms: Pays $5-25 and contributor's copies. Pays on publication. Acquires first North American serial rights.
Advice: "We're looking for high quality work that takes on big issues in a literary way. Please read our back issues before submitting."

☑ $ **NOW & THEN, (IV)**, Center for Appalachian Studies and Services, East Tennessee State University, Box 70556, Johnson City TN 37614-0556. Phone/fax: (423)439-5348. Website: http://www.cass.etsu.edu/n&t/guidelin.htm. **Contact:** Editor. Magazine: 8½×11; 36-52 pages; coated paper and cover stock; illustrations; photographs. Publication focuses on Appalachian culture, present and past. Readers are mostly people in the region involved with Appalachian issues, literature, education." Triannually. Estab. 1984. Circ. 1,000.
Needs: Ethnic, literary, regional, serialized/excerpted novel, prose poem, spiritual and sports. "Absolutely has to relate to Appalachian theme. Can be about adjustment to new environment, themes of leaving and returning, for instance. Nothing unrelated to region." Upcoming themes: "Appalachian Lives" (Summer 1999, deadline March 1, 1999); "Health Care" (Winter 1999, deadline July 1, 1999). Buys 2-3 mss/issue. Publishes ms 3-4 months after acceptance. Published work by Lee Smith, Pinckney Benedict, Gurney Norman, George Ella Lyon; published new writers within the last year. Length: 3,000 words maximum. Publishes short shorts. Also publishes literary essays, poetry.
How to Contact: Send complete ms with cover letter. Reports in 3 months. Include "information we can use for contributor's note." SASE (or IRC). Simultaneous submissions OK, "but let us know when it has been accepted elsewhere right away." Sample copy for $5. Reviews novels and short story collections.
Payment/Terms: Pays up to $75 per story, contributor's copies.
Terms: Holds copyright.
Advice: "We're emphasizing Appalachian culture, which is not often appreciated because analysts are so busy looking at the trouble of the region. We're doing theme issues. Beware of stereotypes. In a regional publication like this one we get lots of them, both good guys and bad guys: salt of the earth to poor white trash. Sometimes we get letters that offer to let us polish up the story. We prefer the author does that him/herself." Send for list of upcoming themes.

[N] **NYX OBSCURA MAGAZINE, Delicate Decadence & Ethereal Music, (II)**, P.O. Box 5554, Atlanta GA 31107. (404)681-1666. E-mail: obscura@mindspring.com. **Editor:** Diana McCrary. Magazine: 6×9; 40 pages; 30 lb. paper; 80 lb. cover stock; illustrations and photos. Annually. Estab. 1994. Circ. 1,500.
Needs: Erotica, fantasy, psychic/supernatural/occult. "Nothing set in the 20th century." Publishes special fiction issues or anthologies. Receives 50-100 unsolicited mss/month. Accepts 2-3 mss/issue; 2-5 mss/year. Publishes ms 6 months after acceptance. Recently published work by Patricia Russo, A.D. Ian and D.F. Lewis. Publishes short shorts. Often critiques or comments on rejected mss.
How to Contact: Query with clips of published work. Reports in 3 weeks on queries; 8 months on mss. Send SASE for reply, return of ms or send disposable copy of ms. Simultaneous and electronic submissions OK. Sample copy for $5. Fiction guidelines for #10 SASE. Reviews novels and short story collections.
Payment/Terms: Pays 1 contributor's copy on publication; additional copies for $2. Acquires one-time rights and rights to reprint on web page.
Advice: Looks for "unusual or archaic themes—fresh, skillful, elegant writing. Scour your manuscript for clichés and eliminate them. Read your manuscript aloud."

🌐 **OASIS**, Oasis Books, 12 Stevenage Rd., London SW6 6ES United Kingdom. **Editor:** Ian Robinson. Published 6 times/year. Circ. 400. Publishes usually 1 story/issue.
Needs: "Innovative, experimental fiction. No science fiction, fantasy, surreal. Wants non-standard, 'experimental' short stories." Recently published work by Sheila E. Murphy, Karen Rosenberg, Gordon Wardman, Frances Pusley, Annie Salager and Anne Bern. Length: 1,800 words maximum.
Payment/Terms: Pays in copies. Sample copy available for $3.50 check (made payable to Robert Vas Dias) and 4 IRCs.

Advice: "Have a look at a copy of the magazine before submitting. We look for originality of thought and expression, and a willingness to take risks."

$ OASIS, A Literary Magazine, (I, II), P.O. Box 626, Largo FL 33779-0626. (813)449-2186. E-mail: oasislit@aol.com. Website: http://members.aol.com/wordthis/schvn.htm (includes writer's guidelines, names of editors, short fiction). **Editor:** Neal Storrs. Magazine: 70 pages. "Literary magazine first, last and always—looking for styles that delight and amaze, that are polished and poised. Next to that, content considerations relatively unimportant—open to all." Quarterly. Estab. 1992. Circ. 500.

Needs: High-quality writing. Receives 150 unsolicited mss/month. Accepts 6 mss/issue; 24 mss/year. Publishes ms 4-6 months after acceptance. Recently published work by Wendell Mayo, Al Masarik and Mark Wisniewski. Publishes 2 new writers/year. Length: no minimum or maximum. Also publishes literary essays and poetry. Occasionally critiques or comments on rejected mss.

How to Contact: Send complete ms with or without a cover letter. Accepts queries/mss by e-mail. Usually reports same day. Send SASE for reply, return of ms or send a disposable copy of ms. Simultaneous, reprint and electronic (e-mail) submissions OK. Sample copy for $7.50. Fiction guidelines for #10 SASE.

Payment/Terms: Pays $15-30 and 1 contributor's copy on publication for first rights.

Advice: "If you want to write good stories, read good stories. Cultivate the critical ability to recognize what makes a story original and true to itself."

☑ OBSIDIAN II: BLACK LITERATURE IN REVIEW, (II, IV), Dept. of English, North Carolina State University, Raleigh NC 27695-8105. (919)515-4153. Fax: (919)515-1836. E-mail: krsassan@unity.ncsu.edu. **Editor:** Afaa M. Weaver. Fiction Editor: Shara McCallum. Magazine: 6×9; 130 pages. "Creative works in English by black writers, scholarly critical studies by all writers on black literature in English." Published 2 times/year (spring/summer, fall/winter). Estab. 1975. Circ. 500.

Needs: Ethnic (pan-African), feminist. All writers on black topics. Upcoming theme: "Prisons, Black Women in Theatre." Accepts 7-9 mss/year. Recently published work by Sean Henry, R. Flowers Rivera, Terrance Hayes, Eugene Kraft and Kwane Dawes. Publishes 20 new writers/year. Length: 1,500-10,000 words.

How to Contact: Send complete ms in duplicate and on disc with SASE. Accepts queries/mss by fax and e-mail. Reports in 3 months. Publishes ms an average of 4-6 months after acceptance. Sample copy for $6.

Payment/Terms: Pays in contributor's copies. Acquires one-time rights. Sponsors contests occasionally; guidelines published in magazine.

Tips: "Following proper format are essential. Your title must be intriguing and clean text. Never give up. Some of the writers we publish were rejected many times before we published them."

☑ $ THE OHIO REVIEW, (II), 209C Ellis Hall, Ohio University, Athens OH 45701-2979. (740)593-1900. Fax: (740)593-2818. **Editor:** Wayne Dodd. Associate Editor: Robert Kinsley. Magazine: 6×9; 200 pages; illustrations on cover. "We attempt to publish the best poetry and fiction written today. For a mainly literary audience." Semiannually. Estab. 1971. Circ. 3,000.

Needs: Contemporary, experimental, literary. "We lean toward contemporary on all subjects." Receives 150-200 unsolicited fiction mss/month. Accepts 5 mss/issue. Does not read mss June 1-September 15. Publishes ms 6 months after acceptance. Also publishes poetry. Sometimes critiques rejected mss and/or recommends other markets.

How to Contact: Query first or send complete ms with cover letter. Reports in 6 weeks. SASE. Sample copy for $6. Fiction guidelines for #10 SASE.

Payment/Terms: Pays $5/page, free subscription to magazine and 2 contributor's copies on publication for first North American serial rights. Sends galleys to author.

Advice: "We feel the short story is an important part of the contemporary writing field and value it highly. Read a copy of our publication to see if your fiction is of the same quality. So often people send us work that simply doesn't fit our needs."

N OHIO TEACHERS WRITE, (I, II, IV), Ohio Council of Teachers of English Language Arts, 1069 Edgewood Dr., Chillicothe OH 45601. (740)775-7494. Fax: (740)634-2890. E-mail: rmcclain@bright.net. **Editor:** Bill Newby. Editors change every 2 years. Magazine: 8½×11; 50 pages; 60 lb. white offset paper; 65 lb. blue cover stock; illustrations and photos. "The purpose of the magazine is threefold: (1) to provide a collection of fine literature for the reading pleasure of teachers and other adult readers; (2) to encourage teachers to compose literary works along with their students; (3) to provide the literate citizens of Ohio a window into the world of educators not often seen by those outside the teaching profession." Annually. Estab. 1995. Circ. 1,000.

- Submissions are limited to Ohio educators.

Needs: Adventure, ethnic/multicultural, experimental, fantasy (science fantasy), feminist, gay, historical, humor/satire, lesbian, literary, mainstream/contemporary, regional, religious/inspirational, romance (contemporary), science fiction (hard science, soft/sociological), senior citizen/retirement, sports, westerns (frontier, traditional), teaching. Receives 2 unsolicited mss/month. Accepts 7 mss/issue. "We read only in May when editorial board meets." Publishes ms 3-4 months after acceptance. Recently published work by Lois Spencer, Harry R. Noden, Linda J. Rice and June Langford Berkley. Length: 2,000 words maximum. Publishes short shorts. Also publishes poetry. Often critiques or comments on rejected ms.

How to Contact: Send 6 copies of complete ms with a cover letter. Include 30-word bio. Reports by July 30th. Send SASE with postage clipped for return of ms or send a disposable copy of ms. Sample copy $6.
Payment/Terms: Pays 2 contributor's copies; additional copies $6. Acquires first rights.

N **OMNIVORE MAGAZINE, (I, II)**, Doublebunny, P.O. Box 3094, Worcester MA 01613. (508)755-LORE. E-mail: bunnyx2@earthlink.net. **Editor:** Sou MacMillan. Magazine: 8½×11; 24-36 pages; 20 lb. paper; 60 lb. vellum cover stock; illustrations and photos. "Our goal is to bring attention to the arts as living and evolving. We are interested in how writing is presented visually on the page, as well as the content, and encourage the original and cutting-edge." Quarterly. Estab. 1995. Circ. 300.
Needs: Erotica, ethnic/multicultural, experimental, gay, humor/satire, lesbian, psychic/supernatural/occult, science fiction (hard science, soft/sociological), serialized novel. No romance, children's/young adult. Receives 4-5 unsolicited mss/month. Accepts 1-2 mss/issue; 6 mss/year. Does not read mss in November/December. Publishes ms 3-9 months after acceptance. Recently published work by Kyria Abrahams, Sean Shea and Eve Stern. Length: 2,200 words average; 500 words minimum; 2,500 words maximum. Publishes short shorts on rare occasion. Also publishes literary essays, literary criticism, poetry. Sometimes critiques or comments on rejected ms.
How to Contact: Query first. Reports in 3 months on queries; 3-6 months on mss. Send SASE for reply, return of ms. Simultaneous submissions OK. Sample copy $5 (will accept in stamps). Fiction guidelines free. Reviews novels and short story collections.
Payment/Terms: Pays 5 contributor's copies; additional copies $2. Acquires one-time rights.

ONIONHEAD, (II), Literary Quarterly, Arts on the Park, Inc., 115 N. Kentucky Ave., Lakeland FL 33801-5044. (941)680-2787. Website: http://www.geocities.com/athens/2031/aotponionhead (includes guidelines, editor and author information, fiction). **Co-Editors:** Susan Crawford and Brenda J. Patterson. Magazine: digest-sized; 40 pages; 20 lb. bond; glossy card cover. "Provocative political, social and cultural observations and hypotheses for a literary audience—an open-minded audience." Estab. 1989. Circ. 250.
Needs: Contemporary, ethnic, experimental, feminist, gay, humor/satire, lesbian, literary, prose poem, regional. "*Onionhead* focuses on provocative political, social and cultural observations and hypotheses. Must have a universal point (international)." Publishes short fiction in each issue. Receives 100-150 unsolicited mss/month. Acquires approximately 28 mss/issue; 100 mss (these numbers include poetry, short prose and essays)/year. Publishes ms within 18 months of acceptance. Recently published work by Robert Cooperman, Brett Hursey and Joan Payne Kincaid. 60% of fiction published is by new writers. Length: 2,500 words average; 3,000 words maximum. Publishes short shorts. Also publishes poetry.
How to Contact: Send complete ms with cover letter that includes brief bio and SASE. Reports in 3 weeks on queries; 2 months on mss. No simultaneous submissions. Sample copy for $3 postpaid. Fiction guidelines for #10 SASE.
Payment/Terms: Pays in contributor's copy. Charge for extras. Acquires first North American serial and electronic rights.
Advice: "Review a sample copy of *Onionhead* and remember *literary quality* is the prime criterion. Avoid heavy-handed approaches to social commentary—be subtle, not didactic. Follow the guidelines and send your best work."

ORACLE STORY, (I, II), Rising Star Publishers, 2105 Amherst Rd., Hyattsville MD 20783-2105. (301)422-2665. Fax: (301)422-2720. **Editorial Director:** Obi H. Ekwonna. Magazine: 5½×8½; 38 pages; white bond paper; 60 lb. Ibs cover. "Didactic well-made stories; basically adults and general public (mass market)." Quarterly. Estab. 1993. Circ. 500.

- *Oracle Story* is a member of the Association of African Writers. The editors are interested in all genres of fiction but with an African-cultural slant.

Needs: Condensed/excerpted novel, ethnic/multicultural, folklore (African), historical, horror, humor/satire, literary, mainstream/contemporary, mystery/suspense (romantic suspense), serialized novel, young adult/teen (horror and mystery). "No erotic, gay or lesbian writings." List of upcoming themes available for SASE. Publishes annual special fiction issue or anthology. Receives 60 unsolicited mss/month. Accepts 8 mss/issue; 26 mss/year. Publishes ms 6-12 months after acceptance. Recently published work by Joseph Manco. Publishes 50 new writers/year. Length: "not more than 20 typewritten pages." Publishes short shorts. Also publishes literary essays, literary criticism and poetry. Sometimes critiques or comments on rejected mss.
How to Contact: Send complete ms with a cover letter. Accepts queries/mss by fax. Include bio with SASE. Reports in 4-6 weeks. SASE for reply or return of ms. No simultaneous submissions. Electronic submissions OK (disks in WordPerfect 5.1, IBM readable format). Sample copy for $5 plus $1.50 postage. Fiction guidelines for SASE. Reviews novels and short story collections.
Payment/Terms: Pays contributor's copy. Acquires first North American seial rights.
Advice: Looks for work that is "well made, well written, and has good language. Take grammar classes." Especially interested in African folklore.

ORANGE COAST REVIEW, (II), Dept. of English, 2701 Fairview Rd., Orange Coast College, Costa Mesa CA 92628-5005. (714)432-5043. Advisor: Raymond Obstfeld. Editors change every 6 months. Magazine: 5½×8½; 70 pages; 60 lb. paper; medium/heavy cover; illustrations and photos. "We look for quality, of course.

The genre, style, and format take second place to intelligence and depth. Our largest audience consists of students and writers." Annually. Estab. 1990. Circ. 750.
Needs: Short stories, poetry, one-act plays, essays, literary criticism and interviews. B&w photography also considered. Publishes ms 3-6 months after acceptance. Length: Open. Publishes short shorts. Sometimes critiques or comments on rejected mss.
How to Contact: Send complete ms with a cover letter. Should include estimated word count, short paragraph bio, list of publications with submission. Reports in 2-3 months on mss. SASE for return ms. Simultaneous submissions OK. Sample copy for $5. Fiction guidelines for #10 SASE.
Payment/Terms: Pays in copies on publication for one-time rights.
Advice: "A manuscript stands out when it actually has a beginning, middle and end; a coherent theme that isn't vague or preachy; and characters that come to life. Check your grammar, punctuation, and spelling—three times. If you don't care about the easy stuff, why should we expect you to have cared about the story or poem. Never single space." Looks for "writing that involves their own voice or style, not Raymond Carver's or whoever else impresses them."

OUTERBRIDGE, (II), English 2S-218, The College of Staten Island (CUNY), 2800 Victory Blvd., Staten Island NY 10314. (718)982-3651. **Editor:** Charlotte Alexander. Magazine: 5½×8½; approximately 110 pages; 60 lb. white offset paper; 65 lb. cover stock. "We are a national literary magazine publishing mostly fiction and poetry. To date, we have had several special focus issues (the 'urban' and the 'rural' experience, 'Southern,' 'childhood,' 'nature and the environment,' 'animals,' 'love and friendship'). For anyone with enough interest in literature to look for writing of quality and writers on the contemporary scene who deserve attention. There probably is a growing circuit of writers, some academics, reading us by recommendations." Annually. Estab. 1975. Circ. 500-700.
Needs: Literary. "No *Reader's Digest* style; that is, very popularly oriented. We like to do interdisciplinary features, e.g., literature and music, literature and science and literature and the natural world." Accepts 8-10 mss/year. Does not read in July or August. Published work by Walter MacDonald, Patricia Ver Ellen, Henry Alley, Kyoko Yoshida and Naomi Rachel. Published new writers within the last year. Length: 10-25 pages. Also publishes poetry. Sometimes recommends other markets.
How to Contact: Query. Send complete ms with cover letter. "Don't talk too much, 'explain' the work, or act apologetic or arrogant. If published, tell where, with a brief bio." SASE (or IRC). Reports in 8-10 weeks on queries and mss. No multiple submissions. Sample copy for $6 for annual issue.
Payment/Terms: Pays 2 contributor's copies. Charges ½ price of current issue for extras to its authors. Acquires one-time rights. Requests credits for further publication of material used by *OB*.
Advice: "Read our publication first. Don't send out blindly; get some idea of what the magazine might want. A *short* personal note with biography is appreciated. Competition is keen. Read an eclectic mix of classic and contemporary literature. Beware of untransformed autobiography, but *everything* in one's experience contributes."

OWEN WISTER REVIEW, (II), Student Publications Board, P.O. Box 3625, University of Wyoming, Laramie WY 82071. (307)766-3819. Fax: (307)766-4027. E-mail: awr@uwyo. Editor: Tony Contento. **Fiction Editors:** "Fiction Selection Committee." Editors change each year, contact selection committee. Magazine: 6×9; 92 pages; 60 lb. matte paper; 80 lb. glossy cover; illustrations; photographs. "Though we are a university publication, our audience is wider than just an academic community. We're looking for fiction, poetry and artwork that captures some portion of the spirit of the American West: of yesterday and today." Semiannually. Estab. 1978. Circ. 600.

- *Owen Wister Review* has won numerous awards and honors far surpassing many student-run publications. Nine poems from *OWR* were nominated for inclusion in the *Pushcart Prize* anthology (1992-1993). The magazine received Best of Show award from the Associated Collegiate Press/College Media Advisors and six individual Gold Circle Awards from the Columbia Scholastic Press Association.

Needs: Ethnic/multicultural, experimental, humor/satire, literary, translations. Receives 12-15 unsolicited mss. Acquires 3 mss/issue; 6-8 mss/year. "Summer months are generally down time for *OWR*." Publishes ms 2-3 months after acceptance. Published work by Jon Billman, Amy Epstein, Pete Fromm, Jill Patterson, Val Pexton and Gary Wallace. Publishes many new writers/year. Length: 1,300 words average; 7,500 words maximum. Publishes short shorts. Also publishes literary essays, literary criticism and poetry.
How to Contact: Send complete ms with cover letter. Accepts queries/submissions by e-mail. Should include bio, list of publications. Reports in 2-3 weeks on queries; 2-3 months on mss. Send SASE for reply, return of ms or send disposable copy of the ms. Sample copy for $5. Free fiction guidelines.
Payment/Terms: Pays 1 contributor's copy. 10% off additional copies. Acquires one-time rights.
Advice: "We seek well-written pieces that break barriers and take readers to new vantage points. Dream, write, revise and share. Fiction only gains life through its readers. We currently are including a distinct, separate Spoken Word CD version of the Owen Wister Review. This allows us to increase our submissions and our audience."

$ THE OXFORD AMERICAN, The Southern Magazine of Good Writing, (II), P.O. Box 1156, Oxford MS 38655. (601)236-1836. **Editor:** Marc Smirnoff. Magazine: 8½×11; 100 pages; glossy paper; glossy cover; illustrations and photos. Bimonthly. Estab. 1992. Circ. 25,000.
Needs: Regional (Southern); stories set in the South. Published work by Lewis Nordan, Julia Reed, Florence

King and Tony Earley. Also publishes literary essays. Sometimes critiques or comments on rejected mss.
How to Contact: Send complete ms. Send SASE for reply, return of ms or send a disposable copy of ms. No simultaneous submissions. Sample copy for $4.50. "We review Southern novels or short story collections only."
Payment/Terms: Pays $100 minimum on publication for first rights; prices vary.
Advice: "I know you've heard it before—but we appreciate those writers who try to get into the spirit of the magazine which they can best accomplish by being familiar with it."

✓ **OXFORD MAGAZINE, (II)**, Bachelor Hall, Miami University, Oxford OH 45056. (513)529-1954 or 529-5221. Editor: David Mitchell Goldberg. Editors change every year. **Send submissions to:** "Fiction Editor." Magazine: 6×9; 85-100 pages; illustrations. Annually. Estab. 1985. Circ. 500-1,000.

- *Oxford* has been awarded two Pushcart Prizes.

Needs: Literary, ethnic, experimental, humor/satire, feminist, gay/lesbian, translations. Receives 50-60 unsolicited mss/month. Reads mss September through January. Published work by Stephen Dixon, André Dubus and Stuart Dybek. Published new writers within the last year. Length: 2,000-4,000 words average. "We will accept long fiction (over 6,000 words) only in cases of exceptional quality." Publishes short shorts. Also publishes literary essays, poetry.
How to Contact: Send complete ms with cover letter, which should include a short bio or interesting information. Simultaneous submissions OK, if notified. Reports in 3-5 months, depending upon time of submissions; mss received after January 1 will be returned. SASE. Sample copy for $5.
Payment/Terms: Pays in contributor's copies. Acquires one-time rights.
Advice: "*Oxford Magazine* is looking for humbly vivid fiction; that is to say, fiction that illuminates, which creates and inhabits an honest, carefully rendered reality populated by believable, three-dimensional characters. We want more stories—from undiscovered writers—that melt hair and offer the heat of a character at an emotional crossroads. Send us work that is uniquely yours; stories we'll wish we'd written ourselves. Send us stories that are unique; we want fiction no one else but you could possibly have written."

OXYGEN, A Spirited Literary Magazine, (II), 535 Geary St., #1010, San Francisco CA 94102-1633. (415)776-9681. E-mail: oxygen@slip.net. **Editor/Publisher:** Richard Hack. Magazine: 5½×8½; 100 pages; 60 lb. vellum paper; laminated cover, perfect-bound. "We are an eclectic, community-spirited magazine looking for vivid, imaginative stories of significance. We welcome fiction and poetry in modes realistic, surreal, expressionist, devotional, erotic, satiric, and invective. We value writers like Algren, Böll, H. Miller, Rabelais and Naylor." Publishes 1-2 issues/year. Estab. 1991. Circ. 350.
Needs: Stories, sketches, tales, novel sections. "Nothing overly commercial, insincere, or mocking, though we enjoy hard satire." Receives 100 unsolicited mss/month. Accepts 5-6 mss/issue; 10-12 mss/year. Publishes ms up to 6 months after acceptance. Recently published work by Eugene Wildman and Mia Stageberg. Publishes 8 previously unpublished writers/year. Length: 500-7,500 words. Also publishes poetry, occasional essays and reviews.
How to Contact: Send complete ms with optional cover letter, bio and list of publications. "Do not submit by e-mail." Reports in 2-8 weeks. Send SASE for reply or return of ms. Simultaneous submissions OK. Sample copy for $5. Fiction guidelines for #10 SASE.
Payment/Terms: Pays 2 contributor's copies. All rights revert to contributors.
Advice: "Efficiency counts, too: delve, don't vacillate. A thicket of non-profound, tone-deaf, superficial academic qualifications will choke off speech and kill feeling and event before they bloom. No simple journalism, column fluff, first-person experiences, diary entries, or stand-up comedy. We are open to many POVs, but we hope for meaningful writing that is community-spirited, rich and suggestive, a style with a nice feel to it. Does it believe in something, does it love life? Or satirize injustice and abuse? What kind of personal quality does it demonstrate?"

OYSTER BOY REVIEW OF FICTION AND POETRY, (I, II), 103B Hanna Street, Carrboro NC 27510. (919)967-1412. E-mail: oyster-boy@sunsite.unc.edu. Website: http://sunsite.unc.edu/ob (includes full contents of all issues; also related links). **Editors:** Damon Sauve and Chad Driscoll. Electronic and print magazine. "An independent literary magazine of poetry and fiction published in North Carolina in print and electronic form. We're interested in the under-rated, the ignored, the misunderstood, and the varietal. We'll make some mistakes. The editors tend to select experimental and traditional narrative fiction. Our audience tends to be young, unpublished writers or writers of considerable talent who have published in the bigger little magazines but like the harder literary edge *Oyster Boy* promotes."
Needs: "Fiction that revolves around characters in conflict with themselves or each other; a plot that has a beginning, a middle, and an end; a narrative with a strong moral center (not necessarily 'moralistic'); a story

SENDING TO A COUNTRY other than your own? Be sure to send International Reply Coupons instead of stamps for replies or return of your manuscript.

with a satisfying resolution to the conflict; and an ethereal something that contributes to the mystery of a question, but does not necessarily seek or contrive to answer it." No genre fiction. Recently published work by Michael Rumaker, Lucy Harrison, Michael McNeilleg and Kevin McGowin. Publishes 15 new writers/year.
How to Contact: Electronic and traditional submissions accepted. "E-mail submissions should be sent as the body-text of the e-mail message, or as an attached ASCII-text file. Attached files of Word 5.1 or later versions are acceptable but not preferred (please indicate version and/or application)."
Advice: "Keep writing, keep submitting, keep revising."

PACIFIC COAST JOURNAL, (I, II), French Bread Publications, P.O. Box 23865, San Jose CA 95153-3868. (408)225-4994. Fax: (408)225-3676. E-mail: paccoastj@juno.com. Website: http://www.bjt.net/~stgraham/pcj (includes guidelines, contest information, past published work). **Editor:** Stillson Graham. Fiction Editor: Stephanie Kylkis. Magazine: 5½×8½; 40 pages; 20 lb. paper; 67 lb. cover; illustrations; b&w photos. "Slight focus toward Western North America/Pacific Rim." Quarterly (or "whenever we have enough money"). Estab. 1992. Circ. 200.
Needs: Ethnic/multicultural, experimental, feminist, historical, humor/satire, literary, science fiction (soft/sociological, magical realism). Receives 30-40 unsolicited mss/month. Accepts 3-4 mss/issue; 10-12 mss/year. Publishes ms 6-18 months after acceptance. Recently published work by Hugh Fox, A.D. Elevitch and Kirby Cangden. Publishes 3-5 new writers/year. Length: 2,500 words preferred; 4,000 words maximum. Publishes short shorts. Also publishes literary essays and poetry. Sometimes critiques or comments on rejected mss. Sponsors contest. Send SASE for details.
How to Contact: Send complete ms with a cover letter. Include 3 other publication titles that are recommended as good for writers. Reports in 2-4 months. Send SASE for reply, return of ms or send a disposable copy of ms. Simultaneous, reprint and electronic submissions OK (Mac or IBM disks or e-mail). Sample copy for $2.50, 6×9 SASE. Reviews novels and short story collections.
Payment/Terms: Pays 1 contributor's copy. Acquires one-time rights.
Advice: "We tend to comment more on a story not accepted for publication when an e-mail address is provided as the SASE. Don't worry about trying to 'say' something. Just write. There are very few quality literary magazines that are not backed by big institutions. We don't have those kinds of resources so publishing anything is a struggle. We have to make each issue count."

☑ **PACIFIC REVIEW, (II)**, Dept. of English and Comparative Lit., San Diego State University, San Diego CA 92182-0295. Contact: Tana Jean Parker, **editor.** Magazine: 6×9; 75-100 pages; book stock paper; paper back, extra heavy cover stock; b&w illustrations, b&w photos. "There is no designated theme. We publish high-quality fiction, poetry, and familiar essays: we accept one in a hundred stories and never print more than 3 stories in one issue, so fiction is not used as filler." Annual. Estab. 1973. Circ. 1,000.
Needs: "We do not restrict or limit our fiction in any way other than quality. We are interested in all fiction, from the very traditional to the highly experimental. Acceptance is determined by the quality of submissions." No mainstream fiction. Published work by Gerald Butler. Publishes 10 new writers/year. Published new writers within the last year. Length: 4,000 words max. Publishes (and prefers) short shorts.
How to Contact: Send original ms with SASE. Reports in 6 months on mss. Sample copy for $3.
Payment/Terms: 1 contributor's copy. "First serial rights are *Pacific Review*'s. All other rights revert to author."
Advice: "The current editor prefers unique work over mainstream/traditional fiction. We accept work that has clearly been composed in the late twentieth century. That is, the author is aware of the differences between this particular era and every other. In an age radically altered by science, most of the stories we receive look like antiques or unconvincing evasions."

☑ **PALO ALTO REVIEW, A Journal of Ideas, (I, II)**, Palo Alto College, 1400 W. Villaret, San Antonio TX 78224. (210)921-5021. Fax: (210)921-5008. E-mail: eshull@accd.edu. **Editors:** Bob Richmond and Ellen Shull. Magazine: 8½×11; 60 pages; 60 lb. natural white paper (50% recycled); illustrations and photographs. "Not too experimental nor excessively avant-garde, just good stories (for fiction). Ideas are what we are after. We are interested in connecting the college and the community. We would hope that those who attempt these connections will choose startling topics and interesting angles with which to investigate the length and breadth of the teaching/learning spectrum." Semiannually (spring and fall). Estab. 1992. Circ. 500-600.
Needs: Adventure, ethnic/multicultural, experimental, fantasy, feminist, historical, humor/satire, literary, mainstream/contemporary, mystery/suspense, regional, romance, science fiction, translations, westerns. Upcoming themes: "Family" (December 1997); "Autobiography" (July 1998). Upcoming themes available for SASE. Receives 100-150 unsolicited mss/month. Accepts 2-4 mss/issue; 4-8 mss/year. Does not read mss March-April and October-November when putting out each issue. Publishes ms 2-15 months after acceptance. Published work by Gayle Silbert, Naomi Chase, Kenneth Emberly, C.J. Hannah, Tom Juvik, Kassie Fleisher and Paul Perry. Publishes 30 new writers/year. Length: 5,000 words maximum. Publishes short shorts. Also publishes articles, interviews, literary essays, literary criticism, poetry. Always critiques or comments on rejected mss.
How to Contact: Send complete ms with a cover letter. "Request sample copy and guidelines." Accepts queries/mss by e-mail. Include brief bio and brief list of publications. Reports in 3-4 months. Send SASE for reply, return of ms or send a disposable copy of ms. Simultaneous and electronic (Macintosh disk) submissions OK. Sample copy for $5. Fiction guidelines for #10 SASE.

Payment/Terms: Pays 2 contributor's copies; additional copies for $5. Acquires first North American serial rights.

Advice: "Good short stories have interesting characters confronted by a dilemma working toward a solution. So often what we get is 'a moment in time,' not a story. Generally, the characters are interesting because the readers can identify with them and know much about them. Edit judiciously. Cut out extraneous verbiage. Set up a choice that has to be made. Then create tension—who wants what and why they can't have it."

PANGOLIN PAPERS, (II), Turtle Press, P.O. Box 241, Nordland WA 98358. (360)385-3626. E-mail: trtlbluf@olympus.net. **Editor:** Pat Britt. Magazine: 5½×8½; 120 pages; 24 lb. paper; 80 lb. cover. "Best quality literary fiction for an informed audience." Triannually. Estab. 1994. Circ. 500.

Needs: Condensed/excerpted novel, experimental, humor/satire, literary, translations. No "genre such as romance or science fiction." Plans to publish special fiction issues or anthologies in the future. Receives 20 unsolicited mss/month. Accepts 7-10 mss/issue; 20-30 mss/year. Does not read mss in July and August. Publishes ms 4-12 months after acceptance. Agented fiction 10%. Published work by Jack Nisbet and Barry Gifford. Publishes 3-4 new writers/year. Length: 3,500 words average; 100 words minimum; 7,000 words maximum. Publishes short shorts. Length: 400 words. Also publishes literary essays. Sometimes critiques or comments on rejected mss.

How to Contact: Send complete ms with a cover letter. Accepts queries/mss by e-mail. Include estimated word count and short bio. Reports in 2 weeks on queries; 2 months on mss. Send SASE for reply, return of ms or send a disposable copy of ms. No simultaneous submissions. Electronic and reprint submissions OK. Sample copy for $5.95 and $1 postage. Fiction guidelines for #10 SAE.

Payment/Terms: Pays 2 contributor's copies. Offers annual $200 prize for best story. Acquires first North American serial rights. Sometimes sends galleys to author.

Advice: "We are looking for original voices. Follow the rules and be honest in your work."

☑ **THE PANNUS INDEX, (IV)**, BGB Press, 158 King St., Northampton MA 01060. (413)584-4776. Fax: (413)584-5674. E-mail: stout@javanet.com. Website: http://www.javanet.com/~stout/pannus/ (includes guidelines, descriptions of past issues, subscription information and links). **Editor:** Vincent Bator. Magazine: 6×10; 120-138 pages; offset/vellum paper; illustrations and photos. "We encourage writers to submit that are working towards the preservation of language and aesthetics. We encourage writers who are anachronistic in their writing, as well as exploring literature's past achievements." Biannual. Estab. 1996. Circ. 200.

Needs: Condensed/Excerpted Novel, historical, humor/satire, nonfiction, translations. List of upcoming themes available with SASE. Publishes special fiction issues or anthologies. Receives 60-75 mss/month. Accepts 5-10 mss/issue; 25-35 mss/year. Publishes ms 3-4 months after acceptance. Recently published work by Steve Tomasula and Ken G. Young. Length: 10,000 words average; no maximum. "We prefer longer pieces." Also publishes literary essays, literary criticism and poetry. Often critiques or comments on rejected mss.

How to Contact: Query with SASE. Include bio. Accepts queries/mss by e-mail. Reports on queries in 2 weeks. Send SASE for reply or send disposable copy of ms. Simultaneous, reprint and disk submissions OK. Sample copy for $8. Fiction guidelines for #10 SASE. Reviews novel and short story collections. Send books to editor.

Payment/Terms: Pays 1 contributor's copy for one-time rights; additional copies $6.

Advice: "We look for quality writing—prose must be technically flawless. To stand out, the writer must have a command of literary history and original non-formulaic ideas."

🍁 ☑ **PAPERPLATES, a magazine for fifty readers," (II)**, Perkolator Kommunikation, 19 Kenwood Ave., Toronto, Ontario M6C 2R8 Canada. (416)651-2551. Fax: (416)651-2910. E-mail: paper@perkolator.com. **Editor:** Bernard Kelly. Magazine: 8½×11; 48 pages; recycled paper; illustrations and photos. Published 2-3 times/year. Estab. 1990. Circ. 500. Member of Toronto Small Press Group and Canadian Magazine Publishers Association.

Needs: Condensed/excerpted novel, ethnic/multicultural, feminist, gay, lesbian, literary, mainstream/contemporary, translations. "No science fiction, fantasy or horror." Receives 2-3 unsolicited mss/month. Accepts 2-3 mss/issue; 6-9 mss/year. Publishes ms 6-8 months after acceptance. Published work by Celia Lottridge, C.J. Lockett, Deirdre Kessler and Marvyne Jenoff. Length: 5,000 words average; 1,500 words minimum; 15,000 words maximum. Publishes short shorts. Also publishes literary essays, literary criticism and poetry.

How to Contact: Send complete ms with a cover letter. Reports in 6 weeks on queries; 3 months on mss. Send SASE for reply, return of ms or send a disposable copy of ms. Simultaneous submissions and electronic submissions OK. Sample copy for $5. Fiction guidelines for #10 SASE.

Payment/Terms: Pays 2 contributor's copies on publication; additional copies for $5. Acquires first North American serial rights.

🏆 **PARAMOUR MAGAZINE, Literary and Artistic Erotica, (IV)**, P.O. Box 949, Cambridge MA 02140-0008. (617)499-0069. E-mail: paramour@paramour.com. Website: http://www.paramour.com/. Publisher/Editor: Amelia Copeland. **Fiction Editor:** Nina Lesser. Magazine: 9×12; 36 pages; matte coated stock; illustrations and photos. "*Paramour* is a quarterly journal of literary and artistic erotica that showcases work by emerging writers and artists. Our goal is to provoke thought, laughter, curiosity and especially, arousal." Quarterly. Estab. 1993. Circ. 12,000.

• Work published in *Paramour* has been selected for inclusion in *Best American Erotica*.

Needs: Erotica. Receives 50 unsolicited mss/month. Accepts 3-5 mss/issue; 12-20 mss/year. Length: 2,000 words average; 1 word minimum; 4,000 words maximum. Publishes short shorts. Also publishes literary essays, literary criticism and poetry.

How to Contact: Request guidelines prior to submissions: call, write or e-mail. Send complete ms with a cover letter. Include estimated word count, name, address and phone number. Reports in 3 weeks on queries; 4 months on mss. SASE for reply only; send disposable copy of ms. No simultaneous submissions. Sample copy for $4.95. Fiction guidelines for #10 SAE and 1 first-class stamp. Reviews novels and short story collections.

Payment/Terms: Pays free subscription to the magazine plus contributor's copies. Acquires first rights.

Advice: "We look for erotic stories which are well-constructed, original, exciting, and dynamic. Clarity, attention to form and image, and heat make a ms stand out. Seek striking and authentic images and make the genre work for you. We see too many derivative rehashes of generic sexual fantasies. We love to see fresh representations that we know will excite readers."

$ THE PARIS REVIEW, (II), 45-39 171 Place, Flushing NY 11358 (*business office only, send mss to address below*). (212)861-0016. Fax: (212)861-4504. **Editor:** George A. Plimpton. Magazine: 5¼×8½; about 260 pages; illustrations and photographs (unsolicited artwork not accepted). "Fiction and poetry of superlative quality, whatever the genre, style or mode. Our contributors include prominent, as well as less well-known and previously unpublished writers. *The Art of Fiction*, *Art of Poetry*, *Art of Criticism* and *Art of Theater* interview series include important contemporary writers discussing their own work and the craft of writing." Quarterly.

Needs: Literary. Receives about 1,000 unsolicited fiction mss each month. Published work by Raymond Carver, Elizabeth Tallent, Rick Bass, John Koethe, Sharon Olds, Derek Walcott, Carolyn Kizer, Tess Gallagher, Peter Handke, Denis Johnson, Bobbie Ann Mason, Harold Brodkey, Joseph Brodsky, John Updike, Andre Dubus, Galway Kinnell, E.L. Doctorow and Philip Levine. Published new writers within the last year. No preferred length. Also publishes literary essays, poetry.

How to Contact: *Send complete ms with SASE to Fiction Editor, 541 E. 72nd St., New York NY 10021.* Reports in 6-8 months. Simultaneous submissions OK. Sample copy for $11. Writer's guidelines for #10 SASE (from Flushing office). Sponsors annual Aga Khan Fiction Contest award of $1,000.

Payment/Terms: Pays up to $600. Pays on publication for all rights. Sends galleys to author.

PARTING GIFTS, (II), 3413 Wilshire, Greensboro NC 27408. E-mail: rbixby@aol.com. Website: http://users.aol.com/marchst (includes guidelines, samples, catalog, news, some artwork and a few java applets just for fun). **Editor:** Robert Bixby. Magazine: 5×7; 60 pages. "High-quality insightful fiction, very brief and on any theme." Semiannually. Estab. 1988.

Needs: "Brevity is the second most important criterion behind literary quality." Publishes ms within one year of acceptance. Recently published work by David Chorlton, Ben Miller, Deborah Bayer, Tessa Dratt, Mary Rohrer-Dann, Peter Markus and Ray Miller. Length: 250 words minimum; 1,000 words maximum. Also publishes poetry. Sometimes critiques rejected mss.

How to Contact: Send complete ms with cover letter. Simultaneous submissions OK. Reports in 1 day on queries; 1-7 days on mss. SASE.

Payment/Terms: Pays in contributor's copies. Acquires one-time rights.

Advice: "Read the works of Amy Hempel, Jim Harrison, Kelly Cherry, C.K. Williams and Janet Kauffman, all excellent writers who epitomize the writing *Parting Gifts* strives to promote. I need more than ever for my authors to be better read. I sense that many unaccepted writers have not put in the hours reading."

PASSAGER, A Journal of Remembrance and Discovery, (I, II, IV), University of Baltimore, 1420 N. Charles St., Baltimore MD 21201-5779. **Editors:** Kendra Kopelke and Mary Azrael. Magazine: 8¼ square; 32 pages; 70 lb. paper; 80 lb. cover; photographs. "We publish stories and novel excerpts, poems, interviews with featured authors. One of our missions is to provide exposure for new older writers; another is to function as a literary community for writers across the country who are not connected to academic institutions or other organized groups." Quarterly. Estab. 1990. Circ. 750.

Needs: "Special interest in discovering new older writers, but publishes all ages." Receives 200 unsolicited mss/month. Accepts 2-3 prose mss/issue; 8-12/year. Does not read mss June through August. Publishes ms up to 18 months after acceptance. Length: 250 words minimum; 4,000 words maximum. Publishes short shorts. Also publishes poetry.

How to Contact: Send complete ms with cover letter. Reports in 3 months on mss. SASE. Simultaneous submissions OK, if noted. Sample copy for $4. Fiction guidelines for #10 SASE. "Send for fiction guidelines and upcoming themes with #10 SASE."

Payment/Terms: Pays subscription to magazine and 2 contributor's copies. Acquires first North American serial rights. Sometimes sends galleys to author.

Advice: "*Get a copy* so you can see the quality of the work we use. We seek powerful images of remembrance and discovery from writers of all ages. No stereotyped images of older people—we are interested in promoting complex images of aging that reveal the imagination and character of this stage of life."

☑ **PASSAGES NORTH, (I, II)**, Northern Michigan University, 1401 Presque Isle Ave., Marquette MI 49855. (906)227-1203. Fax: (906)227-1096. E-mail: jsmolens@nmu.edu. Editor: Anne Ohman Youngs. **Fiction Editors:** Candice Rowe and John Smolens. Magazine: 8×5½; 110-130 pages; 80 lb. paper. "*Passages North* publishes quality fiction, poetry and creative nonfiction by emerging and established writers." Readership: General and literary. Semiannually. Estab. 1979. Circ. 300.

Needs: Ethnic/multicultural, literary, mainstream/contemporary, regional. No science fiction, "typical commercial press work." Receives 100-200 mss/month. Accepts 8-12 fiction mss/year. Does not read May through August. Recently published works by John Epton Sealey, Michael Doherty and Carrie Scarff. 10% of ms published are from new writers. Length: 5,000 words maximum. Critiques returned mss when there is time. Also publishes interviews with authors.

How to Contact: Send complete ms with SASE and estimated word count. Accepts queries/mss by fax. Reports in 6-8 weeks. No simultaneous submissions. Sample copy for $6. Fiction guidelines free.

Payment/Terms: Pays 1 contributor's copy. Rights revert to author on request.

THE PATERSON LITERARY REVIEW, (II), (formerly Footwork), Passaic County Community College, One College Blvd., Paterson NJ 07505. (201)684-6555. **Editor:** Maria Mazziotti Gillan. Magazine: 8½×11; 300 pages; 60 lb. paper; 70 lb. cover; illustrations; photos. Annually.

- *Footwork* was chosen by *Library Journal* as one of the ten best literary magazines in the U.S.

Needs: Contemporary, ethnic, literary. "We are interested in quality short stories, with no taboos on subject matter." Receives about 60 unsolicited mss/month. Publishes ms about 6 months to 1 year after acceptance. Published new writers within the last year. Length: 2,000-3,000 words. Also publishes literary essays, literary criticism, poetry.

How to Contact: Submit no more than 1 story at a time. Submission deadline: March 1. Send SASE for reply or return of ms. "Indicate whether you want story returned." Simultaneous submissions OK. Sample copy for $12. Reviews novels and short story collections.

Payment/Terms: Pays in contributor's copies. Acquires first North American rights.

Advice: Looks for "clear, moving and specific work."

PEARL, A Literary Magazine, (II, IV), Pearl, 3030 E. Second St., Long Beach CA 90803-5163. (562)434-4523. **Editors:** Joan Jobe Smith, Marilyn Johnson and Barbara Hauk. Magazine: 5½×8½; 96 pages; 60 lb. recycled, acid-free paper; perfect-bound; coated cover; b&w drawings and graphics. "We are primarily a poetry magazine, but we do publish some *very short* fiction and nonfiction. We are interested in lively, readable prose that speaks to *real* people in direct, living language; for a general literary audience." Biannually. Estab. 1974. Circ. 600.

Needs: Contemporary, humor/satire, literary, mainstream, prose poem. "We will only consider short-short stories up to 1,200 words. Longer stories (up to 4,000 words) may only be submitted to our short story contest. All contest entries are considered for publication. Although we have no taboos stylistically or subject-wise, obscure, predictable, sentimental, or cliché-ridden stories are a turn-off." Publishes an all fiction issue each year. Receives 10-20 unsolicited mss/month. Accepts 1-10 mss/issue; 12-15 mss/year. Submissions accepted September-May *only*. Publishes ms 6 months to 1 year after acceptance. Recently published work by Patti Munter, Stephanie Dickinson, Denise Duhamel, Lisa Glatt, Gerald Locklin and Thaddeus Rutkowski. Publishes 1-5 new writers/year. Length: 1,000 words average; 500 words minimum; 1,200 words maximum. Also publishes poetry. Sponsors an annual short story contest. Send SASE for complete guidelines.

How to Contact: Send complete ms with cover letter including publishing credits and brief bio. Simultaneous submissions OK. Reports in 6-8 weeks on mss. SASE. Sample copy for $6 (postpaid). Fiction guidelines for #10 SASE.

Payment/Terms: Pays 2 contributor's copies. Acquires first North American serial rights. Sends galleys to author.

Advice: "We look for vivid, *dramatized* situations and characters, stories written in an original 'voice,' that make sense and follow a clear narrative line. What makes a manuscript stand out is more elusive, though—more to do with feeling and imagination than anything else . . ."

☑ **THE PEGASUS REVIEW, (I, IV)**, P.O. Box 88, Henderson MD 21640-0088. (410)482-6736. **Editor:** Art Bounds. Magazine: 5½×8½; 6-8 pages; illustrations. "Our magazine is a bimonthly, entirely in calligraphy, illustrated. Each issue is based on specific themes." Estab. 1980. Circ. 150.

- Because *The Pegasus Review* is done in calligraphy, submissions must be very short. Two pages, says the editor, are the ideal length.

Needs: Humor/satire, literary, prose poem and religious/inspirational. Wants more short-shorts and theme-related fiction. Upcoming themes: "Birth" (January/February); "Spring" (March/April); "The Planets" (May/June); "Summer" (July/August); "Fall" (September/October); "Winter" (November/December). "Themes may be approached by humor, satire, inspirational, autobiographical, prose. Nothing like a new slant on an old theme." Receives 35 unsolicited mss/month. Accepts "about" 50 mss/year. Recently published work by Robert Deluty, Emily C. Long, Hester Dawson and Lawrence W. Thomas. Publishes 15 new writers/year. Published work by 10 new writers within the last year. Publishes short shorts of 2-3 pages; 500 words. Themes are subject to change, so query if in doubt. "Occasional critiques."

How to Contact: Send complete ms. SASE "a must." Brief cover letter with author's background, name and prior credits, if any. Simultaneous submissions acceptable, if so advised. Reports in 1-2 months. Sample copy for $2.50. Fiction guidelines for SAE. Subscription: $12.50/year.
Payment/Terms: Pays 2 contributor's copies. Occasional book awards. Acquires one-time rights.
Advice: "Write on a daily basis, adhere to given guidelines, continuously market your work and heed what an editor might suggest as brief as the suggestion might be. Follow the writing market carefully through publications such as *Writer's Market* and *Novel & Short Story Writer's Market*. Get involved in a writer's group in your area and if none is available, start one."

☑ **PEMBROKE MAGAZINE, (I, II)**, Box 1510, University of North Carolina at Pembroke, Pembroke NC 28372. (910)521-6358. Editor: Shelby Stephenson. **Fiction Editor:** Stephen Smith. Magazine: 6×9; approximately 200 pages; illustrations; photos. Magazine of poems and stories plus literary essays. Annually. Estab. 1969. Circ. 500.
Needs: Open. Receives 120 unsolicited mss/month. Publishes short shorts. Published work by Fred Chappell, Robert Morgan. Published new writers within the last year. Length: open. Occasionally critiques rejected mss and recommends other markets.
How to Contact: Send complete ms. No simultaneous submissions. Reports in up to 3 months. SASE. Sample copy for $8 and 9×10 SAE.
Payment/Terms: Pays 1 contributor's copy.
Advice: "Write with an end for *writing*, not publication."

PENNSYLVANIA ENGLISH, (I), Penn State DuBois, College Place, DuBois PA 15801. (814)375-4814. Fax: (814)375-4784. E-mail: ajv2@psu.edu. Magazine: 5½×8½; up to 180 pages; perfect bound; full color cover featuring the artwork of a Pennsylvania artist. "Our philosophy is quality. We publish literary fiction (and poetry and nonfiction). Our intended audience is literate, college-educated people." Annually. Estab. 1985. Circ. 300.
Needs: Literary, contemporary mainstream. No genre fiction or romance. Publishes ms within 12 months after acceptance. Recently published work by Dave Kress, Dan Leone and Paul West. Length: "no maximum or minimum." 5,000 words maximum. Publishes short shorts. Also publishes literary essays, literary criticism, poetry. Sometimes critiques rejected mss.
How to Contact: Send complete ms with cover letter. Reports in 2 months. SASE. Simultaneous submissions OK.
Payment/Terms: Pays in 2 contributor's copies. Acquires first North American serial rights.
Advice: "Quality of the writing is our only measure. We're not impressed by long-winded cover letters or résumés detailing awards and publications we've never heard of. Beginners and professionals have the same chance with us. We receive stacks of competently written but boring fiction. For a story to rise out of the rejection pile, it takes more than basic competence."

PEREGRINE, The Journal of Amherst Writers & Artists Press, (II), AWA Press, P.O. Box 1076, Amherst MA 01004-1076. (413)253-7764. Fax: (413)253-7764. Website: http://www.javanet.com/~awapress. **Managing Editor:** Nancy Rose. Magazine: 6×9; 120 pages; 60 lb. white offset paper; glossy cover. "*Peregrine* has provided a forum for national and international writers for seventeen years, and is committed to finding excellent work by new writers as well as established authors. We publish what we love, knowing that all editorial decisions are subjective, and that all work has a home somewhere." Annually.
Needs: Poetry and prose—short stories, short short stories, personal essays. No previously published work. No children's stories. Publishes 2 pages in each issue of work in translation. "We welcome work reflecting diversity of voice." Accepts 6-12 fiction mss/issue. Publishes ms an average of 4 months after acceptance. Published work by Marilyn Moriarty, Ruth Hamel, Robert Garner McBrearty and Kevin Markey. Published new writers within the last year. "We like to be surprised. We look for writing that is honest, unpretentious, and memorable." Length: 4,200 words maximum. Short pieces have a better chance of publication. *Peregrine* sponsors an annual contest (The *Peregrine* Prize) and awards $500 each for fiction and poetry, and $100 "Best of the Nest" awarded to a local author.
How to Contact: #10 SASE to "Peregrine Guidelines." Send ms with cover letter; include 40-word biographical note, prior publications and word count. Simultaneous submissions OK. Enclose sufficiently stamped SASE for return of ms; if disposable copy, enclose #10 SASE for response. Deadline for submission: April 1, 1999. Read October-April. Sample copy $8.
Payment/Terms: Pays contributor's copies. All rights return to writer upon publication.
Advice: "We look for heart and soul as well as technical expertise. Trust your own voice. Familiarize yourself with *Peregrine*." Every ms is read by three or more readers.

PHOEBE, An Interdisciplinary Journal of Feminist Scholarship, Theory and Aesthetics, Women's Studies Department, State University of New York, College at Oneonta, Oneonta NY 13820-4015. (607)436-2014. Fax: (607)436-2656. E-mail: phoebe@oneonta.edu. **Editor:** Kathleen O'Mara. Journal: 7×9; 140 pages; 80 lb. paper; illustrations and photos. "Feminist material for feminist scholars and readers." Semiannually. Estab. 1989. Circ. 400.

- Editor would like to see more experimental fiction.

Needs: Feminist: ethnic, experimental, gay, humor/satire, lesbian, literary, translations. Upcoming themes: "Women's Journeys." Receives 25 unsolicited mss/month. "One-third to one-half of each issue is short fiction and poetry." Does not read mss in summer. Publishes ms 3-4 months after acceptance. Recently published work by Elaine Hatfield, Betty A. Wilder, Jenny Potts, Kristan Ruona and Sylvia Van Nooten. Length: 1,500-2,500 words preferred. Publishes short shorts. Sometimes critiques rejected mss and recommends other markets.

How to Contact: Send complete ms with cover letter. Reports in 1 month on queries; 15 weeks on mss. Electronic (WordPerfect/Microsoft Word disk, e-mail) submissions OK. Sample copy for $7.50. Fiction guidelines free.

Payment/Terms: Pays in contributor's copies. Acquires one-time rights.

Advice: "We look for writing with a feminist perspective. *Phoebe* was founded to provide a forum for cross-cultural feminist analysis, debate and exchange. The editors are committed to providing space for all disciplines and new areas of research, criticism and theory in feminist scholarship and aesthetics. *Phoebe* is not committed to any one conception of feminism. All work that is not sexist, racist, homophobic, or otherwise discriminatory, will be welcome. *Phoebe* is particularly committed to publishing work informed by a theoretical perspective which will enrich critical thinking."

PHOEBE, A Journal of Literary Arts, (II), George Mason University, MSN 2D6, 4400 University Dr., Fairfax VA 22030. (703)993-2915. E-mail: phoebe@gmu.edu. Website: http://www.gmu.edu/pubs/phoebe (includes writer's guidelines, fiction and poetry contest guidelines, subscription information, past issue descriptions, etc.). **Fiction Editor:** Renee Sagiv. Editors change each year. Magazine: 6×9; 116 pages; 80 lb. paper; 0-5 illustrations; 0-10 photographs. "We publish mainly fiction and poetry with occasional visual art." Published 2 times/year. Estab. 1972. Circ. 3,000.

Needs: "Looking for a broad range of fiction and poetry. We encourage writers and poets to experiment, to stretch the boundaries of genre." No romance, western, juvenile, erotica. Receives 30 mss/month. Accepts 3-5 mss/issue. Does not read mss in summer. Publishes ms 3-6 months after acceptance. Recently published work by Julie Brossell, Rhonda Claridge, Joseph O'Malley. 75% of work published is by new writers. Length: no more than 35 pages of fiction, no more than 15 pages of poetry.

How to Contact: Send complete ms with cover letter. Include "name, address, phone. Brief bio." SASE. Simultaneous submissions OK. Sample copy for $6.

Payment/Terms: Pays 2 contributor's copies. Acquires one-time rights. All rights revert to author.

Advice: "We are interested in a variety of fiction and poetry. We suggest potential contributors study previous issues. Each year *Phoebe* sponsors fiction and poetry contests, with $500 awarded to the winning short story and poem. The deadline for both the Greg Grummer Award in Poetry and the Phoebe Fiction Prize is December 15. E-mail or send SASE for complete contest guidelines."

$ PIG IRON, (II), Box 237, Youngstown OH 44501. (330)747-6932. Fax: (330)747-0599. **Editor:** Jim Villani. Annual series: 8½×11; 128 pages; 60 lb. offset paper; 85 pt. coated cover stock; b&w illustrations; b&w 120 line photographs. "Contemporary literature by new and experimental writers." Annually. Estab. 1975. Circ. 1,000.

Needs: Literary and thematic. No mainstream. Upcoming themes: "Religion in Modernity" (December 1998); "The 20th Century" (December 1999). Accepts 10-20 mss/issue. Receives approximately 75-100 unsolicited mss/month. Recently published work by Judith Hemschemeyer, Andrena Zowinski, Jim Sanderson, Larry Smith and Wayne Hogan. Length: 8,000 words maximum. Also publishes literary nonfiction, poetry. Sponsors contest. Send SASE for details.

How to Contact: Send complete ms with SASE. No simultaneous submissions. Reports in 4 months. Sample copy for $5.

Payment/Terms: Pays $5/printed page and 2 contributor's copies on publication for first North American serial rights; $5 charge for extras.

Advice: "Looking for work that is polished, compelling and magical."

☑ PIKEVILLE REVIEW, (I), Pikeville College, Sycamore St., Pikeville KY 41501. (606)432-9612. Fax: (606)432-9238. E-mail: eward@pc.edu. Website: http://www.pc.edu (includes writer's guidelines, names of editors, short fiction). **Editor:** Elgin M. Ward. Magazine: 8½×6; 120 pages; illustrations and photos. "Literate audience interested in well-crafted poetry, fiction, essays and reviews." Annually. Estab. 1987. Circ. 500.

Needs: Ethnic/multicultural, experimental, feminist, humor/satire, literary, mainstream/contemporary, regional, translations. Receives 25 unsolicited mss/month. Accepts 3-4 mss/issue. Does not read mss in the summer. Publishes ms 6-8 months after acceptance. Recently published work by Jim Wayne Miller and Robert Morgan. Publishes 1-2 new writers/year. Length: 5,000 words average; 15,000 words maximum. Publishes short shorts. Also publishes literary essays and poetry. Often critiques rejected mss. Sponsors occasional fiction award: $50.

How to Contact: Send complete ms with cover letter. Include estimated word count. Send SASE for reply, return of ms or send a disposable copy of ms. Simultaneous submissions OK. Sample copy for $3. Reviews novels and short story collections.
Payment/Terms: Pays 5 contributor's copies; additional copies for $3. Acquires first rights.
Advice: "Send a clean manuscript with well-developed characters."

PLANET-THE WELSH INTERNATIONALIST, P.O. Box 44, Aberystwyth, Ceredigion, SY23 322 Cymru/ Wales UK. Phone: 01970-611255. Fax: 01970-611197. **Fiction Editor:** John Barnie. Bimonthly. Circ. 1,400. Publishes 1-2 stories/issue.
Needs: "A literary/cultural/political journal centered on Welsh affairs but with a strong interest in minority cultures in Europe and elsewhere." Recently published work by Arthur Winfield Knight, Roger Granelli, Siam James, Jan Morris and Gus Vanderhagle. Length: 1,500-4,000 words maximum.
How to Contact: No submissions returned unless accompanied by an SAE. Writers submitting from abroad should send at least 3 IRCs.
Payment/Terms: Writers receive 1 contributor's copy. Payment is at the rate of £40 per 1,000 words (in the currency of the relevant country if the author lives outside the UK). Sample copy: cost (to USA & Canada) £2.87. Writers' guidelines for SAE.
Advice: "We do not look for fiction which necessarily has a 'Welsh' connection, which some writers assume from our title. We try to publish a broad range of fiction and our main criterion is quality. Try to read copies of any magazine you submit to. Don't write out of the blue to a magazine which might be completely inappropriate to your work. Recognize that you are likely to have a high rejection rate, as magazines tend to favor writers from their own countries."

✓ **THE PLAZA, A Space for Global Human Relations**, U-Kan Inc., Yoyogi 2-32-1, Shibuya-ku, Tokyo 151-0053, Japan. Tel: +81-(3)-3379-3881. Fax: +81-(3)-3379-3882. E-mail: plaza@u-kan.co.jp. Website: http://u-kan.co.jp (includes contribution guide, contents of the current and back issues, representative works by *The Plaza* writers). Editor: Leo Shunji Nishida. **Fiction Editor:** Roger Lakhani. Quarterly. Circ. 4,000. Publishes about 2 stories/issue. "*The Plaza* is an intercultural and bilingual magazine (English and Japanese). Our focus is the 'essence of being human.' All works are published in both Japanese and English (translations by our staff if necessary). The most important criteria is artistic level. We look for works that reflect simply 'being human.' Stories on intercultural (not international) relations are desired. *The Plaza* is devoted to offering a spiritual *Plaza* where people around the world can share their creative work. We introduce contemporary writers and artists as our generation's contribution to the continuing human heritage."
Needs: Length: Less than 1,000 words, minimalist short stories are welcomed. Wants to see more fiction "of not human beings, but being human. Of not international, but intercultural. Of not social, but human relationships." No political themes: religious evangelism; social commentary. Recently published work by Michael Hoffman, Bun'ichirou Chino and Eric T. Forsberg. Publishes 3 new writers/year.
How to Contact: Send complete ms with cover letter. Sample copy and guidelines free. "The most important consideration is that which makes the writer motivated to write. If it is not moral but human, or if it is neither a wide knowledge nor a large computer-like memory, but rather a deep thinking like the quietness in the forest, it is acceptable. While the traditional culture of reading of some thousands of years may be destined to be extinct under the marvellous progress of civilization, *The Plaza* intends to present contemporary works as our global human heritage to readers of forthcoming generations."

✓ $ **PLEIADES, (II)**, Department of English & Philosophy, Central Missouri State University, Martin 336, Warrensburg MO 64093. (660)543-4425. Fax: (660)543-8544. E-mail: rmk8708@cmsu2.cmsu.edu. Website: http://www.cmsu.edu/academics/arts&sciences/Engl/Phil/Pleiades (includes guidelines, editors, sample poetry or prose). **Executive & Fiction Editor:** R.M. Kinder. Co-Editor: Kevin Prufer. Magazine: 5½×8½; 120 pages; 60 lb. paper; perfect-bound; 8 pt. color cover. "*Pleiades* emphasizes cultural diversity, publishes poetry, fiction, literary criticism and reviews for a general educated audience." Semiannually. Estab. 1939. Circ. 500.
Needs: Ethnic/multicultural, experimental, especially cross-genre, feminist, gay, humor/satire, literary, mainstream/contemporary, regional, translations. "No westerns, romance, mystery, etc. Nothing pretentious, didactic or overly sentimental." Receives 40 unsolicited mss/month. Accepts 8 mss/issue; 16 mss/year. "We're slower at reading manuscripts in the summer." Publishes ms 3-8 months after acceptance. Recently published work by Harriet Zinnes, Andrew S. Monson and Vivian Shipley. Length: 3,000-6,000 words average; 800 words minimum; 8,000 words maximum. Also publishes literary essays, literary criticism and poetry. Sometimes critiques or comments on rejected mss.

MARKET CONDITIONS are constantly changing! If you're still using this book and it is 2000 or later, buy the newest edition of *Novel & Short Story Writer's Market* at your favorite bookstore or order from Writer's Digest Books.

How to Contact: Send complete ms with a cover letter. Include 75-100 bio, Social Security number and list of publications. Reports in 3 weeks on queries; 4 months on mss. Send SASE for reply, return of ms or send a disposable copy of ms. Simultaneous submissions OK. Sample copy (including guidelines) for $6.
Payment/Terms: Pays $10 or subscription and 1 contributor's copy on publication. Acquires first North American serial rights.
Advice: Looks for "a blend of language and subject matter that entices from beginning to end. Send us your best work. Don't send us formula stories. While we appreciate and publish well-crafted traditional pieces, we constantly seek the story that risks, that breaks form and expectations and wins us over anyhow."

$ PLOUGHSHARES, (II), Emerson College, 100 Beacon St., Boston MA 02116. (617)824-8753. **Editor:** Don Lee. "Our mission is to present dynamic, contrasting views on what is valid and important in contemporary literature, and to discover and advance significant literary talent. Each issue is guest-edited by a different writer. We no longer structure issues around preconceived themes." Triquarterly. Estab. 1971. Circ. 6,000.

- Work published in *Ploughshares* has been selected continuously for inclusion in the *Best American Short Stories* and *O. Henry Prize* anthologies. In fact the magazine has the honor of having the most stories selected from a single issue (three) to be included in *B.A.S.S.* Guest editors have included Richard Ford, Tim O'Brien and Ann Beattie. *Ploughshares* ranked #20 on *Writer's Digest*'s Fiction 50 list of top markets for fiction writers.

Needs: Literary. "No genre (science fiction, detective, gothic, adventure, etc.), popular formula or commercial fiction whose purpose is to entertain rather than to illuminate." Buys 35 mss/year. Receives 600 unsolicited fiction mss each month. Published work by Rick Bass, Joy Williams and Andre Dubus. Published new writers within the last year. Length: 300-6,000 words.
How to Contact: Reading period: postmarked August 1 to March 31. Cover letter should include "previous pubs." SASE. Reports in 3-5 months on mss. Sample copy for $8. (Please specify fiction issue sample.) Current issue for $9.95. Fiction guidelines for #10 SASE.
Payment/Terms: Pays $25/page, $50 minimum per title; $250 maximum, plus copies and a subscription on publication for first North American serial rights. Offers 50% kill fee for assigned ms not published.
Advice: "Be familiar with our fiction issues, fiction by our writers and by our various editors (e.g., Sue Miller, Tobias Wolff, Rosellen Brown, Richard Ford, Jayne Anne Phillips, James Alan McPherson) and more generally acquaint yourself with the best short fiction currently appearing in the literary quarterlies, and the annual prize anthologies (*Pushcart Prize, O. Henry Awards, Best American Short Stories*). Also realistically consider whether the work you are submitting is as good as or better than—in your own opinion—the work appearing in the magazine you're sending to. What is the level of competition? And what is its volume? (In our case, we accept about one ms in 200.) Never send 'blindly' to a magazine, or without carefully weighing your prospect there against those elsewhere. Always keep a log and a copy of the work you submit."

POETIC SPACE, A Magazine of Poetry & Fiction, (I, II), Poetic Space Press, P.O. Box 11157, Eugene OR 97440. E-mail: poeticspac@aol.com. Editor: Don Hildenbrand. **Fiction Editor:** Thomas Strand. Magazine: 8½×11; 32 pages; bond paper; heavy cover; b&w art. "Social, political, avant-garde, erotic, environmental material for a literary audience." Biannually (summer and winter). Estab. 1983. Circ. 600.
Needs: Erotica, ethnic, experimental, feminist, gay, lesbian, literary. Wants more contemporary, realistic and fantastic fiction. No sentimental, romance, mainstream. Receives about 20 unsolicited mss/month. Accepts 3-4 mss/issue; 8-10 mss/year. Publishes ms 6 months after acceptance. Publishes 5 new writers/year. Recently published work by David Scott Martin, Bruce Holland Rogers, Robert Weaver and Laton Carter. Length: 10 double-spaced pages. Publishes short shorts. Also publishes literary essays, literary criticism, poetry. Often critiques rejected mss and recommends other markets.
How to Contact: Send complete ms with cover letter that includes estimated word count, short bio and list of publications. Queries/mss by e-mail OK. Reports in 1 week on queries; 2 months on mss. SASE. Simultaneous, reprint and electronic submissions OK. Sample copy for $3, 4×9 SAE and 45¢ postage. Fiction guidelines for #10 SAE and 1 first-class stamp (or IRC). Reviews novels and short story collections. Send books to Don Hildenbrand.
Payment/Terms: Pays 1 contributor's copy. Acquires one-time rights or "reserves anthology rights."

POETRY FORUM SHORT STORIES, (I, II), Poetry Forum, 5713 Larchmont Dr., Erie PA 16509. Phone/fax: (814)866-2543 (fax hours 8-10 a.m., 5-8 p.m.). E-mail: 75562.670@compuserve.com. **Editor:** Gunvor Skogsholm. Newspaper: 7×8½; 34 pages; card cover; illustrations. "Human interest themes (no sexually explicit or racially biased or blasphemous material) for the general public—from the grassroot to the intellectual." Quarterly. Estab. 1989. Circ. 400.
Needs: Confession, contemporary, ethnic, experimental, fantasy, feminist, historical, literary, mainstream, mystery/suspense, prose poem, religious/inspirational, romance, science fiction, senior citizen/retirement, young adult/teen. "No blasphemous, sexually explicit material." Publishes annual special fiction issue. Receives 50 unsolicited mss/month. Accepts 12 mss/issue; 40 mss/year. Publishes ms 6 months after acceptance. Agented fiction less than 1%. 80% of work published is by new writers. Length: 2,000 words average; 500 words minimum; 5,000 words maximum. Also publishes literary essays, literary criticism, poetry.
How to Contact: *This magazine charges a "professional members" fee of $36 and prefers to work with*

subscribers. The fee entitles you to publication of a maximum of 3,000 words. Send complete ms with cover letter. Accepts queries/mss by e-mail and fax. Reports in 3 weeks to 2 months on mss. SASE. Simultaneous and reprint submissions OK. "Accepts electronic submissions via disk gladly." Sample copy for $3. Fiction guidelines for SASE. Reviews novels and short story collections.
Payment/Terms: Preference given to submissions by subscribers. Acquires one-time rights.
Advice: "Tell your story with no padding as if telling it to a person standing with one hand on the door ready to run out to a meeting. Have a good lead. This is the 'alpha & omega' of all good story writing. Don't start with 'This is a story about a boy and a girl."

✔ **POET'S FANTASY, (I)**, 227 Hatten Ave., Rice Lake WI 54868-2030. (715)236-3066. E-mail: stardome@chibardwn.net. **Editor:** Gloria Stoeckel. Magazine: 8½×11; 44 pages; 20 lb. paper; colored stock cover; illustrations. *Poet's Fantasy* is a magazine of "fantasy, but not conclusive." Bimonthly. Estab. 1992. Circ. about 400.
Needs: Fantasy (science), literary. No series about sex, love. "Wants to see more fantasy and science fiction." Receives 2-3 unsolicited mss/month. Accepts 6 mss/year. Recently published work by Cath Haftings and Mel Waldman. Publishes "several hundred" new writers/year. Length: 1,000 words average; 500 words minimum; 1,500 words maximum. Publishes short shorts. Also publishes literary essays and poetry.
How to Contact: Send complete ms with a cover letter. Include estimated word count and list of publications. Accepts queries/mss by e-mail. Reports in 3 weeks. Send SASE for reply or return of ms. Simultaneous submissions OK. Sample copy for $5. Fiction guidelines free.
Payment/Terms: Pays $5 coupon on publication toward purchase of subscription for first North American serial rights. Subscribers are given preference.
Advice: "Fiction must include fantasy and have a surprise twist at the end." Wants fiction with "tight writing, action and ending twist. Edit and re-edit before sending."

THE POINTED CIRCLE, (II), Portland Community College-Cascade, 705 N. Killingsworth St., Portland OR 97217. **Editors:** student editorial staff. Magazine: 80 pages; b&w illustrations and photographs. "Anything of interest to educationally/culturally mixed audience." Annually. Estab. 1980.
Needs: Contemporary, ethnic, literary, prose poem, regional. "We will read whatever is sent, but encourage writers to remember we are a quality literary/arts magazine intended to promote the arts in the community." Acquires 3-7 mss/year. Accepts submissions only December 1-February 15, for July 1 issue. Recently published work by Steve Slavin, Ernie Cooper and DC Palter. Publishes several new writers/year. Length: 3,000 words maximum.
How to Contact: Send complete ms with cover letter and brief bio, #10 SASE. "The editors consider all submissions without knowing the identities of the contributors, so please do not put your name on the works themselves." Sample copy for $4.50. Entry guidelines, send #10 SASE. Submitted materials will not be returned unless writer requests and provides SASE with adequate postage.
Payment/Terms: Pays 1 copy. Acquires one-time rights.
Advice: "Looks for quality—topicality—nothing trite. The author cares about language and acts responsibly toward the reader, honors the reader's investment of time and piques the reader's interest."

🏆 **PORCUPINE LITERARY ARTS MAGAZINE, (II)**, P.O. Box 259, Cedarburg WI 53012-0259. (414)375-3128. E-mail: ppine259@aol.com. Website: http://members.aol.com/ppine259 (includes writer's guidelines, cover art, subscription information, table of contents). Editor: W.A. Reed. **Fiction Editor:** Chris Skoczynski. Magazine: 5×8½; 100 pages; glossy color cover stock; illustrations and photos. Publishes "primarily poetry and short fiction. Novel excerpts are acceptable if self-contained. No restrictions as to theme or style." Semiannually. Estab. 1996. Circ. 1,500.

- *Porcupine Literary Arts Magazine* was named Best Literary/Arts Magazine by *Milwaukee Magazine* (1997).

Needs: Condensed/excerpted novel, ethnic/multicultural, literary, mainstream/contemporary. No pornographic or religious. Receives 10 unsolicited mss/month. Accepts 3 mss/issue; 6 mss/year. Publishes ms within 6 months of acceptance. Recently published work by Karen Sharp and Martha Highers. Publishes 4-6 new writers/year. Length: 3,500 words average; 2,000 words minimum; 7,500 words maximum. Publishes literary essays and poetry. Sometimes critiques or comments on rejected mss.
How to Contact: Send complete ms with a cover letter. Accepts queries/mss by e-mail. Include estimated word count, 5-line bio and list of publications. Reports in 2 weeks on queries; 2 months on mss. Send SASE for reply, return of ms or send a disposable copy of ms. No simultaneous submissions. Sample copy for $5. Fiction guidelines for #10 SASE.
Payment/Terms: Pays 1 contributor's copy on publication; additional copies for $8.95. Acquires one-time rights.
Advice: Looks for "believable dialogue and a narrator I can see and hear and smell. Form or join a writers' group. Read aloud. Rewrite extensively."

✔ **POTOMAC REVIEW, The Quarterly with a Conscience—and a Sense of Humor, (I, II)**, Potomac Review, Inc., P.O. Box 354, Port Tobacco MD 25411. (304)258-9122. Website: http://www.meral.com/potomac (includes editor's note, contents page, contact information, some sampling of stories, poems). **Editor:** Eli Flam.

Magazine: 5½×8½; 96 pages; 50 lb. paper; 65 lb. cover; illustrations. *Potomac Review* is "the quarterly with a conscience—and a lurking sense of humor—at the heart of the Mid-Atlantic. We feature a challenging diversity and seek to get at the concealed side of life." Estab. 1994. Circ. 1,500.

Needs: Excerpted novel—"stories with a vivid, individual quality that get at 'the concealed side' of life. Regionally rooted, with an area or theme focus each issue (e.g., 'The Power of Letters,' fall 1998); we also keep an eye on the wider world." Upcoming themes (subject to change): Underground Railroad, Writing Contest Winners, *The Potomac*: Fifty Years Later. Receives 100 unsolicited mss/month, assigns some nonfiction pieces. Accepts 20-30 mss/issue of all sorts; 80-120 mss/year. Publishes ms within a year after acceptance as a rule. Agented fiction 5%. Recently published work by David B. Prather, Audrena Zawinski, Ethel Morgan Smith, Rex Marshall Ellis and Catherine Scherer. Publishes up to 24 new writers/year. Length: 2,000 words average; 100 words minimum; 3,000 words maximum. Publishes short shorts. Length: 250 words. Also publishes poetry, essays and cogent, issue-oriented nonfiction. Humor is welcome.

How to Contact: Send complete ms with a cover letter. Include estimated word count, 2-3 sentence bio, list of publications and SASE. Reports in 2 weeks on queries; 2-3 months on mss. Send SASE for reply, return of ms or send a disposable copy of ms. Simultaneous and reprint submissions OK. Sample copy for $5. Submission guidelines for #10 SASE. Reviews novels, short story collections, other books.

Payment/Terms: Pays 1 contributor's copy; additional copies for $3.

Advice: "Some kind of vision should be inherent in your writing, something to say *inter alia* about life in our times—or other times, for that matter. Read all possible magazines that might take your work; work at your last, first and last, like an old-fashioned shoemaker, daily and with dedication. Learn, above all, to rewrite; and when to stop."

POTPOURRI, (II), P.O. Box 8278, Prairie Village KS 66208. (913)642-1503. Fax: (913)642-3128. E-mail: editor@potpourri.org. Website: Website: http://www.potpourri.com (includes guidelines, contents, reprints of fiction, author profiles). **Senior Editor:** Polly W. Swafford. Magazine: 8×11; 76 pages; glossy cover. "Literary magazine: short stories, verse, essays, travel, prose poetry for a general adult audience." Quarterly. Estab. 1989. Circ. 4,500.

Needs: Adventure, contemporary, ethnic, experimental, fantasy, historical (general), humor/satire, literary, mainstream, suspense, prose poem, romance (contemporary, historical, romantic suspense), science fiction (soft/sociological), western (frontier stories). "*Potpourri* accepts a broad genre; hence its name. Guidelines specify no religious, confessional, racial, political, erotic, abusive or sexual preference materials unless fictional and necessary to plot." Receives 75 unsolicited fiction mss/month. Accepts 10-12 fiction mss/issue; 60-80 prose mss/year. Publishes ms 10-12 months after acceptance. Agented fiction 1%. Recently published work by Walter Cummins, Deborah Shause, Conger Beasley, Theresa Keene and Antonia Clark. Publishes 3-4 new writers/year. Length: 3,500 words maximum. Also publishes poetry and literary essays. Sometimes critiques rejected mss. *Potpourri* offers annual awards (of $100 each) for best of volume in fiction and poetry, more depending on grants received, and sponsors the Annual Council on National Literatures Award of $100 each for poetry and fiction on alternating years. "Manuscripts must celebrate our multicultural and/or historic background." Next fiction entry deadline: August 31, 2000. Reading fee: $5 for 1-3 poems. Send SASE for guidelines.

How to Contact: Send complete ms with cover letter. Accepts queries by e-mail and fax. Include "complete name, address, phone number, brief summary statement about submission, short author bio." Reports in 2-4 months. SASE. Simultaneous submissions OK when advised at time of submission. Sample copy for $4.95 with 9×12 envelope. Fiction guidelines for #10 SASE.

Payment/Terms: Pays contributor's copies. Acquires first rights.

Advice: "We look for well-crafted stories of literary value and stories with reader appeal. First, does the manuscript spark immediate interest and the introduction create the effect that will dominate? Second, does the action in dialogue or narration tell the story? Third, does the conclusion leave something with the reader to be long remembered? We look for the story with an original idea and an unusual twist. We are weary of excessive violence and depressing themes in fiction and are looking for originality in plots and some humorous pieces."

$ POTTERSFIELD PORTFOLIO, (I, II), The Gatsby Press, P.O. Box 27094, Halifax, Nova Scotia B3H 4M8 Canada. Phone/fax: (902)420-0100. E-mail: icolford@is.dal.ca or gaundc@auracom.com. Website: http://www.auracom.com/~saundc/potters.html. Editor: Ian Colford. **Fiction Editor:** Karen Smythe. Magazine: 6×9; 100 pages; recycled acid-free paper and cover; illustrations. "Literary magazine interested in well-written fiction and poetry. No specific thematic interests or biases." Triannually. Estab. 1979. Circ. 500.

Needs: Receives 30-40 fiction mss/month. Buys 4-8 fiction mss/issue. Recently published work by Steven

MARKET CATEGORIES: (I) Open to new writers; **(II)** Open to both new and established writers; **(III)** Interested mostly in established writers; **(IV)** Open to writers whose work is specialized; **(V)** Closed to unsolicited submissions.

Heighton, Sheree Fitch and Jean McMeil. Length: 3,500 words average; 500 words minimum; 5,000 words maximum. Publishes short shorts. Sometimes comments on rejected mss.

How to Contact: Send complete ms with cover letter. Include estimated word count and 50-word bio. No simultaneous submissions. Reports in 3 months. SASE. Sample copy for $7 (US), 10½×7½ SAE and 4 first-class stamps.

Payment/Terms: Pays contributor's copy plus $5 Canadian per printed page to a maximum of $25 on publication for first Canadian serial rights.

Advice: "Provide us with a clean, proofread copy of your story. Include a brief cover letter with biographical note, but don't try to sell the story to us. *Always* include a SASE with sufficient *Canadian* postage, or IRCs, for return of the manuscript or a reply from the editors."

THE PRAIRIE JOURNAL OF CANADIAN LITERATURE, (I, II), Prairie Journal Press, Box 61203, Brentwood Postal Services, Calgary, Alberta T2L 2K6 Canada. **Editor:** A.E. Burke. Journal: 7×8½; 50-60 pages; white bond paper; Cadillac cover stock; cover illustrations. Journal of creative writing and scholarly essays, reviews for literary audience. Semiannually. Published special fiction issue last year. Estab. 1983.

Needs: Contemporary, literary, prose poem, regional, excerpted novel, novella, double-spaced. Canadian authors given preference. Publishes "a variety of types of fiction—fantasy, psychological, character-driven, feminist, etc. We publish authors at all stages of their careers from well-known to first publication." No romance, erotica, pulp. Publishes anthology series open to submissions: *Prairie Journal Poetry II* and *Prairie Journal Fiction III*. Receives 20-40 unsolicited mss each month. Accepts 10-15 mss/issue; 20-30 mss/year. Suggests sample issue before submitting ms. Published work by Nancy Ellen Russell, Carla Mobley, Patrick Quinn. Publishes 20 new writers/year. Length: 2,500 words average; 100 words minimum; 3,000 words maximum. Deadlines: April 1 for spring/summer issue; October 1 for fall/winter. Also publishes literary essays, literary criticism, poetry. Sometimes critiques rejected mss and recommends other markets.

How to Contact: Send complete ms. Reports in 1 month. SASE. Sample copy for $6 (Canadian) and SAE with $1.10 for postage or IRC. Include cover letter of past credits, if any. Reply to queries for SAE with 52¢ for postage or IRC. No American stamps. Reviews novels and short story collections.

Payment/Terms: Pays contributor's copies and modest honoraria. Acquires first North American serial rights. In Canada author retains copyright.

Advice: "We like character-driven rather than plot-centered fiction." Interested in "innovational work of quality. Beginning writers welcome. There is no point in simply republishing known authors or conventional, predictable plots. Of the genres we receive fiction is most often of the highest calibre. It is a very competitive field. Be proud of what you send. You're worth it."

PRAIRIE SCHOONER, (II), University of Nebraska, English Department, 201 Andrews Hall, Lincoln NE 68588-0334. (402)472-0911. E-mail: lrandolp@unlinfo.unl.edu. Website: http://www.unl.edu/schooner/psmain.htm (includes guidelines, editors, table of contents for current issue). **Editor:** Hilda Raz. Magazine: 6×9; 200 pages; good stock paper; heavy cover stock. "A fine literary quarterly of stories, poems, essays and reviews for a general audience that reads for pleasure." Quarterly. Estab. 1926. Circ. 3,200.

- *Prairie Schooner*, one of the oldest publications in this book, has garnered several awards and honors over the years. Work appearing in the magazine has been selected for anthologies including *Pushcart Prizes* and *Best American Short Stories*.

Needs: Good fiction (literary). Accepts 4-5 mss/issue. Receives approximately 500 unsolicited fiction mss each month. Mss are read September through May only. Recently published work by Ursula Hegi, Josip Novakovitch, Rebecca Goldstein, Robin Hemley and Susan Fromberg Schaeffer. Published new writers within the last year. Length: varies. Also publishes poetry. Offers annual prize of $1,000 for best fiction, $500 for best new writer (poetry or fiction), two $500 awards for best poetry (for work published in the magazine in the previous year).

How to Contact: Send complete ms with SASE and cover letter listing previous publications—where, when. Accepts queries/mss by e-mail or fax. Reports in 3-4 months. Sample copy for $5. Reviews novels, poetry and short story collections.

Payment/Terms: Pays in contributor's copies and prize money awarded. Acquires all rights. Will reassign rights upon request after publication.

Advice: "*Prairie Schooner* is eager to see fiction from beginning and established writers. Be tenacious. Accept rejection as a temporary setback and send out rejected stories to other magazines. *Prairie Schooner* is not a magazine with a program. We look for good fiction in traditional narrative modes as well as experimental, metafiction or any other form or fashion a writer might try. Create striking detail, well-developed characters, fresh dialogue; let the images and the situations evoke the stories themes. Too much explication kills a lot of otherwise good stories. Be persistent. Keep writing and sending out new work. Be familiar with the tastes of the magazines where you're sending. We are receiving record numbers of submissions. Prospective contributors must sometimes wait longer to receive our reply."

$ **PRESS, (III)**, Daniel Roberts Inc., 2124 Broadway, Suite 323, New York NY 10023. (212)579-0873. Fax: (212)579-0776. E-mail: pressltd@aol.com. **Editor:** Daniel Roberts. Magazine: 6¾×10; 160 pages; cougap-opaque paper; loe cream cover. Features fiction, poetry and "articles about writing and writers; features that humanize literature, celebrate talent and beauty, and expose fraudulence and pomposity. *Press* will stand not only as the most absolute record of contemporary, American, literary talent, but as a means by which the public can commune with literature." Quarterly. Estab. 1996. Circ. 15,000.

Needs: Receives 800 unsolicited mss/month. Accepts 10 mss/issue; 40 mss/year. Publishes ms 6-10 weeks after acceptance. Agented fiction 10%. Published work by Joyce Carol Oates, Anthony Hecht, Philip Levine, William J. Cobb, James Gallant, Gordon Lish and Harry Mathews. Also publishes poetry. Sometimes comments on or critiques rejected mss.

How to Contact: Send complete ms with a cover letter. Include a short bio and list of publications. Reports in 2 months on queries; 4 months on mss. Send SASE for reply, return of ms or send a disposable copy of ms. Sample copy for $8. Fiction guidelines free.

Payment/Terms: Pays $100 minimum and 1 contributor's copy; additional copies for $6. Pays on acceptance for first rights, first North American serial rights or one-time rights. Sends galleys to the author.

Advice: "While almost all forms are acceptable, prose poems and more experimental writing (stories that don't actually tell a story) are discouraged. We are looking for a strong and specific plot (where 'something' actually happens); one that makes a reader want to turn the page. We want stories where the author's style does not interfere with the plot, but strengthens the expression of that plot."

$ PRISM INTERNATIONAL, (I, II), E462-1866 Main Mall, University of British Columbia, Vancouver, British Columbia V6T 1Z1 Canada. (604)822-2514. E-mail: prism@unixg.ubc.ca. Website: http://www.arts.ubc.ca/prism/. Executive Editor: Emily Snyder. **Editor:** Jerry Aherne. Magazine: 6×9; 72-80 pages; Zephyr book paper; Cornwall, coated one side cover; photos on cover. "An international journal of contemporary writing—fiction, poetry, drama, creative nonfiction and translation." Readership: "public and university libraries, individual subscriptions, bookstores—a world-wide audience concerned with the contemporary in literature." Quarterly. Estab. 1959. Circ. 1,200.

- PRISM *international* has won the Journey Prize Award and stories first published in PRISM have been included in the *Journey Prize Anthology* every year since 1991.

Needs: New writing that is contemporary and literary. Short stories and self-contained novel excerpts. Works of translation are eagerly sought and should be accompanied by a copy of the original. No gothic, confession, religious, romance, pornography, or sci-fi. Also looking for creative nonfiction that is literary, not journalistic, in scope and tone. Buys approximately 70 mss/year. Receives over 100 fiction unsolicted mss each month. PRISM publishes both new and established writers; our contributors have included Franz Kafka, Gabriel Garcia Marquez, Michael Ondaatje, Margaret Laurence, Mark Anthony Jarman, Gail Anderson-Dargatz and Eden Robinson. Submissions should not exceed 5,000 words "though flexible for outstanding work" (only one long story per submission, please). Publishes short shorts. Also publishes poetry and drama. Sponsors annual short fiction contest with $2,000 (Canadian) grand prize: send SASE for details.

How to Contact: Send complete ms with SASE or SAE, IRC and cover letter with bio, information and publications list. Accepts queries/mss by e-mail and fax. "Keep it simple. U.S. contributors take note: Do note send U.S. stamps, they are not valid in Canada. Send International Reply Coupons instead." Reports in 2-6 months. Electronic submissions OK (e-mail, web). Sample copy for $5 (U.S./Canadian).

Payment/Terms: Pays $20 (Canadian)/printed page, 1 year's subscription on publication for first North American serial rights. Selected authors are paid an additional $10/page for digital rights.

Advice: "Read several issues of our magazine before submitting. We are committed to publishing outstanding literary work in all genres. We look for strong, believeable characters; real voices; attention to language; interesting ideas and plots. Send us fresh, innovative work which also shows a mastery of the basics of good prose writing. Poorly constructed or sloppy pieces will not receive serious consideration. We welcome e-mail submissions and are proud to be one of few print literary journals who offer additional payment to select writers for digital publication. Too many e-mail submissions, however, come to us unpolished and unprepared to be published. Writers should craft their work for e-mail submission as carefully as they would for submissions through traditional methods. They should send one piece at a time and wait for our reply before they send another."

PROCREATION: A JOURNAL OF TRUTHTELLING IN POETRY & PROSE, (I), Silent Planet Publishing, Ltd., 6300-138 Creedmoor Rd., Raleigh NC 27612. (919)510-9010. Fax: (919)510-0210. E-mail: editor@procreation.org. Website: http://www.procreation.org (includes writer's guidelines, full issue, editorials, subscription information and links). Editor: Stephen A. West. **Fiction Editor:** Peter Shedor. Journal: digest-sized; 30-36 pages; high-quality paper; matte card cover; photographs. "We are a literary journal dedicated to the pursuit and expression of artfully encapsulated truth. We believe that in creating we echo the Creator's own imaginative and creative activity and, so, become more fully human. We are interested in all kinds of truth, including spiritual truth, but we do not accept propaganda (however truthful), or religious or abstract prose not rooted in real-life experience." Triannually. Estab. 1997. Circ. 500.

Needs: Condensed/excerpted novel, experimental, humor/satire, literary, mainstream/contemporary, religious/inspirational. No erotica, horror, political fiction, graphic violence or "preachy or sentimental fiction." Receives 100 unsolicited mss/month. Accepts 4 mss/issue; 12 mss/year. Publishes ms 3 months after acceptance. Recently published work by Gayle Chaney and John McFarland. Length: 1,500 words average; 250 words minimum; 2,500 words maximum. Publishes short shorts. Length: 250 words. Also publishes poetry. Often critiques or comments on rejected mss.

How to Contact: Send complete ms with a cover letter. Accepts queries/mss by fax. Include estimated word

count, 1 page bio, list of publications "whether, if published, they desire to have contact information listed along with their byline. We seek interaction with the readership, if writers consent, so as to facilitate dialogue and community." Reports in 2 months. SASE for reply, return of ms or send a disposable copy of ms. Sample copy for $5 (US), $8 (foreign) and 5 first-class stamps or 2 IRCs. Fiction guidelines for #10 SASE or SAE and 1 IRC or by e-mail. Reviews novels and short story collections.
Payment/Terms: Pays 1 contributor's copy on publication; additional copies for $4. Acquires first North American serial rights.
Advice: "We look for strong imagery and well-written prose which reveals truth rather than simply states it in a didactic fashion. We are especially interested in fiction that strongly connects to human experience, whether tragic, comic or beautiful, yet which points to a larger truth outside itself, something transcendent. Look for the extraordinary in the ordinary. Write out of experience, with strong attention to the particulars of time, place, and character but at the same time capturing some universal, some shared truth, to which readers can relate."

$ PROVINCETOWN ARTS, (II), Provincetown Arts, Inc., 650 Commercial St., P.O. Box 35, Provincetown MA 02657. (508)487-3167. **Editor:** Christopher Busa. Magazine: 9×12; 184 pages; 60 lb. coated paper; 12 pcs. cover; illustrations and photographs. "*PA* focuses broadly on the artists, writers and theater of America's oldest continuous art colony." Annually. Estab. 1985. Circ. 8,000.

- *Provincetown Arts* is a recipient of a CLMP seed grant. Provincetown Arts Press has an award-winning poetry series.

Needs: Plans special fiction issue. Receives 300 unsolicited mss/year. Buys 5 mss/issue. Publishes ms 3 months after acceptance. Published work by Carole Maso and Hilary Masters. Length: 3,000 words average; 1,500 words minimum; 8,000 words maximum. Publishes short shorts. Also publishes literary essays, literary criticism, poetry. Sometimes critiques rejected mss and recommends other markets.
How to Contact: Send complete ms with cover letter including previous publications. No simultaneous submissions. Reports in 2 weeks on queries; 3 months on mss. SASE. Sample copy for $7.50. Reviews novels and short story collections.
Payment/Terms: Pays $75-300 on publication for first rights. Sends galleys to author.

PUCKERBRUSH REVIEW, (I, II), Puckerbrush Press, 76 Main St., Orono ME 04473. (207)866-4868/581-3832. **Editor:** Constance Hunting. Magazine: 9×12; 80-100 pages; illustrations. "We publish mostly new Maine writers; interviews, fiction, reviews, poetry for a literary audience." Semiannually. Estab. 1979. Circ. approx. 500.
Needs: Belles-lettres, experimental, gay (occasionally), literary. "Wants to see more original, quirky and well-written fiction." No genre fiction. "Nothing cliché." Receives 30 unsolicited mss/month. Accepts 6 mss/issue; 12 mss/year. Publishes ms 1 year after acceptance. Recently published work by Carl Little, Farnham Blair and Peggy Bryant. Publishes 6 new writers/year. Sometimes publishes short shorts. Also publishes literary essays, literary criticism, poetry. Sometimes critiques rejected mss.
How to Contact: Send complete ms with cover letter. Reports in 2 months. SASE. Simultaneous submissions OK. Sample copy for $2. Fiction guidelines for SASE. Sometimes reviews novels and short story collections.
Payment/Terms: Pays in contributor's copies.
Advice: "I don't want to see tired plots or treatments. I want to see respect for language—the right words."

PUERTO DEL SOL, (I), New Mexico State University, Box 3E, Las Cruces NM 88003. (505)646-3931. Fax: (505)646-7725. Editors: Kay West, Antonya Nelson and Kevin McIlvoy. Magazine: 6×9; 200 pages; 60 lb. paper; 70 lb. cover stock; photos sometimes. "We publish quality material from anyone. Poetry, fiction, art, photos, interviews, reviews, parts-of-novels, long poems." Semiannually. Estab. 1961. Circ. 1,500.
Needs: Contemporary, ethnic, experimental, literary, mainstream, prose poem, excerpted novel and translations. Receives varied number of unsolicited fiction mss/month. Acquires 8-10 mss/issue; 12-15 mss/year. Does not read mss March through August. Recently published work by Dagobeuto Gilb, Wendell Mayo and William H. Cobb. Published 8-10 new writers/year. Also publishes poetry. Occasionally critiques rejected mss.
How to Contact: Send complete ms with SASE. Simultaneous submissions OK. Reports in 3 months. Sample copy for $7.
Payment/Terms: Pays 2 contributor's copies. Acquires one-time rights (rights revert to author).
Advice: "We are open to all forms of fiction, from the conventional to the wildly experimental, as long as they

N A $

FOR EXPLANATIONS OF THESE SYMBOLS,
SEE THE INSIDE FRONT AND BACK COVERS OF THIS BOOK.

have integrity and are well written. Too often we receive very impressively 'polished' mss that will dazzle readers with their sheen but offer no character/reader experience of lasting value."

PURPLE PATCH, 8 Beaconview House, Beaconview Rd., West Bromwich B71 3PL England. Phone: 0121-588-6642. **Fiction Editor:** Geoff Stevens. Quarterly. Publishes 1-2 stories/issue. "Prefer a literary style. Bulk of publication is poetry and poetry magazine reviews."

Needs: "Very short stories of a literary nature." Does not want to see fiction with twist endings; poetic and descriptive fiction; or surrealist fiction. Recently published D.F. Lewis, Peter Hawkins and Steve Sreyd. Length: 50-1,000 words maximum.

How to Contact: "Send a short letter introducing yourself. Enclose enough postage (IRC) for reply or return of mss. Sample copy for 5 dollar bill (no checks) or £1."

Terms: Pays contributor's copies to UK writers only.

Tips: "I like to see something different, be it subject, style, or preparation. Although we do like to see beautiful descriptive writings, don't waste words."

QUARTER AFTER EIGHT, A Journal of Prose and Commentary, (II, IV), QAE, Ellis Hall, Ohio University, Athens OH 45701. Editors: Matthew Cooperman, Imad Rahman, Bonnie Proudfoot, Andrew Touhy. **Fiction Editor:** Tom Noyes. Magazine: 6×9; 310 pages; 20 lb. glossy cover stock; photos. "We look to publish work which somehow addresses, in its form and/or content, the boundaries between poetry and prose." Annually.

Needs: Condensed/excerpted novel, erotica, ethnic/multicultural, experimental, gay, humor/satire, lesbian, literary, mainstream/contemporary, translations. Send SASE for list of upcoming themes. Receives 50 unsolicited mss/month. Accepts 10 mss/issue. Does not read mss mid-March to mid-September. Publishes ms 6-9 months after acceptance. Agented fiction 15%. Recently published work by Walter Bargen, Nathaniel Tarn, Diane Glancy and Mary Jane Ryals. Length: 3,000 words average; 10,000 words maximum. Publishes short shorts. Also publishes literary essays, literary criticism, prose poetry. Sometimes critiques or comments on rejected ms.

How to Contact: Send complete ms with a cover letter. Include short bio and list of publications. Reports in 6-8 weeks. Send SASE for return of ms or send a disposable copy of ms. Simultaneous submissions OK. Sample copy for $10, 8×11 SAE and $1.50 postage. Fiction guidelines for #10 SASE. Reviews novels and short story collections. Send books to fiction editor.

Payment/Terms: Pays 2 contributor's copies; additional copies $7. Acquires first North American serial rights. Sponsors contest. Send SASE for guidelines.

Advice: "We're interested in seeing more stories that push language and the traditional form to their limits."

$ QUARTERLY WEST, (II), University of Utah, 200 S. Campus Dr., Room 317, Salt Lake City UT 84112-9109. (801)581-3938. Website: http://chronicle.utah.edu/QW/QW.html (includes novella guidelines, submission guidelines, recent issues with samples of contributors' work). Editor: Margot Schilpp. **Fiction Editors:** Gerry Hart and Becky Lindberg. Editors change every 2 years. Magazine: 6×9; 200 pages; 60 lb. paper; 5-color cover stock; illustrations and photographs rarely. "We try to publish a variety of fiction and poetry from all over the country based not so much on the submitting author's reputation but on the merit of each piece. Our publication is aimed primarily at an educated audience interested in contemporary literature and criticism." Semiannually. "We sponsor a biennial novella competition." (Next competition held in 1998). Estab. 1976. Circ. 1,800.

- *Quarterly West* is a past recipient of grants from the NEA and was awarded First Place for Editorial Content from the American Literary Magazine Awards. Work published in the magazine has been selected for inclusion in the *Pushcart Prize* anthology and *The Best American Short Stories* anthology.

Needs: Literary, contemporary, experimental, translations. Accepts 6-10 mss/issue, 12-20 mss/year. Receives 250 unsolicited fiction mss each month. Recently published work by H.E. Francis, Alan Cheuse, Ron Carlson, Cynthia Baughman, William T. Vollmann, David Kranes and Antonya Nelson. Publishes 3-5 new writers/year. No preferred length; interested in longer, "fuller" short stories, as well as short shorts. Critiques rejected mss when there is time.

How to Contact: Send complete ms. Brief cover letters welcome. Send SASE for reply or return of ms. Simultaneous submissions OK with notification. Reports in 2-3 months; "sooner, if possible." Sample copy for $7.50.

Payment/Terms: Pays $15-500 and 2 contributor's copies on publication for all rights (negotiable).

Advice: "We publish a special section of short shorts every issue, and we also sponsor a biennial novella contest. We are open to experimental work—potential contributors should read the magazine! We solicit occasionally, but tend more toward the surprises—unsolicited. Don't send more than one story per submission, but submit as often as you like."

RAG MAG, (II), Box 12, Goodhue MN 55027-0012. (612)923-4590. **Publisher/Editor:** Beverly Voldseth. Magazine: 6×9; 60-112 pages; varied paper quality; illustrations; photos. "We are eager to print poetry, prose and art work. We are open to all styles." Semiannually. Estab. 1982. Circ. 300.

Needs: Adventure, comics, contemporary, erotica, ethnic, experimental, fantasy, feminist, literary, mainstream, prose poem, regional. "Anything well written is a possibility. It has to be a good adult story, tight, with plot and zip. I also like strange but well done. No extremely violent or pornographic writing." Receives 100 unsolicited mss/month. Accepts 4 mss/issue. Recently published work by Susan Thurston Hamerski, Sigi Leonhard, Paul

Jensi and Steve Lange. Published new writers within the last year. Length: 1,000 words average; 2,200 words maximum. Novel chapters or excerpts 25 pages maximum.
How to Contact: Send short story or excerpt of novel, brief bio and brief cover letter. SASE. Reports in 3-4 weeks. Simultaneous and previously published submissions OK. Single copy for $6.
Payment/Terms: Pays 1 contributor's copy; $4.50 charge for extras. Acquires one-time rights.
Advice: "Submit clean copy on regular typing paper (no tissue-thin stuff). We want fresh images, sparse language, words that will lift us out of our chairs. I like the short story form. I think it's powerful and has a definite place in the literary magazine."

✓ **RAMBUNCTIOUS REVIEW, (I, II)**, Rambunctious Press, Inc., 1221 W. Pratt Blvd., Chicago IL 60626. (773)338-2439. **Editors:** Nancy Lennon, Richard Lennon and Elizabeth Hawsler. Magazine: 10×7; 48 pages; illustrations and photos. Annually. Estab. 1983. Circ. 300.
Needs: Experimental, feminist, humor/satire, literary, mainstream/contemporary. List of upcoming themes available for SASE. Receives 30 unsolicited mss/month. Accepts 4-5 mss/issue. Does not read mss May through August. Publishes ms 5-6 months after acceptance. Published work by Hugh Fox, Lyn Lifshin and Stephen Schroeder. Publishes 6 new writers/year. Length: 12 double-spaced pages. Publishes short shorts. Also publishes poetry. Sometimes critiques or comments on rejected ms. Sponsors contest. Send SASE for details.
How to Contact: Send complete ms with a cover letter. Include estimated word count. Reports in 9 months. Send SASE for reply, return of ms or send a disposable copy of ms. Simultaneous submissions OK. Sample copy for $4.
Payment/Terms: Pays 2 contributor's copies. Acquires one-time rights.

✓ **RASKOLNIKOV'S CELLAR and THE LAMPLIGHT, (I, II)**, The Beggars's Press, 8110 N. 38th St., Omaha NE 68112-2018. (402)455-2615. Editor: Richard Carey. **Fiction Editor:** Danielle Staton. Magazine: 8½×12; 60-150 pages; 20 lb. bond paper; 12pt soft cover. "Our purpose is to encourage writing in the style of the past masters and to hold back illiteracy in our generation." Semiannually. Estab. 1952. Circ. 1,200.

- Member of the International Association of Independent Publishers and the Federation of Literary Publishers.

Needs: Historical, horror, humor/satire, literary, serialized novels, translations. No "religious, sentimental, folksy, science fiction or ultra modern." Publishes special fiction issue or anthologies. Receives 135 unsolicited mss/month. Accepts 15 mss/issue; 30-45 mss/year. Publishes ms 2-6 months after acceptance. Agented fiction 5%. Recently published work by James Scoffield, Richard Davignon and Philip Sparacino. Length: 1,500-2,000 words average; 50 words minimum; 3,000 words maximum. Publishes short shorts. Also publishes literary essays, literary criticism and poetry.
How to Contact: Send complete ms with a cover letter. Include estimated word count and 1 page bio. Reports in 2 months on queries; 4 months on mss. Simultaneous submissions OK. Sample copy for $10 plus 9×12 SAE with 2 first-class stamps. Fiction guidelines for #10 SAE with 2 first-class stamps. Reviews novels or short story collections. Send books to Danielle Staton.
Payment/Terms: Pays 1 contributor's copy for first North American serial rights.
Advice: "We judge on writing style as well as content. If your style of writing and your word usage do not attract us at once, there is faint hope of the content and the plot saving the story. Read and learn from the great writers of the past. Set your stories in the un-computer age, so your characters have time to think, to feel, to react. Use your glorious language to the fullest. Our subscribers can read quite well. The strongest way to say anything is to never quite say it."

N **THE RAW SEED REVIEW, (II)**, P.O. Box 262, Ojai CA 93024. Editor: Sam Taylor. **Fiction Editor:** Stacy Nakell. Magazine; digest-sized; 90-120 pages; quality paper; color card cover; illustrations and photos. "*The Raw Seed Review* aims to be a mecca of imagination, intensity and innovation. We publish poetry, art, fiction and essays that in some way produce a closer encounter with the essence or origin of things—the 'raw seed,' the unknown." Semiannually. Estab. 1999. Circ. 500.
Needs: Condensed/excerpted novel, erotica, experimental, literary. "No genre fiction or anything unoriginal, uninspired or unedited." List of upcoming themes available for SASE. Receives 10 unsolicited mss/month. Accepts 3 mss/issue; 6 mss/year. Publishes ms 1-8 months after acceptance. Length: open, "but shorter pieces stand a better chance." Publishes short shorts. Also publishes literary essays, literary criticism, poetry. Sometimes critiques or comments on rejected ms. Subscribers always receive comments.
How to Contact: Send complete ms with a cover letter. Include estimated word count, bio and list of publications. Reports in 1-12 weeks. SASE for return of ms. Simultaneous submissions OK. Sample copy $6.50. Fiction guidelines for #10 SASE. Reviews novels and short story collections. Send books to editor.
Payment/Terms: Pays 1-3 contributor's copies; additional copies $4. Acquires first rights. Sometimes sends galleys to author.
Advice: "We look for work that springs from inner urgency and/or an inspired original vision; writing that explores and creates the world rather than merely reflecting it. Successful formal innovations are always appreciated, as are pieces that blur the boundaries of reality."

✔ **READER'S BREAK, (I)**, Pine Grove Press, P.O. Box 85, Jamesville NY 13078. (315)423-9268. **Editor:** Gertrude S. Eiler. Annual anthology with an "emphasis on short stories written with style and ability. Our aim has always been to publish work of quality by authors with talent, whether previously published or not."

Needs: "We welcome stories about relationships, tales of action, adventure, science fiction and fantasy, romance, suspense and mystery. Themes and plots may be historical, contemporary or futuristic. No "pornography, sexual perversion, incest or stories for children." Length: 3,500 words maximum. Also publishes "poems to 75 lines in any style or form and on any subject with the above exceptions."

How to Contact: Accepts unsolicited mss. Include SASE. Reports in 3-5 months "since the stories are considered by a number of editorial readers." Reviews novels. SASE for details.

Terms: Pays 1 contributor's copy for one-time rights; additional copies at 20% discount.

Advice: "We prefer fiction with a well-constructed plot and well-defined characters of any age or socio-economic group. Upbeat endings are not required. Please check the sequence of events, their cause-and-effect relationship, the motivation of your characters, and the resolution of plot."

✔ **RE:AL, The Journal of Liberal Arts**, Stephen F. Austin State University, P.O. Box 13007, Nacogdoches TX 75962-3007. (409)468-2059. Fax: (409)468-2614. E-mail: f_real@sfasu.edu. Website: http://www.sfasu.edu (includes writer's guidelines). **Editor:** W. Dale Hearell. Academic journal: 6×10; perfect-bound; 175-225 pages; "top" stock. Editorial content: 30% fiction, 30% poetry, 30% scholarly essays and criticism; an occasional play, book reviews (assigned after query) and interviews. "Work is reviewed based on the intrinsic merit of the scholarship and creative work and its appeal to a sophisticated international readership (U.S., Canada, Great Britain, Ireland, Brazil, Puerto Rico, Italy)." Semiannually. Estab. 1968. Circ. 400.

Needs: Adventure, contemporary, genre, feminist, science fiction, historical, experimental, regional. Receives 1,400-1,600 unsolicited mss/2 issues. Accepts 2-5 fiction mss/issue. Publishes 1-12 months after acceptance. Recently published work by John M. Clarke, Lucas Carpenter, John Dublin and Errol Miller. Publishes 25 new writers/year. Length: 1,000-7,000 words. Occasionally critiques rejected mss and conditionally accepts on basis of critiques and changes.

How to Contact: Send complete ms with cover letter. No simultaneous submissions. Reports in 2 weeks on queries; 3-4 weeks on mss. SASE. Sample copy and writer's guidelines for $5. Guidelines for SASE.

Payment/Terms: Pays 2 contributor's copies; charges for extras. Rights revert to author.

Advice: "Please study an issue. Have your work checked by a well-published writer—who is not a good friend. Also proofread for grammatical and typographical errors. A manuscript must show that the writer is conscious of what he or she is attempting to accomplish in plot, character and theme. A short story isn't written but constructed; the ability to manipulate certain aspects of a story is the sign of a conscious storyteller."

✔ **RED CEDAR REVIEW, (II)**, Dept. of English, 17C Morrill Hall, Michigan State University, East Lansing MI 48824. (517)655-6307. E-mail: presto21@pilot.msu.edu. Website: http://www.msu.edu/~rcreview (includes writer's guidelines, editors' names, subscription information). Editors change. **Fiction Editor:** David Sheridan. Magazine: 5½×8½; 100 pages. Theme: "literary—poetry and short fiction." Biannual. Estab. 1963. Circ. 400.

Needs: Literary. "Good stories with character, plot and style, any genre, but with a real tilt toward literary fiction." Accepts 3-4 mss/issue, 6-10 mss/year. Recently published work by Marc Bookman and Catherine Ryan Hyde. Publishes 10 new writers/year. Length: Open.

How to Contact: Query with unpublished ms with SASE. No simultaneous submissions. Reports in 2-3 months on mss. Publishes ms up to 4 months after acceptance. Sample copy for $5.

Payment/Terms: Pays 2 contributor's copies. $5 charge for extras. Acquires first rights.

Advice: "It would be nice to see more stories that self-confidently further our literary tradition in some way, stories that 'marry artistic vision with moral insight.' What does your story discover about the human condition? What have you done with words and sentences that's new? Hundreds of journals get hundreds of manuscripts in the mail each month. Why does yours need to get printed? I don't want to learn yet again that innocent people suffer, that life is hollow, that the universe is meaningless. Nor do I want to be told that a warm kitten can save one from the abyss. I want an honest, well crafted exploration of where and what we are. Something after which I can no longer see the world in the same way."

N $ **THE REJECTED QUARTERLY, A Journal of Quality Literature Rejected at Least Five Times, (II)**, Black Plankton Press, P.O. Box 1351, Cobb CA 95426. E-mail: bplankton@juno.com. Editor: Daniel Weiss. **Fiction Editors:** Daniel Weiss, Jeff Ludecke. Magazine: 8½×11; 40 pages; 60 lb. paper; 8 pt. Chrome Coat cover stock; illustrations. "We want the best literature possible, regardless of genre. We do, however, have a bias toward the unusual and toward speculative fiction. We aim for a literate, educated audience over 20 years of age." Quarterly. Estab. 1998.

Needs: Experimental, fantasy, historical, humor/satire, literary, mainstream/contemporary, mystery/suspense, romance (futuristic/time travel only), science fiction (soft/sociological), sports. "No vampire fiction." Receives 30 unsolicited mss/month. Accepts 4-6 mss/issue; 16-24 mss/year. Publishes ms 1-12 months after acceptance. Length: 5,000 words average; no mimimum; 8,000 words maximum. Publishes short shorts. Also publishes literary essays, literary criticism, poetry. Often critiques or comments on rejected ms.

How to Contact: Send complete ms with a cover letter. Include estimated word count, 1-paragraph bio and list of publications. Reports in 1-2 weeks on queries; 1-3 months on mss. Send SASE for reply, return of ms or

send a disposable copy of ms. Reprint submissions OK. Sample copy $5 (IRCs for foreign requests). Reviews novels and short story collections.
Payment/Terms: Pays $5 on acceptance and 1 contributor's copy for first rights; additional copies, one at cost, others $5. Sends galleys to author if possible.
Advice: "We are looking for high-quality writing that tells a story or expresses a coherent idea. We want unique stories, original viewpoints and unusual slants."

$ REVIEW: LATIN AMERICAN LITERATURE AND ARTS, 680 Park Ave., New York NY 10021. (212)249-8950, ext. 366. **Editor:** Alfred MacAdam. Managing Editor: Daniel Shapiro. "Magazine of Latin American fiction, poetry and essays in translation for academic, corporate and general audience." Biannual.
Needs: Literary. No political or sociological mss. Receives 5 unsolicited mss/month. Accepts 20 mss/year. Length: 1,500-2,000 words average. Occasionally critiques rejected mss.
How to Contact: "Please submit query before sending any manuscripts. We will request manuscripts if interested." Reports in 3 months. "Submissions must be previously unpublished in English." Simultaneous submissions OK, if notified of acceptance elsewhere. Sample copy free. Reviews novels and short story collections. Send books to Daniel Shapiro, Managing Editor.
Payment/Terms: Pays $50-200 and 2-3 contributor's copies on publication.
Advice: "We are always looking for good translators."

N RHINO, (II), The Poetry Forum, P.O. Box 554, Winnetka IL 60093. Website: http://www.artic.edu/~ageorge/RHINO. **Editors:** Alice George, Deborah Nadler Rosen. Magazine: 5½×7½; 90-120 pages; glossy cover stock; illustrations and photos. "An eclectic magazine looking for strong voices and risk-taking." Annually. Estab. 1976.
Needs: Erotica, ethnic/multicultural, experimental, feminist, humor/satire, literary, mainstream/contemporary, regional. "No long stories—we only print short-shorts/flash fiction." Receives 20-30 unsolicited mss/month. Accepts 1-2 mss/issue. Publishes ms up to 9 months after acceptance. Recently published work by Anne Calcagno and David Starkey. Length: flash fiction/short shorts (under 500 words) only. Also publishes literary essays. Sometimes critiques or comments on rejected ms.
How to Contact: Send complete ms with a cover letter. Include bio. Reports in 1 month on queries; 3 months on mss. Send SASE for reply, return of ms or send a disposable copy of ms. Simultaneous submissions OK. Sample copy and fiction guidelines free.
Payment/Terms: Pays 2 contributor's copies; additional copies $3.50. Acquires one-time rights. Sends galleys to author.

RIO GRANDE REVIEW, UT El Paso's literary magazine, (II), Student publications, 105 E. Union, University of Texas at El Paso, El Paso TX 79968. (915)747-5161. Fax: (915)747-8031. E-mail: rgr@mail.utep.edu. Website: http://www.utep.edu/proscmine/rgr/. **Editors:** Skipper Warson and Magdoline Asfahan. Editors change each year. Magazine: 6×9; approximately 200 pages; 70 lb. paper; 85 lb. cover stock; illustrations and photographs. "We publish any work that challenges writing and reading audiences alike. The intended audience isn't any one sect in particular; rather, the work forcing readers to think as opposed to couch reading is encouraged." Semiannually. Estab. 1984. Circ. 1,000.
Needs: Experimental, feminist, gay, humor/satire, lesbian, mainstream/contemporary, flash fiction, short drama, short fiction. No regional, "anything exclusionarily academic." Receives 40-45 unsolicited mss/month. Accepts 3-4 mss/issue; 6-8 mss/year. Publishes ms approximately 2 months after acceptance. Recently published work by Lawrence Dunning, James J. O'Keeffe and Carole Bubash. Length: 1,750 words average; 1,100 words minimum; 2,000 words maximum. Publishes short shorts. Also publishes poetry. Sometimes critiques or comments on rejected mss.
How to Contact: Send complete ms with a cover letter. Include estimated word count, 40-word bio and list of publications. Reports in 3 months on queries; 4 months on mss. Send SASE for reply and disposable copy of ms. Electronic submissions OK. Sample copy for $5.
Payment/Terms: Pays 2 contributor's copies on publication; additional copies for $5. Acquires "one-time rights that revert back to the author but the *Rio Grande Review* must be mentioned."
Advice: "Be patient. If the beginning fiction writer doesn't make it into the edition the first time, re-submit. Be persistent. One huge category that the *RGR* is branching into is flash fiction. Because the attention span of the nation is dwindling, thereby turning to such no-brain activities as television and movies, literature must change to accommodate as well."

A BULLET INTRODUCES COMMENTS by the editor of *Novel & Short Story Writer's Market* indicating special information about the listing.

$ RIVER STYX, (II), Big River Association, 3207 Washington Ave., St. Louis MO 63103-1218. **Editor:** Richard Newman. Magazine: 6×9; 100 pages; color card cover; perfect-bound; b&w visual art. "No theme restrictions; only high quality, intelligent work." Triannual. Estab. 1975.

Needs: Excerpted novel chapter, contemporary, ethnic, experimental, feminist, gay, satire, lesbian, literary, mainstream, prose poem, translations. No genre fiction, "less thinly veiled autobiography." Receives 150-200 unsolicited mss/month. Accepts 1-3 mss/issue; 3-8 mss/year. Reads only May through November. Recently published work by Richard Burgin, Leslie Pietrzyk and Peggy Shinner. Length: no more than 20-30 manuscript pages. Publishes short shorts. Also publishes poetry. Sometimes critiques rejected mss and recommends other markets.

How to Contact: Send complete ms with name and address on every page. SASE required. Reports in 3-5 months on mss. Simultaneous submissions OK, "if a note is enclosed with your work and if we are notified immediately upon acceptance elsewhere." Sample copy for $7.

Payment/Terms: Pays 2 contributor's copies, 1-year subscription and $8/page "if funds available." Acquires first North American serial rights.

Advice: "We want high-powered stories with well-developed characters. We like strong plots, usually with at least three memorable scenes, and a subplot often helps. No thin, flimsy fiction with merely serviceable language. Short stories shouldn't be any different than poetry–every single word should count. One could argue every word counts more since we're being asked to read 10 to 30 pages."

N ROANOKE REVIEW, (II), English Department, Roanoke College, Salem VA 24153. (703)375-2500. **Editor:** Robert R. Walter. Magazine: 6×9; 40-60 pages. Semiannually. Estab. 1967. Circ. 300.

Needs: Receives 50-60 unsolicited mss/month. Accepts 2-3 mss/issue; 4-6 mss/year. Publishes ms 6 months after acceptance. Length: 2,500 words minimum; 7,500 words maximum. Publishes short shorts. Occasionally critiques rejected mss.

How to Contact: Send complete ms with a cover letter. Reports in 1-2 weeks on queries; 10-12 weeks on mss. SASE for query. Sample copy for $3.

Payment/Terms: Pays in contributor's copies.

✔ $ ROCKET PRESS, (I, II), P.O. Box 730, Greenport NY 11944. E-mail: rocketpress@hotmail.com. Website: http://www.people.delphi.com/rocketusa. **Editor:** Darren Johnson. 16-page newspaper. "A Rocket is a transcendental, celestial traveler—innovative and intelligent fiction and poetry aimed at opening minds—even into the next century." Biannually. Estab. 1993. Circ. 500-2,000.

Needs: Erotica, experimental, humor/satire, literary, special interests (prose poetry). "No historical, romance, academic." Publishes annual special fiction issue or anthology. Receives 20 unsolicited mss/month. Accepts 2-4 mss/issue; 8-16 mss/year. Recently published work by Chris Woods, Roger Lee Kenvin and Ben Ohmart. Publishes 1 new writer/year. Length: 1,000 words average; 500 words minimum; 2,000 words maximum. Publishes short shorts. Length: 400 words. Also publishes poetry. Sometimes critiques or comments on rejected mss.

How to Contact: Reports in 3 months on mss. Send SASE for reply, return of ms or send a disposable copy of ms. Simultaneous submissions OK. Current issue $2, past issue $1.

Payment/Terms: Pays 1¢/word. Acquires one-time rights.

Advice: "We've changed our dateline to 2050 A.D. and publish straight, newspaper-style stories that fit that time frame. Send anything that could also be publishable fifty years from now. Zany is okay. Also, too many writers come off as self-important. When writing a cover letter really try to talk to the editor—don't just rattle off a list of publications you've been in."

THE ROCKFORD REVIEW, (I, II), The Rockford Writers Guild, Box 858, Rockford IL 61105. **Editor-in-Chief:** David Ross. Magazine: 5⅝×8½; 50 pages; b&w illustrations; b&w photos. "We look for prose and poetry with a fresh approach to old themes or new insights into the human condition." Triquarterly. Estab. 1971. Circ. 750.

Needs: Ethnic, experimental, fantasy, humor/satire, literary, regional, science fiction (hard science, soft/sociological). Published work by Kevin Mims, Bill Embly, William Gorman and Melanie Coronetz. Length: Up to 1,300 words. Also publishes one-acts and essays.

How to Contact: Send complete ms. "Include a short biographical note—no more than four sentences." Simultaneous submissions OK. Reports in 6-8 weeks on mss. SASE. Sample copy for $5. Fiction guidelines for SASE.

Payment/Terms: Pays contributor's copies. "Two $25 editor's choice cash prizes per issue." Acquires first North American serial rights.

Advice: "Any subject or theme goes as long as it enhances our understanding of our humanity." Wants more "satire and humor, good dialogue."

$ SALAMANDER, a magazine for poetry, fiction & memoirs, (II), 48 Ackers Ave., Brookline MA 02146. (617)232-0031. Editor: Jennifer Barber. **Fiction Editor:** Peter Brown. Magazine: 5½×8½; 80 pages; illustrations and photos. "We publish outstanding work by new and established writers for a literary audience." Semiannually. Estab. 1992. Circ. 1,000.

• Received grants from the National Endowment for the Arts, Massachusetts Cultural Council and the Brooklin Council on the Arts and Humanities. Member of CLMP.

Needs: Ethnic/multicultural, experimental, feminist, gay, historical, literary, mainstream/contemporary. "Open to most categories." Receives 120 unsolicited mss/month. Accepts 3 mss/issue; 6 mss/year. Publishes ms 3-6 months after acceptance. Agented fiction 1%. Recently published work by Peter Ho Davies, Sean K. Henry, Rebecca McClanahan and Mark Bookman. Length: 10-20 pages. Publishes short shorts. Also publishes literary essays and poetry.

How to Contact: Send complete ms with a cover letter or submit through an agent. Include bio and list of publications. Reports in 1 month on queries, 4 months on mss. Send SASE for return of ms. Sample copy for $3 and 6×9 SAE with $1.47 postage. Fiction guidelines for #10 SASE.

Payment/Terms: Pays $25/two pages printed in magazine plus 2 contributor's copies for one-time rights. Sends galleys to author.

☑ **SALT HILL**, (II), Salt Hill, English Dept., Syracuse University, Syracuse NY 13210. E-mail: jsparker@mailbox.syr.edu. Website: http://www.hypertext.com/sh. Editor: James Wagner. **Fiction Editor:** Caryn Koplik. Editors change each year. Magazine: 5½×8½; 120 pages; 70 lb. paper; 80 lb. 4-color cover; illustrations and photos. Publishes fiction with "fresh imagery, original language and tonal and structural experimentation." Semiannually. Estab. 1994. Circ. 1,000.

• Member of CLMP. Sponsors short short fiction contest. Deadline September 15. Send SASE for details.

Needs: Erotica, ethnic/multicultural, experimental, gay, humor/satire, lesbian, literary, translations. No genre fiction. Receives 40-50 unsolicited mss/month. Accepts 3-5 mss/issue; 6-10 mss/year. Does not read April-June. Publishes ms 2-8 months after acceptance. Recently published work by Lydia Davis, Michael Martone and Elizabeth May. Publishes 0-3 new writers/year. Length: 4,500 words maximum. Publishes short shorts. Also publishes literary essays, literary criticism and poetry.

How to Contact: Send complete ms with a cover letter. Include 3-5 sentence bio and estimated word count. Reports in 2-6 months on mss. Send SASE for reply, return of ms or send disposable copy of ms. Simultaneous submissions OK. Sample copy for $7. Fiction guidelines for #10 SASE. Reviews novels or short story collections. Send books to "Book Review Editor."

Payment/Terms: Pays 2 contributor's copies for first North American serial rights and web rights; additional copies $7. Sends galleys to author.

Tips: "Read everything you can, think about what you read, understand the structures, characters, etc.—then write, and write, and write again."

SALT LICK PRESS, (II), Salt Lick Foundation, Salt Lick Press/Lucky Heart Books, 1900 West Hwy. 6, Waco TX 76712. **Editor:** James Haining. Magazine: 8½×11; 100 pages; 70 lb. offset stock; 65 lb. cover; illustrations and photos. Irregularly. Estab. 1969.

Needs: Contemporary, erotica, ethnic, experimental, feminist, gay, lesbian, literary. Receives 25 unsolicited mss each month. Accepts 4 mss/issue. Length: open. Occasionally critiques rejected mss.

How to Contact: Send complete ms with cover letter. Reports in 2 weeks on queries; 1 month on mss. SASE. Simultaneous and reprint submissions OK. Sample copy for $6, 9×12 SAE and 3 first-class stamps.

Payment/Terms: Pays in contributor's copies. Acquires first North American serial rights. Sends galleys to author.

SAMSARA, The Magazine of Suffering, (IV), P.O. Box 367, College Park MD 20741-0367. Website: http://members.aol.com/rdfgoalie/ (includes writer's guidelines and tips for writers). **Editor:** R. David Fulcher. Magazine: 8½×11; 50-80 pages; Xerox paper; poster stock cover; illustrations. "*Samsara* publishes only stories or poems relating to suffering." Semiannually. Estab. 1994. Circ. 250.

• *Samsara* is a member of the Small Press Genre Association.

Needs: Condensed/excerpted novel, erotica, experimental, fantasy (science fantasy, sword and sorcery), horror, literary, mainstream/contemporary, science fiction (hard science, soft/sociological). Receives 40 unsolicited mss/month. Accepts 17-20 mss/issue; 40 mss/year. "*Samsara* closes to submission after the publication of each issue. However, this schedule is not fixed." Publishes ms 4 months after acceptance. Recently published work by D.F. Lewis, D. Ceder and Christopher Hiuner. Length: 2,000 words average; no minimum or maximum. Publishes short shorts. Also publishes poetry. Sometimes critiques or comments on rejected ms.

How to Contact: Send complete ms with a cover letter. Include estimated word count, 1-page bio and list of publications. Reports in 3 months on queries. Send SASE for reply, return of ms or send a disposable copy of ms. Simultaneous, reprint and electronic submissions OK. Sample copy for $5.50. Fiction guidelines for #10 SASE.

Payment/Terms: Pays 1 contributor's copy. Acquires first North American serial rights and reprint rights.

Advice: "We seek out writers who make use of imagery and avoid over-writing. Symbolism and myth really make a manuscript stand out. Read a sample copy. Too many writers send work which does not pertain to the guidelines. Writers should avoid sending us splatter-punk or gore stories."

SANSKRIT, Literary Arts Magazine of UNC Charlotte, (II), University of North Carolina at Charlotte, Highway 49, Charlotte NC 28223. (704)547-2326. E-mail: sanskrit@email.uncc.edu. Website: http://www.uncc.

edu/stud_organ/sanskrit (includes 1998 edition). Contact: Literary Editor. Magazine: 9×12, 64 pages. "*Sanskrit* is an award-winning magazine produced with two goals in mind: service to the student staff and student body, and the promotion of unpublished and beginning artists. Our intended audience is the literary/arts community of UNCC, Charlotte, other schools and contributors and specifically individuals who might never have read a litarary magazine before." Annually. Estab. 1968.

- *Sanskrit* has received the Pacemaker Award, Associated College Press, Gold Crown Award and Columbia Scholastic Press Award.

Needs: "Not looking for any specific category—just good writing." Receives 6-10 unsolicited mss/month. Acquires 2-3 mss/issue. Publishes in late March. Deadline: first Friday in November. Published work by Chaim Bertman, Kat Meads and Kerry Madden-Lunsford. Length: 250 words minimum;35,000 words maximum. Publishes short shorts. Also publishes poetry. Seldom critiques rejected mss.

How to Contact: Send complete manuscript with cover letter. Accepts queries/mss by e-mail. SASE. Simultaneous submissions OK. Sample copy for $10; additional copies $7. Fiction guidelines for #10 SAE.

Payment/Terms: Pays contributor's copy. Acquires one-time rights. Publication not previously copyrighted.

Advice: "Remember that you are entering a market often saturated with mediocrity—an abundance of cute words and phrases held together by cliques simply will not do."

SATIRE, (I, II), C&K Publications, P.O. Box 340, Hancock MD 21750-0340. (301)678-6999. E-mail: satire@intrepid.net. Website: http://www.intrepid.net/satire (includes guidelines, preview of issues, links for satire, ordering information). **Editor:** Larry Logan. Magazine: 8½×11; 60-70 pages; bond paper; illustrations. "We hope that our quarterly provides a home for contemporary literary satire that might make you laugh . . . make you squirm . . . and make you think." Quarterly. Estab. 1994. Circ. 500.

Needs: Humor/satire, literary. "We will consider all categories as long as a satiric treatment is incorporated. Would like more political satire." Receives 150 unsolicited mss/month. Accepts 20 mss/issue; 80 mss/year. Publishes ms within 6 months after acceptance. Recently published work by Frederick J. McGavran, Mark Gifford, Gene-Michael Higney, Terry Stawar, Barbara Lefcowitz, Dick Lancaster and Leslie Woolf Hedley. Length: 6,000 words maximum. Publishes short shorts. Also publishes literary essays, condensed/excerpted novel, poetry and 3-6 cartoons/issue. Sometimes critiques or comments on rejected mss.

How to Contact: Send complete ms with cover letter. Include estimated word count, a short bio and list of publications. Accepts queries by e-mail. Reports in 3 months on mss. Send SASE for reply, return of ms or send a disposable copy of ms. Simultaneous, reprint and electronic submissions OK. Sample copy for $5 and #10 SASE. Fiction guidelines free.

Payment/Terms: Pays 2 contributor's copies for works over 1 page; additional 5 copies at cost to authors. Acquires one-time rights. Sends galleys to author.

Advice: "When considering fiction, we ask does it make us laugh? Does it make us think? Does it make us say Wow! I never looked at it that way before! Clever humor and wit is prized within a well-developed story/essay/etc."

$ SCARP, New Arts & Writing, % Faculty of Creative Arts, University of Wollongong, Northfields Ave., Wollongong NSW 2522 Australia. Phone: 02 4221 3867. Fax: 02 4221 3301. **Editor:** Ron Pretty. Circ. 1,000. Publishes 3-6 fiction ms annually. Published twice a year.

Needs: "We look for fiction in a contemporary idiom, even if it uses a traditional form." Recently published work by Megan Wynne Jones and Bill Pitt. Preferred length: 2,000 words. We're looking for energy, impact, quality."

How to Contact: "Submit to reach us in April and/or August." Include SASE.

Payment/Terms: Payment: $80 (Australian); contributor's copies supplied.

Advice: "In Australia the beginning writer faces stiff competition—the number of paying outlets is not increasing, but the number of capable writers is."

SCREAMING TOAD PRESS, Dancing with Mr. D. Publications, (II), 809 W. Broad St. #221, Falls-Church VA 22046. E-mail: llcoolj@bellatlantic.net. Website: http://members.bellatlantic.net/~llcoolj. **Editor:** Llori Steinberg. Magazine: 6×9; 20-30 pages; 60 lb. cover; illustrations and photos. "Fiction/nonfiction—usually warped, gore or truelife experience." Quarterly. Estab. 1993. Circ. 500.

Needs: Erotica (horror), experimental, fantasy (children's fantasy, science fantasy), horror, humor/satire, mystery/suspense (amateur sleuth). "Wants to see more reality-oriented fiction with gritty humor." No religion/Christian or Gothic horror. List of upcoming themes available for SASE. Receives 100-350 unsolicited mss/month. Accepts 2 mss/issue; 2-8 mss/year. Published work by George Steinberg, Dave Green and Sharon Aldana. Publishes 22 new writers/year. Length: 1,000 words average; 300-500 words minimum; 1,000 words maximum. Publishes short shorts. Also publishes literary essays and literary criticism. Sometimes critiques or comments on rejected mss.

How to Contact: Send complete ms. Include bio (any length). Reports in 2-6 weeks on queries; 6-12 weeks on mss. Send SASE for reply, return of ms or send a disposable copy of ms. Simultaneous and reprint submissions OK. Sample copy for $5 (payable to Llori Steinberg), #10 SAE and 2 first-class stamps. Fiction guidelines for #10 SAE and 2 first-class stamps.

Payment/Terms: No payment. Copies $5. All rights revert to author.

Advice: "I got to enjoy it—it's gotta be you! Don't copy! I want nothing to do with impersonators! I get too many. Knock me out by being unheard of—in anything you write."

SCRIVENER CREATIVE REVIEW, (II), 853 Sherbrooke St. W., Montreal, Quebec H3A 2T6 Canada. (514)398-6588. Fax: (514)398-8146. E-mail: bqgc@musicb.mcgillica. Coordinating Editors: Konstantine Stavrakos and Michelle Syba. **Fiction Editors:** Michael Bezuhly and Sarah Mynowski. Magazine: 8×9; 100 pages; matte paper; illustrations; b&w photos. "*Scrivener* is a creative journal publishing fiction, poetry, graphics, photography, reviews, interviews and scholarly articles. We publish the best of new and established writers. We examine how current trends in North American writing are rooted in a pervasive creative dynamic; our audience is mostly scholarly and in the writing field." Annually. Estab. 1980. Circ. 500.

Needs: Open, "good writing." Receives 10 unsolicited mss/month. Accepts 20 mss/year. Does not read mss May 1-Sept 1. Publishes ms 2 months after acceptance. Recently published work by Gail Scott, Heather Hermant and Leanne Fitzgerald. Publishes 6 new writers/year. Length: 25 pages maximum. Occasionally publishes short shorts. Also publishes literary essays, literary criticism, poetry. Often critiques rejected mss. Rarely recommends other markets.

How to Contact: Send complete ms with a cover letter and SASE. Include 50-100 word bio and list of publications. Accepts queries/mss by fax. "If piece is in simultaneous circulation, include the titles of the other journals/magazines." Order sample copy ($5); send complete ms with cover letter with "critical statements; where we can reach you; biographical data; education; previous publications." Reports in 4 months on queries and mss. SASE/IRC preferred but not required. Simultaneous and photocopied submissions OK. Accepts computer printouts. Sample copy for $5 (US in USA; Canadian in Canada). Fiction guidelines for SAE/IRC. Reviews novels and short story collections. Send books to Nonfiction Editor.

Payment/Terms: Pays contributor's copies; charges for extras. Rights retained by the author.

Advice: "Send us your best stuff. Don't be deterred by rejections. Sometimes a magazine just isn't looking for your *kind* of writing. Don't neglect the neatness of your presentation."

$ SE LA VIE WRITER'S JOURNAL, (I), Rio Grande Press, P.O. Box 71745, Las Vegas NV 89170. **Editor:** Rosalie Avara. Magazine: 8½×5½; 68-74 pages; bond paper; illustrations. *SLVWJ* accepts work through its short short story contests. "Manuscripts should reflect the 'that's life' (Se La Vie) theme, intended for young adult to adult readers. We also publish *The Story Shop*, an annual anthology of short stories. For *The Story Shop*, we accept any type of wholesome stories (no porn or erotica)." Quarterly. Estab. 1987. Circ. 150.

Needs: Adventure, ethnic/multicultural, humor/satire, literary, mystery/suspense (amateur sleuth, private eye/hardboiled, romantic suspense), regional. "No science fiction, porn or erotica; nothing political or feminist; no alternate lifestyles; no extreme religious (although some spiritual)." Receives 8-10 unsolicited mss/month. Accepts 2 mss/issue for *SLVWJ*; 12-15 mss/issue for *The Story Shop*. Publishes ms 3 months after acceptance; 1 year after acceptance for *The Story Shop*. Published work by Narjura Salam Brax, Edgar H. Thompson and John D. Collins. Publishes 15-20 new writers/year. Length: 500 words average; 300 words minimum; 500 words maximum. Length (for *The Story Shop*): 1,500 words average; 1,000 words minimum; 1,500 words maximum. Also publishes literary essays and poetry. Sometimes critiques or comments on rejected mss.

How to Contact: Send SASE first for guidelines, then send complete ms with cover letter. Include estimated word count. Reports in 2 weeks on queries and mss. Send SASE for reply, return of ms or send a disposable copy of ms. Sample copy for $2. Contest and fiction guidelines for #10 SASE. Reviews short story collections.

Payment/Terms: Pays $5-25 to contest winners; copies of *The Story Shop* available for $6.95 each. Pays on publication. Acquires first North American serial rights.

Advice: *Se La Vie* looks for stories with surprise endings. *The Story Shop* looks for "any story that can hold my interest for the first three pages." For both publications, "believable characters, good dialogue, good description, good plot, etc."

$ THE SEATTLE REVIEW, (II), Padelford Hall Box 354330, University of Washington, Seattle WA 98195. (206)543-9865. **Editor:** Colleen J. McElroy. Fiction Editor: Charles Johnson. Magazine: 6×9. "Includes general fiction, poetry, craft essays on writing, and one interview per issue with a Northwest writer." Semiannual. Published special fiction issue. Estab. 1978. Circ. 1,000.

Needs: Contemporary, ethnic, experimental, fantasy, feminist, gay, historical, horror, humor/satire, lesbian, literary, mainstream, prose poem, psychic/supernatural/occult, regional, science fiction, excerpted novel, mystery/suspense, translations, western. "We also publish a series called Writers and their Craft, which deals with aspects of writing fiction (also poetry)—point of view, characterization, etc., rather than literary criticism, each issue." Does not want to see "anything in bad taste (porn, racist, etc.)." Receives about 100 unsolicited mss/month. Buys about 3-6 mss/issue; about 4-10 mss/year. Does not read mss June through September. Agented fiction 25%. Published work by David Milofsky, Lawson Fusao Inada and Liz Rosenberg; published new writers within the last year. Length: 3,500 words average; 500 words minimum; 10,000 words maximum. Publishes short shorts. Sometimes critiques rejected mss. Occasionally recommends other markets.

How to Contact: Send complete ms. Reports in 6-8 months. SASE. Sample copy "half-price if older than one year." Current issue for $6; some special issues $7.50.
Payment/Terms: Pays 0-$100, free subscription to magazine, 2 contributor's copies; charge for extras. Pays on publication for first North American serial rights. Copyright reverts to writer on publication; "please request release of rights and cite *SR* in reprint publications." Sends galleys to author.
Advice: "Beginners do well in our magazine if they send clean, well-written manuscripts. We've published a lot of 'first stories' from all over the country and take pleasure in discovery."

✓ **SEEMS, (II)**, Lakeland College, Box 359, Sheboygan WI 53082-0359. (920)565-1276. Fax: (920)565-1206. **Editor:** Karl Elder. Magazine: 7×8½; 40 pages. "We publish fiction and poetry for an audience which tends to be highly literate. People read the publication, I suspect, for the sake of reading it." Published irregularly. Estab. 1971. Circ. 300.
Needs: Literary. Accepts 4 mss/issue. Receives 12 unsolicited fiction mss each month. Published work by Sapphire and other emerging writers. Publishes 1-2 new writers/year. Length: 5,000 words maximum. Publishes short shorts. Also publishes poetry. Critiques rejected mss when there is time.
How to Contact: Send complete ms with SASE. Reports in 2 months on mss. Publishes ms an average of 1-2 years after acceptance. Sample copy for $4.
Payment/Terms: Pays 1 contributor's copy; $4 charge for extras. Rights revert to author.
Advice: "Send clear, clean copies. Read the magazine in order to help determine the taste of the editor." Mss are rejected because of "lack of economical expression, or saying with many words what could be said in only a few. Good fiction contains all of the essential elements of poetry; study poetry and apply those elements to fiction. Our interest is shifting to story poems, the grey area between genres."

$ **SENSATIONS MAGAZINE, (I, II)**, 2 Radio Ave., A5, Secaucus NJ 07094-3843. **Founder:** David Messineo. Magazine: 8½×11; 200 pages; 20 lb. paper; full color cover; color photography. "We publish short stories and poetry, no specific theme." Magazine also includes the Rediscovering America in Poetry research series. Semiannually. Estab. 1987.

- *Sensations Magazine* is one of the few markets accepting longer work. They would like to see more mysteries, well-researched historical fiction.

Needs: "We're interested in almost any theme/genre." Wants to see more "well-written mysteries, with great attention to period detail/research." No sexually graphic work. "We're not into gratuitous profanity, pornography, or violence. Sometimes these are needed to properly tell the tale. We'll read anything unusual, providing it is submitted in accordance with our submission policies. No abstract works only the writer can understand." Theme for October 1999 issue: America, 1501-1600. Accepts 2-4 mss/issue. Publishes ms 2 months after acceptance. Recently published work by Susan Caldwell and Gene W. Taylor. Length: 35 pages maximum.
How to Contact: Send SASE for guidelines. Simultaneous submissions OK. Accepts electronic submissions (Macintosh only). *"Do not submit material before reading submission guidelines."* Ask about Summer 1999 contest for top two stories per issue.
Payment/Terms: Pays $100 per story on acceptance for one-time rights.
Advice: "Each story must have a strong beginning that grabs the reader's attention in the first two sentences. Characters have to be realistic and well-described. Readers must like, hate, or have some emotional response to your characters. Setting, plot, construction, attention to detail—all are important. We work with writers to help them improve in these areas, but the better the stories are written before they come to us, the greater the chance for publication. Purchase sample copy first and read the stories."

SEPIA, Poetry & Prose Magazine, Kawabata Press, Knill Cross House, Knill Cross, Millbrook, Nr Torpoint, Cornwall England. **Editor-in-Chief:** Colin David Webb. Published 3 times/year.
Needs: "Magazine for those interested in modern un-clichéd work." No science fiction, detective, "any typical genre." Contains 32 pages/issue. Publishes 5-6 new writers/year. Length: 200-4,000 words (for short stories).
How to Contact: Always include SAE with IRCs. Send $1 for sample copy and guidelines. Subscription $5; "no cheques!"
Payment/Terms: Pays 1 contributor's copy.

✓ $ **THE SEWANEE REVIEW, (III)**, University of the South, Sewanee TN 37383. (931)598-1246. **Editor:** George Core. Magazine: 6×9; 192 pages. "A literary quarterly, publishing original fiction, poetry, essays on

FOR EXPLANATIONS OF THESE SYMBOLS,
SEE THE INSIDE FRONT AND BACK COVERS OF THIS BOOK.

literary and related subjects, book reviews and book notices for well-educated readers who appreciate good American and English literature." Quarterly. Estab. 1892. Circ. 3,200.

Needs: Literary, contemporary. Buys 10-15 mss/year. Receives 100 unsolicited fiction mss each month. Does not read mss June 1-August 31. Published new writers within the last year. Length: 6,000-7,500 words. Critiques rejected mss "when there is time." Sometimes recommends other markets.

How to Contact: Send complete ms with SASE and cover letter stating previous publications, if any. Reports in 6 weeks on mss. Sample copy for $6.25.

Payment/Terms: Pays $10-12/printed page; 2 contributor's copies; $4 charge for extras. Pays on publication for first North American serial rights and second serial rights by agreement. Writer's guidelines for SASE.

Advice: "Send only one story at a time, with a serious and sensible cover letter. We think fiction is of greater general interest than any other literary mode."

N **SHADES OF DECEMBER, (II)**, Box 244, Selden NY 11784. E-mail: eilonwy@innocent.com. **Editor:** Alexander Danner. Magazine: 8½×5½; 60 pages. "Good writing comes in all forms and should not be limited to overly specific or standard genres. Our intended audience is one that is varied in taste and open to the unorthodox." Bimonthly. Estab. 1998. Circ. 200-300. Reading fee of $1 for non-electronic submissions.

Needs: Experimental, fantasy, humor/satire, literary, mainstream/contemporary, psychic/supernatural/occult, romance, science fiction. "We are not limited in the categories of writing that we will consider for publication." Accepts 1-3 mss/issue; 6-18 mss/year. Publishes ms 1-4 months after acceptance. Recently published work by Joe Lucia and Tom Bierowski. Length: 2,500 words maximum. Publishes short shorts. Also publishes literary essays, poetry. Sometimes critiques or comments on rejected ms.

How to Contact: Send complete ms with a cover letter. Include bio (50 words or less) and list of publications. Reports in 6-8 weeks. Send SASE for reply, return of ms or send a disposable copy of ms. Simultaneous and reprint submissions OK. Electronic submissions preferred; $1 reading fee for nonelectronic submissions. Sample copy $3. Fiction guidelines for #10 SASE.

Payment/Terms: Pays 2 contributor's copies. Acquires one-time rights.

Advice: "We like to see work that strays from the conventional. While we print good writing in any form, we prefer to see work that takes risks."

SHATTERED WIG REVIEW, (I, II), Shattered Wig Productions, 425 E. 31st, Baltimore MD 21218. (410)243-6888. **Editor:** Collective. Attn: Sonny Dodkin. Magazine: 8½×8½; 70 pages; "average" paper; cardstock cover; illustrations and photos. "Open forum for the discussion of the absurdo-miserablist aspects of everyday life. Fiction, poetry, graphics, essays, photos." Semiannually. Estab. 1988. Circ. 500.

Needs: Confession, contemporary, erotica, ethnic, experimental, feminist, gay, humor/satire, lesbian, literary, prose poem, psychic/supernatural/occult, regional. Does not want "anything by Ann Beattie or John Irving." Receives 15-20 unsolicited mss/month. Publishes ms 2-4 months after acceptance. Published work by Al Ackerman, Kim Harrison and Mok Hossfeld. Published new writers within the last year. Publishes short shorts. Also publishes literary criticism, poetry. Sometimes critiques rejected mss and recommends other markets.

How to Contact: Send complete ms with cover letter. Reports in 2 months. Send SASE for return of ms. Simultaneous and reprint submissions OK. Sample copy for $4.

Payment/Terms: Pays in contributor's copies. Acquires one-time rights.

Advice: "The arts have been reduced to imploding pus with the only material rewards reserved for vapid stylists and collegiate pod suckers. The only writing that counts has no barriers between imagination and reality, thought and action. Send us at least three pieces so we have a choice."

$ SHENANDOAH, The Washington and Lee Review, (II), 2nd Floor, Troubadour Theater, Lexington VA 24450. (540)463-8765. Fax: (540)463-8461. Website: http://www.wlu.edu/~shenando (includes samples, guidelines and contents). **Editor:** R.T. Smith. Magazine: 6×9; 124 pages. "We are a literary journal devoted to excellence." Quarterly. Estab. 1950. Circ. 2,000.

Needs: Literary. Receives 400-500 unsolicited fiction mss/month. Accepts 4 mss/issue; 16 mss/year. Does not read mss during summer. Publishes ms 6 months to 1 year after acceptance. Published work by Kent Nelson, Barry Gifford, Nicholas Delbanco and Reynolds Price. Publishes 1 new writer/year. Publishes short shorts. Also publishes literary essays, literary criticism and poetry.

How to Contact: Send complete ms with cover letter. Include a 3-sentence bio and list of publications ("just the highlights"). Reports in 10 weeks on mss. Send a disposable copy of ms. Sample copy for $3. Fiction guidelines for #10 SASE. Reviews novels and short story collections.

Payment/Terms: Pays $25/page and free subscription to the magazine on publication. Acquires first North American serial rights. Sends galleys to author. Sponsors contest.

Advice: Looks for "thrift, precision, originality. As Frank O'Connor said, 'Get black on white.' "

SHORT STORIES BIMONTHLY, (I, II), Poetry Forum, 5713 Larchmont Dr., Erie PA 16509. Phone/fax: (814)866-2543. E-mail: 75562.670@compuserve.com. **Editor:** Gunvor Skogsholm. Newsletter: 11×17; 14 pages; 20 lb. paper; illustrations. Estab. 1992. Circ. 400.

Needs: Literary, mainstream. No extreme horror. Receives 30 unsolicited mss/month. Accepts 8-10 mss/issue; 48-60 mss/year. Publishes ms 1-9 months after acceptance. Recently published work by Richard French, Tod

Goldberg and L.B. Sinnat. 70% of work published is by new writers. Length: 1,800 words average; 600 words minimum; 4,000 words maximum. Publishes short shorts. Length: 600 words. Also publishes literary essays and literary criticism.
How to Contact: Send complete ms with a cover letter. Accepts queries/mss by e-mail. Include estimated word count. Reports in 3 weeks to 6 months on mss. Send SASE for reply, return of ms or send a disposable copy of ms. Simultaneous and electronic submissions OK. Sample copy for $3. Fiction guidelines free. Favors submissions from subscribers. "We exist by subscriptions and advertising." Reviews novels and short story collections.
Payment/Terms: Acquires one-time rights. Sponsors contests, awards or grants for fiction writers. Send SASE.
Advice: "Be original, be honest. Write from your deepest sincerity—don't play games with the readers. Meaning: we don't want the last paragraph to tell us we have been fooled."

$ SHORT STUFF MAGAZINE FOR GROWN-UPS, (I, II), Bowman Publications, P.O. Box 7057, Loveland CO 80537. (970)669-9139. **Editor:** Donna Bowman. Magazine: 8½×11; 40 pages; bond paper; enamel cover; b&w illustrations and photographs. "Nonfiction is regional—Colorado and adjacent states. Fiction and humor must be tasteful, but can be any genre, any subject. We are designed to be a 'Reader's Digest' of fiction. We are found in professional waiting rooms, etc." Publishes 6 issues/year.
Needs: Adventure, contemporary, historical, humor/satire, mainstream, mystery/suspense (amateur sleuth, English cozy, police procedural, private eye, romantic suspense), regional, romance (contemporary, gothic, historical), western (frontier). No erotica. "We use holiday themes. Need 3 month lead time. Issues are Valentine (February/March); Easter and St. Patrick's Day (April/May); Mom's and Dad's (June/July); Americana (August/September); Halloween (October/November); and Holiday (December/January). Receives 500 unsolicited mss/month. Accepts 9-12 mss/issue; 76 mss/year. Publishes accepted work immediately. Recently published work by Susanne Shaphren, William Hallstead, Eleanor Sherman, Guy Bellerante, Birdie Etcheson, Guy Belleranti and Jane McBride Choate. Length: 1,000 words average; 1,600 words maximum.
How to Contact: Send complete ms with cover letter. SASE. Reports in 3-6 months. Sample copies for $1.50 and 9×12 SAE with $1.50 postage. Fiction guidelines for SASE.
Payment/Terms: Pays $10-50 "at our discretion" and subscription to magazine on publication for first North American serial rights. $1-5 for fillers (less than 500 words). "We do not pay for single jokes or poetry, but do give free subscription if published."
Advice: "We seek a potpourri of subjects each issue. A new slant, a different approach, fresh viewpoints—all of these excite us. We don't like gore, salacious humor or perverted tales. Prefer third person, past tense. Be sure it is a story with a beginning, middle and end. It must have dialogue. Many beginners do not know an essay from a short story. Essays frequently used if *humorous*. We'd like to see more young (25 and over) humor; 'clean' humor is hard to come by."

$ SIDE SHOW, 8th Short Story Anthology, (II), Somersault Press, P.O. Box 1428, El Cerrito CA 94530-1428. (510)215-2207. E-mail: jisom@crl.com. **Editor:** Shelley Anderson, Kathe Stolz and Marjorie K. Jacobs. Book (paperback): 5½×8½; 300 pages; 50 lb. paper; semigloss card cover with color illustration; perfect-bound. "Quality short stories for a general, literary audience." Annually. Estab. 1991. Circ. 3,000.

- Work published in *Side Show* has been selected for inclusion in the *Pushcart Prize* anthology.

Needs: Contemporary, ethnic, feminist, gay, humor/satire, literary, mainstream. Nothing genre, religious, pornographic. Receives 50-60 unsolicited mss/month. Accepts 25-30 mss/issue. Publishes ms up to 9 months after acceptance. Recently published work by Dorothy Bryant, Susan Welch, Ericka Lutz, Marianne Rogoff and Miguel Rios. 25% of fiction by previously unpublished writers. Publishes 5-10 new writers/year. Length: Open. Critiques rejected mss, if requested.
How to Contact: Accepts queries by e-mail. All submissions entered in contest. *$10 entry fee* (includes subscription to next *Side Show*). No guidelines. Send complete ms with cover letter and entry fee. Reports in 1 month on mss. SASE. Simultaneous submissions OK. Multiple submissions "in same envelope" encouraged. Sample copy for $10 and $2 postage and handling ($.83 sales tax CA residents).
Payment/Terms: Pays $10/printed page on publication for first North American serial rights. Sends galleys to author. All submissions entered in our contest for cash prizes of $500 (1st), $200 (2nd) and $100 (3rd).
Advice: Looks for "readability, vividness of characterization, coherence, inspiration, interesting subject matter, imagination, point of view, originality, plausibility. If your fiction isn't inspired, you probably won't be published by us (i.e., style and craft alone won't do it)."

✓ SIDEWALKS, (II), P.O. Box 321, Champlin MN 55316. (612)571-1390. **Editor:** Tom Heie. Magazine: 5½×8½; 60-75 pages; 60 lb. paper; textured recycled cover. "*Sidewalks* . . . place of discovery, of myth, power, incantation . . . places we continue to meet people, preoccupied, on our way somewhere . . . tense, dark, empty places . . . place we meet friends and strangers, neighborhood sidewalks, place full of memory, paths that bring us home." Semiannually. Estab. 1991. Circ. 500.
Needs: Experimental, humor/satire, literary, mainstream/contemporary, regional. No violent, pornographic kinky material. Accepts 6-8 mss/issue; 12-16 mss/year. Work is accepted for 2 annual deadlines: May 31 and December 31. Publishes ms 10 weeks after deadline. Published work by Sydney Harth, Ben Miller, Robert Haight and W.P. Strange. Length: 2,500 words preferred; 3,000 words maximum. Publishes short shorts. Also publishes poetry.
How to Contact: Send complete ms with cover letter. Include estimated word count, very brief bio, list of

publications. Reports in 1 week on queries; 1 month after deadline on mss. Send SASE for reply, return of ms or send a disposable copy of ms. No simultaneous submissions. Accepts electronic submissions. Sample copy for $5.
Payment/Terms: Pays 1 contributor's copy. Acquires one-time rights.
Advice: "We look for a story with broad appeal, one that is well-crafted and has strong narrative voice, a story that leaves the reader thinking after the reading is over."

SIERRA NEVADA COLLEGE REVIEW, (I, II), Sierra Nevada College, P.O. Box 4269, Incline Village NV 89450. (702)831-1314. **Editor:** June Sylvester. Magazine: 5½×8½; 50-100 pages; coated paper; card cover; saddle-stitched. "We are open to many kinds of work but avoid what we consider trite, sentimental, contrived. . . ." Annually. Estab. 1990. Circ. 200-250 (mostly college libraries).

• The majority of work published in this review is poetry.

Needs: Experimental, literary, mainstream/contemporary, regional. Receives about 50 unsolicited mss/month. Accepts 2-3 mss/year. Does not read mss April 1 through September 1. Work is published by next issue (published in May, annually). Published work by Jamie Andree and James Braziel. Length: 500 words average; 1,000 words maximum. Publishes short shorts. Also publishes literary essays, literary criticism and poetry. Sometimes critiques or comments on rejected mss.
How to Contact: Send complete ms with a cover letter. Include estimated word count and bio. Send SASE for reply, return of ms or send a disposable copy of ms. Simultaneous submissions OK. Sample copy for $2.50.
Payment/Terms: Pays 2 contributor's copies. Acquires one-time rights.
Advice: Looks for "memorable characters, close attention to detail which makes the story vivid. We are interested in flash fiction. Also regional work that catches the flavor of place and time—like strong characters. No moralizing, inspirational work. No science fiction. No children's stories. Tired of trite love stories—cynicism bores us."

$ THE SILVER WEB, A Magazine of the Surreal, (II), Buzzcity Press, Box 38190, Tallahassee FL 32315. (904)385-8948. Fax: (904)385-4063. E-mail: annkl9@mail.idt.net. **Editor:** Ann Kennedy. Magazine: 8½×11; 80 pages; 20 lb. paper; full color; perfect bound; glossy cover; b&w illustrations and photographs. "Looking for unique character-based stories that are off-beat, off-center and strange, but not inaccessible." Semiannually. Estab. 1989. Circ. 2,000.

• *The Silver Web* ranked #25 in *Writer's Digest*'s Fiction 50 list of top markets for fiction writers. Work published in *The Silver Web* has appeared in *The Year's Best Fantasy and Horror* (DAW Books) and *The Year's Best Fantastic Fiction*.

Needs: Experimental, horror, science fiction (soft/sociological). No "traditional storylines, monsters, vampires, werewolves, etc." *The Silver Web* publishes surrealistic fiction and poetry. Work too bizarre for mainstream, but perhaps too literary for genre. This is not a straight horror/sci-fi magazine. No typical storylines." Receives 500 unsolicited mss/month. Accepts 8-10 mss/issue; 16-20 mss/year. Does not read mss October through December. Publishes ms 6-12 months after acceptance. Recently published work by Brian Evenson, Jack Ketchum and Joel Lane. Length: 6,000 words average; 100 words minimum; 8,000 words maximum. Publishes short shorts. Also publishes poetry. Sometimes critiques rejected ms.
How to Contact: Send complete ms with a cover letter. Include estimated word count. Reports in 1 week on queries; 6-8 weeks on mss. Send SASE for reply, return of ms or send a disposable copy of ms plus SASE for reply. Simultaneous and reprint submissions OK. Sample copy for $7.20. Fiction guidelines for #10 SASE. Reviews novels and short story collections.
Payment/Terms: Pays 2-3¢/word and 2 contributor's copies; additional copies for $4. Acquires first North American serial rights, reprint rights or one-time rights.
Advice: "I have a reputation for publishing excellent fiction from newcomers next to talented, established writers, and for publishing cross-genre fiction. No traditional, standard storylines. I'm looking for beautiful writing with plots that are character-based. Tell a good story; tell it with beautiful words. I see too many writers writing for the marketplace and this fiction just doesn't ring true. I'd rather read fiction that comes straight from the heart of the writer." Read a copy of the magazine, at least get the writer's guidelines.

$ SING HEAVENLY MUSE!, Women's Poetry and Prose, (I, II, IV), Box 13320, Minneapolis MN 55411. Contact: Editorial Circle. Magazine: 6×9; 100 pages; 55 lb. acid-free paper; 10 pt. glossy cover stock; illustrations; photos. "We foster the work of women poets, prose writers and artists and work that shows an awareness of women's consciousness." Annually. Estab. 1977. Circ. 300.
Needs: Literary, feminist, prose poem and ethnic/minority. List of upcoming themes and reading periods available for SASE. Receives approximately 30 unsolicited fiction mss each month. Accepts 3-6 mss/issue. Published work by Mary Moore Easter, Mara Kirk Hart and Kay Bache-Snyder. Length: 10,000 words maximum. Publishes short shorts. Also publishes literary essays, poetry. Sometimes critiques or comments on rejected mss.
How to Contact: Query for information on theme issues, reading periods or variations in schedule. No simultaneous submissions. Reports in 1-2 months on queries; 3-9 months on mss. Publishes ms an average of 1 year after acceptance. Sample copy for $4. Fiction guidelines for #10 SASE.
Payment/Terms: Pays 2 contributor's copies and honorarium, depending on funding. Acquires one-time rights. Sends galleys to author.

N **SINISTER WISDOM, (IV)**, Box 3252, Berkeley CA 94703. **Editor:** Margo Mercedes Rivera. Magazine: 5½×8½; 128-144 pages; 55 lb. stock; 10 pt C1S cover; illustrations; photos. Lesbian-feminist journal, providing fiction, poetry, drama, essays, journals and artwork. Quarterly. Past issues included "Lesbians of Color," "Old Lesbians/Dykes" and "Lesbians and Religion." Estab. 1976. Circ. 3,000.

Needs: Lesbian: adventure, contemporary, erotica, ethnic, experimental, fantasy, feminist, historical, humor/satire, literary, prose poem, psychic, regional, science fiction, sports, translations. No heterosexual or male-oriented fiction; nothing that stereotypes or degrades women. Receives 50 unsolicited mss/month. Accepts 25 mss/issue; 75-100 mss/year. Publishes ms 1 month to 1 year after acceptance. Published work by Sapphire, Melanie Kaye/Kantrowitz, Adrienne Rich, Terri L. Jewell and Gloria Anzaldúa; published new writers within the last year. Length: 2,000 words average; 500 words minimum; 4,000 words maximum. Publishes short shorts. Also publishes literary essays, literary criticism, poetry. Occasionally critiques rejected mss. Sometimes recommends other markets.

How to Contact: Send 1 copy of complete ms with cover letter, which should include a brief author's bio to be published when the work is published. Simultaneous submissions OK, if noted. Reports in 2 months on queries; 9 months on mss. SASE. Sample copy for $7.50. Reviews novels and short story collections. Send books to "Attn: Book Review."

Payment/Terms: Pays in contributor's copies. Rights retained by author.

Advice: *Sinister Wisdom* is "a multicultural lesbian journal reflecting the art, writing and politics of our communities."

SKYLARK, (II), Purdue University Calumet, 2200 169th St., Hammond IN 46323. (219)989-2262. Fax: (219)989-2581. E-mail: skylark@nwi.calumet.purdue.edu. **Editor-in-Chief:** Pamela Hunter. Prose Editor: Gordon Stamper. Magazine: 8½×11; 100 pages; illustrations; photos. "*Skylark* presents short stories, essays and poetry which capture a positive outlook on life through vivid imagery, well-developed characterization and unstylized plots. We publish adults, both beginners and professionals, and young authors side be side to complement the points of view of writers of all ages." Annually. Estab. 1971. Circ. 1,000.

Needs: Contemporary, ethnic, experimental, feminist, humor/satire, literary, mainstream, prose poem (gothic), spiritual and sports. Wants to see more experimental and avant garde fiction. No erotica, science fiction, overly-religious stories. Upcoming theme: "Children" (submit by April 1999). Receives 20 mss/month. Accepts 8 mss/issue. Recently published work by Earl Coleman, Shirley Davis and Henry Meyerson. Publishes 8 new writers/year. Length: 4,000 words maximum. Also publishes essays and poetry.

How to Contact: Send complete ms. Send SASE for return of ms. Accepts queries/mss by fax. Reports in 4 months. No simultaneous submissions. Sample copy for $8; back issue for $6.

Payment/Terms: Pays 1 contributor's copy. Acquires first rights. Copyright reverts to author.

Advice: "We seek fiction that presents effective imagery, strong plot, and well-developed characterization. Graphic passages concerning sex or violence are unacceptable. We're looking for dramatic, closely-edited short stories. Please state in your cover letter that the story is not being considered elsewhere."

SLIPSTREAM, (II, IV), Box 2071, New Market Station, Niagara Falls NY 14301. (716)282-2616. Website: http://www.wings.buffalo.edu/libraries/units/pl/slipstream (includes guidelines, editors, current needs, info on current and past releases, sample poems, contest info.). Editor: Dan Sicoli. **Fiction Editors:** R. Borgatti, D. Sicoli and Livio Farallo. Magazine: 7×8½; 80-100 pages; high quality paper; card cover; illustrations; photos. "We use poetry and short fiction with a contemporary urban feel." Estab. 1981. Circ. 500.

Needs: Contemporary, erotica, ethnic, experimental, humor/satire, literary, mainstream and prose poem. No religious, juvenile, young adult or romance. Occasionally publishes theme issues; query for information. Receives over 75 unsolicited mss/month. Accepts 2-4 mss/issue; 6 mss/year. Recently published work by Al Masarik, John Richards, Richard Kostelanetz and B.D. Love. Length: under 15 pages. Publishes short shorts. Rarely critiques rejected mss. Sometimes recommends other markets.

How to Contact: "Query before submitting." Reports within 2 months. Send SASE for reply or return of ms. Sample copy for $5. Fiction guidelines for #10 SASE.

Payment/Terms: Pays 2 contributor's copies. Acquires one-time rights.

Advice: "Writing should be honest, fresh; develop your own style. Check out a sample issue first. Don't write for the sake of writing, write from the gut as if it were a biological need. Write from experience and mean what you say, but say it in the fewest number of words."

✓ **THE SMALL POND MAGAZINE, (II)**, Box 664, Stratford CT 06615. (203)378-4066. **Editor:** Napoleon St. Cyr. Magazine: 5½×8½; 42 pages; 60 lb. offset paper; 65 lb. cover stock; illustrations (art). "Features contemporary poetry, the salt of the earth, peppered with short prose pieces of various kinds. The college educated and erudite read it for good poetry, prose and pleasure." Triannually. Estab. 1964. Circ. 300.

Needs: "Rarely use science fiction or the formula stories you'd find in *Cosmo*, *Redbook*, *Ladies Home Journal*, etc. Philosophy: Highest criteria, originality, even a bit quirky is OK. Don't mind O Henry endings but better be exceptional. Readership: College grads, and college staff, ⅓ of subscribers are college and University libraries." No science fiction, children's. Accepts 10-12 mss/year. Longer response time in July and August. Receives approximately 40 unsolicited fiction mss each month. Recently published work by Peter Baida, Patricia Flynn

and Timothy Reilly. Publishes 3-4 new writers/year. Length: 200-2,500 words. Critiques rejected mss when there is time. Sometimes recommends other markets.
How to Contact: Send complete ms with SASE and short vita. Reports in 2 weeks to 3 months. Publishes ms an average of 2-18 months after acceptance. Sample copy for $4; $3 for back issues.
Payment/Terms: Pays 2 contributor's copies for all rights; $3/copy charge for extras, postage paid.
Advice: "Send for a sample copy first. All mss must be typed. Name and address and story title on front page, name of story on succeeding pages and paginated. I look for polished, smooth progression—no clumsy paragraphs or structures where you know the author didn't edit closely. Also, no poor grammar. Beginning and even established poets read and learn from reading lots of other's verse. Not a bad idea for fiction writers, in their genre, short or long fiction."

$ SNOWY EGRET, (II), The Fair Press, P.O. Box 9, Bowling Green IN 47833. E-mail: pcrepp@wp.bsu.edu. Publisher: Karl Barnebey. **Editor:** Philip Repp. Magazine: 8½×11; 50 pages; text paper; heavier cover; illustrations. "Literary exploration of the abundance and beauty of nature and the ways human beings interact with it." Semiannually. Estab. 1922. Circ. 500.
Needs: Nature writing, including 'true' stories, eye-witness accounts, descriptive sketches and traditional fiction. "We are particularly interested in fiction that celebrates abundance and beauty of nature, encourages a love and respect for the natural world, and affirms the human connection to the environment. No works written for popular genres: horror, science fiction, romance, detective, western, etc." Receives 25 unsolicited mss/month. Accepts up to 6 mss/issue; up to 12 mss/year. Publishes ms 6 months to 1 year after acceptance. Published works by Jane Candia Coleman, Tama Janowitz, David Abrams and Suzanne Kamata. Length: 1,000-3,000 words preferred; 500 words minimum; 10,000 words maximum. Publishes short shorts. Length: 400-500 words. Sometimes critiques rejected mss.
How to Contact: Send complete ms with cover letter. "Cover letter optional: do not query." Reports in 2 months. SASE. Simultaneous (if noted) and electronic (Mac, ASCII) submissions OK. Sample back issues for $8 and 9×12 SAE. Send #10 SASE for writer's guidelines.
Payment/Terms: Pays $2/page and 2 contributor's copies on publication; charge for extras. Acquires first North American serial rights and reprint rights. Sends galleys to author.
Advice: Looks for "honest, freshly detailed pieces with plenty of description and/or dialogue which will allow the reader to identify with the characters and step into the setting. Characters who relate strongly to nature, either positively or negatively, and who, during the course of the story, grow in their understanding of themselves and the world around them."

N SO TO SPEAK, A Feminist Journal of Language and Art, (II, IV), George Mason University, Sub1, Room 254A, 4400 University Dr., Fairfax VA 22030. (703)993-3625. E-mail: sts@gmu.edu. Website: http://www.forthcoming. **Fiction Editor:** Nolde Alexius. Editors change every 2 years. Magazine: 7×10; approximately 70 pages. "We are a feminist journal of high-quality material geared toward an academic/cultured audience." Semiannually. Estab. 1988. Circ. 1,300.
Needs: Ethnic/multicultural, experimental, feminist, lesbian, literary, mainstream/contemporary, regional, translations. "No science fiction, mystery, genre romance, porn (lesbian or straight)." Receives 100 unsolicited mss/month. Accepts 2-3 mss/issue; 6 mss/year. Publishes ms 6 months after acceptance. Recently published work by Deborah J.M. Owen and Sally Chandler. Publishes 2 new writers/year. Length: 4,000 words average; 6,000 words maximum. Publishes short shorts. Also publishes literary essays, literary criticism, book reviews and poetry. Sometimes critiques or comments on rejected mss.
How to Contact: Send complete ms with a cover letter. Include bio (50 words maximum) and SASE. Reports in 6 months on mss. SASE for return of ms or send a disposable copy of ms. Simultaneous submissions OK. Sample copy for $5. Fiction guidelines for #10 SASE.
Payment/Terms: Pays contributor's copies for first North American serial rights.
Advice: "Every writer has something they do exceptionally well; do that and it will shine through in the work. We look for quality prose with a definite appeal to a feminist audience. We are trying to move away from strict genre lines."

THE SOFT DOOR, (I, II), 202 S. Church St., Bowling Green OH 43402. **Editor:** T. Williams. Magazine: 8½×11; 100 pages; bond paper; heavy cover; illustrations and photos. "We publish works that explore human relationships and our relationship to the world." Irregularly.
Needs: Literary, mainstream/contemporary. No science fiction or romance. Upcoming theme: "Custer And The Indians" (deadline October '97). Receives 25 mss/month. Accepts 5 mss/year. Does not read mss November through December. Publishes ms up to 2 years after acceptance. Published work by Mark Sa Franko, Simon Peter Buehrer, E.S. Griggs, Jennifer Casteen and Jim Feltz. Publishes 3 new writers/year. Length: 5,000 words average; 10,000 words maximum. Publishes short shorts. Also publishes poetry. Sometimes critiques or comments on rejected mss.
How to Contact: Send complete ms with a cover letter. Include "short statement about who you are and why you write, along with any successes you have had. Please write to me like I am a human being." Send SASE for reply, return of ms or send a disposable copy of ms. "Please include SASE with all correspondence. Do not send postcards." Simultaneous submissions OK. Sample copy for $12. Make checks payable to T. Williams.

Payment/Terms: Pays 1 contributor's copy. Acquires one-time rights.
Advice: "Read as much contemporary fiction and poetry as you can get your hands on. Write about your deepest concerns. What you write can, and does, change lives. Always interested in works by Native American writers. I also don't get enough work by and about women. Be patient with the small presses. We work under terrific pressure. It's not about money; it's about the literature, caring about ideas that matter."

N SOUNDINGS EAST, (II), English Dept., Salem State College, Salem MA 01970. (508)741-6270. **Advisory Editors:** Joseph Salvatore and Sarah Messer. Magazine: 5½×8½; 64 pages; illustrations; photos. "Mainly a college audience, but we also distribute to libraries throughout the country." Biannual. Estab. 1973. Circ. 2,000.
Needs: Literary, contemporary, prose poem. No juvenile. Publishes 4-5 stories/issue. Receives 30 unsolicited fiction mss each month. Submissions limited to 2 fiction pieces, 5 poems, and/or 5 photos/illustrations. Deadlines: November 20, Fall/Winter issue; April 20, Spring/Summer issue. Recently published work by Antonya Nelson, Philip Gerard and Joe Salvatore; published new writers within the last year. Length: 250-4,000 words. "We are open to short pieces as well as to long works."
How to Contact: Send complete ms with SASE (or IRC). Accepts partial novels and multiple submissions if notified. Reports in 1-3 months on mss. Sample copy for $5.
Payment/Terms: Pays 2 contributor's copies. All publication rights revert to author.
Advice: "We're impressed by an excitement—coupled with craft—in the use of the language. It also helps to reach in and grab the reader by the heart."

✓ SOUTH CAROLINA REVIEW, (I, II), Strode Tower, Clemson University, Clemson SC 29634-1503. (864)656-5399. Fax: (864)656-1345. E-mail: cwayne@clemson.edu. **Editor:** Wayne Chapman. Magazine: 6×9; 200 pages; 60 lb. cream white vellum paper; 65 lb. cream white vellum cover stock. Semiannually. Estab. 1967. Circ. 700.
Needs: Literary and contemporary fiction, poetry, essays, reviews. Receives 50-60 unsolicited fiction mss each month. Does not read mss June through August or December. Published work by Joyce Carol Oates, Rosanne Coggeshall and Stephen Dixon. Published new writers within the last year. Rarely critiques rejected mss.
How to Contact: Send complete ms with SASE. Requires text on disk upon acceptance in WordPerfect or Microsoft Word format. Reports in 3-4 months on mss. "No unsolicited reviews." Sample copy for $5.
Payment/Terms: Pays in contributor's copies.

SOUTH DAKOTA REVIEW, (II), University of South Dakota, Box 111, University Exchange, Vermillion SD 57069. (605)677-5966. Fax: (605)677-5298. E-mail: bbedard@sunbird.usd.edu. Website: http://www.usd.edu/englisdr/index.html (includes masthead page with editors' names and submission/subscription guidelines, sample covers, sample story and essay excerpts and poems). **Editor:** Brian Bedard. Editorial Assistant: Geraldine Sanford. Magazine: 6×9; 160-180 pages; book paper; glossy cover stock; illustrations sometimes; photos on cover. "Literary magazine for university and college audiences and their equivalent. Emphasis is often on the American West and its writers, but will accept mss from anywhere. Issues are generally essay, fiction, and poetry with some literary essays." Quarterly. Estab. 1963. Circ. 500.
Needs: Literary, contemporary, ethnic, excerpted novel, regional. "We like very well-written, thematically ambitious, character-centered short fiction. Contemporary western American setting appeals, but not necessary. No formula stories, horror, or adolescent 'I' narrator." Receives 40 unsolicited fiction mss/month. Accepts about 40 mss/year. Assistant editor accepts mss in June through July, sometimes August. Agented fiction 5%. Publishes short shorts of 5 pages double-spaced typescript. Published work by Steve Heller, H.E. Francis, James Sallis, Ronna Wineberg, Lewis Horne and Rita Welty Bourke. Publishes 3-5 new writers/year. Length: 1,000-1,300 words minimum; 6,000 words maximum. (Has made exceptions, up to novella length.) Sometimes recommends other markets.
How to Contact: Send complete ms with SASE. Accepts queries/mss by fax. "We like cover letters that are not boastful and do not attempt to sell the stories but rather provide some personal information about the writer." Reports in 6-10 weeks. Publishes ms an average of 1-6 months after acceptance. Sample copy for $5.
Payment/Terms: Pays 1-year subscription, plus 2-4 contributor's copies, depending on length of ms; cover price charge for extras while issue is current, $3 when issue becomes a back issue.. Acquires first and reprint rights.
Advice: Rejects mss because of "careless writing; often careless typing; stories too personal ('I' confessional), aimlessness, unclear or unresolved conflicts; subject matter that editor finds clichéd, sensationalized, pretentious or trivial. We are trying to use more fiction and more variety."

✓ SOUTHERN CALIFORNIA ANTHOLOGY, (III), University of Southern California, Waite Phillips Hall, Room 404, Los Angeles CA 90089-4034. (213)740-3252. Fax: (213)740-5775. **Contact:** Editor. Magazine: 5½×8½; 142 pages; semigloss cover stock. "The *Southern California Anthology* is a literary review that is an eclectic collection of previously unpublished quality contemporary fiction, poetry and interviews with established literary people, published for adults of all professions; of particular interest to those interested in serious contemporary literature." Annually. Estab. 1983. Circ. 1,500.
Needs: Contemporary, ethnic, experimental, feminist, historical, humor/satire, literary, mainstream, regional, serialized/excerpted novel. No juvenile, religious, confession, romance, science fiction or pornography. Receives

40 unsolicited fiction mss each month. Accepts 10-12 mss/issue. Does not read February through September. Publishes ms 4 months after acceptance. Recently published work by Stuart Dybek, Larry Heinemann, Aram Saroyan, Susan Fromberg Schaeffer, Robley Wilson and Ross Talarico. Length: 10-15 pages average; 2 pages minimum; 25 pages maximum. Publishes short shorts.
How to Contact: Send complete ms with cover letter or submit through agent. Cover letter should include list of previous publications. Reports on queries in 1 month; on mss in 4 months. Send SASE for reply or return of ms. Sample copy for $4. Fiction guidelines for #10 SASE.
Payment/Terms: Pays in contributor's copies. Acquires first rights.
Advice: "The *Anthology* pays particular attention to craft and style in its selection of narrative writing."

SOUTHERN HUMANITIES REVIEW, (II, IV), Auburn University, 9088 Haley Center, Auburn University AL 36849. **Co-editors:** Dan R. Latimer and Virginia M. Kouidis. Magazine: 6×9; 100 pages; 60 lb. neutral pH, natural paper; 65 lb. neutral pH med. coated cover stock; occasional illustrations and photos. "We publish essays, poetry, fiction and reviews. Our fiction has ranged from very traditional in form and content to very experimental. Literate, college-educated audience. We hope they read our journal for both enlightenment and pleasure." Quarterly. Estab. 1967. Circ. 800.
Needs: Serious fiction, fantasy, feminist, humor and regional. Receives approximately 25 unsolicited fiction mss each month. Accepts 1-2 mss/issue, 4-6 mss/year. Slower reading time in summer. Published work by Anne Brashler, Heimito von Doderer and Ivo Andric; published new writers within the last year. Length: 3,500-15,000 words. Also publishes literary essays, literary criticism, poetry. Critiques rejected mss when there is time. Sometimes recommends other markets.
How to Contact: Send complete ms (one at a time) with SASE and cover letter with an explanation of topic chosen—"special, certain book, etc., a little about author if he/she has never submitted." Reports in 3 months. Sample copy for $5. Reviews novel and short story collections.
Payment/Terms: Pays 2 contributor's copies; $5 charge for extras. Rights revert to author upon publication. Sends galleys to author.
Advice: "Send us the ms with SASE. If we like it, we'll take it or we'll recommend changes. If we don't like it, we'll send it back as promptly as possible. Read the journal. Send typewritten, clean copy carefully proofread. We also award annually the Hoepfner Prize of $100 for the best published essay or short story of the year. Let someone whose opinion you respect read your story and give you an honest appraisal. Rewrite, if necessary, to get the most from your story."

☑ **SOUTHWEST REVIEW, (II)**, P.O. Box 750374, 307 Fondren Library West, Southern Methodist University, Dallas TX 75275-0374. (214)768-1037. **Editor:** Willard Spiegelman. Magazine: 6×9; 144 pages. "The majority of our readers are college-educated adults who wish to stay abreast of the latest and best in contemporary fiction, poetry, literary criticism and books in all but the most specialized disciplines." Quarterly. Estab. 1915. Circ. 1,600.
Needs: "High literary quality; no specific requirements as to subject matter, but cannot use sentimental, religious, western, poor science fiction, pornographic, true confession, mystery, juvenile or serialized or condensed novels." Receives approximately 200 unsolicited fiction mss each month. Published work by Bruce Berger, Thomas Larsen, Alice Hoffman, Matthew Sharpe, Floyd Skloot, Daniel Harris and Daniel Stern. Length: prefers 3,000-5,000 words. Also publishes literary essays and poetry. Occasionally critiques rejected mss.
How to Contact: Send complete ms with SASE. Reports in 6 months on mss. Publishes ms 6-12 months after acceptance. Sample copy for $6. Guidelines for SASE.
Payment/Terms: Payment varies; writers receive 3 contributor's copies. Pays on publication for first North American serial rights. Sends galleys to author.
Advice: "We have become less regional. A lot of time would be saved for us and for the writer if he or she looked at a copy of the *Southwest Review* before submitting. We like to receive a cover letter because it is some reassurance that the author has taken the time to check a current directory for the editor's name. When there isn't a cover letter, we wonder whether the same story is on 20 other desks around the country."

N **SOUTHWESTERN AMERICAN LITERATURE, (II, IV)**, Center for the Study of the Southwest, Southwest Texas State University, San Marcos TX 78666. (512)245-2232. Fax: (512)245-7462. E-mail: mb13@swt.edu. Editors: Mark Busby, D.M. Heaberlin. **Fiction Editor:** Mark Busby. Magazine: 6×9; 125 pages; 80 lb. cover stock. "We publish fiction, nonfiction, poetry, literary criticism and book reviews. Generally speaking, we

MARKET CATEGORIES: (I) Open to new writers; **(II)** Open to both new and established writers; **(III)** Interested mostly in established writers; **(IV)** Open to writers whose work is specialized; **(V)** Closed to unsolicited submissions.

want material concerning the Greater Southwest, or material written by southwestern writers." Semiannually. Estab. 1971. Circ. 300.

- A poem published in *Southwestern American Literature* was selected for the anthology, *Best Texas Writing 2*.

Needs: Ethnic/multicultural, literary, mainstream/contemporary, regional. Receives 10-15 unsolicited mss/month. Accepts 1-2 mss/issue; 4-5 mss/year. Publishes ms up to 6 months after acceptance. Recently published work by Jerry Craven, Paul Ruffin, Robert Flynn and Philip Heldrich. Length: 6,000 words average; 6,250 words maximum. Publishes short shorts. Also publishes literary essays, literary criticism, poetry. Sometimes critiques or comments on rejected ms.
How to Contact: Send complete ms with a cover letter. Include estimated word count, 200-word bio and list of publications. Reports in 1-2 months. SASE for return of ms. Simultaneous submissions OK. Sample copy $7. Fiction guidelines free. Reviews novels and short story collections. Send books to Mark Busby.
Payment/Terms: Pays 2 contributor's copies; additional copies $7. Acquires first rights.
Advice: "We look for crisp language, interesting approach to material; regional emphasis is desired but not required."

$ SPELUNKER FLOPHOUSE, (II), P.O. Box 617742, Chicago IL 60661. E-mail: spelunkerf@aol.com. Website: members.aol.com/spelunkerf/ (includes guidelines, excerpts, magazine history, how to subscribe, etc.). **Editors:** Chris Kubica and Wendy Morgan. Magazine: 8½×7; 96 pages; offset print; perfect-bound; 4-color glossy card cover. "We offer the best poetry, fiction and artwork we can in an inventive, original format. We cooperate regularly with other literary magazines." Quarterly. Estab. 1996. Press run: 1,500.
Needs: Ethnic/multicultural, experimental, feminist, humor/satire, literary, translations. "We are especially interested in fiction and poetry exploring small details of everyday life." No genre fiction. Receives 100 unsolicited mss/month. Accepts 3-6 mss/issue; 12-24 mss/year. Publishes ms 4 months after acceptance. Agented fiction: 5%. Recently published work by Edward Falco, Stephen Dixon, Julie Checkoway, Chris Mazza, W.P. Kinsella, Denise Duhamel and Carolyn Alessio. Publishes 5-20 new writers/year. Length: 100 words minimum; 10,000 words maximum. Publishes short shorts. Also publishes poetry. Often critiques or comments on rejected mss. Sponsors contest. Look for guidelines in the magazine.
How to Contact: Send complete ms with a cover letter. Include bio, list of publications if available and any brief interesting information about yourself. Reports in 4-10 weeks on mss. Send SASE for return of the ms or send a disposable copy of the ms. Simultaneous submissions OK, if noted. Sample copy for $6.95 postpaid. Fiction guidelines free with #10 SASE. Occasionally reviews fiction or poetry in book form.
Payment/Terms: Pays "depending on current cash flow" and 2 contributor's copies. Pays on publication. Acquires first North American serial rights. Sends galleys to author.
Advice: "We are interested in stories that have a strong sense of character, technique, language, realistic dialogue, unique style/voice, and (if possible) a plot. No restrictions on length or subject matter except no genre work or 'statements.' Nothing patently cute. Support this necessary forum for the arts by purchasing copies of literary magazines, reading them, and increasing local awareness of magazines/forums such as ours whenever possible. Study the market; then submit. And keep in touch. We love to hear from members/supporters of the literary community."

$ THE SPIRIT (OF WOMAN IN THE MOON), A New Age Literary Magazine, (I, II), 1409 The Alameda, San Jose CA 95126. (408)279-6626. Fax: (408)279-6636. Magazine: 8×11; 36 pages; 60 lb. white paper; glossy cover stock; illustrations and photos. "*The Spirit*is a positive, upbeat and informative publication. We are particularly interested in material on current New Age feminist topics." Semiannually. Estab. 1993. Circ. 3,000. Member Publishing Triangle. "Every submission must include the reading fee which includes a current issue of *The Spirit*: Poetry (5-poem packet), $12; Fiction and nonfiction, $30 up to 5 pages, $3 for each additional page."
Needs: Ethnic/multicultural, feminist, gay, lesbian, literary, psychic/supernatural/occult, religious/inspirational, science fiction (soft/sociological), serialized novel, African-American, new age views. Likes narrative, futuristic, humanist. Receives 5-30 unsolicited mss/month. Accepts 3-5 mss/issue; 60 mss/year. Publishes mss 2 quarters after acceptance. Recently published work by Wu Hsien. Length: 500-1,500 words average. Publishes short shorts. Also publishes poetry. Always critiques or comments on rejected mss.
How to Contact: Query first. Include word count, 1-paragraph bio, Social Security number, list of publications (10 best) and photo (for publication) with submission. Reports in 2 weeks on queries; 6 weeks on mss. Send SASE for reply, return of ms or send a disposable copy of ms. Simultaneous, reprint and electronic submissions (disk or modem) OK. Sample copy for $4.50 and 6×10 SAE (no IRCs, please). Fiction guidelines free. Reviews novels and short story collections. Send books to Scott Shuker, review editor.
Payment/Terms: Pays $10-100, free subscription to magazine and 2 contributor's copies; additional copies $4.50. Pays on publication. Acquires first North American serial rights or reprint rights.
Advice: "Don't send us things that are meant to be appreciated by the majority culture. We are a niche for new age ideas given the explosive interest in science fiction, psychic phenomenon and angels We want diversity."

SPITBALL, (I), 5560 Fox Rd., Cincinnati OH 45239. (513)385-2268. **Editor:** Mike Shannon. Magazine: 5½×8½; 96 pages; 55 lb. Glatfelter Natural, neutral pH paper; 10 pt. CS1 cover stock; illustrations; photos.

Magazine publishing "fiction and poetry about *baseball* exclusively for an educated, literary segment of the baseball fan population." Biannually. Estab. 1981. Circ. 1,000.

Needs: Confession, contemporary, experimental, historical, literary, mainstream and suspense. "Our only requirement concerning the type of fiction written is that the story be *primarily* about baseball." Receives 100 unsolicited fiction mss/year. Accepts 16-20 mss/year. Published work by Dallas Wiebe, Michael Gilmartin and W.P. Kinsella; published new writers within the last year. Length: 20 typed double-spaced pages. "The longer it is, the better it has to be."

How to Contact: Send complete ms with cover letter and SASE. Include brief bio about author. Reporting time varies. Publishes ms an average of 3 months after acceptance. *First-time submitters are required to purchase a sample copy for $6.*

Payment/Terms: "No monetary payment at present. We may offer nominal payment in the near future." 2 free contributor's copies per issue in which work appears. Acquires first North American serial rights.

Advice: "Our audience is mostly college educated and knowledgeable about baseball. The stories we have published so far have been very well written and displayed a firm grasp of the baseball world and its people. In short, audience response has been great because the stories are simply good as stories. Thus, mere use of baseball as subject is no guarantee of acceptance. We are always seeking submissions. Unlike many literary magazines, we have no backlog of accepted material. Fiction is a natural genre for our exclusive subject, baseball. There are great opportunities for writing in certain areas of fiction, baseball being one of them. Baseball has become the 'in' spectator sport among intellectuals, the general media and the 'yuppie' crowd. Consequently, as subject matter for adult fiction it has gained a much wider acceptance than it once enjoyed."

☑ **SPOUT, (I, II)**, Spout Press, 28 W. Robie St., St. Paul MN 55107. (612)379-7737. E-mail: colb0018@gold.tc.umn.edu. Editors: John Colburn and Michelle Filkins. **Fiction Editor:** Chris Watercott. Magazine: 8½×11; 40 pages; 70 lb. flat white paper; colored cover; illustrations. "We like the surprising, the surreal and the experimental. Our readers are well-read, often writers." Triannually. Estab. 1989. Circ. 300-500.

• *Spout* editors submit work to the *Pushcart* anthology. They would like to see more sudden fiction.

Needs: Condensed/excerpted novel, ethnic/multicultural, experimental, feminist, gay, humor/satire, lesbian, literary, regional, translations. No horror. Publishes special fiction issues or anthologies. Receives 25-30 unsolicited mss/month. Accepts 4-5 mss/issue; 15 mss/year. Publishes ms 1-3 months after acceptance. Agented fiction 5%. Recently published work by Mario Benedetti, Layle Silbert, Stephen Gutierrez and Michael Little.Publishes 5 new writers/year. Length: open. Publishes short shorts and "sudden" fiction. Also publishes poetry. Seldom comments on rejected mss.

How to Contact: Send complete ms with a cover letter. Include short bio and list of publications with submission. Reports in 1 month on queries; 2-3 months on mss. Send SASE for reply, return of ms or send a disposable copy of ms. Simultaneous submissions OK. Sample copy for $3, 8½×11 SAE and 5 first-class stamps. Fiction guidelines for SASE.

Payment/Terms: Pays 1 contributor's copy; additional copies for $3 plus postage. Acquires one-time rights.

Advice: Looks for "imagination, surprise and attention to language. We often publish writers on their third or fourth submission, so don't get discouraged. We need more weird, surreal fiction that lets the reader make his/her own meaning. Don't send moralistic, formulaic work."

$ SPRING FANTASY, (I), Women In The Arts, P.O. Box 2907, Decatur IL 62524. **Contact:** Vice President (newly elected each year). Magazine. "An annual anthology of short stories, juvenile fiction, poetry, essays and black & white artwork; *Spring Fantasy* aims to encourage beginners, especially women." Estab. 1994.

Needs: Adventure, children's/juvenile, fantasy, feminist, historical, horror, humor/satire, literary, mystery/suspense (amateur sleuth, cozy, police procedural, private eye/hardboiled, romantic suspense), romance, science fiction, young adult/teen (adventure, horror, mystery, romance, science fiction, western). Length: 1,500 words maximum.

How to Contact: Send complete ms without a cover letter. Reports in 4 months. Send SASE for reply, return of ms or send a disposable copy of ms. Simultaneous submissions and reprints OK. Sample copy for $6. Guidelines for #10 SASE.

Payment/Terms: Pays $5-30 honorarium on publication and 1 contributor's copy; 20% discount on additional copies. Acquires first and reprint rights. Sponsors annual contest with cash prizes; send SASE for information.

$ SPSM&H, (II, IV), *Amelia* Magazine, 329 "E" St., Bakersfield CA 93304. (805)323-4064. **Editor:** Frederick A. Raborg, Jr. Magazine: 5½×8¼; 24 pages; matte cover stock; illustrations and photos. "*SPSM&H* publishes sonnets, sonnet sequences and fiction, articles and reviews related to the form (fiction may be romantic or Gothic) for a general readership and sonnet enthusiasts." Quarterly. Estab. 1985. Circ. 600.

• This magazine is edited by Frederick A. Raborg, Jr., who is also editor of *Amelia* and *Cicada*.

Needs: Adventure, confession, contemporary, erotica, ethnic, experimental, fantasy, feminist, gay, historical, horror, humor/satire, lesbian, literary, mainstream, mystery/suspense, regional, romance (contemporary, historical), science fiction, senior citizen/retirement, translations and western. All should have romantic element. "We look for strong fiction with romantic or Gothic content, or both. Stories need not have 'happy' endings, and we are open to the experimental and/or avant-garde. Erotica is fine; pornography, no." Receives 30 unsolicited mss/month. Accepts 1 ms/issue; 4 mss/year. Publishes ms 6 months to 1 year after acceptance. Agented fiction 5%.

Published work by Brad Hooper, Mary Louise R. O'Hara and Clara Castelar Bjorlie. Length: 2,000 words average; 500 words minimum; 3,000 words maximum. Critiques rejected ms when appropriate; recommends other markets.
How to Contact: Send complete ms with cover letter. Include Social Security number. Reports in 2 weeks. SASE. Sample copy for $4.95. Fiction guidelines for #10 SASE.
Payment/Terms: Pays $10-25 and contributor's copies on publication for first North American serial rights; charge for extra copies.
Advice: "A good story line (plot) and strong characterization are vital. I want to know the writer has done his homework and is striving to become professional."

STAPLE, Tor Cottage 81, Cavendish Rd., Matlock DE4 3HD United Kingdom. **Fiction Editor:** Don Measham. Published 3 times/year. Circ. up to 600. Publishes up to 50% fiction. *Staple* is "about 90 pages, perfect-bound; beautifully designed and produced."
Needs: "Stories used by *Staple* have ranged from social realism (through autobiography, parody, prequel, parable) to visions and hallucinations. We don't use unmodified genre fiction, i.e., adventure, crime or westerns. We are interested in extracts from larger works—provided author does the extraction." Length: 200 words minimum; 5,000 words maximum.
How to Contact: Adequate IRCs and large envelope for return, if return is required. Otherwise IRC for decision only. Please note that *Staple* requires stories to be previously unpublished worldwide.
Payment/Terms: Pays complimentary copy plus subscription for US contributors. Get a specimen copy of one of the issues with strong prose representation. Send $10 for airmail dispatch, $5 for surface mail.

$ STONE SOUP, The Magazine By Young Writers and Artists, (I, IV), Children's Art Foundation, Box 83, Santa Cruz CA 95063. (408)426-5557. E-mail: gmandel@stonesoup.com. Website: http://www.stonesoup.com (includes writer's guidelines, sample copy, links, curriculum matrix, international children's art). **Editor:** Gerry Mandel. Magazine: 7×10; 48 pages; high quality paper; photos. Stories, poems, book reviews and art by children through age 13. Readership: children, librarians, educators. Published 6 times/year. Estab. 1973. Circ. 20,000.

- This is known as "the literary journal for children." *Stone Soup* has previously won the Ed Press Golden Lamp Honor Award and the Parent's Choice Award.

Needs: Fiction by children on themes based on their own experiences, observations or special interests. Also, some fantasy, mystery, adventure. No clichés, no formulas, no writing exercises; original work only. Receives approximately 1,000 unsolicited fiction mss each month. Accepts approximately 15 mss/issue. Published new writers within the last year. Length: 150-2,500 words. Also publishes literary essays and poetry. Critiques rejected mss upon request.
How to Contact: Send complete ms with cover letter. "We like to learn a little about our young writers, why they like to write, and how they came to write the story they are submitting." SASE. No simultaneous submissions. Reports in 1 month on mss. Does not respond to mss that are not accompanied by an SASE. Publishes ms an average of 3-6 months after acceptance. Sample copy for $4. Guidelines for SASE. Reviews children's books.
Payment/Terms: Pays $10 plus 2 contributor's copies; $2.50 charge for extras. Buys all rights.
Advice: Mss are rejected because they are "derivatives of movies, TV, comic books; or classroom assignments or other formulas."

$ STONEFLOWER LITERARY JOURNAL, (II), Stoneflower Press, 1824 Nacogdoches, Suite 191, San Antonio TX 78209. E-mail: stonflower@aol.com. Editor: Brenda Davidson-Shaddox. Fiction Coordinator: Coley Scott. Journal: 5½×4; 125 pages; 50 lb. white offset paper; 8 pt. carolina C1S cover stock; illustrations (ink drawings only) and photographs (b&w only). Annually. Estab. 1996.

- *Stoneflower Literary Journal* is not currently reading unsolicited manuscripts.

Needs: Recently published work by Carlos Brown, Jane Butkin Roth and Adina Sara. Publishes short shorts, poetry. "We also publish one interview or profile each issue. Subject should be writer, editor, agent, artist, publisher, photographer or other professional whose primary career is creative." Sometimes (but rarely) critiques or comments on rejected mss.
Payment/Terms: "Short story writers receive $10/story; interview $10/work; poetry $5/poem." Pays on publication. Acquires one-time rights. Sponsors contest; "send SASE (9″ envelope with one first-class stamp for guidelines. First place fiction winner $75; 2nd place $25. First place poetry $50; 2nd place $10. All honorable mentions receive free copy of journal. Winners names announced in the journal."
Advice: "Technically correct writing combined with colorful, exciting use of the language helps. A story must draw us in quickly. If we lose interest by the end of the first page, we quit reading. In addition to good writing, clean, professionally prepared manuscripts are a must. Will not read handwritten manuscripts. Don't use clichés. Watch spelling. Stay away from passive verbs. Don't choose an exotic topic; write about what people care about. Above all, study creative writing—either on your own or in classes—and read, read, read. Nothing improves one's writing more than exposure to other good writers."

$ STORY, (II), F&W Publications, 1507 Dana Ave., Cincinnati OH 45207. (513)531-2222. Fax: (513)531-1843. Website: http://www.writersdigest.com (includes guidelines, contest and subscription information, index, preview of current issue, back issue sales). **Editor:** Lois Rosenthal. Magazine: 6¼×9½; 128 pages; uncoated, recycled paper; uncoated index stock. "We publish the finest quality short stories. Will consider unpublished novel excerpts if they are self-inclusive." Quarterly. Estab. 1931.

- STORY won the National Magazine Award for Fiction in 1992 and 1995, and was a finalist in 1994, 1996 and 1997. STORY holds two annual contests, STORY's Short Short Story Competition and the Carson McCullers Prize for the Short Story.

Needs: Literary, experimental, humor, mainstream, translations. No genre fiction—science fiction, detective, young adult, confession, romance, etc. Accepts approximately 12 mss/issue. Agented fiction 50-60%. Published work by Joyce Carol Oates, Carol Shields, Tobias Wolff, Madison Smartt Bell, Rick DeMarinis, Richard Bausch, Rick Bass, Charles Baxter, Tess Gallagher, Rick Moody, Ellen Gilchrist, and Thom Jones; publishes new writers as well as those who are well established. Length: up to 8,000 words.

How to Contact: Send complete ms with or without cover letter, or submit through agent. SASE necessary for return of ms and response. We do not accept fax or electronic submissions. "Will accept simultaneous submissions as long as it is stated in a cover letter." Sample copy for $6.95, 9×12 SAE and $2.40 postage. Fiction guidelines for #10 SASE.

Payment/Terms: Pays $1,000 for stories; $750 for short shorts plus 5 contributor's copies on acceptance for first North American serial rights. Sends galleys to author.

Advice: "We accept fiction of the highest quality, whether by established or new writers. Since we receive more than 300 submissions each week, there is avid competition. We look for original subject matter and fresh voices. Read issues of STORY before trying us."

N 🌐 **STORYBOARD, A Journal of Pacific Imagery, (II, IV)**, Division of English, University of Guam, Mangilao, Guam 96923. Phone: (671)735-2749. Fax: (671)734-0010. E-mail: jtalley@uoga.uog.edu. Website: http://www.uog2.uog.edu/strybrd/STORYBOARD. **Editor:** Jeannine E. Talley. Editors change each year. Magazine: 100 pages; illustrations and photographs. "A multilingual journal with a focus on Pacific writing and writers. We publish short fiction, creative nonfiction and poetry." Annually. Estab. 1991. Circ. 300. Member of Council of Literary Magazines and Presses.

- Material sent to *Storyboard* must relate to the Pacific region or be written by an indigenous Pacific writer.

Needs: Ethnic/multicultural (Pacific region), experimental, family saga, regional (Pacific region). Receives 10-15 unsolicited mss/month. Accepts 30-40 mss/issue. Publishes ms 6-12 months after acceptance. Agented fiction 50-75%. Length: 1,000 words average. Publishes short shorts. Also publishes poetry.

How to Contact: Send complete ms with a cover letter. Accepts queries/mss by e-mail. Include bio. Reports in 1-4 weeks on queries; 4-6 months on mss. Send SASE for reply, return of ms or send a disposable copy of ms. Sample copy $6 and 7×10 SAE. Fiction guidelines free.

Payment/Terms: Pays 2 contributor's copies; additional copies $7.50.

N **STOVEPIPE, A Journal of Little Literary Value, (I, II)**, P.O. Box 1076, Georgetown KY 40324. E-mail: troyteegarden@worldradio.org. **Editor:** Troy Teegarden. Magazine: 8½×5½; 30-60 pages; 70 lb. paper; card stock cover; illustrations. "We like to have a good time with what we read. We publish fiction, nonfiction, poetry and black and white art." Quarterly. Estab. 1995. Circ. 250.

Needs: Comics/graphic novels, experimental, humor/satire, literary, short story collections. No religious, fantasy. Receives 10 unsolicited mss/month. Accepts 1-2 mss/issue; 4-8 mss/year. Publishes ms 1-3 months after acceptance. Publishes 4-8 new writers/year. Recently published work by Ron Whitehead and Charles Chaim Wax. Length: 3,500 words maximum. Publishes short shorts. "We really dig short short stories." Also publishes poetry. Often critiques or comments on rejected ms.

How to Contact: Send complete ms with a cover letter. Accepts queries by e-mail. Include estimated word count, short but informative bio and list of publications. Reports in 1-2 weeks on queries; 1 month on mss. Send SASE for reply, return of ms. Sample copy $2 or send 5½×8½ SAE with 78¢ postage. Fiction guidelines for #10 SASE.

Payment/Terms: Pays 1-3 contributor's copies; additional copies $2. Acquires one-time rights.

Advice: "Stories must be interesting and new and they must offer something original to the reader. We don't see much fiction but would like to publish more."

☑ **$ STREET BEAT QUARTERLY, (I, II)**, Wood Street Commons, 301 Third Ave., Pittsburgh PA 15222. (412)765-3302. Fax: (412)765-2187. **Editor:** Charlene Hoffer. Contact: Sharon Thorp. Magazine: 8½×11; 32 pages; newsprint paper; newsprint cover; illustrations and photos. "*Street Beat Quarterly* publishes (primarily) literary works by those who have experienced homelessness or poverty. We reach those interested in literary magazines and others interested in homelessness issues." Quarterly. Estab. 1990. Circ. 2,000-3,000.

Needs: Adventure, ethnic/multicultural, experimental, fantasy, feminist, historical, humor/satire, literary, mainstream/contemporary, mystery/suspense, stories by children. "No religious." Receives 2 unsolicited mss/month. Accepts 2-5 mss/issue. Publishes ms 1-3 months after acceptance. Published work by Freddy Posco, James Burroughs and Mel Spivak. Length: 750 words average; 100 words minimum; 10,000 words maximum. Publishes short shorts. Also publishes literary essays and poetry. Sometimes critiques or comments on rejected mss.

How to Contact: Send complete ms with a cover letter including bio. Reports in 1 month on mss. Send a disposable copy of ms. Simultaneous, reprint and electronic submissions OK. Sample copy for 3 first-class stamps.
Payment/Terms: Pays $3 plus 1 contributor's copy on publication for one-time rights.
Advice: "We are pretty flexible. Our mission is to publish work by those who have experienced homelessness and poverty; we will consider a limited amount of works by others if it is on the topic (homelessness/poverty). Don't be afraid of us! We are very much a grass-roots publication. Be patient with us; as we sometimes take a short while to respond. We publish some very polished work; we also publish some very 'rough' yet energetic work. We are looking for stories that truly capture the experience of homelessness and poverty on a personal level."

STRUGGLE, A Magazine of Proletarian Revolutionary Literature, (I, II), Box 13261, Detroit MI 48213-0261. (213)273-9039. **Editor:** Tim Hall. Magazine: 5½×8½; 36-72 pages; 20 lb. white bond paper; colored cover; illustrations; occasional photographs. Publishes material related to "the struggle of the working class and all progressive people against the rule of the rich—including their war policies, racism, exploitation of the workers, oppression of women, etc." Quarterly. Estab. 1985.
Needs: Contemporary, ethnic, experimental, feminist, historical (general), humor/satire, literary, prose poem, regional, science fiction, senior citizen/retirement, translations, young adult/teen (10-18). "The theme can be approached in many ways, including plenty of categories not listed here. Would like to see more fiction that depicts the life, work and struggle of the working class of every background; also the struggles of the 1930s and 60s illustrated and brought to life." No romance, psychic, mystery, western, erotica, religious. Receives 10-12 unsolicited fiction mss/month. Publishes ms 6 months or less after acceptance. Recently published work by Alan Bernstein, Bill Embly, Dennis Hammond, Anne Jupiter, Amy Dolejs and Deborah Correnti. Published new writers within the last year. Length: 1,000-3,000 words average; 4,000 words maximum. Publishes short shorts. Normally critiques rejected mss.
How to Contact: Send complete ms; cover letter optional. "Tries to" report in 3-4 months. SASE. Simultaneous and reprint submissions OK. Sample copy for $2.50. Make checks payable to Tim Hall-Special Account.
Payment/Terms: Pays 2 contributor's copies. No rights acquired. Publication not copyrighted.
Advice: "Write about the oppression of the working people, the poor, the minorities, women, and if possible, their rebellion against it—we are not interested in anything which accepts the status quo. We are not too worried about plot and advanced technique (fine if we get them!)—we would probably accept things others would call sketches, provided they have life and struggle. For new writers: just describe for us a situation in which some real people confront some problem of oppression, however seemingly minor. Observe and put down the real facts. Experienced writers: try your 'committed'/experimental fiction on us. We get poetry all the time. We have increased our fiction portion of our content in the last few years. The quality of fiction that we have published has continued to improve. If your work raises an interesting issue of literature and politics, it may get discussed in letters and in my editorial. I suggest ordering a sample."

✔ **SULPHUR RIVER LITERARY REVIEW, (II),** P.O. Box 19228, Austin TX 78760-9228. (512)292-9456. **Editor:** James Michael Robbins. Magazine: 5½×8½; 130 pages; illustrations and photos. "*SRLR* publishes literature of quality—poetry and short fiction with appeal that transcends time. Audience includes a broad spectrum of readers, mostly educated, many of whom are writers, artists and educators." Semiannually. Estab. 1978. Circ. 400.
Needs: Ethnic/multicultural, experimental, feminist, humor/satire, literary, mainstream/contemporary and translations. No "religious, juvenile, teen, sports, romance or mystery." Receives 10-12 unsolicited mss/month. Accepts 2-3 mss/issue; 4-6 mss/year. Publishes ms 1-2 years after acceptance. Recently published work by Aris Fioretos, Ivan A. Bunin, Kevin Meaux and Jamie Brown. Publishes short shorts. Also publishes literary essays, literary criticism and poetry. Often critiques or comments on rejected mss.
How to Contact: Send complete ms with a cover letter. Include short bio and list of publications. Reports in 1 week on queries; 1 month on mss. Send SASE for reply, return of ms or send a disposable copy of ms. No simultaneous submissions. Sample copy for $6.
Payment/Terms: Pays 2 contributor's copies; additional copies for $6. Acquires first North American serial rights.
Advice: Looks for "originality, mastery of the language, imagination. Revise, revise, revise."

✔ **SUN DOG: THE SOUTHEAST REVIEW, (III),** English Department, Florida State University, Tallahassee FL 32306. (904)644-4230. E-mail: mgw0657@mailer.fsu.edu. Website: http://www.english.fsu.edu/sundog/ (includes names of editors, short fiction and writer's guidelines). **Editors:** Miles Garett Watson, Jarret Keene

READ THE BUSINESS OF FICTION WRITING section to learn the correct way to prepare and submit a manuscript.

(fiction) and Ryan G. Van Cleave (poetry). Magazine: 6×9; 60-100 pages; 70 lb. paper; 10 pt. Krome Kote cover; illustrations; photos. Biannually. Estab. 1979. Circ. 2,000.

Needs: "We want stories (under 3,000 words) with striking images, fresh language, and a consistent voice." No genre fiction. Publishes 4-6 new writers/year. We receive approximately 180 submissions per month; we accept less than 5%. Response time averages 2 months. We will comment briefly on rejected mss when time permits.

How to Contact: Send complete ms with SASE and a brief cover letter. Publishes ms an average of 2-6 months after acceptance. Sample copy for $5. Subscriptions for $9.

Payment/Terms: Pays 2 contributor's copies. Acquires first North American serial rights which then revert to author.

Advice: "Avoid trendy experimentation for its own sake (present-tense narration, observation that isn't also revelation). Fresh stories, moving, interesting characters and a sensitivity to language are still fiction mainstays. Also publishes winner and runners-up of the World's Best Short Short Story Contest sponsored by the Florida State University English Department."

THE SUNFLOWER DREAM, (I, II), Sunflower Press, P.O. Box 1883, Galesburg IL 61402-1883. (309)341-1399. **Editor:** M.L. Moeller. Magazine: 8½×11; 100-200 pages; illustrations and photographs. "I want poetry/short stories most people can say, 'Hey, I understand that.' " Quarterly. Estab. 1996. Circ. 200.

Needs: Adventure, fantasy (science fantasy, sword and sorcery), historical, horror, humor/satire, literary, mainstream/contemporary, mystery/suspense (amateur sleuth, romantic suspense), psychic/supernatural/occult, religious/inspirational, romance (contemporary, futuristic/time travel, gothic, historical), science fiction (soft/sociological), westerns (frontier), young adult/teen (adventure, horror, mystery, romance, science fiction). No pornography. Publishes special fiction issues or anthologies. Receives 35 unsolicited mss/month. Accepts 10-15 mss/issue; 40-60 mss/year. Publishes ms 3-4 months after acceptance. Recently published work by Scott Fisher, Marshall Myers, Kevin Ashby and Uncle Mickey. Length: 2,000 words average; 3,000 words maximum. Publishes short shorts. Also publishes literary essays, literary criticism, poetry.

How to Contact: Send complete ms with a cover letter. Include estimated word count, bio and list of publications. Reports in 1-2 months on queries; 4-6 weeks on mss. Send SASE for reply, return of ms or send a disposable copy of ms. Simultaneous submissions and reprints OK. Sample copy for $5. Fiction guidelines free. Reviews novels and short story collections.

Payment/Terms: Acquires first rights or one-time rights. Sponsors contest. "The magazine guidelines include the contest, which is ongoing."

Advice: "I look for quality, pace, and whether it catches my interest and holds it. Write your best . . . and keep on trying. It's very unusual for the first thing you ever write to be accepted. Even very good writers get rejection slips. I see a lot of 'stories' that show how much popular reading the writer does. Reading is very important."

SYCAMORE REVIEW, (II), Department of English, Purdue University, West Lafayette IN 47907. (765)494-3783. Fax: (765)494-3780. E-mail: sycamore@expert.cc.purdue.edu. Website: http://www.sla.purdue.edu/academic/engl/sycamore (includes back and current issues, index, submission guidelines, subscription information, journal library). **Editor-in-Chief:** Sarah Griffiths. Editors change every two years. Send fiction to Fiction Editor, poetry to Poetry Editor, all other correspondence to Editor-in-Chief. Magazine: 5½×8½; 150-200 pages; heavy, textured, uncoated paper; heavy laminated cover. "Journal devoted to contemporary literature. We publish both traditional and experimental fiction, personal essay, poetry, interviews, drama and graphic art. Novel excerpts welcome if they stand alone as a story." Semiannually. Estab. 1989. Circ. 1,000.

- Work published in *Sycamore Review* has been selected for inclusion in the *Pushcart Prize* anthology. The magazine was also named "The Best Magazine from Indiana" by the *Clockwatch Review.*

Needs: Contemporary, experimental, humor/satire, literary, mainstream, regional, translations. "We generally avoid genre literature, but maintain no formal restrictions on style or subject matter. No science fiction, romance, children's." Publishes ms 3 months to 1 year after acceptance. Recently published work by Doris Dörrie, Lucia Perillo and Bill Embly. 10% of material published is by new writers. Length: 3,750 words preferred; 250 words minimum. Also publishes poetry, "this most recently included Charles Wright, Sandra Gilbert and Caroline Knox." Sometimes critiques rejected mss and recommends other markets.

How to Contact: Send complete ms with cover letter. Cover letter should include previous publications and address changes. Does not read mss May through August. Reports in 4 months. SASE. Simultaneous submissions OK. Sample copy for $7. Fiction guidelines for #10 SASE.

Payment/Terms: Pays in contributor's copies; charge for extras. Acquires one-time rights.

Advice: "We publish both new and experienced authors but we're always looking for stories with strong emotional appeal, vivid characterization and a distinctive narrative voice; fiction that breaks new ground while still telling an interesting and significant story. Avoid gimmicks and trite, predictable outcomes. Write stories that have a ring of truth, the impact of felt emotion. Don't be afraid to submit, send your best."

N $ **TAKAHE**, P.O. Box 13-335, Christchurch, New Zealand. **Editors:** Isa Moynihan, Bernadette Hall and Cassandra Fusco. "A literary magazine which appears three or four times a year, and publishes short stories and poetry by both established and emerging writers. The publisher is the Takahe Collective Trust, a charitable trust formed by established writers to help new writers and get them into print. While insisting on correct British spelling (or recognised spellings in foreign languages), smart quotes, and at least internally-consistent punctuation, we, nonetheless, try to allow some latitude in presentation. Any use of foreign languages must be accompanied by an English translation. There is a small payment for work published."

TALKING RIVER REVIEW, (I, II), Lewis-Clark State College, Division of Literature and Languages, 500 8th Ave., Lewiston ID 83501. (208)799-2307. Fax: (208)799-2324. E-mail: triver@lcsc.edu. Editor: Dennis Held. **Fiction Editor:** Claire Davis. Magazine: 6×9; 150 pages; 60 lb. paper; coated, color cover; illustrations and photos. "We publish the best work by well-known and unknown authors; our audience is literary but unpretentious." Semiannually. Estab. 1994. Circ. 500.

Needs: Condensed/excerpted novel, ethnic/multicultural, feminist, historical, humor/satire, literary, mainstream/contemporary, regional. "Wants more well-written, character-driven stories that surprise and delight the reader with fresh, arresting yet unself-conscious language, imagery, metaphor, revelation." No surprise endings; plot-driven stories; or stories that are sexist, racist, homophobic, erotic for shock value, romance. Receives 200 unsolicited mss/month. Accepts 5-8 mss/issue; 10-15 mss/year. Does not read March to September. Publishes ms up to 1 year after acceptance. Agented fiction 10%. Recently published work by Gary Gildner, David Cates, Pete Fromm, Kate Gadbow, David Long, Mary Clearman Blew and Charlene L. Curry. Publishes 10 new writers/year. Length: 3,000 words average; 7,500 words maximum. Rarely publishes short shorts. Also publishes literary essays and poetry. Sometimes critiques or comments on rejected mss.

How to Contact: Send complete manuscript with a cover letter. Include estimated word count, 2-sentence bio, Social Security number and list of publications. Reports in 3 months on mss. Send SASE for reply, return of ms or send disposable copy of ms. Simultaneous submissions OK if indicated. Sample copy for $4. Fiction guidelines for #10 SASE.

Payment/Terms: Pays 2 contributor's copies and a year's subscription for one-time rights; additional copies $4.

Advice: "Revise, revise, revise. Read more widely, including poetry."

N $ TAMEME, (I), New writing from North America/Nueva literatura de Norteamérica, Tameme, Inc., 199 First St., Suite 204, Los Altos CA 94022. (650)941-2037. E-mail: editor@tameme.org. Website: http://www.tameme.org (includes editor, contributors, staff, index of magazine). **Editor:** C.M. Mayo. Magazine: 6×9; 220 pages; good quality paper; heavy cover stock; illustrations; photos. "*Tameme* is an annual fully bilingual magazine dedicated to publishing new writing from North America in side-by-side English-Spanish format. *Tameme*'s goals are to play an instrumental role in introducing important new writing from Canada and the United States to Mexico, and vice versa, and to provide a forum for the art of literary translation." Estab. 1996. Circ. 1,500. Member Council of Literary Magazines and Presses (CLMP).

Needs: Ethnic/multicultural, literary, translations. No genre fiction. Plans special fiction issue or anthology. Receives 10-15 unsolicited mss/month. No romance, mystery or western. Accepts 3-4 mss/issue; 6-8 mss/year, "but we are a new magazine so these numbers may not be indicative of a year from now." Publishes ms 1 year after acceptance. Agented fiction 5%. Recently published work by Fabio Morábito, Margaret Atwood, Juan Villoro, Jaime Sabines, Edwidge Danticat, A. Manette Ansay, Douglas Glover and Marianne Toussaint. Publishes 2-3 new writers/year. Publishes short shorts. Also publishes literary essays and poetry. Sometimes critiques or comments on mss.

How to Contact: Send complete ms with a cover letter. Translators query or submit mss with cover letter, curriculum vita and samples of previous work. Include 1-paragraph bio and list of publications. Reports in 6 weeks on queries; 3 months on mss. Send SASE for reply, return of ms or send a disposable copy of ms. Simultaneous submissions OK, "if we are advised when the manuscript is submitted." Sample copy for $16.95. Fiction guidelines for SASE.

Payment/Terms: Pays 3 contributor's copies to writers; $20 per double-spaced WordPerfect page to translators. Pays on publication. Acquires one-time rights. Sends galleys to author.

Advice: "We're looking for whatever makes us want to stand up and shout YES! Read the magazine, send for guidelines (with SASE), then send only your best, with SASE."

✓ $ TAMPA REVIEW, (I, II), 401 W. Kennedy Blvd., Box 19F, University of Tampa, Tampa FL 33606-1490. (813)253-6266, ext. 6266. Fax: (813)258-7593. E-mail: utpress@alpha.utampa.edu. Editor: Richard Mathews. **Fiction Editors:** Lisa Birnbaum, Kathleen Ochshorn. Magazine: 7½×10½; approximately 70 pages; acid-free paper; visual art; photos. "Interested in fiction of distinctive literary quality." Semiannually. Estab. 1988.

Needs: Contemporary, ethnic, experimental, fantasy, historical, humor/satire, literary, mainstream, prose poem, translations. "We are far more interested in quality than in genre. Nothing sentimental as opposed to genuinely moving, nor self-conscious style at the expense of human truth." Buys 4-5 mss/issue. Publishes ms within 7 months-1 year of acceptance. Agented fiction 60%. Published work by Elizabeth Spencer, Lee K. Abbott, Lorrie Moore, Tim O'Connor and Kit Reed. Length: 250 words minimum; 10,000 words maximum. Publishes short shorts "if the story is good enough." Also publishes literary essays (must be labeled nonfiction), poetry.

How to Contact: Send complete ms with cover letter. Include brief bio. No simultaneous submissions. SASE. Reads September through December; reports January through March. Sample copy for $5 (includes postage) and 9×12 SAE. Fiction guidelines for #10 SASE.

Payment/Terms: Pays $10/printed page on publication for first North American serial rights. Sends galleys to author upon request.
Advice: "There are more good writers publishing in magazines today than there have been in many decades. Unfortunately, there are even more bad ones. In T. Gertler's *Elbowing the Seducer*, an editor advises a young writer that he wants to hear her voice completely, to tell (he means 'show') him in a story the truest thing she knows. We concur. Rather than a trendy workshop story or a minimalism that actually stems from not having much to say, we would like to see stories that make us believe they mattered to the writer and, more importantly, will matter to a reader. Trim until only the essential is left, and don't give up belief in yourself. And it might help to attend a good writers' conference, e.g. Wesleyan or Bennington."

☑ **TAPROOT LITERARY REVIEW, (I, II)**, Taproot Writer's Workshop, Inc., Box 204, Ambridge PA 15003. (724)266-8476. E-mail: taproot10@aol.com. **Editor:** Tikvah Feinstein. Magazine: 5½×8½; 93 pages; #20 paper; card cover; attractively printed; saddle-stitched. "We select on quality, not topic. We have published excellent work other publications have rejected due to subject matter, style or other bias. Variety and quality are our appealing features." Annually. Estab. 1987. Circ. 500.
Needs: Literary. No pornography, religious fiction. The majority of mss published are received through their annual contest. Receives 20 unsolicited mss/month. Accepts 6 fiction mss/issue. Recently published work by Dennis Must, M.A. Boldurian and Kim Honath. Publishes 20 new writers/year. Length: 2,000 words preferred; 250 words minimum; 3,000 words maximum (no longer than 10 pages, double-spaced maximum). Publishes short shorts. Length: 300 words preferred. Sometimes critiques or comments on rejected mss. Also publishes poetry. Sponsors annual contest. Entry fee: $10/story. Deadline: December 31. Send SASE for details.
How to Contact: Send for guidelines first. Send complete ms with a cover letter. Include estimated word count and bio. Accepts queries/mss by e-mail. Reports in 6 months. Send SASE for return of ms or send a disposable copy of ms. No simultaneous submissions. Sample copy for $5, 6×12 SAE and 5 first-class stamps. Fiction guidelines for #10 SASE.
Payment/Terms: Awards $100 in prize money for first place fiction and poetry winners each issue; $25 for 2nd place; 1 contributor's copy. Acquires first rights.
Advice: "*Taproot* is getting more fiction submissions and everyone is read entirely. This takes time, so response can be delayed at busy times of year. Our contest is a good way to start publishing. Send for a sample copy and read it through. Ask for a critique and follow suggestions. Don't be offended by any suggestions—just take them or leave them and keep writing."

☑ **"TEAK" ROUNDUP, The International Quarterly, (I)**, West Coast Paradise Publishing, #5-9060 Tronson Rd., Vernon, British Columbia V1H 1E7 Canada. (250)545-4186. Fax: (250)545-4194. **Editors:** Yvonne and Robert Anstey. Magazine: 5½×8½; 60 pages; 20 lb. copy paper; card stock cover; illustrations and photos. "*'Teak' Roundup* is a general interest showcase for prose and poetry. No uncouth material." Quarterly. Estab. 1994. Circ. 100.
Needs: Adventure, children's/juvenile, condensed/excerpted novel, ethnic/multicultural, historical, humor/satire, literary, mainstream/contemporary, mystery/suspense (police procedural), regional, religious/inspirational, romance (contemporary, historical), sports, westerns, young adult/teen (adventure). "No uncouth or porn." List of upcoming themes available for SASE. Receives 25 unsolicited mss/month. Accepts 20 mss/issue. Publishes ms 3-6 weeks after acceptance. Recently published work by Alice Cundiff and Cynthia Post. Publishes 20 new writers/year. Length: 1,000 words maximum. Also publishes literary essays, literary criticism and poetry. Often critiques or comments on rejected ms.
How to Contact: *Accepts work from subscribers only.* Subscription for $17 (Canadian); $13 (US). Query first or send complete ms with a cover letter. Include estimated word count and brief bio. Reports in 1 week. Send SASE for reply, return of ms or send a disposable copy of ms. Simultaneous, reprint and electronic submissions OK. Sample copy for $5 (Canadian); $3 (US). Fiction guidelines for #10 SASE. Reviews novels and short story collections.
Payment/Terms: Acquires one-time rights (unreserved reprint if "Best of" edition done later.)
Advice: "Subscribe and see popular work which is enjoyed by our growing audience. Many good writers favor us with participation in subscribers-only showcase for prose and poetry. No criticism of generous contributors."

$ **TEARS IN THE FENCE, (II)**, 38 Hod View, Stourpaine, Nr. Blandford Forum, Dorset DT11 8TN England. Phone: 01258-456803. E-mail: poets@inzit.co.uk. **Editor:** David Caddy. Biannual. The editor looks for "the unusual, perceptive and risk-taking as well as the imaginistic and visionary."
Needs: A magazine of poetry, fiction, criticism and reviews, open to a variety of contemporary voices from around the world. Recently published work by Gerald Locklin, Michael Wickinson, Jenny Potts, Jay Merill, Karen Rosenberg and Sarah Connor. Publishes short and long fiction. Publishes 4-5 stories/issue.
Payment/Terms: Pays £7.50 per story plus complimentary copy of the magazine. Sample copy for $5 (US).

THE TEXAS REVIEW, (II), Texas Review Press at Sam Houston University, Huntsville TX 77341. (409)294-1992. **Editor:** Paul Ruffin. Magazine: 6×9; 148-190 pages; best quality paper; 70 lb. cover stock; illustrations; photos. "We publish top quality poetry, fiction, articles, interviews and reviews for a general audience." Semiannually. Estab. 1976. Circ. 1,200.

Needs: Literary and contemporary fiction. "We are eager enough to consider fiction of quality, no matter what its theme or subject matter. No juvenile fiction." Accepts 4 mss/issue. Receives approximately 40-60 unsolicited fiction mss each month. Does not read June-August. Published work by George Garrett, Ellen Gilchrist and Fred Chappell; published new writers within the last year. Length: 500-10,000 words. Critiques rejected mss "when there is time." Recommends other markets.
How to Contact: Send complete ms with cover letter. SASE. Reports in 3 months on mss. Sample copy for $5.
Payment/Terms: Pays contributor's copies plus one year subscription. Acquires first North American serial rights. Sends galleys to author.

TEXTSHOP, A Collaborative Journal of Writing, (I, II), Dept. of English, University of Regina, Regina, Saskatchewan S4S 0A2 Canada. (306)585-4316. **Editors:** Andrew Stubbs, Judy Chapman and Richelle Leonard. Magazine: 8½×11; 50 pages; illustrations. *Textshop* is "eclectic in form and open to fiction, poetry and mixed genres, including creative nonfiction." Annually. Estab. 1993.
Needs: Ethnic/multicultural, experimental, literary. Plans special fiction issues or anthologies. Receives 20-25 unsolicited mss/month. Accepts 15-20 mss/issue. Publishes ms in next issue after acceptance. Publishes 15 new writers/year. Length: 500 words minimum; 1,000 words maximum. Also publishes literary essays, literary criticism and poetry. Sometimes critiques or comments on rejected ms.
How to Contact: Send complete ms with a cover letter. Include estimated word count and 25-word bio with submission. Accepts queries/mss by e-mail. Reports in 1 month on queries; 3 months on mss. SASE. Sample copy for $10. Reviews material published in each issue.
Payment/Terms: Pays 1 contributor's copy; additional copies for $10. Rights remain with the writer.
Advice: Looks for "risk-taking, mixed genre, experimental fiction. Trust your own voice and idiom. Blur the distinction between life and writing."

N **THALIA: Studies in Literary Humor)**, Thalia: Association for the Study of Literary Humor, English Dept., University of Ottawa, Ottawa, Ontario K1N 6N5 Canada. (613)230-9505. Fax: (613)565-5786. **Editor:** J. Tavernier-Courbin. Magazine: illustrations and photos. Semiannually. Estab. 1978. Circ. 500.
Needs: Humor/satire. Upcoming theme: "Humor in the Movies." Publishes short shorts. Also publishes literary essays, literary criticism and poetry. Often critiques or comments on rejected ms.
How to Contact: Send complete ms with a cover letter. Include list of publications. Reports in 4 months on mss. Send SASE for reply. Reviews novels and short story collections.
Payment/Terms: Acquires first rights.

$ **THEMA, (II)**, Box 74109, Metairie LA 70033-4109. **Editor:** Virginia Howard. Magazine: 5½×8½; 200 pages; Grandee Strathmore cover stock; b&w illustrations. "Different specified theme for each issue—short stories, poems, b&w artwork must relate to that theme." Triannually. Estab. 1988.

- Ranked #33 on *Writer's Digest*'s Fiction 50 list of top markets for fiction writers. *Thema* received a Certificate for Excellence in the Arts from the Arts Council of New Orleans.

Needs: Adventure, contemporary, experimental, humor/satire, literary, mainstream, mystery/suspense, prose poem, psychic/supernatural/occult, regional, science fiction, sports, western. "Each issue is based on a specified premise—a different unique theme for each issue. Many types of fiction acceptable, but must fit the premise. No pornographic, scatologic, erotic fiction." Upcoming themes (deadlines for submission in 1999): "On the road to the villa" (March 1); "The wrong cart" (July 1); "Toby came today" (November 1). Publishes ms within 3-4 months of acceptance. Recently published work by Kaye Bache-Snyder, Madonna Dries Christensen, Harold Huber, Becky Mushko and Marvin Thrasher. Publishes 10-15 new writers/year. Length: fewer than 6,000 words preferred. Also publishes poetry. Sometimes critiques rejected mss and recommends other markets.
How to Contact: Send complete ms with cover letter, include "name and address, brief introduction, specifying the intended target issue for the mss." Simultaneous submissions OK. Reports on queries in 1 week; on mss in 5 months after deadline for specified issue. SASE. Sample copy for $8. Free fiction guidelines.
Payment/Terms: Pays $25; $10 for short shorts on acceptance for one-time rights.
Advice: "Do not submit a manuscript unless you have written it for a specified premise. If you don't know the upcoming themes, send for guidelines first, before sending a story. We need more stories told in the Mark Twain/O. Henry tradition in magazine fiction."

✔ **THIRD COAST, (II)**, Dept. of English, Western Michigan University, Kalamazoo MI 49008-5092. (616)387-2675. Fax: (616)387-2562. Website: http://www.umich.edu/thirdcoast (includes guidelines, editors names and samples of past fiction we have published are all available on the website). Managing Editor: Kathleen McGookey. **Fiction Editors:** Darrin Doyle and Janice Robertson. Magazine: 6×9; 150 pages; illustrations and photos. "We will consider many different types of fiction and favor that exhibiting a freshness of vision and approach." Semiannually. Estab. 1995. Circ. 500.

- *Third Coast* has received *Pushcart Prize* nominations. The editors of this publication change with the university year.

Needs: Literary. "While we don't want to see formulaic genre fiction, we will consider material that plays with or challenges generic forms." Receives approximately 100 unsolicited mss/month. Accepts 6-8 mss/issue; 15 mss/year. Publishes ms 3-6 months after acceptance. Recently published work by Peter Ho Davies, Sarah J. Smith, Wang Ping and Sara McAulay. Length: no preference. Publishes short shorts. Also publishes literary essays, poetry and interviews. Sometimes critiques or comments on rejected mss.
How to Contact: Send complete ms with a cover letter. Include list of publications. Reports in 1 month on queries; 2 months on mss. Send SASE for reply, return of ms or send a disposable copy of ms. Simultaneous submissions OK. Sample copy for $6. Fiction guidelines for #10 SASE.
Payment/Terms: Pays 2 contributor's copies as well as 1 year subscription to the publication; additional copies for $4. Acquires one-time rights. Not copyrighted.
Advice: "Of course, the writing itself must be of the highest quality. We love to see work that explores non-western contexts, as well as fiction from all walks of American (and other) experience."

13TH MOON, A Feminist Magazine, (IV), Dept. of English, University at Albany, Albany NY 12222. (518)442-4181. **Editor:** Judith Johnson. Magazine: 6×9; 250 pages; 50 lb. paper; heavy cover stock; photographs. "Feminist literary magazine for feminist women and men." Annually. Estab. 1973. Circ. 2,000.
Needs: Excerpted novel, experimental, feminist, lesbian, literary, prose poem, science fiction, translations. No fiction by men. Plans two volumes on feminist poetics (one volume on narrative forms and one on poetry). Submissions should be accompanied by a statement of the author's poetics (a paragraph to a page long). Accepts 1-3 mss/issue. Does not read mss May-September. Time varies between acceptance and publication. Published work by F.R. Lewis, Jan Ramjerdi and Wilma Kahn. Length: Open. Publishes short shorts. Also publishes poetry. Sometimes critiques rejected mss.
How to Contact: Send complete ms with cover letter and SASE (or IRC); "no queries." Reports in 8 months on mss. SASE. Accepts electronic submissions via disk (WordPerfect 5.1 only). Sample copy for $10.
Payment/Terms: Pays 2 contributor's copies.
Terms: Acquires first North American serial rights.
Advice: Looks for "*unusual* fiction with feminist appeal."

$ 32 PAGES, (I, II), Rain Crow Publishing, 2127 W. Pierce Ave. Apt. 2B, Chicago IL 60622-1824. (773)276-9005. E-mail: 32pp@rain-crow-publishing.com. Website: http://rain-crow-publishing.com/32pp/ (includes writer's guidelines, sample issue, back issue sales, advertising rates). **Editor:** Michael S. Manley. Magazine: 8½×11; 32 pages; 40 lb. white paper; illustrations. "*32 Pages* publishes new and experienced writers in many styles and genres. I look for eclectic, well-crafted, entertaining fiction aimed at those who enjoy literature for its pleasures." 4 to 6 issues per year. Estab. 1997. Circ. 1,000.
Needs: Adventure, erotica, ethnic/multicultural, experimental, fantasy, feminist, gay, historical (general), horror, humor/satire, lesbian, literary, mainstream/contemporary, mystery/suspense, regional, science fiction, translations. "No dogmatically religious, politically propagandistic or formulaic fiction. Not too interested in porn or juvenile, either." Receives 25-50 unsolicited mss/month. Accepts 3-4 mss/issue; 18-24 mss/year. Publishes ms within 6 months after acceptance. Published work by Susan Neville, Stanley Jenkins, William Stuckey, Peter Johnson, Murray Shugars, John McDermott, Carolyn Alessio, Christine Butterworth, Rob Davidson and Maija Kroeger. Publishes several new writers/year. Length: 4,000 words average; 250 words minimum; 8,000 words maximum. Publishes short shorts. Also publishes personal essays, poetry. Sometimes critiques or comments on rejected mss.
How to Contact: Send complete ms with a cover letter. May also e-mail submissions. Include estimated word count and brief bio. Reports in 3 months. Send SASE for reply, return of ms or send a disposable copy of ms. Simultaneous submissions, reprints and electronic submissions OK. Sample copy for $2.50. Fiction guidelines for #10 SASE (1 IRC).
Payment/Terms: Pays $5 per page on publication, free subscription to magazine and 2 contributor's copies; additional copies for $2. Acquires one-time rights and one-time electronic rights. Sends galleys to author. Sponsors "fiction chapbook contest annually. Watch for announcements in writer's publications and on our website."
Advice: "Is it a story I want to read again? Did it keep me locked into its fictional dream? A good manuscript makes me forget I'm reading a manuscript. I look for attention to craft: voice, language, character and plot working together to maximum effect. Unique yet credible settings and situations that entertain will get the most attention. Write to the best of your abilities and submit your best work. Present yourself and your work professionally. Get used to rejections. Literary magazines must change if they are to survive in today's market. Contemporary fiction must do the same."

$ THIS MAGAZINE, (II), Red Maple Foundation, 401 Richmond St. W., Suite 396, Toronto, Ontario M5V 3A8 Canada. (416)979-8400. E-mail: thismag@web.net. Website: http://www.thismag.org (includes writer's guidelines). **Literary Editor:** R.M. Vaughan. Magazine: 8½×11; 48 pages; bond paper; non-coated cover; illustrations and photographs. "Alternative general interest magazine." Bimonthly. Estab. 1966. Circ. 7,000.

• *This Magazine* has won three national Canadian Magazine awards, and was nominated in *Utne Reader's* alternative press awards for cultural coverage. *This Magazine* is not currently accepting unsolicited manuscripts.

Needs: Ethnic, contemporary, experimental, feminist, gay, lesbian, literary, regional. No "commercial/pulp fiction." Published work by Elise Levine, Stuart Ross, Lynn Condy, Allan Barr and Tony Burgess. Length: 2,000 words average; 3,000 words maximum.
How to Contact: "We no longer accept unsolicited poetry or fiction." Accepts queries by e-mail. Sample copy for $4.50 (plus GST). Fiction guidelines for #9 SASE with Canadian stamps or IRC.
Payment/Terms: Pays $150 (Canadian) fiction; $50/poem published for one-time rights.
Advice: "It's best if you're familiar with the magazine when submitting work; a large number of mss that come into the office are inappropriate. Style guides are available. Manuscripts and queries that are clean and personalized really make a difference. Let your work speak for itself—don't try to convince us."

$ THE THREEPENNY REVIEW, (II), P.O. Box 9131, Berkeley CA 94709. (510)849-4545. **Editor:** Wendy Lesser. Tabloid: 10×17; 40 pages; Electrobrite paper; white book cover; illustrations. "Serious fiction." Quarterly. Estab. 1980. Circ. 9,000.

• *The Threepenny Review* ranked #21 on *Writer's Digest*'s Fiction 50 list of top markets for fiction writers, and has received GE Writers Awards, CLMP Editor's Awards, NEA grants, Lila Wallace grants and inclusion of work in the *Pushcart Prize Anthology.*

Needs: Literary. "Nothing 'experimental' (ungrammatical)." Receives 300-400 mss/month. Accepts 3 mss/issue; 12 mss/year. Does *not* read mss June through August. Publishes 6-12 months after acceptance. Agented fiction 5%. Published Sigrid Nunez, Dagoberto Gilb, Gina Berriault and Leonard Michaels. Length: 5,000 words maximum. Publishes short shorts. Also publishes literary essays, literary criticism, poetry.
How to Contact: Send complete ms with a cover letter. Reports in 2-4 weeks on queries;1-2 months on mss. Send SASE for reply, return of ms or send a disposable copy of the ms. No simultaneous submissions. Sample copy for $6. Fiction guidelines for #10 SASE. Reviews novels and short story collections.
Payment/Terms: Pays $200 on acceptance plus free subscription to the magazine; additional copies at half price. Acquires first North American serial rights. Sends galleys to author.

TIMBER CREEK REVIEW, (III), 612 Front St. East, Glendora NJ 08029-1133. (609)863-0610. E-mail: jmfreier@aol.com. **Editor:** J.M. Freiermuth. Newsletter: 5½×8½; 76-84 pages; copy paper; some illustrations and photographs. "Fiction, satire, poetry of all types and travel for a general audience —80% of readers read above the 6th grade level." Quarterly. Circ. 150.
Needs: Adventure, contemporary, ethnic, feminist, historical, humor/satire, mainstream, mystery/suspense (cozy, private eye), regional, western (adult, frontier, traditional). No religion, children's, gay, romance. Plans sixth "All Woman Author" issue (October 1999). Receives 50-60 unsolicited mss/month. Accepts 15-20 mss/issue; 65-75 mss/year. Publishes ms 4-12 months after acceptance. Recently published work by Mark Wisniewski, Dennis Vannatta, Ian Wooler, Willard Rusch and Hugh Fox. Publishes 0-3 new writers/year. Length: 2,500-4,000 words average; 1,200 words minimum; 10,000 words maximum. Publishes short shorts. Length: "Long enough to develop a good bite." Sometimes critiques rejected mss and recommends other markets.
How to Contact: Send complete ms and/or DOS disk (uses MS Word) with cover letter including "name, address, SASE." Accepts queries/mss by e-mail. Reports in 3-6 weeks on mss. SASE. Simultaneous submissions OK. Sample copy for $4 postpaid. Reviews short story collections.
Payment/Terms: Pays subscription to magazine for first publication and contributor's copies for subsequent publications. Acquires one-time rights. Publication not copyrighted.
Advice: "If your story has a spark of life or a degree of humor that brings a smile to my face, you have a chance here. Most stories lack these two ingredients. Write more stories. If you have 20 stories circulating you have a better chance of having one published."

$ TOMORROW Speculative Fiction, (www.tomorrowsf.com) (I), Unifont Co., P.O. Box 6038, Evanston IL 60204. (708)864-3668. E-mail: abudrys@tomorrowsf.com. **Editor and Publisher:** Algis Budrys. Electronic magazine. "Any good science fiction, fantasy and horror, for an audience of fiction readers, plus science articles, poems and cartoons." Bimonthly. Estab. 1992.

• *Tomorrow* has twice been nominated for the Hugo. A collection of articles on writing, originally published in *Tomorrow,* is now available.

Needs: Fantasy, horror, science fiction—any kind. Receives 300 mss/month. Accepts 10-12 mss/issue; 60-82 mss/year. Publishes within 18 months of acceptance. Agented fiction 2%. Published works by Robert Reed, Michael Shea, Nina Kiriki Hoffman, Robert Frazier, Yves Meynard and Elisabeth Vonarburg. Length: 4,000 words average. Publishes short shorts.
How to Contact: On fiction, send complete ms. Include estimated word count and Social Security number. On nonfiction, query. No cover letters. "Creased manuscripts and/or single spaced manuscripts will not be read." Reports in 2 weeks. Send SASE for reply, return of ms if desired. No simultaneous submissions. Sample copy of print issue for $5 plus 9×12 SASE.

Payment/Terms: Pays $75 minimum; 7¢/word maximum. Buys First World electronic English language print rights.
Advice: "Read my book, *Writing to the Point*, $10.50 from Unifont Co."

TOUCHSTONE LITERARY JOURNAL, (II), P.O. Box 8308, Spring TX 77387-8308. Editor/Publisher: William Laufer. Managing Editor: Guida Jackson. **Fiction Editor:** Julia Gomez-Rigas. Magazine: 5½×8½; 56 pages; linen paper; kramkote cover; perfect bound; b&w illustrations; occasional photographs. "Literary and mainstream fiction, but enjoy experimental work and multicultural. Audience middle-class, heavily academic. We are eclectic and given to whims—i.e., two years ago we devoted a 104-page issue to West African women writers." Annually (with occasional special supplements). Estab. 1976. Circ. 1,000.

● Touchstone Press also publishes a chapbook series. Send a SASE for guidelines.

Needs: Humor/satire, literary, translations. No erotica, religious, juvenile, "stories written in creative writing programs that all sound alike." List of upcoming themes available for SASE. Publishes special fiction issue or anthology. Receives 20-30 mss/month. Accepts 3-4 mss/issue. Does not read mss in December. Publishes ms within the year after acceptance. Published work by Ann Alejandro, Lynn Bradley, Roy Fish and Julia Mercedes Castilla. Length: 2,500 words preferred; 250 words minimum; 5,000 words maximum. Publishes short shorts. Length: 300 words. Also publishes literary essays, literary criticism and poetry. Sometimes critiques or comments on rejected mss.
How to Contact: Send complete ms with a cover letter. Include estimated word count and 3-sentence bio. Reports in 6 weeks. Send SASE for return of ms. Simultaneous and electronic submissions OK. Sample copy for $3 or 10 first-class stamps. Fiction guidelines for #10 SASE.
Payment/Terms: Pays 2 contributor's copies; additional copies $5. Acquires one-time rights. Sends galleys to author (unless submitted on disk).
Advice: "We like to see fiction that doesn't read as if it had been composed in a creative writing class. If you can entertain, edify, or touch the reader, polish your story and send it in. Don't worry if it doesn't read like our other fiction."

TRIQUARTERLY, (II), Northwestern University, 2020 Ridge Ave., Evanston IL 60208-4302. (847)491-7614. **Editor:** Susan Hahn. Magazine: 6×9¼; 240-272 pages; 60 lb. paper; heavy cover stock; illustration; photos. "A general literary quarterly especially devoted to fiction. We publish short stories, novellas or excerpts from novels, by American and foreign writers. Genre or style is not a primary consideration. We aim for the general but serious and sophisticated reader. Many of our readers are also writers." Triannual. Estab. 1964. Circ. 5,000.

● Stories from *Triquarterly* have been reprinted in *The Best American Short Stories*, *Pushcart Prizes* and *O'Henry Prize* Anthologies.

Needs: Literary, contemporary and translations. "No prejudices or preconceptions against anything *except* genre fiction (romance, science fiction, etc.)." Accepts 10 mss/issue, 30 mss/year. Receives approximately 500 unsolicited fiction mss each month. Does not read April 1 through September 30. Agented fiction 10%. Recently published work by Steve Fisher, Michael Collins, Hélène Cixous, Charles Baxter, Margot Livesey and Robert Girardi. Publishes 1-5 new writers/year. Length: no requirement. Publishes short shorts.
How to Contact: Send complete ms with SASE. No simultaneous submissions. Reports in 4 months on mss. Publishes ms an average of 6-12 months after acceptance. Sample copy for $5.
Payment/Terms: Pays 2 contributor's copies on publication for first North American serial rights. Cover price less 40% discount for extras. Sends galleys to author. Honoraria vary, depending on grant support.

TUCUMCARI LITERARY REVIEW, (I, II), 3108 W. Bellevue Ave., Los Angeles CA 90026. **Editor:** Troxey Kemper. Magazine: 5½×8½; about 40 pages; 20 lb. bond paper; 67 lb. cover stock; few illustrations; photocopied photographs. "Old-fashioned fiction that can be read and reread for pleasure; no weird, strange pipe dreams and no it-was-all-a-dream endings." Bimonthly. Estab. 1988. Circ. small.
Needs: Adventure, contemporary, ethnic, historical, humor/satire, literary, mainstream, mystery/suspense, regional (southwest USA), senior citizen/retirement, western (frontier stories). "Would like to see more Western, mystery and O. Henry endings." No science fiction, drugs/acid rock, occult, pornography, horror, martial arts or children's stories. Accepts 6 or 8 mss/issue; 35-40 mss/year. Publishes ms 2-6 months after acceptance. Published work by Wilma Elizabeth McDaniel, Ruth Daniels, Andy Peterson and Jim Sullivan. Publishes 10-20 new writers/year. Length: 400-1,200 words preferred. Also publishes rhyming poetry.
How to Contact: Send complete ms with or without cover letter. Reports in 2 weeks. SASE. Simultaneous and reprint submissions OK. Sample copy for $2. Fiction guidelines for #10 SASE.
Payment/Terms: Pays in contributor's copies. Acquires one-time rights. Publication not copyrighted.

READ THE BUSINESS OF FICTION WRITING section to learn the correct way to prepare and submit a manuscript.

Advice: "Computers/printers are 'nice' but sometimes handwritten work on 3-hole lined notebook paper is interesting, too. Don't fall for advice from book doctors or writing experts who recycle the same story over and over. If you've read one, you've read 'em all. Think of some stories you read in English class when you were in grade school/high school. Try something, *but not the same story*, along those lines."

☑ **TURNSTILE, (I)**, 175 Fifth Ave., Suite 2348, New York NY 10010-7848. (212)674-5151. Fax: (212)674-6132. Website: http://www.turnstilepress.com (includes writer's guidelines, staff list, stories, subscription information). **Editor:** Justine Gardner. Magazine: 6×9; 128 pages; 55 lb. paper; 10 pt. cover; illustrations; photos. "Publishing work by new writers." Annual. Estab. 1988. Circ. 1,000.
Needs: "Quality fiction." No genre fiction. Receives approximately 100 unsolicited fiction mss/month. Publishes approximately 5 short story mss/issue. Recently published work by Jane W. Ellis and Lauren Sarat. Publishes 5-7 new writers/year. Length: 2,000 words average; 4,000 words maximum. Also publishes poetry, nonfiction essays, and interviews with well-known writers. Sometimes comments on rejected mss.
How to Contact: Query first or send complete ms with cover letter. Reports on queries in 3-4 weeks; on mss in 2-3 months. SASE. Simultaneous submissions OK. Sample copy for $6.50 and 7×10 SAE; fiction guidelines for #10 SASE.
Payment/Terms: Pays in contributor's copies; charge for extras. Acquires one-time rights.
Advice: "More than ever we're looking for *well-crafted* stories. We look for exceptional characterization and plot. Please do continue to submit new stories even if previous ones were not accepted; however, do not submit more than two stories at one time. Recognizing that the commercial publishing industry takes increasingly few risks on new, unconventional writers, *Turnstile* dedicates itself to encouraging and publishing fresh voices."

$ **THE URBANITE, Surreal & Lively & Bizarre, (II, IV)**, Urban Legend Press, P.O. Box 4737, Davenport IA 52808. Website: http://www.rictus.com/urbanite/index.htm (includes information on current and upcoming issues). **Editor:** Mark McLaughlin. Magazine: 8½×11; 52-80 pages; bond paper; coated cover; saddle-stitched; illustrations. "We look for quality fiction in an urban setting with a surrealistic tone." Each issue includes a featured writer, a featured poet and a featured artist. Published three times a year. Estab. 1991. Circ. 500-1,000.
• *The Urbanite* ranked as No. 22 on the *Writer's Digest* Fiction 50 list.
Needs: Experimental, fantasy (dark fantasy), horror, humor/satire, literary, psychic/supernatural/occult, science fiction (soft/sociological). "We love horror, but please, no tired, gore-ridden horror plots. Horror submissions must be subtle and sly." Upcoming themes: "Strange Nourishment" and "The Zodiac." List of upcoming themes available for SASE. Receives over 800 unsolicited mss/month. Accepts 15 mss/issue; 45 mss/year. Publishes ms 6 months after acceptance. Recently published work by Basil Copper, Wilom Pugmire, Hertzan Chimera, Marni Scofidio Griffin, Pamela Briggs and Thomas Ligotti. Publishes at least 2-3 new writers/year. Length: 2,000 words preferred; 500 words minimum; 3,000 words maximum. Publishes short shorts. Length: 350 words preferred. Also publishes poetry. Sometimes critiques or comments on rejected mss.
How to Contact: Include estimated word count, 4- to 5-sentence bio, Social Security number and list of publications. Reports in 1 month on queries; 3-4 months on mss. Send large SASE for reply and return of ms or send a disposable copy of ms. Sample copy for $5. Fiction guidelines for #10 SASE.
Payment/Terms: Pays 2-3¢/word and 2 contributor's copies for first North American serial rights and nonexclusive rights for public readings. Featured authors receive 3¢/word, 6 contributor's copies and a lifetime subscription to the magazine.
Advice: "The tone of our magazine is unique, and we strongly encourage writers to read an issue to ascertain the sort of material we accept. The number one reason we reject many stories is because they are inappropriate for our publication: in these cases, it is obvious that the writer is not familiar with *The Urbanite*. We are known for publishing quality horror—work from *The Urbanite* has been reprinted in *Year's Best Fantasy & Horror*, *The Year's Best Fantastic Fiction*, and England's *Best New Horror*, volumes 7 and 8. People keep sending amateurish gore-horror, and they are wasting their time and postage. 'Splatter' fiction is on the way out in publishing. We want to see more slipstream fiction and more bizarre (yet urbane and thought-provoking) humor."

VERVE, (I, II), P.O. Box 3205, Simi Valley CA 93093-3025. Editor: Ron Reichick. **Fiction Editor:** Marilyn Hochheiser. Magazine: Digest-sized, 40 pages, 70 lb. paper, 80 lb. cover, cover illustrations or photographs. "Each issue has a theme." Quarterly. Estab. 1989. Circ. 700.
Needs: Contemporary, experimental, fantasy, humor/satire, literary, mainstream, prose poem. No pornographic material. Receives 100 unsolicited fiction mss/month. Accepts 4-6 mss/issue; 8-12 mss/year. Publishes ms 2 months after deadline (March 1 and August 1). Length: 1,000 words maximum. Publishes short shorts. Also publishes literary criticism, poetry.
How to Contact: "Request guidelines before submitting manuscript." Reports 4-6 weeks after deadline. SASE. Simultaneous submissions OK. Sample copy for $3.50. Fiction guidelines for #10 SASE. Reviews short story collections.
Payment/Terms: Pays in contributor's copies. Acquires one-time rights.

🌐 **VIGIL, (II)**, Vigil Publications, 12 Priory Mead, Bruton, Somerset BA10 ODZ England. **Editor:** John Howard Greaves. Estab. 1979. Circ. 250. "Simply the enjoyment of varied forms of poetry and literature with an informed view of poetic technique."

Needs: Needs: experimental, literary, regional. Plans special fiction issue. Length: 500-1,500 words.
Payment/Terms: Pays in contributor's copies. Contributor guidelines available for IRC.
Advice: "Most of the stories we receive are work in progress rather than finished pieces. Well structured, vibrantly expressed work is a delight when it arrives. Freshness and originality must always find an audience."

$ THE VINCENT BROTHERS REVIEW, (II), The Vincent Brothers Company, 4566 Northern Circle, Riverside OH 45424-5733. **Editor:** Kimberly Willardson. Magazine: 5½×8¼; 88-100 perfect-bound pages; 60 lb. white coated paper; 60 lb. Oxford (matte) cover; b&w illustrations and photographs. "We publish at least two theme issues per year. Writers must send SASE for information about upcoming theme issues. Each issue of *TVBR* contains poetry, b&w art, at least six short stories and usually one nonfiction piece. For a mainstream audience looking for an alternative to the slicks." Triannually. Estab. 1988. Circ. 400.

- *TVBR* was ranked #17 in the *Writer's Digest*'s Fiction 50. It has received grants from the Ohio Arts Council for the last six years. Also received grant from the Montgomery County Regional Arts and Cultural District of Ohio for 1998. Won Special Merit Award in 1996 American Literary Magazine Awards sponsored by *Poet* Magazine and Cooper House Publishing. The magazine sponsors a fall fiction contest; deadline in October. Contact them for details.

Needs: Adventure, condensed/excerpted novel, contemporary, ethnic, experimental, feminist, historical, humor/satire, literary, mainstream, mystery/suspense (amateur sleuth, cozy, private eye), prose poem, regional, science fiction (soft/sociological), senior citizen/retirement, serialized novel, translations, western (adult, frontier, traditional). "We focus on the way the story is presented rather than the genre of the story. No racist, sexist, fascist, etc. work." Receives 200-250 unsolicited mss/month. Buys 6-10 mss/issue; 30 mss/year. Publishes ms 2-4 months after acceptance. Published work by Gordon C. Wilson, Tom D. Ellison, Nikolaus Maack, Laurel Jenkins-Crowe and Ariel Smart. Publishes 8-12 new writers/year. Length: 2,500 words average; 250 words minimum; 7,000 words maximum. Maximum 10,000 words for novel condensations. Publishes short shorts. Length: 250-1,000 words. Also publishes literary essays, literary criticism, poetry. Often critiques rejected mss and sometimes recommends other markets.
How to Contact: "Send query letter *before* sending novel excerpts or condensations! *Send only one short story at a time*—unless sending short shorts." Send complete ms. Simultaneous submissions OK, but not preferred. Reports in 3-4 weeks on queries; 2-3 months on mss with SASE. Sample copy for $6.50; back issues for $4.50. Fiction guidelines for #10 SASE. Reviews novels and short story collections.
Payment/Terms: Pays $15-250 on acceptance for first North American serial rights. $200 first place; $100 second; $50 third for annual short story contest. Charge (discounted) for extras.
Advice: "The best way to discover what *TVBR* editors are seeking in fiction is to read at least a couple issues of the magazine. We are typical readers—we want to be grabbed by the first words of a story and rendered unable to put it down until we've read the last word of it. We want stories that we'll want to read again. This doesn't necessarily mean we seek stories that grab the reader via shock tactics; gross-out factors; surface titillation; or emotional manipulation. Good writers know the difference. Research the markets. Read good writing. Dig deep to find original and compelling narrative voices. It's amazing how many dozens and dozens of stories we receive sound/read so very much alike. We've noticed a marked increase in violent and/or socially ill/deviant-themed stories. Hmm. Is this art imitating life or life imitating art or is it just writers desperate to shock the reader into believing this now passes for originality? Incest stories have been done and done well, but that doesn't mean everyone should write one. Same goes for divorce, death-watch, I-killed-my-boss (spouse, etc.) and got-away-with-it stories."

VOX, Pace University Literary Magazine, (I), Pace University, Willcox Hall, Room 43, 4th Floor, 861 Bedford Rd., Pleasantville NY 10570. (914)773-3962. **Editor:** Josh McCuen. Magazine: 5½×8½; perfect-bound; 80-120 pages; illustrations and photos. "*Vox* is made for and by college students and publishes works that, we hope, will appeal to this readership. Funny, sad, everything in between, we want it if it can keep the attention of a collegian with a full course-load. This doesn't mean just the usual beer, sex and drug stories—there's a lot more to life, and that's what *Vox* is interested in giving to our readers. Just make it real, honest, avoid cliches and stereotypes and it'll be considered." Annually (spring). Estab. 1977. Circ. 500-1,000.

- *Vox* received the Columbia Scholastic Press Association Silver Crown Award, 1994, 1995 and 1996.

Needs: College-age interests, condensed/excerpted novel, ethnic/multicultural, feminist, humor/satire, literary, mainstream/contemporary, mystery/suspense (police procedural, private eye/hardboiled, romantic suspense), romance (contemporary). No erotica, horror, senior citizen, juvenile. Does not read mss June, July, August. Recently published work by students from Pace. Length: 1,600 words average; 750 words minimum; 4,000 words maximum. Also publishes literary essays and poetry.
How to Contact: Send complete ms with a cover letter. Include estimated word count and brief bio. Reports in 4-6 weeks. Send SASE for reply; send a disposable copy of ms. Sample copy for $6, 5½×8½ SAE and 4 first-class stamps.
Payment/Terms: Pays 2 contributor's copies; additional copies for $3 and 4 first-class stamps for each copy. Acquires one-time rights. Not copyrighted.
Advice: "Send a neat, proofread manuscript; at least spell check it and let a friend or two read it over. Send an original manuscript—things that sound 'familiar' are the quickest to be forgotten."

☑ **WASHINGTON SQUARE, Literary Review of New York University's Creative Writing Program, (II)**, (formerly Ark/Angel Review), NYU Creative Writing Program, 19 University Place, 3rd Floor, Room 310, New York NY 10003-4556. (212)998-8816. Fax: (212)995-4017. Editor: Stuart Greenhouse. **Fiction Editor:** Eric Ellis. Editors change each year. Magazine: 5½×8½; 144 pages; photographs. "*Washington Square* is the literary review produced by New York University's Graduate Creative Writing Program. We publish outstanding works of fiction and poetry by the students and faculty of NYU as well as the work of writers across the country." Semiannually. Estab. 1996 (we were previously called Ark/Angel Review, estab. 1987). Circ. 1,000.
Needs: Condensed/excerpted novel, ethnic/multicultural, experimental, literary, mainstream/contemporary. No adventure, children's, erotica. Receives 75 unsolicited mss/month. Accepts 10 mss/issue; 20 mss/year. Publishes ms 3-5 months after acceptance. Agented fiction 20%. Published work by Dika Lam, Sarah Inman, Jessica Anya Blau, Irene Korenfield. Length: 5,000 words average; 7,000 words maximum. Publishes short shorts. Also publishes poetry. Sometimes critiques or comments on rejected mss.
How to Contact: Send complete ms with a cover letter. Include estimated word count (only put name on first page). Reports in 2 weeks on queries; 6 weeks on mss. Send SASE for reply, return of ms or send a disposable copy of ms. Simultaneous submissions OK. Sample copy for $6.
Payment/Terms: Pays 3 contributor's copies; additional copies for $6. Acquires first North American serial rights. "Each fall we sponsor a short story contest. Deadline: December 15."
Advice: "We look for compelling, original, outstanding fiction. Please send polished, proofread manuscripts only."

☑ ▣ **WEB DEL SOL, (III)**, E-mail: editor@webdelsol.com. Website: http://webdelsol.com. **Editor:** Michael Neff. Electronic magazine. "The goal of *Web Del Sol* is to use the medium of the Internet to bring the finest in contemporary literary arts to a larger audience. To that end, WDS not only webpublishes collections of work by accomplished writers and poets, but hosts other literary arts publications on the WWW such as *AGNI, Conjunctions, North American Review, Zyzzyva, Flashpoint, Global City Review, The Literary Review* and *The Prose Poem.*

• *Web Del Sol* ranked #31 on *Writer's Digest*'s Fiction 50 list of top markets for fiction writers.

Needs: "WDS publishes work considered to be literary in nature, i.e., non-genre fiction. WDS also publishes poetry, prose poetry, essays and experimental types of writing." Publishes short shorts. Recently published work by Robert Olen Butler, Carole Maso, Michael Martone, Kathleen Hill, Ben Marcus, Bradford Marrow and Diana Abu-Jaber. "Currently, WDS published Featured Writer/Poet websites, approximately 15 per year at this time; but hopes to increase that number substantially in the coming year. WDS also occasionally publishes individual works and plans to do more of these also."
How to Contact: "Submissions by e-mail from September through November and from January through March only. Submissions must contain some brief bio, list of prior publications (if any), and a short work or prortion of that work, neither to exceed 1,000 words. Editors will contact if the balance of work is required."
Advice: "WDS wants fiction that is absolutely cutting edge, unique and/or at a minimum, accomplished with a crisp style and concerning subjects not usually considered the objects of literary scrutiny. Read works in such publications as *Conjunctions* (http://www.conjunctions.com) and *Flashpoint* (http://webdelsol.com/FLASHPOINT) to get an idea what we are looking for."

WEST BRANCH, (II), Bucknell Hall, Bucknell University, Lewisburg PA 17837. **Editors:** Karl Patten and Robert Love Taylor. Magazine: 5½×8½; 96-120 pages; quality paper; coated card cover; perfect-bound; illustrations; photos. Fiction and poetry for readers of contemporary literature. Biannually. Estab. 1977. Circ. 500.
Needs: Literary, contemporary, prose poems and translations. No science fiction. Accepts 3-6 mss/issue. Recently published work by Daniel J. Bingley, Cynthia Elliott, Deborah Hodge, Leslie Pietrzyk, Darby Sanders, Steve Moncada Street, Kathleen Wakefield and Jo-Anne A. Watts. Published new writers within the last year. No preferred length. However, "the fiction we publish usually runs between 12-25 double-spaced pages."
How to Contact: Send complete ms with cover letter, "with information about writer's background, previous publications, etc." SASE. No simultaneous submissions. Reports in 6-8 weeks on mss. Sample copy for $3.
Payment/Terms: Pays 2 contributor's copies and one-year subscription; cover price less 25% discount charge for extras. Acquires first rights.
Advice: "Narrative art fulfills a basic human need—our dreams attest to this—and storytelling is therefore a high calling in any age. Find your own voice and vision. Make a story that speaks to your own mysteries. Cultivate simplicity in form, complexity in theme. Look and listen through your characters."

$ WEST COAST LINE, A Journal of Contemporary Writing & Criticism, (II), 2027 E. Academic Annex, Simon Fraser University, Burnaby, British Columbia V5A 1S6 Canada. (604)291-4287. Fax: (604)291-5737. Website: http://www.sfu.ca/west-coast-line. **Managing Editor:** Jacqueline Larson. Magazine: 6×9; 128-144 pages. "Poetry, fiction, criticism—modern and contemporary, North American, cross-cultural. Readers include academics, writers, students." Triannual. Estab. 1990. Circ. 600.
Needs: Experimental, ethnic/multicultural, feminist, gay, literary. "We do not publish journalistic writing or strictly representational narrative." Receives 30-40 unsolicited mss/month. Accepts 2-3 mss/issue; 3-6 mss/year. Publishes ms 2-10 months after acceptance. Recently published work by Claire Harris, Ashok Matnur, George

Elliot Clarke and Fred Wah. Publishes 3 new writers/year. Length: 3,000-4,000 words. Publishes short shorts. Length: 250-400 words. Also publishes literary essays and literary criticism.
How to Contact: Send complete ms with a cover letter. "We supply an information form for contributors." Reports in 3 months. Send SAE with IRCs, not US postage, for return of ms. No simultaneous submissions. Sample copy for $10. Fiction guidelines free.
Payment/Terms: Pays $3-8/page (Canadian); subscription; 2 contributor copies; additional copies for $6-8/copy, depending on quantity ordered. Pays on publication for one-time rights.
Advice: "Special concern for contemporary writers who are experimenting with, or expanding the boundaries of conventional forms of poetry, fiction and criticism; also interested in criticism and scholarship on Canadian and American modernist writers who are important sources for current writing. We recommend that potential contributors send a letter of enquiry or read back issues before submitting a manuscript."

WEST WIND REVIEW, (I), 1250 Siskiyou Blvd., Ashland OR 97520. (503)552-6518. E-mail: westwind@tao.sou.edu. Website: http://www.sou/stu_affa/westwind.htm. **Editor:** Ramana Lewis (1998-99 school year). Editors change each year. Magazine: 5¾×8½; 150-250 pages; illustrations and photos. "Literary journal publishing prose/poetry/art. Encourages new writers, accepts established writers as well, with an audience of people who like to read anthologies." Annually. Estab. 1980. Circ. 500.
Needs: Adventure, erotica, ethnic/multicultural, experimental, fantasy, feminist, gay, historical (general), horror, humor/satire, lesbian, literary, mainstream/contemporary, mystery/suspense, psychic/supernatural/occult, regional, religious/inspirational, romance, science fiction, senior citizen/retirement, sports, translations—"just about anything." Receives 6-60 unsolicited mss/month. Accepts 15-20 mss/issue. Publishes ms almost immediately after acceptance. Published work by Sharon Doubiago, Tee A. Corinne, Norman Fischer and Sean Brendan-Brown. 50% of work published is by new writers. Length: 3,000 words maximum. Publishes short shorts. Also publishes literary essays and poetry. Sometimes critiques or comments on rejected ms.
How to Contact: Send complete ms with a cover letter. Include estimated word count and short bio. Reports in 2 weeks on queries; by March 1 on mss. Send SASE for reply, return of ms or send a disposable copy of ms. No simultaneous submissions. For fiction guidelines, visit our website.
Payment/Terms: To enter prize contest include $1 with entry. First place winner in fiction wins $25. Accepted authors receive 1 free copy. Authors retain all rights.
Advice: "Good writing stands out. Content is important but style is essential. Clearly finished pieces whose content shows subtle action, reaction and transformation for the character(s) are what we like."

$ WESTERLY, English Dept., University of Western Australia, Nedlands, 6907 Australia. 08 9380 2101. Fax: 08 9380 1030. E-mail: westerly@uniwa.uwa.edu.au. Website: http://www.arts.uwa.edu.au/westerly (includes details of current issue, past issues, forthcoming issues and information about subscribing and contributing). Caroline Horobin, Administrator. Quarterly. Circ. 1,000.
Neds: "A quarterly of poetry, prose, reviews and articles of a literary and cultural kind, giving special attention to Australia and Southeast Asia." No romance, children's science fiction.
How to Contact: Queries by e-mail OK.
Payment/Terms: Pays $50 (AUS) minimum and 1 contributor's copy. Sample copy for $8 (AUS) plus postage.

WESTVIEW, A Journal of Western Oklahoma, (II), Southwestern Oklahoma State University, 100 Campus Dr., Weatherford OK 73096-3098. (405)774-3168. **Editor:** Fred Alsberg. Magazine: 8½×11; 44 pages; 24 lb. paper; slick color cover; illustrations and photographs. Semiannual. Estab. 1981. Circ. 400.
Needs: Contemporary, ethnic (especially Native American), humor, literary, prose poem. No pornography, violence, or gore. No overly sentimental. "We are particularly interested in writers of the Southwest; however, we accept work of quality from elsewhere." Receives 10 unsolicited mss/month. Accepts 5 mss/issue; 10 mss/year. Publishes ms 3-12 months after acceptance. Published work by Diane Glancy, Wendell Mayo, Jack Matthews, Mark Spencer and Pamela Rodgers. Length: 2,000 words average. Also publishes literary essays, literary criticism, poetry. Occasionally critiques rejected mss.
How to Contact: Simultaneous submissions OK. Send complete ms with SASE. Reports in 1-2 months. "We welcome submissions on a 3.5 disk formatted for WordPerfect 5.0, IBM or Macintosh. Please include a hard copy printout of your submission."
Payment/Terms: Pays contributor's copy for first rights.

WHETSTONE, (I, II), English Dept., University of Lethbridge, 4401 University Dr., Lethbridge, Alberta T1K 3M4 Canada. (403)329-2367. Contact: Editorial Board. Magazine: 6×9; 90-140 pages; superbond paper; photos. Magazine publishing "poetry, prose, drama, prints, photographs and occasional music compositions for a general audience." Biannually. Estab. 1971. Circ. 500.
Needs: Experimental, literary, mainstream. "Interested in works by all writers/artists. Interested in multimedia works by individuals or collaborators." Editorial board reads ms September through March. Write for upcoming themes. Accepts 1-2 mss/issue, 3-4 mss/year. Published work by Madeline Sonik, Serenity Bee, Stephen Guppy and Ronnie R. Brown. Published new writers within the last year. Length: maximum 10 pages or 2,500 words. Publishes short shorts. Also publishes poetry, drama and art.
How to Contact: Send 2 short fictions or 6 poems maximum with SASE. Include cover letter with author's

background and experience. No simultaneous submissions. Reports in 6 months on mss. Publishes ms an average of 3-4 months after acceptance. Sample copy for $3 (Canadian) and 7½×10½ or larger SAE and 2 Canadian first-class stamps or IRCs.
Advice: "We seek most styles of quality writing. Follow all submission guidelines, including number of pieces and pages. Avoid moralizing."

WHISKEY ISLAND MAGAZINE, (II), Dept. of English, Cleveland State University, Cleveland OH 44115. (216)687-2056. Fax: (216)687-6943. E-mail: whiskeyisland@popmail.csuohio.edu. Website: http://www.csuohio.edu/whiskey_island (includes writer's guidelines, contest guidelines, staff information, history, short fiction, poetry, subscription information). **Editor:** Pat Stansberry. Editors change each year. Magazine of fiction and poetry, including experimental works, with no specific theme. "We provide a forum for new writers and new work, for themes and points of view that are both meaningful and experimental, accessible and extreme." Biannually. Estab. 1978. Circ. 2,500.
Needs: "Would like to see more short shorts, flesh fiction." Receives 100 unsolicited fiction mss/month. Accepts 4-6 mss/issue. Recently published Vickie A. Carr and John Fulmer. Publishes 5-10 new writers/year. Length: 6,500 words maximum. Also publishes poetry (poetry submissions should contain no more than 10 pages).
How to Contact: Send complete ms with SASE. Accepts queries/mss by e-mail and fax. No simultaneous or previously published submissions. Reports in 2-4 months on mss. Sample copy for $5.
Payment/Terms: Pays 2 contributor's copies. Acquires one-time rights.
Advice: "We seek a different voice, controlled language and strong opening. Also, learn to live with rejection. Even good work is turned away."

✓ **$ THE WILLIAM AND MARY REVIEW, (II)**, P.O. Box 8795, Campus Center, The College of William and Mary, Williamsburg VA 23187-8795. (757)221-3290. E-mail: bbhatl@mail.wm.edu. **Fiction Co-Editors:** Dave Gunton and Amanda Petrusich. Magazine: 110 pages; graphics; photography. "We publish high quality fiction, poetry, interviews with writers, and art. Our audience is primarily academic." Annually. Estab. 1962. Circ. 3,500.

- This magazine has received numerous honors from the Columbia Scholastic Press Association's Golden Circle Awards.

Needs: Literary, contemporary. No horror, hardcore porn, romance. Receives approximately 90 unsolicited fiction mss/month. Accepts 9 mss/issue. Recently published work by Toni de Bonneval, Philip Cioffari and Martha Howard. Publishes 2-3 new writers/year. Length: 7,000 words maximum; no minimum. Also publishes poetry. Usually critiques rejected mss.
How to Contact: Send complete ms with SASE and cover letter with name, address and phone number. "Cover letter should be as brief as possible." Accepts queries by e-mail. Simultaneous submissions OK. Queries by e-mail OK; no mss. Reports in 2-4 months. All departments closed in June, July and August. Sample copy for $5.50. May review novels, poetry and short story collections.
Payment/Terms: Pays 5 contributor's copies; discounts thereafter. Acquires first rights.
Advice: "We look for powerful, tight writing that creates energy. We believe that, first and foremost, a work of fiction must be an entertaining and compelling story. Page allotment to fiction will rise in relation to the quality of fiction received."

✓ 🏆 **$ WILLOW SPRINGS, (II)**, Eastern Washington University, 526 Fifth St., MS-1, Cheney WA 99201. (509)458-6429. **Editor:** Christopher Howell. Magazine: 9×6; 128 pages; 80 lb. glossy cover. "*Willow Springs* publishes literary poetry and fiction of high quality, a mix of new and established writers." Semiannually. Estab. 1977. Circ. 1,200.

- *Willow Springs* is a member of the Council of Literary Magazines and Presses and AWP. The magazine has received grants from the NEA and a CLMP excellence award.

Needs: Parts of novels, short stories, literary, prose poems, poems and translations. "No genre fiction please." Receives 150 unsolicited mss/month. Accepts 2-4 mss/issue; 4-8 mss/year. Does not read mss May 15-September 15. Publishes ms 6 months to one year after acceptance. Recently published work by Alberto Rios, Madeline DeFrees and Robin Hemley; published new writers within the last year. Length: 5,000 words minimum; 11,000 words maximum. Also publishes literary essays, literary criticism and poetry. Rarely critiques rejected mss.
How to Contact: Send complete ms with cover letter. Include short bio. No simultaneous submissions. Reports in 2 weeks on queries. Sample copy for $5.
Payment/Terms: Pays $20-50 and 2 contributor's copies for first North American rights.
Advice: "We hope to attract good fiction writers to our magazine, and we've made a commitment to publish three-four stories per issue. We like fiction that exhibits a fresh approach to language. Our most recent issues, we feel, indicate the quality and level of our commitment."

CHECK THE CATEGORY INDEXES, located at the back of the book, for publishers interested in specific fiction subjects.

WISCONSIN REVIEW, (I, II), University of Wisconsin, Box 158, Radford Hall, Oshkosh WI 54901. (414)424-2267. **Editor:** Debbie Martin. Editors change every year. Send submissions to "Fiction Editor." Magazine: 6×9; 60-100 pages; illustrations. Literary prose and poetry. Triannual. Estab. 1966. Circ. 2,000.
Needs: Literary and experimental. Receives 30 unsolicited fiction mss each month. Publishes 3 new writers/year. Length: up to 5,000 words. Publishes short shorts.
How to Contact: Send complete ms with SASE and cover letter with bio notes. Simultaneous submissions OK. Reports in 2-6 months. Publishes ms an average of 1-3 months after acceptance. Sample copy for $4.
Payment/Terms: Pays 2 contributor's copies. Acquires first rights.
Advice: "We look for well-crafted work with carefully developed characters, plots and meaningful situations. The editors prefer work of original and fresh thought when considering a piece of experimental fiction."

THE WORCESTER REVIEW, (II), Worcester Country Poetry Association, Inc., 71 Pleasant, Worcester MA 01609. (508)797-4770. Website: http://www.geocities.com/paris/leftbank/6433. **Editor:** Rodger Martin. Magazine: 6×9; 100 pages; 60 lb. white offset paper; 10 pt. CS1 cover stock; illustrations and photos. "We like high quality, creative poetry, artwork and fiction. Critical articles should be connected to New England." Annually. Estab. 1972. Circ. 1,000.
Needs: Literary, prose poem. "We encourage New England writers in the hopes we will publish at least 30% New England but want the other 70% to show the best of writing from across the US." Receives 20-30 unsolicited fiction mss/month. Accepts 2-4 mss/issue. Publishes ms an average of 6 months to 1 year after acceptance. Agented fiction less than 10%. Published work by Toni Graham and Carol Glickfeld. Length: 2,000 words average; 1,000 words minimum; 4,000 words maximum. Publishes short shorts. Also publishes literary essays, literary criticism, poetry. Sometimes critiques rejected mss and recommends other markets.
How to Contact: Send complete ms with cover letter. Reports in 6-9 months on mss. SASE. Simultaneous submissions OK if other markets are clearly identified. Sample copy for $5; fiction guidelines free.
Payment/Terms: Pays 2 contributor's copies and honorarium if possible for one-time rights.
Advice: "Send only one short story—reading editors do not like to read two by the same author at the same time. We will use only one. We generally look for creative work with a blend of craftsmanship, insight and empathy. This does not exclude humor. We won't print work that is shoddy in any of these areas."

☑ **WORDS OF WISDOM, (II)**, 3283 UNCG Station, Greensboro NC 27413-1031. (336)334-6970. E-mail: jmfreier@aol.com. **Editor:** Mikhammad Abdel Ishara. Newsletter: 5½×8½; 72-88 pages; copy paper; some illustrations and photographs. "Fiction, satire, humorous poetry and travel for a general audience—80% of readers can read above high school level." Estab. 1981. Circ. 160.
Needs: Adventure, contemporary, ethnic, feminist, historical, humor/satire, mainstream, mystery/suspense (cozy, private eye), regional, western (adult, frontier, traditional). No religion, children's, gay, romance. Fall 1998 issue to feature travel stories in foreign lands. Receives 50-60 unsolicited mss/month. Accepts 15-20 mss/issue; 60-80 mss/year. Publishes ms 2-12 months after acceptance. Recently published work by Tom Glenn, Kate Niles and William McGill. Publishes 0-5 new writers/year. Length: 2,000-3,000 words average; 1,200 words minimum; 7,000 words maximum. Publishes short shorts. Length: "Long enough to develop a good bite." Sometimes critiques rejected mss and recommends other markets.
How to Contact: Send complete manuscript copy and/or DOS floppy (uses MSWord) with cover letter including "name, address, SASE. Include author bio that includes titles of magazines you care enough to send the occasional subscription check. We use those instead of the names of the famous zines that have published you in the past. Submissions without cover letters are not read." Reports in 2-12 weeks on mss. SASE. Simultaneous and electronic (disk) submissions OK. Sample copy for $4 postpaid. Reviews short story collections.
Payment/Terms: Pays subscription to magazine for first publication of story. Acquires one-time rights. Publication not copyrighted.
Advice: "If your story has a spark of life or a degree of humor that brings a smile to my face, you have a chance here. Most stories lack these two ingredients. Don't send something you wrote ten years ago. Don't write your stories as if it were an episode of a TV series. Keep the number of characters down to a manageable number. Try to make everything relate to the plot line."

N $ **works & conversations, creative response in a time of change, (II)**, (formerly The Secret Alameda), P.O. Box 5008, Berkeley CA 94705. (510)653-1146. E-mail: rwhit@jps.net. Website: www.conversations.org. Editor: Richard Whittaker. **Fiction Editor:** Wm. Dudley. Magazine: 8½×11; 64 pages; color cover, 60 lb. coated paper. "We publish art portfolios and interviews, primarily. But we also publish essays, articles, photographs, graphics, a little fiction and poetry, and anything else that strikes our fancy. We're interested in the interior aspects of art and artmaking and the creative process—especially in relation to current values and meaning. Triquarterly. Evolved from earlier publication, *The Secret Alameda*." Estab. 1998.
Needs: Work that reflects upon issues of meaning in light of contemporary conditions. Length: 500-2,000 words. Will consider longer works in special cases. Circ. 2,000-4,000.
How to Contact: Send complete ms with cover letter. Reports in 4-6 weeks. Simultaneous and reprint submissions OK. Sample copy for $5.
Payment/Terms: Pays a small honorarium plus contributor's copies. Acquires one-time rights.
Advice: "Best to get a copy to see what we're up to."

☑ **WRITERS' FORUM, (II)**, University of Colorado at Colorado Springs, Colorado Springs CO 80933-7150. Fax: (719)262-4557. E-mail: kpellow@brain.uccs.edu. **Editor:** C. Kenneth Pellow. "Ten to fifteen short stories or self-contained novel excerpts published once a year along with 25-35 poems. Highest literary quality only: mainstream, avant-garde, with preference to western themes. For small press enthusiasts, teachers and students of creative writing, commercial agents/publishers, university libraries and departments interested in contemporary American literature." Estab. 1974.

Needs: Contemporary, ethnic (Chicano, Native American, not excluding others), literary and regional (West). Receives approximately 50 unsolicited fiction mss each month and will publish new as well as experienced authors. Published fiction by Lanny Ledeboer and Rick Koster. Publishes 2-4 new writers/year. Length: 1,500-8,500 words. Also publishes literary essays, literary criticism, poetry. Critiques rejected mss "when there is time and perceived merit."

How to Contact: Send complete ms and letter with relevant career information with SASE. Prefers submissions July through October. Simultaneous submissions OK. Reports in 5-8 weeks on mss. Publishes ms an average of 6 months after acceptance. Sample back copy $8 to *NSSWM* readers. Current copy $10. Make checks payable to "Writers' Forum."

Payment/Terms: Pays 2 contributor's copies. Cover price less 50% discount for extras. Acquires one-time rights.

Advice: "Read our publication. Be prepared for constructive criticism. We especially seek submissions with a strong voice that show immersion in place (trans-Mississippi West) and development of credible characters. Probably the TV-influenced fiction with trivial dialogue and set-up plot is the most quickly rejected. Our format—a 5½×8½ professionally edited and printed paperback book—lends credibility to authors published in our imprint."

☑ **WRITING FOR OUR LIVES, (I, IV)**, Running Deer Press, 647 N. Santa Cruz Ave., Annex, Los Gatos CA 95030. (408)354-8604. **Editor:** Janet M. McEwan. Magazine: 5¼×8¼; 80 pages; 70 lb. recycled white paper; 80 lb. recycled cover. "*Writing For Our Lives* is a periodical which serves as a vessel for poems, short fiction, stories, letters, autobiographies, and journal excerpts from the life stories, experiences and spiritual journeys of women. Audience is women and friends of women." Semiannually. Estab. 1992. Circ. 600.

Needs: Ethnic/multicultural, experimental, feminist, humor/satire, lesbian, literary, translations, "autobiographical, breaking personal or historical silence on any concerns of women's lives. *Women writers only, please*. We have no preannounced themes." Receives 15-20 unsolicited mss/month. Accepts 10 mss/issue; 20 mss/year. Publishes ms 2-24 months after acceptance. Recently published work by Andrea Allard, Gita Baliga-Savel, JoAnn Cooke, Kelley Jacquez, Jayatta Jones, Ronda Nielson and Karen X. Tulchinsky. Publishes 3-5 new writers/year. Length: 2,100 words maximum. Publishes short shorts. Also publishes poetry. Rarely critiques or comments on rejected mss.

How to Contact: Send complete ms with a cover letter. "Publication dates are May and November. Closing dates for mss are 2/15 and 8/15. Initial report immediate; next report, if any, in 1-18 months." Send 2 SASE's for reply, and one of them must be sufficient for return of ms if desired. Simultaneous and reprint submissions OK. Sample copy for $6-8 (in California add 8.25% sales tax), $9-11 overseas. Fiction guidelines for #10 SASE.

Payment/Terms: Pays 2 contributor's copies; additional copies for 50% discount and 1 year subscription at 50% discount. Acquires one-time rights in case of reprints and first worldwide English language serial rights.

Advice: "It is in our own personal stories that the real herstory of our time is told. This periodical is a place for exploring the boundaries of our empowerment to break long historical and personal silences. While honoring the writing which still needs to be held close to our hearts, we can begin to send some of our heartfelt words out into a wider circle."

XAVIER REVIEW, (I, II), Xavier University, 7325 Palmetto St., Box 110C, New Orleans LA 70125-1098. (504)483-7303. Fax: (504)485-7197. E-mail: rskinner@mail.xula.edu. **Editor:** Thomas Bonner, Jr. Managing Editor: Robert E. Skinner. Assistant Editor: Patrice Melnick. Production Consultant: Mark Whitaker. Magazine: 6×9; 75 pages; 50 lb. paper; 12 pt. CS1 cover; photographs. Magazine of "poetry/fiction/nonfiction/reviews (contemporary literature) for professional writers/libraries/colleges/universities." Semiannually. Estab. 1980. Circ. 500.

Needs: Contemporary, ethnic, experimental, historical (general), literary, Latin American, prose poem, Southern, religious, serialized/excerpted novel, translations. Receives 60 unsolicited fiction mss/month. Accepts 2 mss/issue; 4 mss/year. Does not read mss during the summer months. Published work by Randall Ivey, Rita Porteau, John Goldfine and Christine Wiltz. Length: 10-15 pages. Publishes literary criticism, literary essays, books of creative writing and poetry. Occasionally critiques rejected mss.

How to Contact: Send complete ms. Include 150-word bio and brief list of publications. SASE. Reports in 8-10 weeks. Sample copy for $5.

Payment/Terms: Pays 2 contributor's copies.

☑ **XTREME, The Magazine of Extremely Short Fiction**, P.O. Box 678383, Orlando FL 32825-8383. (407)382-8804. E-mail: rhowiley@aol.com. **Editor:** Rho Wiley. Magazine: 8½×11; 4 pages; heavy bond paper and cover. "Xtreme, the magazine of extremely short fiction, publishes fiction of EXACTLY 250 words. Fiction is considered on the basis of merit only. We feel that the 250 word format affords an opportunity for all writers to push the limits of the language." Semiannually. Estab. 1993. Circ. 500.

Needs: Humor/satire, literary, mainstream/contemporary. Receives 25-30 unsolicited mss/month. Accepts 10 mss/issue; 20 mss/year. Publishes ms 6 months after acceptance. Length: exactly 250 words. Sometimes critiques or comments on rejected mss.

How to Contact: Send complete ms with a cover letter. Reports in 6 weeks on queries; up to 6 months on mss. Send SASE for reply or return of ms. No simultaneous submissions. Sample copy for 9×12 SAE and 2 first-class stamps. Fiction guidelines included with sample copy.

Payment/Terms: Pays 3 contributor's copies for first North American serial rights.

Advice: Looks for "the ability to tell a complete story in the boundaries of the 250 word format. A succinct use of the language always stands out. Work with the form. Try to push the limits of what can happen in only 250 words."

☑ $ **THE YALE REVIEW, (II)**, Yale University/Blackwell Publishers Inc., P.O. Box 208243, New Haven CT 06520-8243. (203)432-0499. Fax: (203)432-0510. E-mail: susanbianochi@yale.edu. Editor: J.D. McClatchy. **Fiction Editor:** Susan Bianconi. Magazine: 9¼×6; 180-190 pages; book stock paper; glossy cover; illustrations and photographs. "*The Yale Review* is meant for the well-read general reader interested in a variety of topics in the arts and letters, in history, and in current affairs." Quarterly. Estab. 1911. Circ. 7,000.

Needs: Mainstream/contemporary. Receives 50-80 unsolicited mss/month. Accepts 1-3 mss/issue; 7-12 mss/year. Publishes ms 3 months after acceptance. Agented fiction 25%. Recently published work by Steven Millhauser, Deborah Eisenberg, Jeffrey Eugenides, Sheila Kohler, Joe Ashby Porter, Julie Orringer, John Barth and James McCourt. Publishes short shorts (but not frequently). Also publishes literary essays, poetry.

How to Contact: Send complete ms with a cover letter. Include estimated word count and list of publications. Reports in 1 month on queries; 2 months on mss. Send SASE for reply, return of ms or send a disposable copy of ms. Always include SASE. No simultaneous submissions. Reviews novels and short story collections. Send books to the editors.

Payment/Terms: Pays $300-400 on publication and 2 contributor's copies; additional copies for $7. Sends galleys to author. "Awards by the editors; cannot be applied for."

Advice: "We find that the most accomplished young writers seem to be people who keep their ears open to other voices; who read widely."

THE YALOBUSHA REVIEW, The Literary Journal of the University of Mississippi, University of Mississippi, P.O. Box 186, University MS 38677-0186. (601)232-7439. E-mail: yalobush@olemiss.edu. Editors change each year. Magazine: 5½×8½; 130 pages; 60 lb. off-white; card cover stock. "We look for high-quality fiction, poetry, and creative essays; and we seek a balance of regional and national writers." Annually. Estab. 1995. Circ. 500.

Needs: Literary. "No genre or formula fiction." List of upcoming themes available for SASE. Receives 30 unsolicited mss/month. Accepts 6 mss/issue. Does not read mss April through August. Published work by Larry Brown, Cynthia Shearer and Eric Miles Williamson. Length: 15 pages average; 35 pages maximum. Publishes short shorts. Also publishes literary essays and poetry. Sometimes critiques or comments on rejected mss.

How to Contact: Send complete ms with a cover letter. Reports in 1 month on queries; reporting time on mss varies. Send SASE for reply, return of ms or send a disposable copy of ms. Electronic submissions OK. Fiction guidelines for #10 SASE.

Payment/Terms: Pays 2 contributor's copies and $100 to the Editor's Choice winner for each issue. Pays on publication. Acquires first North American serial rights.

Advice: "We look for writers with a strong, distinct voice and good stories to tell." Would like to see more "good endings!"

YEMASSEE, The literary journal of the University of South Carolina, (II), Department of English, University of South Carolina, Columbia SC 29208. (803)777-4204. Fax: (803)777-9064. **Editor:** Melissa Johnson. Magazine: 5½×8½; 60-80 pages; 60 lb. natural paper; 65 lb. cover; cover illustration. "We are open to a variety of subjects and writing styles. *Yemassee* publishes primarily fiction and poetry, but we are also interested in one-act plays, brief excerpts of novels, essays, reviews and interviews with literary figures. Our essential consideration for acceptance is the quality of the work." Semiannually. Estab. 1993. Circ. 375.

Needs: Condensed/excerpted novel, ethnic/multicultural, experimental, feminist, gay, historical, humor/satire, lesbian, literary, regional. No romance, religious/inspirational, young adult/teen, children's/juvenile, erotica. Receives 10 unsolicited mss/month. Accepts 1-3 mss/issue; 2-6 mss/year. "We hold manuscripts until our reading periods—October 1 to November 15 and March 15 to April 30." Publishes ms 2-4 months after acceptance. Published work by Gene Able, Thomas David Lisk, Chris Railey, Robert B. Kennedy, Nichole Potts and Michael Cody. Length: 4,000 words or less. Publishes short shorts. Also publishes literary essays and poetry.

How to Contact: Send complete ms with a cover letter. Include estimated word count, brief bio, Social Security number and list of publications. Reports in 2 weeks on queries, 2-4 months after deadlines on mss. Send SASE for reply, return of ms or send disposable copy of ms. Simultaneous submissions OK. Sample copy for $5. Fiction guidelines for #10 SASE.

Payment/Terms: Pays 2 contributor's copies for first rights; additional copies $2.75. All submissions are considered for the *Yemassee* awards—$200 each for the best poetry and fiction in each issue when funding permits.

Advice: "Our criteria are generally based on what we perceive as quality. Generally that is work that is literary. We are interested in subtlety and originality, interesting or beautiful language; craft and precision. Read more, write more and revise more. Read our journal and any other journal before you submit to see if your work seems appropriate. Send for guidelines and make sure you follow them. Don't suck up in the cover letter. Be honest."

☑ **$ ZERO HOUR, "Where Culture Meets Crime," (I)**, Box 766, Seattle WA 98111. (206)282-5712. Fax: (206)405-2851. **Editor:** Jim Jones. Newsprint paper; illustrations and photos. "We are interested in fringe culture. We publish fiction, poetry, essays, confessions, photos, illustrations and interviews, for young, politically left audience interested in current affairs, non-mainstream music, art, culture." Semiannually. Estab. 1988. Circ. 3,000.

Needs: Confessions, erotica, ethnic, experimental, feminist, gay, humor/satire, psychic/supernatural/occult and translations. "Each issue revolves around an issue in contemporary culture: cults and fanaticism, addiction, pornography, etc." No romance, inspirational, juvenile/young, sports, science fiction, western. Receives 5 unsolicited mss/month. Accepts 3 mss/issue; 9 mss/year. Publishes ms 2-3 months after acceptance. Published work by Billy Childish, Billie Livingston and Peter Toliver. Publishes 20 new writers/year. Length: 1,200 words average; 400 words minimum; 5,000 words maximum. Publishes short shorts. Length: 400 words. Sometimes critiques rejected mss.

How to Contact: Query first. Reports in 2 weeks on queries; 1 month on mss. SASE. Simultaneous submissions OK. Sample copy for $3, 9×12 SAE and 5 first-class stamps. Fiction guidelines free. Reviews novels and short story collections.

Payment/Terms: Pays $25 per short story, $650 for novels for one-time rights. Sends galleys to author.

Advice: Looking for "straight-forward narrative prose—true-to-life experiences told about unique experiences or from an unusual perspective. Ask yourself does it fit our theme? Is it well written, from an unusual point of view or on an unexplored/underexplored topic? In terms of styles we are specifically seeking narrative prose that tells us a story, gives us a glimpse of a bigger picture, but not one that leaves us going, 'Huh?' It can't be too 'literary' or 'high brow' (some of us are refugees from academia), and it shouldn't be too experimental or too heavy on language over substance ('literary masturbation'). Some authors we like are: Jim Thompson, Graham Greene, Cookie Meuller, Dennis Cooper, Flannery O'Connor, Katherine Porter, Paul Bowles, and Harry Crews. Our audience is young, hip and not necessarily people who normally read books."

$ ZOETROPE, All Story, (II), AZX Publications, 260 Fifth Ave., Suite 1200, New York NY 10001. (212)696-5720. Fax: (212)696-5845. **Editor:** Adrienne Brodeur. Magazine: 10½×14; 60 pages; illustrations and photos. Triannual. Estab. 1997. Circ. 40,000.

- *Zoetrope: All Story* was ranked #6 on the *Writer's Digest*'s Fiction 50 list of top markets for fiction writers.

Needs: Literary, mainstream/contemporary, one act plays. Receives 500 unsolicited mss/month. Accepts 7-8 mss/issue; 21-24 mss/year. Publishes ms 2-6 months after acceptance. Agented fiction 15%. Length: 7,000 words maximum.

How to Contact: Send complete manuscript (no more than 2) with a cover letter. Include estimated word count and list of publications. Simultaneous submissions OK. Sample copy for $5 and 9×12 SAE and $1.70 postage. Fiction guidelines for #10 SASE. *No unsolicited submissions from June 1-August 31.*

Payment/Terms: Pays $1,000 for 2 year option on movie rights for unsolicited submissions; $5,000 for commissioned works.

$ ZYZZYVA, the last word: west coast writers & artists, (II, IV), 41 Sutter St., Suite 1400, San Francisco CA 94104. (415)752-4393. Fax: (415)752-4391. E-mail: zyzzyvainc@aol.com. Website: http://www.webdelsol.com/ZYZZYVA (includes guidelines, names of editors, selections from current issues, editor's note). Editor: Howard Junker. Magazine: 6×9; 208 pages; graphics; photos. "Literate" magazine featuring West Coast writers and artists. Triquarterly. Estab. 1985. Circ. 4,000.

- *Zyzzyva* ranked #10 on *Writer's Digest*'s Fiction 50 list of top markets for fiction writers, and was recently profiled in *Poet's & Writer's* magazine.

Needs: Contemporary, experimental, literary, prose poem. West Coast US writers only. Receives 400 unsolicited mss/month. Accepts 5 fiction mss/issue; 20 mss/year. Agented fiction: 10%. Recently published work by Justin Chin, Jewelle Gomez and Jess Mowry. Publishes 20 new writers/year. Length: varies. Also publishes literary essays.

How to Contact: Send complete ms. "Cover letters are of minimal importance." Reports in 2 weeks on mss. SASE. No simultaneous or reprint submissions. Sample copy for $5. Fiction guidelines on masthead page.
Payment/Terms: Pays $50 on acceptance for first North American serial rights.
Advice: "Search out the right market for you—not your dream market, but the magazine that needs and wants your manuscript. It is out there. As the education level of the general population increases—and as the number of avowed writers increases, too, we are finding more exciting work, especially by writers never published before."

Small Circulation Magazines

This section of *Novel & Short Story Writer's Market* contains general interest, special interest, regional and genre magazines with circulations of under 10,000. Although these magazines vary greatly in size, theme, format and management, the editors are all looking for short stories for their respective publications. Their specific fiction needs present writers of all degrees of expertise and interests with an abundance of publishing opportunities.

Although not as high-paying as the large-circulation consumer magazines, many of the publications listed here do pay writers 1-5¢/word or more. Also unlike the big consumer magazines, these markets are very open to new writers and relatively easy to break into. Their only criteria is that your story be well written, well presented, and suitable for their particular readership.

DIVERSITY IN OPPORTUNITY

Among the diverse publications in this section are magazines devoted to almost every topic, every level of writing and every type of writer. Paying genre magazines include *Marion Zimmer Bradley's Fantasy Magazine* (3-10¢/word); *Weird Tales* (3¢/word minimum); and *Mystery Time* (¼-1¢/word).

Some of the markets listed here publish fiction about a particular geographic area or by authors who live in that locale. A few of those regional publications are *Italian Americana*; *Big Sky Stories*; and *Texas Young Writers' Newsletter.*

Publications with even more specialized editorial needs than genre and regional fiction include *The Healing Inn*, "geared to encouraging Christians who have been wounded by a church or religious cult"; *Mentor & Protege* wanting stories that are mentoring related; and *Rosebud, For People Who Enjoy Writing*.

SELECTING THE RIGHT MARKET

Your chance for publication begins as you zero in on those markets most likely to be interested in your work. If you write genre fiction, check out specific sections for lists of magazines publishing in that genre (mystery, page 74; romance, page 92; science fiction and fantasy, page 103). For other types of fiction, begin by looking at the Category Index starting on page 632. If your work is more general, or, in fact, very specialized, you may wish to browse through the listings, perhaps looking up those magazines published in your state or region. Also check the Zine section for other specialized and genre publications.

In addition to browsing through the listings and using the Category Index, check the ranking codes at the beginning of listings to find those most likely to be receptive to your work. This is especially true for beginning writers, who should look for magazines that say they are especially open to new writers (**I**) and for those giving equal weight to both new and established writers (**II**). For more explanation about these codes, see the end of this introduction.

Once you have a list of magazines you might like to try, read their listings carefully. Much of the material within each listing carries clues that tell you more about the magazine. How to Use This Book to Publish Your Fiction starting on page 3 describes in detail the listing information common to all the markets in our book.

The physical description appearing near the beginning of the listings can give you clues about the size and financial commitment to the publication. This is not always an indication of quality, but chances are a publication with expensive paper and four-color artwork on the cover has more prestige than a photocopied publication featuring a clip art self-cover. For more information on some of the paper, binding and printing terms used in these descriptions, see Printing and Production Terms Defined on page 627.

FURTHERING YOUR SEARCH

It cannot be stressed enough that reading the listing is only the first part of developing your marketing plan. The second part, equally important, is to obtain fiction guidelines and read the actual magazine. Reading copies of a magazine helps you determine the fine points of the magazine's publishing style and philosophy. There is no substitute for this type of hands-on research.

Unlike commercial magazines available at most newsstands and bookstores, it requires a little more effort to obtain some of the magazines listed here. You may need to send for a sample copy. We include sample copy prices in the listings whenever possible.

FOR MORE INFORMATION

See The Business of Fiction Writing for the specific mechanics of manuscript submission. Above all, editors appreciate a professional presentation. Include a brief cover letter and send a self-addressed envelope for a reply or a self-addressed envelope in a size large enough to accommodate your manuscript, if you would like it returned. Be sure to include enough stamps or International Reply Coupons (for replies from countries other than your own) to cover your manuscript's return. Many publishers today appreciate receiving a disposable manuscript, eliminating the cost to writers of return postage and saving editors the effort of repackaging manuscripts for return.

Most of the magazines listed here are published in the US. You will also find some English-speaking markets from around the world. These foreign publications are denoted with a 🌐 symbol at the beginning of listings. To make it easier to find Canadian markets, we include a 🍁 symbol at the start of those listings. The ★ symbol indicates markets that offer writers greater opportunities by buying a large amount of freelance/unagented manuscripts, or by otherwise being very open to new writers.

The following is the ranking system we have used to categorize the listings in this section.

- **I Publication encourages beginning or unpublished writers to submit work for consideration and publishes new writers regularly.**
- **II Publication accepts work by established writers and by writers of exceptional talent.**
- **III Publication does not encourage beginning writers; prints mostly writers with previous publication credits; very few new writers.**
- **IV Special-interest or regional publication, open only to writers in certain genres or on certain subjects or from certain geographical areas.**
- **V Closed to unsolicited submissions.**

ABOVE THE BRIDGE, (IV), Third Stone Publishing, P.O. Box 416, Marquette MI 49855. (906)494-2458. E-mail: classen@mail.portup.com. Website: http://www.portup.com/ABOVE. **Editor:** Mikel B. Classen. Magazine: 8½×11; 56 pages; 80 lb. text paper; 80 lb. LOE cover stock; illustrations and photos. "For and about the Upper Peninsula of Michigan." Bimonthly. Estab. 1985. Circ. 5,000.

Needs: Regional. "Any stories pertaining to the Upper Peninsula of Michigan." Family-oriented magazine. "We appreciate disk submissions, using fiction online." Receives 15-20 unsolicited mss/month. Accepts 12-13 mss/year. Publishes ms up to 2 years after acceptance. Length: 800-1,000 words average; 300 words minimum; 2,000 words maximum. Publishes short stories and short venues. Length: 300-400 words. Also publishes literary essays and literary criticism.

How to Contact: Send complete ms with a cover letter. Should include estimated word count, bio, name, address, phone number. Reports in 6-8 months. Send SASE for reply, return of ms or send a disposable copy of ms. Simultaneous and reprint submissions OK. Sample copy for $3.50. Fiction guidelines free.
Payment/Terms: Pays 2¢/word on publication. "If your material is used online, you will be paid double (online plus in print)." Buys one-time rights.
Advice: "Make certain that the manuscript pertains to the Upper Peninsula of Michigan. If you've never been there, don't fake it."

ALTAIR, Alternative Airings in Speculative Fiction, (II), Altair Publishing, P.O. Box 475, Blackwood, South Australia 5051. +61 (8)8278 8995. Fax: +61 (8)8278 5585. E-mail: altair@senet.com.au. **Editor/Fiction Editor:** Robert N. Stephenson. **Fiction Editor:** Jason Bleckly. Magazine: A5; 152 pages; 80ssm bond paper; 250ssm glossy cover stock; illustrations. "We publish speculative fiction with a focus on science fiction and fantasy; a good mix of the two encouraged. We like character-driven stories."

- At press time, DNA Publications was being licensed to publish an American edition of this magazine. Contact DNA Publications at P.O. Box 2988, Radford VA 24143-2988 for updated guidelines.

Needs: Fantasy (science fantasy), mystery/suspense, science fiction (hard science, soft/sociological, some cyberpunk). Accepts 6-10 mss/issue; 12-70/year. Length: 5,000 words average; 2,000 words minimum; 6,500 words maximum. Publishes short shorts (length: 1,500 words). Sometimes critiques or comments on rejected mss.
How to Contact: Send complete ms with a cover letter. Include estimated word count and 5-line bio. "Return postage is essential or e-mail address; not read otherwise." Reports in 2 months on mss. SASE (or IRCs) for reply or return of ms.
Payment/Terms: Pays 3 cents/word and 1 contributor's copy; additional copies $10. Acquires first world serial rights. Issue #1 is a large international competition open to all writers. Information available from website.
Advice: "We want strong characters, good, clear ideas and a believable plot. We are not interested in single-faceted work; localized slang is not good for an international audience. We are looking for cultural influences and this will show through the writer's talent."

AMMONITE, 12 Priory Mead, Bruton Somerset BA100DZ United Kingdom. **Fiction Editor:** John Howard-Greaves. Published occasionally. Circ. 200.
Needs: "Myth, legend, science fiction to do with the current passage of evolution towards the possibilities of the Aquarian Age." Publishes 3-7 stories/issue. Length: no minimum; 2,500 words maximum.
Payment/Terms: Pays 1 contributor copy.

ANTHOLOGY, (I, II), Inkwell Press, P.O. Box 4411, Mesa AZ 85211-4411. (602)461-8200. E-mail: anthology@juno.com. Website: http://www.primenet.com/~inkwell. **Editor:** Sharon Skinner. Magazine: 8½×11; 20-28 pages; 20 lb. paper; 60-100 lb. cover stock; illustrations and photos. "Our intended audience is anyone who likes to read." Bimonthly. Estab. 1994. Circ. 500-1,000.
Needs: Adventure, children's/juvenile (5-9 and 10-12 years); fantasy (science fantasy, sword and sorcery), humor/satire, literary, mystery/suspense (amateur sleuth, police procedural, private eye/hardboiled), science fiction (hard science, soft/sociological). *Anthology* maintains an ongoing series of short stories based in the Mythical City of Haven. Information in guidelines. Receives 10-20 unsolicited mss/month. Accepts 2 mss/issue; 12 mss/year. Publishes ms 6-12 months after acceptance. Length: 3,000-6,000 words average; Haven stories 3,000-5,000 words. Publishes short shorts. Also publishes poetry.
How to Contact: Send complete ms with a cover letter. Include estimated word count. Reports in 4 weeks on queries; 2 months on mss. Send SASE for reply, return of ms or send disposable copy of ms. Simultaneous, reprint and electronic (disk or modem) submissions OK. Sample copy for $3.95. Fiction guidelines for 4½×9½ SASE. Reviews chapbooks and audio books.
Payment/Terms: Pays 1 contributor's copy; additional copies $2. Haven stories pay $5. Acquires one-time rights. *Anthology* retains rights to reprint any Haven story, however, author may submit the story elsewhere for simultaneous publication.
Advice: "Is there passion in the writing? Is there forethought? Will the story make an emotional connection to the reader? Send for guidelines and a sample issue. If you see that your work would not only fit into, but add something to *Anthology*, then send it."

**FOR EXPLANATIONS OF THESE SYMBOLS,
SEE THE INSIDE FRONT AND BACK COVERS OF THIS BOOK.**

ARACHNE, INC., (II), Arachne, hanging by a thread, Inc., 2363 Page Rd., Kennedy NY 14747-9717. **Editor:** Susan L. Leach. Chapbook: 8½×5; 25 pages; 20 lb. paper; 20 lb. cover; illustrations; b&w photos. Semiannually. Estab. 1980. Circ. 500.

Needs: Regional. "No obscenity, no pornography." List of upcoming themes available for SASE. Receives 50 unsolicited mss/month. Buys 4 mss/issue; 8-10 mss/year. Does not read mss during Christmas. Publishes ms 3 months after acceptance. Published work by Anne Thore Beacham. Length: 1,500 words average; 1,200 words minimum; 1,800 words maximum. Also publishes literary criticism, poetry. Sometimes critiques or comments on rejected ms.

How to Contact: Query with or without clips of published work or send complete ms with a cover letter. Should include estimated word count, bio. Reports in 2 weeks on queries; 2 months on mss. Send SASE for reply, return of ms or send a disposable copy of ms. No simultaneous submissions. Sample copy for $2.50.

Payment/Terms: Pays 2 contributor's copies; additional copies for $2. Acquires first rights. Sends galleys to author. Not copyrighted.

Advice: "Send clean laser-printed copy using a simple font—only a few poems at a time. I am not interested in reading seductive poetry or conquer-the-world poetry—so please, read a copy of *Arachne* first."

AUGURIES, Morton Publishing, P.O. Box 23, Gosport, Hants P012 2XD England. **Editor:** Nik Morton. Circ. 300.

Needs: "Science fiction and fantasy, maximum length 4,000 words." Averages 15 stories/year. Publishes 6 new writers/year.

Payment/Terms: Pays £2 per 1,000 words plus complimentary copy. "Buy back issues, then try me!" Sample copy for $10. Subscription (2 issues) $30 to 'Morton Publishing.' Member of the New SF Alliance.

Advice: "Rewrite, put it away, rewrite. Be self-critical. Ask yourself: What am I saying—what do I mean?"

$ AUREALIS, Australian Fantasy and Science Fiction, P.O. Box 2164, Mt. Waverley, Victoria 3149 Australia. Website: http://aurealis.hl.net (includes writer's guidelines, names of editors, interviews with authors, chat line, competitions, market news, online ordering, online bookshop). Fiction Editors: Dirk Strasser and Stephen Higgins. Zine specializing in science fiction, fantasy and horror. Semiannually. Circ. 2,500.

Needs: Publishes 7 stories/issue: science fiction, fantasy and horror short stories. Recently published work by Terry Dowling and Sean McMullen. Publishes 4 new writers/year. Length: 2,000 words minimum; 8,000 words maximum.

How to Contact: "No reprints; no stories accepted elsewhere. Send one story at a time."

Payment/Terms: Pays 2-6¢ (Australian)/word and contributor's copy. Sample copy for $10 (Australian). Writer's guidelines available for SAE with IRC.

Advice: "Read the magazine. It is available in the UK and North America."

BANGTALE INTERNATIONAL, (II), Wild Horse Press, P.O. Box 83984, Phoenix AZ 85071. (602)993-4989. E-mail: bangtale@primenet.com. **Editor:** William Dudley. Magazine: 8½×5½; 64 pages; 70 lb. paper; 80 lb. cover. "To publish work from and about as many different cultures and countries as we can." Semiannually. Estab. 1994. Circ. 500.

Needs: Adventure, children's/juvenile (1-4, 5-9, 10-12 years), condensed/excerpted novel, ethnic/multicultural, historical, humor/satire, literary, mystery/suspense, regional, romance, translations, westerns, young adult/teen. Receives 50 unsolicited mss/month. Accepts 4 mss/issue; 8 mss/year. Publishes ms 4-6 months after acceptance. Recently published work by Gabrielle Banks and Molly Caldwell. Length: 1,500 words average; 500 words minimum; 2,000 words maximum. Publishes short shorts. Also publishes literary essays, literary criticism and poetry. Sometimes critiques or comments on rejected mss.

How to Contact: Send complete ms with a cover letter. Include estimated word count, and bio. Reports in 4-6 months on mss. Send SASE for reply, return of ms or send disposable copy of ms. Simultaneous and electronic submissions OK. Sample copy for $5 and 8½×11 envelope with $1.50 postage. Fiction guidelines for #10 SASE.

Payment/Terms: Pays $10 minimum; $25 maximum on publication for one-time rights. Sometimes sends galleys to author. Not copyrighted.

Advice: "Write what you know and that which you feel strongly about. We want work that can be understood, work that has feeling, as opposed to work that is obscure and evasive."

BARDIC RUNES, (I, IV), 424 Cambridge St, Ottawa, Ontario K1S 4H5 Canada. (613)231-4311. E-mail address: bn872@freenet.carleton.ca. **Editor:** Michael McKenny. Magazine. Estab. 1990.

Needs: Fantasy. "Traditional or high fantasy. Story should be set in pre-industrial society either historical or of author's invention." Recently published work by Frida Westford, D.K. Latta, Cherith Baldry, Ross G. Kouhi, Ceri Jordan and Jeanny Driscoll. Length: 3,500 words or less.

How to Contact: Electronic submissions OK. For e-mail, send plain unencoded ASCII. "Others may not reach me and, if they do, I may not even reply." For disk, send WordPerfect or ASCII. "No need to unencode."

Payment/Terms: Pays ½¢/word on acceptance. Reports in 2 weeks.

Advice: "Writers, pay keen attention to our stated needs or your story will probably be rejected, however good it may be. We now have more subscribers and more contributors from around the world. Read on every continent except Antarctica."

BIG SKY STORIES, (II), P.O. Box 477, Choteau MT 59422. (406)466-5300. Editor: Happy Feder. 8½×11; 48 pages; heavy bond paper; illustrations and photos. "We publish fiction set in Big Sky Country (Montana, Wyoming, North and South Dakota) prior to 1950. Don't fake the history or geography. Our readers want to be entertained and educated!" Bimonthly. Estab. 1996. Circ. 4,000.

- *Big Sky Stories* is not accepting unsolicited mss in 1999.

Needs: Historical. Publishes special fiction issues or anthologies. Accepts 2-4 mss/issue. Also publishes literary essays. Recently published work by Johnny D. Boggs, Richard Wheeler, Stan Lynde and Gwen Petersen. Publishes 6-10 new writers/year. Often critiques or comments on rejected ms.
How to Contact: Send complete ms with a cover letter. Should include estimated word count and list of publications with submission. Reports in 1-2 months. Send SASE for reply, return of ms or send a disposable copy of ms. Simultaneous and reprint submissions OK. Sample copy for $4, 8½×11 SAE and 2 first-class stamps. Fiction guidelines for SASE. Reviews novels and short story collections.
Payment/Terms: Pays minimum 1¢/word on publication for first publication rights.
Advice: "Your first paragraph should introduce where, when, who and what, and the story must be set in Big Sky Country. Don't bluff or offer 'soft' history, i.e., a story that, with a few name/place changes, could take place in Ohio or Maryland or Okinawa. Know your Big Sky history."

BLACK BOOKS BULLETIN: WORDSWORK, (IV), Third World Press, P.O. Box 19730, Chicago IL 60619-0730. (773)651-0700. Fax: (773)651-7286. **Editor:** Haki R. Madhubuti. Magazine: 80 pages. "*Black Books Bulletin: WordsWork* publishes progressive material related to an enlightened African-American audience." Annually.

- In addition to publishing fiction, *Black Books Bulletin: WordsWork* is primarily a review publication covering nonfiction, fiction and poetry books by African-American authors.

Needs: Condensed/excerpted novel, ethnic/multicultural, feminist, historical (general). Receives 40 unsolicited mss/month. Accepts 2 mss/issue. Does not read mss January through June. Publishes ms 1 year after acceptance. Agented fiction 20%. Published work by Amiri Baraka, Keorapetse Kgositsile. Also publishes literary essays, literary criticism, poetry. Sometimes critiques or comments on rejected mss.
How to Contact: Query first. Include estimated word count and bio. Reports in 3 weeks on queries; 3 months on mss. Simultaneous and reprint submissions OK. Reviews novels and short story collections. Send books to Assistant Editor Melissa Moore.
Payment/Terms: Pays on publication. Acquires all rights.

BLACKFIRE, (I, IV), BLK Publishing Co., P.O. Box 83912, Los Angeles CA 90083-0912. (310)410-0808. Fax: (310)410-9250. E-mail: newsroom@blk.com. Website: http://www.blk.com. **Editor:** Alan Bell. Magazine: 8⅛×10⅞; 68 pages; color glossy throughout; illustrations and photographs. Bimonthly magazine featuring the erotic images, experiences and fantasies of black gay and bisexual men. Estab. 1992.

- BLK is a member of COSMEP.

Needs: Ethnic/multicultural, gay. No interracial stories or idealized pornography. Accepts 4 mss/issue. Recently published work by Terrance 'Kenji' Evans, Geoff Adams, Shawn Hinds, Stefan Collins and Robert Wesley. Publishes short shorts. Also publishes poetry.
How to Contact: Query first, query with clips of published work or send complete ms with a cover letter. Should include bio (3 sentences). Send a disposable copy of ms. Simultaneous and electronic submissions OK. Sample copy for $7. Fiction guidelines free.
Payment/Terms: Pays $50-100, 5 contributor's copies. Acquires first North American serial rights and right to anthologize.
Advice: "*Blackfire* seeks erotic material of the highest quality. The most important thing is that the work be erotic and that it features black gay men or themes. Study the magazine to see what we do and how we do it. Some fiction is very romantic, other is highly sexual. Most articles in *Blackfire* cater to black gay/bisexual men between these two extremes."

$ BOY'S QUEST, (II), The Bluffton News Publishing & Printing Co., P.O. Box 227, Bluffton OH 45817. (419)358-4610. Fax: (419)358-5027. **Editor:** Marilyn Edwards. Magazine: 7×9; 50 pages; enamel paper; illustrations and photos. Bimonthly. Estab. 1994.

- *Boy's Quest* received an EDPRESS Distinguished Achievement Award for Excellence in Educational Journalism, and a Silver Award-Gallery of Superb Printing.

Needs: Adventure, children's/juvenile (5-9 years, 10-12 years), ethnic/multicultural, historical, sports. Upcoming

MARKET CATEGORIES: (I) Open to new writers; **(II)** Open to both new and established writers; **(III)** Interested mostly in established writers; **(IV)** Open to writers whose work is specialized; **(V)** Closed to unsolicited submissions.

themes: astronomy, states, US presidents, weather, inventions, Indians. List of upcoming themes available for SASE. Receives 300-400 unsolicited mss/month. Accepts 20-40 mss/year. Agented fiction 2%. Published work by Jean Patrick, Eve Marar and Linda Herman. Length: 300-500 words average; 500 words maximum. Publishes short shorts. Length: 250-400 words. Also publishes poetry. Always critiques or comments on rejected mss.
How to Contact: Send complete ms with a cover letter. Include estimated word count, 1 page bio, Social Security number, list of publications. Reports in 2-4 weeks on queries; 6-10 weeks on mss. Simultaneous and reprint submissions OK. Sample copy for $3. Fiction guidelines for #10 SASE. Reviews novels and short story collections.
Payment/Terms: Pays 5¢/word and 1 contributor's copy on publication for first North American serial rights; additional copies $3, $2 for 10 or more.
Advice: Looks for "wholesome material. Follow our theme list and study copies of the magazine."

☑ $ **MARION ZIMMER BRADLEY'S FANTASY MAGAZINE, (II, IV)**, Box 249, Berkeley CA 94701-0249. (510)644-9222. Fax: (510)644-9222. E-mail: mzbfm@well.com. Website: http://www.mzbfm.com (includes writer's guidelines, articles on writing, back issue index). **Editor:** Mrs. Marion Bradley. Magazine: 8½×11; 64 pages; 60 lb. text paper; 10 lb. cover stock; b&w interior and 4-color cover illustrations. "Fantasy only; strictly family oriented." Quarterly.

- This magazine is named for and edited by one of the pioneers of fantasy fiction. Bradley is perhaps best known for the multi-volume Darkover series.

Needs: Fantasy. May include adventure, contemporary, humor/satire, mystery/suspense and young adult/teen (10-18) (all with fantasy elements). "No avant-garde or romantic fantasy. No computer games!" Receives 50-200 unsolicited mss/week. Accepts 8-10 mss/issue; 36-40 mss/year. Publishes ms 3-12 months after acceptance. Agented fiction 5%. Recently published work by India Edghill, Steven Piziks, Jo Clayton, Karen Anderson, Marion Zimmer Bradley and Dorothy J. Heydt. Publishes 10 new writers/year. Length: 3,000-4,000 words average; 5,500 words maximum. Publishes short shorts.
How to Contact: Send #10 SASE for guidelines *before* sending ms. Send complete ms. SASE. Reports in 90 days. No simultaneous submissions. Sample copy for $4.
Payment/Terms: Pays 3-10¢/word on acceptance and contributor's copies for first North American serial rights.
Advice: "If I want to finish reading it—I figure other people will too. A manuscript stands out if I care whether the characters do well, if it has a rhythm. Make sure it has characters I will know *you* care about. If you don't care about them, how do you expect me to? Read guidelines *before* sending ms. Beware of 'dime-a-dozen' subjects such as dragons, elves, unicorns, wizards, vampires, writers, sea creatures, brute warriors, ghosts, adventuring sorcerers/sorceresses, thieves/assassins, or final exams for wizards. We get dozens of these kinds of stories every week, and we reject all but the truly unusual and well-written ones."

$ **CHALLENGING DESTINY, New Fantasy & Science Fiction, (I)**, Crystalline Sphere Publishing, R.R. #6, St. Marys Ontario N4X 1C8 Canada. (519)884-7557. E-mail: csp@golden.net. Website: http://www.golden.net/~csp/ (includes previews of published and upcoming magazines, writer's guidelines, reviews of books, movies, soundtracks and games, links to other websites). **Editors:** David M. Switzer and Robert P. Switzer. Magazine: 8×5¼; 100 pages; Kallima 10 pt cover; illustrations. "We publish all kinds of science fiction and fantasy short stories." Quarterly. Estab. 1997. Circ. 500.
Needs: Fantasy, science fiction. No horror, short short stories. Receives 40 unsolicited mss/month. Accepts 6 mss/issue, 24 mss/year. Publishes ms 1-3 months after acceptance. Recently published work by Michael Mirolla, Stefano Donati, D. Sandy Nielsen, Bonnie Blake, Robert Arthur Vanderwoode and Erik Allen Elness. Publishes 12 new writers/year. Length: 6,000 words average; 2,000 words minimum; 10,000 words maximum. Also publishes literary essays, literary criticism and poetry. Often critiques or comments on rejected mss.
How to Contact: Send complete ms with a cover letter. Accepts queries/mss by e-mail. Include estimated word count. Reports in 1 month on queries, 2 months on mss. Send SASE for reply, return of ms or send disposable copy of ms. Simultaneous, reprint and electronic submissions OK. Sample copy for $5.50. Guidelines for 1 IRC. Reviews novels and short story collections. Send books to James Schellenberg, R.R. #1, 4421 Spring Creek Rd., Vineland Ontario L0R 2C0 Canada.
Payment/Terms: Pays 1¢/word plus 2 contributor's copies for first North American serial rights. Sends galleys to author.
Advice: "Manuscripts with a good story and interesting characters stand out. We look for fiction that entertains and makes you think. If you're going to write short fiction, you need to read lots of it. Don't reinvent the wheel. Use your own voice. We've been on the Web since the beginning and are accepting submissions over e-mail. A lot of action is happening online these days."

THE CHINOOK QUARTERLY, (II), Chinook Press, 1432 Yellowstone Ave., Billings MT 59102. (406)245-7704. **Editor:** Mary Ellen Westwood. Magazine: 7×8½; 60-80 pages; acid-free paper; card cover stock; illustrations; photos. "*The Chinook Quarterly* will be a catalyst for human change and understanding. We want forward-looking and challenging submissions that will be of use to readers in the West." Quarterly. Estab. 1996.
Needs: Adventure, children's/juvenile (10-12 years), condensed/excerpted novel, ethnic/multicultural, experimental, fantasy (science fantasy), feminist, historical, humor/satire, literary, mainstream/contemporary, mystery/

suspense (all kinds), regional, romance (contemporary, futuristic/time travel), science fiction (hard science, soft/sociological), sports, translations, westerns, young adult/teen (all kinds). Especially interested in stories about the contemporary West. "No fiction that degrades or discounts human beings." Accepts 4-6 mss/issue; 16-24 mss/year. Publishes ms 1-12 months after acceptance. Length: 1,600 words average; 300 words minimum; 2,000 words maximum. Publishes short shorts. Also publishes literary essays, literary criticism and poetry. Often critiques or comments on rejected mss.
How to Contact: Send complete ms with a cover letter. Include estimated word count, 250-word bio, Social Security number, list of publications and explanation of the piece submitted (why did you write it?)." Send SASE for return of ms. Reprints OK. Sample copy for $7. Fiction guidelines for #10 SASE. Reviews novels and short story collections.
Payment/Terms: Pays $2/printed page and 4 contributor's copies on publication. Acquires one-time rights. Sends galleys to the author.
Advice: "I am looking for a fresh and daring approach and a thinking view of the world. I admire risk takers. I want writing about real people, not just academic musings. I want the true life experiences of humans, not some shallow misinterpretations. Edit, edit, edit . . . after you rewrite, of course."

☑ $ **CLUBHOUSE MAGAZINE, Focus on the Family, (IV)**, 8605 Explorer Dr., Colorado Springs CO 80920. (719)531-3400, ext. 1750. Fax: (719)531-3499. **Editor:** Jesse Florea. Associate Editor: Annette Brashler Bourland. Magazine: 24 pages; illustrations and photos. Christian children's magazine. Monthly. Estab. 1987. Circ. 100,000.

- *Clubhouse Magazine* has received Evangelical Press Association awards for fiction and art.

Needs: Adventure, children's/juvenile (10-12 years), religious/inspirational, sports. No animal fiction or where the main character is not between the ages of 10-12 and dealing with issues appropriate to the age level. Would like to see more historical fiction with Bible-believing/Christian protagonist. Receives 30 unsolicited mss/month. Accepts 1 ms/issue; 12 mss/year. Recently published work by Nancy N. Rue, Sigmund Brouwer and Katherine Bond. Publishes 8 new writers/year. Length: 400-600 words average. Publishes short shorts. Often critiques or comments on rejected mss.
How to Contact: Send complete ms with a cover letter. Include estimated word count, Social Security number and list of publications. Reports in 4-6 weeks on queries and mss. Send SASE for reply, return of ms or send disposable copy of ms. Simultaneous submissions OK. Sample copy free. Fiction guidelines for $1.50.
Payment/Terms: Pays $25 minimum; $250 maximum on acceptance and 3 contributor's copies for first rights.
Advice: "*Clubhouse* readers are 8- to 12-year-old boys and girls who desire to know more about God and the Bible. Their parents (who typically pay for the membership) want wholesome, educational material with scriptural or moral insight. The kids want excitement, adventure, action, humor or mystery. Your job as a writer is to please both the parent and child with each article."

☑ **COCHRAN'S CORNER, (I)**, 1003 Tyler Court, Waldorf MD 20602-2964. Phone/fax: (301)870-1664. President: Ada Cochran. **Editor:** Jeanie Saunders. Magazine: 5½×8; 52 pages. "We publish fiction, nonfiction and poetry. Our only requirement is no strong language." For a "family" audience. Quarterly magazine. Estab. 1986. Circ. 500.
Needs: Adventure, children's/juvenile, historical, horror, humor/satire, mystery/suspense, religious/inspirational, romance, science fiction, young adult/teen (10-18 years). Would like to see more mystery and romance fiction. "Mss must be free from language you wouldn't want your/our children to read." Plans a special fiction issue. Receives 50 mss/month. Accepts 4 mss/issue; 8 mss/year. Publishes ms by the next issue after acceptance. Recently published work by James Hughes, Ellen Sandry, James Bennet, Susan Lee and Judy Demers. Publishes approximately 30 new writers/year. Length: 500 words preferred; 300 words minimum; 1,000 words maximum. Also publishes literary essays, literary criticism, poetry.
How to Contact: "Right now we are forced to limit acceptance to *subscribers only.*" Send complete ms with cover letter. Reports in 3 weeks on queries; 6-8 weeks on mss. SASE for manuscript. Simultaneous and reprint submissions OK. Sample copy for $5, 9×12 SAE and 90¢ postage. Fiction guidelines for #10 SASE.
Payment/Terms: Pays in contributor's copies. Acquires one-time rights.
Advice: "I feel the quality of fiction is getting better. The public is demanding a good read, instead of having sex or violence carry the story. I predict that fiction has a good future. We like to print the story as the writer submits it if possible. This way writers can compare their work with their peers and take the necessary steps to improve and go on to sell to bigger magazines. Stories from the heart desire a place to be published. We try to fill that need. Be willing to edit yourself. Polish your manuscript before submitting to editors."

☑ **COLD-DRILL MAGAZINE, (IV)**, English Dept., Boise State University, 1910 University Dr., Boise ID 83725. (208)385-1999. **Editor:** Tamara Shores. Faculty Advisor: Dr. Mitchell Wieland. Magazine: box format;

READ THE BUSINESS OF FICTION WRITING section to learn the correct way to prepare and submit a manuscript.

various perfect and non-perfect bound inserts; illustrations and photos. Material submitted *must be by Idaho authors or deal with Idaho*. For adult audiences. Annually. Estab. 1970. Circ. 500.
Needs: "The 1997-98 issue will not have a theme; it will be open to all forms of writing and artwork." Length: determined by submissions.
How to Contact: Query first. SASE.
Payment/Terms: Pays in contributor's copies. Acquires first rights.

COMMUNITIES MAGAZINE, (I, IV), P.O. Box 169, Masonville CO 80541-0169. Phone/fax: (970)593-5615. E-mail: communities@ic.org. Website: http://www.ic.org/ (includes samples of articles, ads, from current and back issues). **Editor:** Diana Christian. Guest editors change with each issue. "Articles on intentional communities—cohousing, ecovillages, urban group houses, student co-ops, rural communes, land-trust communities, and other forms of community (including non-residential)—as well as worker co-ops and workplace democracy. Written for people generally interested in intentional community and cooperative ventures, current and former community members, and people seeking to form or join an intentional community or co-op venture." Quarterly magazine. Estab. 1973. Circ. 4,000.
Needs: "Utopian" stories, science fiction (soft/sociological). "Stories set in intentional communities or cooperatively run organizations." Each issue focused around a theme. Accepts "1-2 mss/year (more if we got them)." Publishes 25-30 new writers/year. Length: 750 words minimum; 3,000 words maximum.
How to Contact: "To submit an article, please first send for writer's guidelines." Accepts queries/mss by e-mail and fax. Reports in 1 month on queries; 6-8 weeks on mss. Simultaneous and previously published submissions OK. Sample copy for $5. *Communities Magazine*, 138 Twin Oaks Rd., Louisa VA 23093.
Payment/Terms: Pays 1 year subscription (4 issues) or 4 contributor's copies. Acquires first North American rights.
Advice: "We receive too many articles and stories which are completely off topic (in which the writer assumes we are about community in the generic sense, i.e., "community spirit," a neighborhood or town), by people who have no idea what an intentional community is, and/or who have never seen the magazine. We ask that writers read a sample issue first. We like the personal touch; concrete, visual, tightly written, upbeat, or offbeat message; short. No abstract, negative or loosely written, long fiction."

☑ **THE COMPLEAT NURSE, A Voice of Independent Nursing, (I)**, Dry Bones Press, P.O. Box 640345, San Francisco CA 94164-0345. Phone/fax: (415)292-7371. E-mail: jrankin@drybones.com. Website: http://www.drybones.com (includes current listings, guest book, online order placement, delays in publication schedule). **Editor/Publisher:** Jim Rankin. Newsletter: 8½×11; 4-6 pages; 60 lb. paper; illustrations and photographs. "We publish themes, ideas, and subjects of interest to nurses and their patients—a definition we view very broadly. Nurses seen as cultural individuals, who practice as well in a profession." Monthly. Estab. 1990.

- Member of PMA, SPAN.

Needs: Adventure, children's/juvenile, erotica, ethnic/multicultural, fantasy (sexuality and sexual issues), feminist, gay, historical, humor/satire, lesbian, mainstream/contemporary, mystery/suspense, regional, religious/inspirational (historical), science fiction, senior citizen/retirement, translations, young adult/teen, nurse or patient issues. Impact of health care infrastructure changes. Publishes special fiction issues or anthologies. Receives 2-3 unsolicited mss/month. Fiction mss accepted varies; 3-5 mss/year. Publishes ms almost immediately to 1 year after acceptance. Length: 1,500 words average; 3,000 words maximum. Publishes short shorts. Also publishes literary essays, literary criticism, poetry. Always critiques or comments on rejected mss.
How to Contact: Query first with clips of published work. Include estimated word count, bio, Social Security number and list of publications. Reports in 1 month on queries; 1-2 months on mss. Send SASE for reply, return of ms or send a disposable copy of ms. Simultaneous submissions, reprints and electronic submissions OK. Reviews novels and short story collections. Send books to editor.
Payment/Terms: Pays in contributor's copies on publication. Rights acquired negotiable. Sends galleys to author.
Advice: "Please consider basic human issues including humor and personal experience and write about those things. We are a shoestring small press—and authors need to work with us to build markets. But we can consider good things others pass up, or unique things."

THE COZY DETECTIVE, Mystery Magazine, (I), Meager Ink Publishing, 686 Jakes Ct., McMinnville OR 97128. (503)435-1212. Fax: (503) 472-4896. E-mail: detectivemag@onlinemac.com. Editor: David Workman. **Fiction Editor:** Charlie Bradley. Magazine: 8½×5½; 80 pages; illustrations and photos. Publishes mystery/suspense fiction and true crime stories for mystery buffs. Quarterly. Estab. 1994. Circ. 2,000.
Needs: Condensed/excerpted novel, mystery/suspense (amateur sleuth, cozy, police procedural, private eye/hardboiled), science fiction (mystery), serialized novel, young adult (mystery). No "sex, violence or vulgarity." Publishes special fiction issues or anthologies. Receives 15-25 unsolicited mss/month. Accepts 5 mss/issue; 20 mss/year. Does not read mss June-August. Recently published work by Kris Neri, Wendy Dager, Ruth Latta, James Geisert, C. Lester Bradley and Robert W. Kreps. Length: 6,000 words maximum; will consider longer stories for two-part series. Publishes short shorts. Also publishes poetry. Sometimes critiques or comments on rejected ms.
How to Contact: Send complete ms with a cover letter. Include 1-paragraph bio and estimated word count.

Reports in 2 months on queries; 1-6 months on mss. Send SASE for reply, return of ms or send disposable copy of ms. Simultaneous, reprint and electronic submissions OK. Sample copy for $2.95. Fiction guidelines for #10 SASE. Reviews novels and short story collections. Send books to "Review Editor."
Payment/Terms: Pays 2 contributor's copies for first North American serial rights; additional copies $1.50.
Advice: "Do your best work—don't rush. Try to make your plot secondary to characters in the story. We look for action, crisp dialogue and original use of old ideas. We love a good mystery."

CZ'S MAGAZINE, (I, II), CZA, 10035 Douglas Ct., St. Ann MO 63074. (314)890-2060. E-mail: cz@cza.com. Website: http://www.cza.com/ (includes guidelines, reader participation in giving comments on stories and poems). **Editor:** Loretta Nichols. Magazine: 8×10; 20-25 pages; illustrations and photos. "This publication is produced for writers who want to be published in a general subject magazine. We publish general topics and wholesome plots. Family reading. Inspirational type stories and poems." Monthly. Estab. 1997. Circ. 200.
Needs: Adventure, children's/juvenile (10-12 years), experimental, fantasy (science fantasy, sword and sorcery), feminist, humor/satire, literary, mainstream/contemporary, mystery/suspense (amateur sleuth, police procedural, romantic suspense), psychic/supernatural/occult, religious/inspirational, romance (contemporary, futuristic/time travel, gothic), young adult/teen (adventure, mystery, romance, science fiction), interviews. Would like to see more inspirational and romance fiction. Receives 20 unsolicited mss/month. Accepts 3 mss/issue; 36 mss/year. Publishes ms "up to 3 months" after acceptance. Recently published work by Kenneth Goldman and Jack Fisher. Publishes 50 new writers/year. Length: 1,500 words average; 500 words minimum; 3,000 words maximum. Publishes short shorts. Also publishes literary essays, literary criticism and poetry. Sometimes critiques or comments on rejected mss.
How to Contact: Limits acceptance to subscribers only. Send complete ms with a cover letter. Accepts queries/mss by e-mail. Include estimated word count, bio and list of publications. Reports in 3 weeks on queries; 2 months on mss. Send SASE for reply, return of ms or send a disposable copy of ms. Simultaneous submissions and reprints OK. Sample copy for $2. Fiction guidelines free. Reviews novels and short story collections. Send books to editor.
Payment/Terms: Pays contributor's copies for one-time rights.
Advice: "Send your work with SASE. I always publish unpublished authors first (unless their work is not fitting)."

☑ **$ DAGGER OF THE MIND, Beyond The Realms Of Imagination, (II)**, K'yi-Lih Productions (a division of Breach Enterprises), 1317 Hookridge Dr., El Paso TX 79925-7808. (915)591-0541. **Executive Editor:** Arthur William Lloyd Breach. Magazine. 8½×11; 62-86 pages; hibright paper; high glossy cover; from 5-12 illustrations. "Our aim is to provide the reading, educated public with thought-provoking, intelligent fiction without graphic sex, violence and gore. We publish science fiction, fantasy, horror, mystery and parapsychological/fortean nonfiction material." Quarterly. Estab. 1990. Circ. 5,000.

- Do not send this publication "slasher" horror. The editor's preferences lean toward *Twilight Zone* and similar material. He says he added mystery to his needs but has received very little quality material in this genre.

Needs: Lovecraftian, *Twilight Zone* fiction. Intelligent, well-crafted and thought provoking exactly like the television series. Adventure, experimental, fantasy, horror, mystery/suspense (private eye, police procedural), science fiction (hard science, soft/sociological). Nothing sick and blasphemous, vulgar, obscene, racist, sexist, profane, humorous, weak, exploited women stories and those with idiotic puns. No westerns or slasher. Plans special paperback anthologies. Receives 500 unsolicited mss/month. Accepts 8-15 mss/issue; 90-100 mss/year depending upon length. Publishes ms 2 years after acceptance. Agented fiction 30%. Published work by Sidney Williams, Jessica Amanda Salmonson and Donald R. Burleson. Publishes 1-2 new writers/year. All lengths are acceptable; from short shorts to novelette lengths. Also publishes literary essays, literary criticism, poetry. Sometimes comments on rejected mss.
How to Contact: All mail should be addressed to Arthur Breach. Send complete manuscript with cover letter. "Include a bio and list of previously published credits with tearsheets. I also expect a brief synopsis of the story." Reports in 6 months on mss. SASE. Simultaneous submissions OK "as long as I am informed that they are such." Accepts electronic submissions. Sample copy for $3.50, 9×12 SAE and 5 first-class stamps. Fiction guidelines for #10 SASE.
Payment/Terms: Pays ½-1¢/word plus 1 contributor's copy on publication for first rights (possibly anthology rights as well).
Advice: "I'm a big fan of the late H.P. Lovecraft. I love reading through Dunsanian and Cthulhu Mythos tales. I'm constantly on the lookout for this special brand of fiction. If you want to grab my attention immediately, write on the outside of the envelope 'Lovecraftian submission enclosed.' There are a number of things which make submissions stand out for me. Is there any sensitivity to the tale? I like sensitive material, so long as it doesn't become mushy. Another thing that grabs my attention are characters which leap out of the pages at you. Move me, bring a tear to my eye; make me stop and think about the world and people around me. Frighten me with little spoken of truths about the human condition. In short, show me that you can move me in such a way as I have never been moved before."

N **DARK MATTER, The Magazine of Dark Fantasy and Science Fiction, (II)**, Sign of the Celtic Cross Press, 2222 Foothill Blvd., Suite E-216, La Crescenta CA 91011-1456. **Editor:** Christopher Hennessey-DeRose. Magazine: digest sized; 30-40 pages; 24 lb. paper; gloss cover stock; illustrations. "*TwilightZone*-esque stories/art for a mature (not xxx-rated) audience." Publishes 3 times/year. Estab. 1998. Circ. 100.
Needs: Horror, humor/satire, psychic/supernatural/occult, science fiction (hard science, soft/sociological). "No fantasy, splatterpunk." Receives 50 unsolicited mss/month. Accepts 4-5 mss/issue; 15-20 mss/year. Publishes ms 6-12 months after acceptance. Recently published work by D.F. Lewis, Charlee Jacob, D. Sandy Nielsen and John B. Rosenman. Length: 2,000 words average; 250 words minimum; 3,000 words maximum. Publishes short shorts. Also publishes literary essays. Sometimes critiques or comments on rejected ms.
How to Contact: Send complete ms with a cover letter. Include estimated word count, 50-word bio, social security number and list of publications. Reports in 3 months. Send SASE for return of ms or send a disposable copy of ms. Simultaneous and reprint submissions OK. Sample copy for $4.95. Fiction guidelines free.
Payment/Terms: Pays $2 on acceptance and 1 contributor's copy; additional copies $3. Acquires first North American serial rights and non-exclusive anthology reprint rights.
Advice: "Use proper manuscript format."

DREAM INTERNATIONAL/QUARTERLY, (I, II, IV), U.S. Address: Charles I. Jones, #H-1, 411 14th St., Ramona CA 92065-2769. **Editor-in-Chief:** Charles I. Jones. Magazine: 5×7; 80-135 pages; Xerox paper; parchment cover stock; some illustrations and photos. "Publishes fiction and nonfiction that is dream-related or clearly inspired by a dream. Also dream-related fantasy." Quarterly. Estab. 1981. Circ. 80-100.
Needs: Adventure, confession, contemporary, erotica, ethnic, experimental, fantasy, historical, horror, humor/satire, literary, mainstream, mystery/suspense, prose poem, psychic/supernatural/occult, romance, science fiction, translations, young adult/teen (10-18). "We would like to see submissions that deal with dreams that have an influence on the person's daily waking life. Suggestions for making dreams beneficial to the dreamer in his/her waking life. We would also like to see more submissions dealing with lucid dreaming." Receives 20-30 unsolicited mss/month. Publishes ms 8 months to 2 years after acceptance. Publishes 40-50 new writers/year. Length: 1,000 words minimum; 2,000 words maximum. Publishes short shorts. Recently published work by Cristopher Clutter, Judith Klass, Florence McGinn, Scott McFarlane and Dawn Goodrich. Also publishes literary essays, poetry (poetry submissions to Carmen M. Pursifull, 809 W. Maple St., Champaign IL 61820-2810. Hard copy only for poetry . . . no electronic submissions please! Send SASE for poetry guidelines).
How to Contact: Submit ms. Reports in 6 weeks on queries; 3 months on mss. SASE. Simultaneous and reprint submissions OK. Electronic submissions preferred (except poetry). "If you really want something to have the best chance, send an MS-DOS format IBM-compatible file on a 3.5 disk in MS-Word for Windows format (ASCII and WordPerfect also acceptable). Hardcopy must accompany disk." Sample copy for $13. Guidelines $2 with SAE and 2 first-class stamps. Subscription: $50 (1-year); $100 (2-year). "Accepted mss will not be returned unless requested at time of submission."
Payment/Terms: Pays in contributor's copies (contributors must pay $3 for postage and handling). Offers magazine subscription. Acquires one-time rights.
Advice: "Write about what you know. Make the reader 'stand up and take notice.' Avoid rambling and stay away from chichés in your writing unless, of course, it is of a humorous nature and is purposefully done to make a point."

$ DREAMS & VISIONS, New Frontiers in Christian Fiction, (II), Skysong Press, 35 Peter St. S., Orillia, Ontario L3V 5AB Canada. Website: http://www.bconnex.net/~skysong. **Editor:** Steve Stanton. Magazine: 5½×8½; 56 pages; 20 lb. bond paper; glossy cover. "Contemporary Christian fiction in a variety of styles for adult Christians." Triannually. Estab. 1989. Circ. 200.
Needs: Contemporary, experimental, fantasy, humor/satire, literary, religious/inspirational, science fiction (soft/sociological). "All stories should portray a Christian world view or expand upon Biblical themes or ethics in an entertaining or enlightening manner." Receives 20 unsolicited mss/month. Accepts 7 mss/issue; 21 mss/year. Publishes ms 2-6 months after acceptance. Length: 2,500 words; 2,000 words minimum; 6,000 words maximum.
How to Contact: Send complete ms with cover letter. "Bio is optional: degrees held and in what specialties, publishing credits, service in the church, etc." Reports in 1 month on queries; 2-4 months on mss. SASE. Simultaneous submissions OK. Sample copy for $4.95. Fiction guidelines for SASE or on website.
Payment/Terms: Pays ½¢/word and contributor's copy. Acquires first North American serial rights and one-time, non-exclusive reprint rights.
Advice: "In general we look for work that has some literary value, that is in some way unique and relevant to Christian readers today. Our first priority is technical adequacy, though we will occasionally work with a beginning writer to polish a manuscript. Ultimately, we look for stories that glorify the Lord Jesus Christ, stories that build up rather than tear down, that exalt the sanctity of life, the holiness of God, and the value of the family."

ELDRITCH TALES, (II, IV), Yith Press, 1051 Wellington Rd., Lawrence KS 66049. (913)843-4341. **Editor-in-Chief:** Crispin Burnham. Magazine: 6×9; 120 pages (average); glossy cover; illustrations; "very few" photos. "The magazine concerns horror fiction in the tradition of the old *Weird Tales* magazine. We publish fiction in the tradition of H.P. Lovecraft, Robert Bloch and Stephen King, among others, for fans of this particular genre." Semiannually. Estab. 1975. Circ. 1,000.

Needs: Horror and psychic/supernatural/occult. "No mad slasher stories or similar nonsupernatural horror stories." Receives about 8 unsolicited fiction mss/month. Accepts 12 mss/issue, 24 mss/year. Published work by J.N. Williamson, William F. Wu, Ron Dee and Charles Grant. Published new writers within the last year. Length: 50-100 words minimum; 20,000 words maximum; 10,000 words average. Occasionally critiques rejected mss.
How to Contact: Send complete ms with SASE and cover letter stating past sales. Previously published submissions OK. Prefers letter-quality submissions. Reports in 4 months. Publication could take up to 5 years after acceptance. Sample copy for $7.25.
Payment/Terms: ¼¢/word; 1 contributor's copy. $1 minimum payment. Pays in royalties on publication for first rights.
Advice: "Buy a sample copy and read it thoroughly. Most rejects with my magazine are because people have not checked out what an issue is like or what type of stories I accept. Most rejected stories fall into one of two categories: non-horror fantasy (sword & sorcery, high fantasy) or non-supernatural horror (mad slasher stories, 'Halloween' clones, I call them). When I say that they should read my publication, I'm not whistling Dixie. We hope to up the magazine's frequency to a quarterly. We also plan to be putting out one or two books a year, mostly novels, but short story collections will be considered as well."

THE ELOQUENT UMBRELLA, (I, II, IV), Linn-Benton Community College, 6500 SW Pacific Blvd., Albany OR 97321-3779. (541)753-3335. **Contact:** Linda Smith. Magazine: illustrations and photos. "*The Eloquent Umbrella*'s purpose is to showcase art, photography, poetry and prose of Linn and Benton Counties in Oregon." Annually. Estab. 1990. Circ. 500.
Needs: Regional. "No slander, pornography or other material unsuitable for community reading." Accepts 50-100 mss/issue. Deadline January 15 each year. Reads mss during winter term only; publishes in spring. Length: 2,000 words maximum. Publishes short shorts. Also publishes literary essays, literary criticism and poetry.
How to Contact: Send complete ms with cover letter. Include 1- to 5-line bio. Reports in 6 weeks on mss. SASE for return of ms or send a disposable copy of ms. Simultaneous submissions OK. Sample copy for $2 and 8½×11 SAE.
Payment/Terms: Rights remain with author.
Advice: "The magazine is created by a collective editorial board and production team in a literary publication class."

EYES, (I, II), Apt. 301, 2715 S. Jefferson Ave., Saginaw MI 48601-3830. (517)752-5202. Website: http://members.aol.com/fjm3eyes/index.html (includes guidelines). **Editor:** Frank J. Mueller, III. Magazine: 8½×11; 40 pages; 20 lb. paper; Antiqua parchment, blue 65 lb. cover. "No specific theme. Speculative fiction and surrealism most welcome. For a general, educated, not necessarily literary audience." Estab. 1991. Circ. 30-40.
Needs: Contemporary, horror (psychological), mainstream, ghost story. "Especially looking for speculative fiction and surrealism. Would like to see more ghost stories, student writing. Dark fantasy OK, but not preferred." No sword/sorcery, no overt science fiction. Nothing pornographic; no preachiness; children's fiction discouraged. Accepts 4-8 mss/issue. Publishes ms up to 1 year or longer after acceptance. Publishes 14-20 new fiction writers/year. Length: up to 6,000 words. Sometimes critiques rejected mss.
How to Contact: Query first or send complete ms. Reports in 1 month (or less) on queries; 3 months or longer on mss. SASE. No simultaneous submissions. Sample copy for $4; extras $4. Subscriptions $14. (Checks to Frank J. Mueller III.) Fiction guidelines for #10 SASE.
Payment/Terms: Pays one contributor's copy. Acquires one-time rights.
Advice: "Pay attention to character. A strong plot alone, while important, may not be enough to get you in *Eyes*. Atmosphere and mood are also important. Please proofread. If you have a manuscript you like enough to see it in *Eyes*, send it to me. Above all, don't let rejections discourage you. I would encourage the purchase of a sample to get an idea of what I'm looking for."

🌐 **$ THE FIRST WORD BULLETIN, (I, II)**, Domingo Fernandez 5, Box 500, 28036 Madrid, Spain. United States address: **c/o Mary Swain,** 2046 Lothbury Dr., Fayetteville NC 28304-5666. (910)426-0134. Fax: (910)426-5240. E-mail: gw83@correo.interlink.es. Website: http://www.interlink.es/peraso/first (includes names and addresses of editors, addressses for subscriptions, list of types of stories). Managing Editor: G.W. Amick. Magazine: 15 cm×21cm; 64 pages; slick paper; 160 grams, slick cover; illustrations. "We want to make the public acutely aware of problems concerning pollution of air, earth and water. Also man's inhumanity to man and animal." Publishes material on environment, ecology, nature, alternative medicine; young adult, retirement articles. Quarterly. Estab. 1995. Circ. 5,000.
Needs: Adventure, historical, humor/satire, literary, mainstream/contemporary, senior citizen/retirement, young

MARKET CONDITIONS are constantly changing! If you're still using this book and it is 2000 or later, buy the newest edition of *Novel & Short Story Writer's Market* at your favorite bookstore or order from Writer's Digest Books.

adult/teen (adventure, western). No pornography, smut, dirty language; no mystery, science fiction (unless related to the world environment), detective stories or romance. Would like to see more "down-to-earth grass-roots stories; more alternatives to helping the poor." Receives 15-20 unsolicited mss/month. Accepts 6-8 mss/issue; 24-32 mss/year. Publishes ms 1-2 months after acceptance. Agented fiction 10%. Recently published work by Evelyn Horan (Israel-American), Richard Reeve (UK), May Lenzer (USA), Dorothy Eker (Canada) and Joyce Vath (Mexico). Publishes 8 new writers/year. Length: 800 words minimum; 4,000 words maximum. Publishes short shorts. Also publishes literary essays, literary criticism and poetry. Often critiques or comments on rejected mss.

How to Contact: Send complete ms with a cover letter or submit through an agent. Include estimated word count, short bio, Social Security number, list of publications. Reports in 6 weeks on queries; 3-4 months on mss. Send disposable copy of ms. Sample copy for $6.50. Fiction guidelines for $2. "We use only overseas airmail postage as surface mail is far too slow."

Payment/Terms: Pays 25¢/word minimum, $50 maximum plus 1 contributor's copy (writer pay postage, 4 IRCs) for one-time world rights.

Advice: "In fiction I like to see the two dogs and a bone theory, well crafted with attention to clarity and precision of language, that is a seamless read. We want to give exposure to emerging writers. First, write from the heart and then revise and revise until it is acceptable. You don't always have to write what you know about but if different pay close attention to detail from research. Study the market you are writing for. Most manuscripts that land on an editor's desk are not suitable because of not being familiar with the magazine or the editor's needs. Some are too long or of the wrong genre. Buy a copy and know the magazine."

FORESIGHT, (IV), 44 Brockhurst Rd., Hodge Hill, Birmingham B36 8JB England. 0121.783.0587. Editor: John Barklam. **Fiction Editor:** Judy Barklam. Quarterly.

Needs: Magazine including "new age material, world peace, psychic phenomena, research, occultism, spiritualism, mysticism, UFOs, philosophy, etc. Shorter articles required on a specific theme related to the subject matter of *Foresight* magazine." Length: 300-1,000 words.

How to Contact: Send SAE with IRC for return of ms.

Payment/Terms: Pays in contributor's copies. Sample copy for 75p and 50p postage.

$ FREE FOCUS/OSTENTATIOUS MIND, Wagner Press, (I, II), Bowbridge Press, P.O. Box 7415, JAF Station, New York NY 10116-7415. **Editor:** Patricia Denise Coscia. Editors change each year. Magazine: 8×14; 10 pages; recycled paper; illustrations and photos. "*Free Focus* is a small-press magazine which focuses on the educated women of today, and *Ostentatious Mind* is designed to encourage the intense writer, the cutting reality." Bimonthly. Estab. 1985 and 1987. Circ. 100 each.

Needs: Experimental, feminist, humor/satire, literary, mainstream/contemporary, mystery/suspense (romantic), psychic/supernatural/occult, westerns (traditional), young adult/teen (adventure). "X-rated fiction is not accepted." List of upcoming themes available for SASE. Plans future special fiction issue or anthology. Receives 1,000 unsolicited mss/month. Does not read mss February to August. Publishes ms 3-6 months after acceptance. Published work by Edward Janz. Publishes 200 new writers/year. Length: 500 words average; 1,000 words maximum. Publishes short shorts. Also publishes literary essays, literary criticism and poetry. Always critiques or comments on rejected mss. Sponsors contest for work submitted to *Free Focus*.

How to Contact: Query with clips of published work or send complete ms with a cover letter. Should include 100-word bio and list of publications. Reports in 3 months. Send SASE for reply. Simultaneous submissions OK. Sample copy for $3, #10 SAE and $1 postage. Fiction guidelines for #10 SAE and $1 postage. Reviews novels and short story collections.

Payment/Terms: Pays $2.50-5 and 2 contributor's copies on publication for all rights; additional copies for $2. Sends galleys to author.

Advice: "This publication is for beginning writers. Do not get discouraged; submit your writing. We look for imagination and creativity; no x-rated writing."

GAY CHICAGO MAGAZINE, (II), Gernhardt Publications, Inc., 3121 N. Broadway, Chicago IL 60657-4522. (773)327-7271. Publisher: Ralph Paul Gernhardt. Associate Publisher: Jerry Williams. **Entertainment Editor:** Jeff Rossen. Magazine: 8½×11; 80-144 pages; newsprint paper and cover stock; illustrations; photos. Entertainment guide, information for the gay community.

Needs: Erotica (but no explicit hard core), lesbian, gay and romance. Receives "a few" unsolicited mss/month. Acquires 10-15 mss/year. Published new writers within the last year. Length: 1,000-3,000 words.

How to Contact: Send all submissions Attn: Jeff Rossen. Send complete ms with SASE. Accepts 3.5 disk submissions and Macintosh or ASCII Format, "also accepts floppies and zips." Reports in 4-6 weeks on mss. Free sample copy for 9×12 SAE and $1.45 postage.

Payment/Terms: Minimal. 5-10 free contributor's copies; no charge for extras "if within reason." Acquires one-time rights.

GLOBAL TAPESTRY JOURNAL, (II), BB Books, 1 Spring Bank, Longsight Rd., Copster Green, Blackburn, Lancashire BB1 9EU England. **Editor:** Dave Cunliffe. Magazine. Limited press run: 1,000-1,500/issue.

Needs: "Post-underground with avant-garde, experimental, alternative, counterculture, psychedelic, mystical,

anarchist etc. fiction for a bohemian and counterculture audience." Published fiction by Andy Darlington, Sir Darren Subarton and A.D. Winans. Published work by new writers within the last year.
How to Contact: Accepts unsolicited mss. SAE, IRCs. Reports in 2-6 weeks.
Payment/Terms: Pays contributor's copy. Sample copy for $4 (Sterling Cheque, British Money Order or dollar currency).

N ✓ $ **GRUE MAGAZINE, (II, IV)**, Hell's Kitchen Productions, P.O. Box 370, New York NY 10108-0370. Phone/fax: (212)245-2329. E-mail: nadramia@panix.com. **Editor:** Peggy Nadramia. Magazine: 5½×8½; 96 pages; 60 lb. paper; 10 pt. C1S film laminate cover; illustrations; photos. "We look for quality short fiction centered on horror and dark fantasy—new traditions in the realms of the gothic and the macabre for horror fans well read in the genre, looking for something new and different, as well as horror novices looking for a good scare." Triannually. Estab. 1985.
Needs: Horror, psychic/supernatural/occult. No fantasy or science fiction. Receives 250 unsolicited fiction mss/month. Accepts 10 mss/issue; 25-30 mss/year. Publishes ms 1-2 years after acceptance. Recently published work by Wayne Allen Sallee, Kevin Filan, A.R. Morlan and Denise Dumars. Publishes 10-15 new writers/year. Length: 4,000 words average; 6,500 words maximum. Sometimes critiques rejected ms.
How to Contact: Send complete ms with cover letter. "I like to hear where the writer heard about *Grue*, his most recent or prestigious sales, and maybe a word or two about himself." Reports in 3 weeks on queries; 6 months on mss. Send SASE for return of ms. Sample copy for $5. Fiction guidelines for #10 SASE.
Payment/Terms: Pays ½¢/word on publication and 2 contributor's copies for first North American serial rights.
Advice: "Remember that readers of *Grue* are mainly seasoned horror fans, and *not* interested or excited by a straight vampire, werewolf or ghost story—they'll see all the signs, and guess where you're going long before you get there. Throw a new angle on what you're doing; put it in a new light. How? Well, what scares *you*? What's *your* personal phobia or anxiety? When the writer is genuinely, emotionally involved with his subject matter, and is totally honest with himself and his reader, then we can't help being involved, too, and that's where good writing begins and ends."

$ **THE GRYPHON SCIENCE FICTION AND FANTASY READER, The Paperback Magazine of Science Fiction-Science Fantasy, (II)**, (formerly *Other Worlds*), Gryphon Publications, Box 209, Brooklyn NY 11228. **Editor:** Gary Lovisi. Magazine: 5×8; 150 pages; offset paper; card cover; perfect-bound; illustrations and photographs. "Adventure—or action-oriented SF—stories that are fun to read." Annually. Estab. 1988. Circ. 500.
Needs: Science fiction, fantasy or sword and sorcery. Receives 24 unsolicited mss/month. Accepts 4-6 mss/issue. Publishes ms 1-2 years (usually) after acceptance. Length: 3,000 words maximum. Publishes short shorts. Length: 500 words. Sometimes critiques rejected mss and recommends other markets.
How to Contact: Query first. Do not send ms as most of issues are filled with staff/contract authors. Simultaneous submissions OK. Reports in 2 weeks on queries; 2 months on mss. SASE. Sample copy for $15 (150 pages perfect bound).
Payment/Terms: Pays $5-50/story and 1 contributor's copy. Acquires first North American serial rights. Copyright reverts to author.
Advice: Looks for classic style science fiction and fantasy.

N **HARD ROW TO HOE DIVISION, (II)**, Misty Hill Press, P.O. Box 541-I, Healdsburg CA 95448. (707)433-9786. **Editor:** Joe Armstrong. Newsletter: 8½×11; 12 pages; 60 lb. white paper; illustrations and photos. "Book reviews, short story and poetry of rural USA including environmental and nature subjects." Triannually. Estab. 1982. Circ. 150.

- *Hard Row to Hoe* was called "one of ten best literary newsletters in the U.S." by *Small Press* magazine.

Needs: Rural America. Receives 8-10 unsolicited mss/month. Acquires 1 ms/issue; 3-4 mss/year. Publishes ms 6-9 months after acceptance. Length: 1,500 words average; 2,000-2,200 words maximum. Publishes short shorts. Sometimes critiques rejected mss.
How to Contact: Send complete ms with cover letter. Reports in 3-4 weeks on mss. SASE. No simultaneous submissions. Sample copy for $2. Fiction guidelines for legal-size SASE.
Payment/Terms: Pays 2 contributor's copies. Acquires one-time rights.
Advice: "Be certain the subject fits the special need."

$ **HARDBOILED, (I, II)**, Gryphon Publications, P.O. Box 209, Brooklyn NY 11228-0209. **Editor:** Gary Lovisi. Magazine: Digest-sized; 100 pages; offset paper; color cover; illustrations. Publishes "cutting edge, hard, noir fiction with impact! Query on nonfiction and reviews." Quarterly. Estab. 1988.

- By "hardboiled" the editor does not mean rehashing of pulp detective fiction from the 1940s and 1950s but, rather, realistic, gritty material. Lovisi could be called a pulp fiction "afficionado," however. He also publishes *Paperback Parade* and holds an annual vintage paperback fiction convention each year.

Needs: Mystery/suspense (private eye, police procedural, noir). Receives 40-60 mss/month. Accepts 20-25 mss/year. Publishes ms within 6 months-2 years of acceptance. Published work by Andrew Vachss, Joe Lansdale, Bill Nolan, Richard Lupoff, Bill Pronzini and Eugene Izzi. Published many new writers within the last year.

Length: 2,000 words minimum; 3,000 words maximum. Sometimes critiques rejected mss and recommends other markets.
How to Contact: Query first or send complete ms with cover letter. Query with SASE only on anything over 3,000 words. No full-length novels. Reports in 1 month on queries; 1-2 months on mss. SASE. Simultaneous submissions OK, but query first. Sample copy for $7.
Payment/Terms: Pays $5-50 on publication and 2 contributor's copies for first North American serial rights. Copyright reverts to author.

☑ **THE HEALING INN, An Ointment of Love for the Wounded Heart, (I, IV)**, Christian Airline Personnel Missionary Outreach, 3908 NE 140th St., Seattle WA 98125. Phone/fax: (206)440-3382. **Editor:** June Shafhid. Magazine: 8×10; 20 pages. "*The Healing Inn* is geared to encouraging Christians that have been wounded by a church or religious cult. The content or message is to draw people back to God and a balance of healthy Christianity, using fiction stories to encourage their hearts and testimonies to teach them to be individuals before God and man." Estab. 1995. Circ. 8,000.
Needs: Adventure, humor/satire, religious/inspirational. "All stories must have an inspirational message. No judgmental or harsh stories." Publishes ms 3-6 months after acceptance. Length: 2,000 words average; 500 words minimum; 3,000 words maximum. Publishes short shorts. Also publishes poetry.
How to Contact: Send complete ms with a cover letter. Include estimated word count, a short bio and Social Security number. Reports in 2-4 weeks on mss. Send SASE for return of ms. Simultaneous submissions and reprints OK. Sample copy free.
Payment/Terms: Pays free subscription to the magazine and contributor's copies. Acquires first North American serial rights.
Advice: "I look for well-written stories that touch the heart—whether it be humorous or drama. Heartfelt, heartwrenching, life-changing themes catch my eye. Write from your heart; be expressive and honest."

$ HOPSCOTCH: THE MAGAZINE FOR GIRLS, (II), The Bluffton News Publishing & Printing Co., P.O. Box 164, Bluffton OH 45817. (419)358-4610. Fax: (419)358-5027. **Editor:** Marilyn Edwards. Magazine: 7×9; 50 pages; enamel paper; pen & ink illustrations; photographs. Publishes stories for and about girls ages 5-12. Bimonthly. Estab. 1989. Circ. 9,000.

- *Hopscotch* is indexed in the *Children's Magazine Guide* and *Ed Press* and has received a Parents' Choice Gold Medal Award and Ed Press Awards.

Needs: Children's/juvenile (5-9, 10-12 years): adventure, ethnic/multicultural, fantasy, historical (general), sports. Upcoming themes: "Good Health"; "Summertime"; "Pets"; "Different Kinds of Schools"; "Cats"; "Poetry"; "Friends"; "Inventions;" "Dolls." Receives 300-400 unsolicited mss/month. Accepts 20-40 mss/year. Agented fiction 2%. Published work by Lois Grambling, Betty Killion, Jean Patrick and VaDonna Jean Leaf. Length: 500-750 words preferred; 300 words minimum; 750 words maximum. Publishes short shorts. Length: 250-400 words. Also publishes poetry, puzzles, hidden pictures and crafts. Always comments on rejected mss.
How to Contact: Send complete ms with cover letter. Include estimated word count, 1-page bio, Social Security number and list of publications. Reports in 2-4 weeks on queries; 6-10 weeks on mss. Send SASE for reply, return of ms or send disposable copy of the ms. Simultaneous and reprint submissions OK. Sample copy for $3. Fiction guidelines for #10 SASE. Reviews novels and short story collections.
Payment/Terms: Pays 5¢/word (extra for usable photos or illustrations) before publication and 1 contributor's copy for first North American serial rights; additional copies $3; $2 for 10 or more.
Advice: "Make sure you have studied copies of our magazine to see what we like. Follow our theme list. We are looking for wholesome stories. This is what our publication is all about."

HURRICANE ALICE, A Feminist Quarterly, (II), Hurricane Alice Fn., Inc., Dept. of English, Rhode Island College, Providence RI 02908. (401)456-8377. E-mail: mreddy@grog.ric.edu. **Executive Editor:** Maureen Reddy. Fiction is collectively edited. Tabloid: 11×17; 12-16 pages; newsprint stock; illustrations and photos. "We look for feminist fictions with a certain analytic snap, for serious readers, seriously interested in emerging forms of feminist art/artists." Quarterly. Estab. 1983. Circ. 600-700.
Needs: Experimental, feminist, gay, humor/satire, lesbian, science fiction, translations, work by young women. No coming-out stories, defloration stories, abortion stories, dreary realism. Would like to see more speculative and experimental fiction. Upcoming themes: "Working class women" and "young women." Receives 100 unsolicited mss/month. Publishes 8-10 stories annually. Publishes mss up to 1 year after acceptance. Recently published work by Vickie Nelson, Mary Sharratt and Kathryn Duhamel. Publishes 4-5 new writers/year. Length: up to 3,000 words maximum. Publishes short shorts. Occasionally critiques rejected mss.

- **A BULLET INTRODUCES COMMENTS** by the editor of *Novel & Short Story Writer's Market* indicating special information about the listing.

How to Contact: Send complete ms with cover letter. "A brief biographical statement is never amiss. Writers should be sure to tell us if a piece was commissioned by one of the editors." Reports in 3-4 months. SASE for ms. Simultaneous submissions OK, but must be identified as such. Sample copy for $2.50, 11×14 SAE and 2 first-class stamps.
Payment/Terms: Pays 6 contributor's copies. Acquires one-time rights.
Advice: "Fiction is a craft. Just because something happened, it isn't a story; it becomes a story when you transform it through your art, your craft."

$ IN THE FAMILY, The Magazine for Lesbians, Gays, Bisexuals and their Relations, (I, II, IV), P.O. Box 5387, Takoma Park MD 20913. (301)270-4771. Fax: (301)270-4660. E-mail: helenalips@aol.com. Website: http://www.inthefamily.com (includes writer's guidelines, bulletin board, back issues and current issue descriptions). Editor: Laura Markowitz. **Fiction Editor:** Helena Lipstadt. Magazine: 8½×11, 32 pages; coated paper; coated cover; illustrations and photos. "We use a therapy lens to explore the diverse relationships and families of lesbians, gays, bisexuals and their straight relations." Quarterly. Estab. 1995. Circ. 2,000.

- Received 1997 Excellence in Media Award from the American Association for Marriage and Family Therapy. Member of IPA.

Needs: Ethnic/multicultural, feminist, gay, humor/satire, lesbian. No erotica. Would like to see more short stories. List of upcoming themes available for SASE. Receives 25 unsolicited mss/month. Accepts 1 ms/issue; 4 mss/year. Publishes ms 3-6 months after acceptance. Published work by Ellen Hawley, Daniel Cox, Shoshana Daniel and Martha Davis. Publishes 2 new writers/year. Length: 2,000 words average; 2,500 words maximum. Publishes short shorts. Also publishes literary essays and poetry. Sometimes critiques or comments on rejected mss.
How to Contact: Send complete ms with a cover letter. Include estimated word count and 40-word bio. Reports in 6 weeks on queries and mss. Send SASE for reply, return of ms or send disposable copy of ms. Sample copy for $5.50. Fiction guidelines free. Reviews novels and short story collections. Send books to Wayne Scott, Book Review Editor.
Payment/Terms: Pays $25 minimum; $50 maximum plus free subscription to magazine and 5 contributor's copies for first rights.
Advice: "Story must relate to our theme of gay/lesbian/bi relationships and family in some way. Read a few issues and get a sense for what we publish. Shorter is better. Go deep, write from the gut, but not just your pain; also your joy and insight."

ITALIAN AMERICANA, (I, II, IV), URI/CCE 80 Washington St., Providence RI 02903-1803. (401)277-5306. Fax: (401)277-5100. Website: http://www.uri.edu/prov/italian/italian.html (includes writer's guidelines, names of editors). **Editor:** Carol Bonomo Albright. Poetry Editor: Dana Gioia. Magazine: 6×9; 200 pages; varnished cover; perfect-bound; photographs. "*Italian Americana* contains historical articles, fiction, poetry and memoirs, all concerning the Italian experience in the Americas." Semiannually. Estab. 1974. Circ. 1,200.
Needs: Italian American: literary. No nostalgia. Receives 10 mss/month. Accepts 3 mss/issue; 6-7 mss/year. Publishes up to 1 year after acceptance. Agented fiction 5%. Recently published work by Mary Caponegro and Tony Ardizzone. Publishes 1-2 new writers/year. Length: 20 double-spaced pages. Publishes short stories. Also publishes literary essays, literary criticism, poetry. Sometimes critiques rejected mss. Sponsors $500-1,000 literature prize annually.
How to Contact: Send complete ms (in triplicate) with a cover letter. Accepts queries/mss by fax. Include 3-5 line bio, list of publications. Reports in 1 month on queries; 2-4 months on mss. Send SASE for reply, return of ms or send a disposable copy of ms. No simultaneous submissions. Sample copy for $6. Fiction guidelines for SASE. Reviews novels and short story collections. Send books to Professor John Paul Russo, English Dept., Univ. of Miami, Coral Gables, FL 33124.
Payment/Terms: Awards $250 to best fiction of year and 1 contributor's copy; additional copies $7. Acquires first North American serial rights.
Advice: "Please individualize characters, instead of presenting types (i.e., lovable uncle, etc.). No nostalgia."

JEWISH CURRENTS MAGAZINE, (IV), 22 E. 17th St., New York NY 10003-1919. Phone/fax: (212)924-5740. **Editor-in-Chief:** Morris U. Schappes. Magazine: 5½×8½; 48 pages. "We are a secular, progressive, independent Jewish monthly, pro-Israel though not Zionist, printing fiction, poetry articles and reviews on Jewish politics and history, Holocaust/Resistance; mideast peace process, Black-Jewish relations, labor struggles, women's issues. Audience left/progressive, Jewish." Monthly. Estab. 1946. Circ. 2,200.

- This magazine may be slow to respond. They continue to be backlogged.

Needs: Contemporary, ethnic, feminist, historical, humor/satire, literary, senior citizen/retirement, translations. "We are interested in *authentic* experience and readable prose; humanistic orientation. Must have Jewish theme. Could use more humor; short, smart, emotional and intellectual impact. No religious, political sectarian; no porn or hard sex, no escapist stuff. Go easy on experimentation, but we're interested." Upcoming themes (submit at least 3 months in advance): "Black-Jewish Relations" (February); "Holocaust/Resistance" (April); "Israel" (May); "Jews in the USSR & Ex-USSR" (July-August). Receives 6-10 unsolicited fiction mss/month. Accepts 0-1 ms/issue; 8-10 mss/year. Published work by Grace Paley, Paul Robeson, Jr., Robert Meeropol and Andrew Furman. Publishes 9-12 new writers/year. Length: 1,000 words minimum; 3,000 words maximum; 1,800 words average. Also publishes literary essays, literary criticism, poetry.

How to Contact: Send complete ms with cover letter. "Writers should include brief biographical information, especially their publishing histories." SASE. No simultaneous submissions. Reports in 2 months on mss. Publishes ms 2-24 months after acceptance. Sample copy for $3 with SAE and 3 first-class stamps. Reviews novels and short story collections.
Payment/Terms: Pays complimentary one-year subscription and 6 contributor's copies. "We readily give reprint permission at no charge." Sends galleys to author.
Advice: Noted for "stories with Jewish content and personal Jewish experience—e.g., immigrant or Holocaust memories, assimilation dilemmas, dealing with Jewish conflicts OK. Space is increasingly a problem. Be intelligent, imaginative, intuitive and absolutely honest. Have a musical ear, and an ear for people: how they sound when they talk, and also hear what they don't say."

🌐 ☑ $ **JEWISH QUARTERLY,** P.O. Box 2078, London W1A1JR England. E-mail: jewish.quarterly@ort.org. Website: http://www.ortnet.ort.org/communit/jq/start.htm (includes magazine info, covers, excerpts from articles). **Editor:** Matthew Reisz. Quarterly. Publishes 1-3 contribution of fiction/issue.
Needs: "It deals in the broadest sense with all issues of Jewish interest." Length: 1,500 words minimum; 7,000 words maximum.
Payment/Terms: Payment for accepted items £50.
Advice: "Work should have either a Jewish theme in the widest interpretation of that phrase or a theme which would interest our readership. The question which contributors should ask is 'Why should it appear in the *Jewish Quarterly* and not in another periodical?' "

JOURNAL OF POLYMORPHOUS PERVERSITY, (I), Wry-Bred Press, Inc., 10 Waterside Plaza, Suite 20-B, New York NY 10010. (212)689-5473. E-mail: info@psychohumor.com. Website: http://www.psychohumor.com. **Editor:** Glenn Ellenbogen. Magazine: 6¾×10; 24 pages; 60 lb. paper; antique india cover stock; illustrations with some articles. "*JPP* is a humorous and satirical journal of psychology, psychiatry, and the closely allied mental health disciplines." For "psychologists, psychiatrists, social workers, psychiatric nurses, *and* the psychologically sophisticated layman." Semiannally. Estab. 1984.
Needs: Humor/satire. "We only consider materials that are funny or that relate to psychology *or* behavior." Receives 50 unsolicited mss/month. Accepts 8 mss/issue; 16 mss/year. Most writers published last year were previously unpublished writers. Length: 1,500 words average; 4,000 words maximum. Comments on rejected mss.
How to Contact: Send complete ms *in triplicate*. Include cover letter and SASE. Reports in 1-3 months on mss. SASE. Sample copy for $7. Fiction guidelines for #10 SASE.
Payment/Terms: Pays 2 contributor's copies; additional copies $7.
Advice: "We will *not* look at poetry. We only want to see intelligent spoofs of scholarly psychology and psychiatry articles written in scholarly scientific language. Take a look at *real* journals of psychology and try to lampoon their *style* as much as their content. There are few places to showcase satire of the social sciences, thus we provide one vehicle for injecting a dose of humor into this often too serious area. Occasionally, we will accept a piece of creative writing written in the first person, e.g. 'A Subjective Assessment of the Oral Doctoral Defense Process: I Don't Want to Talk About It, If You Want to Know the Truth' (the latter being a piece in which Holden Caulfield shares his experiences relating to obtaining his Ph.D. in Psychology). Other creative pieces have involved a psychodiagnostic evaluation of The Little Prince (as a psychiatric patient) and God being refused tenure (after having created the world) because of insufficient publications and teaching experience."

LEFT CURVE, (II), P.O. Box 472, Oakland CA 94604. (510)763-7193. E-mail: leftcurv@wco.com. Website: http://www.wco.com/~leftcurv. **Editor:** Csaba Polony. Magazine: 8½×11; 130 pages; 60 lb. paper; 100 pt. C1S Durosheen cover; illustrations; photos. "*Left Curve* is an artist-produced journal addressing the problem(s) of cultural forms emerging from the crises of modernity that strive to be independent from the control of dominant institutions, based on the recognition of the destructiveness of commodity (capitalist) systems to all life." Published irregularly. Estab. 1974. Circ. 2,000.
Needs: Contemporary, ethnic, experimental, historical, literary, prose poem, regional, science fiction, translations, political. "We publish critical, open, social/political-conscious writing." Upcoming theme: "Cyber-space and Nature." Receives approximately 12 unsolicited fiction mss/month. Accepts approximately 1 ms/issue. Publishes ms a maximum of 12 months after acceptance. Published work by Pēter Lengyel and Michael Filas. Length: 1,200 words average; 500 words minimum; 2,500 words maximum. Publishes short shorts. Sometimes comments on rejected mss.

MARKET CATEGORIES: (I) Open to new writers; **(II)** Open to both new and established writers; **(III)** Interested mostly in established writers; **(IV)** Open to writers whose work is specialized; **(V)** Closed to unsolicited submissions.

How to Contact: Send complete ms with cover letter. Include "statement of writer's intent, brief bio and reason for submitting to *Left Curve*." Electronic submissions OK; "prefer 3½ disk and hard copy, though we do accept e-mail submissions." Reports in 3-6 months. SASE. Sample copy for $8, 9×12 SAE and $1.24 postage. Fiction guidelines for 1 first-class stamp.
Payment/Terms: Pays in contributor's copies. Rights revert to author.
Advice: "Dig deep; no superficial personalisms, no corny satire. Be honest, realistic and gorge out the truth you wish to say. Understand yourself and the world. Have writing be a means to achieve or realize what is real."

LOST WORLDS, The Science Fiction and Fantasy Forum, (I, IV), HBD Publishing, P.O. Box 605, Concord NC 28026-0605. Phone/fax: (704)933-7998. **Editor:** Holley B. Drye. Newsletter: 8½×11; 48 pages; 24 lb. bond paper; full-color cover; b&w illustrations. "General interest science fiction and fantasy, as well as some specialized genre writing. For broad-spectrum age groups, anyone interested in newcomers." Monthly. Estab. 1988. Circ. 150.
Needs: Experimental, fantasy, horror, psychic/supernatural/occult, science fiction (hard science, soft/sociological), serialized novel. Publishes annual special fiction issue. Receives 35-45 unsolicited mss/month. Accepts 10-14 mss/issue; 100 and up mss/year. Publishes ms 1 year after acceptance (unless otherwise notified). Length: 3,000 words preferred; 2,000 words minimum; 5,500 words maximum. Publishes short shorts. Sometimes critiques rejected mss and recommends other markets. "Although we do not publish every type of genre fiction, I will, if asked, critique anyone who wishes to send me their work. There is no fee for reading or critiquing stories."
How to Contact: Query first. "Cover letters should include where and when to contact the author, a pen name, if one is preferred, as well as their real name, and whether or not they wish their real names to be kept confidential. Due to overwhelming response, we are currently unable to predict response time to mss or queries. Phone calls are welcome to check on manuscripts." SASE for return of ms. Simultaneous and reprint submissions OK. Accepts electronic submissions via disk or modem. Sample copy for $5. Fiction guidelines free.
Payment/Terms: Pays contributor's copies. Acquires one-time rights.
Advice: "I look for originality of story, good characterization and dialogue, well-written descriptive passages, and over-all story quality. The presentation of the work also makes a big impression, whether it be good or bad. Neat, typed manuscripts will always have a better chance than hand-written or badly typed ones. All manuscripts are read by either three or four different people, with an eye towards development of plot and comparison to other material within the writer's field of experience. Plagiarism is not tolerated, and we do look for it while reading a manuscript under consideration. If you have any questions, feel free to call—we honestly don't mind. Never be afraid to send us anything, we really are kind people."

MAIL CALL JOURNAL, Keeping the Spirit of the Civil War Soldier Alive!, Distant Frontier Press, P.O. Box 5031, Dept. N, South Hackensack NJ 07606. (201)296-0419. E-mail: mcj@historyonline.net. Website: http://www.historyonline.net (includes sample issues, latest editorials, writer's guidelines, poetry and writer's contest information). **Managing Editor:** Anna Pansini. Newsletter: 8½×11; 8 pages; 20 lb. paper; illustrations. *Mail Call Journal* focuses on the soldiers' lives during the Civil War and publishes Civil War soldiers' letters, diaries, memoirs and stories of the individual soldiers as well as poems. Bimonthly. Estab. 1990. Circ. 500.
Needs: Historical (American Civil War). Receives 20 unsolicited mss/month. Accepts 1 mss/issue; 6 mss/year. Publishes ms up to 1½ years after acceptance. Publishes 10 new writers/year. Length: 500 words minimum; 1,500 words maximum. Also publishes literary essays, literary criticism and poetry. Sometimes critiques or comments on rejected ms.
How to Contact: Send complete ms with a cover letter mentioning "any relations from the Civil War period for reference only, not a determining factor." Accepts queries/mss by e-mail. Reports in 1 year. SASE for return of ms. Simultaneous, reprint and electronic (disk) submissions OK. Sample copy and fiction guidelines are included in a writer's packet for $5.
Payment/Terms: Pays in contributor's copies. Acquires one-time rights for print and Internet publication.
Advice: Wants more "personal accounts" and no "overused themes. Write from your heart but use your head. Our readers are knowledgeable about the basics of the Civil War, so go beyond that."

MAJESTIC BOOKS, (I, IV), P.O. Box 19097A, Johnston RI 02919-0097. Fiction Editor: Cindy MacDonald. Bound softcover short story anthologies; 5½×8½; 192 pages; 60 lb. paper; C1S cover stock. "Majestic Books is a small press which was formed to give children an outlet for their work. We publish softcover bound anthologies of fictional stories by children, for children and adults who enjoy the work of children." Triannually. Estab. 1993. Circ. 250.

- Although Majestic Books is a small publisher, they are in the market for short fiction for their anthologies. They do a book of stories by children.

Needs: Stories written on any subject by children (under 18) only. Children's/juvenile (10-12 years), young adult (13-18 years). Receives 50 unsolicited mss/month. Accepts 100 mss/year. Publishes ms 1 year maximum after acceptance. Recently published work by Jennie Alpert, Gregory Miller and Brian Freeman. Publishes 100 new writers/year. Length: 100 words minimum; 2,000 words maximum. Publishes short shorts. Also publishes literary essays.
How to Contact: Send complete ms with a cover letter. Include estimated word count and author's age. Reports

in 3 weeks. Send SASE for reply. Simultaneous submissions OK. Sample copy for $3. Fiction guidelines for #10 SASE.
Payment/Terms: Pays 10% royalty for all books sold due to the author's inclusion.
Advice: "We love stories that will keep a reader thinking long after they have read the last word. Be original. We have received some manuscripts of shows we have seen on television or books we have read. Write from inside you and you'll be surprised at how much better your writing will be. Use *your* imagination."

$ MASQUERADE, An Erotic Journal, (II, IV), 801 Second Ave., New York NY 10017. (212)661-7878, ext. 331. Fax: (212)986-7355. E-mail: mhohmann@crespub.com. Website: http://www.masqueradebooks.com (includes writer's guidelines, names of editors, short fiction, interviews with authors, chat line, etc.). **Editor-in-Chief:** Marti Hohmann. Magazine: 8½×11; gloss paper; gloss cover; illustrations and photos. "*Masquerade* is a pansexual, sex-positive publication expressly interested in work by artists and writers outside the mainstream."
Needs: Erotica or stories generally concerned with sex and relationships. "Stories should contain explicit sexual content. Keep characters and relationships legal: please do not refer to the sexual thoughts, feelings, or actions of characters under eighteen years of age. We do not publish representations of incest or bestiality." No soft, "hearts and flowers" erotica, unless authentically felt and brilliantly executed; no work by men using female pseudonyms because they believe they "deeply" understand a "female point of view." Recently published work by Pierre Bourgeade, Pat Califia, Terence Sellers, Florence Dugas and Cecilia Tan. Length: 3,000 words average; 5,000 words maximum.
How to Contact: Send complete ms with a cover letter. Accepts queries by e-mail. Reports in 2-3 weeks on mss. Send SASE for reply; prefer disposable mss. No simultaneous submissions or reprints. Reviews novels and short story collections. Send books to editor.
Payment/Terms: Pays 3 cents/word; $100 maximum on publication for first North American serial rights.
Advice: "All departments are open to freelance writers, and those new to the genre are especially encouraged to try. Don't wait for theme anthologies or calls for submissions from our house; we have several large collections in the works and are always screening material."

MEDICINAL PURPOSES, Literary Review, (I, II), Poet to Poet Inc., 86-37 120 St., #2D, % Catterson, Richmond Hill NY 11418. (718)776-8853, (718)847-2150. E-mail: scarptp@worldnet.att.com. Website: http://wsite.com/poettopoet (includes writer's guidelines, samples of published work and announcements for open readings). **Editors:** Robert Dunn and Thomas M. Catterson. Fiction Editor: Andrew Clark. Magazine: 8½×5½; 64 pages; illustrations. "*Medicinal Purposes* publishes quality work that will benefit the world, though not necessarily through obvious means." Tri-annually. Estab. 1995. Circ. 1,000.
Needs: Adventure, erotica, ethnic/multicultural, experimental, fantasy, feminist, gay, historical, horror, humor/satire, lesbian, literary, mainstream/contemporary, mystery/suspense, psychic/supernatural/occult, regional, romance, science fiction, senior citizen/retirement, sports, westerns, young adult/teen. "Please no pornography, or hatemongering." Receives 15 unsolicited mss/month. Accepts 2-3 mss/issue; 8 mss/year. Publishes ms up to four issues after acceptance. Recently published work by Lisa Meyer and David Huberman. Publishes 100 new writers/year. Length: 2,000 words average; 50 words minimum; 3,000 words maximum. "We prefer maximum of 10 double-spaced pages." Publishes short shorts. Also publishes literary essays, literary criticism, poetry. Sometimes critiques or comments on rejected mss.
How to Contact: Send complete ms with a cover letter. Include estimated word count, brief bio, Social Security number. Reports in 6 weeks on queries; 8 weeks on mss. SASE. Simultaneous and electronic submissions (modem through e-mail) OK. Sample copy for $6, 6×9 SAE and 4 first-class stamps. Fiction guidelines free for #10 SASE.
Payment/Terms: Pays 2 contributor's copies. Acquires first rights.
Advice: "One aspect of the better stories we've seen is that the writer enjoys (or, at least, believes in) the tale being told. Also, learn the language—good English can be a beautiful thing. We long for stories that only a specific writer can tell, by virtue of experience or style. Expand our horizons. Clichés equal death around here."

MEDIPHORS, A Literary Journal of the Health Professions, (I, II, IV), P.O. Box 327, Bloomsburg PA 17815. E-mail: mediphor@ptd.net. Website: http://www.mediphors.org (includes writer's guidelines, names of editors, samples of short stories, essays, poetry, photography, covers and current contents, art and more). **Editor:** Eugene D. Radice, MD. Magazine: 8½×11; 73 pages; 20 lb. white paper; 70 lb. cover; illustrations and photos. "We publish broad work related to medicine and health including essay, short story, commentary, fiction, poetry. Our audience: general readers and health care professionals." Semiannually. Estab. 1993. Circ. 900.
Needs: "Short stories related to health." Adventure, experimental, historical, humor/satire, literary, mainstream/contemporary, science fiction (hard science, soft/sociological), medicine. "No religious, romance, suspense, erotica, fantasy." Receives 50 unsolicited mss/month. Accepts 14 mss/issue; 28 mss/year. Publishes ms 10 months after acceptance. Agented fiction 2%. Publishes 10 new writers/year. Length: 2,500 words average; 4,500 words maximum. Publishes short shorts. Also publishes literary essays and poetry. Sometimes critiques or comments on rejected mss.
How to Contact: Send complete ms with a cover letter. Include estimated word count, bio (paragraph) and any experience/employment in the health professions. Reports in 4 months on mss. Send SASE for reply, return

of ms or send a disposable copy of ms. No simultaneous submissions. Sample copy for $6. Fiction guidelines for #10 SASE.
Payment/Terms: Pays 2 contributor's copies; additional copies for $5.50 Acquires first North American serial rights.
Advice: Looks for "high quality writing that shows fresh perspective in the medical and health fields. Accurate knowledge of subject material. Situations that explore human understanding in adversity. Order a sample copy for examples of work. Start with basic quality writing in short story and create believable, engaging stories concerning medicine and health. Knowledge of the field is important since the audience includes professionals within the medical field. Don't be discouraged. We enjoy receiving work from beginning writers."

MENTOR & PROTEGE, Accelerating Personal & Professional Development Through the Art and Practice of Mentoring and Coaching, (I, IV), P.O. Box 4382, Overland Park KS 66204. (913)362-7889. **Editor:** Maureen Waters. Newsletter: 8½×11; 12 pages. Quarterly. Estab. 1989. Circ. 250.
Needs: "Submissions must be mentoring, coaching or wisdom related." Receives 1 unsolicited ms/month. "I would run more fiction if I received more." Recently published work by Charles Chaim Wax. Publishes 1 new writer/year. Length: 1,200-3,000 words. Also publishes literary essays. Sometimes critiques or comments on rejected mss.
How to Contact: Query first or send complete ms with a cover letter. Include bio with submission. Reports in 1 month on queries; 2 months on mss. Send SASE for reply, return of ms or send a disposable copy of ms. Simultaneous, reprint and electronic submissions (Mac, IBM disks) OK. Sample copy for $6. Fiction guidelines for #10 SASE.
Payment/Terms: Pays 2 contributor's copies and automatic entry in The Mentor Award (prize $250).
Advice: "The writer should understand the concept of wisdom and how that manifests through mentoring and coaching. Readers are professionals involved in mentoring programs, so the fiction we print has to paint a picture that is relevant to them—perhaps helps them understand a new aspect of wisdom or moves them into a new way of thinking. If it's a good or fixable story, I'll work with the writer."

$ MINDSPARKS, The Magazine of Science and Science Fiction, (I, II, IV), Molecudyne Research, P.O. Box 1302, Laurel MD 20725-1302. (410)715-1703. E-mail: asaro@sff.net. Website: http://www.sff.net/people/asaro/ (includes interviews, reviews, information on the Skolian Empire/Ruby Dynasty books, science articles). **Editor:** Catherine Asaro. Magazine: 8½×11; 44 pages; 20 lb. white paper; 60 lb. cover; illustrations and photos. "We publish science fiction and science articles." Published on a varied schedule. Estab. 1993. Circ. 1,000.

- *Mindsparks* is in the process of changing from a paper magazine to an electronic publication. For more information, either write the above editorial address or check the website.

Needs: Science fiction (hard science, soft/sociological), young adult (science fiction). "No pornography." Receives 50 unsolicited submissions/month. Accepts 2-4 mss/issue; 12-14 mss/year. Publishes ms 1-24 months after acceptance. Published work by Hal Clement, G. David Nordley, Lois Gresh and Paul Levinson. Publishes an average of 10 new writers/year. Length: 4,000 words average; 8,000 words maximum. Publishes short shorts. Also publishes literary essays, literary criticism and poetry. Often critiques or comments on rejected mss.
How to Contact: Send complete ms with a cover letter. Include estimated word count and list of publications. "Prefers initial contact be made by mail." Reports in 2-3 months. Send SASE for reply, return of ms or send a disposable copy of ms. Simultaneous submissions OK. Sample copy for $4.50, 8½×11 SAE and $1 postage or 2 IRCs. Fiction guidelines for #10 SASE. Reviews novels and short story collections.
Payment/Terms: Pays 2¢/word on publication for first North American serial rights. Sends galleys to author.
Advice: Looks for "well-written, well-researched, interesting science ideas with good characterization and good plot. Read a copy of the magazine. We receive many submissions that don't fit the intent of *Mindsparks*."

THE MIRACULOUS MEDAL, (IV), The Central Association of the Miraculous Medal, 475 E. Chelten Ave., Philadelphia PA 19144. (215)848-1010. **Editor:** Rev. William J. O'Brien, C.M. Magazine. Quarterly.
Needs: Religious/inspirational. Receives 25 unsolicited fiction mss/month. Accepts 2 mss/issue; 8 mss/year. Publishes ms up to two years or more after acceptance.
How to Contact: Query first with SASE. Sample copy and fiction guidelines free.
Payment/Terms: Pays 2¢/word minimum. Pays on acceptance for first rights.

☑ MOUNTAIN LUMINARY, (I), P.O. Box 1187, Mountain View AR 72560-1187. (870)585-2260. Fax: (870)269-4110. E-mail: ecomtn@mvtel.net. **Editor:** Anne Thiel. Magazine; photos. "*Mountain Luminary* is dedicated to bringing information to people about the Aquarian Age; how to grow with its new and evolutionary energies and how to work with the resultant changes in spirituality, relationships, environment and the planet. *Mountain Luminary* provides a vehicle for people to share ideas, philosophies and experiences that deepen understanding of this evolutionary process and humankind's journey on Earth." International quarterly. Estab. 1985.
Needs: Humor/satire, metaphor/inspirational/Aquarian-Age topics. Accepts 8-10 mss/year. Publishes ms 6 months after acceptance. Recently published work by Gerald Lewis, Robert L. Mayne and Anne Brewer. Publishes 6 new writers/year.

How to Contact: Query with clips of published work. SASE for return of ms. Accepts queries/mss by fax and e-mail. Simultaneous and electronic submissions (Mac IIci, Quark XP) OK. Sample copy and writer's guidelines free.
Payment/Terms: Pays 1 contributor's copy. "We may offer advertising space as payment." Acquires first rights.
Advice: "We look for stories with a moral—those with insight to problems on the path which raise the reader's awareness. Topical interests include: New Age/Aquarian Age, astrology, crystals, cultural and ethnic concerns, dreams, ecosystems, the environment, extraterrestrials, feminism, folklore, healing and health, holistic and natural health, inspiration, juvenile and teen issues, lifestyle, meditation, men's issues, metaphysics, mysticism, nutrition, parallel dimensions, prayer, psychic phenomenon, self-help, spirituality and women's issues."

$ MURDEROUS INTENT, Mystery Magazine, (I, IV), Madison Publishing Company, P.O. Box 5947, Vancouver WA 98668-5947. (360)695-9004. Fax: (360)693-3354. E-mail: madison@teleport.com. Website: http://www.teleport.com/~madison (includes writer's guidelines, short fiction, articles, interviews, table of contents, minisynopsis corner, subscription and convention information). **Editor:** Margo Power. Magazine: 8½×11; 64 pages; newsprint; glossy 2-color cover; illustrations; photos, cozy/soft boiled mystery magazine publishing fiction, nonfiction and interviews. Quarterly. Estab. 1995. Circ. 7,000.

- *Murderous Intent* was rated 9th in *Writer's Digest* Fiction Top 50, 1998. Several authors have been short fiction Derringer Award recipients.

Needs: Mystery/suspense (amateur sleuth, cozy, police procedural, private eye), psychic/supernatural/occult, science fiction (with mystery) "occasionally." No true crime, no cannibal stories, no stories with excessive violence, language or sex. (Nothing but mystery/suspense with a little ghostly presence now and then). Receives 200 unsolicited mss/month. Accepts 10-14 mss/issue; 40-48 mss/year. Publishes ms up to 1 year after acceptance. Recently published work by Jeremiah Healy, Toni L.P. Kelner, Carol Cail, Michael Mallory, Seymour Shubin and John Herrmann. Publishes 10 or more new writers/year. Publishes 30% new writers/year. Length: 2,000-4,000 words average; 250 words minimum; 5,000 words maximum. Publishes short shorts. Length: 250-400 words. Also publishes mystery-related essays and poetry. Sometimes critiques or comments on rejected mss. Annual contest, 2,000 words, mystery. Deadline: August 1. $10 entry fee. SASE.
How to Contact: Send complete ms with a cover letter; only 1 story/submission. Include estimated word count, brief bio name of story and telephone number and e-mail address. Reports in 3 months on queries, 3-6 months on mss. Send SASE for reply or send a disposable copy of ms. Simultaneous submissions OK. Sample copy for $5, 9×12 SAE and 4 first-class stamps. Guidelines for #10 SASE. "Minisynopsis Corner" for authors to submit minisynopses of their new mystery novels (free).
Payment/Terms: Pays $10 and 2 contributor's copies on acceptance; additional copies for $3.50 (issue their story appears in). Acquires first North American serial rights.
Advice: "The competition is tough so write the mystery you love—build characters people will remember—and surprise us."

MY LEGACY, (I, II), Weems Concepts, HCR-13, Box 21AA, Artemas PA 17211-9405. (814)458-3102. **Editor:** Kay Weems. Magazine: digest size; 125-150 pages; white paper; 20 lb. colored paper cover; illustrations. "Work must be in good taste. No bad language. Audience is from all walks of life," adults and children. Quarterly. Estab. 1991. Circ. 200.
Needs: Adventure, children's/juvenile (10-12 years), fantasy (children's fantasy, science fantasy), historical, horror, humor/satire, mainstream/contemporary, mystery/suspense (amateur sleuth, cozy, police procedural, private eye/hardboiled, romantic suspense), regional, religious/inspirational, romance (contemporary, futuristic/time travel, gothic, historical), science fiction (hard science, soft/sociological), senior citizen/retirement, westerns (frontier, traditional), young adult/teen (adventure, mystery, science fiction, western). No porno. List of upcoming themes available for SASE. Publishes special fiction issues or anthologies. Receives 15-30 unsolicited mss/month. Accepts 30-35 mss/issue; 120-140 mss/year. Publishes ms within 6 months after acceptance. Published work by Peter Gauthier, Jel D.Lewis (Jones); Brucie Jacobs, Joseph Farley, Mark Scott and Gerri George. Length: 2,500 words average. Publishes short shorts. Very seldom critiques or comments on rejected mss; "usually don't have time."
How to Contact: Send complete ms with a cover letter. Include estimated word count, bio (short paragraph) and list of publications. Reports within 6 months on mss. Send SASE for reply, return of ms or send a disposable copy of ms (preferable). Simultaneous and reprint submissions OK. Sample copy for $3.50, 9×6½ SAE and $1.70 postage. Fiction guidelines for #10 SASE.
Payment/Terms: Acquires one-time rights.
Advice: Looks for "a good beginning, tight writing, good conversations, believable characters and believable ending."

MYSTERY TIME, An Anthology of Short Stories, (I), Hutton Publications, P.O. Box 2907, Decatur IL 62524. **Editor:** Linda Hutton. Booklet: 5½×8½; 52 pages; bond paper; illustrations. "Biannual collection of short stories with a suspense or mystery theme for mystery buffs, with an emphasis on women writers and women protagonists." Estab. 1983.
Needs: Mystery/suspense only. Features older women as protagonists. Receives 10-15 unsolicited fiction mss/

month. Accepts 20-24 mss/year. Published work by Patricia Crandall, Marian Poe and Vera Searles. Published new writers within the last year. Length: 1,500 words maximum. Occasionally critiques rejected mss and recommends other markets.
How to Contact: Send complete ms with SASE. "No cover letters." Simultaneous and previously published submissions OK. Reports in 1 month on mss. Publishes ms an average of 6-8 months after acceptance. Reprint submissions OK. Sample copy for $4. Fiction guidelines for #10 SASE.
Payment/Terms: Pays ¼-1¢/word and 1 contributor's copy; additional copies $2.50. Acquires one-time rights.
Advice: "Study a sample copy and the guidelines. Too many amateurs mark themselves as amateurs by submitting blindly."

$ NEW ENGLAND WRITERS' NETWORK, (I, II), P.O. Box 483, Hudson MA 01749-0483. (978)562-2946. Fax: (978)568-0497. E-mail: newn4u@aol.com. Editor: Glenda Baker. **Fiction Editor:** Liz Aleshire. Poetry Editor: Judy Adourian. Magazine: 8½×11; 24 pages; coated cover. "We are devoted to helping new writers get published and to teaching through example and content. We are looking for well-written stories that grab us from the opening paragraph." Quarterly. Estab. 1994. Circ. 200.

- *New England Writers' Network* has a new feature called First Fiction. A story by a previously unpublished fiction writer is spotlighted under the heading First Fiction.

Needs: Adventure, condensed/excerpted novel, ethnic/multicultural, humor/satire, literary, mainstream/contemporary, mystery/suspense, religious/inspirational, romance. "We will consider anything except pornography or extreme violence." Accepts 5 mss/issue; 20 mss/year. Reads mss only from June 1 through September 1. Publishes ms 4-12 months after acceptance. Recently published work by Arline Chase, James Calandrillo, Edward Allen Faine, Nick Hubacker and Steve Burt. Publishes 4-6 new writers/year. Length: 2,000 words maximum. Publishes short shorts. Also publishes poetry and 3-4 personal essays per issue. Always critiques or comments on rejected mss.
How to Contact: Send complete ms with a cover letter. Include estimated word count. Bio on acceptance. Reports in 4 months. SASE for return of ms. No simultaneous submissions. Sample copy for $5. Fiction guidelines free. "We do not review story collections or novels. We do publish 2,000 words (maximum) novel excerpts. Writer picks the excerpt—do not send novel."
Payment/Terms: Pays $10 for fiction, $5 for personal essays, $3 per poem on publication and 1 contributor's copy. Acquires first North American serial rights.
Advice: "Give us a try! Please send for guidelines and a sample."

NEW METHODS, The Journal of Animal Health Technology, (IV), P.O. Box 22605, San Francisco CA 94122-0605. (415)379-9065. **Editor:** Ronald S. Lippert, AHT. Newsletter ("could become magazine again"): 8½×11; 2-4 pages; 20 lb. paper; illustrations; "rarely" photos. Network service in the animal field educating services for mostly professionals in the animal field; e.g., animal health technicians. Monthly. Estab. 1976. Circ. 5,608.
Needs: Animals: contemporary, experimental, historical, mainstream, regional. No stories unrelated to animals. Receives 12 unsolicited fiction mss/month. Accepts one ms/issue; 12 mss/year. Length: Open. "Rarely" publishes short shorts. Occasionally critiques rejected mss. Recommends other markets.
How to Contact: Query first with theme, length, expected time of completion, photos/illustrations, if any, biographical sketch of author, all necessary credits or send complete ms. Report time varies (up to 4 months). SASE for query and ms. Simultaneous submissions OK. Sample copy and fiction guidelines for $2.90.
Payment/Terms: No payment. Acquires one-time rights. Back issue and fiction guidelines only with SASE for $2, must mention Writer's Digest Books.
Advice: Sponsors contests: theme changes but generally concerns the biggest topics of the year in the animal field. "Emotion, personal experience—make the person feel it. We are growing."

$ NEWFANGLED FAIRY TALES and GIRLS TO THE RESCUE, (II), Meadowbrook Press, 5451 Smetana Dr., Minnetonka MN 55343. (612)930-1100. **Editor:** Bruce Lansky. Assistant Editor: Jason Sanford. Anthology series for children ages 8-12. Each book is published semiannually.
Needs: Children's/juvenile short stories (8-12 years). No novels or picture books. Receives 50-60 unsolicited submissions/month for each series. Accepts 10 mss/issue; 20 mss/year/book. Publishes ms 1 year after acceptance. Publishes 10-15 new writers/year. Length: 1,200-1,500 words average; 1,800 words maximum. Sometimes comments on or critiques rejected mss.
How to Contact: Query first. Include estimated word count and list of publications. Reports in 3 months. Send SASE for reply, return of ms or send disposable copy of ms. Simultaneous submissions and reprints OK. Fiction guidelines for #10 SASE. Address all submissions to Jason Sanford, assistant editor.

INTERESTED IN A PARTICULAR GENRE? Check our new sections for: **Mystery/Suspense**, page 57; **Romance**, page 77; **Science Fiction & Fantasy**, page 95.

Payment/Terms: Pays $500 on publication for nonexclusive worldwide rights. Sends galleys to author.
Advice: "Read our guidelines before submitting. All our anthology series for children have very strict guidelines. Also, please read the books to get a feel for what types of stories we publish. Our series consistently feature short stories by previously unpublished writers—we consider stories on their own merits, not on the reputations of the authors."

$ NIGHT TERRORS, (II), 1202 W. Market St., Orrville OH 44667-1710. (330)683-0338. E-mail: ded3548@aol.com. Website: http://users.aol.com/NTMagazine/ (includes updated guidelines, bios of the editor and writers, short fiction, order info, links to other sites of interest to writers and readers of horror). **Editor/Publisher:** D.E. Davidson. Magazine: 8½×11; 52 pages; 80 lb. glossy cover; illustrations and photographs. *Night Terrors* publishes quality horror fiction for literate adults. Quarterly. Estab. 1996. Circ. 1,000.

- *Night Terrors* has had seven stories listed in the Honorable Mention section of *The Year's Best Fantasy and Horror, Eleventh Annual Collection.* Two *Night Terror* stories were nominated for the Horror Writer's Association's Bram Stoker Award for Short Fiction.

Needs: Horror, psychic/supernatural/occult. "Night Terrors does not accept stories involving abuse, sexual mutilation or stories with children as main characters. We publish traditional supernatural/psychological horror for a mature audience. Our emphasis is on literate work with a chill." Receives 50 unsolicited mss/month. Accepts 12 mss/issue; 46 mss/year. Publishes ms 2-6 months after acceptance. Recently published work by A.R. Morlan, J.N. Williamson, Hugh B. Cave, Don D'Ammassa and Dominick Cancilla. Publishes 2 new writers/year. Length: 3,000 words average; 2,000 words minimum; 5,000 words maximum. Often critiques or comments on rejected mss.
How to Contact: Send complete ms with a cover letter. Include estimated word count, 50-word bio and list of publications. Reports in 1 week on queries; 2 months on mss. Send SASE for reply, return of ms or send a disposable copy of ms. Simultaneous submissions and reprints OK. Sample copy for $6 (make checks to D.E. Davidson). Fiction guidelines free for #10 SASE.
Payment/Terms: Pays up to $100 on publication and 1-2 contributor's copy; additional copies for $4.50. Acquires first North American serial rights or second rights for reprints. Sends galleys to author.
Advice: "I publish what I like. I like stories which involve me with the viewpoint character and leave me with the feeling that his/her fate could have or might be mine. Act professionally. Check your work for typos, spelling, grammar, punctuation, format. Send your work flat. And if you must, paper clip it, don't staple. Include a brief, to-the-point cover letter."

THE NOCTURNAL LYRIC, (I, IV), Box 115, San Pedro CA 90733. (310)519-9220. E-mail: nlyric@webtv.net. Website: http://www.Angelfire.com/ca/nocturnallyric (includes fiction guidelines, upcoming authors, sample poetry and links to similar sites). **Editor:** Susan Moon. Digest: 5½×8½; 40 pages; illustrations. "We are a non-profit literary journal, dedicated to printing fiction by new writers for the sole purpose of getting read by people who otherwise might have never seen their work." Bimonthly. Estab. 1987. Circ. 400.
Needs: Experimental, horror, humor/satire, psychic/supernatural/occult, bizarre, poetry. Nothing graphically pornographic. "We will give priority to unusual, creative pieces. We would like to see more thought-provoking fiction." Receives 50 unsolicited mss/month. Publishes ms 10-12 months after acceptance. Recently published work by Janice Knapp, Cath Haftings, Brian Freeman, Jake Aurelian and Nancy L'enz Hogan. Publishes 20 new writers/year. Length: 2,000 words maximum. Publishes short shorts. Also publishes poetry.
How to Contact: Send complete ms with cover letter. Accepts queries by e-mail. Include "something about the author, areas of fiction he/she is interested in." Reports in 2 weeks on queries; 6-8 months on mss. SASE. Simultaneous and reprint submissions OK. Sample copy for $3 (checks to Susan Moon). Fiction guidelines for #10 SASE.
Payment/Terms: Pays in gift certificates for subscription discounts. Publication not copyrighted.
Advice: "Please stop wasting your postage sending us things that are in no way bizarre. Do send us your weirdest, most unique creations. Don't pretend you've read us when you haven't! I can usually tell! We're getting more into strange, surrealistic horror and fantasy, or silly, satirical horror. If you're avant-garde, we want you! We're mainly accepting things that are bizarre all the way through, as opposed to ones that only have a surprise bizarre ending."

THE OAK, (I, II), 1530 Seventh St., Rock Island IL 61201. (309)788-3980. **Editor:** Betty Mowery. Magazine: 8½×11; 8-20 pages. "To provide a showcase for new authors while showing the work of established authors as well; to publish wholesome work, something with a message." Bimonthly. Estab. 1991. Circ. 300.
Needs: Adventure, contemporary, experimental, fantasy, humor, mainstream, prose poem. No erotica or mainstream fantasy. Receives 25 mss/month. Accepts up to 12 mss/issue. Publishes ms within 3 months of acceptance. Published 25 new writers/year. Publishes 10 new writers/year. Length: 500 words maximum. Publishes short shorts. Length: 200 words.
How to Contact: Send complete ms. Reports in 1 week. SASE. Simultaneous and reprint submissions OK. Sample copy for $2. Subscription $10 for 4 issues.
Payment/Terms: None, but not necessary to buy a copy in order to be published. Acquires first rights.
Advice: "I do not want erotica, extreme violence or killing of humans or animals the sake of killing. Just be yourself when you write. Please include SASE or manuscripts will be destroyed. Be sure name and address are

on the manuscript. Study the markets for length of manuscript and what type of material is wanted."

ON SPEC, more than just science fiction, (II), The Copper Pig Writers' Society, Box 4727, Edmonton, Alberta T6E 5G6 Canada. Phone/fax: (403)413-0215. E-mail: onspec@earthling.net. Website: http://www.icomm.ca/onspec (includes writer's guidelines, editor names and credits, past editorials, Robert J. Sawyer's columns on writing, excerpts from published fiction, links to writer's Internet resources). **Contact:** The Editors. Magazine: 5×8; 96 pages; illustrations. "Provides a venue for Canadian speculative writing—science fiction, fantasy, horror, magic realism." Quarterly. Estab. 1989. Circ. 2,000.

Needs: Fantasy and science fiction. No condensed or excerpted novels, no religious/inspirational stories. "We would like to see more horror, fantasy, science fiction—well-developed stories with complex characters and strong plots." Receives 50 mss/month. Buys 10 mss/issue; 40 mss/year. "We read manuscripts during the month after each deadline: February 28/May 31/August 31/November 30. Please note that we want manuscripts in competition format." Publishes ms 6 months after acceptance. Recently published work by Allan Weiss, Edo Van Belkom, Gerald Truscott, John Graham, Laurie Channer and David Nickle. Publishes new writers, number varies. Length: 4,000 words average; 1,000 words minimum; 6,000 words maximum. Also publishes poetry. Always critiques or comments on rejected mss.

How to Contact: Send complete ms with a cover letter. Accepts queries only by e-mail. Include estimated word count, 2-sentence bio and phone number. Reports in 5 months on mss. SASE for return of ms or send a disposable copy of ms plus #10 SASE for response. No simultaneous submissions. Sample copy for $6. Fiction guidelines for #10 SASE.

Payment/Terms: Pays $40-180 and 2 contributor's copies; additional copies for $4. Pays on acceptance for first North American serial rights. Sends galleys to author.

Advice: "Please note we prefer Canadian writers. Tend to prefer character-driven stories. Don't be afraid of rejection, it happens to all of us."

PARADOXISM, Anti-literary Journal, (IV) (formerly The Paradoxist Literary Movement), University of New Mexico, Gallup NM 87301. E-mail: smarand@unm.edu. Website: http://www.gallup.unm.edu/~smarandache/manif3@unm.txt. **Editor:** Florentin Smarandache. Magazine: 8½×11; 100 pages; illustrations. "The paradoxist literary movement is an avant-garde movement set up by the editor in the 1980s in Romania. It tries to generalize the art, to make the unliterary become literary." Annually. Estab. 1993. Circ. 500.

Needs: "Crazy, uncommon, experimental, avant-garde"; also ethnic/multicultural. Plans specific themes in the next year. Publishes annual special fiction issue or anthology. Receives 3-4 unsolicited mss/month. Accepts 10 mss/issue. Published work by Dan Topa and Anatol Cioeanu. Length: 500 words minimum; 1,000 words maximum. Publishes short shorts. Also publishes literary essays, literary criticism and poetry.

How to Contact: Query with clips of unpublished work. Reports in 2 months on mss. Send a disposable copy of ms. Sample copy for $19.95 and 8½×11 SASE.

Payment/Terms: Pays 1 contributor's copy. Not copyrighted.

Advice: "The Basic Thesis of the paradoxism: everything has a meaning and a non-meaning in a harmony each other. The Essence of the paradoxism: a) the sense has a non-sense, and reciprocally b) the non-sense has a sense. The Motto of the paradoxism: 'All is possible, the impossible too!' The Symbol of the paradoxism: (a spiral—optic illusion, or vicious circle)."

$ PARSEC, Canada's Sci-Fi Source, (II), Parsec Publishing Company, ℅ Plaza 69, 1935 Paris St., P.O. Box 21019, Sudbury Ontario P3E 6G6 Canada. (705)523-1831. Fax: (705) 523-5276. E-mail: parsec@vianet.on.ca. **Editor:** Chris Krejlgaard. Magazine: 8×10¾; 60 pages; newsprint; illustrations and photos. "We accentuate the Canadian content in science fiction, fantasy and horror media projects." Quarterly. Estab. 1995. Circ. 4,000.

- Member of the Canadian Magazine Publishers Association.

Needs: Fantasy (science fantasy, sword and sorcery), horror, science fiction. "No first-person narratives." Publishes special fiction issues or anthologies. Accepts 16 mss/issue. Publishes ms 6-9 months after acceptance. Length: 2,500 words average; 1,500 words minimum; 5,000 words maximum. Often critiques or comments on rejected mss.

How to Contact: Query first; no unsolicited mss accepted. Include estimated word count. Reports in 3 months on queries. Include SASE for reply. Simultaneous and electronic submissions OK. Sample copy for $3. Fiction guidelines for 4×9 SASE. Reviews novels and short story collections. Send books to editor.

Payment/Terms: Pays $75 minimum; $125 maximum on publication plus 2 contributor's copies for first rights.

Advice: "The writer has four paragraphs to hook me. After that it's an uphill climb. A story must be compelling and relevant. Psuedo-science is frowned upon, but well-researched work that follows current work or trends through to a logical end is applauded. Read and know what type of work appears in *Parsec*. Too many authors submit work that clearly isn't suitable in terms of style and genre."

THE PIPE SMOKER'S EPHEMERIS, (I, II, IV), The Universal Coterie of Pipe Smokers, 20-37 120 St., College Point NY 11356-2128. **Editor:** Tom Dunn. Magazine: 8½×11; 84-96 pages; offset paper and cover; illustrations; photos. Pipe smoking and tobacco theme for general and professional audience. Irregular quarterly. Estab. 1964.

Needs: Pipe smoking related: historical, humor/satire, literary. Publishes ms up to 1 year after acceptance. Length: 2,500 words average; 5,000 words maximum. Also publishes short shorts. Occasionally critiques rejected mss.
How to Contact: Send complete ms with cover letter. Reports in 2 weeks on mss. Simultaneous and reprints OK. Sample copy for 8½×11 SAE and 6 first-class stamps.
Payment/Terms: Acquires one-time rights.

$ PIRATE WRITINGS, Tales of Fantasy, Mystery & Science Fiction, (II), Pirate Writings Publishing, P.O. Box 329, Brightwaters NY 11718-0329. E-mail: pwpubl@aol.com. **Editor:** Edward J. McFadden. Assistant Editor: Tom Piccirilli. Magazine: full size, saddle stapled. "We are looking for poetry and short stories that entertain." Quarterly. Estab. 1992. Circ. 6,000.
Needs: Fantasy (dark fantasy, science fantasy, sword and sorcery), mystery/suspense, science fiction (all types). Receives 300-400 unsolicited mss/month. Accepts 8 mss/issue; 30-40 mss/year. Publishes ms 1-2 years after acceptance. Length: 3,000 words average; 750 words minimum; 8,000 words maximum. Also publishes poetry. Sometimes critiques or comments on rejected mss.
How to Contact: Send complete ms with cover letter. Include estimated word count, 1 paragraph bio, Social Security number, list of publications with submission. Reports in 1 week on queries; 2 months on mss. Send SASE for reply or return of ms or disposable copy of ms. Will consider simultaneous submissions. Sample copy for $5 (make check payable to Pirate Writings Publishing). Fiction guidelines for #10 SAE.
Payment/Terms: Pays 1-5¢/word for first North American serial rights.
Advice: "My goal is to provide a diverse, entertaining and thought-provoking magazine featuring all the above stated genres in every issue. Hints: I love a good ending. Move me, make me laugh, surprise me, and you're in. Read *PW* and you'll see what I mean."

N THE PORTABLE WALL, (II), Basement Press, 215 Burlington, Billings MT 59101. (406)256-3588. **Editor:** Daniel Struckman. Magazine: 6×9¼; 64 pages; cotton rag paper; best quality cover; line engravings; illustrations. "We consider all kinds of material. Bias toward humor." Semiannually. Estab. 1977. Circ. 400.
Needs: Adventure, contemporary, ethnic, experimental, feminist, historical, humor/satire, literary, mainstream, prose poem, regional, science fiction, senior citizen, sports, translations. Upcoming themes: "Human Rights" (1996); "Household Pets" (1997). "We favor short pieces and poetry." Receives 5-10 unsolicited mss/month. Accepts 3-4 mss/issue; 6-8 mss/year. Publishes ms 6-12 months after acceptance. Published works by Gray Harris and Wilbur Wood. Length: 2,000 words preferred. Publishes short shorts. Also publishes literary essays, literary criticism, poetry. Sometimes critiques rejected mss.
How to Contact: Send complete ms with cover letter. No simultaneous submissions. Reports within 3 months on mss. SASE. Sample copy for $6.50.
Payment/Terms: Pays subscription to magazine. Acquires one-time rights.
Advice: "We like language that evokes believable pictures in our minds and that tells news. We are definitely leaning toward idiomatic voices."

POSKISNOLT PRESS, Yesterday's Press, (I, II, IV), Yesterday's Press, JAF Station, Box 7415, New York NY 10116-4630. **Editor:** Patricia D. Coscia. Magazine: 7×8½; 20 pages; regular typing paper. Estab. 1989. Circ. 100.
Needs: Contemporary, erotica, ethnic, experimental, fantasy, feminist, gay, humor/satire, lesbian, literary, mainstream, prose poem, psychic/supernatural/occult, romance, senior citizen/retirement, western, young adult/teen (10-18 years). "X-rated material is not accepted!" Plans to publish a special fiction issue or anthology in the future. Receives 50 unsolicited mss/month. Accepts 30 mss/issue; 100 mss/year. Publishes ms 6 months after acceptance. Length: 200 words average; 100 words minimum; 500 words maximum. Publishes short shorts. Length: 100-500 words. Sometimes critiques rejected mss and recommends other markets.
How to Contact: Query first with clips of published work or send complete ms with cover letter. Reports in 1 week on queries; 6 months on mss. SASE. Accepts simultaneous submissions. Sample copy for $5 with #10 SAE and $2 postage. Fiction guidelines for #10 SAE and $2 postage.
Payment/Terms: Pays with subscription to magazine or contributor's copies; charges for extras. Acquires all rights, first rights or one-time rights.

THE POST, (II), Publishers Syndication International, P.O. Box 6218, Charlottesville VA 22906-6218. (804)964-1194. Fax: (804)964-0096. E-mail: asam@hombuslib.com. Website: http://www.hombuslib.com/. **Editor:** A.P. Samuels. Magazine: 8½×11; 32 pages. Monthly. Estab. 1988.
Needs: Adventure, mystery/suspense (private eye), romance (romantic suspense, historical, contemporary), west-

ern (traditional). "No explicit sex, gore, weird themes, extreme violence or bad language." Receives 35 unsolicited mss/month. Accepts 1 ms/issue; 12 mss/year. Time between acceptance and publication varies. Agented fiction 10%. Publishes 1-3 new writers/year. Length: 10,000 words average.
How to Contact: Send complete ms with cover letter. Reports on mss in 5 weeks. No simultaneous submissions. Fiction guidelines for #10 SASE.
Payment/Terms: Pays ½¢ to 4¢/word on acceptance for all rights.
Advice: "Manuscripts must be for a general audience."

$ PRISONERS OF THE NIGHT, An Adult Anthology of Erotica, Fright, Allure and . . . Vampirism, (II, IV), MKASHEF Enterprises, P.O. Box 688, Yucca Valley CA 92286-0688. E-mail: alayne@inetworld.net. **Editor:** Alayne Gelfand. Magazine: 9×6; 50-80 pages; 20 lb. paper; slick cover; illustrations. "An adult, erotic vampire anthology of original character stories and poetry. Heterosexual and homosexual situations." Annually. Estab. 1987. Circ. 5,000.
Needs: "All stories must be erotic vampire stories, with unique characters, unusual situations." Adventure, contemporary, erotica, fantasy, feminist, gay, lesbian, literary, mystery/suspense, prose poem, psychic/supernatural/occult, science fiction (soft/sociological). No fiction that deals with anyone else's creations, i.e., no "Dracula" stories. No traditional Gothic, humor. Receives 100-150 unsolicited fiction mss/month. Buys 5-12 mss/issue. Publishes ms 1-11 months after acceptance. Published work by Nancy Kilpatrick, Adam Meyer, Charlee Jacob and Tom Piccirilli. Publishes 1-5 new writers/year. Length: under 10,000 words. Publishes short shorts. Sometimes critiques rejected mss.
How to Contact: Send complete ms with short cover letter. "A brief introduction of author to the editor; name, address, *some* past credits if available." Reports in 1-3 weeks on queries; 2-4 months on mss. Reads *only* September through March. SASE. No simultaneous submissions. Accepts electronic submissions via Word, Word for Windows, ASCII disk. Sample copy #1-4, $15; #5, $12; #6-#9, $9.95, #10, $7.95. Fiction guidelines for #10 SASE.
Payment/Terms: Pays 1¢/word for fiction on acceptance for first North American serial rights.
Advice: Looks for "clean, professional presentation. Interesting writing style that flows from word-one and sucks the reader in. An interesting idea/concept that appears at the beginning of a story. Read at least the most current issue of the publication to which you submit and read the guidelines before submitting. Know your market!"

$ PSI, (I, II), P.O. Box 6218, Charlottesville VA 22906-6218. (804)964-1194. Fax: (804)964-0096. E-mail: asam@esinet.net. **Editor:** A.P. Samuels. Magazine: 8½×11; 32 pages; bond paper; self cover. "Mystery and romance." Bimonthly. Estab. 1987.
Needs: Adventure, romance (contemporary, historical, young adult), mystery/suspense (private eye), western (traditional). No ghoulish, sex, violence. Wants to see more believable stories. Receives 35 unsolicited mss/month. Accepts 1-2 mss/issue. Publishes 1-3 new writers/year. Length: 10,000 (stories) and 30,000 (novelettes) words average. Critiques rejected mss "only on a rare occasion."
How to Contact: Send complete ms with cover letter. Reports in 2 weeks on queries; 4-6 weeks on mss. SASE. No simultaneous submissions. Accepts electronic submissions via disk.
Payment/Terms: Pays 1-4¢/word plus royalty on acceptance for all rights.
Advice: "Manuscripts must be for a general audience. Just good plain story telling (make it compelling). No explicit sex or ghoulish violence."

☑ QUEEN OF ALL HEARTS, (II), Queen Magazine, Montfort Missionaries, 26 S. Saxon Ave., Bay Shore NY 11706-8993. (516)665-0726. Fax: (516)665-4349. E-mail: pretre@worldnet.att.net. **Managing Editor:** Roger M. Charest, S.M.M. Magazine: 7¾×10¾; 48 pages; self cover stock; illustrations and photos. Magazine of "stories, articles and features on the Mother of God by explaining the Scriptural basis and traditional teaching of the Catholic Church concerning the Mother of Jesus, her influence in fields of history, literature, art, music, poetry, etc." Bimonthly. Estab. 1950. Circ. 2,500.

- *Queen of Hearts* received a Catholic Press Award for General Excellence (third place) and a Prayer and Spirituality Journalism Award.

Needs: Religious/inspirational. "No mss not about Our Lady, the Mother of God, the Mother of Jesus." Recently published work by Richard O'Donnell and Jackie Clements-Marenda. Publishes 6 new writers/year. Length: 1,500-2,000 words. Sometimes recommends other markets.
How to Contact: Send complete ms with SASE. Accepts queries/mss by e-mail and fax (mss by permission only). No simultaneous submissions. Reports in 1 month on mss. Publishes ms 6-12 months after acceptance. Sample copy for $2.50 with 9×12 SAE.
Payment/Terms: Varies. Pays 6 contributor's copies.
Advice: "We are publishing stories with a Marian theme."

$ QUEEN'S QUARTERLY, A Canadian Review, (I, IV), Queen's University, Kingston, Ontario K7L 3N6 Canada. Phone/fax: (613)545-2667. Fax: (613)545-6822. E-mail: qquartly@post.queensu.ca. Website: http://info.queensu.ca./quarterly. **Editor:** Boris Castel. Magazine: 6×9; 800 pages/year; illustrations. "A general inter-

est intellectual review, featuring articles on science, politics, humanities, arts and letters. Book reviews, poetry and fiction." Quarterly. Estab. 1893. Circ. 3,000.
Needs: Adventure, contemporary, experimental, fantasy, historical, humor/satire, literary, mainstream, science fiction and women's. "*Special emphasis on work by Canadian writers*." Accepts 2 mss/issue; 8 mss/year. Published work by Gail Anderson-Dargatz, Mark Jarman, Rick Bowers and Dennis Bock; published new writers within the last year. Length: 2,000-3,000 words. Also publishes literary essays, literary criticism, poetry.
How to Contact: "Send complete ms with SASE." No simultaneous or multiple submissions. Reports within 3 months. Sample copy for $6.50. Reviews novels and short story collections. Electronic submissions OK.
Payment/Terms: Pays $100-300 for fiction, 2 contributor's copies and 1-year subscription; $5 charge for extras. Pays on publication for first North American serial rights. Sends galleys to author.

RESPONSE, A Contemporary Jewish Review, (II, IV), 114 W. 26th St., Suite 1004, New York NY 10001-6812. (212)620-0350. Fax: (212)929-3459. E-mail: response@panix.com. **Editors:** David R. Adler, Chanita Baumheft and Michael Steinberg. Magazine: 6×9; 120 pages; 70 lb. paper; 10 pt. CS1 cover; illustrations; photos. "Fiction, poetry and essays with a Jewish theme, for Jewish students and young adults." Quarterly. Estab. 1967. Circ. 6,000.
Needs: Contemporary, ethnic, experimental, feminist, historical (general), humor/satire, literary, prose poem, regional, religious, spirituals, translations. "Stories in which the Holocaust plays a major role must be exceptional in quality. The shrill and the morbid will not be accepted." Receives 10-20 unsolicited mss/month. Accepts 5-10 mss/issue; 10-15 mss/year. Publishes ms 2-4 months after acceptance. Length: 15-20 pages (double spaced). Publishes short shorts. Sometimes recommends other markets.
How to Contact: Send complete ms with cover letter; include brief biography of author. SASE. No simultaneous submissions. Sample copy for $6; free guidelines.
Payment/Terms: Pays in contributor's copies. Acquires all rights.
Advice: "In the best pieces, every word will show the author's conscious attention to the craft. Subtle ambiguities, quiet ironies and other such carefully handled tropes are not lost on *Response*'s readers. Pieces that also show passion that is not marred by either shrillness or pathos are respected and often welcomed. Writers who write from the gut or the muse are few in number. *Response* personally prefers the writer who thinks about what he or she is doing, rather than the writer who intuits his or her stories."

RFD, A Country Journal for Gay Men Everywhere, (I, II, IV), Short Mountain Collective, P.O. Box 68, Liberty TN 37095. (615)536-5176. **Contact:** The Collective. Magazine: 8½×11; 64-80 pages. "Focus on radical faeries, gay men's spirituality—country living." Quarterly. Estab. 1974. Circ. 3,600.
Needs: Gay: Erotica, ethnic/multicultural, experimental, fantasy, feminist, humor/satire, literary, mainstream/contemporary, mystery/suspense, psychic/supernatural/occult, regional, romance. Receives 10 unsolicited mss/month. Accepts 3 mss/issue; 12 mss/year. Length: open. Publishes short shorts. Also publishes literary essays, literary criticism and poetry.
How to Contact: Send complete ms with cover letter and estimated word count. Usually reports in 6-9 months. Send SASE for reply, return of ms or send disposable copy of ms. Sample copy for $6. Free fiction guidelines.
Payment/Terms: Pays 1 or 2 contributor's copies. Not copyrighted.

ROMANTIC HEARTS, A Magazine Dedicated to Short Romantic Fiction, (I, II, IV), P.O. Box 450669, Westlake OH 44145-0612. **Editor:** Debra L. Krauss. Magazine: 5¼×8; 48 pages; 20 lb. paper; 20 lb. color cover; illustrations and photographs. "Romantic Hearts is dedicated to publishing the finest romantic short fiction written today. Our audience is romance readers and writers. We also publish short romantic essays (500-1,500 words) and love poems of 25 lines of less." Bimonthly. Estab. 1996.
Needs: Romance (contemporary, futuristic/time travel, gothic, historical, all types). Wants more historical fiction. No erotica or pornography. Receives 25 unsolicited mss/month. Accepts 5-7 mss/issue; 36-40 mss/year. Publishes ms 8-14 months after acceptance. Recently published work by Holly J. Fuhrmann, Penelope A. Marzec, Reia Parks and Sheri Cobb South. Publishes 20 new writers/year. Length: 3,000 words average; 1,500 words minimum; 4,000 words maximum. Also publishes literary essays (must have a romantic theme), poetry. Often critiques or comments on rejected mss.
How to Contact: Send complete ms with a cover letter. Include estimated word count. Reports in 6-8 weeks. Send SASE for reply, return of ms or send a disposable copy of ms. No simultaneous submissions. Sample copy for $4 ppd. Fiction guidelines free for #10 SASE.
Payment/Terms: Pays 3 contributor's copies on publication; additional copies for $2. Acquires first North American serial rights. "Send #10 SASE with request for contest guidelines."
Advice: "The stories I select are uplifting and positive. They must also be a 'romance.' A standout manuscript is one that contains strong characterization and lots of emotion. Always include a cover letter and correctly format your manuscript. Please be sure your story is a romance with a happy ending or the promise of one."

$ ROSEBUD™, For People Who Enjoy Writing, (I, II), P.O. Box 459, Cambridge WI 53523. Phone/fax: (608)423-9609. Website: http://www.hyperionstudio.com/rosebud (includes writer's guidelines, contests, preview, *Rosebud* bulletin board, teachers guide to current issue, outreach programs and advertising rates). **Editor:** Roderick Clark. Magazine: 7×10; 136 pages; 60 lb. matte; 100 lb. cover; illustrations. Quarterly. Estab. 1993. Circ. 10,000.

• *Rosebud* was selected for inclusion in the *Writer's Digest* "Fiction 50" list of top fiction markets.

Needs: Adventure, condensed/excerpted novel, ethnic/multicultural, experimental, historical (general), humor/satire, literary, mainstream/contemporary, psychic/supernatural/occult, regional, romance (contemporary), science fiction (soft/sociological), serialized novel, translations. Each submission must fit loosely into one of the following categories to qualify: City and Shadow (urban settings), Songs of Suburbia (suburban themes), These Green Hills (nature and nostalgia), En Route (any type of travel), Mothers, Daughters, Wives (relationships), Ulysses' Bow (manhood), Paper, Scissors, Rock (childhood, middle age, old age), The Jeweled Prize (concerning love), Lost and Found (loss and discovery), Voices in Other Rooms (historic or of other culture), Overtime (involving work), Anything Goes (humor), I Hear Music (music), Season to Taste (food), Word Jazz (wordplay), Apples to Oranges (miscellaneous, excerpts, profiles). Publishes annual special fiction issue or anthology. Receives 1,200 unsolicited mss/month. Accepts 16 mss/issue; 64 mss/year. Publishes ms 1-3 months after acceptance. Published work by Seamus Heany, Louis Simpson, Allen Ginsberg and Philip Levine. 70% of work published is by new writers. Length: 1,200-1,800 words average. Occasionally uses longer pieces and novel excerpts (prepublished). Publishes short shorts. Also publishes literary essays. Often critiques or comments on rejected mss.

How to Contact: Send complete ms with a cover letter. Include estimated word count and list of publications. Reports in 3 months on mss. SASE for return of ms. Simultaneous and reprints submissions OK. Sample copy for $5.95. Fiction guidelines for legal SASE.

Payment/Terms: Pays $45 and 3 contributor's copies on publication for one-time rights; additional copies for $4.40.

Advice: "Each issue will have six or seven flexible departments (selected from a total of sixteen departments that will rotate). We are seeking stories, articles, profiles, and poems of: love, alienation, travel, humor, nostalgia and unexpected revelation. Something has to 'happen' in the pieces we choose, but what happens inside characters is much more interesting to us than plot manipulation. We like good storytelling, real emotion and authentic voice."

N **SHIVER MAGAZINE, The Magazine for Active Minds Bent on Twisting Others, (I, II)**, Shiver Publications, P.O. Box 178, Surrey, British Columbia V3T 4W8 Canada. (604)581-9111. E-mail: shiver@clubtek.com. Website: http://www.clubtek.com/shiver (includes writer's guidelines). Editor: T.L. Craigen. Fiction Editor: L.K. Mason. Magazine: 8½×11; 56 pages; 20 lb. bond paper; glossy cover stock; illustrations. "*Shiver* is a shared-world magazine. We publish fantasy, horror and science fiction and our intended audience is 17 and up." Semiannually. Estab. 1995. Circ. 1,200.

Needs: Fantasy (children's, science fantasy, sword and sorcery), horror, science fiction (hard science, soft/sociological). "No gratuitous sex or profanity." Receives 40 unsolicited mss/month. Accepts 6 mss/issue; 12 mss/year. Publishes ms 3-6 months after acceptance. Recently published work by Dietmar Trommeshauser, Cathy Buburuz and Alan M. Clark. Length: 5,000 words average; 1,000 words minimum; 10,000 words maximum. Publishes short shorts. Length: 500 words. Also publishes poetry. Always critiques or comments on rejected ms.

How to Contact: Send complete ms with a cover letter. Include estimated word count and 50-word bio. Reports in 2 weeks on queries; 2 months on mss. Send SASE for reply, return of ms or send a disposable copy of ms. Reprint submissions OK. Sample copy $5 (US). Fiction guidelines for #10 SASE.

Payment/Terms: Pays $10-100 on acceptance and 1 contributor's copy; additional copies $3. Acquires first North American serial rights. Sponsors contests. Send SASE for details.

Advice: "We tend to stay away from overly traditional pieces. Writers have a greater chance of being published if they participate in our shared-world theme."

SKIPPING STONES: A Multicultural Children's Magazine, (I, II), P.O. Box 3939, Eugene OR 97403-0939. (541)342-4956. E-mail: skipping@efn.org. Website: http://www.nonviolence.org/skipping (includes writer's guidelines). **Executive Editor:** Arun N. Toké. Magazine: 8½×11; 36 pages; recycled 50 lb. halopaque paper; 100 lb. text cover; illustrations and photos. "*Skipping Stones* is a multicultural, international, nature awareness magazine for children 8-16, and their parents and teachers." Published 5 times a year. Estab. 1988. Circ. 3,000.

• *Skipping Stones* received the 1997 National Association for Multicultural Education, Name Award.

Needs: Children's/juvenile (8-16 years): ethnic/multicultural, feminist, religious/inspirational, young adult/teen, international, nature. No simplistic, fiction for the sake of fiction, mystery, violent or abusive language, science fiction. "We want more authentic pieces based on truly multicultural/intercultural/international living experiences of authors. We welcome works by people of color." Upcoming themes for 1998: "Living Abroad," "Crosscultural Communications," "Humor Unlimited, Int'l," "Folktales," "Turning Points in Life . . .," "Raising Children: Rewards, Punishments." List of upcoming themes available for SASE. Receives 50 mss/month. Accepts 5-8 mss/issue; 25-30 mss/year. Publishes ms 3-6 months after acceptance. Published work by Victoria Collett, Charles Curatalo, Anjali Amit, Lily Hartmann and Peter Chase. Publishes up to 100 new writers/year. Length: 750 words average; 250 words minimum; 1,000 words maximum. Publishes short shorts. Also publishes literary essays and poetry (by youth under 19). Often critiques or comments on rejected mss. Sponsors contests and awards for fiction writers under 17 years of age.

How to Contact: Send complete ms with a cover letter. Accepts queries/mss by e-mail. Include 50- to 100-

word bio with background, international or intercultural experiences. Reports in 1 month on queries; 3 months on mss. Send SASE for reply, return of ms or send a disposable copy of ms. Simultaneous submissions OK. Sample copy for $5, 9×12 SAE and 4 first-class stamps. Fiction guidelines for #10 SASE.
Payment/Terms: Pays 1-3 contributor's copies; additional copies for $3. Acquires first North American serial rights and nonexclusive reprint rights.
Advice: Looking for stories with "multicultural/multiethnic theme, use of other languages when appropriate. Realistic and suitable for 8 to 16 year olds. Promoting social and nature awareness. In addition to encouraging children's creativity, we also invite adults to submit their own writing and artwork for publication in *Skipping Stones*. Writings and artwork by adults should challenge readers to think and learn, cooperate and create."

☑ **SLATE AND STYLE, Magazine of the National Federation of the Blind Writers Division, (I, IV)**, NFB Writer's Division, 2704 Beach Dr., Merrick NY 11566. (516)868-8718. Fax: (516)868-9076. E-mail: loristay@aol.com. **Fiction Editor:** Loraine Stayer. Newsletter: 8×10; 32 print/40 Braille pages; cassette and large print. "Articles of interest to writers, and resources for blind writers." Quarterly. Estab. 1982. Circ. 200. "We publish fiction only as a result of our contests. Contest entries should be sent to ℅ Tom Stevens, 1203 S. Fairview Rd., Columbia MO 65203. There is a $5 entry fee and the contest runs from September 1 to May 1. Write for details."
Needs: Adventure, contemporary, fantasy, humor/satire, blindness. No erotica. "Avoid theme of death." Does not read mss in June or July. Recently published work by Dave Taub, Marie Anna Pape and Lois Wencil. Publishes 8-10 new writers/year. Length: 3,000 words maximum. Publishes short shorts. Also publishes literary criticism and poetry. Critiques rejected mss only if requested.
How to Contact: Reports in 3-6 weeks. Accepts queries by e-mail. Large print sample copy for $2.50.
Payment/Terms: Pays in contributor's copies. Acquires one-time rights. Publication not copyrighted. Sponsors contests for fiction writers.
Advice: "Keep a copy. Editors can lose your work. Consider each first draft as just that and review your work before you send it. SASE a must. Although we circulate to blind writers, I do not wish to see articles on blindness by sighted writers unless they are married to, or the son/daughter/parent of a blind person. In general, we do not even print articles on blidness, preferring to publish articles on alternate techniques a blind writer can use to surmount his blindness."

SPACE AND TIME, (I, II), 138 W. 70th St. (4B), New York NY 10023-4468. Website: http://www.bway.net/~natalia/space&time.html (includes guidelines, staff, current and future contents, back issues/books for sale, schedule of our reading series). Editor: Gordon Linzner. **Fiction Editor:** Tom Piccirilli. Magazine: 8½×11; 48 pages; 50 lb. paper; index card cover stock; illustrations and photos. "We publish science fiction, fantasy, horror and our favorite, that-which-defies-categorization." Biannually. Estab. 1966. Circ. 2,000. Member of the Small Press Center and the Small Press Genre Organization.
Needs: Fantasy (science, sword and sorcery, undefinable), horror, science fiction (hard science, soft/sociological, undefinable). Receives 100 unsolicited mss/month. Accepts 12 mss/issue; 24 mss/year. Publishes ms 6-18 months after acceptance. Recently published work by Don Webb, Sue Storm, Mary Soon Lee and Stephen Dedhan. Length: 5,000 words average; 10,000 words maximum. Publishes short shorts. Also publishes literary essays, literary criticism and poetry. Send poems to Lawrence Greenberg. Often critiques or comments on rejected mss.
How to Contact: Send complete ms. Include estimated word count. Reports in 1 week on queries; 2-3 months on mss. Send SASE for reply, return of ms or send a disposable copy of ms. Sample copy for $5 and 9×12 SAE with $1.25 postage or 3 IRCs. Fiction guidelines for #10 SASE or SAE and 1 IRC.
Payment/Terms: Pays 1¢/word, $5 minimum and 2 contributor's copies on acceptance; additional copies $3. Acquires first North American serial rights and option to reprint in context of magazine.
Advice: Looks for "good writing, strong characterization and unusual plot or premise."

SPACEWAYS WEEKLY, The E-mail Magazine of Science Fiction & Fantasy, (I), P.O. Box 3023, London Ontario N6A 4H9 Canada. E-mail: spaceways@mirror.org. Website: http://www.mirror.org/spaceways/index.html (includes subscription information, resources and links, list of writers, guidelines, sample of current story, general information). **Editor:** Rigel D. Chiokis. Electronic magazine. "We publish science fiction and fantasy short stories in an electronic format. We publish one story per week. Our audience is mostly adults with e-mail and is increasingly international." Weekly. Estab. 1997.
Needs: Experimental, fantasy (science fantasy, sword and sorcery), feminist (science fiction and fantasy), gay (science fiction and fantasy), lesbian (science fiction and fantasy), science fiction (hard science, soft/sociological). No erotica or pornographic. Receives 8-12 unsolicited mss/month. Accepts 1 ms/issue; 52 mss/year. Publishes

ms 4-6 months after acceptance. Recently published work by Jane Mitchell, Magee Gilks, Darren Latta, Mark Budman, F. Alexander Brejcha and Barb Soutar. Publishes 45-50 new writers/year. Length: 2,000-3,000 words average; 5,000 words maximum. Publishes short shorts. Often critiques or comments on rejected mss.
How to Contact: Send complete ms with a cover letter by e-mail in ASCII text. Accepts queries/mss by e-mail. Include estimated word count and copyright notice. Simultaneous submissions OK. Guidelines for #10 SASE.
Payment/Terms: Pays .01/word CDN plus 1 year subscription on acceptance for first Canadian rights.
Advice: "A story must have good characterization first; a good plot, second. Send for my guidelines or read them on our webpage. Follow those guidelines to the letter."

N SPIRIT TO SPIRIT, (I, II, IV), (formerly *Merlana's Magickal Messages*), Navarro Publications/Literary Services, P.O. Box 1107, Blythe CA 92226-1107. (888)922-0833. **Managing Editor:** Marjorie E. Navarro. Executive Editor: Richard Navarro. Magazine: digest-sized; 35-75 pages; "desk-top published;" soft cover. "*STS* is a New-Age style pagan publication featuring short stories, articles and poetry." Published 3 times/year (March, July, October).
Needs: New Age, pagan, goddess/god related works. Short stories up to 3,500 words, "with positive uplifting material." No mystery or science fiction; no organized religious, anything with violence or gratuitous sex. Recently published work by Allison M. Shade, Derrick Corley, James Thomas Romano, Paris Flammonde and Hugh Fox.
How to Contact: *Charges reading fee to nonsubscribers: $1/article, $1/6 poems, $3/short story (refundable).* Send complete ms with cover letter. "I like to know a little bit about the author, including publishing credits. (Don't worry if you have none; we enjoy discovering new talent.) Also, what prompted you to write this particular story?" Reports in 6-10 weeks. SASE. Sample copy for $6 (payable to Navarro Publications). Fiction guidelines for #10 SASE.
Payment/Terms: Pays 1 contributor's copy. Tearsheets available on request for SASE.
Advice: "Looking for fresh originality! Give me an uplifting/healing message of the spirit and together we shall create real magick in ours and others' lives."

✔ **THE STORYTELLER, For Amateur Writers, (I)**, 2441 Washington Rd., Maynard AR 72444. (870)647-2137. **Editor:** Regina Williams. Tabloid: 8½×11; 50-60 pages; typing paper; illustrations. "This magazine is open to all new writers regardless of age. I will accept short stories in any genre and poetry in any type. Please keep in mind, this is a family publication." Quarterly. Estab. 1996.
Needs: Adventure, historical, humor/satire, literary, mainstream/contemporary, mystery/suspense, regional, religious/inspirational, romance, science fiction (soft/sociological), senior citizen/retirement, sports, westerns, young adult/teen. "I will not accept pornography, erotica, foul language, horror or graphic violence." Wants more well-plotted mysteries. Publishes ms 3-9 months after acceptance. Recently published work by Randy Offner, Otis Lawson, Bryan Byrd and Gracie Cauble. Publishes approximately 100 new writers/year. Length: 1,500 words maximum; 200 words minimum. Publishes short shorts. Also publishes literary essays and poetry. Sometimes critiques or comments on rejected mss.
How to Contact: Nonsubscribers must pay reading fee: $1/poem, $2/short story. Send complete ms with a cover letter. Include estimated word count and 5-line bio. Reports 2-4 weeks on queries; 1-2 months on mss. Send SASE for reply, return of ms or send a disposable copy of ms. Simultaneous and reprint submissions OK. Sample copy for $6. Fiction guidelines for #10 SASE.
Payment/Terms: "Readers vote quarterly for their favorites in all categories. Winning authors receive certificate of merit and free copy of issue in which their story or poem appeared."
Advice: Looks for "professionalism, good plots and unique characters. Purchase a sample copy so you know the kind of material we look for. Even though this is for amateur writers, don't send us something you would not send to paying markets." Would like more "well-plotted mysteries and suspense and a few traditional westerns. Avoid sending anything that children or young adults would not (or could not) read, such as really bad language."

N THE STRAND MAGAZINE, Box 1418, Birmingham, MI 48012-1418. (800)300-6657. Fax: (248)874-1046. E-mail: strandmag@worldnet.att.net. **Editor:** A. F. Gullie. Quarterly mystery magazine. Estab. 1998. "After an absence of nearly half a century, the magazine known to millions for bringing Sir Arthur Conan Doyle's ingenious detective, Sherlock Holmes, to the world has once again appeared on the literary scene. First launched in 1891, *The Strand* included in its pages the works of some of the greatest writers of the 20th century: Agatha Christie, Dorothy Sayers, Margery Allingham, W. Somerset Maugham, Graham Greene, P.G. Wodehouse, H.G. Wells, Aldous Huxley and many others. In 1950, economic difficulties in England caused a drop in circulation which forced the magazine to cease publication."
Needs: Mysteries, detective stories, tales of terror and the supernatural "written in the classic tradition of this century's great authors. Stories can be set in any time or place, provided they are well written and the plots interesting and well thought out. We are NOT interested in submissions with any sexual content." Length: 2,000-6,000 words, "however, we may occasionally publish short shorts of 1,000 words or sometimes go as long as a short novella."
How to Contact: Send complete ms, typed, double-spaced on one side of each page. SASE (IRCs if outside

the US). Reports in 4 months.
Payment/Terms: Pays $25-$50 on acceptance for first North American serial rights.

STUDIO: A JOURNAL OF CHRISTIANS WRITING, (II), 727 Peel St., Albury 2640 Australia. **Managing Editor:** Paul Grover. Circ. 300. Quarterly. Averages 20-30 stories/year.
Needs: "*Studio* publishes prose and poetry of literary merit, offers a venue for new and aspiring writers, and seeks to create a sense of community among Christians writing." Length: 500-5,000 words.
Payment/Terms: Pays in copies. Sample copy available for $8 (Australian). Subscription $40 (Australian) for 4 issues (1 year). International draft in Australian dollars and IRC required.

$ TALEBONES, Fiction on the Dark Edge, (II), Fairwood Press, 10531 SE 250th Place, #104, Kent WA 98031. (253)813-6814. E-mail: talebones@nventure.com. Website: http://www.nventure.com/talebones (includes guidelines, submission requirements, excerpts, news about the magazine, bios). **Editors:** Patrick and Honna Swenson. Magazine: digest size; 68 pages; standard paper; glossy cover stock; illustrations and photos. "We like stories that have punch, but still entertain. We like dark science fiction and dark fantasy, humor, psychological and experimental works." Quarterly. Estab. 1995. Circ. 400.

- *Talebones* received over 15 Honorable Mentions in the Year's Best anthologies over the past 2 years.

Needs: Fantasy (dark), humor/satire, science fiction (hard science, soft/sociological, dark). "No straight slash and hack horror. No cat stories or stories told by young adults. Would like to see more science fiction." Receives 200 mss/month. Accepts 6-7 mss/issue; 24-28 mss/year. Publishes ms 3-4 months after acceptance. Recently published work by Patrick O'Leary, Bruce Boston, Leslie What, Mark Rich, Trey R. Barker and Uncle River. Publishes 2-3 new writers/year. Length: 3,000-4,000 words average; 500 words minimum; 6,000 words maximum. Publihses short shorts. Length: 1,000 words. Also publishes poetry.
How to Contact: Send complete ms with a cover letter. Accepts queries/mss by e-mail. Include estimated word count and 1-paragraph bio. Reports in 1 week on queries; 1-3 weeks on mss. Send SASE for reply, return of ms or send a disposable copy of ms. No simultaneous submissions. No reprints. Electronic submissions (e-mail) OK. Sample copy for $4.50. Fiction guidelines for SASE. Reviews novels and short story collections.
Payment/Terms: Pays $10-100 on acceptance and 1 contributor's copy; additional copies for $3. Acquires first North American serial rights. Sends galleys to author.
Advice: "The story must be entertaining, but should blur the boundary between science fiction and horror. All our stories have a dark edge to them, but often are humorous or psychological. Be polite and know how to properly present a manuscript. Include a cover letter, but keep it short and to the point."

TEXAS YOUNG WRITERS' NEWSLETTER, (I, II, IV), Texas Young Writers' Association, P.O. Box 942, Adkins TX 78101-0942. **Editor:** Susan Currie. Newsletter: 8½×11; 8 pages; 20 lb. white paper; illustrations. "*TYWN* teaches young writers about the art and business of writing, and also gives them a place to publish their best work. We publish articles by adults with experience in publishing, and poetry and short stories by young writers 12-19." Bimonthly. Estab. 1994. Circ. 300.
Needs: Open to authors ages 12-19 only. Adventure, ethnic/multicultural, fantasy (children's fantasy, science fantasy), historical, humor/satire, literary, mainstream/contemporary, mystery/suspense, romance, science fiction, young adult/teen. "Anything by young writers, 12-19. No erotica, horror, gay/lesbian or occult." List of upcoming themes available for SASE. Receives 6 unsolicited mss/month. Accepts 1 ms/issue; 9 mss/year. Publishes ms 6 months after acceptance. Published work by Sarah Elezian, Lillette Hill, Caroline Beever and Anthony Twistt. Length: 900 words average; 500 words minimum; 1,100 words maximum. Publishes short shorts. Also publishes poetry. Always critiques or comments on rejected ms.
How to Contact: Send complete ms with a cover letter. Include estimated word count and 50-100 word bio. Reports in 6 weeks. Send SASE for reply, return of ms. Sample copy for $1. Guidelines for #10 SASE, "please specify adult or young writer's guidelines."
Payment/Terms: Pays 2 contributor's copies for poetry, 5 for articles and short stories. Acquires first North American serial rights. Not copyrighted.
Advice: "Please read back issues and study the sort of fiction we publish, and make sure it fits our newsletter. Since *TYWN* is sent to schools and young people, we prefer upbeat, nonviolent stories. I look for work that is highly original, creative, and appropriate for our audience. Manuscripts that are professional and striking stand out. I haven't seen enough stories with strong characters and involving plots. I don't want to see dull stories with dull characters. We want to show our young writers terrific examples of stories that they can learn from."

✓ THE THRESHOLD, (I, II), Crossover Press, P.O. Box 101362, Pittsburgh PA 15237. (412)635-8334. E-mail: lazarro@aol.com. Website: http://members.aol.com/lazarro/Threshold/home.htm. **Editors:** Don H. Laird and Michael Carricato. Magazine: 8½×11; 48 pages; colored bond paper; card cover; illustrations. "We truly are a magazine 'for writers, by writers.' We always give constructive criticism, not a form letter. Our audience is both young and old and they are in search of one thing: imaginative stories and poetry." Quarterly. Estab. 1996. Circ. 1,000.
Needs: Adventure, condensed/excerpted novel, erotica, experimental, fantasy, gay, horror, humor/satire, lesbian, literary, mainstream/contemporary, mystery/suspense, psychic/supernatural/occult, romance (contemporary, futuristic/time travel/gothic), science fiction, serialized novel, westerns. Publishes special fiction issues or antholog-

ies. Receives 20 unsolicited mss/month. Accepts 6-8 mss/issue, 24-32 mss/year. Publishes ms up to 5 months after acceptance. Recently published work by Timothy Egan, Paul Perry, Nikki Prescott, Doina N. Locke, Ari Cetron and Danielle Langevin. Length: 3,000-5,000 words average; 8,000 words maximum. Publishes short shorts. Also publishes poetry. Always critiques or comments on rejected mss.

How to Contact: Send complete ms with a cover letter. Include estimated word count and 2-paragraph bio. Reports in 2 weeks on queries; 4-6 months on mss. Send SASE for reply, return of ms or send disposable copy of ms. Simultaneous, reprint and electronic submissions OK. Sample copy for $5.95. Fiction guidelines for #10 SASE.

Payment/Terms: Pays 1 contributor's copy for one-time rights.

Advice: "If we like it, we print it. Period. If it needs some changes, we send a letter recommending where some revisions would help. It is an open forum between writer and editor. Send in the work. Don't be discouraged by form rejection letters."

THRESHOLDS QUARTERLY, School of Metaphysics Associates Journal, (I, II, IV), SOM Publishing, School of Metaphysics National Headquarters, HCR1, Box 15, Windyville MO 65783. (417)345-8411. Fax: (417)345-6688 (call first, computerized). Website: http://www.som.org. **Editor:** Dr. Barbara Condron. Senior Editor: Dr. Laurel Fuller Clark. Magazine: 7×10; 32 pages; line drawings and b&w photos. "The School of Metaphysics is a nonprofit educational and service organization invested in education and research in the expansion of human consciousness and spiritual evolution of humanity. For all ages and backgrounds. Themes: dreams, healing, science fiction, personal insight, morality tales, fables, humor, spiritual insight, mystic experiences, religious articles, creative writing with universal themes." Quarterly. Estab. 1975. Circ. 5,000.

Needs: Adventure, fantasy, humor, psychic/supernatural, religious/inspirational, science fiction. Upcoming themes: "Dreams, Visions, and Creative Imagination" (February); "Health and Wholeness" (May); "Intuitive Arts" (August); "Man's Spiritual Consciousness" (November). Receives 5 unsolicited mss/month. Length: 4-10 double-spaced typed pages. Publishes short shorts. Also publishes literary essays and poetry. Often critiques or comments on rejected mss.

How to Contact: Query with outline; will accept unsolicited ms with cover letter; no guarantee on time length to respond. Include bio (1-2 paragraphs). Send SASE for reply, return of ms or send a disposable copy of ms. Sample copy for 9×12 SAE and $1.50 postage. Fiction guidelines for #10 SASE.

Payment/Terms: Pays up to 5 contributor's copies. Acquires all rights.

Advice: "We encourage works that have one or more of the following attributes: uplifting, educational, inspirational, entertaining, informative and innovative."

N 🌐 **TOGETHER WITH CHILDREN, Christian Resources and Inspiration for Leaders**, The National Society, Church House, Great Smith St., London SW1P 3NZ England. Phone/fax: 0171-739-9823. **Editor:** Mrs. P. Macnaughton. Magazine of forward-looking Christian education for children up to age 13. Short stories, plays, services, projects, etc. Also songs, carols, occasional poems. Readers are church children's group leaders, primary school and Sunday school teachers, clergy. Publishes 50% new writers.

Needs: Stories are usually intended to be read aloud. Length: 1,000 words preferred, 2,000 words maximum. Can be stories for use in church services, or school assemblies, or with smaller groups and can be for a specific age-group, or for all ages. They should have some Christian content, either implicit or explicit. If you are hoping to re-tell a Bible story, it is helpful to try to put a fresh angle on it, like seeing it through the eyes of one of the characters, or putting it in a contemporary setting. Note intended audience.

How to Contact: Accepts queries/mss by fax.

VINTAGE NORTHWEST, (I, IV), Box 193, Bothell WA 98041. (425)823-9189. **Editors:** Jane Kaake and Sylvia Tacker. Magazine: 7×8½; 68 pages; illustrations. "We are a senior literary magazine, published by Northshore Senior Center, but our focus is to appeal to all ages. All work done by volunteers except printing." Published winter and summer. Estab. 1980. Circ. 500.

Needs: Adventure, comedy, fantasy, historical, humor/satire, inspirational, mystery/suspense, nostalgia, poetry, western (frontier). No religious or political mss. Receives 10-12 unsolicited mss/month. Publishes as many new writers as possible. Length: 1,000 words maximum. Also publishes literary essays. Occasionally critiques rejected mss.

How to Contact: Send complete ms. SASE. Simultaneous and previously published submissions OK. Reports in 3-6 months. Sample copy for $4.25 (postage included). Guidelines with SASE.

Payment/Terms: Pays 1 contributor's copy.

Advice: "Our only requirement is that the author be over 50 when submission is written."

$ VIRGINIA QUARTERLY REVIEW, (I, II), One West Range, Charlottesville VA 22903. (804)924-3124. Fax: (804)924-1397. E-mail: jco7e@virginia.edu. **Editor:** Staige Blackford. "A national magazine of literature and discussion. A lay, intellectual audience; people who are not out-and-out scholars but who are interested in ideas and literature." Quarterly. Estab. 1925. Circ. 4,000.

Needs: Adventure, contemporary, ethnic, feminist, humor, literary, romance, serialized novels (excerpts) and translations. "No pornography." Buys 3 mss/issue, 20 mss/year. Length: 3,000-7,000 words.

How to Contact: Query or send complete ms. SASE. No simultaneous submissions. Reports in 2 weeks on

queries, 2 months on mss. Sample copy for $5.
Payment/Terms: Pays $10/printed page on publication for all rights. "Will transfer upon request." Offers Emily Clark Balch Award for best published short story of the year.
Advice: Looks for "stories with a somewhat Southern dialect and/or setting. Humor is welcome; stories involving cancer and geriatrics are not."

VOLCANO QUARTERLY, The Village Square of Volcanodom, (I, II, IV), 420 SE Evans Lane, Issaquah WA 98027. (425)392-7858. E-mail: vqjantan@aol.com. Website: http://memberes.aol.com/vqjantan. Editor: Janet Tanaka.

- *Volcano Quarterly* has ceased print publication, and plans to publish online in late 1999 or 2000. Please contact for updated writer's guidelines.

$ WEIRD TALES, (II), (formerly *Worlds of Fantasy & Horror*), DNA Publications, 123 Crooked Lane, King of Prussia PA 19406-2570. (610)275-4463. E-mail: owlswick@netaxs.com. **Editors:** George H. Scithers and Darrell Schweitzer. Magazine: 8½×11; 68 pages; white, non-glossy paper; glossy 4-color cover; illustrations. "We publish fantastic fiction, supernatural horror for an adult audience." Quarterly. Estab. 1923. Circ. 10,000.
Needs: Fantasy (science, sword and sorcery), horror, psychic/supernatural/occult, translations. "We want to see a wide range of fantasy, from sword and sorcery to supernatural horror. We can use some unclassifiables." No hard science fiction or non-fantasy. Receives 400 unsolicited mss/month. Accepts 8 mss/issue; 32 mss/year. Publishes ms 6-18 months after acceptance. Agented fiction 10%. Published work by Tanith Lee, Thomas Ligotti, Ian Watson and Lord Dunsany. Publishes 6 new writers/year. Length: 4,000 words average; 10,000 words maximum (very few over 8,000). "No effective minimum. Shortest we ever published was about 100 words." Publishes short shorts. Also publishes poetry. Always critiques or comments on rejected mss.
How to Contact: Send complete ms. Include estimated word count. Reports in 2-3 weeks on mss. Send SASE for reply, return of ms or send a disposable copy of ms with SASE. No simultaneous submissions. No reprint submissions, "but will buy first North American rights to stories published overseas." Sample copy for $4.95. Fiction guidelines for #10 SASE. Reviews novels and short story collections relevant to the horror/fantasy field.
Payment/Terms: Pays 3¢/word minimum and 2 contributor's copies for first North American serial rights plus anthology option. Sends galleys to author.
Advice: "We look for imagination and vivid writing. Read the magazine. Get a good grounding in the contemporary horror and fantasy field through the various 'best of the year' anthologies. Avoid the obvious cliches of technicalities of the hereafter, the mechanics of vampirism, generic Tolkien-clone fantasy. In general, it is better to be honest and emotionally moving rather than clever. Avoid stories which have nothing of interest save for the allegedly 'surprise' ending."

WESTERN DIGEST, Crossbow Publications, 400 Whiteland Dr. NE, Calgary, Alberta T1Y 3M7 Canada. (403)280-3424. E-mail: crossbow@cadvision.com. Website: http://www.westerndigest.com (includes sample issue, 2 short stories, profile and links, comment page). **Publisher:** Douglas Sharp. Newsletter: 8½×11; 20 pages. Publishes Western fiction and cowboy poetry only. Estab. 1995. Circ. 200.
Needs: Westerns (frontier, traditional). "Do not combine westerns with science fiction. Would like to see more humorous stories." Receives 4 unsolicited mss/month. Accepts 5-8 mss/issue; 50 mss/year. Publishes ms 18 months after acceptance. Recently published work by C.F. Eckhart, Jonny Boggs, A.J. Arnold and Emery Mohok. Publishes 10 new writers/year. Length: 3,000 words average; 1,000 words minimum; 5,000 words maximum. Publishes short shorts. Length: 1,000 words. Also publishes literary criticism and poetry. Always critiques or comments on rejected mss.
How to Contact: Send complete ms with a cover letter. Accepts queries/mss by e-mail. Include 10- to 30-word bio. Reports in 1 week on queries; 2 weeks on mss. Send SAE and 2 IRCs for return of ms. Simultaneous submissions, reprints and electronic (Macintosh disk, WordPerfect 5.1) submissions OK. Sample copy for $4. Fiction guidelines free. Reviews novels or short story collections.
Payment/Terms: Pays $10-60 (Canadian funds) and free subscription to the magazine on publication. Acquires one-time rights.
Advice: "I enjoy stories with humorous, ironic or surprise endings. I would like to read more humorous stories. Avoid shoot-'em-ups. One gets tired of reading stories where the fastest gun wins in the end. There are other stories to be told of the pioneers. Rewrite your story until it is perfect. Do not use contractions in narration unless

**FOR EXPLANATIONS OF THESE SYMBOLS,
SEE THE INSIDE FRONT AND BACK COVERS OF THIS BOOK.**

the story is written in first person. Do not send three consecutive pages of dialogue. Be sure to identify the speaker after three or four paragraphs. A reader should not have to reread a passage to understand it. Please, no sex or heavy duty swearing."

☑ **WISCONSIN ACADEMY REVIEW, (IV)**, Wisconsin Academy of Sciences, Arts & Letters, 1922 University Ave., Madison WI 53705-4099. (608)263-1692. Fax: (608)265-3039. **Editorial Director:** Faith B. Miracle. Magazine: 8½×11; 48-52 pages; 75 lb. coated paper; coated cover stock; illustrations; photos. "The *Review* reflects the focus of the sponsoring institution with its editorial emphasis on Wisconsin's intellectual, cultural, social and physical environment. It features short fiction, poetry, essays, nonfiction articles and Wisconsin-related art and book reviews for people interested in furthering regional arts and literature and disseminating information about sciences." Quarterly. Estab. 1954. Circ. approximately 1,800.

Needs: Experimental, historical, humor/satire, literary, mainstream, prose poem. "Author must have a Wisconsin connection or fiction must be set in Wisconsin." Receives 5-6 unsolicited fiction mss/month. Accepts 1-2 mss/issue; 6-8 mss/year. Published new writers within the last year. Length: 1,000 words minimum; 3,500 words maximum. Also publishes poetry; "will consider" literary essays, literary criticism.

How to Contact: Send complete ms with SAE and state author's connection to Wisconsin, the prerequisite. Sample copy for $3. Fiction guidelines for SASE. Reviews books on Wisconsin themes.

Payment/Terms: Pays 3-5 contributor's copies. Acquires first rights on publication.

Advice: "Manuscript publication is at the discretion of the editor based on space, content and balance. We prefer previously unpublished poetry and fiction. We publish emerging as well as established authors; fiction and poetry, without names attached, are sent to reviewers for evaluation."

🌐 N **WORKS**, 12 Blakestones Rd., Slaithwaite, Huddersfield HD7 5UQ England. **Fiction Editor:** D. W. Hughes. Circ. 2,000. 70% of content is fiction. "A4, 40 pages speculative and imaginative fiction (science fiction) with poetry, illustrated." Quarterly. Member of the New Science Fiction Alliance.

Needs: Science fiction. Usual maximum is 4,500-5,000 words.

How to Contact: "All manuscripts should be accompanied by a SASE (in the UK). USA send 2 IRCs with ms, if disposable or 4 IRCs, if not." Price: £5 *cash only or cheque in sterling* for 1 issue, £10 *cash* or cheque in sterling for 2 issues; £20 *cash* or check in pounds sterling for 4 issues; enclose IRC.

Payment/Terms: Pays in copies.

☑ **WRITERS' INTL. FORUM, (I, II)**, Bristol Services International, P.O. Box 516, Tracyton WA 98393-0516. **Editor:** Sandra E. Haven. Website: http://www.bristolservicesintl.com (includes writer's guidelines; competition rules, prizes and deadlines; free tips and techniques). "*Writers' Intl. Forum—For Those Who Write to Sell*, features markets listing, lessons on writing, features about the writing craft and a 'Featured Manuscript' section in which a short story or essay is published with author bio and with a free professional critique of that manuscript." Magazine. Monthly. Estab. 1990.

Needs: Adventure, childrens/juvenile (8-12 years), fantasy, historical, humor/satire, inspirational, mainstream/contemporary, mystery/suspense, psychic/supernatural/occult, regional, religious, romance (contemporary, young adult), science fiction, senior citizen/retirement, sports, westerns, young adult/teen. "No graphic sex, violence, vignettes or experimental formats." Accepts 20-40 mss/year. Publishes ms an average of 4 months after acceptance. Recently published work by Artsun Akopian (Russian author) and Marianna Heusler. Publishes 20-40 new writers/year. Length: 1,000 words maximum. Publishes short shorts.

How to Contact: Send complete ms with a cover letter. Include brief bio. Reports in 2 months on mss. Send SASE for reply. Fiction guidelines and competition information for #10 SASE or available on website.

Payment/Terms: Pays $30 plus 2 contributor's copies on acceptance and free professional critique; additional copies for authors at discounted rates. Acquires first rights. Sample copy for $3.

Advice: "The fastest way to know if your story might be suitable for our unique 'Featured Manuscript' column is to read a copy first. If your story is written for children, state the intended age group. If a manuscript is submitted by a young author, please so note so it can can be considered for our parallel publication, *Writers' Intl. Forum for Young Authors*. Guidelines and contest information available for SASE or from website."

YARNS AND SUCH, (I, IV), Creative With Words Publications, Box 223226, Carmel CA 93922. Fax: (408)655-8627. E-mail: cwwpub@usa.net. Website: http://members.tripod.com/~CreativeWithWords (includes themes, guidelines, submittal form, cost of back issues, advertising rates, editorial statement; editing tips of current issue; best of the month salute and winning writing). **Editors:** Brigitta Geltrich (General Editor) and Bert Hower (Nature Editor). Booklet: 5½×8½; 60-90 pages; bond paper; illustrations. Folklore. 12-14 issues annually. Estab. 1975. Circ. varies.

Needs: Ethnic, humor/satire, mystery/suspense (amateur sleuth, private eye), regional, folklore. "Twice a year we publish an anthology of the writings of young writers, titled: *We are Writers Too!*" No violence or erotica, overly religious fiction or sensationalism. List of animal themes available for SASE. Receives 500 unsolicited fiction mss/month. Publishes ms 1-2 months after deadline. Recently published work by Toni Collins, Joe Ritter, Lisa Alexander; published new writers within the last year. Length: 1,500 words average; limits poetry to 20 lines or less. 46 characters per line or less. Critiques rejected mss "when requested, *then we charge $20/prose, up to 1,000 words*."

How to Contact: Query first or send complete ms with cover letter and SASE. Accepts queries/mss by e-mail with writer's e-mail address given. "Reference has to be made to which project the manuscript is being submitted. Unsolicited mss without SASE will be destroyed after holding them 1 month." Reports in 2 weeks on queries; 2 months on mss; longer on specific seasonal anthologies. No simultaneous submissions. Accepts electronic (disk) submissions via Macintosh and IBM/PC. Sample copy for $6. Fiction guidelines for #10 SASE.
Payment/Terms: No payment. Acquires one-time rights. 20% reduction on each copy ordered; 30% reduction on each copy on orders of 10 or more. Offers "Best of the Month" one free copy and publishing on the web.
Advice: "We have increased the number of anthologies we are publishing to 12-14 per year and offer a greater variety of themes. We look for clean family-type fiction. Also, we ask the writer to look at the world from a different perspective, research topic thoroughly, be creative, apply brevity, tell the story from a character's viewpoint, tighten dialogue, be less descriptive, proofread before submitting and be patient. We will not publish every manuscript we receive. It has to be in standard English, well-written, proofread. We do not appreciate receiving manuscripts where we have to do the proofreading and the correcting of grammar."

YOUNG JUDAEAN, (IV), Hadassah Zionist Youth Commission, 50 W. 58th St., New York NY 10019. (212)303-4575. **Editor:** Debra Neufeld. National Education Supervisor: Mel Sobell. Magazine: 8½×11; 16 pages; illustrations. "*Young Judaean* is for members of the Young Judaea Zionist youth movement, ages 8-13." Quarterly. Estab. 1910. Circ. 4,000.
Needs: Children's fiction including adventure, ethnic, fantasy, historical, humor/satire, juvenile, prose poem, religious, science fiction, suspense/mystery and translations. "All stories must have Jewish relevance." Receives 10-15 unsolicited fiction mss/month. Publishes ms up to 2 years after acceptance. Accepts 1-2 mss/issue; 10-20 mss/year. Length: 750 words minimum; 1,000 words maximum.
How to Contact: Send complete ms with SASE. Reports in 3 months on mss. Sample copy for 75¢. Free fiction guidelines.
Payment/Terms: Pays five contributor's copies.
Advice: "Stories must be of Jewish interest—lively and accessible to children without being condescending."

THE ZONE, Pigasus Press, 13 Hazely Combe, Arreton, Isle of Wight, PO30 3AJ England. **Editor:** Tony Lee. Magazine. "A magazine of quality science fiction plus articles and reviews." Publishes up to 6 stories/issue. Biannually.
Needs: Science fiction (hard, contemporary science fiction/fantasy). No sword and sorcery, supernatural horror. Length: 1,000 words minimum; 5,000 words maximum.
How to Contact: "Study recent issues of the magazine. Unsolicited submissions are always welcome but writers must enclose SAE/IRC for reply, plus adequate postage to return ms if unsuitable."
Payment/Terms: Pays in copies. "Token payment for stories and articles of 2,000 words and over." Sample copies available for $9 (cash, US dollars) or 9 IRCs; for UK, £3.20; EC countries, £5 (cheques/eurocheques, should be made payable to Tony Lee).

Zines

Vastly different from one another in appearance and content, the common source of zines seems to be a need for self-expression. Although this need to voice opinions has always been around, it was not until the '70s, and possibly beginning with the social upheaval of the '60s, that the availability of photocopiers and computers provided an easy, cheap way to produce the self-published and usually self-written "zines." And now, with the cyberspace explosion, an overwhelming number of "e-zines" are springing up in an electronic format.

SELF-EXPRESSION AND ARTISTIC FREEDOM

The editorial content of zines runs the gamut from traditional and genre fiction to personal rants and highly experimental work. Artistic freedom, however, is a characteristic of all zines. Although zine editors are open to a wide range of fiction that more conventional editors might not consider, don't make the mistake of thinking they expect any less from writers than the editors of other types of publications. Zine editors look for work that is creative and well presented and that shows the writer has taken time to become familiar with the market. And since most zines are highly specialized, familiarity with the niche markets they offer is extremely important.

Some of the zines listed here have been published since the early '80s, but many are relatively new and some were just starting publication as they filled out the questionnaire to be included in this edition of *Novel & Short Story Writer's Market*. Unfortunately, due to the waning energy and shrinking funds of their publishers (and often a lack of material), few last for more than several issues. Fortunately, though, some have been around since the late '70s and early '80s, and hundreds of new ones are launched every day.

While zines represent the most volatile group of publications in *Novel & Short Story Writer's Market*, they are also the most open to submissions by beginning writers. As mentioned above, the editors of zines are often writers themselves and welcome the opportunity to give others a chance at publication.

SELECTING THE RIGHT MARKET

Your chance for publication begins as you zero in on the zines most likely to be interested in your work. Begin by browsing through the listings. This is especially important since zines are the most diverse and specialized markets listed in this book. If you write genre fiction, check out the specific sections for lists of magazines publishing in that genre (mystery, page 74; romance, page 92; science fiction and fantasy, page 103). For other types of fiction, check the Category Index (starting on page 632) for the appropriate subject heading.

In addition to browsing through the listings and using the Category Index, check the ranking codes at the beginning of listings to find those most likely to be receptive to your work. Most all zines are open to new writers (**I**) or to both new and established writers (**II**). For more explanation about these codes, see the end of this introduction.

Once you have a list of zines you might like to try, read their listings carefully. Zines vary greatly in appearance as well as content. Some paper zines are photocopies published whenever the editor has material and money, while others feature offset printing and regular distribution schedules. And a few have evolved into four-color, commercial-looking, very slick publications. The physical description appearing near the beginning of the listings gives you clues about the size and financial commitment to the publication. This is not always an indication of quality, but chances are a publication with expensive paper and four-color artwork on the cover has more prestige than a photocopied publication featuring a clip art self-cover. If you're a new writer or your work is considered avant garde, however, you may be more interested in the photocopied zine or one of the electronic zines. For more information on some of the paper, binding and printing terms used in these descriptions, see Printing and Production Terms Defined on page 627. Also, How to Use This Book to Publish Your Fiction, starting on page 3, describes in detail the listing information common to all markets in our book.

FURTHERING YOUR SEARCH

Reading the listings is only the first part of developing your marketing plan. The second part, equally important, is to obtain fiction guidelines and a copy of the actual zine. Reading copies of the publication helps you determine the fine points of the zine's publishing style and philosophy. Especially since zines tend to be highly specialized, there is no substitute for this hands-on, eyes-on research. With e-zines, all the information you need is available on their websites.

Unlike commercial periodicals available at most newsstands and bookstores, it requires a little more effort to obtain most of the paper zines listed here. You will probably need to send for a sample copy. We include sample copy prices in the listings whenever possible.

For a comprehensive listing of zines in a number of categories and reviews of each, check out Seth Friedman's *Factsheet Five* (P.O. Box 170099, San Francisco CA 94117-0099) published twice every year. *Scavenger's Newsletter* (519 Ellinwood, Osage City KS 66523) also lists markets for science fiction, fantasy, horror and mystery. More zines and information on starting your own zine can be found in *The World of Zines: A Guide to the Independent Magazine Revolution*, by Mike Gunderloy and Cari Goldberg Janice (Penguin Books, 375 Hudson St., New York NY 10014). Also check the Websites of Interest section on page 629 for leads to finding great markets on the Internet.

The following is the ranking system used to categorize the listings in this section:

I Publication encourages beginning or unpublished writers to submit work for consideration and publishes new writers regularly.
II Publication accepts outstanding work by beginning and established writers.
III Hard to break into; publishes mostly previously published writers.
IV Special-interest or regional publication, open only to writers in certain genres or on certain subjects or from certain geographical areas.

☑ $ **ABSOLUTE MAGNITUDE, Science Fiction Adventures, (I, II, IV)**, DNA Publications, P.O. Box 2988, Radford VA 24143-2988. (413)772-0725. **Editor:** Warren Lapine. Zine: 8½×11; 96 pages; newsprint; color cover; illustrations. "We publish technical science fiction that is adventurous and character driven." Quarterly. Estab. 1993. Circ. 9,000.

• *Absolute Magnitude* ranked #15 on *Writer's Digest's* Fiction 50 list of top fiction markets.

Needs: Science fiction: adventure, hard science. No fantasy, horror, funny science fiction. Receives 300-500 unsolicited mss/month. Accepts 7-10 mss/issue; 28-40 mss/year. Publishes ms 3-6 months after acceptance. Agented fiction 5%. Published work by Hal Clement, Chris Bunch, C.J. Cherryh, Barry B. Longyear and Harlan Ellison. Length: 5,000-12,000 words average; 1,000 words minimum; 25,000 words maximum. Publishes very little poetry. Often critiques or comments on rejected ms.

How to Contact: Do NOT query. Send complete ms with a cover letter. Should include estimated word count and list of publications. Send SASE for reply, return of ms or send a disposable copy of ms. Simultaneous and reprint submissions OK. Sample copy for $5. Reviews novels and short story collections.

Payment/Terms: Pays 1-5¢/word on publication for first North American serial rights; 1¢/word for first reprint rights. Sometimes sends galleys to author.

Advice: "We want good writing with solid characterization, also character growth, story development, and plot resolution. We would like to see more character-driven stories."

N **AFFABLE NEIGHBOR, (I, II)**, P.O. Box 3635, Ann Arbor MI 48106-3635. Editor: Joel Henry-Fisher. **Fiction Editors:** Joel Henry-Fisher, Leigh Chalmers. Zine: size/pages vary; usually photocopy paper and cover

stock; illustrations and photos. "Counter-culture zine publishing high and low art and experimentation of all forms, advocating the Affable Neighbor Worldview®." Estab. 1994. Circ. under 500.
Needs: Adventure, comics/graphic novels, erotica, ethnic/multicultural, experimental, fantasy, feminist, gay, glitz, historical, horror, humor/satire, lesbian, literary, psychic/supernatural/occult, romance ("kamp/sleaze perhaps"), science fiction, short story collections, translations, collage/text. "No pro-religious—unless, perhaps, fringe related; no tired, formulaic writings." Receives 15 unsolicited mss/month. Accepts 1-2 mss/issue. Length: short. Publishes short shorts (under 500 words). Also publishes literary essays, literary criticism, poetry. Sometimes critiques or comments on rejected ms.
How to Contact: Send complete ms with a cover letter. Reports in 1 week. Send SASE for reply, return of ms or send a disposable copy of ms. Simultaneous and reprint submissions OK. Sample copy for 3 first-class stamps. Reviews novels, short story collections and nonfiction books of interest to writers. Send books to Leigh Chalmers, Assistant Editor, Affable Neighbor, 729 E. Burnside #210, Portland OR 97214. Send disposable copies or SASE.
Payment/Terms: Pays free subscription if requested and contributor's copies. Not copyrighted.
Advice: "We like interesting and exciting works—experimental, brash, and sometimes dead-serious."

ART:MAG, (II), P.O. Box 70896, Las Vegas NV 89170. (702)734-8121. **Editor:** Peter Magliocco. Zine: 5½×8½, 8½×14, also 8½×11; 70-90 pages; 20 lb. bond paper; b&w pen and ink illustrations and photographs. Publishes "irreverent, literary-minded work by committed writers," for "small press, 'quasi-art-oriented' " audience. Annually. Estab. 1984. Circ. under 500.
Needs: Condensed/excerpted novel, confession, contemporary, erotica, ethnic, experimental, fantasy, feminist, gay, historical (general), horror, humor/satire, lesbian, literary, mainstream, mystery/suspense, prose poem, psychic/supernatural/occult, regional, science fiction, translations and arts. Wants to see more "daring and thought-provoking" fiction. No "slick-oriented stuff published by major magazines." Receives 1 plus ms/month. Accepts 1-2 mss/year. Does not read mss July-October. Publishes ms within 3-6 months of acceptance. Recently published work by David Lefkowitz, Ralph Greco, Jr., Fernand Roqueplan, Albert Huffstickler, George Keithley, Paul Andrew E. Smith and Elizabeth Rose. Publishes 2 new writers/year. Length: 2,000 words preferred; 250 words minimum; 3,000 words maximum. Also publishes literary essays "if relevant to aesthetic preferences," literary criticism "occasionally," poetry. Sometimes critiques rejected mss.
How to Contact: Send complete ms with cover letter. Reports in 3 months. SASE for ms. Simultaneous submissions OK. Sample copy for $5, 6×9 SAE and 79¢ postage. Fiction guidelines for #10 SASE.
Payment/Terms: Pays contributor's copies. Acquires one-time rights.
Advice: "Seeking more novel and quality-oriented work, usually from solicited authors. Magazine fiction today needs to be concerned with the issues of fiction writing itself—not just with a desire to publish or please the largest audience. Think about things in the fine art world as well as the literary one and keep the hard core of life in between."

☑ **ATROCITY, Publication of the Absurd Sig of Mensa, (II)**, 2419 Greensburg Pike, Pittsburgh PA 15221. E-mail: rollh@juno.com. Website: http://www.geocities.com/Eureka/Park/3517 (includes samples). Editor: Hank Roll. **Editorial contact:** Tinker. Zine: 5½×8½; 30 pages; offset 20 lb. paper and cover; illustrations. Humor and satire for "high IQ-Mensa" members. Monthly. Estab. 1976. Circ. 250.
Needs: Humor/satire: Liar's Club, parody, jokes, funny stories, comments on the absurdity of today's world. Receives 30 unsolicited mss/month. Accepts 2 mss/issue. Publishes ms 6-12 months after acceptance. Published work by John Smethers, Sheryll Watt, Dolph Wave and Ellen Warts. Publishes 12 new writers/last year. Length: 50-150 words preferred; 650 words maximum.
How to Contact: Send complete ms. "No cover letter necessary if ms states what rights (e.g. first North American serial/reprint, etc.) are offered." Accepts queries/mss by e-mail. Reports in 1 month. SASE. Simultaneous and reprint submissions OK. Sample copy for $1.
Payment/Terms: Pays contributor's copies. Acquires one-time rights.
Advice: Do not submit mss exceeding 650 words. Manuscript should be single-spaced and copy ready in a horizontal format to fit on one 5½×8½ sheet. "If you don't read the specs, you get it back. Don't waste our time."

☑ ▣ **AURICULAR IMMERSION MEDIA ONLINE MAGAZINE, (I, II)**, 2434 21st Ave., San Francisco CA 94116. (415)664-6302. E-mail: aherrick@auricular.com. Website: http://www.auricular.com/AIM. **Editor:** Alan Herrick. Electronic zine. "An online magazine fueled mostly by submissions and developed as a support mechanism for beginning and experienced writers and reporters. Very little editorial discretion is exercised making this sort of an open forum, or testing ground for many contributors. Intended audience is 18-45. Magazine offers fiction, serial fiction, reviews (film and music) political articles, rants, raves and the like. Much of the reported material has a sarcastic edge."
Needs: "Completely open. Nothing offensively hateful. We would like to see more women writers' works." Recently published work by Ted Rosen, Ben Ohmart, Henry Warwick, John Humphries, Alan Herrick, Cliff Neighbors. Publishes as many new writers "as are willing to contribute material."
How to Contact: Electronic submissions only. Send mss via email in ASCII format or as a MS word RTF attachment.
Advice: "Be open minded, have an edge, and be willing to see your material presented in a fashion that is

unconventional to other publications in attitude and appearance. Quite a few of our writers have scored weekly columns and paid publishing ventures with their submission to AIM on their CV. Although we can't afford to pay . . . we update the publication online regularly . . . all past submissions are available as archived material and we do our best to get word of our publication out to the masses without cluttering it with advertising and fluff."

babysue, (II), P.O. Box 8989, Atlanta GA 31106-8989. (404)875-8951. Website: http://www.babysue.com (includes comics, poetry, fiction and a wealth of music reviews). **Editor:** Don W. Seven. Zine: 8½×11; 32 pages; illustrations and photos. "*babysue* is a collection of music reviews, poetry, short fiction and cartoons for anyone who can think and is not easily offended." Biannually. Estab. 1983. Circ. 5,000.

- Sometimes funny, very often perverse, this 'zine featuring mostly cartoons and "comix" definitely is not for the easily offended.

Needs: Erotica, experimental and humor/satire. Receives 5-10 mss/month. Accepts 3-4 mss/year. Publishes ms within 3 months of acceptance. Recently published work by Daniel Lanette, Massy Baw, Andrew Taylor and Barbara Rimshaw. Publishes short shorts. Length: 1-2 single-spaced pages.
How to Contact: Query with clips of published work. SASE. Simultaneous submissions OK. No submissions via e-mail.
Payment/Terms: Pays 1 contributor's copy.
Advice: "Create out of the love of creating, not to see your work in print!"

THE BITTER OLEANDER, (II), 4983 Tall Oaks Dr., Fayetteville NY 13066-9776. (315)637-3047. Fax: (315)637-5056. E-mail: bones44@ix.netcom.com. Website: http://www.bitteroleander.com. **Editor:** Paul B. Roth. Zine specializing in poetry and fiction: 6×9; 128 pages; 55 lb. paper; 12 pt. CIS cover stock; photos. "We're interested in the surreal; deep image; particularization of natural experiences." Semiannually. Estab. 1974. Circ. 1,500.

- In 1998 *The Bitter Oleander* received a Hemingway grant from the French Ministry of Culture.

Needs: Experimental, new age/mystic/spiritual, translations. "No pornography; no confessional; no romance." Receives 12 unsolicited mss/month. Accepts 1-2 mss/issue; 2-4 mss/year. Does not read mss in July. Publishes ms 4-6 months after acceptance. Recently published work by Robert Bly, Charles Wright, Louis Simpson, Marjorie Agosín, Duane Cocke, Alan Britt and John Shepley. Length: 2,000 words minimum; 3,000 words maximum. Publishes short shorts. Length: 1,500 words. Also publishes literary essays, poetry. Always critiques or comments on rejected ms.
How to Contact: Send complete ms with a cover letter. Include estimated word count, 50-word bio and list of publications. Reports in 1 week on queries; 1 month on mss. Send SASE for reply, return of ms. Sample copy for $8, 4½×10½ SAE with 4 first-class stamps. Fiction guidelines for #10 SASE.
Payment/Terms: Pays 1 contributor's copy; additional copies $8. Acquires first rights.
Advice: "We're interested in originality."

$ THE BLACK LILY, Fantasy and Medieval Review, (I, II, IV), Southern Goblin Productions, 8444 Cypress Circle, Sarasota FL 34243-2006. (941)351-4386. E-mail: gkuklews@ix.netcom.com. Editor: Vincent Kuklewski. **Fiction Editor:** Michael Nauton. Zine specializing in Pre-1600 A.D. World: 64 pages; 50 lb. paper; card cover; illustrations and photos. Quarterly. Estab. 1996. Circ. 475.
Needs: Ethnic/Multicultural, fantasy (sword and sorcery), gay, horror, humor/satire, lesbian, literary, mystery/suspense (police procedural, magic/wizard), serialized novel, translations, folktales. No science fiction or gratuitous gore. Upcoming themes: "Byzantine Empire" (January); "1001 Arabian Nights" (August). List of upcoming themes available for SASE. Publishes special fiction issues or anthologies. Receives 20-30 unsolicited mss/month. Accepts 3-5 mss/issue; 25-30 mss/year. Publishes ms 4-10 months after acceptance. Recently published work by Scott Urban, Jim Lee, D.F. Lewis, Lori J. Paxton, Nancy Bennett, Jones Rada, Jr., Uncle River and Ken Goldman. Length: 3,000-4,000 words average; 1,500 words minimum; 60,000 words maximum. Publishes short shorts. Also publishes literary essays, literary criticism and poetry. Often critiques or comments on rejected manuscripts.
How to Contact: Send complete manuscript with a cover letter or e-mail submission with cover letter. Include estimated word count and 2-line bio. Reports in 1 month on queries; 3 months on mss. Send SASE for reply and send a disposable copy of ms. Reprints and electronic submissions OK. Reviews novels and short story collections. Send books to Vincent Kuklewski.
Payment/Terms: Pays $5 minimum; $50 maximum on acceptance and 1 contributor's copy for one-time or first international serial rights.
Advice: "Avoid tales in which Evil is unbelievably unopposed, in which the characters are so flat they are interchangeable, in which there are elements of magic (overt or implied). A glut of goth and vampire themes is making dark fiction cliché and far too many beginning writers are jumping on the bandwagon. We try to keep open markets for heroic fiction by steering new writers to h.f. themes and other h.f. zines. We also try in each issue to publish a folktale from all of the world's cultures, from Africa to Asia to the Americas. But they must have a pre-1600 A.D. setting."

BLACK PETALS, (I, II, III), 1319 Marshall St., Manitowoc WI 54220. (920)684-7901. **Editor:** D.M. Yortom. Zine specializing in horror/fantasy: full size; 40-60 pages; photocopied; illustrations; movie and book reviews. "A little something special for those special readers of oddity and terror." Bimonthly. Estab. 1997. Circ. 200.
Needs: Experimental, fantasy (sword and sorcery, fairies, elves), horror, psychic/supernatural/occult; science fiction (soft/sociological). Wants more hard core horror. No children's or romance. Contests every issue. Receives 20-40 unsolicited mss/month. Accepts 8-10 mss/issue. Recently published work by June Harmon, C.B. Thatcher, James Patterson and Greg Gifune. Publishes 10 new writers/year. Length: 1,500 words average; no minimum; 2,500 words maximum. Publishes short shorts. Also publishes poetry. Always critiques or comments on rejected mss.
How to Contact: Send complete ms. Include estimated word count and list of publications. Reports in 2-4 weeks on queries and mss. Send 10×13 SASE for return of ms. Simultaneous submissions and reprints OK. Sample copy for $2. Fiction guidelines for #10 SASE.
Payment/Terms: Pays contributor's copies; additional copies $1.
Advice: "My best advice—submit! How do you know if you'll get published unless you submit! Also, obtain a sample copy, follow guidelines and don't watch the mailbox. New unpublished writers are high on my list. If I have time I'll even held edit a manuscript. If I reject a manuscript, I encourage writers to send something else. Don't ever be discouraged, and don't wallpaper your office with rejection notes—toss them!"

N ▣ **BLAST@EXPLODE.COM, (I, II)**, E-mail: blaststory@aol.com. Website: http://www.Blast@explode.com. **Editor:** Martha Ross. Electronic zine. "As a new publication, our philosophy is evolving, but we founded *Blast* with the idea of providing a forum for talented new writers to get published."
Needs: "We're open to any style or genre—mystery, science fiction, experimental, political, philosophical. However, we want our fiction geared toward a general audience, so a writer of, say, a science fiction piece would need to explain technical references." Recently published work by Willy Morris, Amy Pang, Joann Back and Barb Natividad. Publishes several new writers/year.
How to Contact: Contact by e-mail only. Send story in an attachment. If possible, try to convert story to Microsoft Word before sending.
Payment/Terms: No payment.
Advice: "The story should come first. It cannot be overwhelmed by a writer wanting to be clever with style or to push forth a statement or political agenda. We would like to see more fiction with strong storylines and use of language, intriguing characters."

N **BLOODSONGS**, 1921 E. Colonial Dr., 2nd Floor, Orlando FL 32803. E-mail: bloodsongs@implosion-mag.com. Website: http://www.bloodsongs.com. **Fiction Editor:** David G. Barnett. Magazine: 8½×11; 64 pages; 60 lb. glossy color paper; self-cover; illustrations and photos. "Bloodsongs searches for the most extreme horror out there—stories to make readers shudder and cringe." Quarterly. Estab. 1992. Circ. 15,000.
Needs: Horror. "Other genres, such as fantasy, occult, adventure and even western are OK, but the base must be horror." Receives 100 mss/month. Accepts 5-7 mss/issue; 20-30 mss/year. Publishes ms 4-7 months after acceptance. Published work by Edward Lee, Lucy Taylor and Charlie Jacob. Length: 2,500 average; 6,500 words maximum. Also publishes literary criticism. Sometimes critiques or comments on rejected mss.
How to Contact: Send complete ms with cover letter. Include estimated word count and list of publications. Reports in 1-3 months on mss. Send SASE for reply, return of ms or send a disposable copy of ms. Simultaneous and reprint submissions OK. Sample copy for $5. Guidelines for SASE. Reviews novels and short story collections. Send books to editor Cynthia Conlin.
Payment/Terms: Pays $15-20/story within 30 days of publication and 4 contributor's copies; additional copies $3. Acquires first or one-time rights. Sends galleys to author if requested.
Tips: "Your opening paragraphs are the most important. Make sure your plot and characters are well developed, and be careful when chossing subject matter such as vampires, deals with the devil, werewolves, etc,; they are cliché magnets. Have someone proofread your story before you submit."

▣ **THE BRINK, (I)**. E-mail: sandy@brink.com. Website: http://brink.com/brink. **Editor:** Sandy Wilder. Electronic zine. Publishes "marginal writing with extreme energy for a kinky neurotic audience."
Needs: "Fiction, poetry, astronomy, porn. We'll look at anything, but we may not read it." Would like to see more "real stories about people, their pets and their cars." Recently published work by George Rosenburg, Danny Vinik and Craig Baldwin. Publishes 6-10 new writers/year.
How to Contact: "Send attachments in Microsoft Word if possible. Manuscripts in HTML are given strong preference for publication."

Advice: "Bombard us with your poop. Send naked pictures of yourselves."

THE BROBDINGNAGIAN TIMES, (I, II), 96 Albert Rd., Cork, Ireland. Phone: (21)311227. **Editor:** Giovanni Malito. Zine specializing in short international work: 6×8½; 8 pages; 80 gramme paper; illustrations. "There are no obvious editorial slants. We are interested in any prose from anyone anywhere provided it is short (1,000 words maximum)." Quarterly. Estab. 1996. Circ. 250.
Needs: Ethnic/multicultural, experimental, horror, humor/satire, literary, romance (contemporary), science fiction (hard science/technological, soft/sociological). "No ghost stories/dysfunctional family stories/first sex stories." Receives 4-6 unsolicited mss/month. Accepts 2 mss/issue; 8 mss/year. Publishes ms in next issue after acceptance. Publishes 2-3 new writers/year. Recently published work by D.F. Lewis, Christopher Woods, Michael Wynne, Laura Lush, Ruba Neda and Ian Rourke. Length: 600 words average; 50 words minimum; 1,000 words maximum. Publishes short shorts. Length: 500 words. Also publishes literary essays, poetry. Always critiques or comments on rejected ms.
How to Contact: Send complete ms with a cover letter. Include estimated word count, 3-line bio. Reports in 1 week on queries; 3 weeks on mss. Send SASE (IRCs) for reply, return of ms or send a disposable copy of ms. Simultaneous and reprint submissions OK. Sample copy for #10 SAE and 2 IRCs. Fiction guidelines for #10 SAE and 1 IRC.
Payment/Terms: Pays 2 contributor's copies; additional copies for postage. Acquires one-time rights for Ireland/U.K. Sends galleys to author if required. Copyrighted Ireland/U.K.
Advice: "Crisp language. Economy of language. These are important, otherwise almost anything goes."

THE CAT'S EYE, (I). (615)228-8639. E-mail: Thecatseye@aol.com. Website: http://members.aol.com/thecatseye/index.htm. **Editor:** Lysa Fuller. Electronic zine. "A literary e-zine to provide readers and writers a place to submit their creations for possible web publication."
Needs: "Poetry, short fiction and some non-fiction." Would like to see more romance, science fiction and fantasy. No pornography. Recently published work by Ben Stivers and Toni Visage. Publishes 80-100 new writers/year.
How to Contact: Electronic submissions only. "Send submission either in the e-mail itself or attached in a .doc file."
Advice: "Just be yourself, write about what you know and like. We like to help young authors and new authors get a break."

CETERIS PARIBUS, (I, II). E-mail: ceteris@intrepid.net. Website: http://www.intrepid.net/ceteris/paribus.htm. **Editor:** Roger Jones. Electronic zine. "Good writing with heart. Works by a circle of core writers, supplemented by select unsolicited contributions, have sustained a warm and entertaining intellectual and cultural exchange. The magazine strives to be unique, not bizarre; thought provoking, not iconoclastic; hospitable, not factional; literate, but not pedantic." Bimonthly.
Needs: "Fiction, poetry, personal narratives, topical essays, reviews and criticism for the discerning reader. Our editors are not usually enthusiastic about experimental fiction or writing that is weird for weird's sake. We will consider any well written story with the almost hypnotic ability to transport the reader into its world. We favor traditional literary fiction, but we also welcome genre fiction." Publishes at least 6 new writers/year.
How to Contact: Electronic and traditional submissions accepted. "Manuscripts should be copied and pasted into e-mail. Don't use attachments! For the internet-impaired, paper manuscripts can be sent to Ceteris Paribus/1410 N. Quinn St. #3/Arlington, Virginia 22209—but the response time will unavoidably be longer for such submissions."
Advice: "First, send only material that has not appeared previously. We are a unique Web magazine, not a recycling center. Second, we look for more than clever word-spinning. Style should be cultivated to enhance content; it can never compensate the lack. Write about what matters to you, not what might excite others. We look for writers who, through humor or drama, have something of value to say about the human experience."

A COMPANION IN ZEOR, (I, II, IV), 307 Ashland Ave., Egg Harbor Township NJ 08234-5568. (606)645-6938. Fax: (606)645-8084. E-mail: klitman323@aol.com or karenlitman@juno.com. Website: http://www.geocities.com/~rmgiroux/CZ (includes guidelines, back issue flyers, etc.). **Editor:** Karen Litman. Fanzine: 8½×11; 60 pages; "letter" paper; heavy blue cover; b&w line illustrations; occasional b&w photographs. Publishes science fiction based on the various Universe creations of Jacqueline Lichtenberg. Occasional features on Star Trek, and other interests, convention reports, reviews of movies and books, recordings, etc. Published irregularly. Estab. 1978. Circ. 300.

- *Companion in Zeor* is one fanzine devoted to the work and characters of Jacqueline Lichtenberg. Lichtenberg's work includes several future world, alien and group culture novels and series including the Sime/Gen Series and The Dushau trilogy. She's also penned two books on her own vampire character and she co-authored *Star Trek Lives*.

Needs: Fantasy, humor/satire, prose poem, science fiction. "No vicious satire. Nothing X-rated. Homosexuality prohibited unless *essential* in story. We run a clean publication that anyone should be able to read without fear." Occasionally receives one manuscript a month." Publication of an accepted ms "goes to website posting." Occasionally critiques rejected mss and recommends other markets.

How to Contact: Query first or send complete ms with cover letter. "Prefer cover letters about any writing experience prior, or related interests toward writing aims." Reports in 1 month. SASE. Simultaneous submissions OK. Sample copy price depends on individual circumstances. Fiction guidelines for #10 SASE. "I write individual letters to all queries. No form letter at present." SASE for guidelines required. Reviews science fiction/fantasy collections or titles. "We can accept e-mail queries and manuscripts through AOL providers."
Payment/Terms: Pays in contributor's copies. Acquires first rights. Acquires website rights as well.
Advice: "Send concise cover letter asking what the author would like me to do for them if their manuscript can not be used by my publication. They should follow guidelines of the type of material I use, which is often not done. I have had many submissions I can not use as it is general fiction which was sent instead. Ask for guidelines before submitting to a publication. Write to the best of your ability and work with your editor to develop your work to a higher point than your present skill level. Take constructive criticism and learn from it. Electronic web publishing seems the way the industry is heading. I would not have thought of a website a few years ago. Guidelines can be sent by e-mail. Receipt of manuscripts can only be through klitman323@aol.com. Juno cannot handle attachments. People can learn more through the domain—www.simegen.com/index.html."

✓ 🏆 **CROSSROADS . . . Where Evil Dwells, (I, II)**, 911 Haw Branch Rd., Beaulaville NC 28518-9539. (910)324-5395. Fax: (910)324-2657. E-mail: patnielsen@earthlink.net. Website: http://www.members.aol.com/evildwells. **Editor/Publisher:** Pat Nielsen. Zine: digest-sized; approximately 68 pages; 20 lb. paper; 64 lb. index cover. "All stories must be about people at a *Crossroad* in their lives, or set at the crossroads themselves—or both. I strongly encourage writers to do research about the crossroad legends. This is an *adult* horror magazine." Triannually. (Published February, June and October.) Estab. 1992. Circ. 100.

- Work appearing in *Crossroads* received three Honorable Mentions in *The Year's Best Horror and Fantasy.*

Needs: Horror, psychological, psychic/supernatural/occult for adults. "No futuristic or fiction set in the past. No science fiction/fantasy; no "nightly news" horror. No sex or violence involving small children. Every October issue is the Halloween issue—all material must have a Halloween theme," deadline: October 15. Receives 20 unsolicited mss/month. Accepts 10-15 mss/issue; 30 mss/year. Publishes ms 1-6 months after acceptance. Recently published work by Charlee Jacob, John Everson, Deidra Cox and Wayne Edwards. Publishes 4-6 new writers/year. Length: 1,500 words average; 500 words minimum; 3,500 words maximum. Also publishes literary criticism and poetry. "I also need good artists." Often critiques or comments on rejected mss.
How to Contact: Send complete ms with a cover letter. Include estimated word count. Accepts queries by e-mail and fax (no mss). Reports in 2 weeks on queries; 2-4 weeks on mss. Send SASE for reply, return of ms or send a disposable copy of ms. "I don't like IRCs—please use US stamps whenever possible." No simultaneous submissions. Reprints OK. Sample copy for $4.50. Fiction guidelines for #10 SASE.
Payment/Terms: Pays 1 contributor's copy; additional copies for $3.50 plus postage for multiple copies. Acquires first North American serial rights. Sends galleys to author (time permitting).
Advice: "I publish many kinds of horror, from the mild to the hard core horror. Don't copy well-known or any other writers. Find your own voice and style and go with it to the best of your ability. I don't go by any trends. I know what I like and I publish as I see fit. Do not send science fiction or fantasy in any form."

CURRICULUM VITAE, (I), Simpson Publications, Grove City Factory Stores, P.O. Box 1309, Grove City PA 16127. (814)671-1361. E-mail: simpub@hotmail.com. Website: http://www.geocities.com/soho/cafe/2550 (includes guidelines, contacts, fiction, interviews). **Editor:** Michael Dittman. Zine: digest-sized; 75-100 pages; standard paper; card cover stock; illustrations. "We are dedicated to new, exciting writers. We like essays, travelogues and short stories filled with wonderful, tense, funny work by writers who just happen to be underpublished or beginners. Our audience is young and overeducated." Quarterly. Estab. 1995. Circ. 2,000.
Needs: Condensed/excerpted novel, erotica, ethnic/multicultural, experimental, humor/satire, literary, mainstream/contemporary, serialized novel, sports, translations. Wants to see more hyper realism, magic realism and translations. "No sentimental 'weepers' or Bukowski-esque material." List of upcoming themes available for SASE. Publishes special fiction issues or anthologies. Receives 45 unsolicited mss/month. Accepts 7 mss/issue; 28 mss/year. Publishes mss 12 months after acceptance. Recently published work by Amber Meadow Adams and Carl Hoffman. Publishes 25 new writers/year. Publishes short shorts. Also publishes literary essays, literary criticism, poetry. Often critiques or comments on rejected mss.
How to Contact: Send complete ms with cover letter. Accepts queries/mss by e-mail. Reports in 1 month on queries and mss. Send SASE for reply, return of ms or send a disposable copy of ms. Simultaneous, reprint and electronic submissions OK. Sample copy for $3. Fiction guidelines for #10 SASE. Reviews novels and short story collections. Send books to Amy Kleinfelder.
Payment/Terms: Pays minimum 2 contributor's copies to $125 maximum on publication. Acquires one-time rights.
Advice: "Looks for quality of writing, a knowledge of past works of literature and a willingness to work with our editors. Submit often and take criticism with a grain of salt."

DARK STARR, (I, II, IV), Navarro Publications, P.O. Box 1107, Blythe CA 92226-1107. (888)922-0835. Executive Editor: Richard Navarro. **Managing Editor:** Marjorie Navarro. Zine specializing in horror/sci-fi/mystery/occult: digest size; 30-50 pages; laminated cover. Quarterly. Estab. 1998. Circ. 200.

Needs: Condensed/excerpted novel, erotica, fantasy (science fantasy, sword and sorcery), horror, mystery/suspense (private eye/hardboiled, romantic suspense), psychic/supernatural/occult, science fiction (hard science). Publishes special fiction issues or anthologies. Receives 100 unsolicited mss/month. Accepts 8-10 mss/issue, 32 mss/year. Publishes ms 3 months after acceptance. Agented fiction 5%. "We brought back a publication last published in 1990, so most writers/authors will be new to this publication." Recently published work by C. Weaver, Derrick Corley, Barbara J. Less, James Lee, Alex Bledsoe and Cheré Taylor. Length: 2,500 word average; 300 words minimum; 8,500 words maximum. Publishes short shorts. Also publishes poetry. Sometimes critiques or comments on rejected mss.
How to Contact: Send ms with a cover letter. Include estimated word count and bio. Reports in 2 months on mss. Send SASE for reply, return of ms or send disposable copy of ms. Simultaneous and reprint submissions OK. Sample copy for $7 and 6×9 envelope with 2 first-class stamps. Fiction guidelines for #10 SASE.
Payment/Terms: Pays 1 contributor's copy.
Advice: Looks for "excellence in the genre submitted. If it's horror scare me; if it's fantasy let me live it; if it's sci-fi take me there; if it's supernatural give me 'goosebumps.' Please make sure manuscript is clean/legible and check spelling/sentence structure. Read the resource books, pay attention to guidelines, keep your work circulating."

N DEADLY NIGHTSHADE, (I, II), P.O. Box 50174, Minneapolis MN 55405. (612)822-4252. E-mail: femmegothique@interzone.org. **Editor:** Angela M. Bacon. Zine: 5½×8½; 40-50 pages; regular paper; 67 lb. cover stock; illustrations and photos. "A zine for the darker side of life. *Deadly Nightshade* specializes in publishing horror, themes based on the gothic/industrial subculture, but will accept other literary work outside the genre based on quality." Quarterly. Estab. 1997. Circ. 50-100.
Needs: Fantasy (sword and sorcery), horror, psychic/supernatural/occult. "No sexually explicit (bordering on porn) material; no sports-related, children's/juvenile, religious." Receives 1-2 unsolicited mss/month. Accepts 1-2 mss/issue. Publishes ms 1-3 months after acceptance. Recently published work by Greg Moore and Alexander Bledsoe. Length: 2,500 words average; 500 words minimum; 2,500 words maximum. Publishes short shorts. Also publishes poetry.
How to Contact: Query first with or without clips of published work. Include estimated word count, 1-page bio. Reports in 2-3 weeks. Send SASE for reply, return of ms or send a disposable copy of ms. Simultaneous and reprint submissions OK. Electronic submissions (disk or modem) OK. Sample copy for $4 (U.S. currency only; contact for Canada/Mexico/overseas pricing). Fiction guidelines for #10 SASE.
Payment/Terms: Pays 1 contributor's copy; additional copies $4 (Canada/Mexico/overseas prices are higher).

DIXIE PHOENIX, Exploration in Spirituality, Silliness, the Civil War and So Much More, (I, II, IV), 3888 N. 30th St., Arlington VA 22207. E-mail: srimichel@delphi.com. Website: http://www.concentric.net/~yamyak/DixiePhoenix/Frontporch.html (includes writer's guidelines, zine history, selected articles, collected reviews, a few recipes and a growing number of links). **Editors:** Mike & Bjorn Munson. Zine specializing in literature/essays: 5½×8½; 40-52 pages; 60 lb. standard paper; 60-70 lb. color cover; illustrations, photographs. "Our audience appears to be of all religious and political persuasions from fringe to mainstream. We try to make each issue intriguing, informative, edifying and entertaining. We're a 'Mom & Pop publication' not a corporate operation." Semiannually. Estab. 1992. Circ. 500.
Needs: Historical (general), humor/satire, literary, mainstream/contemporary, regional, religious/inspirational, translations, travel essays, Celtic and Southern themes, Southern ghost stories, regional from all walks of life; folklore from around the world. Wants more "transcendental, regional" fiction. No children's/juvenile, erotica (no profanity in general), psychic/occult, romance. Receives 8-10 unsolicited mss/month. Accepts 1-2 mss/issue; 3-4 mss/year. Publishes ms 6-18 months after acceptance. Recently published Errol Miller, Angela S. Jones and James C. Sullivan. Length: 1,500 words average; 250 words minimum; 7,000 words maximum. Publishes short shorts. Also publishes literary essays, literary criticism, poetry. "We have regular columns concerning history, culture and spirituality." Sometimes critiques or comments on rejected mss.
How to Contact: Query first or e-mail. Include a "nice friendly letter telling us about themselves and/or their writing." Reports in 1 month on queries; e-mail queries are often quicker; 3-4 months on mss. Send a disposable copy of ms. Simultaneous submissions, reprints and electronic submissions OK. Sample copy for $2. Reviews novels and short story collections (also music).
Payment/Terms: Pays 3 contributor's copies on publication; additional copies for $2. Acquires one-time rights.
Advice: "We value sincerity over shock value. Fiction with a 'Phoenix Flavor' has a subject of personal exploration/discovery/epiphany/subjectivity whether spiritual, emotional, intellectual, etc. Definitely get a sample copy of our publication to get an idea of what we're about. Do many drafts and learn to critique your own work. Polish, polish, polish. No work is ever completely done."

✔ $ DREAMS OF DECADENCE, Vampire Poetry and Fiction, (I, II, IV), DNA Publications, Inc., P.O. Box 2988, Radford VA 24143-2988. E-mail: dreams@shaysnet.com. **Editor:** Angela G. Kessler. Zine: digest size; 80 pages; illustrations. Specializes in "vampire fiction and poetry for vampire fans." Quarterly. Estab. 1995. Circ. 5,000.
Needs: Vampires. "I am not interested in seeing the clichés redone." Receives 300 unsolicited mss/month. Accepts 4 mss/issue; 12 mss/year. Publishes ms 1-6 months after acceptance. Length: 4,000 words average; 1,000

words minimum; 7,000 maximum. Also publishes poetry. Always critiques or comments on rejected mss.
How to Contact: Send complete ms with cover letter. Include estimated word count, 1-paragraph bio and list of publications. Reports in 2 months on mss. Send SASE for reply, return of ms or send a disposable copy of ms. Simultaneous submissions OK. Sample copy for $5. Fiction guidelines for #10 SASE. Reviews novels and short story collections.
Payment/Terms: Pays 1-5¢/word on publication and 1 contributor's copy; additional copies for $2.50. Acquires first North American serial rights.
Advice: "I like stories that take the traditional concept of the vampire into new territory, or look at it (from within or without) with a fresh perspective. Don't forget to include a SASE for reply or return of manuscript. Also, to see what an editor wants, *read an issue*."

✔ ▣ THE DRINKIN' BUDDY MAGAZINE: A Magazine for Art and Words, (I), Pimperial Productions, P.O. Box 720608, San Jose CA 95172. (408)397-8226. E-mail: editor@drinkinbuddy.com. Website: http://www.drinkinbuddy.com (includes names of editors, short fiction, interviews with authors, interviews with bands, reviews, fashion, food, movies, art, poetry, games). **Editor:** Mike. Webzine. Weekly. Estab. 1994. Circ. Worldwide.
Needs: Adventure, condensed/excerpted novel, erotica, ethnic/multicultural, fantasy, gay, historical, horror, humor, lesbian, literary, mainstream, mystery/suspense, psychic/supernatural, regional, romance, science fiction, sports, westerns. They would like to see more "drug-induced fiction. No father/son stories." Receives 30-40 unsolicited mss/month. Publishes short shorts.
How to Contact: Send 8-10 typewritten pgs. maximum. Send a disposable copy of the ms. Simultaneous, electronic submissions OK.
Payment/Terms: Acquires one-time rights.
Advice: "Looking for submissions in avant-garde, macabre, banal. Good characters and a snappy title make a manuscript stand out."

N THE EDGE, TALES OF SUSPENSE, (I, II, III), Thievin' Kitty Publications, P.O. Box 341, Marion MA 02738. E-mail: theedge@capecod.net. **Editor:** Greg F. Gifune. Associate Editors: Carla S. Gifune, Chuck A. Deude. Zine specializing in varied genre suspense: digest-sized; 60-80 pages; heavy stock paper; heavy card cover. "We publish a broad range of genres, subjects and styles. While not an easy magazine to break into, we offer thrilling, 'edge of your seat' fiction from both seasoned and newer writers. We focus on the writing, not illustrations or distracting bells and whistles. Our goal is to present a quality, entertaining publication." Triannually. Estab. 1998. Circ. 1,000.
Needs: Adventure, erotica, gay, horror, lesbian, mystery/suspense (police procedural, private eye/hardboiled, noir), psychic/supernatural/occult, science fiction (hard science, soft/sociological), westerns with supernatural or horror element only. "Emphasis is on horror, crime and science fiction." No children's, young adult, romance, humor. Receives 30-40 unsolicited mss/month. Accepts 10-12 mss/issue; 30-36 mss/year. Publishes ms 1-4 months after acceptance. Agented fiction 1-2%. Recently published work by Ken Goldman, John Roux, Phyllis Pyle, Stefano Donati, Christopher Hivner, Jeff Allency and Lida Broadhurst. Length: 2,500-4,500 words average; 700 words minimum; 8,000 words maximum. Also publishes poetry. Always critiques or comments on rejected mss.
How to Contact: Send complete ms with a cover letter. Include estimated word count, brief bio and list of publications. Reports in 1-8 weeks. Send SASE for reply, return of ms or send a disposable copy of ms. Simultaneous submissions OK but not preferred. Sample copy for $6 U.S., $7 elsewhere (includes postage). Fiction guidelines for #10 SASE.
Payment/Terms: Pays 1 contributor's copy; additional copies $5. Acquires one-time rights.
Advice: "We look for taut, tense thrillers with realistic dialogue, engaging characters, strong plots and endings that are both powerful and memorable. Graphic violence, sex and profanity all have their place but do not have to be gratuitous. We will not accept anything racist, sexist, sacrilegious, or stories that depict children or animals in violent or sexual situations!"

EIDOS: Sexual Freedom and Erotic Entertainment for Consenting Adults, (IV), P.O. Box 96, Boston MA 02137-0096. (617)262-0096. Fax: (617)364-0096. E-mail: eidos@eidos.org. Website: http://www.eidos.org (includes feature articles, interviews, poetry, short fiction, photos). **Editor:** Brenda Loew. Magazine: 8½×11; 40 pages; offset lithography; illustrations and photos. Magazine specializing in erotica for women, men and couples of all sexual orientations, preferences and lifestyles. "Explicit material regarding language and behavior formed in relationships, intimacy, moment of satisfaction—sensual, sexy, honest. For an energetic, well informed, international erotica readership." Quarterly. Estab. 1984. Circ. 12,000.
Needs: Erotica. Upbeat erotic fiction is especially wanted. Publishes at least 10-12 pieces of fiction/year. Recently published work by Mykola Dementuk, Jennifer Cole and Cliff Burns. Length: 1,000 words average; 500 words minimum; 2,000 words maximum. Also publishes literary criticism, poetry. Occasionally critiques rejected mss.
How to Contact: Send complete ms with SASE. "Cover letter with history of publication or short bio is welcome." Accepts queries/mss by e-mail. Reports in 1 month on queries; 1 month on mss. Simultaneous

submissions OK. Sample copy for $5. Fiction guidelines for #10 SASE. Reviews novels and short story collections, "if related to subject of erotica (sex, politics, religion, etc.)."

Payment/Terms: Pays in contributor's copies. Acquires first North American serial rights.

Advice: "We receive more erotic fiction manuscripts now than in the past. Most likely because both men and women are more comfortable with the notion of submitting these manuscripts for publication as well as the desire to see alternative sexually-explicit fiction in print. Therefore we can publish more erotic fiction because we have more material to choose from. There is still a lot of debate as to what erotic fiction consists of. This is a tough market to break into. Manuscripts must fit our editorial needs and it is best to order a sample issue prior to writing or submitting material. Honest, explicitly pro-sex, mutually consensual erotica lacks unwanted power, control and degradation—no unwanted coercion of any kind."

ENTERZONE, (I). E-mail: editor@ezone.org. Website: http//ezone.org/ez. **Story Editor:** Martha Conway. "*Enterzone* is a hyperzine of writing, art and new media publishing fiction and nonfiction stories, essays, criticism, personal commentary, poetry, computer-generated and scanned artwork, photography, audio art, comics, and cartoons for the internet-enabled adult reading public." Recently published work by David Alexander, Levi Asher, Frederick Barthelme, Milorad Pavic and Lisa Solod. Publishes 4-8 new writers/year.

- Work from *Enterzone* was anthologized in a 1997 book titled *Coffeehouse: Writings from the Web.*

Needs: Would like to see more short stories and hyperfiction. No science fiction or fantasy.

How to Contact: Query through e-mail: query@ezone.org.

Advice "We like stories that ring true. We like nonfiction that transcends the personal. We like our prose poetic and our poetry focused."

N **ETERNITY MAGAZINE, An online journal of the speculative imagination, (I, II)**, Eternity Press, P.O. Box 930068, Norcross GA 30003. E-mail: eternityol@aol.com. Website: http://members.aol.com/eternityol/main.htm. **Editor:** Steve Algieri. Electronic zine specializing in science fiction, fantasy and horror. Illustrations. "Cutting-edge speculative fiction and poetry that matters. Embraces controversy, alternative views and new styles." Monthly. Estab. 1997. Circ. 3,000 page hits.

Needs: Ethnic/multicultural, experimental, fantasy (children's, science, sword and sorcery), horror, psychic/supernatural/occult, romance (futuristic/time travel, gothic), science fiction (hard science, soft/sociological), young adult/teen (horror, science fiction). "No pornographic, senseless violence and gore, child abuse and stories that perpetuate hate. We would like to see more gay/lesbian and ethnic fiction with a fantastic theme." List of upcoming themes for SASE. Receives 100 unsolicited mss/month. Accepts 6-7 mss/issue; 80 mss/year. Publishes ms 4 months after acceptance. Recently published work by Brian A. Hopkins, Loren W. Cooper, Elizabeth Barrette and Stella Atrium. Length: 2,000-5,000 words average; 15,000 maximum. Publishes short shorts. Also publishes literary essays, literary criticism, poetry. Always critiques or comments on rejected ms.

How to Contact: Send complete ms with a cover letter. Include estimated word count, bio (under 100 words) and list of publications. Reports in 2 weeks on queries; 10 weeks on mss. SASE for reply. Send a disposable copy of ms. Electronic submissions (disk or modem) OK. Reviews novels and short story collections.

Payment/Terms: Pays $2-30 on publication for first electronic rights. Sends galleys to author. Not copyrighted.

Advice: "We like clean manuscripts that start strong and end with a bang. We tend to select stories with strong conflict and that deal with issues. We love controversy and unique styles."

$ **THE FIFTH DI/THE SIXTH SENSE/STAR/JUST BECAUSE, (II)**, Promart Writing Lab's Small Press Family, P.O. Box 1094, Carmichael CA 95609-1094. (916)973-1020. E-mail: promartian@earthlink.net. Website: http://www.angelfire.com/ca2/promart/mwindex.html (includes writer's guidelines, subscription information, sample fiction). **Editor:** James B. Baker. Four anthologies; $8\frac{1}{2} \times 12$; 176 pages per anthology; 20 lb. paper; 24 lb. cover stock. Specializes in science fiction. "My intended audience is made up of those desiring to see man going to the stars. *The Fifth Di* is adult; *The Sixth Sense* is family (no excessive sex or bad language); and *Star* is our feature anthology; *Just Because* is for the thinking man. Also, online magazine called *Martian Wave*." Estab. 1995. Circ. 192. Member of The Writers' Alliance and The National Writer's Association.

Needs: Science fiction, serialized novel. "No horror and only minimal fantasy." Receives 15-20 unsolicited mss/month. Accepts 10 mss/issue; 180 mss/year. Publishes ms 6-12 months after acceptance. Recently published work by James S. Dorr, Brian A. Hopkins, Joan Tobin, Paul Gates and Gail Hayden. Publishes 10 new writers/year. Length: 3,500 words average. Publishes short shorts. Also publishes literary essays and poetry. Always critiques or comments on rejected mss. Sponsors "Novette" contest (25,000 words or more). Entry fee: $19. Send SASE for information.

How to Contact: Send complete ms with cover letter. Include estimated word count and bio. Reports in days on queries; weeks on mss. SASE or SAE and IRCs if out of U.S. No simultaneous submissions. Sample copy for $7.50 and 5×9 SASE.

Payment/Terms: Pays $5-40 (.0115/word) on publication and contributor's copy; additional copies for $1.50. Acquires first rights.

Advice: "Do your own thing—ignore the trends. You must do your own editing—too many glitches and your excellent manuscript will be rejected."

N **FUEL MAGAZINE, (II)**, Anaconda Press, P.O. Box 08979, Chicago IL 60640. E-mail: alowry@chireader.com. **Editor:** Andy Lowry. Zine: 5½×8½; 40 pages; 60 lb. offset paper; 110 lb. cover stock; illustrations. "*Fuel* is a very eccentric, eclectic magazine. We do not consider ourselves an academic publication; rather, we prefer to publish underground lesser-known writers." Quarterly. Estab. 1992. Circ. 1,500.

- *Fuel*'s fiction needs have gone from 50% of the magazine to 75-80%. The magazine is best known for dark, realistic fiction.

Needs: Ethnic/multicultural, experimental, feminist, literary. No science fiction, romance, horror, humor/satire. List of upcoming themes available for SASE. Receives 50 unsolicited mss/month. Accepts 5 mss/issue; 20-25 mss/year. Publishes ms 3-5 months after acceptance. Published work by Nicole Panter, Gerald Locklin, Alan Catlin and Sesshu Foster. Length: 2,500 words preferred; 500 words minimum; 3,000 words maximum. Publishes short shorts. Length: 250 words. Also publishes poetry.
How to Contact: Query first. Include estimated word count and list of publications. Reports in 4 weeks on queries; 6 weeks on mss. SASE. No simultaneous submissions. Reprint and electronic submissions OK. Sample copy for $3. Fiction guidelines for #10 SASE.
Payment/Terms: Pays contributor's copies; additional copies at cost. Rights revert to authors.
Advice: "We are not your normal publication—we want intelligent, cutting edge, strongly written works. Persistence pays off—keep trying."

GERBIL, A Queer Culture Zine, (II), P.O. Box 10692, Rochester NY 14610. E-mail: gerbil@rpa.net. **Editors:** Tony Leuzzi and Brad Pease. Zine specializing in queer culture: 9½×7½; 32 pages; opaque quality paper; opaque cover stock; illustrations and photos. "We provide a forum for queer-identified writers who want to express ideas, views, aesthetics that aren't covered in the mainstream gay press." Quarterly. Estab. 1994. Circ. 2,800.
Needs: Condensed/excerpted novel, erotica, ethnic/multicultural, gay, humor/satire, lesbian, literary, mainstream/contemporary, psychic/supernatural/occult. Receives 20 unsolicited mss/month. Accepts 1 ms/issue; 5 mss/year. Publishes ms 4-6 months after acceptance. Published work by Kevin Killian, Bo Huston, Lawrence Braithwaite, Liam Brosnaham and Gysbert Menninga. Length: 250 words minimum; 5,000 words maximum. Publishes short shorts. Also publishes literary essays and poetry. Always critiques or comments on rejected mss.
How to Contact: Send complete ms with a cover letter. Include brief bio. Reports in 2 weeks on queries; 3-5 months on mss. Send SASE for return of ms or send disposable copy of ms. No simultaneous submissions. Electronic submissions OK. Sample copy for $4. Fiction guidelines for #10 SASE. Reviews novels or short story collections. Send books to editor.
Payment/Terms: Pays 3 contributor's copies for one-time rights.
Advice: "Always keep in mind a strong sense of story. Keep an open mind and always read. If you're honest and work hard, someone somewhere will accept your work."

GOTTA WRITE NETWORK LITMAG, (I, II), Maren Publications, 515 E. Thacker, Hoffman Estates IL 60194-1957. E-mail: netera@aol.com. **Editor:** Denise Fleischer. Magazine: 8½×11; 48-64 pages; saddle-stapled ordinary paper; matte card or lighter weight cover stock; illustrations. Magazine "serves as an open forum to discuss new markets, successes and difficulties. Gives beginning writers their first break into print and promotionally supports established professional novelists." Distributed through the US, Canada and England. Semiannually. Estab. 1988. Circ. 200.

- In addition to publishing fiction, *Gotta Write Network Litmag* includes articles on writing techniques, small press market news, writers' seminar reviews, science fiction convention updates, and features a "Behind the Scenes" section in which qualified writers can conduct mail interviews with small press editors and professional writers. Writers interviewed in this manner in the past have included Frederik Pohl, Jody Lynn Nye, Lawrence Watt-Evans and artist Michael Whelan.

Needs: Adventure, contemporary, fantasy, historical, humor/satire, literary, mainstream, prose poem, romance (gothic), science fiction (hard science, soft/sociological). "Currently seeking work with a clear-cut message or a twist at the very end. All genres accepted with the exception of excessive violence, sexual overtones or obscenity." Receives 75-150 unsolicited mss per month. Accepts 1-6 mss per issue; up to 20 mss a year. Publishes mss 6-12 months after acceptance. Recently published Debora Ann Belardino, Guilford Barton, Richard Geha, Damian Cohen and J. Spencer Dreischarf. Length: 10 pages maximum for short stories. Also publishes poetry.
How to Contact: Send complete ms with cover letter. Include "who you are, genre, previous publications and focused area of writing." Reports in 2-4 months (later during publication months). SASE ("no SASE, no repsonse"). Reports on fax submissions within days. Responds by fax. No simultaneous submissions or reprints. Electronic (e-mail) submissions OK. Sample copy for $5. Fiction guidelines for SASE.
Payment/Terms: Pays $10 or 2 contributor's copies for first North American serial rights.
Advice: "If I still think about the direction of the story after I've read it, I know it's good. Organize your

CHECK THE CATEGORY INDEXES, located at the back of the book, for publishers interested in specific fiction subjects.

thoughts on the plot and character development (qualities, emotions) before enduring ten drafts. Make your characters come alive by giving them a personality and a background, and then give them a little freedom. Let them take you through the story."

✔ ▣ **HERETIC HOLLOW, (I, II, IV)**, Box 5511, Pasadena CA 91117. (626)584-0008. E-mail: draigeye@earthlink.net. Website: http://www.home.earthlink.net/~draigeye. **Editor:** Draigeye. Online zine specializing in occult, magic and metaphysical: 8½×11; 8 pages; white stock paper; grey stock cover; illustrations and photographs. Themes include occult, magical, metaphysical, shamanic, wiccan, psychic. Monthly. Estab. 1996. Circ. 250.

Needs: Erotica, experimental, feminist, gay, horror, lesbian, psychic/supernatural/occult, romance (futuristic/time travel), science fiction. No religious/inspirational. Receives 0-1 unsolicited mss/month. Accepts 0-1 mss/issue. Publishes ms within 3 months after acceptance. Publishes 6-10 new writers/year. Length: 500 words average; 250 words minimum; 5,000 words maximum. Publishes short shorts. Also publishes literary essays, poetry. Always critiques or comments on rejected mss.

How to Contact: Send complete ms with a cover letter. Include half page bio and phone number. Send disposable copy of ms. Simultaneous submissions, reprints and electronic submissions OK. Guidelines free.

Payment/Terms: Acquires first rights. Sends galleys to author if local.

Advice: "We look for uniqueness and off-the-wall temporal irony. Beginners should send some. Don't hold back. You really are a good writer. We just haven't met—yet!"

✔ ▣ **I LIKE MONKEYS, (I)**. (909)624-2525. E-mail: arango@bigfoot.com. Website: http://www.angelfire.com/il/ikemonkeys. **Editor:** Padgett Arango. Electronic zine. "A wide range of fiction that runs from absurdism to fairly middle-of-the-road postmodernism. A sense of humor is always a plus, but a good grasp of innate futility of modern existence will more than make up for that."

Needs: "Prose of every length is preferred, but poetry is also accepted." No non-experimental genre fiction. Recently published work by Andrew Wood, Anne Paulsen and Alex Cabrera. Publishes as many new writer as possible/year.

How to Contact: Electronic submissions only.

Advice: "It's not hard. Write something vaguely interesting and it will probably be published."

IN CELEBRATION OF TREES, (I, II, IV). E-mail: FTFD57A@prodigy.com. Website: http://www.geocities.com/RainForest/9899. **Editor:** Sheila Barrera. Electronic zine. "The trees give us so much: paper, wood, shade, cleaner fresher air, but how often do we really see them? The trees pages are dedicated to reminding the world that a world without trees just might not be that great. In fact, it might be downright unsurvivable." Monthly to bimonthly.

Needs: Poetry, short stories, paintings and computer art, quotes, ponderings and thoughts. "Anything about trees." No "erotica or smut." Would like to see more personal stories relating some kind of relationship with a tree or trees. "Alice Pero is probably our most famous contributor, having been performing on the NYC live poetry beat for years. Gym Nasium-Saldutti, award winning poet and artist, is another, his website having won many awards for being in the top % of the web as well as a wonderful one from the Dali Museum for his tribute to the artist."

How to Contact: Electronic submissions only.

Advice: "If you know HTML coding, please do this, and that will save me time trying to figure out where the stanzas end and begin if your server has scrambled them."

✔ ▣ **THE INDITER, (I)**. (250)386-1663. Fax: (250)995-1872 E-mail: editor@lnditer.com. Website: http://www.inditer.com. **Editor:** Bill Loeppky. Electronic zine. "*The Inditer* is an online magazine dedicated to the encouragement of new writers and essayists. Those wishing to submit material of political or social editorial comment are also welcome to submit their work. Our intended audience would include readers, publishers and editors, secondary school and college creative writing departments."

- The editor would like to see more historical and science fiction. He is also interested in contemporary life essays and political commentary.

Needs: "Fiction, non-fiction, lifestyle articles, sci-fi, political or social articles intended to evoke response and alternative views. I do not want to see smut for the sake of smut. If course language is required to portray a character, so be it. Course language used simply for shock value will not be published. I do not want to see radical political or religious philosophy, nor do I want to see proselytism. I do not want to see material which could be deemed to be defaming or derogatory. I do not want to see writing which is esoteric to the point of being inane." Recently published work by Carline Zarlengo Sposto (Memphis), Larry Lynch (New Brunswick, Canada), Victor Wee (Singapore), Moira Moss (Michigan) and Amy Mueller (Iowa). Publishes 40-50 new writers/year.

How to Contact: Electronic submissions only. Send ms an e-mail attachment in ASCII text. Short pieces can also be sent as part of the body of an e-mail.

Payment/Terms: "There is no pay for manuscripts used, nor is there a charge to the writer. *The Inditer* is intended to be a vehicle which new writers can use to showcase their work. A number of writers who have published with me have found subsequent markets for their work, and two of them earned university credit for published works. Several universities and colleges have made use of *The Inditer*, both to critique its contents, and for students to avail themselves of it."

Advice: "You can either e-mail your submissions or you can use the form on the website. If you'd like to run an idea by us before sending it in, check one of the department categories on the form and type a brief description of your idea in the box."

INTERTEXT, (I, II). (415)789-1010. E-mail: editors@intertext.com. Website: http://www.intertext.com. **Editor:** Jason Snell. Electronic zine. "Our readers are computer literate (because we're online only) and appreciate entertaining fiction. They're usually accepting of different styles and genres—from mainstream to historical to science fiction to fantasy to horror to mystery—because we don't limit ourselves to one genre. They just want to read a story that makes them think or transports them to an interesting new place."

Needs: "Well-written fiction from any genre or setting." Especially looking for intelligent science fiction. No "exploitative sex or violence. We will print stories with explicit sex or violence, but not if it serves no purpose other than titillation." Recently published work by E. Jay O'Connell, Richard Kadrey, Levi Asher, Marcus Eubanks and William Routhier. Publishes 16 new writers/year.

How to Contact: Electronic submissions only. Stories should be in ASCII, HTML, or Microsoft Word (v. 5 or 6) formats.

Advice: "Have a clear writing style—the most clever story we've seen in months still won't make it if it's written badly. Try to make our readers think in a way they haven't before, or take them to a place they've never thought about before. And don't be afraid to mix genres—our readers have come to appreciate stories that aren't easily labeled as being part of one genre or another."

JACK MACKEREL MAGAZINE, (I, II), Rowhouse Press, P.O. Box 23134, Seattle WA 98102-0434. **Editor:** Greg Bachar. Zine: 5½×8½; 40-60 pages; Xerox bond paper; glossy card cover stock; b&w illustrations and photos. "We publish unconventional art, poetry and fiction." Quarterly. Estab. 1993. Circ. 1,000.

Needs: Condensed/excerpted novel, erotica, experimental, literary, surreal, translations. Publishes occasional chapbooks and anthologies. Receives 20-100 unsolicited mss/month. Accepts 10-20 mss/issue; 40-75 mss/year. Recently published work by David Berman, William Waltz, Heather Hayes, Brett Ralph, Ann Miller, Paul Dickinson and John Rose. Length: 250 words minimum; 5,000 words maximum. Publishes short shorts. Also publishes literary essays, literary criticism and poetry.

How to Contact: Send complete ms with a cover letter. Include bio with submission. Send SASE for reply, return of ms or send a disposable copy of ms. Sample copy for $5 (make checks or money order out to Greg Bachar). Reviews novels and short story collections.

Payment/Terms: Pays in contributor's copies.

N JUICY BRITCHES MAGAZINE, A Quarterly Anthology of Erotica, (II), Juicy Britches Publications, 675 Fairview Dr., Suite 246, Carson City NV 89701. (702)629-0575. E-mail: juicy@reno.quik.com. **Editor:** Carol Bardelli. Zine specializing in erotica: 8½×11; 120 pages; 25 lb. bond; 110 lb. cover stock; illustrations and photos. "We publish a wide variety of erotica and some non-erotic fiction, poetry, comics and novel excerpts. Our philosophy is sexuality is normal adult behavior and enhanced by reading well-written erotica." Quarterly. Estab. 1997. Circ. 200 print copies.

Needs: Condensed/excerpted novel, erotica, experimental, humor/satire, lesbian, serialized novel. "No child abuse or violence." Receives 50-75 unsolicited mss/month. Accepts 15-30 mss/issue; 60-120 mss/year. Publishes ms 2-4 months after acceptance. Recently published work by Ernest Slyman, David Sutherland, Erin Klee and Ralph Greco Jr. Length: 1,500 words average; 200 words minimum; 2,000 words maximum. Publishes short shorts. Also publishes literary essays, literary criticism, poetry. Sometimes critiques or comments on rejected ms.

How to Contact: Send complete ms with a cover letter. "We prefer contact by e-mail, but accept snail mail submissions." Include estimated word count. Send SASE for reply, return of ms or send a disposable copy of ms. Simultaneous and reprint submissions OK. Electronic submissions (disk or modem) OK. Sample copy for $8.50 and 10×12 SAE. Fiction guidelines for #10 SASE. Reviews novels and short story collections.

Payment/Terms: Pays $3-25 on publication for one-time rights.

Advice: "Tight, fast-paced plotting and believable characters are a must. Erotica should appeal to the emotions as well as the senses. Sex should be secondary to story and adventure."

THE LETTER PARADE, (I), Bonnie Jo Enterprises, P.O. Box 52, Comstock MI 49041-0052. **Editor:** Bonnie Jo. Zine: legal/letter-sized; 6 pages. Quarterly. Estab. 1985. Circ. 113. "The Letter Parade is a humble, mild-mannered newsletter which publishes short essays, stories, letters, and artwork which are enjoyable or thought-provoking to read or view—humorous essays or letters are our favorite."

Needs: "Anything short. We print very little fiction, actually. We print more essays. But we're open to the fun little story." Receives 25-30 unsolicited mss/month. Accepts 1-2 mss/issue. Publishes ms up to a year after acceptance. Recently published work by Heidi Bell and Carla Vissers. Publishes about 2 new writers/year. Length: 250-750 words preferred; 2,000 words maximum. Publishes short shorts. Also publishes any kind of essays.
How to Contact: Send complete ms with a cover letter. "Please single space so I can publish pieces in the form I receive them." Send disposable copy of ms. Reports in 4 months. Simultaneous and reprint submissions OK. Sample copy for $1. Reviews novels or short story collections. Send review copies to Christopher Magson.
Payment/Terms: Pays subscription to magazine. Not copyrighted.
Advice: "We're predisposed to stories about animals so long as the stories aren't sentimental. No stories ending in suicide. We like humor that's not too light, not too dark. What ridiculous thing happened on the way to the hardware store? What did you do when your cows got loose? What makes you think your husband is in love with Maggie Thatcher?"

LIQUID OHIO, Voice of the Unheard, (I), Blue Fish Publications, P.O. Box 60265, Bakersfield CA 93386-0265. (805)871-0586. E-mail: liquidohio@aol.com. **Editor:** Amber Goddard. Magazine: 8×11; 13-25 pages; copy paper; illustrations and photos. "*Liquid Ohio* is a fairly new publication whose goal is to publish new writers that others might toss in the trash. Our main audience is creatively eccentric people who feel what they do." Quarterly. Estab. 1995. Circ. 500.
Needs: Experimental, humor/satire, literary. "No erotica, vampires or any combination of the two." Receives 15-20 unsolicited mss/month. Accepts 2 mss/issue; 24-30 mss/year. Publishes ms 1-3 months after acceptance. Recently published work by Janet Kuypers, Peter Gorman and Christine Brandel. Publishes 40-60 new writers/year. Length: 1,500-1,800 words average; 2,500-3,000 words maximum. Publishes short shorts. Also publishes literary essays, literary criticism, poetry.
How to Contact: Send complete ms with a cover letter. Should include estimated word count. Reports in 3-4 weeks on queries; 3 months on mss. Send SASE for reply, return of ms or send a disposable copy of ms. Simultaneous submissions, reprint and electronic submissions OK. Sample copy for $3, 11×14 SAE and 3 first-class stamps. Fiction guidelines for #10 SASE.
Payment/Terms: Pays 3 contributor's copies. Acquires one-time rights.
Advice: "We like things that are different, but not too abstract or 'artsy' that one goes away saying, 'huh?' Write what you feel, not necessarily what sounds deep or meaningful—it will probably be that naturally if it's real. Send in anything you've got—live on the edge. Stories that are relatable, that deal with those of us trying to find a creative train in the world. We also love stories that are extremely unique e.g., talking pickles, etc."

THE MONTHLY INDEPENDENT TRIBUNE TIMES JOURNAL POST GAZETTE NEWS CHRONICLE BULLETIN, The Magazine to Which No Superlatives Apply, (I), 80 Fairlawn Dr., Berkeley CA 94708-2106. Editor: T.S. Child. **Fiction Editor:** Denver Tucson. Zine: 5½×8; 8 pages; 60 lb. paper; 60 lb. cover; illustrations and photographs. "We publish short stories, short short stories, plays, game show transcriptions, pictures made of words, teeny-weeny novelinis." Published irregularly. Estab. 1983. Circ. 500.

• The editor would like to see more "discombobulating" stories.

Needs: Adventure, experimental, humor/satire, mystery/suspense (amateur sleuth, private eye), psychic/supernatural/occult. "If it's serious, literary, perfect, well-done or elegant, we don't want it. If it's bizarre, unclassifiable, funny, cryptic or original, we might." Nothing "pretentious; important; meaningful; honest." Receives 20 unsolicited mss/month. Accepts 3-4 mss/issue. Accepted manuscripts published in next issue. Length: 400 words preferred; 1,200 words maximum. Publishes short shorts. Length: 400 words. Sometimes critiques rejected mss.
How to Contact: Send complete ms with cover letter. Reports in 1 month. SASE. "May" accept simultaneous submissions. Sample copy for 50¢, and SASE.
Payment/Terms: Pays subscription (2 issues); 3 contributor's copies. Not copyrighted.
Advice: "First of all, stories must be *short*—1,200 words maximum, but the shorter the better. They must make us either laugh or scream or scratch our heads, or all three. Things that are slightly humorous, or written with any kind of audience in mind, are returned. If you can think of another magazine that might publish your story, send it to them, not us. Send us your worst, weirdest stories, the ones you're too embarrassed to send anywhere else."

☑ ▣ **moonbomb press, (I, II)**, (formerly the moonbomb writer's syndicate). E-mail: moonbomb@hooked.net. Website: http://www.hooked.net/users/moonbomb. **Editor:** Paul C. Choi. Electronic zine. "We are contemporary, urban, irreverent, ethnic, random."
Needs: Short stories, poetry, short plays, any fictional format, autobiographical non-fiction, fictional journalism.

A BULLET INTRODUCES COMMENTS by the editor of *Novel & Short Story Writer's Market* indicating special information about the listing.

No children's fiction. Recently published work by Paul Rossi and Sheryl Ridenour. Publishes 3-4 new writers/year.
How to Contact: Electronic submissions only.
Advice: "Be bold."

MYSTERY AND MANNERS QUARTERLY, (I, II). E-mail: brandt8@indy.net. Website: http://www.indy.net/-brandt8/mysman/mysman.htm. **Editor:** Brandt Judson Ryan. Electronic zine. "To provide realistic, short fiction to the world online—fiction that includes all the five senses, forcing the reader to see something they might not have before."
Needs: "Short fiction only—no genre stories, no mysteries (the title of the zine is misleading)." Would like to see more literary fiction. Recently published work by Alex Keegan, Tom Harper and Sylvia Petter. Publishes 3 new writers/year.
How to Contact: Electronic submissions only. Send ms as an e-mail attachment or in the body of the message.
Advice: "In a realistic way, attempt to bring the other-worldly, right down into the worldly."

THE NEBULA, (I, II). (412)381-1146. E-mail: drow.queen@nebula.nauticom.net or lance@nebula.nauticom.net. Website: http://nebula.nauticom.net/nebula. **Editors:** Cindy Henderson and Lance Williams. "It is The Nebulous Association's mission to publish the highest quality special interest fanzine in the Ohio Valley region. We want to provide our subscribers with the most accurate and up-to-date information on the gaming, science fiction and fantasy genres. It is also our mission to hold highly organized and interesting gaming events for the lowest cost possible to the consumer."
Needs: Gaming, science fiction, fantasy, horror. Recently published work by Cindy Henderson, Hugh Barnes, Lance Williams, Owen McPhee, Pat Beck, James Dodd and Rob Burton. Publishes 6-12 new writers/year.
How to Contact: Electronic submissions only. Send ms at text file in e-mail.

NUTHOUSE, Essays, Stories and Other Amusements, (II), Twin Rivers Press, P.O. Box 119, Ellenton FL 34222. E-mail: nuthous499@aol.com. Website: http://members.aol.com/Nuthous499/index.html (includes writer's guidelines, readers' letters, excerpts). **Chief of Staff:** Dr. Ludwig "Needles" Von Quirk. Zine: digest-sized; 12-16 pages; bond paper; illustrations and photos. "Humor of all genres for an adult readership that is not easily offended." Published every 6 weeks. Estab. 1993. Circ. 100.
Needs: Humor/satire: erotica, experimental, fantasy, feminist, historical (general), horror, literary, main-stream/contemporary, mystery/suspense, psychic/supernatural/occult, romance, science fiction and westerns. Plans annual "Halloween Party" issue featuring humorous verse and fiction with a horror theme. Receives 12-30 unsolicited mss/month. Accepts 3-5 mss/issue; 30 mss/year. Publishes ms 6-12 months after acceptance. Published work by Dale Andrew White, Mitchell Nathanson, Rob Loughran, Vanessa Dodge, Ken Rand, Don Hornbostel and Michael McWey. Length: 500 words average; 100 words minimum; 1,000 words maximum. Publishes short shorts. Length: 100-250 words. Also publishes literary essays, literary criticism and poetry. Often critiques or comments on rejected mss.
How to Contact: Send complete ms with a cover letter. Include estimated word count, bio (paragraph) and list of publications. Reports in 2-4 weeks on mss. SASE for return of ms or send disposable copy of ms. Simultaneous and reprint submissions OK. Sample copy for $1 (payable to Twin Rivers Press). Fiction guidelines for #10 SASE.
Payment/Terms: Pays 1 contributor's copy. Acquires one-time rights. Not copyrighted.
Advice: Looks for "laugh-out-loud prose. Strive for original ideas; read the great humorists—Saki, Woody Allen, Robert Benchley, Garrison Keillor, John Irving—and learn from them. We are turned off by sophomoric attempts at humor built on a single, tired, overworked gag or pun; give us a story with a beginning, middle and end."

$ OF UNICORNS AND SPACE STATIONS, (I, II, IV), %Gene Davis, P.O. Box 97, Bountiful UT 84011-0097. Website: http://www.genedavis.com/magazine. **Senior Editor:** Gene Davis. Zine: 5½×8½; 60 pages; 20 lb. white paper; card cover stock; illustrations. "We want science fiction and fantasy of a positive nature, that gives us ideas, that warns us about the future and gives potential answers. It should be for adults, though graphic sex, violence and offensive language are not considered." Biannual. Estab. 1994. Circ. 100.
Needs: Fantasy (science fantasy, sword and sorcery), science fiction (hard science, soft/sociological, utopian). Wants "clear writing that is easy to follow." Receives 20 unsolicited mss/month. Accepts 9-13 mss/issue; approximtely 25 mss/year. Publishes ms 6-12 months after acceptance. Recently published work by Jackie Shank and L.J. Coleman. Publishes approximately 5 new writers/year. Length: 3,000 words average. Publishes short shorts. Also publishes poetry. Sometimes critiques or comments on rejected mss.

How to Contact: Send complete ms (clean, well-written, not stapled) with a cover letter. Include estimated word count, bio (75 words or less) and writer's classification of the piece (science fiction, fantasy, poetry). Reports in 3 months. Send SASE for reply, return of ms or send a disposable copy of ms. Simultaneous, reprint and electronic (disk only) submissions OK. If a subscriber, e-mail submissions OK. Sample copy for $4. Fiction guidelines for #10 SASE.
Payment/Terms: Pays 1¢/word and 1 contributor's copy for stories; $5/poem and 1 contributor's copy for poetry; additional copies for $4. Acquires one-time rights.
Advice: "Keep trying. It may take several tries to get published. Most stories I see are good. You just need to find an editor that goes ga-ga over your style."

OUTER DARKNESS, Where Nightmares Roam Unleashed, (I, II), Outer Darkness Press, 1312 N. Delaware Place, Tulsa OK 74110. (918)832-1246. **Editor:** Dennis Kirk. Zine: 8½×5½; 60-80 pages; 20 lb. paper; 90 lb. glossy cover; illustrations. Specializes in imaginative literature. "Variety is something I strive for in *Outer Darkness*. In each issue we present readers with great tales of science fiction and horror along with poetry, cartoons and interviews/essays. I seek to provide readers with a magazine which, overall, is fun to read." Quarterly. Estab. 1994. Circ. 500.

- Fiction published in *Outer Darkness* has received honorable mention in *The Year's Best Fantasy and Horror*.

Needs: Fantasy (science), horror, mystery/suspense (with horror slant), psychic/supernatural/occult, romance (gothic), science fiction (hard science, soft/sociological). No straight mystery, pure fantasy—works which do not incorporate elements of science fiction and/or horror. Wants more "character driven tales—especially in the genre of science fiction." "I do not publish works with children in sexual situations and graphic language should be kept to a minimum." Occasionally publishes theme issues. Send SASE for details. Receives 50-75 unsolicited mss/month. Accepts 7-9 mss/issue; 20-50 mss/year. Recently published work by D.F. Lewis, Scott Thomas, Deborah Hunt, Charlee Jacob and Ken Abner. Publishes 4-6 new writers/year. . Length: 3,000 words average; 1,000 words minimum; 5,000 words maximum. Also publishes literary essays and poetry. Always critiques or comments on rejected mss.
How to Contact: Send complete ms with a cover letter. Include estimated word count, 50- to 75-word bio, list of publications and "any awards, honors you have received." Reports in 1 week on queries; 1-2 months on mss. Send SASE for reply, return of ms or send a disposable copy of ms. Simultaneous submissions OK. Sample copy for $3.95. Fiction guidelines for #10 SASE.
Payment/Terms: Pays 3 contributor's copies for fiction, 2 for poetry and art. Pays on publication. Acquires one-time rights.
Advice: "Suspense is one thing I look for in stories. I want stories which grab the reader early on . . . and don't let go. I want stories which start off on either an interesting or suspenseful note. Read the works of Alan Dean Foster. Don't be discouraged by rejections. The best writers have received their share of rejection slips. Be patient. Take time to polish your work. Produce the best work you can and continue to submit, regardless of rejections. New writers now have more markets than ever before. I believe readers are searching for more 'traditional' works—and less 'experimental' styles. And while I have published works of an experimental nature, I like to give readers good, solid traditional fiction, for which I feel there is a definite demand."

THE OUTPOST, (I, II). (609)587-4821. Fax: (609)586-8795. E-mail: thepost@concentric.net. Website: http://www.cris.com/~Thepost/index.htm. **Editor:** Tom Julian. Electronic zine. "We want writers and artists to take part in the things going on at *The Outpost*."
Needs: Fantasy, science fiction. Would like to see more comedies, plays and stories about relationships. "No copy-cats. No just like the *Hitchhikers Guide* stuff, please." Recently published work by Victor Martin Ivers, John McGerr and Kenneth Newquist. Publishes as many new writers "as cut the mustard."
How to Contact: Electronic submissions only. Send ms by e-mail.
Advice: "Give me something that puts me there and make it a place I'd want to go."

PABLO LENNIS, The Magazine of Science Fiction, Fantasy and Fact, (I, II, IV), Etaoin Shrdlu Press, Fandom House, 30 N. 19th St., Lafayette IN 47904. **Editor:** John Thiel. Zine: 8½×11; 26 pages; standard stock; illustrations and "occasional" photos. "Science fiction, fantasy, science, research and mystic for scientists and science fiction and fantasy appreciators." Monthly.
Needs: Fantasy, science fiction. Receives 50 unsolicited mss/year. Accepts 4 mss/issue; 48 mss/year. Publishes ms 4 months after acceptance. Recently published work by Michael Lohr, Arthur Winfield Knight, Joanne Tolson and C.B. Thatcher. Publishes 36 new writers/year. Length: 1,500 words average; 3,000 words maximum. Also publishes literary criticism, poetry. Occasionally critiques rejected mss and recommends other markets.
How to Contact: "Method of submission is author's choice but he might prefer to query. No self-statement is necessary." No simultaneous submissions. Reports in 2 weeks. Does not accept computer printouts.
Payment/Terms: Pays 1 contributor's copy. Publication not copyrighted.
Advice: "I have taboos against unpleasant and offensive language and want material which is morally or otherwise elevating to the reader. I prefer an optimistic approach and favor fine writing. With a good structure dealt with intelligently underlying this, you have the kind of story I like. I prefer stories that have something to say to those which have something to report."

PBW, (I, II), 130 W. Limestone, Yellow Springs OH 45387. (513)767-7416. E-mail: rianca@aol.com. **Editor:** Richard Freeman. Electronic disk zine: 700 pages; illustrations. "*PBW* is an experimental floppy disk that 'prints' strange and 'unpublishable' in an above-ground-sense writing." Quarterly electronic zine. Featuring avant-garde fiction and poetry. Estab. 1988.

- *PBW* is an electronic zine which can be read on a Macintosh or available over modem on BBS. Write for details.

Needs: Erotica, experimental, gay, lesbian, literary. No "conventional fiction of any kind." Receives 3 unsolicited mss/month. Accepts 40 mss/issue; 160 mss/year. Publishes ms within 3 months after acceptance. Published work by Dave Castleman, Marie Markoe and Henry Hardee. Publishes 10-15 new writers/year. Length: open. Publishes short shorts and novels in chapters. Publishes literary essays, literary criticisms and poetry. Always critiques or comments on rejected mss.
How to Contact: Send complete ms with a cover letter. Accepts queries by e-mail. "Manuscripts are only taken if sent on disk." Reports in 2 weeks. Send SASE for reply, return of ms or send a disposable copy of ms. Simultaneous, reprint and electronic (Mac or modem) submissions OK. Sample copy for $2. Reviews novels and short story collections.
Payment/Terms: Pays 1 contributor's copy. All rights revert back to author. Not copyrighted.

PEGASUS ONLINE, the Fantasy and Science Fiction Ezine, (I, II). E-mail: editors@pegasusonline.com or scottMarlow@pegasusonline.com. Website: http://www.pegasusonline.com. **Editor:** Scott F. Marlowe. Electronic zine. "*Pegasus Online* focuses upon the genres of science and fantasy fiction. We look for original work which inspires and moves the reader, writing which may cause him or her to think, and maybe even allow to pause for a moment to consider the how's and why's of those things around us."
Needs: Fantasy, science fiction. "More specifically, fantasy is to be of the pure fantastic type: dragons, goblins, magic and everything else you can expect from something not of this world. Science fiction can or cannot be of the 'hard' variety." No "excessive profanity or needless gore." Recently published work by Allen Woods, Jonathan Lowe, Kate Thornton and Stephen Dixon. Publishes 12 new writers/year.
How to Contact: Electronic submissions only. Send mss by e-mail.
Advice: "Tell a complete tale with strong characters and a plot which draws the reader in from the very first sentence to the very last. The key to good fiction writing is presenting readers with characters they can identify with at some level. Your characters certainly can be larger than life, but they should not be all-powerful. Also, be careful with grammar and sentence structure. We get too many submissions which have good plot lines, but are rejected because of poor English skills. The end-all is this: we as humans read because we want to escape from reality for a short time. Make us feel like we've entered your world and make us want to see your characters succeed (or not, depending on your plot's angle), and you've done your job and made us happy at the same time."

PEN & SWORD, (I). (415)626-5179. E-mail: jag@rahul.net. Website: http://www.rahul.net/jag/. **Editor:** Jim Gardner. Electronic zine. "The best in modern and post-modern fiction, poetry, essays, criticism and reviews."
Needs: "*Pen & Sword* is an equal opportunity publisher and especially welcomes work from the gay/lesbian/bisexual community." Recently published work by Aldo Alvarez and Jim Tushinski. Publishes 6-10 new writers/year.
How to Contact: "Electronic submissions to the editor in MS Word, FrameMaker, HTML (preferred) or ASCII text are acceptable."

PENNY DREADFUL, Tales & Poems of Fantastic Terror, (II, IV), Pendragon Publications, 407 West 50th St., #16, Hell's Kitchen NY 10019. **Editor:** Michael Pendragon. Zine specializing in horror: 8½×5½; 40 pages; illustrations and photos. Publication to "celebrate the darker aspects of man, the world and their creator. We seek to address a highly literate audience who appreciate horror as a literary art form." Triannually. Estab. 1996. Circ. 500.

- Penny Dreadful won an Honorable Mention in St. Martin's Press's *The Year's Best Fantasy and Horror* competition.

Needs: Fantasy (dark symbolist), horror, psychic/supernatural/occult. Wants more "tales set in and in the style of the 19th century." No modern science fiction "constantly referring to 20th century persons, events, products, etc." List of upcoming themes available for SASE. Receives 50 unsolicited mss/month. Accepts 3-5 mss/issue; 9-15 mss/year. "*Penny Dreadful* reads all year until we have accepted enough submissions to fill more than one year's worth of issues." Recently published work by James S. Dorr, Scott Thomas, D.M. Yorton, Paul Bradshaw, Nancy Bennett and John Light. Publishes 6 new writers/year. Length: 500 words minimum; 2,500 words maximum. Publishes short shorts. Also publishes poetry. Always critiques or comments on rejected mss.
How to Contact: Send complete ms with a cover letter. Include estimated word count, bio and list of publications. Reports in up to 3 months on queries and mss. Send SASE for reply, return of ms or send disposable copy of ms. Simultaneous submissions and reprints OK. Sample copy for 9×6 SASE with 3 first-class stamps. Fiction guidelines for #10 SASE.
Payment/Terms: Pays free subscription to magazine plus 2 contributor's copies for one-time rights. Sends galleys to author. Not copyrighted.
Advice: Looks for "literary dark horror in the tradition of Poe, M.R. James, Shelley and LeFanu—dark, disquiet-

ing tales designed to challenge the readers' perceptions of human nature, morality and man's place within the Darkness. Stories should be set prior to 1910 or possess a timeless quality. Avoid graphic sex, strong language, references to 20th century people, excessive gore and shock elements. Be prepared to spend significant amounts of time and money. Whenever possible, try to submit to independent zines specializing in your genre. Expect only one copy as payment. Over time—if you're exceptionally talented and/or lucky—you may begin to build a small following."

PEOPLENET DISABILITY DATENET HOME PAGE, "Where People Meet People," (IV), Box 897, Levittown NY 11756-0897. (516)579-4043. E-mail: mauro@idt.net. Website: http://idt.net/~mauro (includes writer's guidelines, articles, stories, poems). **Editor:** Robert Mauro. "Romance stories featuring disabled characters." Estab. 1995.
Needs: Romance, contemporary and disabled. Main character must be disabled. Upcoming theme: "Marriage between disabled and non-disabled." Accepts 3 mss/year. Publishes immediately after acceptance. Publishes 21 new writers/year. Length: 1,500 words. Publishes short shorts. Length: 750 words. Also publishes poetry. Especially looking for book reviews on books dealing with disabled persons and sexuality.
How to Contact: Send complete ms by e-mail. No simultaneous submissions. Fiction guidelines online.
Payment/Terms: Acquires first rights.
Advice: "We are looking for romance stories of under 1,000 words on romance with a disabled man or woman as the main character. No sob stories or 'super crip' stories. Just realistic romance. No porn. Erotica okay. Love, respect, trust, understanding and acceptance are what I want."

PHRASE ONLINE, (I). Fax: (352)629-3367. E-mail: tsprang@phrase.org. Website: http://www.phrase.org. **Editor:** Todd Sprang. Electronic zine, "*Phrase* is an open forum for any and all writers who wish to release their work for the world to read." Bimonthly.
Needs: Short and long fiction, poetry. Other media are considered. Would like to see more satire. Recently published work by Jae H. Lee, Robert Brower and Jason Stelzer. Published 3 new writers in last issue.
How to Contact: Provides form on website for electronic submissions.
Advice: "Proofread. Proofread proofread. Proofread some more."

PIF, (I). (360)493-0596. E-mail: editor@pifmagazine.com. Website: http://www.pifmagazine.com. **Editor:** Richard Luck. Electronic zine. "Starting point for the Literary E-press, *Pif* believes that electronic publishing will revolutionize the industry as profoundly as the printing press did, and we aim to usher in this new era with the best and the brightest the Net has to offer. Our audience is a cross-section of the global community. We're read in over 87 different countries. The majority of our readers tend to be educated, culturally aware and open-minded. Quite a few of our readers are writers as well."
Needs: "We publish a wide range of material, including: poetry, fiction, commentary and original artwork. We also include book, movie and music reviews. We are open to most anything, as long as it is well-written and shows a real love for the craft. We especially seek contemporary literary-quality fiction in the style of Douglas Coupland, Erica Jong, Henry Miller, et al. We're particularly interested in writers who are willing to break boundaries, who are honest and believe in themselves and the characters they create." Recently published work by Amy Hempel, Richard K. Weems, Gail Hoskins Gilberg, Liam Rector and David Lehman. "We are the premier publisher of new and unpublished writers on the Net. Several of the writers we originally introduced have, as a result of appearing in *Pif*, subsequently published novels or collections of poetry with mainstream publishers." Publishes 30 new fiction writers and 40-50 new poets/year.
How to Contact: Electronic submissions only. "Submit via e-mail, including the story/poem as a MIME attachment in Word for Windows format (PC-based), or cut and paste into the body of the e-mail. Always send submissions to the proper editor. E-mail subs@pifmagazine.com for a complete listing of e-mail addresses."
Advice: "Be honest and be yourself. Take a chance and see where it leads you. Above all, believe in your characters and the story you're telling. If you're bored while writing the piece, chances are we'll be bored reading it. So be enthusiastic. Be brave. Be willing to go out on a limb."

$ PLAY THE ODDS, (I), The Big Dog Press, 11614 Ashwood, Little Rock AR 72211. (501)224-9452. Editor: Tom Raley. **Fiction Editor:** Barbra Stone. Zine specializing in gaming/gambling: 8½×11; 16 lb. paper; illustrations and photos. "We cover gambling activities all across the country. We offer tips, reviews, instructions and advice. We also cover cruise lines since most have casinos on board." Monthly. Estab. 1997.

- Sponsors several contests both annual and ongoing. Details are printed in each issue. *Play the Odds* ranked #2 on *Writer's Digest's* Fiction 50 list of top fiction markets.

Needs: Adventure, fantasy (science fantasy), horror, mystery/suspense (cozy, private eye/hardboiled, romantic suspense), science fiction (soft sociological), senior citizen/retirement, sports, westerns (traditional). Receives 20-25 unsolicited mss/month. Accepts 1-2 mss/issue; 12-20 mss/year. Publishes ms 2-4 months after acceptance.

Published work by Jennifer Sinclair and Gary Lewis. Length: 600 words average; 800 words maximum. Publishes short shorts. Also publishes literary criticism and poetry. Always critiques or comments on rejected mss.
How to Contact: Send complete ms with a cover letter. Include estimated word count and 100 word bio. Reports in 2 weeks on queries; 4-6 weeks on mss. Send SASE for reply, return of ms or send disposable copy of ms. Simultaneous submissions OK. Sample copy for $2. Fiction guidelines for #10 SASE. Reviews novels and short story collections. Send books to D.A. Rogers.
Payment/Terms: Pays $1,500 minimum; $3,000 maximum on acceptance for one-time rights.
Advice: "We look for fast paced stories with real characters. The stories should be fun, enjoyable and the main character doesn't need to be trying to save the world. Few, if any of us, do that. We do however get in bad situations. You must write what you enjoy writing about. If you don't want to write a story about gambling or a gambler, it will show in your work. If it is something you do want, that will also show in your work and we will notice it."

N **PURPLE MIST, (I, II, IV)**, 1319 Marshall St., Manitowoc WI 54220. (920)684-7901. **Editor:** Nell Harmon. Zine specializing in fantasy/adult fairy tales: digest-sized; 20-40 pages; illustrations. "We publish magical tales—tales with fairies, trolls, ogres, wizards, dragons and genies. Adult fairy tales: bringing back the old favorites of childhood but with more of an adult theme." Triannually. Estab. 1998.
Needs: Erotica (soft), fantasy (science fantasy, sword and sorcery, adult fairy tales), science fiction (fantasy). "No hard science fiction; no strong horror; no children's or romance." Receives 5-8 unsolicited mss/month. Accepts 6-12 mss/issue. Publishes ms 1-6 months after acceptance. Agented fiction 1%. Recently published work by Wayne Wilkinson, Gary Jurechka, Linney Teague McCall and D.M. Yorton. Length: 1,200 words maximum. Publishes short shorts. Also publishes poetry. Always critiques or comments on rejected ms.
How to Contact: Send complete ms with a cover letter. Include estimated word count, 1-paragraph bio and list of publications. Reports in 2 weeks on queries; 1-4 weeks on mss. Send SASE for reply, return of ms or send a disposable copy of ms. Simultaneous and reprint submissions OK. Sample copy for $2. Fiction guidelines for #10 SASE.
Payment/Terms: Pays 1 contributor's copy; additional copies $2. Acquires one-time rights. Not copyrighted.

QECE, Question Everything Challenge Everything, (II, IV), 406 Main St. #3C, Collegeville PA 19426. E-mail: qece@aol.com. **Editor:** Larry Nocella. Zine: 5½×8½; 44 pages; copy paper; copy paper cover; illustrations and photographs. Zine "seeking to inspire free thought and action by encouraging a more questioning mentality. Intended for dreamers and quiet laid-back rebels." Triannually. Estab. 1996. Circ. 300.
Needs: Experimental. "Anything that inspires others to question and challenge conventions of fiction. Aggressive, compelling, short, fun is OK too. No lame stuff. Be wary of anything too foo-foo literary." No genre fiction, no formulas. Receives 15 unsolicited mss/month. Accepts 1 ms/issue; 3 mss/year. Publishes ms 6 months after acceptance. Recently published work by Digby Idz, Michael P. Smith, Andy Rant and C.H. Tuck. Publishes 12 new writers/year. Length: 1,000 words average. Publishes short shorts. Always critiques or comments on rejected mss.
How to Contact: Send complete ms with a cover letter. Include estimated word count and 25 words or less bio. Reports in 4 months. Send SASE for reply, return of ms or send a disposable copy of ms. Simultaneous and e-mail submissions OK. Sample copy for $3. Fiction guidelines free for #10 SASE.
Payment/Terms: Pays 2 contributor's copies; additional copies for $3. Acquires one-time rights.
Advice: "Ignore 'trends'; be yourself as much as possible and you'll create something unique. Be as timeless as possible. Avoid obscure, trendy references. Tie comments about a current trend to timeless observation. If it's in the 'news' chances are it won't be in QECE, The 'news' is a joke. Tell me something I need to know. Favor anecdotes and philosophy over intense political opinions. I'd prefer to hear about personal experiences and emotions everyone can relate to. Criticism is welcome, though. QECE can be negative, but remember it is positive too. Just go for it! Send away and let me decide! Get busy!"

R'N'R, (I). E-mail: glbeke@panix.com. Website: http://www.panix.com/-glbeke. **Editor:** George L. Beke. Electronic zine. "Literate writing with a musical bent. Write with attitude."
Needs: "Poems, memoirs, fiction, musings, confessions, critiques that are smart, evocative and surprising. Nothing boring." Publishes "as many new writers as possible."
How to Contact: Electronic submissions only.
Advice: "Send it."

MARKET CATEGORIES: (I) Open to new writers; **(II)** Open to both new and established writers; **(III)** Interested mostly in established writers; **(IV)** Open to writers whose work is specialized; **(V)** Closed to unsolicited submissions.

RALPH'S REVIEW, (I), RC Publications, 129A Wellington Ave., Albany NY 12203-2637. (518)459-0883. Fax: (518)442-5811. E-mail: rcpub@juno.com. **Editor:** Ralph Cornell. Zine: 8½×11; 20-35 pages; 20 lb. bond paper and cover. "To let as many writers as possible get a chance to publish their works, fantasy, sci-fi, horror, poetry. We are adding home remedies and gardening tips. Audience: adult, young adult, responsible, self contained, conscious human beings." Quarterly. Estab. 1988. Circ. 200.
Needs: Adventure, fantasy (science fantasy), horror, humor/satire, literary, psychic/supernatural/occult, science fiction, stamp and coin collecting, dinosaurs, environmental, fishing. No extreme violence, racial, gay/lesbian/x-rated. Publishes annual special fiction issue or anthology. Receives 10-15 unsolicited mss/month. Accepts 1-2 mss/issue; 12-15 mss/year. Publishes ms 2-4 months after acceptance. Recently published work by Ralph Cornell, Celeste Plowden, Bob Holmes and Renese Carlisle. Publishes 10-20 previously unpublished writer's/year. Length: 500-1,000 words average; 50 words minimum; 2,000 words maximum. $2 reading fee for all stories over 500 words. Publishes short shorts. Also publishes poetry. Sometimes critiques or comments on rejected mss.
How to Contact: Send complete ms with a cover letter. Include 1-paragraph bio and list of publications. Reports in 2-3 weeks on queries; 2-3 months on mss. Send SASE for reply, return of ms or send a disposable copy of ms. Simultaneous and reprint submissions OK. Sample copy for $2, 9×12 SAE and 5 first-class stamps. Fiction guidelines for #10 SASE. Reviews novels or short story collections.
Payment/Terms: Pays 1 contributor's copy; additional copies for $2. Acquires first North American serial rights.
Advice: Looks for manuscripts "that start out active and continue to grow until you go 'Ahh!' at the end. Something I've never read before. Make sure spelling is correct, content is crisp and active, characters are believable. Must be horrific, your worst nightmare, makes you want to look in the corner while sitting in your own living room."

✓ ▣ **RENAISSANCE MAGAZINE, (I, II)**, (formerly *Growing Pains* Magazine), 168 Orient Ave., Pawtucket RI 02861. E-mail: kridolfi@efortress.com. Website: http://users.efortress.com/kridolfi/. **Editor:** Kevin Ridolfi. Electronic zine. "*Renaissance* provides an open forum and exchange for an online community seeking for diversity on the jumbled and stagnant Internet. Works should be well-written and should deal with the effective resolution of a problem."
Needs: Short fiction, serial fiction, poetry, essays, humor, young adult. "No lewd, adult fiction." Recently published work by George Kashdan, Jennifer Maine, Elizabeth Dumont and Bonnie Nay. Publishes 24 new writers/year. Length: 3,000 words maximum.
How to Contact: Electronic and traditional submissions accepted, electronic (e-mail) submissions preferred.
Advice: "Browse through *Renaissance*'s past issues for content tendencies and submission requirements. Don't be afraid to go out on a short limb, but please limit yourself to our already existing categories."

S.L.U.G. FEST, LTD., A Magazine of Free Expression, (I), SF, Ltd., P.O. Box 1238, Simpsonville SC 29681-1238. Editor: M.T. Nowak. **Fiction Editor:** M. Tatlow. Zine: 8½×11; 70 pages; 20 lb. paper; 30 lb. cover stock; illustrations. "We are dedicated to publishing the best poetry and fiction we can find from writers who have yet to be discovered." Quarterly. Estab. 1991. Circ. 1,000.
Needs: Adventure, ethnic/multicultural, experimental, feminist, historical, humor/satire, literary, mainstream/contemporary, regional, "philosophies, ramblings." "No poor writing." Receives 30 unsolicited mss/month. Accepts 5-10 mss/issue; 20-40 mss/year. Publishes mss 3 months after acceptance. 50% of material published is by new writers. Length: 7,000-10,000 words preferred. Publishes short shorts. Also publishes literary essays, literary criticism and poetry. Often critiques and comments on rejected mss.
How to Contact: Send complete ms with a cover letter. Include estimated word count. Reports in 5 weeks. Send SASE for reply, return of ms or send a disposable copy of ms. Simultaneous, reprint and electronic submissions OK. Sample copy for $5. Fiction guidelines free. Reviews novels and short story collections.
Payment/Terms: Pays 1 contributor's copy. Rights revert to author upon publication.
Advice: "We look for humor, quality of imagery. Get our interest. Style and content must grab our editors. Strive for a humorous or unusual slant on life."

🌐 **SCRIPTIO UK/EUROPE, (IV)**, E-mail: scriptiouk@geocities.com or scriptiouk@rocketmail.com. Website: http://www.geocities.com/Athens/Forum/9212. Electronic zine. Estab. 1996.
Needs: All kinds of fiction by European writers. Length: 15,000 words maximum. Publishes short shorts. Also publishes literary essays, literary criticism and poetry.
How to Contact: Query first by e-mail. Include list of publications. Reports in 2 weeks on queries. Simultaneous, reprint and electronic submissions OK.
Advice: "Do your best work."

N **SEDUCTIVE TORTURE, Vampire Tales, (I, II, IV)**, Vamp, Inc., 1319 Marshall St., Manitowoc WI 54220. (920)684-7901. **Editor:** D.M. Yorton. Zine specializing in vampire tales: digest-sized, 20-40 pages; illustrations. "Dark moody stories dealing with vampires." Adult audience. Triannually. Estab. 1998.
Needs: Erotica (soft!), fantasy, horror (soft), psychic/supernatural/occult. Receives 12-20 unsolicited mss/month. Accepts 4-8 mss/issue. Publishes ms 1-6 months after acceptance. Recently published work by Alex Bledsoe,

Gary Jurechka and L. Fowler. Length: 1,100 words average; 1,500 words maximum. Publishes short shorts. Also publishes poetry. Always critiques or comments on rejected ms.
How to Contact: Send complete ms with a cover letter. Include estimated word count, 1-paragraph bio and list of publications. Reports in 1 week on queries; 1-4 weeks on mss. Send SASE for reply, return of ms or send a disposable copy of ms. Simultaneous and reprint submissions OK. Sample copy for $3. Fiction guidelines for #10 SASE.
Payment/Terms: Pays 1 contributor's copy; additional copies $3.25. Acquires one-time rights. Not copyrighted.
Advice: "We're looking for more new age and present-time vampire stories, not gothic unless well written."

☑ **SEPULCHRE, (I, IV)**, Koshkovich Press, 5037 Worchester Dr., Dayton OH 45431-1137. (937)253-6517. E-mail: vannar@bigfoot.com. Website: http://www.members.aol.com/sepulch862/sepulchre1.htm (includes writer's guidelines, links to contributors' websites, graphic of current issue's cover, along with contributor list). **Editor:** Scot H.P. Drew. Zine: digest size; approximately 40 pages; 28 lb. paper; 67 lb. coverstock; illustrations and photos. "Quarterly zine devoted to bringing new writers of dark fantasy and imaginative horror out into the sunlight of the small press literary scene." Publishes fiction and poetry. Estab. 1997.
Needs: Fantasy (dark), horror, psychic/supernatural/occult. "No urban horror, sociological science fiction. We would like to see more classic horror akin to Poe, Lovecraft, Bierce." Receives 10 unsolicited mss/month. Accepts 5 mss/issue; 20 mss/year. Recently published work by Charlee Jacob, D.F. Lewis and S.C. Virtes. Publishes approximately 10 new writers/year. Length: 2,000-5,000 words average; 10,000 words maximum. Publishes short shorts. Also publishes poetry. Sample copy for $3.00. Fiction guidelines for #10 SASE.
How to Contact: Send complete ms with a cover letter. Accepts queries by e-mail. Include 2-5 line bio for inclusion with piece. Send disposable copy of ms. Reports in 1 month on mss. Simultaneous submissions OK.
Payment/Terms: Pays 1 contributor's copy.
Advice: "Send your darkest, most disturbing pieces. Use what I call the clusterbomb approach: simply innundate the target market with your work."

☑ **SORCEROUS MAGAZINE, Sword & Sorcery, Epic Fantasy, (I, IV)**, P.O. Box 292474, Sacramento CA 95829-2474. **Editor:** Rebecca Treadway. Zine: digest size; 60-70 pages; 20 lb. bond paper. Specializes in sword & sorcery and medieval renaissance-based fantasy, heroic fantasy, gritty fantasy, adventure, epic fantasy and dark fantasy. Annually. Estab. 1994. Circ. 200.
Needs: Fantasy (sword and sorcery, epic). "No parody, short shorts, romance, science fiction or hybrid genres such as fantasy westerns and urban fantasy." Receives 20-30 unsolicited mss/month. Accepts 7-8 mss/issue; 24-30 mss/year. Publishes 3-6 months after acceptance. Length: 7,000 words maximum. Often critiques or comments on rejected mss.
How to Contact: Send complete ms with a cover letter. Include estimated word count and 1-paragraph bio. Reports in 2 weeks on queries; 1 month on mss. Send SASE for reply, return of ms or send a disposable copy of ms. Simultaneous submissions and reprints OK if indicated. Sample copy for $6. Fiction guidelines for #10 SASE.
Payment/Terms: Pays 1-2 contributor's copies; additional copies $3. Acquires one-time rights.
Advice: "When magic is the primary focus of the tale, I notice a manuscript more than the typical 'Barbarian Adventure.' Realistic, details in background and well-developed characters stand out. Read the guidelines thoroughly. This publication is very specific on this matter. If not purchasing a sample copy, be familiar with styles of authors I prefer—Tolkien, Howard, Eddings, etc. Don't listen to anyone but your own instincts—too many people today try to discourage writers, especially young genre-writers. I don't follow industry trends, neither should the writer. I'm not soft-skinned, I'm not easy to offend, but too many of my submissions have been light hearted with pouty women! I *don't* need that!"

☑ **SPUNK, The Journal of Spontaneous Creativity, (I, II)**, P.O. Box 55336, Hayward CA 94945. (510)278-6689. **Editor:** Sean Reinhart. Zine: 5½×8½; 30 pages; photocopied; illustrations and photos. "*Spunk* is dedicated to the publication of short creative outbursts with no pretensions or apprehensions—somewhere along the fine line between matter and energy lies *Spunk*." Semiannually. Estab. 1997. Circ. 500.
Needs: Experimental, literary. List of upcoming themes available for SASE. Receive 20 unsolicited mss/month. Accepts to 4-8 mss/issue; 10-20 mss/year. Publishes ms 6-12 months after acceptance. Recently published work by Violet Jones and Stephen Gutierrez. Length: 1,000 words average. "We love really good one-pagers." Also publishes literary essays and poetry. Sometimes critiques or comments on rejected mss.
How to Contact: Send complete ms with a cover letter. Reports in 6 months on mss. Send SASE for reply, return of ms. Simultaneous submissions OK. Sample copy for $2. Fiction guidelines for #10 SASE. Reviews novels and short story collections. Send books to editor.
Payment/Terms: Pays 1 contributor's copy for first North American serial rights.
Advice: "All work should be short, unique and above all Spunky. Obtain a sample copy, not necessarily to emulate our style, but to know if we're on the same planet or not."

☑ **STARK RAVING SANITY, (I, II)**. E-mail: srsmail@usa.net. Website: http://www.unf.edu/coas/lang-lit/srs. **Editor:** Mike S. Dubose. Electronic zine. "We have published short stories, poems, novel excerpts, prose poems, poetic prose, micro-fiction and everything in between. Our intended audience is anyone looking for an entertaining work of substance."

Needs: "Anything goes, as long as it fits our eclectic, ever changing tastes. We want works that illustrate a variant view of reality—but then again all works do just that. So anything of quality is what we like. No hate prose or porn." Recently published work by Joe Flowers, R.N. Friedland, Jonathan Lowe and Len Kruger. Publishes 2-3 new writers/year.

How to Contact: Electronic submissions accepted only. "Send 2-20 pages in the body of an e-mail message or as a text-only attachment (DOS or MS Word). Please read the guidelines (available online)."

Advice: "In taking fiction, I like (and look for) characters who act as if they are real, situations that are interesting, and writing that sings. I will accept first-time writers if the writing does not look like it came from a first-timer. In other words, I want quality. Please be professional. Read the journal. Read and follow the guidelines. And keep in mind also that we too are real people on schedules. Mutual respect, please."

☑ $ **STARSHIP EARTH, (I, II, IV)**, Black Moon Publishing, P.O. Box 484, Bellaire OH 43906. (740)671-3253. E-mail: shadowhors@aol.com. Editor: Kirin Lee. **Fiction Editor:** Silver Shadowhorse. Zine specializing in the sci-fi universe: 8½×11; 60 pages; glossy paper and cover; illustrations and photos. "We are mostly non-fiction with one piece of fiction per month." Monthly. Estab. 1995. Circ. 30,000.

- Sponsors contest. Send SASE for details.

Needs: Fantasy (science fantasy), science fiction (hard science, soft/sociological, historical). Wants more hard science fiction. No "sword and sorcery, religious, mystery or comedy." Publishes special fiction issues or anthologies. Receives 100-200 unsolicited mss/month. Accepts 1 ms/issue; 12 mss/year. Publishes ms 16-18 months after acceptance. Recently published work by Christy Malcovic, Duane Davis and Jonston Furgeson. Publishes 9 new writers/year. Length: 2,000-3,000 words average; 3,000 words maximum. Publishes short shorts. Sometimes critiques or comments on rejected mss.

How to Contact: Query or send complete ms with a cover letter. Include estimated word count, short bio and list of publications. Reports in 3 weeks on queries; 3-4 months on mss. Send SASE for reply, return of ms or send disposable copy of ms. Fiction guidelines for #10 SASE. Reviews novels and short story collections. Send books to Jenna Dawson.

Payment/Terms: Pays 1 cent/word minimum; 3 cents/word maximum plus 1 contributor's copy for first rights.

Advice: "Get our guidelines. Submit in the correct format. Send typed or computer printed manuscripts only. Avoid bad language, explicit sex and violence. Do not include any religious content. Manuscripts stand out when they are professionally presented."

STRONG COFFEE, (I, II), 5412 N. Clark Street, Chicago, IL 60640. (773) 989-0799. Fax: (773)989-5934. E-mail: coffee@strong-coffee.com. Website: http://www.strong-coffee.com. **Editor:** Martin Northway. Electronic and print zine. "*Strong Coffee* is a coffeehouse publication. Everything one would find in a coffeehouse, one can find in *Strong Coffee*: Art, poetry, fiction, photography, music, humor, politics, coffee, satire, whimsy and conversation, in no particular order or proportion. Like a coffeehouse habitué, each time our readers visit they may find old friends and acquaintances, interesting characters, a celebrity or two, or a whole new crop of faces. There is no agenda, only a forum for community and culture." 20,000 copies distributed free to 220 Chicago-area locations. Monthly.

Needs: Fiction; poetry; art; photography; essay; humor; satire; whimsy; interviews; book, music, art, dance and drama reviews; and "anything else we like." No genre fiction.Recently published work by Achy Obejas, Terry Jacobus, Vincent Tinguely, Witold Gombrowicz (Greg Pekala, trans.), Allen Ginsberg, Henry Hardee and Timothy Quinn. Publishes 10-30 new writers/year.

How to Contact: Send complete ms with SASE or send "as e-mail attachment, MS Word 6.0 or lower, WordPerfect 5.2 or lower, or RTF. If none of the above are available, then e-mail text is OK. In all cases, name, address and telephone must be included. Also, the submission must specify whether it is made for electronic publication only, print publication only or both forms of our publication. Those submitted for use in both media are more likely to be accepted."

Advice: "Short pieces are more likely to be published than long pieces, but we publish those too. Usually, nothing over 10 double-spaced pages gets published, but sometimes it does. We are more interested in quality than subject matter, length or genre. We publish conventional, experimental and non-categorizable fiction. If the piece makes us laugh or cry or think, it has a good chance. If it does all three, it's a shoo-in."

SWAGAZINE, (I, II), E-mail: swagazine@jamesclark.com. Website: http://www.swagazine.com. **Editor:** Jim Clark. Electronic zine. "*Swagazine* originated within the online community in Santa Barbara at a now defunct BBS we knew as Swagland. The personalities who graced our electronic medium shared messages of such considerable talent that we decided to pool our efforts, take on the world, and start a magazine of our own. Now, several years later, the BBS world has migrated to the Internet and so has our publication."

Needs: "There is no limitation on style, content or subject matter. *Swagazine* focuses on prose and poetry both as art forms and entertainment media. Social, philosophical and liberal political themes are dealt with, but not in a way that mimics news magazines or purely didactic writing. It is not our goal to educate our readers; we presume they are already educated. *Swagazine* attempts to examine the dynamic relationship between the mindand the voice; between the conscience of people and the standards of mass society; between the message of the endangered individual and the moronic giant of popular opinion." Recently published work by Colin Campbell, Jillian Firth, Ricky Garni, Michael Hoerman, AidanButler and Bryan Zepp Jamieson. Publishes 3-4 new writers/year.

How to Contact: Electronic submission only. "Submissions of poetry and prose should be in standard ASCII format as part of the message body. Attachments in alternate word-processor formats will be sent to the bottom of the consideration pile."

Payment/Terms: "Our electronic magazines are vehicles for aesthetic experiments and entertainment; we are not making money, so we cannot offer any to our submitters. What we do offer is participation in an artistic endeavor that will bring writers and artists together and into opposition; the artist becomes the art and the art is let out of the closet, the disk drive, and the soul."

Advice: "While it is our intent to spotlight our local talent, we are open to submissions from anyone, anywhere. If you would like to submit your prose, poetry, dramatic dialogue, or artwork to us, create freely and honestly. Trendiness is not valued; we probably wouldn't even recognize a fashionable approach if we saw it. Take all the risks you want; no subject matters are forbidden prima facie."

$ SYNAESTHESIA PRESS CHAPBOOK SERIES, (II), P.O. Box 641083, San Francisco CA 94164-1083. (415)908-6797. E-mail: books@synaethesia.com. Website: http://www.synaethesia.com (includes publication, bookstore, links). **Editor:** Jim Camp. Zine specializing in fiction: 16 pages; 50 lb. paper; card cover. Publishes fiction by new and established authors "writing outside the margin." Quarterly. Estab. 1995. Circ. 500.

Needs: Erotica, experimental, literary. No romance, children's, westerns, science fiction. Receives 10 unsolicited mss/month. Accepts 10 mss/year. Publishes ms 1-6 months after acceptance. Recently published work by Barry Gifford, Jack Micheline and A.D. Michele. Publishes 1 new writer/year. Length: 2,500 words maximum. Publishes short shorts. Also publishes literary essays, literary criticism and poetry.

How to Contact: Query first. Accepts queries/mss by e-mail. Include estimated word count. Reports in 1 week on queries. Send SASE for reply. Simultaneous, reprint and electronic submissions OK. Sample copy for $5. Fiction guidelines free. Reviews novels or short story collections. Send books to editor.

Payment/Terms: Pays $50 plus 3 contributor's copies. Sends galleys to author.

Advice: "Make it stand out. Hopefully, you are over 'anxiety of influence.' "

TELETALE, a Playground for Writers, (I). E-mail: campbell@highfiber.com. Website: http://www.us1.net/campbell. **Editor:** Harlen Campbell. Electronic zine. "*TeleTale* offers writers an opportunity to experiment with electronic media and publishing—everything from traditional through post-modernist, experimental and hypertext fiction, poetry or new forms. My desire is to provide a virtual work-bench upon which artists can prototype the literature of the 21st century—whatever that may turn out to be."

Needs: "Anything of interest to a literate, wired mind. Hypertext, linear or any other form. No hard-core porn. Recently published work by Walter Sorrels and Robert Weber.

How to Contact: Electronic submissions only. See website for details.

Advice: "For a work to be valuable, the reader must be more important to the writer than him or herself."

TRANSCENDENT VISIONS, (II), Toxic Evolution Press, 251 S. Olds Blvd., 84-E, Fairless Hills PA 19030-3426. (215)547-7159. **Editor:** David Kime. Zine: letter size; 24 pages; xerox paper; illustrations. "*Transcendent Visions* is a literary zine by and for people who have been labeled mentally ill. Our purpose is to illustrate how creative and articulate mental patients are." Quarterly. Estab. 1992. Circ. 200.

• *Transcendent Visions* has received excellent reviews in many underground publications.

Needs: Experimental, feminist, gay, humor/satire, lesbian. Especially interested in material dealing with mental illness. "I do not like stuff one would find in a mainstream publication. No porn." Receives 5 unsolicited mss/month. Accepts 7 mss/issue; 20 mss/year. Publishes ms 3-4 months after acceptance. Published work by Jim Reagan and Mike Stickel. Length: under 10 pages typed, double-spaced. Publishes short shorts. Also publishes poetry.

How to Contact: Send complete ms with cover letter. Include half-page bio. Reports in 2 weeks on queries; 1 month on mss. Send disposable copy of ms. Simultaneous submissions and reprints OK. Sample copy for $2.

Payment/Terms: Pays 1 contributor's copy on publication. Acquires one-time rights.

Advice: "We like unusual stories that are quirky. Please do not go on and on about what zines you have been published in or awards you have won, etc. We just want to read your material, not know your life story. Please don't swamp me with tons of submissions. Send up to five stories. Please print or type your name and address."

✓ THE UNKNOWN WRITER, (I, II), 5 Pothat St., Sloatsburg NY 10974. (914)753-8363. Fax: (914)753-6562. E-mail: dsdaviswriter@worldnet.att.net. **Editor:** D.S. Davis. Zine specializing in fiction, poetry, environ-

SENDING TO A COUNTRY other than your own? Be sure to send International Reply Coupons instead of stamps for replies or return of your manuscript.

mental issues: digest size; 40 pages; 24 lb. fiber paper; 80 lb. fiber cover stock; illustrations and photos. "*The Unknown Writer* is a forum for new writers and artists. Any subject matter and style goes as long as it's interesting." Triannually. Estab. 1995. Circ. 500.
Needs: Adventure, erotica, ethnic/multicultural, experimental, feminist, gay, historical (general), humor/satire, lesbian, literary, mainstream/contemporary, regional, sports, environmental issues. "Our zine is not really appropriate for children or young adults. We have little interest in science fiction or horror, religious and little room for condensed or serialized novels." Receives 20 unsolicited mss/month. Accepts 10 mss/issue; 30 mss/year. Publishes ms 3-5 months after acceptance. Recently published work by Satig Mesropian, Frank Scozzari and W. Royce Adams. Publishes 10 new writers/year. Length: 2,500 words average; 5,000 words maximum. Publishes short shorts. Also publishes literary essays, literary criticism and poetry.
How to Contact: Send complete ms with a cover letter. Include 100-word bio and list of publications. Accepts queries/mss by e-mail. Reports in 3 months. Send a disposable copy of ms. Simultaneous and electronic (disk or modem) submissions OK. Sample copy for $3, Writer's guidelines for #10 SASE. Reviews novels and short story collections.
Payment/Terms: Pays 2 contributor's copies; additional copies for $3. Acquires one-time rights. Not copyrighted.
Advice: "Almost anything goes but we prefer tightly written stories with good dialogue that are not impossible to follow. Write, rewrite and keep writing. When submitting your work, start with small stories and small publications and build your way up. If you're good, publishers will notice."

VIRGIN MEAT, (I), 2325 W.K 15, Lancaster CA 93536. (805)722-1758. E-mail: virginmeat@aol.com. **Editor:** Steve Blum. Gothic interactive computer e-zine. Published irregularly. Estab. 1987. Circ. 5,000.
Needs: Horror. Receives 3-4 mss/day. Length: 2,000 words maximum. Also publishes poetry, art, sound and QTM's.
How to Contact: Request writers' guidelines before your first submission. Submit mss via e-mail address above. Sample copy for $5.
Payment/Terms: Pays in contributor's copies. Acquires one-time rights. Publication not copyrighted.
Advice: "Horror fiction should be horrific all the way through, not just at the end. Avoid common settings, senseless violence and humor."

N **VOIDING THE VOID™, (I)**, 9 Menlo St., Brighton MA 02135. (617)783-4503. E-mail: mail@vvoid.com. Website: http://www.vvoid.com. **Editor:** E. Lippincott. Electronic zine and hard copy specializing in personal world views: 8½×11; 1 page; mock newsprint for hard copy. "A small reader specializing in individuals' fictional and nonfictional views of the world around them—as they personally experience it." Published every third Friday. Estab. 1997. Circ. 100 both in US and UK.
Needs: All categories. "We will consider anything the potential contributor feels is appropriate to the theme 'tangibility.' All fiction genres OK." Publishes holiday issues; submit at least 1 month prior to holiday. Receives 10-20 unsolicited mss/month. Accepts 3-10 mss/issue; 120 mss/year. Publishes ms immediately to 2 months after acceptance. Recently published work by Andrew Tiffen (UK), Brian Stuss, Barbara Lopez, Carey Lippincott, Erik Seims, Dan Budnik and Jenny Wu. Length: 2,000 words maximum. Publishes short shorts. Also publishes literary essays, literary criticism, poetry. Always critiques or comments on rejected ms.
How to Contact: Send complete ms with a cover letter; send electronic submissions via website or direct e-mail. Include estimated word count. Report in 2 weeks on queries; 6 weeks on mss. Send SASE for reply or return of ms. Simultaneous and reprint (with date and place indicated) submissions OK. Sample copy and fiction guidelines for #10 SASE. Reviews novels and short story collections
Payment/Terms: Pays 5 contributor's copies; additional copies 25¢. Acquires one-time rights. Not copyrighted.
Advice: "*Voiding the Void* is very small and has a very particular slant. This publication is not about the 'writing' or the 'art' so much as it is about the human being behind it all."

VOX, Because reaction is a sound, (I, II), Cleave Press, 1603 Hazeldine SE, Albuquerque NM 87106. Phone/fax: (505)764-8443. **Editor:** Robbyn Sanger. Zine: 8½×11; 64 pages; newsprint paper; illustrations and photos. "Say it like it is. (Enough said.)" Quarterly. Estab. 1994. Circ. 1,000.
Needs: Erotica, ethnic/multicultural, experimental, feminist, gay, humor/satire, lesbian, literary, opinions, translations. "No formula fiction." Upcoming themes: "Revenge" (deadline January 1999); "Sacrifice" (deadline May 1999); "Herspective" (deadline December 1999). Receives 50 mss/month. Buys 30 mss/issue; 60 mss/year. Publishes ms 4-24 months after acceptance. Published work by Jim Pritchard, Kevin Sampsell and Noel Franklin. Publishes 25 new writers/year. Length: 500 words average; 5 words minimum; 1,000 words maximum. Publishes short shorts. Length: 25 plus words. Sometimes critiques or comments on rejected ms.
How to Contact: Send complete ms with a cover letter. Include estimated word count and brief bio. Reports in 2-4 weeks on queries; 1-2 months on mss. Send SASE for reply, return of ms or send a disposable copy of ms. Simultaneous, reprint and electronic submissions OK. Sample copy for $2. Fiction guidelines free for legal SASE.
Payment/Terms: Pays 2 copies. Acquires one-time rights. Sends galleys to author (if requested). Not copyrighted.
Advice: "Get a sample copy before submitting! I love short shorts. Nothing plot-driven. Have a clearly defined

writing voice. Interesting characters, too. I see a lot of writing that seems self-important, stuff that says, 'I'm the author, look at what I know and what I can do.' I think writing should be about the piece itself, to make the writing stand out, not the author. If a reader is impressed by the piece, that in itself will draw attention to the author. Manuscripts stand out when they are actually thematically appropriate and within the word limit. A clean style helps a piece be selected. Write like you talk. Or like you think. (Don't write like you're writing . . . sometimes that brings an unnatural tension. Loosen up!)"

WIT'S END LITERARY CYBERZINE, (I, II). Fax: (702)648-7296. E-mail: myrddin@skylink.net. Website: http://www.geocities.com/WestHollywood/4128/index.htm. **Editor:** Richard A. Vanaman. Electronic zine. "To promote and encourage creativity amongst the Gay/Lesbian/Bisexual/Transgendered community."

Needs: Poetry, short stories, non-fiction, photography, art, comic strips targeted to the G/L/B/T community. No content containing hate, bigotry or prejudice. Recently published work by Hassan Galadari, Jameson Currier and Eric Hansen. Publishes 100 new writers/year.

How to Contact: Electronic submissions only. Ms should be sent as an e-mail attachment.

Advice: "Be creative, be yourself. And don't forget to include your copyright statement."

ZOTHIQUE, The Gargoyle Society Journal, (I, II). E-mail: lwild@viper.net.au. Website: http://www.viper.net.au/~/wild/zothique.html. Editor: Leon D. Wild. Electronic zine that publishes dark fantasy, weird horror, artificial mythology and the gothic imaginary.

Needs: Very short prose, poetry, articles and reviews. Recently published work by Don Webb, Marie Buckner and Azra Medea. Publishes 9 new writers/year.

How to Contact: Electronic submissions only. Send ms by e-mail.

Advice: "Write it from the perspective of 'the dark side.' Read some earlier issues to get an idea of what we are striving for."

READ THE BUSINESS OF FICTION WRITING section to learn the correct way to prepare and submit a manuscript.

Consumer Magazines

In this section of *Novel & Short Story Writer's Market* are consumer magazines with circulations of more than 10,000. Many have circulations in the hundreds of thousands or millions. Among the oldest magazines listed here are ones not only familiar to us, but also to our parents, grandparents and even great-grandparents: *The Atlantic Monthly* (1857); *Christian Century* (1900); *Redbook* (1903); *The New Yorker* (1925); *Analog Science Fiction & Fact* (1930); *Esquire* (1933); and *Jack and Jill* (1938).

Consumer periodicals make excellent markets for fiction in terms of exposure, prestige and payment. Because these magazines are well-known, however, competition is great. Even the largest consumer publications buy only one or two stories an issue, yet thousands of writers submit to these popular magazines.

Despite the odds, it is possible for talented new writers to break into print in the magazines listed here. Editors at *Redbook*, a top fiction market which receives up to 600 unsolicited submissions a month, say, "We are interested in new voices and buy up to a quarter of our stories from unsolicited submissions." The fact that *Redbook* and other well-respected publications such as *The Atlantic Monthly* and *The New Yorker* continue to list their fiction needs in *Novel & Short Story Writer's Market* from year to year indicates they are open to both new and established writers. Your keys to breaking into these markets are careful research, professional presentation and, of course, top-quality prose.

TYPES OF CONSUMER MAGAZINES

In this section you will find a number of popular publications, some for a broad-based, general-interest readership and others for large but select groups of readers—children, teenagers, women, men and seniors. Just a few of these publications include *Boys' Life*, *American Girl*, *Seventeen*, *Esquire*, *Harper's*, *Ladies' Home Journal* and *Mature Years*. You'll also find regional publications such as *Florida Wildlife*, *Georgia Journal*, *Yankee Magazine* and *Portland Magazine*.

Religious and church-affiliated magazines include *The Friend Magazine*, *New Era Magazine* and *Guideposts for Kids*. Other magazines are devoted to the interests of particular cultures and outlooks such as *African Voices*, publishing "enlightening and entertaining literature on the varied lifestyles of people of color," and *India Currents*, specializing in the "arts and culture of India as seen in America for Indians and non-Indians with a common interest in India."

Top markets for genre fiction include *Ellery Queen's Mystery Magazine*, *Alfred Hitchcock Mystery Magazine*, *Analog Science Fiction & Fact* and *Asimov's Science Fiction*. These magazines are known to book publishers as fertile ground for budding genre novelists.

SELECTING THE RIGHT MARKET

Unlike smaller journals and publications, most of the magazines listed here are available at newsstands and bookstores. Many can also be found in the library, and guidelines and sample copies are almost always available by mail. Start your search, then, by familiarizing yourself with the fiction included in the magazines that interest you.

Don't make the mistake of thinking, just because you are familiar with a magazine, that their fiction isn't any different today than when you first saw it. Nothing could be further from the truth—consumer magazines, no matter how well established, are constantly revising their fiction needs as they strive to reach new readers and expand their audience base.

In a magazine that uses only one or two stories an issue, take a look at the nonfiction articles and features as well. These can give you a better idea of the audience for the publication and clues to the type of fiction that might appeal to them.

If you write genre fiction, check out the specific sections for lists of magazines publishing in that genre (mystery, page 74; romance, page 92; science fiction and fantasy, page 103). For other types of fiction look in the Category Index beginning on page 632. There you will find a list of markets that say they are looking for a particular subject.

You may want to use our ranking codes as a guide, especially if you are a new writer. At the end of this introduction is a list of the Roman numeral codes we use and what they mean.

FURTHERING YOUR SEARCH

See How to Use This Book to Publish Your Fiction (page 3) for information about the material common to all listings in this book. In this section in particular, pay close attention to the number of submissions a magazine receives in a given period and how many they publish in the same period. This will give you a clear picture of how stiff your competition can be. Also, the ☆ symbol before a listing identifies markets that offer writers greater opportunities by buying a large amount of freelance/unagented manuscripts.

While many of the magazines listed here publish one or two pieces of fiction in each issue, some also publish special fiction issues once or twice a year. We have indicated this in the listing information. We also note if the magazine is open to novel excerpts as well as short fiction and we advise novelists to query first before submitting long work.

The Business of Fiction Writing, beginning on page 121, covers the basics of submitting your work. Professional presentation is a must for all markets listed. Editors at consumer magazines are especially busy, and anything you can do to make your manuscript easy to read and accessible will help your chances of being published. Most magazines want to see complete manuscripts, but watch for publications in this section that require a query first. Also read Queries That Made It Happen, beginning on page 107.

As in the previous section, we've included our own comments in many of the listings, set off by a bullet (●). Whenever possible, we list the publication's recent awards and honors. We've also included any special information we feel will help you in determining whether a particular publication interests you.

The maple leaf symbol (🍁) identifies our Canadian listings. You will also find some English-speaking markets from around the world. These foreign magazines are denoted with 🌐 at the beginning of the listings. Remember to use International Reply Coupons rather than stamps when you want a reply from a country other than your own.

FOR MORE INFORMATION

For more on consumer magazines, see issues of *Writer's Digest* and *Fiction Writer* (both by F&W Publications) and industry trade publications available in larger libraries.

For news about some of the genre publications listed here and information about a particular field, there are a number of magazines devoted to genre topics, including *The Mystery Review*, *Locus* (for science fiction) and *Science Fiction Chronicle*. Addresses for these and other industry magazines can be found in the Publications of Interest to Fiction Writers section of this book.

Membership in the national groups devoted to specific genre fields is not restricted to novelists and can be valuable to writers of short fiction in these fields. Many include awards for "Best Short Story" in their annual contests. For information on organizations for genre writers, see For Mystery Writers, page 76; For Romance Writers, page 94; and For Science Fiction & Fantasy Writers, page 106. Also see the Organizations section of this book.

The following is the ranking system we have used to categorize the periodicals in this section:

I Periodical encourages beginning or unpublished writers to submit work for consideration and publishes new writers regularly.
II Periodical accepts outstanding work by beginning and established writers.
III Hard to break into; periodical publishes mostly previously published writers.
IV Special-interest or regional magazine, open only to writers in certain genres or on certain subjects or from certain geographic areas.
V Periodical closed to unsolicited submissions.

$ AFRICAN VOICES, The Art and Literary Publication With Class & Soul, (I, II), African Voices Communications, Inc., 270 W. 96th St., New York NY 10025. (212)865-2982. Editor: Carolyn A. Butts. Managing Editor: Layding Kaliba. **Fiction Editor**: Gail Sharbaan. Magazine: 32 pages; illustrations and photos. "*AV* publishes enlightening and entertaining literature on the varied lifestyles of people of color." Quarterly. Estab. 1993. Circ. 20,000.

Needs: African-American: children's/juvenile (10-12 years), condensed/excerpted novel, erotica, ethnic/multicultural, gay, historical (general), horror, humor/satire, literary, mystery/suspense, psychic/supernatural/occult, religious/inspirational, science fiction, young adult/teen (adventure, romance). List of upcoming themes available for SASE. Publishes special fiction issue. Receives 20-50 unsolicited mss/month. Accepts 20 mss/issue. Publishes ms 3-6 months after acceptance. Agented fiction 5%. Published work by Junot Díaz, Michel Marriott and Carol Dixon. Length: 2,000 words average; 500 words minimum; 3,000 words maximum. Occasionally publishes short shorts. Also publishes literary essays and poetry.

How to Contact: Query with clips of published work. Include short bio. Reports in 6-12 weeks depending on backlog of queries; 2-3 months on mss. Send SASE for return of ms. Simultaneous, reprint and electronic submissions OK. Sample copy for $3 and 9×12 SASE. Free fiction guidelines. Reviews novels and short story collections. Send books to Book Editor.

Payment/Terms: Pays $25 maximum on publication for first North American serial rights, free subscription and 5 contributor's copies.

Advice: "A manuscript stands out if it is neatly typed with a well-written and interesting story line or plot. Originality encouraged. We are interested in more horror, erotic and drama pieces. *AV* wants to highlight the diversity in our culture. Stories must touch the humanity in us all."

✔ $ AIM MAGAZINE, (I, II), P.O. Box 1174, Maywood IL 60153. (773)874-6184. Fax: (206)543-2746. Editor: Myron Apilado, EdD. **Fiction Editor:** Mark Boone. Magazine: 8½×11; 48 pages; slick paper; photos and illustrations. Publishes material "to purge racism from the human bloodstream through the written word—that is the purpose of *Aim Magazine*." Quarterly. Estab. 1973. Circ. 10,000.

- *Aim* sponsors an annual short story contest.

Needs: Open. No "religious" mss. Published special fiction issue last year; plans another. Receives 25 unsolicited mss/month. Buys 15 mss/issue; 60 mss/year. Published work by Clayton Davis, Kenneth Nunn, Charles J. Wheelan, Estelle Lurie and Jesus Diaz. Publishes 40 new writers/year. Length: 800-1,000 words average. Publishes short shorts. Sometimes comments on rejected mss.

How to Contact: Send complete ms. Include SASE with cover letter and author's photograph. Simultaneous submissions OK. Reports in 1 month. Sample copy for $4 with SAE (9×12) and $1.80 postage. Fiction guidelines for #10 SASE.

Payment/Terms: Pays $15-25 on publication for first rights.

Advice: "Search for those who are making unselfish contributions to their community and write about them. Write about your own experiences. Be familiar with the background of your characters." Known for "stories with social significance, proving that people from different ethnic, racial backgrounds are more alike than they are different."

N $ AMAZING® STORIES, (II), Wizards of the Coast, P.O. Box 707, Renton WA 98057-0707. (425)204-6500. Website: http://www.wizards.com/Corporate_Info/Submissions_Amazing_Stories.html (includes fiction guidelines). **Editor:** Mr. Kim Mohan. Magazine: 8⅜×10¾; 96 pages; perfect-bound; color illustrations; rarely photos. Magazine of science fiction and fantasy stories for adults and young adults. Quarterly. Estab. 1926. Circ. 30,000.

Needs: Science fiction (hard science, soft/sociological), occasionally fantasy, rarely horror. "We prefer science fiction to dominate our content, but we will not turn away a well-written fantasy or horror piece. Low priority to heroic, pseudo-Medieval fantasy and stories derivative of folk tales; no gratuitous gore or offensive language."

Receives 250-300 unsolicited fiction mss/month. Accepts 6-8 mss/issue. Publishes ms 4-8 months after acceptance. Agented fiction less than 5%. Published work by Orson Scott Card, Kristine Kathryn Rusch, Ben Bova, Ursula K. Le Guin, Neal Barrett, Jr. and Jack Williamson; published new writers within the last year. Length: 1,000 words minimum; 8,000 words maximum; can go to 10,000 words for work of exceptional merit. Not actively seeking serializations or excerpts from longer works. Usually critiques rejected ms.
How to Contact: Send complete ms with a cover letter. Include list of other professional credits in the genre. Reports in 60 days. SASE. No simultaneous submissions. Sample copy for $8 (includes first-class postage and handling). Fiction guidelines for #10 SASE or available at website.
Payment/Terms: Pays 6-10¢/word on acceptance for first worldwide rights in the English language. Sends galleys to author.
Advice: "*AMAZING® Stories* has recently resumed publication after a three-year suspension. This incarnation of the magazine contains some media-related fiction based on properties such as *Star Trek* and *Babylon 5*, but we are not open to unsolicited submissions of this type of material. The bulk of the magazine continues to be devoted to original, non-media-related science fiction. Our taste is eclectic, but our standards are high—we appreciate innovations in style or content, as long as the work is internally consistent and comprehensible."

☑ $ **AMERICAN GIRL, (III)**, Pleasant Company Publications, 8400 Fairway Place, Middleton WI 53562. (608)836-4848. E-mail: readermail.ag.pleasantco.com. **Editor:** Sarah Jane Brian. Magazine: 8½×11; 52 pages; illustrations and photos. "Four-color bimonthly magazine for girls age 8-12." Estab. 1991. Circ. 700,000.

- Pleasant Company is known for its series of books featuring girls from different periods of American history.

Needs: Children's/juvenile (girls 8-12 years): "contemporary, realistic fiction, adventure, historical, problem stories." No romance, science fiction, fantasy. Receives 100 unsolicited mss/month. Accepts 1 ms/year. Length: 2,300 words maximum. Publishes short shorts. Also publishes literary essays and poetry (if age appropriate).
How to Contact: Query with published samples. Include bio (1 paragraph). Send SASE for reply, return of ms or send a disposable copy of ms. Simultaneous submissions OK. Sample copy for $3.95 plus $1.93 postage.
Payment/Terms: Pays in cash; amount negotiable. Pays on acceptance for first North American serial rights. Sends galleys to author.

☑ 🏆 $ **ANALOG SCIENCE FICTION & FACT, (II)**, Dell Magazines, 1270 Avenue of the Americas, New York NY 10020. (212)698-1381. Fax: (212)698-1198. E-mail: analogsf@erols.com. Website: http://www.sfsite.com. **Editor:** Stanley Schmidt. Magazine: 5⅜×8½; 140 pages; illustrations (drawings); photos. "Well-written science fiction based on speculative ideas and fact articles on topics of the present and future frontiers of research. Our readership includes intelligent laymen and/or those professionally active in science and technology." Published 11 times yearly. Estab. 1930. Circ. 60,000.

- *Analog* is considered one of the leading science fiction publications. The magazine has won a number of Hugos, Chesleys and Nebula Awards. *Analog* ranked #34 on the *Writer's Digest*'s Fiction 50 list of top markets for fiction writers.

Needs: Science fiction (hard science, soft sociological) and serialized novels. "No stories which are not truly science fiction in the sense of having a plausible speculative idea *integral to the story.* We would like to see good humor that is also good, solid science fiction. We do one double-size issue per year (July)." Receives 300-500 unsolicited fiction mss/month. Accepts 4-8 mss/issue. Agented fiction 20%. Recently published work by Joan Slonczewski, Ben Bova, Maya Kaathryn Bonnhoff, Jerry Oltion, Paul Levinson and Timothy Zahn. Publishes 5-10 new writers/year. Length: 2,000-80,000 words. Publishes short shorts. Critiques rejected mss "when there is time." Sometimes recommends other markets.
How to Contact: Send complete ms with SASE. Include cover letter with "anything that I need to know before reading the story, e.g. that it's a rewrite I suggested or that it incorporates copyrighted material. Otherwise, no cover letter is needed." Query with SASE only on serials. Reports in 1 month on both query and ms. No simultaneous submissions. Fiction guidelines for SASE. Sample copy for $4. Reviews novels and short story collections. Send books to Tom Easton.
Payment/Terms: Pays 5-8¢/word on acceptance for first North American serial rights and nonexclusive foreign rights. Sends galleys to author.
Advice: Mss are rejected because of "inaccurate science; poor plotting, characterization or writing in general. We literally only have room for 1-2% of what we get. Many stories are rejected not because of anything conspicuously *wrong*, but because they lack anything sufficiently *special*. What we buy must stand out from the crowd. Fresh, thought-provoking ideas are important. Familiarize yourself with the magazine—but don't try to imitate what we've already published."

🍁 $ **THE ANNALS OF ST. ANNE DE BEAUPRÉ, (II)**, Redemptorist Fathers, P.O. Box 1000, St. Anne de Beaupré, Quebec G0A 3C0 Canada. (418)827-4538. Fax: (418)827-4530. **Editor:** Father Roch Achard, C.Ss.R. Magazine: 8×11; 32 pages; glossy paper; photos. "Our aim is to promote devotion to St. Anne and Catholic family values." Monthly. Estab. 1878. Circ. 50,000.
Needs: Religious/inspirational. "We only wish to see something inspirational, educational, objective, uplifting. Reporting rather than analysis is simply not remarkable." Receives 50-60 unsolicited mss/month. Published work

by Beverly Sheresh, Eugene Miller and Aubrey Haines. Publishes short stories. Length: 1,500 maximum. Always critiques or comments on rejected ms.
How to Contact: Send complete ms with a cover letter. Include estimated word count. Reports in 3 weeks. Send SASE for reply or return of ms. No simultaneous submissions. Free sample copy and guidelines.
Payment/Terms: Pays 3-4¢/word on acceptance and 3 contributor's copies on publication for first North American serial rights.

APPALACHIA JOURNAL, (II, IV), Appalachian Mountain Club, 5 Joy St., Boston MA 02108. (617)523-0636. Editor: Sandy Stott. Magazine: 6×9; 160 pages; 60 lb. recycled paper; 10 pt. CS1 cover; 5-10 illustrations; 20-30 photographs. "*Appalachia* is the oldest mountaineering and conservation journal in the country. It specializes in backcountry recreation and conservation topics (hiking, canoeing, cross-country skiing, etc.) for outdoor (including armchair) enthusiasts." Semiannually (June and December). Estab. 1876. Circ. 15,000.
Needs: Prose, poem, sports. Receives 5-10 unsolicited mss/month. Accepts 1-2 mss/issue; 2-4 mss/year. Publishes ms 6-12 months after acceptance. Length: 500-4,000 words average. Publishes short shorts.
How to Contact: Send complete ms with cover letter. No simultaneous submissions. Reports in 1 month on queries; 3 months on mss. SASE (or IRC) for query. Sample copy for $5. Fiction guidelines for #10 SAE.
Payment/Terms: Pays contributor's copies. Occasionally pays $100-300 for a feature—usually assigned.
Advice: "All submissions should be related to conservation, mountaineering, and/or backcountry recreation both in the Northeast and throughout the world. Most of our journal is nonfiction. The fiction we publish is mountain-related and often off-beat. Send us material that says, I went to the wilderness and *thought* this; not I went there and did this."

N $ ART TIMES, A Literary Journal and Resource for All the Arts, (II), P.O. Box 730, Mt. Marion NY 12456. Phone/fax: (914)246-6944. **Editor:** Raymond J. Steiner. Magazine: 12×15; 20 pages; Jet paper and cover; illustrations; photos. "Arts magazine covering the disciplines for an over-40, affluent, arts-conscious and literate audience." Monthly. Estab. 1984. Circ. 18,000.
Needs: Adventure, contemporary, ethnic, fantasy, feminist, gay, historical, humor/satire, lesbian, literary, mainstream and science fiction. "We seek quality literary pieces. Nothing violent, sexist, erotic, juvenile, racist, romantic, political, etc." Receives 30-50 mss/month. Accepts 1 ms/issue; 11 mss/year. Publishes ms within 48-60 months of acceptance. Publishes 1-5 new writers/year. Length: 1,500 words maximum. Publishes short shorts.
How to Contact: Send complete ms with cover letter. Simultaneous submissions OK. Reports in 6 months. SASE. Sample copy for $1.75, 9×12 SAE and 3 first-class stamps. Fiction guidelines for #10 SASE.
Payment/Terms: Pays $25, free one-year subscription to magazine and 6 contributor's copies on publication for first North American serial rights.
Advice: "Competition is greater (more submissions received), but keep trying. We print new as well as published writers."

☆ $ ASIMOV'S SCIENCE FICTION, (II), 1270 Avenue of the Americas, New York NY 10020. (212)698-1313. E-mail: asimovs@erols.com. Website: http://www.asimovs.com (includes guidelines, names of editors, short fiction, interviews with authors, editorials, and more). **Editor:** Gardner Dozois. Executive Editor: Sheila Williams. Magazine: 5⅜×8½ (trim size); 144 pages; 30 lb. newspaper; 70 lb. to 8 pt. C1S cover stock; illustrations; rarely photos. Magazine consists of science fiction and fantasy stories for adults and young adults. Publishes "the best short science fiction available." Estab. 1977. Circ. 50,000. 11 issues/year (one double issue).

- Named for a science fiction "legend," *Asimov's* regularly receives Hugo and Nebula Awards. Editor Gardner Dozois has received several awards for editing including Hugos and those from *Locus* and *Science Fiction Chronicle* magazines. This publication ranked #14 on *Writer's Digest*'s Fiction 50 list of top markets for fiction writers.

Needs: Science fiction (hard science, soft sociological), fantasy. No horror or psychic/supernatural. Receives approximately 800 unsolicited fiction mss each month. Accepts 10 mss/issue. Publishes ms 6-12 months after acceptance. Agented fiction 10%. Published work by Robert Silverberg, Connie Willis and Greg Egan. Publishes 6 new writers/year. Length: up to 20,000 words. Publishes short shorts. Critiques rejected mss "when there is time."
How to Contact: Send complete ms with SASE. No simultaneous submissions. Reports in 2-3 months. Fiction guidelines for #10 SASE. Sample copy for $3.50 and 9×12 SASE. Reviews novels and short story collections. Send books to Book Reviewer.
Payment/Terms: Pays 6-8¢/word for stories up to 7,500 words; 5¢/word for stories over 12,500; $450 for stories between those limits. Pays on acceptance for first North American serial rights plus specified foreign rights, as explained in contract. Very rarely buys reprints. Sends galleys to author.
Advice: "We are looking for character stories rather than those emphasizing technology or science. New writers will do best with a story under 10,000 words. Every new science fiction or fantasy film seems to 'inspire' writers—and this is not a desirable trend. Be sure to be familiar with our magazine and the type of story we like; workshops and lots of practice help. Try to stay away from trite, cliched themes. Start in the middle of the action, starting as close to the end of the story as you possibly can. We like stories that extrapolate from up-to-date scientific research, but don't forget that we've been publishing clone stories for decades. Ideas must be fresh."

$ THE ASSOCIATE REFORMED PRESBYTERIAN, (II, IV), The Associate Reformed Presbyterian, Inc., 1 Cleveland St., Greenville SC 29601. (864)232-8297. **Editor:** Ben Johnston. Magazine: 8½×11; 32-48 pages; 50 lb. offset paper; illustrations; photos. "We are the official magazine of our denomination. Articles generally relate to activities within the denomination—conferences, department work, etc., with a few special articles that would be of general interest to readers." Monthly. Estab. 1976. Circ. 6,100.

Needs: Contemporary, juvenile, religious/inspirational, spiritual, young adult/teen. "Stories should portray Christian values. No retelling of Bible stories or 'talking animal' stories. Stories for youth should deal with resolving real issues for young people." Receives 30-40 unsolicited fiction mss/month. Accepts 10-12 mss/year. Publishes ms within 1 year after acceptance. Published work by Lawrence Dorr, Jan Johnson and Deborah Christensen. Length: 300-750 words (children); 1,250 words maximum (youth). Sometimes critiques rejected mss.

How to Contact: Include cover letter. Reports in 6 weeks on queries and mss. Simultaneous submissions OK. Sample copy for $1.50; fiction guidelines for #10 SASE.

Payment/Terms: Pays $20-75 for first rights and contributor's copies.

Advice: "Currently we are seeking stories aimed at the 10 to 15 age group. We have an oversupply of stories for younger children."

$ THE ATLANTIC MONTHLY, (I, II), 77 N. Washington St., Boston MA 02114. (617)854-7700. Editor: William Whitworth. **Senior Editors:** Michael Curtis, Jack Beatty, Barbara Wallraff and Corby Kummer. Managing Editor: Cullen Murphy. General magazine for the college educated with broad cultural interests. Monthly. Estab. 1857. Circ. 450,000.

- Work published in *The Atlantic Monthly* has been selected for inclusion in Best American Short Stories and O. Henry Prize anthologies for 1995. The *Atlantic Monthly* ranked #1 on *Writer's Digest*'s Fiction 50 list of top markets for fiction writers.

Needs: Literary and contemporary. "Seeks fiction that is clear, tightly written with strong sense of 'story' and well-defined characters." Accepts 15-18 stories/year. Receives 1,000 unsolicited fiction mss each month. Published work by Alice Munro, E.S. Goldman, Charles Baxter and T.C. Boyle; published new writers within the last year. Preferred length: 2,000-6,000 words.

How to Contact: Send cover letter and complete ms with SASE. Reports in 2 months on mss.

Payment/Terms: Pays $2,500/story on acceptance for first North American serial rights.

Advice: When making first contact, "cover letters are sometimes helpful, particularly if they cite prior publications or involvement in writing programs. Common mistakes: melodrama, inconclusiveness, lack of development, unpersuasive characters and/or dialogue."

$ BALLOON LIFE, The Magazine for Hot Air Ballooning, (II, IV), 2336 47th Ave., SW, Seattle WA 98116. (206)935-3649. Fax: (206)935-3326. E-mail: tom@balloonlife.com. Website: http://www.balloonlife.com/ (includes guidelines, sample issues). **Editor:** Tom Hamilton. Magazine: 8½×11; 48 pages; color, b&w photos. Publishes material "about the sport of hot air ballooning. Readers participate in hot air ballooning as pilots, crew, official observers at events and spectators."

Needs: Humor/satire, related to hot air ballooning. "Manuscripts should involve the sport of hot air ballooning in any aspect. Prefer humor based on actual events; fiction seldom published." Accepts 4-6 mss/year. Publishes ms within 3-4 months after acceptance. Length: 800 words minimum; 1,500 words maximum; 1,200 words average. Publishes short shorts. Length: 400-500 words. Sometimes critiques rejected mss and recommends other markets.

How to Contact: Send complete ms with cover letter that includes Social Security number. Accepts queries/mss by e-mail and fax (ms by permission only). Reports in 3 weeks on queries; 2 weeks on mss. SASE. Simultaneous and reprint submissions OK. Sample copy for 9×12 SAE and $1.94 postage. Guidelines for #10 SASE.

Payment/Terms: Pays $25-75 and contributor's copies on publication for first North American serial, one-time or other rights.

Advice: "Generally the magazine looks for humor pieces that can provide a light-hearted change of pace from the technical and current event articles. An example of a work we used was titled 'Balloon Astrology' and dealt with the character of a hot air balloon based on what sign it was born (made) under."

$ THE BEAR DELUXE MAGAZINE, (I, II) (formerly *The Bear Essential Magazine*), ORLO, 2516 NW 29th, P.O. Box 10342, Portland OR 97296. (503)242-1047. Fax: (503)243-2645. E-mail: bear@orlo.org. **Editor:** Thomas L. Webb. Magazine: 11×14; 72 pages; newsprint paper; Kraft paper cover; illustrations and photos. "*The Bear Deluxe* has an environmental focus, combining all forms and styles. Fiction should have environmental thread to it and should be engaging to a cross-section of audiences. The more street-level, the better." Quarterly. Estab. 1993. Circ. 17,000.

- *The Bear Deluxe* has received a publishing grant from the Oregon Council for the Humanities.

Needs: Environmentally focused: humor/satire, literary, science fiction. "We would like to see more nontraditional forms." List of upcoming themes available for SASE. Receives 10-20 unsolicited mss/month. Accepts 2-3 mss/issue; 4-6 mss/year. Publishes ms 2 months after acceptance. Recently published work by David James Duncan, Robert Michael Pyle and Judith Barrington. Publishes 3-5 new writers/year. Length: 2,500 words average; 900 words minimum; 4,500 words maximum. Publishes short shorts. Also publishes literary essays, literary criticism, poetry, reviews, opinion, investigative journalism, interviews and creative nonfiction. Sometimes critiques or comments on rejected mss.

How to Contact: Send complete ms with a cover letter. Include estimated word count, 10 to 15-word bio, list of publications, copy on disk, if possible. Accepts queries/mss by e-mail (mss by permission only). Reports in 1 month on queries; 3 months on mss. Send a disposable copy of mss. Simultaneous and electronic (disk is best, then e-mail) submissions OK. Sample copy for $3, 7½×11 SAE and 5 first-class stamps. Fiction guidelines for #10 SASE. Reviews novels and short story collections. Send SASE for "Edward Abbey" fiction contest.

Payment/Terms: Pays free subscription to the magazine, contributor's copies and 5¢ per published word; additional copies for postage. Acquires first or one-time rights. Sends galleys to author. Not copyrighted. Sponsors contests and awards for fiction writers.

Advice: "Keep sending work. Write actively and focus on the connections of man, nature, etc., not just flowery descriptions. Urban and suburban environments are grist for the mill as well. Have not seen enough quality humorous and ironic writing. Juxtaposition of place welcome. Action and hands-on great. Not all that interested in environmental ranting and simple 'walks through the park.' Make it powerful, yet accessible to a wide audience."

$ BOMB MAGAZINE, (II), New Art Publications, 594 Broadway, Suite 905, New York NY 10012. (212)431-3943. Fax: (212)431-5880. E-mail: bomb@echonyc.com. **Editor-in-Chief:** Betsy Sussler. Associate Editor: Suzan Sherman. Magazine: 11×14; 104 pages; 70 lb. glossy cover; illustrations and photographs. Publishes "work which is unconventional and contains an edge, whether it be in style or subject matter." Quarterly. Estab. 1981.

Needs: Contemporary, experimental, serialized novel. No genre: romance, horror, western. Receives 50 unsolicited mss/week. Accepts 6 mss/issue; 24 mss/year. Publishes ms 3-6 months after acceptance. Agented fiction 70%. Published work by Jim Lewis, AM Homes, Sandra Cisneros and Leslie Dick. Publishes 8 new writers/year. Length: 10-12 pages average. Publishes interviews.

How to Contact: Send complete ms up to 25 pages in length with cover letter. Reports in 4 months on mss. SASE. Sample copy for $4.50 with $1.67 postage.

Payment/Terms: Pays $100 and contributor's copies on publication for first or one-time rights. Sends galleys to author.

Advice: "We are committed to publishing new work that commercial publishers often deem too dangerous or difficult. The problem is, a lot of young writers confuse difficult with dreadful. Read the magazine before you even think of submitting something."

$ BOSTON REVIEW, A political and literary forum, (II), Boston Critic Inc., E53-407, MIT, Cambridge MA 02139. (617)253-3642. Fax: (617)252-1549. E-mail: bostonreview@mit.edu. Website: http://www-polisci.mit.edu/bostonreview/ (includes full issue 1 month after publication, poetry and fiction links page, guidelines and contests guidelines, bookstore listing and subscription info). Editor: Joshua Cohen. **Fiction Editor:** Jodi Daynard. A bimonthly magazine "providing a forum of ideas in politics, literature and culture. Essays, reviews, poetry and fiction are published in every issue. Audience is well educated and interested in under recognized writers." Magazine: 10¾×14¾; 56 pages; newsprint. Estab. 1975. Circ. 30,000.

• *Boston Review* is the recipient of a Pushcart Prize in poetry.

Needs: Contemporary, ethnic, experimental, literary, prose poem, regional, translations. No romance, erotica, genre fiction. Receives 150 unsolicited fiction mss/month. Buys 4-6 mss/year. Publishes ms an average of 4 months after acceptance. Published work by Harry Mathews and W.D. Wetherell. Length: 4,000 words maximum; 2,000 words average. Occasionally critiques rejected ms.

How to Contact: Send complete ms with cover letter and SASE. "You can almost always tell professional writers by the very thought-out way they present themselves in cover letters. But even a beginning writer should find some link between the work (its style, subject, etc.) and the publication—some reason why the editor should consider publishing it." Accepts queries by e-mail. Reports in 2-4 months. Simultaneous submissions OK (if noted). Sample copy for $4.50. Reviews novels and short story collections. Send books to Matthew Howard, managing editor.

Payment/Terms: Pays $50-100 and 5 contributor's copies after publication for first rights.

Advice: "I'm looking for stories that are emotionally and intellectually substantive and also interesting on the level of language. Things that are shocking, dark, lewd, comic, or even insane are fine so long as the fiction is *controlled* and purposeful in a masterly way. Subtlety, delicacy and lyricism are attractive too. Work tirelessly

FOR EXPLANATIONS OF THESE SYMBOLS,
SEE THE INSIDE FRONT AND BACK COVERS OF THIS BOOK.

to make the work truly polished before you send it out. Make sure you know the publication you're submitting to—don't send blind."

$ BOWHUNTER MAGAZINE, The Number One Bowhunting Magazine, (IV), Cowles Enthusiast Media Inc., 6405 Flank Dr., Harrisburg PA 17112. (717)657-9555. Fax: (717)657-9526. Founder/Editor-in-Chief: M.R. James. Associate Publisher/Editorial Director: Richard Cochran. **Editor:** Dwight Schuh. Magazine: 8×10½; 150 pages; 75 lb. glossy paper; 150 lb. glossy cover stock; illustrations and photographs. "We are a special interest publication for people who hunt with the bow and arrow. We publish hunting adventure and how-to stories. Our audience is predominantly male, 30-50, middle income." Bimonthly. Circ. 200,000.

• Themes included in most fiction considered for *Bowhunter* are pro-conservation as well as pro-hunting.

Needs: Bowhunting, outdoor adventure. "Writers must expect a very limited market. We buy only one or two fiction pieces a year. Writers must know the market—bowhunting—and let that be the theme of their work. No 'me and my dog' types of stories; no stories by people who have obviously never held a bow in their hands." Receives 25 unsolicited fiction mss/month. Accepts 30 mss/year. Publishes ms 3 months to 2 years after acceptance. Length: 1,500 words average; 500 words minimum; 2,000 words maximum. Publishes short shorts. Length: 500 words. Sometimes critiques rejected mss and recommends other markets.

How to Contact: Query first or send complete ms with cover letter. Reports in 2 weeks on queries; 1 month on mss. Sample copy for $2 and 8½×11 SAE with appropriate postage. Fiction guidelines for #10 SASE.

Payment/Terms: Pays $100-350 on acceptance for first worldwide serial rights.

Advice: "We have a resident humorist who supplies us with most of the 'fiction' we need. But if a story comes through the door which captures the essence of bowhunting and we feel it will reach out to our readers, we will buy it. Despite our macho outdoor magazine status, we are a bunch of English majors who love to read. You can't bull your way around real outdoor people—they can spot a phony at 20 paces. If you've never camped out under the stars and listened to an elk bugle and try to relate that experience without really experiencing it, someone's going to know. We are very specialized; we don't want stories about shooting apples off people's heads or of Cupid's arrow finding its mark. James Dickey's *Deliverance* used bowhunting metaphorically, very effectively . . . while we don't expect that type of writing from everyone, that's the kind of feeling that characterizes a good piece of outdoor fiction."

✓ $ BOYS' LIFE, For All Boys, (II), Boy Scouts of America, Magazine Division, Box 152079, 1325 W. Walnut Hill Lane, Irving TX 75015-2079. (214)580-2000. **Fiction Editor:** Shannon Lowry. Magazine: 8×11; 68 pages; slick cover stock; illustrations; photos. "*Boys' Life* covers Boy Scout activities and general interest subjects for ages 8 to 18, Boy Scouts, Cub Scouts and others of that age group." Monthly. Estab. 1911. Circ. 1,300,000.

• Boy's Life ranked #3 on *Writer's Digest*'s Fiction 50 list of top fiction markets for writers.

Needs: Adventure, humor/satire, mystery/suspense (young adult), science fiction, sports, western (young adult), young adult. "We publish short stories aimed at a young adult audience and frequently written from the viewpoint of a 10- to 16-year-old boy protagonist." Receives approximately 150 unsolicited mss/month. Buys 12-18 mss/year. Published work by Donald J. Sobol, Geoffrey Norman, G. Clifton Wisler and Marlys Stapelbroek; published new writers within the last year. Length: 500 words minimum; 1,500 words maximum; 1,200 words average. "Very rarely" critiques rejected ms.

How to Contact: Send complete ms with SASE. "We'd much rather see manuscripts than queries." Reports in 6-8 weeks. No simultaneous submissions. For sample copy "check your local library." Writer's guidelines available; send SASE.

Payment/Terms: Pays $750 and up ("depending on length and writer's experience with us") on acceptance for one-time rights.

Advice: "*Boys' Life* writers understand the readers. They treat them as intelligent human beings with a thirst for knowledge and entertainment. We tend to use some of the same authors repeatedly because their characters, themes, etc., develop a following among our readers. Read at least a year's worth of the magazine. You will get a feeling for what our readers are interested in and what kind of fiction we buy."

$ BUGLE, Journal of Elk and the Hunt, (II, IV), Rocky Mountain Elk Foundation, P.O. Box 8249, Missoula MT 59807-8249. (406)523-4570. Fax: (406)523-4550. E-mail: lcromrich@rmef.org. Website: http://www.rmef.org. **Editor:** Dan Crockett. Editorial Assistant: Lee Cromrich. Magazine: 8½×11; 114-172 pages; 55 lb. Escanaba paper; 80 lb. sterling cover; b&w, 4-color illustrations and photographs. "The Rocky Mountain Elk Foundation is a nonprofit conservation organization established in 1984 to help conserve critical habitat for elk and other wildlife. *BUGLE* specializes in research, stories (fiction and nonfiction), art and photography pertaining to the world of elk and elk hunting." Bimonthly. Estab. 1984.

Needs: Elk-related adventure, children's/juvenile (5-9 years, 10-12 years), historical, human interest, natural history, scientific. "We would like to see more humor. No formula outdoor or how-to writing." Upcoming themes; "Bowhunting" and "Women in the Outdoors." Receives 10-15 unsolicited mss/month. Accepts 5 mss/issue; 18-20 mss/year. Publishes ms 6 months after acceptance. Published work by Don Burgess and Mike Logan. Publishes 10 new writers/year. Length: 2,500 words preferred; 1,500 words minimum; 5,000 words maximum. Publishes short shorts. Also publishes literary essays and poetry.

How to Contact: Query first or send complete ms with a cover letter. Accepts queries/mss by e-mail and fax

(ms by permission only). Include estimated word count and bio (100 words). Reports in 2-4 weeks on queries; 4-6 weeks on ms. Send SASE for reply, return of ms or send a disposable copy of ms. Sample copy for $5. Writers guidelines free.
Payment/Terms: Pays 25¢/word maximum on acceptance for one-time rights.
Advice: "We accept fiction and nonfiction stories about elk that show originality, and respect for the animal and its habitat."

$ CALLIOPE, World History for Young People, (II, IV), Cobblestone Publishing, Inc., 30 Grove St., Suite C, Peterborough NH 03458. (603)924-7209. **Editor:** Rosalie Baker. Department. Magazine. "*Calliope* covers world history (east/west) and lively, original approaches to the subject are the primary concerns of the editors in choosing material. For 8-14 year olds." Monthly except June, July, August. Estab. 1990. Circ. 11,000.

- Cobblestone Publishing also publishes the children's magazines *Cobblestone, Faces, Odyssey* and *Appleseeds* listed in this book. *Calliope* has received the Ed Press Golden Lamp and One-Theme Issue awards.

Needs: Material must fit upcoming theme; write for themes and deadlines. Childrens/juvenile (8-14 years). "Authentic historical and biographical fiction, adventure, retold legends, etc. relating to the theme." Send SASE for guidelines and theme list. Published after theme deadline. Recently published work by Duane Damon and Amita V. Sarin. Publishes 5-10 new writers/year. Length: 800 words maximum. Publishes short shorts. Also publishes poetry.
How to Contact: Query first or query with clips of published work (if new to *Calliope*). Include a brief cover letter stating estimated word count and 1-page outline explaining information to be presented, extensive bibliography of materials used. Reports in several months (if interested, response 5 months before publication date). Send SASE (or IRC) for reply (writers may send a stamped reply postcard to find out if query has been received). Sample copy for $4.50, 7½×10½ SAE and $1.05 postage. Guidelines for #10 SAE and 1 first-class stamp.
Payment/Terms: Pays 20-25¢/word.
Terms: Pays on publication for all rights.
Advice: "We look for fiction that exhibits a grasp of details; the ability to include fact and fiction without on over-abundance of description. Research your topic/theme well, read and reread your query, and make sure your facts are accurate."

$ CAMPUS LIFE MAGAZINE, (II), Christianity Today, Inc., 465 Gundersen Dr., Carol Stream IL 60188. (630)260-6200. Fax: (630)260-0114. E-mail: cledit@aol.com. Website: http://www.christianity.net/campuslife. **Managing Editor:** Christopher Lutes. Magazine: 8¼×11¼; 100 pages; 4-color and b&w illustrations; 4-color and b&w photos. "General interest magazine with a Christian point of view." Articles "vary from serious to humorous to current trends and issues, for high school and college age readers." Bimonthly. Estab. 1942. Circ. 100,000.

- *Campus Life* regularly receives awards from the Evangelical Press Association.

Needs: "All fiction submissions must be contemporary, reflecting the teen experience in the '90s. We are a Christian magazine but are *not* interested in sappy, formulaic, sentimentally religious stories. We *are* interested in well-crafted stories that portray life realistically, stories high school and college youth relate to. Writing must reflect a Christian world view. If you don't understand our market and style, don't submit." Accepts 5 mss/year. Reading and response time slower in summer. Published work by Barbara Durkin and Tracy Dalton. Published new writers within the last year. Length: 1,000-2,000 words average, "possibly longer."
How to Contact: Query with short synopsis of work, published samples and SASE. Does not accept unsolicited mss. Reports in 4-6 weeks on queries. Sample copy for $2 and 9½×11 envelope.
Payment/Terms: Pays "generally" 15-20¢/word; 2 contributor's copies on acceptance for one-time rights.
Advice: "We print finely-crafted fiction that carries a contemporary teen (older teen) theme. First person fiction often works best. Ask us for sample copy with fiction story. Fiction communicates to our reader. We want experienced fiction writers who have something to say to or about young people without getting propagandistic."

$ CAPPER'S, (II), Ogden Publications, Inc. 1503 S.W. 42nd St., Topeka KS 66609-1265. (785)274-4346. Fax: (785)274-4305. E-mail: cappers@kspress.com. Website: http://www.cappers.com (includes sample items from publication and subscription information). **Editor:** Ann Crahan. Magazine: 32-48 pages; newsprint paper and cover stock; photos. A "clean, uplifting and nonsensational newspaper for families, from children to grandparents." Biweekly. Estab. 1879. Circ. 250,000.

- *Capper's* is interested in longer works, 7,000 words or more. They would like to see more stories with older characters.

Needs: Serialized novels suitable for adults to seniors. "We accept novel-length stories for serialization. No fiction containing violence, sexual references or obscenity. We would like to see more western romance, pioneer stories." Receives 2-3 unsolicited fiction mss each month. Accepts 4-6 stories/year. Recently published work by C.J. Sargent and Mona Exinger. Published new writers within the last year. Length: 7,000 words minimum; 40,000 words maximum.
How to Contact: Send complete ms with SASE. Cover letter and/or synopsis helpful. Reports in 6-8 months on ms. Sample copy for $1.50.

Payment/Terms: Pays $75-300 for one-time serialization and contributor's copies (1-2 copies as needed for copyright) on acceptance for second serial (reprint) rights and one-time rights.
Advice: "Since we publish in serialization, be sure your manuscript is suitable for that format. Each segment needs to be compelling enough so the reader remembers it and is anxious to read the next installment. Please proofread and edit carefully. We've seen major characters change names partway through the manuscript."

$ CHAT, King's Reach Tower, Stamford St., London SE1 9LS England. **Fiction Editor:** Olwen Rice. Weekly. Circ. 550,000.
Needs: Publishes mysteries, thrillers, science fiction and romance. Publishes 1 story/issue; 1 Christmas issue; 1 Summer special. Length: 700 words maximum.
How to Contact: "I accept and buy fiction from anyone, anywhere. Send material with reply coupons if you want your story returned."
Payment/Terms: Payment "negotiated with the fiction editor and made by cheque." Call or write editor for sample copy. Writer's guidelines available for SAE and IRCs.

$ CHICKADEE, (II), Owl Communications, 179 John St., Suite 500, Toronto, Ontario M5T 3G5 Canada. (416)340-2700. Fax: (416)340-9769. E-mail: chickadeenet@owl.on.ca. Website: http://www.owl.on.ca. **Editor:** Kat Mototsone. Magazine: 8½×11¾; 32 pages; glossy paper and cover stock; illustrations and photographs. "*Chickadee* is created to give children aged 6-9 a lively, fun-filled look at the world around them. Each issue has a mix of activities, puzzles, games and stories." Published 9 times/year. Estab. 1979. Circ. 110,000.

- *Chickadee* has won several awards including the Ed Press Golden Lamp Honor award and the Parents' Choice Golden Seal awards.

Needs: Juvenile. No religious material. Accepts 1 ms/issue; 9 mss/year. Publishes ms an average of 1 year after acceptance. Published new writers within the last year. Length: 300-900 words.
How to Contact: Send complete ms and cover letter with $1 or IRC to cover postage and handling. Simultaneous submissions OK. Reports in 2 months. Sample copy for $4.50. Fiction guidelines for SAE and IRC.
Payment/Terms: Pays $25-250 (Canadian); 2 contributor's copies on acceptance for all rights. Occasionally buys reprints.
Advice: "Read back issues to see what types of fiction we publish. Common mistakes include loose, rambling, and boring prose; stories that lack a clear beginning, middle and end; unbelievable characters; and overwriting."

$ CHILDREN'S DIGEST, (II, IV), Children's Better Health Institute, P.O. Box 567, 1100 Waterway Blvd., Indianapolis IN 46206. Magazine: 7×10⅛; 36 pages; reflective and preseparated illustrations; color and b&w photos. Magazine with special emphasis on health, nutrition, exercise and safety for preteens.

- Other magazines published by Children's Better Health Institute and listed in this book are *Children's Playmate*, *Humpty Dumpty*, *Jack and Jill* and *Turtle*.

Needs: "Realistic stories, short plays, adventure and mysteries. Humorous stories are highly desirable. We especially need stories that *subtly* encourage readers to develop better health or safety habits. Stories should not exceed 1,500 words." Receives 40-50 unsolicited fiction mss each month. Published work by Judith Josephson, Pat McCarthy and Sharen Liddell; published new writers within the last year.
How to Contact: Send complete ms with SASE. "A cover letter isn't necessary unless an author wishes to include publishing credits and special knowledge of the subject matter." Reports in 3 months. Sample copy for $1.25. Fiction guidelines for SASE.
Payment/Terms: Pays 12¢/word minimum with up to 10 contributor's copies on publication for all rights.
Advice: "We try to present our health-related material in a positive—not a negative—light, and we try to incorporate humor and a light approach wherever possible without minimizing the seriousness of what we are saying. Fiction stories that deal with a health theme need not have health as the primary subject but should include it in some way in the course of events. Most rejected health-related manuscripts are too preachy or they lack substance. Children's magazines are not training grounds where authors learn to write 'real' material for 'real' readers. Because our readers frequently have limited attention spans, it is very important that we offer them well-written stories."

$ CHILDREN'S PLAYMATE, (IV), Children's Better Health Institute, P.O. Box 567, 1100 Waterway Blvd., Indianapolis IN 46206. (317)636-8881. **Editor:** Terry Harshman. Magazine: 7½×10; 48 pages; preseparated and reflective art; b&w and color illustrations. Juvenile magazine for children ages 6-8 years. Published 8 times/year.

- *Children's Digest*, *Humpty Dumpty Jack and Jill* and *Turtle* magazines are also published by Children's Better Health Institute and listed in this book.

Needs: Juvenile with special emphasis on health, nutrition, safety and exercise. "Our present needs are for short, entertaining stories with a subtle health angle. Seasonal material is also always welcome." No adult or adolescent fiction. Receives approximately 150 unsolicited fiction mss each month. Published work by Batta Killion, Ericka Northrop, Elizabeth Murphy-Melas; published new writers within the last year. Length: 300-700 words.
How to Contact: Send complete ms with SASE. Indicate word count on material and date sent. Reports in 8-10 weeks. Sample copy for $1.25. Writer's guidelines for SASE.
Payment/Terms: Pays up to 17¢/word and 10 contributor's copies on publication for *all* rights.

Advice: "Stories should be kept simple and entertaining. Study past issues of the magazine—be aware of vocabulary limitations of the readers."

$ THE CHRISTIAN CENTURY, An Ecumenical Weekly, (I, IV), 407 S. Dearborn St., Chicago IL 60605. (312)427-5380. Fax: (312)427-1302. **Editor:** James Wall. Magazine: 8¼ × 10⅞; 24-40 pages; illustrations and photos. "A liberal Protestant magazine interested in the public meaning of Christian faith as it applies to social issues, and in the individual appropriation of faith in modern circumstances." Weekly (sometimes bi-weekly). Estab. 1884. Circ. 35,000.

- *Christian Century* has received many awards each year from the Associated Church Press, including: best critical review, best written humor, best feature article, best fiction, etc.

Needs: Religious/inspirational: feminist, mainstream/contemporary. "We are interested in articles that touch on religious themes in a sophisticated way; we are not interested in simplistic pietistic pieces." Receives 80 unsolicited mss/month. Accepts 10% of unsolicited mss. Publishes ms 1-3 months after acceptance. Published work by David Borofka and Doris Betts. Length: 2,500 words average; 1,500 words minimum; 3,000 words maximum. Also publishes literary essays and poetry.
How to Contact: Send complete ms with a cover letter. Include bio (100 words). Reports in 1 week on queries; 1 month on mss. Send a disposable copy of ms. No simultaneous submissions. Sample copy for $3. Reviews novels and short story collections.
Payment/Terms: Pays $200 maximum and 1 contributor's copy (additional copies for $1) on publication for all rights. Sends galleys to author.

$ CLUBHOUSE, Focus on the Family, (II, III), 8605 Explorer Dr., Colorado Springs CO 80920. (719)531-3400. **Editor:** Jesse Florea. Associate Editor: Annette Brashler Bourland. Magazine: 8 × 11; 24 pages; illustrations and photos. Publishes literature for kids aged 8-12. "Stories must have moral lesson included. *Clubhouse* readers are 8- to 12-year-old boys and girls who desire to know more about God and the Bible. Their parents (who typically pay for the membership) want wholesome, educational material with Scriptual or moral insight. The kids want excitement, adventure, action, humor or mystery. Your job as a writer is to please both the parent and child with each article." Monthly. Estab. 1989. Circ. 100,000.
Needs: Children's/juvenile (8-12 years), religious/inspirational, young adult/teen (adventure, western). No science fiction. Receives 150 unsolicited ms/month. Accepts 3-4 mss/issue. Agented fiction 15%. Published work by Sigmund Brower and Nancy Rue. Length: 1,200 words average; 400 words minimum; 2,500 words maximum. "Sometimes we'll run two-part fiction."
How to Contact: Send complete ms with cover letter. Include estimated word count, bio and list of publications. Reports in 8-10 weeks. Send SASE for reply, return of ms or send a disposable copy of ms. Sample copy for $1.50. Guidelines free.
Payment/Terms: Pays $400 maximum on acceptance and 2 contributor's copies; additional copies for $1.50. Acquires all rights, first rights, first North American serial rights or one-time rights.
Advice: Looks for "humor with a point, historical fiction featuring great Christians or Christians who lived during great times; contemporary, exotic settings; holiday material (Christmas, Thanksgiving, Easter, President's Day); parables; fantasy (avoid graphic descriptions of evil creatures and sorcery); mystery stories; choose-your-own adventure stories and westerns. No contemporary, middle-class family settings (we already have authors who can meet these needs) or stories dealing with boy-girl relationships."

$ COBBLESTONE, Discover American History, (I, II), 30 Grove St., Suite C, Peterborough NH 03458. **Editor:** Meg Chorlian. Magazine. "Historical accuracy and lively, original approaches to the subject are primary concerns of the editors in choosing material. For 8-14 year olds." Monthly (except June, July and August). Estab. 1979. Circ. 36,000.

- *Cobblestone* has received Ed Press and Parent's Choice awards.

Needs: Material must fit upcoming theme; write for theme list and deadlines. Childrens/juvenile (8-14 years). "Authentic historical and biographical fiction, adventure, retold legends, etc., relating to the theme." Upcoming themes available for SASE. Published after theme deadline. Accepts 1-2 fiction mss/issue. Length: 800 words maximum. Publishes short shorts. Also publishes poetry.
How to Contact: Query first or query with clips of published work (if new to *Cobblestone*). Include estimated word count. "Include detailed outline explaining the information to be presented in the article and bibliography of material used." Reports in several months. If interested, responds to queries 5 months before publication date. Send SASE (or IRC) for reply or send self-addressed postcard to find out if query was received. Electronic submissions (disk, Microsoft Word or MS-DOS) OK. Sample copy for $4.95, 7½ × 10½ SAE and $1.05 postage. Fiction guidelines for #10 SAE and 1 first-class stamp.

INTERESTED IN A PARTICULAR GENRE? Check our new sections for: **Mystery/Suspense**, page 57; **Romance**, page 77; **Science Fiction & Fantasy**, page 95.

Payment/Terms: Pays 20-25¢/word on publication for all rights.
Advice: Writers may send $8.95 plus $3 shipping for *Cobblestone*'s index for a listing of subjects covered in back issues.

N **$ COMPANION MAGAZINE, (II)**, Conventual Franciscan Friars, 695 Cotwell Ave., Suite 600, Toronto, Ontario M4C 5R6 Canada. (416)690-5611. Fax: (416)690-3320. **Editor:** Fr. Phil Kelly, OFM. Conv. Managing Editor: Betty McCrimmon. Publishes material "emphasizing religious and human values and stressing Franciscan virtues—peace, simplicity, joy." Monthly. Estab. 1936. Circ. 5,000.
Needs: Adventure, humor, mainstream, religious. Canadian settings preferred. Receives 50 unsolicited fiction mss/month. Accepts 2 mss/issue. Time varies between acceptance and publication. Length: 1,200 words maximum. Publishes short shorts.
How to Contact: Send complete mss. Accepts mss by fax. Reports in 3 weeks to 1 month on mss. SAE with "cash to buy stamps" or IRC. Sample copy and fiction guidelines free.
Payment/Terms: Pays 6¢/word (Canadian funds) on publication for first North American serial rights.

$ CONTACT ADVERTISING, (IV), Box 3431, Ft. Pierce FL 34948. (561)464-5447. E-mail: nietzche@cadv.com. **Editor:** Herman Nietzche. Magazines and newspapers. Publications vary in size, 56-80 pages. "Group of 26 erotica, soft core publications for swingers, single males, married males, gay males, transgendered and bisexual persons." Bimonthly, quarterly and monthly. Estab. 1975. Circ. combined is 2,000,000.

- This a group of regional publications with *very* explicit sexual content, graphic personal ads, etc. Not for the easily offended.

Needs: Erotica, fantasy, swinger, fetish, gay, lesbian. Receives 8-10 unsolicited mss/month. Accepts 1-2 mss/issue; 40-50 mss/year. Publishes ms 1-3 months after acceptance. Length: 2,000 words minimum; 3,500 words maximum. Sometimes critiques rejected mss.
How to Contact: Query first, query with clips of published work or send complete ms with cover letter. SASE. Simultaneous and reprint submissions OK. Sample copy for $6. Fiction guidelines with SASE.
Payment/Terms: First submission, free subscription to magazine; subsequent submissions $25 on publication for all rights or first rights; all receive 3 contributor's copies.
Advice: "Know your grammar! Content must be of an adult nature but well within guidelines of the law. Fantasy, unusual sexual encounters, swinging stories or editorials of a sexual bend are acceptable. Read Henry Miller!"

$ CORNERSTONE MAGAZINE, (I, II), Cornerstone Communications, Inc., 939 W. Wilson Ave., Chicago IL 60640. (773)561-2450 ext. 2394. Fax (773)989-2076. Editor: Jon Trott. **Fiction Editor:** Nanci Mortimer. Magazine: 8½×11; 64 pages; 35 lb. coated matie paper; self cover; illustrations and photos. "For adults, 18-45. We publish nonfiction (essays, personal experience, religious), music interviews, current events, film and book reviews, fiction, poetry. *Cornerstone* challenges readers to look through the window of biblical reality. Known as avant-garde, yet attempts to express orthodox belief in the language of the nineties." Approx. quarterly. Estab. 1972. Circ. 38,000.

- *Cornerstone Magazine* has won numerous awards from the Evangelical Press Association.

Needs: Ethnic/multicultural, fantasy (science fantasy), humor/satire, literary, mainstream/contemporary, religious/inspirational. Special interest in "issues pertinent to contemporary society, seen with a biblical worldview." No "pornography, cheap shots at non-Christians, unrealistic or syrupy articles." Receives 60 unsolicited mss/month. Accepts 1 mss/issue; 3-4 mss/year. Does not read mss during Christmas/New Year's week and the month of July. Published work by Dave Cheadle, C.S. Lewis and J.B. Simmonds. Length: 1,200 words average; 250 words minimum; 2,500 words maximum. Publishes short shorts. Length: 250-450 words. Also publishes literary essays, literary criticism and poetry.
How to Contact: Send complete ms. Include estimated word count, bio (50-100 words), list of publications, and name, address, phone and fax number on every item submitted. Send disposable copy of the ms. Will consider simultaneous submissions, reprints and electronic (disk or modem) submissions. Reports in up to 6 months, only on acceptance. Sample copy for 8½×11 SAE and 6 first-class stamps. Reviews novels and short story collections.
Payment/Terms: Pays 8-10¢/word maximum; also 6 contributor's copies on publication. Purchases first serial rights.
Advice: "Articles may express Christian world view but shouldn't be unrealistic or syrupy. We're looking for high-quality fiction with skillful characterization and plot development and imaginative symbolism." Looks for "mature Christian short stories, as opposed to those more fit for church bulletins. We want fiction with bite and an edge but with a Christian worldview."

$ COSMOPOLITAN MAGAZINE, (III), The Hearst Corp., 224 W. 57th St., New York NY 10019. (212)649-2000. Editor: Kate White. **Books Editor:** Alison Brower. "Most novel excerpts feature young, contemporary female protagonists and traditional plots, characterizations." Single career women (ages 18-34). Monthly. Circ. just under 3 million.
Needs: Adventure, contemporary, mystery and romance. Buys current novel or book excerpts. Agented fiction 98%. Published excerpts by Danielle Steel, Mario Puzo, Louise Erdrich and Lisa Scottoline.
How to Contact: Accepts submissions from agents and publishers only. Guidelines for #10 SASE. Reports in 8-10 weeks.

Payment/Terms: Open to negotiation with author's agent or publisher.

$ COUNTRY WOMAN, (IV), Reiman Publications, Box 643, Milwaukee WI 53201. (414)423-0100. Editor: Ann Kaiser. Managing Editor: Kathleen Pohl. Magazine: 8½×11; 68 pages; excellent quality paper; excellent cover stock; illustrations and photographs. "Articles should have a rural theme and be of specific interest to women who live on a farm or ranch, or in a small town or country home, and/or are simply interested in country-oriented topics." Bimonthly. Estab. 1971.

Needs: Fiction must be upbeat, heartwarming and focus on a country woman as central character. "Many of our stories and articles are written by our readers!" Published work by Edna Norrell, Millie Thomas Kearney and Rita Peterson. Published new writers within last year. Publishes 1 fiction story/issue. Length: 1,000 words.

How to Contact: Send $2 and SASE for sample copy and writer's guidelines. All manuscripts should be sent to Kathy Pohl, Managing Editor. Reports in 2-3 months. Include cover letter and SASE. Simultaneous and reprint submissions OK.

Payment/Terms: Pays $90-125 on acceptance for one-time rights.

Advice: "Read the magazine to get to know our audience. Send us country-to-the-core fiction, not yuppie-country stories—our readers know the difference! Very traditional fiction—with a definite beginning, middle and end, some kind of conflict/resolution, etc. We do not want to see contemporary avant-garde fiction—nothing dealing with divorce, drugs, etc., or general societal malaise of the '90s."

CREATIVE KIDS, (I, IV), Prufrock Press, P.O. Box 8813, Waco TX 76714-8813. (800)998-2208. Fax: (800)240-0333. E-mail: creative_kids@prufrock.com. Website: http://www.prufrock.com (includes catalog, submission guidelines and information about our staff). **Editor:** Libby Lindsey. Magazine: 7×10½; 36 pages; illustrations; photos. Material by children for children. Published 4 times/year. Estab. 1980. Circ: 45,000.

- *Creative Kids* featuring work by children has won Ed Press and Parents' Choice Gold and Silver Awards.

Needs: "We publish work by children ages 8-14." Publishes short stories, essays, games, puzzles, poems, opinion pieces and letters. Accepts 3-4 mss/issue; 12-16 mss/year. Publishes ms up to 2 years after acceptance. Published new writers within the last year. No novels.

How to Contact: Send complete ms with cover letter, include name, age, birthday, home address, school name and address, grade, statement of originality signed by teacher or parent. Must include SASE for response. Do not query. Reports in 1 month on mss. SASE. No simultaneous submissions. Sample copy for $3. Guidelines for SASE.

Payment/Terms: Pays 1 contributor's copy. Acquires all rights.

Advice: "*Creative Kids* is designed to entertain, stimulate and challenge the creativity of children ages 8 to 14, encouraging their abilities and helping them to explore their ideas, opinions and world. We would like more opinion pieces."

$ CRICKET MAGAZINE, (II), Carus Corporation, P.O. Box 300, Peru IL 61354. (815)224-6656. **Editor-in-Chief:** Marianne Carus. Magazine: 8×10; 64 pages; illustrations; photos. Magazine for children, ages 9-14. Monthly. Estab. 1973. Circ. 83,000.

- *Cricket* has received a Parents Choice Award, a Paul A. Witty Short Story Award and awards from Ed Press. *Cricket* ranked #11 on *Writer's Digest*'s Fiction 50 list of top markets for fiction writers. Carus Corporation also publishes *Spider, the Magazine for Children*, also listed in this book.

Needs: Adventure, contemporary, ethnic, fantasy, historic fiction, folk and fairytales, humorous, juvenile, mystery, science fiction and translations. No adult articles. All issues have different "mini-themes." Receives approximately 1,100 unsolicited fiction mss each month. Publishes ms 6-24 months or longer after acceptance. Accepts 180 mss/year. Agented fiction 1-2%. Published work by Peter Dickinson, Mary Stolz and Jane Yolen. Published new writers within the last year. Length: 500-2,000 words.

How to Contact: Do not query first. Send complete ms with SASE. List previous publications. Reports in 3 months on mss. Sample copy for $4; guidelines for SASE.

Payment/Terms: Pays up to 25¢/word; 2 contributor's copies; $2 charge for extras on publication for first rights. Sends edited mss for approval. Buys reprints.

Advice: "Do not write *down* to children. Write about well-researched subjects you are familiar with and interested in, or about something that concerns you deeply. Children *need* fiction and fantasy. Carefully study several issues of *Cricket* before you submit your manuscript." Sponsors contests for readers of all ages.

✔ $ CRUSADER MAGAZINE, (II), Calvinist Cadet Corps, Box 7259, Grand Rapids MI 49510-7259. (616)241-5616. Fax: (616)241-5558. E-mail: cccorders@aol.com. **Editor:** G. Richard Broene. Magazine: 8½×11; 24 pages; 50 lb. white paper and cover stock; illustrations; photos. Magazine "for boys (ages 9-14) who are members of the Calvinist Cadet Corps. *Crusader* publishes stories and articles that have to do with the interests and concerns of boys, teaching Christian values subtly." 7 issues/year. Estab. 1958. Circ. 12,000.

Needs: Adventure, comics, juvenile, religious/inspirational, spiritual and sports. No fantasy, science fiction, fashion, horror or erotica. List of upcoming themes available for SASE. Receives 60 unsolicited fiction mss/month. Buys 3 mss/issue; 18 mss/year. Publishes ms 4-11 months after acceptance. Published work by Sigmund Brouwer, Douglas DeVries and Betty Lou Mell. Publishes 0-1 new writers/year. Length: 800 words minimum; 1,500 words maximum; 1,200 words average. Publishes short shorts.

How to Contact: Send complete ms and SASE with cover letter including theme of story. Accepts queries by fax and e-mail. Reports in 4-8 weeks. Simultaneous and previously published submissions OK. Sample copy with a 9×12 SAE and 4 first-class stamps. Fiction guidelines for #10 SASE.
Payment/Terms: Pays 2-5¢/word and 1 contributor's copy. Pays on acceptance for one-time rights. Buys reprints.
Advice: "On a cover sheet, list the point your story is trying to make. Our magazine has a theme for each issue, and we try to fit the fiction to the theme. All fiction should be about a young boy's interests—sports, outdoor activities, problems—with an emphasis on a Christian multiracial perspective. No simple moralisms. Avoid simplistic answers to complicated problems."

$ DIALOGUE, A World of Ideas for Visually Impaired People of All Ages, (I, II), Blindskills Inc., P.O. Box 5181, Salem OR 97304-0181. (800)860-4224. (503)581-4224. Fax: (503)581-0178. E-mail: blindskl@teleport.com. **Editor/Publisher:** Carol McCarl. Magazine: 9×11; 130 pages; matte stock. Publishes information of general interest to visually impaired. Quarterly. Estab. 1961. Circ. 15,000.
Needs: Contemporary, humor/satire, literary, mainstream, senior citizen/retirement. No erotica, religion, confessional or experimental. Receives approximately 10 unsolicited fiction mss/month. Accepts 3 mss/issue, 12 mss/year. Publishes ms an average of 6 months after acceptance. Published work by Kim Rush, Diana Braun and Eric Cameron. Published new writers within the last year. Length: 1,000 words average; 500 words minimum; 1,300 words maximum. Publishes short shorts. Occasionally critiques rejected mss. Sometimes recommends other markets. "We give top priority to blind or visually impaired (legally blind) authors."
How to Contact: Query first or send complete ms with SASE. Also send statement of visual disability. Reports in 2 weeks on queries; 6 weeks on mss. Reprint submissions OK. Accepts electronic submissions on disk; IBM and compatible; Word Perfect 5.1 or 6.0 preferred. Sample copy for $6 and #10 SAE with 1 first-class stamp. Fiction guidelines free.
Payment/Terms: Pays $5-25 and contributor's copy on acceptance for first rights.
Advice: "Authors should be blind or visually impaired. We prefer contemporary problem stories in which the protagonist solves his or her own problem. We are looking for strongly-plotted stories with definite beginnings, climaxes and endings. Characters may be blind, sighted or visually in-between. Because we want to encourage any writer who shows promise, we may return a story for revision when necessary."

$ DISCOVERIES, (II), WordAction Publishing Company, 6401 The Paseo, Kansas City MO 64131. (816)333-7000 ext. 2359. Fax: (816)333-4439. Contact: Assistant Editor. Story paper: 8½×11; 4 pages; illustrations. "Committed to reinforce the Bible concept taught in Sunday School curriculum, for ages 8-10 (grades 3-4)." Weekly.
Needs: Religious, puzzles, Bible trivia, 100-200 words. "Avoid fantasy, science fiction, personification of animals and cultural references that are distinctly American." Accepts 1-2 stories and 1-2 puzzles/issue. Publishes ms 1-2 years after acceptance. Publishes 5-10 new writers/year. Length: 500 words.
How to Contact: Send complete ms with cover letter and SASE. Send SASE for sample copy and guidelines.
Payment/Terms: Pays 5¢/word for multiple rights on acceptance or on publication.
Advice: "Stories should vividly portray definite Christian emphasis or character building values, without being preachy."

☑ **$ DISCOVERY TRAILS (I, II)**, (formerly *Junior Trails*), Gospel Publishing House, 1445 Boonville Ave., Springfield MO 65802-1894. (417)862-2781. **Upper Elementary Editor:** Sinda S. Zinn. Magazine: 8×10; 4 pages; coated offset paper; art illustrations; photos. "A Sunday school take-home paper of articles and fictional stories that apply Christian principles to everyday living for 10- to 12-year-old children." Weekly. Estab. 1954. Circ. 40,000.
Needs: Contemporary, juvenile, religious/inspirational, spiritual, sports. Adventure stories and serials are welcome. No Biblical fiction or science fiction. Accepts 2 mss/issue. Published work by Melissa Knight, O.B. Comer, Russell Lewis and Theresa E. Calvin. Published new writers within the last year. Length: 800-1,000 words. Publishes short shorts.
How to Contact: Send complete ms with SASE. Reports in 4-6 weeks. Free sample copy and guidelines with SASE.
Payment/Terms: Pays 8-10¢/word and 3 contributor's copies on acceptance for first rights.
Advice: "Know the age level and direct stories or articles relevant to that age group. Since junior-age children (grades 5 and 6) enjoy action, fiction provides a vehicle for communicating moral/spiritual principles in a dramatic framework. Fiction, if well done, can be a powerful tool for relating Christian principles. It must, however, be realistic and believable in its development. Make your children be children, not overly mature for their age. We would like more stories with a *city* setting. Write for contemporary children, using setting and background that includes various ethnic groups."

$ EMPHASIS ON FAITH AND LIVING, (IV), Missionary Church, Inc., P.O. Box 9127, Fort Wayne IN 46899-9127. (219)747-2027. Fax: (219)747-5331. **Editor:** Robert L. Ransom. Magazine: 8½×11; 16 pages; offset paper; illustrations and photos. "Religious/church oriented." Bimonthly. Estab. 1969. Circ. 14,000.
Needs: Religious/inspirational. Receives 10-15 unsolicited mss/month. Accepts 2 mss/year. Publishes ms 3-6

months after acceptance. Published work by Debra Wood and Denise George. Length: 500 words average; 200 words minimum; 1,000 words maximum. Publishes short shorts. Length: 200-250 words.
How to Contact: Send complete ms with a cover letter. Include estimated word count, bio and Social Security number. Reports in 2-3 months on mss. Send SASE for reply, return of ms or send a disposable copy of ms. Simultaneous reprint and electronic submissions OK. Sample copy for 9×12 SAE.
Payment/Terms: Pays $10-50 and 5 contributor's copies on publication.

$ ESQUIRE, The Magazine for Men, (III), Hearst Corp., 250 W. 55th St., New York NY 10019. (212)649-4020. Editor: David Granger. **Literary Editor:** Adrienne Miller. Magazine. Monthly. Estab. 1933. Circ. 750,000. General readership is college educated and sophisticated, between ages 30 and 45.

- *Esquire* is well-respected for its fiction and has received several National Magazine Awards. Work published in *Esquire* has been selected for inclusion in the *Best American Short Stories* anthology.

Needs: No "pornography, science fiction or 'true romance' stories." Publishes special fiction issue in July. Receives "thousands" of unsolicited mss/year. Rarely accepts unsolicited fiction. Published work by David Foster Wallace, Tony Earley, Elizabeth McCracken, Heidi Jularits, Martin Amis, Don DeLillo.
How to Contact: Send complete ms with cover letter or submit through an agent. Simultaneous submissions OK. Fiction guidelines for SASE.
Payment/Terms: Pays in cash on acceptance, amount undisclosed. Publishes ms an average of 2 months after acceptance.
Advice: "Submit one story at a time. Worry a little less about publication, a little more about the work itself."

$ EVANGEL, (I, II, IV), Light & Life Communications, P.O. Box 535002, Indianapolis IN 46253-5002. (317)244-3660. **Editor:** Julie Innes. Sunday school take-home paper for distribution to adults who attend church. Fiction involves couples and singles coping with everyday crises, making decisions that show growth. Magazine: 5½×8½; 8 pages; 2- and 4-color illustrations; color and b&w photos. Weekly. Estab. 1897. Circ. 22,000.
Needs: Religious/inspirational. "No fiction without any semblance of Christian message or where the message clobbers the reader." Receives approximately 300 unsolicited fiction mss/month. Accepts 3-4 mss/issue, 156-200 mss/year. Recently published work by Karen Leet and Dennis Hensley. 40% of work published is by new writers. Length: 1,000-1,200 words.
How to Contact: Send complete ms with SASE. Reports in 2 months. Electronic submissions (3½ inch disk-WordPerfect) OK; send hard copy with disk. Sample copy and writer's guidelines with #10 SASE.
Payment/Terms: Pays 4¢/word and 2 contributor's copies on publication; charge for extras.
Advice: "Choose a contemporary situation or conflict and create a good mix for the characters (not all-good or all-bad heroes and villains). Don't spell out everything in detail; let the reader fill in some blanks in the story. Keep him guessing." Rejects mss because of "unbelievable characters and predictable events in the story."

$ FACES, People, Places and Cultures, A Cobblestone Publication, (II, IV), Cobblestone Publishing, Inc., 30 Grove St., Suite C, Peterborough NH 03458. (603)924-7209. Fax: (603)924-7380. E-mail: faces@cobblestonepub.com. **Managing Editor:** Denise Babcock. Magazine. *Faces* is a magazine about people and places in the world for 8 to 14-year-olds. Estab. 1984. Circ. 15,000. Monthly, except June, July and August.
Needs: All material must relate to theme; send for theme list. Children's/juvenile (8-14 years), "retold legends, folk tales, stories from around the world, etc., relating to the theme." Length: 800 words preferred. Publishes short shorts.
How to Contact: Query first or query with clips of published work (send query 6-9 months prior to theme issue publication date). Include estimated word count and bio (2-3 lines). Reports 4 months before publication date. Send SASE for reply. Sample copy for $4.95, 7½×10½ SAE and $2 postage. Fiction guidelines for SASE.
Payment/Terms: Pays 20-25¢/word on publication for all rights.

$ FIRST HAND, Experiences for Loving Men, (II, IV), First Hand Ltd., Box 1314, Teaneck NJ 07666. (201)836-9177. Fax: (201)836-5055. E-mail: firsthand3@aol.com. **Editor:** Bob Harris. Magazine: digest size; 130 pages; illustrations. "Half of the magazine is made up of our readers' own gay sexual experiences. Rest is fiction and columns devoted to health, travel, books, etc." Publishes 16 times/year. Estab. 1980. Circ. 60,000.

- First Hand Ltd. also publishes *Guys* and *Manscape*, listed in this book.

Needs: Erotica, gay. "Should be written in first person." No science fiction or fantasy. Erotica should detail experiences based in reality. Receives 75-100 unsolicited mss/month. Accepts 6 mss/issue; 72 mss/year. Publishes ms 9-18 months after acceptance. Length: 3,000 words preferred; 2,000 words minimum; 3,750 words maximum. Sometimes critiques rejected mss.
How to Contact: Send complete ms with cover letter. Include name, address, telephone and Social Security number and "advise on use of pseudonym if any. Also whether selling all rights or first North American rights." No simultaneous submissions. Reports in 1-2 months. SASE. Sample copy for $5. Fiction guidelines for #10 SASE.
Payment/Terms: Pays $100-150 on publication for all rights or first North American serial rights.
Advice: "Avoid the hackneyed situations. Be original. We like strong plots."

$ FLORIDA WILDLIFE, (IV), Florida Game & Fresh Water Fish Commission, 620 S. Meridian St., Tallahassee FL 32399-1600. (850)488-5563. Fax: (850)488-1961. Website: http://www.state.Fl.us/gfc/gfchome. **Editor:** Dick Sublette. Associate Editor: James Call. Magazine: 8½×11; 32 pages. "Conservation-oriented material for an 'outdoor' audience." Bimonthly. Estab. 1947. Circ. 26,000.

- *Florida Wildlife* has received the Florida Magazine Association and Association of Conservation Information awards.

Needs: "Florida-related adventure, natural history, volunteers and conservation/environmental work." Accepts 24 mss/year. Length: 1,200 words average; 500 words minimum; 2,000 words maximum.
How to Contact: Send complete ms, double spaced, with cover letter including Social Security number. "We prefer to review article. Response time varies with amount of material on hand." Sample copy for $3.50. Will send writer's guidelines and how to submit memo upon request.
Payment/Terms: Pays minimum of $50 per published page on publication for one-time rights.
Advice: "Send your best work. It must *directly* concern Florida wildlife."

$ THE FRIEND MAGAZINE, (II), The Church of Jesus Christ of Latter-day Saints, 50 E. North Temple, 23rd Floor, Salt Lake City UT 84150. (801)240-2210. **Editor:** Vivian Paulsen. Magazine: 8½×10½; 50 pages; 40 lb. coated paper; 70 lb. coated cover stock; illustrations; photos. Publishes for 3- to 11-year-olds. Monthly. Estab. 1971. Circ. 275,000.
Needs: Children's/juvenile: adventure, ethnic, some historical, humor, mainstream, religious/inspirational, nature. Length: 1,000 words maximum. Publishes short shorts. Length: 250 words.
How to Contact: Send complete ms. "No query letters please." Reports in 6-8 weeks. SASE. Sample copy for $1.50 with 9½×11 SAE and four 32¢ stamps.
Payment/Terms: Pays 9-13¢/word on acceptance for all rights.
Advice: "The *Friend* is particularly interested in stories with substance for tiny tots. Stories should focus on character-building qualities and should be wholesome without moralizing or preaching. Boys and girls resolving conflicts is a theme of particular merit. Since the magazine is circulated worldwide, the *Friend* is interested in stories and articles with universal settings, conflicts and character. Other suggestions include rebus, picture, holiday, sports, and photo stories, or manuscripts that portray various cultures. Very short pieces (up to 250 words) are desired for younger readers and preschool children. Appropriate humor is a constant need."

$ THE GEM, (II), Churches of God, General Conference, Box 926, Findlay OH 45839. (419)424-1961. E-mail: cggc@bright.net. Website: http://www.rareyroth.com/cggc. **Editor:** Evelyn Sloat. Magazine: 6×9; 8 pages; 50 lb. uncoated paper; illustrations (clip art). "True-to-life stories of healed relationships and growing maturity in the Christian faith for senior high students through senior citizens who attend Churches of God, General Conference Sunday Schools." Weekly. Estab. 1865. Circ. 7,000.
Needs: Adventure, humor, mainstream, religious/inspirational, senior citizen/retirement. Nothing that denies or ridicules standard Christian values. Prefers personal testimony or nonfiction short stories. Receives 30 unsolicited fiction mss/month. Accepts 1 ms every 2-3 issues; 20-25 mss/year. Publishes ms 4-12 months after submission. Published work by Betty Steele Everett, Todd Lee and Betty Lou Mell. Length: 1,500 words average; 500 words minimum; 1,700 words maximum.
How to Contact: Send complete ms with cover letter ("letter not essential, unless there is information about author's background which enhances story's credibility or verifies details as being authentic"). Reports in 6 months. SASE. Simultaneous and reprint submissions OK. Sample copy and fiction guidelines for #10 SASE. "If more than one sample copy is desired along with the guidelines, will need 2 oz. postage."
Payment/Terms: Pays $10-15 and contributor's copies on publication for one-time rights. Charge for extras (postage for mailing more than one).
Advice: "Competition at the mediocre level is fierce. There is a dearth of well-written, relevant fiction which wrestles with real problems involving Christian values applied to the crisis times and 'passages' of life. Humor which puts the daily grind into a fresh perspective and which promises hope for survival is also in short supply. Write from your own experience. Avoid religious jargon and stereotypes. Conclusion must be believable in terms of the story—don't force a 'Christian' ending. Avoid simplistic solutions to complex problems. Listen to the storytelling art of Garrison Keillor. Feel how very particular experiences of small town life in Minnesota become universal."

$ GENT, (II), Dugent Publishing Corp., 14411 Commerce Way, Suite 420, Miami Lakes FL 33016. (305)557-0071. **Editor:** Bruce Arthur. "Men's magazine designed to have erotic appeal for the reader. Our publications are directed to a male audience, but we do have a certain percentage of female readers. For the most part, our

audience is interested in erotically stimulating material, but not exclusively." Monthly. Estab. 1959. Circ. 175,000.
Needs: Erotica: contemporary, science fiction, horror, mystery, adventure, humor. *Gent* specializes in "D-Cup cheesecake," and fiction should be slanted accordingly. "Most of the fiction published includes several sex scenes. No fiction that concerns children, religious subjects or anything that might be libelous." Receives 30-50 unsolicited fiction mss/month. Accepts 2 mss/issue; 26 mss/year. Publishes ms an average of 3 months after acceptance. Agented fiction 10%. Published new writers within the last year. Length: 2,000-3,500 words. Critiques rejected mss "when there is time."
How to Contact: Send complete ms with SASE. Reports in 1 month. Sample copy for $7. Fiction guidelines for #10 SASE.
Payment/Terms: Pays $200 minimum on publication and 1 contributor's copy for first North American serial rights.
Advice: "Since *Gent* magazine is the 'Home of the D-Cups,' stories and articles containing either characters or themes with a major emphasis on large breasts will have the best chance for consideration. Study a sample copy first." Mss are rejected because "there are not enough or ineffective erotic sequences, plot is not plausible, wrong length, or not slanted specifically for us."

N ★ $ GIRLFRIENDS MAGAZINE, Lesbian Culture, Politics, and Entertainment (II, III, IV), 3415 Cesar Chavez St., Suite 101, San Francisco CA 94110. Fax: (415)648-4705. E-mail: staff@gfriends.com. Website: http://www.gfriends.com (online content plus web-only interviews). Editor: Heather Findlay. Fiction Editor: Kathleen Hildenbrand. Lesbian lifestyle magazine: 48 pages; glossy paper; illustrations and photos. "We publish very short (1,400-word) fiction and humor pieces that are relevant to our lesbian audience." Monthly. Estab. 1994. Circ. 80,000.
Needs: Feminist, gay, humor/satire, lesbian, literary, mainstream/contemporary, romance (contemporary) "No fiction that's too long, cliché or that doesn't keep our lesbian audience in mind. (No first-time, coming-out stories, or stories with lesbians sleeping with men.)" Receives 20 unsolicited mss/month. Accepts 1 ms/issue; 12 mss/year. Publishes ms 4-6 months after acceptance. Agented fiction 50%. Publishes 2-3 new writers/year. Length: 1,400 words. Doesn't usually publish short shorts. Sometimes critiques or comments on rejected ms.
How to Contact: Query with clips of published work or send complete ms with a cover letter. Accepts queries/mss by e-mail and fax. Reports in 6-8 weeks. Send SASE for reply, return of ms or send a disposable copy of ms. Simultaneous and reprint submissions OK. Sample copy for $5 and $3 postage. Fiction guidelines free. Reviews novels, short story collections and nonfiction books of interest to writers. Send books to fiction editor.
Payment/Terms: Pays $100-150, free subscription and 2 contributor's copies on publication. Rights acquired vary.
Advice: "We're looking for engaging, high-quality pieces that are relevant to someone besides the author. We get so many love poems or stories about how someone fell in love, which just aren't relevant to a wider audience."

★ $ GOLF JOURNAL, (II), United States Golf Assoc., Golf House, P.O. Box 708, Far Hills NJ 07931-0708. (908)234-2300. Fax: (908)781-1112. **Editor:** Brett Avery. Managing Editor: Rich Skyzinski. Magazine: 48-56 pages; self cover stock; illustrations and photos. "The magazine's subject is golf—its history, lore, rules, equipment and general information. The focus is on amateur golf and those things applying to the millions of American golfers. Our audience is generally professional, highly literate and knowledgeable; they read *Golf Journal* because of an interest in the game, its traditions, and its noncommercial aspects." Published 9 times/year. Estab. 1948. Circ. 650,000.
Needs: Poignant or humorous essays and short stories. "Golf jokes will not be used." Accepts 12 mss/year. Published new writers within the last year. Length: 1,000-2,000 words. Recommends other markets.
How to Contact: Send complete ms with SASE. Reports in 2 months on mss. Sample copy for SASE.
Payment/Terms: Pays $500-1,000 on acceptance and 5 contributor's copies.
Advice: "Know your subject (golf); familiarize yourself first with the publication." Rejects mss because "fiction usually does not serve the function of *Golf Journal*, which, as the official magazine of the United States Golf Association, deals chiefly with the history, lore and rules of golf."

$ GOOD HOUSEKEEPING, (II), 959 Eighth Ave., New York NY 10019. **Contact:** Fiction Editor. "It is now our policy that all submissions of unsolicited fiction received in our offices will be read and, if found to be unsuitable for us, destroyed by recycling. If you wish to introduce your work to us, you will be submitting material that will not be critiqued or returned. The odds are long that we will contact you to inquire about publishing your submission or to invite you to correspond with us directly, so please be sure before you take the time and expense to submit it that it is our type of material."
Advice: "We welcome short fiction submissions (1,000-3,000 words). We look for stories with strong emotional interest—stories revolving around, for example, courtship, romance, marriage, family, friendships, personal growth, coming of age. The best way to gauge whether your story might be appropriate for us is to read the fiction in several of our recent issues. (We are sorry but we cannot furnish sample copies of the magazine.) We prefer double-spaced, typewritten (or keyboarded) manuscripts, accompanied by a short cover letter listing any previous writing credits. (We're sorry, but no e-mailed or faxed submissions will be accepted.) Make sure that your name and address appear on the manuscript and that you retain a copy for yourself."

$ GRIT, American Life & Traditions, (II), Ogden Publications, Inc., 1503 S.W. 42nd St., Topeka KS 66609-1265. (913)274-4300. Fax: (785)274-4305. E-mail: grit@kspress.com. Website: http://www.grit.com (includes cover story from current issue plus titles of other features and book and products store). **Editor-in-Chief:** Donna Doyle. Assistant Editor: Jim Baker. Note on envelope: Attn: Fiction Department. Tabloid: 50 pages; 30 lb. newsprint; illustrations and photos. "*Grit* is a 'good news' publication and has been since 1882. Fiction should be 1,200 words or more and interesting, inspiring, perhaps compelling in nature. Audience is *conservative*; readers tend to be 40+ from smaller towns, rural areas." Biweekly. Estab. 1882. Circ. 400,000.

• *Grit* is considered one of the leading family-oriented publications.

Needs: Adventure, nostalgia, condensed novelette, mainstream/contemporary (conservative), mystery/suspense, light religious/inspirational, romance (contemporary, historical), science fiction, westerns (frontier, traditional). "No sex, violence, drugs, obscene words, abuse, alcohol, or negative diatribes." Upcoming themes: "Gardening" (January/February); "Love & Romance (February); "Presenting the Harvest" (June); "Back to School" (August); "Health Issue" (September); "Home for the Holidays" (November); "Christmas Theme" (December). Buys 1 mss/issue; 26 mss/year. Recently published work by Tim Myers, Gayle Brown, Laura Altom and George Chaffee. Publishes 20 new writers/year. Length: 1,500 words average; 1,200 words minimum; 2,500 words maximum for serials. Also publishes poetry.

How To Contact: Send complete ms with cover letter. Include estimated word count, brief bio, Social Security number, list of publications with submission. Reports in 6 months. Send SASE for return of ms. No simultaneous submissions. Sample copy for $4 postage/appropriate SASE.

Payment/Terms: Negotiable.

Terms: Purchases first North American serial or one-time rights.

Advice: Looks for "well-written, fast-paced adventures, lessons of life, wholesome stories with heart."

$ GUIDEPOSTS FOR KIDS, (II), P.O. Box 638, Chesterton IN 46304. Editor: Mary Lou Carney. Magazine: 8¼ × 10¾; 32 pages. "Value-centered bimonthly for kids 7-12 years old. Not preachy, concerned with contemporary issues." Bimonthly. Estab. 1990. Circ. 200,000.

• The magazine publishes many new writers but is primarily a market for writers who have already been published. *Guideposts for Kids* received Awards of Excellence from the Ed Press Association in 1995-1998, and also has received from SCBWI the Angel Awards.

Needs: Children's/juvenile: fantasy, historical (general), humor, mystery/suspense, religious/inspirational, westerns, holidays. "No 'adult as hero' or 'I-prayed-I-got' stories." Upcoming themes: Choices, Animals, Humor, Courage. Receives 200 unsolicited mss/month. Accepts 1-2 mss/issue; 6-10 mss/year. Recently published work by Lurlene McDaniel and Lisa Harkrader. Length: 1,300 words preferred; 600 words minimum; 1,400 words maximum. Publishes short shorts. Also publishes small amount of poetry. Sometimes critiques rejected mss; "only what shows promise."

How to Contact: Send complete ms with cover letter. Include estimated word count, Social Security number, phone number and SASE. Reports in 6-8 weeks. Send SASE for reply, return of ms or send disposable copy of ms. Simultaneous submissions OK. Sample copy for $3.25. Fiction guidelines for #10 SASE.

Payment/Terms: $250-600 on acceptance for all rights; 2 contributor's copies. Additional copies available.

Advice: "We're looking for the good stuff. Fast-paced, well-crafted stories aimed at kids 8-12 years of age. Stories should reflect strong traditional values. Don't preach. This is not a Sunday School handout, but a good solid piece of fiction that reflects traditional values and morality. Build your story around a solid principle and let the reader gain insight by inference. Don't let adults solve problems. While adults can appear in stories, they can't give the characters life's answers. Don't make your kid protagonist grateful and awed by sage, adult advice. Be original. We want a good mix of fiction—contemporary, historical, fantasy, sci-fi, mystery—centered around things that interest and concern kids. A kid reader should be able to identify with the characters strongly enough to think. '*I know just how he feels*!' Create a plot with believable characters. Here's how it works: the story must tell what happens when someone the reader likes (character) reaches an important goal (climax) by overcoming obstacles (conflict). Let kids be kids. Your dialogue (and use plenty of it!) should reflect how the kids sound, think and feel. Avoid slang, but listen to how real kids talk before you try and write for them. Give your characters feelings and actions suitable for the 4th to 6th grader."

$ GUYS, (I, II), FirstHand Ltd., Box 1314, Teaneck NJ 07666. (201)836-9177. Fax: (201)836-5055. E-mail: firsthand3@aol.com. **Editor:** William Spencer. Magazine: digest size; 130 pages; illustrations; photos. "Fiction and informative departments for today's gay man. Fiction is of an erotic nature, and we especially need short shorts and novella-length stories." Estab. 1988.

Needs: Gay. "Should be written in first person. No science fiction or fantasy. No four-legged animals. All

MARKET CATEGORIES: **(I)** Unpublished entries; **(II)** Published entries nominated by the author; **(III)** Published entries nominated by the editor, publisher or nominating body; **(IV)** Specialized entries.

characters must be over 18. Stories including members of ethnic groups are especially welcome. Erotica should be based on reality." Accepts 6 mss/issue; 66 mss/year. Publishes ms 6-12 months after acceptance. Published work by Robert H. Fletcher, Davem Verne and Biff Cole. Published new writers within the last year. Length: 3,000 words average; 2,000 words minimum; 3,750 words maximum. For novellas: 7,500-8,600 words. Publishes short shorts. Length: 750-1,250 words. Sometimes critiques rejected mss and recommends other markets.
How to Contact: Send complete ms with cover letter, include writer's name, address, telephone number and Social Security number and whether selling all rights or first North American serial rights. Reports in 6-8 weeks on ms. SASE. Accepts diskette or e-mail submissions. Sample copy for $5.50. Fiction guidelines for #10 SASE. Reviews novels and short story collections.
Payment/Terms: Pays $100-150; $75 for short shorts (all rights); $250 for novellas (all rights). Acquires all rights or first North American serial rights.
Advice: "Keep it simple, keep it sexy. If it turns you on, it will turn the reader on."

$ HARPER'S MAGAZINE, (II, III), 666 Broadway, 11th Floor, New York NY 10012. (212)614-6500. Website: http://www.harpers.org (includes submission guidelines). **Editor:** Lewis H. Lapham. Magazine: 8×10¾; 80 pages; illustrations. Magazine for well-educated, widely read and socially concerned readers, college-aged and older, those active in political and community affairs. Monthly. Circ. 218,000.

- This is considered a top but tough market for contemporary fiction.

Needs: Contemporary and humor. Stories on contemporary life and its problems. Receives 600 unsolicited fiction mss/year. Accepts 1 ms/year. Recently published work by David Guterson, David Foster Wallace, Johnathan Franzen, Steven Millhauser, Lisa Roney, Rick Moody and Steven Dixon. Published new writers within the last year. First published David Foster Wallace. Length: 1,000-5,000 words.
How to Contact: Query to managing editor, or through agent. Reports in 6 weeks on queries.
Payment/Terms: Pays $500-1,000 on acceptance for rights, which vary on each author materials and length. Sends galleys to author.
Advice: Buys very little fiction but *Harper's* has published short stories traditionally.

$ HIGHLIGHTS FOR CHILDREN, 803 Church St., Honesdale PA 18431. (717)253-1080. Editor: Kent L. Brown, Jr. Address fiction to: Beth Troop, **Manuscript Coordinator**. Magazine: 8½×11; 42 pages; uncoated paper; coated cover stock; illustrations; photos. Monthly. Circ. 2.8 million.

- *Highlights* is very supportive of writers. The magazine sponsors a contest and a workshop each year at Chautauqua (New York). Several authors published in *Highlights* have received SCBWI Magazine Merit Awards. *Highlights* ranked #5 on *Writer's Digest*'s Fiction 50 list of top markets for fiction writers.

Needs: Juvenile (ages 2-12). Unusual stories appealing to both girls and boys; stories with good characterization, strong emotional appeal, vivid, full of action. "Begin with action rather than description, have strong plot, believable setting, suspense from start to finish." Length: 400-900 words. "We also need easy stories for very young readers (100-400 words)." No war, crime or violence. Receives 600-800 unsolicited fiction mss/month. Accepts 6-7 mss/issue. Also publishes rebus (picture) stories of 125 words or under for the 3- to 7-year-old child. Published work by Virginia Kroll, Harriett Diller and Vashanti Rahaman; published new writers within the last year. Critiques rejected mss occasionally, "especially when editors see possibilities in story."
How to Contact: Send complete ms with SASE and include a rough word count and cover letter "with any previous acceptances by our magazine; any other published work anywhere." Reports in 1 month. Free guidelines on request.
Payment/Terms: Pays 14¢ and up/word on acceptance for all rights. Sends galleys to author.
Advice: "We accept a story on its merit whether written by an unpublished or an experienced writer. Mss are rejected because of poor writing, lack of plot, trite or worn-out plot, or poor characterization. Children *like* stories and learn about life from stories. Children learn to become lifelong fiction readers by enjoying stories. Feel passion for your subject. Create vivid images. Write a child-centered story; leave adults in the background."

$ ALFRED HITCHCOCK MYSTERY MAGAZINE, (I, II), Dell Magazines, 1270 Avenue of the Americas, 10th Floor, New York NY 10020. (212)698-1313. **Editor:** Cathleen Jordan. Mystery fiction magazine: 5½×8½; 144 pages; 28 lb. newsprint paper; 60 lb. machine-/coated cover stock; illustrations; photos. Published 11 times/year, including 1 double issue. Estab. 1956. Circ. 615,000 readers.

- Stories published in *Alfred Hitchcock Mystery Magazine* have won Edgar Awards for "Best Mystery Story of the Year," Shamus Awards for "Best Private Eye Story of the Year" and Robert L. Fish Awards for "Best First Mystery Short Story of the Year."

Needs: Mystery and detection (amateur sleuth, private eye, police procedural, suspense, etc.). No sensationalism. Number of mss/issue varies with length of mss. Length: up to 14,000 words. Also publishes short shorts.
How to Contact: Send complete ms and SASE. Reports in 2 months. Guideline sheet for SASE.
Payment/Terms: Pays 8¢/word on acceptance.

$ HOME TIMES, (I, II, IV), Neighbor News, Inc., 3676 Collin Dr. #12, West Palm Beach FL 33406. (561)439-3509. E-mail: hometimes@aol.com. **Editor:** Dennis Lombard. Newspaper: tabloid; 24 pages; newsprint; illustrations and photographs. "Conservative news, views, fiction, poetry, sold to general public." Weekly. Estab. 1980. Circ. 5,000.

• The publisher offers "101 Reasons Why I Reject Your Manuscript," a 120-page report for a cost of $19.

Needs: Adventure, historical (general), humor/satire, literary, mainstream, religious/inspirational, sports. No romance. "All fiction needs to be related to the publication's focus on current events and conservative perspective—we feel you must examine a sample issue because *Home Times* is *different*." Nothing "preachy or doctrinal, but Biblical worldview needed." Receives 40 unsolicited mss/month. Accepts 2-4 mss/issue. Publishes ms 1-9 months after acceptance. Published work by Cal Thomas, Chuck Colson, Armstrong Williams and Bruce Bartlett. Publishes 5-10 new writers/year. Length: 700 words average; 500 words minimum; 800 words maximum.

How to Contact: Send complete manuscript with cover letter including word count. "Absolutely no queries." Include in cover letter "One to two sentences on what the piece is and who you are." Reports on mss in 1 month. SASE. Simultaneous and reprint submissions OK. Sample current issues for $3. Guidelines for #10 SASE.

Payment/Terms: Pays $5-25 for one-time rights.

Advice: "We are very open to new writers, but read our newspaper—get the drift of our rather unusual conservative, pro-Christian, but non-religious content. Looks for "historical, issues, or family orientation; also like creative nonfiction on historical and issues subjects." Send $10 for a writer's 1-year subscription (12 current issues).

☆ $ HORIZONS, The Magazine of Presbyterian Women, (II, IV), 100 Witherspoon St., Louisville KY 40202-1396. (502)569-5379. Fax: (502)569-8085. E-mail: lbradley@ctr.pcusa.org. **Associate Editor:** Leah Bradley. Magazine: 8×11; 40 pages; illustrations and photos. Magazine owned and operated by Presbyterian Women featuring "information, inspiration and education from the perspectives of women committed to Christ, the church and faithful discipleship." Bimonthly. Estab. 1988. Circ. 25,000.

Needs: Ethnic/multicultural, feminist, historical, humor/satire, literary, mainstream/contemporary, religious/inspirational, senior citizen/retirement, translations. "No sex/violence or romance." List of upcoming themes available for SASE. Receives 50 unsolicited mss/month. Accepts 1 ms/issue. Publishes ms 4 months after acceptance. Publishes 6 new writers/year. Length: 800-1,200 words maximum. Publishes short shorts. Length: 500 words. Also publishes literary essays, fiction and poetry. Sometimes critiques or comments on rejected mss.

How to Contact: Send complete ms with cover letter. Include estimated word count and Social Security number. Accepts queries and mss by e-mail and fax (mss by permission only). Reports in 1 week on queries; 2 weeks on mss. SASE or send a disposable copy of ms. Simultaneous submissions OK. Sample copy for 9×12 SAE. Fiction guidelines for #10 SASE. Reviews novels and short story collections. Send books to Leah Bradley.

Payment/Terms: Pays $50/page and 2 contributor's copies on publication for all rights; additional copies for $2.50.

Advice: "We are most interested in stories or articles that focus on current issues—family life, the mission of the church, and the challenges of culture and society—from the perspective of women committed to Christ."

✔ ☆ $ HUMPTY DUMPTY'S MAGAZINE, (II), Children's Better Health Institute, Box 567, 1100 Waterway Blvd., Indianapolis IN 46206. (317)636-8881. Fax: (317)684-8094. Website: http://www.satevepost.org/kidsonline. **Editor:** Nancy S. Axelrad. Magazine: 7⅝×10⅛; 36 pages; 35 lb. paper; coated cover; illustrations; some photos. Children's magazine "seeking to encourage children, ages 4-6, in healthy lifestyle habits, especially good nutrition and fitness." Publishes 8 issues/year.

• The Children's Better Health Institute also publishes *Children's Digest, Children's Playmate, Jack and Jill* and *Turtle,* also listed in this publication.

Needs: Juvenile health-related material and material of a more general nature. No inanimate talking objects, animal stories and science fiction. Rhyming stories should flow easily with no contrived rhymes. Receives 100-200 unsolicited mss/month. Accepts 2-3 mss/issue. Publishes 6-8 new writers/year. Length: 300 words maximum.

How to Contact: Send complete ms with SASE. No queries. Reports in 3 months. Sample copy for $1.75. Editorial guidelines for SASE.

Payment/Terms: Pays up to 22¢/word for stories plus 10 contributor's copies on publication for all rights. (One-time book rights returned when requested for specific publication.)

Advice: "In contemporary stories, characters should be up-to-date, with realistic dialogue. We're looking for health-related stories with unusual twists or surprise endings. We want to avoid stories and poems that 'preach.' We try to present the health material in a positive way, utilizing a light humorous approach wherever possible." Most rejected mss "are too wordy. Need short, short nonfiction."

$ HUSTLER BUSTY BEAUTIES, (I, IV), HG Publications, Inc., 8484 Wilshire Blvd., Suite 900, Beverly Hills CA 90211. (213)651-5400. **Editor:** N. Morgen Hagen. Magazine: 8×11; 100 pages; 60 lb. paper; 80 lb. cover; illustrations and photographs. "Adult entertainment and reading centered around large-breasted women for an over-18 audience, mostly male." Published 13 times/year. Estab. 1988. Circ. 150,000.

Needs: Adventure, erotica, fantasy, mystery/suspense. All must have erotic theme. Receives 25 unsolicited fiction mss/month. Accepts 1 ms/issue; 6-12 mss/year. Publishes mss 3-6 months after acceptance. Published work by Mike Dillon and H.H. Morris. Length: 1,600 words preferred; 1,000 words minimum; 2,000 words maximum.

How to Contact: Query first. Then send complete ms with cover letter. Reports in 2 weeks on queries; in 2-4 weeks on mss. SASE. Sample copy for $5. Fiction guidelines free.

Payment/Terms: Pays $350-500 (fiction) and $50 (erotic letters) on publication for all rights.

Advice: Looks for "1. plausible plot, well-defined characters, literary ingenuity; 2. hot sex scenes; 3. readable, coherent, grammatically sound prose."

☑ ✪ $ IMPLOSION, A Journal of the Bizarre and Eccentric, (II), P.O. Box 533653, Orlando FL 32853. (407)246-6515. E-mail: cynthia@implosion-mag.com. Website: http://www.implosion-mag.com (includes guidelines, content samples, subscription info). **Editor:** Cynthia Conlin. Magazine: 8½×11; 64 pages; 50 lb. glossy paper; 80 lb. glossy cover stock; illustrations and photos. "*Implosion* explores the bizarre and eccentric. Publishes nonfiction features on travel, culture, art, film, music and more." Quarterly. Estab. 1995. Circ. 18,000.
Needs: Adventure, experimental (science fantasy), horror, humor, psychic/supernatural/occult, science fiction (hard science, soft/sociological). Especially interested in "material with weird and bizarre themes and overtones." No porn, children's. Receives 100 mss/month. Accepts 2-3 mss/issue; 8-15 mss/year. Publishes ms 4-7 months after acceptance. Published work by J. Spencer Dreischarf, Bert Benmeyer, D.F. Lewis and Rick Reed. Publishes 5-8 new writers/year. Length: 2,000 words average; 6,000 words maximum. Publishes short shorts. Also publishes literary criticism. Sometimes critiques or comments on rejected mss.
How to Contact: Send complete ms with cover letter. Include estimated word count and list of publications. Reports in 2-6 months on mss. Send SASE for reply, return of ms or send a disposable copy of ms. Simultaneous and reprint submissions OK. Sample copy for $5. Guidelines for SASE. Reviews novels and short story collections. Send books to editor.
Payment/Terms: Pays $15-30/story within 30 days of publication and 4 contributor's copies; additional copies for $3. Acquires first or one-time rights. Sends galleys to author if requested.
Advice: "We want new ideas and concepts, not clichéd rehashes of 'Twilight Zone' plots. A bit of humor doesn't hurt, either. Remember that 'bizarre' doesn't mean silly or pointless. Check your work for grammatical errors and the like—there's no greater turnoff than poorly constructed manuscripts."

☑ ✪ $ IN TOUCH FOR MEN, (I, IV), 13122 Saticoy St., North Hollywood CA 91605-3402. (818)764-2288. Fax: (818)764-2307. E-mail: info@intouchformen.com. Website: http://www.intouchformen.com (includes information about current issues, subscription rates, hyperfiction, back issues and video reviews). **Editor:** Alan W. Mills. Magazine: 8×10¾; 100 pages; glossy paper; coated cover; illustrations and photographs. "*In Touch* is a magazine for gay men. It features five to six nude male centerfolds in each issue, but is erotic rather than pornographic. We include fiction. We also publish two other magazines, *Indulge* and *Blackmale*." Monthly. Estab. 1973. Circ. 70,000.
Needs: Confession, gay erotica, romance (contemporary, historical). All characters must be over 18 years old. Stories must have an explicit erotic content. No heterosexual or internalized homophobic fiction. Accepts 7 mss/month; 80 mss/year. Publishes ms 6 months after acceptance. Publishes 20 new writers/year. Length: 2,500 words average; up to 3,500 words maximum. Sometimes critiques rejected mss and recommends other markets.
How to Contact: Send complete ms with cover letter, name, address and Social Security number. Accepts queries and mss by e-mail and fax (mss by permission only). Reports in 2 weeks on queries; 2 months on mss. SASE. Simultaneous and reprint submissions, if from local publication, OK. Disk submissions OK (call before sending by modem). Sample copy for $6.95. Fiction guidelines free. Reviews novels and short story collections.
Payment/Terms: Pays $25-75 (except on rare occasions for a longer piece) on publication for one-time rights.
Advice: Publishes "primarily erotic material geared toward gay men. We sometimes run nonfiction or features about gay issues. I personally prefer (and accept) manuscripts that are not only erotic/hardcore, but show a developed story, plot and a concise ending (as opposed to just sexual vignettes that basically lead nowhere). If it has a little romance, too, that's even better. Emphasis still on the erotic, though. We now only use 'safe sex' depictions in fiction, hoping that it will prompt people to act responsibly. We have a new interest in experimental fiction as long as it does not violate the standards of the homoerotic genre. All fiction must conform to the basic rules of the genre. Beyond that, we look for inventive use of language, unique content, exciting themes and, on occasion, experimental structures or subversive issues. If you're writing for a genre, know that genre, but don't be afraid to twist things around just enough to stand out from the crowd. Our website is becoming increasingly important to us. We have our eyes open for interesting hyperfiction because we want people to keep returning to our site, hoping that they might subscribe to the magazine."

✪ INDIA CURRENTS, (II,IV), The Complete Indian American Magazine, Box 21285, San Jose CA 95151. (408)274-6966. Fax: (408)274-2733. **Managing Editor:** Vandana Kumar. E-mail: editor@indiacur.com. Magazine: 8½×11; 104 pages; newsprint paper; illustrations and photographs. "The arts and culture of India as seen in America for Indians and non-Indians with a common interest in India." Monthly. Estab. 1987. Circ. 25,000.
Needs: All Indian content: contemporary, ethnic, feminist, historical (general), humor/satire, literary, mainstream, regional, religious/inspirational, romance, translations (from Indian languages). "We seek material with insight into Indian culture, American culture and the crossing from one to another." Receives 12 unsolicited mss/month. Accepts 1 ms/issue; 12 mss/year. Publishes ms 2-6 months after acceptance. Published work by Chitra Divakaruni, Jyotsna Sreenivasan and Rajini Srikanth. Published new writers within the last year. Length: 1,800 words.
How to Contact: Send complete ms with cover letter and clips of published work. Reports in 2-3 months on mss. SASE. Simultaneous and reprint submissions OK. Accepts electronic submissions. Sample copy for $3.
Payment/Terms: Pays in subscriptions on publication for one-time rights.

Advice: "Story must be related to India and subcontinent in some meaningful way. The best stories are those which document some deep transformation as a result of an Indian experience, or those which show the humanity of Indians."

$ IRELAND'S OWN, (IV), 1 North Main St., Wexford Ireland. **Editors:** Gerry Breen and Margaret Galvin. Weekly. Circ. 50,000. Publishes 3 stories/issue. "*Ireland's Own* is a homey family-oriented weekly magazine with a story emphasis on the traditional values of Irish society. Short stories must be written in a straightforward nonexperimental manner with an Irish orientation." Length: 1,800-2,000 words. Pays £40-50 on publication. "Study and know the magazine's requirements, orientation and target market. Guidelines and copies sent out on request."

$ JACK AND JILL, (II, IV), The Children's Better Health Institute, P.O. Box 567, 1100 Waterway Blvd., Indianapolis IN 46206. (317)636-8881. **Editor:** Daniel Lee. Children's magazine of articles, stories and activities, many with a health, safety, exercise or nutritional-oriented theme, ages 7-10 years. Monthly except January/February, April/May, July/August, October/November. Estab. 1938.
Needs: Science fiction, mystery, sports, adventure, historical fiction and humor. Health-related stories with a subtle lesson. Published new writers within the last year. Length: 500-800 words.
How to Contact: Send complete ms with SASE. Reports in 3 months on mss. Sample copy for $1.25. Fiction guidelines for SASE.
Payment/Terms: Pays up to 20¢/word on publication for all rights.
Advice: "Try to present health material in a positive—not a negative—light. Use humor and a light approach wherever possible without minimizing the seriousness of the subject. We need more humor and adventure stories."

$ JIVE, BLACK CONFESSIONS, BLACK ROMANCE, BRONZE THRILLS, BLACK SECRETS, TRUE BLACK EXPERIENCE, (I, II), Sterling/Mcfadden, 233 Park Ave. S., Fifth Floor, New York NY 10003. (212)780-3500. **Editor:** Marcia Mahan. Magazine: 8½×11; 72 pages; newsprint paper; glossy cover; 8×10 photographs. "We publish stories that are romantic and have romantic lovemaking scenes in them. Our audience is basically young. However, we have a significant audience base of housewives. The age range is from 18-49." Bimonthly (*Jive* and *Black Romance* in odd-numbered months; *Black Confessions* and *Bronze Thrills* in even-numbered months). 6 issues per year. Estab. 1962. Circ. 100,000.
Needs: Confession, romance (contemporary, young adult). No "stories that are stereotypical to black people, ones that do not follow the basic rules of writing, or ones that are too graphic in content and lack a romantic element." Receives 20 or more unsolicited fiction mss/month. Accepts 6 mss/issue (2 issues/month); 144 mss/year. Publishes ms an average of 2-3 months after acceptance. Published work by Linda Smith; published new writers within the last year. Length: 18-24 pages.
How to Contact: Query with clips of published work or send complete ms with cover letter. "A cover letter should include an author's bio and what he or she proposes to do. Of course, address and phone number." Reports in 3 months. SASE. Simultaneous submissions OK. "Please contact me if simultaneously submitted work has been accepted elsewhere." Sample copy for 9×12 SAE and 5 first-class stamps; fiction guidelines for #10 SAE and 2 first-class stamps.
Payment/Terms: Pays $75-100 on publication for all rights.
Advice: "Our five magazines are a great starting point for new writers. We accept work from beginners as well as established writers. Please study and research black culture and lifestyles if you are not a black writer. Stereotypical stories are not acceptable. Set the stories all over the world and all over the USA—not just down south. We are not looking for 'the runaway who gets turned out by a sweet-talking pimp' stories. We are looking for stories about all types of female characters. Any writer should not be afraid to communicate with us if he or she is having some difficulty with writing a story. We are available to help at any stage of the submission process. Also, writers should practice patience. If we do not contact the writer, that means that the story is being read or is being held on file for future publication. If we get in touch with the writer, it usually means a request for revision and resubmission. Do the best work possible and don't let rejection slips send you off 'the deep end.' Don't take everything that is said about your work so personally. We are buying all of our work from freelance writers."

$ LADIES' HOME JOURNAL, (III), Published by Meredith Corporation, 125 Park Ave., New York NY 10017. (212)557-6600. Editor-in-Chief: Myrna Blyth. **Books/Fiction Editor:** Mary Moklev. Managing Editor: Carolyn Noyes. Magazine: 190 pages; 34-38 lb. coated paper; 65 lb. coated cover; illustrations and photos.

- *Ladies' Home Journal* has won several awards for journalism.

Needs: Book mss and short stories, *accepted only through an agent*. Return of unsolicited material cannot be guaranteed. Published work by Fay Weldon, Anita Shreve, Jane Shapiro and Anne Rivers Siddons. Length: approximately 2,000-2,500 words.

How to Contact: Send complete ms with cover letter (credits). Simultaneous submissions OK. Publishes ms 4-12 months after acceptance.
Payment/Terms: Acquires First North American rights.
Advice: "Our readers like stories, especially those that have emotional impact. Stories about relationships between people—husband/wife—mother/son—seem to be subjects that can be explored effectively in short stories. Our reader's mail and surveys attest to this fact: Readers enjoy our fiction and are most keenly tuned to stories dealing with children. Fiction today is stronger than ever. Beginners can be optimistic; if they have talent, I do believe that talent will be discovered. It is best to read the magazine before submitting."

$ LADYBUG, (II, IV), The Cricket Magazine Group, P.O. Box 300, Peru IL 61354. (815)224-6656. Editor-in-Chief: Marianne Carus. **Editor:** Paula Morrow. Magazine: 8×10; 36 pages plus 4-page pullout section; illustrations. "*Ladybug* publishes original stories and poems and reprints written by the world's best children's authors. For young children, ages 2-6." Monthly. Estab. 1990. Circ. 130,000.

• *Ladybug* has received the Parents Choice Award; the Golden Lamp Honor Award and the Golden Lamp Award from Ed Press, and Magazine Merit awards from the Society of Children's Book Writers and Illustrators.

Needs: Fairy tales, fantasy (children's), folk tales, juvenile, picture stories, preschool, read-out-loud stories. Length: 300-750 words preferred. Publishes short shorts.
How to Contact: Send complete ms with cover letter. Include word count on ms (do not count title). Reports in 3 months. SASE. Reprints are OK. Fiction guidelines for SASE. Sample copy for $4. For guidelines *and* sample send 9×12 SAE (no stamps required) and $4.
Payment/Terms: Pays up to 25¢/word (less for reprints) on publication for first publication rights or second serial (reprint) rights. For recurring features, pays flat fee and copyright becomes property of The Cricket Magazine Group.
Advice: Looks for "well-written stories for preschoolers: age-appropriate, not condescending. We look for rich, evocative language and sense of joy or wonder."

✓ $ LIGUORIAN, (I, IV), "A Leading Catholic Magazine," Liguori Publications, 1 Liguori Dr., Liguori MO 63057-9998. (800)464-2555. Fax: (800)325-9526. E-mail: 104626.1547@compuserve.com. **Editor-in-Chief:** Allan Weinert, CSS.R. Magazine: 5×8½; 64 pages; b&w illustrations and photographs. "*Liguorian* is a Catholic magazine aimed at helping our readers to live a full Christian life. We publish articles for families, young people, children, religious and singles—all with the same aim." Monthly. Estab. 1913. Circ. 330,000.

• *Liguorian* received Catholic Press Association awards for 1997 including Best Special Issue (September 1997); Best Short Story (*Across the Clothesline*, by Kay Hogan); and an honorable mention (*In the Shadow of the Willows*, by Molly Glissner).

Needs: Religious/inspirational, young adult and senior citizen/retirement (with moral Christian thrust), spiritual. "Stories submitted to *Liguorian* must have as their goal the lifting up of the reader to a higher Christian view of values and goals. We are not interested in contemporary works that lack purpose or are of questionable moral value." Receives approximately 25 unsolicited fiction mss/month. Accepts 12 mss/year. Recently published work by Sharon Helgens and Jon Ripslinger. Publishes 3-4 new writers/year. Length: 1,500-2,000 words preferred. Also publishes short shorts. Occasionally critiques rejected mss "if we feel the author is capable of giving us something we need even though this story did not suit us."
How to Contact: Send complete ms with SASE. Accepts disk submissions compatible with IBM, using a WordPerfect 5.1 program; prefers hard copy with disk submission. Reports in 10-12 weeks on mss. Sample copy and guidelines for #10 SASE.
Payment/Terms: Pays 10-12¢/word and 5 contributor's copies on acceptance for all rights. Offers 50% kill fee for assigned mss not published.
Advice: "First read several issues containing short stories. We look for originality and creative input in each story we read. Since most editors must wade through mounds of manuscripts each month, consideration for the editor requires that the market be studied, the manuscript be carefully presented and polished before submitting. Our publication uses only one story a month. Compare this with the 25 or more we receive over the transom each month. Also, many fiction mss are written without a specific goal or thrust, i.e., an interesting incident that goes nowhere is *not a story*. We believe fiction is a highly effective mode for transmitting the Christian message and also provides a good balance in an unusually heavy issue."

LILITH MAGAZINE, The Independent Jewish Women's Magazine, (I, II, IV), 250 W. 57th St., Suite 2432, New York NY 10107. (212)757-0818. E-mail: lilithmag@aol.com. Editor: Susan Weidman Schneider. **Fiction Editor:** Faye Moskowitz. Magazine: 48 pages; 80 lb. cover; b&w illustrations; b&w and color photos.

 **A BULLET INTRODUCES COMMENTS** by the editor of *Novel & Short Story Writer's Market* indicating special information about the listing.

Publishes work relating to Jewish feminism, for Jewish feminists, feminists and Jewish households. Quarterly. Estab. 1976. Circ. 25,000.

Needs: Ethnic, feminist, lesbian, literary, prose poem, religious/inspirational, spiritual, translation, young adult. "Nothing that does not in any way relate to Jews, women or Jewish women." Receives 15 unsolicited mss/month. Accepts 1 ms/issue; 4 mss/year. Publishes ms up to 1 year after acceptance. Published work by Lesléa Newman, Marge Piercy and Gloria Goldreich. Publishes short shorts.

How to Contact: Send complete ms with cover letter, which should include a 2-line bio. Reports in 2 months on queries; 2-6 months on mss. SASE. Simultaneous and reprint submissions OK but must be indicated in cover letter. Sample copy for $6. Writer's guidelines for #10 SASE. Reviews novels and short story collections. Send books to Susan Weidman Schneider.

Payment/Terms: Varies. Acquires first rights.

Advice: "Read the magazine to be familiar with the kinds of material we publish."

$ LIVE, (II, IV), Assemblies of God, 1445 Boonville, Springfield MO 65802-1894. (417)862-2781. **Editor:** Paul W. Smith. "A take-home story paper distributed weekly in young adult/adult Sunday school classes. *Live* is a story paper primarily. Stories in both fiction and narrative style are welcome. Poems, first-person anecdotes and humor are used as fillers. The purpose of *Live* is to present in short story form realistic characters who utilize biblical principles. We hope to challenge readers to take risks for God and to resolve their problems scripturally." Weekly. Circ. 130,000.

Needs: Religious/inspirational, prose poem and spiritual. "Inner city, ethnic, racial settings." No controversial stories about such subjects as feminism, war or capital punishment. Accepts 2 mss/issue. Recently published work by M.G. Baldwin, Robert Robeson, Clarence Trowbridge, Alan Cliburn, Kevin Dawson, Betty Lou Mell, Linda Hutton and Rhonda Stapleton. Publishes 40 new writers/year. Length: 500-1,700 words.

How to Contact: Send complete ms. Social Security number and word count must be included. Simultaneous submissions OK. Reports in 6-8 weeks. Sample copy and guidelines for SASE.

Payment/Terms: Pays 10¢/word (first rights); 7¢/word (second rights) on acceptance.

Advice: "Study our publication and write good, inspirational true to life or fiction stories that will encourage people to become all they can be as Christians. Stories should go somewhere! Action, not just thought—life; interaction, not just insights. Heroes and heroines, suspense and conflict. Avoid simplistic, pietistic conclusions, preachy, critical or moralizing. We don't accept science or Bible fiction. Stories should be encouraging, challenging, humorous. Even problem-centered stories should be upbeat." Reserves the right to change titles, abbreviate length and clarify flashbacks for publication.

N $ LONDON REVIEW OF BOOKS, 28 Little Russell St., London WC1A England. **Editor:** Mary-Kay Wilmers. Circ. 16,000. Publishes 2-3 stories annually. Publishes "book reviews with long essay-length reviews. Also publishes the occasional short story."

Payment/Terms: Pays £200 per story and 6 contributor's copies.

N $ THE LUTHERAN JOURNAL, (II), Macalester Park Publishing, 7317 Cahill Rd., Minneapolis MN 55439. (612)941-6830. **Editor:** Rev. A.U. Deye. "A family magazine providing wholesome and inspirational reading material for the enjoyment and enrichment of Lutherans." Quarterly. Estab. 1936. Circ. 125,000.

Needs: Literary, contemporary, religious/inspirational, romance (historical), senior citizen/retirement and young adult. Must be appropriate for distribution in the churches. Buys 3-6 mss/issue. Length: 1,000-1,500 words.

How to Contact: Send complete ms with SASE. Sample copy for SAE with 59¢ postage.

Payment/Terms: Pays $10-25 and 6 contributor's copies on publication for all and first rights.

$ MAGAZINE OF FANTASY AND SCIENCE FICTION, (II), P.O. Box 1806, New York NY 10159-1806. Phone/fax: (212)982-2676. E-mail: gordonfsf@aol.com. Website: http://www.fsfmag.com (includes writer's guidelines, nonfiction features, current issue, information on back issues and links). **Editor:** Gordon Van Gelder. Magazine: illustrations on cover only. Publishes "science fiction and fantasy. Our readers are age 13 and up who are interested in science fiction and fantasy." Monthly. Estab. 1949. Circ. 50,000.

- *Magazine of Fantasy and Science Fiction* has won numerous awards including two Nebulas in 1997 and one in 1998. The magazine ranks #4 on the latest *Writer's Digest* Fiction 50 list.

Needs: Fantasy and science fiction. Receives 500-600 unsolicited fiction submissions/month. Buys 8 fiction mss/issue ("on average"); 100-140 mss/year. Time between acceptance and publication varies; up to 3 years. Published work by Ray Bradbury, Esther M. Friesner, Stephen King and Gene Wolfe. Publishes 3-8 new writers/year. Length: 25,000 words maximum. Publishes short shorts. Critiques rejected ms, "if quality warrants it." Sometimes recommends other markets.

How to Contact: Send complete ms with cover letter. Reports in 1 month on queries; 6-8 weeks on mss. SASE (or IRC). No simultaneous submissions. Sample copy for $5. Fiction guidelines for SASE.

Payment/Terms: Pays 5-8¢/word.

Terms: Pays on acceptance for first North American serial rights; foreign, option on anthology if requested.

$ MANSCAPE, (I, IV), First Hand Ltd., Box 1314, Teaneck NJ 07666. (201)836-9177. Fax: (201)836-5055. E-mail: firsthand3@aol.com. **Editor:** Mick Cody. Magazine: digest sized; 98 pages; illustrations. "Magazine is devoted to gay male sexual fetishes; publishes fiction and readers' letters devoted to this theme." Monthly. Estab. 1985. Circ. 60,000.

Needs: Erotica, gay. Should be written in first person. No science fiction or fantasy. Erotica must be based on real life. Receives 25 unsolicited fiction mss/month. Accepts 5 mss/issue; 60 mss/year. Publishes ms an average of 12-18 months after acceptance. Published new writers within the last year. Length: 3,000 words average; 2,000 words minimum; 3,750 words maximum. Sometimes critiques rejected ms.
How to Contact: Send complete ms with cover letter. SASE. Sample copy for $5; guidelines for #10 SASE.
Payment/Terms: Pays $100-150 on publication for all rights or first North American serial rights.
Advice: "Keep story interesting by exhibiting believability and sexual tension."

$ MATURE LIVING, (II), Lifeway Christian Resources of the Southern Baptist Convention, MSN 140, 127 Ninth Ave. North, Nashville TN 37234-0140. (615)251-2191. Fax: (615)251-5008. E-mail: maturel iving@bssb.com. **Editor:** Al Shackleford. Magazine: 8½×11; 52 pages; non-glare paper; slick cover stock; full color illustrations and photos. "Our magazine is Christian in content and the material required is what would appeal to 55 and over age group: inspirational, informational, nostalgic, humorous. Our magazine is distributed mainly through churches (especially Southern Baptist churches) that buy the magazine in bulk and distribute it to members in this age group." Monthly. Estab. 1977. Circ. 360,000.

• *Mature Living* received the gold award in the 1998 National Mature Media Awards.

Needs: Humor, religious/inspirational and senior citizen/retirement. Avoid all types of pornography, drugs, liquor, horror, science fiction and stories demeaning to the elderly. Receives 10 mss/month. Buys 1-2 mss/issue. Publishes ms an average of 1 year after acceptance. Published work by Burndean N. Sheffy, Pearl E. Trigg, Joyce M. Sixberry; published new writers within the last year. Length: 800-1,200 words (prefers 1,000).
How to Contact: Send complete ms with SASE. Include estimated word count and Social Security number. Reports in 2 months. Sample copy for $1. Guidelines for SASE.
Payment/Terms: Pays $75 on acceptance; 3 contributor's copies. $1 charge for extras. First rights if requested.
Advice: Mss are rejected because they are too long or subject matter unsuitable. "Our readers seem to enjoy an occasional short piece of fiction. It must be believable, however, and present senior adults in a favorable light."

$ MATURE YEARS, (II, IV), United Methodist Publishing House, 201 Eighth Ave. S., Nashville TN 37202. (615)749-6292. Fax: (615)749-6512. **Editor:** Marvin W. Cropsey. Magazine: 8½×11; 112 pages; illustrations and photos. Magazine "helps persons in and nearing retirement to appropriate the resources of the Christian faith as they seek to face the problems and opportunities related to aging." Quarterly. Estab. 1953.
Needs: Humor, intergenerational relationships, nostalgia, older adult issues, religious/inspirational, spiritual (for older adults). "We don't want anything poking fun at old age, saccharine stories or anything not for older adults. Must show older adults (age 55 plus) in a positive manner." Accepts 1 ms/issue, 4 mss/year. Publishes ms 1 year after acceptance. Published work by Ann S. Gray, Betty Z. Walker and Vickie Elaine Legg. Published new writers within the last year. Length: 1,000-1,800 words.
How to Contact: Send complete ms with SASE and Social Security number. No simultaneous submissions. Reports in 2 months. Sample copy for 10½×11 SAE and $5.
Payment/Terms: Pays 6¢/word on acceptance.
Advice: "Practice writing dialogue! Listen to people talk; take notes; master dialogue writing! Not easy, but well worth it! Most inquiry letters are far too long. If you can't sell me an idea in a brief paragraph, you're not going to sell the reader on reading your finished article or story."

$ MESSENGER OF THE SACRED HEART, (II), Apostleship of Prayer, 661 Greenwood Ave., Toronto, Ontario M4J 4B3 Canada. (416)466-1195. **Editors:** Rev. F.J. Power, S.J. and Alfred DeManche. Magazine: 7×10; 32 pages; coated paper; self-cover; illustrations; photos. Magazine for "Canadian and U.S. Catholics interested in developing a life of prayer and spirituality; stresses the great value of our ordinary actions and lives." Monthly. Estab. 1891. Circ. 14,000.
Needs: Religious/inspirational. Stories about people, adventure, heroism, humor, drama. No poetry. Accepts 1 ms/issue. Length: 750-1,500 words. Recommends other markets.
How to Contact: Send complete ms with SAE. No simultaneous submissions. Reports in 1 month. Sample copy for $1.50 (Canadian).
Payment/Terms: Pays 4¢/word, 3 contributor's copies on acceptance for first North American serial rights. Rarely buys reprints.
Advice: "Develop a story that sustains interest to the end. Do not preach, but use plot and characters to convey the message or theme. Aim to move the heart as well as the mind. If you can, add a light touch or a sense of humor to the story. Your ending should have impact, leaving a moral or faith message for the reader."

$ MIDSTREAM, A Monthly Jewish Review, (II, IV), Theodor Herzl Foundation, 110 E. 59th St., New York NY 10022-1304. (212)339-6046. **Editor:** Joel Carmichael. Magazine: 8½×11; 48 pages; 50 lb. paper; 65 lb. white smooth cover stock. "We are a Zionist journal; we publish material with Jewish themes or that would appeal to a Jewish readership." Published 8 times/year. Estab. 1954. Circ. 10,000.

• Work published in *Midstream* was included in the *O. Henry Award* prize anthology.

Needs: Historical (general), humor/satire, literary, mainstream, translations. Receives 15-20 unsolicited mss/

month. Accepts 1 mss/issue; 10 mss/year. Publishes ms 6-18 months after acceptance. Agented fiction 10%. Published work by I. B. Singer, Anita Jackson and Enid Shomer. Length: 2,500 words average; 1,500 words minimum; 4,500 words maximum. Sometimes critiques rejected mss.
How to Contact: Send complete ms with cover letter, which should include "address, telephone, or affiliation of author; state that the ms is fiction." Reports in "up to 6 months." SASE.
Payment/Terms: Pays 5¢/word and contributor's copies on publication for first rights.
Advice: "Be patient—we publish only one piece of fiction per issue and we have a backlog."

$ MONTANA SENIOR NEWS, (II,IV), Barrett-Whitman Co., Box 3363, Great Falls MT 59403. (406)761-0305. Fax: (406)761-8358. E-mail: montsrnews@imt.net. **Editor:** Jack Love. Tabloid: 11×17; 60-80 pages; newsprint paper and cover; illustrations; photos. Publishes "everything of interest to seniors, except most day-to-day political items like Social Security and topics covered in the daily news. Personal profiles of seniors, their lives, times and reminiscences." Bimonthly. Estab. 1984. Circ. 27,000.
Needs: Historical, senior citizen/retirement, western (historical or contemporary). No fiction "unrelated to experiences to which seniors can relate." Buys 1 or fewer mss/issue; 4-5 mss/year. Publishes ms within 6 months of acceptance. Length: 500-800 words preferred. Publishes short stories. Length: under 500 words.
How to Contact: Send complete ms with cover letter and phone number. Only responds to selected mss. SASE. Simultaneous and reprint submissions OK. Accepts electronic submission via WordPerfect disk. Sample copy for 9×12 SAE and $2 postage and handling.
Payment/Terms: Pays 4¢/word on publication for first rights or one-time rights.

$ MY FRIEND, The Catholic Magazine for Kids, (II), Pauline Books & Media, 50 St. Paul's Ave., Boston MA 02130. (617)522-8911. **Editor:** Sister Anne Joan. Magazine: 8½×11; 32 pages; smooth, glossy paper and cover stock; illustrations; photos. Magazine of "religious truths and positive values for children in a format which is enjoyable and attractive. Each issue contains Bible stories, lives of saints and famous people, short stories, science corner, contests, projects, etc." Monthly during school year (September-June). Estab. 1979. Circ. 12,000.

• *My Friend* received third place in the Catholic Press Association's Best Short Story competition in 1997.

Needs: Juvenile, religious/inspirational, spiritual (children), sports (children). Receives 60 unsolicited fiction mss/month. Accepts 3-4 mss/issue; 30-40 mss/year. Published work by Rita Robinson, Mary Elizabeth Anderson and Sandra Humphrey. Published new writers within the past year. Length: 200 words minimum; 900 words maximum; 600 words average.
How to Contact: Send complete ms with SASE. Accepts queries/mss by e-mail and fax. Reports in 1-2 months on mss. Publishes ms an average of 1 year after acceptance. Sample copy for $2 and 9×12 SAE ($1.24 postage).
Payment/Terms: Pays $20-150 (stories, articles).
Advice: "We are looking for stories that immediately grab the imagination of the reader. Good dialogue, realistic character development, current lingo are necessary. Fiction can entertain, inspire or teach. Fiction stories do not have to do all three. We have a need for each of these types at different times. We prefer child-centered stories in a real-world setting. We are particularly interested in media-related articles and stories that involve healthy choices regarding media use. Try to write visually—be 'graphics-friendly.' "

$ NA'AMAT WOMAN, Magazine of NA'AMAT USA, The Women's Labor Zionist Organization of America, (IV), 200 Madison Ave., New York NY 10016-3903. (212)725-8010. **Editor:** Judith A. Sokoloff. "Magazine covering a wide variety of subjects of interest to the Jewish community—including political and social issues, arts, profiles; many articles about Israel; and women's issues. Fiction must have a Jewish theme. Readers are the American Jewish community." Published 5 times/year. Estab. 1926. Circ. 20,000.
Needs: Contemporary, ethnic, literary. Receives 10 unsolicited fiction mss/month. Accepts 3-5 fiction mss/year. Length: 1,500 words minimum; 3,000 words maximum. Also buys nonfiction.
How to Contact: Query first or send complete ms with SASE. Reports in 3 months on mss. Free sample copy for 9×11½ SAE and $1.20 postage.
Payment/Terms: Pays 10¢/word and 2 contributor's copies on publication for first North American serial rights; assignments on work-for-hire basis.
Advice: "No maudlin nostalgia or romance; no hackneyed Jewish humor and no poetry."

$ NEW ERA MAGAZINE, (I, II, IV), The Church of Jesus Christ of Latter-day Saints, 50 E. North Temple St., Salt Lake City UT 84150. (801)532-2951. Fax: (801)240-5997. **Editor:** Larry A. Hiller. Magazine: 8×10½; 51 pages; 40 lb. coated paper; illustrations and photos. "We will publish fiction on any theme that strengthens and builds the standards and convictions of teenage Latter-day Saints ('Mormons')." Monthly. Estab. 1971. Circ. 220,000.

READ THE BUSINESS OF FICTION WRITING section to learn the correct way to prepare and submit a manuscript.

• *New Era* is a recipient of the Focus on Excellence Award from Brigham Young University. The magazine also sponsors a writing contest.

Needs: Stories on family relationships, self-esteem, dealing with loneliness, resisting peer pressure and all aspects of maintaining Christian values in the modern world. "All material must be written from a Latter-day Saint ('Mormon') point of view—or at least from a generally Christian point of view, reflecting LDS life and values. Would like to see more fiction with a lighthearted approach to self-esteem or peer pressure." No science fiction or fantasy. Receives 30-35 unsolicited mss/month. Accepts 1 ms/issue; 12 mss/year. Publishes ms 3 months to 3 years after acceptance. Published work by A.E. Cannon, on Smurthwaite, Jack Weyland and Alma Yates. Publishes 2-3 new writers/year. Length: 1,500 words average; 250 words minimum; 2,000 words maximum.

How to Contact: Send complete ms. Reports in 6-8 weeks. SASE. Disk submissions (WordPerfect, MacIntosh) OK. Sample copy for $1.50 and 9×12 SAE with 2 first-class stamps. Fiction guidelines for #10 SASE.

Payment/Terms: Pays $50-375 and contributor's copies on acceptance for all rights (will reassign to author on request).

Advice: "Each magazine has its own personality—you wouldn't write the same style of fiction for *Seventeen* that you would write for *Omni*. Very few writers who are not of our faith have been able to write for us successfully, and the reason usually is that they don't know what it's like to be a member of our church. You must study and research and know those you are writing about. We love to work with beginning authors, and we're a great place to break in if you can understand us." Sponsors contests and awards for LDS fiction writers. "We have an annual contest; entry forms are in each October issue. Deadline is January; winners published in September."

$ NEW MYSTERY, (III), The Best New Mystery Stories, 175 Fifth Ave., #2001, New York NY 10010-7703. (212)353-1582. E-mail: newmyste@erols.com. Website: http://www.NewMystery.com (includes book reviews and short shorts). **Editor:** Charles Raisch III. Magazine: 8½×11; 96 pages; illustrations and photographs. "Mystery, suspense and crime." Quarterly. Estab. 1990. Circ. 90,000.

• Fiction published in *New Mystery* has been nominated for Edgar, Macavity and Anthony awards. Response time for this magazine seems to be slower in summer months. The mystery included here is varied and realistic.

Needs: Mystery/suspense (cozy to hardboiled). No horror or romance. Plans special annual anthology. Receives 350 unsolicited mss/month. Buys 6-10 ms/issue. Agented fiction 50%. Published work by Stuart Kaminsky, Andrew Greeley and Rosemary Santini. Publishes 1 new writer/issue. Length: 3,000-5,000 words preferred. Also buys short book reviews 500-3,000 words. Sometimes critiques rejected mss.

How to Contact: *New Mystery charges a $7 fee for purchase of a contributor's packet, which includes guidelines and 2 sample copies.* Send complete ms with cover letter. "We cannot be responsible for unsolicited manuscripts." Reports on ms in 1 month. SASE. Sample copy for $5, 9×12 SAE and 4 first-class stamps.

Payment/Terms: Pays $25-1,000 on publication for negotiated rights.

Advice: Stories should have "believable characters in trouble; sympathetic lead; visual language." Sponsors "Annual First Story Contest."

$ NEW SPY, (II, IV), New Spy, Inc., 175 Fifth Ave., Suite 2001, New York NY 10010-7703. **Contact:** Editorial Committee. Magazine: 8½×11; 56 pages; illustrations and photos. Publishes "the world's best spy, thriller, intrigue and adventure short stories and book reviews." Quarterly. Estab. 1997. Circ. 70,000.

Needs: "Modern and historical spy fiction of the highest quality. Most international theaters acceptable, especially Europe, the Middle East and Asia. Offbeat situations and characters encouraged, but the use of solid principles of foreign intelligence intrigue is a central consideration. Military themes okay, as long as at some point, the uniform comes off and secretive plainclothes work carries the day." Published work by Leslie Horvitz and Josh Pachter. Length: 3,000-7,000 words preferred. Also buys short book reviews of 250-2,000 words. "See examples in our coverage of Ambler, DeMille, Harris, Ludlum, Truscott and others, I#1."

How to Contact: Send complete ms with a cover letter. If no report in 60 days, consider ms rejected. "*New Spy* magazine is not responsible for unsolicited manuscripts, drawings or other material." Sample copy for $5, 9×12 SAE and 4 first-class stamps.

Payment/Terms: Pays $25-1,000 on publication for negotiable rights.

$ THE NEW YORKER, (III), The New Yorker, Inc., 20 W. 43rd St., New York NY 10036. (212)536-5800. **Contact:** Fiction Department. A quality magazine of interesting, well-written stories, articles, essays and poems for a literate audience. Weekly. Estab. 1925. Circ. 750,000.

How to Contact: Send complete ms with SASE. Reports in 10-12 weeks on mss. Publishes 1 ms/issue.

Payment/Terms: Varies. Pays on acceptance.

Advice: "Be lively, original, not overly literary. Write what you want to write, not what you think the editor would like. Send poetry to Poetry Department."

$ NUGGET, (II), Firestone Publishing Inc., 14411 Commerce Way, Suite 420, Miami Lakes FL 33016. (305)557-0071. **Editor-in-Chief:** Christopher James. A newsstand magazine designed to have erotic appeal for a fetish-oriented audience. Published 12 times a year. Estab. 1956. Circ. 100,000.

Needs: Offbeat, fetish-oriented material encompassing a variety of subjects (B&D, TV, TS, spanking, amputee-

ism, golden showers, infantalism, catfighting, etc.). Most of fiction includes several sex scenes. No fiction that concerns children or religious subjects. Accepts 2 mss/issue. Agented fiction 5%. Length: 2,000-3,500 words.
How to Contact: Send complete ms with SASE. Reports in 1 month. Sample copy for $3.50. Guidelines for legal-sized SASE.
Payment/Terms: Pays minimum $200 and 1 contributor's copy on publication for first rights.
Advice: "Keep in mind the nature of the publication, which is fetish erotica. Subject matter can vary, but we prefer fetish themes."

✔ $ **ODYSSEY, Adventures in Science**, Cobblestone Publishing, Inc., 30 Grove St., Suite C, Peterborough NH 03458. (603)924-7209. **Senior Editor:** Elizabeth E. Lindstrom. Magazine. "Scientific accuracy, original approaches to the subject are primary concerns of the editors in choosing material. For 10-16 year olds." Monthly (except July and August). Estab. 1991. Circ. 30,000.
Needs: Material must match theme; send for theme list and deadlines. Children's/juvenile (10-16 years), "authentic historical and biographical fiction, science fiction, retold legends, etc., relating to theme." List of upcoming themes available for SASE. Length: 750-1,000 words maximum.
How to Contact: Query first or query with clips of published work (if new to *Odyssey*). "Include estimated word count and a detailed 1-page outline explaining the information to be presented; an extensive bibliography of materials authors plan to use." Reports in several months. Send SASE for reply or send stamped postcard to find out if ms has been received. Sample copy for $4.50, 9×12 SAE and $1.05 postage. Fiction guidelines for SASE.
Payment/Terms: Pays 20-25¢/word on publication for all rights.
Advice: "We also include in-depth nonfiction, plays and biographies."

✔ ✪ $ **ON THE LINE, (II)**, Mennonite Publishing House, 616 Walnut Ave., Scottdale PA 15683-1999. (724)887-8500. **Editor:** Mary Meyer. Magazine: 7×10; 28 pages; illustrations; b&w photos. "A religious magazine with the goal of helping children grow in their understanding and appreciation of God, the created world, themselves and other people." For children ages 9-14. Weekly. Estab. 1970. Circ. 6,000.
Needs: Adventure and problem-solving stories with Christian values for older children and young teens (9-14 years). Receives 50-100 unsolicited mss/month. Accepts 52 mss/year. Published work by Terry Miller Shannon, Sandra Smith and Eleanor F. Kane. Published new writers within the last year. Length: 800-1,500 words.
How to Contact: Send complete ms noting whether author is offering first-time or reprint rights. Reports in 1 month. SASE. Simultaneous and previously published work OK. Free sample copy and fiction guidelines.
Payment/Terms: Pays on acceptance for one-time rights.
Advice: "We believe in the power of story to entertain, inspire and challenge the reader to new growth. Know children and their thoughts, feelings and interests. Be realistic with characters and events in the fiction. Stories do not need to be true, but need to *feel* true."

✔ $ **OPTIONS, The *Bi*-Monthly, (I, IV)**, AJA Publishing, Box 170, Irvington NY 10533. E-mail: dianaeditr@aol.com. **Associate Editor:** Diana Sheridan. Magazine: digest-sized; 114 pages; newsprint paper; glossy cover stock; illustrations and photos. Sexually explicit magazine for and about bisexuals. "Please read our Advice subhead." 10 issues/year. Estab. 1982. Circ. 100,000.
Needs: Erotica, bisexual, gay, lesbian. "First person as-if-true experiences." Accepts 6 unsolicited fiction mss/issue. "Very little" of fiction is agented. Published new writers within the last year. Length: 2,000-3,000 words. Sometimes critiques rejected mss.
How to Contact: Send complete ms with or without cover letter. No simultaneous submissions. Reports in approximately 3 weeks. SASE. Electronic submissions (disk or e-mail as textfiles) OK. "Submissions on Macintosh disk welcome and can often use IBM submissions, but please include hard copy too." Sample copy for $2.95 and 6×9 SAE with 5 first-class stamps. Fiction guidelines for SASE.
Payment/Terms: Pays $100 on publication for all rights. Will reassign book rights on request.
Advice: "Read a copy of *Options* carefully and look at our spec sheet before writing anything for us. That's not new advice, but to judge from some of what we get in the mail, it's necessary to repeat. We only buy two bi/lesbian pieces per issue; need is greater for bi/gay male mss. Though we're a bi rather than gay magazine, the emphasis is on same-sex relationships. If the readers want to read about a male/female couple, they'll buy another magazine. Gay male stories sent to *Options* will also be considered for publication in *Beau*, our gay male magazine. Must get into the hot action by 1,000 words into the story. (Sooner is fine too!) *Most important:* We *only* publish male/male stories that feature 'safe sex' practices unless the story is clearly something that took place pre-AIDS."

✔ $ **ORANGE COAST MAGAZINE, The Magazine of Orange County, (IV)**, 3701 Birch St., Suite 100, Newport Beach CA 92660. (949)862-1133. Fax: (949)862-0133. E-mail: ocmag@aol.com. Website: http://www.orangecoast.com. **Editor:** Patrick Mott. Managing Editor: Sharon Chan. Magazine: 8½×11; 175 pages; 50 lb. Sonoma gloss paper; Warrenflo cover; illustrations and photographs. *Orange Coast* publishes articles offering insight into the community for its affluent, well-educated Orange County readers. Monthly. Estab. 1974. Circ. 38,000.
Needs: Fiction rarely published. Fiction submissions must have Orange County setting or characters or be

relevant to local sensibilities. Receives 30 unsolicited mss/month. Accepts 2 mss/year. Publishes ms 4-6 months after acceptance. Length: 2,500 words average; 1,500 words minimum; 3,000 words maximum.
How to Contact: Send complete ms with cover letter that includes Social Security number. Electronic submissions OK. Reports in 3 months. SASE. Simultaneous submissions OK. Sample copy for 9×12 SASE.
Payment/Terms: Pays $25-800 on acceptance for first North American serial rights.
Advice: "Read the magazine. Tell us why a specific piece of fiction belongs there. Convince us to make an exception. We're looking for lean, punchy writing free of clichés or overwriting. Show a thorough understanding of Southern California life."

$ PEOPLE'S FRIEND, 80 Kingsway East, Dundee DD4 8SL Scotland. 01382 223131. Fax: 01382 452491. **Fiction Editor:** Margaret McCoy. Weekly. Circ. 470,000.
Needs: Specializes in women's fiction. "British backgrounds preferred (but not essential) by our readership. Quite simply, we aim to entertain. Stories should have believable, well-developed characters in situations our readers can relate to. Our readers tend to be traditionalists." No stories of the supernatural, or extreme sex or violence. Recently published work by Betty McInnes, Shirley Worral and Christina Jones. "We actively encourage new authors and do our best to help and advise." Publishes 5 stories/issue. Length: 1,000-4,000 words.
Payment/Terms: Pays $75-85 and contributor's copies. Sample copy and guidelines available on application.
Advice: Looks for manuscript with "emotional content and characterization."

PLAYBOY MAGAZINE, 680 N. Lake Shore Dr., Chicago IL 60611. (312)751-8000. Contact: Fiction Editor. Monthly magazine. "As the world's largest general-interest lifestyle magazine for men, *Playboy* spans the spectrum of contemporary men's passions. From hard-hitting investigative journalism to light-hearted humor, the latest in fashion and personal technology to the cutting edge of the popular culture, *Playboy* is and always has been both guidebook and dream book for generations of American men . . . the definitive source of information and ideas for over 10 million readers each month. In addition, *Playboy*'s 'Interview' and '20 Questions' present profiles of politicians, athletes and today's hottest personalities." Estab. 1953, Circ. 3,283,000.

- At time of publication, *Playboy* was not accepting unsolicited submissions.

$ POCKETS, Devotional Magazine for Children, (II), The Upper Room, 1908 Grand Ave., Box 189, Nashville TN 37202. (615)340-7333. E-mail: pockets@upperroom.org. Website: http://www.upperroom.org/pockets (includes themes, guidelines and contest guidelines). **Editor-in-Chief:** Janet R. Knight. Magazine: 7×9; 48 pages; 50 lb. white econowrite paper; 80 lb. white coated, heavy cover stock; color and 2-color illustrations; some photos. Magazine for children ages 6-12, with articles specifically geared for ages 8 to 11. "The magazine offers stories, activities, prayers, poems—all geared to giving children a better understanding of themselves as children of God." Published monthly except for January. Estab. 1981. Estimated circ. 99,000.

- *Pockets* has received honors from the Educational Press Association of America. The magazine's fiction tends to feature children dealing with real-life situations "from a faith perspective." *Pockets* ranked #41 on *Writer's Digest*'s Fiction 50.

Needs: Adventure, contemporary, ethnic, historical (general), juvenile, religious/inspirational and suspense/mystery. No fantasy, science fiction, talking animals. "All submissions should address the broad theme of the magazine. Each issue will be built around one theme with material which can be used by children in a variety of ways. Scripture stories, fiction, poetry, prayers, art, graphics, puzzles and activities will all be included. Submissions do not need to be overtly religious. They should help children experience a Christian lifestyle that is not always a neatly-wrapped moral package, but is open to the continuing revelation of God's will. Seasonal material, both secular and liturgical, is desired. No violence, horror, sexual and racial stereotyping or fiction containing heavy moralizing." No talking animal stories or fantasy. Receives approximately 200 unsolicited fiction mss/month. Accepts 4-5 mss/issue; 44-60 mss/year. Publishes short shorts. A peace-with-justice theme will run throughout the magazine. Published work by Peggy King Anderson, Angela Gibson and John Steptoe. Published new writers last year. Length: 600 words minimum; 1,600 words maximum; 1,200 words average.
How to Contact: Send complete ms with SASE. Previously published submissions OK, but no simultaneous or faxed submissions. Reports in 1 month on mss. Publishes ms 1 year to 18 months after acceptance. Sample copy free with SAE and 4 first-class stamps. Fiction guidelines and themes with SASE. "Strongly advise sending for themes before submitting."
Payment/Terms: Pays 14¢/word and up and 2-5 contributor's copies on acceptance for first North American serial rights. $1.95 charge for extras; $1 each for 10 or more.
Advice: "Listen to children as they talk with each other. Please send for a sample copy as well as guidelines and themes. Many ms we receive are simply inappropriate. Each issue is theme-related. Please send for list of themes. New themes published in December of each year. Include SASE." Sponsors annual fiction writing contest. Deadline: Aug. 15. Send for guidelines. $1,000 award and publication.

$ PORTLAND MAGAZINE, Maine's City Magazine, (I, II), 578 Congress St., Portland ME 04101. (207)775-4339. **Editor:** Colin Sargent. Magazine: 56 pages; 60 lb. paper; 80 lb. cover stock; illustrations and photographs. "City lifestyle magazine—style, business, real estate, controversy, fashion, cuisine, interviews and art relating to the Maine area." Monthly. Estab. 1986. Circ. 100,000.
Needs: Contemporary, historical, literary. Receives 20 unsolicited fiction mss/month. Accepts 1 mss/issue; 10

mss/year. Publishes short shorts. Published work by Janwillem van de Wetering, Sanford Phippen and Mame Medwed. Length: 3 double-spaced typed pages.
How to Contact: Query first. "Fiction below 700 words, please." Send complete ms with cover letter. Reports in 6 months. SASE. Accepts electronic submissions.
Payment/Terms: Pays on publication for first North American serial rights.
Advice: "We publish ambitious short fiction featuring everyone from Frederick Barthelme to newly discovered fiction by Edna St. Vincent Millay."

✔ ★ $ **POWER AND LIGHT, (I, II)**, Word Action Publishing Company, 6401 The Paseo, Kansas City MO 64131-1284. (816)333-7000. Fax: (816)333-4439. E-mail: mhammer@nazarene.org. **Editor:** Beula J. Postlewait. Associate Editor: Matt Price. Story paper: 5½×8; 8 pages; storypaper and newsprint; illustrations and photos. "Relates Sunday School learning to preteens' lives. Must reflect theology of the Church of the Nazarene." Weekly. Estab. 1993. Circ. 740,000.

- *Power and Light* would like to see fiction with more natural, contemporary, positive situations.

Needs: Children's/juvenile (1-4 years; 10-12 years): adventure, fantasy (children's fantasy), religious/inspirational. List of upcoming themes available for SASE. Receives 40 mss/month. Accepts 10 mss/year. Publishes ms 2 years after acceptance. Recently published work by Bob Hostetler and Evelyn Horan. Publishes 10 new writers/year. Length: 700 words average; 650-700 words minimum; 750 words maximum. Often critiques or comments on rejected mss.
How to Contact: Query first ("E-mail response is much quicker and more convenient for queries"). Include estimated word count and Social Security number. Reports in 1 month on queries; 3 months on mss. SASE for reply or return or ms. Simultaneous, reprint and electronic (IBM disk or e-mail) submissions OK. Sample copy for #10 SASE. Fiction guidelines for #10 SASE.
Payment/Terms: Pays 5¢/word and 4 contributor's copies on publication for multi-use rights.
Advice: Looks for "creativity—situations relating to preteens that are not trite such as shoplifting, etc."

★ $ **PURPOSE, (I, II)**, Herald Press, 616 Walnut Ave., Scottdale PA 15683-1999. (412)887-8500. Fax: (412)887-3111. **Editor:** James E. Horsch. Magazine: 5⅜×8⅜; 8 pages; illustrations; photos. "Magazine focuses on Christian discipleship—how to be a faithful Christian in the midst of tough everyday life complexities. Uses story form to present models and examples to encourage Christians in living a life of faithful discipleship." Weekly. Estab. 1968. Circ. 12,200.
Needs: Historical, religious/inspirational. No militaristic/narrow patriotism or racism. Receives 100 unsolicited mss/month. Accepts 3 mss/issue; 140 mss/year. Published work by Kayleen Reusser, Crane Delbert Bennett and Margaret Hook. Length: 600 words average; 800 words maximum. Occasionally comments on rejected mss.
How to Contact: Send complete ms only. Reports in 2 months. Simultaneous and previously published work OK. Sample copy for 6×9 SAE and 2 first-class stamps. Writer's guidelines free with sample copy only.
Payment/Terms: Pays up to 5¢/word for stories and 2 contributor's copies on acceptance for one-time rights.
Advice: Many stories are "situational—how to respond to dilemmas. Write crisp, action moving, personal style, focused upon an individual, a group of people, or an organization. The story form is an excellent literary device to use in exploring discipleship issues. There are many issues to explore. Each writer brings a unique solution. Let's hear them. The first two paragraphs are crucial in establishing the mood/issue to be resolved in the story. Work hard on developing these."

★ 🏆 $ **ELLERY QUEEN'S MYSTERY MAGAZINE, (II)**, Dell Magazines, 1270 Avenue of the Americas, New York NY 10020. (212)698-1313. Fax: (212)698-1198. Website: http://www.elknet.net/mysterypages (includes writer's guidelines, short fiction, book reviews and magazine's history and awards). **Editor:** Janet Hutchings. Magazine: 5⅜×8½; 144 pages with special 240-page combined September/October issue. Magazine for lovers of mystery fiction. Published 11 times/year. Estab. 1941. Circ. 500,000 readers.

- *EQMM* has won numerous awards and sponsors its own award for Best Stories of the Year, nominated by its readership.

Needs: "We accept only mystery, crime, suspense and detective fiction." Receives approximately 400 unsolicited fiction mss each month. Accepts 10-15 mss/issue. Publishes ms 6-12 months after acceptance. Agented fiction 50%. Published work by Peter Lovesey, Anne Perry, Marcia Muller and Ruth Rendell. Publishes 11 new writers/year. Length: up to 7,000 words, occasionally longer. Publishes 1-2 short novels of up to 17,000 words/year by established authors; minute mysteries of 250 words; short, humorous mystery verse. Critiques rejected

FOR EXPLANATIONS OF THESE SYMBOLS,
SEE THE INSIDE FRONT AND BACK COVERS OF THIS BOOK.

mss "only when a story might be a possibility for us if revised." Sometimes recommends other markets.
How to Contact: Send complete ms with SASE. Cover letter should include publishing credits and brief biographical sketch. Simultaneous submissions OK. Reports in 3 months or sooner on mss. Fiction guidelines with SASE. Sample copy for $2.95.
Payment/Terms: Pays 3¢/word and up on acceptance for first North American serial rights. Occasionally buys reprints.
Advice: "We have a Department of First Stories and usually publish at least one first story an issue—i.e., the author's first published fiction. We select stories that are fresh and of the kind our readers have expressed a liking for. In writing a detective story, you must play fair with the reader, providing clues and necessary information. Otherwise you have a better chance of publishing if you avoid writing to formula."

$ R-A-D-A-R, (I, II), Standard Publishing, 8121 Hamilton Ave., Cincinnati OH 45231-9943. (513)931-4050. **Editor:** Gary Thacker. Magazine: 12 pages; newsprint; illustrations; a few photos. "*R-A-D-A-R* is a take-home paper, distributed in Sunday school classes for children in grades 3-4. The stories and other features reinforce the Bible lesson taught in class. Boys and girls who attend Sunday school make up the audience. The fiction stories, Bible picture stories and other special features appeal to their interests." Weekly. Estab. 1978.

- *R-A-D-A-R* ranked #32 on *Writer's Digest*'s Fiction 50 list of top markets for fiction writers. At the time of publication, R-A-D-A-R was being reorganized. Query for current guidelines.

Needs: Fiction—The hero of the story should be an 9-11-year-old in a situation involving one or more of the following: history, mystery, animals, sports, adventure, school, travel, relationships with parents, friends and others. Stories should have believable plots and be wholesome, Christian character-building, but not "preachy." No science fiction. List of upcoming themes available for SASE. Published new writers within the last year. Length: 900-1,000 words average.
How to Contact: Send complete ms. Prefers for authors to send business-size SASE and request theme sheet. "Writing for a specific topic on theme sheet is much better than submitting unsolicited." Reports in 6-8 weeks on mss. SASE for ms. Simultaneous submissions permitted but not desired; reprint submissions OK. Sample copy and guidelines with SASE.
Payment/Terms: Pays 3-7¢/word on acceptance for first rights, reprints, etc.; 4 contributor's copies sent on publication.
Advice: "Send SASE with two first-class stamps for sample copy, guidelines and theme list. Follow the specifics of guidelines. Keep your writing current with the times and happenings of our world. Our needs change as the needs of 3rd-4th graders change. Writers must keep current."

$ RADIANCE, The Magazine for Large Women, (II), Box 30246, Oakland CA 94604. (510)482-0680. Website: http://www.radiancemagazine.com. **Editor:** Alice Ansfield. Fiction Editors: Alice Ansfield and Catherine Taylor. Magazine: 8½×11; 60 pages; glossy/coated paper; 70 lb. cover stock; illustrations; photos. "Theme is to encourage women to live fully now, whatever their body size. To stop waiting to live or feel good about themselves until they lose weight." Quarterly. Estab. 1984. Circ. 17,000. Readership: 80,000.
Needs: Adventure, contemporary, erotica, ethnic, fantasy, feminist, historical, humor/satire, mainstream, mystery/suspense, prose poem, science fiction, spiritual, sports, young adult/teen. "Want fiction to have a larger-bodied character; living in a positive, upbeat way. Our goal is to empower women." Receives 150 mss/month. Accepts 40 mss/year. Publishes ms within 1 year of acceptance. Published work by Marla Zarrow, Sallie Tisdale and Mary Kay Blakely. Publishes 10 new writers/year. Length: 2,000 words average; 1,000 words minimum; 5,000 words maximum. Publishes short shorts. Sometimes critiques rejected mss.
How to Contact: Query with clips of published work and send complete ms with cover letter. Reports in 3-4 months. SASE. Reprint submissions OK. Sample copy for $3.50. Guidelines for #10 SASE. Reviews novels and short story collections "with at least one large-size heroine."
Payment/Terms: Pays $35-100 and contributor's copies on publication for one-time rights. Sends galleys to the author if requested.
Advice: "Read our magazine before sending anything to us. Know what our philosophy and points of view are before sending a manuscript. Look around within your community for inspiring, successful and unique large women doing things worth writing about. At this time, prefer fiction having to do with a larger woman (man, child). *Radiance* is one of the leading resources in the size-acceptance movement. Each issue profiles dynamic large women from all walks of life, along with articles on health, media, fashion and politics. Our audience is the 30 million American women who wear a size 16 or over. Feminist, emotionally-supportive, quarterly magazine."

$ RANGER RICK MAGAZINE, (II), National Wildlife Federation, 8925 Leesburg Pike, Vienna VA 22184. (703)790-4000. Editor: Gerald Bishop. **Fiction Editor:** Deborah Churchman. Magazine: 8×10; 48 pages; glossy paper; 60 lb. cover stock; illustrations; photos. "*Ranger Rick* emphasizes conservation and the enjoyment of nature through full-color photos and art, fiction and nonfiction articles, games and puzzles, and special columns. Our audience ranges in ages from 7-12, with the greatest number in the 7 and up. We aim for a fourth grade reading level. They read for fun and information." Monthly. Estab. 1967. Circ. 650,000.

- *Ranger Rick* has won several Ed Press awards. The editors say the magazine has had a backlog of stories recently, yet they would like to see more *good* mystery and science fiction stories (with nature themes).

Needs: Adventure, fantasy, humor, mystery (amateur sleuth), science fiction and sports. "Interesting stories for kids focusing directly on nature or related subjects. Fiction that carries a conservation message is always needed, as are adventure stories involving kids with nature or the outdoors. Moralistic 'lessons' taught children by parents or teachers are not accepted. Human qualities are attributed to animals only in our regular feature, 'Adventures of Ranger Rick.' " Receives about 150-200 unsolicited fiction mss each month. Accepts about 6 mss/year. Published fiction by Leslie Dendy. Length: 900 words maximum. Critiques rejected mss "when there is time."
How to Contact: Query with sample lead and any clips of published work with SASE. May consider simultaneous submissions. Reports in 3 months on queries and mss. Publishes ms 8 months to 1 year after acceptance, but sometimes longer. Sample copy for $2. Guidelines for legal-sized SASE.
Payment/Terms: Pays $600 maximum/full-length ms on acceptance for all rights. Very rarely buys reprints. Sends galleys to author.
Advice: "For our magazine, the writer needs to understand kids and that aspect of nature he or she is writing about—a difficult combination! Manuscripts are rejected because they are contrived and/or condescending—often overwritten. Some manuscripts are anthropomorphic, others are above our readers' level. We find that fiction stories help children understand the natural world and the environmental problems it faces. Beginning writers have a chance equal to that of established authors *provided* the quality is there. Would love to see more science fiction and fantasy, as well as mysteries."

⊘ **REDBOOK, (II)**, The Hearst Corporation, 224 W. 57th St., New York NY 10019. (212)649-2000. **Fiction Editor:** Dawn Raffel. Magazine: 8×10¾; 150-250 pages; 34 lb. paper; 70 lb. cover; illustrations; photos. "*Redbook*'s readership consists of American women, ages 25-44. Most are well-educated, married, have children and also work outside the home." Monthly. Estab. 1903. Circ. 3,200,000.
Needs: *Redbook* was not accepting unsolicited mss at the time of publication.

$ REFORM JUDAISM, (II, IV), Union of American Hebrew Congregations, 838 5th Ave., New York NY 10021. (212)650-4240. Website: http://www.uchc.org/rjmag/ (includes writer's guidelines, general information, past issues, and more). **Editor:** Aron Hirt-Manheimer. Managing Editor: Joy Weinberg. Magazine: 8×10¾; 96 pages; illustrations; photos. "We cover subjects of Jewish interest in general and Reform Jewish in particular, for members of Reform Jewish congregations in the United States and Canada." Quarterly. Estab. 1972. Circ. 295,000.

- Recipient of The Simon Rockower Award for Excellence in Jewish Journalism for feature writing, graphic design and photography. The editor says they would publish more stories if they could find excellent, sophisticated, contemporary Jewish fiction.

Needs: Humor/satire, religious/inspirational. Receives 75 unsolicited mss/month. Buys 3 mss/year. Publishes ms 6 months after acceptance. Recently published work by Frederick Fastow and Bob Sloan. Length: 1,500 words average; 600 words minimum; 3,500 words maximum.
How to Contact: Send complete ms with cover letter. Reports in 6 weeks. SASE for ms. For quickest response send self addressed stamped postcard with choices: "Yes, we're interested in publishing; Maybe, we'd like to hold for future consideration; No, we've decided to pass on publication." Simultaneous submissions OK. Sample copy for $3.50.
Payment/Terms: Pays 30¢/word on publication for first North American serial rights.

$ ST. ANTHONY MESSENGER, (I, II), 1615 Republic St., Cincinnati OH 45210-1298. E-mail: stanthony@americancatholic.org. Website: http://www.AmericanCatholic.org (includes Saint of the day, selected articles, product information). **Editor:** Norman Perry, O.F.M. Magazine: 8×10¾; 56 pages; illustrations; photos. "*St. Anthony Messenger* is a Catholic family magazine which aims to help its readers lead more fully human and Christian lives. We publish articles which report on a changing church and world, opinion pieces written from the perspective of Christian faith and values, personality profiles, and fiction which entertains and informs." Monthly. Estab. 1893. Circ. 346,000.

- This is a leading Catholic magazine, but has won awards for both religious and secular journalism and writing from the Catholic Press Association, the International Association of Business Communicators and the Cincinnati Editors Association.

Needs: Contemporary, religious/inspirational, romance, senior citizen/retirement and spiritual. "We do not want mawkishly sentimental or preachy fiction. Stories are most often rejected for poor plotting and characterization; bad dialogue—listen to how people talk; inadequate motivation. Many stories say nothing, are 'happenings' rather than stories." No fetal journals, no rewritten Bible stories. Receives 70-80 unsolicited fiction mss/month. Accepts 1 ms/issue; 12 mss/year. Publishes ms up to 1 year after acceptance. Recently published work by Arthur Powers, Barbara Tylla and Susan McElwain. Length: 2,000-3,000 words. Critiques rejected mss "when there is time." Sometimes recommends other markets.
How to Contact: Send complete ms with SASE. No simultaneous submissions. Accepts queries/mss by e-mail and fax. Reports in 6-8 weeks. Sample copy and guidelines for #10 SASE. Reviews novels and short story collections. Send books to Barbara Beckwith, book review editor.
Payment/Terms: Pays 15¢/word maximum and 2 contributor's copies on acceptance for first serial rights; $1 charge for extras.
Advice: "We publish one story a month and we get up to 1,000 a year. Too many offer simplistic 'solutions' or

answers, Pay attention to endings. Easy, simplistic, deus ex machina endings don't work. People have to feel characters in the stories are real and have a reason to care about them and what happens to them. Fiction entertains but can also convey a point in a very telling way just as the Bible uses stories to teach."

$ SATURDAY NIGHT, Saturday Night Magazine Ltd., 184 Front St. E, Suite 400, Toronto, Ontario M5A 4N3 Canada. (416)368-7237. Fax: (416)368-5112. E-mail: editorial@saturdaynight.ca. Editor: Kenneth Whyte. **Contact:** Tara Ariano, assistant to the editor. Monthly magazine. Readership is urban concentrated. Well-educated, with a high disposable income. Average age is 43. Estab. 1887. Circ. 410,000.
Needs: Publishes novel excerpts.
How to Contact: Submit seasonal material 3-4 months in advance. Accepts simultaneous submissions. Sample copy for $3.50. Writer's guidelines free.
Payment/Terms: Pays on receipt of a publishable ms. Buys first North American serial rights.

$ SEEK, (II), Standard Publishing, 8121 Hamilton Ave., Cincinnati OH 45231-2396. (513)931-4050. Fax: (513)931-0950. **Editor:** Eileen H. Wilmoth. Magazine: 5½×8½; 8 pages; newsprint paper; art and photos in each issue. "Inspirational stories of faith-in-action for Christian young adults; a Sunday School take-home paper." Weekly. Estab. 1970. Circ. 40,000.

- *Seek* ranked #40 on *Writer's Digest*'s Fiction 50 list of top markets for fiction writers.

Needs: Religious/inspirational. Accepts 150 mss/year. Publishes ms an average of 1 year after acceptance. 20% of work published is by new writers. Length: 500-1,200 words.
How to Contact: Send complete ms with SASE. No simultaneous submissions. Reports in 2-3 months. Free sample copy and guidelines.
Payment/Terms: Pays 5-7¢/word on acceptance. Buys reprints.
Advice: "Write a credible story with Christian slant—no preachments; avoid overworked themes such as joy in suffering, generation gaps, etc. Most manuscripts are rejected by us because of irrelevant topic or message, unrealistic story, or poor character and/or plot development. We use fiction stories that are believable."

$ SEVENTEEN, (I, II), III Magazine Corp., 850 Third Ave., New York NY 10022-6258. **Fiction Editor:** Ben Schrank. Magazine: 8½×11; 125-400 pages; 40 lb. coated paper; 80 lb. coated cover stock; illustrations; photos. A general interest magazine with fashion; beauty care; pertinent topics such as current issues, attitudes, experiences and concerns of teenagers. Monthly. Estab. 1944. Circ. 2.5 million.

- *Seventeen* sponsors an annual fiction contest for writers age 13-21. *Seventeen* ranked #7 on *Writer's Digest*'s Fiction 50 list of top fiction markets.

Needs: High-quality literary fiction. No science fiction, action/adventure or pornography. Receives 200 unsolicited fiction mss/month. Accepts 6-12 mss/year. Agented fiction 50%. Published work by Margaret Atwood, Edna O'Brien, Blake Nelson, Joyce Carol Oates, Ellen Gilchrist and Pagan Kennedy. Publishes 4-5 new writers/year. Length: approximately 750-3,500 words.
How to Contact: Send complete ms with SASE and cover letter with relevant credits. Reports in 3 months on mss. Guidelines for submissions with SASE.
Payment/Terms: Pays $700-2,500 on acceptance for one-time rights.
Advice: "Respect the intelligence and sophistication of teenagers. *Seventeen* remains open to the surprise of new voices. Our commitment to publishing the work of new writers remains strong; we continue to read every submission we receive. We believe that good fiction can move the reader toward thoughtful examination of her own life as well as the lives of others—providing her ultimately with a fuller appreciation of what it means to be human. While stories that focus on female teenage experience continue to be of interest, the less obvious possibilities are equally welcome. We encourage writers to submit literary short stories concerning subjects that may not be immediately identifiable as 'teenage,' with narrative styles that are experimental and challenging. Too often, unsolicited submissions possess voices and themes condescending and unsophisticated. Also, writers hesitate to send stories to *Seventeen* which they think too violent or risqué. Good writing holds the imaginable and then some, and if it doesn't find its home here, we're always grateful for the introduction to a writer's work. We're more inclined to publish cutting edge fiction than simple, young adult fiction."

$ SHOFAR, For Jewish Kids On The Move, (II, IV), 43 Northcote Dr., Melville NY 11747-3924. (516)643-4598. Fax: (516)643-4598. **Editor:** Gerald H. Grayson, Ph.D. Magazine: 8½×11; 32 pages; 60 lb. paper; 80 lb. cover; illustration; photos. Audience: Jewish children in fourth through eighth grades. Monthly (October-May). Estab. 1984. Circ. 10,000.
Needs: Children's/juvenile (middle reader): cartoons, contemporary, humorous, poetry, puzzles, religious, sports. "All material must be on a Jewish theme." Receives 12-24 unsolicited mss/month. Accepts 3-5 mss/issue; 24-40 mss/year. Published work by Caryn Huberman, Diane Claerbout and Rabbi Sheldon Lewis. Length: 500-700 words. Occasionally critiques rejected mss. Recommends other markets.
How to Contact: Send complete ms with cover letter. Reports in 6-8 weeks. SASE. Simultaneous and reprint submissions OK. Sample copy for 9×12 SAE and $1.01 first-class postage. Fiction guidelines for 3½×6½ SASE.
Payment/Terms: Pays 10¢/word and 5 contributor's copies on publication for first North American serial rights.

Advice: "Know the magazine and the religious-education needs of Jewish elementary-school-age children. If you are a Jewish educator, what has worked for you in the classroom? Write it out; send it on to me; I'll help you develop the idea into a short piece of fiction. A beginning fiction writer eager to break into *Shofar* will find an eager editor willing to help."

$ SOJOURNER, The Women's Forum, (I, IV), 42 Seaverns, Jamaica Plain MA 02130. (617)524-0415. E-mail: info@sojourner.org. Website: http://www.sojourner.org. **Editor:** Stephanie Poggi. Magazine: 11×17; 48 pages; newsprint; illustrations; photos. "Feminist journal publishing interviews, nonfiction features, news, viewpoints, poetry, reviews (music, cinema, books) and fiction for women." Published monthly. Estab. 1975. Circ. 40,000.

Needs: "Writing on race, sex, class and queerness." Experimental, fantasy, feminist, lesbian, humor/satire, literary, prose poem and women's. Upcoming themes: Fiction/Arts Issue; Annual Health Supplement; Women and Aging; Sports/Travel; Pride; and Women in the Labor Movement (January). Receives 20 unsolicited fiction mss/month. Accepts 10 mss/year. Agented fiction 10%. Published work by Ruth Ann Lonardelli and Janie Adams. Published new writers within the last year. Length: 1,000 words minimum; 4,000 words maximum; 2,500 words average.

How to Contact: Send complete ms with SASE and cover letter with description of previous publications; current works. Simultaneous submissions OK. Reports in 6-8 months. Publishes ms an average of 6 months after acceptance. Sample copy for $3 with 10×13 SASE. Fiction guidelines for SASE.

Payment/Terms: Pays subscription to magazine and 2 contributor's copies, $15 for first rights. No extra charge up to 5 contributor's copies; $1 charge each thereafter.

Advice: "Pay attention to appearance of manuscript! Very difficult to wade through sloppily presented fiction, however good. Do write a cover letter. If not cute, it can't hurt and may help. Mention previous publication(s)."

$ SPIDER, The Magazine for Children, (II), Carus Publishing Co./The Cricket Magazine Group, P.O. Box 300, Peru IL 61354. 1-800-588-8585. **Editor-in-Chief:** Marianne Carus. Associate Editor: Laura Tillotson. Magazine: 8×10; 33 pages; illustrations and photos. "*Spider* publishes high-quality literature for beginning readers, mostly children ages 6 to 9." Monthly. Estab. 1994. Circ. 85,000.

- *Spider* was ranked #50 on *Writer's Digest*'s Fiction 50 list of top markets for fiction writers. Carus Publishing also publishes *Cricket* magazine, also listed in this publication.

Needs: Children's/juvenile (6-9 years), fantasy (children's fantasy). "No religious, didactic, or violent stories, or anything that talks down to children." Accepts 4 mss/issue. Publishes ms 1-2 years after acceptance. Agented fiction 2%. Published work by Lissa Rovetch, Ursula K. LeGuin and Eric Kimmel. Length: 775 words average; 300 words minimum; 1,000 words maximum. Publishes short shorts. Also publishes poetry. Often critiques or comments on rejected ms.

How to Contact: Send complete ms with a cover letter. Include exact word count. Reports in 3 months. Send SASE for return of ms. Simultaneous and reprint submissions OK. Sample copy for $4. Fiction guidelines for #10 SASE.

Payment/Terms: Pays 25¢/word and 2 contributor's copies on publication for first rights or one-time rights; additional copies for $2.

Advice: "Read back issues of *Spider*." Looks for "quality writing, good characterization, lively style, humor. We would like to see more multicultural fiction."

$ SPIRIT, (I), Good Ground Press, 1884 Randolph Ave., St. Paul MN 55105. (612)690-7012. Fax: (612)690-7039. Website: http://www.goodgroundpress.com. **Editor:** Joan Mitchell. Magazine: 8 ½×11; 4 pages; 50 lb. paper. Religious education magazine for Roman Catholic teens. "Stories must be realistic, not moralistic or pietistic. They are used as catalysts to promote teens' discussion of their conflicts." Biweekly (28 issues). Estab. 1988. Circ. 25,000.

Needs: Feminist, religious/inspirational, young adult/teen. Upcoming themes: Christmas and Easter. List of upcoming themes available for SASE. Receives 20 unsolicited mss/month. Accepts 1 mss/issue; 12 mss/year. Publishes ms 6-12 months after acceptance. Published work by Margaret McCarthy, Kathleen Y Choi, Heather Klassen, Kathleen Cleberg, Bob Bartlett and Ron LaGro. Length: 1,000 words minimum; 1,200 words maximum. Sometimes critiques or comments on rejected mss.

How to Contact: Send complete ms with a cover letter. Include estimated word count. Reports in 6 months on mss. SASE for return of ms or send a disposable copy of ms. Simultaneous submissions and reprints OK. Sample copy and fiction guidelines free.

Payment/Terms: Pays $200 minimum on publication and 5 contributor's copies. Acquires first North American serial rights.

CHECK THE CATEGORY INDEXES, located at the back of the book, for publishers interested in specific fiction subjects.

Advice: Looks for "believable conflicts for teens. Just because we're religious, don't send pious, moralistic work."

$ STANDARD, (I, II, IV), Nazarene International Headquarters, 6401 The Paseo, Kansas City MO 64131. (816)333-7000. **Editor:** Everett Leadingham. Magazine: 8½×11; 8 pages; illustrations; photos. Inspirational reading for adults. Weekly. Estab. 1936. Circ. 165,000.

● *Standard* ranked #26 on *Writer's Digest*'s Fiction 50 list of top markets for fiction writers.

Needs: "Looking for stories that show Christianity in action." Publishes ms 14-18 months after acceptance. Published new writers within the last year. Length: 1,200-1,500 words average; 500 words minimum; 1,200 words maximum.

How to Contact: Send complete ms with name, address and phone number. Reports in 2-3 months on mss. SASE. Simultaneous submissions OK but will pay only reprint rates. Sample copy and guidelines for SAE and 2 first-class stamps.

Payment/Terms: Pays 3½¢/word; 2¢/word (reprint) on acceptance; contributor's copies on publication.

✔ ✪ $ STORY FRIENDS, (II), Mennonite Publishing House, 616 Walnut Ave., Scottdale PA 15683-1999. (724)887-8500. Fax: (724)887-3111. E-mail: rstutz@mph.org. **Editor:** Rose Mary Stutzman. A magazine which portrays Jesus as a friend and helper. Nonfiction and fiction for children 4-9 years of age. Monthly.

● The Mennonite Publishing House also published *On the Line*, *Purpose* and *With* magazines.

Needs: Juvenile. Stories of everyday experiences at home, in church, in school or at play, which provide models of Christian values. "Wants to see more fiction related to Mennonites, set in African-American, Latino or Hispanic settings. No stories about children and their grandparents or children and their elderly neighbors. I have more than enough." Recently published work by Virginia Kroll and Lisa Harkrader. Publishes 10-12 new writers/year. Length: 300-800 words.

How to Contact: Send complete ms with SASE. Seasonal or holiday material should be submitted 6 months in advance. Free sample copy with SASE.

Payment/Terms: Pays 3-5¢/word on acceptance for one-time rights. Buys reprints. Not copyrighted.

Advice: "I am buying more 500-word stories since we switched to a new format. It is important to include relationships, patterns of forgiveness, respect, honesty, trust and caring. Prefer exciting yet plausible short stories which offer varied settings, introduce children to wide ranges of friends and demonstrate joys, fears, temptations and successes of the readers. Read good children's literature, the classics, the Newberry winner and the Caldecott winners. Respect children you know and allow their resourcefulness and character to have a voice in your writing."

✪ $ STRAIGHT, (II), Standard Publishing Co., 8121 Hamilton Ave., Cincinnati OH 45231. (513)931-4050. **Editor:** Heather Wallace. "Publication helping and encouraging teens to live a victorious, fulfilling Christian life. Distributed through churches and some private subscriptions." Magazine: 6½×7½; 12 pages; newsprint paper and cover; illustrations (color); photos. Quarterly in weekly parts. Estab. 1951. Circ. 30,000.

● *Straight* ranked #27 on *Writer's Digest*'s Fiction 50 list of top markets for fiction writers.

Needs: Contemporary, religious/inspirational, romance, spiritual, mystery, adventure and humor—all with Christian emphasis. "Stories dealing with teens and teen life, with a positive message or theme. Topics that interest teenagers include school, family life, recreation, friends, church, part-time jobs, dating and music. Main character should be a Christian teenager and regular churchgoer, who faces situations using Bible principles." No science fiction. Themes available on a quarterly basis for SASE. Receives approximately 100 unsolicited fiction mss/month. Accepts 2-3 mss/issue; 100-125 mss/year. Publishes ms an average of 1 year after acceptance. Less than 1% of fiction is agented. Published work by Alan Cliburn, Betty Steele Everett and Teresa Cleary. Published new writers within the last year. Length: 900-1,500 words. Recommends other markets.

How to Contact: Send complete ms with SASE and cover letter (experience with teens especially preferred from new writers). Reports in 1-2 months. Sample copy and guidelines for SASE.

Payment/Terms: Pays 5-7¢/word on acceptance for first and one-time rights. Buys reprints.

Advice: "Get to know us before submitting, through guidelines and sample issues (SASE). And get to know teenagers. A writer must know what today's teens are like, and what kinds of conflicts they experience. In writing a short fiction piece for the teen reader, don't try to accomplish too much. If your character is dealing with the problem of prejudice, don't also deal with his/her fights with sister, desire for a bicycle, or anything else that is not absolutely essential to the reader's understanding of the major conflict."

✪ 🏆 $ THE SUN, (II), The Sun Publishing Company, Inc., 107 N. Roberson St., Chapel Hill NC 27516. (919)942-5282. **Editor:** Sy Safransky. Magazine: 8½×11; 40 pages; offset paper; glossy cover stock; illustrations; photos. "*The Sun* is a magazine of ideas. While we tend to favor personal writing, we're open to just about anything—even experimental writing, if it doesn't make us feel stupid. Surprise us; we often don't know what we'll like until we read it." Monthly. Estab. 1974. Circ. 35,000.

● *The Sun* ranked #44 on *Writer's Digest*'s Fiction 50 list of top markets for fiction writers.

Needs: Open to all fiction. Receives approximately 500 unsolicited fiction mss each month. Accepts 3 ms/issue. Recently published work by Poe Ballantine, Robin Hemley and Nance Van Winckel. Publishes 2-3 previously unpublished writers/year. Publishes 2-3 new writers/year. Length: 7,000 words maximum. Also publishes poetry.

How to Contact: Send complete ms with SASE. Reports in 3 months. Publishes ms an average of 6-12 months after acceptance. Sample copy for $5

Payment/Terms: Pays up to $500 on publication, plus 2 contributor's copies and a complimentary one-year subscription for one-time rights. Publishes reprints.

Advice: "We favor honest, personal writing with an intimate point of view."

$ TROIKA MAGAZINE, Wit, Wisdom, and Wherewithal, (I, II), Lone Tout Publications, Inc., P.O. Box 1006, Weston CT 06883. (203)227-5377. Fax: (203)222-9332. E-mail: troikamag@aol.com. Editor: Celia Meadow. **Fiction Editor:** Gregory Cowles. Magazine: 8⅛×10⅝; 100 pages; 45 lb. Expression paper; 100 lb. Warren cover; illustrations and photographs. "Our general interest magazine is geared toward an audience aged 30-50 looking to balance a lifestyle of family, community and personal success." Quarterly. Estab. 1994. Circ. 100,000.

- *Troika* received 1995 *Print Magazine* Awards for Excellence (design) and two Ozzie Silver Awards for Excellence (design).

Needs: Humor/satire, literary, mainstream/contemporary. No genre, experimental or children's. List of upcoming themes available for SASE. Receives 200 unsolicited mss/month. Accepts 2-5 mss/issue; 8-20 mss/year. Publishes ms 3-6 months after acceptance. Recently published work by Nelson DeMille, Gene Perret, Craig Furnals and Chris Boal. Length: 2,000-3,000 words. Also publishes literary essays and literary criticism. Sometimes critiques or comments on rejected ms.

How to Contact: Send complete ms with a cover letter giving address, phone/fax number and e-mail address. Include estimated word count, brief bio, SASE and list of publications with submission. Reports in 1-3 months. Send SASE for reply to query. Send a disposable copy of ms. Simultaneous and electronic submissions OK. Sample copy for $5. Guidelines for #10 SASE.

Payment/Terms: Pays $250 maximum on publication for first North American serial rights.

Advice: "What makes a manuscript stand out? An authentic voice, an original story, a strong narrative, a delight in language, a sharp eye for detail, a keen intelligence. But proper grammar and spelling don't hurt either."

$ TURTLE MAGAZINE FOR PRESCHOOL KIDS, (II), Children's Better Health Institute, Benjamin Franklin Literary & Medical Society, Inc., Box 567, 1100 Waterway Blvd., Indianapolis IN 46206. (317)636-8881. **Editor:** Terry Harshman. Magazine of picture stories and articles for preschool children 2-5 years old.

- The Children's Better Health Institute also publishes *Children's Digest, Children's Playmate, Jack and Jill* and *Humpty Dumpty*, also listed in this section.

Needs: Juvenile (preschool). Special emphasis on health, nutrition, exercise and safety. Also has need for "action rhymes to foster creative movement, very simple science experiments, and simple food activities." Receives approximately 100 unsolicited fiction mss/month. Published new writers within the last year. Length: 300 words for bedtime or naptime stories.

How to Contact: Send complete ms with SASE. No queries. Reports in 8-10 weeks. Send SASE for Editorial Guidelines. Sample copy for $1.25.

Payment/Terms: Pays up to 22¢/word (approximate); varies for poetry and activities; includes 10 complimentary copies of issue in which work appears. Pays on publication for all rights.

Advice: "Become familiar with recent issues of the magazine and have a thorough understanding of the preschool child. You'll find we are catering more to our youngest readers, so think simply. Also, avoid being too heavy-handed with health-related material. First and foremost, health features should be fun! Because we have developed our own turtle character ('PokeyToes'), we are not interested in fiction stories featuring other turtles."

N VISTA, (II), Wesleyan Publishing House, Box 50434, Indianapolis IN 46953. (317)595-4144. **Editor:** Kelly Trennepohl. Magazine: 8½×11; 8 pages; offset paper and cover; illustrations and photos. "*Vista* is our adult take-home paper." Weekly. Estab. 1906. Circ. 40,000.

Needs: Religious/inspirational, convictional.

How to Contact: Sample copy for 9×12 SAE.

$ WITH: The Magazine for Radical Christian Youth (II, IV), Faith & Life Press, Box 347, Newton KS 67114-0347. (316)283-5100. Fax: (316)283-0454. E-mail: deliag@gcmc.org. **Editor:** Carol Duerksen. Editorial Assistant: Delia Graber. Magazine: 8½×11; 32 pages; 60 lb. coated paper and cover; illustrations and photos. "Our purpose is to help teenagers understand the issues that impact them and to help them make choices that reflect Mennonite-Anabaptist understandings of living by the Spirit of Christ. We publish all types of material—fiction, nonfiction, teen personal experience, etc." Published 8 times/year. Estab. 1968. Circ. 6,100.

• *With* won several awards from the Associated Church Press and the Evangelical Press Association, including the 1997 Award of Excellence in Youth Category for best youth magazine. *With* ranked #36 on *Writer's Digest*'s Fiction 50 list of top markets for fiction writers.

Needs: Contemporary, ethnic, humor/satire, mainstream, religious, young adult/teen (15-18 years). "We accept issue-oriented pieces as well as religious pieces. No religious fiction that gives 'pat' answers to serious situations." Would like to see more humor. Receives about 50 unsolicited mss/month. Accepts 1-2 mss/issue; 10-12 mss/year. Publishes ms up to 1 year after acceptance. Recently published work by Shirley Byers Lalonde. Publishes 1-3 new writers/year. Length: 1,500 words preferred; 400 words minimum; 2,000 words maximum. Rarely critiques rejected mss.

How to Contact: Send complete ms with cover letter, include short summary of author's credits and what rights they are selling. Reports in 1-2 months on mss. SASE. Simultaneous and reprint submissions OK. Sample copy for 9×12 SAE and $1.21 postage. Fiction guidelines for #10 SASE.

Payment/Terms: Pays 4¢/word for reprints; 6¢/word for simultaneous rights (one-time rights to an unpublished story); 6-10¢/word for assigned stories (first rights). Supplies contributor's copies; charge for extras.

Advice: "Each story should make a single point that our readers will find helpful through applying it in their own lives. Request our theme list and detailed fiction guidelines (enclose SASE). All our stories are theme-related, so writing to our themes greatly improves your odds."

🌐 $ **WOMAN'S WEEKLY**, IPC Magazines, King's Reach, Stamford St., London SE1 9LS England. **Fiction Editor:** Gaynor Davies. Circ. 700,000. Publishes 1 serial and at least 2 short stories/week. "Short stories can be on any theme, but must have warmth. No explicit sex or violence. Serials need not be written in installments. They are submitted as complete manuscripts and we split them up, or send first installment of serial (6,000 words) and synopsis of the rest." Length: 1,000-3,500 words for short stories; 12,000-36,000 words for serials. Short story payment starts at £230 and rises as writer becomes a more regular contributor. Serial payments start at around £600/installment. Writers also receive contributor's copies. "Read the magazine concerned and try to understand who the publication is aimed at." Writers' guidelines available. Write to "Fiction Department."

✔ ★ $ **WOMAN'S WORLD MAGAZINE, The Woman's Weekly, (I)**, 270 Sylvan Ave., Englewood Cliffs NJ 07632. E-mail: wwweekly@aol.com. **Fiction Editor:** Deborah Dragovic. Magazine; 9½×11; 54 pages. We publish short romances and mini-mysteries for all women, ages 18-68." Weekly. Estab. 1980. Circ. 1.5 million.

Needs: Romance (contemporary), mystery. "We buy contemporary romances of 1,500 words. Stories must revolve around a compelling, true-to-life relationship dilemma; may feature a male or female protagonist, and may be written in either the first or third person. We are *not* interested in stories of life-or-death, or fluffy, fly-away style romances. When we say romance, what we really mean is relationship, whether it's just beginning or is about to celebrate its 50th anniversary." Receives 2,500 unsolicited mss/month. Accepts 2 mss/issue; 104 mss/year. Publishes mss 2-3 months after acceptance. Recently published work by Linda S. Reilly, Linda Yellin and Tim Myers. Length: romances—1,500 words; mysteries—1,000 words.

How to Contact: Send complete ms, "double spaced and typed in number 12 font." Cover letter not necessary. Include name, address, phone number and fax on first page of mss. *No queries*. Reports in 4-8 months. SASE. Fiction guidelines free.

Payment/Terms: Romances—$1,000, mysteries—$500. Pays on acceptance for first North American serial rights only.

Advice: "Familiarize yourself totally with our format and style. Read at least a year's worth of *Woman's World* fiction. Analyze and dissect it. Regarding romances, scrutinize them not only for content but tone, mood and sensibility."

N ✔ $ **WONDER TIME, (II)**, WordAction Publications, 6401 The Paseo, Kansas City MO 64131. (816)333-7000. Fax: (816)333-4439. **Editor:** Donna Fillmore. Magazine: 8¼×11; 4 pages; self cover; color illustrations. Hand-out story paper published through WordAction Publications; stories follow outline of Sunday School lessons for 6-8 year-olds. Weekly. Circ. 45,000.

Needs: Religious/inspirational and juvenile. Wants more "really good Christian fiction with a true story line, not just a narration of moralistic events." Stories must have first- to second-grade readability. No fairy tales or science fiction. Receives 50-75 unsolicited fiction mss/month. Accepts 1 ms/issue. Recently published work by Ruth Blount and Shirley Smith. Length: 250-350 words.

How to Contact: Send complete ms with SASE. Reports in 6 weeks. Sample copy and curriculum guide with SASE.

Payment/Terms: Pays $25 minimum on acceptance for multi-use rights.

Advice: "Basic themes reappear regularly. Please write for a theme list. Also, be familiar with what *Wonder Time* is all about. Ask for guidelines, sample copies, theme list before submitting."

N ★ **WY'EAST HISTORICAL JOURNAL, (II)**, Crumb Elbow Publishing, P.O. Box 294, Rhododendron OR 97049. (503)622-4798. Editor: Michael P. Jones. Journal: 5½×8½; 60 pages; top-notch paper; hardcover and softbound; illustrations and photographs. "The journal is published for Cascade Georgraphic Society, a nonprofit educational organization. Publishes historical or contemporary articles on the history of Oregon's Mt.

Hood, the Columbia River, the Pacific NW, or the Old Oregon Country that includes Oregon, Washington, Idaho, Wyoming, Montana, Alaska, Northern California and British Columbia and sometimes other areas. For young adults to elderly." Quarterly. Estab. 1992. Circ. 2,500.

Needs: Open. Special interests include wildlife and fisheries, history of fur trade in Pacific Northwest, the Oregon Trail and Indians. "All materials should relate—somehow—to the region the publication is interested in." Publishes annual special fiction issue in winter. Receives 10 unsolicited mss/month. Accepts 1-2 mss/issue; 22-24 mss/year. Publishes ms up to one year after acceptance. Published work by Joel Palmer. Publishes 5-10 new writers/year. Publishes short shorts. Recommends other markets. "We have several other publications through Crumb Elbow Publishing where we can redirect the material."

How to Contact: Query with clips of published work or send complete ms with cover letter. Reports in 2 months "depending upon work load." SASE (required or material will *not* be returned). Simultaneous and reprint submissions OK. Sample copy for $7. Fiction guidelines for #10 SASE.

Payment/Terms: Pays contributor's copies on publication. Acquires one-time rights.

Advice: "A manuscrip has to have a historical or contemporary tie to the Old Oregon Country, which was the lands that lay west of the Rocky Mountains to the Pacific Ocean, south to and including Northern California, and north to and including Alaska. It has to be about such things as nature, fish and wildlife, the Oregon Trail, pioneer settlement and homesteading, the Indian wars, gold mining, wild horses—which are only a few ideas. It has to be written in a non-offensive style, meaning please remove all four-letter words or passages dealing with loose sex. Do not be afraid to try something a little different. If you write for the marketplace you might get published, but you lose something in the creative presentation. Write to please yourself and others will recognize your refreshing approach."

★ $ **YANKEE MAGAZINE, (II, III)**, Yankee Publishing Inc., P.O. Box 520, Dublin NH 03444. (603)563-8111. Fax: (603)563-8252. E-mail: queries@yankeepub.com. Editor: Judson D. Hale. Managing Editor: Tim Clark. **Contact:** Jeanne Wheaton, editorial assistant. Magazine: 6×9; 176 pages; glossy paper; 4-color glossy cover stock; illustrations; color photos. "Entertaining and informative New England regional on current issues, people, history, antiques and crafts for general reading audience." Monthly. Estab. 1935. Circ. 700,000.

• *Yankee* ranked #19 in *Writer's Digest*'s Fiction 50 list of top fiction markets.

Needs: Literary. Fiction is to be set in New England or compatible with the area. No religious/inspirational, formula fiction or stereotypical dialect, novels or novellas. Accepts 3-4 mss/year. Published work by Andre Dubus, H. L. Mountzoures and Fred Bonnie. Published new writers within the last year. Length: 2,500 words. Publishes short shorts.

How to Contact: Send complete ms with SASE and previous publications. "Cover letters are important if they provide relevant information: previous publications or awards; special courses taken; special references (e.g. 'William Shakespeare suggested I send this to you . . . .')" Simultaneous submissions OK, "within reason." Reports in 2-8 weeks.

Payment/Terms: Pays $1,000 on acceptance; rights negotiable. Makes "no changes without author consent." Supplies contributor copies; sends galleys to authors.

Advice: "Read previous ten stories in *Yankee* for style and content. Fiction must be realistic and reflect life as it is—complexities and ambiguities inherent. Our fiction adds to the 'complete menu'—the magazine includes many categories—humor, profiles, straight journalism, essays, etc. Listen to the advice of any editor who takes the time to write a personal letter. Go to workshops; get advice and other readings before sending story out cold."

N ★ ✓ $ **YOUNG SALVATIONIST, (II, IV)**, The Salvation Army, P.O. Box 269, 615 Slaters Lane, Alexandria VA 22313. (703)684-5500. Fax: (703)684-5539. E-mail: ys@usn.salvationarmy.org. **Managing Editor:** Tim Clark. Magazine: 8×11; 16 pages; illustrations and photos. Christian emphasis articles for youth members of The Salvation Army. 10 issues/year. Estab. 1984. Circ. 50,000.

Needs: Religious/inspirational, young adult/teen. Receives 150 unsolicited mss/month. Buys 9-10 ms/issue; 90-100 mss/year. Publishes ms 3-4 months after acceptance. Publishes 10 new writers/year. Length: 1,000 words preferred; 750 words minimum; 1,200 words maximum. Publishes short shorts. Sometimes critiques rejected mss and recommends other markets.

How to Contact: Send complete ms. Accepts queries/mss by fax and e-mail. Reports in 1-2 weeks on queries; 2-4 weeks on mss. SASE. Simultaneous and reprint submissions OK. Sample copy for 9×12 SAE and 3 first-class stamps. Fiction guidelines and theme list for #10 SASE. Address submissions to Tim Clark.

Payment/Terms: Pays 10¢/word on acceptance for all rights, first rights, first North American serial rights and one-time rights.

Advice: "Don't write about your high school experience. Write about teens now."

Small Press

The term "small press" is often used in the broadest sense within the publishing industry. Depending on the person you're talking with, small press can mean one- and two-person operations, small or mid-size independent presses or university presses and other nonprofit publishers. *This market section contains only micropresses, small presses publishing three or fewer books per year.*

MICROPRESSES

The very small presses listed here are owned or operated by one to three people, often friends or family members. Some are cooperatives of writers and most of these presses started out publishing their staff members' books or books by their friends. Even the most successful of these presses are unable to afford the six-figure advances, lavish promotional budgets and huge press runs possible in the large, commercial houses. These presses can easily be swamped with submissions, but writers published by them are usually treated as "one of the family."

SELECTING YOUR MARKET

Reading the listing should be just your first step in finding markets that interest you. It's best to familiarize yourself with a press's focus and line. Most produce catalogs or at least fliers advertising their books. Whenever possible, obtain these and writers' guidelines.

If possible, read some of the books published by a press that interests you. It is sometimes difficult to locate books published by micropress publishers. Some sell only through the mail.

In How to Use This Book to Publish Your Fiction we discuss how to use the Category Index located near the end of this book. If you've written a particular type of novel, look in the Category Index under the type of fiction you write to find presses interested in your specific subject.

We've also included Roman numeral ranking codes placed at the start of each listing to help you determine how open the press is to new writers. The explanations of these codes appear at the end of this introduction.

In addition to the N symbol indicating new listings, we include other symbols to help you in narrowing your search. English-speaking foreign markets are denoted by a 🌐 symbol. The maple leaf symbol (🍁) identifies Canadian presses. If you are not a Canadian writer, but are interested in a Canadian press, check the listing carefully. Many small presses in Canada receive grants and other funds from their provincial or national government and are, therefore, restricted to publishing Canadian authors.

There are no subsidy book publishers listed in *Novel & Short Story Writer's Market*. By subsidy, we mean any arrangement in which the writer is expected to pay all or part of the cost of producing, distributing and marketing his book. We feel a writer should not be asked to share in any cost of turning his manuscript into a book. All the book publishers listed here told us that they do not charge writers for publishing their work. *If any of the publishers listed here ask you to pay any part of publishing or marketing your manuscript, please let us know.*

Keep in mind most of the presses listed here have very small staffs. We asked them to give themselves a generous amount of response time in their listing, but note it is not unusual for a small press to get behind. Add three or four weeks to the reporting time listed before checking on the status of your submission.

As with commercial book publishers, we ask small presses to give us a list of recent titles each year. If they did not change their title list from last year, it may be that, because they do so few fiction titles, they have not published any or they may be particularly proud of certain titles published earlier. If the recent titles are unchanged, we've altered the sentence to read "Published" rather than "Recently published."

The Business of Fiction Writing gives the fundamentals of approaching book publishers. The listings include information on what the publisher wishes to see in a submission package: sample chapters, an entire manuscript or other material.

Our editorial comments are set off by a bullet (●) within the listing. We use this feature to include additional information on the type of work published by the press, the awards and honors received by presses and other information we feel will help you make an informed marketing decision.

FOR MORE INFORMATION

For more small presses see the *International Directory of Little Magazines and Small Presses* published by Dustbooks (P.O. Box 100, Paradise CA 95967). To keep up with changes in the industry throughout the year, check issues of two small press trade publications: *Small Press Review* (also published by Dustbooks) and *Independent Publisher* (Jenkins Group, Inc., 121 E. Front St., 4th Floor, Traverse City MI 49684).

The ranking codes used in this section are as follows:

- **I Publisher encourages beginning or unpublished writers to submit work for consideration and publishes new writers frequently.**
- **II Publisher accepts outstanding work by beginning and established writers.**
- **III Hard to break into; publishes mostly writers with extensive previous publication credits or agented writers.**
- **IV Special-interest or regional publisher, open only to writers in certain genres or on certain subjects or from certain geographic areas.**
- **V Closed to unsolicited submissions.**

ACME PRESS, (I, II), P.O. Box 1702, Westminster MD 21158. (410)848-7577. **Acquisitions**: Ms. E.G. Johnston, managing editor. Estab. 1991. "We operate on a part-time basis and publish 1-2 novels/year." Publishes hardcover and paperback originals. Published new writers within the last year. Averages 1-2 novels/year.
Needs: Humor/satire. "We publish only humor novels, so we don't want to see anything that's not funny." Published *She-Crab Soup*, by Dawn Langley Simmons (fictional memoir/humor); *Biting the Wall*, by J. M. Johnston (humor/mystery); and *Hearts of Gold*, by James Magorian (humor/mystery).
How to Contact: Accepts unsolicited mss. Query first, submit outline/synopsis and first 50 pages or submit complete ms with cover letter. Include estimated word count with submission. SASE for reply, return of ms or send a disposable copy of ms. Agented fiction 25%. Reports in 1-2 weeks on queries; 4-6 weeks on mss. Simultaneous submissions OK. Always comments on rejected mss.
Terms: Provides 25 author's copies; pays 50% of profits. Sends galleys to author. Publishes ms 1 year after acceptance. Writer's guidelines and book catalog for #10 SASE.

AGELESS PRESS, (II, IV), P.O. Box 5915, Sarasota FL 34277-5915. Phone/fax: (941)952-0576. E-mail: irishope@juno.com. Website: http://members.home.net/irishope/ageless.htm (includes contest winners, articles, book excerpts). **Acquisitions**: Iris Forrest, editor. Estab. 1992. Independent publisher. Publishes paperback originals. Books: acid-free paper; notched perfect binding; no illustrations; average print order: 5,000; first novel print order: 5,000. Published new writers within the last year. Averages 1 title each year.
Needs: Experimental, fantasy, humor/satire, literary, mainstream/contemporary, mystery/suspense, New Age/mystic/spiritual, science fiction, short story collections, thriller/espionage. Looking for material "based on personal computer experiences." Stories selected by editor. Published *Computer Legends, Lies & Lore*, by various (anthology); and *Computer Tales of Fact & Fantasy*, by various (anthology).
How to Contact: Query first. Does not accept unsolicited mss. Unsolicited queries/correspondence by e-mail and fax OK. Send SASE for reply, return of ms or send a disposable copy of ms. Reports in 1 week. Simultaneous and electronic (disk, 5¼ or 3.5 IBM) submissions in ASCII format OK. Sometimes comments on rejected mss.

Terms: Offers negotiable advance. Publishes ms 6-12 months after acceptance.

ANVIL PRESS, (I, II), Bentall Centre, P.O. Box 1575, Vancouver, British Columbia V6C 2P7 Canada; or Lee Building, #204-A, 175 E. Broadway, Vancouver, British Columbia V5T 1W2 Canada. (604)876-8710. Fax: (604)879-2667. E-mail: subter@pinc.com. **Acquisitions**: Brian Kaufman and Dennis E. Bolen, fiction editors. Estab. 1988. "1½ person operation with volunteer editorial board. Anvil Press publishes contemporary fiction, poetry and drama, giving voice to up-and-coming Canadian writers, exploring all literary genres, discovering, nurturing and promoting new Canadian literary talent." Publishes paperback originals. Books: offset or web printing; perfect-bound. Average print order: 1,000-1,500. First novel print order: 1,000. Plans 2 first novels this year. Averages 2-3 fiction titles each year. Often comments on rejected mss. Also offers a critique service for a fee.

- Anvil Press's *Monday Night Man*, by Grant Buday, was nominated for the City of Van Conver Book Prize. *Ivanhoe Station*, by Lyle Neff, was nominated for the British Columbia Book Prize in 1998.

Needs: Experimental, contemporary modern, literary, short story collections. Recently published *Monday Night Man*, by Grant Buday (short stories); and *Salvage King, Ya*, by Mark Jarman (novel). Published new writers within the last year. Publishes the Anvil Pamphlet series: shorter works (essays, political tracts, polemics, treatises and works of fiction that are shorter than novel or novella form).
How to Contact: Canadian writers only. Accepts unsolicited mss. Query first or submit outline/synopsis and 1-2 sample chapters. Include estimated word count and bio with submission. Send SASE for reply, return of ms or a disposable copy of ms. Reports in 1 month on queries; 2-4 months on mss. Simultaneous submissions OK (please note in query letter that manuscript is a simultaneous submission).
Terms: Pays royalties of 15% (of final sales). Average advance: $200-400. Sends galleys to author. Publishes ms within contract year. Book catalog for 9×12 SASE and 2 first-class stamps.
Advice: "We are only interested in writing that is progressive in some way—form, content. We want contemporary fiction from serious writers who intend to be around for awhile and be a name people will know in years to come."

ARIADNE PRESS, (I), 4817 Tallahassee Ave., Rockville MD 20853-2144. Phone/fax: (301)949-2514. **Acquisitions**: Carol Hoover, president. Estab. 1976. "Our purpose is to promote the publication of emerging fiction writers." Shoestring operation—corporation with 4 directors who also act as editors. Publishes hardcover and paperback originals. Books: 50 lb. alkaline paper; offset printing; Smyth-sewn binding. Average print order 1,000. First novel print order 1,000. Plans 1 first novel this year. Averages 1 total title each year; only fiction. Distributes titles through mail-order; Seven Hills Book Distributors, Cincinnati, OH. Promotes titles through *Voice* literary supplement, *New York Review of Books*, *Boston Consortium*, *Book Reader* and *Rapport*.
Needs: Adventure, contemporary, feminist, historical, humor/satire, literary, mainstream, psychological, family relations, marital, war. Looking for "literary-mainstream" fiction. Novels only. No poetry, short stories or fictionalized biographies; no science fiction, horror or mystery. Published *The Greener Grass*, by Paul Bourguignon; *A Rumor of Distant Tribes*, by Eugene Jeffers; *Cross a Dark Bridge*, by Deborah Churchman (psychological suspense) and *Steps of the Sun*, bu Eva Thaddeus (love and conflict in a university town).
How to Contact: *Query first*. SASE. Agented fiction 5%. Reports in 1 month on queries; 2 months on mss. Simultaneous submissions OK. Sometimes critiques rejected mss. "We comment on selected mss of superior writing quality, even when rejected."
Terms: Pays royalties of 10%. No advance. Sends galleys to author. Writer's guidelines and list of books in stock for #10 SASE.
Advice: "We exist primarily for nonestablished writers. Try large, commercial presses first. Novels from 175-350 double-spaced pages have the best chance with us. Characters and story must fit together so well that it is hard to tell which grew out of the other. Send query letter with SASE in advance! Never send an unsolicited manuscript without advance clearance."

ARTEMIS CREATIONS PUBLISHING, 3395 Nostrand Ave., 2-J, Brooklyn NY 11229-4053. Fax: (718)648-8215. **Acquisitions**: Shirley Oliveira, president. Publishes trade paperback originals and reprints. Publishes 3-4 titles/year.
Imprint(s): Fem Suprem; *Matriarch's Way* (journal).
Needs: Erotica, experimental, fantasy, feminist, gothic, horror, mystery, occult, religious, science fiction. Recently published *Welts*, by Gloria and Dave Wallace (erotica).

FOR EXPLANATIONS OF THESE SYMBOLS,
SEE THE INSIDE FRONT AND BACK COVERS OF THIS BOOK.

How to Contact: Query or submit synopsis and 3 sample chapters with SASE. Reports in 3 days. Simultaneous submissions OK. *Charges $15 reading fee.*
Terms: No advance. Publishes ms 18 months after acceptance. Writer's guidelines for #10 SASE.
Advice: "Our readers are looking for strong, powerful feminine archetypes in fiction and nonfiction—goddess, matriarchy, etc."

ATTIC PRESS, (IV), Crawford Business Park, Crosses Green, Cork, Ireland. Contact: Managing Editor. E-mail: s.wilbourne@ucc.ie. Website: http://www.iol.ie/~atticirl/. Averages 2-3 fiction titles/year. "Attic Press is an independent, export-oriented, Irish-owned publishing house with a strong international profile. The press specializes in the publication of fiction and nonfiction books for and about women by Irish and international authors." Publishes an award-winning series of teenage fiction, Bright Sparks. Send cover letter, synopsis, brief summary, sample chapters. Pays advance on signing contract and royalties. Write for catalog.

BEGGAR'S PRESS, (II), 8110 N. 38th St., Omaha NE 68112-2018. (402)455-2615. Publisher: Richard R. Carey. Imprints are Lamplight, Raskolnikov's Cellar, Beggar's Review. Estab. 1952. Small independent publisher. "We are noted for publishing books and periodicals in the styles of the great masters of the past. We publish three periodicals (literary) and novels, poetry chapbooks, and collections of short stories." Publishes paperback originals. Books: 20 lb. paper; offset; perfect binding; some illustrations. Average print order: 500-700. First novel print order: 500. Published new writers within the last year. Plans 2 first novels this year. Averages 3-5 total titles, 4 fiction titles/year. Charges "reasonable rate" for complete ms critique. Member of International Association of Independent Publishers and Federation of Literary Publishers.
Needs: Adventure, historical (general, 1800's), horror (psychological), humor/satire, literary, mystery/suspense, romance (gothic, historical), short story collection. Recently published *An Evening Studying the Anatomy of Jena Kruger*, by Richard Carey; *My Doorknob Is Female*, by Diane Jensen; and *Seduction of An Olive*, by Debra Knight. Plans series.
How to Contact: "We are not accepting queries or manuscripts at the present time. We are completely scheduled for the next two years."
Payment/Terms: Pays royalties of 10% minimum; 15% maximum; provides 2 author's copies

BILINGUAL PRESS/EDITORIAL BILINGÜE, (II, IV), Hispanic Research Center, Arizona State University, Tempe AZ 85287-2702. (602)965-3867. Editor: Gary Keller. Estab. 1973. "University affiliated." Publishes hardcover and paperback originals, and reprints. Books: 60 lb. acid-free paper; single sheet or web press printing; case-bound and perfect-bound; illustrations sometimes; average print order: 4,000 copies (1,000 case-bound, 3,000 soft cover). Published new writers within the last year. Plans 2 first novels this year. Averages 12 total titles, 6 fiction each year. Sometimes comments on rejected ms.
Needs: Ethnic, literary, short story collections, translations. "We are always on the lookout for Chicano, Puerto Rican, Cuban-American or other U.S.-Hispanic themes with strong and serious literary qualities and distinctive and intellectually important themes. We have been receiving a lot of fiction set in Latin America (usually Mexico or Central America) where the main character is either an ingenue to the culture or a spy, adventurer or mercenary. We don't publish this sort of 'Look, I'm in an exotic land' type of thing. Also, novels about the Aztecs or other pre-Columbians are very iffy." Published *MotherTongue*, by Demetria Martinez (novel); *Rita and Los Angeles*, by Leo Romero (short stories); and *Sanctuary Stories*, by Michael Smith (stories and essays).
How to Contact: Query first. SASE. Reports in 3 weeks on queries; 2 months on mss. Simultaneous submissions OK.
Terms: Pays royalties of 10%. Average advance $500. Provides 10 author's copies. Sends galleys to author. Publishes ms 1 year after acceptance. Writer's guidelines available. Book catalog free.
Advice: "Writers should take the utmost care in assuring that their manuscripts are clean, grammatically impeccable, and have perfect spelling. This is true not only of the English but the Spanish as well. All accent marks need to be in place as well as other diacritical marks. When these are missing it's an immediate first indication that the author does not really know Hispanic culture and is not equipped to write about it. We are interested in publishing creative literature that treats the U.S.-Hispanic experience in a distinctive, creative, revealing way. The kinds of books that we publish we keep in print for a very long time irrespective of sales. We are busy establishing and preserving a U.S.-Hispanic canon of creative literature."

BOOKS FOR ALL TIMES, INC., (III), Box 2, Alexandria VA 22313. Website: http://www.bfat.com. **Acquisitions**: Joe David, publisher/editor. Estab. 1981. One-man operation. Publishes hardcover and paperback originals. Books: 60 lb. paper; offset printing; perfect binding. Average print order: 1,000. "No plans for new writers at present." Has published 2 fiction titles to date.
Needs: Contemporary, literary, short story collections. "No novels at the moment; hopeful, though, of someday soon publishing a collection of quality short stories. No popular fiction or material easily published by the major or minor houses specializing in mindless entertainment. Only interested in stories of the Victor Hugo or Sinclair Lewis quality."

How to Contact: Query first with SASE. Simultaneous submissions OK. Reports in 1 month on queries. Occasionally critiques rejected mss.
Terms: Pays negotiable advance. "Publishing/payment arrangement will depend on plans for the book." Book catalog free with SASE.
Advice: Interested in "controversial, honest books which satisfy the reader's curiosity to know. Read Victor Hugo, Fyodor Dostoyevsky and Sinclair Lewis, for example. I am actively looking for short articles (up to 3,000 words) on contemporary education. I prefer material critical of the public schools when documented and convincing."

N **BROWNOUT LABORATORIES, (I)**, RD 2, Box 5, Little Falls NY 13365. **Acquisitions:** Michael Hanna, fiction editor. Estab. 1994. "Brownout Laboratories publishes the works of the young intelligentsia." Publishes paperback originals. Books: 100% recycled, 75% post-consumer content paper; high-quality photocopying; hand-sewn saddle-stitch binding. Average print order: 50. Plans 1-2 first novels in 1999. Averages 2-3 total titles, 1 fiction title/year.
Needs: Erotica (no gratuitous violence), ethnic/multicultural, experimental, feminist, gay and bisexual (but not queer), lesbian and bisexual (but not queer), literary, mystery/suspense (hardboiled), science fiction (must be of high enough quality to be of interest to critics who have no particular penchant for science fiction), short story collections, translations (if translated by the author from French, German, Spanish or Croatian/Bosnian).
How to Contact: Accepts unsolicited mss. Query with outline/synopsis and first 10 pages. Send SASE for reply, return of ms or send a disposable copy of ms. Reports in 3 weeks on queries; 2 months on mss. Simultaneous submissions OK. Always critiques or comments on rejected ms.
Terms: Pays royalty of 20%. "We publish the book and then pay royalties on each copy sold." Publishes ms 1-3 months after acceptance. Book catalog free.

✓ **CALYX BOOKS, (I, II)**, P.O. Box B, Corvallis OR 97339-0539. (503)753-9384. Fax: (541)753-0515. E-mail: calyx@proaxis.com. **Acquisitions**: M. Donnelly, editor; Micki Reaman, fiction editor. Estab. 1986. "Calyx exists to publish women's literary and artistic work and is committed to publishing the works of all women, including women of color, older women, working-class women, and other voices that need to be heard." Publishes hardcover and paperback originals. Books: offset printing; paper and cloth binding. Average print order: 5,000-10,000 copies. First novel print order: 5,000. **Publishes approximately 1 previously unpublished writer/year.** Averages 3 total titles each year. Distributes titles through Consortium Book Sales and Distribution. Promotes titles through author reading tours, print advertising (trade and individuals), galley and review copy mailings, presence at trade shows, etc.

- Past anthologies include *Forbidden Stitch: An Asian American Women's Anthology*; *Women and Aging*, and *Present Tense: Writing and Art by Young Women*.

Needs: Contemporary, ethnic, experimental, feminist, lesbian, literary, short story collections, translations. Published *Second Sight*, by Rickey Gard Diamond; *Into the Forest*, by Jean Hegland (women's literature); and *Switch*, by Carol Guess (lesbian literature).
How to Contact: Query first. Send SASE for reply. Reports in 4 months on queries. E-mail query for guidelines OK.
Terms: Pays royalties of 10% minimum, author's copies, (depends on grant/award money). Average advance: $200-500. Sends galleys to author. Publishes ms 2 years after acceptance. Writer's guidelines for #10 SASE. Book catalog free on request.
Advice: "Read our book catalog and journal. Be familiar with our publications. Follow our guidelines (which can be requested with a SASE) and be patient. Our process is lengthy."

N **CHRISTCHURCH PUBLISHERS LTD.**, 2 Caversham St., London S.W.3, 4AH UK. Fiction Editor: James Hughes. Averages 25 fiction titles/year. "Miscellaneous fiction, also poetry. More 'literary' style of fiction, but also thrillers, crime fiction etc." Length: 30,000 words minimum. Send a cover letter, synopsis, brief summary. "Preliminary letter and *brief* synopsis favored." Pays advance and royalties. "We have contacts and agents worldwide."

CREATIVITY UNLIMITED PRESS, (II), 30819 Casilina, Rancho Palos Verdes CA 90274. (310)377-7908. **Acquisitions**: Rochelle Stockwell. Estab. 1980. One-person operation with plans to expand. Publishes paperback originals and self-hypnosis cassette tapes. Books: perfect binding; illustrations; average print order: 1,000; first novel print order 1,000. Averages 1 title (fiction or nonfiction) each year.
Needs: Published *Insides Out*, by Shelley Stockwell (plain talk poetry); *Sex and Other Touchy Subjects*, (poetry

and short stories); *Timetravel: Do-It Yourself Past Life Regression Handbook*; *Denial is Not a River in Egypt* and *Everything You Ever Wanted to Know About Everything*.
Advice: Write for more information.

CROSS-CULTURAL COMMUNICATIONS, (I, IV), 239 Wynsum Ave., Merrick NY 11566-4725. (516)868-5635. Fax: (516)379-1901. Editorial Director: Stanley H. Barkan. Estab. 1971. "Small/alternative literary arts publisher focusing on the traditionally neglected languages and cultures in bilingual and multimedia format." Publishes chapbooks, magazines, anthologies, novels, audio cassettes (talking books) and video cassettes (video books, video mags); hardcover and paperback originals. Publishes new women writers series, Holocaust series, Israeli writers series, Dutch writers series, Asian-, African- and Italian-American heritage writers series, Native American writers series, Latin American writers series.

- Authors published by this press have received international awards including Nat Scammacca who won the National Poetry Prize of Italy and Gabriel Preil who won the Bialik Prize of Israel.

Needs: Contemporary, literary, experimental, ethnic, humor/satire, juvenile and young adult folktales, and translations. "Main interests: bilingual short stories and children's folktales, parts of novels of authors of other cultures, translations; some American fiction. No fiction that is not directed toward other cultures. For an annual anthology of authors writing in other languages (primarily), we will be seeking very short stories with original-language copy (other than Latin script should be print quality 10/12) on good paper. Title: *Cross-Cultural Review Anthology: International Fiction 1*. We expect to extend our *CCR* series to include 10 fiction issues: *Five Contemporary* (Dutch, Swedish, Yiddish, Norwegian, Danish, Sicilian, Greek, Israeli, etc.) *Fiction Writers*." Published *Sicilian Origin of the Odyssey*, by L.G. Pocock (bilingual English-Italian translation by Nat Scammacca); *Sikano L'Americano!* and *Bye Bye America*, by Nat Scammacca; and *Milkrun*, by Robert J. Gress.
How to Contact: Accepts unsolicited mss. Query with SAE with $1 postage to include book catalog. "Note: Original language ms should accompany translations." Simultaneous and photocopied submissions OK. Reports in 1 month.
Terms: Pays "sometimes" 10-25% in royalties and "occasionally" by outright purchase, in author's copies—"10% of run for chapbook series," and "by arrangement for other publications." No advance.
Advice: "Write because you want to or you must; satisfy yourself. If you've done the best you can, then you've succeeded. You will find a publisher and an audience eventually. Generally, we have a greater interest in nonfiction novels and translations. Short stories and excerpts from novels written in one of the traditional neglected languages are preferred—with the original version (i.e., bilingual). Our kinderbook series will soon be in production with a similar bilingual emphasis, especially for folktales, fairy tales, and fables."

✓ **GRIFFON HOUSE PUBLICATIONS**, 1401 Pennsylvania Ave., Wilmington DE 19806. Phone/fax: (302)656-3230. President: Frank D. Grande. Estab. 1976. Small press. Publishes paperback originals and reprints.
Needs: Contemporary, drama, ethnic (open), experimental, literary, multinational theory, poetry, reprints, theory, translations.
How to Contact: Query with SASE. No simultaneous submissions. Reports in 1 month.
Terms: Pays in author's copies. No advance.

HANDSHAKE EDITIONS, Atelier A2, 83 rue de la Tombe Issoire, 75014 Paris France. Fax: 33-1-4320-4195. E-mail: jim_haynes@wanadoo.jr. Editor: Jim Haynes. Publishes 4 story collections or novels/year. "Only face-to-face submissions accepted. More interested in 'faction' and autobiographical writing." Pays in copies. Writers interested in submitting a manscript should "have lunch or dinner with me in Paris."

HEMKUNT, Publishers A-78 Naraina Industrial Area Ph.I, New Delhi India 110028. **Acquisitions**: G.P. Singh, managing director; Deepinder Singh/Arvinder Singh, export directors.
Needs: "We would be interested in novels, preferably by authors with a published work. Would like to have distribution rights for US, Canada and UK beside India."
How to Contact: Send a cover letter, brief summary, 3 sample chapters (first, last and one other chapter). "Writer should have at least 1-2 published novels to his/her credit."
Terms: Catalog on request.

✓ **HOLLOW EARTH PUBLISHING, (II)**, P.O. Box 1355, Boston MA 02205-1355. (617)746-3130. E-mail: hep2@aol.com. **Acquisitions**: Helian Grimes, editor/publisher. Estab. 1983. "Small independent publisher." Publishes hardcover and paperback originals and reprints. Books: acid-free paper; offset printing; Smythe binding.
Needs: Comics/graphic novels, fantasy (sword and sorcery), feminist, gay, lesbian, literary, New Age/mystic/spiritual, translations. Looking for "computers, Internet, Norse mythology, magic." Publishes various computer application series.
How to Contact: Contact by e-mail only. Does not accept unsolicited mss. Include estimated word count, 1-2 page bio, list of publishing credits. Agented fiction 90%. Reports in 2 months. Accepts disk submissions.
Terms: Pays in royalties. Sends galleys to author. Publishes ms 6 months after acceptance.
Advice: Looking for "less fiction, more computer information."

ILLUMINATION PUBLISHING CO., (II, IV), P.O. Box 1865, Bellevue WA 98009. (425)646-3670. Fax: (425)646-4144. E-mail: liteinfo@illumin.com. Website: http://www.illumin.com. **Acquisitions**: Ruth Thompson, editorial director. Estab. 1987. "Illumination Arts is a small company publishing high quality, enlightened children's picture books with spiritual and inspirational values." Publishes hardcover originals. Publishes 2 children's picture book/year. **Publishes 1-2 previously unpublished writers/year.** Distributes titles through Book World, New Leaf, De Vorss, Book People, Quality, Ingram, Baker & Taylor, Koen Pacific and bookstores. Promotes titles through direct mailings, website, book shows, flyers and posters, catalogs. Also arranges author and illustrators signings and enters many book award events. Member of Book Publishers of the Northwest.

- Illumination Publishing's *SAI Prophecy* was selected as best novel and *Dreambirds* was selected as best children's book by The Coalition of Visionary Retailers at The International New Age Trade Show, 1998. *The Right Touch* was a finalist in 1998 Small Press Awards.

Needs: Children's/juvenile (adventure, inspirational, preschool/picture books). Recently published *The Right Touch*, by Sandy Kleven and *Dreambirds*, by David Ogden (children's picture books); and *The SAI Prophecy*, by Barbara Gardner (adult novel).
How to Contact: Accepts unsolicited mss. Query first or submit complete ms with cover letter. Unsolicited queries/correspondence by e-mail and fax OK. Include estimated word count, Social Security number and list of publishing credits. Send SASE for reply or return of ms. Reports in 1 week on queries; 1 month on mss. Simultaneous submissions OK. Often critiques or comments on rejected mss.
Terms: Pays royalties. Sends galleys to author. Publishes ms 18 months-2 years after acceptance. Writer's guidelines for SASE.
Advice: "Submit full manuscripts, neatly typed without grammatical or spelling errors. Expect to be edited many times. Be patient. We are very *painstaking*."

IVY LEAGUE PRESS, INC., (II), P.O. Box 3326, San Ramon CA 94583-8326. (925)736-0601 or 800-IVY-PRESS. Fax: (925)736-0602. E-mail: ivyleaguepress@worldnet.att.net. **Acquisitions**: Maria Thomas, editor. Publishes hardcover and paperback originals. Specializes in medical thrillers. Books: perfect binding. First novel print order: 5,000. Plans 1 novel this year. Averages 2 total titles, 1-2 fiction titles/year. Distributes titles through Baker & Taylor and Ingram. Promotes titles through TV, radio and print.
Needs: Mystery/suspense(medical). Published *Allergy Shots*, by Litman.
How to Contact: Accepts unsolicited mss. Query with outline/synopsis. Include estimated word count, bio and list of publishing credits. Send SASE or a disposable copy of the ms. Reports in 2 months on queries. Electronic submissions OK. Always critiques or comments on rejected mss.
Payment/Terms: Royalties vary. Sends galleys to author.
Advice: "If you tell a terrific story of medical suspense, one which is hard to put down, we may publish it."

JESPERSON PRESS LTD., (I), 39 James Lane, St. John's, Newfoundland A1E 3H3 Canada. (709)753-0633. Editor: JoAnne Soper-Cook. Midsize independent publisher. Publishes hardcover and paperback originals. Averages 7-10 total titles, 1-2 fiction titles each year. Sometimes comments on rejected mss.
Needs: Solid contemporary fiction by Newfoundland authors about Newfoundland, preferably novel-length or short story collection. Not interested in young adult, childrens' or poetry of any kind.
How to Contact: Query with synopsis and SASE (Canadian postage or IRCs, please) only. No unsolicited mss. Reports in 3 months or less.
Terms: Pays negotiable royalties. Sends galleys to author. Book catalog free.

KAWABATA PRESS, (II), Knill Cross House, Knill Cross, Millbrook, Torpoint, Cornwall PL10 1DX England. Fiction Editor: Colln Webb.
Needs: "Mostly poetry—but prose should be realistic, free of genre writing and clichés and above all original in ideas and content." Length: 200-4,000 words (for stories).
How to Contact: "Don't forget return postage (or IRC)."
Terms: Writers receive half of profits after print costs are covered. Write for guidelines and book list.
Advice: "Avoid clichés; avoid obnoxious plots; avoid the big themes (life, death, etc.); be original; find a new angle or perspective; try to be natural rather than clever; be honest."

LEAPFROG PRESS, (I, II), P.O. Box 1495, 110 Commercial St., Wellfleet MA 02667-1495. (508)349-1925. Fax: (508)349-1180. E-mail: leapfrog@capecod.net. Website: http://www.leapfrogpress.com (includes description of press, mission statement, writer's guidelines, e-mail link, description of books, sample poems, link to distributor, cover designs). **Acquisitions:** Ira Wood and Marge Piercy, publishers. Estab. 1996. "We publish book-length literary fiction and literate nonfiction that reflects a strong personal story. We publish books that are referred to by the large publishers as midlist but which we believe to be the heart and soul of literature. We're a small shop—two editors and an office manager." Publishes hardcover and paperback originals and paperback reprints. Books: acid-free paper; sewn binding. Average print order: 1,000-3,000. First novel print order: 1,500 (average). Plans up to 3 first novels this year. Averages 2-3 total titles, 1-2 fiction titles/year. Distributes titles through Consortium Book Sales and Distribution, St. Paul, MN. Promotes titles through all national review media, bookstore readings, author tours, website, radio shows.

- Member of the Publishers Marketing Association, Bookbuilders of Boston and PEN.

Needs: Erotica, ethnic (Jewish), feminist, gay, humor/satire, lesbian, literary, mainstream/contemporary, regional (Cape Cod), religious (Jewish). "Genres often blur; we're interested in good writing. We'd love to see memoirs as well as fiction that comments on the world through the lens of personal, political or family experience." Recently published *The Dangerous Age*, by Annette Williams Jaffee; *The Kitchen Man*, by Ira Wood; and *Leo G. Fergus.com*, by Anne Taugherlini (all mainstream).
How to Contact: Query first with outline/synopsis and 2-4 sample chapters (50 pages). Does not accept unsolicited mss. Unsolicited queries/correspondence by e-mail OK. Include bio, list of publishing credits and a brief description of the book with submission. Send SASE for reply, return of ms or send a disposable copy of ms. Reports in 6 weeks on queries; 6 months on mss. Simultaneous submissions OK. Sometimes critiques or comments on rejected mss.
Payment/Terms: Pays royalties of 5% minimum; 8% maximum. Offers negotiable advance. Provides negotiable number of author's copies. Sends galleys to author. Publishes ms 1-2 years after acceptance.
Advice: "Send us a manuscript that educates us somewhat about our world and does not dwell on personal problems only. And, it must be well written. We are willing to work with writers who are less experienced but who can accept editing advice. We strongly push sales of secondary rights (translations, foreign sales) and expect the author and publisher to participate equally in the proceeds. Writers must be willing to accept and incorporate editorial advice and cannot shirk their responsibility to publicize their own work by giving readings, contacting book stores, drumming up local media attention, etc. We believe in strong marketing with an author who can publicize him/herself."

LEMEAC EDITEUR INC., (I, II), 1124 Marie Anne Est, Montreal, Québec H2J 2B7 Canada. (514)524-5558. Fax: (514)524-3145. Directeur Littéraire: Pierre Filion. Estab. 1957. Publishes paperback originals. Books: offset #2 paper; offset printing; allemand binding; color/cover illustration. Average print order: 1,000. First novel print order: 1,000. Published new writers within the last year. Plans 1 first novel this year. Averages 25 total titles, 20 fiction titles each year. Often critiques or comments on rejected mss.
Needs: Literary, romance (contemporary, futuristic/time travel, historical), short story collections, translations. Writers submit to editor. Recently published *Un objet de beauté*, by Michel Tremblay (novel); and *L'Emprinte de l'ange*, by Nancy Huston (novel).
How to Contact: Accepts unsolicited mss. Submit complete ms with cover letter. Send a disposable copy of ms. Agented fiction 10%. Reports in 3 months on queries; 6 months on mss. No simultaneous submissions.
Terms: Pays royalties of 10%. Sends galleys to author. Publishes ms 1-2 years after acceptance.

LUCKY HEART BOOKS, (II), Subsidiary of Salt Lick Press, Salt Lick Foundation, Inc., 1900 West Hwy. 6, Waco TX 76712. **Acquisitions**: James Haining, editor/publisher. Estab. 1969. Small press with significant work reviews in several national publications. Publishes paperback originals and reprints. Books: offset/bond paper; offset printing; hand-sewn or perfect-bound; illustrations. Average print order: 500. First novel print order: 500.
Needs: Open to all fiction categories. Published *Catch My Breath*, by Michael Lally.
How to Contact: Accepts unsolicited mss. SASE. Agented fiction 1%. Reports in 2 weeks to 4 months on mss. Sometimes critiques or comments on rejected mss.
Terms: Pays 10 author's copies. Sends galleys to author.
Advice: "Follow your heart. Believe in what you do. Use the head, but follow the heart."

THE LUTTERWORTH PRESS, P.O. Box 60, Cambridge CB1 2NT England. Fax: +44(0)1223 366951. E-mail: lutterworth.pr@dial.pipex.com. Website: http://dialspace.dial.pipex.com/lutterworth.pr/ (includes catalogs, company résumé, order forms, selection of books with extra details). **Acquisitions:** Adrian Brink, fiction editor. "Two hundred-year-old small press publishing wide range of adult nonfiction, religious and children's books."
Imprint(s): Acorn Editions.
Needs: The only fiction we publish is for children: picture books (with text from 0-10,000 words), educational, young novels, story collections. Also nonfiction as well as religious children's books."
How to Contact: Send synopsis and sample chapter. Unsolicited queries/correspondence by e-mail and fax OK. "Send IRCs. English language is universal, i.e., mid-Atlantic English."
Terms: Pays royalty.

MID-LIST PRESS, (I, II), Jackson, Hart & Leslie, Inc., 4324-12th Ave. S., Minneapolis MN 55407-3218. (612)822-3733. Fax: (612)823-8387. E-mail: guide@midlist.org. Website: http://www.midlist.org (includes writer's guidelines, history/mission, authors and titles, ordering information). **Acquisitions**: Marianne Nora, associate publisher; Lane Stiles, senior editor. Estab. 1989. Nonprofit literary small press. Publishes hardcover originals

READ THE BUSINESS OF FICTION WRITING section to learn the correct way to prepare and submit a manuscript.

and paperback originals and hardcover reprints. Books: acid-free paper; offset printing; perfect or Smyth-sewn binding. Average print order: 2,000. **Publishes 2 previously unpublished authors/year.** Plans 1 first novel this year. Averages 3 fiction titles each year. Rarely comments on rejected mss. Distributes titles through National Book Network. Promotes titles through publicity, direct mail, catalogs, sales reps, BEA, author's events.

• The publisher's philosophy is to nurture "mid-list" titles—books of literary merit that may not fit "promotional pigeonholes"—especially by writers who were previously unpublished.

Needs: General fiction. No children's/juvenile, romance, young adult, religious. Published *Part of His Story*, by Alfred Corn (novel); *Women and Children First*, by Bill Oliver (short fiction collection); and *The Latest Epistle of Jim*, by Roy Shepard (novel). Publishes First Series Award for the Novel and First Series Award for Short Fiction.

How to Contact: Accepts unsolicited mss. Query first for guidelines or visit website at www.midlist.org. Include #10 SASE. Send SASE for reply, return of ms or send a disposable copy of the ms. Agented fiction less than 10%. Reports in 1-3 weeks on queries; 1-3 months on mss. Simultaneous submissions OK.

Terms: Pays royalty of 40% minimum; 50% maximum of profits. Average advance: $1,000. Sends galleys to author. Publishes ms 6-12 months after acceptance. Writer's guidelines for #10 SASE.

Advice: "Write first for guidelines before submitting a query, proposal or manuscript. And take the time to read some of the titles we've published."

MILKWEEDS FOR YOUNG READERS, Imprint of Milkweed Editions, 430 First Ave. N., Suite 400, Minneapolis MN 55401-1743. (612)332-3192. Fax: (612)332-6248. **Acquisitions:** Elisabeth Fitz, children's reader. Estab. 1984. "Milkweeds for Young Readers are works that embody humane values and contribute to cultural understanding." Publishes hardcover and trade paperback originals. Publishes 25% previously unpublished writers/year. Publishes 3 titles/year.

Needs: For ages 8-12: adventure, animal, fantasy, historical, humor, juvenile, mainstream/contemporary, religious, romance, sports. Recently published *Behind the Bedroom Wall*, by Laura E. Williams (historical); *The Boy with Paper Wings*, by Susan Lowell; and *Summer of the Bonepile Monster*, by Aileen Kilgore Henderson (adventure).

How to Contact: Query with 2-3 sample chapters and SASE. Agented fiction 30%. Reports in 2 months on queries, 6 months on mss. Simultaneous submissions OK.

Terms: Pays 7½% royalty on retail price. Advance varies. Publishes ms 1 year after acceptance. Writer's guidelines for #10 SASE. Book catalog for $1.50.

MISTY HILL PRESS, (II), 5024 Turner Rd., Sebastopol, CA 95472. (707)823-7437. **Acquisitions**: Sally S. Karste, managing editor. Estab. 1985. Two person operation on a part-time basis. Publishes paperback originals. Books: illustrations; average print order: 2,000; first novel print order: 500-1,000. Plans 1 first novel this year. Publishes 1 title each year.

Needs: Juvenile (historical). Looking for "historical fiction for children, well researched for library market." Published *Trails to Poosey*, by Olive R. Cook (historical fiction); and *Tales Fledgling Homestead*, by Joe Armstrong (nonfiction portraits).

How to Contact: Accepts unsolicited mss. Submit outline/synopsis and sample chapters. Reports within weeks. Simultaneous submissions OK. Sometimes critiques rejected mss; *$15/hour charge for critiques*.

Terms: Pays royalties of 5%. Sends prepublication galleys to author. Writer's guidelines and book catalog for SASE (or IRC).

N **NICETOWN, (II, III)**, 1460 N. 52nd St., Philadelphia PA 19131. (215)477-1435. Fax: (215)473-7575. E-mail: tedcam@aol.com. Imprints are Nicetown Audio Tapes. Editor: Theodore W. Wing. Estab. 1986. Publishes hardcover and paperback originals and paperback reprints. Averages 4 total titles each year. Often critiques or comments on rejected mss.

Needs: Horror, romance, science fiction, short story collections, thriller/espionage.

How to Contact: Accepts unsolicited mss. Query with outline/synopsis and 2 sample chapters. Include estimated word count, 1-page bio, Social Security number and list of publishing credits. Reports in 3 weeks on queries; 2 months on mss. Simultaneous and electronic submissions OK.

Terms: Offers negotiable advance; provides author's copies.

OUR CHILD PRESS, P.O. Box 74, Wayne PA 19087-0074. (610)964-0606. CEO: Carol Hallenbeck. Estab. 1984. Publishes hardcover and paperback originals and reprints. Plans 2 first novels this year. Plans 2 titles this year.

Needs: Adventure, contemporary, fantasy, juvenile (5-9 yrs.), preschool/picture book and young adult/teen (10-18 years). Especially interested in books on adoption or learning disabilities. Published *Don't Call Me Marda*, by Sheila Welch (juvenile); *Oliver—An Adoption Story*, by Lois Wickstrom; and *Blue Ridge*, by Jon Patrick Harper.

How to Contact: Query first. Does not accept unsolicited mss. Reports in 2 weeks on queries; 2 months on mss. Simultaneous submissions OK. Sometimes comments on rejected mss.

Terms: Pays royalties of 5% minimum. Publishes ms up to 6 months after acceptance. Book catalog free.

✓ **OUTRIDER PRESS, (I, II)**, 937 Patricia Lane, Crete IL 60417. (708)672-6630. Fax: (708)672-5820. E-mail: outriderpr@aol.com. **Acquisitions**: Phyllis Nelson, president; Whitney Scott, fiction editor. Estab. 1988. "Small operation to support the voices of freedom and equality regardless of race, gender, orientation. Known for publishing new authors." Publishes trade paper originals. Books: offset printing; perfect binding; average print order: under 5,000. Averages 2-3 total titles, 1 fiction title each year. Distributes titles through Baker & Taylor, amazon.com. Promotes titles through readings, book fairs, publishing parties, book stores, amazon.com and paid ads.

Needs: Feminist, literary, New Age/mystic/spiritual, gay, lesbian, short story collection. No Christian/religious work. Publishes anthologies. "Our anthologies are contests with cash prizes in addition to publication and high-profile readings. Therefore, we charge a $16 reading fee for poetry and fiction." Guidelines for SASE. Recently published *Freedom's Just Another Word* (poetry and short fiction on freedoms earned and yearned for). Scheduled for 1999 publication: *Feathers, Fins & Fur* (anthology of poetry, short fiction and essays on animals); and *Scratching It Out—A Slightly Irreverent Writer's Manual*.

How to Contact: Accepts unsolicited mss with SASE. Submit complete ms with cover letter (with short stories). Include estimated word count and list of publishing credits. SASE for return of ms. Reports in 1 month on queries; 2 months on mss. Simultaneous submissions OK. Accepts electronic submissions (3.5 IBM compatible—WordPerfect 5.0, 5.1, 5.2 or 6.0 for DOS; Microsoft Word '97; Rich Text format. No ASCII, no Macs). Sometimes comments on rejected mss; *charges $2 double-spaced pages with 10-page minimum, prepaid and SASE for return.*

Terms: Payment depends on award money. Writer's guidelines for SASE.

Advice: "We have a need for short and super-short fiction with pace and flair and poetry with texture and imagery. Give me fresh, honest writing that reflects craft, focus and sense of place; character-driven writing that studies the terrain of human hearts exploring the non-traditional. Take risks, but know your craft. We favor work that's well-crafted, tightly-written and smoothly flowing. Read our publications to familiarize yourself with our preferences."

PAGES PUBLISHING GROUP, (I, II), Division of PAGES Book Fairs, Inc., 801 94th Ave. N., St. Petersburg FL 33702-2426. (813)578-7600. Address material to Acquisitions Editor. Estab. 1984. "Children's mid-size press." Publishes paperback originals for children. Published new writers within the last year.

Imprint(s): Willowisp Press, Worthington Press, Hamburger Press, Riverbank Press.

Needs: "Children's fiction and nonfiction, K-8." Adventure, contemporary, romance, for grades 5-8. No "violence, sex; romance must be very lightly treated." Riverbank Press is specifically for professional storytellers." Recently published *Funny Money*, by Florence Temko (activity book); and *Real-Life Strange Encounters*, by Tracey Dils (nonfiction).

How to Contact: Accepts unsolicited mss. Query (except picture books) with outline/synopsis and 3 sample chapters. Must send SASE. Reporting time on queries varies; 2 months on mss. Simultaneous submissions OK. "Prefer hard copy for original submissions; prefer disk for publication."

Terms: Pay "varies." Publishes ms 6-12 months after acceptance. Writer's guidelines for #10 SASE.

Advice: "We need *fresh* ideas that speak to children. Our consumer is *the child*, so the story must appeal to him or her at a kid's level. 'Fun' and 'engaging' are the watchwords."

⊘ **PAPYRUS PUBLISHERS & LETTERBOX LITERARY SERVICE, (II)**, P.O. Box 27383, Las Vegas NV 89126-1383. (702)256-3838. Publicity and Promotion Director: Anthony Wade. **Acquisitions**: Geoffrey Hutchison-Cleaves, editor-in-chief; Jessie Rosé, fiction editor. Estab. London 1946; USA 1982. Mid-size independent press. Publishes hardcover originals. Audio books; average print order 2,500. Averages 3 total titles each year. Promotes titles through mail, individual author fliers, author tours.

Imprint(s): Letterbox Literary Service.

Needs: No erotica, gay, feminist, children's, spiritual, lesbian, political. Published *Is Forever Too Long?* by Heather Latimer (romantic fiction); *Violet*, by Joan Griffith; and *Louis Wain—King of the Cat Artists 1860-1939*, by Heather Latimer (dramatized biography).

How to Contact: "Not accepting right now. Fully stocked."

Terms: Pays royalties of 10% minimum. Advance varies. Publishes ms 1 year after acceptance.

Advice: "Don't send it, unless you have polished and polished and polished. Absolutely no established author sends off a piece that has just been 'written' once. That is the first draft of many!"

DAVID PHILIP PUBLISHERS, P.O. Box 23408, Claremont 7735 South Africa. Fax: (21)643358. E-mail: dpp@iafrica.com.

Needs: "Fiction with Southern African concern or focus. Progressive, often suitable for school or university prescription, literary, serious."

How to Contact: Send synopsis and 1 sample chapter.

Terms: Pays royalties. Write for guidelines.

Advice: "Familiarize yourself with list of publisher to which you wish to submit work."

N **PIG IRON PRESS, (IV)**, 26 N. Phelps, Box 237, Youngstown OH 44501. (330)747-6932. Fax: (330)747-0599. **Acquisitons:** Jim Villani, editor/publisher. Small independent publisher. Publishes hardcover originals,

paperback originals and reprints. Books: 60 lb. offset paper; offset lithography; paper/casebound; illustration on cover only. Average print order: 1,000. First novel print order: 800. Plans to publish 2 first novels in 1999. Averages 2 total titles, 1 fiction title/year.
Needs: Adventure, experimental, science fiction, short story collections. Recently published *The Harvest*, by Judith Hemschemeyer (social realism); and *Gamma Connection*, by Charles Darling (science fiction).
How to Contact: Include estimated word count and list of publishing credits. Send SASE for reply, return of ms or send a disposable copy of ms. Reports in 1 month on queries; 3 months on mss.
Terms: Pays royalties of 5% minimum; 10% maximum. Provides 20 author's copies. Sends galleys to author. Writer's guidelines for #10 SASE. Book catalog for SASE.

N **PLEASURE BOAT STUDIO, (II)**, 802 E. 6th, Port Angeles WA 98362. Phone/fax: (888)810-5308. E-mail: pbstudio@pbstudio.com. Website: http://www.pbstudio.com (includes sample works; writer's guidelines; company philosophy; names of authors, titles). **Acquisitions:** William Slaughter and Jack Estes, fiction editors. Estab. 1996. "We publish high-quality literary (not mainstream) fiction in original or in translation." Publishes paperback originals. Books: 55 lb. paper; perfect binding. Average print order: 1,500. First novel print order: 1,000. **Publishes 1 new writer/year.** Averages 2-3 total titles; 1 fiction title/year.
Needs: Erotica, ethnic/multicultural, feminist, gay, historical, humor/satire, literary, regional, short story collections, translations. Recently published *In Memory of Hawks*, by Irving Warner (short story collection); and *Setting Out: The Education of Li-li*, by Tung Nien (English translation).
How to Contact: Accepts unsolicited mss. Query with outline/synopsis and 1-2 sample chapters. Unsolicited queries/correspondence by e-mail and fax OK. Include estimated word count, 1-page bio and list of publishing credits. Send SASE for reply, return of ms or send a disposable copy of ms. Reports in 3-4 weeks on queries; 3-4 months on mss. Simultaneous submissions OK. *"Negotiable charge for ms critique."*
Terms: Pays royalty of 10%. Provides 25 author's copies. "Payment by individual arrangement." Sends galleys to author. Publishes ms 1-2 years after acceptance.

✓ ⊘ **THE POST-APOLLO PRESS, (I, II)**, 35 Marie St., Sausalito CA 94965. (415)332-1458. Fax: (415)332-8045. E-mail: tpapress@dnai.com. Website: http://www.dnai.com/~tpapress/ (includes excerpts, catalog, reviews and ordering links). **Acquisitions**: Simone Fattal, publisher. Estab. 1982. Specializes in "women writers published in Europe or the Middle East who have been translated into English for the first time." Publishes paperback originals. Book: acid-free paper; lithography printing; perfect-bound. Average print order: 2,000. First novel print order: 2,000. Published new writers within the last year. Averages 2 total titles, 1 fiction title each year. Distributes titles through Small Press Distribution, Berkeley, California. Promotes titles through advertising in selected literary quarterlies, SPD catalog, Feminist Bookstore News & Catalog, ALA and ABA and SF Bay Area Book Festival participation.
Needs: Feminist, lesbian, literary, spiritual, translations. No juvenile, horror, sports or romance. "Many of our books are first translations into English." Recently published *Josef Is Dying*, by Ulla Berkéwicz (novel); and *A Beggar At Damascus Gate*, by Yasmine Zahran.
How to Contact: "The Post-Apollo Press is not accepting manuscripts or queries currently due to a full publishing schedule."
Terms: Pays royalties of 6½% minimum or by individual arrangement. Sends galleys to author. Publishes ms 1½ years after acceptance. Book catalog free.
Advice: "We want to see serious, literary quality, informed by an experimental aesthetic."

N 🍁 ✓ **THE PRAIRIE PUBLISHING COMPANY**, Box 2997, Winnipeg, Manitoba R3C 4B5 Canada. (204)837-7499. Publisher: Ralph Watkins. Estab. 1969. Buys juvenile mss with illustrations. Books: 60 lb. high-bulk paper; offset printing; perfect-bound; line-drawings. Average print order: 2,000. Published work by previously unpublished authors within the last year. First novel print order: 2,000. **Published work by previously unpublished authors within the last year.**
Needs: Open. Published: *The Homeplace*, (historical novel); *My Name is Marie Anne Gaboury*, (first French-Canadian woman in the Northwest); and *The Tale of Jonathan Thimblemouse*.
How to Contact: Query with SASE or IRC. No simultaneous submissions. Reports in 1 month on queries, 6 weeks on mss. Publishes ms 4-6 months after acceptance. Free book catalog.
Terms: Pays 10% in royalties. No advance.
Advice: "We work on a manuscript with the intensity of a Max Perkins. A clean, well-prepared manuscript can go a long way toward making an editor's job easier. On the other hand, the author should not attempt to anticipate the format of the book, which is a decision for the publisher to make. In order to succeed in today's market, the story must be tight, well written and to the point. Do not be discouraged by rejections."

PRESS GANG PUBLISHERS, (II, IV), 1723 Grant St., Vancouver, British Columbia V5L 2Y6 Canada. (604)251-3315. Fax: (604)251-3329. Website: http://www.pressgang.bc.ca. Estab. 1974. Feminist press, 3 full-time staff. Publishes paperback originals and reprints. Books: paperback; offset printing; perfect-bound. Average print order: 3,500. First novel print order: 2,000.

- Press Gang Publishers received the Lambda Literary Award 1997 for *Beyond the Pale* by Elana Dykewoman and the Ferro-Grumley Prize 1997 for *Sunnybrook: A True Story with Lies* by Persimmon Blackbridge.

Needs: Feminist fiction, nonfiction, mystery, short stories. Subjects and themes include lesbian, women and psychiatry, women and the law, native studies, women of color, erotica, literary. No children/young adult/teen. No poetry. Priority given to Canadian writers. Recently published *Prozac Highway*, by Persimmon Blackridge; *Love Ruins Everything*, by Karen X. Tulchinsky; and *When Fox Is A Thousand*, by Larissa Lai.
How to Contact: Accepts unsolicited mss. Query first. SASE. Reports in 2 months on queries; 3-4 months on mss. Simultaneous submissions OK.
Terms: Pays 8-10% royalties. Sends galleys to author. Book catalog free on request.

PUBLISHERS SYNDICATION, INTERNATIONAL, (II), P.O. Box 6218, Charlottesville VA 22906-6218. (804)964-1194. Fax: (804)964-0096. **Acquisitions:** A. Samuels. Estab. 1979.
Needs: Adventure, mystery/suspense (amateur sleuth, police procedural), thriller/espionage, western (frontier saga).
How to Contact: Accepts unsolicited mss. Submit complete ms with a cover letter. Include estimated word count. Send SASE for reply, return of ms. Reports in 3-4 weeks on mss.
Terms: Pays royalties of .05% minimum; 2% maximum. Advance is negotiable. Writer's guidelines for SASE.
Advice: "The type of manuscript we are looking for is devoid of references which might offend. Remember you are writing for a general audience."

PUCKERBRUSH PRESS, (I, II), 76 Main St., Orono ME 04473. (207)581-3832 or 866-4808. **Acquisitions**: Constance Hunting, publisher/editor. Estab. 1971. Small, independent press. Publishes paperback originals. Books: laser printing; perfect-bound; sometimes illustrations. Average print order: 1,000. Published new writers within the last year. Publishes 1 previously unpublished writer/year. Averages 3 total titles each year. Distributes titles through MWPA and mail order. Promotes titles through advertising in Maine in Print.
Needs: Contemporary, experimental, literary, high-quality work. Published *An Old Pub Near the Angel*, by James Kelman (short stories); *A Stranger Here, Myself*, by Tema Nason (female stories); and *Dorando*, by James Boswell (novel).
How to Contact: Accepts unsolicited mss. Submit complete ms with cover letter. SASE. Reports in 2 weeks on queries; 2 months on mss. Sometimes comments on rejected mss. *If detailed comment, $500.*
Terms: Pays royalties of 10%; 20 author's copies. Sends galleys to author. Publishes ms usually 1 year after acceptance. Writer's guidelines for #10 SASE. "I have a book list and flyers."
Advice: "Write for yourself."

PUDDING HOUSE PUBLICATIONS, (II), 60 N. Main St., Johnstown OH 43031. (614)967-6060. E-mail: pudding@johnstown.net. Website: http://www.puddinghouse.com (includes staff, departments, photos, guidelines, books for direct and wholesale purchase, publications list, writing games, poem of the month, Unitarian Universalist poets page, calls, etc.). **Acquisitions**: Jennifer Bosveld, editor. Estab. 1979. "Small independent publisher seeking outrageously fresh short shorts stories." Publishes paperback originals. Books: paper varies; side stapled; b&w illustrations. Published new writers within the last year. Promotes titles through direct mail, conference exhibits, readings, workshops.
Needs: Ethnic/multicultural, experimental, humor/satire, literary, the writing experience, liberal/alternative politics or spirituality, new approaches. Recently published *Karmic 4-Star Buckaroo*, by John Bennett (short stories); and *Maggie Lynn & Her Perpetual State of Fulfillment in Johnstown Ohio*, by Jennifer Bosweld (novella).
How to Contact: Accepts unsolicited mss. Submit complete ms with cover letter and ample SASE. Include short bio and list of publishing credits. Send SASE for return of ms. Reports in 1 week. No simultaneous submissions. Sometimes critiques or comments on rejected mss for various fee, if close.
Terms: Pays in author's copies. Sends galleys to author for chapbooks. Publishes ms 2-24 months after acceptance. Writer's guidelines free for SASE. Publication list available.
Advice: "Send dense, rich, pop-culture-placed pieces that sound like the best poetry (gives us an economy of words)."

RED SAGE PUBLISHING, INC., (II), P.O. Box 4844, Seminole FL 33775-4844. Phone/fax: (727)391-3847. Website: http://www.RedSagePub.com. **Acquisitions:** Alexandria Kendall, editor (romance erotica). Estab. 1955. Publishes "romance erotica or ultra-sensual romance novellas written by romance writers." Publishes paperback originals. Books: perfect binding. **Published 3 new writers within the last year.** Averages 1 total title, 1 fiction title/year.

- Red Sage Publishing received the Fallot Literary Award for Fiction.

Imprint(s): The Secrets Volumes (romance erotica), edited by Alexandria Kendall.
Needs: Romance (erotica) novellas for The Secrets Volumes: The Best in Women's Sensual Fiction anthology.

Length: 20,000-30,000 words. Writers may submit to anthology editor. Recently published *Secrets Volume 3*, edited by Alexandria Kendall (romance erotica).
How to Contact: Accepts unsolicited mss. Query with outline/synopsis and 10 sample pages. Include estimated word count and list of publishing credits. Send SASE for return of ms. Reports in 3 months. Sometimes critiques or comments on rejected ms.
Terms: Pays advance and royalty. Sends galleys to author. Publishes ms 1-2 years after acceptance. Writer's guidelines for SASE.

RENDITIONS, (IV), Research Centre for Translation, Institute of Chinese Studies, Chinese University of Hong Kong, Shatin, New Territories, Hong Kong. Phone: 852-26097399. Fax: 852-26035110. E-mail: renditions@cuhk.edu.hk. Website: http://www.cuhk.edu.hk/renditions (includes sections about Research Centre for Translation, the Chinese University of Hong Kong, *Renditions* magazines, Renditions paperbacks, Renditions books, forthcoming, ordering information and related sites). **Acquisitions:** Dr. Eva Hung, editor. Averages 2-3 fiction titles annually. "Academic specialist publisher. Distributes titles through local and overseas distributors and electronically via homepage and amazon.com. Promotes titles through homepage, by exchange ads with *China Now* and *China Review International* and paid ads in *Feminist Bookstone News* and *Journal of Asian Studies* of AAS.
Needs: Will only consider English translations of Chinese fiction, prose, drama and poetry. Fiction published either in semiannual journal (*Renditions*) or in the Renditions Paperback series. Recently published *The Cockroach and Other Stories*, by Liu Yichang; *A Girl Like Me and Other Stories* and *Marvels of a Floating City*, by Xi Xi (Hong Kong stories).
How to Contact: For fiction over 5,000 words in translation, sample is required. Sample length: 1,000-2,000 words. Send sample chapter. "Submit only works in our specialized area. One copy of translation accompanied by one copy of original Chinese text." Fax and e-mail requests for information and guidelines OK.
Terms: Pays honorarium for publication in *Renditions*; royalties for paperback series.

RONSDALE PRESS, (II, IV), 3350 W. 21 Ave., Vancouver, British Columbia V6S 1G7 Canada. (604)738-4688. Fax: (604)731-4548. E-mail: ronhatch@pinc.com. Website: http://www.ronsdalepress.com (includes guidelines, catalog, events). **Acquisitions**: Ronald B. Hatch, president. Estab. 1988. Ronsdale Press is "dedicated to publishing books that give Canadians new insights into themselves and their country." Publishes paperback originals. Books: 60 lb. paper; photo offset printing; perfect binding. Average print order: 1,000. **Publishes 1-2 previously unpublished writers/year.** First novel print order: 1,000. Plans 1 first novel this year. Averages 3 fiction titles each year. Distributes titles through General Distribution, LPC/Inbook and Partners West. Promotes titles through ads in BC Bookworld and Globe & Mail, and interviews on radio.
Needs: Experimental and literary. Published *The Ghouls' Night Out*, by Janice MacDonald (children's); *Willobe of Wuzz*, by Sandra Glaze (children's); and *Daruma Days*, by Terry Watada (short stories).
How to Contact: *Canadian authors only.* Accepts unsolicited mss. Submit outline/synopsis and first 100 pages. SASE. Unsolicited queries/correspondence by e-mail and fax OK. Short story collections must have some magazine publication. Reports in 2 weeks on queries; 2 months on mss. Sometimes comments on rejected mss.
Terms: Pays royalties of 10%. Provides author's copies. Sends galleys to author. Publishes ms 6 months after acceptance.
Advice: "We publish both fiction and poetry. Authors *must* be Canadian. We look for writing that shows the author has read widely in contemporary and earlier literature. Ronsdale, like other literary presses, is not interested in mass-market or pulp materials."

ST. AUGUSTINE SOCIETY PRESS, (I, IV), 68 Kingsway Crescent, Etobicoke, Ontario M8X 2R6 Canada. (416)239-1670. **Acquisitions**: Frances Breckenridge, editor. Estab. 1994. "We are a small press, independent of any church. We seek manuscripts which can expand the circle of light detailed by St. Augustine, either fiction or nonfiction." Publishes paperback originals. Average print order: 500 (depends on the type of final product). Averages 1 total title, variable number of fiction titles each year. Member of Toronto Small Press Group.
Needs: Literary, mainstream/contemporary. Published *Maledetti (The Forsaken)*, by Michael Gualtieri (novel).
How to Contact: Accepts unsolicited mss. Query with outline/synopsis and 2 sample chapters. Send SASE for reply, return of ms or send a disposable copy of ms. Reports in 3 weeks on queries. Simultaneous submissions OK.
Payment/Terms: Negotiable. Sends galleys to author. Publishes ms 6 months after acceptance. Free writer's guidelines.
Advice: "We welcome works by writers who have, through years of study, gained insights into the human condition. A book that is just a 'good read' is of no interest to us."

INTERESTED IN A PARTICULAR GENRE? Check our new sections for: **Mystery/Suspense**, page 57; **Romance**, page 77; **Science Fiction & Fantasy**, page 95.

THE SAVANT GARDE WORKSHOP, (II, IV), a privately-owned affiliate of The Savant Garde Institute, Ltd., P.O. Box 1650, Sag Harbor NY 11963-0060. Phone/fax: (516)725-1414. **Acquisitions**: Vilna Jorgen II, publisher; Charles Collins, editor, literary futurist; Artemis Smith, editor, multimedia philosophy, long poems. Estab. 1953. "Literary multiple-media publisher." Publishes hardcover and paperback originals and reprints. First novel print order: 1,000. Averages 2 total titles. Promotes titles through listing in R.R. Bowker, amazon.com, Baker & Taylor, word-of-mouth in world literary circles and academic/scientific conferences.

- Be sure to look at this publishers' guidelines first. Works could best be described as avant-garde/post modern, experimental.

Needs: Contemporary, futuristic, humanist, literary, philosophical. "We are open to the best, whatever it is." No "mediocrity or pot boilers." Published *01 or a Machine Called SKEETS*, by Artemis Smith (avant-garde). Series include "On-Demand Desktop Collectors' Editions," "Artists' Limited Editions," "Monographs of The Savant Garde Institute."

How to Contact: Do not send unsolicited mss. Query first with SASE, outline, sample pages and complete vita. Agented fiction 1%. Reports in 6 weeks on queries ("during academic year"); 2 months on invited mss. Sometimes comments on rejected mss. Critiques rejected mss for $50.

Terms: Average advance: $500, provides author's copies, honorarium (depends on grant/award money). Terms set by individual arrangement with author depending on the book and previous professional experience. Sends galleys to author. Publishes ms 18 months after acceptance. Writer's guidelines free.

Advice: "Most of the time we recommend authors to literary agents who can get better deals for them with other publishers, since we are looking for extremely rare offerings. We are not interested in the usual commercial submissions. Convince us you are a real artist, not a hacker." Would like to see more "thinking for the 21st Century of Nobel Prize calibre. We're expanding into multimedia CD-ROM co-publishing and seek multitalented authors who can produce and perform their own multimedia work for CD-ROM release. We are overbought and underfunded—don't expect a quick reply or fast publication date."

N **THE SENIORS MARKET, (I, II, IV)**, 652 Treece Gulch, Stevensville MT 59870. (406)777-5191. Fax: (406)777-7206. E-mail: cotton@bigsky.net. Website: http://www.Missoula.BigSky.net/coveandcloister. **Acquisitions:** James L. Cotton, editor. "We will consider other submissions, but strongly prefer material written *by* seniors (over 50) *for* seniors."

Needs: Adventure, historical, humor/satire, literary, mainstream/contemporary, mystery/suspense (amateur sleuth, cozy), regional, religious/inspirational, romance (contemporary, gothic, historical, frontier), senior citizen/retirement, sports, westerns (frontier, traditional). Publishes ms 1 year after acceptance. Will consider short story collection for anthology. *"Always comments on rejected ms. Will critique or line edit for a fee."*

How to Contact: Query first. Include estimated word count, 1-page, single-spaced bio and social security number. "Authors must submit a marketing/promotion plan. Don't submit if you expect us to do this without your involvement." Reports in 3 weeks on queries; 2 months on mss. Send SASE for reply; send a disposable copy of ms. Simultaneous submissions OK.

Terms: Pays advance and royalty. Sends galleys to author. Publishes ms 1 year after acceptance.

Advice: "Remember we prefer senior writers. Whether literary or genre, your work must be genuine, not imitative nor trendy. Time is precious, and if you ask seniors to spend it with your work, it must add meaning and pleasure to their lives."

N **SERPENT'S TAIL**, 4 Blackstock Mews, London N4 2BT UK. Fiction Editor: Peter Ayrton. Averages 30 fiction titles/year. "We are an up-market literary house whose tastes are well out of the mainstream. We see our audience as young and urban-based. Translations, literary fiction and cultural studies are our forte." Length: 30,000 words minimum; 100,000 words maximum.

How to Contact: "Send query letter first, and only after you have looked at the books we publish." Send cover letter; enclose IRC or postage. Write office for catalog.

Terms: Pays advance plus royalties.

Tips: "For us, writers need not give extra background to their work, its context, etc. regarding the fact that they are not British. We are a cosmopolitan bunch."

SNOWAPPLE PRESS, (I, II), P.O. Box 66024, Heritage Postal Outlet, Edmonton, Alberta T6J 6T4 Canada. (403)437-0191. **Acquisitions**: Vanna Tessier, editor. Estab. 1991. "We focus on topics that are interesting, unusual and controversial." Small independent literary press. Publishes hardcover and paperback originals. Books: non-acid paper; offset printing; perfect binding; illustrations. Average print order: 500. First novel print order: 500. Plans 1 first novel this year. Averages 3-4 total titles, 1-2 fiction titles each year. Distributes titles through bookseller and library wholesalers. Promotes titles through press releases and reviews.

Needs: Adventure, children's/juvenile (adventure, fantasy, mystery), experimental, historical, literary, mainstream/contemporary, short story collections, translations, young adult/teen (adventure, mystery/suspense). Recently published *Gypsy Drums*, by Vanna Tessier (short stories); *Salamander Moon*, by Cecelia Frey (short stories); and *Missing Bones*, by Vanna Tessier (young adult).

How to Contact: Does not accept unsolicited mss. Query first with 1-page cover letter. Include estimated word count, 300-word bio and list of publishing credits. SASE with sufficient IRCs. Reports in 3-4 weeks on queries; 3 months on mss. Simultaneous submissions OK.

Terms: Pays honorarium; provides 10-25 author's copies. Sends galleys to author. Publishes ms 12-18 months after acceptance.
Advice: "Query first to obtain guidelines with proper SASE and IRCs."

THE SPIRIT THAT MOVES US PRESS, (II), P.O. Box 720820-N, Jackson Heights NY 11372-0820. (718)426-8788. E-mail: msklar@mindspring.com. **Acquisitions**: Morty Sklar, editor/publisher. Estab. 1974. Small independent literary publisher. Publishes hardcover and paperback originals. "We do, for the most part, simultaneous clothbound and trade paperbacks for the same title." Books: 60 lb. natural acid-free paper; mostly photo-offset, some letterpress; cloth and perfect binding; illustrations. Average print order: 3,000. Published new writers within the last year. **Publishes 75% previously unpublished writers/year.** Averages 2 fiction titles, mostly multi-author. Distributes titles directly and through wholesalers. Promotes titles through direct mail and review copies, as well as advertisements in trade and consumer publications.

- *Patchwork Of Dreams*, was awarded a grant by New York City Council representative to place this book in several schools for classroom use. The Spirit That Moves Us Press is known for our having been the first U.S. publisher of Jaroslav Seifert, who won the Nobel Prize a year after they published his *The Casting Of Bells*.

Needs: Literary. "Our choice of 'literary' does not exclude almost any other category—as long as the writing communicates on an emotional level, and is involved with people more than things. Nothing sensational or academic." Published *Patchwork of Dreams: Voices from the Heart of the New America*, a multiethnic collection of fiction and other genres; *Editor's Choice III: Fiction, Poetry & Art from the U.S. Small Press*, biennally, and *Free Parking*, all edited by Morty Sklar.
How to Contact: Accepts unsolicited mss. "We are undergoing major changes. Please query before sending work." Query letter only first "unless he/she sees an announcement that calls for manuscripts and gives a deadline." Include estimated word count, bio and whether or not ms is a simultaneous submission. SASE for reply or return of ms. Reports on mss "if rejected, soon; if under consideration, from 1-3 months." Comments on rejected mss "when author requests that or when we are compelled to by the writing (good or bad)."
Terms: Pays royalties of 10% net and authors copies, also honorarium, depends on finances. Sends galleys to author. Publishes up to 1 year after acceptance. Plans and time-frames for #10 SASE "but the guidelines are only for certain books; we don't use general guidelines." Catalog for 6×9 SAE and 2 first-class stamps.
Advice: "We are interested in work that is not only well written, but that gets the reader involved on an emotional level. No matter how skilled the writing is, or how interesting or exciting the story, if we don't care about the people in it, we won't consider it. Also, we are open to a great variety of styles, so just be yourself and don't try to second-guess the editor. You may have our newest collection *Patchwork of Dreams* as a sample, for $10 (regularly $14.50 with postage).

STORMLINE PRESS, (I, II), P.O. Box 593, Urbana IL 61801. Publisher: Raymond Bial. Estab. 1985. "Small independent literary press operated by one person on a part-time basis, publishing one or two books annually." Publishes hardcover and paperback originals. Books: acid-free paper; paper and cloth binding; b&w illustrations. Average print order: 1,000-2,000. First novel print order: 1,000-2,000. Published new writers within the last year. Averages 1-2 total titles, all fiction each year.

- Stormline's title, *First Frost*, was selected for a Best of the Small Presses Award.

Needs: Literary. Looks for "serious literary works, especially those which accurately and sensitively reflect rural and small town life." Published *Silent Friends: A Quaker Quilt*, by Margaret Lacey (short story collection).
How to Contact: No longer considers unsolicited submissions.
Terms: Pays royalties of 10% maximum. Provides author's copies. Sends galleys to author. Publishes ms 6-12 months after acceptance. Writer's guidelines for SASE. Book catalog free.
Advice: "We look for a distinctive voice and writing style. We are always interested in looking at manuscripts of exceptional literary merit. We are not interested in popular fiction or experimental writing. Please review other titles published by the press, notably *Silent Friends: A Quaker Quilt*, to get an idea of the type of books published by our press."

THIRD SIDE PRESS, INC., (II), 2250 W. Farragut, Chicago IL 60625-1863. (773)271-3029. Fax: (773)271-0459. E-mail: thirdside@aol.com. **Acquisitions**: Midge Stocker, publisher. Estab. 1991. "Small, independent press, feminist." Publishes paperback originals. "Experimental and contemporary lesbian novels." Books: 50 lb. recycled, acid-free paper; offset-web or sheet printing; perfect binding. Average print order: 3,000. First novel print order: 2,000. Published new writers within the last year. Averages 4 total titles, 2 fiction titles each year. Distributes titles through Consortium Book Sales & Distribution.
Needs: Lesbian: feminist, literary, mainstream/contemporary. No "collections of stories; horror; poetry; homophobic" material. Recently published *Not So Much the Fall*, by Kerry Hart (first novel); *Speaking in Whispers*, by Kathleen Morris (erotica); and *The Mayor of Heaven*, by Lynn Kanter.
How to Contact: Query first. Queries by e-mail OK. Include bio (1-2 paragraphs) and synopsis. Send SASE for reply, return of ms or send a disposable copy of ms. Reports in 2-3 weeks on queries; 3-6 months on mss. Simultaneous submissions OK with notice. Sometimes comments on rejected mss.
Terms: Pays royalties (varies). Provides 10 author's copies. Publishes ms 6-18 months after acceptance. Writer's guidelines for 9×12 SAE and 2 first-class stamps. Book catalog for 2 first-class stamps.

Advice: "Look at our catalog and read one or two of our other books to get a feel for how your work will fit with what we've been publishing. Plan book readings and other appearances to help sell your book. And don't quit your day job."

THIRD WORLD PRESS, P.O. Box 19730, Chicago IL 60619. (773)651-0700. Fax: (773)651-7286. Publisher/Editor: Haki Madhubuti. Fiction Editors: Gwendolyn Mitchell, Melissa Moore. Estab. 1967. Black-owned and operated independent publisher of fiction and nonfiction books about the black experience throughout the Diaspora. Publishes paperback originals. Plans 1 first novel this year, as well as short story collections. Averages 10 total titles, 3 fiction titles each year. Average first novel print order 15,000 copies. Distributes titles through Partners, Baker & Taylor and bookstores. Promotes titles through direct mail, catalogs and newspapers.
Needs: Ethnic, historical, juvenile (animal, easy-to-read, fantasy, historical, contemporary), preschool/picture book, short story collections, and young adult/teen (easy-to-read/teen, folktales, historical). Recently published *In the Shadow of the Son*, by Michael Simanga. "We primarily publish nonfiction, but will consider fiction by and about blacks."
How to Contact: Accepts unsolicited mss January and July only. Query or submit outline/synopsis and 1 sample chapter with SASE. Reports in 6 weeks on queries; 5 months on mss. Simultaneous submissions OK. Accepts computer printout submissions.
Terms: Individual arrangement with author depending on the book, etc.

THISTLEDOWN PRESS, (II, IV), 633 Main St., Saskatoon, Saskatchewan S7H 0J8 Canada. (306)244-1722. Fax: (306)244-1762. E-mail: thistle@sk.sympatico.ca. Website: http://www.thistledown.sk.ca (includes guidelines, catalog, teaching materials). Editor-in-Chief: Patrick O'Rourke. **Acquisitions**: Jesse Stothers. Estab. 1975. Publishes paperback originals—literary fiction, young adult fiction, poetry. Books: Quality stock paper; offset printing; perfect-bound; occasional illustrations. Average print order 1,500-2,000. First novel print order: 1,000-1,500. **Publishes 4 previously unpublished writers/year.** Publishes 12 titles, 6 or 7 fiction, each year. Distributes titles through General Distribution Services. Promotes titles through intensive school promotions, online, advertising, special offers.

- Thistledown received a Saskatchewan Book Award-Publishing in Education in 1998 for *Tales: Stories for Young Adults*, by R.P. MacIntyre, editor.

Needs: Literary, experimental, short story collections, novels.
How to Contact: Query first with SASE. No unsolicited mss. Unsolicited queries/correspondence by e-mail and fax OK. "We *only* want to see Canadian-authored submissions. We will *not* consider multiple submissions." Photocopied submissions OK. Reports in 2 months on queries. Publishes anthologies. "Stories are nominated." Recently published *The Serpent Bride*, by K.V. Johansen (Danish folk stories); *The Secret of the Northern Lights*, by W.P. Kinsella (short fiction-Hubbeman stories); and *The Crying Jesus*, by R.P. MacIntyre (young adult fiction). Also publishes The Mayer Mystery Series (mystery novels for young adults) and The New Leaf Series (first books for poetry and fiction).
Payment/Terms: Pays standard royalty on retail price. Publishes ms 2 years after acceptance. Writer's guidelines and book catalog for #10 SASE.
Advice: "We are primarily looking for quality writing that is original and innovative in its perspective and/or use of language. Thistledown would like to receive queries first before submission—perhaps with novel outline, some indication of previous publications, periodicals your work has appeared in. *We publish Canadian authors only.* We are continuing to publish more fiction and are looking for new fiction writers to add to our list. New Leaf Editions line is first books of poetry or fiction by emerging Saskatchewan authors. Familiarize yourself with some of our books before submitting a query or manuscript to the press."

TURNSTONE PRESS, (II), 607-100 Arthur St., Winnipeg, Manitoba R3B 1H3 Canada. (204)947-1555. Fax: (204)942-1555. E-mail: editor@turnstonepress.mb.ca. **Acquisitions**: Manuela Dias, editor. Estab. 1976. "Turnstone Press is a literary press that publishes Canadian writers with an emphasis on writers from, and writing on, the Canadian west." Canadian literary press focusing on eclectic new writing, prairie writers and travel writing. Books: Offset paper; perfect-bound; average first novel print order: 1,500. **Publishes 3 previously unpublished writers/year.** Averages 8-10 total titles/year. Distributes titles through General Distribution Services (Canada and US). Promotes titles through Canadian national and local print media and select US print advertising.

- Turnstone Press received the Manitoba Book Design of the Year Award. *Summer of My Amazing Luck*, by Miriam Toews was nominated for the Stephen Leacock Award for Humor and the John Hirsch Award for Most Promising Writer.

Needs: Experimental, literary, regional (Western Canada), mystery, gothic, noir. "We will be doing only 2-3 fiction titles a year. Interested in new work exploring new narrative/fiction forms, travel/adventure writing of a literary nature and writing that pushes the boundaries of genre." Published *How to Get There From Here*, by Michelle Berry (short stories); *A Blue and Golden Year*, by Alison Preston (mystery); and *Summer of My Amazing Luck*, by Miriam Toews (comic novel).
How to Contact: *Canadian authors only.* Accepts unsolicited mss. Query first with 20-40 sample pages and SASE. Include estimated word count and list of publishing credits. Reports in 6 weeks on queries; 2-4 months on mss.

Terms: Pays royalties of 10%; 10 author's copies. Average advance: $500. Publishes ms 1 year after acceptance. Sends galleys to author. Book catalog free with SASE. Simultaneous submissions OK if notified.
Advice: "Like most Canadian literary presses, we depend heavily on government grants which are not available for books by non-Canadians. Do some homework before submitting work to make sure your subject matter/genre/writing style falls within the publishers area of interest. Specializes in experimental literary and prairie writing."

N **ULTRAMARINE PUBLISHING CO., INC., (V)**, Box 303, Hastings-on-the-Hudson NY 10706. (914)478-1339. Fax: (914)478-1365. Publisher: Christopher P. Stephens. Estab. 1973. Small publisher. "We have 200 titles in print. We also distribute for authors where a major publisher has dropped a title." Averages 15 total titles, 12 fiction titles each year. Buys 90% agented fiction. Occasionally critiques rejected mss.
Needs: Experimental, fantasy, mainstream, science fiction, short story collections. No romance, westerns, mysteries.
How to Contact: Does not accept unsolicited mss.
Terms: Pays royalties of 10% minimum; advance is negotiable. Publishes ms an average of 8 months after acceptance. Free book catalog.

✓ **UNIVERSITY OF MISSOURI PRESS, (II)**, 2910 LeMone Blvd., Columbia MO 65201-8227. (573)882-7641. Fax: (573)884-4498. E-mail: willcoxc@ext.missouri.edu. Website: www.system.missouri.edu.upress (includes authors, titles, book descriptions). **Acquisitions**: Clair Willcox, editor. Estab. 1958. "Mid-size university press." Publishes paperback originals and reprints (short story collections only). Published new writers within the last year. Publishes 1 previously unpublished writer/year. Averages 52 total titles, 4 short story collections each year. Distributes titles through direct mail, bookstores, sales reps.

• The University of Missouri Press is a member of the Association of American University Presses.

Needs: Short story collections. No children's fiction. Recently published *The Palace of Wasted Footsteps*, by Cary Holladay; *Veneer*, by Steve Yarbrough; *The Buddha in Malibu*, by William Harrison; and *Joe Baker is Dead*, by Mary Troy (all short story collections).
How to Contact: Accepts unsolicited mss. Query first. Queries/correspondence by e-mail and fax OK. Submit cover letter and sample story or two. Include bio/publishing credits. SASE for reply. Reports in 2 weeks on queries; 3 months on mss. Simultaneous submissions OK. Sometimes comments on rejected ms.
Terms: Pays royalties of 6%. Sends galleys to author. Publishes ms 1-1½ years after acceptance. Book catalogs are free.

UNIVERSITY OF NEVADA PRESS, (II, IV), MS 166, Reno NV 89557-0076. (702)784-6573. Fax: (702)784-6200. E-mail: dalrympl@scs.unr.edu. Director: Ronald E. Latimer. Editor-in-Chief: Margaret Dalrymple. Estab. 1961. "Small university press. Publishes fiction that focuses primarily on the American West." Publishes hardcover and paperback originals and paperback reprints. Books: acid-free paper. Publishes approximately 25 total titles, 1 fiction title/year. Member AAUP.
Needs: Ethnic/multicultural (general), family saga, historical (American West), humor/satire, mystery/suspense (U.S. West), regional (U.S. West). Published *Wild Indians & Other Creatures*, by Adrian Louis (short stories); *Bad Boys and Black Sheep*, by Robert Franklin Gish (short stories); and *The Measurable World*, by Katharine Coles (novel). "We have series in Basque Studies, Gambling Studies, history and humanities, ethnonationalism, Western literature."
How to Contact: Accepts unsolicited mss. Query with outline/synopsis and 2-4 sample chapters. E-mail and fax OK. Include estimated word count, 1-2 page bio and list of publishing credits. Send SASE for reply, return of ms or send a disposable copy of ms. Agented fiction 20%. Reports in 2-3 weeks on queries; 2-4 months on mss. Sometimes critiques or comments on rejected mss.
Payment/Terms: Pays royalties; negotiated on a book-by-book basis. Sends galleys to author. Publishes ms 9-24 months after acceptance. Writer's guidelines for #10 SASE.
Advice: "We are not interested in genre fiction."

✓ 🏆 **UNIVERSITY PRESS OF COLORADO, (IV)**, P.O. Box 849, Niwot CO 80544. (303)530-5337. Fax: (303)530-5306. E-mail: hallein@spot.colorado.edu. **Acquisitions**: Yashja Hallein, acquisitions editor; Luther Wilson, director. Estab. 1965. "Small, independent, scholarly publisher, nonprofit." Publishes hardcover and paperback originals and reprints. Books: acid-free paper; offset printing; case bound. Average print order: 1,000. First novel print order: 1,500. **Publishes 1 previously unpublished writer/year.** Averages 30 total titles, 2 fiction titles each year. Member of The Association of American University Presses.

● *Mari: A Novel*, by Jane Valentine Barker, published by the University of Colorado Press, received the 1998 Colorado Book Award in Fiction and the Colorado Author's League 1997 and the Top Hand Award for Best Fiction.

Needs: Regional (western), western (modern). Recently published *The Circle Leads Home*, by Mary Anderson Parks (20th century Native American); *The Meade Solution*, by Robert Conley (contemporary fiction); and *Roll On Columbia I, II, & III*, by Bill Gulick (western history).

How to Contact: Query with outline/synopsis and 3 sample chapters. Include estimated word count, bio and list of publishing credits. Unsolicited queries/correspondence by e-mail and fax OK. Send SASE for reply, return of ms or send disposable copy of ms. Agented fiction 90%. Reports in 3 weeks on queries; 4 months on mss. Sometimes critiques or comments on rejected mss.

Terms: Pays royalties of 12% maximum. Provides 10 author's copies. Sends galleys to author. Publishes ms within 2 years after acceptance. Writer's guidelines and book catalog free.

Advice: "We look for high quality fiction that might not appeal to the larger trade houses. We are interested in publishing fiction that fits into our series *Women's West*. Generally, our authors are responsible for proofreading and indexing their own manuscripts. If they do not wish to do so, we will hire proofreaders and/or indexers at the author's expense."

VAN NESTE BOOKS, (I, II), 12836 Ashtree Rd., Midlothian VA 23113-3095. Phone/fax: (804)897-3568. E-mail: kvno@aol.com. **Acquisitions**: Karen Van Neste Owen, publisher. Estab. 1996. "We are a small independent publisher interested in publishing serious fiction." Publishes hardcover originals. Books: 55 lb. acid-free paper; cloth binding; illustrations (cover only). Average print order: 1,500. **Publishes 2 previously unpublished writers/year.** Plans 2 first novels for 1999 and 2-4 novels per year thereafter. Averages 2-4 total titles, 2-4 fiction titles each year. Distributes titles through The Permanent Press, Sag Harbor, NY. Promotes titles through bound galleys mailed to book reviewers throughout the U.S. and representation by the Permanent Press's foreign and Hollywood agents.

Needs: Feminist, historical, humor/satire, literary, mainstream/contemporary, mystery/suspense, regional (southern), thriller/espionage. Recently published *Styll in Love*, by Rob Schultz and *One August Day*, by Charlotte Morgan (mainstream contemporary).

How to Contact: Accepts unsolicited mss. Query with "brief" synopsis and 3 sample chapters. Include estimated word count, 2-paragraph bio, Social Security number and list of publishing credits. Unsolicited queries/correspondence by e-mail OK. Send SASE for reply, return of ms or send disposable copy of ms. Reports in 2 months on queries; 6 months on mss. Sometimes critiques or comments on rejected mss.

Terms: Pays royalties of 10-15% minimum on print runs of more than 2,500 copies; half that on print runs under 2,500 copies. Average advance: $500 for finished disk. Sends galleys to author. Publishes ms 12-18 months after acceptance.

Advice: "I am looking for serious, mainstream contemporary fiction and will consider first-time novelists. However, because the business is so small, I need the copy to be as clean (free of mistakes) as possible. No collections of short stories, poetry or juvenile fiction, please."

W.W. PUBLICATIONS, (IV), Subsidiary of A.T.S., Box 373, Highland MI 48357-0373. (813)585-0985. Also publishes *Minas Tirith Evening Star*. **Acquisitions**: Philip Helms, editor. Estab. 1967. One-man operation on part-time basis. Publishes paperback originals and reprints. Books: typing paper; offset printing; staple-bound; black ink illustrations. Average print order: 500. First novel print order: 500. Averages 1 title (fiction) each year.

● The publisher is an arm of the American Tolkien Society.

Needs: Fantasy, science fiction, young adult/teen (fantasy/science fiction). "Specializes in Tolkien-related or middle-earth fiction." Published *The Adventures of Fungo Hafwirse*, by Philip W. Helms and David L. Dettman.

How to Contact: Accepts unsolicited mss. Submit complete ms with SASE. Reports in 1 month. Simultaneous submissions OK. Occasionally critiques rejected mss.

Terms: Individual arrangement with author depending on book, etc.; provides 5 author's copies. Free book catalog.

Advice: "We are publishing more fiction and more paperbacks. The author/editor relationship: a friend and helper."

☑ **WOMAN IN THE MOON PUBLICATIONS, (I, IV)**, 1409 The Alameda, San Jose CA 95126. (408)279-6626. Fax: (408)279-6636(*). E-mail: womaninmoon@earthlink.net. Publisher: Dr. SDiane A. Bogus. Editor-in-Chief: Mary Pascual. Estab. 1979. "We are a small press with a primary publishing agenda for poetry, New Age fiction and reference books of no more than 1,000 words biannually. For our news magazine *The Spirit* we accept short story manuscripts." Averages 2-4 total titles each year.

Needs: Contemporary, ethnic, fantasy, gay, lesbian, psychic/supernatural/occult, prisoner's stories, short story collections.

How to Contact: Accepts unsolicited mss between January 1-April 30 only up to 100 mss. Query first or submit outline/synopsis and sample chapters. Query by letter, phone, fax or e-mail. SASE for query. Acknowledges in 1 week; reports during or at end of season. Simultaneous submissions OK. Comments on rejected mss.

Terms: *$125 reading fee required.* Pays royalties of 5% minimum; 10% maximum. Pays $30 plus 2 copies for

short stories in quarterly newsletter. Publishes ms within 6 months after acceptance. Writer's guidelines for #10 SASE. Book sample for 6×9 SAE and $4 postage. Book catalog for $5.
Advice: "To the short story writer, write us a real life lesbian gay set of stories. Tell us how life is for an African American person in an enlightened world. Create a possibility, an ideal that humanity can live toward. Write a set of stories that will free, redeem and instruct humanity. The trends in fiction by women have to do with the heroine as physical and capable and not necessarily defended by or romantically linked to a male." Sponsors fiction and nonfiction prose contest in the name of Audre Lorde. Awards two $250 prizes. Contest runs from September 1 to November 30. Winners announced in February.

✓ **WOODLEY MEMORIAL PRESS, (IV)**, English Dept., Washburn University, Topeka KS 66621. (785)234-1032. E-mail: zzlaws@washburn.edu. Website: http://www.wuacc.edu/reference/woodley-press/index.html (includes writer's guidelines, editors, authors, titles). Editor: Robert N. Lawson. Estab. 1980. "Woodley Memorial Press is a small, nonprofit press which publishes book-length poetry and fiction collections by Kansas writers only; by 'Kansas writers' we mean writers who reside in Kansas or have a Kansas connection." Publishes paperback originals. Averages 2 titles each year.
Needs: Contemporary, experimental, literary, mainstream, short story collection. "We do not want to see genre fiction, juvenile, or young adult." Published *Rudolph, Encouraged by His Therapist*, by Eugene H. Bales.
How to Contact: *Charges $5 reading fee.* Accepts unsolicited mss. Accepts unsolicited queries and correspondence by e-mail. Send complete ms. SASE. Reports in 2 weeks on queries; 2 months on mss. Sometimes comments on rejected ms.
Terms: "Terms are individually arranged with author after acceptance of manuscript." Publishes ms one year after acceptance. Writer's guidelines available at above website address.
Advice: "We only publish one work of fiction a year, on average, and definitely want it to be by a Kansas author. We are more likely to do a collection of short stories by a single author."

FOR EXPLANATIONS OF THESE SYMBOLS,
SEE THE INSIDE FRONT AND BACK COVERS OF THIS BOOK.

Book Publishers

In this section, you will find many of the "big-name" book publishers—Avon, The Berkley Publishing Group, Harcourt Brace & Company, Harlequin, Alfred A. Knopf, and Little Brown and Company, to name a few. Many of these publishers remain tough markets for new writers or for those whose work might be considered literary or experimental. Indeed, some only accept work from established authors, and then often only through an author's agent.

Also listed here are "small presses" publishing four or more titles annually. Included among them are small and mid-size independent presses, university presses and other nonprofit publishers. Introducing new writers to the reading public has become an increasingly more important role of these smaller presses at a time when the large conglomerates are taking less chances on unknown writers. Many of the successful small presses listed in this section have built their reputations and their businesses in this way and have become known for publishing prize-winning fiction.

These smaller presses also tend to keep books in print longer than larger houses. And, since small presses publish a smaller number of books, each title is equally important to the publisher, and each is promoted in much the same way and with the same commitment. Editors also stay at small presses longer because they have more of a stake in the business—often they own the business. Many smaller book publishers are writers themselves and know first-hand the importance of a close editor-author or publisher-author relationship. (See the Small Press Advantage on page 421 for more reasons to submit your manuscript to a small press.)

However, although having your novel published by one of the big commercial publishers listed in this section is difficult, it is not impossible. The trade magazine *Publisher's Weekly* regularly features interviews with writers whose first novels are being released by top publishers. Many editors at large publishing houses find great satisfaction in publishing a writer's first novel. For perspective from inside a large commercial publishing house, see the interview with Simon & Schuster vice president Chuck Adams (page 44).

TYPES OF BOOK PUBLISHERS

Large or small, the publishers in this section publish books "for the trade." That is, unlike textbook, technical or scholarly publishers, trade publishers publish books to be sold to the general consumer through bookstores, chain stores or other retail outlets. Within the trade book field, however, there are a number of different types of books.

The easiest way to categorize books is by their physical appearance and the way they are marketed. Hardcover books are the more expensive editions of a book, sold through bookstores and carrying a price tag of around $20 and up. Trade paperbacks are soft-bound books, also sold mostly in bookstores, but they carry a more modest price tag of usually around $10 to $20. Today a lot of fiction is published in this form because it means a lower financial risk than hardcover.

Mass market paperbacks are another animal altogether. These are the smaller "pocket-size" books available at bookstores, grocery stores, drug stores, chain retail outlets, etc. Much genre or category fiction is published in this format. This area of the publishing industry is very open to the work of talented new writers who write in specific genres such as science fiction, romance and mystery.

At one time publishers could be easily identified and grouped by the type of books they do. Today, however, the lines between hardcover and paperback books are blurred. Many publishers known for publishing hardcover books also publish trade paperbacks and have paperback imprints. This enables them to offer established authors (and a very few lucky newcomers) hard-soft deals in which their book comes out in both versions. Thanks to the mergers of the past decade, too, the same company may own several hardcover and paperback subsidiaries and imprints, even though their editorial focuses may remain separate.

THE SMALL PRESS ADVANTAGE

Hefty advances, media hype, glamorous parties. When the big publishing houses start calling, sometimes the siren songs are hard for authors to ignore. But not all authors are clamoring for seven-figure advances and multi-book contracts. Small presses are alive and kicking, and certainly they have something to offer.

"At Four Walls Eight Windows you work directly with us," says publisher John Oakes. "An author has direct input into how the book's edited, presented and marketed, and that's hugely important to people. If they don't think it is, they find out it is. Many of our authors were at larger houses." (An Insider Report with John Oakes appears on page 456.)

Unless the advance is inordinately large, an author can still see the same money at a small house over time that they would get elsewhere. At Four Walls, the writer gets personal attention from a single editor, consultation on cover art and other artistic decisions, and an enduring work. Small presses typically rely more on backlist sales, so they're less likely to let a book go out of print. Oakes also stresses the advantage of having your book edited by an editor rather than an agent. Too often at big publishers, overworked editors rely heavily on agents to have a book in publishable form before it comes in.

But smaller houses can look to conglomeration as a means of consolidating the sound of sirens. Having fewer publishers will translate into fewer books released and in turn fewer authors, helping to mop up a flooded book market. Oakes predicts that big publishers will invest more into individual titles, consequently retreating to lower-risk books with thick profit margins. As big houses wring out books from their lists that can't sell 20,000 copies, small presses are free to pick up the more promising titles. The market is becoming leaner, the quality of writing is improving and mediocre authors are getting cast out to sea. When they wash ashore, they'd better watch out for the seductive sea nymphs.

—Brad Crawford

CHOOSING A BOOK PUBLISHER

In addition to checking the bookstores and libraries for books by publishers that interest you, you may want to refer to the Category Index at the back of this book to find publishers divided by specific subject categories. If you write genre fiction, check our new genre sections for lists of book publishers: (mystery, page 74; romance, page 92; science fiction and fantasy, page 103). The subjects listed in the Indexes are general. Read individual listings to find which subcategories interest a publisher. For example, you will find several romance publishers listed in the For Romance Writers Section, but read the listings to find which type of romance is considered—gothic, contemporary, Regency or futuristic. See How to Use This Book to Publish Your Fiction for more on how to refine your list of potential markets.

The Roman numeral ranking codes appearing after the names of the publishers will also help you in selecting a publisher. These codes are especially important in this section, because many of the publishing houses listed here require writers to submit through an agent. A numeral **III** identifies those that mostly publish established and agented authors, while a numeral **I** points to publishers most open to new writers. See the end of this introduction for a complete list of ranking codes.

IN THE LISTINGS

As with other sections in this book, we identify new listings with a symbol. In this section, most with this symbol are not new publishers, but instead are established publishers who decided to list this year in the hope of finding promising new writers.

In addition to the symbol indicating new listings, we include other symbols to help you in narrowing your search. English-speaking foreign markets are denoted by a . The maple leaf symbol identifies Canadian presses. If you are not a Canadian writer, but are interested in a Canadian press, check the listing carefully. Many small presses in Canada receive grants and other funds from their provincial or national government and are, therefore, restricted to publishing Canadian authors.

We continue to include editorial comments set off by a bullet (•) within listings. This is where we include information about any special requirements or circumstances that will help you know even more about the publisher's needs and policies. The symbol identifies publishers who have recently received honors or awards for their books. And the symbol indicates that a publisher accepts agented submissions only.

Each listing includes a summary of the editorial mission of the house, an overarching principle that ties together what they publish. Under the heading **Acquisitions**: we list one or more editors, often with their specific area of expertise. An imprint listed in boldface type means there is an independent listing arranged alphabetically within this section.

Book editors asked us again this year to emphasize the importance of paying close attention to the Needs and How to Contact subheads of listings for book publishers. Unlike magazine editors who want to see complete manuscripts of short stories, most of the book publishers listed here ask that writers send a query letter with an outline and/or synopsis and several chapters of their novel. The Business of Fiction Writing, beginning on page 121 of this book, outlines how to prepare work to submit directly to a publisher.

There are no subsidy book publishers listed in *Novel & Short Story Writer's Market*. By subsidy, we mean any arrangement in which the writer is expected to pay all or part of the cost of producing, distributing and marketing his book. We feel a writer should not be asked to share in any cost of turning his manuscript into a book. All the book publishers listed here told us that they *do not charge writers* for publishing their work. *If any of the publishers listed here ask you to pay any part of publishing or marketing your manuscript, please let us know.*

A NOTE ABOUT AGENTS

Many publishers are willing to look at unsolicited submissions, but most feel having an agent is to the writer's best advantage. In this section more than any other, you'll find a number of publishers who prefer submissions from agents. That's why this year we've included a section of agents open to submissions from fiction writers (page 131). And to help you find the right agent for you—and for your fiction—read Agent Targeting, beginning on page 118.

For listings of more agents and additional information on how to approach and deal with them, see the 1999 *Guide to Literary Agents*, published by Writer's Digest Books. The book separates nonfee- and fee-charging agents. While many agents do not charge any fees up front, a few charge writers to cover the costs of using outside readers. Be wary of those who charge large sums of money for reading a manuscript. Reading fees do not guarantee representation. Think of an agent as a potential business partner and feel free to ask tough questions about his or her credentials, experience and business practices.

FOR MORE INFORMATION

Some of the mystery, romance and science fiction publishers included in this section are also included in *Mystery Writer's Sourcebook*, *Romance Writer's Sourcebook* or *Science Fiction and Fantasy Writer's Sourcebook* (all published by Writer's Digest Books). These books include in-depth interviews with editors and publishers. Also check issues of *Publishers Weekly* for publishing industry trade news in the U.S. and around the world or *Quill & Quire* for book publishing news in the Canadian book industry.

For more small presses see the *International Directory of Little Magazines and Small Presses* published by Dustbooks (P.O. Box 100, Paradise CA 95967). To keep up with changes in the industry throughout the year, check issues of two small press trade publications: *Small Press Review* (also published by Dustbooks) and *Independent Publisher* (formerly *Small Press*) (Jenkins Group, Inc., 121 E. Front St., 4th Floor, Traverse City MI 49684).

The ranking system we've used for listings in this section is as follows:

I Publisher encourages beginning or unpublished writers to submit work for consideration and publishes new writers frequently.
II Publisher accepts outstanding work by beginning and established writers.
III Hard to break into; publishes mostly writers with extensive previous publication credits or agented writers.
IV Special-interest or regional publisher, open only to writers in certain genres or on certain subjects or from certain geographic areas.
V Closed to unsolicited submissions.

ABSEY & CO., INC., (II), 5706 Root Rd., Suite #5, Spring TX 77389. (281)257-2340. Fax: (281)251-4676. E-mail: abseyandco@aol.com. **Acquisitions:** Trey Hall, editor-in-chief. "We are interested in book-length fiction of literary merit with a firm intended audience." Publishes hardcover and paperback originals. Publishes 6-10 titles/year. Receives 900-1,000 submissions/year. Accepts 50% of books from first-time authors and unagented writers.

- Two Absey books were named to the American Library Association's Best Books for Young Adults for 1998.

Needs: Juvenile, mainstream/contemporary, short story collections. Also publishes poetry.
How to Contact: Query with SASE. Reports in 3 months on queries, 6 months on mss. No e-mail submissions. Simultaneous submissions OK.
Terms: Pays 8-15% royalty on wholesale price. Publishes ms 1 year after acceptance. Writer's guidelines for #10 SASE.
Advice: "Since we are a small, new press looking for good manuscripts with a firm intended audience, we tend to work closely and attentively with our authors."

ACADEMY CHICAGO PUBLISHERS, (II), 363 W. Erie St., Chicago IL 60610. (312)751-7302. **Acquisitions**: Anita Miller, senior editor. Estab. 1975. Midsize independent publisher. Publishes hardcover and paperback originals and paperback reprints.
Needs: Biography, history, academic and anthologies. Only the most unusual mysteries, no private-eyes or thrillers. No explicit sex or violence. Serious fiction, not romance/adventure. "We will consider historical fiction that is well researched. No science fiction/fantasy, no religious/inspirational, no how-to, no cookbooks. In general, we are very conscious of women's roles. We publish very few children's books." Published *The Man Who Once Played Catch with Nellie Fox*, by John Mandarino; *Glass Hearts*, by Terri Paul; and *Murder at Heartbreak Hospital*, by Henry Slesar.
How to Contact: Accepts unsolicited queries. Query and submit first three consecutive chapters, triple spaced, with SASE and a cover letter briefly describing the content of your work. No simultaneous submissions. "Manuscripts without envelopes will be discarded. *Mailers* are a *must*."
Terms: Pays 5-10% on net in royalties; no advance. Publishes ms 18 months after acceptance. Sends galleys to author.
Advice: "At the moment we are swamped with manuscripts and anything under consideration can be under consideration for months."

☑ **ACE SCIENCE FICTION, (II)**, Berkley Publishing Group, 375 Hudson St., New York NY 10014. (212)366-2000. **Acquisitions**: Susan Allison, editor-in-chief; Anne Sowards, editorial assistant. Estab. 1948. Publishes paperback originals and reprints and 6-10 hardcovers per year. Number of titles: 6/month. Buys 85-95% agented fiction.

Needs: Science fiction and fantasy. No other genre accepted. No short stories. Published *Forever Peace*, by Joe Haldeman; and *Neuromancer*, by William Gibson.

How to Contact: Submit outline/synopsis and 3 sample chapters with SASE. No simultaneous submissions. Reports in 2 months minimum on mss. "Queries answered immediately if SASE enclosed." Publishes ms an average of 18 months after acceptance.

Terms: Standard for the field. Sends galleys to author.

Advice: "Good science fiction and fantasy are almost always written by people who have read and loved a lot of it. We are looking for knowledgeable science or magic, as well as sympathetic characters with recognizable motivation. We are looking for solid, well-plotted science fiction: good action adventure, well-researched hard science with good characterization and books that emphasize characterization without sacrificing plot. In fantasy we are looking for all types of work, from high fantasy to sword and sorcery." Submit fantasy and science fiction to Anne Sowards.

ACROPOLIS BOOKS, INC., (I, II, III), 747 Sheridan Blvd., #1A, Lakewood CO 80214-2551. (303)231-9923. Fax: (303)231-0492. E-mail: acropolisbooks@worldnet.att.net. Website: acropolisbooks.com. **Acquisitions:** Constance J. Wilson, vice president of operations. Midsize trade publisher; full (national) distribution. "It is the mission of Acropolis Books to publish books at the highest level of consciousness, commonly referred to as mysticism. This was the consciousness demonstrated by revelators of every religion in the world." Publishes hardcover and paperback originals and reprints. Publishes 20 titles/year. Imprint publishes 5-10 titles/year.

Imprint(s): I-Level, Awakening and Flashlight.

Needs: Mysticism/inspirational. "Our books encompass the spiritual principles of Omnipresence, Omnipotence and Omniscience; and further bring home the mystical realization that everyone in this world is an individual instrument of God in expression." Recently published *Invisible Leadership*, by Robert Rabbin; and *Secret Splendor*, by Charles Essert.

How to Contact: Submit 4 sample chapters with SASE. Include estimated word count, 1 page bio, social security number and list of publishing credits. Reports in 1 month on queries, 3 months on mss.

Terms: Royalties or outright purchases negotiable. Advances negotiable. Publishes ms an average of 1 year after acceptance. Writer's guidelines for #10 SASE.

Advice: "Clearly understand our focus by reading or understanding books that we have published."

ADAEX EDUCATIONAL PUBLICATIONS, (IV), P.O. Box AK188, Kumasi, Ghana. Fax: 233-51-30282. **Acquisitions**: Asare Konadu Yamoah, publisher, George Apraku Dentu, fiction editor. Distributes titles through bookstores. Promotes titles through advertising, direct mail.

Needs: Looks for cultural development, romance, literary translators and copyright brokers. "Publication development organization for Ghanaian, African and world literature: novels, workbooks, language development, etc." Recently published *Strange Happenings* and *Creatures of Circumstance*, by Asare Konadu. Average 5-10 fiction titles/year. Length: 8-250 typed pages.

How to Contact: Send brief summary and first and last chapter.

Terms: Pays advance and royalties.

ADVOCACY PRESS, (IV), Box 236, Santa Barbara CA 93102-0236. (805)962-2728. Fax: (805)963-3580. E-mail: advpress@rain.org. **Acquisitions**: Lin Jean Chiriaco, curriculum specialist. Estab. 1983. "We promote gender equity and positive self-esteem through our publications." Small publisher with 3-5 titles/year. Hardcover and paperback originals. Books: perfect or Smyth-sewn binding; illustrations; average print order: 5,000-10,000 copies; first novel print order: 5,000-10,000. Averages 2 children's fiction (32-48 pg.) titles per year. Promotes titles through catalogs, distributors, schools and bookstores.

- **Advocacy Press is not accepting submissions for 1999.** Advocacy Press books have won the Ben Franklin Award and the Friends of American Writers Award. The press also received the Eleanor Roosevelt Research and Development Award from the American Association of University Women for its significant contribution to equitable education.

Needs: Juvenile. Wants only feminist/nontraditional messages to boys or girls—picture books; self-esteem issues. Published *Minou*, by Mindy Bingham (picture book); *Kylie's Song*, by Patty Sheehan (picture book); *Nature's Wonderful World in Rhyme*, by William Sheehan. Publishes the World of Work Series (real life stories about work).

How to Contact: Submit complete manuscript with SASE for return. Reports in 10 weeks on queries. Simultaneous submissions OK.

Terms: Pays in royalties of 5-10%. Book catalog for SASE.

Advice: Wants "only fictional stories for children 4-12-years-old that give messages of self-sufficiency for little girls; little boys can nurture and little girls can be anything they want to be, etc. Please review some of our publications *before* you submit to us. For layout and writing guidelines, we recommend that you read *The*

Children's Book: How to Write It, How to Sell It by Ellen Roberts, Writers Digest Books. *Because of our limited focus, most of our titles have been written inhouse.*"

ALASKA NATIVE LANGUAGE CENTER, (IV), University of Alaska, P.O. Box 757680, Fairbanks AK 99775-7680. (907)474-7874. **Acquisitions**: Tom Alton, editor. Estab. 1972. Small education publisher limited to books in and about Alaska native languages. Generally nonfiction. Publishes hardcover and paperback originals. Books: 60 lb. book paper; offset printing; perfect binding; photos, line art illustrations; average print order: 500-1,000 copies. Averages 6-8 total titles each year.
Needs: Ethnic. Publishes original fiction only in native language and English by Alaska native writers. Published *A Practical Grammar of the Central Alaskan Yup'ik Eskimo Language*, by Steven A. Jacobson; *One Must Arrive With a Story to Tell*, by the Elders of Tununak, Alaska.
How to Contact: Does not accept unsolicited mss. Electronic submissions via ASCII for modem transmissions or Macintosh compatible files on 3.5 disk.
Terms: Does not pay. Sends galleys to author.

☑ **ALEXANDER BOOKS, (II, IV)**, Subsidiary of Creativity, Inc., 65 Macedonia Rd., Alexander NC 28701. (828)252-9515. E-mail: barbara@abooks.com. Website: http://www.abooks.com (includes writer's guidelines, authors and titles). **Acquisitions:** Barbara Blood, executive editor. Publishes hardcover originals, and trade paperback and mass market paperback originals and reprints. Publishes primarily reprints; "very little" new fiction. Publishes 8-10 titles/year. **Publishes "maybe one" previously published author every other year.**
Imprint(s): Farthest Star (Barbara Blood, editor).
Needs: Historical, mainstream/contemporary, mystery, science fiction, western. "We prefer local or well-known authors or local interest settings." Recently published *Birthright: The Book of Man*, by Mike Resnick (science fiction); and *Compleat Chance Perdue*, by Ross H. Spencer (mystery).
How to Contact: Query or submit synopsis and 3 sample chapters with SASE. Reports in 1-2 months on queries.
Terms: Pays 12-15% royalty on wholesale price. Advances seldom given (minimum $100). Publishes ms 1-2 years after acceptance. Book catalog and writer's guidelines for 8½×11 SASE with $1.01 in first-class stamps.
Advice: "Your cover letter is very important. Most acquisition editors don't get past the letter. Make sure the letter makes the editor want to go further into the query package."

ALYSON PUBLICATIONS, INC., (II), 6922 Hollywood Blvd., Suite 1000, Los Angeles CA 90028. (213)871-1225. Fax: (213)467-6805. **Acquisitions**: Julie K. Trevelyan, fiction editor. Estab. 1979. Medium-sized publisher specializing in lesbian- and gay-related material. Publishes paperback originals and reprints. Books: paper and printing varies; trade paper, perfect-bound; average print order: 8,000; first novel print order: 6,000. Published new writers within the last year. Plans 40 total titles, 18 fiction titles each year.
Imprint(s): Alyson Wonderland, Alyson Classics Library.

- In addition to adult titles, Alyson Publications has been known for its line of young adult and children's books.

Needs: "We are interested in all categories; *all* materials must be geared toward lesbian and/or gay readers. No poetry." Recently published *3 Plays by Mart Crowley*; *Swords of the Rainbow*, edited by Eric Garber and Jewelle Gomez; and *Daddy's Wedding*, Michael Willhoite. Publishes anthologies. Authors may submit to them directly.
How to Contact: Query first with SASE. Reports in 3-12 weeks.
Terms: "We prefer to discuss terms with the author. Gay and/or lesbian nonfiction and excellent fiction are our focal points." Sends galleys to author. Book catalog for SAE and 3 first-class stamps.

☑ **AMERICAN DIABETES ASSOCIATION, (II)**, 1660 Duke St., Alexandria VA 22314. (703)549-1500. Website: http://www.diabetes.org. **Acquisitions:** Robert J. Anthony, acquisitions editor. "The mission of the American Diabetes Association is to prevent and cure diabetes and to improve the lives of all people affected by diabetes." Publishes hardcover originals and trade paperback originals. Publishes 15 titles/year.
Needs: Juvenile. "We publish very little fiction—all for juveniles with diabetes." Recently published *The Dinosaur Tamer*, by Marcia Levine Mazur (juvenile fiction).
How to Contact: Query with synopsis and 2 sample chapters. Reports in 2 months.
Terms: Pays 7-10% royalty on retail price. Offers $3,000 advance. Publishes ms 9 months after acceptance. Book catalog free.
Advice: "Our audience consists primarily of consumers with diabetes who want to better manage their illness. Obtain a few of our books to better understand our target audience and appropriate reading level."

ANNICK PRESS LTD., (IV), 15 Patricia Ave., Willowdale, Ontario M2M 1H9 Canada. (416)221-4802. Publisher of children's books. Publishes hardcover and paperback originals. Books: offset paper; full-color offset printing; perfect and library bound; full-color illustrations. Average print order: 9,000. First novel print order: 7,000. Plans 18 first picture books this year. Averages approximately 25 titles each year, both fiction and nonfiction. Average first picture book print order 2,000 cloth, 12,000 paper copies. Distributes titles through Firefly Books Ltd.
Needs: Children's books only.

How to Contact: "Annick Press publishes only work by Canadian citizens or residents." Does not accept unsolicited mss. Query with SASE. Free book catalog. Occasionally critiques rejected mss.
Terms: No terms disclosed.

✓ **ARCADE PUBLISHING, (III)**, 141 Fifth Ave., New York NY 10010. (212)475-2633. Fax: (212)353-8148. President, Editor-in-Chief: Richard Seaver. **Acquisitions**: Cal Barksdale, Richard Seaver, Jeannette Seaver, Tim Bent, Sean McDonald and Coates Bateman. Estab. 1988. Independent publisher. Publishes hardcover originals and paperback reprints. Books: 50-55 lb. paper; notch, perfect-bound; illustrations; average print order: 10,000; first novel print order: 3,000-5,000. Published new writers within the year. Averages 40 total titles, 12-15 fiction titles each year. Distributes titles through Little, Brown & Co.
Needs: Literary, mainstream/contemporary, mystery/suspense, translations. No romance, science fiction, young adult. Recently published *Trying to Save Piggy Sneed*, by John Irving; *Europa*, by Tim Parks; *Dreams of My Russian Summers*, by Andrei Makine; *The Brush-Off*, by Shane Maloney; and *The Secret Diary of Anne Boleyn*, by Robin Maxwell.
How to Contact: No unsolicited mss; unsolicited mss will be returned (SASE or IRC). Submit through an agent only. Agented fiction 100%. Reports in 2 weeks on queries; 3-4 months on mss. Does not comment on rejected ms.
Terms: Pays negotiable advances and royalties and 10 author's copies. Writer's guidelines and book catalog for SASE.

ARCHWAY PAPERBACKS/MINSTREL BOOKS, (II), Imprint of Pocket Books for Young Readers, 1230 Avenue of the Americas, New York NY 10020. (212)698-7669. **Acquisitions**: Patricia MacDonald, vice president/editorial director. Published by Pocket Books. Publishes paperback originals and reprints. Published new writers this year.
Imprint(s): Minstrel Books (ages 7-12); and **Archway** (ages 12 and up).
Needs: Young adult: mystery, suspense/adventure, thrillers. Young readers (80 pages and up): adventure, animals, humor, family, fantasy, friends, mystery, school, etc. No picture books. Published *Fear Street: The New Boy*, by R.L. Stine; and *Aliens Ate My Homework*, by Bruce Coville.
How to Contact: Submit query first with outline; SASE "mandatory. If SASE not attached, query letter will not be answered."
Payment/Terms: Pays royalties of 6% minimum; 8% maximum. Publishes ms 2 years after acceptance.

ARTE PUBLICO PRESS, (II, IV), University of Houston, 4800 Calhoun, Houston TX 77204-2090. (713)743-2847. **Acquisitions**: Dr. Nicolás Kanellos, publisher. Estab. 1979. "Small press devoted to the publication of contemporary U.S.-Hispanic literature. Mostly trade paper; publishes 4-6 clothbound books/year. Publishes fiction and belles lettres." Publishes 36 paperback originals and occasionally reprints. Average print order 2,000-5,000. First novel print order 2,500-5,000.
Imprint(s): Piñata Books featuring children's and young adult literature by U.S.-Hispanic authors and ***The Americas Review***.

- Arte Publico Press received the 1994 American Book Award for *In Search of Bernabé*, by Graciela Limón; the Thorpe Menn Award for Literary Achievement; the Southwest Book Award and others. Arte Publico Press is the oldest and largest publisher of Hispanic literature for children and adults in the United States.

Needs: Childrens/juvenile, contemporary, ethnic, feminist, literary, short story collections, young adult written by US-Hispanic authors. Recently published *A Perfect Silence*, by Alba Ambert; *Song of the Hummingbird*, by Graciela Limón; and *Little Havana Blues: A Cuban-American Literature Anthology.*
How to Contact: Accepts unsolicited mss. Submit outline/synopsis and sample chapters or complete ms with cover letter and SASE. Agented fiction 1%. Reports in 1 month on queries; 4 months on mss. Sometimes critiques rejected mss.
Terms: Offers $1,000-3,000 advance. Pays 10% royalty on wholesale price. Provides 20 author's copies; 40% discount on subsequent copies. Sends galleys to author. Publishes ms minimum 2 years after acceptance. Guidelines for SASE; book catalog free on request.
Advice: "Include cover letter in which you 'sell' your book—why should we publish the book, who will want to read it, why does it matter, etc."

FOR EXPLANATIONS OF THESE SYMBOLS,
SEE THE INSIDE FRONT AND BACK COVERS OF THIS BOOK.

☑ 🏆 **ATHENEUM BOOKS FOR YOUNG READERS, (II)**, Imprint of the Simon & Schuster Children's Publishing Division, 1230 Avenue of the Americas, New York NY 10022. (212)698-2721. Vice President/Editorial Director: Jonathan J. Lanman. Editorial Coordinator: Howard Kaplan. **Acquistions**: Marcia Marshall, executive director; Caitlyn Dlouhy, senior editor; Anne Schwartz, editorial director, Anne Schwartz Books. Second largest imprint of large publisher/corporation. Publishes hardcover originals. Books: Illustrations for picture books, some illustrated short novels. Average print order: 6,000-7,500. First novel print order: 5,000. Averages 50 total titles, 25 middle grade and YA fiction titles each year.

- Books published by Atheneum Books for Children have received the Newbery Medal (*The View From Saturday*, by E.L. Konigsburg) and the Christopher Award (*The Gold Coin*, by Alma Flor Ada, illustrated by Neal Waldman). Because of the merger of Macmillan and Simon & Schuster, Atheneum Books has absorbed the Scribners imprint of Macmillan.

Needs: Juvenile (adventure, animal, contemporary, fantasy, historical, sports), preschool/picture book, young adult/teen (fantasy/science fiction, historical, mystery, problem novels, sports, spy/adventure). No "paperback romance type" fiction. Published *Lottie's New Beach Towel*, by Petra Matthers (3-8, picture book); *Achingly Alice*, by Phyllis Reynolds Naylor (10-14, middle grade novel); and *Rearranging*, by David Gifaldi (12 & up young adult fiction).
How to Contact: Accepts queries only. SASE. Agented fiction 40%. Reports in 4-6 weeks on queries. Simultaneous submissions OK "if we are so informed and author is unpublished." Very rarely critiques rejected mss.
Terms: Pays in royalties of 10%. Average advance: $3,000 "along with advance and royalties, authors receive ten free copies of their book and can purchase more at a special discount." Sends galleys to author. Writer's guidelines for #10 SASE.
Advice: "We publish all hardcover originals, occasionally an American edition of a British publication. Our fiction needs have not varied in terms of quantity—of the 50-60 titles we do each year, 25 are fiction in different age levels. We are less interested in specific topics or subject matter than in overall quality of craftsmanship. First, know your market thoroughly. We publish only children's books, so caring for and *respecting* children is of utmost importance. Also, fad topics are dangerous, as are works you haven't polished to the best of your ability. (Why should we choose a 'jewel in the rough' when we can get a manuscript a professional has polished to be ready for publication?) The juvenile market is not one in which a writer can 'practice' to become an adult writer. In general, be professional. We appreciate the writers who take the time to find out what type of books we publish by visiting the libraries and reading the books. Neatness is a pleasure, too."

AVALON BOOKS, (I, II, IV), Imprint of Thomas Bouregy Company, Inc., 401 Lafayette St., New York NY 10003. (212)598-0222. **Editorial**: Ms. Dale Jagemann. Publishes hardcover originals. Averages 60 titles/year.
Needs: "Avalon Books publishes wholesome romances, mysteries, westerns. Intended for family reading, our books are read by adults as well as teenagers, and their characters are all adults. There is no graphic sex in any of our novels. Currently, we publish five books a month: two romances, one mystery, one career romance and one western. All the romances are contemporary; all the westerns are historical." Published *Ride the Rainbow Home*, by Susan Aylworth (career romance); *The Hydrogen Murder*, by Camille Minichino (mystery); *The Mysterious Cape Cod Manuscript*, by Marie Lee (mystery); and *Hannah and the Horseman*, by Johnny D. Boggs (western). Books range in length from a minimum of 40,000 words to a maximum of 50,000 words.
How to Contact: Submit the first three chapters. "We'll contact you if we're interested." Publishes many first novels. Enclose ms-size SASE. Reports in about 3 months. "Send SASE for a copy of our tip sheet."
Terms: The first half of the advance is paid upon signing of the contract; the second within 30 days after publication. Usually publishes within 6 to 8 months.

AVON BOOKS, (II), The Hearst Corporation, 1350 Avenue of the Americas, New York NY 10019. (212)261-6800. Senior Vice President/Publisher: Lou Aronica. Estab. 1941. Large hardcover and paperback publisher. Publishes hardcover and paperback originals and reprints. Averages more than 400 titles a year.
Imprint(s): Bard, **EOS**, Twilight, Spike, Avon, Camelot and **Flare.**
Needs: Literary fiction and nonfiction, health, history, mystery, science fiction, romance, young adult, pop culture.
How to Contact: Query letters only. SASE to insure response.
Terms: Vary.

AVON EOS, (II, V), Imprint of Avon Books, 1350 Avenue of the Americas, New York NY 10019. (212)261-6821. Fax: (212)261-6895. **Acquisitions:** Jennifer Brehl, senior editor. Diana Gill, assistant editor. Imprint estab. 1998. Science fiction and fantasy imprint for serious readers. Imprint of major general trade publisher. Publishes trade hardcover, trade paperback (original and reprint), mass market paperback (original and reprint). Published new writers within the last year. Publishes 70 total titles/year, all fiction.
Needs: Fantasy, science fiction. Recently published *Full Tide of Night*, by J.R. Dunn; *Shards of a Broken Crown*, by Raymond E. Feist; and *Six Moon Dance*, by Sheri S. Tepper.
How to Contact: Does not accept unsolicited mss. Send query with outline/synopsis and 3 sample chapters. Do not send full ms. Include estimated word count, bio and list of publishing credits. Send SASE for reply. Agented fiction 99%. Reports in 1 month on queries. Simultaneous submissions OK.
Terms: Pays negotiable advance. Sends galleys to author.

INSIDER REPORT

Shooting straight from the hip: writing and publishing the western novel

Johnny Boggs

How does the night operations managing editor of the *Fort Worth Star-Telegram*'s sports copy desk keep himself busy during the daylight hours? He keeps busy with cattle drives, gunfights and Indian skirmishes, of course. At least that's how managing editor and author Johnny Boggs occupies his free time since discovering his interest in, and talent for, the Western genre.

Beginning with short story writing in high school to publishing stories in literary magazines in college to making the national scene in 1995 by publishing in *Louis L'Amour Western Magazine* and *Boy's Life*, Boggs has remained with the genre he enjoys most. Says Boggs, "I published a few contemporary Southern stories when I was experimenting to discover what I wrote best, but most of the short stories I've published are Westerns." Boggs also prefers the Western genre because he thinks being from the South (he's originally from South Carolina) and writing Southern fiction tends to lead readers to believe the work is autobiographical. "That's not exactly what I want people to think—it isn't me, it's just my crazy imagination."

Truth be told, the Western genre takes much more than imagination. It also takes research skills. Boggs avidly researches the Old West to maintain historical accuracy in his work, spending as much of his "off-duty" time researching as he does writing. "When I read something in a Western that isn't right—a town that wasn't founded until 1880 in a novel set in the 1860s or a gun inaccurately described for the period—I'm always irritated as a reader. So, as a writer, I don't want to screw up."

Frequently, Boggs uses old newspapers and catalogs as sources. "I've found a wealth of information in old period newspapers. But it's not so much the news you can get from these newspapers as the ads. My two biggest reference books are old Bloomingdale's and Montgomery Ward catalogs." The catalogs provide Boggs with two things—the merchandise available at the time and the brand names sold. Boggs says just thumbing through old catalogs provides historically accurate information that can add creditability to your work.

Also, Boggs gains valuable research information through organizations dedicated to the preservation of the Old West. One such organization is the National Congress of Old West Shootists (NCOWS). NCOWS is associated with a growing sport called Cowboy Action Shooting where people dress in Old West clothing and shoot at targets using replica or original period firearms. Boggs became a member of NCOWS after he sold a short story to NCOWS's newsletter, *The Shootist*, and received membership as part of the payment. "It's a good group and a good resource for information on firearms and clothing. I

INSIDER REPORT, *Boggs*

might even go out shooting with them, though I doubt I'll hit a whole lot of my targets."

Boggs's association with NCOWS not only introduced him to target shooting but also to the idea of expanding into novel writing. In fact, it was a friend he met who suggested Boggs make the jump from short stories to novels. "My friend Bruce Thorstad had just sold his first novel, a Western, when we met in 1990 at a Cowboy Shooting Meet and began corresponding. (I'd send him a short story to critique then he'd send me a couple of chapters from his latest novel.) At some point, Bruce suggested I try writing a novel. He even offered suggestions on how he wrote his."

However, the transition from short story writing to novel writing does not happen overnight. "My first novel was about a cattle drive, a fairly traditional Western," says Boggs. "I'd work on it, then I would set it aside for a month or longer. Finally, I finished. But when I looked up, three years had passed." Knowing a 68,000-word manuscript shouldn't take three years to write, Boggs determined he needed to discipline himself to just sit down and write. With this in mind, he turned his attention to a new manuscript. "I said, this is the time for you to bear down."

Not yet comfortable with the dictates of the 90,000-plus-word manuscripts required by traditional novels, Boggs began his next manuscript with a specific publisher in mind, Avalon Books. Boggs was attracted to Avalon's maximum length requirement of 50,000 words. He says, "I figured the shorter novel was a kind of a stepping stone from the short story. You get the 2,000-word short story nailed down, then you move up to a short novel. Once you get comfortable with the short novel, then you work up to the larger historical novel."

After completing three chapters of the manuscript, titled *Hannah and the Horseman*, Boggs queried Avalon. He sent a standard query letter with a brief description of the manuscript and an offer to send the first three chapters with a synopsis. After only a few weeks, Boggs received a request for the three chapters and synopsis. "With the standard response time for sample chapters being two to three months, I mailed the package thinking 'I have two months to finish a half-complete manuscript.' "

However, the strict deadline—a normal component of his job at the copy desk—gave him the focus he needed to dedicate himself to the project. When Marcia Markland, then vice president and publisher of Avalon, called and asked to see the rest of the manuscript, Boggs had just completed the last chapter. He says, "It worked for me, but I wouldn't recommend it." Since then, the writing has come a lot easier for Boggs. "I realized if you sit down and write, you will get *something* accomplished. It's just a matter of discipline."

Less than a week from receiving *Hannah and the Horseman*, Markland called wanting to buy the novel, but with two stipulations. She wanted Boggs to change the ending and make this manuscript the first in a series of stories revolving around the same characters. "I didn't even know Avalon was doing series," says Boggs. He told Markland he was already at work on another novel—an idea he had developed while researching *Hannah and the Horseman*—and he needed time to think about her request. "She said, 'Go ahead and keep at the manuscript you're working on now. But, while you're working, think about doing something else [with the ending of *Hannah*]."

Instead of rewriting the ending of *Hannah*, Boggs wrote Markland with another suggestion—he'd begin the next novel in the series where the first left off. That suggestion became *The Courtship of Hannah and the Horseman*. "In a lot of ways I think *The Courtship of Hannah and the Horseman* was one of the best novels I have written because, basically, it wasn't my idea," says Boggs. "I really didn't want to do a series. When I

INSIDER REPORT, *continued*

finished *Hannah and the Horseman*, I was ready to try something new, but I'm still at it. The characters grow on you and you get used to them. Also, you can expand the characters in a series and have more fun with them. When you are writing 50,000 words, character development is something you usually don't get to do because the publisher wants strong action. You can't have everything. But you can expand and grow with a series, so it's worked well."

Since the publication of *Hannah and the Horseman* in April of 1997, Boggs has published four more books with Avalon, three in the *Hannah and the Horseman* series—*The Courtship of Hannah and the Horseman*, *Riding with Hannah and the Horseman*, and *Hannah and the Horseman at the Gallows Tree*—and *This Man Colter*, the book he had begun when first contacted by Markland. Boggs also has his sixth novel, *The Curse of Dunbar's Gold*, under consideration at Avalon and is at work on his seventh, another story in the *Hannah* series. With each of his submissions, both for the *Hannah and the Horseman* series and the non-series manuscripts, Boggs queries Avalon and then sends the three sample chapters and a synopsis. "I don't have a mega book deal or anything. It's one book at a time."

With seven books under his gun belt, Boggs now finds himself being sought out by other writers at conferences. He says, "When people discover you are a published writer, they throw ideas at you. The biggest obstacle these people have is not coming up with ideas to write about, but actually doing the writing. You have to sit down and write. The book doesn't write itself. Most people have a book or a novel in them. But what I've learned is you need to have the discipline to take your idea, sit down and actually write it."

—*Chantelle Bentley*

Advice: "Get an agent."

✓ **AVON FLARE BOOKS, (II)**, Imprint of Avon Books, Division of the Hearst Corp., 1350 Avenue of the Americas, New York NY 10019. (212)261-6800. Fax: (212)261-6895. **Acquisitions:** Elise Howard, editor-in-chief. Publishes mass market paperback originals and reprints. Imprint publishes 115 new titles/year.

Needs: Adventure, ethnic, humor, mainstream, mystery, romance, suspense, contemporary. "Very selective with mystery." Manuscripts appropriate to ages 12-18. Recently published *Key to the Indian*, by Lynne Reid Banks; and the *Making Out* series by Katherine Applegate.

How to Contact: Query with sample chapters and synopsis. Reports in 4 months. Simultaneous submissions OK.

Terms: Pays 6-8% royalty. Offers $2,500 minimum advance. Publishes ms 2 years after acceptance. Writer's guidelines and book catalog for 8×10 SAE with 5 first-class stamps.

Advice: "The YA market is not as strong as it was five years ago. We are very selective with young adult fiction. *Avon does not publish picture books,* nor do we use freelance readers."

N **AVON TWILIGHT, (II)**, Imprint of Avon Books, 1350 Avenue of the Americas, New York NY 10019. (212)261-6800. Fax: (212)261-6895. Website: http://www.avonbooks.com/avon/mystery.html. **Acquisitions:** Jennifer Sawyer Fisher, senior editor (series detective mysteries). Publishes hardcover and mass market paperback originals, trade and mass market paperback reprints.

Needs: Mystery. "We are looking for mainstream series mystery novels." Recently published *The Ape Who Guards the Balance*, by Elizabeth Peters; *No Hiding Place*, by Valerie Wilson Wesley; and *Yankee Doodle Dead*, by Carolyn Hart (mysteries).

How to Contact: Query or submit synopsis, 2 sample chapters and SASE. Simultaneous submissions OK.

Terms: Pays royalty of 7½% minimum, 15% maximum on retail price depending on format.

Advice: "Mystery series with a strong regional base are a plus."

BAEN BOOKS, (II), P.O. Box 1403, Riverdale NY 10471. (718)548-3100. Website: http://www.baen.com (includes writer's guidelines, chat line, annotated catalog, author bios, tour information). Publisher and Editor: Jim Baen. **Acquisitions**: Toni Weisskopf, executive editor. Estab. 1983. "We publish books at the heart of science fiction and fantasy." Independent publisher. Publishes hardcover and paperback originals and paperback reprints. Published new writers within the last year. Plans 2-3 first novels this year. Averages 60 fiction titles each year. Distributes titles through Simon & Schuster.
Imprint(s): Baen Science Fiction and Baen Fantasy.
Needs: Fantasy and science fiction. Interested in science fiction novels (based on real science) and fantasy novels "that at least strive for originality." Recently published *Komarr*, by Lois McMaster Bugold; *Four and Twenty Blackbirds*, by Mercedes Lachey; and *Echoes of Honor*, by David Weber.
How to Contact: Accepts unsolicited mss. Submit ms or outline/synopsis and 3 consecutive sample chapters with SASE (or IRC). Reports in 6-9 months. Will consider simultaneous submissions, "but grudgingly and not as seriously as exclusives." Occasionally critiques rejected mss.
Terms: Pays in royalties; offers advance. Sends galleys to author. Writer's guidelines for SASE.
Advice: "Keep an eye and a firm hand on the overall story you are telling. Style is important but less important than plot. Good style, like good breeding, never calls attention to itself. Read *Writing to the Point*, by Algis Budrys. We like to maintain long-term relationships with authors."

☑ **BAKER BOOKS, (II, IV)**, a division of Baker Book House, P.O. Box 6287, Grand Rapids MI 49516-6213. (616)676-9185. Fax: (616)676-9573. Website: http://www.bakerbooks.com (includes guidelines, "Meet Our Editors," book excerpts and features, company history, advance info. on future releases). **Acquisitions**: Rebecca Cooper, editorial associate, Trade Books. Estab. 1939. "Midsize Evangelical publisher." Publishes hardcover and paperback originals. Books: web offset print; average print order: 5,000-10,000; first novel print order: 5,000. Averages 130 total titles.
Needs: "We are mainly seeking Christian fiction of two genres: contemporary women's fiction and mystery." No fiction that is not written from a Christian perspective or of a genre not specified. Recently published *Praise Jerusalem!*, by Augusta Trobaugh (contemporary women's fiction); and *The Secrets of Barneveld Calvary*, by James Schaap (contemporary women's fiction).
How to Contact: Does not accept unsolicited mss. Submit query letter, outline/synopsis and 3 sample chapters. SASE. Agented fiction 80% (so far). Reports in 4-8 months on queries. Simultaneous submissions OK. Sometimes comments on rejected ms.
Terms: Pays royalties of 14% (of net). Sometimes offers advance. Sends galleys to author. Publishes ms 1 year after acceptance. Writer's guidelines for #10 SASE. Book catalog for 9½×12½ SAE and 3 first-class stamps.
Advice: "We are not interested in historical fiction, romances, science fiction, Biblical narratives, or spiritual warfare novels. Please write for further information regarding our fiction lines. Send a cover letter describing your novel and your credentials as an author. Do not call to 'pass by' your idea. Do not send complete manuscripts."

BALLANTINE BOOKS, (II), 201 E. 50th St., New York NY 10022. Subsidiary of Random House. **Acquisitions**: Doug Grad, editor (historical, thriller); Leona Nevler, editor (all fiction); Peter Borland, executive editor (commercial fiction); Elisa Wares, senior editor (romance, mystery); Joe Blades, associate publisher (mystery); Andrea Schulz, senior editor (literary fiction). Publishes originals (general fiction, mass-market, trade paperback and hardcover). Published new writers this year. Averages over 120 total titles each year.
Needs: Major historical fiction, women's mainstream and general fiction.
How to Contact: Submit query letter or brief synopsis and first 100 pages of ms. SASE required. Reports in 2 months on queries; 4-5 months on mss.
Terms: Pays in royalties and advance.

BANKS CHANNEL BOOKS, (IV), P.O. Box 4446, Wilmington NC 28406. (910)762-4677. Fax (910)762-4677. E-mail: bankschan@aol.com. Managing Editor: E.R. Olefsky. Estab. 1993. "We are a regional press doing books by Carolina authors only. We look at fiction through our novel contest only." Publishes hardcover and paperback originals and paperback reprints. Books: 50-60 lb. paper; perfect or hardcase bound; illustrations sometimes. Average print order: 3,000. First novel print order: 2,000-3,000. Published new writers within the last year. Plans 3 novels this year.
Needs: Literary. Published *How Close We Come*, by Susan S. Kelly; *All We Know of Heaven*, by Sue Ellen Bridgers; and *Festival in Fire Season* (reprint), by Ellyn Bache.
How to Contact: Charges entry fee for contest. Send query letter first. Include 1-paragraph bio and list of publishing credits with submission. SASE for reply or return of ms. Reports in 1 week on queries; 2 months on mss. No simultaneous submissions.
Payment/Terms: Pays royalties of 6% minimum; 10% maximum. Sends galleys to author. Publishes ms 1 year after acceptance. Contest guidelines for #10 SASE.
Advice: "We are seeing work that ten years ago would have been snapped up by the big New York presses—and we are delighted to have it. Send a beautifully crafted piece of literary fiction to our contest. It doesn't need to have a Carolina setting, but it helps."

INSIDER REPORT

Pearl Cleage: find your own voice, trust your vision

Pearl Cleage isn't worried about being typecast, either as a person, or an author. But she refuses to accept restrictions on her politics, her personal life, or the way she writes. "Too many authors get caught up in finding the right formula," says the playwright-turned-essayist and first-time novelist. "But if you have something to say, you'll find the right form."

Cleage, a nationally known playwright, is accustomed to crossing boundaries to make her point. Many of her works, including *Flyin' West*, *Blues for an Alabama Sky*, and *Bourbon at the Border*, show the struggles facing women, especially African-American women. Her 1994 book of essays, *Deals with the Devil: And Other Reasons to Riot* (One World/Ballantine Books), confronted those issues in a more personal voice. When she sat down to write what became her first novel, *What Looks Like Crazy on an Ordinary Day* (Avon Books), she had some specific objectives.

"I wanted to tell a love story," she says. But the novel is hardly a cookie-cutter romance. Cleage's heroine is HIV positive, a woman who plans a brief trip to her hometown before moving on to the more supportive environment of San Francisco. "I wanted to show that becoming HIV-positive doesn't mean your world comes to an end," Cleage says. And while AIDS is an issue, the novel also tackles joblessness, teenage motherhood, family relationships and problems that are increasingly commonplace in America. The novel is set in Idlewild, Michigan, a former all-black resort town. Cleage says Idlewild is a small rural town, facing all the big-city pressures of nearby Detroit—the perfect place to describe what she sees happening around her.

Cleage also deliberately chose the novel as a format for her message because she wanted to focus on her characters' thoughts and emotions. "With plays, you can show interactions," she says, "but it's more difficult to show the inner workings." Despite her experience as an author, Cleage confesses she made some false starts in the new format.

"I sat down and wrote 30 pages that were awful," she says. "It's very different from writing for the theater." Cleage says writing plays is a communal experience because the work is made real by the interaction of the actors. But novels are a one-to-one communication between reader and author. Cleage says it took her some time to find her feet in the new format, but even the false starts were helpful. And she found the format made some things easier. "In a play you have to use stage directions and lighting cues and suggestions to let the audience know it's morning in Atlanta," Cleage notes. "But in a novel, you simply say, 'it's morning in Atlanta.' "

Cleage wrote the bulk of her novel before taking it to an editor. Although many of her friends have an editor review work as they write, Cleage prefers to work on her own. There is no right or wrong way to write, she says, but writers have to find a style they are comfortable with. "The important thing is to be authentic." While an editor can

INSIDER REPORT, *Cleage*

help fine-tune a project, Cleage says that's no substitute for "finding your own voice." And she says writers need to have the confidence to stand behind their work.

When Cleage took the manuscript for *What Looks Like Crazy* to her editor at Ballantine, the editor recommended several major changes. So Cleage decided to go to another publisher. "That can be a little scary," she admits, especially for first-time authors who are reluctant to disagree with editors. But she says writing is a solo pursuit, and a good piece, whether it's a play, an essay or a novel, needs to have a single vision. Learning to trust yourself is the most important lesson an author can learn. "You have to be confident of your voice, in what you have to say," Cleage says.

Cleage has found herself part of a growing wave of African-American women writers, like Alice Walker and Terry McMillan. She says publishers are paying more attention to these women, in part to capture a new reader's market. But she isn't worried about being lumped into some category. "I certainly don't mind being grouped with writers like Alice Walker," she laughs. And she thinks there is enough diversity of message, method and approach to go around. "This is a segment of the population that traditionally hasn't been heard from, and we have a lot to say." Regardless of publishers' motivations, she says it's refreshing to see a wider range of people being published.

It's still not an easy market, Cleage warns. And even though publishers are considering a wider range of authors, the market as a whole is shrinking. "You have a situation where publishers are reluctant to take a chance," she says. She advises authors to be open to criticism and to new ideas. "What works for one writer won't necessarily work for another," she says, "and you need to keep working at it, to find what works for you, for your voice."

Cleage advises writers to be persistent and patient. But she hopes more people will find their voice and share it with others. "There are a million stories about people in this country," she says. "And we need to eliminate barriers and extend our vision."

—Alison Holm

Editor's Note: As this book was going to press, Cleage's novel What Looks Like Crazy on an Ordinary Day *was chosen as an Oprah's Book Club™ selection.*

BANTAM BOOKS, (II), Division of Bantam Dell Doubleday Publishing Group, Inc. 1540 Broadway, New York NY 10036. (212)354-6500. Fax: (212)782-9523. **Acquisitions:** Toni Burbank, Ann Harris, executive editors. Estab. 1945. Complete publishing: hard-cover, trade, mass market. Publishes 350 titles/year.
Imprint(s): Crime Line, Domain, **Fanfare**, **Loveswept**, **Spectra**.
Needs: Contemporary, literary, mystery, historical, western, romance, science fiction, fantasy, adventure, horror, gay, lesbian. Recently published *The Story of B*, by Daniel Quinn; and *The Burning Man*, by Phillip M. Margolin.
How to Contact: Query letter only first. No unsolicited mss. Include estimated word count and list of publishing credits. Simultaneous submissions OK. Reports on queries in 2-3 months.
Terms: Individually negotiated. Publishes ms 1 year after acceptance. Writer's guidelines (for romance only) free for SASE.

BANTAM/DOUBLEDAY/DELL BOOKS FOR YOUNG READERS DIVISION, (III), Bantam/Doubleday/Dell, 1540 Broadway, New York NY 10036. **Acquisitions**: Michelle Poploff, editorial director. Editor-in-Chief to the Young Readers Division: Beverly Horowitz. Estab. 1945. Complete publishing: hardcover, trade, mass market.
Imprint(s): Delacorte, **Doubleday Adult Trade**, Doubleday Picture Books; Paperback line: Dell Yearling, Laurel-Leaf, Skylark, Star Fire, Little Rooster, Sweet Dreams, Sweet Valley High.

- The Young Readers Division offers two contests, the Delacorte Press Annual Prize for a First Young Adult Novel and the Marguerite DeAngeli Prize.

Needs: Childrens/juvenile, young adult/teen. Published *Baby*, by Patricia MacLachlan; *Whatever Happened to Janie*, by Caroline Cooney; *Nate the Great and the Pillowcase*, by Marjorie Sharmat.
How to Contact: Does not accept unsolicited mss. Submit through agent. Agented fiction 100%. Reports on queries "as soon as possible." Simultaneous submissions OK.
Terms: Individually negotiated; offers advance.

BEACH HOLME PUBLISHERS LTD., (II), 226-2040 W. 12th Ave., Vancouver, British Columbia V6J 2G2 Canada. (604)773-4868. Fax: (604)733-4860. E-mail: bhp@beachholme.bc.ca. Website: http://www.beachholme.bc.ca. **Acquisitions:** Joy Gugeler, managing editor; Teresa Bubela, editor. Estab. 1971. Publishes trade paperback originals. Publishes 10 titles/year. "Accepting only Canadian submissions." **Publishes 40% previously unpublished writers/year.**
Needs: Adult literary fiction from authors published in Canadian literary magazines. Young adult (Canada historical/regional). "Interested in excellent quality, imaginative writing." Recently published *Inappropriate Behavior*, by Irene Mock (short fiction).
How to Contact: Send cover letter, SASE, outline and two chapters. Reports in 2 months. Simultaneous submissions OK, if so noted.
Terms: Pays 10% royalty on retail price. Offers $500 average advance. Publishes ms 1 year after acceptance. Writer's guidelines free.
Advice: "Make sure the manuscript is well written. We see so many that only the unique and excellent can't be put down. Prior publication is a must. This doesn't necessarily mean book length manuscripts, but a writer should try to publish his or her short fiction."

BEACON HILL PRESS OF KANSAS CITY, (II), Book Division of Nazarene Publishing House, P.O. Box 419527, Kansas City MO 64141. Fax: (816)753-4071. E-mail: bjp@bhillkc.com. **Acquisitions:** Kelly Gallagher, director. Estab. 1912. "Beacon Hill Press is a Christ-centered publisher that provides authentically Christian resources that are faithful to God's word and relevant to life." Publishes hardcover and paperback originals. Publishes 30 titles/year. Accent on holy living; encouragement in daily Christian life.
Needs: Wholesome, inspirational. Considers historical and Biblical fiction, Christian romance, but no teen or children's. Recently published *Turn Northward, Love*, by Ruth Glover; and *Fly Away*, by Lynn Austin.
How to Contact: Query or proposal preferred. Reports in 3 months. Average ms length: 30,000-60,000 words.
Terms: Standard contract is 12% royalty on net sales for first 10,000 copies and 14% on subsequent copies. (Sometimes makes flat rate purchase.) Publishes ms within 1 year after acceptance.

FREDERIC C. BEIL, PUBLISHER, INC., (II), 609 Whitaker St., Savannah GA 31401. E-mail: beilbook@beil.com. Website: http://www.beil.com. **Acquisitions**: Frederic C. Beil III, president; Mary Ann Bowman, editor. Estab. 1983. "Our objectives are (1) to offer to the reading public carefully selected texts of lasting value; (2) to adhere to high standards in the choice of materials and in bookmarking craftsmanship; (3) to produce books that exemplify good taste in format and design; and (4) to maintain the lowest cost consistent with quality." General trade publisher. Publishes hardcover originals and reprints. Books: acid-free paper; letterpress and offset printing; Smyth-sewn, hardcover binding; illustrations. Average print order: 3,000. First novel print order: 3,000. Plans 2 first novels this year. Averages 14 total titles, 4 fiction titles each year.
Imprint(s): The Sandstone Press, Hypermedia, Inc.
Needs: Historical, literary, regional, short story collections, translations. Published *A Woman of Means*, by Peter Taylor; *An Exile*, by Madison Jones; and *A Master of the Century Past*, by Robert Metzger.
How to Contact: Does not accept unsolicited mss. Query first. Reports in 1 week on queries.
Terms: Payment "all negotiable." Sends galleys to author. Book catalog free on request.

✓ **THE BERKLEY PUBLISHING GROUP, (III)**, Subsidiary of G.P. Putnam's Sons, 375 Hudson St., New York NY 10014. (212)366-2000. Publisher/Editor-in-Chief: Leslie Gelbman. Associate Director, Editorial: Susan Allison. Fiction Editors: Natalee Rosenstein, Judith Palais, Tom Colgan, Gail Fortune, Ginjer Buchanan, Lisa Considine, Denise Silvestro and Hillary Cige. Nonfiction: Lisa Considine, Denise Silvestro and Hillary Cige. Large commercial category line. Publishes paperback originals, trade paperbacks and hardcover and paperback reprints. Books: Paperbound printing; perfect binding; average print order: "depends on position in list." Plans approx. 10 first novels this year. Averages 1,180 total titles, 1,000 fiction titles each year.
Imprint(s): Berkley, Jove, Boulevard, **Ace Science Fiction.**
Needs: Fantasy, mainstream, mystery/suspense, romance (contemporary, historical), science fiction. Published works by Tom Clancy and Patricia Cornwell.
How to Contact: *Strongly* recommends agented material. Queries answered if SASE enclosed. Accepts simulta-

INTERESTED IN A PARTICULAR GENRE? Check our new sections for: **Mystery/Suspense**, page 57; **Romance**, page 77; **Science Fiction & Fantasy**, page 95.

neous submissions. Reports in 3 months minimum on mss.
Terms: Pays royalties of 4-10%. Provides 10 author's copies. Publishes ms 2 years after acceptance. Writer's guidelines and book catalog not available.
Advice: "Aspiring novelists should keep abreast of the current trends in publishing by reading *The New York Times* Bestseller Lists, trade magazines for their desired genre and *Publishers Weekly.*"

BETHANY HOUSE PUBLISHERS, (II, IV), Subsidiary of Bethany Fellowship, Inc., 11300 Hampshire Ave. S., Minneapolis MN 55438. (612)829-2500. **Acquisitions:** Sharon Madison, review department. "The purpose of Bethany House Publishers' publishing program is to relate biblical truth to all areas of life, whether in the framework of a well-told story, a challenging book for spiritual growth, or a Bible reference work." Publishes hardcover and trade paperback originals, mass market paperback reprints. Publishes 120-150 titles/year.
Imprint(s): Portraits (Barbara Lilland, editor).
Needs: Adventure, historical, mainstream/contemporary, religious (romance), young adult. Recently published *The Tender Years*, by Janette Oke; *The Shunning*, by Beverly Lewis; and *Mandie & the Courtroom Battle*, by Lois Gladys Leppard.
How to Contact: Submit proposal package including synopsis, 3 sample chapters, author information, educational background and writing experience with SASE. Reports in 3 months. Simultaneous submissions OK.
Terms: Pays negotiable royalty on wholesale price. Offers negotiable advance. Publishes ms 1 year after acceptance. Writer's guidelines free. Book catalog for 9×12 SAE with 5 first-class stamps.

☑ **BIRCH BROOK PRESS, (IV)**, P.O. Box 81, Delhi NY 13753. (212)353-3326. Fax: (607)746-7453. **Acquisitions**: Tom Tolnay, publisher. Estab. 1982. Small publisher of popular culture and literary titles in handcrafted letterpress editions. Publishes fiction anthologies with specific theme. Books: 80 lb. vellum paper; letter press printing; illustrations. Average print order: 500-1,000. Plans 1 first novel this year. Averages 4-6 total titles, 2 fiction titles each year. Distributes titles through Ingram, Baker and Taylor, Barnes & Noble On-Line, amazon.com. Promotes titles through catalogs and direct mail.
Imprint(s): Persephone Press.
Needs: Literary. "We make specific calls for fiction when we are doing an anthology." Plans to publish literary-quality anthology of mystery short stories. Recently published *Magic & Madness in the Library*, edited by Eric Graeber (short story collection); *Kilimanjaro Burning*, by John Robinson (novella); *Autobiography of Maria Callas: A Novel*, by Alma Bond.
How to Contact: Does not seek unsolicited mss. Query first. SASE. Reports on queries in 2-6 weeks; mss 2-4 months. Simultaneous submissions OK. Sometimes critiques or comments on rejected mss.
Terms: Modest flat fee as advance against royalties. Writers guidelines for SASE.
Advice: "We mostly generate our own anthologies and print notices to request submissions."

BkMk PRESS, (II), UMKC, University House, 5100 Rockhill Rd., Kansas City MO 64110-2499. (816)235-2558. Fax: (816)235-2611. E-mail: freemank@smtpgate.ssb.umkc.edu. **Acquisitions**: James McKinley, director. Estab. 1971. Small independent press. "Mostly short story collections." Publishes hardback and paperback originals. Books: standard paper; offset printing; perfect- and case-bound; average print order: 600. **Publishes 0-1 previously unpublished authors/year.** Averages 6 total titles, 1 fiction title each year. Distributes titles through direct mail and wholesalers (Books in Print). Promotes titles through Books in Print, some magazine/journal advertising, brochure mailings, readings and appearances.
Needs: Contemporary, ethnic, experimental, literary, translations. "Fiction publishing limited to short stories and novellas. Ordinarily prints anthologies or collections by one writer. BkMk Press does not publish commercial novels." Published *Drive Dive Dance & Fight*, by Thomas E. Kennedy (short stories); *Body and Blood*, by Philip Russell (episodic novel); and *Mustaches & Other Stories*, by G.W. Clift (short stories).
How to Contact: Query first or submit 2 sample chapters with SASE. Reports in 2-3 months on queries; 6 months on mss.
Terms: Pays royalties of 10% and 20 author's copies. Sends galleys to author. Free book catalog.
Advice: "We value the exceptional, rare, well-crafted and daring. Please pursue magazine/journal publication of individual stories before you query us. The object is to hone your craft before you place it before a publication." Especially interested in Midwestern writers.

BLACK HERON PRESS, (I, II), P.O. Box 95676, Seattle WA 98145. **Acquisitions**: Jerry Gold, publisher. Estab. 1984. One-person operation; no immediate plans to expand. "We're known for literary fiction. We've done several Vietnam War titles and several surrealistic fictions." Publishes paperback and hardback originals. Average print order: 2,000; first novel print order: 1,500. Averages 4 fiction titles each year. Distributes titles nationally.

- Three books published by Black Heron Press have won awards from King County Arts Commission. This press received Bumbershoot Most Significant Contribution to Literature in 1996. Black Heron Press will not be looking at new material until winter 1999.

Needs: Adventure, contemporary, experimental, humor/satire, literary, science fiction. Vietnam war novel—literary. "We don't want to see fiction written for the mass market. If it sells to the mass market, fine, but we don't see ourselves as a commercial press." Recently published *Charlie & The Children*, by Joanna C. Scott;

The Fruit 'N Food, by Leonard Chang; and *In A Cold Open Field*, by Sheila Solomon Klass.
How to Contact: Query and sample chapters only. Reports in 3 months on queries. Simultaneous submissions OK.
Terms: Pays standard royalty rates. No advance.
Advice: "A query letter should tell me: 1) number of words; 2) number of pages; 3) if ms is available on floppy disk; 4) if parts of novel have been published; 5) if so, where?"

JOHN F. BLAIR, PUBLISHER, (II, IV), 1406 Plaza Dr., Winston-Salem NC 27103. (910)768-1374. Fax: (910)768-9194. **Acquisitions**: Carolyn Sakowski, president. Estab. 1954. Small independent publisher. Publishes hardcover and paperback originals. Books: Acid-free paper; offset printing; illustrations. Average print order: 5,000. Number of titles: 17 in 1996, 20 in 1997. "Among our 17-20 books, we do one novel a year."
Needs: Prefers regional material dealing with southeastern U.S. No confessions or erotica. "Our editorial focus concentrates mostly on nonfiction." Published *The Big Ear*, by Robin Hemley (short story collection); *How to Get Home*, by Bret Lott; and *Cape Fear Rising*, by Philip Gerard.
How to Contact: Query or submit with SASE. Simultaneous submissions OK. Reports in 1 month. Publishes ms 1-2 years after acceptance. Free book catalog.
Terms: Negotiable.
Advice: "We are primarily interested in nonfiction titles. Most of our titles have a tie-in with North Carolina or the southeastern United States. Please enclose a cover letter and outline with the manuscript. We prefer to review queries before we are sent complete manuscripts. Queries should include an approximate word count."

BLUE MOON BOOKS, INC., (II), 61 Fourth Ave., New York NY 10003. (212)505-6880. Fax: (212)673-1039. E-mail: bluoff@aol.com. **Acquisitions:** Barney Rosset, editor. "Blue Moon Books is strictly an erotic press; largely fetish-oriented material, B&D, S&M, etc." Publishes trade paperback and mass market paperback originals. Publishes 30-40 titles/year.
Imprint(s): North Star Line.
Needs: Erotica. Recently published *Ironwood Revisited*, by Dan Winslow; and *Sundancer*, by Briony Shilton.
How to Contact: Query or submit synopsis and 1-2 sample chapters with SASE. Reports in 2 months. Simultaneous submissions OK.
Terms: Pays 7½-10% royalty on retail price. Offers $500 and up advance. Publishes ms 1 year after acceptance. Book catalog free.

⊘ **THE BLUE SKY PRESS, (V)**, Imprint of Scholastic Inc., 555 Broadway, New York NY 10012. (212)343-6100. Fax: (212)343-4535. Website: http://www.scholastic.com. **Acquisitions:** The Editors. Blue Sky Press publishes primarily juvenile picture books. Publishes hardcover originals. Publishes 15-20 titles/year.

- Because of a long backlog of books, The Blue Sky Press is not accepting unsolicited submissions.

Needs: Juvenile: adventure, fantasy, historical, humor, mainstream/contemporary, picture books, multicultural, folktales. Recently published *Second Cousins*, by Virginia Hamilton (novel); *No, David!*, by David Shannon (picture book); and *To Every Thing There is a Season*, by Leo and Diane Dillon (multicultural/historical).
How to Contact: Agented fiction 25%. Reports in 6 months on queries.
Terms: Pays 10% royalty on wholesale price, between authors and illustrators. Publishes ms 2½ years after acceptance.

BLUE STAR PRODUCTIONS, (II, IV), Division of Bookworld, Inc., 9666 E. Riggs Rd., #194, Sun Lakes AZ 85248. (602)895-7995. Fax: (602)895-6991. E-mail: bkworld@aol.com. Website: http://www.bkworld.com. **Acquisitions:** Barbara DeBolt, editor. Blue Star Productions publishes metaphysical fiction and nonfiction titles on specialized subjects. "Our mission is to aid in the spiritual growth of mankind." Publishes trade and mass market paperback originals. Publishes 10-12 titles/year.
Needs: Fantasy, visionary fiction, spiritual (metaphysical), UFO's. Recently published *The Best Kept Secrets*, by Charles Wright; and *The Antilles Incident*, by Donald Todd.
How to Contact: Query or submit synopsis and the first 3 chapters. No phone queries. SASE a must. Reports in 1 month on queries, 6 months on mss.
Terms: Pays 10% royalty on retail price; 15% royalty on wholesale price. No advance. Writer's guidelines for #10 SASE. Book catalog free.
Advice: "Know our guidelines."

✔ 🏆 **BOOKCRAFT, INC., (I)**, 2405 W. Orton Circle, West Valley City UT 84119. (801)908-3400. **Acquisitions**: Cory H. Maxwell, editorial manager. Publishes hardcover and softcover originals. Books: 60 lb. stock

MARKET CATEGORIES: (I) Unpublished entries; **(II)** Published entries nominated by the author; **(III)** Published entries nominated by the editor, publisher or nominating body; **(IV)** Specialized entries.

paper; sheet-fed and web press; average print order: 5,000-7,000; 3,000 for reprints. Published new writers within the last year. "We are always open for creative, fresh ideas."

Imprint(s): Parliament.

- Books published by Bookcraft have received several awards from the Association of Mormon Letters and the 1994 John and Frankie Orton Award for LDS Lierature went to *The Work and the Glory*, by Gerald N. Lund.

Needs: Contemporary, family saga, historical, mystery/suspense (private eye, romantic suspense, young adult), romance (gothic), religious/inspirational, thriller/espionage and western (traditional frontier, young adult). Recently published *The Work and the Glory: Thy Gold to Refine* (vol. 4), by Gerald N. Lund; *A Face in the Shadows*, by Susan Evans McCloud; and *Two Roads*, by Chris Crowe.

How to Contact: Query, submit outline/synopsis and sample chapters, or submit complete ms with SASE (or IRC). Reports in 2 months.

Terms: Pays royalties; no advance. Sends galleys to author. Free book catalog and writer's guidelines.

Advice: "Our principal market is the membership of The Church of Jesus Christ of Latter-Day Saints (Mormons) and manuscripts should relate to the background, doctrines or practices of that church. The tone should be fresh, positive and motivational, but not preachy. We do not publish anti-Mormon works."

BOOKS IN MOTION, (II), 9212 E. Montgomery, Suite #501, Spokane WA 99206. (509)922-1646. **Acquisitions**: Gary Challender, president. Estab. 1980. "Audiobook company, national marketer. Publishes novels in audiobook form *only*." Published new writers within the last year. Averages 70 total titles, 65 fiction titles each year.

- Books in Motion is known for its audio westerns and mysteries. The publisher has received favorable reviews from *Library Journal*, *Kliatt Magazine* and *Audio-File* magazine.

Needs: Action/adventure, westerns, mystery, science fiction (non-technical), some romance. Recently published *Kiahawk*, by Craig Fraley; *The Isle of Venus Mystery*, by Tom Neet; and *Name Witheld*, by J.A. Jance. Have published over 140 new authors in last 3 years.

How to Contact: Accepts unsolicted mss. Submit synopsis and sample chapters (first and middle). SASE for ms. Agented fiction 10%. Reports within 3 weeks to 3 months. Simultaneous submissions OK.

Terms: Pays royalties of 10%. "We pay royalties every 6 months. Royalties that are received are based on the gross sales that any given title generates during the 6-month interval. Authors must be patient since it usually takes a minimum of one year before new titles will have significant sales." Publishes ms 6-12 months after acceptance. Book catalog free on request.

Advice: "Our audience is 20% women, 80% men. Many of our audience are truck drivers, who want something interesting to listen to. We prefer a minimum of profanity and no gratuitous sex. We want novels with a strong plot. The fewer the characters, the better it will work on tape. Six-tape audiobooks sell and rent better than any other size in the unabridged format. One hour of tape is equal to 40 pages of double-spaced, 12 pitch, normal margin, typed pages. Manuscript should be between 200 and 400 pages."

BOREALIS PRESS, (I, IV), 9 Ashburn Dr., Nepean, Ontario K2E 6N4 Canada. Fax: (613)829-7783. E-mail: borealis@istar.ca. Website: http://www.borealispress.com (includes names of editors, authors, titles). **Acquisitions**: Frank Tierney, editor; Glenn Clever, fiction editor. Estab. 1970. "Publishes Canadiana, with an emphasis on titles suitable for adoption at senior high school/university levels." Publishes hardcover and paperback originals and reprints. Books: standard book-quality paper; offset printing; perfect and cloth binding. Average print order: 1,000. Buys juvenile mss with b&w illustrations. Averages 4 total titles each year. Promotes titles through website, catalogue distribution, fliers for titles, ads in media.

Imprint(s): *Journal of Canadian Poetry*, Tecumseh Press Ltd., Canadian Critical Editions Series.

- Borealis Press has a "New Canadian Drama," with six books in print. The series won Ontario Arts Council and Canada Council grants.

Needs: Contemporary, literary, juvenile, young adult. "Must have a Canadian content or author; query first." Recently published *Alphabet Soup*, by Kerry Rauch; *Jamie of Fort William*, by Elizabeth Kouhi; and *Sunshine Sketches of a Little Town*, by Stephen Leacock.

How to Contact: Submit query with SASE (Canadian postage). No simultaneous submissions. Reports in 2 weeks on queries, 3-4 months on mss. Publishes ms 1-2 years after acceptance.

Terms: Pays 10% royalties and 3 free author's copies; no advance. Sends galleys to author. Publishes ms 18 months after acceptance. Free book catalog with SASE.

Advice: "Have your work professionally edited. Our greatest challenge is finding good authors, i.e., those who submit innovative and original material."

THOMAS BOUREGY & COMPANY, INC., 401 Lafayette St., New York NY 10003. Small category line. See Avalon Books.

MARION BOYARS PUBLISHERS INC., (II), 237 E. 39th St., New York NY 10016. Editorial Office (all submissions): 24 Lacy Road, London SW15 1NL England. Fiction Editor: Marion Boyars. Publishes 15 novels or story collections/year. "A lot of American fiction. Authors include Ken Kesey, Eudora Welty, Stephen Koch, Samuel Charters, Page Edwards, Viatia Spiegelman, Kenneth Gangemi, Tim O'Brien, Julian Green. British and Irish fiction. Translations from the French, German, Turkish, Arabic, Italian, Spanish." Send cover letter and entire manuscript "always with sufficient return postage by check." Pays advance against royalties. "Most fiction working *well* in one country does well in another. We usually have world rights, i.e. world English plus translation rights." Enclose return postage by check, minimum $3, for catalog. "No manuscripts to New York office."

BOYDS MILLS PRESS, (II), Subsidiary of Highlights for Children, 815 Church St., Honesdale PA 18431. (800)490-5111. Fax: (717)253-0179. **Acquisitions**: Beth Troop, manuscript coordinator. Estab. 1990. "Independent publisher of quality books for children of all ages." Publishes hardcover. Books: Coated paper; offset printing; case binding; 4-color illustrations; average print order varies. Plans 4 fiction titles (novels). Distributes titles through independent sales reps and via order line directly from Boyds Mills Press. Promotes titles through sales and professional conferences; sales reps; reviews. **Publishes 1 previously unpublished writer/year.**

- Boyds Mills Press author Jan Cheripko won the Young Adults Choices for 1998 and the 1997 Joan Fassler Memorial Book Award for *Imitate the Tiger.*

Needs: Juvenile, young adult (adventure, animal, contemporary, ethnic, historical, sports). Recently published *Navajo Summer*, by Jennifer Owings Dewey; *Sharp Horns on the Moon*, by Carole Crowe; and *Joyride*, by Gretchen Olson.

How to Contact: Accepts unsolicited mss. Send first three chapters and synopsis. Reports in 1 month. Simultaneous submissions OK.

Terms: Pays standard rates. Sends pre-publication galleys to author. Time between acceptance and publication depends on "what season it is scheduled for." Writer's guidelines for #10 SASE.

Advice: "Read through our recently published titles and review our catalogue. If your book is too different from what we publish, then it may not fit our list. Feel free to query us if you're not sure."

BRANDEN PUBLISHING CO., (I, II), Subsidiary of Branden Press, Box 843, 17 Station St., Brookline Village MA 02447. Fax: (617)734-2046. E-mail: branden@branden.com. Website: http://www.branden.com. **Acquisitions**: Adolph Caso, editor. Estab. 1967. Publishes hardcover and paperback originals and reprints. Books: 55-60 lb. acid-free paper; case- or perfect-bound; illustrations; average print order: 5,000. Plans 5 first novels this year. Averages 15 total titles, 5 fiction titles each year.

Imprint(s): I.P.L.

Needs: Ethnic, historical, literary, military/war, short story collections and translations. Looking for "contemporary, fast pace, modern society." No porno, experimental or horror. Published *I, Morgain*, by Harry Robin; *The Bell Keeper*, by Marilyn Seguin; and *The Straw Obelisk*, by Adolph Caso.

How to Contact: Does not accept unsolicited mss. Query *only* with SASE. Reports in 1 week on queries.

Terms: Pays royalties of 5-10% minimum. Advance negotiable. Provides 10 author's copies. Sends galleys to author. Publishes ms "several months" after acceptance.

Advice: "Publishing more fiction because of demand. *Do not make phone, fax or e-mail inquiries.* Do not oversubmit; single submissions only; do not procrastinate if contract is offered. Our audience is a well-read general public, professionals, college students, and some high school students. We like books by or about women."

GEORGE BRAZILLER, INC., (II), 171 Madison Ave., Suite 1103, New York NY 10016. (212)889-0909. **Acquisitions:** Mary Taveros, production editor. Publishes hardcover and trade paperback originals and reprints. Publishes 25 titles/year.

Needs: Ethnic, gay, lesbian, literary. "We rarely do fiction but when we have published novels, they have mostly been literary novels." Recently published *Blindsight*, by Herve Guibert; and *Papa's Suitcase*, by Gerhard Kopf (literary fiction).

How to Contact: Submit 4-6 sample chapters with SASE. Agented fiction 20%. Reports in 3 months on proposals.

Terms: Pays standard royalty: 8% paperback; 10-15% hardback. Publishes ms 10 months after acceptance. Writer's guidelines and book catalog free.

BRIDGE WORKS PUBLISHING CO., (I, II), 221 Bridge Lane, Box 1798, Bridgehampton NY 11932. (516)537-3418. Fax: (516)537-5092. E-mail: bap@hamptons.com. **Acquisitions**: Barbara Phillips, editorial director. Estab. 1992. "We are very small (3 full-time employees) doing only 4-6 books a year. We publish quality fiction and nonfiction. Our books are routinely reviewed in such papers as *The New York Times*, *Newsday*, *The Washington Post* and *The Boston Globe*." Publishes hardcover originals. Average print order: 5,000. Published new writers within the last year. Plans 4 novels and 2 nonfiction titles this year. Averages 4-6 total titles (75% fiction) each year. Distributes titles through National Book Network.

Needs Humor/satire, literary, translations. Recently published *Fear*, by Simon Lane; and *Boondocking*, by Tricia Bauer.

How to Contact: Accepts unsolicited mss, but "must send query letter first." Query with outline/synopsis and 4 sample chapters. "If you are a first-time writer, do not query or send manuscripts unless work has been edited by a freelance editor." Include estimated word count and list of publishing credits. Send SASE for reply, return of ms or send a disposable copy of ms. Agented fiction 50%. Reports in 2 weeks on queries; 2 months on mss. Sometimes critiques or comments on rejected mss.

Payment/Terms: Pays royalties of 10% maximum "based on cover price with a reserve against returns." Average advance: $1,000. Sends galleys to author. Publishes ms 1 year after acceptance.
Advice: "We publish the so-called 'mid-list' book although we have had bestsellers. We are more interested in discovering great new writers than in making millions. We work closely with our authors in both the editorial and marketing processes. We publish only six books a year, literary fiction and nonfiction. We receive thousands of submissions. Please do not query or send manuscripts if your work has not been seen by a freelance editor first."

BROADWAY BOOKS, (V), Division of Random House, Inc. 1540 Broadway, New York NY 10036. (212)354-6500. Publisher: William Shinker. **Acquisitions:** John Sterling, senior vice president and editor-in-chief (literary fiction, nonfiction). Broadway publishes general interest nonfiction and fiction for adults. Publishes hardcover and trade paperback originals and reprints.
Needs: Publishes commercial literary fiction. Recently published *Freedomland*, by Richard Price.
How to Contact: This publisher accepts agented fiction only.

CAMELOT BOOKS, (II), Imprint of Avon Books, Division of The Hearst Corp., 1350 Avenue of the Americas, New York NY 10019. (212)261-6800. Fax: (212)261-6895. **Acquisitions**: Elise Howard, editorial director; Stephanie Seigel, assistant editor. Camelot publishes fiction for children ages 8-12. Publishes paperback originals and reprints. Publishes 80-100 titles/year.
Imprint(s): Avon Flare (for ages 12 and up).
Needs: Subjects include adventure, humor, juvenile (Camelot, 8-12) mainstream, mystery, ("very selective with mystery"), suspense. Avon does not publish picture books. Recently published *Honus & Me*, by Dan Gutman; and *Christie & Company*, by Katherine Hall Page (mystery).
How to Contact: Submit query letter *only*. Reports back in 3 months.
Terms: Pays 6-8% royalty on retail price. Offers $2,000 minimum advance. Publishes ms 2 years after acceptance. Writer's guidelines and book catalog for 8×10 SAE with 5 first-class stamps.

CANADIAN INSTITUTE OF UKRAINIAN STUDIES PRESS, (IV), CIUS Toronto Publications Office, University of Toronto, Dept. of Slavic Languages and Literatures, 21 Sussex Ave., Toronto, Ontario M5S 1A1 Canada. (416)978-8240. Fax: (416)978-2672. E-mail: cius@chass.utoronto.ca. Website: http://www.utoronto.ca/cius. **Acquisitions**: Maxim Tarnawsky, director. Estab. 1976. "We publish scholarship about Ukraine and Ukrainians in Canada." Publishes hardcover and trade paperback originals and reprints. Publishes 5-10 titles/year.
Needs: Ukrainian literary works. "We do not publish fiction except for use as college textbooks." Recently published *Recreations*, by Yuri Andrukhouych.
How to Contact: Query or submit complete ms. Reports in 1 month on queries, 3 months on mss.
Terms: Nonauthor-subsidy publishes 20-30% of books. Pays 0-2% royalty on retail price. Publishes ms 2 years after acceptance. Writer's guidelines and book catalog free.
Advice: "We are a scholarly press and do not normally pay our authors. Our audience consists of university students and teachers and the general public interested in Ukrainian and Ukrainian-Canadian affairs."

CANDLEWICK PRESS, (II, IV), Subsidiary of Walker Books Ltd. (London), 2067 Massachusetts Ave., Cambridge MA 02140. (617)661-3330. Fax: (617)661-0565. **Acquisitions:** Liz Bicknell, editor-in-chief (nonfiction/fiction); Mary Lee Donovan, senior editor (nonfiction/fiction); Gale Pryor, editor (nonfiction/fiction); Amy Ehrlich, editor at large (picture books/fiction). Candlewick Press publishes high-quality illustrated children's books for ages infant through young adult. "We are a truly child-centered publisher." Estab. 1991. Publishes hardcover originals, trade paperback originals and reprints. Publishes 200 titles/year.
Needs: Juvenile. Recently published *What Do Fish Have To Do With Anything*, by Avi; and *Thirsty*, by M.T. Anderson.
How to Contact: Agented submissions only. Reports in 10 weeks on mss. Simultaneous submissions OK, if so noted.
Terms: Pays 10% royalty on retail price. Advance varies. Publishes ms 3 years after acceptance for illustrated books, 1 year for others.

CAROLRHODA BOOKS, INC., (II, IV), Imprint of Lerner Publications Co., 241 First Ave. N., Minneapolis MN 55401. (612)332-3344. Fax: (612)332-7615. Website: http://www.lernerbooks.com. **Acquisitions:** Rebecca Poole, submissions editor. Estab. 1969. Carolrhoda Books seeks creative children's nonfiction and historical fiction with unique and well-developed ideas and angles. Publishes hardcover originals. Publishes 50-60 titles/year.
Needs: Juvenile, historical, picture books. "We continue to add fiction for middle grades and 1-2 picture books per year. Not looking for folktales or anthropomorphic animal stories." Recently published *Come Morning*, by Leslie Davis Guccione (historical); *Fire in the Sky*, by Candice Ransom (historical); and *Fire at the Triangle Factory*, by Holly Littlefield (easy reader historical).
How to Contact: Query with SASE or send complete ms for picture books. Include SASE for return of ms. Reports in 3 months on queries; 5 months on mss. Simultaneous submissions OK.

Terms: Pays royalty on wholesale price, makes outright purchase or negotiates payments of advance against royalty. Advance varies. Publishes ms 18 months after acceptance. Writer's guidelines and book catalog for 9×12 SASE with $3 in postage. No phone calls.
Advice: "Our audience consists of children ages four to eleven. We publish very few picture books. We prefer manuscripts that can fit into one of our series. Spend time developing your idea in a unique way or from a unique angle; avoid trite, hackneyed plots and ideas."

CARROLL & GRAF PUBLISHERS, INC., (III), 260 Fifth Ave., New York NY 10001. (212)889-8772. Fax: (212)545-7909. **Acquisitions**: Kent Carroll, publisher/executive editor. Estab. 1983. "Carroll and Graf is one of the few remaining independent trade publishers and is therefore able to publish successfully and work with first-time authors and novelists." Publishes hardcover and paperback originals and paperback reprints. Plans 5 first novels this year. Averages 120 total titles, 75 fiction titles each year. Average first novel print order 7,500 copies.
Needs: Contemporary, erotica, fantasy, science fiction, literary, mainstream and mystery/suspense. No romance.
How to Contact: Does not accept unsolicited mss. Query first or submit outline/synopsis and sample chapters. SASE. Reports in 2 weeks. Occasionally critiques rejected mss.
Terms: Pays in royalties of 6% minimum; 15% maximum; advance negotiable. Sends galleys to author. Publishes ms 9 months after acceptance. Free book catalog on request.

☑ 🅰 **CARTWHEEL BOOKS, (V)**, Imprint of Scholastic, Inc., 555 Broadway, New York NY 10012. (212)343-6100. Fax: (212)343-4444. Website: http://www.scholastic.com. **Acquisitions:** Gina Shaw, editor; Sonia Black, editor; Diane Muldrow, editor. Estab. 1991. "Cartwheel Books publishes innovative books for children, ages 3-9. We are looking for 'novelties' that are books first, play objects second. Even without its gimmick, a Cartwheel Book should stand alone as a valid piece of children's literature." Publishes hardcover originals. Publishes 85-100 titles/year.
Needs: Fantasy, humor, juvenile, mystery, picture books, science fiction. "The subject should have mass market appeal for very young children. Humor can be helpful, but not necessary. Mistakes writers make are a reading level that is too difficult, a topic of no interest or too narrow, or manuscripts that are too long." Recently published *Little Bill (series)*, by Bill Cosby (picture book); *Dinofours* (series), by Steve Metzger (picture book); and *The Haunted House*, by Fiona Conboy (3-D puzzle storybook).
How to Contact: Agented submissions or previously published authors only. Reports in 2 months on queries; 6 months on mss. Simultaneous submissions OK.
Terms: Pays royalty on retail price. Offers advance. Publishes ms 2 years after acceptance. Book catalog for 9×12 SAE. Writer's guidelines free.
Advice: Audience is young children, ages 3-9. "Know what types of books the publisher does. Some manuscripts that don't work for one house may be perfect for another. Check out bookstores or catalogs to see where your writing would 'fit' best."

☑ **CATBIRD PRESS, (II)**, 16 Windsor Rd., North Haven CT 06473-3015. E-mail: catbird@pipeline.com. Publisher: Robert Wechsler. **Acquisitions**: Rosie Tighe, editor. Estab. 1987. Small independent trade publisher. "Catbird Press specializes in quality, imaginative prose humor and Central European literature in translation." Publishes cloth and paperback originals. Books: acid-free paper; offset printing; paper binding; illustrations (where relevant). Average print order: 4,000. First novel print order: 3,000. **Publishes 0-1 previously unpublished writers/year.** Averages 4 total titles, 1-2 fiction titles each year. Promotes books through reviews, publicity, advertising, readings and signings.

- Catbird Press's *It Came With the House*, by Jeffrey Shaffer, was a finalist in the Best Humor Book category of the Small Press Book Awards.

Needs: Humor (specialty); literary, translations (specialty Czech, French and German read in-house). No thriller, historical, science fiction, or other genre writing; only writing with a fresh style and approach. Recently published *The Third Lion*, by Floyd Kemske; *It Came With the House*, by Jeffrey Shaffer; and *The Cornerstone*, by Randall Beth Platt.
How to Contact: Accepts unsolicited mss but no queries. Submit outline/synopsis with sample chapter. Accepts queries (but no mss) by e-mail. SASE. Reports in 2-4 weeks on mss. Simultaneous submissions OK, "but let us know if simultaneous."
Terms: Pays royalties of 7½-10%. Average advance: $2,000; offers negotiable advance. Sends galleys to author. Publishes ms approximately 1 year after acceptance. Terms depend on particular book. Writer's guidelines for #10 SASE.
Advice: "Book publishing is a business. If you're not willing to learn the business and research the publishers, as well as learn the craft, you should not expect much from publishers. It's a waste of time to send genre or other

AN IMPRINT LISTED IN BOLDFACE TYPE means there is an independent listing arranged alphabetically within this section.

derivative writing to a quality literary press. We are interested in novelists who combine a sense of humor with a true knowledge of and love for language, a lack of ideology, care for craft and self-criticism."

CENTENNIAL PUBLICATIONS, (II), 256 Nashua Ct., Grand Junction CO 81503. (970)243-8780. **Acquisitions:** Dick Spurr, publisher. Publishes hardcover and trade paperback originals and reprints. Publishes 4-5 titles/year.
Needs: Humor, mystery. "We are very selective in this market." Recently published *In Over My Waders*, by Jack Sayer (humor).
How to Contact: Submit synopsis. Reports in 1 week on queries, 1 month on mss.
Terms: Pays 8-10% royalty on retail price. Offers average of $1,000 advance. Publishes ms 8 months after acceptance. Book catalog free.

CHARIOT CHILDREN'S BOOKS, (III), Imprint of Chariot Victor Publishing, 4050 Lee Vance View, Colorado Springs CO 80918. (719)536-3271. Fax: (719)536-3269. **Acquisitions:** Liz Duckworth, managing editor. "Chariot Children's Books publishes works of children's inspirational titles, ages 1-12, with a strong underlying Christian theme or clearly stated Biblical value." Publishes hardcover and trade paperback originals. Publishes 40 titles/year.

- Chariot Children's Books is not accepting unsolicited submissions at this time.

Needs: Historical, juvenile, picture books, religious. "Our age range is 8-12 years old. We're particularly interested in historical Christian juvenile fiction and series." Does not want teen fiction; currently overwhelmed with contemporary fiction. Recently published *Dance of Darkness*, by Sigmund Brouwer (Winds of Light series).
How to Contact: Queries from previously published authors only. Query with SASE. Reports in 4 months on queries. Simultaneous submissions OK if so noted.
Terms: Pays variable royalty on retail price. Offers advance, $1,000 for picture books, $2,500 for juvenile fiction. Publishes ms 2 years after acceptance. Writer's guidelines for #10 SASE. Book catalog on request.

CHARIOT VICTOR PUBLISHING, (V), 4050 Lee Vance View, Colorado Springs CO 80918. (719)536-3280. Fax: (719)536-3269. **Acquisitions**: Lee Hough, senior acquisitions editor; Karl Schaller, editorial director; Kathy Davis (children), editorial assistant; Dave Horton (adult), acquisitions editor. Estab. 1875. Publishes hardcover and paperback originals. Number of fiction titles: 35-40 juvenile, 4-6 adult. Encourages new writers.
Imprint(s): Chariot Books, Victor Books, Lion Publishing.
Needs: Religious/inspirational, juvenile, young adult and adult; sports, animal, spy/adventure, historical, Biblical, fantasy/science fiction, picture book and easy-to-read. Published *California Pioneer* series, by Elaine Schulte; *The Patriots*, by Jack Cavanaugh. Published new writers within the last year.
How to Contact: No unsolicited mss. Only accepts agented and requested submissions. All unsolicited mss are returned unopened.
Terms: Royalties vary ("depending on whether it is trade, mass market or cloth" and whether picture book or novel). Offers advance. Writer's guidelines with SASE.
Advice: "Focus on Christians, not Christianity. Chariot Victor Publishing publishes books for toddlers through adults which help people better understand their relationship with God, and/or the message of God's book, the Bible. Interested in seeing contemporary novels (*not* Harlequin-type) adventure, romance, suspense with Christian perspective."

CHARLESBRIDGE PUBLISHING, (III), 85 Main St., Watertown MA 02472. (617)926-0329, ext. 140. Website: http://www.charlesbridge.com (includes writer's guidelines, names of editors, authors, titles, chat lines). **Acquisitions:** Elena Dworkin Wright, editorial director. Estab. 1980. "We are looking for fiction to use as literature in the math and physical science curriculum." **Published 1 previously unpublished writer/year.** Publishes school programs and hardcover and trade paperback originals. Publishes 20 books/year. Promotes titles through catalogs, trade shows, education conventions, author presentations through our speaker's bureau.
Imprint: ***Talewinds*** (fiction).
Needs: Math concepts in nonrhyming story. Recently published *Sir Cumference and the First Round Table*, by Cindy Neuschwander (a math adventure/picture book); *We Are a Rainbow*, by Nancy Maria Grande Tabor; and *Alice in Pastaland*, by Alexandra Wright (picture books).
How to Contact: Reports in 2 months.
Terms: Publishes ms 1 year after acceptance.
Advice: "We market through schools, book stores and specialty stores at museums, science centers, etc."

CHINOOK PRESS, (II), 1432 Yellowstone Ave., Billings MT 59102. (406)245-7704. Editor/Publisher: Mary Ellen Westwood. Estab. 1996. "One-person operation on a part-time basis just starting out. I hope to have a catalog of equal parts fiction, nonfiction and poetry." Publishes paperback originals. Books: acid-free paper; printing and binding suitable to product; illustrations. Average print order: 2,000-5,000. First novel print order: 2,000-5,000. Plans 1 first novel this year. Averages 4 total titles, 2 fiction titles each year. Sometimes critiques or comments on rejected mss.
Needs: Adventure, childrens/juvenile (all types), ethnic/multicultural, experimental, family saga, fantasy (all types), feminist, historical, humor/satire, literary, mainstream/contemporary, mystery/suspense (all types), re-

gional (the West), science fiction (all types), short story collections, translations, young adult/teen (all types). "I want fiction that educates and uplifts, that shows real human beings in real or imagined situations that aid in human advancement. I do not want fiction that titillates for the sole purpose of titillation. I want fiction with a definite message and purpose."
How to Contact: Accepts unsolicited mss. Submit complete ms with cover letter. Include estimated word count, 1-page bio, Social Security number, list of publishing credits and "brief explanation of why you wrote what you wrote." Send SASE for return of ms. Reports in 2 months on queries and mss. Simultaneous submissions OK "if identified as such."
Terms: "We make individual arrangements with each author depending on book, but author must provide promotion time." Sends galleys to author. Publishes ms 2 months to 2 years after acceptance. Writer's guidelines for #10 SASE.
Advice: "I am a well-trained and well-practiced editor with 29 years experience in both journalism and law. Bad spelling, incorrect grammar and muddy thinking will not sell your work to me. But your best effort will receive attentive and enthusiastic handling here. I want more new and creative solutions to the human condition. I want fewer 'Oh, woe is me! I just can't do anything with my life.' stories."

✔ **CHRONICLE BOOKS, (II)**, Chronicle Publishing Co., 85 Second St., 6th Floor, San Francisco CA 94105. (415)537-3730. Fax: (415)537-4440. E-mail: frontdesk@chronbooks.com. Website: http://www.chronbooks.com. President: Jack Jensen. Publishing Director: Caroline Herter. Associate Publishers: Nion McEvoy, Victoria Rock, Christine Carswell. **Acquisitions**: Jay Schaefer, editor (fiction); Victoria Rock, editor (children's). Estab. 1966. Publishes hardcover and trade paperback originals. Averages 200 total titles, 10 fiction titles each year.
Needs: Open. Looking for novellas, collections and novels. No romances, science fiction, or any genre fiction: no category fiction. Publishes anthologies. Published *Griffin & Sabine*, by Nick Bantock; *Lies of the Saints*, by Erin McGraw; *Spirits of the Ordinary*, by Kathleen Alcalá and *The Lonliest Road in America*, by Roy Parvin.
How to Contact: Accepts unsolicited mss. Submit complete ms with synopsis and cover letter. "No queries, please." Send SASE for reply and return of ms. Agented fiction 50%. Prefers no simultaneous submissions. Sometimes comments on rejected ms.
Terms: Standard rates. Sends galleys to author. Publishes ms 9-12 months after acceptance. Writer's guidelines available on website.

CHRONICLE BOOKS FOR CHILDREN, (II, IV), Imprint of Chronicle Books, 85 Second St., San Francisco CA 94105. (415)537-3730. Fax: (415)537-4460. E-mail: frontdesk@chronbooks.com. Website: http://www.chronbooks.com. **Acquisitions:** Victoria Rock, director of Children's Books (nonfiction/fiction); Amy Novesky, assistant editor (nonfiction/fiction plus middle grade and young adult). "Chronicle Books for Children publishes an eclectic mixture of traditional and innovative children's books. We're looking for quirky, bold artwork and subject matter." Publishes hardcover and trade paperback originals. Publishes 40-50 titles/year.
Needs: Fiction picture books, middle grades fiction, young adult projects. Mainstream/contemporary, multicultural, picture books, young adult, chapter books. Recently published *The Eyes of Graywolf*, by Jonathan London; *Dem Bones*, by Bob Banner; and *Hush Little Baby*, by Sylvia Long.
How to Contact: Query with synopsis and SASE. Send complete ms for picture books. Reports in 2-18 weeks on queries; 5 months on mss. Simultaneous submissions OK, if so noted.
Terms: Pays 8% royalty. Advance varies. Publishes ms 18 months after acceptance. Writer's guidelines for #10 SASE. Book catalog for 9×12 SAE and 8 first-class stamps.
Advice: "We are interested in projects that have a unique bent to them—be it in subject matter, writing style, or illustrative technique. As a small list, we are looking for books that will lend our list a distinctive flavor. Primarily we are interested in fiction and nonfiction picture books for children ages up to eight years, and nonfiction books for children ages up to twelve years. We publish board, pop-up, and other novelty formats as well as picture books. We are also interested in early chapter books, middle grade fiction, and young adult projects."

CIRCLET PRESS, (IV), 1770 Massachusetts Ave., #278, Cambridge MA 02140. (617)864-0492 (noon-6p.m. EST). Fax: (617)864-0663, call before faxing. E-mail: circlet-info@circlet.com. Website: http://www.circlet.com/ (includes previews of upcoming books, catalog of complete books in print, links to authors' web pages and other publishers). **Acquistions**: Cecilia Tan, publisher. Estab. 1992. Small, independent specialty book publisher. "We are the only book publisher specializing in science fiction and fantasy of an erotic nature." Publishes paperback originals. Books: perfect binding; illustrations sometimes; average print order: 2,500. **Publishes 50 previously unpublished writers/year.** Averages 6-8 anthologies each year. Distributes titles through the LPC Group in the US/Canada, Turnaround UK in the UK and Bulldog Books in Australia. Promotes titles through reviews in book trade and general media, mentions in Publishers Weekly, Bookselling This Week and regional radio/TV.

- Nominated titles from Circlet Press were finalists in the Small Press Book Award, Firecracker Alternative Book Award and Lambda Literary Award in 1998.

Needs: "We publish only short stories of erotic science fiction/fantasy, of all persuasions (gay, straight, bi, feminist, lesbian, etc.). No horror! No exploitative sex, murder or rape. No degradation." No novels. All books are anthologies of short stories. Recently published *Things Invisible to See*, edited by Lawrence Schimel (anthology); *Fetish Fantastic* and *Cherished Blood*, both edited by Cecilia Tan (anthologies).

How to Contact: Accepts unsolicited mss between April 1 and August 31. Accepts queries (no mss) by e-mail. "Any manuscript sent other than this time period will be returned unread or discarded." Submit complete short story with cover letter. Include estimated word count, 50-100 word bio, list of publishing credits. Send SASE for reply, return of ms or send a disposable copy of ms. Agented fiction 5%. Reports in 6-12 months. Simultaneous submissions OK. Always critiques or comments on rejected mss.
Terms: Pays minimum ½¢/word for 1-time anthology rights only, plus 2 copies; author is free to sell other rights. Sends galleys to author. Publishes ms 1-24 months after acceptance. Writer's guidelines for #10 SASE. Book catalog for #10 SAE and 2 first-class stamps.
Advice: "Read what we publish, learn to use lyrical but concise language to portray sex positively. Make sex and erotic interaction integral to your plot. Stay away from genre stereotypes. Use depth of character, internal monologue and psychological introspection to draw me in." Note: "We do not publish novels."

CITADEL PRESS, (II), Carol Publishing Group, 120 Enterprise Ave., Secaucus NJ 07094. (212)736-1141. Fax: (201)866-8159. E-mail: info@citadelpublishing.com. Website: http://www.citadelpublishing.com. **Acquisitions**: Allan J. Wilson, executive editor; Hillel Black, associate editor. Estab. 1942. Publishes hardcover and paperback originals and paperback reprints. Specializes in biography and film. Averages 65 total titles, 4-7 fiction titles each year. Occasionally critiques rejected mss.
Needs: No religious, romantic or detective fiction. Published *The Last Empress*, by Alexandra Romanov and *Marquis De Sade* (biography).
How to Contact: Accepts unsolicited mss. Query first with SASE (or IRC). Reports in 6 weeks on queries; 2 months on mss. Simultaneous submissions OK.
Terms: Pays in royalties of 10% minimum; 15% maximum; 12-25 author's copies. Advance is more for agented ms; $4,000 and up.

CITY LIGHTS BOOKS, (II), 261 Columbus Ave., San Francisco CA 94133. (415)362-1901. Fax: (415)362-4921. **Acquisitions:** Robert Sharrard, editor. Estab. 1955. Publishes paperback originals. Plans 1-2 first novels this year. Averages 12 total titles, 4-5 fiction titles/year.
How to Contact: Accepts unsolicited mss with SASE. Query letter only first. Unsolicited queries/correspondence by fax OK. Send SASE for reply, return of ms or send a disposable copy of ms.

CLARION BOOKS, (V), Imprint of Houghton Mifflin Company, 215 Park Ave. S., New York NY 10003. **Acquisitions**: Dorothy Briley, editor/publisher; Dinah Stevenson, executive editor; Nina Ignatowicz, senior editor. Estab. 1965. Clarion is a strong presence when it comes to books for young readers. Publishes hardcover originals. Publishes 50 titles/year.

- Clarion is swamped with submissions and is not accepting manuscripts at this time.

CLEIS PRESS, (II), P.O. Box 14684, San Francisco CA 94114. E-mail: sfcleis@aol.com. **Acquisitions**: Frederique Delacoste, editor. Estab. 1980. Midsize independent publisher. Publishes paperback originals. Published new writers within the last year. Plans 1 first novel every other year. Averages 15 total titles, 5 (3 are anthologies) fiction titles/year.

- Cleis Press has received the Best Lesbian Fiction Lambda Literary Award for *Memory Mambo*, by Achy Obejas, the Fab Award, Firecracker for Outstanding Press; and several Canada Award nominations.

Needs: Comics/graphic novels, erotica, ethnic/multicultural (gay/lesbian), feminist, gay, historical (gay/lesbian), horror (vampire), humor/satire, lesbian, short story collection, thriller/espionage, translations. Recently published *The Woman Who Knew Too Much*, by B. Reece Johnson (novel); and *A Fragile Union*, by Joan Nestle (essays).
How to Contact: Accepts unsolicited mss with SASE. Accepts unsolicited queries by E-mail. Submit complete ms with a cover letter. Include 1- or 2-page bio, list of publishing credits. Send SASE for reply or send a disposable copy of ms. Agented fiction 25%. Reports in 6 weeks. No simultaneous submissions.
Payment/Terms: Pays royalty of 7%. Advance is negotiable. Sends galleys to author. Publishes ms 12-18 months after acceptance. Catalogue for SASE and 2 first-class stamps.

COFFEE HOUSE PRESS, (II), 27 N. Fourth St., Minneapolis MN 55401. (612)338-0125. **Acquisitions**: Allan Kornblum and Chris Fischbach, editors. Estab. 1984. "Nonprofit publisher with a small staff. We publish literary titles: fiction and poetry." Publishes paperback originals. Books: acid-free paper; Smyth-sewn binding; cover illustrations; average print order: 2,500. First novel print order: 3,000-4,000. Published new writers within the last year. Plans 2 first novels this year. Averages 12 total titles, 6 fiction titles each year.

- This successful nonprofit small press has received numerous grants from various organizations including NEA, the Mellon Foundation and Lila Wallace/Readers Digest.

Needs: Contemporary, ethnic, experimental, satire, literary. Looking for "non-genre, contemporary, high quality, unique material." No westerns, romance, erotica, mainstream, science fiction or mystery. Publishes anthologies, but they are closed to unsolicited submissions. Also publishes a series of short-short collections called "Coffee-to-Go." Published *Ex Utero*, by Laurie Foos (first novel); *Gunga Din Highway*, by Frank Chin (novel); and *A .38 Special & a Broken Heart*, by Jonis Agee (short short stories).
How to Contact: Accepts unsolicited mss. Submit samples with cover letter. SASE. Agented fiction 10%. Reports in 2 months on queries; 7 months on mss.
Terms: Pays royalties of 8%. Average advance: $3,000. Provides 15 author's copies. Writer's guidelines for #10 SASE with 55¢ postage.

✔ **CONCORDIA PUBLISHING HOUSE, (II)**, 3558 S. Jefferson Ave., St. Louis MO 63118-3968. (314)268-3698. Fax: (314)268-1329. Children's Editor: Jane Wilke. Adult and Youth Editor: Rachel Hoyer. Estab. 1869. "We publish Protestant, inspirational, theological, family and juvenile books. All manuscripts should conform to the doctrinal tenets of The Lutheran Church—Missouri Synod." Publishes hardcover and trade paperback originals. Publishes 160 titles/year.

- Concordia has increased their number of books published from 80 to 160 in the past year.

Needs: Juvenile novels. "We will consider fiction for the following age ranges: 4-7, 6-9, 8-12, 10-14, and children's picture books. All books must contain Christian content. No adult Christian fiction." Recently published *The Presidential Mystery*, by Dandi Daley Mackall; and *Hail to the Chump*, by Paul Buchanan.
How to Contact: No phone queries, please. Send a query with SASE first. Reports in 2-3 months on queries. Simultaneous submissions discouraged.
Terms: Pays royalty or makes outright purchase. Publishes ms 18 months after acceptance. Writer's guidelines for #10 SASE.
Advice: "Our needs have broadened to include writers of books for lay adult Christians."

N 🌐 **CONSTABLE AND COMPANY, (IV)**, 3 The Lanchesters, 162 Fulham Palace Rd., London W6 9ER England. Editorial Director: Carol O'Brien. Averages 34 fiction titles/year. Publishes "crime fiction (mysteries)." Length: 60,000 words minimum; 100,000 words maximum. Send brief summary, 3 sample chapters and return postage. Pays advance and royalties. Write to publishers for catalog.

🍁 ✔ 🏆 **COTEAU BOOKS, (IV)**, Thunder Creek Publishing Co-operative Ltd., 401-2206 Dewdney Ave., Regina, Saskatchewan S4R 1H3 Canada. (306)777-0170. Fax: (306)522-5152. E-mail: nik@coteau.unibase.com. Website: http://coteau.unibase.com. **Acquisitions**: Barbara Sapergia, acquisitions editor. Estab. 1975. "Coteau Books publishes the finest Canadian fiction, poetry drama and children's literature, with an emphasis on western writers." Independent publisher. Publishes paperback originals. Books: #2 offset or 60 lb. hi-bulk paper; offset printing; perfect bound; 4-color illustrations. Average print order: 1,500-3,000; first novel print order: approx. 1,500. Published new writers within the last year. Publishes 14 total titles, 6-8 fiction titles each year. Distributed by General Distribution Services.

- Books published by Coteau Books have received awards including the City of Edmonton Book Prize for *Banjo Lessons*, Jubilee Fiction Award for *In the Misleading Absence of Light*, and the Danuta Gleed Literary Award for *The Progress of an Object in Motion.*

Needs: Novels, short fiction, middle years and young adult fiction. No science fiction. No children's picture books. Publishes Canadian authors only.
How to Contact: *Canadian writers only.* Send submissions with query letter and résumé to Acquisitions Editor. SASE. No simultaneous or multiple submissions. Fiction 10%. Responds to e-mail queries. Reports on queries in 2-3 months; 2-3 months on mss. Sometimes comments on rejected mss.
Terms: "We're a co-operative and receive subsidies from the Canadian, provincial and local governments. We do not accept payments from authors to publish their works." Sends galleys to author. Publishes ms 1-2 years after acceptance. Book catalog for 8½×11 SASE.
Advice: "We publish short-story collections, novels, drama, nonfiction and poetry collections, as well as literary interviews and children's books. This is part of our mandate. The work speaks for itself! Be bold. Be creative. Be persistent!"

A **COUNTERPOINT, (V)**, 1627 I St. NW, Suite 850, Washington DC 20006. Fax: (202)887-0562. **Acquisitions**: Jack Shoemaker, editor-in-chief. "Counterpoint publishes serious literary work, with particular emphasis on natural history, science, philosophy and contemporary thought, history, art, poetry and fiction. All of our books are printed on acid-free paper, with cloth bindings sewn. In this multimedia age, we are committed to the significant readership that still demands and appreciates well-published and well-crafted books." Publishes hardcover and trade paperback originals and reprints. Publishes 20-25 titles/year.
Needs: Historical, humor, literary, mainstream/contemporary, religious, short story collections. Recently published *Women in Their Beds*, by Gina Berriault (short stories).
How to Contact: Agented submissions only. Reports in 2 months. Simultaneous submissions OK.
Terms: Pays 7½-15% royalty on retail price. Publishes ms 18 months after acceptance.

CREATIVE WITH WORDS PUBLICATIONS, (I), Box 223226, Carmel CA 93922. Fax: (408)655-8627. E-mail: cwwpub@usa.net. Website: http://members.tripod.com/~CreativeWithWords (includes guidelines, themes, submittal form, catalog, editor's notes, editing tips, mission statement, "Best of the month" salute to writers and winning entry). **Acquisitions**: Brigitta Geltrich (general); Bert Hower (nature), fiction editor. Estab. 1975. Staff works on part-time basis "with guest editors, artists and readers from throughout the U.S. We try to publish clean prose and poetry with family appeal." Books: bond and stock paper; mimeographed printing; saddle-stitched binding; illustrations and photographs. 50-70% of fiction published is by new writers. Average print order varies. Publishes paperback anthologies of new and established writers. Averages 12-14 anthologies each year. Distributes titles through author, schools and libraries.

Needs: Humor/satire, juvenile (easy-to-read, fantasy), nature. "Editorial needs center on folkloristic items (according to themes): tall tales and such for annual anthologies." Needs seasonal short stories, stories on values and human relationships appealing to general public; "tales" of folklore nature, appealing to all ages, poetry, prose and language art works by children. Recently published anthologies, *Humor, School, Love, Folklore*."

How to Contact: Accepts unsolicited mss. Query first; submit complete ms (prose no more than 1,500 words) with SASE and cover letter. Electronic submissions (3.5 diskette) OK. Reports in 1 month on queries; 2-4 weeks on mss after deadline. Publishes ms 1-2 months after deadline. Writer's guidelines and theme list (1 oz.) for SASE. No simultaneous submissions, "no previously published material." *Critiques rejected mss; $10 for short stories (less than 1,000 words); $20 for longer stories, folklore items; $5 for poetry* (up to 20 lines).

Terms: Pays in 20% reduced author copies (20%: 1-9 copies; 30%: 10 copies); Best of the Month (1 free copy) and winning entry published on the Web.

Advice: "Our fiction appeals to general public: children—senior citizens. Follow guidelines and rules of Creative With Words Publications and not those the writer feels CWW should have. We only consider fiction along the lines of folklore, seasonal genres and annual themes set by CWW. Be brief, sincere, well-informed, patient and proficient! Look at the world from a different perspective, research your topic thoroughly, apply brevity, and write your story through a viewpoint character, whether antagonist, protagonist or narrator."

N 🌐 **CRESCENT MOON, (I, II)**, Box 393, Maidstone, Kent ME14 5XY England. Subsidiaries: Joe's Press, *Passion Magazine*. **Acquisitions:** J. Robinson, director. Estab. 1988. Small independent publisher. Publishes hardcover and paperback originals. Published new writers within the last year. Plans 1-2 first novels in 1999. Averages 25 total titles, 1-2 fiction titles/year. Sometimes critiques or comments on rejected ms.

Needs: Erotica, experimental, feminist, gay, lesbian, literary, New Age/mystic/spiritual, short story collections, translations. Plans anthology. Send short stories to editor.

How to Contact: Accepts unsolicited mss. Query with outline/synopsis and 2 sample chapters. Include estimated word count, list of publishing credits. Send SASE (IRCs) for reply, return of ms or send a disposable copy of ms. Agented fiction 10%. Reports in 1 month on queries; 4 months on mss. Simultaneous submissions OK.

Terms: Negotiable. Sends galleys to author. Publishes ms 12-18 months after acceptance. Writer's guidelines for SASE (2 IRCs); book catalog for SASE (2 IRCs).

Advice: "We publish a small amount of fiction, and mainly in *Pagan Magazine* and *Passion Magazine*."

🏆 **CROSSWAY BOOKS, (II, IV)**, Division of Good News Publishers, 1300 Crescent, Wheaton IL 60187-5800. Fax: (630)682-4785. **Acquisitions**: Jill Carter. Estab. 1938. " 'Making a difference in people's lives for Christ' as its maxim, Crossway Books lists titles written from an evangelical Christian perspective." Midsize independent evangelical religious publisher. Publishes paperback originals. Average print order 5,000-10,000 copies. Averages 60 total titles, 10-15 fiction titles each year. Distributes through Christian bookstores and catalogs.

- Crossway Books is known as a leader in Christian fiction. Several of their books have received "Gold Medallion" awards from the Evangelical Christian Publishers Association.

Needs: Contemporary, adventure, historical, literary, religious/inspirational, young adult. "All fiction published by Crossway Books must be written from the perspective of evangelical Christianity. It must understand and view the world through a Christian worldview." No sentimental, didactic, "inspirational" religious fiction, heavy-handed allegorical or derivative fantasy. Recently published *The Stain*, by Harry Lee Kraus (medical suspense); *Sweet Carolina*, by Stephen Bly (historical western); and *In Shadow of Love*, by Sally John (contemporary).

How to Contact: Does not accept unsolicited mss. Send query with synopsis and sample chapters only. Reports in 6-8 weeks on queries. Publishes ms 1-2 years after acceptance.

Terms: Pays in royalties and negotiates advance. Writer's guidelines for SASE. Book catalog for 9×12 SAE and 6 first-class stamps.

Advice: "We feel called to publish fiction in the following categories: supernatural fiction, Christian realism, historical fiction, intrigue, western fiction and children's fiction. All fiction should include explicit Christian content, artfully woven into the plot, and must be consistent with our statements of vision, purpose and commitment. Crossway can successfully publish and market *quality* Christian novelists. Also read John Gardner's *On Moral Fiction*. We require a minimum word count of 25,000 words."

✔ **CUMBERLAND HOUSE PUBLISHING, (II)**, 431 Harding Industrial Dr., Nashville TN 37211. (615)832-1171. Fax: (615)832-0633. E-mail: cumbhouse@aol.com. **Acquisitions:** Ron Pitkin, president. "We look for unique titles with clearly defined audiences." Publishes hardcover and trade paperback originals, and

hardcover and trade paperback reprints. Publishes 35 titles/year. Imprint publishes 5 titles/year.
Imprint(s): Cumberland House Hearthside; Julia M. Pitkin, editor-in-chief.
Needs: Mystery, western. Recently published *A Rumor of Bones*, by Beverly Connor (mystery); and *The Broncbuster*, by Mike Flanagan.
How to Contact: Query first. Writers should know "the odds are really stacked against them." Agented fiction 20%. Reports in 2 months on queries; 4 months on mss. Simultaneous submissions OK.
Terms: Pays 10-20% royalty on wholesale price. Offers $1,000-10,000 advance. Publishes ms an average of 8 months after acceptance. Book catalog for 8×10 SAE and 4 first-class stamps. Writer's guidelines free.
Advice: Audience is "adventuresome people who like a fresh approach to things. Writers should tell what their idea is, why it's unique and why somebody would want to buy it—but don't pester us."

✓ **DANTE UNIVERSITY OF AMERICA PRESS, INC., (II)**, P.O. Box 843, Brookline Village MA 02147-0843. Fax: (617)734-2046. E-mail: danteu@usa1.com. Website: http://www.danteuniversity.org/dpress.html. **Acquisitions**: Adolph Caso, president. "The Dante University Press exists to bring quality, educational books pertaining to our Italian heritage as well as the historical and political studies of America. Profits from the sale of these publications benefit the Foundation, bringing Dante University closer to a reality." Estab. 1975. Publishes hardcover and trade paperback originals and reprints. Publishes 5 titles/year. Average print order for a first book is 3,000.
Needs: Translations from Italian and Latin. Recently published *Rogue Angel*, by Carol Damioli.
How to Contact: Query first with SASE. Agented fiction 50%. Reports in 2 months.
Terms: Pays royalty. Negotiable advance. Publishes ms 10 months after acceptance.

DARK HORSE COMICS, INC., (I, IV), 10956 SE Main St., Milwaukie OR 97222. (503)652-8815. Fax: (503)654-9440. E-mail: bena@dhorse.com. Website: http://www.dhorse.com (includes overview of titles). Estab. 1986. "Dark Horse publishes all kinds of comics material, and we try not to limit ourselves to any one genre or any one philosophy. Most of our comics are intended for readers 15-40, though we also publish material that is accessible to younger readers." Comic books: newsprint or glossy paper, each title 24-28 pages. Averages 10-30 total titles each year. Publishes 3-5 new writers/year. Distributes through direct market, bookstores and newsstands.

- Dark Horse Press's comics have won several awards including the Eisner, Harvey and Parent's Choice awards.

Needs: Comics: adventure, childrens/juvenile, fantasy (space fantasy, super hero, sword and sorcery), horror, humor/satire, mystery/suspense (private eye/hardboiled), psychic/supernatural, romance (contemporary), science fiction (hard science, soft/sociological), western (traditional). Plans anthology. Recently published comics by Stan Sakai, Jay Stephens and Paul Pope. Published short story comic anthologies: *Dark Horse Presents*.
How to Contact: Does not accept unsolicited mss. Query letter first. Also accepts queries by e-mail. Include one-page bio, list of publishing credits. Send SASE or disposable copy of ms. Reports in 1-2 months. Simultaneous submissions OK.
Terms: Pays $25-100/page and 5-25 author's copies. "We usually buy first and second rights, other rights on publication." Writer's guidelines free for #10 SASE.
Advice: "Read comics. Know comics. Understand comics. Have a reason to want to publish your story as a comic, beyond it not working as a novel or screenplay. Obtain copies of our Writer's Guidelines before making a query."

✓ **MAY DAVENPORT, PUBLISHERS, (II)**, 26313 Purissima Rd., Los Altos Hills CA 94022. (650)948-6499. Fax: (650)947-1373. E-mail: robertd@whidbey.com. Website: http://www.maydavenportpublishers.com (includes catalog, author information). **Acquisitions:** May Davenport, editor/publisher. Estab. 1976. "We prefer books which can be *used* in high schools as supplementary readings in English or creative writing courses. Reading skills have to be taught, and novels by humorous authors can be more pleasant to read than Hawthorne's or Melville's novels, war novels, or novels about past generations. Humor has a place in literature." Publishes hardcover and trade paperback originals. Publishes 4 titles/year. Distributes titles through direct mail order.
Imprint(s): md Books (nonfiction and fiction).
Needs: Humor, literary. "We want to focus on novels junior and senior high school teachers can share with their reluctant readers in their classrooms." Recently published *Grandpa McKutcheon's Kangaroomatic Rocking Chair*, by Jonathan Middleton (read-and-color book); and *The Ghost, The Gold and The Whippoorwill*, by Frank J. Nucklos (preteen novel).
How to Contact: Query with SASE. Reports in 1 month.
Terms: Pays 15% royalty on retail price. No advance. Publishes ms 1 year after acceptance. Book catalog and writer's guidelines for #10 SASE.
Advice: "Just write humorous fictional novels about today's generation with youthful, admirable, believable characters to make young readers laugh. TV-oriented youth need role models in literature, and how a writer uses descriptive adjectives and similes enlightens youngsters who are so used to music, animation, special effects with stories."

DAW BOOKS, INC., (I), Distributed by Penguin Putnam Inc., 375 Hudson St., New York NY 10014. Fax: (212)366-2090. Publishers: Elizabeth R. Wollheim and Sheila E. Gilbert. **Acquisitions**: Peter Stampfel, submissions editor. Estab. 1971. Publishes paperback originals and hardcover originals. Books: Illustrations sometimes; average print and number of first novels published per year vary widely. Averages 40 new titles plus 40 or more reissues, all fiction, each year. Occasionally critiques rejected mss.
Needs: Science fiction (hard science, soft sociological), fantasy and mainstream thrillers only. Recently published *Owl Sight*, by Mercedes Lackey; *Retribution*, by Elizabeth Forrest; and *This Alien Shore*, by C.S. Friedman. Publishes many original anthologies including *Sword & Sorceress* (edited by Marion Zimmer Bradley); *Cat Fantastic* (edited by Andre Norton and Martin H. Greenberg). "You may write to the editors (after looking at the anthology) for guidelines % DAW."
How to Contact: Submit complete ms with return postage and SASE. Usually reports in 3-5 months on mss, but in special cases may take longer. "No agent required."
Terms: Pays an advance against royalities. Sends galleys to author.
Advice: "We strongly encourage new writers. Research your publishers and submit only appropriate work."

DEAD LETTER, (II), Imprint of St. Martin's Press, 175 Fifth Ave., New York NY 10010. (212)674-5151. **Acquisitions:** Joe Veltre, editor. Publishes trade hardcover and paperback originals and reprints, literary fiction and mass market paperback originals and reprints. Publishes 36 titles/year.
Needs: Mystery.
How to Contact: Query with synopsis, 3 sample chapters and SASE. Agented fiction 98%. Simultaneous submissions OK.
Terms: Pays variable royalty on net price. Advance varies.

DEL REY BOOKS, (II), Subsidiary of Ballantine Books, 201 E. 50 St., New York NY 10022-7703. (212)572-2677. E-mail: delray@randomhouse.com. Website: http://www.randomhouse.com/delrey/. Executive Editor: Shelly Shapiro. Senior Editor: Jill Benjamin. Estab. 1977. "In terms of mass market, we basically created the field of fantasy bestsellers. Not that it didn't exist before, but we put the mass into mass market." Publishes hardcover originals and paperback originals and reprints. Plans 6-7 first novels this year. Publishes 60 titles each year, all fiction. Sometimes critiques rejected mss.
Needs: Fantasy and science fiction. Fantasy must have magic as an intrinsic element to the plot. No flying-saucer, Atlantis or occult novels. Published *First King of Shamara*, by Terry Brooks; *The Demon Awakens*, by R.A. Salvatore; *The Chronicles of Pern*, by Anne McCaffrey (science fiction/hardcover original); *The Shining Ones*, by David Eddings (fantasy/hardcover original); and *Jack the Bodiless*, by Julian May (science fiction/paperback reprint).
How to Contact: Query first to Jill Benjamin with detailed outline and synopsis of story from beginning to end. No unsolicited mss. Reports in 6 months, occasionally longer.
Terms: Pays royalty on retail price; "advance is competitive." Publishes ms 1 year after acceptance. Sends galleys to author. Writer's guidelines for #10 SASE.
Advice: Has been publishing "more fiction and hardcovers, because the market is there for them. Read a lot of science fiction and fantasy, such as works by Anne McCaffrey, David Eddings, Larry Niven, Arthur C. Clarke, Terry Brooks, Frederik Pohl, Barbara Hambly. When writing, pay particular attention to plotting (and a satisfactory conclusion) and characters (sympathetic and well-rounded) because those are what readers look for."

DELACORTE PRESS, (II), Imprint of Dell Publishing, Division of Bantam Doubleday Dell, 1540 Broadway, New York NY 10036. (212)354-6500. Editor-in-Chief: Leslie Schnur. **Acquisitions**: (Ms.) Jackie Cantor (women's fiction); Steve Ross (commercial nonfiction and fiction). Publishes hardcover and trade paperback originals. Publishes 36 titles/year.
Needs: Mainstream/contemporary. No mss for children's or young adult books accepted in this division. Published *Killing Time in St. Cloud*, by Judith Guest; *The Horse Whisperer*, by Nicholas Evans; *Hardcase*, by Bill Pronzin; and *The Magic Bullet*, by Harry Stein.
How to Contact: Query with outline, first 3 chapters or brief proposal. Accepts simultaneous submissions. Reports in 4 months.
Terms: Pays 7½-12½ royalty. Advance varies. Publishes ms 2 years after acceptance, but varies. Guidelines for 9×12 SASE.

DELACORTE/DELL BOOKS FOR YOUNG READERS/DOUBLEDAY, (II, III, IV), Division of Bantam Doubleday Dell Publishing Group, Inc., 1540 Broadway, New York NY 10036. See listing for Bantam/Doubleday/Dell Books for Young Readers.

READ THE BUSINESS OF FICTION WRITING section to learn the correct way to prepare and submit a manuscript.

DELL PUBLISHING ISLAND, (II), Imprint of Dell Publishing, Division of Bantam Doubleday Dell, 1540 Broadway, New York NY 10036. (212)354-6500. **Acquisitions**: Leslie Schnur, editor-in-chief. Publishes trade paperback originals and reprints. Publishes bestseller fiction and nonfiction. Publishes 12 titles/year.
Needs: Mystery, romance, suspense. Published *Runaway Jury*, by John Grisham (suspense).
How to Contact: Reports in 4-6 months on queries. Agented fiction 95%. Simultaneous submissions OK.
Terms: Pays 7½-12½% royalty on retail price. Advance varies. Simultaneous submissions OK. Publishes ms 1 year after acceptance. Book catalog for 9×12 SAE and 3 first class stamps.

DELTA TRADE PAPERBACKS, (II), Imprint of Dell Publishing, Division of Bantam Doubleday Dell, 1540 Broadway, New York NY 10036. (212)354-6500. **Acquisitions**: Leslie Schnur, editor-in-chief. Publishes trade paperback originals, mostly light, humorous material and books on pop culture. Publishes 36 titles/year.
Needs: Erotica, literary, short story collections. Recently published *Fast Greens*, by Turk Pipkin; *Last Days of the Dog Men*, by Brad Watson (stories); and *Sacred Dust*, by David Hill.
How to Contact: Query with synopsis, 2-3 sample chapters or complete ms and SASE. Agented fiction 95%. Reports in 4-6 months on queries. Simultaneous submissions OK.
Terms: Pays 7½-12½% royalty on retail price. Advance varies. Publishes ms 1 year after acceptance. Book catalog for 9×12 SAE and 3 first class stamps.

DIAL BOOKS FOR YOUNG READERS, (V), Division of Penguin Putnam Inc., 375 Hudson St., New York NY 10014. (212)366-2000. Editor-in-Chief/Pres./Publisher: Phyllis Fogelman. Editorial Assistant: Victoria Wells. **Acquisitions**: Submissions Editor. Estab. 1961. Trade children's book publisher, "looking for agented picture book mss and novels." Publishes hardcover originals. Plans 1 first novel this year. Averages 100 titles, mainly fiction.
Imprint(s): Pied Piper Books, Easy-to-Read Books.
Needs: Juvenile (1-9 yrs.) including: animal, fantasy, spy/adventure, contemporary and easy-to-read; young adult/teen (10-16 years) including: fantasy/science fiction, literary and commercial mystery and fiction. Published *Sam and the Tigers*, by Julius Lester and Jerry Pinckney; *Language of Doves*, by Rosemary Wells; and *Great Interactive Dream Machine*, by Richard Peck.
How to Contact: Does not accept unsolicited mss. Query with SASE. Occasionally critiques or comments on rejected ms.
Terms: Pays advance against royalties.
Advice: "To agents: We are publishing more fiction books than in the past, and we publish only hardcover originals, most of which are fiction. At this time we are particularly interested in both fiction and nonfiction for the middle grades, and innovative picture book manuscripts. We also are looking for easy-to-reads for first and second graders. Plays, collections of games and riddles, and counting and alphabet books are generally discouraged. Before submitting a manuscript to a publisher, it is a good idea to request a catalog to see what the publisher is currently publishing. We will send a catalog to anyone who sends 4 first-class stamps with a self-addressed, 9×12 envelope."

DIAL PRESS, (V), Imprint of Dell Publishing, 1540 Broadway, New York NY 10036. (212)354-6500. Fax: (212)782-9698. Website: http://www.bbd.com. **Acquisitions:** Susan Kamil, vice president, editorial director. Estab. 1924. "Dial Press is dedicated to the publication of quality fiction and nonfiction." Publishes 6-12 titles/year.
Needs: Ethnic, literary. Recently published *Pack of Two*, by Caroline Knapp (memoir); *Animal Husbandry*, by Laura Zigman (humorous novel); and *Kanterkill Falls*, by Allegra Goodman (literary novel).
How to Contact: Agented submissions only. Reports in 2 months. Simultaneous submissions OK.
Terms: Pays royalty on retail price. Publishes ms 1-2 years after acceptance.

DOUBLEDAY ADULT TRADE, (III), a division of Bantam Doubleday Dell Publishing Group, Inc., 1540 Broadway., New York NY 10036. (212)782-9911. Fax: (212)782-9700. Website: http://www.bdd.com. **Acquisitions**: Patricia Mulcahy, vice president/editor-in-chief. Estab. 1897. Publishes hardcover and paperback originals and paperback reprints.
Imprint(s): Anchor Press (contact Gerald Howard); Currency (contact Roger Scholl); Main Street (contact Gerald Howard); **Nan A. Talese** (contact Nan A. Talese); Religious Division (contact Eric Major); Image (contact Trace Murphy).
Needs: "Doubleday is not able to consider unsolicited queries, proposals or manuscripts unless submitted through a bona fide literary agent."
Terms: Pays in royalties; offers advance. Publishes ms 1 year after acceptance.

DOUBLEDAY CANADA LIMITED, 105 Bond St., Toronto, Ontario M5B 1Y3 Canada. No unsolicited submissions. Prefers not to share information.

DOWN EAST BOOKS, (II), Division of Down East Enterprise, Inc., P.O. Box 679, Camden ME 04843-0679. Fax: (207)594-7215. E-mail: adevine@downeast.com. Senior Editor: Karin Womer. **Acquisitions:** Acquisitions Editor. Estab. 1954. "We are primarily a regional publisher concentrating on Maine or New England."

Publishes hardcover and trade paperback originals and trade paperback reprints. Publishes 20-24 titles/year. Average print order for a first book is 3,000.

• Down East Books has published Elisabeth Ogilvie, Michael McIntosh, Louise Dickinson Roch and John N. Cole.

Imprint(s): Silver Quill (outdoor sportsmen market).

Needs: Juvenile, regional. "We publish 1-2 juvenile titles/year (fiction and non-fiction), and 1-2 adult fiction titles/year." Recently published *Tides of the Heart*, by Thomas M. Sheehan (novel); *Day Before Winter*, by Elisabeth Ogilvie (novel); and *My Brothers' Keeper*, by Nancy Johnson (young adult novel).

How to Contact: Query first with small sample of text, outline and SASE. Reports in 2 months. Simultaneous submissions OK.

Terms: Pays 10-15% on receipts. Offers $200 average advance. Publishes ms 1 year after acceptance. Writer's guidelines for 9×12 SAE with 3 first-class stamps.

[N] **DUCKWORTH PRESS, (I, IV)**, 3005 66th St., Lubbock TX 79413-5707. Phone/fax: (806)799-3706. E-mail: msuniver@swbell.net. **Acquisitions:** Ann Phillips, fiction editor (romance, detective/mystery); L.K. Thompson, fiction editor (action, mainstream). Estab. 1991. "We prefer writers who live in Texas and New Mexico who are well established and known in the areas where they live since we apply a regional approach to marketing. We do small editions and intense marketing in an author's region. We don't do very much business in major metropolitan areas." Publishes some hardcover originals, mostly paperback originals. Books: 20 lb. paper; electronic press; perfect binding; a few illustrations. Average print order: 250. First novel print order: 100-500. Published 2 new writers within the last year. Plans 2 first novels in 1999. Averages 4 total titles, 2 fiction titles/year.

Needs: Adventure, children's/juvenile (adventure, easy-to- read, fantasy, historical, mystery), family saga, historical, humor/satire, mainstream/contemporary, mystery/suspense (amateur sleuth, police procedural), regional (Texas, New Mexico), romance (contemporary, historical, romantic suspense), western (traditional). Recently published *The Bonners*, by John W. Curry (historical fiction); and *Thorns on the Laurel*, by Katherine Gonzales (historical romance).

How to Contact: Query letter only first. Unsolicited queries/correspondence by e-mail OK. Include estimated word count and bio (3 pages or less). Send SASE for reply, return of ms or send a disposable copy of ms. Reports in 3-4 weeks on queries; 1-2 months on mss. Simultaneous and electronic submissions (disk) OK. Often critiques or comments on rejected ms.

Terms: Pays royalties of 10% minimum; 25% maximum. Small advance. Provides 5 author's copies and pays royalties on gross sales. "If the author helps with legwork, we pay a higher royalty." Sends galleys to author. Publishes ms up to 2 months after acceptance. Writer's guidelines for #10 SASE.

Advice: "We like material that is familiar to small town readers, material that is easy to read, material that families will buy simply because they 'know' the author or they recognize place of references."

✓ **DUFOUR EDITIONS, (II,IV)**, P.O. Box 7, Chester Springs PA 19425. (610)458-5005. Fax: (610)458-7103. E-mail: dufour8023@aol.com. **Acquisitions:** Thomas Lavoie, associate publisher. Estab. 1940s. Small independent publisher, tending toward literary fiction. Publishes hardcover and paperback originals and reprints. Publishes 6-7 total titles/year; 1-2 fiction titles. Promotes titles through catalogs, reviews, direct mail, sales reps, Book Expo and wholesalers.

Needs: Literary, short story collections, translations. Recently published *Last Love in Constantinople*, by Milorad Pavic.

How to Contact: Send query letter only first. Include estimated word count, bio and list of publishing credits. Include SASE for reply. Reports in 2-3 weeks on queries; 2-3 months on mss.

THOMAS DUNNE BOOKS, Imprint of St. Martin's Press, 175 Fifth Ave., New York NY 10010. (212)674-5151. **Acquisitions:** Tom Dunne. Publishes wide range of fiction and nonfiction. Publishes hardcover originals, trade paperback originals and reprints. Publishes 90 titles/year.

Needs: Mainstream/contemporary, mystery/suspense, "women's" thriller. Recently published *Brandenburg*, by Glenn Meade (thriller); and *Birds of Prey*, by Wilbur Smith.

How to Contact: Query or submit synopsis and 100 sample pages with SASE. Reports in 2 months on queries. Simultaneous submissions OK.

Terms: Pays 10-15% royalty on retail price for hardcover, 7½% for paperback. Advance varies with project. Publishes ms 1 year after acceptance. Book catalog and writer's guidelines free.

[A] **DUTTON, (III)**, Division of Penguin Putnam Inc., 375 Hudson St., New York NY 10014. (212)366-2000. **Acquisitions**: Michaela Hamilton, vice president/publisher (fiction), Signet and Onyx; Arnold Dolin, associate publisher, Dutton, publisher, Plume; Laura Gilman, editorial director, Roc; Rosemary Ahern, senior editor (literary fiction); Joe Pittman, editor (mystery); Diedre Mullane, senior editor (multicultural literary fiction); Audrey LeFehr, executive editor (women's fiction). Estab. 1948. Publishes hardcover and paperback originals and paperback reprints. Published new writers within the last year.

Imprint(s): Onyx, Topaz, Mentor, Signet Classic, Plume, Plume Fiction, Meridian, **Roc**.
Needs: "All kinds of commercial and literary fiction, including mainstream, historical, Regency, New Age, western, thriller, science fiction, fantasy, gay. Full length novels and collections." Published *Trial by Fire*, by Nancy Taylor Rosenberg; *Black Cross*, by Greg Iles; and *The Takeover*, by Stephen Frey.
How to Contact: Agented mss only. Queries accepted with SASE. "State type of book and past publishing projects." Simultaneous submissions OK. Reports in 3 months.
Terms: Pays in royalties and author's copies; offers advance. Sends galleys to author. Publishes ms 18 months after acceptance. Book catalog for SASE.
Advice: "Write the complete manuscript and submit it to an agent or agents. We publish The Trailsman, Battletech and other western and science fiction series—all by ongoing authors. Would be receptive to ideas for new series in commercial fiction."

✔ **DUTTON CHILDREN'S BOOKS, (II)**, Imprint of Penguin Putnam Inc., 345 Hudson St., New York NY 10014. (212)414-3700. **Acquisitions:** Lucia Monfried, associate publisher and editor-in-chief. Estab. 1852. Dutton Children's Books publishes fiction and nonfiction for readers ranging from preschoolers to young adults on a variety of subjects. Publishes hardcover originals. Publishes 70 titles/year.
Needs: Dutton Children's Books has a complete publishing program that includes picture books; easy-to-read books; and fiction for all ages, from "first-chapter" books to young adult readers. Published *The Iron Ring*, by Lloyd Alexander.
How to Contact: Query with SASE.
Terms: Pays royalty on retail price.

✔ **E.M. PRESS, INC., (I, IV)**, P.O. Box 4057, Manassas VA 20108. (540)439-0304. E-mail: empress2@erols.com. Website: http://www.empressinc.com. **Acquisitions**: Phoebe Tufts, fiction editor. Estab. 1991. "Expanding small press." Publishes paperback and hardcover originals. Books: 50 lb. text paper; offset printing; perfect binding; illustrations. Average print order: 1,200-5,000. Averages 8 total titles, fiction, poetry and nonfiction, each year. Distributes titles through wholesalers and direct sales. Promotes titles through radio and TV, Interview Report, direct mailings and Ingram's catalogs.
Needs: "We are focusing more on Virginia/Maryland/DC authors and subject matter. We're emphasizing nonfiction and we're launching a new children's line, though we still consider 'marketable' fiction. Recently published *The Relationship*, by John Hyman (young adult); *Santa's New Reindeer*, by Judie Schrecker; *I, Anna Kerry*, by William Giannini (literary); and *How Will They Get That Heart Down Your Throat*, by Karen Walton.
How to Contact: Accepts unsolicited mss. Submit outline/synopsis and sample chapters or complete ms with cover letter. Include estimated word count. Send a SASE for reply, return of ms or send a disposable copy of the ms. Agented fiction 10%. Reports in 3 months on queries; 3 months on mss. Simultaneous submissions OK.
Terms: Amount of royalties and advances varies. Sends galleys to author. Publishes ms 18 months after acceptance. Writer's guidelines for SASE.
Advice: Publishing "less fiction, more regional work, though we look for fiction that will do well in secondary rights sales."

EAKIN PRESS, (II, IV), P.O. Box 90159, Austin TX 78709-0159. (512)288-1771. Fax: (512)288-1813. **Acquisitions**: Edwin M. Eakin, editorial director; Melissa Roberts, Virginia Messer. Estab. 1978. Eakin specializes in Texana and Western Americana for adults and juveniles. Publishes hardcover originals. Books: Old style (acid-free); offset printing; case binding; illustrations. Average print order 2,000. First novel print order 5,000. Published new writers within the last year. Plans 2 first novels this year. Averages 80 total titles each year.
Imprint(s): Nortex.
Needs: Juvenile. Specifically needs historical fiction for school market, juveniles set in Southwest for Southwest grade schoolers. Published *Wall Street Wives*, by Ande Ellen Winkler; *Jericho Day*, by Warren Murphy; and *Blood Red Sun*, by Stephen Mertz.
How to Contact: Prefers queries, but accepts unsolicited mss. Send SASE for guidelines. Agented fiction 5%. Simultaneous submissions OK. Reports in 3 months on queries.
Terms: Pays royalties; average advance: $1,000. Sends galleys to author. Publishes ms 1-1½ years after acceptance. Writers guidelines for #10 SASE. Book catalog for 75¢.
Advice: "Juvenile fiction only with strong Southwest theme. We receive around 600 queries or unsolicited mss a year."

✔ **THE ECCO PRESS, (II)**, 100 W. Broad St., Hopewell NJ 08525. (609)466-4748. **Acquisitions**: Daniel Halpern, editor-in-chief. Estab. 1970. Small publisher. Publishes hardcover and paperback originals and reprints.

Books: acid-free paper; offset printing; Smythe-sewn binding; occasional illustrations. Averages 60 total titles, 20 fiction titles each year. Average first novel print order: 3,000 copies.
Needs: "We can publish possibly one or two original novels a year." No science fiction, romantic novels, western (cowboy) or historical novels. Recently published *Summer at Gaglow*, by Esther Freud; *Hell*, by Kathryn Davis; and *Vast Emotions and Imperfect Thoughts*, by Ruben Fonseca.
How to Contact: Accepts unsolicited mss. Query first with SASE and 1-page bio. Send all queries to submissions editor. Reports in 3-6 months, depending on the season.
Terms: Pays in royalties. Advance is negotiable. Publishes ms 1 year after acceptance. Writer's guidelines for SASE. Book catalog free on request.
Advice: "We are always interested in first novels and feel it's important they be brought to the attention of the reading public."

EDGE BOOKS, (II), Imprint of Henry Holt & Co., 115 W. 18th St., New York NY 10011. (212)886-9200. **Acquisitions:** Marc Aronson, executive editor. Publishes hardcover originals. Publishes 4-5 titles/year.
Needs: Young adult. Recently published *Shizko's Daughter*, by Kyoko Mori; and *The Long Season of Rain*, by Helen Kim (novels).
How to Contact: Query or submit complete ms. Reports in 4 months on queries. Simultaneous submissions OK.
Terms: Pays 6-7½% royalty on retail price. Advance varies. Publishes ms 18 months after acceptance. Book catalog free from Henry Holt (same address).
Advice: "All our titles are international or multicultural coming-of-age fiction and nonfiction. We are very open to new authors, but because we publish so few titles, the standards are very high. The emphasis is on voice and literary quality, rather than subject."

ÉDITIONS LA LIBERTÉ INC., (II), 3020 Chemin Ste-Foy, Ste-Foy, Quebec G1X 3V6 Canada. Phone/fax: (418)658-3763. **Acquisitions**: Nathalie Roy, director of operations. Publishes trade paperback originals. **Publishes 75% previously unpublished writers/year.** Publishes 4-5 titles/year.
Needs: Historical, juvenile, literary, mainstream/contemporary, short story collections, young adult. Recently published *L'espace Montauban/Le Dernier Roman Scout*, by Jean Désy.
How to Contact: Query with synopsis. Simultaneous submissions OK.
Terms: Pays 10% royalty on retail price. Accepts only mss written in French. Publishes ms 4 months after acceptance. Book catalog free.

WM. B. EERDMANS PUBLISHING CO., (II), 255 Jefferson Ave. SE, Grand Rapids MI 49503-4570. (800)253-7521. Fax: (616)459-6540. **Acquisitions**: Jon Pott, editor-in-chief, fiction editor (adult fiction); Judy Zylstra, fiction editor (children). Estab. 1911. "Although Eerdmans publishes some regional books and other nonreligious titles, it is essentially a religious publisher whose titles range from the academic to the semi-popular. Our children's fiction is meant to help a child explore life in God's world and to foster a child's exploration of her or his faith. We are a midsize independent publisher. We publish a few adult novels a year, and these tend to address spiritual issues from a Christian perspective." Publishes hardcover and paperback originals and reprints. **Publishes 1 previously unpublished writer/year.** Averages 200 total titles, 10-15 fiction titles (mostly for children) each year. Sometimes critiques or comments on rejected ms.
Imprint(s): Eerdmans Books for Young Readers.
- Wm. B. Eerdmans Publishing Co.'s titles have won awards from the American Library Association and The American Bookseller's Association.

Needs: Religious (children's, general, fantasy). Recently published *God's Little Seeds*, by Bijou Le Tord (children's); *Forgive the River, Forgive the Sky*, by Gloria Whelan; and *A Traitor Among Us*, by Elizabeth Von Steenwyk (both middle readers).
How to Contact: Accepts unsolicited mss. Query with outline/synopsis and 2 sample chapters. Accepts unsolicited queries and correspondence by fax. Include 150- to 200-word bio and list of publishing credits. SASE for reply or send a disposable copy of ms. Agented fiction 25%. Reports in 3-4 weeks on queries; 2-3 months on mss. Simultaneous submissions OK, "if notified." Electronic submission (fax) OK.
Terms: Pays royalties of 7% minimum. Offers negotiable advance. Sends galleys to author. Publishes ms 12-18 months after acceptance. Writer's guidelines and book catalog free.
Advice: "Our readers are educated and fairly sophisticated, and we are looking for novels with literary merit."

EMPYREAL PRESS, (II), P.O. Box 1746, Place Du Parc, Montreal, Quebec H2W 2R7 Canada. Website: http://www.generation.net/~talisher/empyreal. **Acquisitions**: Geof Isherwood, publisher. "Our mission is the publishing of Canadian and other literature which doesn't fit into any standard 'mold'—writing which is experimental yet grounded in discipline, imagination." Publishes trade paperback originals. Publishes 50% previously unpublished writers/year. Publishes 1-4 titles/year.
- Empyreal Press is not currently accepting unsolicited manuscripts.

How to Contact: Query first. No unsolicited mss.
Terms: Pays 10% royalty on wholesale price. Offers $300 (Canadian) advance. Book catalog for #10 SASE.

✓ PAUL S. ERIKSSON, PUBLISHER, (II), P.O. Box 125, Forest Dale VT 05745. (802)247-4210 Fax: (802)247-4256. **Acquisitions**: Paul S. Eriksson, editor; Peggy Eriksson, associate publisher/co-editor. Estab. 1960. "We look for intelligence, excitement and saleability." Publishes hardcover and paperback originals. First novel print order: 3,000-5,000.
Needs: Mainstream. Published *The Headmaster's Papers*, by Richard A. Hawley; *The Year that Trembled*, by Scott Lax; and *Hand in Hand*, by Tauno Yliruusi.
How to Contact: Query first. Publishes ms an average of 6 months after acceptance.
Terms: Pays 10-15% in royalties; advance offered if necessary. Free book catalog.
Advice: "Our taste runs to serious fiction."

M. EVANS & CO., INC., (II), 216 E. 49th St., New York NY 10017. (212)688-2810. Fax: (212)486-4544. E-mail: mevans@spiynet.com. Contact: Editor. Estab. 1960. Publishes hardcover and trade paper nonfiction and a small fiction list. Publishes 30-40 titles each year.
Needs: "Small general trade publisher specializing in nonfiction titles on health, nutrition, diet, cookbooks, parenting, popular psychology." Published *A Fine Italian Hand*, by William Murray; and *Presumption*, by Julia Barnett.
How to Contact: Query first with outline/synopsis and 3 sample chapters. SASE. Agented fiction: 100%. Simultaneous submissions OK.
Terms: Pays in royalties and offers advance; amounts vary. Sends galleys to author. Publishes ms 6-12 months after acceptance.

FABER AND FABER, INC., (II), 53 Shore Rd., Winchester MA 01890.

- Farrar, Straus & Giroux purchased a majority stake in Faber & Faber, Inc., the US subsidiary of the British publisher Faber & Faber Ltd. Faber & Faber, Inc. no longer originates its own titles, but will publish and distribute titles acquired on the British side by Faber & Faber, Ltd.

✓ A FANFARE, (V), Imprint of Bantam Books, Division of Bantam Doubleday Dell, 1540 Broadway, New York NY 10036. (212)354-6500. Fax: (212)782-9523. **Acquisition:** Beth de Guzman, senior editor; Wendy McCurdy, senior editor; Stephanie Kip, editor. Fanfare's mission is "to publish a range of the best voices in women's fiction from brand new to established authors." **Publishes 10-15% previously unpublished writers/year.** Publishes 30 titles/year.
Needs: Publishes only romance and women's contemporary fiction. Adventure/romance, historical/romance, suspense/romance, western/romance. Length: 90,000-120,000 words. Recently published *The Unlikely Angel*, by Betina Krahn (historical romance); *Long After Midnight*, by Iris Johansen (romantic suspense); and *Stolen Hearts*, by Michelle Martin (contemporary romance).
How to Contact: Agented submissions only. Agented fiction 95%. Reports in 2-3 months on queries; 3-4 months on mss (accepted only upon request). Simultaneous submissions OK.
Terms: Royalty and advance negotiable. Publishes ms 12 months after acceptance.
Advice: "Be aware of what we publish and what our needs are in terms of length and content of manuscripts."

FANTAGRAPHICS BOOKS, (II, IV), 7563 Lake City Way NE, Seattle WA 98115. (206)524-1967. Fax: (206)524-2104. Publisher: Gary Groth. Estab. 1976. Publishes comic books, comics series and graphic novels. Books: offset printing; saddle-stitched periodicals and Smythe-sewn books; heavily illustrated. Publishes originals and reprints. Publishes 25 titles each month.
Needs: Comic books and graphic novels (adventure, fantasy, horror, mystery, romance, science, social parodies). "We look for subject matter that is more or less the same as you would find in mainstream fiction." Published *Blood of Palomar*, by Gilbert Hernandez; *The Dragon Bellows Saga*, by Stan Sakai; *Death of Speedy*; *Housebound with Rick Geary*; and *Little Nemo in Slumberland*.
How to Contact: Send a plot summary, pages of completed art (photocopies only) and character sketches. May send completed script if the author is willing to work with an artist of the publisher's choosing. Include cover letter and SASE. Reports in 1 month.
Terms: Pays in royalties of 8% (but must be split with artist) and advance.

✓ FARRAR, STRAUS & GIROUX, (III), 19 Union Square W., New York NY 10003. (212)741-6900. Fax: (212)633-2427. **Acquisitions**: Jonathan Galassi, editor-in-chief; Elisabeth Sifton, publisher, Hill & Wang (European literature, German literature in translation); John Glusman, executive editor (literary fiction); Rebecca Saleton, editorial director, North Point Press; Elisabeth Dyssegard, executive editor, Noonday; Ethan Nosowsky, editor (literary fiction); Rebecca Kurson, assistant editor (fiction). Publishes hardcover originals. Published new

CHECK THE CATEGORY INDEXES, located at the back of the book, for publishers interested in specific fiction subjects.

writers within the last year. Plans 2 first novels this year. Averages 120 hardcover titles/year. Receives 5,000 submissions/year.
Imprint(s): Hill & Wang, **The Noonday Press**, North Point Press and Farrar, Straus & Giroux Books for Young Readers (Sunburst Books, Aerial Fiction, Mirasol).
Needs: Open. No genre material. Publishes Alice McDermott, Nadine Gordimer, Mario Vargas Llosa, Richard Powers, Tom Wolfe, Deborah Eisenberg, Scott Turow and Susan Sontag.
How to Contact: Does not accept unsolicited mss. Query first (outline/synopsis and sample chapters). "Vast majority of fiction is agented." Reports in 2-3 months. Simultaneous submissions OK.
Terms: Pays royalties (standard, subject to negotiation). Offers advance. Sends galleys to author. Publishes ms 18 months after acceptance. Catalog for 9×12 SAE with 3 first class stamps.
Tips: "Study our style and list."

☑ **FARRAR, STRAUS & GIROUX/CHILDREN'S BOOKS, (I)**, 19 Union Square W., New York NY 10003. (212)741-6900. Fax: (212)633-2427. E-mail: remayes@fsgee.com. **Acquisitions**: Jonathan Galassi, editor-in-chief. Estab. 1946. "We publish original and well-written material for all ages." Number of titles: 50. Published new writers within the last year. Buys 25% agented fiction.
Needs: Children's picture books, juvenile novels, nonfiction. Published *Sheep in Wolves' Clothing*, by Satoshi Kitamura; *Remembering Mog*, by Colby Rodowsky; and *Starry Messenger*, by Peter Sis.
How to Contact: Submit outline/synopsis and 3 sample chapters, summary of ms and any pertinent information about author, author's writing, etc. Reports in 2 months on queries, 3 months on mss. Publishes ms 18-24 months after acceptance.
Terms: Pays in royalties; offers advance. Publishes ms 18 months after acceptance. Book catalog with 9×12 SASE and 96¢ postage.
Advice: "Study our list to avoid sending something inappropriate. Send query letters for long manuscripts; don't ask for editorial advice (just not possible, unfortunately); and send SASEs!"

☑ **FARTHEST STAR, (II)**, Imprint of Alexander Books, 65 Macedonia Rd., Alexander NC 28701. (828)252-9515. Fax: (828)255-8719. E-mail: barbara@obooks.com. Website: http://www.obooks.com (includes titles). **Acquisitions:** Barbara Blood, editor. Publishes trade paperback originals and reprints. Publishes 4 titles/year. Distributes titles through major distributors, mail order catalog and on the Web.
Needs: Science fiction. Recently published *Birthright: The Book of Man*, by Mike Resnick (science fiction reprint); and *Compleat Chance Purdue*, by Ross H. Spencer (mystery).
How to Contact: Query or submit 3 sample chapters with SASE. Reports in 1-2 months on queries. Simultaneous submissions OK.
Terms: Pays 12-15% royalty on wholesale price. Seldom offers advance. Publishes ms 1-2 years after acceptance. Writer's guidelines for #10 SASE with 2 first-class stamps. Book catalog for 8½×11 SASE with $1.01 first-class stamps.
Tips: "Your cover letter is very important. Most acquisition editors don't go past the cover letter."

FAWCETT, (I, II, III), Division of Random House/Ballantine, 201 E. 50th St., New York NY 10022. (212)751-2600. **Acquisitions**: Leona Nevler, editor-in-chief. Estab. 1955. Major publisher of mass market and trade paperbacks. Publishes paperback originals and reprints. Prints 160 titles annually. Encourages new writers. "Always looking for *great* first novels."
Imprint(s): Ivy, Crest, Gold Medal, Columbine and Juniper.
Needs: Mysteries. Published *Noelle*, by Diana Palmer; *Writing for the Moon*, by Kristin Hannah.
How to Contact: Query with SASE. Send outline and sample chapters for adult mass market. If ms is requested, simultaneous submissions OK. Prefers letter-quality. Reports in 2-4 months.
Terms: Pays usual advance and royalties. Publishes ms 1 year after acceptance.
Advice: "Gold Medal list consists of four paperbacks per month—usually three are originals."

FC2/BLACK ICE BOOKS, (I), Unit for Contemporary Literature, Illinois State University, Normal IL 61790-4241. (309)438-3582. Fax: (309)438-3523. E-mail: ckwhite@rs6000.cmp.ilstu.edu. Co-director: Curtis White. Estab. 1974. "Publisher of innovative fiction." Publishes hardcover and paperback originals. Books: perfect/Smyth binding; illustrations. Average print order: 2,200. First novel print order: 2,200. Published new writers within the last year. Plans 2 first novels this year. Averages 10 total titles, 10 fiction titles each year. Often critiques or comments on rejected mss.
Needs: Feminist, gay, literary, science fiction (cyberpunk), short story collections. Published *Cares of the Day*, by Ivan Webster (minority); *Angry Nights*, by Larry Fondation (literary); and *Little Sisters of the Apocalypse*, by Kit Reed (science fiction).
How to Contact: Accepts unsolicited mss. Query with outline/synopsis. Include 1-page bio, list of publishing credits. SASE. Agented fiction 5%. Reports on queries in 3 weeks. Simultaneous submissions OK.
Terms: Pays royalties of 8-10%; offers $100 advance. Sends galleys to author. Publishes ms 1 year after acceptance. Writer's guidelines for SASE.
Advice: "Be familiar with our list."

✔ **THE FEMINIST PRESS AT THE CITY UNIVERSITY OF NEW YORK**, City College, Wingate Building, Convent Ave. at 138th St., New York NY 10031. (212)650-8890. Fax: (212)650-8869. Website: http://www.web.gsvc.cuny.edu/feministpress (includes writer's guidelines, online catalog, teacher's resources). **Acquisitions**: Jean Casella, senior editor; Florence Howe, publisher; Sara Clough, assistant editor; Denise Maynard, children's. Estab. 1970. "Nonprofit, tax-exempt, education and publishing organization interested in changing the curriculum, the classroom and consciousness." Publishes hardcover and paperback reprints. "We use an acid-free paper, perfect-bind our books, four color covers; and some cloth for library sales if the book has been out of print for some time; we shoot from the original text when possible. We always include a scholarly and literary afterword, since we are introducing a text to a new audience. Average print run: 4,000." Publishes no original fiction; exceptions are anthologies and international works. Averages 10-15 total titles/year; 4-8 fiction titles/year (reprints of feminist classics only). Distributes titles through Consortium Book Sales and Distribution. Promotes titles through author tours, advertising, exhibits and conferences.

Needs: Children's, contemporary, ethnic, feminist, gay, lesbian, literary, regional, science fiction, translations, women's. Recently published *Apples From the Desert*, by Savyon Liebrecht (short stories, translation); *Confessions of Madame Psyche*, by Dorothy Bryant (novel); and *Mulberry and Peach*, by Hualing Nen (novel, translation).

How to Contact: Accepts unsolicited mss. Query first. Submit outline/synopsis and 1 sample chapter. Accepts queries/correspondence by fax. SASE. Reports in 1 month on queries; 3 months on mss. Simultaneous submissions OK.

Terms: Pays royalties of 10% of net sales; $100 advance; 10 author's copies. Sends galleys to author. Book catalog free on request.

🏆 **FIREBRAND BOOKS, (II)**, 141 The Commons, Ithaca NY 14850. (607)272-0000. Website: http://www.firebrandbooks.com. **Acquisitions**: Nancy K. Bereano, publisher. Estab. 1985. "Our audience includes feminists, lesbians, ethnic audiences, and other progressive people." Independent feminist and lesbian press. Publishes quality trade paperback originals. Averages 6-8 total titles each year.

- Firebrand has won the Lambda Literary Award Organization's Publisher's Service Award.

Needs: Feminist, lesbian. Published *The Gilda Stories*, by Jewelle Gomez (novel); and *Stone Butch Blues*, by Leslie Feinberg (novel).

How to Contact: Accepts unsolicited mss. Submit outline/synopsis and sample chapters or send complete ms with cover letter. SASE. Reports in 2 weeks on queries; 2 months on mss. Simultaneous submissions OK with notification.

Terms: Pays royalties. Publishes ms 1 year after acceptance.

FJORD PRESS, (II), P.O. Box 16349, Seattle WA 98116. (206)935-7376. Fax: (206)938-1991. E-mail: fjord@halcyon.com. Website: http://www.fjordpress.com/fjord. **Acquisitions:** Steven T. Murray, editor-in-chief. Estab. 1981. "We publish only literary novels of the highest quality." Publishes paperback originals and reprints. Books: acid-free paper; offset printing; perfect bound. Average print order: 2-3,000. First novel print order: 1,500-2,000. Published new writers within the last year. Plans 2 first novels this year. Publishes 4-6 total titles/year; 4 fiction titles.

Needs: Ethnic/multicultural (general, African-American), feminist, gay, lesbian, literary, mainstream/contemporary, mystery suspense (amateur sleuth only), regional (contemporary west), translations. Recently published *Runemaker*, by Tiina Nunnally (ethnic amateur sleuth); *Plenty Good Room*, by Teresa McClain-Watson (African-American mainstream); *Love Like Gumbo*, by Nancy Rawles (Creole family saga).

How to Contact: Send Query letter or query with synopsis and 1 sample chapter (20 pages maximum). Unsolicited queries/correspondence by e-mail OK. Include estimated word count and list of publishing credits. Include SASE for reply, return of ms. Reports in 1-2 months on queries; 2-3 months on mss. Simultaneous submissions OK.

Terms: Pays royalties of 8% minimum; 10% maximum. Pays advance; negotiable. Sends galleys to author. Publishes ms 7-24 months after acceptance. Guidelines and book catalog for #10 SASE or on website.

Advice: "We are picking up midlist authors who have been dumped by large corporate houses—we love it. Check your market carefully. Don't send us anything until you have looked at our books in your local or university library."

FLARE BOOKS, (II), Imprint of Avon Books, Div. of the Hearst Corp., 1350 Avenue of the Americas, New York NY 10019. (212)261-6800. Editor-in-Chief: Elise Howard. Estab. 1981. Small, young adult line. Publishes paperback originals and reprints. Plans 2-3 first novels this year. Averages 24 titles, all fiction each year.

Needs: Young adult (easy-to-read [hi-lo], problem novels, historical romance, spy/adventure), "very selective." Looking for contemporary fiction. No science fiction/fantasy, heavy problem novels, poetry. Published *Nothing But the Truth, A Documentary Novel*, by Avi; *Night Cries*, by Barbara Steiner; and *The Weirdo*, by Theodore Taylor.

How to Contact: Accepts unsolicited mss. Submit complete ms with cover letter (preferred) or outline/synopsis and 3 sample chapters. Agented fiction 75%. Reports in 3-4 weeks on queries; 3-4 months on mss. Simultaneous submissions OK.

Terms: Royalties and advance negotiable. Sends galleys to author. Writer's guidelines for #10 SASE. Book catalog for 9×12 SAE with 98¢ postage. "We run a young adult novel competition each year."

✓ **FOCUS PUBLISHING, INC., (II)**, 502 Third St. N.W., Bemidji MN 56601. (218)759-9817. Website: http://www.paulbunyan.net/focus. **Acquisitions:** Jan Haley, president. "Focus Publishing is a small press primarily devoted to Christian books appropriate to children and home-schooling families." Publishes hardcover and trade paperback originals and reprints. Publishes 4-6 titles/year.
Needs: Juvenile, picture books, religious, young adult. "We are looking for Christian books for men and young adults. Be sure to list your target audience." Recently published *The Gift*, by Jan Haley.
How to Contact: Query and submit synopsis with SASE. Reports in 2 months.
Terms: Pays 7-10% royalty on retail price. Publishes ms 1 year after acceptance. Book catalog free.
Advice: "I prefer SASE inquiries, synopsis and target markets. Please don't send 5 lbs. of paper with no return postage."

FORGE BOOKS, (I), Tom Doherty Associates, St. Martin's Press, 175 5th Ave., New York NY 10010. (212)388-0100. Fax: (212)388-0191. **Acquisitions**: Melissa Ann Singer, senior editor; Natalia Aponte, editor; Stephen de las Heras, assistant editor. Estab. 1993. "Midsize company that specializes in genre fiction, mainly thrillers, historicals and mysteries." Publishes hardcover and paperback originals. Published new writers within the last year. Plans 2-3 first novels this year. Averages 130 total titles, 129 fiction titles each year. Sometimes critiques or comments on rejected mss.
Imprint(s): TOR Books, Orb.
Needs: Erotica, historical, horror, mainstream/contemporary, mystery/suspense (amateur sleuth, cozy, police procedural, private eye/hardboiled), thriller/espionage, western (frontier saga, traditional). Plans anthology. Published *Relic*, by Douglas Preston and Lincoln Child (thriller); *Mirage*, by Soheir Khashoggi (contemporary fiction); *1812*, by David Nevin (historical); and *Billy Gashade*, by Loren D. Estleman.
How to Contact: Accepts unsolicited mss. Query with outline/synopsis and 5 sample chapters. Include estimated word count, bio and list of publishing credits. SASE for reply. Agented fiction 90%. Reports in 4 months on proposals. Simultaneous submissions OK.
Terms: Pays royalties. Advance $7,000 and up. Sends galleys to author. Publishes ms 9 months after acceptance.
Advice: "The writing mechanics must be outstanding for a new author to break in to today's market."

[A] **FOUL PLAY, (V)**, Imprint of W.W. Norton, 500 Fifth Ave., New York NY 10110. (212)354-5500. Fax: (212)869-0856. Website: http://www.wwnorton.com. **Acquisitions:** Candace Watt, editor. Estab. 1996. Publishes hardcover originals and paperback reprints. Publishes 6 titles/year.
Needs: Mystery, suspense.
How to Contact: Agented mss only.

FOUR WALLS EIGHT WINDOWS, (II), 39 W. 14th St., #503, New York NY 10011. (212)206-8965. E-mail: eightwind@aol.com. Website: http://www.fourwallseightwindows.com (includes complete catalog, featured books and ordering information). **Acquisitions**: John Oakes, publisher. Estab. 1986. "We are a small independent publisher." Publishes hardcover and paperback originals and paperback reprints. Books: quality paper; paper or cloth binding; illustrations sometimes. Average print order: 3,000-7,000. First novel print order: 3,000-5,000. Plans 1 first novel this year. Averages 18 total titles/year; approximately 9 fiction titles/year.

- Four Walls Eight Windows' books have received mention from the *New York Times* as "Notable Books of the Year" and have been nominated for *L.A. Times* fiction and nonfiction prizes.

Needs: Literary, nonfiction.
How to Contact: Does not accept unsolicited submissions. "Query letter accompanied by sample chapter, outline and SASE is best. Useful to know if writer has published elsewhere, and if so, where." Agented fiction 70%. Reports in 2 months. Simultaneous submissions OK. No electronic submissions.
Terms: Pays standard royalties; advance varies. Sends galleys to author. Publishes ms 1-2 years after acceptance. Book catalog free on request.
Advice: "We get 3,000 or so submissions a year: 1. Learn what our taste is, first; 2. Be patient."

✓ **FRIENDS UNITED PRESS, (I)**, 101 Quaker Hill Dr., Richmond IN 47374-1980. (765)962-7573. Fax: (765)966-1293. Website: http://www.fum.org. **Acquisitions**: Barbara Bennett Mays, editor/manager. Estab. 1973. "Friends United Press commits itself to energize and equip Friends and others through the power of the Holy Spirit to gather people into fellowship where Jesus Christ is known, loved and obeyed as teacher and Lord." Quaker Denominated House. Publishes paperback originals. Books: 60 lb. paper; perfect bound. Average print

INTERESTED IN A PARTICULAR GENRE? Check our new sections for: **Mystery/Suspense**, page 57; **Romance**, page 77; **Science Fiction & Fantasy**, page 95.

INSIDER REPORT

Four Walls Eight Windows: home for a few of today's most original voices

John Oakes

It's a good time for small presses. Despite the movement toward conglomeration and multi-national publishing, many small presses are posting record profits, and some have even outgrown the small press label. These scrappy publishers have embraced the merger climate by cultivating tight niches and picking up the books bigger houses won't carry. And the results at Four Walls Eight Windows have been no different.

In the push to concentrate subject matter, publisher John Oakes has been working extensively with writers who deal in what he calls "cutting edge speculative fiction." The term refers to writing that presents an imaginative alternative reality in a modern context, a genre savvy readers will note used to be labeled science fiction. Paul Di Filippo and *Slaughtermatic* author Steve Aylett embody this style at Four Walls.

"You have writers like George Orwell or William S. Burroughs who get deemed acceptable because they're not really science fiction," Oakes says. "But in fact they are science fiction. They deal with a world that's not our current one. I think any interesting writer takes reality and plays with it."

In 1996, Oakes's focus in this area led him to sign a contract with Gordon Lish, whom *Publishers Weekly* defines as having an "in-your-face eccentricity." The ten-book package included seven of Lish's previously released titles and three new books. Four Walls released the new works in the fall of each year, starting with *Epigraph* in 1996. The third book, *Arcade*, was released last fall.

The press's newest discovery is Steven Kotler, who is working with Four Walls editor JillEllyn Riley to produce *Angle Quickest for Flight*, a thriller due out in the spring of 1999. Of the 16 to 20 books Four Walls publishes in a year, typically only a few have first-time authors. To improve their odds, writers must be able to set themselves apart. As Oakes says, "We generally can't afford to groom authors. They've got to come to us with their hair cut."

Toward that end, aspiring authors should keep in mind how Oakes personally assesses a manuscript's potential. Liabilities include informality in correspondence, indirect cover letters, ignorance of Four Walls' specialties, and synopses of stories' plots.

"If you have to describe, 'Billy is a farmer . . .', already it's not for us," he says. "If you tried to describe the plots of many of our books, it would be impossible because the plot isn't about much. The writing and how writers present it is much more interesting to me."

Oakes's philosophy has worked. Since he and Dan Simon launched the small New York-based publishing house 12 years ago, it has gone from releasing 4 titles a year to 18. Four Walls' popular list, solid distribution and emphasis on subsidiary rights deals made 1998 its most successful year to date. Simon left Four Walls in October of 1995 to found Seven Stories Press, but Oakes has continued to guide Four Walls in a more competitive direction.

INSIDER REPORT, *Oakes*

The press's specialties include newer forays into popular science and business and an old reliable: politics. Last fall it released the Barney Rosset-edited *Evergreen Review Reader*, a compilation from the 1960s magazine on social criticism and counterculture politics.

"When we started out in 1987, we were trying to do a little bit of everything, always with a progressive underpinning," says Oakes. "I think our politics haven't changed one drop. But as far as publishing goes, we have gotten a little more focused."

And they've done it by necessity. In today's fiction market, having well-known authors is a must. The timing and the market are crucial. If an author's name isn't readily recognizable, a publisher must have exceptional publicity and distribution to release a successful book.

"Currently one of the problems is that you do a wonderful book and you can't get reviewed," Oakes says. "You can't find a spot on the shelves. There are 50,000 other titles that are demanding people's attention."

In this situation, small presses often find themselves in a catch-22. Books with enough critical acclaim and publicity to get noticed often risk getting picked up by a big house or co-opted. But books too far on the fringe, the ones safe from adoption by larger publishers, get ignored in the press and never make it off the shelves. Oakes estimates that 80 percent of his releases could be done at a large house: books such as the 500+-page cyclist's resource *Bike Cult* or *Fermat's Last Theorem* by Amir Aczel (see The Small Press Advantage in the introduction to this section).

After Four Walls released Aylett's *Slaughtermatic*, the hype spread quickly. *The New York Times Book Review* covered it, and the publicity put Aylett on the map. But *Slaughtermatic* didn't sell more than 10,000 copies, and the result sent a message to Oakes that no book is safe.

"Larger houses would have picked it up if they had known what kind of reviews he would get, but they wouldn't have signed him in the first place," Oakes says. "They wouldn't have realized that this is somebody really great."

Oakes also sifts through reviews and journals to find writers with original voices and styles relevant to the Four Walls catalogue. The most important consideration for success is the appropriateness of each author and subject for the house. A small press cannot risk publishing a book that's not right for it.

It can sound discouraging: the sheer number of books, the esoteric etiquette of individual publishers and the battle for known authors while developing writers get overlooked. But realize that not all publishers are created equal. In a dynamic market, Four Walls will continue to rely on both new and established voices to shape edifying books and delight its readers.

—*Brad Crawford*

order: 1,000. Averages 7 total titles, 1-2 fiction titles each year. Member of Protestant Church Publishers Association. Promotes titles through magazines.

Needs: Historical (Friends' history), religious (children's, inspirational). Recently published *For The Gift of A Friend*; *For the Love of a Friend*; and *For the Call of a Friend*, by Susan McCracken.

How to Contact: Accepts unsolicited mss. Submit complete ms with cover letter. Send SASE for reply, return of ms or send disposable copy of ms. Agented fiction 1%. Reports in 3 months. Simultaneous submissions OK. Sometimes critiques or comments on rejected mss.

Terms: Pays royalties of 7½% maximum. Sends galleys to author. Publishes ms 1 year after acceptance. Writer's guidelines for #10 SASE.

Advice: "Membership in the Society of Friends (Quakers) is preferred. Manuscript should be about Quakers,

Quaker history or theology, or about theology or spirituality that is in the realm of the theology and spirituality of Friends."

GAY SUNSHINE PRESS AND LEYLAND PUBLICATIONS, (IV), P.O. Box 410690, San Francisco CA 94141. Fax: (415)626-1802. Website: http://www.gaysunshine.com. **Acquisitions**: Winston Leyland, editor. Estab. 1970. Midsize independent press. Publishes hardcover and paperback originals. Books: natural paper; perfect-bound; illustrations. Average print order: 5,000-10,000.

- Gay Sunshine Press has received a Lambda Book Award for *Gay Roots* (volume 1), named "Best Book by a Gay or Lesbian Press."

Needs: Literary, experimental, translations—all gay male material only. "We desire fiction on gay themes of *high* literary quality and prefer writers who have already had work published in literary magazines. We also publish erotica—short stories and novels." Published *Partings at Dawn: An Anthology of Japanese Gay Literature from the 12th to the 20th Centuries*; and *Out of the Blue: Russia's Hidden Gay Literature—An Anthology.*
How to Contact: "Do not send an unsolicited manuscript." Query with SASE. Reports in 3 weeks on queries; 2 months on mss. Send $1 for catalog.
Terms: Negotiates terms with author. Sends galleys to author. Pays royalties or by outright purchase.
Advice: "We continue to be interested in receiving queries from authors who have book-length manuscripts of high literary quality. We feel it is important that an author know exactly what to expect from our press (promotion, distribution, etc.) before a contract is signed. Before submitting a query or manuscript to a particular press, obtain critical feedback on your manuscript from knowledgeable people. If you alienate a publisher by submitting a manuscript shoddily prepared/typed, or one needing very extensive rewriting, or one which is not in the area of the publisher's specialty, you will surely not get a second chance with that press."

LAURA GERINGER BOOKS, (II), Imprint of HarperCollins Children's Books, 10 E. 53rd St., New York NY 10022. (212)207-7000. Website: http://www.harpercollins.com. **Acquisitions:** Laura Geringer, editorial director. "We look for books that are out of the ordinary, authors who have their own definite take, and artists that add a sense of humor to the text." Publishes hardcover originals. **Published 5% previously unpublished writers/year.** Publishes 15-20 titles/year.
Needs: Adventure, fantasy, historical, humor, literary, picture books, young adult. Recently published *Zoe Rising*, by Pam Conrad (novel); and *The Leaf Men*, by William Joyce (picture book).
How to Contact: Query with SASE for picture books; submit complete ms with SASE for novels. Agented fiction 75%. Reports in 4 months on queries.
Terms: Pays 10-12½% on retail price. Advance varies. Publishes ms 6-12 months after acceptance for novels, 1-2 years after acceptance for picture books. Writer's guidelines for #10 SASE. Book catalog for 8×10 SAE with 3 first-class stamps.
Advice: "A mistake writers often make is failing to research the type of books an imprint publishes, therefore sending inappropriate material."

GESSLER PUBLISHING COMPANY, (IV), 10 E. Church Ave., Roanoke VA 24011. (703)345-1429. Fax: (540)342-7172. E-mail: gesslerco@aol.com. Website: http://www.gessler.com (includes company info., teacher activities, links). **Acquisitions**: Richard Kurshan, CEO. Estab. 1932. "Publisher/distributor of foreign language educational materials (primary/secondary schools)." Publishes paperback originals and reprints, videos and software. Averages 75 total titles each year. Distributes titles through education dealers and catalog.
Needs: "Foreign language or English as a Second Language." Needs juvenile, literary, preschool/picture book, short story collections, translations. Published *Don Quixote de la Mancha* (cartoon version of classic, in Spanish); *El Cid* (prose and poetry version of the classic, In Spanish); and *Les Miserables* (simplified version of Victor Hugo classic, in French).
How to Contact: Query first, then send outline/synopsis and 2-3 sample chapters; complete ms with cover letter. Agented fiction 10%. Reports on queries in 1 month; on mss in 6 weeks. Simultaneous and electronic (e-mail, fax) submissions OK. Sometimes comments on rejected ms.
Terms: Pay varies with each author and contract. Sends galleys to author. "Varies on time of submission and acceptance relating to our catalog publication date." Publishes ms 9 months after acceptance. Writer's guidelines not available. Book catalog free on request.
Advice: "We specialize in the foreign language market directed to teachers and schools. A book that would interest us has to be attractive to the market. A teacher would be most likely to create a book for us."

GODDESS DEAD PUBLICATIONS, (I,II), Damage, Inc., P.O. Box 46277, Los Angeles CA 90046. (213)850-0067. Fax (213)850-5894. **Acquisitions:** Tracey Lee Williams, owner. Estab. 1996. Publishes paperback originals. Books: perfect binding. Average print order: 500. First novel print order: 500. Averages 3-5 total titles, 3 fiction titles/year.
Needs: Experimental, feminist, literary, mainstream/contemporary.
How to Contact: Accepts unsolicited mss. Query with outline/synopsis. Unsolicited queries/correspondence by fax OK. Include bio and list of publishing credits. SASE for reply or return of ms. Reports in 2 months on queries; up to 6 months on mss. Simultaneous submissions OK.
Payment/Terms: Royalties and advance negotiable; pays author's copies. Sends galleys to author. Publishes

ms 6 months minimum after acceptance. Writer's guidelines free.
Advice: "Don't try to please me—just write your best stuff. Be unique, be unafraid."

GOOSE LANE EDITIONS, (II, IV), 469 King St., Fredericton, New Brunswick E3B 1E5 Canada. (506)450-4251. **Acquisitions**: Laurel Boone, acquisitions editor. Estab. 1957. Publishes hardcover and paperback originals and occasional reprints. Books: some illustrations. Average print run: 2,000. First novel print order: 1,500. Averages 14 total titles, 4-5 fiction titles each year. Distributes titles through General Distribution Services, Literary Press Group (Canada); Stoddart (US).

- Goose Lane author Lynn Coady won the Canadian Author's Association Air Canada Award for most promising author under 30 for her novel *Strange Heaven*. Goose Lane has won the Atlantic Booksellers' Association Booksellers' Choice Award and the Friends of American Writers Book Award for *English Lessons*, by Shauna Singh Baldwin and the Small Press Book Awards for *Season of Apples*, by Ann Copeland.

Needs: Contemporary, historical, literary, short story collections. "Not suitable for mainstream or mass-market submissions. No genres i.e.: modern and historical adventure, crime, modern and historical romance, science fiction, fantasy, westerns, confessional works (fictional and autobiographical), and thrillers and other mystery books." Recently published *Strange Heaven*, by Lynn Coady; *Man of Bone*, by Alan Cumyn; and *Brennen Siding Trilogy*, by Herb Curtis.
How to Contact: Considers unsolicited mss; outline or synopsis and 30-50 page sample. Query first. SASE "with Canadian stamps, International Reply Coupons, cash, check or money order. No U.S. stamps please." Reports in 6 months. Simultaneous submissions OK.
Terms: Pays royalties of 8% minimum; 12% maximum. Average advance: $100-200, negotiable. Sends galleys to author. Writers guidelines for 9×12 SAE and IRC.
Advice: "We do not usually consider submissions from outside Canada."

GRAYWOLF PRESS, (III), 2402 University Ave., Suite 203, St. Paul MN 55114. (612)641-0077. Fax: (612)641-0036. Website: http://www.graywolfpress.org. Editor/Publisher: Fiona McCrae. **Acquisitions**: Jeffrey Shotts. Estab. 1974. "Graywolf Press is an independent, nonprofit publisher dedicated to the creation and promotion of thoughtful and imaginative contemporary literature essential to a vital and diverse culture." Growing small literary press, nonprofit corporation. Publishes hardcover and paperback originals and paperback reprints. Books: acid-free quality paper; offset printing; hardcover and soft binding; illustrations occasionally. Average print order: 3,000-10,000. First novel print order: 2,000-6,000. Averages 18-20 total titles, 6-8 fiction titles each year.

- Graywolf Press books have won numerous awards.

Needs: Literary, and short story collections. Literary fiction; no genre books (romance, western, science fiction, suspense). Published *The Apprentice*, by Lewis Libby (novel); *Watershed*, by Percival Everett (novel); and *Rainy Lake*, by Mary François Rockcastle (novel).
How to Contact: Query with SASE. Reports in 3 months. Simultaneous submissions OK. Occasionally critiques rejected mss.
Terms: Pays in royalties of 7½-10%; negotiates advance and number of author's copies. Sends galleys to author. Publishes ms 18 months after acceptance. Free book catalog. Guidelines for #10 SASE.

GREENE BARK PRESS, (II), P.O. Box 1108, Bridgeport CT 06601. (203)372-4861. E-mail: greenebark@aol.com. Website: http://www.bookworld.com/greenebark. **Acquisitions:** Michele Hofbauer, associate publisher. "We only publish children's fiction—all subjects, but in reading picture book format appealing to ages 3-9 or all ages." Publishes hardcover originals. **Publishes 60% previously unpublished writers/year.** Publishes 5 titles/year. Distributes titles through Baker & Taylor, Partners Book Distributing and Quality Books. Promotes titles through ads, trade shows (national and regional), direct mail campaigns.
Needs: Juvenile. Recently published *Molly Meets Mona & Friends*, by Gladys Walker (hardcover picture book).
How to Contact: Submit complete ms with SASE. Does not accept queries or ms by e-mail. Reports in 3 months on mss. Simultaneous submissions OK.
Terms: Pays 10-15% royalty on wholesale price. Publishes ms 1 year after acceptance. Writer's guidelines and book catalog with SASE.
Advice: Audience is "children who read to themselves and others. Mothers, fathers, grandparents, godparents who read to their respective children, grandchildren. Include SASE, be prepared to wait, do not inquire by telephone."

GREENWILLOW BOOKS, (III), Imprint of William Morrow & Co., Division of Hearst Books, 1350 Avenue of the Americas, New York NY 10019. (212)261-6500. Website: http://www.williammorrow.com. Estab. 1974. "Greenwillow Books publishes quality hardcover books for children." Publishes hardcover originals and reprints. **Publishes 1% previously unpublished writers/year.** Publishes 70-80 titles/year.
Needs: Juvenile, picture books: fantasy, historical, humor, literary, mystery. Recently published *The Cuckoo's Child*, by Suzanne Freeman; *No Pretty Pictures: A Child of War*, by Anita Lobel; and *Mud Flat April Fool*, by James Stevenson.
How to Contact: Reports in 3 months on mss. Agented fiction 70%. Simultaneous submissions OK.

INSIDER REPORT

Josip Novakovich: on the enjoyment of writing fiction

Josip Novakovich's writing is compared to the work of Tolstoy, Gogol, Nabokov and Kafka. According to *The New York Times Book Review*, this is not merely due to the gravity of its subject matter (life in the war-torn Balkans) and his own life (as an emigre in the U.S.), but because it combines "originality, experience and insight."

Credit: Jeanette Novakovich

Josip Novakovich

Novakovich's latest collection of short stories, *Salvation and Other Disasters* (Graywolf Press, 1998), offers an honest and much needed perspective on life in his native Croatia—a part of the world most of us know only through news of its violence. In addition to being poignant and, at times, disturbing, the stories reinforce Novakovich's reputation as one of the great short story writers of our time.

Novakovich has published another story collection called *Yolk* (Graywolf Press, 1995); and a book of essays entitled *Apricots from Chernobyl* (Graywolf Press, 1995). He's also written two instructional books on writing fiction—*Fiction Writer's Workshop* (Story Press, 1995) and *Writing Fiction Step by Step* (Story Press, 1998). He won the 1997 Whiting Writers' Award, an Ingram Merrill Award, the Richard Margolis Prize for Socially Important Writing, and a NEA Fellowship for Fiction Writing. Currently he teaches writing at the University of Cincinnati.

Can you describe your writing practice?
I wish I had one. I usually write three or four days a week, but I can't predict which ones. You know, I have kids and I teach so it's difficult. I write in spurts, as I know a lot of writers do. This ideology that you have to write every day is really just a Protestant work ethic and I don't think it needs to be taken that seriously.

Where do find most of your story ideas?
I used to get my story ideas from memory, but I've pretty much exhausted that source. Now I hunt for stories artificially, through observation or when I hear something unusual. Sometimes if I have two separate stories that aren't working I'll put them together and try to work with them that way. And I need more than just a story idea. I also need character sketches, setting ideas, etc., and so I combine all of those elements with the idea and form a story that way.

Many people take writing very seriously. Can you suggest ways that a person can make writing more enjoyable?
In the beginning of a story it's easy to be playful and carefree. Then later on when all of the elements of the story are laid out and need to be harmonized, it becomes more difficult

INSIDER REPORT, *Novakovich*

to have fun with the writing. As the story progresses, it's easy for the writer to worry and writing becomes a labor rather than enjoyment. It's hard not to take it seriously sometimes, especially when you've been working on a story for a while and you are involved with it.

Often I tell my students to take several ideas that don't have much to do with each other and put them together to write a story. The absurdity of putting those two ideas together leads to enjoyment. It's good even in the middle of the story to start playing and trying new ideas. And especially now, since we have the stories on disks or on our computers, there's no reason to feel unsafe or worry about experimenting with a story.

What is the most enjoyable part of writing fiction for you?
I used to enjoy the final revision because there is a sensation of safety in revision. You already have the ideas and structure and other elements down, and revision is the time to put the finishing touches on the work. Now I enjoy the original drafts the most, the experimenting with new ideas.

Which part of writing fiction is your least favorite?
I hate spell checking and I hate getting rejections. Though I get fewer of those now because I don't send as many things out. And maybe I write better than I used to.

How has getting your work published changed your writing and the way you feel about your writing?
Getting published means dealing with editors. And they've clipped my wings in some ways, made it less fun. I try to forget about what editors want so the writing is fun, but that is hard to do. I do write best when I have fun and when I don't worry about it as much.

What's the biggest writing problem you hear about from your students? And what's your advice to them?
Usually I have more complaints about their work than they do about their own. Honestly though, beginning writers' stories usually move too fast. If I say it takes me two weeks to write a story, beginning writers usually say, "It takes that long?" And more advanced writers usually say, "That's all?" Most beginning writers' scenes are not developed enough—they summarize a lot, psychologize a lot. Professional writers on the other hand linger on detail. So I suggest to beginning writers that they slow down and have patience with their scenes.

—*Wendy Knerr*

Terms: Pays 10% royalty on wholesale price for first-time authors. Advance varies. Publishes ms 2 years after acceptance. Writer's guidelines for #10 SASE. Book catalog for $2 and 9×12 SAE.

GREYCLIFF PUBLISHING CO., (II, IV), P.O. Box 1273, Helena MT 59722. (406)443-1888. Fax: (406)443-0788. **Acquisitions:** Gary LaFontaine, partner. Estab. 1985. "Small independent publisher with Montana novel series." Publishes hardcover and paperback originals and hardcover and paperback reprints. Books: 60 lb. paper; illustrations in nonffiction. Average print order: 2,000. First novel print order: 3,000. Published new writers within the last year. Averages 6 total titles, 2 fiction titles/year. Member of SPAN and the Rocky Mountain Booksellers Association.

Needs: Montana only. Adventure, ethnic/multicultural (Native American), family saga, historical, literary, mainstream/contemporary, mystery/suspense, regional (Montana), short story collections, western. Recently published *Queen of the Legal Tender Saloon*, by Eileen Clarke. Publishes the Greycliff Montana novel series.
How to Contact: Accepts unsolicited mss. Submit complete manuscript with cover letter. Unsolicited queries/correspondence by fax OK. Include estimated word count, 100-word bio, Social Security number and list of publishing credits. Send SASE for reply or return of mss. Reports in 1 month on queries; 2 months on mss. Simultaneous submissions OK. Sometimes comments on rejected mss.
Payment/Terms: Pays in royalities. Average advance: $500. Sends galleys to author. Publishes ms 18 months after acceptance. Book catalog for $1 plus SASE.
Advice: "We love Montana. We publish for a large group of people who also believe that this state is special. We want engrossing novels set in Montana."

GROLIER PUBLISHING, (II), Grolier Inc., Sherman Turnpike, Danbury CT 06813. (203)797-3500. Fax: (203)797-3197. Estab. 1895. "Grolier Publishing is a leading publisher of reference, educational and children's books. We provide parents, teachers and librarians with the tools they need to enlighten children to the pleasure of learning and prepare them for the road ahead." Publishes hardcover and trade paperback originals.
Imprint(s): Children's Press, Franklin Watts, **Orchard Books**.
Needs: Juvenile, picture books.
How to Contact: Prefers to work with unagented authors. Reports in 4 months on proposals. Simultaneous submissions OK.
Terms: Pays royalty for established authors; makes outright purchase for first-time authors. Advance varies. Publishes ms 18 months after acceptance. Writer's guidelines free. Book catalog for 9×12 SAE and $3 postage.

GRYPHON PUBLICATIONS, (I, II), P.O. Box 209, Brooklyn NY 11228. (718)646-6126 (after 6 pm EST). **Acquisitions**: Gary Lovisi, owner/editor. Estab. 1983. Publishes hardcover and paperback originals and trade paperback reprints. Books: bond paper; offset printing; perfect binding. Average print order: 500-1,000. Published new writers within the last year. Plans 2 first novels this year. Averages 10-15 total titles, 12 fiction titles each year.
Imprint(s): Gryphon Books, Gryphon Doubles.
Needs: Mystery/suspense (private eye/hardboiled, crime), science fiction (hard science/technological, soft/sociological). No horror, romance or westerns. Published *The Dreaming Detective*, by Ralph Vaughn (mystery-fantasy-horror); *The Woman in the Dugout*, by Gary Lovisi and T. Arnone (baseball novel); and *A Mate for Murder*, by Bruno Fischer (hardboiled pulp). Publishes Gryphon Double novel series.
How to Contact: "I am not looking for novels now but will see a *1-page synopsis* with SASE." Include estimated word count, 50-word bio, short list of publishing credits, "how you heard about us." Send SASE. Do not send ms. Agented fiction 5-10%. Reports in 2-4 weeks on queries; 1-2 months on mss. Simultaneous and electronic submissions OK (with hard copy—disk in ASCII). Often critiques or comments on rejected mss.
Terms: For magazines, $5-45 on publication plus 2 contributor's copies; for novels/collections payment varies and is much more. Sends galleys to author. Publishes ms 1-3 years after acceptance. Writers guidelines and book catalog for SASE.
Advice: "I am looking for better and better writing, more cutting-edge material with *impact*! Keep it lean and focused."

GUERNICA EDITIONS, (III, IV), P.O. Box 117, Toronto, Ontario M63 2WC Canada. (416)658-9888. Fax: (416)657-8885. Website: http://www.ourworld.compuserve.com/Homepages/Guernica (includes authors, titles). **Acquisitions**: Antonio D'Alfonso, editor. Umberto Claudio, fiction editor. Estab. 1978. Publishes paperback originals. Books: offset printing; perfect binding. Average print order: 1,500. Average first novel print order: 1,000. **Publishes 1 previously unpublished writer/year.** Plans to publish 1 first novel this year. Publishes 16-20 total titles each year. Promotes titles through direct mail and advertising.
Needs: Contemporary, ethnic, literary, translations of foreign novels. Looking for novels about women and ethnic subjects. No unsolicited works. Recently published *Feast of the Dead*, by Anthony Fragola (short stories); *Impala*, by Carole David (novel); and *A House on the Piazza*, by Kenny Marotta (short stories).
How to Contact: Query first. Does not accept or return unsolicited mss. IRCs. 100% of fiction is agented. Reports in 6 months. Electronic submissions via IBM WordPerfect disks.
Terms: Pays royalties of 7-10% and 10 author's copies. Book catalog for SAE and $5 postage. (Canadian stamps only).
Advice: Publishing "short novels (150 pages or less)."

ROBERT HALE LIMITED, (II), Clerkenwell House, 45/47 Clerkenwell Green, London EC1R 0HT England. Fax: 0171-490-4958. Publishes hardcover and trade paperback originals and hardcover reprints. **Publishes approximately 50 previously unpublished writers/year.**

Needs: Historical (not U.S. history), mainstream and western. Length: 40,000-150,000 words. Recently published *The Big Brown Bear*, by Roben Alegant (mainstream); *Mexican Hat*, by Michael McGarrety (crime); and *Mischief*, by Amanda Quick (historical romance).

How to Contact: Send cover letter, synopsis or brief summary and 2 sample chapters. Unsolicited queries/correspondence by fax OK.

Advice: "Write well and have a strong plot!"

HAMPTON ROADS PUBLISHING COMPANY, INC., (II, IV), 134 Burgess Ln., Charlottesville VA 22902. (804)296-2772. Fax: (804)296-5096. E-mail: hrpc@hrpub.com. Website: http://www.hrpub.com (includes writer's guidelines, authors, titles, synopsis of books, message board, guest book). **Acquisitions**: Frank DeMarco, chairman and chief editor. Estab. 1989. Small company that publishes and distributes hardcover and paperback originals on subjects including metaphysics, health, complementary medicine, visionary fiction and other related topics. "We work as a team to produce the best books we are capable of producing which will impact, uplift and contribute to positive change in the world. We publish what defies or doesn't quite fit the usual genres. We are noted for visionary fiction." Average print order: 3,000-5,000. **Publishes 6-10 previously unpublished writers/year.** Averages 30 total titles/year, 5-6 fiction titles/year. Distributes titles through distributors. Promotes titles through advertising, representatives, author signings and radio-TV interviews with authors.

Needs: Literary, New Age/mystic/spiritual, psychic/supernatural/occult. Looking for "visionary fiction, past-life fiction, based on actual memories." Recently published *The Mt. Pelée Redemption*, by Stephen Hawley Martin (visionary); *Northumberland Dreaming*, by Mary Rhees Mercker (past-life); and *The Mole and the Owl*, by Charles Duffie (visionary).

How to Contact: Accepts unsolicited mss. Query first. Unsolicited queries/correspondence by e-mail and fax OK. Include description of book. Send SASE for reply, return of ms or send disposable copy of ms (preferred). Agented fiction 5%. Reports in 3-4 weeks on queries; 3-5 months on mss. Simultaneous submissions OK.

Terms: Pays in royalties; advance is negotiable. Sends galleys to author.

Advice: "Send us something new and different. Be patient. Sometimes we are slow."

HARCOURT BRACE & COMPANY, (III), 525 B St., Suite 1900, San Diego CA 92101. (619)699-6810. Fax: (619)699-6777. Publisher: Louise Pelan. **Acquisitions**: Diane D'Andrade, executive editor (general fiction); Jeannette Larson, editor (general fiction); Allyn Johnston, editorial director of Harcourt Brace Children's Books; Linda Zuckerman, editorial director of Browndeer Press; Elizabeth Van Doren, editorial director of Gulliver Books; Anne Davies, editor of Gulliver Books; Paula Wiseman, editorial director of Silver Whistle. Publishes hardcover originals and paperback reprints. Averages 150 titles/year. Publishes "very few" new writers/year.

Imprint(s): Harcourt Brace Children's Books, Gulliver Books, Browndeer Press, Red Wagon Books and Silver Whistle.

- Books published by Harcourt Brace & Co. have received numerous awards including the Caldecott and Newbery medals and selections as the American Library Association's "Best Books for Young Adults." Note that the publisher only accepts manuscripts through an agent. Unagented writers may query only.

Needs: Nonfiction for all ages, picture books for very young children, historical, mystery. Recently published *To Market, To Market*, by Ann Miranda; *Antarctic Antics*, by Judy Sierra; *Armageddon Summer*, by Bruce Coville and Jan Yolen; and *Count On Me*, by Alice Provensen.

How to Contact: Query first. Submit through agent only. No unsolicited mss.

Terms: Terms vary according to individual books; pays on royalty basis. Catalog for 9×12 SASE.

Advice: "Read as much current fiction as you can; familiarize yourself with the type of fiction published by a particular house; interact with young people to obtain a realistic picture of their concerns, interests and speech patterns."

HARCOURT BRACE & COMPANY, Children's Books Division, (II), 525 B St., Suite 1900, San Diego CA 92101. (619) 231-6616. Fax: (619)699-6777. E-mail: lpelan@harcourtbrace.com. **Acquisitions:** Manuscript Submissions. "Harcourt Brace & Company owns some of the world's most prestigious publishing imprints—which distinguish quality products for the juvenile, educational, scientific, technical, medical, professional and trade markets worldwide." Publishes hardcover originals and trade paperback reprints.

Imprint(s): Harcourt Brace Children's Books, Gulliver Books, Gulliver Green, Browndeer Press, Silver Whistle, Red Wagon, Voyager and Odyssey Paperbacks, Magic Carpet and Libros Viajeros.

Needs: Childrens/juvenile, young adult. Recently published *The Many Troubles of Andy Russell*, by David Adler (middle grade); *Armageddon Summer*, by Bruce Coville and Jane Yolen (young adult); and *Pictures 1918*, by Jeanette Ingold (young adult).

How to Contact: Query first. No phone calls.

HARLEQUIN ENTERPRISES, LTD., (II, IV), 225 Duncan Mill Rd., Don Mills, Ontario M3B 3K9 Canada. (416)445-5860. Website: http://www.romance.net (includes product listings, author information, a full

range of related information). Chairman and CEO: Brian E. Hickey. President and COO: Stuart J. Campbell. Vice President Editorial: Isabel Swift. Editorial Director Harlequin, Gold Eagle, MIRA, Worldwide Library: Randall Toye; Silhouette, Steeple Hill: Tara Gavin. Estab. 1949. Publishes paperback originals and reprints. Books: Newsprint paper; web printing; perfect-bound. Published new writers within the last year. Number of titles: Averages 700/year. Distributes titles through retail market, direct mail market and overseas through operating companies. Promotes titles through trade and consumer advertising: print, radio, TV. Buys agented and unagented fiction.
Imprint(s): Harlequin, Silhouette, MIRA, Gold Eagle, Worldwide Mysteries, Steeple Hill.
Needs: Romance, heroic adventure, mystery/suspense (romantic suspense *only*). Will accept nothing that is not related to the desired categories.
How to Contact: Send query letter or send outline and first 50 pages (2 or 3 chapters) or submit through agent with SASE (Canadian). No simultaneous submissions. Reports in 6 weeks on queries; 2 months on mss.
Terms: Offers royalties, advance. Must return advance if book is not completed or is unacceptable. Sends galleys to author. Publishes ms 1 year after acceptance. Guidelines available.
Advice: "The quickest route to success is to follow directions for submissions: Query first. We encourage first novelists. Before sending a manuscript, read as many current Harlequin titles as you can. It's very important to know the genre and the series most appropriate for your submission." Submissions for Harlequin Romance and Harlequin Presents should go to: Mills & Boon Limited Eton House, 18-24 Paradise Road, Richmond, Surrey TW9 1SR United Kingdom, Attn: Karin Stoecker; Superromances: Paula Eykelhof, senior editor, (Don Mills address above); Temptation: Birgit Davis-Todd, senior editor (Don Mills address). American Romances and Intrigue: Debra Matteucci, senior editor and editorial coordinator, Harlequin Books, 6th Floor, 300 E. 42 Street, New York, NY 10017. Silhouette and Steeple Hill submissions should also be sent to the New York office, attention Tara Gavin. MIRA submissions to Dianne Moggy, senior editor (Don Mills address); Gold Eagle and Worldwide Mysteries submissions to Feroze Mohammed, senior editor (Don Mills address). "The relationship between the novelist and editor is regarded highly and treated with professionalism."

✔ **HARPERCOLLINS CHILDREN'S BOOKS, (II)**, HarperCollins Publishers, 10 E. 53rd St., New York NY 10022. (212)207-7000. Senior Vice President/Publisher: Susan Katz. Senior Vice President/Associate Publisher/Editor-in-Chief: Kate Jackson. **Acquisitions**: Joanna Cotler, vice president/editorial director, Joanna Cotler Books; Michael di Capua, vice president/publisher, Michael di Capua Books; Laura Geringer, vice president/editorial director, Laura Geringer Books; Mary Alice Moore, vice president/editorial director, HarperFestival; Ginee Seo, editorial director, Harper Trophy; Executive Editors: Sally Doherty, Kate M. Jackson, Ginee Seo, Phoebe Yen and Robert O. Warren. Publishes hardcover trade titles and paperbacks.
Needs: Picture books, easy-to-read, middle-grade, teenage and young adult novels; fiction, fantasy, animal, sports, spy/adventure, historical, science fiction, problem novels and contemporary. Published Harper: *Walk Two Moons*, by Sharon Creech (ages 8-12); *The Best School Year Ever*, by Barbara Robinson (ages 8 up); Harper Trophy (paperbacks): *Catherine, Called Birdy*, by Karen Cushman (ages 12 and up). Also publishes The Danger Guys series by Tony Abbott (ages 7-10).
How to Contact: Query; submit complete ms; submit outline/synopsis and sample chapters; submit through agent. SASE for query, ms. Please identify simultaneous submissions. Reports in 2-3 months.
Terms: Average 10% in royalties. Royalties on picture books shared with illustrators. Offers advance. Publishes novel 1 year; picture books 2 years after acceptance. Writer's guidelines and book catalog for SASE.
Advice: "Write from your own experience and the child you once were. Read widely in the field of adult and children's literature. Realize that writing for children is a difficult challenge. Read other young adult novelists as well as adult novelists. Pay attention to styles, approaches, topics. Be willing to rewrite, perhaps many times. We have no rules for subject matter, length or vocabulary but look instead for ideas that are fresh and imaginative. Good writing that involves the reader in a story or subject that has appeal for young readers is also essential. One submission is considered by all imprints."

HARPERCOLLINS PUBLISHERS, (V), 10 E. 53rd St., New York NY 10022. (212)207-7000. Website: http://www.harpercollins.com. **Acquisitions**: Joelle Delbourgo, senior vice president, associate publisher, editor-in-chief. "HarperCollins, one of the largest English language publishers in the world, is a broad-based publisher with strengths in academic, business and professional, children's, educational, general interest, and religious and spiritual books, as well as multimedia titles." Publishes hardcover and paperback originals and paperback reprints. Trade publishes more than 500 titles/year.

FOR EXPLANATIONS OF THESE SYMBOLS,
SEE THE INSIDE FRONT AND BACK COVERS OF THIS BOOK.

Imprint(s): Harper Adult Trade; Harper Audio, Harper Business, **HarperLibros**, **HarperPaperbacks**, **Harper-Perennial**, **Harper Children's Books**, HarperSan Francisco, Regan Books, Cliff Street Books, HarperEntertainment, HarperResource, Westview Press, **Zondervan Publishing House**.
Needs: Adventure, fantasy, gothic, historical, mystery, science fiction, suspense, western, literary. "We look for a strong story line and exceptional literary talent." Recently published *The Tennis Partner*, by Abraham Verghese; *The Professor and the Madman*, by Simon Winchester; *I Know This Much Is True*, by Wally Lamb; *The Antelope Wife*, by Louise Erdrich; *Cloudsplitter*, by Russell Banks; and *The Soul of Sex*, by Thomas Moore.
How to Contact: *No unsolicited queries or mss.* Agented submissions only. Reports on solicited queries in 6 weeks.
Terms: Pays standard royalties. Advance negotiable.
Advice: "We do not accept any unsolicited material."

HARPERCOLLINS PUBLISHERS (CANADA) LIMITED, (II), 55 Avenue Rd., Suite 2900, Toronto, Ontario M5R 3L2 Canada. (416)975-9334. **Acquisitions**: Iris Tupholme, vice president/publisher/editor-in-chief. Publishes hardcover originals and reprints, trade paperback originals and reprints, mass market paperback reprints. Publishes 40-60 titles/year.
Needs: Ethnic, experimental, feminist, juvenile, literary, mainstream/contemporary, picture books, religious, short story collections, young adult. Recently published *Any Known Blood*, by Lawrence Hill (novel).
How to Contact: "Query first, including a self-addressed envelope with appropriate Canadian postage or international postal coupons. We do not accept unsolicited mss."
Terms: Offers from $1,500 to over six figures advance. Publishes book 18 months after acceptance.

HARPERCOLLINS PUBLISHERS (NEW ZEALAND) LIMITED, (IV), P.O. Box 1, Auckland, New Zealand. **Acquisitions**: Ian Watt, publisher. Averages 4-6 fiction titles/year (20-25 nonfiction).
Imprint(s): Flamingo.
Needs: Adult fiction: Flamingo imprint; Junior fiction: 8-11 years. Length: Flamingo: 40,000 + words; Junior: 15-17,000 words.
How to Contact: Full ms preferred.
Terms: Pays royalties. "Write and ask for guidelines."
Advice: "It helps if the author and story have New Zealand connections/content."

HARPERLIBROS, (III), Imprint of HarperCollins Publishers, 10 E. 53rd St., New York NY 10022. (212)207-7000. Fax: (212)207-7145. Website: http://www.harpercollins.com. **Acquisitions:** Terry Karten, editorial director. Estab. 1994. "HarperLibros offers Spanish language editions of selected HarperCollins titles, sometimes reprints, sometimes new books that are published simultaneously in English and Spanish. The list mirrors the English-language list of HarperCollins in that we publish both literary and commercial fiction and nonfiction titles including all the different HarperCollins categories, such as self-help, spirituality, etc." Publishes hardcover and trade paperback originals. Publishes 10 titles/year.
Imprint(s): Harper Arco Iris (Jennifer Pasanen) (children's).
Needs: Literary.
How to Contact: Query. *No unsolicited mss.*
Terms: Pays variable royalty on net price. Advance varies. Publishes ms 1 year after acceptance.

HARPERPAPERBACKS, (V), Division of HarperCollins Publishers, 10 E. 53rd St., New York NY 10022. (212)207-7000. Fax: (212)207-7759. **Acquisitions**: Carolyn Marino, editorial director; Jessica Lichtenstein, fiction editor; Laura Cifelli, fiction editor (romantic fiction); Leslie Stern, fiction editor. Publishes paperback originals and reprints. Published new writers within the last year.
Imprint(s): HarperChoice.
Needs: Mainstream/contemporary, mystery/suspense, romance (contemporary, historical, romantic suspense), thriller/espionage.
How to Contact: Query by letter or agent. No unsolicited mss accepted. Unsolicited queries/correspondence by fax OK.
Terms: Pays advance and royalties.

HARPERPERENNIAL, (V), Imprint of HarperCollins Publishers, 10 E. 53rd St., New York NY 10036. (212)207-7000. Website: http://www.harpercollins.com. **Acquisitions:** Susan Weinberg, senior vice president/publisher. Estab. 1963. "HarperPerennial publishes a broad range of adult fiction and nonfiction paperbacks." Publishes trade paperback originals and reprints. Publishes 100 titles/year.
Needs: Ethnic, feminist, literary. "Don't send us novels—go through hardcover." Published *Lying On the Couch*, by Irwin D. Yalom (psycho-thriller novel); *American Pie*, by Michael Lee West (novel); and *Bird Girl and the Man Who Followed the Sun*, by Velma Wallis (fiction/native American studies).
How to Contact: Agented submissions only. Reports in 2 weeks on queries; 1 month on mss.
Terms: Pays 5-7½% royalty. Advance varies. Publishes ms 6 months after acceptance. Book catalog free.
Advice: Audience is general reader—high school, college. "Call and get the name of an editor and they will

look at it. Usually an editor is listed in a book's acknowledgments. You should address your submission to an editor or else it will probably be returned."

☑ **HARVEST HOUSE PUBLISHERS, (II, IV)**, 1075 Arrowsmith, Eugene OR 97402-9197. (541)343-0123. Editorial Manager: LaRae Weikert. Editorial Director: Carolyn McCready. Estab. 1974. "The foundation of our publishing program is to publish books that 'help the hurts of people' and nurture spiritual growth." Midsize independent publisher. Publishes hardcover and paperback originals and reprints. Books: 40 lb. ground wood paper; offset printing; perfect binding; average print order: 10,000; first novel print order: 10,000-15,000. Averages 120 total titles, 6 fiction titles each year.

How to Contact: No longer accepting unsolicited ms. Recommends using Evangelical Christian Publishers Association website (www.ecpa.org) or the Writer's Edge.

HELICON NINE EDITIONS, (I, II), Subsidiary of Midwest Center for the Literary Arts, Inc., P.O. Box 22412, Kansas City MO 64113. (816)753-1095. **Acquisitions**: Gloria Vando Hickok, publisher/editor. Estab. 1990. Small press publishing poetry, fiction, creative nonfiction and anthologies. Publishes paperback originals. Books: 60 lb. paper; offset printing; perfect-bound; 4-color cover. Average print order: 1,000-5,000. Plans 4 total titles, 2-4 fiction titles this year. Also publishes one-story chapbooks called *feuillets*, which come with envelope, 250 print run. Distributes titles through Baker & Taylor, The Booksource, Brodart, Ingrams, Follett (library acquisitions), Midwest Library Service. Promotes titles through reviews, readings, radio and television interviews.

- Helicon Nine Editions sponsors the annual Willa Cather Fiction Prize—a $1,000 prize plus publication. Send a SASE for guidelines. Helicon Nine author Anne Whitney Pierce won the O'Henry Award for *Galaxy Girls: Wonder Woman*.

Needs: Contemporary, ethnic, experimental, literary, short story collections, translations. "We're only interested in fine literature." Nothing "commercial." Published *Knucklebones*, by Annabel Thomas (short story collection); *Return to Sender*, by Ann Slegman (novel); and *Eternal City*, by Molly Shapiro (short story collection). Published new writers within the last year.

How to Contact: Does not accept unsolicited mss. Query first. SASE. Reports in 1 week on queries.

Terms: Pays advance and royalties, author's copies. "Individual arrangement with author." Sends galleys to author. Publishes ms 6-12 months after acceptance.

Advice: "We accept short story collections. We welcome new writers and first books. Submit a clean, readable copy in a folder or box—paginated with title and name on each page. Also, do not pre-design book, i.e., no illustrations. We'd like to see books that will be read 50-100 years from now."

HOHM PRESS, (II), P.O. Box 2501, Prescott AZ 86302. (520)717-1779. E-mail: pinedr@goodnet.com. **Acquisitions:** Regina Sara Ryan, managing editor. "Our offerings include a range of titles in the areas of psychology and spirituality, herbistry, alternative health methods and nutrition, as well as distinctive children's books. Hohm Press is proud to present authors from the U.S. and Europe who have a clarity of vision and the mastery to communicate that vision." Publishes hardcover and trade paperback originals. Publishes 6-8 titles/year. **50% of books from first-time authors.**

How to Contact: Reports in 3 months on queries. Simultaneous submissions OK.

Terms: Pays 10-15% royalty on net sales. No advance. Publishes ms 18 months after acceptance. Book catalog for $1.50.

HOLMES PUBLISHING GROUP, (II), P.O. Box 623, Edmonds WA 98020. E-mail: jdh@jdh.seanet.com. CEO: J.D. Holmes. **Acquisitions:** L.Y. Fitzgerald. Holmes publishes informative spiritual health titles on philosophy, metaphysical and religious subjects. Publishes hardcover and trade paperback originals and reprints. Publishes 40 titles/year.

Imprint(s): Alchemical Press, Sure Fire Press, Contra/Thought, Alexandria Press.

Needs: Metaphysical, occult.

How to Contact: Query first with SASE. Reports in 2 months.

Terms: Pays 10% royalty on wholesale price. Publishes ms 4 months after acceptance.

☑ **HENRY HOLT & COMPANY, (III)**, 115 W. 18th St., 6th Floor, New York NY 10011. (212)886-9200. Editor-in-Chief: William Strachan. **Acquisitions**: Sara Bershtel, editorial director (Metropolitan Books); Allen Peacock, senior editor (fiction). Publishes hardcover and paperback originals and reprints. Averages 80-100 total original titles, 35% of total is fiction each year.

Imprint(s): Owl (paper).

- Henry Holt is publishing more titles and more fiction.

How to Contact: Accepts queries; no unsolicited mss. Agented fiction 95%.

Terms: Pays in royalties of 10% minimum; 15% maximum; advance. Sends galleys to author.

☑ **HENRY HOLT & COMPANY BOOKS FOR YOUNG READERS, (II)**, Imprint of Henry Holt & Co., Inc., 115 W. 18th St., New York NY 10011. (212)886-9200. Fax: (212)633-0748. **Acquisitions:** Laura Godwin, vice president and associate publisher. Marc Aronson, senior editor (young adult nonfiction and fiction); Christy Ottaviano, senior editor (picture books, middle grade fiction). Estab. 1866 (Holt). Henry Holt Books for Young

Readers publishes excellent books of all kinds (fiction, nonfiction, illustrated) for all ages, from the very young to the young adult. Publishes hardcover and trade paperback originals. Publishes 50-60 titles/year.
Imprint(s): Edge Books (Marc Aronson, senior editor, "a high caliber young adult fiction imprint"); Red Feather Books ("covers a range between early chapter and younger middle grade readers"); Owlet Paperbacks.
Needs: Juvenile: adventure, animal, contemporary, fantasy, history, humor, multicultural, religion, sports, suspense/mystery. Picture books: animal, concept, history, humor, multicultural, religion, sports. Young adult: contemporary, fantasy, history, multicultural, nature/environment, problem novels, sports. Recently published *Smack*, by Melvin Burgess; and *Whirligig*, by Paul Fleischman (both young adult).
How to Contact: Query with SASE. Reports in 5 months on queries and mss. No longer accepts multiple simultaneous submissions.
Terms: Pays royalty and advance. Publishes ms 18 months after acceptance. Book catalog and writer's guidelines upon request with SASE.

HOUGHTON MIFFLIN BOOKS FOR CHILDREN, (II), Imprint of Houghton Mifflin Company, 222 Berkeley St., Boston MA 02116-3764. (617)351-5000. Fax: (617)351-1111. E-mail: hmco.com. Website: http://www.hmco.com (includes titles, job postings, etc.) **Acquisitions:** Sarah Hines-Stephens, assistant editor; Margaret Raymo, senior editor; Ann Rider, senior editor; Amy Flynn, associate editor. "Houghton Mifflin gives shape to ideas that educate, inform, and above all, delight." Publishes hardcover and trade paperback originals and reprints. **Publishes 12 previously unpublished writers/year.** Firm publishes approximately 60 titles/year. Promtoes titles through author visits, advertising, reviews.
Imprint(s): Clarion Books, New York City (contact: Dinah Stevenson); Walter Lorraine Books (contact: W. Lorraine).

- Houghton Mifflin Books for Children received Caldecott and Newbery awards in 1998.

Needs: Adventure, ethnic, historical, humor, juvenile (early readers), literary, mystery, picture books, suspense, young adult, board books. Recently published *Checkers*, by John Marsden (young adult); *Martha Walks the Dog*, by Susan Meddaugh (picture book); and *What Do You See When You Shut Your Eyes*, by Cynthia Zarin (picture book).
How to Contact: Submit complete ms with appropriate-sized SASE. Reports in 2 months. Simultaneous submissions OK. Mss and proposals in the following format are not considered: e-mail, fax, disk, website.
Terms: Pays 5-10% royalty on retail price. Advance dependent on many factors. Publishes ms 18 months after acceptance. For writer's guidelines need small SASE. For book catalog need 9×12 SASE with 3 first-class stamps.

HOUGHTON MIFFLIN COMPANY, (III), 222 Berkeley St., Boston MA 02116. (617)351-5000. Fax: (617)351-1202. Website: http://www.hmco.com. **Acquisitions**: Christina Coffin, managing editor. Estab. 1832. Publishes hardcover and paperback originals and paperback reprints. Averages 100 total titles, 50 fiction titles each year.
Needs: None at present.
Terms: Pays royalties of 10% minimum; 15% maximum. Advance varies. Publishes ms 1-2 years after acceptance.
How to Contact: Does not accept unsolicited mss. Buys virtually 100% agented fiction.

HUMANITAS, (II), 990 Croissant Picard, Brossard, Quebec J4W 1S5 Canada. Phone/fax: (450)466-9737. **Acquisitions**: Constantin Stoiciu, president. Publishes hardcover originals. Publishes 20% previously unpublished writers/year. Publishes 20 titles/year.

- Humanitas publishes novels in French only.

Needs: Fantasy, romance, short story collections. Recently published *L'Adolescent Qui Regardait Passer La Vie*, by Gary Klang (roman).
How to Contact: Query first. Simultaneous submissions OK.
Terms: Pays 10-12% royalty on wholesale price. Publishes ms 2 months after acceptance. Writer's guidelines and book catalog free on request.

HYPERION BOOKS FOR CHILDREN, (V), Imprint of Hyperion, 114 Fifth Ave., New York NY 10011. (212)633-4400. Fax: (212)633-4833. **Acquisitions:** Editorial Director. "The aim of Hyperion Books for Children is to create a dynamic children's program informed by Disney's creative vision, direct connection to children,

MARKET CATEGORIES: (I) Open to new writers; **(II)** Open to both new and established writers; **(III)** Interested mostly in established writers; **(IV)** Open to writers whose work is specialized; **(V)** Closed to unsolicited submissions.

and unparallelled marketing and distribution." Publishes hardcover and trade paperback originals. Publishes 210 titles/year.
Needs: Juvenile, picture books, young adult. Recently published *McDuff*, by Rosemary Wells and Susan Jeffers (picture book); and *Split Just Right*, by Adele Griffin (middle grade).
How to Contact: Agented submissions only. Reports in 1 month. Simultaneous submissions OK.
Terms: Pays royalty, "varies too widely to generalize." Advance varies. Publishes ms 1 year after acceptance. Writer's guidelines and book catalog free.
Advice: "Hyperion Books for Children are meant to appeal to an upscale children's audience. Study your audience. Look at and research current children's books. Who publishes what you like? Approach them. We are Disney and are always looking for Disney material."

✔ 🅰 **IDEALS CHILDREN'S BOOKS, (V)**, Imprint of Hambleton-Hill Publishing, Inc., 1501 County Hospital Rd., Nashville TN 37218. **Acquisitions:** Bethany Snyder, copy editor. Ideals Children's Books publishes some fiction and nonfiction for toddlers to 8-year-olds. Publishes children's hardcover and trade paperback originals. Publishes 40 titles/year.
Needs: Childrens/juvenile. Recently published *Molly*, by Joseph S. Bonsall, illustrated by Erin M. Mauterer; and *Arianna and the Strawberry Tea*, by Maria Fasal Faulconer, illustrated by Katy Keck Arnsteen.
How to Contact: This publisher only accepts unsolicited mss from agents and members of the Society of Children's Book Writers & Illustrators, and previously published book authors may submit with a list of writing credits.
Terms: Pay determined by individual contract. Publishes ms up to 2 years after acceptance. Writer's guidelines for #10 SASE.
Advice: Audience is children in the toddler to 8-year-old range. "We are seeking original, child-centered fiction for the picture book format. We do not publish chapter books. We are not interested in alphabet books or anthropomorphism."

INTERCONTINENTAL PUBLISHING, (I,II,IV), 6451 Steeple Chase Ln., Manassas VA 20111-2611. (703)369-4992. Fax: (703)670-7825. E-mail: icpub@worldnet.att.net. Publisher: H.G. Smittenaar. Estab. 1992. Small press publisher of hardcover and paperback originals. Average print order: 5,000. **Publishes 1-3 previously unpublished writers/year.** Publishes 6 total titles/year; 6 fiction titles. Promotes titles through space advertising, posters, distributor catalog, personal appearances, direct mail.
Needs: Mystery/suspense (amateur sleuth, cozy, police procedural, private eye/hardboiled). Recently published *The Cop Was White As Snow*, by Spizer (mystery); *Dekok and Murder in Ecstasy*, by Baantjer (police procedural).
How to Contact: Query with outline/synopsis and 1-3 sample chapters. Include estimated word count. Send SASE for reply, return of ms or send disposable copy of ms. Reports in 1-2 months on queries and mss. Simultaneous submissions OK.
Terms: Pays royalties of 5% minimum. Sends galleys to author.
Advice: "Be original, write proper English, be entertaining."

✔ **INTERLINK PUBLISHING GROUP, INC., (V)**, 46 Crosby St., Northampton MA 01060-1804. (413)582-7054. Fax: (413)582-7057. E-mail: interpg@aol.com. Contemporary fiction in translation published under Emerging Voices: New International Fiction. **Acquisitions**: Michel Moushabeck, publisher; Pam Thompson, fiction editor. Estab. 1987. "Midsize independent publisher specializing in world travel, world literature, world history and politics." Publishes hardcover and paperback originals. Books: 55 lb. Warren Sebago Cream white paper; web offset printing; perfect binding; average print order: 5,000; first novel print order: 5,000. Distributes titles through distributors such as Baker & Taylor. Promotes titles through book mailings to extensive, specialized lists of editors and reviewers, authors read at bookstores and special events across the country. Published new writers within the last year. **Publishes 0-2 previously unpublished writers/year.** Plans 2 first novels this year. Averages 30 total titles, 2-6 fiction titles each year.
Imprint(s): Interlink Books, Olive Branch Press and Crocodile Books USA.
Needs: "Adult translated fiction from around the world." Recently published *House of the Winds*, by Mia Yun (first novel, first translation in English); *The Gardens of Light*, by Amin Maalouf (novel translated from French); and *War in the Land of Egypt*, by Yusef Al-Qaid (novel translated from Arabic). Publishes the International Folk Tales series.
How to Contact: Does not accept unsolicited mss, e-mail or fax queries. Submit query letter and brief sample only. SASE. Reports within 6 weeks on queries.
Terms: Pays royalties of 6% minimum; 7% maximum. Sends galleys to author. Publishes ms 1-1½ years after acceptance.
Advice: "Our Emerging Voices Series is designed to bring to North American readers the once-unheard voices of writers who have achieved wide acclaim at home, but were not recognized beyond the borders of their native lands. We are also looking for folktale collections (for adults) from around the world that fit in our International Folk Tale Series."

✔ **IRONWEED PRESS, (II)**, P.O. Box 754208, Parkside Station, Forest Hills NY 11375. (718)544-1120. Fax: (718)268-2394. E-mail: iwpress@aol.com. **Acquisitions**: Jin Soo Kang, publisher; Robert Giannetto, manag-

ing editor (literary). Estab. 1996. Small independent publisher. Publishes hardcover and paperback originals. Plans 1 first novel this year. Averages 4 total titles, 4 fiction titles/year. Distributes titles through national wholesalers.
Needs: Ethnic/multicultural (Asian-American), experimental, humor/satire, literary. Recently published *Best Short Stories of Frank Norris* (literature).
How to Contact: Accepts unsolicited mss. Unsolicited queries/correspondence by e-mail OK. Submit complete ms with a cover letter. Include list of publishing credits. SASE for return of ms. Reports in 1 month on queries; 2-3 months on mss. Simultaneous submissions OK. Sometimes critiques or comments on rejected mss.
Payment/Terms: Pays royalties of 8% minimum; offers advance; provides author's copies. Sends galleys to author. Publishes ms 6-12 months after acceptance.

ITALICA PRESS, (II, IV), 595 Main St., #605, New York NY 10044. (212)935-4230. Fax: (212)838-7812. E-mail: italica@idt.net. Website: http://www.italica.com (includes authors, titles). **Acquisitions**: Eileen Gardiner and Ronald G. Musto, publishers. Estab. 1985. Small independent publisher of Italian fiction in translation. Publishes paperback originals. Books: 50-60 lb. natural paper; offset printing; Smythe-sewn binding; illustrations. Average print order: 1,500. "First time translators published. We would like to see translations of Italian writers well-known in Italy who are not yet translated for an American audience." Publishes 6 total titles each year; 2 fiction titles. Distributes titles through direct mail. Promotes titles through catalogs and website.
Needs: Translations of 20th Century Italian fiction. Published *Bakunin's Son*, by Sergio Atzeni (experimental); *Otronto*, by Maria Corti; and *Sparrow*, by Giovanni Verga.
How to Contact: Accepts unsolicited mss. Query first. Queries by e-mail and fax OK. Reports in 3 weeks on queries; 2 months on mss. Simultaneous submissions OK. Electronic submissions via Macintosh disk. Sometimes critiques rejected mss.
Terms: Pays in royalties of 5-15% and 10 author's copies. Sends pre-publication galleys to author. Publishes ms 1 year after acceptance. Book catalog free on request.
Advice: "Remember we publish *only* fiction that has been previously published in Italian. A *brief* call saves a lot of postage. 90% of the proposals we receive are completely off base—but we are very interested in things that are right on target. Please send return postage if you want your manuscript back."

JAMESON BOOKS, (I, II, IV), Jameson Books, Inc., The Frontier Library, 722 Columbus St., Ottawa IL 61350. (815)434-7905. Fax: (815)434-7907. E-mail: 72557.3635@compuserve.com. **Acquisitions**: Jameson G. Campaigne, Jr., publisher/editor Estab. 1986. "Jameson Books publishes conservative/libertarian politics and economics and pre-cowboy frontier novels (1750-1840)." Publishes hardcover and paperback originals and reprints. Books: free sheet paper; offset printing; average print order: 10,000; first novel print order: 5,000. Plans 6-8 novels this year. Averages 12-16 total titles, 4-8 fiction titles each year. Distributes titles through LPC Group/Chicago (book trade). Occasionally critiques or comments on rejected mss.
Needs: Very well-researched western (frontier pre-1850). No cowboys, no science fiction, mystery, poetry, et al. Published *Yellowstone Kelly*, by Peter Bowen; *Wister Trace*, by Loren Estelman; and *One-Eyed Dream*, by Terry Johnston.
How to Contact: Does not accepted unsolicited mss. Submit outline/synopsis and 3 consecutive sample chapters. SASE. Agented fiction 50%. Reports in 2 weeks on queries; 2-5 months on mss. Simultaneous submissions OK.
Terms: Pays royalties of 5% minimum; 15% maximum. Average advance: $1,500. Sends galleys to author. Publishes ms 1-12 months after acceptance.

JOURNEY BOOKS FOR YOUNG READERS, (I, II), (formerly Bob Jones University Press), a division of Bob Jones University Press, Greenville SC 29614. (864)242-5100, ext. 4316. Website: http://www.bju.edu/press/freelnce.html. **Acquisitions**: Mrs. Gloria Repp, editor. Estab. 1974. "Small independent publisher." Publishes paperback originals and reprints. Books: 50 lb. white paper; Webb lithography printing; perfect-bound binding. Average print order: 5,000. First novel print order: 5,000. Published new writers within the last year. Plans 3 first novels this year. Averages 12 total titles, 10 fiction titles each year.
Needs: Children's/juvenile (adventure, animal, easy-to-read, historical, mystery, series, sports), young adults (adventure, historical, mystery/suspense, series, sports, western). Published *The Rivers of Judah*, by Catherine Farnes (contemporary teen fiction); *Arby Jenkins*, by Sharon Hambric (contemporary ages 9-12); and *The Treasure Keeper*, by Anita Williams, (adventure ages 6-10).
How to Contact: Accepts unsolicited mss. Query with outline and 5 sample chapters. Submit complete ms with cover letter. Include estimated word count, short bio, Social Security number and list of publishing credits. Send SASE for reply, return of ms or send a disposable copy of ms. Reports in 3 weeks on queries; 6 weeks on mss. Simultaneous and disk submissions (IBM compatible preferred) OK. "Check our webpage for guidelines." Sometimes comments on rejected mss.

SENDING TO A COUNTRY other than your own? Be sure to send International Reply Coupons instead of stamps for replies or return of your manuscript.

Terms: "Pay flat fee for first-time authors; royalties for established authors." Sends final ms to author. Publishes ms 12-18 months after acceptance. Writer's guidelines and book catalog free.
Advice: Needs "more upper-elementary adventure/mystery or a good series. No picture books. No didactic stories. Read guidelines carefully. Send SASE if you wish to have ms returned. Give us original, well-developed characters in a suspenseful plot with good moral tone."

N **KAEDEN BOOKS, (II)**, 19915 Lake Rd., Box 16190, Rocky River OH 44116. (440)356-0030. Fax: (440)356-5081. E-mail: kaeden01@aol.com. **Acquisitions:** Kathleen Urmston, fiction editor (children's K-3); Karen Tabak, fiction editor (children's grades 3-6). Estab. 1990. "Children's book publisher for education K-6 market: reading stories, science, math and social studies materials, also poetry." Publishes paperback originals. Books: offset printing; saddle binding; illustrations. Average print order: 5,000. First novel print order: 5,000. **Published more than 20 new writers within the last year.** Plans 2 first novels in 1999. Averages 50 total titles, 40 fiction titles/year.
Needs: Adventure, children's/juvenile (adventure, animal, easy-to-read, fantasy, historical, mystery, preschool/picture book, series, sports), ethnic/multicultural, fantasy (space fantasy), historical (general), humor/satire, mystery/suspense (amateur sleuth), romance (romantic suspense), science fiction (soft/sociological), short story collections, thriller/espionage. Plans a poetry anthology/associated stories. Submit stories and poetry to editor.
How to Contact: Accepts unsolicited mss. Query with outline/synopsis. Include 1-page bio and list of publishing credits. Send a disposable copy of ms. Reports in 1 year.
Terms: Negotiable, either royalties or flat fee by individual arrangement with author depending on book. No advance. Publishes ms 6-24 months after acceptance.
Advice: "Our line is expanding with particular interest in poetry and fiction/nonfiction for grades three to six. Material must be suitable for use in the public school classroom, be multicultural and be high interest with appropriate word usage for the respective grade."

✔ **KAYA PRODUCTION, (II)**, 132 W. 22th St., 4th Floor, New York NY 10011. (212)352-9220. Fax: (212)352-9221. E-mail: kaya@kaya.com. Website: http://www.kaya.com. **Acquisitions:** Sunyoung Lee, associate editor. "Kaya is a small independent press dedicated to the publication of innovative literature from the Asian diaspora." Publishes hardcover originals and trade paperback originals and reprints.
Needs: Ethnic, regional. "Kaya publishes Asian, Asian-American and Asian diasporic materials. We are looking for innovative writers with a commitment to quality literature." Recently published *East Goes West*, by Younghill Kang (novel reprint).
How to Contact: Submit synopsis and 2-4 sample chapters with SASE. Reports in 6 months on mss. Simultaneous submissions OK.
Terms: Writer's guidelines for #10 SASE. Book catalog free.
Advice: Audience is people interested in a high standard of literature and who are interested in breaking down easy approaches to multicultural literature.

✔ A **KENSINGTON PUBLISHING CORP., (II)**, 850 Third Ave., 16th Floor, New York NY 10022. (212)407-1500. Fax: (212)935-0699. **Acquisitions**: Karen Thomas, senior editor (Arabesque); Tracy Bernstein, executive editor (Kensington Trade Paperbacks); Paul Dinas, executive editor (Pinnacle Books); Ann La Farge, executive editor (Zebra Books and Kensington Mass Market). Estab. 1975. "Kensington focuses on profitable niches and uses aggressive marketing techniques to support its books." Publishes hardcover originals, trade paperbacks and mass market originals and reprints. Averages 300 total titles/year.
Needs: Adventure, contemporary, erotica, mysteries, nonfiction, romance (contemporary, historical, regency, multicultural), thrillers, true crime, women's. No science fiction. Published *Destiny Mine*, by Janelle Taylor; *The Fall Line*, by Mark T. Sullivan; *Cemetary of Angels*, by Noel Hynd; and "Bride Price," in *Irish Magic II*, by Roberta Gellis. Ms length ranges from 100,000 to 125,000 words.
How to Contact: Contact with agent. Reports in 3-5 months.
Terms: Pays royalties and advances. Publishes ms 18 months after acceptance. Free book catalog.
Advice: "We want fiction that will appeal to the mass market and we want writers who want to make a career."

✔ ⊘ **ALLEN A. KNOLL, PUBLISHERS, (V)**, 200A W. Victoria St., Suite 3, Santa Barbara CA 93101-3627. Fax: (805)966-6657. E-mail: aaknoll@aol.com. Estab. 1990. Small independent publisher. "We publish books for intelligent people who read for fun." Publishes hardcover originals. Books: Offset printing; sewn binding. Member PMA, SPAN, ABA. Distributes titles through Ingram, Baker & Taylor, Brodart, Sunbelt. Promotes titles through advertising in specialty publications, direct mail, prepublication reviews and advertising.
Needs: Recently published *Flip Side*, by Theodore Roosevelt Gardner II (suspense); *The Unlucky Seven*, by Alistair Boyle (mystery); and *Nobody Roots for Goliath*, by David Champion (courtroom drama). Publishes A Bomber Hanson Mystery (courtroom drama series) and A Gil Yates Private Investigator Novel (P.I. series).
How to Contact: Does not accept unsolicited mss. Book catalog free.

ALFRED A. KNOPF, (II), Division of Random House, 201 E. 50th St., New York NY 10022. (212)751-2600. Vice President: Judith Jones. **Acquisitions**: Senior Editor. Estab. 1915. Publishes hardcover originals. Number

of titles: approximately 46 each year. Buys 75% agented fiction. Published new writers in the last year. Also publishes nonfiction.
Needs: Contemporary, literary, suspense and spy. No western, gothic, romance, erotica, religious or science fiction. Published *Silent Witness*, by Richard North Patterson; *Mystery Ride*, by Robert Boswell; *The Night Manager*, by John Le Carre; and *Lasher*, by Anne Rice. Published new writers within the last year.
How to Contact: Submit outline or synopsis with SASE. Reports within 1 month on mss. Publishes ms an average of 1 year after acceptance.
Terms: Pays 10-15% in royalties; offers advance. Must return advance if book is not completed or is unacceptable. Publishes ms 1 year after acceptance.
Advice: Publishes book-length fiction of literary merit by known and unknown writers.

KNOPF BOOKS FOR YOUNG READERS, (II), Division of Random House, 201 E. 50th St., New York NY 10022. (212)751-2600. Website: http://www.randomhouse.com/Knopf/index. **Acquisitions**: Sinion Boughton, publishing director. "Knopf is known for high quality literary fiction, and is willing to take risks with writing styles. It publishes for children ages 5 and up." Publishes hardcover and paperback originals and reprints. Averages 30 total titles, approximately 7 fiction titles each year.
Imprint(s): Dragonfly Books (picture books) and Knopf paperbacks (fiction).
Needs: "High-quality contemporary, humor, picture books, middle grade novels." Published *Merl and Jasper's Supper Caper*, by Laura Rankin, *The Squiggle*, by Carole Lexa Shaefer and Piers Morgan; *Crash*, by Jerry Spinelli; and *The Golden Compass*, by Philip Pullman.
How to Contact: Query with outline/synopsis and 2 sample chapters with SASE. Simultaneous submissions OK. Reports in 6-8 weeks on queries.
Terms: Pays royalties of 4% minimum; 10% maximum. Average advance: $3,000 and up. Sends galleys to author. Publishes ms 1-2 years after acceptance.

N **LAUGHING OWL PUBLISHING, INC., (IV)**, 12610 Highway 90, Grand Bay AL 36541. (334)865-5177. Fax: (334)865-6252. E-mail: laughingowl@juno.com. Website: http://www.laughingowl.com (includes online bookstore, catalog, first chapters, writer's guidelines). **Acquisitions:** Heather Wilkinson, fiction editor. "Publisher of multi-genre fiction with a fresh new voice." Publishes paperback originals. Books: 50 lb. paper; offset printing; perfect binding. Average print order: 3,000-5,000. First novel print order: 2,000-3,000. Published 4 new writers within the last year. Plans 3 first novels in 1999. Averages 5 fiction titles/year.
Needs: Adventure, historical, horror (dark fantasy), psychic/supernatural/occult, regional (Southern), romance (contemporary). *"Fully contracted until 2003."* Recently published *Angel Fire*, by Ron Franscell (contemporary literary fiction); *Glencoe, A Romance of Scotland*, by Muireall Donald (historical); and *The Beloved*, by M.D. Gray (occult suspense).
How to Contact: Query with outline synopsis. Unsolicited queries/correspondence by e-mail and fax OK. Include exact word count. Send SASE for reply. Agented fiction 25%. Reports in 2 months on queries; 3-6 months on mss. Electronic submissions (disk or modem) OK. Always critiques or comments on rejected ms.
Terms: Pays royalties of 6% minimum; 12% maximum; standard royalty contract. Sends galleys to author. Writer's guidelines and book catalog free; available on website.
Advice: "Follow our writer's guidelines. We give equal consideration to first-time writers as to established writers. Be professional; take the query letter seriously. A synopsis is not the first 20 pages. We want work that is available on disk to save on typesetting costs."

LAUREL BOOKS, (II), Imprint of Dell Publishing, Division of Bantam Doubleday Dell, 1540 Broadway, New York NY 10036. (212)354-6500. **Acquisitions:** Leslie Schnur, editor-in-chief. Publishes trade paperback originals, mostly light, humorous material and books on pop culture. Publishes 4 titles/year.
Needs: Literary.
How to Contact: Query with synopsis, 2-3 sample chapters or complete ms and SASE. Reports in 4-6 months on queries. Simultaneous submissions OK.
Terms: Pays 7½-12½% royalty on retail price. Advance varies. Publishes ms 1 year after acceptance. Book catalog for 9×12 SAE and 3 first class stamps.

✔ **LEE & LOW BOOKS, (I, II)**, 95 Madison Ave., New York NY 10016. (212)779-4400. Fax: (212)683-1894. Publisher: Philip Lee. **Acquisitions**: Renee Schultz. Estab. 1991. "Our goals are to meet a growing need for books that address children of color, and to present literature that all children can identify with. We only consider multicultural children's picture books. Of special interest are stories set in contemporary America." Publishes hardcover originals—picture books only. Averages 8-10 total titles each year.
Needs: Children's/juvenile (historical, multicultural, preschool/picture book for children ages 4-10). "We do not consider folktales, fairy tales or animal stories." Published *Dear Ms. Parks: A Dialogue With Today's Youth*, by Rosa Parks (collection of correspondence); *Giving Thanks: A Native American Good Morning Message*, by Chief Jake Swamp (picture book); and *Sam and the Lucky Money*, by Karen Chinn (picture book).

INSIDER REPORT

Ron Franscell: finding a home for his first novel

Ron Franscell

For months, newspaper editor Ron Franscell chipped away at *Angel Fire*, his powerful first novel and award-winning story of two Wyoming brothers separated body, mind and spirit by the war in Vietnam. The 41-year-old writer's ten-hour days at his daily newspaper in Gillette, Wyoming, were shadowed by another three hours at home as a novelist. And he admits, the transition was often a challenge.

"After a life of writing newspaper articles, I thought it would be easy," Franscell says, "but long fiction is a completely different mind-set than newspaper writing. There is a distinction between being a writer and a newspaperman in the same way there is a difference between being a poet and a news anchor. When writing for a newspaper we tell the most important thing first, make nothing up, get it done fast, eviscerate detail, and ignore our own emotions."

But novel-length fiction, according to Franscell, is the antithesis of journalism. "We tell the most important things last, we make everything up, we deliberate, go slowly. We ornament the story with details and explore and exploit emotions—we use every ounce of them. The difference may not be immediately recognizable to people who don't write. But to writers, it's obvious."

For Franscell, a newspaperman for almost 20 years, meeting the challenge was the only conceivable option. "I couldn't grant myself the title of 'real' writer until I wrote a novel," he says. "That's not true for all newspaper people, but it was for me. I wanted to tell a story that was mine and no one else's. I carried *Angel Fire* around in me for 15 years before I actually started to write it. It grew up with me. And I think it's a better, wiser story for the gestation."

Winning the Wyoming Art Council's $2,000 Literary Fellowship in 1996 told Franscell his faith in *Angel Fire* was well invested. "It was like a new tank of gas," he says. "It made me feel there was a reason to keep writing." If winning was fuel for Franscell's creative fires, comments like those of Fellowship judge and author Melissa Pritchard surely kicked up the octane. Pritchard says of *Angel Fire*: "Ron Franscell's narrative powers so effortlessly persuade us of the reality of Cassidy and Daniel McLeod, of their father Archimedes, of their town, West Canaan, Wyoming, in 1957. We gladly forego our more comfortable, habit-drenched world for his more compelling and emotionally provocative one."

Hamilton Boudreaux, President of Alabama's Laughing Owl Publishing, agrees with Pritchard's assessment entirely. "Our submissions editor got *Angel Fire* first," Boudreaux says. "She came to me with tears in her eyes, saying this book had changed her life. I thought I should give it a serious read." Boudreaux, and in fact the entire editorial board

INSIDER REPORT, *Franscell*

at Laughing Owl, leapt at the chance to publish *Angel Fire*, after that first, emotionally charged review.

But not all of Franscell's professional dealings were so life affirming. "Thirty-eight big-house editors hadn't been so eager to take a chance on a first 'literary' novel," Franscell says. "As a result, I think I was chronically discouraged with the process. Here I was getting these glowing rejections, which was more frustrating. One editor said, 'This is the best book to land on my desk in three years, but I'm not buying fiction these days.' "

In time, Franscell learned the contractual end of publishing was more business than art. "They were saying, 'We like your art, but we don't know if we'll be able to sell enough of it to make our investment back.' Big publishing houses have become schools of gray-suit fish following a pretty lure," he says. "New York lusts for Hollywood's glitter."

Boudreaux agrees. "It is becoming harder and harder for new artists to break into the market. A first-time writer is a very risky commodity. And the large publishing corporations are risk-averse. Small houses print small runs, and risk less capital. We are also extremely cost efficient."

Simply put, smaller publishers like Laughing Owl have stepped in to gather wheat inadvertently cast out with the chaff. "You see parallel developments in film and music," Boudreaux says. "Do you get the IFC or Sundance channels? Have you seen the explosion of new record labels? We are not unique in recognizing a business opportunity. What makes us unique is our vision, and our business plan. We love book sellers, but we would like to sell directly to readers via mail order or, even better, through the Internet." Case in point, the *Angel Fire* web page: (http://www.laughingowl.com/angelfire.htm). Within three weeks after his agent finalized contractual negotiations, Laughing Owl had a web page in place to herald the publication of Franscell's book.

Smaller houses can also afford to indulge more personal literary leanings than larger publishers. "Laughing Owl Publishing is owned by writers who happen to believe readers are willing and hungry to read life-changing fiction," Boudreaux says. "We believe we're filling a niche."

"All the people who have all the big money—people who could do something for the art—are setting it aside," Franscell says. "It's fortunate that small publishers like Laughing Owl are stepping in, doing it more economically, and probably doing a better job at the art. It's not likely to make literary writers rich. But if wealth was our primary purpose, we probably wouldn't be writing that kind of book."

With a new novel coming out and others in production, does Franscell plan to phase journalism out of his immediate future? "Nope. Not a chance," the veteran editor says. "I've been in Gillette nine years. In that time, *The News-Record* has continued as one of the best small dailies in the country. It was named one of the seven best-designed small dailies in the world by the Society of Newspaper Design's magazine last fall. One of the things I've learned is you don't need a lot of resources to be resourceful. I know there is not a thing the bigger papers can do that we can't do as well or better. I have no plan or desire to stop being a newspaperman. I know my place in the world. Writing literary fiction is just another element of storytelling. It's another aspect of who I am as a writer."

—Kelly Milner Halls

How to Contact: Accepts unsolicited mss. Send complete ms with cover letter or through an agent. Send SASE for reply, return of ms or send a disposable ms. Agented fiction 30%. Reports in 1-4 months. Simultaneous submissions OK. Sometimes critiques or comments on rejected mss.
Terms: Pays royalties. Offers advance. Sends galleys to author. Publishes ms 18 months after acceptance. Writer's guidelines for #10 SASE. Book catalog for SASE with $1.01 postage.
Advice: "Writers should familiarize themselves with the styles and formats of recently published children's books. Lee & Low Books is a multicultural children's book publisher. We would like to see more contemporary stories set in the U.S. Animal stories and folktales are not considered at this time."

LEISURE BOOKS, (I, II), Division of Dorchester Publishing Co., Inc., 276 Fifth Ave., Suite 1008, New York NY 10001. (212)725-8811. Fax: (212)532-1054. E-mail: timdy@aol.com. Website: http://www.dorchesterpub.com (includes writer's guidelines, names of editors, authors, titles, etc.). **Acquisitions**: Jennifer Bonnell, fiction editor; Gretchen Comba, fiction editor. Mass-market paperback publisher—originals and reprints. Books: Newsprint paper; offset printing; perfect-bound; average print order: variable; first novel print order: variable. Plans 25 first novels this year. Averages 150 total titles, 145 fiction titles each year. Promotes titles through ads in *Romantic Times*, author readings, promotional items.
Imprint(s): Leisure Books (contact: Alicia Condon), **Love Spell Books** (contact: Christopher Kesslar).
Needs: Historical romance, horror, techno-thriller, western. Looking for "historical romance (90,000-115,000 words)." Published *Pure Temptation*, by Connie Mason (historical romance); and *Frankly My Dear*, by Sandra Hill (time-travel romance).
How to Contact: Accepts unsolicited mss. Query first. SASE. Agented fiction 70%. Reports in 1 month on queries; 3-4 months on mss. "All mss must be typed, double-spaced on one side and left unbound." Comments on rejected ms "only if requested ms requires it."
Terms: Offers negotiable advance. Payment depends "on category and track record of author." Sends galleys to author. Publishes ms within 2 years after acceptance. Romance guidelines for #10 SASE.
Advice: Encourages first novelists "if they are talented and willing to take direction, *and* write the kind of genre fiction we publish. Please include a brief synopsis if sample chapters are requested."

LERNER PUBLICATIONS COMPANY, (II), 241 First Ave. N., Minneapolis MN 55401. (612)332-3344. **Acquisitions**: Jennifer Martin, editor. Estab. 1959. "Midsize independent *children's* publisher." Publishes hardcover originals and paperback reprints. Books: Offset printing; reinforced library binding; perfect binding; average print order: 5,000-7,500; first novel print order: 5,000. Averages 70 total titles, 1-2 fiction titles each year.
Imprint(s): First Avenue Editions.

- **Not accepting submissions until September 1999.** Lerner Publication's joke book series is recommended by "Reading Rainbow" (associated with the popular television show of the same name).

Needs: Young adult: general, problem novels, sports, adventure, mystery (young adult). Looking for "well-written middle grade and young adult. No *adult fiction* or single short stories." Recently published *Dancing Pink Flamigos and Other Stories*, by Maria Testa.
How to Contact: Accepts unsolicited mss. Query first or submit outline/synopsis and 2 sample chapters. Reports in 1 month on queries; 2 months on mss. Simultaneous submissions OK.
Terms: Pays royalties. Offers advance. Provides author's copies. Sends galleys to author. Publishes ms 12-18 months after acceptance. Writer's guidelines for #10 SASE. Book catalog for 9×12 SAE with $1.90 postage.
Advice: Would like to see "less gender and racial stereotyping; protagonists from many cultures."

LINTEL, (II), 24 Blake Lane, Middletown NY 10940. (212)674-4901. Editorial Director: Walter James Miller. Estab. 1977. Two-person organization on part-time basis. Books: 90% opaque paper; photo offset printing; perfect binding; illustrations. Average print order: 1,000. First novel print order: 1,200. Publishes hardcover and paperback originals. Occasionally comments on rejected mss.
Needs: Experimental, feminist, gay, lesbian, regional short fiction. Published second edition (fourth printing) of *Klytaimnestra Who Stayed at Home*, mythopoeic novel by Nancy Bogen; and *The Mountain,* by Rebecca Rass.
How to Contact: Accepts unsolicited mss. Query with SASE. Simultaneous and photocopied submissions OK. Reports in 2 months on queries; 3 months on mss. Publishes ms 6-8 months after acceptance.
Terms: Negotiated. No advance. Sends galleys to author. Free book catalog.
Advice: "Lintel is devoted to the kinds of literary art that will never make The Literary Guild or even the Book-of-the-Month Club: that is, literature concerned with the advancement of literary art. We still look for the innovative work ignored by the commercial presses. We consider any ms on its merits alone. We encourage first novelists. Be innovative, advance the *art* of fiction, but still keep in mind the need to reach reader's aspirations

as well as your own. Originality is the greatest suspense-building factor. Consistent misspelling errors, errors in grammar and syntax can mean only rejection."

LIONHEARTED PUBLISHING, INC., (II), P.O. Box 618, Zephyr Cove NV 89448-0618. (702)588-1388. Fax: (702)588-1386. E-mail: admin@lionhearted.com. Website: http://www.LionHearted.com (includes writer's guidelines, authors, titles, articles and writing tips for authors). **Acquisitions**: Historical or Contemporary Acquisitions Editor. Estab. 1994. Independent. "We publish entertaining, fun, romantic genre fiction—single title releases." Publishes paperback originals. Books: mass market paperback; perfect binding. Published new writers within the last year. Plans 12 first novels this year. Averages 12-72 fiction titles/year. Distributes titles through amazon.com; all Barnes & Noble store computer systems. Promotes titles through direct mail and advertising.

- LionHearted Publishing is mentioned in the *Wall Street Journal's 1998 Almanac for Women Entrepreneurs*.

Needs: Romance (contemporary, futuristic/time travel, historical, regency period, romantic suspense; over 65,000 words only). Recently published *Isn't It Romantic?*, by Ronda Thompson (romance); and *Oracle*, by Katherine Greyle (romance).
How to Contact: Accepts unsolicited mss. Query with outline/synopsis and 3 sample chapters. Include estimated word count, list of publishing credits, cover letter and 1 paragraph story summary in cover or query letter. Send SASE for reply, return of ms or send disposable copy of ms. Agented fiction less than 10%. Reports in 1 month on queries; 3 months on mss. No simultaneous submissions. Always critiques or comments on rejected mss.
Terms: Pays royalties of 10% maximum on paperbacks; 10-25% on electronic books. Average advance: $1,000. $5,000 minimum guarantee on royalties. Sends galleys to author. Publishes ms 18-24 months after acceptance. Writer's guidelines free for #10 SASE. Book catalog available for SASE.
Advice: "If you are not an avid reader of romance, don't attempt to write romance, and don't waste your time or an editor's by submitting to a publisher of romance."

THE LITERATURE BUREAU, P.O. Box CY749 Causeway, Harare Zimbabwe. **Acquisitions**: B.C. Chitsike, fiction editor. Publishes 8 previously unpublished writers/year. Averages 12 fiction titles/year. Distributes titles through booksellers and our tours to schools. Promotes titles through radio programs and book reviews.
Needs: "All types of fiction from the old world novels to the modern ones with current issues. We publish these books in association with commercial publishers but we also publish in our own right. We specialize in Shona and Ndebele, our local languages in Zimbabwe. Manuscripts in English are not our priority." Recently published *Madirativhang*, edited by E. Mari (poetry); *Emdangweni*, edited by E. Bhala (poetry); and *Ndakazvibaya*, by D. Phiri (short stories). Length: 7,000-30,000 words.
How to Contact: Send entire manuscript. Reports in 6 months on mss.
Terms: Pays royalties. Obtain guidelines by writing to the Bureau.
Advice: "Send the complete manuscript for assessment. If it is a good one it is either published by the Bureau or sponsored for publication. If it needs any correction, a full report will be sent to the author. We have 'Hints to New Authors,' a pamphlet for aspiring authors. These can be obtained on request."

LITTLE, BROWN AND COMPANY, (II, III), 1271 Avenue of the Americas, New York NY 10020 and 3 Center Plaza, Boston MA 02108. (212)522-8700 and (617)227-0730. Fax: (212)522-2067. **Acquisitions**: Editorial Department. Estab. 1837. "The general editorial philosophy for all divisions continues to be broad and flexible, with high quality and the promise of commercial success always the first considerations." Medium-size house. Publishes adult and juvenile hardcover and paperback originals. Averages 200-225 total adult titles/year. Number of fiction titles varies.
Imprint(s): Little, Brown; Back Bay; Bulfinch Press.

- Send children's submissions to Submissions Editor, Children's Books, at Boston address. Send Bulfinch submissions to Submissions Editor, Bulfinch Press, at Boston address. Include SASE.

Needs: Open. No science fiction. Published *Along Came a Spider*, by James Patterson; *The Poet*, by Michael Connelly; *The Pugilist at Rest: Stories*, by Thom Jones. Published new writers within the last year.
How to Contact: Does not accept unsolicited adult mss. "We accept submissions from authors who have published before, in book form, magazines, newspapers or journals. No submissions from unpublished writers." Reports in 4-6 months on queries. Simultaneous and photocopied submissions OK.
Terms: "We publish on a royalty basis, with advance."

LITTLE, BROWN AND COMPANY CHILDREN'S BOOKS, (III), Trade Division; Children's Books, 34 Beacon St., Boston MA 02108. (617)227-0730. Fax: (617)227-8344. Website: http://www.littlebrown.com. Maria Modugno, editor-in-chief. **Acquisitions**: Erica Stahler, assistant editor; Megan S. Tingley, senior editor; Stephanie Peters, editor. Estab. 1837. Books: 70 lb. paper; sheet-fed printing; illustrations. Sometimes buys juvenile mss with illustrations "if by professional artist." Published "a few" new writers within the last year. Distributes titles through sales representatives. Promotes titles through author tours, book signings, posters, press kits, magazine and newspapers and Beacon Hill Bookbay.

- *Maniac Magee*, by Jerry Spinelli and published by Little, Brown and Company Children's Books, received a Newbery Award. *The Tulip Touch*, by Anne Fine received the Whitbread Award. *The Day Gogo Went to Vote*, by Elinor Sisulu received a 1997 ALA Notable Children's Books award. *Lunch Bunnies*, by Kathryn Lasky was listed in *Publishers Weekly* "Best Books '96."

Needs: Middle grade fiction and young adult. Recently published *Edward and the Pirates*, by David McPhail (picture book); *One of Each*, by Mary Ann Hoberman (picture book); and *The Tulip Touch*, by Anne Fine (young adult). Publishes 3 previously unpublished writers/year.

How to Contact: Submit through agent; authors with previous credits in children's book or magazine publishing may submit directly (include list of writing credits). Inquiries by fax OK.

Terms: Pays on royalty basis. Sends galleys to author. Publishes ms 1-2 years after acceptance.

Advice: "We are looking for trade books with bookstore appeal. We are especially looking for young children's (ages 3-5) picture books. New authors should be aware of what is currently being published. We recommend they spend time at the local library and bookstore familiarizing themselves with new publications." Known for "humorous middle grade fiction with lots of kid appeal. Literary, multi-layered young adult fiction with distinctive characters and complex plots."

LITTLE SIMON, (III), Imprint of Simon & Schuster Children's Publishing Division, 1230 Avenue of the Americas, New York NY 10022. (212)698-7200. Website: http://www.simonandschuster.com. **Acquisitions**: Submissions Editor. "Our goal is to provide fresh material in an innovative format for pre-school age. Our books are often, if not exclusively, illustrator driven." Averages 120 total titles/year. This imprint publishes novelty books only (pop-ups, lift-the-flaps board books, etc).

How to Contact: Query for more information. Does not accept unsolicited mss. Reports in 8 months. Accepts simultaneous submissions.

Terms: Pays royalties of 2% minimum; 5% maximum. Publishes ms 6 months after acceptance.

☑ **LITTLE TIGER PRESS**, % XYZ Distributors, N16 W23390 Stoneridge Dr., Waukesha WI 53188. (414)466-6900. **Acquisitions**: Amy Mascillino. Publishes hardcover originals. Publishes 8-10 titles/year. Receives 100 queries and 1,200 mss/year.

Needs: Humor, juvenile, picture books. "Humorous stories, stories about animals, children's imagination, or realistic fiction are especially sought." Recently published *Commotion in the Ocean*, by Giles Andreae and David Wojtowycz; and *Beware of the Bears!*, written by Alan MacDonald and illustrated by Gwyneth Williamson.

How to Contact: Send ms with SASE. Agented fiction 15%. Reports in 2 months on queries and proposals, 3 months on mss. Simultaneous submissions OK.

Terms: Pays 7½-10% royalty on retail price or for first-time authors makes outright purchase of $800-2,500. Offers $2,000 minimum advance. Publishes ms 1 year after acceptance. Writer's guidelines for #10 SASE. Book catalog for #10 SASE with 3 first-class stamps.

Advice: "Audience is children 3-8 years old. We are looking for simple, basic picture books, preferably humorous, that children will enjoy again and again. We do not have a multicultural or social agenda."

LIVING THE GOOD NEWS, (II), a division of the Morehouse Group, 600 Grant St., Suite #400. Denver CO 80203. Fax: (303)832-4971. **Acquisitions:** Liz Riggleman, editorial administrator. "Living the Good News is looking for books on practical, personal, spiritual growth for children, teens, families and faith communities." Publishes hardcover and trade paperback originals. Publishes 15 titles/year.

Needs: Juvenile, picture books, religious, young adult.

How to Contact: Query first. Submit synopsis with SASE. Reports in 2 months on proposals. Simultaneous submissions OK.

Terms: Pays royalty. Publishes ms 1 year after acceptance. Book catalog for 9×12 SAE and 4 first-class stamps. Writer's guidelines for #10 SASE.

Advice: Audience is those seeking to enrich their spiritual journey, typically from mainline and liturgical church backgrounds. "We look for original, creative ways to build connectedness with self, others, God and the earth."

LIVINGSTON PRESS, (II), Station 22, University of Alabama, Livingston AL 35470. Fax: (205)652-3717. E-mail: jwt@uwamail.westal.edu. Website: http://www.livingstonpress (includes catalog). **Acquisitions**: Joe Taylor, editor. Estab. 1982. "Literary press. We publish offbeat and/or southern literature. Emphasis on offbeat." Publishes hardcover and paperback originals. Books: acid-free paper; offset printing; perfect binding. Average print order: 1,500. First novel print order: 1,500. Published new writers within the last year. Plans 2 first novels this year. Averages 4-6 total titles, 5 fiction titles each year. Distributes titles through Yankee Book, Baker & Taylor, Blackwell North America. Promotes titles through catalogs, readings, postcards, 75-100 review copies. Sometimes critiques or comments on rejected mss.

Imprint(s): Swallows Tale Press.

Needs: Literary, short story collections. No genre. Recently published *Microgravity*, by Beth Partin (novel).

How to Contact: Does not accept unsolicited mss. Query first. Include bio, list of publishing credits. Send SASE for reply, return of ms or send a disposable copy of ms. Reports in 3 weeks on queries; 6 months on mss. Simultaneous submissions OK.

Terms: Pays 12% of press run in contributor's copies. Sends galleys to author. Publishes ms 1-2 years after acceptance. Book catalog free.

☑ **LLEWELLYN PUBLICATIONS, (IV)**, Llewellyn Worldwide, Ltd., P.O. Box 64383, St. Paul MN 55164-0383. (612)291-1970. Fax: (612)291-1908. Website: http://www.llewellyn.com. **Acquisitions:** Nancy Mostad, acquisitions and development manager. Midsize publisher of New Age/occult fiction and nonfiction. Publishes paperback originals. Plans 1-2 first novels this year. Publishes 100 total titles/year; 10 fiction titles/year.
Needs: New Age/mystic/spiritual, psychic/supernatural/occult. Recently published *Soothsayer*, by D.J. Conway (occult); and *Ronin*, by D.A. Heeley (fantasy).
How to Contact: Query with outline/synopsis and 3 sample chapters or submit complete ms with a cover letter. Include estimated word count and bio. Send SASE for reply, return of ms or send disposable copy of ms. Replies in 1 week on queries; 2 weeks to 2 months on mss. Simultaneous submissions OK.
Terms: Pays 10% royalty on money received both retail and wholesale. Sends galleys to author. Publishes ms 1 year after acceptance. Fiction guidelines free. Book catalog $3.

☑ **JAMES LORIMER & CO., PUBLISHERS, (II)**, 35 Britain St., Toronto, Ontario M5A 1R7 Canada. (416)362-4762. Fax: (416)362-3939. E-mail: jlc@sympatico.ca. **Acquisitions**: Diane Young, editor-in-chief. "James Lorimer & Co. publishes Canadian authors only, on Canadian issues/topics. For juvenile list, realistic themes only, especially mysteries and sports." Publishes trade paperback originals. **Publishes 10% previously unpublished writers/year.** Publishes 30 titles/year.
Needs: Juvenile, young adult. "No fantasy, science fiction, talking animals; realistic themes only. Currently seeking chapter books for ages 7-11 and sports novels for ages 9-13 (Canadian writers only)."
How to Contact: Submit synopsis and 2 sample chapters. Reports in 4 months.
Terms: Pays 5-10% royalty on retail price. Offers negotiable advance. Publishes ms about 1 year after acceptance. Book catalog for #10 SASE.

LOTHROP, LEE & SHEPARD BOOKS, (III), William Morrow & Co., 1350 Sixth Ave., New York NY 10019. (212)261-6641. Fax: (212)261-6648. Website: http://www.williammorrow.com. **Acquisitions**: Susan Pearson, vice president/editor-in-chief (young adult); Melanie Donovan, senior editor (young adult, middle grade). Estab. mid 19th century. "We publish children's books for all ages—about 25 books a year—primarily picture books. We are known for multicultural fiction." Publishes hardcover originals. **Publishes 0-1 previously unpublished writers/year.** Averages 25 total titles, 2-3 fiction titles each year. Promotes titles through industry journals and with counter displays.
Imprint(s): Morrow Junior Books (Contact: Diana Capriotti), **Greenwillow Books** (Contact: Barbara Trueson).
- The press received the Pura Belpre Honor Award for *Gathering the Sun*.

Needs: "Our needs are not by category but by quality—we are interested only in fiction of a superlative quality." Recently published *Moaning Bones: African American Ghost Stories*, by James Haskins.
How to Contact: Accepts unsolicited mss. SASE for return of ms. Agented fiction 100%. Reports in 3-6 months on mss. Sometimes comments on rejected mss.
Terms: Pays royalties of 10% minimum; negotiable advance. Sends galleys to author. Publishes ms within 2 years after acceptance.
Advice: "I'd like to see more quality. More mss that move me to out-loud laughter or real tears—i.e. mss that touch my heart. Find an agent. Work on the craft. We are less able to work with beginners with an eye to the future; mss must be of a higher quality than ever before in order to be accepted."

LOVE SPELL, (I, II), Leisure Books, Division of Dorchester Publishing Co., Inc., 276 Fifth Ave., Suite 1008, New York NY 10001-0112. (212)725-8811. **Acquisitions**: Christopher Kessler, editor; Jennifer Bonnell and Mira Son, editorial assistants. "Love Spell publishes quirky sub-genres of romance: time-travel, paranormal, futuristic. Despite the exotic settings, we are still interested in character-driven plots." Mass market paperback publisher—originals and reprints. Books: newsprint paper; offset printing; perfect-bound; average print order: varies; first novel print order: varies. Plans 15 first novels this year. Averages 45 titles/year.
Needs: Romance (futuristic, time travel, paranormal, historical). Looking for romances of 90,000-115,000 words. Recently published *Hidden Heart*, by Anne Avery (futuristic romance).
How to Contact: Accepts unsolicited mss. Query first. "All mss must be typed, double-spaced on one side and left unbound." SASE for return of ms. Agented fiction 70%. Reports in 1 month on queries; 4 months on mss. Comments "only if requested ms requires it."
Terms: Offers negotiable advance. "Payment depends on category and track record of author." Sends galleys to author. Publishes ms within 2 years after acceptance. Writer's guidelines for #10 SASE.
Advice: "The best way to learn to write a Love Spell Romance is by reading several of our recent releases. The best written stories are usually ones writers feel passionate about—so write from your heart! Also, the market is very tight these days so more than ever we are looking for refreshing, standout original fiction."

THE LYONS PRESS, (II), 31 W. 21st St., New York NY 10010. (212)929-1836. **Acquisitions**: Lilly Golden and Bryan Oettel. Estab. 1984. Publishes hardcover and paperback originals and paperback reprints. Published new writers within the last year. Averages 70 total titles.
Needs: Adventure (sports), short story collections, western, outdoors. Published *Guiding Elliott*, by Robert Lee (fiction); *Travers Corners*, by Scott Waldie (short stories); and *Dry Rain*, by Pete Fromm (short stories).
How to Contact: Accepts unsolicited mss. Query with outline/synopsis. Include bio and list of publishing

credits. Send SASE for reply. Agented fiction 60%. Reports in 2 months. Simultaneous submissions OK. Critiques or comments on rejected mss.
Terms: Pays royalties; offers advance. Sends galleys to author.

MACMURRAY & BECK, INC., (II), 1649 Downing St., Denver CO 80218. (303)832-2152. Fax: (303)832-2158. E-mail: ramey@macmurraybeck.com. Website: http://www.macmurraybeck.com (includes writer's guidelines, authors, titles). **Acquisitions**: Frederick Ramey, executive editor. Estab. 1991. "We are interested in reflective personal narrative of high literary quality." Publishes hardcover and paperback originals. Books: average print order: 4,000; first novel print order: 4,000. Published new writers within the last year. Plans 3-4 novels this year. Averages 8 total titles, 2-3 fiction titles each year. Distributes titles through major wholesalers and the Internet. Promotes titles through national advertising, direct mail and the Internet.
Imprint(s): Divina—a speculative fiction imprint (contact Leslie Koffler).
Needs: Contemporary, literary, short story collections, translations. Looking for "reflective fiction with high literary quality and commercial potential. No genre fiction, plot-driven, traditional, frontier western or mainstream." Recently published *Horace Afoot*, by Frederick Reuss; *Celibates and Other Lovers*, by Walter Keady; and *Perdido*, by Rick Collignon.
How to Contact: Does not accept unsolicited mss. Query first with outline/synopsis and 15 sample pages. Include 1-page bio, list of publishing credits, any writing awards or grants. SASE for reply. Agented fiction 75%. Reports in 3 months on queries. Simultaneous submissions OK. Sometimes critiques or comments on rejected mss.
Terms: Pays royalties; offers negotiable advance. Publishes ms 18 months after acceptance. Book catalog for $2.
Advice: "We are most interested in manuscripts that reflect carefully and emotionally on the ways we live our lives, on the things that happen to us, on what we know and believe. Our editors are also drawn to works that contemplate the roles that geography, culture, family and tradition play in all our efforts to define ourselves. We search for works that are free of the modern habit of accepting the world without thought. We publish a very limited number of novels each year and base our selection on literary quality first. Submit a concise, saleable proposal. Tell us why we should publish the book, not just what it is about."

⊘ **JOHN MACRAE BOOKS, (III)**, Imprint of Henry Holt & Co., Inc., 115 W. 18th St., New York NY 10011. (212)886-9200. Estab. 1991. "We publish literary fiction and nonfiction. Our primary interest is in language; strong, compelling writing." Publishes hardcover originals. Publishes 20-25 titles/year.
Needs: Literary, mainstream/contemporary. Recently published *Burning Their Boats*, by Angela Carter (novel).
How to Contact: Does not accept unsolicited mss or queries.
Terms: Pays standard hardcover royalty. Advance varies. Publishes ms 1 year after acceptance.

MAGE PUBLISHERS, (IV), 1032 29th St. NW, Washington DC 20007. (202)342-1642. Fax: (202)342-9269. E-mail: info@mage.com. Website: http://www.mage.com. **Acquisitions**: Amin Sepehri, assistant to publisher. Estab. 1985. "Small independent publisher." Publishes hardcover originals. Averages 4 total titles, 1 fiction title each year.
Needs: "We publish only books on Iran and Persia and translations of Iranian fiction writers." Ethnic (Iran) fiction. Recently published *My Uncle Napolean*, by Iraj Pezeshkzad; *King of the Benighted*, by M. Irani; and *Sutra and Other Stories*, by Simon Daneshvar.
How to Contact: Query first. SASE. Reports in 3 months on queries. Simultaneous and electronic submissions OK.
Terms: Pays royalties. Publishes ms 1 year after acceptance. Writer's guidelines for SASE. Book catalog free.
Advice: "If it isn't related to Persia/Iran, don't waste our time or yours."

✔ Ⓐ **MAIN STREET BOOKS, (V)**, Imprint of Doubleday Adult Trade, 1540 Broadway, New York NY 10036. (212)354-6500. **Acquisitions:** Gerald Howard, editor-in-chief. Estab. 1992. "Main Street Books continues the tradition of Dolphin Books of publishing backlists, but we are focusing more on 'up front' books and big sellers in the areas of self-help, fitness and popular culture." Publishes hardcover originals, trade paperback originals and reprints. Publishes 20-30 titles/year.
Needs: Literary, pop, commercial. Recently published *Outside Providence*, by Peter Farrelly; and *Beeperless Remote*, by Van Whitfield.
How to Contact: Agented submissions only. Reports in 1 month on queries; 6 months on mss. Simultaneous submissions OK, if so noted.
Terms: Offers advance and royalties. Publishes ms 18 months after acceptance. Doubleday book catalog and

AN IMPRINT LISTED IN BOLDFACE TYPE means there is an independent listing arranged alphabetically within this section.

writer's guidelines free.
Advice: "We have a general interest list."

MARCH STREET PRESS, (II), 3413 Wilshire, Greensboro NC 27408-2329. Phone/fax: (336)282-9754. E-mail: rbixby@aol.com. Website: http://users.aol.com/marchst (includes writer's guidelines; names of editors, authors, titles). **Acquisitions:** Robert Bixby, editor/publisher. Estab. 1988. Publishes paperback originals. Books: vellum paper; photocopy; saddle-stitch binding. Averages 4-6 total titles, 1 or fewer fiction titles/year.
Needs: Literary. Short story collections.
How to Contact: *"Accepts unsolicited mss if $10 reading fee enclosed."* Submit complete ms with a cover letter and reading fee. Send SASE for reply, return of ms or send a disposable copy of ms. Reports in 1 week on queries; 6 months on mss. Simultaneous submissions OK. Sometimes critiques or comments on a rejected ms.
Terms: Pays royalty of 15%. Provides 10 author's copies. Sends galleys to author. Publishes ms 6-12 months after acceptance. Writer's guidelines for #10 SASE; also on website.

MARINER BOOKS, (III), Imprint of Houghton Mifflin, 222 Berkeley St., Boston MA 02116. (617)351-5000. Fax: (617)351-1202. Website: http://www.hmco.com. **Acquisitions:** John Radziewicz. Estab. 1997. Publishes trade paperback originals and reprints.

- Mariner Books' *The Blue Flower*, by Penelope Fitzgerald, received the National Book Critics Circle Award.

Needs: Literary, mainstream/contemporary. Recently published *The Blue Flower*, by Penelope Fitzgerald (historical fiction).
How to Contact: Query first. Prefers agented submissions.
Terms: Pays royalty on retail price or makes outright purchase. Advance varies. Book catalog free.

MARIPOSA, (II), Imprint of Scholastic Inc., 555 Broadway, New York NY 10012. (212)343-6100. Website: http://www.scholastic.com. **Acquisitions:** Susana Pasternac, editor. "There is a great need for children's Spanish-language literature, work that is well done and authentic, that fills a *need*, not just a space." Publishes trade paperback originals and reprints. Publishes 20-25 titles/year (2-3 original titles/year).
Needs: Juvenile, picture books, young adult. "We do Spanish-language translations of the Magic School Bus and Goosebumps series." Recently published *Abuela and the Three Bears*, by Jerry Gello and Anna Lopez Escriva (bilingual picture book).
How to Contact: Query with completed ms and SASE. Reports in 3 months on mss. Simultaneous submissions OK.
Terms: Pays royalty on retail price, varies. Publishes ms 1 year after acceptance. Book catalog for #10 SASE.

MARITIMES ARTS PROJECTS PRODUCTIONS, (V), Box 596, Stn. A, Fredericton, New Brunswick E3B 5A6 Canada. Phone/fax: (506)454-5127. E-mail: jblades@nbnet.nb.ca. **Acquisitions**: Joe Blades, publisher. "We are a small, mostly literary Canadian publishing house. We accept only Canadian authors." Publishes Canadian-authored trade paperback originals and reprints. **Publishes 1 previously unpublished writer/year.** Publishes 8-12 titles/year, plus *New Muse of Contempt* magazine. Distributes titles through General Distribution Services Ltd. (Toronto, Vancouver and Buffalo).

- Maritimes Arts Projects Productions is not currently accepting unsolicited submissions or queries. Only accepting mss or queries pertaining to the contest for first book for unpublished fiction writers (New Muse Award). Query with SASE for details.

Imprint(s): Broken Jaw Press, Book Rat, SpareTime Editions, Dead Sea Physh Products.
Needs: Literary. Recently published *Rum River*, by Raymond Fraser; and *Herbarium of Souls*, by Vladimar Tasic.
How to Contact: Not currently accepting unsolicited book mss or queries.
Terms: Pays 10% royalty on retail price. Offers $0-100 advance. Publishes ms 1 year after acceptance. Writer's guidelines for #10 SASE (Canadian postage or IRC). Book catalog for 6½×9½ SAE with 2 first-class Canadian stamps or IRC.

MARLOWE & COMPANY, (III), Avalon Publishing Group, 841 Broadway, 4th Floor, New York NY 10003. (212)614-7880. **Acquisitions**: Jeri T. Smith, acquisitions editor. "We feature challenging, entertaining and topical titles in our extensive publishing program." Publishes hardcover and trade paperback originals and reprints. Publishes 50 titles/year.
Needs: Literary. "We are looking for literary, rather than genre fiction." Recently published *Fata Morgana*, by William Kotzwinkle; and *Heart's Journey In Winter*, by James Buchaw (winner of the Guardian Fiction Prize).
How to Contact: Query with SASE. "We do not accept unsolicited submissions." Reports in 2 months on queries. Simultaneous submissions OK.
Terms: Pays 10% royalty on retail price for hardcover, 6% for paperback. Offers advance of 50% of anticipated first printing. Publishes ms 1 year after acceptance. Book catalog free.

MASQUERADE BOOKS, (IV), Crescent Publishing, 801 Second Ave., New York NY 10017. (212)661-7878. Fax: (212)986-7355. E-mail: masqbks@aol.com. **Acquisitions:** Marti Hohmann, editor-in-chief; Jennifer

Rent, managing editor. Nation's largest erotic press. Publishes hardcover and paperback originals and paperback reprints. Published new writers within the last year. Plans 25 first novels next year. Publishes 125 total titles; 115 fiction titles.

Needs: Erotica, fantasy, gay, historical, horror, lesbian, psychic/supernatural/occult, romance, science fiction, short story collections, thriller/espionage. No children's, young adult, religious. "All manuscripts must contain explicit sexual content. No children, incest, bestiality." Prefers SM/fetish erotica. Recently published *The Slave*, by Laura Antoniou (novel); *Flashpoint: Gay Male Sexual Writing*, by Michael Bronski (anthology); and *The Mad Man*, by Samuel Delany (novel).

How to Contact: Accepts unsolicited submissions. Query or send complete ms with a cover letter. Unsolicited correspondence by e-mail and fax OK. Include estimated word count and list of publishing credits. Send SASE for reply, return of ms or send disposable copy of ms. Agented fiction: 20%. Reports in 2 weeks on queries; 2 months on mss.

Terms: Pays royalties of 5% minimum plus negotiable advance and author's copies. Publishes ms 5-6 months after acceptance. Guideline and catalog free.

Advice: "We are always in the market for well-written, mass-market fiction. Gay market is saturated; no new material until 1999. By contrast, lesbian authors encouraged to submit. Familiarize yourself with our imprints and order a sample copy of our bimonthly magazine before sending us material. Imprints are as follows: Masquerade: straight erotica; Badboy: erotica for gay men; Rosebud: erotica for lesbians; Hard Candy: literary works by gay men with a strong emphasis on sexuality; Rhinoceros: pansexual literary words with a strong emphasis on sexuality."

MARGARET K. McELDERRY BOOKS, (V), Imprint of the Simon & Schuster Children's Publishing Division, 1230 Sixth Ave., New York NY 10020. (212)698-2761. **Acquisitions**: Emma D. Dryden, senior editor. Estab. 1971. Publishes hardcover originals. Books: High quality paper; offset printing; cloth and three-piece bindings; illustrations; average print order: 10,000; first novel print order: 6,000. Published new writers within the last year. Averages 25 total titles each year. Buys juvenile and young adult mss, agented or non-agented. Query first.

- Books published by Margaret K. McElderry Books have received numerous awards including the Newbery and the Caldecott Awards, and a *Boston Globe/Horn Book* honor award. Because of the merger between Macmillan and Simon & Schuster this imprint (still intact) is under a new division (see above).

Needs: All categories (fiction and nonfiction) for juvenile and young adult: adventure, contemporary, early chapter books, fantasy, literary, mystery and picture books. "We will consider any category. Results depend on the quality of the imagination, the artwork and the writing." Recently published *A Summertime Song*, written and illustrated by Irene Haas; *Dog Friday*, by Hilary McKay; and *The Moorchild*, by Eloise McGraw.

Terms: Pays in royalties; offers advance. Publishes ms 18 months after acceptance.

Advice: "Imaginative writing of high quality is always in demand; also picture books that are original and unusual. Picture book manuscripts written in prose are totally acceptable. Keep in mind that McElderry Books is a very small imprint which only publishes 12 or 13 books per season, so we are very selective about the books we will undertake for publication. The YA market is tough right now, so we're being very picky. We try not to publish any 'trend' books. Be familiar with our list and with what is being published this year by all publishing houses."

McGREGOR PUBLISHING, (II), 118 S. Westshore Blvd., Suite 233, Tampa FL 33609. (813)254-2665 or (888)405-2665. Fax: (813)254-6177. E-mail: mcgregpub@aol.com. **Acquisitions:** Dave Rosenbaum, acquisitions editor. Publishes hardcover and trade paperback originals. Publishes 4-6 titles/year.

Needs: Mystery/suspense.

How to Contact: Query or submit synopsis with 2 sample chapters. Reports in 1 month on queries, 2 months on mss. Simultaneous submissions OK.

Terms: Pays 10-12% on retail price; 13-16% on wholesale price. Advances vary. Publishes ms 1 year after acceptance. Writer's guidelines and book catalog free.

Advice: "We work closely with an author to produce quality product with strong promotional campaigns."

MEADOWBROOK PRESS, (II), 5451 Smetana Dr., Minnetonka MN 55343. (612)930-1100. Fax: (612)930-1940. **Acquisitions:** Jason Sanford, fiction editor. Estab. 1975. Publishes trade paperback originals. Publishes 20 titles/year.

Needs: Childrens/juvenile. "We have very specific guidelines for children's fiction. Send for guidelines before submitting. We do not accept unsolicited picture books or novel-length submissions." Recently published *Girls to the Rescue*, Book #5, edited by Bruce Lansky (a collection of stories featuring courageous, clever and determined girls); and *Newfangled Fairy Tales*.

How to Contact: Query first. Reports in 3 months on queries. Simultaneous submissions OK.

Terms: Publishes ms 1 year after acceptance. Writer's guidelines and book catalog for #10 SASE.

Advice: "We publish several fiction anthologies for children and are always on the lookout for quality short stories. We are especially willing to work with new writers—we consider stories on their own merits, not on the reputations of the authors."

MERCURY HOUSE, (V), 336 Clementina St., Suite 300, San Francisco CA 94103. (415)626-7874. Fax: (415)626-7875. Website: http://www.wenet.net/~mercury/. **Acquisitions**: K. Janene-Nelson, managing editor; Tom Christensen, executive director. Estab. 1985. Small nonprofit literary house publishing outstanding work overlooked by mainstream presses, especially with a minority viewpoint. Publishes paperback originals. Books: acid-free paper; notch binding; some illustrations. Average print order: 4,000; first novel print order: 3,500. Averages 8 total titles, 2 fiction titles/year. Member of Consortium Book Sales & Distribution.

- Recent recognition of Mercury House includes a 1998 PEN Oakland Josephine Miles Award for *House With A Blue Bed*, by Alfred Arteaga, and a 1997 French/American Translation Award finalist for *Masters & Servants*, by Pierre Michon, translated by Wyatt Alexander Mason.

Needs: Ethnic/multicultural, experimental, feminist, gay, lesbian, literary, regional (western), translations. Publishes a sacred view of work; black view of jazz anthologies. Recently published *Masters and Servants*, by Pierre Michon, translated by Wyatt A. Mason; *Manhattan Music*, by Meena Alexander (multicultural); and *Ring of Fire: A Pacific Basin Journey*, by James D. Houston (literary travel).
How to Contact: Does not accept unsolicited mss.
Terms: Pays royalties of 10% minimum. Average advance is low. Provides 10 author's copies. Sends galleys to author. Publishes ms in the same season after acceptance. Writer's guidelines free for #10 SASE. Book catalog for 6½×8½ SAE and $1.01 postage.

MILKWEED EDITIONS, (II), 430 First Ave. N., Suite 400, Minneapolis MN 55401-1743. (612)332-3192. Fax: (612)332-6248. E-mail: books@milkweed.org. Website: http://www.milkweededitions.org (includes writer's guidelines, mission statement, catalog, poem of day, excerpts from titles). **Acquisitions**: Emilie Buchwald, publisher; Elisabeth Fitz, manuscript coordinator. Estab. 1984. Nonprofit publisher with the intention of transforming society through literature. Publishes hardcover and paperback originals. Books: book text quality—acid-free paper; offset printing; perfect or hardcover binding. Average print order: 4,000. First novel print order depends on book. Averages 14 total titles/year. Number of fiction titles "depends on manuscripts." Large orders distributed through Publishers Group West, individual orders handled in-house. Promotes titles through author tours, readings, reviews in media publications, mass and individual mailings of catalogs, trade shows.

- Milkweed Editions books have received numerous awards, including Finalist, *LMP* Individual Achievement Award for Editor Emilie Buchwald, awards from the American Library Association, and several Pushcarts.

Needs: For adult readers: literary fiction, nonfiction, poetry, essays; for children (ages 8-12): fiction and biographies. Translations welcome for both audiences. No legends or folktales for children. No romance, mysteries, science fiction.
How to Contact: Send for guidelines first, then submit complete ms. Reports in 1 month on queries; 6 months on mss. Simultaneous submissions OK. "Send for guidelines. Must enclose SASE."
Terms: Authors are paid in royalties of 7%; offers negotiable advance; 10 author's copies. Sends galleys to author. Publishes ms 1 year after acceptance. Book catalog for $1.50 postage.
Advice: "Read good contemporary literary fiction, find your own voice, and persist. Familiarize yourself with our list before submitting."

MINSTREL BOOKS, (II), Imprint of Pocket Books for Young Readers, Imprint of Simon & Schuster, 1230 Avenue of the Americas, New York NY 10020. (212)698-7000. Website: http://www.simonandschuster.com. Editorial director: Patricia McDonald. **Acquisitions:** Attn: Manuscript proposals. Estab. 1986. "Minstrel publishes fun, kid-oriented books, the kinds kids pick for themselves, for middle grade readers, ages 8-12." Publishes hardcover originals and reprints, trade paperback originals. Publishes 125 titles/year.
Needs: Middle grade fiction for ages 8-12: animal stories, fantasy, humor, juvenile, mystery, suspense. No picture books. "Thrillers are very popular, and 'humor at school' books." Recently published *R.L. Stine's Ghosts of Fear Street*, by R.L. Stine; and *Aliens Ate My Homework*, by Bruce Coville.
How to Contact: Query with synopsis/outline, sample chapters and SASE. Reports in 3 months on queries. Simultaneous submissions OK.
Terms: Pays 6-8% royalty on retail price. Advance varies. Publishes ms 2 years after acceptance. Writer's guidelines and book catalog free.
Advice: "Hang out with kids to make sure your dialogue and subject matter are accurate."

MOREHOUSE PUBLISHING CO., (II), 4475 Linglestown Rd., Harrisburg PA 17112. Fax: (717)541-8136. Website: http://www.morehousegroup.com. **Acquisitions:** Debra K. Farrington, editorial director. Estab.

MARKET CATEGORIES: (I) Open to new writers; **(II)** Open to both new and established writers; **(III)** Interested mostly in established writers; **(IV)** Open to writers whose work is specialized; **(V)** Closed to unsolicited submissions.

1884. Morehouse publishes a wide variety of religious nonfiction and fiction with an emphasis on the Anglican faith. Publishes hardcover and paperback originals. Publishes 15 titles/year.
Needs: Juvenile, picture books, religious, young adult. Small children's list. Artwork essential. Recently published *Bless All Creatures Here Below*, by Judith Gwyn Brown; and *Angel and Me*, by Sara Maitland.
How to Contact: Query with synopsis, 2 chapters, intro and SASE. Note: Manuscripts from outside the US will not be returned. Please send copies only. Reports in 4 months. Simultaneous submissions OK.
Terms: Pays 7-10% royalty. Offers $500-1,000 advance. Publishes ms 8 months after acceptance. Book catalog for 9×12 SAE with $1.01 in postage stamps.

WILLIAM MORROW AND COMPANY, INC., (II), 1350 Avenue of the Americas, New York NY 10019. (212)261-6500. Fax: (212)261-6595. **Acquisitions**: Elizabeth Nichols Kelly, vice president and editor-in-chief (William Morrow); Amy Cohn (Beech Tree Books, Mulberry Books); Susan Pearson, editor-in-chief (Lothrop, Lee & Shepard Books); David Reuther, editor-in-chief (Morrow Junior Books); Toni Sciarra, editor (Quill Trade Paperbacks); Elizabeth Shub (Greenwillow Books). Estab. 1926. Approximately one fourth of books published are fiction.
Imprint(s): Greenwillow Books; Hearst Books; Hearst Marine Books; **Lothrop, Lee & Shepard**; Morrow; **Morrow Junior Books**; Mulberry Books; Quill Trade Paperbacks; Tambourine Books; Tupelo Books and Rob Weisbach Books.
Needs: "Morrow accepts only the highest quality submissions" in contemporary, literary, experimental, adventure, mystery/suspense, spy, historical, war, feminist, gay/lesbian, science fiction, horror, humor/satire and translations. Juvenile and young adult divisions are separate.
How to Contact: Submit through agent. All unsolicited mss are returned unopened. "We will accept queries, proposals or mss only when submitted through a literary agent." Simultaneous submissions OK.
Terms: Pays in royalties; offers advance. Sends galleys to author. Publishes ms 2 years after acceptance. Free book catalog.
Advice: "The Morrow divisions of Greenwillow Books; Lothrop, Lee & Shepard; Mulberry Books and Morrow Junior Books handle juvenile books. We do five to ten first novels every year and about one-fourth of the titles are fiction. Having an agent helps to find a publisher."

MORROW JUNIOR BOOKS, (III), 1350 Avenue of the Americas, New York NY 10019. (212)261-6691. **Acquisitions**: Barbara Lalicki, editor-in-chief; Meredith Charpentier, executive editor; Rosemary Brosnan, executive editor; Andrea Curley, senior editor. Publishes hardcover originals. Plans 1 first novel this year. Averages 55 total titles each year.
Needs: Juvenile (5-9 years) including animal, easy-to-read, fantasy (very little), spy/adventure, preschool/picture book, young adult/teen (10-18 years) including historical, sports. Published *I Lost My Bear*, by Jules Feiffer; *My Own Two Feet*, by Beverly Cleary; and *Ghost Canoe*, by Will Hobbs.
How to Contact: Does not accept unsolicited mss.
Terms: Authors paid in royalties; offers variable advance. Books published 12-18 months after acceptance. Book catalog free on request.
Advice: "Our list is very full at this time. No unsolicited manuscripts."

MULTNOMAH PUBLISHERS, INC., (II), P.O. Box 1720, Sisters OR 97759. (541)549-1144. Fax: (541)549-2044. **Acquisitions**: Editorial Dept. Estab. 1987. Midsize independent publisher of evangelical fiction and nonfiction. Publishes paperback originals. Books: perfect binding; average print order: 12,000. Averages 120 total titles, 20-25 fiction titles each year.

- Multnomah Books has received several Gold Medallion Book Awards from the Evangelical Christian Publishers Association.

Needs: Literary, religious/inspirational issue or thesis fiction. Recently published *Virtually Eliminated*, by Jefferson Scott (technothriller); and *A Gathering of Finches*, by Jane Kirkpatrick (historical novel).
How to Contact: Submit outline/synopsis and 3 sample chapters. "Include a cover letter with any additional information that might help us in our review." Send SASE for reply, return of ms or send a disposable copy of ms. Reports in 10 weeks. Simultaneous submissions OK.
Terms: Pays royalties. Provides 100 author's copies. Sends galleys to author. Publishes ms 1-2 years after acceptance. Writer's guidelines for SASE.
Advice: "Looking for clean, moral, uplifting fiction. We're particularly interested in contemporary women's fiction, historical fiction, superior romance, and thesis fiction."

THE MYSTERIOUS PRESS, (III), Crime and mystery fiction imprint for Warner Books, 1271 Avenue of the Americas, New York NY 10120. (212)522-7200. Website: http://www.warnerbooks.com. (includes authors, titles, guidelines, bulletin board, tour info., contests). **Acquisitions**: William Malloy, editor-in-chief. Sara Ann Freed, executive editor. Estab. 1976. Publishes hardcover originals and paperback reprints. Books: Hardcover (some Smythe-sewn) and paperback binding; illustrations rarely. Average first novel print order: 5,000 copies. Published new writers within the last year.

- The Mysterious Press's *Up Jumps the Devil*, by Margaret Maron, won the Agatha Award for Best Mystery Novel.

Needs: Mystery/suspense. Published *The Two-Bear Mambo*, by Joe R. Lansdale; *Both Ends of the Night*, by Marcia Muller; *The Ax* by Donald Westlake; and *Never Street*, by Loren D. Estleman.
How to Contact: Agented material only. Critiques "only those rejected writers we wish to encourage."
Terms: Pays in royalties of 10% minimum; offers negotiable advance. Sends galleys to author. Buys hard and softcover rights. Publishes ms 1 year after acceptance.
Advice: "Write a strong and memorable novel, and with the help of a good literary agent, you'll find the right publishing house. Don't despair if your manuscript is rejected by several houses. All publishing houses are looking for new and exciting crime novels, but it may not be at the time your novel is submitted. Hang in there, keep the faith—and good luck."

THE NAIAD PRESS, INC., (I, II, IV), P.O. Box 10543, Tallahassee FL 32302. (904)539-5965. Fax: (904)539-9731. E-mail: naiadpress@aol.com. Website: http://www.naiadpress.com (includes complete and detailed catalog, order capacity). **Acquisitions**: Barbara Grier, editorial director. Estab. 1973. "Oldest and largest lesbian publishing company. We are scrupulously honest and we keep our books in print for the most part." Books: 50 lb. offset paper; sheet-fed offset; perfect-bound. Average print order: 12,000. First novel print order: 12,000. Publishes 34 total titles each year. Distributes titles through distributors, direct sales to stores and individuals and over the Web. Promotes titles through a first class mailing to over 26,000 lesbians monthly; 2,800 bookstores on mailing list.

- The Naiad Press is one of the most successful and well-known lesbian publishers. They have also produced eight of their books on audio cassette.

Needs: Lesbian fiction, all genres. Recently published *Love in the Balance*, by Marianne K. Martin; *Bad Moon Rising*, by Barbara Johnson; and *Endless Love*, by Lisa Shapiro.
How to Contact: Query first only. SASE. Include outline/synopsis, estimated word count, 2-sentence bio. Reports in 3 weeks on queries; 3 months on mss. No simultaneous submissions.
Terms: Pays 15% royalties using a standard recovery contract. Occasionally pays 7½% royalties against cover price. "Seldom gives advances and has never seen a first novel worthy of one. Believes authors are investments in their own and the company's future—that the best author is the author who produces a book every 12-18 months forever and knows that there is a *home* for that book." Publishes ms 1-2 years after acceptance. Book catalog for legal-sized SASE and $1.50 postage and handling.
Advice: "We publish lesbian fiction primarily and prefer honest work (i.e., positive, upbeat lesbian characters). Lesbian content must be accurate . . . a lot of earlier lesbian novels were less than honest. No breast beating or complaining. Our fiction titles are becoming increasingly *genre* fiction, which we encourage. Original fiction in paperback is our main field, and its popularity increases. We publish books BY, FOR AND ABOUT lesbians. We are not interested in books that are unrealistic. You know and we know what the real world of lesbian interest is like. Don't even try to fool us. Short, well-written books do best. Authors who want to succeed and will work to do so have the best shot."

THE NAUTICAL & AVIATION PUBLISHING CO. OF AMERICA INC., (IV), 8 W. Madison St., Baltimore MD 21201. (410)659-0220. Fax: (410)539-8832. President: Jan Snouck-Hurgronje. **Acquisitions**: Rebecca Irish, editor. Estab. 1979. Small publisher interested in quality military history and literature. Publishes hardcover originals and reprints. Averages 10 total titles, 1-4 fiction titles each year.
Needs: Military/war (especially military history and Civil War). Looks for "novels with a strong military history orientation." Published *Normandy*, by VADM William P. Mack (military fiction); *Straits of Messina*, by VADM William P. Mack (military fiction); and *The Captain*, by Jan De Hartog (military fiction).
How to Contact: Accepts unsolicited mss. Query first or submit complete mss with cover letter. SASE necessary for return of mss. Agented fiction "miniscule." Reports on queries in 2-3 weeks; on mss in 3 weeks. Simultaneous submissions OK. Sometimes comments on rejected mss.
Terms: Pays royalties of 10-15% on selling price. Advance negotiable. After acceptance publishes ms "as quickly as possible—next season." Book catalog free on request.
Advice: Publishing more fiction. Encourages first novelists. "We're interested in good writing—first novel or last novel. Keep it historical, put characters in a historical context. Professionalism counts. Know your subject. *Convince us.*"

NAVAL INSTITUTE PRESS, (II), Imprint of U.S. Naval Institute, 118 Maryland Ave., Annapolis MD 21402-5035. Fax: (410)269-7940. E-mail: esecunda@usni.org. Website: http://www.usni.org. Press Director: Ronald Chambers. **Acquisitions:** Paul Wilderson, executive editor; Mark Gatlin, senior acquisitions editor; Scott Belliveau, acquisitions editor. Estab. 1873. The U.S. Naval Institute Press publishes general and scholarly books of professional, scientific, historical and literary interest to the naval and maritime community. Publishes 80 titles/year. Average print order for a first book is 2,000.
Imprint(s): Bluejacket Books (paperback reprints).
Needs: Limited fiction on military and naval themes. Recently published *Rising Wind*, by Dick Couch (modern military thriller).
How to Contact: Query letter strongly recommended.
Terms: Pays 5-10% royalty on net sales. Publishes ms 1 year after acceptance. Writer's guidelines for #10 SASE. Book catalog free with 9×12 SASE.

✔ **THOMAS NELSON PUBLISHERS, (IV)**, Thomas Nelson, Inc., 404 BNA Dr., Bldg. 200, Suite 508, Nashville TN 37217. (615)902-2415. Website: http://www.tommynelson.com. Estab. 1798. **Acquisitions:** Laura Minchew, acquisitions editor. "Largest Christian book publishers." Publishes hardcover and paperback originals. Averages 50-75 total titles each year.
Imprint(s): Word Kids.
Needs: Adventure, children's/juvenile (adventure), mystery/suspense, religious/inspirational (general), western (frontier saga, traditional). "All work must be Christian in focus." No short stories. Published *A Skeleton in God's Closet*, by Paul Maier (suspense/mystery); *The Twilight of Courage*, by Brock and Bodie Thoene (historical suspense); and *The Secrets of the Roses*, by Lila Peiffer (romance).
How to Contact: Corporate office does not accept unsolicited mss. "No phone queries." Send brief prosaic résumé, 1 page synopsis, an SASE and one sample chapter. Reports on queries in 1 month; 3 months on mss.
Terms: Pays royalty on wholesale price or makes outright purchase. Offers negotiable advance. Sends galleys to author. Publishes ms 1-2 years after acceptance. Writer's guidelines for #10 SASE. Simultaneous submissions OK if so stated in cover letter.
Advice: "We are a conservative publishing house and want material which is conservative in morals and in nature."

✔ **NEW VICTORIA PUBLISHERS, (II, IV)**, P.O. Box 27, Norwich VT 05055-0027. Phone/fax: (802)649-5297. E-mail: newvic@aol.com. Website: http://www.opendoor.com/NewVic/ (includes list of titles). **Acquisitions**: Claudia Lamperti, editor; ReBecca Béguin, editor. Estab. 1976. Small, three-person operation. Publishes trade paperback originals. Plans 2-5 first novels this year. **Publishes approximately 3 previously unpublished writers/year.** Averages 8-10 titles/year. Distributes titles through Inbook/LPC Group.

- Books published by New Victoria Publishers have been nominated for Lambda Literary Awards and the Vermont Book Publishers Special Merit Award.

Needs: Lesbian/feminist: adventure, fantasy, historical, humor, mystery (amateur sleuth), romance. Looking for "strong feminist characters, also strong plot and action. We will consider most anything if it is well written and appeals to a lesbian/feminist audience; mostly mysteries." Publishes anthologies or special editions. Query for guidelines. Recently published *Rafferty Street*, by Lee Lynch (novel); *Killing At the Cat*, by Carlene Miller (mystery); and *Skin to Skin*, by Martha Miller (erotic short fiction).
How to Contact: Submit outline/synopsis and sample chapters. SASE. Unsolicited queries/correspondence by e-mail and fax OK. Reports in 2 weeks on queries; 1 month on mss.
Terms: Pays royalties of 10%. Publishes ms 1 year after acceptance. Book catalog free.
Advice: "We are especially interested in lesbian or feminist mysteries, ideally with a character or characters who can evolve through a series of books. Mysteries should involve a complex plot, accurate legal and police procedural detail, and protagonists with full emotional lives. Pay attention to plot and character development. Read guidelines carefully."

✔ **NEW YORK UNIVERSITY PRESS**, 70 Washington Square, New York NY 10012. (212)998-2575. Fax: (212)995-3833. E-mail: nyupmark@elmer2.bobst.nyu.edu. Website: http://www.nyu.edu/pages/nyupress/index.html. **Acquisitions:** Jennifer Hammer (psychology, religion); Eric Zinner (cultural studies, media, anthropology); Niko Pfund (business, history, law); Stephen Mayro (social science). Estab. 1916. "New York University Press embraces ideological diversity. We often publish books on the same issue from different poles to generate dialogue, engender and resist pat categorizations." Hardcover and trade paperback originals. **Publishes 30% previously unpublished writers/year.**
Needs: Literary. "We publish only 1 fiction title per year and don't encourage fiction submissions." Recently published *Bird-Self Accumulated*, by Don Judson (novella).
How to Contact: Submit synopsis and 1 sample chapter with SASE. Reports in 1 month. Simultaneous submissions OK.
Terms: Advance and royalty on net receipts varies. Publishes ms 8 months after acceptance.

🍁 ✔ **NEWEST PUBLISHERS LTD., (IV)**, 201, 8540-109 St., Edmonton, Alberta T6G 1E6 Canada. (403)432-9427. Fax: (403)433-3179. E-mail: newest@planet.eon.net. **Acquisitions**: Liz Grieve, general manager. Estab. 1977. Publishes trade paperback originals. Published new writers within the last year. Averages 8 total titles, fiction and nonfiction. Distributes titles through General Distribution Services. Promotes titles through book launches, media interviews, review copy mailings and touring.
Needs: Literary. "Our press is interested in western Canadian writing." Recently published *The Widows*, by Suzette Mayr (novel); *The Blood Girls*, by Meira Cook (novel); and *Baser Elements*, by Murray Malcolm (crime fiction). Publishes the Nunatak New Fiction Series.

● **A BULLET INTRODUCES COMMENTS** by the editor of *Novel & Short Story Writer's Market* indicating special information about the listing.

How to Contact: Accepts unsolicited mss. Query first or submit outline/synopsis and 3 sample chapters. Accepts queries/mss by e-mail. SASE necessary for return of ms. Reports in 2 months on queries; 4 months on mss. Rarely offers comments on rejected mss.
Terms: Pays royalties of 10% minimum. Sends galleys to author. Publishes ms at least 1 year after acceptance. Book catalog for 9×12 SASE.
Advice: "*We publish western Canadian writers only or books about western Canada.* We are looking for excellent quality and originality."

NIGHTSHADE PRESS, (II), Ward Hill, Troy ME 04987-0076. (207)948-3427. Fax: (207)948-5088. E-mail: potatoeyes@uninets.net. Website: http://www.litline.org (includes guidelines, newsletter, book list). Contact: Carolyn Page or Roy Zarucchi, editors. Estab. 1988. "Fulltime small press publishing literary magazine, poetry chapbooks, plus 1 or 2 nonfiction projects per year. Short stories or essays for *Potato Eyes only, no novels please*." Publishes paperback originals. Books: 60 lb. paper; offset printing; saddle-stitched or perfect-bound; illustrations. Average print order: 400. Published new writers within the last year. Averages 4 total titles (all poetry) plus 2 issues of the literary magazine *Potato Eyes*. *Potato Eyes* sometimes uses guest editors. Promotes titles through mailing lists and independent book stores.
Needs: Contemporary, feminist, humor/satire, literary, mainstream, regional. No religious, romance, preschool, juvenile, young adult, psychic/occult. Published *Two If By Sea*, by Edward M. Holmes; *Nightshade Nightstand Short Story Reader*, foreward by Fred Chappell; and *Every Day A Visitor*, by Richard Abrons.
How to Contact: Accepts unsolicited mss—short stories only. "Willing to read agented material." Unsolicited queries by e-mail OK. Reports in 1 month on queries; 3-4 months on mss. Sometimes comments on rejected mss.
Terms: Pays 2 author's copies. Publishes ms about 1 year after acceptance. Writer's guidelines and book catalog for SASE. Individual contracts negotiated with authors.
Advice: "Would like to see more real humor; less gratuitous violence—the opposite of TV. We have overdosed on heavily dialected southern stories which treat country people with a mixture of ridicule and exaggeration. We prefer treatment of characterization which offers dignity and respect for folks who make do with little and who respect their environment. We are also interested in social criticism, in writers who take chances and who color outside the lines. We also invite experimental forms. Read us first. An investment of $5 may save the writer twice that in postage."

NOONDAY PRESS, (II), Imprint of Farrar Straus Giroux, Inc., 19 Union Square W., New York NY 10003. (212)741-6900. Fax: (212)633-2427. **Acquisitions:** Judy Klein, executive editor. Noonday emphasizes literary nonfiction and fiction, as well as fiction and poetry reprints. Publishes trade paperback originals and reprints.
Needs: Literary. Mostly reprints of classic authors. Recently published *Annie John*, by Jamaica Kincaid; and *Enemies: A Love Story*, by Isaac Bashevis Singer.
How to Contact: Query with outline. Reports in 2 months on queries. Simultaneous submissions OK.
Terms: Pays 6% royalty on retail price. Advance varies. Publishes ms 1 year after acceptance. Writer's guidelines free.

NORTHLAND PUBLISHING CO., INC., (II), P.O. Box 1389, Flagstaff AZ 86002-1389. (520)774-5251. Fax: (520)774-0592. E-mail: emurphy@northlandpub.com. Website: http://www.northlandpub.com. **Acquisitions:** Erin Murphy, editor-in-chief. Estab. 1958. "We seek authoritative manuscripts on our specialty subjects; no mainstream, general fiction or nonfiction." Publishes hardcover and trade paperback originals. **Publishes 30% previously unpublished writers/year.** Averages 10 titles/year.

- This publisher has received the following awards: National Cowboy Hall of Fame Western Heritage Award for Outstanding Juvenile Book (*The Night the Grandfathers Danced*); Colorado Book Awards—Best Children's Book (*Goose and the Mountain Lion*); Reading Rainbow Book (*It Rained on the Desert Today*).

Imprint(s): Rising Moon (books for young readers).
Needs: Unique children's picture book and middle reader chapter book stories, especially those with Southwest/West regional theme; Native American folktales (retold by Native Americans only, please). Picture book mss should be 350-1,500 words; chapter book mss should be approximately 20,000 words. Does not want to see "mainstream" stories. Northland does not publish general trade fiction. Recently published *The Night the Grandfathers Danced*, by Linda Theresa Raczek, illustrated by Katalin Ohla Ehling; and *My Name is York*, by Elizabeth Van Steenwyk, illustrated by Bill Farnsworth (children's book).
How to Contact: Query or submit outline and 3 sample chapters. Reports in 1 month on queries; 3 months on mss. No fax or e-mail submissions. Simultaneous submissions OK if so noted.
Terms: Pays 5-12% royalty on net receipts, depending upon terms. Offers $4,000-5,000 average advance. Publishes ms 2 years after acceptance. Writer's guidelines and book catalog for 9×12 SAE with $1.50 in postage.
Advice: "Our audience is composed of general interest readers and those interested in specialty subjects such as Native American culture and crafts. It is not necessarily a scholarly market, but it is sophisticated."

NORTH-SOUTH BOOKS, (V), affiliate of Nord-Sud Verlag AG, 1123 Broadway, Suite 800, New York NY 10010. (212)463-9736. Website: http://www.northsouth.com. **Acquisitions:** Julie Amper. Estab. 1985. "The aim of North-South is to build bridges—bridges between authors and artists from different countries and between readers of all ages. We believe children should be exposed to as wide a range of artistic styles as possible with universal themes." Publishes 5% previously unpublished writers/year. Publishes 100 titles/year.

• North-South Books is the publisher of the international bestseller, *The Rainbow Fish*.

Needs: Picture books, easy-to-read. "We are currently accepting only picture books; all other books are selected by our German office." Recently published *The Rainbow Fish & the Big Blue Whale*, by Marcus Pfister (picture); *The Other Side of the Bridge*, Wolfram Hänel (easy-to-read); and *A Mouse in the House*, by G. Wagener.
How to Contact: Agented fiction only. Query. Does not respond unless interested. All unsolicited mss returned unopened. Returns submissions accompanied by SASE.
Terms: Pays royalty on retail price. Publishes ms 2 years after acceptance.

W.W. NORTON & COMPANY, INC., (II), 500 Fifth Ave., New York NY 10110. (212)354-5500. Website: http://www.norton.com. Estab. 1924. Midsize independent publisher of trade books and college textbooks. Publishes literary fiction. Publishes hardcover originals. Occasionally comments on rejected mss.

• *Ship Fever*, by Andrea Barrett, published by W.W. Norton & Company, Inc., won the National Book Award.

Needs: High-quality literary fiction. No occult, science fiction, religious, gothic, romances, experimental, confession, erotica, psychic/supernatural, fantasy, horror, juvenile or young adult. Recently published *Ship Fever*, by Andrea Barrett; *Oyster*, by Jannette Turner Hospital; and *Power*, by Linda Hogan.
How to Contact: Submit query letter to "Editorial Department" listing credentials and briefly describing ms. SASE. Simultaneous submissions OK. Reports in 8-10 weeks. Packaging and postage must be enclosed to ensure safe return of materials.
Advice: "We will occasionally encourage writers of promise whom we do not immediately publish. We are principally interested in the literary quality of fiction manuscripts. A familiarity with our current list of titles will give you an idea of what we're looking for. If your book is good and you have no agent you may eventually succeed; but the road to success will be easier and shorter if you have an agent backing the book."

ONE WORLD, (II), Imprint of Ballantine Publishing, 201 E. 50th St., New York NY 10022. (212)572-2620. Fax: (212)940-7539. Website: http://www.randomhouse.com. **Acquisitions:** Cheryl Woodruff, associate publisher; Gary Brozek, associate editor. Estab. 1992. "One World's list includes books written by and focused on African Americans, Native Americans, Asian Americans and Latino Americans. We concentrate on *American* multicultural experiences." Publishes hardcover and trade paperback originals, trade and mass market paperback reprints. **Publishes 25% previously unpublished writers/year;** 5% from unagented writers.
Needs: Historical. "We are looking for good contemporary fiction. In the past, topics have mostly been 'pre-Civil rights era and before.' " Published *Kinfolks*, by Kristin Hunter Lattany (novel).
How to Contact: Query with synopsis, 3 sample chapters (100 pages) and SASE. Reports in 4 months.
Terms: Pays 8-12% royalty on retail price, varies from hardcover to mass market. Advance varies. Publishes ms 2 years after acceptance. Writer's guidelines and book catalog for #10 SASE.
Advice: "For first-time authors, have a completed manuscript. You won't be asked to write on speculation."

ORCA BOOK PUBLISHERS LTD., (I, IV), P.O. Box 5626, Station B, Victoria, British Columbia V8R 6S4 Canada. (250)380-1229. Fax: (250)380-1892. E-mail: orca@pinc.com. Website: http://www.pinc.com/orca. Publisher: R.J. Tyrrell. Estab. 1984. **Acquisitions**: Ann Featherstone, children's book editor. "Regional publisher of West Coast-oriented titles." Publishes hardcover and paperback originals. Books: quality 60 lb. book stock paper; illustrations Average print order: 3,000-5,000. First novel print order: 2,000-3,000. Plans 1-2 first novels this year. Averages 20-25 total titles, 1-2 fiction titles each year. Sometimes comments on rejected mss.
Needs: Contemporary, juvenile (5-9 years), literary, mainstream, young adult/teen (10-18 years). Looking for "contemporary fiction." No "romance, science fiction."
How to Contact: Query first, then submit outline/synopsis and 1 or 2 sample chapters. SASE. Agented fiction 20%. Reports in 2 weeks on queries; 1-2 months on mss. Publishes Canadian authors only.
Terms: Pays royalties of 10%; $500 average advance. Sends galleys to author. Publishes ms 6 months-1 year after acceptance. Writer's guidelines for SASE. Book catalog for 8½×11 SASE.
Advice: "We are looking to promote and publish Canadians."

ORCHARD BOOKS, (II), A Grolier Publishing Company, 95 Madison Ave., New York NY 10016. (212)951-2600. **Acquisitions:** Sarah Caguiat, editor; Ana Cerro, editor; Dominic Barth, associate editor. Orchard specializes in children's illustrated and picture books. Publishes hardcover and trade paperback originals. **Publishes 25% previously unpublished writers/year.**
Needs: Picture books, young adult, middle reader, board book, novelty. Published *Silver Packages*, by Rylant and Soentpiet; and *Mysterious Thelonius*, by Raschka.
How to Contact: Query with SASE. Reports in 3 months on queries.
Terms: Pays 7½-10% royalty on retail price. Advance varies. Publishes ms 1 year after acceptance.
Advice: "Go to a bookstore and read several Orchard Books to get an idea of what we publish. Write what you feel and query us if you think it's 'right.' It's worth finding the right publishing match."

ORIENT PAPERBACKS, (II), A division of Vision Books Pvt Ltd., Madarsa Rd., Kashmere Gate, Delhi 110 006 India. Editor: Sudhir Malhotra. Publishes 10-15 novels or story collections/year. "We are one of the largest paperback publishers in S.E. Asia and publish English fiction by authors from this part of the world."
Needs: Length: 40,000 words minimum.
Terms: Pays royalty on copies sold.
How to Contact: Send cover letter, brief summary, 1 sample chapter and author's bio data. "We send writers' guidelines on accepting a proposal."

ORPHEUS ROMANCE, (I, II), Red Merle Ltd., Pinegrove Box 64004, Oakville, Ontario L6K 2C0 Canada. (905)337-2188. Fax: (905)337-0999. E-mail: info@orpheusromance.com. Website: http://www.OrpheusRomance.com and http://www.iReadRomance.com (includes submission guidelines; online/downloadable romance short stories; online zine; "Orpheus Romancer"; chat rooms; forums; profiles; etc.). **Acquisitions:** Marybeth O'Halloran, fiction editor (Orpheus Romance—classic/modern/chimeric/period, including Bittersweets); Maralyn Ellis, fiction editor (Retrospective Romance [1900-1960s]); Kirsten Jarvis, fiction editor (Orpheus Romancer—Bedtime Bites). Estab. 1966. "Orpheus Romance publishes fresh, first-rate romantic fiction, including: Bittersweets (less traditional endings); Retrospectives (1900-1960s romances) and all other traditional romance categories in both novel and shorter lengths." Publishes paperback originals and online/downloadable originals. Books: 50 lb. book newsprint; sheet-fed offset; perfect binding; cover duotone illustrations. Published 5 new writers within the last year. Plans 6 first novels in 1999. Averages 6 fiction titles/year.
Needs: Romance (contemporary, futuristic/time travel, gothic, historical, regency period, romantic suspense), young adult/teen (romance). Especially looking for Retrospective (1900-1960s), Bittersweets, Generationals (sagas) and Englightenments. Recently published *True Love*, by Flora Kidd and *Cheyenne Moon*, by Karlyn Thayer (online short stories); and *Stand & Deliver*, by Kat McBride (novelette). Publishes Generationals series (family sagas; stories through time).
How to Contact: Accepts unsolicited mss. Query with outline/synopsis and 3 sample chapters. Unsolicited queries/correspondence by e-mail and fax OK. Include estimated word count, 200-word bio and list of publishing credits. Send SASE for reply; send a disposable copy of ms. Reports in 6 weeks on queries; 2 months on mss. Electronic submissions (disk or modem) OK. Sometimes critiques or comments on rejected ms.
Terms: Pays royalties for novels. Advance negotiable. Pays 5¢/word for short stories. "Payment by individual arrangement with author." Sends galleys to author. Publishes ms up to one year after acceptance. Writer's guidelines for SASE (1 IRC). Book catalog for #10 SASE (1 IRC).
Advice: "We are looking for professional, polished manuscripts with strong elements of characterization, setting, plot and resolution. We are publishing topics and themes that are a little broader than traditional mainstream romance but the romance must still be central."

✓ **RICHARD C. OWEN PUBLISHERS INC., (II)**, P.O. Box 585, Katonah NY 10536. Fax: (914)232-3903. **Acquisitions:** Janice Boland, director of children's books. "Our focus is literacy education with a meaning-centered perspective. We believe students become enthusiastic, independent, life-long learners when supported and guided by skillful teachers. The professional development work we do and the books we publish support these beliefs." Publishes hardcover and paperback originals. **Publishes 4 previously unpublished writers/year.** Distributes titles to schools via mail order. Promotes titles through data base mailing, reputation, catalog, brochures, appropriate publications—magazines, etc.

- "We are also seeking manuscripts for our new collection of short, snappy stories for 8-10-year-old children (3rd and 4th grades). Subjects include humor, careers, mysteries, science fiction, folktales, women, fashion trends, sports, music, myths, journalism, history, inventions, planets, architecture, plays, adventure, technology, vehicles."

Needs: Picture books. "Brief, strong story line, real characters, natural language, exciting—child-appealing stories with a twist. No lists, alphabet or counting books." Recently published *Play Ball*, by Gail Fleagle; *The Old Train*, by Rick Latta; and *The Children of Sierra Leone*, by Arama Christiana (picture storybooks).
How to Contact: Send for ms guidelines, then submit full ms with SASE. Reports in 1 month on queries; 2 months on mss. Simultaneous submissions OK, if so noted.
Terms: Pays 5% royalty on wholesale price. Publishes ms 3 years after acceptance. Writer's guidelines for SASE with 52¢ postage.
Advice: "We don't respond to queries. Because our books are so brief it is better to send entire ms."

✓ **OWL BOOKS, (II)**, Imprint of Henry Holt & Co., Inc., 115 W. 18th St., New York NY 10011. (212)886-9200. **Acquisitions:** David Sobel, senior editor. Estab. 1996. "We are looking for original, great ideas that have commercial appeal, but that you can respect." **Publishes 30% previously unpublished writers/year.**

INTERESTED IN A PARTICULAR GENRE? Check our new sections for: **Mystery/Suspense**, page 57; **Romance**, page 77; **Science Fiction & Fantasy**, page 95.

Needs: Literary mainstream/contemporary. Published *White Boy Shuffle*, by Paul Beatty; and *The Debt to Pleasure*, by John Lanchester.
How to Contact: Query with synopsis, 1 sample chapter and SASE. Reports in 2 months. Simultaneous submissions OK.
Terms: Pays 6-7½% royalty on retail price. Advance varies. Publishes ms 1 year after acceptance.

OWL CREEK PRESS, (II), 2693 SW Camano Dr., Camano Island WA 98292. **Acquisitions:** Rich Ives, editor. "We publish selections on artistic merit only." Publishes hardcover originals, trade paperback originals and reprints. Publishes 4-6 titles/year. **50% from previously unpublished writers.**
Needs: Literary, short story collections. Recently published *The Body of Martin Aguilera*, by Percival Everett; and *Beasts of the Forest, Beasts of the Field*, by Matt Pavelich.
How to Contact: Submit 1 sample chapter. Reports in 3 months.
Terms: Pays 10-15% royalty, makes outright purchase or with a percentage of print run. Publishes ms 2 years after acceptance. Book catalog for #10 SASE.

✓ **PANTHEON BOOKS, (III)**, Subsidiary of Random House, 201 E. 50th St., 25th Floor, New York NY 10022. (212)751-2600. Fax: (212)572-6030. Editorial Director: Dan Frank. Editor: Claudine O'Hearn. Senior Editor: Shelley Wagner. Executive Editor: Erroll McDonald. **Acquisitions**: Editorial Department. Estab. 1942. "Small but well-established imprint of well-known large house." Publishes hardcover and trade paperback originals and trade paperback reprints. Averages 75 total titles, about one-third fiction, each year.
Needs: Quality fiction and nonfiction. Published *Crooked Little Heart*, by Anne Lamott.
How to Contact: Query letter and sample material. SASE.
Payment/Terms: Pays royalties; offers advance.

✓ 🏆 **PAPIER-MACHE PRESS, (II)**, 627 Walker St., Watsonville CA 95076-4119. (408)763-1420. Fax: (408)763-1422. Website: http://www.ReadersNdex.com/papiermache. **Acquisitions**: Shirley Coe, acquisitions editor. Estab. 1984. "Small women's press." Publishes anthologies, novels. Books: 60-70 lb. offset paper; perfect-bound or case-bound. Average print order: 25,000. Published new writers within the last year. Publishes 6-10 total titles/year.

- Papier-Mache Press author Molly Giles won the Small Press Book Award for Fiction and the California Book Award for Fiction for *Creek Walk and Other Stories*.

Needs: Contemporary, short stories on announced themes. Recently published *At Our Core: Women Writing About Power*, by Sandra Martz (anthology); and *Generation to Generation*, by Sandra Martz and Shirley Coe (anthology).
How to Contact: Send SASE for current submission guidelines.
Terms: Standard royalty agreements and complimentary copy. Publishes ms 18 months after acceptance. Writer's guidelines and book catalog free.
Advice: "Request submission guidelines regarding upcoming anthology themes and submission periods."

PASSEGGIATA PRESS, INC., (III, IV), P.O. Box 636, Pueblo CO 81002. (719)544-1038. Fax: (719)546-7889. **Acquisitions**: Donald Herdeck, publisher/editor-in-chief. Estab. 1973. "We search for books that will make clear the complexity and value of non-Western literature and culture." Small independent publisher with expanding list. Publishes hardcover and paperback originals and reprints. Books: library binding; illustrations. Average print order: 1,000-1,500. First novel print order: 1,000. Averages 15 total titles, 6-8 fiction titles each year. **15% of books from first-time authors; 99% from unagented writers.**
Needs: "We publish original fiction only by writers from Africa, the Caribbean, the Middle East, Asia and the Pacific. No fiction by writers from North America or Western Europe." Published *Lina: Portrait of a Damascene Girl*, by Samar Altar; *The Native Informant*, by Ramzi Salti (stories); and *Repudiation*, by Rachid Boudjedra.
How to Contact: Query with outline/synopsis and sample pages with SASE. State "origins (non-Western), education and previous publications." Reports in 1 month on queries; 2 months on mss. Simultaneous submissions OK. Occasionally critiques ("a few sentences") rejected mss.
Terms: "Send inquiry letter first and ms only if so requested by us. We are not a subsidy publisher, but do a few specialized titles a year with grants. In those cases we accept institutional subventions. Foundation or institution receives 20-30 copies of book and at times royalty on first printing. We pay royalties twice yearly (against advance) as a percentage of net paid receipts." Royalties of 5% minimum; 10% maximum. Offers negotiable advance, $300 average. Provides 10 author's copies. Sends galleys to author. Free book catalog available; inquiry letter first and ms only if so requested by us.
Advice: "Submit professional work (within our parameters of interest) with well worked-over language and clean manuscripts prepared to exacting standards."

🏆 **PEACHTREE PUBLISHERS, LTD., (IV)**, 494 Armour Circle NE, Atlanta GA 30324. (404)876-8761. Fax: (404)875-2578. Website: http://www.peachtree-online.com (includes writer's guidelines, current catalog of titles, upcoming promotional events, behind-the-scenes look at creating a book). President: Margaret Quinlin. **Acquisitions**: Sarah Smith, fiction editor. Estab. 1977. Small, independent publisher specializing in general interest publications, particularly of Southern origin. Publishes hardcover and paperback originals and hardcover

reprints. Average first novel print run 5,000-8,000. Averages 18-20 total titles, 1-2 fiction titles each year. **Publishes 2 previously unpublished writers/year.** Plans 3 first novels this year. Promotes titles through review copies to appropriate publications, press kits and book signings at local bookstores.
Imprint(s): Freestone and Peachtree Jr.

- Peachtree has received the 1998 Books for the Teen Age and the 1998 Oklahoma Book Award for *Hero*, by S.L. Rottman. They recently put a stronger emphasis on books for children and young adults.

Needs: Young adult and juvenile fiction. Contemporary, literary, mainstream, regional. "We are primarily seeking Southern fiction: Southern themes, characters, and/or locales, and children's books." No adult science fiction/fantasy, horror, religious, romance, historical or mystery/suspense. "We are seeking YA and juvenile works including mystery and historical fiction, however." Published *Hero*, by S.L. Rottman; *Over What Hill?* and *Out to Pasture*, by Effie Wilder.
How to Contact: Accepts unsolicited mss. Query, submit outline/synopsis and 50 pages, or submit complete ms with SASE. Reports in 1 month on queries; 3 months on mss. Simultaneous submissions OK.
Terms: Pays in royalties. Sends galleys to author. Free writer's guidelines. Publishes ms 2 years after acceptance. Book catalog for 2 first-class stamps.
Advice: "We encourage original efforts in first novels."

PEEPAL TREE PRESS, (II), 17 King's Ave., Leeds LS6 1QS England. E-mail: submissions@peepal.demon.co.uk. **Acquisitions**: Jeremy Poynting, fiction editor. Publishes 3 previously unpublished writers/year. Averages 12-14 fiction titles/year.
Needs: "Peepal Tree publishes primarily Caribbean and Black British fiction, though it has begun to expand into African and South Asian writing. We publish both novels and collections of short stories." Recently published *Uncle Obadiah & the Alien*, by Geoffrey Philp (Caribbean); *The View from Belmon*, by Kevyn Alan Arthur (Caribbean/historical); and *Excavation*, by Jean Goulbourne (Caribbean/adventure). Length: 25,000 words minimum; 100,000 words maximum.
How to Contact: Send a cover letter, synopsis and 3 sample chapters.
Terms: Pays 10% royalties, in general no advances.
Advice: "We suggest that authors send for a copy of our catalog to get some sense of the range and parameters of what we do." Peepal Tree publishes an annual catalog from the address above. Catalog is also available by e-mail: hannah@peepal.demon.co.uk.

PELICAN PUBLISHING COMPANY, (IV), Box 3110, Gretna LA 70054-3110. (504)368-1175. Website: http://www.pelicanpub.com (includes writer's guidelines, featured book, index of Pelican books). **Acquisitions**: Nina Kooij, editor-in-chief. Estab. 1926. "We seek writers on the cutting edge of ideas. We believe ideas have consequences. One of the consequences is that they lead to a bestselling book." Publishes paperback reprints and hardcover originals. Books: Hardcover and paperback binding; illustrations sometimes. Buys juvenile mss with illustrations. Distributes titles internationally through distributors, bookstores, libraries. Promotes titles at reading and book conventions, in trade magazines, in radio interviews, print reviews and TV interviews.
Needs: Juvenile fiction, especially with a regional and/or historical focus. No young adult fiction, contemporary fiction or fiction containing graphic language, violence or sex. Also no "psychological" novels. Recently published *A Coat of Blue and a Coat of Gray*, by Harold Bell Wright (middle reader Civil War novel).
How to Contact: Prefers query. May submit outline/synopsis and 2 sample chapters with SASE. No simultaneous submissions. "Not responsible if writer's only copy is sent." Reports in 1 month on queries; 3 months on mss. Publishes ms 12-18 months after acceptance. Comments on rejected mss "infrequently."
Terms: Pays 10% in royalties; 10 contributor's copies; advance considered. Sends galleys to author. Publishes ms 18 months after acceptance. Catalog of titles and writer's guidelines for SASE.
Advice: "Research the market carefully. Request our catalog to see if your work is consistent with our list. For ages 8 and up, story must be planned in chapters that will fill at least 90 double-spaced manuscript pages. Topic should be historical and, preferably, linked to a particular region or culture. We look for stories that illuminate a particular place and time in history and that are clean entertainment. The only original adult work we might consider is historical fiction, preferably Civil War (not romance). For middle readers, regional historical or regional adventure could be considered. Please don't send three or more chapters unless solicited. Follow our guidelines listed under 'How to Contact.' "

✔ **PEMMICAN PUBLICATIONS, (II, IV)**, 1635 Burrows Ave., Unit 2, Winnipeg, Manitoba R2X 3B5 Canada. (204)589-6346. Fax: (204)589-2063. E-mail: pemmican@pemmican.mb.ca. Website: http://www.pemmican.mb.ca. **Acquisitions**: Sue Maclean, managing editor. Estab. 1980. Metis and Aboriginal children's books, some adult. Publishes paperback originals. Books: stapled binding and perfect-bound; 4-color illustrations. Average print order: 2,500. First novel print order: 1,000. Published new writers within the last year. Averages 9 total titles each year. Distributes titles through Pemmican Publications. Promotes titles through press releases, fax, catalogues and book displays.
Needs: Children's/juvenile (American Indian, easy-to-read, preschool/picture book); ethnic/multicultural (Native American). Recently published *Red Parka Mary*, by Peter Eyvindson (children's); *Nanabosho & Kitchie Odjig*, by Joe McLellan (native children's legend); and *Jack Pine Fish Camp*, by Tina Umpherville (children's). Also publishes the Builders of Canada series.

How to Contact: Accepts unsolicited mss. Submit complete ms with cover letter. Send SASE (or IRC) for reply, return of ms or send a disposable copy of ms. Reports in 1 year. Simultaneous submissions OK.
Terms: Pays royalties of 10% minimum. Average advance: $350. Provides 10 author's copies.

PENGUIN PUTNAM INC., 375 Hudson St., New York NY 10014. Website: http://www.penguinputnam.com. See the listing for Dutton Signet.

PERFECTION LEARNING CORP., (I, II, IV), 10520 New York Ave., Des Moines IA 50322. (515)278-0133. Fax: (515)278-2980. E-mail: perflern@netins.net. **Acquisitions:** Sue Thies, senior editor K-12 books—Cover-to-Cover imprint. Midsize, supplemental publisher of educational materials. Publishes hardcover and paperback originals. **Publishes 10-15 previously unpublished writers/year.** Publishes 50-75 total titles/year, fiction and nonfiction. Distributes titles through catalog and sales reps. Promotes titles through educational conferences, brochures, sales calls.
Imprint(s): Cover-to-Cover (contact: Sune Thies, senior editor, all genres).
Needs: Hi/lo mss in all genres. Readability of ms should be at least second grade levels below interest level. Please do not submit mss with fewer than 4,000 words or more than 20,000 words. Recently published *Tall Shadow*, by Bonnie Highsmith Taylor (Native American); *The Rattlesnack Necklace*, by Linda Baxter (historical fiction); and *Tales of Mark Twain*, by Peg Hall (retold short stories)."
How to Contact: Query with outline/synopsis and 3-4 sample chapters or submit complete ms with a cover letter. Unsolicited queries/correspondence by e-mail or fax OK. Include 1-page bio, estimated word count and list of publishing credits. Send SASE for reply, return of ms or send a disposable copy of the ms. Reports in 1-2 months on queries; 3-4 months on mss. Simultaneous submissions OK.
Terms: Publishes ms 6-8 months after acceptance. Fiction guidelines free.
Advice: "We are an educational publisher. Check with educators to find out their needs, their students' needs and what's popular.

✓ **PHILOMEL BOOKS, (II)**, Imprint of Penguin Putnam Inc., 345 Hudson St., New York NY 10014. (212)414-3610. **Acquisitions**: Patricia Gauch, editorial director; Michael Green, senior editor. Estab. 1980. "A high-quality oriented imprint focused on stimulating picture books, middle-grade novels, and young adult novels." Publishes hardcover originals and paperback reprints. Averages 25 total titles, 5-7 novels/year.
Needs: Adventure, ethnic, family saga, fantasy, historical, juvenile (5-9 years), literary, preschool/picture book, regional, short story collections, translations, western (young adult), young adult/teen (10-18 years). Looking for "story-driven novels with a strong cultural voice but which speak universally." No "generic, mass-market oriented fiction." Recently published *The Long Patrol*, by Brian Jacques; *I Am Mordred*, by Nancy Springer; and *Choosing Up Sides*, by John H. Ritter.
How to Contact: Accepts unsolicited mss. Query first or submit outline/synopsis and first 3 chapters. SASE. Agented fiction 40%. Reports in 8-10 weeks on queries; 12-16 weeks on mss. Simultaneous submissions OK. Sometimes comments on rejected ms.
Terms: Pays royalties, negotiable advance and author's copies. Sends galleys to author. Publishes ms anywhere from 1-3 years after acceptance. Writer's guidelines for #10 SASE. Book catalog for 9×12 SASE.
Advice: "We are not a mass-market publisher and do not publish short stories independently. In addition, we do just a few novels a year."

PICADOR USA, (II), Imprint of St. Martin's Press, 175 Fifth Ave., New York NY 10010. **Acquisitions:** George Witte. Estab. 1994. "We publish high-quality literary fiction and nonfiction. We are open to a broad range of subjects, well written by authoritative authors." Publishes hardcover originals and trade paperback originals and reprints. **Publishes 30% previously unpublished writers/year.**
Needs: Literary. Recently published *Leaving Small's Hotel*, by Eric Kraft; *Mr. White's Confession*, by Robert Clark; and *At Home in the World*, by Joyce Maynard.
How to Contact: Query only with SASE. Reports in 2 months on queries. Simultaneous submissions OK.
Terms: Pays 7½-12½% royalty on retail price. Advance varies. Publishes ms 18 months after acceptance. Writer's guidelines for #10 SASE. Book catalog for 9×12 SASE and $2.60 postage.

PIÑATA BOOKS, (II), Imprint of Arte Publico Press, University of Houston, Houston TX 77204-2090. (713)743-2841. Fax: (713)743-2847. **Acquisitions:** Nicolas Kanellos, president. Estab. 1994. "We are dedicated to the publication of children's and young adult literature focusing on U.S. Hispanic culture." Publishes hardcover and trade paperback originals. **Publishes 60% previously unpublished writers/year.**
Needs: Adventure, juvenile, picture books, young adult. Recently published *The Secret of Two Brothers*, by Irene Beltran Hernandez (ages 11-adult); *Pepita Talks Twice*, by Ofelia Dumas Lachtman (picture book, ages 3-7); and *Jumping Off to Freedom*, by Anilu Bernardo (young adult).
How to Contact: Query with synopsis, 2 sample chapters and SASE. Reports in 1 month on queries, 6 months on mss. Simultaneous submissions OK.
Terms: Pays 10% royalty on wholesale price. Offers $1,000-3,000 advance. Publishes ms 2 years after acceptance. Writer's guidelines for #10 SASE. Book catalog free.
Advice: "Include cover letter with submission explaining why your manuscript is unique and important, why

we should publish it, who will buy it, etc."

PINEAPPLE PRESS, (II, IV), P.O. Box 3899, Sarasota FL 34230-3899. (941)953-2797. E-mail: info@pineapplepress.com. Website: http://www.pineapplepress.com (includes searchable database of titles, news events, featured books, company profile, and option to request a hard copy of catalog). **Acquisitions**: June Cussen, executive editor. Estab. 1982. Small independent trade publisher. Publishes hardcover and paperback originals and paperback reprints. Books: quality paper; offset printing; Smyth-sewn or perfect-bound; illustrations occasionally. Average print order: 5,000. First novel print order: 2,000-5,000. Published new writers within the last year. Plans 1-2 first novels this year. Averages 20 total titles each year. Distributes titles through Pineapple, Ingram and Baker & Taylor. Promotes titles through reviews, advertising in print media, direct mail, author signings and the World Wide Web.
Needs: "We prefer to see only novels set in Florida." Recently published *Power in the Blood*, by Michael Lister (ecclesiastical mystery); *My Brother Michael*, by Janis Owens (Southern drama); *The Thang That Ate My Granddaddy's Dog*, by John Calvin Rainey (African-American); and *Conflict of Interest*, by Terry Lewis (legal thriller).
How to Contact: Prefers query, cover letter listing previous publications, outline or one-page synopsis with sample chapters (including the first) and SASE. Then if requested, submit complete ms with SASE. Reports in 2 months. Simultaneous submissions OK.
Terms: Pays royalties of 7½-15%. Advance is not usually offered. "Basically, it is an individual agreement with each author depending on the book." Sends galleys to author. Publishes ms 18 months after acceptance. Book catalog sent if label and $1.24 postage enclosed.
Advice: "Quality first novels will be published, though we usually only do one or two novels per year. We regard the author/editor relationship as a trusting relationship with communication open both ways. Learn all you can about the publishing process and about how to promote your book once it is published."

PIPPIN PRESS, (II), 229 E. 85th Street, Gracie Station Box 1347, New York NY 10028. (212)288-4920. Fax: (732)225-1562. **Acquisitions**: Barbara Francis, publisher; Joyce Segal, senior editor. Estab. 1987. "Small, independent children's book company, formed by the former editor-in-chief of Prentice Hall's juvenile book division." Publishes hardcover originals. Books: 135-150 GSM offset-semi-matte paper (for picture books); offset, sheet-fed printing; Smythe-sewn binding; full color, black and white line illustrations and half tone, b&w and full color illustrations. Averages 5-6 titles each year. Sometimes comments on rejected mss.
Needs: Juvenile only (5-12 yrs. including animal, easy-to-read, fantasy, science, humorous, spy/adventure). "I am interested in humorous novels for children of about 7-12 and in picture books with the focus on humor. Also interested in autobiographical novels for 8-12 year olds and selected historical fiction for the same age group."
How to Contact: No unsolicited mss. Query first. SASE. Reports in 2-3 weeks on queries. Simultaneous submissions OK.
Terms: Pays royalties. Sends galleys to author. Publication time after ms is accepted "depends on the amount of revision required, type of illustration, etc." Writer's guidelines for #10 SASE.

PLEASANT COMPANY PUBLICATIONS, (II), Subsidiary of Pleasant Company, 8400 Fairway Place, Middleton WI 53528. (608)836-4848. Fax: (608)836-1999. **Acquisitions:** Jennifer Hirsch, submissions editor. Estab. 1986. Midsize independent publisher. "We are best known for our historical fiction for girls ages 8-12." Publishes hardcover and paperback originals. Averages 10-15 total titles, 3 fiction titles/year.
Imprints: The American Girls Collection and American Girl Library.
Needs: Children's/juvenile (historical, mystery, contemporary for girls 8-12). Pleasant Company Publications also seeks mss for its forthcoming contemporary fiction imprint. "Novels should capture the spirit of contemporary American girls and also illuminate the ways in which their lives are personally touched by issues and concerns affecting America today. We are looking for thoughtfully developed characters and plots, and a discernible sense of place." Stories must feature an American girl, aged 10-12; reading level 4th-5th grade. No science fiction or first-romance stories. Recently published *Meet Josefina*, *Josefina Learns a Lesson*, and *Josefina's Surprise*, all by Valerie Tripp (historical middle grade). Publishes The American Girls Collection series; "also, possibly other historical fiction and contemporary fiction for girls 8-12."
How to Contact: Accepts unsolicited mss. Query with outline/synopsis and 3 sample chapters or send entire ms. Include list of publishing credits. "Tell us why the story is right for us." Send SASE for reply, return of ms or send a disposable copy of ms. Agented fiction 5%. Reports in 8-10 weeks on queries; 3-4 months on mss. Simultaneous submissions OK.
Payment/Terms: Vary. Publishes ms 3-12 months after acceptance. Writer's guidelines for SASE.

Advice: For historical fiction "your story *must* have a girl protagonist age 8-12. No early reader. Our readers are girls 8-12, along with parents and educators. We want to see character development and strong plotting."

POCKET BOOKS, (II), Division of Simon & Schuster, 1230 Avenue of the Americas, New York NY 10020. (212)698-7000. **Acquisitions**: Emily Bestler, executive vice president/editorial director; Patricia McDonald, editorial director. Publishes paperback and hardcover originals and reprints. Published new writers within the last year. Averages 300 titles each year. Buys 90% agented fiction. Promotes books through print advertising, radio, TV ads, readings and book signings.
Imprint(s): Washington Square Press, MTV Fiction and Star Trek.
Needs: Adventure, contemporary, erotica, ethnic, fantasy, feminist, gothic, historical, horror, humor/satire, literary, mainstream, military/war, psychic/supernatural, romance, spy, suspense/mystery, western. Published *Waiting to Exhale*, by Terry McMillan; *The Way Things Ought To Be*, by Rush Limbaugh (hardcover and paperback); *Harvest*, by Tess Gerritsen; and *She's Come Undone*, by Wally Lamb.
How to Contact: Query with SASE (or IRC). No unsolicited mss. Reports in 6 months on queries only. Publishes ms 12-18 months after acceptance. Sometimes critiques rejected mss.
Terms: Pays in royalties and offers advance. Sends galleys to author. Writer must return advance if book is not completed or is not acceptable. Publishes ms 2 years after acceptance. Writer's guidelines for #10 SASE.

PRAIRIE JOURNAL PRESS, (I, IV), Prairie Journal Trust, P.O. Box 61203, Brentwood Postal Services, Calgary, Alberta T2L 2K6 Canada. **Acquisitions**: Anne Burke, literary editor. Estab. 1983. Small-press, noncommercial literary publisher. Publishes paperback originals. Books: bond paper; offset printing; stapled binding; b&w line drawings. **Publishes 8-10 previously unpublished writers/year.** Averages 2 total titles or anthologies/year. Promotes titles through direct mail and in journals.
Needs: Literary, short stories. No romance, horror, pulp, erotica, magazine type, children's, adventure, formula, western. Published *Prairie Journal Fiction*, *Prairie Journal Fiction II* (anthologies of short stories); *Solstice* (short fiction on the theme of aging); and *Prairie Journal Prose*.
How to Contact: Accepts unsolicited mss. Query first and send Canadian postage or IRCs and $6 for sample copy, then submit 1-2 stories with SAE and IRCs. Reports in 6 months or sooner. Occasionally critiques or comments on rejected mss if requested.
Terms: Pays 1 author's copy; honorarium depends on grant/award provided by the government or private/corporate donations. Sends galleys to author. Book catalog free on request to institutions; SAE with IRC for individuals. "No U.S. stamps!"
Advice: "We wish we had the means to promote more new writers. We often are seeking theme-related stories. We look for something different each time and try not to repeat types of stories if possible."

PREP PUBLISHING, (I, II), PREP Inc., 1110½ Hay St., Fayetteville NC 28305. (910)483-6611. Fax: (910)483-2439. E-mail: preppub@aol.com. Website: http://www.prep-pub.com (includes bookstore, author guidelines, chat line for authors, etc.). **Acquisitions**: Anne McKinney, editor (career/religion/mystery); Frances Sweeney, editor (juvenile/literary fiction); Janet Abernethy, editor (biography/romance, other). Estab. 1994. "We publish books that aim to enrich people's lives and help them optimize the human experience." Publishing division affiliated with a 20-year-old company. Publishes hardcover and paperback originals. Books: acid free paper; offset printing; perfect binding; illustrations. Average print order: 5,000. First novel print order: 5,000. Averages up to 15 total titles, 10 fiction titles each year. Distributes titles through Ingram, Baker & Taylor, Quality Books, Unique Books and others. Promotes titles through advance reader's copies to bookstores, reviews, author signings at booksellers' convention, etc.

• **At press time we learned that Prep Publishing charges writers a $100 "reading fee."**

Needs: Children's/juvenile (adventure, mystery), religious/inspirational, romance (contemporary, romantic suspense), thriller/espionage, young adult (adventure, mystery/suspense, romance, sports). "Spiritual/inspirational novels are most welcome." Published *Second Time Around*; and *Back in Time*, by Patty Sleem (mysteries); and *A Gentle Breeze From Gossamer Wings*, by Gordon Beld (historical fiction).
How to Contact: Send SASE for author's guidelines and current catalog. Often comments on rejected mss.
Terms: Pays negotiable royalties. Advance is negotiable. Individual arrangement with author depending on the book. Sends galleys to author. Publishes ms 1-2 years after acceptance.
Advice: "Rewrite and edit carefully before sending manuscript. We look for quality fiction that will appeal to future generations."

PRESIDIO PRESS, (IV), 505B San Marin Dr., Suite 300, Novato CA 94945. (415)898-1081, ext. 125. Fax: (415)898-0383. **Acquisitions**: E.J. McCarthy, editor-in-chief. Estab. 1976. Small independent general trade—specialist in military. Publishes hardcover originals. Publishes an average of 2 works of fiction per list under its Lyford Books imprint. Regularly publishes new writers. Averages 24 new titles each year.
Imprint(s): Lyford Books.
Needs: Historical with military background, war, thriller/espionage. Recently published *Synbat*, by Bob Mayer; *Proud Legions*, by John Antal; and *A Murder of Crows*, by Steve Shepard.
How to Contact: Accepts unsolicited mss. Query first. SASE. Reports in 2 weeks on queries; 2-3 months on mss. Simultaneous submissions OK. Critiques or comments on rejected ms.

Terms: Pays in royalties of 15% of net minimum; advance: $1,000 average. Sends edited manuscripts and page proofs to author. Publishes ms 12-18 months after acceptance. Book catalog and guidelines free on request. Send 9×12 SASE with $1.30 postage.
Advice: "Think twice before entering any highly competitive genre; don't imitate; do your best. Have faith in your writing and don't let the market disappoint or discourage you."

PRIDE PUBLICATIONS AND IMPRINTS, (I, II), P.O. Box 148, Radnor OH 43066. (888)902-5983. E-mail: pridepblsh@aol.com. **Acquisitions:** Cris Newport, senior editor. Large independent publisher specializing in cutting edge novels and children's books. Publishes paperback originals and reprints. Average and first novel print orders: 5,000. Published new writers within the last year. Plans 2 first novels this year. Averages 10 total titles/year, 8 fiction titles/year.

- Chosen as the "Best Example of an Independent Publisher" by BookWatch (Midwest Book Review).

Needs: Adventure, children's/juvenile (adventure, easy-to-read, fantasy, historical, mystery, series), comics/graphic novels, erotica, ethnic/mulitcultural, experimental, fantasy (space fantasy, sword and sorcery), feminist, gay, historical, horror (dark fantasy, futuristic, psychological, supernatural), humor/satire, lesbian, literary, mainstream/contemporary, mystery/suspense (amateur sleuth), New Age/mystic/spiritual, psychic/supernatural/occult, religious (children's, general, inspirational, fantasy, mystery/suspense, thriller), science fiction (hard science, soft/sociological, cyberfiction), young adult/teen (adventure, easy-to-read, fantasy/science fiction, historical, horror, mystery/suspense, problem novels, series). Published *Still Life with Buddy*, by Leslie Newman (novel told in poetry); *Shadows of Aggar*, by Chris Anne Wolfe (fantasy); and *The White Bones of Truth*, by Cris Newport (future fiction). Publishes mystery and science fiction series.
How to Contact: Accepts unsolicited mss. Query with outline/synopsis and 3 sample chapters. Unsolicited queries/correspondence by e-mail OK. Include estimated word count, 100 word bio, list of publishing credits. Send SASE for reply, return of ms. Agented fiction 20%. Reports in 2 weeks on queries; 3 months on mss. Simultaneous submissions OK.
Terms: Pays royalties of 10% minimum; 60% maximum. Publishes ms 12 months after acceptance. Fiction guidelines for #10 SASE. Catalog for #10 SAE with 2 first-class stamps.
Advice: "We feel there is a lot of poor quality work being published, and so are careful to choose work that is revolutionary and cutting edge. Read our books before you even query us."

PUFFIN BOOKS, (II), Imprint of Penguin Putnam Inc., 345 Hudson St., New York NY 10014-3657. (212)414-3481. Website: http://www.penguinputnam.com. **Acquisitions:** Sharyn November, senior editor; Julie Koffman, editorial assistant. "Puffin Books publishes high-end trade paperbacks and paperback reprints for preschool children, beginning and middle readers, and young adults." Publishes trade paperback originals and reprints.
Needs: Picture books, young adult novels, middle grade and easy-to-read grades 1-3. "We publish mostly paperback reprints. We do few original titles." Recently published *A Gift for Mama*, by Esther Hautzig (Puffin chapter book).
How to Contact: Submit picture book ms or 3 sample chapters with SASE. Reports in 4 months on mss. Simultaneous submissions OK, if so noted.
Terms: Royalty and advance vary. Publishes ms 1 year after acceptance. Book catalog for 9×12 SASE with 7 first-class stamps; send request to Marketing Department.
Advice: "Our audience ranges from little children 'first books' to young adult (ages 14-16). An original idea has the best luck."

G.P. PUTNAM'S SONS, (III), Imprint of Penguin Putnam Inc., 375 Hudson St., New York NY 10016. (212)951-8405. Fax: (212)951-8694. Website: http://www.putnam.com. **Acquisitions**: Maya Rao, editorial assista nt. Publishes hardcover originals. Published new writers within the last year.
Imprint(s): Grosset, **Philomel**, Price Stern Sloan, Putnam, **Riverhead**, Jeremy P. Tarcher.
Needs: Adventure, mainstream/contemporary, mystery/suspense, science fiction. Recently published *Executive Orders*, by Tom Clancy (adventure); *Small Vices*, by Robert B. Parker (mystery/thriller); and *Chromosome 6*, by Robin Cook (medical thriller).
How to Contact: Does not accept unsolicited mss. Reports in 6 months on queries. Simultaneous submissions OK.
Payment/Terms: Pays variable royalties on retail price. Advance varies. Writer's guidelines free.

MARKET CATEGORIES: (I) Open to new writers; **(II)** Open to both new and established writers; **(III)** Interested mostly in established writers; **(IV)** Open to writers whose work is specialized; **(V)** Closed to unsolicited submissions.

QUARTET BOOKS LIMITED, (IV), 27 Goodge Street, London W1P1FD England. Fax: 0171 637 1866. E-mail: quartetbooks@easynet.co.uk. Publishing Director: Stella Kane. Publishes "cutting-edge, avante-garde literary fiction." **Publishes 2-5 previously unpublished writers/year.** Publishes 30 novels/year. Distributes titles through Plymbridge Distribution Services. Promotes titles through trade advertising mostly.

Needs: Contemporary literary fiction including translations, popular culture, biographies, music, history and politics. *No* romantic fiction, science fiction or poetry."Recently published *Brand New Cherry Flavor*, by Todd Grimsal (literary-black comic); *Pope John*, by Donna Woolfolk Cross (historical literary); and *The Romance Reader*, by Pearl Abraham (rites of passage-literary).

How to Contact: "Send brief synopsis and sample chapters. Unsolicited queries/correspondence by e-mail and fax OK."

Terms: Payment is: advance—half on signature, half on delivery or publication.

RAGWEED PRESS INC./gynergy books, (I), P.O. Box 2023, Charlottetown, Prince Edward Island C1A 7N7 Canada. (902)566-5750. Fax: (902)566-4473. E-mail: editor@ragweed.com. **Acquisitions**: Managing Editor. Estab. 1980. "Independent Canadian-owned feminist press." Publishes paperback originals. Books: 60 lb. paper; perfect binding. Average print order: 3,000. Averages 10 total titles, 3 fiction titles each year. Published new writers within the last year.

Needs: *Canadian-authors only.* "We do accept submissions to anthologies from U.S. writers." Children's/juvenile (adventure, picture book, girl-positive), feminist, lesbian, young adult. Recently published *The Memory Stone*, by Anne Louise MacDonald (children's picture book); and *Mothering Teens*, by Miriam Kaufman.

How to Contact: Accepts unsolicited mss with cover letter, brief bio, list of publishing credits. SASE for reply. Reports in 6 months. Simultaneous submissions OK.

Terms: Pays royalties of 10%; offers negotiable advance. Provides 5 author's copies. Sends galleys to author. Publishes ms 1-2 years after acceptance. Writer's guidelines for #10 SASE. Book catalog for large SAE and 2 first-class stamps.

Advice: "Send us your full manuscript, and be patient. Please remember SASE—no phone calls or e-mail."

RAINBOW BOOKS, INC., (I, II), P.O. Box 430, Highland City, FL 33846. (800)613-BOOK. Fax: (941)648-4420. E-mail: naip@aol.com. **Acquisitions:** Besty Lampe, editorial director. Estab. 1979. Midsize press. Publishes trade paperback originals. Books: 60 lb. paper; perfect binding. Average print order: 15,000. First novel print order: 2,000-5,000. **Published 2 previously unpublished writers in 1998.** Plans 2 first novels for January 1999. Distributes titles through Ingram Books, Baker & Taylor Books, amazon.com, barnesandnoble.com, as well as other regional distributors. Promotes titles through advance bound galleys to hi-profile reviewers well in advance of publication, advertising.

Imprints: Rainbow Mystery (book-length mysteries), Deadlines (short fiction mysteries).

- Member of Publishers Association of the South, Florida Publishers Association, National Association of Independent Publishers, Association of American Publishers, Publishers Marketing Association.

Needs: Mystery/suspense (amateur sleuth, cozy, police procedural). "We would like to see well-written mysteries." Recently published *Pharmacology Is Murder*, by Dirk Wyle (mystery); and *Path to Ariquera*, by Mark Jacoby (adventure).

How to Contact: Accepts unsolicited mss. Query first for guidelines. Include estimated word count, bio of 3 pages or less, Social Security number and list of publishing credits. Send SASE for reply, return of ms or send disposable copy of ms. "But tell us." Reports in 2-3 weeks on queries; 8-10 weeks on mss. Simultaneous submissions OK.

Terms: Pays in royalties plus advance and 50 author's copies. Negotiates all arrangements. Sends galleys to author. Publishes ms 1-2 years after acceptance.

Advice: "Since we are just beginning to publish fiction, the future is hard to read. However, we expect to stick with trade softcover, since it covers the most territory. We feel that the very large publishers have closed their doors to the unpublished author—that poor soul who writes well but doesn't have a track record. We'd like to find those folks and give them an opportunity to be published and perhaps find an audience that would follow them through the years. In other words, we're going to look very carefully at each manuscript we call for. Be professional. Come in with that manuscript looking like a pro's manuscript. Please don't tell us, 'I have a great idea for a novel and I've got it on paper. You can clean it up however you want.' That's not to say that we won't help the author that's 'almost there'; we will. Meanwhile, be prepared. If we decide to take on the novel, provide a PC compatible diskette of the book."

RANDOM HOUSE CHILDREN'S PUBLISHING, (V), (formerly Random House Books for Young Readers), Imprint of Random House, 201 E. 50th St., New York NY 10022. (212)751-2600. Fax: (212)940-7685. Website: http://www.randomhouse.com/kids (includes catalog, contests, new books, author information, CD-ROM store, Arthur the Aardvark & Seussville websites.) Publishing Director: Kate Klimo. **Acquisitions:** Lisa Banim, editor (young adult); Ruth Koeppel, editor (Stepping Stones series); Heidi Kilgras, editor (Step-Into-Reading series). Estab. 1935. Publishes hardcover, trade paperback, and mass market paperback originals and reprints. **Publishes 1-5 previously unpublished writers/year.** "Random House Children's Books aims to create books that nurture the hearts and minds of children, providing and promoting quality books and a rich variety of media that entertain and educate readers from 6 months to 12 years." Distributes titles to trade and mass markets. Promotes titles through magazine ads, in-store promotions.

- Random House Children's Publishing received American Bookseller, Children's Pick of the Lists award for *Toots & the Upside Down House*, 1997.

Needs: Humor, juvenile, mystery, picture books, young adult. Recently published *Arthur's Boo-Boo Book*, by Marc Brown (board book with stickers, ages 0-4); *Day of the Dragon-King*, by Mary Pope Osborne (Stepping Stone series ages 5-8); and *A Dollar for Penny*, by Dr. Julie Glass (Step-Into-Reading & Math ages 5-8).
How to Contact: Agented fiction only. Reports in 3-24 weeks. Simultaneous submissions OK.
Terms: Pays 1-6% royalty or makes outright purchase. Advance varies. Publishes ms 1-3 years after acceptance.
Advice: "Familiarize yourself with our list. We look for original, unique stories. Do something that hasn't been done."

RANDOM HOUSE, INC., (II), 201 E. 50th St., 11th Floor, New York NY 10022. (212)751-2600. **Acquisitions**: Sandy Fine, submissions coordinator. Estab. 1925. Publishes hardcover and paperback originals. Encourages new writers.
Imprint(s): Pantheon Books, **Vintage Books**, Times Books, Villard Books and **Knopf**.
Needs: Adventure, contemporary, experimental, fantasy, historical, horror, humor, literary, mainstream, short story collections, mystery/suspense. "We publish fiction of the highest standards." Authors include James Michener, Robert Ludlum, Mary Gordon.
How to Contact: Query with SASE. Simultaneous submissions OK. Reports in 4-6 weeks on queries, 2 months on mss. Rarely comments on rejected mss.
Terms: Payment as per standard minimum book contracts. Free writer's guidelines and book catalog.
Advice: "Please try to get an agent because of the large volume of manuscripts received, agented work is looked at first."

RANDOM HOUSE, INC. JUVENILE BOOKS, (V), 201 E. 50th St., New York NY 10022. (212)572-2600. **Acquisitions**: (Juvenile Division): Kate Klimo, publishing director, Random House; Lisa Banim, creative director, digest and rack. Simon Boughton, vice president/publishing director, Andrea Cascardi, associate publishing director, Crown/Knopf. Managing Editor (all imprints): Sue Malone Barber. Publishes hardcover, trade paperback and mass market paperback originals, mass market paperback reprints.
Imprint(s): Random House Books for Young Readers, **Alfred A. Knopf**, Crown Children's Books, Dragonfly Paperbacks.
Needs: Adventure, young adult (confession), fantasy, historical, horror, humor, juvenile, mystery/suspense, picture books, science fiction (juvenile/young adult), young adult.
How to Contact: Agented fiction only.

RANDOM HOUSE OF CANADA, (III), Division of Random House, Inc., 33 Yonge St., Suite 210, Toronto, Ontario M5E 1G4 Canada. Publishes hardcover and paperback originals. Publishes 56 titles/year. No unsolicited mss. Agented fiction only. All unsolicited mss returned unopened. "We are *not* a mass market publisher."
Imprint(s): Vintage Canada.

RED DEER COLLEGE PRESS, (II, IV), Box 5005, Red Deer, Alberta T4N 5H5 Canada. (403)342-3321. Fax: (403)357-3639. E-mail: cdearden@rdc.ab.ca. **Acquisitions**: Dennis Johnson, managing editor; Aritha van Herk, editor (general literary fiction). Estab. 1975. Publishes adult and young adult hardcover and paperback originals "focusing on books by, about, or of interest to Western Canadians." Books: offset paper; offset printing; hardcover/perfect-bound. Average print order: 5,000. First novel print order: 2,500. Averages 14-16 total titles, 2 fiction titles each year. Distributes titles in Canada, the US and the UK.
Imprint(s): Roundup Books (edited by Ted Stone), Inprints (fiction reprint series, edited by Aritha van Herk).

- Red Deer College Press has received numerous honors and awards from the Book Publishers Association of Alberta, Canadian Children's Book Centre, the Governor General of Canada and the Writers Guild of Alberta. *Mamie's Children: Three Generations of Prairie Women*, by Judy Schultz received the Georges Bugnet Award for Best Novel.

Needs: Contemporary, experimental, literary, young adult. No romance, science fiction. Published anthologies under Roundup Books imprint focusing on stories/poetry of the Canadian and American West. Recently published

**FOR EXPLANATIONS OF THESE SYMBOLS,
SEE THE INSIDE FRONT AND BACK COVERS OF THIS BOOK.**

Cowgirls, by Thelma Poirier; and *The Complete Cowboy Reader*, by Ted Stone (anthologies).

How to Contact: *Canadian authors only.* Does not accept unsolicited mss in children's and young adult genres. Query first or submit outline/synopsis and 2 sample chapters. SASE. Reports in 6 months on queries; in 6 months on mss. Simultaneous submissions OK. Final mss must be submitted on Mac disk in MS Word.

Terms: Pays royalties of 8-10%. Advance is negotiable. Sends galleys to author. Publishes ms 1 year after acceptance. Book catalog for 9×12 SASE.

Advice: "We're very interested in literary and experimental fiction from Canadian writers with a proven track record (either published books or widely published in established magazines or journals) and for manuscripts with regional themes and/or a distinctive voice. We publish Canadian authors almost exclusively."

☑ **RED DRAGON PRESS, (II)**, 433 Old Town Court, Alexandria VA 22314-3545. **Acquisitions**: Laura Qa, publisher. David Alan, editor. Estab. 1993. "Small independent publisher of innovative, progressive and experimental works." Publishes paperback originals. Books: quality paper; offset printing; perfect binding; some illustrations. Average print order: 500. **Publishes 2-3 previously unpublished writers/year.** Plans 1 first novel this year. Averages 4 total titles, 1-2 fiction titles/year. Member of Women's National Book Association. Distributes titles through amazon.com, Borders, Barnes & Noble, retail and wholesale, special order and direct mail order. Promotes titles through arts reviews, journals, newsletters, special events, readings and signings.

Needs: Experimental, fantasy (space fantasy), feminist, gay, horror (dark fantasy, futuristic, psychological, supernatural), lesbian, literary, psychic/supernatural/occult, science fiction (hard science/technological, soft/sociological), short story collections. Recently published *True Stories: Fiction by Uncommon Women*, by Grace Cavalieri, Susan Cole, Jean Russell, Laura Qa and Dee Snyder.

How to Contact: Accepts unsolicited mss. Submit query letter. Unsolicited queries/correspondence by fax OK. Include 1 page bio, list of publishing credits and 1-3 sample stories (up to 36 pages). Send SASE for reply, return of ms or send disposable copy of ms. Reports in 6 weeks. Simultaneous submissions OK. Often critiques or comments on rejected mss *for various fee*.

Terms: Publishes ms 6-12 months after acceptance. Writer's guidelines free for #10 SASE. Book catalog for #10 SASE.

Advice: "Be familiar with the work of one or more of our previously published authors."

REVELL PUBLISHING, (III), Subsidiary of Baker Book House, P.O. Box 6287, Grand Rapids MI 49516-6287. (616)676-9185. Fax: (616)676-9573. E-mail: lholland@bakerbooks.com or petersen@bakerbooks.com. Website: http://www.bakerbooks.com. **Acquisitions**: Linda Holland, editorial director; Bill Petersen, senior acquisitions editor; Jane Campbell, senior editor (Chosen Books). Estab. 1870. Midsize publisher. "Revell publishes to the heart (rather than to the head). For 125 years, Revell has been publishing evangelical books for personal enrichment and spiritual growth of general Christian readers." Publishes hardcover, trade paperback and mass market originals and reprints. Average print order: 7,500. Published new writers within the last year. Plans 1 first novel this year. Averages 60 total titles, 8 fiction titles each year. 10% of books from first-time authors.

Imprint(s): Spire Books.

Needs: Religious/inspirational (general). Published *Ordeal at Iron Mountain*, by Linda Rae Rao (historical); *A Time to Weep*, by Gilbert Morris (historical); and *The End of the Age*, by David Dolan (suspense).

How to Contact: Query with outline/synopsis. Include estimated word count, bio and list of publishing credits. Send SASE for reply, return of ms or send a disposable copy of ms. Agented fiction 20%. Reports in 3 weeks on queries; 2 weeks on mss. Simultaneous submissions OK. Sometimes comments on rejected mss.

Terms: Pays royalties. Sends galleys to author. Publishes ms 1 year after acceptance. Writer's guidelines for SASE.

☑ **REVIEW AND HERALD PUBLISHING ASSOCIATION, (II)**, 55 W. Oak Ridge Dr., Hagerstown MD 21740. (301)393-3000. **Acquisitions**: Jeannette R. Johnson, editor. "Through print and electronic media, the Review and Herald Publishing Association nurtures a growing relationship with God by providing products that teach and enrich people spiritually, mentally, physically and socially as we near Christ's soon second coming." Publishes hardcover, trade paperback and mass market paperback originals and reprints. **Publishes 50% previously unpublished writers/year.**

Needs: Adventure, historical, humor, juvenile, mainstream/contemporary, religious, all Christian-living related. Recently published *Shadow Creek Ranch*, by Charles Mills (juvenile adventure series); *The Liberation of Allyson Brown*, by Helen Godfrey Pyke (inspirational); and *The Appearing*, by Penny Estes Wheeler (inspirational).

How to Contact: Submit synopsis and complete ms or 3 sample chapters. Reports in 1 month on queries; 2 months on mss. Simultaneous submissions OK.

Terms: Pays 7-15% royalty. Offers $500-1,000 advance. Publishes ms 18 months after acceptance. Writer's guidelines for #10 SASE. Book catalog for 10×13 SASE.

Advice: "We publish for a wide audience, preschool through adult."

THE RIEHLE FOUNDATION, (II), P.O. Box 7, Milford OH 45150. Fax: (513)576-0022. **Acquisitions:** Mrs. B. Lewis, general manager. "We are only interested in materials which are written to draw the reader to a deeper love for God." Publishes trade paperback originals and reprints. **Publishes 50% previously unpublished writers/year.**

Needs: Religious, short story collections; all with Roman Catholic subjects. Published *Six Short Stories on the Via Dolorosa*, by Ernesto V. Laguette (devotional short stories).
How to Contact: Submit entire ms with SASE. Reports in 3 months. Simultaneous submissions OK.
Terms: Pays royalty. Publishes ms 6 months after acceptance. Writer's guidelines and book catalog for #10 SASE.

✓ **RISING TIDE PRESS, (II)**, 3831 N. Oracle Rd., Tucson AZ 85705. (520)888-1140. E-mail: rtpress@aol.com. **Acquisitions**: Lee Boojamra, editor; Alice Frier, senior editor (romance, literary and erotica); Lee Boojamra, editor (mystery/adventure); Lee Ferris, editor (science fiction/fantasy/horror). Estab. 1988. "Independent women's press, publishing lesbian nonfiction and fiction—novels only—no short stories." Publishes paperback trade originals. Books: 60 lb. vellum paper; sheet fed and/or web printing; perfect-bound. Average print run: 5,000. First novel print run: 4,000-6,000. **Publishes 4-5 previously unpublished writers/year.** Plans 10-12 first novels this year. Averages 12 total titles. Distributes titles through Bookpeople, Koen Books, Baker & Taylor, Alamo Square, Marginal (Canada), Turnaround (UK) and Banyon Tree (Pacific Basin). Promotes titles through magazines, journals, newspapers, *PW*, Lambda Book Report, distributor's catalogs, special publications.

- Rising Tide plans two anthologies: *Women Cruising Women* (short stories) and *How I Met My True Love* (lesbian romance). Deadline is June 1, 1999. SASE for guidelines.

Needs: Lesbian adventure, contemporary, erotica, fantasy, feminist, romance, science fiction, suspense/mystery, western. Looking for romance and mystery. "Minimal heterosexual content." Recently published *Deadly Gamble*, by Diane Davidson (mystery); *Cloud Nine Affair*, by Katherine Kreuter (mystery); and *Coming Attractions*, by Bobbi Marolt (romance). Developing a dark fantasy and erotica line.
How to Contact: Accepts unsolicited mss with 1-page outline/synopsis and SASE. Reports in 1 week on queries; 2-3 months on mss. Comments on rejected mss.
Terms: Pays 10-15% royalties. "*We will assist writers who wish to self-publish for a nominal fee.*" Sends galleys to author. Publishes ms 6-18 months after acceptance. Writer's guidelines for #10 SASE. Book catalog for $1.
Advice: "Outline your story to give it boundaries structure, find creative ways to introduce your characters and begin the story in the middle of some action and dialogue. Our greatest challenge is finding quality manuscripts that are well plotted and not predictable, with well-developed, memorable characters."

ROC, (II, III), Imprint of Dutton Signet, a division of Penguin Putnam, Inc., 375 Hudson St., New York NY 10014. (212)366-2000. Fax: (212)366-2888. **Acquisitions**: Laura Anne Gilman, executive editor. Publishes hardcover, trade paperback and mass market originals and hardcover, trade paperback (and mass market) reprints. Published new writers within the last year. Averages 48 (all fiction) titles each year.
Needs: Fantasy, horror (dark fantasy) and science fiction. Publishes science fiction, horror and fantasy anthologies. Anthologies by invitation only. Published *Deathstalker War*, by Simon Green (science fiction); *Dragon at World's End*; by Christopher Rowley (fantasy); and *Silk*, by Caitlin Kiernan (horror). Publishes the Battletech® and Shadowrun® series.
How to Contact: Query with outline/synopsis and 3 sample chapters. Include list of publishing credits. Not responsible for return of submission if no SASE is included. Agented fiction 99%. Reports in 1 month on queries; 4-6 months on mss. Simultaneous submissions OK. Sometimes comments on rejected ms.
Terms: "Competitive with the field."

RUSSIAN HILL PRESS, (II,III), 1250 17th St., 2nd Floor, San Francisco CA 94107. (415)487-0480. Fax: (415)487-0290. E-mail: editors@russianhill.com. **Acquisitions:** Kit Cooley, assistant editor. Estab. 1996. "Small (but growing) independent publisher. Focus: West Coast, irreverent, youthful." Publishes hardcover originals. Average print order 5,000. First novel print order 2,000. **Publishes 25% of books from first-time authors.** Averages 6-10 total titles, 5-9 fiction titles/year. Member of PMA, IPN.
Needs: Erotica, ethnic/multicultural, feminist, gay, humor/satire, lesbian, literary, mainstream/contemporary, mystery/suspense, regional (west of the Rockies), thriller/espionage. Especially looking for literary, Generation X, thriller, humor. Published *Tainted Million*, by Susan Trott (mystery); *Swamp Cats*, by Jeff Love (humorous); and *Funerals for Horses*, by Catherine Ryan Hyde (literary).
How to Contact: Does not accept unsolicited mss. Query letter only first. Unsolicited queries/correspondence by e-mail and fax OK. Include estimated word count, 1-page bio and list of publishing credits with submission. SASE for reply. Agented fiction 90%. Reports in 2 months on queries; 4 months on mss. Simultaneous submissions OK. Sometimes critiques or comments on rejected mss.
Payment/Terms: Pays royalties of 10% minimum; 15% maximum. Offers negotiable advance. Sends galleys to author. Publishes ms 8 months after acceptance. Writer's guidelines for #10 SASE. Book catalog for $2.
Advice: "Get an agent. Pay attention to the types of fiction we publish."

ST. MARTIN'S PRESS, (II), 175 Fifth Ave., New York NY 10010. (212)674-5151. Chairman and CEO: John Sargent. President: Roy Gainsburg. Publishes hardcover and paperback reprints and originals.
Imprint(s): Thomas Dunne, Picador USA.
Needs: Contemporary, literary, experimental, adventure, mystery/suspense, spy, historical, war, gothic, romance, confession, feminist, gay, lesbian, ethnic, erotica, psychic/supernatural, religious/inspirational, science fiction, fantasy, horror and humor/satire. No plays, children's literature or short fiction. Published *The Silence of the*

Lambs, by Thomas Harris; *The Shell Seekers* and *September* by Rosamunde Pilcher.
How to Contact: Query or submit complete ms with SASE. Simultaneous submissions OK (if declared as such). Reports in 2-3 weeks on queries, 4-6 weeks on mss.
Terms: Pays standard advance and royalties.

SARABANDE BOOKS, INC., (II), 2234 Dundee Rd., Suite 200, Louisville KY 40205-1845. Fax: (502)458-4065. E-mail: sarabandek@aol.com. Website: http://www.SarabandeBooks.org (includes authors, forthcoming titles, backlist, writer's guidelines, names of editors, author interviews and excerpts from their work and ordering and contest information). **Acquisitions**: Sarah Gorham, editor-in-chief (short fiction); Kirkby Tiltle, fiction editor. Estab. 1994. "Small literary press publishing poetry and short fiction." Publishes hardcover and paperback originals. **Publishes 1-2 previously unpublished writers/year.** Averages 6 total titles, 2-3 fiction titles each year. Distributes titles through Consortium Book Sales & Distribution. Promotes titles through advertising in national magazines, sales reps, brochures, newsletters, postcards, catalogs, press release mailings, sales conferences, book fairs, author tours and reviews.

- Books published by Sarabande Books have received the following awards: 1997/98 Society of Midland Authors Award and 1997 Carl Sandburg Award—Sharon Solwitz, *Blood & Milk*; 1997 Poetry Center Book Award and First Annual Levis Reading Prize—Belle Waring, *Dark Blonde*.

Needs: Short story collections, 300 pages maximum (or collections of novellas, or single novellas of 150 pages). "Short fiction *only*. We do not publish full-length novels." Recently published *Where She Went*, by Kate Walbert (interconnected short stories); *A Gram of Mars*, by Becky Hagenston (short stories); and *Sparkman in the Sky & Other Stories*, by Brian Griffin (short stories).
How to Contact: Submit (in September only). Query with outline/synopsis and 1 sample story or 10-page sample. Include 1 page bio, listing of publishing credits. SASE for reply. Reports in 3 months on queries; 6 months on mss. Simultaneous submissions OK.
Terms: Pays in royalties, author's copies. Sends galleys to author. Writer's guidelines available for contest only. Send #10 SASE. Book catalog available.
Advice: "Make sure you're not writing in a vacuum, that you've read and are conscious of your competition in contemporary literature. Have someone read your manuscript, checking it for ordering, coherence. Better a lean, consistently strong manuscript than one that is long and uneven. Old fashioned as it sounds, we like a story to have good narrative, or at least we like to be engaged, to find ourselves turning the pages with real interest."

SCHOLASTIC INC., (II), 555 Broadway, New York NY 10012-3999. (212)343-6100. Website: http://www.scholastic.com (includes general information about Scholastic). Scholastic Inc. **Acquisitions**: Jean Feiwel, senior vice president/publisher, Book Group Scholastic Inc. Estab. 1920. Publishes books for children ages 4-young adult. "We are proud of the many fine, innovative materials we have created—such as classroom magazines, book clubs, book fairs, and our new literacy and technology programs. But we are most proud of our reputation as 'The Most Trusted Name in Learning.' " Publishes juvenile hardcover picture books, novels and nonfiction. Distributes titles through Scholastic Book Clubs, Scholastic Book Fairs, bookstores and other retailers.
Imprint(s): Blue Sky Press (contact: Bonnie Verberg, editorial director); **Cartwheel Books** (contact: Bernette Ford, editorial director); **Arthur Levine Books** (contact: Arthur Levine, editorial director); **Mariposa** (Spanish language contact: Susana Pasternac, editorial director); **Scholastic Press** (contact: editorial director); Scholastic Professional Books (contact: Terry Cooper, editorial director); Scholastic Trade Paperbacks (contact: Craig Walker, editorial director; Maria Weisbin, assistant to Craig Walker); Scholastic Reference (contact: Wendy Barish, editorial director).

- Scholastic published *Out of the Dust*, by Karen Hesse winner of the Newbery Medal.

Needs: Hardcover—open to all subjects suitable for children. Paperback—family stories, mysteries, school, friendships for ages 8-12, 35,000 words. Young adult fiction, romance, family and mystery for ages 12-15, 40,000-45,000 words for average to good readers. Published *Her Stories: African American Folktales, Fairy Tales and True Tales*, by Virginia Hamilton, illustrated by Leo and Diane Dillon; and *Pigs in the Middle of the Road*, by Lynn Plourde.
How to Contact: Queries welcome; unsolicited manuscripts discouraged. Submissions (agented) may be made to the Editorial Director or to Jean Feivel. Reports in 6 months.
Terms: Pays advance and royalty on retail price. Writer's guidelines for #10 SASE.
Advice: "Be current, topical and get an agent for your work."

SCHOLASTIC PRESS, (V), Imprint of Scholastic Inc., 555 Broadway, New York NY 10012. (212)343-6100. Website: http://www.scholastic.com. **Acquisitions:** Attn. Editorial Director. Scholastic Press publishes a range of picture books, middle grade and young adult novels. Publishes hardcover originals. **Publishes 5% previously unpublished writers/year.**
Needs: Juvenile, picture books. Recently published *Perloo the Bold*, by Ari; and *Riding Freedom*, by Pam Nuñoz Ryan.
How to Contact: Agented submissions only. Reports in 6 months on queries from previously published authors.
Terms: Pays royalty on retail price. Royalty and advance vary. Publishes ms 18 months after acceptance.

SCOTTISH CULTURAL PRESS, (II, IV), Unit 14, Leith Walk Business Centre, 130 Leith Walk, Edinburgh EH6 5DT Scotland. (0131)555-5950. Fax: +44(0)131555-5018. E-mail: scp@sol.co.uk. Website: http://www.taynet.co.uk/users/scp (includes catalog, order form, new book details). Director: Jill Dick. Estab. 1992. Small independent publisher of paperback originals. Publishes Scottish contemporary fiction. Mainly concentrates on Scottish authors or Scottish content. Average print order: 1,000-2,000. **Publishes 1-2 previously unpublished writers/year.** Plans 1-2 first novels this year. Averages 35 total titles/year, 5 fiction titles/year. Distributes titles through Scottish Book Source, direct mail. Promotes titles through TV, radio, newspapers, magazines, exhibitions, including London Book Fair, ABA, etc., catalog mailings.
Imprint(s): Scottish Children's Press (contact: Avril Gray, Scottish fiction only).
Needs: Children's/juvenile (all), mainstream/contemporary, short story collections, young adult/teen (adventure, fantasy/science fiction, historical, horror, mystery/suspense, problem novels, romance, series, sports). All should be by a Scottish author or have Scottish content. Recently published *Special Deliverance*, by Donald Murray (short stories); and *Night Visits*, by Ron Butkin (novel).
How to Contact: Accepts unsolicited submissions. Query with outline/synopsis and 2 sample chapters. Unsolicited queries/correspondence by e-mail and fax OK. Include 1 page bio and list of publishing credits. Send SASE for return of ms or send disposable copy of ms. Agented fiction 4%. Reports in 3 weeks on queries; 4 months on mss. Simultaneous submissions OK.
Terms: Pays royalties of 10% minimum. Sends galleys to author. Publishes ms 12 months after acceptance. Book catalog free.

SCRIBNER'S, (V), Unit of Simon & Schuster, 1230 Avenue of the Americas, New York NY 10020. (212)698-7000. **Acquisitions**: Jillian Blake, editor. Publishes hardcover originals. Published new writers within the last year. Averages 70-75 total titles/year.
Imprint(s): Rawson Associates (contact Eleanor Rawson); Lisa Drew Books (contact Lisa Drew).
Needs: Literary, mystery/suspense. Recently published *Accordion Crimes*, by E. Annie Proulx (novel, Pulitzer Prize winning author); *Underworld*, by Don Delillo; and *Go Now*, by Richard Hell (novel).
How to Contact: Submit through agent. Reports in 3 months on queries. Simultaneous submissions OK.
Terms: Pays royalties of 7½% minimum; 12½% maximum. Advance varies. Publishes ms 9 months after acceptance.

SEAL PRESS, (I, IV), 3131 Western Ave., Suite 410, Seattle WA 98121. (206)283-7844. Fax: (206)285-9410. E-mail: sealprss@cn.org. Website: http://www.sealpress.com. **Acquisitions**: Faith Conlon, president. Estab. 1976. "Midsize independent feminist book publisher interested in original, lively, radical, empowering and culturally diverse books by women." Publishes hardcover and trade paperback originals. Books: 55 lb. natural paper; Cameron Belt, Web or offset printing; perfect binding; illustrations occasionally; average print order: 6,500; first novel print order: 4,000-5,000. Averages 15 total titles, 6 fiction titles each year. Receives 500 queries and 250 mss/year. **25% of books from first-time authors; 80% from unagented writers.** Sometimes critiques rejected ms "very briefly."

- Seal has received numerous awards including Lambda Literary Awards for mysteries, humor and translation.

Needs: Ethnic, feminist, humor/satire, lesbian, literary, mystery (amateur sleuth, cozy, private eye/hardboiled), young adult (easy-to-read, historical, sports). "We publish women only. Work must be feminist, non-racist, non-homophobic." Publishes anthologies. Send SASE for list of upcoming projects. Published *An Open Weave*, by Devorah Major (literary novel); *Faint Praise*, by Ellen Hart (mystery novel); and *The Lesbian Parenting Book*, by D. Menlee Clunis and G. Dorsey Green.
How to Contact: Query with outline/synopsis and 2 sample chapters. SASE. Reports in 2 months.
Terms: Pays royalties; offers negotiable advance. Publishes ms 1-2 years after acceptance. Writer's guidelines and book catalog are free.

SECOND CHANCE PRESS AND THE PERMANENT PRESS, (I, II), 4170 Noyac Rd., Sag Harbor NY 11963. (516)725-1101. **Acquisitions**: Judith and Martin Shepard, publishers. Estab. 1977. Mid-size, independent publisher of literary fiction. Publishes hardcover originals. Books: hardcover. Average print order: 1,500-2,000. First novel print order: 1,500-2,000. Published new writers within the last year. **Publishes 75% previously unpublished writers/year.** Averages 12 total titles, all fiction, each year. Distributes titles through Ingram, Baker & Taylor and Brodart. Promotes titles through reviews.

- This publisher received a Literary Marketplace Award for Editorial Excellence and a Small Press Book Award for Best Gay/Lesbian Title for Elise O'Haene's *Licking Our Wounds*.

Needs: Contemporary, erotica, ethnic/multicultural, experimental, family saga, literary, mainstream. "We like

READ THE BUSINESS OF FICTION WRITING section to learn the correct way to prepare and submit a manuscript.

novels with a unique point of view and a high quality of writing." No genre novels. Recently published *The Handsome Sailor*, by Larry Duberstein; *Rhonda the Rubber Woman*, by Norma Peterson; and *The Last Days of Il Duce*, by Domonic Stansberry.

How to Contact: Query with outline and no more than 2 chapters. SASE. Agented fiction 35%. Reports in 6 weeks on queries; 6 months on mss. Simultaneous submissions OK.

Terms: Pays royalties of 10-20%. Advance: $1,000. Sends galleys to author. Book catalog for $3.

Advice: "We are looking for good books, be they tenth novels or first ones, it makes little difference. The fiction is more important than the track record. Send us the beginning of the story, it's impossible to judge something that begins on page 302. Also, no outlines and very short synopsis—let the writing present itself."

SERENDIPITY SYSTEMS, (I, II, IV), P.O. Box 140, San Simeon CA 93452. (805)927-5259. E-mail: bookware@thegrid.net. Website: http://www.thegrid.net/bookware/bookware.htm (includes guidelines, sample books, writer's manuscript help, catalog). **Acquisitions**: John Galuszka, publisher. Estab. 1985. "Electronic publishing for IBM-PC compatible systems." Publishes "electronic editions originals and reprints." Books on disk. Published new writers within the last year. Averages 36 total titles, 15 fiction titles each year (either publish or distribute). Often comments on rejected mss.

Imprint(s): Books-on-Disks™ and Bookware™.

Needs: "Works of fiction which use, or have the potential to use, hypertext, multimedia or other computer-enhanced features. We cannot use on-paper manuscripts." No romance, religion, New Age, children's, young adult, occult. Published *Costa Azul*, by C.J. Newton (humor); *Sideshow*, by Marian Allan (science fiction); and *Silicon Karma*, by Tom Easton (science fiction).

How to Contact: Query by e-mail. Submit complete ms with cover letter and SASE. *IBM-PC compatible disk required.* ASCII files required unless the work is hypertext or multimedia. Send SASE for reply, return of ms or send disposable copy of ms. Reports in 2 weeks on queries; 1 month on mss.

Terms: Pays royalties of 25%. Publishes ms 2 months after acceptance. Writer's guidelines for SASE.

Advice: "We are interested in seeing multimedia works suitable for Internet distribution. Would like to see: more works of serious literature—novels, short stories, plays, etc. Would like to not see: right wing adventure fantasies from 'Tom Clancy' wanna-be's."

SEVEN BUFFALOES PRESS, (II), Box 249, Big Timber MT 59011. **Acquisitions**: Art Cuelho, editor/publisher. Estab. 1975. Publishes paperback originals. Averages 4-5 total titles each year.

Needs: Contemporary, short story collections, "rural, American Hobo, Okies, Native-American, Southern Appalachia, Arkansas and the Ozarks. Wants farm- and ranch-based stories." Published *Rig Nine*, by William Rintoul (collection of oilfield short stories).

How to Contact: Query first with SASE. Reports in 1 month. Sample copy $6.75.

Terms: Pays royalties of 10% minimum; 15% on second edition or in author's copies (10% of edition). No advance. Writer's guidelines and book catalog for SASE.

Advice: "There's too much influence from TV and Hollywood, media writing I call it. We need to get back to the people, to those who built and are still building this nation with sweat, blood and brains. More people are into it for the money, instead of for the good writing that is still to be cranked out by isolated writers. Remember, I was a writer for ten years before I became a publisher."

SEVEN STORIES PRESS, (II), 140 Watts St., New York NY 10013. (212)995-0908. Fax: (212)995-0720. Website: http://www.sevenstories.com. **Acquisitions**: Daniel Simon. Estab. 1995. "Publishers of a distinguished list of authors in fine literature, journalism, contemporary culture and alternative health." Publishes hardcover and paperback originals and paperback reprints. Average print order: 5,000. **Publishes 15% of books from first-time authors.** Averages 20 total titles, 10 fiction titles/year. Sometimes critiques or comments on rejected mss.

- Seven Stories Press received the Firecracker Alternative Book Award (nonfiction), 1996 and 1997; the Will Eisner Comic Industry Award (Best Graphic Album-New) 1997; nomination for Best Books for Young Adults by ALA 1997; Nebula Award Finalist, 1995, 1996.

Needs: Literary. Plans anthologies. Ongoing series of short story collections from other cultures (e.g., *Contemporary Fiction from Central America*; from Vietnam, etc. Published *The House of Moses All-Stars*, by Charley Rosen (novel); *. . . And Dreams Are Dreams*, by Vassilis Vassilikos (novel); and *Exteriors*, by Annie Ernaux (novel).

How to Contact: Query with outline/synopsis and 1 sample chapter. Include list of publishing credits. SASE for reply. Agented fiction 60%. Reports in 1 month on queries; 4 months on mss. Simultaneous submissions OK.

Payment/Terms: Pays standard royalty; offers advance. Sends galleys to author. Publishes ms 1-2 years after acceptance. Free book catalog.

Advice: "Writers should only send us their work after they have read some of the books we publish and find our editorial vision in sync with theirs."

SEVERN HOUSE PUBLISHERS, (V), 9-15 High St., Sutton, Surrey SM1 1DF United Kingdom. (0181)770-3930. Fax: (0181)770-3850. **Acquisitions**: Sara Short, editorial director. Publishes hardcover and trade paperback originals and reprints. Publishes 120 titles/year.

Needs: Adventure, fantasy, historical, horror, mainstream/contemporary, mystery/suspense, romance, science fiction, short story collections. Published *Tender Warrior*, by Fern Michaels (historical romance); *Second Time Around*, by Julie Ellis (romance); *Devil May Care*, by Elizabeth Peters (crime and mystery); and *Blood and Honor*, by W.E.B. Griffin (war fiction).
How to Contact: *Agented submissions only.* Submit synopsis and 3 sample chapters. Reports in 3 months on proposals.
Terms: Pays 7½-15% royalty on retail price. Offers $750-2,500. Simultaneous submissions OK. Book catalog free.

HAROLD SHAW PUBLISHERS, (II, IV), Box 567, 388 Gundersen Dr., Wheaton IL 60189. (603)665-6700. **Acquisitions**: Joan Guest, managing editor. Literary Editor: Lil Copan. Estab. 1968. "Small, independent religious publisher with expanding fiction line." Publishes trade paperback originals and reprints. Average print order: 5,000. Averages 40 total titles, 1-2 fiction titles each year. Receives 1,000 submissions/year. **10-20% of books from first-time authors; 90% from unagented writers.**
Needs: Literary, religious/inspirational. Looking for religious literary novels for adults. No short stories, romances, children's fiction. Recently published *The Other Side of the Sun* and *Love Letters*, by Madeleine L'Engle; and *The Tower, the Mask, and the Grave*, by Betty Smartt Carter (mystery). Published new writers within the last year.
How to Contact: Accepts unsolicited mss. Query first. Submit outline/synopsis and 2-3 sample chapters. SASE. Reports in 4-6 weeks on queries; 3-4 months on mss. No simultaneous submissions. Sometimes critiques rejected mss.
Terms: Pays royalties of 5-10%. Provides 10 author's copies. Sends pages to author. Publishes ms 12-18 months after acceptance. Writer's guidelines for #10 SASE. Book catalog for 9×12 SAE and 5 first-class stamps.
Advice: "Character and plot development are important to us. We look for quality writing in word and in thought. 'Sappiness' and 'pop-writing' don't go over well at all with our editorial department."

SILHOUETTE BOOKS, (I, II, IV), 300 E. 42nd St., 6th Floor, New York NY 10017. (212)682-6080. Fax: (212)682-4539. Website: http://www.romance.net. Editorial Manager: Tara Gavin. Executive Senior Editor and Editorial Coordinator (SIM/SYT): Leslie J. Wainger. **Acquisitions:** Mary-Theresa Hussey, senior editor (Silhouette Romance); Joan Marlow Golan, senior editor (Silhouette Desire); Karen Taylor Richman, senior editor (Silhouette Special Edition); Tracy Farrell, Senior Editor and Editorial Coordinator (Harlequin Historicals). Editors: Gail Chasan, Melissa Jeglinski, Karen Kosztolnyik, Margaret Marbury. Estab. 1979. Publishes paperback originals. Published 10-20 new writers within the last year. Buys agented and unagented adult romances. Averages 360 total titles each year.
Imprint(s): Silhouette Romance, Silhouette Special Edition, Silhouette Desire, Silhouette Intimate Moments, Silhouette Yours Truly, Harlequin Historicals.

- Books published by Silhouette Books have received numerous awards including Romance Writers of America's Rita Award, awards from Romantic Times and best selling awards from Walden and B. Dalton bookstores.

Needs: Contemporary romances, historical romances. Recently published *Unforgettable Bride*, by Annette Broadrick (SR); *A Baby in His In-Box*, by Jennifer Greene (SD); *Wild Mustang Woman*, by Lindsay McKenna (SSE); *The Proposal*, by Linda Turner (SIM); *Big Bad Daddy*, by Christie Ridgway (SYT); *Lion's Lady*, by Suzanne Barclay (HH); and *Decidedly Married*, by Carole Gift Page (LI).
How to Contact: Submit query letter with brief synopsis and SASE. No unsolicited or simultaneous submissions. Publishes ms 9-36 months after acceptance. Occasionally comments on rejected mss.
Terms: Pays in royalties; offers advance (negotiated on an individual basis). Must return advance if book is not completed or is unacceptable. Publishes ms 3 years after acceptance.
Advice: "You are competing with writers that love the genre and know what our readers want—because many of them started as readers. Please note that the fact that our novels are fun to read doesn't make them easy to write. Storytelling ability, clean compelling writing and love of the genre are necessary."

SIMON & SCHUSTER BOOKS FOR YOUNG READERS, (V), Subsidiary of Simon & Schuster Children's Publishing Division, 1230 Avenue of the Americas, New York NY 10020. (212)698-2851. Fax: (212)698-2796. Website: http://www.simonsayskids.com. **Acquisitions:** Stephanie Owens Lurie, vice president/editorial director; David Gale, executive editor; Kevin Lewis, editor; Michele Coppola, editor. "We're looking for complex, challenging YA novels and middle-grade fiction with a fresh, unique slant." Publishes hardcover originals. **Publishes 2-3 previously unpublished writers/year.** Plans 4 first novels this year. Averages 80 total titles, 20 fiction titles each year. Promotes titles through trade magazines, conventions and catalog.

- Books from Simon & Schuster Books for Young Readers have received the following awards: *School Library Journal* Best Book of 1997 for *The Fat Man*, by Maurice Gee; ALA Notable and Best Book for Young Adults for *Habibi*, by Naomi Shihab Nye; and the ALA Best Book for Young Adults and Quick Pick for the Reluctant YA Reader for *Doing Time*, by Rob Thomas; and *1 Horn Book*-Fanfare List.

Needs: Children's/juvenile, young adult/teen (adventure, historical, mystery, contemporary fiction). No problem novels. No anthropomorphic characters. Publishes anthologies; editor solicits from established writers. Recently

published *The Year of the Sawdust Man*, by A. LaFaye (middle-grade fiction); *Satellite Down*, by Rob Thomas (young adult fiction); and *Heaven*, by Angela Johnson (young adult fiction).
How to Contact: *Does not accept unsolicited mss*. Submit query letter and SASE. Agented fiction 90%. Reports in 2 months on queries. Simultaneous submissions OK.
Terms: Pays royalties. Offers negotiable advance. Sends galleys to author. Publishes ms within 2 years of acceptance. Writer's guidelines for #10 SASE. Book catalog available in libraries.
Advice: "Study our catalog and read books we have published to get an idea of our list. The fiction market is crowded and writers need a strong, fresh, original voice to stand out."

SINCLAIR-STEVENSON, (II), 20 Vanthall Bridge Rd., London SW1 V 2SA England. Fiction Editor: Penelope Hoare. Averages 30 fiction titles/year. "Trade hardbacks of quality fiction from new and established authors: Jane Gardam, Rose Tremain, Susan Hill, Peter Ackroyd." Length: open. Send a cover letter. Pays advance and royalties. Contact sales manager for catalog. No guidelines available.

GIBBS SMITH, PUBLISHER/PEREGRINE SMITH, (II, IV), P.O. Box 667, Layton UT 84041. (801)544-9800. Fax: (801)544-5582. Website: http://www.gibbs~smith.com. **Acquisitions**: Gail Yngve, fiction editor; Theresa Desmond, children's editor; Madge Baird, editorial director (westerns). Estab. 1969. Small independent press. "We publish books that make a difference." Publishes hardcover and paperback originals and reprints. Averages 40-60 total titles, 1-2 fiction titles each year. Receives 1,500-2,000 submissions/year. **Publishes 8-10% of books from first-time authors; 50% from unagented writers.**

- Gibbs Smith is the recipient of a Western Writers Association Fiction Award.

Needs: Children's (preschool/picture books), comics/graphic novels, ethnic/multicultural, feminist, humor/satire, literary, mainstream/contemporary, New Age/mystic/spiritual, science fiction (hard science/technological, soft/sociological), short story collections. Publishes *The Peregrine Reader*, a series of anthologies based upon a variety of themes. Published *The White Rooster and Other Stories*, by Robert Bausch (literary); and *Last Buckaroo*, by Mackey Hedges (western).
How to Contact: Accepts unsolicited mss. Query with outline/synopsis and 2 sample chapters. Include estimated word count, 1-paragraph bio and list of publishing credits. SASE for reply. Reports in 3-4 weeks on queries; 2-4 months on mss. Simultaneous submissions OK. Sometimes critiques or comments on rejected mss.
Terms: Pays royalties; amount depends on author and author's publishing history. Provides 10 author's copies. Sends galleys to author. Publishes ms 1-2 years after acceptance. Writer's guidelines and book catalog for #10 SASE.
Advice: "The fiction editor also holds several other positions within the company. Please be patient about response time."

SOHO PRESS, (I, II), 853 Broadway, New York NY 10003. (212)260-1900. Website: http://www.sohopress.com. **Acquisitions**: Juris Jurjevics, Laura M.C. Hruska and Melanie Fleishman, editors. "Soho Press publishes discerning authors for discriminating readers." Publishes hardcover originals and trade paperback reprints. **Publishes 7-10 previously unpublished writers/year.** Averages 25 titles/year. Distributes titles through Farrar, Straus & Giroux. Promotes titles through readings, tours, print ads, reviews, interviews, advance reading copies, postcards and brochures.
Imprint(s): Soho Crime, edited by Laura Hruska and Juris Jurjevics (mystery); and Hera, edited by Laura Hruska (women's historical fiction).
Needs: Ethnic, literary, mainstream, mystery/espionage, suspense. "We do novels that are the very best of their kind." Recently published *The Farming of Bones*, by Edwidge Danticat; *Madam Fate*, by Marcia Douglas; and *All Saints*, by Karen Palmer (literary). Also publishes the Hera series (serious historical fiction reprints with strong female leads).
How to Contact: Submit query with SASE. Reports in 1 month on queries; 6 weeks on mss. Simultaneous submissions OK.
Terms: Pays royalties of 10-15% on retail price. For trade paperbacks pays 7½%. Offers advance. Publishes ms 1 year after acceptance. Book catalog plus $1 for SASE.
Advice: Greatest challenge is "introducing brand new, untested writers. We do not care if they are agented or not. Half the books we publish come directly from authors. We look for a distinctive writing style, strong writing skills and compelling plots. We are not interested in trite expression of mass market formulae."

☑ **SOUNDPRINTS, (II)**, Division of Trudy Corporation, 353 Main Ave., Norwalk CT 06851. Fax: (203)846-1776. E-mail: sndprnts@ix.netcom.com. Website: http://www.soundprints.com. **Acquisitions**: Cassia Farkas, editor. "Soundprints takes you on an Odyssey of discovery, exploring an historical event or a moment in time that affects our every day lives. Each Odyssey is approved by a Smithsonian Institution curator, so readers experience the adventures as if they were really there." Publishes hardcover originals. **Publishes 20% previously unpublished writers/year.** Publishes 10-14 titles/year.
Needs: Juvenile.
How to Contact: Query first. Reports on queries in 3 months. Simultaneous submissions OK.
Terms: Makes outright purchase. No advance. Publishes ms 2 years after acceptance. Book catalog for 9×12 SAE with $1.05 postage. Writer's guidelines for #10 SASE.
Advice: "Our books are written for children from ages 4-8. Our most successful authors can craft a wonderful story which is derived from authentic wildlife facts. First inquiry to us should ask about our interest in publishing a book about a specific animal or habitat. We launched a new series in fall of 1996. Stories are about historical events that are represented by exhibits in the Smithsonian Institution's museums. When we publish juvenile fiction, it will be about wildlife and all information in the book *must* be accurate."

SOUTHERN METHODIST UNIVERSITY PRESS, (I, II), P.O. Box 415, Dallas TX 75275. (214)768-1433. Fax: (214)768-1428. **Acquisitions**: Kathryn M. Lang, senior editor. Estab. 1936. "Small university press publishing in areas of film/theater, Southwest life and letters, religion/medical ethics and contemporary fiction." Publishes hardcover and paperback originals and reprints. Books: acid-free paper; perfect-bound; some illustrations. Average print order 2,000. **Publishes 2 previously unpublished writers/year.** Averages 10-12 total titles; 3-4 fiction titles each year. Sometimes comments on rejected mss. Distributes titles through Texas A&M University Press Consortium. Promotes titles through writers' publications.
Needs: Contemporary, ethnic, literary, regional, short story collections. "We are always willing to look at 'serious' or 'literary' fiction." No "mass market, science fiction, formula, thriller, romance." Recently published *The Earth & the Sky*, by Debbie Lee Wesselmann; *Lost and Old Rivers*, by Dean Chauser; and *Polonaise*, by Tony Bukoski (short story collections).
How to Contact: Accepts unsolicited mss. Query first. Submit outline/synopsis and 3 sample chapters. SASE. Reports in 3 weeks on queries; 6-12 months on mss. No simultaneous submissions.
Terms: Pays royalties of 10% net, negotiable small advance, 10 author's copies. Publishes ms 1 year after acceptance. Book catalog free.
Advice: "We view encouraging first time authors as part of the mission of a university press. Send query describing the project and your own background. Research the press before you submit—don't send us the kinds of things we don't publish." Looks for "quality fiction from new or established writers."

SPECTRA BOOKS, (II, IV), Subsidiary of Bantam Doubleday Dell Publishing Group, 1540 Broadway, New York NY 10036. (212)782-9418. Fax: (212)782-9523. Website: http://www.bdd.com. Executive Editor: Jennifer Hershey. Senior Editor: Tom Dupree. **Acquisitions:** Anne Groell, associate editor. Estab. 1985. Large science fiction, fantasy and speculative fiction line. Publishes hardcover originals, paperback originals and trade paperbacks. Averages 60 total titles, all fiction.

- Many Bantam Spectra Books have received Hugos and Nebulas.

Needs: Fantasy, humor (fantasy, science fiction), literary, science fiction. Needs include novels that attempt to broaden the traditional range of science fiction and fantasy. Strong emphasis on characterization. Especially well written traditional science fiction and fantasy will be considered. No fiction that doesn't have at least some element of speculation or the fantastic. Published *Game of Thrones*, by George R. Martin (medieval fantasy); *Assassin's Quest*, by Robin Hobb (coming of age fantasy); and *Blue Mars*, by Stanley Robinson (science fiction).
How to Contact: Query first with 3 chapters and a short (no more than 3 pages double-spaced) synopsis. SASE. Agented fiction 90%. Reports in 6 months. Simultaneous submissions OK if noted.
Terms: Pays in royalties; negotiable advance. Sends galleys to author. Writer's guidelines for #10 SASE.
Advice: "Please follow our guidelines carefully and type neatly."

☑ **SPINSTERS INK, (II, IV)**, 32 E. First St., #330, Duluth MN 55802. Fax: (218)727-3119. E-mail: spinster@spinsters-ink.com. Website: http://www.spinsters-ink.com (includes online catalog, writer's guidelines, staff list, chat rooms, excerpts from books, discussion forums). **Acquisitions**: Nancy Walker. Estab. 1978. Moderate-size women's publishing company growing steadily. "We are committed to publishing works by women writing from the periphery: fat women, Jewish women, lesbians, poor women, rural women, women of color, etc." Publishes paperback originals and reprints. Books: 55 lb. acid-free natural paper; photo offset printing; perfect-bound; illustrations when appropriate. Average print order: 5,000. Published new writers within the last year. Plans 2 first novels this year. Averages 6 total titles, 3-5 fiction titles each year. Distributes titles through Words Distributing and all wholesalers. Promotes titles through Women's Review of Books, Feminist Bookstore News, regional advertising, author interviews and reviews.

- Spinsters Ink won a 1997 Minnesota Women's Consortium Award. They published *Silent Words*, by Joan Drury, which received a 1997 Minnesota Book Award, a 1997 PMA Benjamin Franklin Award and a 1997 Northeastern Minnesota Book Award.

Needs: Feminist, lesbian. Wants "full-length quality fiction—thoroughly revised novels which display deep

characterization, theme and style. We *only* consider books by women. No books by men, or books with sexist, racist or ageist content." Published *Silent Words*, by Joan Drury (feminist mystery); *The Activist's Daughter*, by Ellyn Bache (feminist); and *Living at Night*, by Mariana Romo-Carmona (lesbian). Publishes anthologies. Writers may submit directly. Series include: "Coming of Age Series" and "Forgotten Women's Series."
How to Contact: Query or submit outline/synopsis and 2-5 sample chapters not to exceed 50 pages with SASE. Reports in 1 month on queries; 3 months on mss. Simultaneous submissions OK. Prefers hard copy submission. Occasionally critiques rejected mss.
Terms: Pays royalties of 7-10%, plus 10 author's copies; unlimited extra copies at 40% discount. Publishes ms 18 months after acceptance. Free book catalog.
Advice: "In the past, lesbian fiction has been largely 'escape fiction' with sex and romance as the only required ingredients; however, we encourage more complex work that treats the lesbian lifestyle with the honesty it deserves. Look at our catalog and mission statement. Does your book fit our criteria?"

☑ **STARBURST PUBLISHERS, (II)**, P.O. Box 4123, Lancaster PA 17604. (717)293-0939. Fax: (717)293-1945. E-mail: starburst@starburstpublishers.com. Website: http://www.starburstpublishers.com (includes writer's guidelines, authors, titles, editorial information, catalog, rights, distribution, etc.). **Acquisitions**: David A. Robie, editorial director. Estab. 1982. Midsize independent press specializing in inspirational and self-help books. Publishes trade paperback and hardcover originals and trade paperback reprints. Receives 1,000 submission/year. 60% of books by first-time authors. **Publishes 1-2 previously unpublished writers/year.** Averages 10-15 total titles each year. Distributes titles through all major distributors and sales reps. Promotes titles through print, radio, and major distributors.
Needs: Religious/inspirational: Adventure, contemporary, fantasy, historical, horror, military/war, psychic/supernatural/occult, romance (contemporary, historical), spiritual, suspense/mystery, western. Wants "inspirational material." Published *The Fragile Thread*, by Aliske Webb; and *The Miracle of the Sacred Scroll*, by Johan Christian.
How to Contact: Submit outline/synopsis, 3 sample chapters, bio and SASE. Unsolicited queries/correspondence by e-mail OK. Agented fiction less than 25%. Reports in 6-8 weeks on manuscripts; 1 month on queries. Accepts electronic submissions via disk and modem, "but also wants clean double-spaced typewritten or computer printout manuscript."
Terms: Pays royalties of 6% minimum; 16% maximum. "Individual arrangement with writer depending on the manuscript as well as writer's experience as a published author." Publishes ms up to one year after acceptance. Writer's guidelines for #10 SASE. Book catalog for 9×12 SAE and 4 first-class stamps.
Advice: "50% of our line goes into the inspirational marketplace; 50% into the general marketplace. We are one of the few publishers that has direct sales representation into both the inspirational and general marketplace."

☑ **STEEPLE HILL, (II)**, 300 E. 42nd Street, 6th Floor, New York NY 10017. (212)682-6080. Fax: (212)682-4539. Steeple Hill publishes Love Inspired, a line of inspirational contemporary romances with stories designed to lift readers spirits and gladden their hearts. These books feature characters facing the challenge of today's world and learning important lessons about life, love and faith. Editorial Manager: Tara Gavin. **Acquisitions**: Tracy Farrell, senior editor and editorial coordinator; Anne Canadeo, freelance editor. Melissa Jeglinski, editor. Publishes paperback originals and reprints. Buys agented and unagented inspirational love stories.

- Authors who write for Steeple Hill are a combination of celebrated authors in the Christian women's fiction market such as Jane Peart, Carole Gift Page, Roger Elwood, Sara Mitchell and Irene Brand, as well as talented newcomers to the field of inspirational romance.

Needs: "Wholesome contemporary tales of inspirational romance that include strong family values and high moral standards. Drama, humor and a touch of mystery all have a place in the series." To be published: *The Risk of Loving*, by Jane Peart; *In Search of her Own*, by Carole Gift Page; *Promises*, by Roger Elwood; *Night Music*, by Sara Mitchell; and *Child of Her Heart*, by Irene Brand.
How to Contact: Submit query letter with brief synopsis and SASE or write for detailed submission guidelines/tip sheets. No unsolicited or simultaneous submissions. Publishes 9-36 months after acceptance. Occasionally comments on rejected mss.
Terms: Royalties paid twice-yearly; offers advance (negotiated on an individual basis). Must return advance if book is not completed or unacceptable. Writer's guidelines for #10 SASE.
Advice: "Although the element of faith must be clearly present, it should be well-integrated into the characterizations and plot. Children and humor are welcome; family values and traditional morals are imperative. While there is no premarital sex between characters, a vivid, exciting romance that is presented with a mature prespective is essential."

☑ **STILL WATERS POETRY PRESS, (II)**, 459 Willow Ave., Galloway Township NJ 08201. Website: http://www2.netcom.com/~salake/stillwaterspoetry.html. **Acquisitions**: Shirley A. Lake, editor. "Dedicated to significant poetry for, by or about women, we want contemporary themes and styles set on American soil. We don't want gay, patriarchal religion, lesbian, simple rhyme or erotic themes." Publishes trade paperback originals and chapbooks. Publishes 4 titles/year. Receives 50 queries and 500 mss/year. **Publishes 80% previously unpublished writers/year.**
Needs: Literary, women's interests. "We seldom publish fiction. Don't send the same old stuff." No long books.

Published *Grain Pie*, by Anne Lawrence (chapbook).
How to Contact: Short stories only with SASE. Reports in 1 month on queries; 3 months on mss. Simultaneous submissions OK.
Terms: Pays in copies for first press run; 10% royalty for additional press runs. No advance. Publishes ms 4 months after acceptance. Writer's guidelines and book catalog for #10 SASE.
Advice: "Audience is adults with literary awareness. Don't send manuscripts via certified mail."

STONE BRIDGE PRESS, (IV), P.O. Box 8208, Berkeley CA 94707. (510)524-8732. Fax: (510)524-8711. E-mail: sbpedit@stonebridge.com. Website: http://www.stonebridge.com (includes complete catalog, contact information, related features, submission guidelines and excerpts). **Acquisitions**: Peter Goodman, publisher. Estab. 1989. "Independent press focusing on books about Japan in English (business, language, culture, literature)." Publishes paperback originals and reprints. Books: 60-70 lb. offset paper; web and sheet paper; perfect-bound; some illustrations. Averages 6 total titles, 2 fiction titles, each year. Distributes titles through Consortium. Promotes titles through Internet announcements, special-interest magazines and niche tie-ins to associations.
Imprint(s): Rock Spring Collection of Japanese Literature, edited by Peter Goodman.

- Stone Bridge Press received a PEN West Literary Award for Translation and a Japan-U.S. Friendship Prize for *Still Life*, by Junzo Shono, translated by Wayne P. Lammers.

Needs: Japan-themed. No poetry. If not translation, interested in the expatriate experience. "Primarily looking at material relating to Japan. Mostly translations, but we'd like to see samples of work dealing with the expatriate experience." Also Asian- and Japanese-American. Recently published *The Broken Bridge*, edited by Suzanne Kamata (anthology).
How to Contact: Accepts unsolicited mss. Query first. Unsolicited queries/correspondence by e-mail and fax OK. Submit 1-page cover letter, outline/synopsis and 3 sample chapters. SASE. Agented fiction 25%. Reports in 1 month on queries; 6-8 months on mss. Simultaneous submissions OK. Sometimes comments on rejected ms.
Terms: Pays royalties, offers negotiable advance. Publishes ms 18-24 months after acceptance. Catalog for 1 first-class stamp.
Advice: "As we focus on Japan-related material there is no point in approaching us unless you are very familiar with Japan. We'd especially like to see submissions dealing with the expatriate experience. Please, absolutely no commercial fiction."

STONEWALL INN, (II), Imprint of St. Martin's Press, 175 Fifth Ave., New York NY 10010. (212)674-5151. Website: http://www.stonewallinn.com. **Acquisitions:** Keith Kahla, general editor. "Stonewall Inn is the only gay and lesbian focused imprint at a major house . . . and is more inclusive of gay men than most small presses." Publishes trade paperback originals and reprints. Publishes 20-23 titles/year. Receives 3,000 queries/year. **Publishes 40% previously unpublished writers/year.**
Needs: Gay, lesbian, literary, mystery. Recently published *Love Alone*, by Paul Monette; and *Buddies*, by Ethan Mordden.
How to Contact: Query with SASE. Reports in 6 months on queries. Simultaneous submissions OK.
Terms: Pays standard royalty on retail price. Pays $5,000 advance (for first-time authors). Publishes ms 1 year after acceptance. Book catalog free.
Advice: "Anybody who has any question about what a gay novel is should go out and read half a dozen. For example, there are hundreds of 'coming out' novels in print."

STORY LINE PRESS, (II), Three Oaks Farm, P.O. Box 1108, Ashland OR 97520. (541)512-8792. Fax: (541)512-8793. E-mail: slp@teleport.com. Website: http://www.teleport.com/~slp. **Acquisitions**: Robert McDowell, editor. Estab. 1985. "Nonprofit literary press." Publishes hardcover and paperback originals and hardcover and paperback reprints. Published new writers within the last year. Plans 1 first novel this year. Averages 12 total titles, 3 fiction titles each year.

- Story Line Press books have received awards including the Oregon Book Award.

Needs: Adventure, ethnic/multicultural, literary, mystery/suspense, regional, short story collections, translations. Recently published *Of Una Jeffers, A Memoir*, by Edith Greenan; and *The Ghost of Tradition, Expansive Poetry and Post Modernism*, by Kevin Walzer. Publishes Stuart Mallory Mystery series.
How to Contact: Accepts unsolicited mss. Returns mss "if postage is included." Query with outline. Include bio, list of publishing credits and description of work. Send SASE for reply, return of ms or send a disposable copy of ms. Agented fiction 2.7%. Reports in 9-12 weeks on queries; 6-9 months on mss. Simultaneous submissions OK. No electronic submissions.
Terms: Provides author's copies; payment depends on grant/award money. Sends galleys to author. Publishes ms 1-3 years after acceptance. Book catalog for 7×10 SASE.
Advice: "Patience . . . understanding of a nonprofit literary presses' limitations. Be very familiar with our list and only submit accordingly."

THE SUMMIT PUBLISHING GROUP, (II), 2000 E. Lamar Blvd., Suite 600, Arlington TX 76006. (817)588-3013. **Acquisitions:** Jill Bertolet, publisher. Summit Publishing Group seeks contemporary books with a nationwide appeal. Publishes hardcover originals, trade paperback originals and reprints. Publishes 35 titles/year. **Publishes 40% previously unpublished writers/year.**

Needs: Literary, religious. Recently published *The Gospel of Elvis*, by Louie Ludwig (humor).

How to Contact: Submit synopsis, 2 sample chapters and SASE. Reports in 1 month on queries, 3 months on mss. Simultaneous submissions OK.

Terms: Pays 5-20% royalty on wholesale price. Offers $2,000 and up advance. Publishes ms 6 months after acceptance.

SUNSTONE PRESS, (IV), P.O. Box 2321, Santa Fe NM 87504-2321. (505)988-4418. Contact: James C. Smith, Jr. Estab. 1971. Midsize publisher. Publishes hardcover and paperback originals. Average first novel print order: 2,000. Published new writers within the last year. Plans 2 first novels this year. Averages 16 total titles, 2-3 fiction titles, each year.

- Sunstone Press published *Ninez*, by Virginia Nylander Ebinger which received the Southwest Book Award from the Border Regional Library Association.

Needs: Western. "We have a Southwestern theme emphasis. Sometimes buys juvenile mss with illustrations." No science fiction, romance or occult. Published *Apache: The Long Ride Home*, by Grant Gall (Indian/Western); *Sorrel*, by Rita Cleary; and *To Die in Dinetah*, by John Truitt.

How to Contact: Accepts unsolicited mss. Query first or submit outline/synopsis and 2 sample chapters with SASE. Reports in 2 weeks. Simultaneous submissions OK. Publishes ms 9-12 months after acceptance.

Terms: Pays royalties, 10% maximum, and 10 author's copies.

TAB BOOK CLUB, (TEEN AGE BOOK CLUB), (II), Scholastic Inc., 555 Broadway, New York NY 10012. Senior Editor: Greg Holch. Published new writers within the last year.

Needs: "TAB Book Club publishes novels for young teenagers in seventh through ninth grades. At the present time these novels are all reprints from Scholastic's trade division or from other publishers. The Tab Book Club is not currently publishing original novels."

How to Contact: "We are not looking at new manuscripts this year."

Advice: "The books we are publishing now are literary works that we hope will become the classics of the future. They are novels that reveal the hearts and souls of their authors."

NAN A. TALESE, (V), Imprint of Doubleday, 1540 Broadway, New York NY 10036. (212)782-8918. Fax: (212)782-9261. Website: http://www.bdd.com. **Acquisitions:** Nan A. Talese, editorial director. "Nan A. Talese publishes nonfiction with a powerful guiding narrative and relevance to larger cultural trends and interests, and literary fiction of the highest quality." Publishes hardcover originals. Publishes 15 titles/year. Receives 400 queries and mss/year.

Needs: Literary. Published *The Dancer Upstairs*, by Nicholas Shakespeare (novel); *Alias Grace*, by Margaret Atwood (novel); and *Into the Great Wide Open*, by Kevin Carty (first novel).

How to Contact: Agented fiction only. Reports in 1 week on queries, 1 month on mss. Simultaneous submissions OK.

Terms: Pays royalty on retail price, varies. Advance varies. Publishes ms 8 months after acceptance.

Advice: "We're interested in everything literary—we're not interested in genre fiction. No low-market stuff. Audience is highly literate people interested in literary books. We want well-written material."

TEXAS CHRISTIAN UNIVERSITY PRESS, (III), P.O. Box 298300, TCU, Fort Worth TX 76129. (817)257-7822. Fax: (817)257-7333. Director: Judy Alter. **Acquisitions:** Tracy Row, editor. Estab. 1966. Texas Christian publishes "scholarly monographs, other serious scholarly work and regional titles of significance focusing on the history and literature of the American." Publishes hardcover originals, some reprints. **Publishes 10% previously unpublished writers/year.** Publishes 10 titles/year. Receives 100 submissions/year.

Needs: Regional fiction. Published *Hunter's Trap*, by C.W. Smith; *Tales from the Sunday House*, by Minetta Altgelt Goyne (history); and *The Coldest Day in Texas*, by Peggy Pursy Freeman (juvenile).

How to Contact: Considers mss by invitation only. Please do not query. Reports in 3 months.

Terms: Nonauthor-subsidy publishes 10% of books. Pays 10% royalty on net price. Publishes ms 16 months after acceptance.

Advice: "Regional and/or Texana nonfiction or fiction have best chance of breaking into our firm."

THORNDIKE PRESS, (IV), Division of Macmillan U.S.A., Box 159, Thorndike ME 04986. (800)223-6121. **Acquisitions**: Jamie Knobloch. Estab. 1979. Midsize publisher of hardcover and paperback large print *reprints*. Books: alkaline paper; offset printing; Smythe-sewn library binding; average print order: 1,000. Publishes 660 total titles each year.

Needs: *No fiction that has not been previously published.*

How to Contact: Does not accept unsolicited mss. Query.

Terms: Pays 10% in royalties.

Advice: "We do not accept unpublished works."

TIDEWATER PUBLISHERS, (II), Imprint of Cornell Maritime Press, Inc., P.O. Box 456, Centreville MD 21617-0456. (410)758-1075. Fax: (410)758-6849. **Acquisitions:** Charlotte Kurst, managing editor. Estab. 1938. "Tidewater Publishers issues adult nonfiction works related to the Chesapeake Bay area, Delmarva or Maryland in general. The only fiction we handle is juvenile and must have a regional focus." Publishes hardcover and paperback originals. **Publishes 41% previously unpublished writers/year.** Publishes 7-9 titles/year.
Needs: Regional juvenile fiction only. Published *Toulouse: The Story of a Canada Goose*, by Priscilla Cummings (picture book); and *Oyster Moon*, by Margaret Meacham (adventure).
How to Contact: Query or submit outline/synopsis and sample chapters. Reports in 2 months.
Terms: Pays 7½-15% royalty on retail price. Publishes ms 1 year after acceptance. Book catalog for 10×13 SAE with 5 first-class stamps.
Advice: "Our audience is made up of readers interested in works that are specific to the Chesapeake Bay and Delmarva Peninsula area."

TOR BOOKS, (II), Tom Doherty Associates, 175 Fifth Ave., New York NY 10010. (212)388-0100. **Acquisitions**: Patrick Nielsen Hayden, manager of science fiction; Melissa Singer (Forge Books). Estab. 1980. Publishes hardcover and paperback originals, plus some paperback reprints. Books: 5 point Dombook paper; offset printing; Bursel and perfect binding; few illustrations. Averages 200 total titles, mostly fiction, each year. Some nonfiction titles.
Imprint(s): Forge Books.
Needs: Fantasy, mainstream, science fiction and horror. Published *The Path of Daggers*, by Robert Jordan; *1916*, by Morgan Llywelyn; *The Predators*, by Harold Robbins; and *Darwinia*, by Robert Charles Wilson.
How to Contact: Agented mss preferred. Buys 90% agented fiction. No simultaneous submissions. Address manuscripts to "Editorial," *not* to the Managing Editor's office.
Terms: Pays in royalties and advance. Writer must return advance if book is not completed or is unacceptable. Sends galleys to author. Free book catalog on request. Publishes ms 1-2 years after acceptance.

✓ **TSR, INC.**, Wizards of the Coast, P.O. Box 707, Renton WA 98057-0707. (425)226-6500. Executive Editor: Mary Kirchoff. **Acquisitions**: Submissions Editor. Estab. 1974. "We publish original paperback and hardcover novels and 'shared world' books." TSR publishes games as well, including the Dungeons & Dragons® role-playing game. Books: standard paperbacks; offset printing; perfect binding; b&w (usually) illustrations; average first novel print order: 75,000. Averages 20-30 fiction titles each year. Receives 600 queries and 300 mss/year. **Publishes 10% previously unpublished writers.**
Imprint(s): Dragonlance® series, Forgotten Realms™ series, Dungeons & Dragons® Books, Dark Sun Books, **TSR™ Books**, Ravenloft™ Books.

- TSR also publishes the magazine *Amazing Stories* listed in this book.

Needs: "We most often publish character-oriented fantasy and science fiction; all horror must be suitable for line of Ravenluff™ Books. We work with authors who can deal in a serious fashion with the genres we concentrate on and can be creative within the confines of our work-for-hire contracts." Published *The Legacy*, by R.A. Salvatore; *The Valorian*, by Mary H. Herbert; and *Before the Mask*, by Michael and Teri Williams.
How to Contact: "Because most of our books are strongly tied to our game products, we expect our writers to be very familiar with those products."
Terms: Pays royalties of 4% of cover price. Offers advances. "Commissioned works, with the exception of our TSR™ Books line, are written as work-for-hire, with TSR, Inc., holding all copyrights." Publishes ms 1 year after acceptance.
Advice: "With the huge success of our Dragonlance® series and Forgotten Realms™ books, we expect to be working even more closely with TSR-owned fantasy worlds. Be familiar with our line and query us regarding a proposal."

TYNDALE HOUSE PUBLISHERS, (II, IV), P.O. Box 80, 351 Executive Drive, Wheaton IL 60189-0080. (630)668-8300. Fax: (630)668-8311. E-mail: kv@tyndale.com. Website: http://www.tyndale.com. Vice President of Editorial: Ron Beers. **Acquisitions**: Ken Petersen, acquisition director. Manuscript Review Committee. Estab. 1962. Privately owned religious press. Publishes hardcover and trade paperback originals and paperback reprints. Averages 100 total titles, 20-25 fiction titles each year. Average first novel print order: 5,000-15,000 copies. Distributes titles through catalog houses, rackers and distributors. Promotes titles through prints ads in trade publications, radio, point of sale materials and catalogs.
Imprint(s): Lining Books.

- Three books published by Tyndale House have received the Gold Medallion Book Award. They include *An Echo in the Darkness*, by Francine Rivers; *The Sword of Truth*, by Gilbert Morris; and *A Rose Remembered*, by Michael Phillips.

CHECK THE CATEGORY INDEXES, located at the back of the book, for publishers interested in specific fiction subjects.

Needs: Religious: historical, romance. "We primarily publish Christian historical romances, with occasional contemporary, suspense or standalones." Published *Treasure of Zanzibar*, by Catherine Palmer (adventure romance); *The Atonement Child*, by Francine Rivers (general); and *Left Behind* series, by Jerry Jenkins and Tim Lattaye (prophecy fiction). Publishes 1 previously unpublished writer/year.
How to Contact: Does not accept unsolicited mss. Queries only. Reports in 6-10 weeks. Publishes ms an average of 9-18 months after acceptance.
Terms: Royalty and advance negotiable. Publishes ms 18 months after acceptance. Writer's guidelines and book catalog for 9×12 SAE and $2.40 for postage.
Advice: "We are a religious publishing house with a primarily evangelical Christian market. We are looking for spiritual themes and content within established genres."

☑ **UNITY BOOKS, (II)**, Unity School of Christianity, 1901 NW Blue Parkway, Unity Village MO 64065-0001. (816)524-3550 ext. 3190. Fax: (816)251-3552. E-mail: sprice@unityworldhq.org. Website: http://www.unityworldhq.org. **Acquisitions**: Michael Maday, editor; Raymond Teague, associate editor. "We are a bridge between traditional Christianity and New Age spirituality. Unity School of Christianity is based on metaphysical Christian principles, spiritual values and the healing power of prayer as a resource for daily living." Publishes hardcover and trade paperback originals and reprints. **Publishes 50% previously unpublished writers/year.** Publishes 16 titles/year.
Needs: Spiritual, inspirational, metaphysical.
How to Contact: Query with synopsis and sample chapter. Reports in 1 month on queries; 2 months on mss.
Terms: Pays 10-15% royalty on net receipts. Publishes ms 13 months after acceptance of final ms. Writer's guidelines and book catalog free.

UNIVERSITY OF GEORGIA PRESS, (II), 330 Research Dr., Athens GA 30602-4901. (706)369-6130. Fax: (706)369-6131. E-mail: ugapress@uga.edu. **Acquisitions:** David Dejardines, acquisition editor. Estab. 1938. University of Georgia Press is a midsized press. "We publish one or two original works of fiction/year. Those with which we have had the greatest success are literary novels, with southern settings and themes. We do not publish mainstream fiction in general, particularly historical or adventure/action novels. We publish short fiction (two collections/year) *only* through our Flannery O'Connor award for short fiction competition." Occasionally publishes previously unpublished authors. Publishes 85 titles/year.
Imprint(s): Brown Thrasher Books, David Dejardines, acquisition editor (paperback originals and reprints, Southern history, literature and culture).
Needs: Literary. Recently published *Daughters of My People*, by James Kilgo; *Virgin Forest*, by Eric Zencey; and *Battlegrounds of Memory*, by Clay Lewis.
How to Contact: Query with 1-2 sample chapters and SASE. Reports in 2 months on queries.
Terms: Pays 7-10% royalty on net price. Rarely offers advance; amount varies. Publishes ms 1 year after acceptance. Writer's guidelines for #10 SASE. Book catalog free.

☑ **UNIVERSITY OF IOWA PRESS, (II)**, 119 W. Park Rd., Iowa City IA 52242-1000. (319)335-2000. Fax: (319)335-2055. Website: http://www.uiowa.edu/~uipress. **Acquisitions:** Holly Carver, interim director. Estab. 1969. Publishes hardcover and paperback originals. **Publishes 30% previously unpublished writers/year.** Publishes 35 titles/year. Average print order for a first book is 1,000-1,200.
Needs: Currently publishes the Iowa Short Fiction Award selections.
How to Contact: Query first. Reports within 4 months.
Terms: Pays 7-10% royalty on net price. Publishes ms 1 year after acceptance. Writer's guidelines and book catalog free.

☑ **UNIVERSITY OF NEBRASKA PRESS, (IV)**, 312 N. 14th St., P.O. Box 880484, Lincoln NE 68588-0484. (402)472-3581. Fax: (402)472-0308. E-mail: press@unlinfo.unl.edu. Website: http://www.unl.edu./UP/home.htm. **Acquisitions:** Daniel Ross, director. Estab. 1941. "The University of Nebraska Press seeks to encourage, develop, publish and disseminate research, literature and the publishing arts. The Press maintains scholarly standards and fosters innovations guided by referred evaluations." Publishes hardcover and paperback originals and reprints. **Publishes 25% previously unpublished writers/year.** Average print order for a first book is 1,200.
Imprint(s): Bison Books (paperback reprints).

- University of Nebraska Press has published such authors as N. Scott Momaday and Diane Glancy.

Needs: Accepts fiction translations but no original fiction. Published *School Days*, by Patrick Chamoiseau (Caribbean childhood memoir); *Rue Ordener, Rue Labat*, Sarah Kofman (France-Judaism, 20th century); and *Celebration in the Northwest*, by Ana Maria Matute (contemporary Spanish women's fiction).
How to Contact: Query first with outline/synopsis, 1 sample chapter and introduction. Reports in 4 months.
Terms: Pays graduated royalty from 7% on original books. Occasional advance. Writer's guidelines and book catalog for 9×12 SAE with 5 first-class stamps.

THE UNIVERSITY OF TENNESSEE PRESS, (II), 293 Communications Bldg., Knoxville TN 37996-0325. Fax: (423)974-3724. E-mail: utpress2@utk.edu. Website: http://www.sunsite.utk.edu/utpress. **Acquisitions:** Joyce Harrison, acquisitions editor; Jenifer Siler, director. Estab. 1940. **Publishes 35% previously unpublished**

writers/year. Publishes 30 titles/year. Average print order for a first book is 1,000.
Needs: Regional. Recently published *Sharpshooter*, by David Madden (Civil War novel).
How to Contact: Query with SASE first. Reports in 2 months.
Terms: Nonauthor-subsidy publishes 10% of books. Pays negotiable royalty on net receipts. Publishes ms 1 year after acceptance. Writer's guidelines for SASE. Book catalog for 12×16 SAE with 2 first-class stamps.
Advice: "Our market is in several groups: scholars; educated readers with special interests in given scholarly subjects; and the general educated public interested in Tennessee, Appalachia and the South. Not all our books appeal to all these groups, of course, but any given book must appeal to at least one of them."

UNIVERSITY OF TEXAS PRESS, (II), P.O. Box 7819, Austin TX 78713-7819. Fax: (512)320-0668. E-mail: castiron@mail.utexas.edu. Website: http://www.utexas.edu/utpress/. **Acquisitions:** Theresa May, assistant director/executive editor (social sciences, Latin American studies); James Burr, acquisitions editor (humanities, classics). Contact: Acquisitions Editor (science). Estab. 1952. **Publishes 50% previously unpublished writers/year.** Publishes 80 titles/year. Average print order for a first book is 1,000.
Needs: Latin American and Middle Eastern fiction only in translation. Recently published *Lost in the City: Tree of Desire* and *Serafin*, by Ionacio Solares (novels).
How to Contact: Query or submit outline and 2 sample chapters. Reports in up to 3 months.
Terms: Pays royalty usually based on net income. Offers advance occasionally. Publishes ms 18 months after acceptance. Writer's guidelines and book catalog free.
Advice: "It's difficult to make a manuscript over 400 double-spaced pages into a feasible book. Authors should take special care to edit out extraneous material. Looks for sharply focused, in-depth treatments of important topics."

UNIVERSITY PRESS OF NEW ENGLAND, (II), (includes Wesleyan University Press), 23 S. Main St., Hanover NH 03755-2048. (603)643-7100. Fax: (603)643-1540. E-mail: university.press@dartmouth.edu. Website: http://www.dartmouth.edu/acad-inst/upne/ (includes writer's guidelines, names of editors, authors, titles, etc.). Director: Peter Gilbert. **Acquisitions:** Phil Pochoda, editorial director (literary, New England); Phyliss Deutsch, editor. Estab. 1970. "University Press of New England is a consortium of six university presses. Some books—those published for one of the consortium members—carry the joint imprint of New England and the member: Wesleyan, Dartmouth, Brandeis, Tufts, University of New Hampshire and Middlebury College. Associate member: Salzburg Seminar." Publishes hardcover originals; New England settings only. Publishes 80 titles/year; 4 fiction titles/year. Promotes titles through catalog, magazine advertisements, trade journal ads, mailings.
Imprint(s): HardScrabble.

- University Press of New England books received the Bakeless Literary Publication Prize for *Tell Me Everything and Other Stories*, by Joyce Minnefeld; and the Strauss Living Award/A.A. of Arts & Letters for *Wherever That Great Heart May Be*, by W.D. Wetherell.

Needs: Literary, regional (New England) novels and reprints. Recently published *Weird Women, Wired Woman*, by Kit Reed (literary); *Judgment Hill*, by Castle Freeman Jr. (novel); and *Tell Me Everything*, by Joyce Hinnefeld (literary, short stories).
How to Contact: Query first. Unsolicited queries/correspondence by e-mail and fax OK. Submit outline, list of publishing credits, 1-2 sample chapters with SASE. Agented fiction 50%. Simultaneous submissions OK. Reports in 2 months. Sometimes comments on rejected mss.
Terms: Nonauthor-subsidy publishes 80% of books. Pays standard royalty. Offers advance occasionally. Writer's guidelines and book catalog for 9×12 SAE with 5 first-class stamps.

VANWELL PUBLISHING LIMITED (II), 1 Northrup Crescent, P.O. Box 2131, St. Catharines, Ontario L2R 7S2 Canada. (905)937-3100. Fax: (905)937-1760. **Acquisitions:** Angela Dobler, general editor; Simon Kooter, editor (military). Estab. 1983. Publishes trade originals and reprints. **Publishes 85% previously unpublished writers/year.** Publishes 5-7 titles/year.

- Vanwell Publishing Ltd. has received awards from Education Children's Book Centre and Notable Education Libraries Association.

Needs: Historical, military/war. Recently published *The Stone Orchard*, by Susan Merritt (historical fiction); *The Wagner Whacker*, by Joseph Romain (baseball, historical fiction).
How to Contact: Query first with SASE. Reports in 6 months on queries.
Terms: Pays 8-15% royalty on wholesale price. Offers $200 average advance. Publishes ms 1 year after acceptance. Book catalog free.
Advice: "The writer has the best chance of selling a manuscript to our firm which is in keeping with our publishing program, well written and organized. Our audience: older male, history buff, war veteran; regional tourist; students. *Canadian* only military/aviation, naval, military/history and children's nonfiction have the best chance with us."

VIKING, (V), Imprint of Penguin Putnam Inc., 375 Hudson St., New York NY 10014. (212)366-2000. **Acquisitions:** Barbara Grossman, publisher. Publishes a mix of academic and popular fiction and nonfiction. Publishes hardcover and trade paperback originals.
Needs: Literary, mainstream/contemporary, mystery, suspense. Published *Out to Canaan*, by John Karon (novel).

How to Contact: Agented fiction only. Reports in 4-6 months on queries. Simultaneous submissions OK.
Terms: Pays 10-15% royalty on retail price. Advance negotiable. Publishes ms 1 year after acceptance.
Advice: "Looking for writers who can deliver a book a year (or faster) of consistent quality."

VIKING CHILDREN'S BOOKS, (II), Imprint of Penguin Putnam Inc., 375 Hudson St., New York NY 10014-3657. (212)366-2000. Fax: (212)414-3399. Website: http://www.penguinputnam.com (includes online catalog of all imprints, feature articles and interviews, young readers site, order information, education and teacher's resources). **Acquisitions:** Melanie Cecka, editor. "Viking Children's Books publishes the highest quality trade books for children including fiction, nonfiction, and novelty books for pre-schoolers through young adults." Publishes hardcover originals. **Publishes 1-5 previously unpublished writers/year.** Publishes 80 books/year. Promotes titles through press kits, institutional ads.
Needs: Juvenile, young adult. Recently published *Someone Like You*, by Sarah Dessen (novel); *Window Music*, by Anastasia Suen/Wade Zahares (picture book); and *Spotlight on Cody*, by Betsy Duffey (chapter book).
How to Contact: Query with synopsis, one sample chapter. Picture books submit entire ms. Reports in 2-3 months on queries. Simultaneous submissions OK. SASE mandatory for return of materials.
Terms: Pays 10% royalty on retail price. Advance negotiable. Publishes ms 12-18 months after acceptance.
Advice: No "cartoony" or mass-market submissions for picture books.

VISION BOOKS PVT LTD., (II), Madarsa Rd., Kashmere Gate, Delhi 110006 India. **Acquisitions**: Sudhir Malhotra, fiction editor. Publishes 25 titles/year.
Needs: "We are a large multilingual publishing house publishing fiction and other trade books."
How to Contact: "A brief synopsis should be submitted initially. Subsequently, upon hearing from the editor, a typescript may be sent."
Terms: Pays royalties.

VISTA PUBLISHING, INC., (I, IV), 422 Morris Ave., Suite One, Long Branch NJ 07740-5901. (732)229-6500. Fax: (732)229-9647. E-mail: czagury@vistapubl.com. Website: http://www.vistapubl.com (includes titles, authors, editors, pricing and ordering information). **Acquisitions**: Carolyn Zagury, president. Estab. 1991. "Small, independent press, owned by women and specializing in fiction by nurses and allied health professional authors." Publishes paperback originals. **Publishes 3 previously unpublished writers/year.** Plans 3 first novels this year. Averages 12 total titles, 6 fiction titles each year. Distributes titles through catalogs, wholesalers, distributors, exhibits, website, trade shows, book clubs and bookstores. Promotes titles through author signings, press releases, author speakings, author interviews, exhibits, website, direct mail and book reviews.
Needs: Adventure, humor/satire, mystery/suspense, romance, short story collections. Recently published *Broken Butterflies*, by Jodi Lalone (short stories); *By Prescription Only*, by Nancy Lamoeeux (suspense); and *Yesterday's Nightmare*, by Donna Harland (mystery).
How to Contact: Accepts unsolicited mss. Query with complete ms. E-mail and fax query letter/correspondence OK. Include bio. Send SASE for reply, return of ms or send disposable copy of ms. Reports in 2 months on mss. Simultaneous submissions OK. Comments on rejected mss.
Terms: Pays royalties. Sends galleys to author. Publishes ms 2 years after acceptance. Writer's guidelines and book catalog for SASE.
Advice: "We prefer to read full mss. Authors should be nurses or allied health professionals."

WALKER AND COMPANY, (I), 435 Hudson St., New York NY 10014. Fax: (212)727-0984. **Acquisitions**: Michael Seidman (mystery), Jacqueline Johnson (western), Soyung Pak (young adult). Estab. 1959. Midsize independent publisher with plans to expand. Publishes hardcover and trade paperback originals. Average first novel print order: 2,500-3,500. Number of titles: 70/year. Published many new writers within the last year.

- Books published by Walker and Company have received numerous awards including the Spur Award (for westerns) and the Shamus Awards for Best First Private Eye Novel and Best Novel.

Needs: Nonfiction, sophisticated, quality mystery (amateur sleuth, cozy, private eye, police procedural), traditional western and children's and young adult nonfiction. Published *The Killing of Monday Brown*, by Sandra West Prowell; *Murder in the Place of Anubis*, by Lynda S. Robinson; and *Who In Hell Is Wanda Fuca*, by G.M. Ford.
How to Contact: *Does not accept unsolicited mss*. Submit outline and chapters as preliminary. Query letter should include "a concise description of the story line, including its outcome, word length of story (we prefer 70,000 words), writing experience, publishing credits, particular expertise on this subject and in this genre. Common mistakes: Sounding unprofessional (i.e. too chatty, too braggardly). Forgetting SASE." Agented fiction

A BULLET INTRODUCES COMMENTS by the editor of *Novel & Short Story Writer's Market* indicating special information about the listing.

50%. Notify if multiple or simultaneous submissions. Reports in 3-5 months. Publishes ms an average of 1 year after acceptance. Occasionally comments on rejected mss.
Terms: Negotiable (usually advance against royalty). Must return advance if book is not completed or is unacceptable.
Advice: "As for mysteries, we are open to all types, including suspense novels and offbeat books that maintain a 'play fair' puzzle. We are always looking for well-written western novels that are offbeat and strong on characterization. Character development is most important in all Walker fiction. We expect the author to be expert in the categories, to know the background and foundations of the genre. To realize that just because some subgenre is hot it doesn't mean that that is the area to mine—after all, if everyone is doing female p.i.s, doesn't it make more sense to do something that isn't crowded, something that might serve to balance a list, rather than make it top heavy? Finally, don't tell us why your book is going to be a success; instead, show me that you can write and write well. It is your writing, and not your hype that interests us."

WARNER ASPECT, (V), Imprint of Warner Books, 1271 Avenue of the Americas, New York NY 10020. Fax: (212)522-5113. Website: http://warnerbooks.com (includes each month's new titles, advice from writers, previous titles and interviews with authors, "hot news," contests). **Acquisitions**: Betsy Mitchell, editor-in-chief. "We're looking for 'epic' stories in both fantasy and science fiction." Publishes hardcover, trade paperback, mass market paperback originals and mass market paperback reprints. **Publishes 2 previously unpublished writers/year.** Distributes titles through nationwide sales force.

- Warner Aspect published *Reclamation*, by Sarah Zettel, winner of Locus Award for Best First Novel.

Needs: Fantasy, science fiction. Recently published *The Reality Dysfunction*, by Peter F. Hamilton (science fiction); *Brown Girl in the Ring*, by Nalo Hopkinson (science fiction); and *The Barbed Coil*, by J.V. Jones (fantasy).
How to Contact: Agented fiction only. Reports in 10 weeks on mss.
Terms: Pays royalty on retail price. Offers $5,000-up advance. Publishes ms 14 months after acceptance of ms.
Advice: "Think epic! Our favorite stories are big-screen science fiction and fantasy, with plenty of characters and subplots. Sample our existing titles—we're a fairly new list and pretty strongly focused." Mistake writers often make is "hoping against hope that being unagented won't make a difference. We simply don't have the staff to look at unagented projects."

WARNER BOOKS, (V), Time & Life Building, 1271 Avenue of the Americas, New York NY 10020. (212)522-7200. Publishes hardcover, trade paperback and mass market paperback originals and reprints. Warner publishes general interest fiction. Averages 350 total titles/year.
Imprint(s): Mysterious Press, **Warner Aspect**.
Needs: Fantasy, horror, mainstream, mystery/suspense, romance, science fiction, thriller. Published *The Celestine Prophecy*, by James Redfield; *Nocturne*, by Ed McBain (mystery); *Mail*, by Mameve Medwed; *Fat Tuesday*, by Sandra Brown; and *The Notebook*, by Nicholas Sparks.

DANIEL WEISS ASSOCIATES, INC., (II), 33 W. 17th St., New York NY 10011. Fax: (212)633-1236. **Acquisitions**: Jennifer Klein, editorial assistant; Kieran Scott, editor (YA romance); Lisa Papademetriou, editor (middle grade); Laura Burns, editor (middle grade horse series). Estab. 1987. "Packager of 140 titles a year including juvenile, young adult, and adult fiction as well as nonfiction titles. We package for a range of publishers within their specifications." Publishes paperback originals. All titles by first-time writers are commissioned for established series.
Needs: Juvenile (ballet, friendship, horse, mystery), mainstream, preschool/picture book, beginning readers and young adult (continuity series, romance, romantic suspense, thriller). Publishes Sweet Valley Twins, Sweet Valley High and Sweet Valley University series. "We cannot acquire single-title manuscripts that are not submitted specifically according to our guidelines for an established series." Recently published *Sweet Valley High (#140)* and *Sweet Valley University (#29)*, by Francine Pascal (young adult series); *Thoroughbred*, by Joanna Campbell (juvenile horse series); *Love Stories (#27)*, by Kieran Scott (YA romance series); and *Mindwarp*, by Chris Archer (middle grade science fiction series).
How to Contact: Send SASE for guidelines to series currently in production. Unsolicited queries/correspondence by fax OK.
Terms: Pays advance royalty. Advance is negotiable. Publishes ms 1 year after acceptance. Writer's guidelines for #10 SASE.
Advice: "We are always happy to work with and encourage first-time novelists. Being packagers, we often create and outline books by committee. This system is quite beneficial to writers who may be less experienced."

WESLEYAN UNIVERSITY PRESS, (II), 110 Mount Vernon St., Middletown CT 06459. (860)685-2420. **Acquisitions:** Suzanna Tamminen, editor-in-chief. "We are a scholarly press with a focus on cultural studies." Publishes hardcover originals. Publishes 10% previously unpublished writers/year. Publishes 20-25 titles/year.
Needs: Science fiction. "We publish very little fiction." Recently published *Dhalgren*, by Samuel R. Delany.
How to Contact: Submit outline. Reports in 1 month on queries, 3 months on mss. Simultaneous submissions OK.
Terms: Pays 10% royalty. Offers up to $3,000 advance. Publishes ms 1 year after acceptance. Writer's guidelines

for #10 SASE. Book catalog free.
Advice: Audience is the informed general reader to specialized academic reader.

WHISPERING COYOTE PRESS, INC., (II), 300 Crescent Court, Suite 860, Dallas TX 75201. Fax: (214)871-5577, (214)319-7298. **Acquisitions**: Mrs. Lou Alpert, publisher. Publishes picture books for children ages 3-10. Publishes 20% previously unpublished writers/year. Publishes 6 titles/year.
Needs: Adventure, fantasy, juvenile picture books. "We only do picture books." Published *The Red Shoes*, retold and illustrated by Barbara Bazilian, adapted from a story by Hans Christian Anderson; *Cats on Judy*, by JoAnn Early Macken, illustrated by Judith DuFour Love; and *Hush! A Gaelic Lullaby*, by Carole Gerber, illustrated by Mary Husted.
How to Contact: Submit complete ms. If author is illustrator also, submit sample art. Send photocopies, no original art. Agented fiction 10%. Reports in 3 months. Simultaneous submissions OK.
Terms: Pays 8% royalty on retail price of first 10,000 copies, 10% after (combined author and illustrator). Offers $2,000-8,000 advance (combined author, illustrator). Publishes ms 2 years after acceptance. Writer's guidelines and book catalog for #10 SASE.

☑ **WHITE PINE PRESS, (II)**, 10 Village Square, Fredonia NY 14063-1763. (716)672-5743. Website: http://www.netsync.net/users/wpine (includes writer's guidelines, authors, titles). **Acquisitions**: Dennis Maloney, director; Elaine La Mattina, fiction editor. Estab. 1973. "White Pine Press is your passport to a world of voices, emphasizing literature from around the world." Small literary publisher of multicultural works, mostly translations. Publishes paperback originals and reprints. Books: 60 lb. natural paper; offset; perfect binding. Average print order: 2,000-3,000. First novel print order: 2,000. **Publishes 2-3 previously unpublished writers/year.** Averages 8-10 total titles, 6-7 fiction titles each year. Distributes titles through Consortium Book Sales & Distribution. Promotes titles through reviews, advertising, direct mailing, readings and signings.
Needs: Ethnic/multicultural, literary, short story collections, translations. Looking for "strong novels." No romance, science fiction. Publishes anthologies. Editors select stories. Recently published *A Bowl of Sour Cherries*, by Yelena Franklin (literary); *Ximena at the Crossroads*, by Laura Riesco (literary translation); and *In Lithuanian Wood*, by Wendell Mayo (literary). Publishes Dispatches series (international fiction), a Human Rights series, and Secret Weavers series (writing by Latin American Women) and New American Voices Series (first novels by American writer).
How to Contact: Accepts unsolicited mss. Query letter with outline/synopsis and 2 sample chapters. Include estimated word count and list of publishing credits. SASE for reply or return of ms. Agented fiction 10%. Reports in 2 weeks on queries; 3 months on mss. Simultaneous submissions OK.
Terms: Pays royalties of 5% minimum; 10% maximum. Offers negotiable advance. Pays in author's copies; payment depends on grant/award money. Sends galleys to author. Publishes 1-2 years after acceptance. Book catalog free.
Advice: "Follow our guidelines."

☑ **WILLOW CREEK PRESS, (II)**, P.O. Box 147, 9931 Highway 70 W., Minocqua WI 54548. (715)358-7010. Fax: (715)358-2807. E-mail: ljevert@newnorth.net. Website: http://www.willowcreekpress.com. **Acquisitions:** Laura Evert, managing editor. Publishes 15% previously unpublished writers. Publishes hardcover and trade paperback originals and reprints. Publishes 15% previously unpublished writers/year. Publishes 25 titles/year. Receives 400 queries and 150 mss/year.
Needs: Adventure, humor, picture books, short story collections. Recently published *Cold Noses and Warm Hearts*, edited by Laurie Morrow (short story collection); *Flashes in the River*, by Ed Gray (illustrated fiction); and *Poetry for Guys*, by Kathy Schmook.
How to Contact: Submit synopsis and 2 sample chapters. Reports in 2 months. Simultaneous submissions OK.
Terms: Pays 6-15% royalty on wholesale price. Offers $2,000-5,000 advance. Publishes ms 10 months after acceptance. Book catalog for $1.

WILSHIRE BOOK CO., (II), 12015 Sherman Rd., North Hollywood CA 91605-3781. (818)765-8579. Fax: (818)765-2922. E-mail: mpowers@mpowers.com. Website: http://www.mpowers.com (includes types of books published). **Acquisitions:** Melvin Powers, publisher. Marcia Powers, senior editor (adult fables). Estab. 1947. "You are not only what you are today, but also what you choose to become tomorrow. We are looking for adult fables that teach principles of psychological growth." Publishes trade paperback originals and reprints. **Publishes 80% previously unpublished writers/year.** Publishes 15 titles/year. Distributes titles through wholesalers, bookstores and mail order. Promotes titles through author interviews on radio and television.
Needs: Allegories that teach principles of psychological/spiritual growth or offer guidance in living. Min. 30,000 words. Published *The Princess Who Believed in Fairy Tales*, by Marcia Grad; *The Knight in Rusty Armor*, by Robert Fisher. Allegories only. No standard novels or short stories.
How to Contact: Requires synopsis, 3 sample chapters and SASE. Accepts complete mss. Unsolicited queries/correspondence by e-mail OK. Reports in 2 months.
Terms: Pays standard royalty. Publishes ms 6 months after acceptance.
Advice: "We are vitally interested in all new material we receive. Just as you hopefully submit your manuscript for publication, we hopefully read every one submitted, searching for those that we believe will be successful in

the marketplace. Writing and publishing must be a team effort. We need you to write what we can sell. We suggest that you read the successful books mentioned above or others that are similar: *Greatest Salesman in the World*, *Illusions*, *Way of the Peaceful Warrior*, *Celestine Prophecy*. Analyze them to discover what elements make them winners. Duplicate those elements in your own style, using a creative new approach and fresh material, and you will have written a book we can successfully market."

WISDOM PUBLICATIONS, (II), 199 Elm St., Somerville MA 02144. (617)776-7416, ext. 25. Fax: (617)776-7844. E-mail: editorial@wisdompubs.org. Website: http://www.wisdompubs.org. Publisher: Timothy McNeill. **Acquisitions:** Editorial Director. "Wisdom Publications is a nonprofit publisher for works on Buddhism, Tibet and East-West themes." Publishes hardcover originals, trade paperback originals and reprints. **Publishes 50% previously unpublished writers/year.** Publishes 12-15 titles/year.
Needs: Children's books with Buddhist themes. Published *Her Father's Garden*, by James Vollbracht; and *The Gift*, by Isia Osuchowska.
How to Contact: Query first with SASE.
Terms: Pays 4-8% royalty on wholesale price (net). Publishes ms 2 years after acceptance. Writer's guidelines and book catalog free.
Advice: "We are now publishing children's books with Buddhist themes and contemplative/Buddhist poetry."

THE WOMEN'S PRESS, (IV), 34 Great Sutton St., London EC1V 0DX England. **Acquisitions**: Helen Windrath, Kirsty Dunseath and Charlotte Cole, fiction editors. Publishes approximately 50 titles/year.
Needs: "Women's fiction, written by women. Centered on women. Theme can be anything—all themes may be women's concern—but we look for political/feminist awareness, originality, wit, fiction of ideas. Includes literary fiction, crime, and teenage list *Livewire*."
Terms: Writers receive royalty, including advance.
Advice: Writers should ask themselves, "Is this a manuscript which would interest a feminist/political press?"

THE WONDERLAND PRESS, INC., 160 Fifth Avenue, Suite 723, New York NY 10010. (212)989-2550. Fax: (212)989-2321. E-mail: litraryagt@aol.com. Contact: John Campbell. Estab. 1985. Member of the American Book Producers Association. Represents 24 clients. Specializes in high-quality nonfiction, illustrated, reference, how-to and entertainment books. "We welcome submissions from new authors, but proposals must be unique, of high commercial interest and well written." Currently handles: 90% nonfiction books; 10% novels.

- The Wonderland Press is also a book packager and "in a very strong position to nurture strong proposals all the way from concept through bound books."

Represents: Interested in reviewing nonfiction books, novels. Considers these nonfiction areas: art/architecture/design; biography/autobiography; enthnic/cultural interests; gay/lesbian issues; health/medicine; history; how-to; humor; interior design/decorating; language/literature/criticism; photography; popular culture; psychology; self-help/personal improvement. Considers these fiction areas: action/adventure; literary; picture book; thriller.
How to Contact: Send outline/proposal with SASE. Reports in 3-5 days on queries; 1-2 weeks on mss.
Needs: Does not want to receive poetry, memoir, children or category fiction.
Recent Sales: Sold titles in the last year. *Portraits of Hope*, by Nora Feller/Marcia Sherrill (Smithmark/Stewart Tabori & Chang); *The Essential Jackson Pollock*, by Justin Spring (Harry N. Abrams, Inc.); *501 Great Things About Being Gay*, by Edward Taussig (Andrews McMeel); *The Dictionary of Science Fiction Places*, by Brian Stableford (Simon & Schuster); *Infinite Worlds*, by Vincent Fate (Penguin Studio). "Almost all of our new authors come to us by referral. Often they 'find' us by researching the books we have sold for our other clients."
Terms: Agent receives 15% commission on domestic sales. Offers written contract. 30-90 days notice must be given to terminate contract. Offers criticism service, included in 15% commission. Charges for photocopying, long-distance telephone, overnight express-mail, messengering.
Tips: "Follow your talent. Write with passion. Know your market. Submit work in final form; if you feel a need to apologize for its mistakes, typos, or incompleteness, then it is not ready to be seen. We want to see your best work."

WORLDWIDE LIBRARY, (II), Division of Harlequin Books, 225 Duncan Mill Rd., Don Mills, Ontario M3B 3K9 Canada. (416)445-5860. **Acquisitions**: Feroze Mohammed, senior editor/editorial coordinator. Estab. 1979. Large commercial category line. Publishes paperback originals and reprints. Averages 72 titles, all fiction, each year. "Mystery program is reprint; no originals please."
Imprint(s): Worldwide Mystery; Gold Eagle Books.
Needs: "We publish action-adventure series; future fiction." A new future fiction series, *Outlanders*, was recently published.

SENDING TO A COUNTRY other than your own? Be sure to send International Reply Coupons instead of stamps for replies or return of your manuscript.

How to Contact: Query first or submit outline/synopsis/series concept or overview and sample chapters. SAE. U.S. stamps do not work in Canada; use International Reply Coupons or money order. Reports in 10 weeks on queries. Simultaneous submissions OK. Sometimes critiques rejected ms.
Terms: Advance and sometimes royalties; copyright buyout. Publishes ms 1-2 years after acceptance.
Advice: "Publishing fiction in very selective areas. As a genre publisher we are always on the lookout for innovative series ideas, especially in the men's adventure area."

WRITE WAY PUBLISHING, (I, II), Suite 210, 10555 E. Dartmouth, Aurora CO 80014. (303)695-0001. Fax: (303)368-8004. E-mail: writewy@aol.com. Website: http://www.writewaypub.com (includes first chapter, reviews and sales information on every title). **Acquisitions**: Dorrie O'Brien, owner/editor. Estab. 1993. "Write Way is a book-only, fiction-only small press concentrating on genre publications such as mysteries, soft science fiction, fairy tale/fantasy and horror/thrillers. Small press. Publishes hardcover originals. Average print order: 2,500. First novel print order: 1,000. Published new writers within the last year. **Publishes 60% previously unpublished writers/year.** Averages 10-12 total titles, all fiction, each year. Distributes titles through Midpoint Trade Books. Promotes titles through newspapers, magazines and trade shows.
Needs: Fantasy/fairy tale, horror (soft), mystery/suspense (amateur sleuth, cozy, police procedural, private eye/hardboiled), psychic/supernatural, science fiction (soft/sociological, space trilogy/series). Recently published *The Dead Past*, by Tom Piccirilli (mystery); *Fury's Children*, by Seymour Shubin (psychological suspense); and *Cheat the Devil*, by Jane Rubino (mystery).
How to Contact: Query with short outline/synopsis and 1-2 sample chapters. Include estimated word count, bio (reasonably short) and list of publishing credits. Send SASE for reply, return of ms or send a disposable copy of ms. Agented fiction 10%. Reports in 2-4 weeks on queries; 6-8 months on mss. Simultaneous submissions OK. Often comments on rejected mss.
Terms: Pays royalties of 8% minimum; 10% maximum. Does not pay advances. Sends galleys to author. Publishes ms within 3 years after acceptance. Writer's guidelines for SASE.
Advice: "Always have the query letter, synopsis and the first chapters edited by an unbiased party prior to submitting them to us. Remember: first impressions are just as important to a publisher as they might be to a prospective employer."

WRITERS PRESS, (II), 5278 Chinden Blvd., Boise ID 83714. (208)327-0566. Fax: (208)327-3477. E-mail: writers@cyberhighway.net. Website: http://www.writerspress.com. **Acquisitions:** John Ybarra, editor. "Our philosophy is to show children how to help themselves and others. By publishing high-quality children's literature that is both fun and educational, we are striving to make a difference in today's educational world." Publishes hardcover and trade paperback originals. **Publishes 60% previously unpublished writers/year.** Publishes 6 titles/year.
Needs: Adventure, historical, juvenile, picture books, young adult, inclusion, special education. Published *Eagle Feather*, by Sonia Gardner, illustrated by James Spurlock (picture book).
How to Contact: Query first. Reports in 1 month on queries, 4 months on mss.
Terms: Pays 4-12% royalty or makes outright purchase of up to $1,500. Publishes ms 6 months after acceptance. Writer's and catalog guidelines free.

YORK PRESS LTD., (II), 77 Carlton St., Suite 305, Toronto, Ontario M5B 2J7 Canada. (416)599-6652. Fax: (416)599-2675. **Acquisitions:** Dr. S. Elkhadem, general manager/editor. Estab. 1975. "We publish scholarly books and creative writing of an experimental nature." Publishes trade paperback originals. **Publishes 10% previously unpublished writers/year.** Publishes 10 titles/year.
Needs: "Fiction of an experimental nature by well-established writers." Recently published *The Moonhare*, by Kirk Hampton (experimental novel).
How to Contact: Query first. Reports in 2 months.
Terms: Pays 10-20% royalty on wholesale price. Publishes ms 6 months after acceptance.

ZEBRA BOOKS, (II), Imprint of Kensington, 850 Third Ave., 16th Floor, New York NY 10022. (212)407-1500. Publisher: Lynn Brown. **Acquisitions**: Ann Lafarge, editor. "Zebra Books is dedicated to women's fiction, which includes, but is not limited to romance." Publishes hardcover originals, trade paperback and mass market paperback originals and reprints. **Publishes 5% previously unpublished writers/year.** Publishes 140-170 titles/year.
Needs: Romance, women's fiction. Published *By Candelight*; *Love With a Stranger*, by Janell Taylor (romance); and *Darling Jasmine*, by Bertrice Small.
How to Contact: Query with synopsis and SASE. Not accepting unsolicited submissions. Reports in 1 month on queries, in 3 months on mss. Simultaneous submissions OK.
Terms: Pays variable royalty and advance. Publishes ms 18 months after acceptance. Book catalog for #10 SASE.

ZOLAND BOOKS, INC., (II, III), 384 Huron Ave., Cambridge MA 02138. (617)864-6252. Fax: (617)661-4998. **Acquisitions**: Roland Pease, publisher/editor. Managing Editor: Michael Lindgren. Marketing Director/Nonfiction Editor: Stephen Hull. Estab. 1987. "We are a literary press, publishing poetry, fiction, nonfiction, photography, and other titles of literary interest." Publishes hardcover and paperback originals and reprints. Books: acid-free paper; sewn binding; some with illustrations. Average print order: 2,000-5,000. **Publishes 1-2 previously unpublished writers/year.** Averages 14 total titles each year. Distributes titles through Consortium Book Sales and Distribution. Promotes titles through catalog, publicity, advertisements, direct mail.

- Recent awards include: Hemmingway/PEN Award, Kafka Prize for Women's Fiction, National Book Award finalist, New York Times Notable Book, Publishers Weekly Best Book of the Year.

Needs: Contemporary, feminist, literary, African-American interest. Recently published *Glorie*, by Caryn James; *The Old World*, by Jonathan Strong; and *Boyne's Lassie*, by Dick Wimmer.
How to Contact: Accepts unsolicited mss. Query first, then send complete ms with cover letter. SASE. Reports in 4-6 weeks on queries; 3-6 months on mss.
Terms: Pays royalties of 5-8%. Average advance: $1,500; negotiable (also pays author's copies). Sends galleys to author. Publishes ms 1-2 years after acceptance. Book catalog for 6×9 SAE and 2 first-class stamps.

ZONDERVAN, (III, IV), Division of HarperCollins Publishers, 5300 Patterson SE, Grand Rapids MI 49530. (616)698-6900. E-mail: @zph.com. Website: http://www.zondervan.com. **Acquisitions**: Manuscript Review Editor. Estab. 1931. "Our mission is to be the leading Christian communication company meeting the needs of people with resources that glorify Jesus Christ and promote biblical principles." Large evangelical Christian publishing house. Publishes hardcover and paperback originals and reprints, though fiction is generally in paper only. Published new writers in the last year. Averages 150 total titles, 15-20 fiction titles each year. Average first novel: 5,000 copies.
Needs: Adult fiction, (mainstream, biblical, historical, romance, adventure, mystery), "Inklings-style" fiction of high literary quality and juvenile fiction (primarily mystery/adventure novels for 8-12-year-olds). Christian relevance necessary in all cases. Will *not* consider collections of short stories. Published *Every Hidden Thing*, by Athol Dickson (mystery); *Byzantium*, by Steven Lawhead (historical); and *Threshold*, by Bill Myers (suspense).
How to Contact: Accepts unsolicited mss. Write for writer's guidelines first. Include #10 SASE. Query or submit outline/synopsis and 2 sample chapters. Reports in 6-8 weeks on queries; 3-4 months on mss.
Terms: "Standard contract provides for a percentage of the net price received by publisher for each copy sold, usually 14-17% of net."
Advice: "Almost no unsolicited fiction is published. Send plot outline and one or two sample chapters. Editors will *not* read entire manuscripts. Your sample chapters will make or break you."

Screenwriting

BY KIRSTEN HOLM

Practically everyone you meet in Los Angeles, from your airport cabbie on, is writing a script. It might be a feature film, movie of the week, TV series or documentary, but the sheer amount of competition can seem overwhelming. Some will never make a sale, while others make a decent living on sales and options without ever having any of their work produced. But there are those writers who make a living doing what they love and see their names roll by on the credits. How do they get there? How do *you* get there?

First, work on your writing. You'll improve with each script, so there is no way of getting around the need to write and write some more. It's a good idea to read as many scripts as you can get your hands on. Check your local bookstores and libraries. Script City (8033 Sunset Blvd., Suite 1500, Hollywood CA 90046, (800)676-2522) carries thousands of movie and TV scripts, classics to current releases, as well as books, audio/video seminars and software in their $2 catalog. Book City (6631 Hollywood Blvd., Hollywood CA 90028, (800)4-CINEMA) has film and TV scripts in all genres and a large selection of movie books in their $2.50 catalog.

There are lots of books that will give you the "rules" of format and structure for writing for TV or film. Samuel French (7623 Sunset Blvd., Hollywood CA 90046 (213)876-0570) carries a number of how-to books and reference materials on these subjects. The correct format marks your script as a professional submission. Most successful scriptwriters will tell you to learn the correct structure, internalize those rules—and then throw them away and write intuitively.

WRITING FOR TV

To break into TV you must have spec scripts—work written for free that serves as a calling card and gets you in the door. A spec script showcases your writing abilities and gets your name in front of influential people. Whether a network has invited you in to pitch some ideas, or a movie producer has contacted you to write a first draft for a feature film, the quality of writing in your spec script got their attention and that may get you the job.

It's a good idea to have several spec scripts, perhaps one each for three of the top five shows in the format you prefer to work in, whether it's sitcom (half-hour comedies), episodic (one hour series) or movie of the week (two hour dramatic movies). Perhaps you want to showcase the breadth of your writing ability; some writers have a portfolio of a few eight o'clock type shows (i.e., *Friends*, *Mad About You*, *Home Improvement*), a few nine-o'clock shows (i.e., *Ellen*, *Seinfeld*, *The X Files*) and one or two episodics (i.e., *Homicide*, *Law and Order*, *NYPD Blue*). These are all "hot" shows for writers and can demonstrate your abilities to create believable dialogue for characters already familiar to your intended readers. For TV and cable movies you should have completed original scripts (not sequels to existing movies) and you might also have a few for episodic TV shows.

In choosing the shows you write spec scripts for you must remember one thing: don't write a script for a show you want to work on. If you want to write for *NYPD Blue*, for example, you'll send a *Law and Order* script and vice versa. It may seem contradictory, but it is standard practice. It reduces the chances of lawsuits, and writers and producers can feel very proprietary about their show and their stories. They may not be objective enough to fairly evaluate your

---

KIRSTEN HOLM *is editor of* Writer's Market.

writing. In submitting another similar type of show you'll avoid those problems while demonstrating comparable skills.

In writing your TV script you must get *inside* the show and understand the characters' internal motivations. You must immerse yourself in how the characters speak, think and interact. Don't introduce new characters in a spec script for an existing show—write believable dialogue for the characters as they are portrayed. Be sure to choose a show that you like—you'll be better able to demonstrate your writing ability through characters you respond to.

You must also understand the external factors. How the show is filmed bears on how you write. Most sitcoms are shot on videotape with three cameras, on a sound stage with a studio audience. Episodics are often shot on film with one camera and include on-location shots. *Mad About You* has a flat, evenly-lit look and takes place in a limited number of locations. *Law and Order* has a gritty realism with varying lighting and a variety of settings from McCord's office to outside a bodega on East 135th.

Another important external influence in writing for TV is the timing of commercials in conjunction with the act structure. There are lots of sources detailing the suggested content and length of acts, but generally a sitcom has a teaser (short opening scene), two acts and a tag (short closing scene), and an episodic has a teaser, four acts and a tag. Each act closes with a turning point. Watching TV analytically and keeping a log of events will reveal some elements of basic structure. *Successful Scriptwriting*, by Wolff & Cox (Writer's Digest Books), offers detailed discussions of various types of shows.

WRITING FOR THE MOVIES

With feature films you may feel at once more liberated and more bound by structure. An original movie script contains characters you have created, with storylines you design, allowing you more freedom than you have in TV. However, your writing must still convey believable dialogue and realistic characters, with a plausible plot and high-quality writing carried through the roughly 120 pages. The characters must have a problem that involves the audience. When you go to a movie you don't want to spend time watching the *second* worst night of a character's life. You're looking for the big issue that crystallizes a character, that portrays a journey with important consequences.

At the same time you are creating, you should also be constructing. Be aware of the basic three act structure for feature films. Scenes can be of varying lengths, but are usually no longer than three to three and a half pages. Some writers list scenes that must occur, then flesh them out from beginning to end, writing with the structure of events in mind. The beginning and climactic scenes are the easiest; it's how they get there from here that's difficult.

Many novice screenwriters tend to write too many visual cues and camera directions into their scripts. Your goal should be to write something readable, like a "compressed novella." Write succinct resonant scenes and leave the camera technique to the director and producer. In action/adventure movies, however, there needs to be a balance since the script demands more visual direction.

It seems to be easier for TV writers to cross over to movies. Cable movies bridge the two, and are generally less derivative and more willing to take chances with a higher quality show designed to attract an audience not interested in network offerings. Cable is also less susceptible to advertiser pullout, which means it can tackle more controversial topics.

Feature films and TV are very different and writers occupy different positions. TV is a medium for writers and producers; directors work for them. Many TV writers are also producers. In feature films the writers and producers work for the director and often have little or no say about what happens to the work once the script has been sold. For TV the writer pitches the idea; for feature films generally the producer pitches the idea and then finds a writer.

MARKETING YOUR SCRIPTS

If you intend to make writing your profession you must act professionally. Accepted submission practices should become second nature.

- The initial pitch is made through a query letter, which is no longer than one page with a one paragraph synopsis and brief summary of your credits if they are relevant to the subject of your script.
- Never send a complete manuscript until it is requested.
- Almost every script sent to a producer, studio or agent must be accompanied by a release form. Ask for that company's form when you receive an invitation to submit the whole script. Mark your envelope "release form enclosed" to prevent it being returned unread.
- Always include a self-addressed stamped envelope (SASE) if you want your work returned; a disposable copy may be accompanied by a self-addressed stamped postcard for reply.
- Allow four to six weeks from receipt of your manuscript before writing a follow-up letter.

When your script is requested, be sure it's written in the appropriate format. Unusual binding, fancy covers or illustrations mark an amateur. Three brass brads with a plain or black cover indicate a pro.

There are a limited number of ideas in the world, so it's inevitable that similar ideas occur to more than one person. Hollywood is a buyer's market and a release form states that pretty clearly. An idea is not copyrightable, so be careful about sharing premises. The written expression of that idea, however, can be protected and it's a good idea to do so. The Writers Guild of America can register scripts for television and theatrical motion pictures, series formats, storylines and step outlines. You need not be a member of the WGA to use this service. Copyrighting your work with the Copyright Office of the Library of Congress also protects your work from infringement. Contact either agency for more information and an application form.

If you are a writer, you should write—all the time. When you're not writing, read. There are numerous books on the art, craft and business of screenwriting. Industry trade papers such as *Daily Variety* and *Hollywood Reporter* can keep you in touch with the day to day news and upcoming events. Specialty newsletters such as *Hollywood Scriptwriter* (P.O. Box 10277, Burbank CA 91510, (818)845-5525, http://www.hollywoodscriptwriter.com) offer tips from successful scriptwriters and agents. The *Hollywood Creative Directory* (3000 W. Olympic Blvd., Suite 2525, Santa Monica CA 90404, (800)815-0503, fax: (310)315-4816, e-mail: hcd@hollyvision.com, website: http://www.hollyvision.com) is an extensive list of production companies, studios and networks that also lists companies and talent with studio deals. Excellent resources on the craft of screenwriting include *Successful Scriptwriting*, by Jurgen Wolff and Kerry Cox (Writer's Digest Books, 1507 Dana Ave., Cincinnati OH 45207, (800)289-0963) and *Screenplay: The Foundations of Screenwriting*, by Syd Field (Bantam Doubleday Dell Publishing Group, Inc., 1540 Broadway, New York NY 10036).

Computer services have various bulletin boards and chat hours for scriptwriters that provide contact with other writers and a chance to share information and encouragement.

It may take years of work before you come up with a script someone is willing to take a chance on. Those years need to be spent learning your craft and understanding the business. Polishing scripts, writing new material, keeping current with the industry and networking constantly will keep you busy. When you do get that call you'll be confident in your abilities and know that your hard work is beginning to pay off.

N **ALEXANDER/ENRIGHT AND ASSOCIATES**, 201 Wilshire Blvd., 3rd Floor, Santa Monica CA 90401. Contact: Sarah Koepple, development associate. Produces for a general television audience. Buys 3 scripts/year. Works with many writers/year. Buys TV and film rights only. Accepts previously produced material. Reports in 1 month on queries; 6 weeks on submissions. Query with synopsis. Pays in accordance with Writer's Guild standards.

Needs: Women driven dramas, but will accept others. No extreme violence, horror or stalkers.

N **ALPHAVILLE**, 555 Melrose Ave., Los Angeles CA 90038. Director of Development: Ray Lee. Estab. 1987. General audience. Buys 5-10 scripts/year. Buys all rights. Accepts previously produced material. Reports in 1-2 months on queries. "I'd like to read a catalog without having to contact writer unless I like an idea." Pays in accordance with Wrtier's Guild standards.
Needs: Films. Adventure/action, thrillers.

N **THE AMERICAN MOVING PICTURE COMPANY INC.**, 838 N. Doheny Dr., #904, Los Angeles CA 90069. (310)276-0750. Contact: Isabel Casper, vice president, creative affairs. Estab. 1979. Theatrical motion picture audience. Buys screenplay rights and ancillaries. Produced four theatrical motion pictures. Does not return submissions. Reports in 1 month. Query with synopsis. Pays in accordance with Writers Guild standards or more.
Needs: Films (35mm), commercial. "We want commercial and unique material."

N **AMERICAN WORLD PICTURES INC.**, 21800 Oxnard St., Suite 480, Studio City CA 91367. Development/Acquisitions: Brian Etting/Terese Linden. Estab. 1991. Video/television market-Adults. Buys 4 scripts/year. Works with 5 writers/year. Buys all rights. Accepts previously produced material. Reports in 1-2 months on queries; 2-3 months on submissions. Query.
Needs: Films (35mm). Action, suspense, thriller genres only.
Tips: Strong characters, strong dialogue.

N **ANGEL FILMS**, 967 Highway 40, New Franklin MO 65274-9778. (573)698-3900. Fax: (573)698-3900. E-mail: angelfilm@aol.com. Vice President Production: Matthew Eastman. Estab. 1980. Produces material for feature films, television. Buys 10 scripts/year. Works with 20 writers/year. Buys all rights. Accepts previously published material (if rights available). Reports in 1 months on queries; 1-2 months on scripts. Query with synopsis. Makes outright purchase. Our company is a low-budget producer, which means people get paid fairly, but don't get rich."
Needs: Films (35mm), videotapes. "We are looking for projects that can be used to produce feature film and television feature film and series work. These would be in the areas of action adventure, comedy, horror, thriller, science fiction, animation for children." Also looking for direct to video materials.
Tips: "Don't copy others. Try to be original. Don't overwork your idea. As far as trends are concerned, don't pay attention to what is 'in.' By the time it gets to us it will most likely be on the way 'out.' And if you can't let your own grandmother read it, don't send it. Slow down on western submissions. They are not selling. If you wish material returned, enclose proper postage with all submissions. Send SASE for response to queries and return of scripts."

N **ANGEL'S TOUCH PRODUCTIONS**, 22906 Calabash St., Woodland Hills CA 91364. Contact: Phil Nemy, director of development. Estab. 1986. Professional screenplays and teleplays. Send synopsis. Reports in 8 months. Rights negotiated between production company and author. Payment negotiated.
Needs: All types, all genres, only full-length teleplays and screenplays—no one-acts.
Tips: "We only seek feature film screenplays, television screenplays, and episodic teleplays. No phone calls!"

N **THE BADHAM COMPANY**, 4035 Goodland Ave., Studio City CA 91604. (818)623-2929. Estab. 1991. Theatrical audience. Buys 1 script/year. Works with 2-3 writers/year. Buys first rights. Accepts previously produced material. Reports in 1 month. Query with synopsis. We go to studio and they purchase option.
Needs: Films (35mm).
Tips: "It's too easy to write action and ignore characters."

N **BARNSTORM FILMS**, 73 Market St., Venice CA 90291. (310)396-5937. Estab. 1969. Produces feature films. Buys 2-3 scripts/year. Works with 4-5 writers/year.
Tips: Looking for strong, character-based commercial scripts. Not interested in science fiction or fantasy. Must send SASE with query letter. Query first, do not send script unless we request it!"

N **BIG EVENT PICTURES**, (formerly StoneRoad Production, Inc.), 11288 Ventura Blvd., #909, Studio City CA 91604. E-mail: stoweroad1@aol.com. Contact: Michael Cargile, president. Produces feature films for theaters, cable TV and home video. PG, R, and G-rated films. Buys/options 10 scripts/year. Reports in 1 month on queries if interested; 2 months requested on submissions. Query with SASE and synopsis. Pay varies greatly.

FOR EXPLANATIONS OF THESE SYMBOLS,
SEE THE INSIDE FRONT AND BACK COVERS OF THIS BOOK.

Needs: Films. All genres. Looking for good material from writers who have taken the time to learn the unique and difficult craft of scriptwriting.
Tips: "Interesting query letters intrigue us—and tell us something about the writer. Query letter should include a short 'log line' or 'pitch' encapsulating 'what this story is about'. We look for unique stories and strong characters. We would like to see more action and science fiction submissions. We make movies that we would like to see. Producers are known for encouraging new (e.g. unproduced) screenwriters and giving real consideration to their scripts."

N **BIG STAR MOTION PICTURES LTD.**, 13025 Yonge St., #201, Richmond Hill, Ontario L4E 1Z5 Canada. (416)720-9825. Fax: (905)773-3153. E-mail: bigstar@pathcom.com. Contact: Frank A. Deluca. Estab. 1991. Buys 5 scripts/year. Works with 5-10 writers/year. Reports in 3 months on queries; 3 months on scripts. Submit synopsis first. Scripts should be submitted by agent or lawyer.
Needs: Films (35mm). "We are very active in all medias, but are primarily looking for television projects, cable, network, etc. Family Films are of special interest."

N **BOZ PRODUCTIONS**, 10960 Wilshire Blvd., Suite 734, Los Angeles CA 90024. (310)235-5401. Fax: (310)235-5766. E-mail: boz51@aol.com. Director of Development: Jeff Monarch. Estab. 1987. All audiences. Buys 3-5 scripts/year. Works with several writers/year. Buys all rights. Accepts previously produced material. Reports in 1 month on queries; 1-2 months on scripts. Query with synopsis and résumé. Pay varies.
Needs: Films (35mm). Feature-length film scripts or rights to real stories for MOW's.

N **CANVAS HOUSE FILMS**, 3671 Bear St., #E, Santa Ana CA 92704. Contact: Mitch Teemley, producer. Estab. 1994. General audience. Buys 2-3 scripts/year. Works with 10-15 writers/year. Buys first rights, all rights. Accepts previously produced material. Reports in 1 month on queries; 4 months on submissions. Query with detailed (2-4 page) synopsis and résumé or list of credits. Pays in accordance with Writers Guild standards.
Needs: Films (35mm). "Quality feature-length filmscripts—all types, but no lurid, 'hard-R'-rated material."
Tips: "Know proper formatting and story structure. There is a need for 'family' material that can appeal to *grown-ups* as well as children."

N **CAPITAL ARTS ENTERTAINMENT, INC.**, 23315 Clifton, Valencia CA 91354. President of Development: Rob Kerchner. Estab. 1994. Family audiences. Buys 5 scripts/year. Works with 20 writers/year. Buys all rights. No previously produced material. No submissions will be returned. Reports in 1 month on queries; 1-24 months on submission. Query with synopsis only. No scripts or they will be destroyed. Pay outright purchase $1,000-15,000.
Tips: Send only family pitches (especially high concept) for completed spec scripts.

N **ALLAN CARR ENTERPRISES**, P.O. Box 15568, Beverly Hills CA 90209-1568. (310)278-2490. Producer: Rob Bonet. Estab. 1977. Buys 15-20 scripts/year. Works with 10 writers/year. Buys rights depending on film or theater. Accepts previously produced material. Reports in 1 month. Catalog for #10 SASE. Query with synopsis. Pays in accordance with Writer's Guild standards.
Needs: Films (35mm, 70mm), VHS tapes 20 minutes or less. Romantic comedy, adventure, dramantic black comedy.

N **CINE/DESIGN FILMS, INC.**, P.O. Box 6495, Denver CO 80206. (303)777-4222. E-mail: jghusband@aol.com. Producer/Director: Jon Husband. Produces educational material for general, sales-training and theatrical audiences. 75% freelance written; 90% unagented submissions. "Original, solid ideas are encouraged." Rights purchased vary.
Needs: Films (16, 35mm). "Motion picture outlines in the theatrical and documentary areas. We are seeking theatrical scripts in the low-budget area that are possible to produce for under $2 to 3 million. We seek flexibility and personalities who can work well with our clients." Send 8-10-page outline before submitting ms. Pays $100-200/screen minute on 16mm productions. Theatrical scripts negotiable.
Tips: "Understand the marketing needs of film production today. Materials will not be returned."

N **CLARK FILM PRODUCTION CHARITY, INC.**, P.O. Box 773, Balboa CA 92661. Contact: Mr. Steven Clark, president. Estab. 1987. General audience. Buys 1 script/year. Works with 4 writers/year. Buys first rights. Accepts previously produced material. Reports in 6 months. Submit synopsis/outline. Pays in accordance with Writers Guild of America west standards.
Needs: Family-oriented, general audience materials, with universal appeal.
Recent Production: "Currently working with King Kigel V, His Majesty the King of Rwanda, Africa, on a public service announcement through United Nations UNICEF for His Majesty's children and orphans with relief. Although now accepting general audience material, as always."

N **CLC PRODUCTIONS**, 1223 Wilshire Blvd., Suite 404, Santa Monica CA 90403. (310)454-0664. Contact: Susan Roberts. Estab. 1984. T.V. and film. "We are interested in suspense, comedy. Action/adventure with a strong female role age 35-45." Buys 4-5 scripts/year. Works with 5-10 writers/year. Buys all rights. Accepts previously produced materials. Reports in 1 month on submissions.

N **CODIKOW FILMS**, 8899 Beverly Blvd., #719, Los Angeles CA 90048. (310)246-9388. Fax: (310)246-9877. Website: http://www.codikowfilms.com. Director of Development: Diana Williams. Estab. 1990. Buys 6 scripts/year. Works with 12 writers/year. Buys all rights. Reports in 2 months on submissions. Query or résumé. Pays in accordance with Writer's Guild standards.
Needs: Films (35mm). Commercial and independent screenplays; good writing—all subjects.

N **CPC ENTERTAINMENT**, 840 N. Larrabee St., #2322, Los Angeles CA 90069. (310)652-8194. Fax: (310)652-4998. E-mail: 74151.1117@compuserve.com. Producer/Director: Peggy Chene. Vice President, Creative Affairs: Meri Howard. Development Associate: Eileen Aronas. Feature and TV. Buys 15 scripts/year. Works with 24 writers/year. Buys all rights. Recent production: "In the Eyes of a Stranger," CBS-TV thriller starring Richard Dean Anderson, CBS-TV. Reports in 2 months on queries; 3 months on submissions. Query with 1 sentence premise, 3 sentence synopsis and résumé. Outright purchase WGA minimum; and up.

● CPC Entertainment is looking for scripts of wider budget range, from low independent to high studio.

Needs: Needs feature and TV movie screenplays: small independent, or any budget for thrillers, true stories, action/adventure, character driven stories of any genre.

N **DAYDREAM PRODS., INC.**, 8969 Sunset Blvd., Los Angeles CA 90069. (310)285-9677. E-mail: dydream@earthlink.net. Contact: Sheryl Schwartz. Estab. 1995. Buys 2 scripts/year. Works with 3-4 writers/year. Buys all rights. Previously produced material OK. Reports in 4 months on submissions. Query with synopsis. Pays in accordance with Writer's Guild standards.
Needs: Films (35mm).
Tips: "Looking for television projects, MOW's sitcoms and children's programming."

N **EARTH TRACKS PRODUCTIONS**, 4809 Avenue N, Suite 286, Brooklyn NY 11234. Contact: David Krinsky. Estab. 1985. Produces material for independent studios. Buys 1-3 scripts/year. Buys all rights. No books, no treatments, no plays, no articles. *Only* completed movie scripts. Reports in 6 weeks on queries.

● This producer notes a high rate of inappropriate submissions. Please read and follow guidelines carefully.

Needs: Commercial, well-written, low budget, high concept scripts in the drama, dark comedy and thriller genres. No other genre scripts. Query with 1-page synopsis and SASE. No treatments. *Do not send any scripts unless requested.* Also looking for writers to script existing projects in development.
Tips: "Writers should be flexible and open to suggestions. Material with interest (in writing) from a known actor is a *major plus* in the consideration of the material. Any submissions of more than two pages will *not* be read or returned. We have recently reorganized and are only seeking quality, *low budget* scripts for inhouse production. Controversial, with strong lead characters (dialogue), are preferred." (Examples: 'Natural Born Killers,' 'From Dusk Till Dawn,' 'Pulp Fiction.') Do not send queries by certified/registered mail. They will be rejected. Note: Due to new postal regulations requested scripts are no longer returned. We do not have personnel to send to post office to wait on line to return your scripts. Sorry. They can no longer be dropped in mailboxes for return. Writers who insist their scripts be returned must pay a fee for our time and labor of $15 per script. No exceptions. There is no fee to read requested material. Writers must submit signed release forms with submission."

N **EAST EL LAY FILMS**, 12041 Hoffman St., Studio City CA 91604. (818)769-4565. (818)769-1917. Contact: Daniel Kuhn, president. Co-President: Susan Coppola (director). Estab. 1992. Low-budget feature films for television markets. Buys 2 scripts/year. Works with many writers/year. Buys first rights and options for at least 1 year with refusal rights. Reports in 3-4 weeks on queries. Query with synopsis and résumé. Pays royalty, makes outright purchase or option fee.
Needs: Film loops (35mm), videotapes.

N **ENTERTAINMENT PRODUCTIONS, INC.**, 2118 Wilshire Blvd., Suite 744, Santa Monica CA 90403. (310)456-3143. Fax: (310)456-8950. Producer: Edward Coe. Contact: Story Editor. Estab. 1971. Produces films for theatrical and television (worldwide) distribution. Reports in 1 month only if SASE enclosed.
Needs: Screenplay originals. Query with synopsis and SASE. Price negotiated on a project-by-project basis. Writer's release in any form will be acceptable.
Tips: "State why script has great potential."

N **EPIPHANY PRODUCTIONS INC.**, 10625 Esther Ave., Los Angeles CA 90064. Fax: (310)815-1269. E-mail: roadog@concentric.net. Contact: Scott Frank, president. Estab. 1983. Film and TV audiences. Buys 12 scripts/year. Works with 18 writers/year. Reports in 3 months on submissions. Query with synopsis. Produced 2 Showtime movies in 1995. Produced feature, *Roaddogs* in 1997.
Tips: We are seeking compelling human stories with rich characters that can be shot on a modest budget, 3-10 million."

[N] **JOSEPH FEVRY ENTERTAINMENT**, 230 West 41st St., Suite 1400, New York NY 10036. (212)221-9090. Executive Producer: Joseph Fevry. Estab. 1982. Buys all rights. Accepts previously produced material. Reports in 1 month. Query with synopsis or completed script. Pays negotiated option.
Needs: Films.

[N] **FORRESTER FILMS**, 2803 Forrester Dr., Los Angeles CA 90064. President: Barbara Klein. Estab. 1992. Theatrical audience. Buys 2 scripts/year. Works with 20 writers/year. Buys all rights. Accepts previously produced material. No submissions will be returned. Reports in 1 month on queries; 3 months on submissions. Query with synopsis. Pays in accordance with Writer's Guild standard.
Needs: Films (35mm).
Tips: "Individual market getting tougher and tougher. So material has to be better and better."

[N] **BETH GROSSBARD PRODUCTIONS**, 5168 Otis Ave., Tarzana CA 91356. Contact: Beth Grossbard, producer. Estab. 1994. Buys 6 scripts/year. Works with 20 writers/year. First rights and true life story rights. Reports in 3 months on queries; 4 months on submissions. Query with synopsis, treatment/outline and completed script. Pays in accordance with Writer's Guild standards.
Needs: Films (35mm).
Tips: "Looking for unique, high-concept stories; family dramas; personal accounts; true stories; social issues."

[N] **HANDPRINT ENTERTAINMENT**, 8436 W. 3rd St., Suite #650, Los Angeles CA 90036. Estab. 1997. Young adult to adult 18-40. Buys 10 scripts/year. Works with 40 writers/year. Buys first or all rights. "We are submit to 20th Century Fox to buy or seek our own means." Accepts previously produced material. Reports in 1 month. Query with synopsis. Pays in accordance with Writer's Guild standards.
Needs: Television films.
Tips: "Commerically-minded material with an edge—thrillers, dramas, action. Push the envelope of your genre."

[N] **NICHOLAS HASSITT FILMS**, 1345 N. Hayworth Ave., Suite 210, West Hollywood CA 90046. Contact: Simon Ledworth, director of development. Estab. 1994. Material intended for general audience. Buys 4 scripts/year. Works with 15 writers/year. Buys all rights. Accepts previously produced material. Reports in 1 month. Query with synopsis. Pays in accordance with Writer's Guild standards.
Needs: Films (35mm). "Looking for screenplays and novels that can be developed in feature film."

[N] ☐ **HBO PICTURES**, 2049 Century Park E., Suite 3600, Los Angeles CA 90067. (310)201-9302. Fax: (310)201-9552. Contact: Bettina Moss, story editor. Reports in 1 month. Query with synopsis one page or shorter. Payment varies.
Needs: Features for TV. Looks at all genres except family films or films with children as main protagonists. Focus on socially relevant material.

[N] ☐ **HELIOS PRODUCTIONS**, 5514 Wilshire Blvd., 11th Floor, Los Angeles CA 90036. (213)934-5454. Contact: Tyler Steele. Estab. 1984. Television (network & cable). Buys 12-15 scripts/year. Works with 6-10 writers/year. Buys all rights, film rights & serial. Accepts previously produced material. Reports in 1 month on queries; 1-2 months on submissions. Catalog for SAE with 2 first-class stamps. Query or phone query/pitch. Pays outright in accordance with Writer's Guild standards.
Needs: Films, movies for television.

[N] ☐ **IFM FILM ASSOCIATES INC.**, 1541 N. Gardner St., Los Angeles CA 90046. (213)874-4249. Executive Vice President: Ann Lyons. Estab. 1994. Film and television all media world wide. Buys 10 scripts/year. Works with 30 writers/year. Buys all rights. No previously produced material. No submissions will be returned. Reports in 1 month on queries; 1-3 months on submissions. Catalog for SAE with $3. Query with synopsis. Pays in accordance with Writer's Guild standards, or so otherwise negotiated.
Needs: Film (35mm). Thrillers, family, action.

[N] **INTERNATIONAL HOME ENTERTAINMENT**, 1440 Veteran Ave., Suite 650, Los Angeles CA 90024. (213)460-4545. Contact: Jed Leland, Jr., assistant to the president. Estab. 1976. Buys first rights. Reports in 2 months. Query. Pays in accordance with Writers Guild standards.

- Looking for material that is international in scope.

Tips: "Our response time is faster on average now (3-6 weeks), but no replies without a SASE. *No unsolicited scripts*.We do not respond to unsolicited phone calls."

MARTY KATZ PRODUCTIONS, 1250 6th St., Suite 205, Santa Monica CA 90401. (310)260-8501. Contact: Fred Levy. Estab. 1992. Produces material for all audiences. Buys first, all and film rights. Accepts previously produced material. Reports in 1 month.
Needs: Films (35mm).

KJD TELEPRODUCTIONS, 30 Whyte Dr., Voorhees NJ 08043. (609)751-3500. Fax: (609)751-7729. E-mail: mactoday@ios.com. President: Larry Scott. Estab. 1989. Broadcast audience. Buys 6 scripts/year. Works with 3 writers/year. Buys all rights. No previously produced material. Reports in 1 month. Catalog free. Query. Makes outright purchase.
Needs: Films, videotapes, multimedia kits.

ADAM KLINE PRODUCTIONS, 11925 Wilshire Blvd., 3rd Floor, Los Angeles CA 90025. (310)312-4814. Producer: Adam Kline. Estab. 1994. Features. Buys 20 scripts/year. Works with 200+ writers/year. Buys all rights. Accepts previously produced material. Report in 1 week on queries; 1-2 months on submissions. Query with synopsis or 5-7 sentence summary of finished feature length screenplay(s) of any genre or budget. All negotiable in all types of options or purchases.
Needs: "I needs scripts. I look for commercial mainstream material."

KN'K PRODUCTIONS INC., 5230 Shira Dr., Valley Village CA 91607-2300. (818)760-3106. Fax: (818)760-2478 or (818)760-3106. Creative Director: Katharine Kramer. Estab. 1992. "Looking for film material with strong roles for mature women (ages 40-55 etc.). Also roles for young women and potential movie musicals, message movies." Buys 3 scripts/year. Works with 5 writers/year. Buys all rights. No previously produced material. Reports in 2-3 months. Catalog for #10 SASE. Submit synopsis, complete script and résumé. Pays in accordance with Writers Guild standards or partnership.
Needs: Multimedia kits. "Doing more partnerships with writers as opposed to just Writers Guild minimum. Concentration on original vehicles for the mature actress to fill the gap that's missing from mainstream cinema."
Tips: "We are primarily looking for women's projects, for female-driven vehicles for mature actresses, 45-55, but we are emphasizing music-driven projects more and more. We are also looking for strong male-driven vehicles (emphasis on mature actors.) We are focusing on character-driven, original material."

THE JONATHON KRANE GROUP, 9255 Sunset Blvd., #1111, Los Angeles CA 90069. Contact: Kimberlyn Lucken. Estab. 1981. Produces material for all audiences. Works with 15 writers/year. Have first look with Fox 2000. Accepts previously produced material. Reports in 1 month on queries; 2 months on submissions. Query with synopsis.
Needs: Films (35mm). "All genre and budget ranges."

LANCASTER GATE ENTERTAINMENT, 4702 Hayvenhurst Ave., Encino CA 91436. (818)995-6000. Contact: Brian K. Schlichter, director of development. Estab. 1989. Theatrical and television. Works with dozens of writers/year. Rights purchased negotiable. Recently produced projects: *Grumpy Old Men*, *Grumpier Old Men*, *Angel Flight Down*, *Deadly Web*, *December.* Reports in 1 month on queries. Query. Pays in accordance with Writer's Guild standards.
Needs: Films (35mm-70mm). Feature and long form television scripts.

THE LANDSBURG COMPANY, 11811 W. Olympic Blvd., Los Angeles CA 90064-1113. (310)478-7878. Contact: Gloria Morris, development manager. Estab. 1972. Produces for a general television audience. Options 5 scripts/year. Works with 20 writers/year. Buys first, book and life rights. Accepts previously produced work. Reports in 2 weeks on queries; 2 months on submissions. Query with synopsis. Pays in accordance with Writer's Guild standards.
Tips: "We concentrate on long form projects for network and cable television. Stories that follow trends, that have a feature feel and that have a universal appeal."

ANDREW LAUREN PRODUCTIONS, 114 E. 70th St., Suite #3, New York City NY 10021. (212)639-1975. Director of Development: Jordon Hoffman. Estab. 1996. Produces for theatrical audiences. Buys all rights. Reports in 1 month on queries; 4 months on submissions. Query. Pays in accordance with Writer's Guild standards.
Needs: Films (35mm). "We are looking for original feature length screenplays or a writer who can adapt one."

LICHT/MUELLER FILM CORP., 132A S. Lasky Dr., Suite #200, Beverly Hills CA 90212. Creative Assistant: David Blackman. Estab. 1983. Produces material for all audiences. Accepts previously produced material. Reports in 1 month on queries; 3 months on submissions. Query with synopsis.
Needs: Films (35mm). "Scripts for feature films."

LOCKWOOD FILMS (LONDON) INC., 2569 Boston Dr., RR #41, London, Ontario N6H 5L2 Canada. (519)434-6006. Fax: (519)645-0507. E-mail: mark.mccurdy@odyssey.on.ca. President: Nancy Johnson. Estab. 1974. Audience is entertainment and general broadcast for kids 9-12 and family viewing. Works with 5-6 writers/year. Submit query with synopsis, résumé or sample scripts. "Submissions will not be considered unless a

proposal submission agreement is signed. We will send one upon receiving submissions." Negotiated fee.
Needs: Family entertainment: series, seasonal specials, mini-series, and movies of the week. Also feature films, documentaries.
Tips: "Potential contributors should have a fax machine and should be prepared to sign a 'proposal submission agreement.' We are in development with national broadcaster on live-action family drama series. Looking for international co-production opportunities."

N LONGFELLOW PICTURES, 145 Hudson St., 12th Floor, New York NY 10013. (212)431-5550. Fax: (212)431-5822. E-mail: longpics@aol.com. Contact: Tara Connaughton, director of creative development. All audiences. Buys 4-8 scripts/year. Works with 4-6 writers/year. Buys all rights. Accepts previously produced material. Reports in 1 month on queries, 8 months on submissions. Query with synopsis.
Needs: Films.

N LOIS LUGER PRODUCTIONS, 800 South Carson Ave., Los Angeles CA 90036. (213)937-8996. Vice President Current Affairs: Wendy Arthur. Estab. 1986. Buys 6 scripts/year. Works with 20 writers/year. Buys all rights, excluding book publishing rights. Accepts previously produced material. Reports in 1 month on queries; 2-3 months on submissions. Query with synopsis. Pays in accordance with Writer's Guild standards.
Needs: Films.

N A LUMIERE, 8442 Melrose Place, Los Angeles CA 90069. (213)653-7878. Chief Executive Officer: Randolph Pitts. Estab. 1984. Produces material for the general audience. Buys 5 scripts/year. Works with 10 writers/year. Accepts previously produced material. Reports in 2 months. Query through known agent or attorney. Pays negotiated on case by case bases.
Needs: Films (35mm). "Screenplays which will attract major directing and acting talent, regardless of genre or perceived commerciality."

N LEE MAGID PRODUCTIONS, P.O. Box 532, Malibu CA 90265. (213)463-5998. President: Lee Magid. Produces material for all markets: adult, commercial—even musicals. 90% freelance written. 70% of scripts produced are unagented submissions. Works with many unpublished/unproduced writers. Buys all rights or will negotiate. No previously produced material. Does not return unsolicited material.
Needs: Films, sound filmstrips, phonograph records, television shows/series and videotape presentations. Currently interested in film material, either for video (television) or theatrical. "We deal with cable networks, producers, live-stage productions, etc." Works with musicals for cable TV. Prefers musical forms for video comedy. "We're interested in comedy material. Forget drug-related scripts." Submit synopsis/outline and résumé. Pays royalty, in accordance with Writers Guild standards, makes outright purchase or individual arrangement depending on author.

N MEDIACOM DEVELOPMENT CORP., P.O. Box 6331, Burbank CA 91510-6331. (818)594-4089. Contact: Felix Girard, director/program development. Estab. 1978. 80% freelance written. Buys 8-12 scripts/year from unpublished/unproduced writers. 50% of scripts produced are unagented submissions. Query with samples. Reports in 1 month. Buys all rights or first rights. Written query only. Please do not call.
Needs: Produces films, multimedia kits, tapes and cassettes, slides and videotape with programmed instructional print materials, broadcast and cable television programs. Publishes software ("programmed instruction training courses"). Negotiates payment depending on project. Looking for new ideas for CD-ROM titles.
Tips: "Send short samples of work. Especially interested in flexibility to meet clients' demands, creativity in treatment of precise subject matter. We are looking for good, fresh projects (both special and series) for cable and pay television markets. A trend in the audiovisual field that freelance writers should be aware of is the move toward more interactive video disc/computer CRT delivery of training materials for corporate markets."

N MILWAUKEE FILMWORKS, 4218 Whitsett Ave., Suite 4, Studio City CA 91604. (818)762-9080. Fax: (310)278-2632. Contact: Douglas Gardner. Estab. 1991. Film and TV audience. Works with 6 writers/year. Buys screenplays-option. *Feature scripts only.* Returns submissions on a case to case basis. Reports in 3 months. Query with complete script. Pay varies in accordance with Writers Guild standards.
Tips: "Looking for good action scripts to be submitted."

N MNC FILMS, P.O. Box 16195, Beverly Hills CA 90209-2195. E-mail: mncfilms@aol.com. Contact: Mark Cohen, producer. Estab. 1991. Feature film audience. Buys 2 scripts/year. Works with 3 writers/year. Buys all

rights or purchases option on screenplay. Accepts previously produced material. Reports in 2 months. Query with synopsis. Pays in accordance with Writers Guild standards (work for hire) or variable fee for option of material.
Needs: Film (35mm). Feature length films. "I'm looking for story-driven films with well-developed characters. Screenplays or books easily adaptable for lower budget (few locations, stunts, special effects)."
Tips: "In the past I have received many submissions from writers who do not pay attention to the type of material that I am looking for. I am looking for character-driven stories with an emphasis on individuals and relationships."

N **MONAREX HOLLYWOOD CORPORATION**, 9421½ W. Pico Blvd., Los Angeles CA 90035. (310)552-1069. Contact: Chris D. Nebe, president. Estab. 1978. Award-winning producers of theatrical and television motion pictures and miniseries; also international distributors. Buys 5-6 scripts/year. Buys all rights. Reports in 2 months.
Needs: "We are seeking action, adventure, comedy and character-oriented love stories, dance, horror and dramatic screenplays." First submit synopsis/outline with SASE. After review of the synopsis/outline, the screenplay will be requested. Pays in accordance with Writers Guild standards.
Tips: "We look for exciting visuals with strong characters and a unique plot."

N **MONTIVAGUS PRODUCTIONS**, 13930 Burbank Blvd., Suite 100, Sherman Oaks CA 91401-5003. (818)782-1212. Fax: (818)782-1931. Contact: Douglas Coler, VP Creative Affairs. Estab. 1990. Buys 3 scripts/year. Works with 3-4 writers/year. Buys all rights. Query with synopsis only. Responds if interested in synopsis; 1 month on scripts. Encourages submissions from new and emerging writers. Also interested in novels, short stories and plays for adaptation to the big screen. Pays in accordance with Writers Guild standards. Also accepts plays for theatrical staging under it's stageWorks! program.
Needs: Films (35mm).
Tips: Looking for character-driven scripts; no big budget action films. Keep query short and to the point. Synopsis should be a half to three-quarters of a page. No longer. "Please don't tell me how funny, or how good or how exciting your script is. I'll find out. It's the story I want to know first." Unsolicited scripts will be returned unread. Proper script format a must. Coverage will be shared with the writer.

N **MORROW-HEUS PRODUCTIONS**, 8800 Venice Blvd., #209, Los Angeles CA 90034. (310)815-9973. Website: http://www.members.aol.com/MorrowHeus/pagel.html.Contact: Paul Shrater, director of development. Estab. 1989. Intended for the worldwide film and television audience. Buys film and television option. Accepts previously produced material. Reports in 1 month. Send query with synopsis. Pays negotiated option (standard industry practice).
Needs: Films (35mm). Feature film, television mow, drama, comedy, romance, adventure, action, thriller, family.

N ☐ **MOUNTAIN DRIVE**, 625 Arizona Ave., Santa Monica CA 90401. (310)395-6200. Development Director: John G. Otto. Estab. 1980. Film and TV audience. Works with 10-15 writers/year. Buys all rights. Accept previously produced material. Reports in 1-2 months on queries; 1 month on submissions. Catalog for #10 SASE. Query with synopsis or completed script. Pays by royalty, outright purchase or in accordance with Writer's Guild standards.
Needs: Films (35mm), videotapes. "Mini-series-historical, contemporary dramas. Children's programming, family films, as well as Satuday morning. Sci-fi stories. Action-adventure-syndication."
Tips: "Please ensure that script/treatment is registered. Receive thousands of scripts each year with no return information. Trends seem to go with character-driven material. Effects important in some respect, but good story is what counts."

N **MOVIE REPS INTERNATIONAL**, 7135 Hollywood Blvd., #104, Los Angeles CA 90046. (213)876-4052. Contact: Krishna Shah, president/CEO. Fax: (213)876-4052. Estab. 1989. US and foreign audiences. Buys 4 scripts/year. Works with 2 writers/year. Buys first or all rights. No previously produced material. Reports in 1 month on queries. Free catalog. Query with synopsis. Pays royalty or makes outright purchase.
Needs: Films (35mm). Feature film script, minimum 100 pages. Genres: action/thriller, romantic comedy, adventure, art type of film. Looking for: fresh ideas, no holds barred kind of script, extremely original.
Tips: Originality is key; and combine it with high concept.

N **MWG PRODUCTIONS**, 2317 Vasanta Way, Los Angeles CA 90068. (213)469-8290. Contact: Max Goldenson, executive producer. Estab. 1981. Buys 3 scripts/year. Works with 10 writers/year. Buys all rights. Accepts previously produced material. Reports in 1 month on queries; 3 months on submissions. Query with synopsis and résumé. Pays in accordance with Writer's Guild standards.
Needs: Films, multimedia kits and videotapes.

N **NEW & UNIQUE VIDEOS**, 2336 Sumac Dr., San Diego CA 92105. (619)282-6126. E-mail: videos@concentric.net. Website: http://www.concentric.net/~videos. Contact: Candace Love, creative director. Estab. 1982. General TV and videotape audiences. Buys 10-15 scripts/year. Buys first rights, all rights. No previously produced material. Reports in 1-2 months. Catalog for #10 SASE. Query with synopsis. Makes outright purchase, negotiable.

INSIDER REPORT

Author Rob Thomas takes a novel approach to screenwriting

Rob Thomas lined up a publisher for his first book *Rats Saw God* on his own, unagented, despite its controversial content. Four or five publishing houses turned Thomas's book down before Simon & Schuster Books for Young Readers scooped it up and signed Thomas to write three more young adult novels.

That was 1996 and, as Thomas will attest, a lot can happen in three years. He followed publication of that first book with *Slave Day*, *Doing Time: Notes from the Undergrad* and *Satellite Down*. Both *Slave Day* and *Satellite Down* are being considered for motion pictures, and Thomas has moved on to writing for television: after his debut as a screenwriter for *Dawson's Creek*, he moved on to his own series, *Cupid*, which premiered in September 1998 on ABC.

"I knew nothing about the publishing business and no one in the publishing business," Thomas says. "When I finished *Rats Saw God*, I went out and bought *Writer's Market* and *Guide to Literary Agents*. I used the information I found there and ended up getting a book deal. So it can happen. The thing about writing, at least from my experience, is I was given a fair shake. You're judged by what's on the page, and there's nothing else they can judge you by."

As you progressed through your book contract, did you find the process got easier?

The need to write faster didn't necessarily mean I was writing better books. After the first book, I quit my day job, and my advances were so small I was literally writing to eat. So not only was I doing the novels, but I was also ghostwriting anything I could get. I wrote *Rats Saw God* writing a page a day for a year. Since then, I've been writing five pages a day, and immediately after quitting my job it became necessary to write very fast. I think I became a better writer, but probably a less observant editor. With *Rats Saw God* I would let myself stay on one sentence forever; by the time I was writing *Doing Time*, I didn't have that luxury.

How do your skills in fiction writing translate to screenwriting?

What I enjoy most in writing is voice, and that's essentially what screenwriting is—having a voice and writing dialogue. In screenplays you don't spend a page describing the dew on the grass by the barn, or whatever, which is stuff that I'm not that good at anyway. So it plays to my strengths, I think.

Do you plan to return to novels or stay with television?

I really look forward to writing another novel, because a novel is all you, where writing for television and film is a collaboration, a democracy. I miss knowing that what I put

INSIDER REPORT, *Thomas*

down on the page is going to be what people read. In television, you write something and then the studio puts in their two cents, the network puts in their two cents, the director puts in his two cents, and . . . I've had to please a lot of different masters. You don't have to do that with books, and I miss that. However, I can make more on one television script than I can on a novel, and a television script takes me two weeks. A novel will take five months. I could write two feature screenplays in the time it takes me to write a novel, and it would pay me ten times what I make on a novel.

So is it love or is it money?

The good news is it can be both. I just wrote the adaptation of *Slave Day* for Universal, and the nice thing there is I get paid not only for screenwriting but for the book. So at the end of a day it can be real possible. And I do have an offer for *Satellite Down* as well. I love writing books, but it's tough to say, "Okay, for the next four or five months I'm not going to take any of this money people are offering me."

Did you expect before *Rats Saw God* was published that your career would head in this direction?

No, not at all. It amazes me on a daily basis—I'm in Chicago right now where we film the *Cupid* series, and if I go downstairs there are 200 employees, and all these sets built that essentially I wrote. There are famous actors who are doing lines that I wrote. There's a chair that has my name stitched to it down there. All of these things, really. Thirteen months ago I lived in Texas and I was ghostwriting *X-Files* novels. It boggles my mind sometimes.

—*Anne Bowling*

Needs: Videotapes.
Tips: "First and foremost, read these tips very carefully. We are seeking unique slants on interesting topics in 60-90 minute special-interest videotape format, preferably already produced, packaged and ready for distribution. Currently distributed titles include 'Massage for Relaxation'; 'Ultimate Mountain Biking' and 'Full Cycle: World Odyssey.' No movies or movie treatments. We concentrate on sports, health and other educational home-video titles. Please study the genre and get an understanding of what 'special interest' means. Send a SASE for our catalog to see what kinds of titles we produce. This will save you time and resources. Video distribution has become highly competitive. Doing adequate homework at the beginning will prevent heartache down the road. Study your market. Determine the need for (yet another?) video on your topic. The elements for success are: intensive market research, passion, humor, imagination and a timely or timeless quality."

N **OMEGA ENTERTAINMENT**, 8760 Shoreham Dr., Los Angeles CA 90069. Vice President: Christy L. Pokarney. Estab. 1979. Produces material for film (worldwide). Buys 1 scripts/year. Works with 4 writers/year. Buys all rights. Accepts previously produced material. Query with synopsis. Pays royalty or outright purchase.
Needs: Films (35mm).

N **OPEN DOOR ENTERTAINMENT**, 1519 Glencoe Ave., Venice CA 90291. (310)664-9876. President: Kai Schoenhals. Estab. 1997. Feature films. Global distribution all ages. Buys 4-7 scripts/year. Works with 15-20 writers/year. Buys first rights, all rights and film rights, limited options. Accept previously produced material. Reports in 1 month, depending on where we are in terms of production and travel. Query with synopsis, completed script or resume. Pays 2-5% dependent, once we begin principle photography.
Needs: Films (35mm).
Tips: "We have offices in LA, NYC, London, Copenhagen and Warsaw. We are interested in crossing the Atlantic gap. We are most interested in bringing projects to Poland to be put into production there. (i.e., genre, sci-fi, fantasy, horror, epic, comedy, drama, action)."

TOM PARKER MOTION PICTURES, 3941 S. Bristol, #285, Santa Ana CA 92704. (714)545-2887. Fax: (714)545-9775. President: Tom Parker. Contact: Yvonne Ortega, script/development. Produces and distributes feature-length motion pictures worldwide for theatrical, home video, pay and free TV. Also produces short subject special interest films (30, 45, 60 minutes). Works with 5-10 scripts/year. Previously produced and distributed "Amazing Love Secret" (R), and "The Sturgis Story" (R). Reports in 6 months. "Follow the instructions herein and do not phone for info or to inquire about your script."

Needs: "Complete script *only* for low budget (under $1 million) "R" or "PG" rated action/thriller, action/adventure, comedy, adult romance (R), sex comedy (R), family action/adventure to be filmed in 35mm film for the theatrical and home video market. (Do not send TV movie scripts, series, teleplays, stage plays). *Very limited dialogue.* Scripts should be action-oriented and fully described. Screen stories or scripts OK, but no camera angles please. No heavy drama, documentaries, social commentaries, dope stories, weird or horror. Violence or sex OK, but must be well motivated with strong story line." Submit synopsis and description of characters with finished scripts. Makes outright purchase: $5,000-25,000. Will consider participation, co-production.

Tips: "Absolutely will not return scripts or report on rejected scripts unless accompanied by SASE."

PAULIST PRODUCTION, 17575 Pacific Coast Hwy., P.O. Box 1057, Pacific Palisades CA 90272-4148. (310)454-0688. Director of Development: Barbara R. Nicolos. Estab. 1964. General public-domestic and international audiences. Buys 2-3 scripts/year. Buys all rights or film/tv rights for published works. Accepts previously produced material. Report in 1 month on queries; 2 months on submissions. Query with synopsis. Pays in accordance with Writer's Guild standards.

Needs: Films (35mm). "We are looking for material to develop into television/cable movies. Our criterion are powerful narratives with well-drawn characters which shed light on man's search for meaning and personal growth. We want spiritual themes which are not necessarily overtly Christian, but which do not reject traditional Christian values."

Tips: "Would be screenwriters should be very careful to adhere to the industry standards for formatting a screenplay. A brilliant narrative is no substitute for the wrong margins or typeface. Synopsis should be more about the theme of the work and why it should be made than all the details of the story. . . . If a script is ailing violence and gratuitous sex aren't going to cure it. Don't add artificial sub plots just because it seems to be what sells."

PHASE I PRODUCTIONS, 429 Santa Monica Blvd., Suite #610, Santa Monica CA 90401. Vice President: Kristin Schwarz. Estab. 1995. Film and TV audiences. Buys 12 scripts/year. Works with 3 dozen scripts in-house. Buys all rights. No previously produced material. Reports in 1-2 weeks on queries; 1-2 months on submissions. Submissions must not be unsolicited. Must come through agent or attorney or will be returned. Pays in accordance with Writer's Guild standards.

Needs: Films. Feature film and television and cable movies.

POP/ART FILM FACTORY, 513 Wilshire Blvd., #215, Santa Monica CA 90401. Contact: Daniel Zirilli. Estab. 1990. Produces material for "all audiences/features films." Query with synopsis. Pays on per project basis.

Needs: Film (35mm), documentaries, multimedia kits. "Looking for interesting productions of all kinds. We are producing 3 feature films per year, and 15-20 music-oriented projects. Also looking for exercise and other special interest videos."

Tips: "Be original. Do not play it safe. If you don't receive a response from anyone you have ever sent your ideas to, or you continually get rejected, don't give up if you believe in yourself. Good luck and keep writing!"

PORTAGE ROAD ENTERTAINMENT INC., 4040 Alta Mesa Dr., Studio City CA 91604. President: Jeff Wollnough. Estab. 1994. Film and television features. Buys 3-7 scripts/year. Works with 3-7 writers/year. Buys all rights. Accept previously produced material. Reports in 1 month on queries; 3 months on submissions. Query with synopsis or completed script.

Needs: Films (35mm). We are seeking viable feature film and movie of the week television. Properties—all genres.

PROMARK ENTERTAINMENT GROUP, 3599 Cahuenga Blvd. W., Los Angeles CA 90026. (213)878-0404. Fax: (213)878-0486. Contact: Gil Adrienne Wishnick, vice president Creative Affairs. Promark is a foreign sales company, producing theatrical films for the foreign market, domestic theatrical and cable as well as for video. Buys 8-10 scripts/year. Works with 8-10 writers/year. Buys all rights. Reports in 1 month on queries, 2 months on submissions. Query with synopsis. Makes outright purchase.

- Promark is concentrating on action-thrillers in the vein of *The Net* or *Marathon Man*. They are not looking for science fiction/action as much this year, as they have a rather full production slate with many sci-fi and techno-thrillers.

Needs: Film (35mm). "We are looking for screenplays in the action, action-adventure, thriller and science fiction/action genres. Our aim is to produce lower budget (3 million and under) films that have a solid, novel premise—a smart but smaller scale independent film. Our films are male-oriented, urban in setting and hopefully smart. We try to find projects with a fresh premise, a clever hook and strong characters. We will also consider a family film, but not a drama or a comedy. Again, these family films need to have an element of action or suspense. We are not interested in comedies, dramas or erotic thrillers. Our budgets are lower, approximately three million and under. Among the films we produced are: *A Breed Apart*, a psychological thriller with Andrew McCarthy; *The Invader*, a sci-fiction action/drama, starring Sean Young, Ben Cross and Nick Mancuso; *The Shadowmen* with Eric Roberts, Sherilyn Fenn and Dean Stockwell; and a sci-fi thriller about cloning entitled *Johnny 2.0*, which stars Jeff Fahey."

Tips: "Check on the genres any potential production company accepts and slant your submissions accordingly. Do your homework before you send a query or call. Find out who to contact, what their title is and what the production company tends to make in terms of genre, budget and style. Find the address yourself—don't ask the production executive for it, for example. It's insulting to the executive to have to inform a caller of the company name or address. We are currently looking for suspenseful thrillers with interesting, even quirky characters. We are also looking for family films, specifically adventure yarns for and about kids (ages 8-13) in which the kids are the action heroes. The budgets are low (750,000), so special effects are out. Otherwise, our needs remain roughly the same."

N THE PUPPETOON STUDIOS, P.O. Box 80141, Las Vegas NV 89180. Website: http://www.scifistation.com. Contact: Arnold Leibovit, vice president of production. Estab. 1987. "Broad audience." Works with 2 writers/year. Reports in 1 month on queries; 2 months on scripts. Query with synopsis. Submit complete script. A Submission Release *must* be included with all queries. Currently producing the animated feature, "Moby Dick: The Whale's Tale." SASE required for return of all materials. Pays in accordance with Writers Guild standards. No novels, plays, poems, treatments; no submissions on computer disk. Unsolicited scripts must have release. Must include release form.

Needs: Films (35mm). "We are seeking animation properties including presentation drawings and character designs. The more detailed drawings with animation scripts the better. Always looking for fresh broad audience material."

N REEL LIFE WOMEN, 10158 Hollow Glew Cir., Bel Air CA 90077. (310)271-4722. Co-President: Joanne Parrent. Estab. 1997. Mass audiences. Buys 3-4 scripts/year. Accepts previously produced material. Reports in 1 month on queries; 2 months on submissions. Query with synopsis, resume or SASE for response to query. Pays in accordance with Writer's Guild standards.

Needs: Films. Looking for full-length scripts for feature films or television movies only. (No series or episode TV scripts.) Must be professionally formatted (courier 12pt.) and under 130 pages. All genres considered particularly drama, comedy, action, suspense.

Tips: "We are particularly interested in stories with strong female main characters."

N RICHULCO, INC., 11041 Santa Monica Blvd., Suite 511, Los Angeles CA 90025. Contact: Richard Hull. Estab. 1993. All audiences. Buys 2 scripts/year. Works with 10-15 writers/year. Buys all rights. Accepts previously produced material. Reports in 1 month on queries; 3 month on submissions. Query with synopsis or resume.

Needs: Films (35mm), videotapes. High concept, excellent dialogue, screenplays.

N ROBERT SCHAFFEL/SHARON ROESLER, (formerly Eclectic Films, Inc.), 5750 Wilshire Blvd., Suite 580, Los Angeles CA 90036. Producers: Robert Schaffel/Sharon Roesler. Feature film audience—worldwide. Reports in 2 months on script. Call or write to request permission to submit completed screenplays.

N THE SHELDON/POST COMPANY, 1437 Rising Glen Rd., Los Angeles CA 90069. Contact: Mark Wright, director of development. Producers: David Sheldon, Ira Post. Estab. 1989. Produces theatrical motion pictures, movies and series for television. Options and acquires all rights. Reports in 2 months. Query with 1-2 page synopsis, 2-3 sample pages and SASE. "Do not send scripts or books until requested. If the synopsis is of interest, you will be sent a release form to return with your manuscript. No phone inquiries." Pays in accordance with Writers Guild standards.

Needs: "We look for all types of material, including women's stories, children's and family stories, suspense dramas, horror, sci-fi, thrillers, action-adventure." True stories should include news articles or other documentation.

Tips: "A synopsis should tell the entire story with the entire plot—including a beginning, a middle and an end. During the past three years, the producers have been in business with 20th Century Fox, Paramount Pictures,

FOR EXPLANATIONS OF THESE SYMBOLS,
SEE THE INSIDE FRONT AND BACK COVERS OF THIS BOOK.

Columbia Pictures and currently have contracts with Dick Clark Productions. Most recent productions: "Grizzly Adams and the Legend of Dark Mountain" and "Secrets of a Small Town."

N **DARRYL SILVER**, 8050-4 Canby, Reseda CA 91335. Contact: Darryl Silver. Estab. 1995. Feature and TV. Buys 7 scripts/year. Works with 15-25 writers/year. Buys all rights. No previously produced material. Reports in 1 month. Query with synopsis. Buys option first.
Needs: Films (35mm) and TV.

N **SKYLARK FILMS**, 1123 Pacific St., Santa Monica CA 90405. (310)396-5753. Fax: (310)396-5753. E-mail: skyfilm@aol.com. Contact: Brad Pollack, producer. Estab. 1990. Buys 6 scripts/year. Buys first or all rights. Accepts previously produced material. Reports in 2-4 weeks on queries; 1-2 months on submissions. Query with synopsis. Option or other structures depending on circumstances. Pays in accordance with Writer's Guild standards.
Needs: Films (TV, cable, feature).

- Skylark Films is now seeking action, suspense, thrillers and science fiction.

Tips: "Generally, we look for the best material we can find, other than the horror genre. Particular new areas of focus are romantic comedy, true stories for TV mow's and low-budget quirky material. No response unless we want to see material. Will also look at material for ½ weekly television syndication possibilities."

N **SKYLINE PARTNERS**, 10550 Wilshire Blvd., #304, Los Angeles CA 90024. Contact: Fred Kuehuert. Estab. 1990. Produces material for theatrical, television, video audiences. Buys 3 scripts/year. Buys all rights. Accepts previously produced material. Reports in 2 months on queries. Buys all rights. Accepts previously produced material. Reports in 2 months on queries. Query with synopsis. Pays per negotiation.
Needs: Films (35mm).

N ☐ **ALAN SMITHEE FILMS**, 7510 Sunset Blvd., Suite #525, Hollywood CA 90046. Director: Fred Smythe. Estab. 1990. Mass, cable television and theatrical releases. Buys 2 scripts/year. Works with 10 writers/year. Buys first time rights, all rights or options short-term. No previously produced material. No submissions will be returned. Reports in 2 months. Query with synopsis. Pays in accordance with Writer's Guild standards.
Needs: Films (35mm), videotapes. No specific needs. Varies constantly with market.
Tips: "Strong dialogue. Fresh angles in storylines. It's all been told before, so tell it well."

N **SPECTACOR FILMS**, 9000 Sunset Blvd., #1550, West Hollywood CA 90069. Director of Development: Jonathan Mundale. Estab. 1988. HBO audiences. Buys 3-4 scripts/year. Works with 10-12 writers/year. Buys all rights. No previously produced material. Reports in 1 month on queries; 3 months on submissions. Query with synopsis or completed script. Pays small option money applicable to $40-50,000 purchase price.
Needs: Films. Low budget action scripts. Should be 105 pages or less. Cop/action stories, buddy action stories. Unique hook or idea. Hero should be male in his 30's.
Tips: "Don't think you are the only one writing the great 'millenium' script or the great 'cloning' script. There are thousands of them."

N **STARMIST DEVELOPMENT, INC.**, P.O. Box 6006, Torrance CA 90504-0006. Contact: Arnold Lütz, CEO. Estab. 1995. Film, video and television audience. Buys 5-6 scripts/year. Buys all rights. Reports in 6 months. Completed script and treatment. Pays $1,000-100,000.
Needs: Also accepting original 35mm films and videotapes for distributor. Pays $100,000-300,000.
Tips: "Be patient. The movie industry is a slow beast, but the rewards are beautiful. Take your time writing your treatment and screenplay. We're looking for all types of material, including women's stories, suspense dramas, family stories, horror, sci-fi, thrillers, action-adventure and more. Enclose postage if you want your script returned."

N **STEVENS & ASSOCIATES**, 9454 Wilshire Blvd., Beverly Hills CA 90212. (310)275-7541. President: Neal Stevens. Estab. 1995. All demographics. Buys 15 scripts/year. Works with 75 writers/year. Accepts previously produced material. Sometimes returns submissions with SASE. "Everything has to come through letter." Reports in 3-4 weeks on queries; 2-3 weeks on submissions. Query or query with synopsis. Pays varies depending on the project.
Needs: Films.
Tips: "Looking for 'splashy' material that jumps off the page. Good stay, dialogue and plot. We're very particular. Company is two years old and about to make third film."

N **STORY BROOKE FILMS**, 10380 Tennessee Ave., Los Angeles CA 90064. (310)553-9642. Owner: James Brooke. Estab. 1990. Buys 5 scripts/year. Works with 20 writers/year. Buys all rights. Accepts previously produced material. Reports in 1 month. Query with synopsis. Pays in accordance with Writer's Guild standards.
Needs: Films. Feature length screenplays.

N STRATUM ENTERTAINMENT, 747 Tearwood Rd., Los Angeles CA 90049. (310)472-4217. President: Dianne Mandell. Estab. 1995. Buys 2-3 scripts/year. Works with 20 writers/year. Buys first and all rights. Accepts previously produced material. Reports immediately on queries; 1 month on submissions. Complete script. Pays in accordance with Writer's Guild standards.
Needs: Films.

N A STUDIO MERRYWOOD, 85 Putnam Ave., Hamden CT 06517-2827. Phone/fax: (203)407-1834. E-mail: merrywood@compuserve.com. Website: http://ourworld.compuserve.com/homepages/Merrywood. Contact: Raul daSilva, creative director. Estab. 1984. Produces animated motion pictures for entertainment audiences. "We are planning to severely limit but not close out freelance input. Will be taking roughly 5-7%. We will accept only material which we request from agent. Cannot return material or respond to direct queries."

- The Merrywood Studio is no longer producing children's animation of any kind.

Needs: Proprietary material only. Human potential themes woven into highly entertaining drama, high adventure, comedy. This is a new market for animation with only precedent in the illustrated novels published in France and Japan. Cannot handle unsolicited mail/scripts and will not return mail. Open to *agented* submissions of credit sheets, concepts and synopses only. Profit sharing depending upon value of concept and writer's following. Pays at least Writers Guild levels or better, plus expenses.
Tips: "This is *not a market for beginning writers*. Established, professional work with highly unusual and original themes is sought. If you love writing, it will show and we will recognize it and reward it in every way you can imagine. We are not a 'factory' and work on a very high level of excellence."

N TALKING RINGS ENTERTAINMENT, P.O. Box 80141, Las Vegas NV 89180. E-mail: director@scifistation.com. Website: http://www.scifistation.com. President/Artistic Director: Arnold Leibovit. Contact: Barbara Schimpf, vice president, production. Estab. 1988. "Produces material for motion pictures and television. Works with 5 writers/year. Reports on submissions in 2 months. No treatments, novels, poems or plays, no submissions on computer disk. Query with logline and synopsis. A Submission Release *must* be included with all queries. Produced and directed "The Fantasy Film Worlds of George Pal," "The Puppetoon Movie." Currently producing a remake of "The Time Machine," "7 Faces of Dr. Lao." SASE required for return of all materials. Pays in accordance with Writers Guild Standards.
Needs: "Prefers high concept, mixed genres, comedy, adventure, sci-fi/fantasy, as well as unusual visually rich character driven smaller works with unusual twists, comic sensibility, pathos and always always the unexpected." Films (35mm), videotapes. No unsolicited unagented material. Must include release form.
Tips: "New policy: submission of logline and synopsis for evaluation first. Do not send scripts until we ask for them. A Talking Rings Entertainment release form must be completed and returned with material. Accepting loglines via e-mail at director@scifistation.com."

N THREE GUYS FROM VERONA INC., 12423 Ventura Ct., Studio City CA 91604. (818)509-2288. Partner: Clancy Grass. Estab. 1993. Buys 3 scripts/year. Works with 7-8 writers/year. Buys first and all rights. Accepts previously produced material. Reports in 1 month on queries; 3 months on submissions. Catalog for #10 SASE. Query with synopsis. Pays in accordance with Writer's Guild standards excluding synopsis.
Needs: Films (16 & 35mm), videotapes. Looking for great idea, nothing specific.

N U.S. FILM CORP., 2029 Century Park E., #1260, Los Angeles CA 90067. (310)475-4547. Contact: Robert Nau, president. Estab. 1993. Action audience. Buys 5 scripts/year. Works with 10 writers/year. Buys all rights. Reports in 1 month. Query with synopsis. Pays per negotiation.
Needs Films (35mm). Action adventure, thrillers—feature length.

N RONI WEISBERG PRODUCTIONS, 10960 Wilshire Blvd., 7th Floor, Los Angeles CA 90024. (310)235-5478. Executive Producer: Roni Weisberg. Estab. 1985. Television, film and cable. Buys 4 scripts/year. Works with 20 writers/year. Buys rights as necessary. Accepts previously produced material. Reports in 1 month. Query with synopsis. Pays in accordance with Writer's Guild standards.
Needs: Films (35mm), videotapes. Female appeal/drama, thrillers, contoversial subject, kid/family comedy.
Tips: "Promotable concept driven material regardless of genre."

N WONDERLAND ENTERTAINMENT GROUP, 1712 Anacapa St., Santa Barbara CA 93101. (805)569-0733. Fax: (818)769-5391. E-mail: wl1@gte.net. Contact: Emmanuel Itier, president. Estab. 1989. Produces material for any audience. Buys 5 scripts/year. Works with 4 writers/year. Buys all rights. Accepts previously produced material. Reports in 1 month. Submit complete script and résumé. Pays in accordance with Writers Guild standards.
Needs: Films. "We are seeking any screenplay for full-length motion pictures."
Tips: "Be patient but aggressive enough to keep people interested in your screenplay."

N WORLD FILM SERVICES, 630 Fifth Ave., Suite 1505, New York NY 10111. (212)632-3456. Director of Development: David Laserson. Estab. 1963. Mainstream, family, adult. Buys 5 scripts/year. Works with 5-20

writers/year. Buys all rights. No previously produced material. Reports in 1 month on queries; 2 months on submissions. Query. Pays in accordance with Writer's Guild standards.
Needs: Films (35mm). "We are looking for beautifully written, character-driven screenplays that can play big. Scripts A-list talent would give their *** to star in."
Tips: "Never assume the director will ameliorate the weak spots in your script. Try to really write a film on paper, to the tiniest detail. Leave the reader reeling from your VISION."

N **ZANIMO PRODUCTIONS USA, INC.**, 6308 W. 89th St., Suite 211, Los Angeles CA 90045. Contact: Tambre Hemstreet, president. Estab. 1991. Produces for a feature film or cable audience. Options 5-10 scripts/year. Works with 10 writers/year. Reports in 1 month on queries; 2 months on submissions. Query with synopsis. Payment depends entirely on each individual submission.
Needs: Films (35mm). Action, dramatic or thrillers—feature screenplays (like "The Grifters"). No period pieces. Length: under 120 pages.
Tips: High concept is not enough. There must be depth to the story and the characters. Must send query letter with synopsis first. Scripts by request only please."

N **ZIDE ENTERTAINMENT/ZIDE/PERRY FILMS**, 9100 Wilshire Blvd., Suite 615E, Beverly Hills CA 90212. (310)887-2990. Contact: J.C. Spink. Estab. 1994. All audiences. "We set up about 20 projects a year, 1998 should be even bigger." Works with 50 writers/year. Buys management/production company rights. Reports in 1 month. Query with synopsis. We keep a management percentage.
Needs: Films (35mm). Scripts, books, comic books, treatments.

Contests & Awards

In addition to honors and, quite often, cash awards, contests and awards programs offer writers the opportunity to be judged on the basis of quality alone without the outside factors that sometimes influence publishing decisions. New writers who win contests may be published for the first time, while more experienced writers may gain public recognition of an entire body of work.

On page 548, Linda Burmeister Davies, co-editor of *Glimmer Train Stories*, talks about the three annual fiction contests that prestigious literary journal sponsors. On page 550, Christine Byl shares her experience of entering and winning the 1998 Short-Story Award for New Writers.

Listed here are contests for almost every type of fiction writing. Some focus on form, such as STORY's Short Short Fiction Contest, for stories up to 1,500 words. Others feature writing on particular themes or topics including The Isaac Asimov Award for science fiction, the ASF Translation Prize and the Arthur Ellis Awards for crime fiction. Still others are prestigious prizes or awards for work that must be nominated such as the Pulitzer Prize in Fiction and the Whiting Writers' Awards. Chances are no matter what type of fiction you write, there is a contest or award program that may interest you.

SELECTING AND SUBMITTING TO A CONTEST

Use the same care in submitting to contests as you would sending your manuscript to a publication or book publisher. Deadlines are very important and where possible we've included this information. At times contest deadlines were only approximate at our press deadline, so be sure to write or call for complete information.

Follow the rules to the letter. If, for instance, contest rules require your name on a cover sheet only, you will be disqualified if you ignore this and put your name on every page. Find out how many copies to send. If you don't send the correct amount, by the time you are contacted to send more it may be past the submission deadline. An increasing number of contests invite writers to query by e-mail and many post contest information on their websites. Check listings for e-mail and website addresses.

One note of caution: Beware of contests that charge entry fees that are disproportionate to the amount of the prize. Contests offering a $10 prize, but charging $7 in entry fees, are a waste of your time and money.

If you are interested in a contest or award that requires your publisher to nominate your work, it's acceptable to make your interest known. Be sure to leave the publisher plenty of time, however, to make the nomination deadline.

The Roman numeral coding we use to rank listings in this section is different than that used in previous sections. The following is our ranking system:

- **I Contest for unpublished fiction, usually open to both new and experienced writers.**
- **II Contest for published (usually including self-published) fiction, which may be entered by the author.**
- **III Contest for fiction, which must be nominated by an editor, publisher or other nominating body.**
- **IV Contest limited to residents of a certain region, of a certain age or to writing on certain themes or subjects.**

ABIKO QUARTERLY INTERNATIONAL FICTION CONTEST/TSUJINAKA AWARD (I), 8-1-8 Namiki, Abiko-shi, Chiba-ken 270-11 Japan. E-mail: alp@db3.so-net.or.jp. Contact: Laurel Sicks, editor. Award to "best short story in English of up to 5,000 words." Award: 100,000 yen. Competition receives 100 submissions. Entry fee $12. Guidelines available after September 1 for SASE. Inquiries by e-mail OK. Open September 1-December 31 each year. Previously unpublished submissions. Word length: up to 5,000 words. "Winners will be announced in *Poets & Writers*. Do not send IRCs for notification. No American postage. Send two copies of manuscript. We keep master copy which we treat like gold. The other copy is remailed to judge." Winners announced July 1999. Winners notified by mail.

N _ADVENTURES IN STORYTELLING MAGAZINE_'S NATIONAL STORIES INTO PRINT WRITING CONTEST, (I, IV), *Adventures in Storytelling Magazine*, 1702 Eastbrook Dr., Columbus OH 43223. Contact: Chris Irvin. Annual competition with theme for stories 500 words or less. Two categories: one for adults 13 years or older, one for children under age 13. Prizes: 1st, 2nd and 3rd place winner and 3 honorable mentions in each category. Cash awards are given based on total entry fees. First place will receive 25% of total entry fees; 2nd place, 15%; and 3rd place, 10%. Entry fee $3 per entry for adults, $1 per entry for children. Guidelines for SASE.

✓ _AIM MAGAZINE_ SHORT STORY CONTEST, (I), P.O. Box 20554, Chicago IL 60620. (773)874-6184. Fax: (206)543-2746. Contact: Myron Apilado, publisher/editor; Ruth Apilado, associate editor; Mark Boone, fiction editor. Estab. 1984. "To encourage and reward good writing in the short story form. The contest is particularly for new writers." Contest offered annually if money available. Award: $100 plus publication in fall issue. Competition receives 40 submissions. "Judged by *Aim*'s editorial staff." Sample copy for $4. Contest rules for SASE. Deadline: August 15. Unpublished submissions. "We're looking for compelling, well-written stories with lasting social significance." Winners announced September 1.

✓ AKRON MANUSCRIPT CLUB ANNUAL FICTION CONTEST (I), Akron Manuscript Club and A.U., Falls Writer's Workshop, and Taylor Memorial Library, P.O. Box 1101, Cuyahoga Falls OH 44223-0101. (330)923-2094. Contest Director: M.M. LoPiccolo. Award to "encourage writers with cash prizes and certificates and to provide in-depth critique that most writers have never had the benefit of seeing." Annual competition for short stories. Award: certificates to $50 (1st Prize in three fiction categories dependent on funding); certificates for 2nd and 3rd Prizes. Competition receives 20-50 submissions per category. Judge: M.M. LoPiccolo. Entry/critique fee $25 for each entry in one category. Guidelines will be sent *only* with SASE. Inquiries by e-mail OK. Deadline: January 1-March 15. Unpublished submissions. Word length: 2,500 words (12-13 pages). Send all mail to: Fiction Contest, P.O. Box 1101, Cuyahoga Falls OH 44223-0101, Attn: M.M. LoPiccolo. "Send *no* manuscript without obtaining current guidelines. *Nothing* will be returned without SASE." Winners announced May 1999. Winners notified by mail. List of winners available after May for SASE.

ALABAMA STATE COUNCIL ON THE ARTS INDIVIDUAL ARTIST FELLOWSHIP, (II, IV), 201 Monroe St., Montgomery AL 36130. (205)242-4076 ext. 226. E-mail: becky@arts.state.al.us. Contact: Becky Mullen. "To recognize the achievements and potential of Alabama writers." Semiannual awards: $5,000 and $10,000 grants awarded in even-numbered years (2000-2002). Guidelines available January 2000 by e-mail or phone. Inquiries by fax and e-mail OK. Competition receives approximately 30 submissions annually. Judges: Independent peer panel. Deadline: May 1. Two-year Alabama residency required. Winners announced in September. Winners notified by letter. List of winners available by e-mail, phone or fax.

N ALLIGATOR JUNIPER NATIONAL WRITING CONTEST, (I, IV), Prescott College, 220 Grove Ave., Prescott AZ 86301. (520)776-5231. Fax: (520)776-5137. Annual competition with theme for fiction, creative nonfiction, poetry. "We aim to publish work that is original, graceful, skillful, authentic, moving, and memorable. We encourage submissions by members of protected classes: women, minorities, gay and lesbian." Award: $500 for 1st place in each category. Fiction is judged by editors and staff of *Alligator Juniper*. Entry fee $10 for each story up to 30 pages. Additional entries require additional fee. All entrants receive the next issue. Guidelines available for SASE.

AMELIA MAGAZINE AWARDS, (I), 329 "E" St., Bakersfield CA 93304. (805)323-4064. Contact: Frederick A. Raborg, Jr., editor. The Reed Smith Fiction Prize; The Willie Lee Martin Short Story Award; The Cassie Wade Short Fiction Award; The Patrick T. T. Bradshaw Fiction Award; and four annual genre awards in science fiction, romance, western and fantasy/horror. Estab. 1984. Annual. "To publish the finest fiction possible and reward the writer; to allow good writers to earn some money in small press publication. *Amelia* strives to fill that gap between major circulation magazines and quality university journals." Unpublished submissions. Length: The Reed Smith—3,000 words maximum; The Willie Lee Martin—3,500-5,000 words; The Cassie Wade—4,500 words maximum; The Patrick T. T. Bradshaw—25,000 words; the genre awards—science fiction, 5,000 words; romance, 3,000 words; western, 5,000 words; fantasy/horror, 5,000 words. Award: "Each prize consists of $200 plus publication and two copies of issue containing winner's work." The Reed Smith Fiction Prize offers two additional awards when quality merits of $100 and $50, and publication; Bradshaw Book Award: $250, 2 copies. Deadlines: The Reed Smith Prize—September 1; The Willie Lee Martin—March 1; The Cassie Wade—June 1; The Patrick T. T. Bradshaw—February 15; *Amelia* fantasy/horror—February 1; *Amelia* western—April 1; *Amelia* romance—October 1; *Amelia* science fiction—December 15. Entry fee: $5. Bradshaw Award fee: $10. Contest rules for SASE. Looking for "high quality work equal to finest fiction being published today."

***AMERICAN FICTION* AWARDS, (I)**, New Rivers Press, Moorhead State University, P.O. Box 229, Moorhead MN 56563. (218)236-4681. Fax: (218)236-2168. E-mail: davisa@mhdl.moorhead.msus.edu. Contact: Alan Davis, editor. "To find and publish short fiction by emerging writers." Annual award for short stories. Award: $1,000 (1st Prize), $500 (2nd Prize), $250 (3rd Prize). Competition receives approximately 1,000 submissions. Editor chooses finalists: guest judge chooses winners; past judges have included Antonya Nelson, Robert Boswell and Joyce Carol Oates. Entry fee $7.50. Guidelines available December 1998 for SASE. Inquiries by e-mail OK. Deadline: May 1. Unpublished submissions. Word length: up to 10,000 words. "We are looking for quality literary or mainstream fiction—all subjects and styles." No genre fiction. For a sample copy, contact your bookstore or New Rivers Press, 420 N. Fifth St., Suite 910, Minneapolis MN 55401. Send ms and cover letter with bio "after reading our ads in *AWP* and *Poets and Writers* each spring." (Previous editions published by Birch Lane Press/Carol Publishing Groups.) Winners announced in September/October 1999. Winners notified by phone/mail. List of winners available for SASE.

N ***ANALECTA* COLLEGE FICTION CONTEST, (I, IV)**, The Liberal Arts Council, FAC 17, Austin TX 78712. (512)471-6563. Editor: David Michaelsen. Award to "give student writers, at the University of Texas and universities across the country, a forum for publication. We believe that publication in a magazine with the quality and reputation of *Analecta* will benefit student writers." Annual competition for short stories, poetry, drama, nonfiction, visual art. Award: $100. Competition receives approximately 1,500 submissions. Judges: Student editiorial board of approximately 25 people. No entry fee. Guidelines for SASE. Deadline: mid-October. Unpublished submissions. Limited to college students. Length: 15 pages or less. "*Analecta* is distributed to 300 university writing programs across the country."

ANAMNESIS FICTION AWARD, (I), Anamnesis Press, P.O. Box 51115, Palo Alto CA 94303. (415)255-8366. Fax: (415)255-3190. E-mail: anamnesis@compuserve.com. Website: http://ourworld.compuserve.com/homepages/anamnesis. Contact: Keith Allen Daniels, president. Award to "recognize quality writers of short fiction in an era when the novel has become far too commercial and serious short fiction is in short supply." Annual competition for short stories. Award: $1,000 and an award certificate plus chapbook publication of the winning story. Judges: 3 anonymous literary experts. Entry fee $20. Guidelines for SASE or on webpage. Inquiries by fax and e-mail OK. Deadline: March 15. Unpublished submissions. Word length: 7,500 words or less. "We want to see stories with emotional/intellectual depth, sensitivity, imaginative ideas and strong characters." Winners notified by mail by June 30. List of winners available on webpage.

SHERWOOD ANDERSON SHORT FICTION PRIZE, (I), *Mid-American Review*, Dept. of English, Bowling Green State University, Bowling Green OH 43403. (419)372-2725. Contact: Michael Czyzniejewski, fiction editor. "Contest is judged by an anonymous judge, who is a well-known fiction writer. Only stories accepted for publication by *Mid-American Review* are considered." Award frequency is subject to availability of funds. Competition receives 4,000 submissions. "To encourage the writer of quality short fiction." No entry fee. Guidelines available for SASE. Inquiries by e-mail OK. Deadline: May 1999. Unpublished material. Winners announced in the fall issue. Winners notified by phone or mail.

ANDREAS-GRYPHIUS-PREIS (LITERATURPREIS DER KÜNSTLERGILDE), (II, IV), Die Künstlergilde e.V., Hafenmarkt 2, D-73728 Esslingen a.N., Germany. Phone: 0049/711/3969010. Fax: 0049/711/39690123. Chief Secretary: Ramona Rauscher-Steinebrunner. "The prize is awarded for the best piece of writing or for complete literary works." Annual competition for short stories, novels, story collections, translations. Award: 1 prize of DM 25,000; 1 prize of DM 7,000. Competition receives 50 entries. Inquiries by fax OK. Judges: Jury members (7 persons). Guidelines available. Inquiries by fax OK. Fiction should be published in German in the last 5 years. Deadline: October. "The prize is awarded to writers who are dealing with the particular problems of the German culture in eastern Europe." Winners announced beginning of 1998. Winners notified by mail.

ANISFIELD-WOLF BOOK AWARDS, The Cleveland Foundation, 1422 Euclid Ave., Suite 1400, Cleveland OH 44115-2001. (216)861-3810. Fax: (216)861-6754. E-mail: lwoodman@clevefdn.org. Director of Communications: Lynne E. Woodman. Award to recognize recent books which have made important contributions to our understanding of racism or our appreciation of the rich diversity of human cultures. Annual award for novels and story collections. Award: $10,000, divided equally if multiple winners. Judges: panel of jurors. No entry fee. Guidelines available for SASE. Deadline: January 31, 1999 for books published in 1998. Previously published submissions between January 1, 1998 and December 31, 1998. "Only books written in English and published in the preceding calendar year are eligible. Plays and screenplays are not eligible, nor are works in progress. No grants are made for the completion or publication of manuscripts." Winners notified by phone. Call for list of winners.

THE ANNUAL/ATLANTIC WRITING COMPETITIONS, (I, IV), Writers' Federation of Nova Scotia, 1809 Barrington St., Suite 901, Halifax, Nova Scotia B3J 3K8 Canada. (902)423-8116. E-mail: writers1@fox.nstn.ca. Website: http://www.chebucto.ns.ca/Culture/WFNS/. Executive Director: Jane Buss. "To recognize and encourage unpublished writers in the region of Atlantic Canada. (Competition only open to residents of Nova Scotia, Newfoundland, Prince Edward Island and New Brunswick, the four Atlantic Provinces.)" Annual competition for short stories, novels, poetry, children's writing and drama. Award: Various cash awards. Competition receives approximately 10-12 submissions for novels; 75 for poetry; 75 for children's; 75 for short stories; 10 for nonfiction. Judges: Professional writers, librarians, booksellers. Entry fee $15/entry. Guidelines available after May 1999 for SASE. Inquiries by fax or e-mail OK. Deadline: August 1999. Unpublished submissions. Winners announced February 2000. Winners notified by mail. List of winners available by request from office.

ANTHOLOGY ANNUAL CONTEST, (I), P.O. Box 4411, Mesa AZ 85201. (602)461-8200. E-mail: tavara@juno.com. Contest Coordinator: Sharon Skinner. Annual competition for short stories. Awards: 1st Prize $100, *Anthology* T-shirt, 1-year subscription; 2nd Prize, *Anthology* T-shirt, 1-year subscription; 3rd Prize, 1-year subscription. All prize-winning stories are published in January/February of following year. Entry fee $5/short story. Maximum number of entries: 2/writer. "All stories submitted to contest are eligible to be printed in upcoming issues of *Anthology*, regardless of finish, unless author specifies otherwise. We ask for one-time rights. All copyrights are held by their original owner." Guidelines for SASE. Simultaneous and prepublished submissions OK. Any subject, any genre. Word length: 1,000-6,000 words.

ANVIL PRESS 3-DAY NOVEL WRITING CONTEST, (I), Anvil Press, 204-A 175 E. Broadway, Vancouver, British Columbia V5T 1W2 Canada. (604)876-8710. Fax: (604)879-2667. E-mail: subter@pinc.com. Editorial Assistant: Johanne Provencal. Annual prize for best novel written in 3 days, held every Labor Day weekend. Award: Offer of publication with percentage of royalties (grand prize); $500 Canadian (1st runner up); $250 Canadian (2nd runner up). Competition receives 1,000 submissions. Judges: Anvil Press Editorial Board. Entry fee: $25. Guidelines for SASE. Inquiries by fax and e-mail OK. Deadline: September 4. "Runner up categories may not be offered every year. Please query." Winners announced November 30. Winners notified by phone and mail. List of winners available September 30 for SASE.

ARIZONA COMMISSION ON THE ARTS CREATIVE WRITING FELLOWSHIPS, (I, IV), 417 W. Roosevelt St., Phoenix AZ 85003. (602)255-5882. E-mail: artscomm@primenet.com. Website: http://az.arts.asu.edu/artscomm. Contact: Jill Bernstein, literature director. Fellowships awarded in alternate years to fiction writers and poets. Award: $5,000-7,500. Competition receives 120-150 submissions. Judges: Out-of-state writers/editors. Guidelines available for SASE. Inquiries by fax and e-mail OK. Deadline: September 17. Arizona resident poets and writers over 18 years of age only. Winners announced April 1999. Winners notified in writing. List of winners available for SASE.

ARTIST TRUST ARTIST FELLOWSHIPS; GAP GRANTS, (I, II, IV), Artist Trust, 1402 Third Ave., Suite 404, Seattle WA 98101-2118. (206)467-8734. Fax: (206)467-9633. E-mail: arttrust@eskimo.com. Program Director: Heather Dwyer. Artist Trust has 2 grant programs for generative artists in Washington State; the GAP and Fellowships. The GAP (Grants for Artist's Projects) is an annual award of up to $1,200 for a project proposal. The program is open to artists in all disciplines. The Fellowship grant is an award of $5,000 in unrestricted funding. Fellowships for Craft, Media, Literature and Music will be awarded in 1999, and Fellowships for Dance, Design, Theater and Visual Art will be awarded in 1998. Competition receives 600 (GAP) submissions; 500 (Fellowship 1999). Judges: Fellowship—Peer panel of 3 professional artists and arts professionals in each discipline; GAP—Interdisciplinary peer panel of 5 artists and arts professionals. Guidelines available in December for GAP grants; April for Fellowship for SASE. Inquiries by fax and e-mail OK. Deadline: February 28 (GAP), mid-June (Fellowship). Winners announced December (Fellowship), May (GAP). Winners notified by mail. List of winners available by mail.

ASF TRANSLATION PRIZE, (II, IV), American-Scandinavian Foundation, 725 Park Ave., New York NY 10021. (212)879-9779. Fax: (212)249-3444. E-mail: agyongy@amscan.org. Website: http://www.amscan.org. Contact: Publishing office. Estab. 1980. "To encourage the translation and publication of the best of contemporary Scandinavian poetry and fiction and to make it available to a wider American audience." Annual competition for poetry, drama, literary prose and fiction translations. Award: $2,000, a bronze medallion and publication in *Scandinavian Review*. Competition receives 20-25 submissions. Competition rules and entry forms available with SASE. Inquiries by fax and e-mail OK. Deadline: June 1, 1999. Submissions must have been previously published in the original Scandinavian language. No previously translated material. Original authors should have been born within past 200 years. Winners announced in September. Winners notified by letter. List of winners available for SASE. "Select a choice literary work by an important Scandinavian author."

THE ISAAC ASIMOV AWARD, (I, IV), International Association for the Fantastic in the Arts and *Asimov's* magazine, School of Mass Communications, U. of South Florida, 4202 E. Fowler, Tampa FL 33620. (813)974-6792. Fax: (813)974-2592. E-mail: rwilber@chuma.cas.usf.edu. Administrator: Rick Wilber. "The award honors the legacy of one of science fiction's most distinguished authors through an award aimed at undergraduate writers." Annual award for short stories. Award: $500 and consideration for publication in *Asimov's*. Competition receives 200 submissions. Judges: *Asimov*'s editors. Entry fee $5. Guidelines available for SASE. Inquiries by fax and e-mail OK. Deadline: December 15. Unpublished submissions. Full-time college undergraduates only. Winners announced in March. Winners notified by telephone. List of winners available in February for SASE.

ASTED/GRAND PRIX DE LITTERATURE JEUNESSE DU QUEBEC-ALVINE-BELISLE, (III, IV), Association pour l'avancement des sciences et des techniques de la documentation, 3414 Avenue du Parc, Bureau 202, Montreal, Quebec H2X 2H5 Canada. (514)281-5012. Fax: (514)281-8219. E-mail: info@asted.org. Website: http://www.asted.org. President: Josée Valiquette. "Prize granted for the best work in youth literature edited in French in the Quebec Province. Authors and editors can participate in the contest." Annual competition for fiction and nonfiction for children and young adults. Award: $500. Deadline: June 1. Contest entry limited to editors of books published during the preceding year. French translations of other languages are not accepted.

THE ATHENAEUM LITERARY AWARD, (II, IV), The Athenaeum of Philadelphia, 219 S. Sixth St., Philadelphia PA 19106. (215)925-2688. Contact: Literary Award Committee. Annual award to recognize and encourage outstanding literary achievement in Philadelphia and its vicinity. Award: A bronze medal bearing the name of the award, the seal of the Athenaeum, the title of the book, the name of the author and the year. Judged by committee appointed by Board of Directors. Deadline: December. Submissions must have been published during the preceding year. Nominations shall be made in writing to the Literary Award Committee by the author, the publisher or a member of the Athenaeum, accompanied by a copy of the book. The Athenaeum Literary Award is granted for a work of general literature, not exclusively for fiction. Juvenile fiction is not included.

AUTHORS IN THE PARK/*FINE PRINT* CONTEST, (I), P.O. Box 85, Winter Park FL 32790-0085. (407)658-4520. Fax: (407)275-8688. E-mail: foley@magicnet.net. Contact: David Foley. Annual competition. Award: $1,000 (1st Prize), $500 (2nd Prize), $250 (3rd Prize). Competition receives 200 submissions. Guidelines for SASE. Read guidelines before sending ms. Deadline: April 31. Word length: 5,000 words maximum. Winners announced in short story collection, *Fine Print*, before December.

AWP AWARD SERIES IN THE NOVEL, POETRY, CREATIVE NONFICTION AND SHORT FICTION, (I), The Associated Writing Programs, Tallwood House, Mail Stop 1E3, George Mason University, Fairfax VA 22030. (703)993-4301. Fax: (703)993-4302. E-mail: awp@gmu.edu. Website: http://www.gmu.edu/departments/awp. Annual award. The AWP Award Series was established in cooperation with several university presses in order to publish and make fine fiction available to a wide audience. The competition is open to all authors writing in English. Winners receive $2,000. Awards: $2,000 honorarium and publication with a university press. In addition, AWP tries to place mss of finalists with participating presses. Judges: Distinguished writers in each genre. Entry fee $20 nonmembers, $10 AWP members. Contest/award rules and guidelines for business-size SASE or visit our website. No phone calls please. Mss must be postmarked between January 1-February 28. Only book-length mss in the novel and short story collections are eligible. Manuscripts previously published in their entirety, including self-publishing, are not eligible. No mss returned. Winners notified by phone or mail.

AWP INTRO JOURNALS PROJECT, (I, IV), Tallwood House, Mail Stop 1E3, George Mason University, Fairfax VA 22030. Contact: David Sherwin. "This is a prize for students in AWP member university creative writing programs only. Authors are nominated by the head of the creative writing department. Each school may send 2 nominated short stories." Annual competition for short stories and poetry. Award: $50 plus publication in participating journal. 1998 journals included *Puerto del Sol*, *Quarterly West*, *Mid-American Review*, *Cimmaron Review*, *The Metropolitan Review*, *Willow Springs* and *Hayden's Ferry Review*. Judges: AWP. Deadline: December. Unpublished submissions only.

EMILY CLARK BALCH AWARDS, (I), *The Virginia Quarterly Review*, One West Range, Charlottesville VA 22903. Editor: Staige D. Blackford. Annual award "to recognize distinguished short fiction by American writers." For stories published in *The Virginia Quarterly Review* during the calendar year. Award: $500.

BARRINGTON AREA ARTS COUNCIL/WHETSTONE PRIZES, (I), Box 1266, Barrington IL 60010-1266. (847)382-5626. Fax: (847)382-3685. Co-editors: Sandra Berris, Marsha Portnoy and Jean Tolle. Annual competition "to encourage and reward works of literary excellence." Awards: The Whetstone Prize,

FOR EXPLANATIONS OF THESE SYMBOLS, SEE THE INSIDE FRONT AND BACK COVERS OF THIS BOOK.

usually $500 to a single author for best fiction, nonfiction or poetry selected for publication in *Whetstone* (an annual literary journal); The John Patrick McGrath Award, $250 to a single author, for fiction. Competition receives hundreds of entries; all submissions to *Whetstone* are eligible. Judges: co-editors of *Whetstone*. Guidelines available by mail or fax query. Deadline: open until publication; "we read all year." Unpublished submissions. Length: prose up to 25 pages; poetry, 3-5 poems. Sample copies with guidelines $5 postpaid. Winners announced December. Winners notified by letter. List of winners available in January for SASE. Winners announced in front of *Whetstone* as well as press releases, etc.

BCLT/BCLA TRANSLATION COMPETITION, British Centre for Literary Translation/British Comparative Literature Association, % BCLT/EUR, University of East Anglia, Norwich NR4 7TJ England. Phone/fax: +44 1603 592785. E-mail: c.c.wilson@uea.ac.uk. Contact: Christine Wilson, publicity coordinator. Annual competition for translations. Award: £500. Judges: a panel. Entry fee £5 cheque or cash. Guidelines available for SASE. Deadline: early 1999. Word length: 25 double-spaced A4 single-sided pages. Winners announced July or August. Winners notified by mail.

***BELLETRIST REVIEW* ANNUAL FICTION CONTEST, (I)**, Belletrist Review, P.O. Box 596, Plainville CT 06062-0596. (860)747-2058. E-mail: mrlene@aol.com. Contact: Marlene Dube, editor. "To provide an incentive for writers to submit quality fiction for consideration and recognition." Annual competition for short stories. Award: $200. Competition receives approximately 100-150 submissions. Judges: Editorial panel of *Belletrist Review*. Entry fee $5. Guidelines available for SASE. Inquiries by e-mail OK. Deadline: July 15. Unpublished submissions. Word length: 2,500-5,000 words. Winners announced in September. Winners notified by phone and mail. List of winners available for SASE. "An interview with the winning author will also be published with the winning story in the September issue. No simultaneous submissions."

GEORGE BENNETT FELLOWSHIP, (I), Phillips Exeter Academy, 20 Main St., Exeter NH 03833-2460. Coordinator, Selection Committee: Charles Pratt. "To provide time and freedom from monetary concerns to a person contemplating or pursuing a career as a professional writer." Annual award of writing residency. Award: A stipend ($6,000 at present), plus room and board for academic year. Competition receives approximately 150 submissions. Judges are a committee of the English department. Entry fee $5. Application form and guidelines for SASE. Deadline: December 1. Winners announced in March. Winners notified by letter or phone. List of winners available in March. All applicants will receive an announcement of the winner.

BEST FIRST PRIVATE EYE NOVEL CONTEST, (I, IV), Private Eye Writers of America, Thomas Dunne Books, St. Martin's Press, 175 Fifth Ave., New York NY 10010. Annual award. To publish a writer's first "private eye" novel. Award: Publication of novel by St. Martin's Press. Advance: $10,000 against royalties (standard contract). Judges are selected by sponsors. Guidelines for #10 SASE. Deadline: August 1. Unpublished submissions. "Open to any professional or nonprofessional writer who has never published a 'private eye' novel and who is not under contract with a publisher for the publication of a 'private eye' novel. As used in the rules, 'private eye' novel means: a novel in which the main character is an independent investigator who is not a member of any law enforcement or government agency, and who receives a fee for his or her investigative services."

"BEST OF OHIO WRITERS" CONTEST, (I, IV), *Ohio Writer Magazine*, P.O. Box 91801, Cleveland OH 44101. (216)932-8444. Executive Director: Darlene Montonaro. Award "to encourage and promote the work of writers in Ohio." Annual competition for short stories. Awards: $100 (1st Prize), $50 (2nd Prize), $25 (3rd Prize). Competition receives 250-300 submissions. Judges: "a selected panel of prominent Ohio writers." Entry fee $10; includes subscription to *Ohio Writer*. Guidelines available after January 1 for SASE. Deadline: June 30. Unpublished submissions. Ohio writers only. Length: 2,500 words. "No cliché plots; we're looking for fresh, unpublished voices." Winners announced November 1. Winners are notified by phone; confirmed by mail. List of winners available November 1 for SASE.

THE GEOFFREY BILSON AWARD FOR HISTORICAL FICTION FOR YOUNG PEOPLE, (II, IV), The Canadian Children's Book Centre, 35 Spadina Rd., Toronto, Ontario M5R 2S9 Canada. (416)975-0010. Fax: (416)975-1839. E-mail: ccbc@sympatico.ca. Website: http://www3.sympatico.ca/ccbc. Contact: Judi McCallum, librarian. "Award given for best piece of historical fiction for young people." Annual competition for novels. Award: $1,000 (Canadian). Competition receives approximately 8-12 submissions. Judged by a jury of five people from the children's literature community. Previously published submissions. Canadian authors only. "Publishers of Canadian children's books regularly submit copies of their books to the Centre for our library collection. From those books, selections are made for inclusion in the Our Choice list of recommended Canadian children's books each year. The shortlist for the Bilson Award is created after the selections have been made for Our Choice, as the book must first be selected for Our Choice to be part of the Bilson shortlist."

IRMA S. AND JAMES H. BLACK CHILDREN'S BOOK AWARD, (II), Bank Street College, 610 W. 112th St., New York NY 10025-1898. (212)875-4450. Fax: (212)875-4558. E-mail: lindag@bnkst.edu. Website: http://www.bnkst.edu/library/clib/isb.html. Award Director: Linda Greengrass. Annual award "to honor the young children's book published in the preceding year judged the most outstanding in text as well as in art. Book must be published the year preceding the May award." Award: Press function at Harvard Club, a scroll and seals by Maurice Sendak for attaching to award book's run. Judges: adult children's literature experts and children 6-10 years old. No entry fee. Inquiries by fax and e-mail OK. Deadline: December 15. "Write to address above. Usually publishers submit books they want considered, but individuals can too. No entries are returned." Winners announced in May. Winners notified by phone.

✓ **JAMES TAIT BLACK MEMORIAL PRIZES, (III, IV)**, Department of English Literature, University of Edinburgh, Edinburgh EH8 9JX Scotland. Phone: 44 131 650 3617. Fax: 44 131 650 6898. E-mail: information.office@ed.ac.uk. Website: http://www.ed.ac.uk. Contact: Anne McKelvie, Deputy Director of Information and PR Services. "Two prizes are awarded: one for the best work of fiction, one for the best biography or work of that nature, published during the calendar year: October 1st to September 30th." Annual competition. Award: £3,000 each. Competition receives approximately 300 submissions. Judge: Professor R.D.S. Jack, Dept. of English Literature. Guidelines for SASE or SAE and IRC. Guildlines available Sept. 30. Deadline: September 30. Previously published submissions. "Eligible works are those written in English, originating with a British publisher, and first published in Britain in the year of the award. Works should be submitted by publishers." Winners announced in January. Winners notified by phone, via publisher. Contact Department of English Literature for list of winners.

***THE BLACK WARRIOR REVIEW* LITERARY AWARD, (II, III)**, P.O. Box 862936, Tuscaloosa AL 35486-0277. (205)348-4518. Website: http://www.sa.ua.edu/osm/bwr. Editor: Christopher Chambers. "Award is to recognize the best fiction published in *BWR* in a volume year. Only fiction accepted for publication is considered for the award." Competition is for short stories and novel chapters. Award: $500. Competition receives approximately 3,000 submissions. Prize awarded by an outside judge. Guidelines available for SASE. Winners announced in the Fall. Winners notified by phone or mail. List of winners available for purchase in Fall issue.

🌐 **BOARDMAN TASKER PRIZE, (III, IV)**, 14 Pine Lodge, Dairyground Rd., Bramhall, Stockport, Cheshire SK7 2HS United Kingdom. Phone/fax: 0161 439 4624. Contact: Mrs. Dorothy Boardman. "To reward a book which has made an outstanding contribution to mountain literature. A memorial to Peter Boardman and Joe Tasker, who disappeared on Everest in 1982." Award: £2,000. Competition receives approx. 18 submissions. Judges: A panel of 3 judges elected by trustees. Guidelines for SASE. Deadline: August 15. Limited to works published or distributed in the UK for the first time between November 1 and October 31. Publisher's entry only. "May be fiction, nonfiction, poetry or drama. Not an anthology. Subject must be concerned with a mountain environment. Previous winners have been books on expeditions, climbing experiences; a biography of a mountaineer; novels." Winners announced October or November. Winners notified by mail. Short list, available in September, will be sent to all publishers who have entered books.

✓ **BOOK PUBLISHERS OF TEXAS AWARD, (II, IV), The Texas Institute of Letters**, TCU Press, TCU Box 298300, Fort Worth TX 76129. (817)257-7822. Fax: (817)257-5075. E-mail: j.alter@tcu.edu. Website: http://www.prs.tcu.edu/prs/til/. Secretary: Judy Alter. "Award to honor the best book written for children or young people that was published the year prior to that in which the award is given." Annual competition for children's literature. Award: $250. Competition receives approximately 40 submissions. Judges: Committee selected by TIL. Guidelines available after June 30 for SASE sent to P.O. Box 39800, Fort Worth TX 76129. Inquiries by e-mail OK. Deadline: January 4. Previously published submissions from January 1 through December 31 of the year prior to the award. "To be eligible, the writer must have been born in Texas or have lived in the state for two years at some time, or the subject matter of the work must be associated with Texas." Winners announced in April. Winners notified by mail or phone. List of winners available for SASE.

***BOSTON GLOBE-HORN BOOK* AWARDS, (III)**, *Horn Book Magazine, Inc.*, 11 Beacon St., Suite 1000, Boston MA 02108. (617)523-0299. (617)227-1555. Fax: (617)523-0299. E-mail: info@hbook.com. Contact: Karen Walsh, marketing manager. Annual award. "To honor excellence in children's fiction or poetry, picture and nonfiction books published within the US." Award: $500 and engraved silver bowl first prize in each category; engraved silver plate for the 2 honor books in each category. Competition receives 2,000 submissions. No entry fee. Guidelines available after January for SASE. Inquiries by fax and e-mail OK. Entry forms or rules for SASE. Deadline: May 15. Previously published material between June 1, 1998-May 31, 1999. Books are submitted by publishers. Winners announced in August. List of winners available by telephone or e-mail.

✓ **BRAZOS BOOKSTORE (HOUSTON) AWARD (SINGLE SHORT STORY), (II, IV)**, The Texas Institute of Letters, % TCU Press, TCU Box 298300, Ft. Worth TX 76129. (817)257-7822. (817)257-5075. E-mail: j.alter@tcu.edu. Website: http://www.prs.tcu.edu/prs/til/. Awards Coordinator: Judy Alter. Award to "honor the writer of the best short story published for the first time during the calendar year before the award is given." Annual competition for short stories. Award: $750. Competition receives approximately 40-50 submissions. Judges: Panel selected by TIL Council. Guidelines for SASE sent to P.O. Box 39800, Fort Worth TX 76129. Inquiries by e-mail OK. Deadline: January 2. Previously published submissions. Entries must have appeared in print between January 1 and December 31 of the year prior to the award. "Award available to writers who, at some time, have lived in Texas at least two years consecutively or whose work has a significant Texas theme. Entries must be sent directly to the three judges. Their names and addresses are available from the TIL office. Include SASE."

BRONX RECOGNIZES ITS OWN (B.R.I.O.), (I, IV), Bronx Council on the Arts, 1738 Hone Ave., Bronx NY 10461-1486. (718)931-9500. Fax: (718)409-6445. E-mail: bronxart@artswire.org. Website: http://www.bronxarts.org. Arts Services Associate: Evelyn Collazo. Award to "recognize local artistic talent in Bronx County." Annual competition for novels. Award: $1,500 fellowship (awards 15/year in visual, media, performing and literary arts). Competition receives approximately 15 literary submissions. Judges: peer panel of non-Bronx based artists. Guidelines available mid-December by a phone call, written request or on website. Inquiries by fax and e-mail OK. Deadline: March. Only Bronx-based individual artists may apply. Proof of Bronx residency required. Word length: 20 typed pages of ms. Winners announced in May. Winners notified 2 months after deadline by mail. List of winners available for SASE.

GEORGES BUGNET AWARD FOR THE NOVEL, (II, IV), Writers Guild of Alberta, 3rd Floor, Percy Page Centre, 11759 Groat Rd., Edmonton, Alberta T5M 3K6 Canada. (403)422-8174. Fax: (403)422-2663. Contact: Darlene Diver, assistant director. "To recognize outstanding books published by Alberta authors each year." Annual competition for novels. Award: $500 (Canadian) and leather-bound book. Competition receives 20-30 submissions. Judges: selected published writers across Canada. Guidelines for SASE. Deadline: December 31. Previously published submissions. Must have appeared in print between January 1 and December 31. Open to Alberta authors only.

✓ **BURNABY WRITERS' SOCIETY ANNUAL COMPETITION, (I, IV)**, 6584 Deer Lake Ave., British Columbia V5G 377 Canada. (604)435-6500. Annual competition to encourage creative writing in British Columbia. "Category varies from year to year." Award: $200, $100 and $50 (Canadian) prizes. Receives 400-600 entries for each award. Judge: "independent recognized professional in the field." Entry fee $5. Contest requirements after March for SASE. Deadline: May 31. Open to British Columbia authors only. Winners announced in September. Winners notified by phone or mail. List of winners available for SASE.

✓ **BUSH ARTIST FELLOWSHIPS, (I, IV)**, The Bush Foundation, E-900 First Nat'l Bank Building, 332 Minnesota St., St. Paul MN 55101-1387. (651)227-0891. Fax: (651)297-6485. E-mail: kpolley@bushfound.org. Program Assistant: Kathi Polley. Award to "provide support for artists to work in their chosen art forms." Annual grant. Award: $40,000 for 12-18 months. Competition receives 400 submissions. Literature (fiction, creative nonfiction, poetry) offered every other year. Next offered 1999 BAF. Applications available August. Inquiries by fax OK. Deadline: October. Must meet certain publication requirements. Judges: a panel of artists and arts professionals who reside outside of Minnesota, South Dakota, North Dakota or Wisconsin. Applicants must be at least 25 years old, and Minnesota, South Dakota, North Dakota or Western Wisconsin residents. Students not eligible. Winners announced in May. Winners notified by letter. List of winners available in May; will be sent to all applicants.

***BYLINE* MAGAZINE LITERARY AWARDS, (I, IV)**, P.O. Box 130596, Edmond OK 73013-0001. (405)348-5591. E-mail: bylinemp@aol.com. Website: http://www.bylinemag.com. Contact: Marcia Preston, executive editor/publisher. "To encourage our subscribers in striving for high quality writing." Annual awards for short stories and poetry. Award: $250 in each category. Competition receives 200 submissions. Judges are published writers not on the *ByLine* staff. Entry fee $5 for stories; $3 for poems. Guidelines available for SASE. Postmark deadline: November 1. "Judges look for quality writing, well-drawn characters, significant themes. Entries should be unpublished and not have won money in any previous contest. Winners announced in February issue and published in February or March issue with photo and short bio. Open to subscribers only."

✓ **CALIFORNIA WRITERS' CLUB CONTEST, (I)**, California Writers' Club, P.O. Box 1281, Berkeley CA 94701. E-mail: calwriters@ndti.net. Contact: Contest Coordinator. Cash awards "to encourage writing." Competition is held annually. Competition receives varying number of submissions. Judges: Professional writers, members of California Writers' Club. Entry fee to be determined. Guidelines available January 1 through March 30 by mail or on website. Inquiries by fax or e-mail OK. Deadline: May 1. Unpublished submissions. "Open to all." Winners announced at annual conference. Winners notified by mail, fax or phone. List of winners available July 1.

MARKET CATEGORIES: (I) Unpublished entries; **(II)** Published entries nominated by the author; **(III)** Published entries nominated by the editor, publisher or nominating body; **(IV)** Specialized entries.

✓ JOHN W. CAMPBELL MEMORIAL AWARD FOR THE BEST SCIENCE-FICTION NOVEL OF THE YEAR; THEODORE STURGEON MEMORIAL AWARD FOR THE BEST SCIENCE FICTION SHORT FICTION, (II, III), Center for the Study of Science Fiction, English Dept., University of Kansas, Lawrence KS 66045. (785)864-3380. Fax: (785)864-4298. E-mail: jgunn@falcon.cc.ukans.edu. Website: http://www.falcon.cc.ukans.edu/~sfcenter/. Professor and Director: James Gunn. "To honor the best novel and short science fiction of the year." Annual competition for short stories and novels. Award: Certificate. "Winners' names are engraved on a trophy." Campbell Award receives approximately 200 submissions. Judges: 2 separate juries. Inquiries by e-mail and fax OK. Deadline: December 31. For previously published submissions. "Ordinarily publishers should submit work, but authors have done so when publishers would not. Send for list of jurors." Entrants for the Sturgeon Award are selected by nomination only. Winners announced July 9. List of winners available for SASE.

N CANADA COUNCIL GOVERNOR GENERAL'S LITERARY AWARDS, (III, IV), Canada Council for the Arts, 350 Albert St., P.O. Box 1047, Ottawa, Ontario K1P 5V8 Canada. (613)566-4414, ext. 5576. E-mail: josiane.polidori@canadacouncil.ca. Contact: Writing and Publishing Section. "Awards of $10,000 each are given annually to the best English-language and best French-language Canadian work in each of seven categories: children's literature (text) and children's literature (illustration), drama, fiction, poetry, nonfiction and translation." Canadian authors, illustrators and translators only. Books must be submitted by publishers (4 copies must be sent to the Canada Council) and accompanied by a Publisher's Submissions Form, available from the Writing and Publishing Section. Self-published books are not eligible.

✓ CAPTIVATING BEGINNINGS CONTEST, (I), *Lynx Eye*, 1880 Hill Dr., Los Angeles CA 90041-1244. (213)550-8522. Co-editor: Pam McCully. Annual award for stories "with engrossing beginnings, stories that will enthrall and absorb readers." Award: $100 plus publication, 1st Prize; $10 each for 4 honorable mentions plus publication. Competition receives 600 submissions. Entry fee $5/story. Guidelines available for SASE. Unpublished submissions. Length: 7,500 words or less. "The stories will be judged on the first 500 words." Deadline: January 31. Winners announced March 15. Winners notified by phone or e-mail. List of winners available March 30 for SASE.

RAYMOND CARVER SHORT STORY CONTEST, (I, IV), Dept. of English, Humboldt State University, Arcata CA 95521-4957. (707)826-5946, ext. 1. Website: http://www.humboldt.edu/~ams20/carver/. Contact: Student Coordinator. Annual award for previously unpublished short stories. Award: $1,000 and publication in *Toyon* (1st Prize). $500 and honorable mention in *Toyon* (2nd Prize). Honorable mention in *Toyon* (3rd Prize). Competition receives 600 submissions. Entry fee $10/story. Guidelines available June 1 for #10 SASE. Deadline: December 1. For US citizens only. Send 2 copies of story; author's name, address, phone number and title of story on separate cover page only. Story must be no more than 6,000 words. For notification of receipt of ms, include self-addressed, stamped postcard. For Winners List include SASE. For a copy of the *Toyon*, send $2. "Follow directions and have faith in your work." Winners announced June 1. Winners notified by mail. List of winners available June 1.

✓ THE *CHELSEA* AWARDS, (II), P.O. Box 773, Cooper Station, New York NY 10276-0773. E-mail: rafoerster@aol.com. *Mail entries to*: Chelsea Awards, %Richard Foerster, Editor, P.O. Box 1040, York Beach ME 03910-1040. Annual competition for short stories. Award: $1,000 and publication in *Chelsea* (all entries are considered for publication). Competition receives 300 submissions. Judges: the editors. Entry fee $10 (for which entrants also receive a subscription). Guidelines available for SASE. Deadline: June 15. Unpublished submissions. Manuscripts may not exceed 30 typed pages or about 7,500 words. The stories must not be under consideration elsewhere or scheduled for book publication within 8 months of the competition deadline. Include separate cover sheet; no name on ms. Mss will not be returned; include SASE for notification of results. Winners announced August 15. Winners notified by telephone. List of winners available August 20 for SASE.

CHEVRON AWARD AND WRITERS UNLIMITED AWARD, Writers Unlimited, 910 Grant Ave., Pascagoula MS 39567-7222. (601)762-4230. Contest Chairman: Nina Mason. "Part of an annual contest to encourage first-class writing of poetry and prose." Annual competition for short stories. Prize amounts vary with $50 being the maximum. Competition receives 100 submissions. Guidelines available after July 1. Inquiries by e-mail OK. Deadline: September 1. Guidelines available after July 1 for SASE. Winners announced by mail in October. List of winners available October 15.

N CHICANO/LATINO LITERARY CONTEST, (I, IV), Dept. of Spanish & Portuguese, University of California-Irvine, Irvine CA 92697. (949)824-5443. Fax: (949)824-2803. E-mail: rubyt@uci.edu. Website: http://www.hnet.uci.edu/spanishandportuguese/contest.html. Coordinator: Ruby Trejo. Annual award for novels, short stories, poetry and drama (different genre every year). Award: Usually $1,000. Guidelines for SASE. Deadline: May 15. Inquiries by fax and e-mail OK. Unpublished submissions. Winners notified by letter in October.

THE CHILDREN'S BOOK AWARD, (II), Federation of Children's Book Groups, The Old Malt House, Aldbourne, Marlborough, Wilts SN8 2DW England. Award to "promote good quality books for children."

Annual award for short stories, novels, story collections and translations. Award: "Portfolio of children's writing and drawings and a magnificent trophy of silver and oak." Judges: Thousands of children from all over the United Kingdom. Guidelines for SASE or SAE and IRC. Deadline: December 31. Published and previously unpublished submissions (first publication in UK). "The book should be suitable for children."

THE CHRISTOPHER AWARD, (II), The Christophers, 12 E. 48th St., New York NY 10017. (212)759-4050. Contact: Ms. Peggy Flanagan, awards coordinator. Annual award "to encourage creative people to continue to produce works which affirm the highest values of the human spirit in adult and children's books." Published submissions only. Award: Bronze medallion. "Award judged by a grassroots panel and a final panel of experts. Juvenile works are 'children tested.' " Examples of books awarded: *The Silver Balloon*, by Susan Bonners, and *Minty: A Story of Young Harriet Tubman*, by Alan Schroeder.

CNW/FFWA FLORIDA STATE WRITING COMPETITION, (I), Florida Freelance Writers Association, P.O. Box A, North Stratford NH 03590. (603)922-8338. Fax: (603)922-8339. E-mail: danakcnw@moose.ncia.net. Executive Director: Dana K. Cassell. Award "to recognize publishable writing." Annual competition for short stories and novels. Awards: $75, books, certificate or membership. Competition receives 50-100 submissions. Judges: published authors, teachers, editors. Entry fee varies with membership status. Guidelines available after March 15 for SASE. Deadline: March 15. Previously unpublished submissions. Winners will be notified by mail by May 31.

N **COMMUNITY WRITERS ASSOCIATION NATIONAL WRITING COMPETITION, (I)**, P.O. Box 12, Newport RI 02840-0001. Annual competition for short stories and poems. Short stories, any subject, up to 2,500 words. Award (each category): 1st Prize, $500 plus publication of winning entry in special chapbook and on CWA official website; 2nd Prize, 3 free CWA workshops/events plus publication of winning entry in special chapbook; 3rd Prize, 2 free CWA workshops/events plus publication of winning entry in special chapbook. Judging by panel of writing professionals. Entry fee $5/short story. No limit of entries. Fees non-refundable. Guidelines for SASE. Entrant must be 18 or over. Submissions must be original, unpublished. Winners will be notified by telephone or mail.

CONNECTICUT COMMISSION ON THE ARTS ARTIST FELLOWSHIPS, (I, II, IV), One Financial Plaza, Hartford CT 06103-2601. (203)566-4770. Fax: (860)566-6462. E-mail: kdemeo@csunet.ctstateu.edu. Website: http://www.cslnet.ctstateu.edu/cca/. Program Manager: Linda Dente. "To support the creation of new work by creative artists *living in Connecticut*." Biennial competition for the creation or completion of new works in literature, i.e., short stories, novels, story collections, poetry and playwriting. Awards: $5,000 and $2,500. Competition receives 75-100 submissions. Judges: Peer professionals (writers, editors). Guidelines available in May. Inquiries by fax and e-mail OK. Deadline: September. Writers may send either previously published or unpublished submissions—up to 20 pages of material. Connecticut residents only. "Write to please yourself. If you win, that's a bonus." Winners announced in January. Winners notified by mail.

N **CONSEIL DE LA VIE FRANCAISE EN AMÉRIQUE/PRIX CHAMPLAIN, (II, IV)**, Conseil de la vie Française en Amérique, 150 Gaul René-Lévesque Est, Rez-De-Chaussee, Quebec G1R 2B2 Canada. (418)646-9117. Fax: (418)644-7670. E-mail: cufa@cufa.ca. Website: http://www.cufa.ca. Prix Champlain estab. 1957. Annual award to encourage literary work in novel or short story in French by Francophiles living outside Quebec and in the US or Canada. "There is no restriction as to the subject matter. If the author lives in Quebec, the subject matter must be related to French-speaking people living outside of Quebec." Award: $1,500 in Canadian currency. The prize will be given alternately; one year for fiction, the next for nonfiction. Next fiction award in 1999. 3 different judges each year. Guidelines for SASE or IRC. Deadline: December 31. For previously published or contracted submissions, published no more than 3 years prior to award. Author must furnish 4 examples of work, curriculum vitae, address and phone number.

✓ **COTTONWOOD FICTION FELLOWSHIP, (IV)**, Cottonwood Cooperative, 1124 Columbia NE, Albuquerque NM 87106. (505)255-1544. E-mail: cottonwood@geocities.com. Website: http://www.geocities.com/~cottonwood. Director: Charli Buono de Valdez. Award "to honor and enable a Southwestern, mid-career writer." Annual competition for short stories, novels and story collections. Award: $1,000. 1997 Cottonwood Awards received only 50 submissions. Judges: Panel of Southwestern writers. Entry fee $16. Include SASE for return of ms. Guidelines for SASE. Published or unpublished submissions. Limited to writers from Southwest region (Arizona, Colorado, New Mexico, Oklahoma, Texas, Nevada, California—south of and including Bakersfield and San Luis Obispo—and Utah) who have never published a novel or collection of stories. Any genre. "There is particular interest in stories inspired by the Southwest and dealing in some manner with the substance of the Southwest although this preference is by no means definitive." Word length: "Interested authors should submit portfolios—suggested length between 3 and 50 pages. Portfolio may include any number of individual stories and/or a novel excerpt." Deadline: December 31.

✓ **DANA AWARD IN SPECULATIVE FICTION, (IV)**, 7207 Townsend Forest Court, Browns Summit NC 27214-9634. (336)656-7009. E-mail: danaawards@pipeline.com. Website: http://danaawards.home.pipeline.

Chair, Dana Awards: Mary Elizabeth Parker. Award "to reward work that has been previously unrecognized in the area of speculative fiction (fantasy, futuristic, time travel, psychological suspense/horror). No work for children/young adults. Let authors be aware work must meet standards of literary complexity and excellence. That is, character development, excellence of style are as important as the plot line." Annual competition for short stories. Awards: $500. Competition receives 100-200 submissions. Entry fee $10/short story. Make checks payable to Dana Awards. Guidelines for SASE or on website. Inquiries by fax and e-mail OK. Unpublished submissions and not under contract to any publisher. Word length: no minimum, but no longer than 12 double-spaced pages or 3,000 words. Postmark deadline: October 31. Winners announced early Spring. Winners notified by phone; then by letter. List of winners available for SASE in early Spring.

☑ **DANA AWARD IN THE NOVEL**, 7207 Townsend Forest Court, Browns Summit NC 27214-9634. (336)656-7009. E-mail: danaawards@pipeline.com. Website: http://danaawards.home.pipeline.com. Chair, Dana Awards: Mary Elizabeth Parker. Award to "reward work that has not yet been recognized, since we know from firsthand experience how tough the literary market is." Annual competition for novels. No genre fiction, please. Award: $1,000. Competition receives 200-300 submissions. Judges: nationally-published novelists. Entry fee $20 for each submission. Guidelines for SASE. Postmark deadline October 31. Unpublished submissions and not under contract to be published. "Novelists should submit first 50 pages only of a novel either completed or in progress. No novels for children/young adults. In-progress submissions should be as polished as possible. Multiple submissions accepted, but each must include a separate $20 entry fee. Make checks payable to Dana Awards. Winners announced early Spring. Winners notified by phone; then by letter. List of winners available early Spring for SASE.

THE DOROTHY DANIELS ANNUAL HONORARY WRITING AWARD, National League of American Pen Women, Simi Valley Branch, P.O. Box 1485, Simi Valley CA 93062. Contest Chair: Diane Reichick. Award "to honor excellent writing." Annual competition for short stories. Award: $100 (1st Place). Judges: Pen Women members. Competition receives approximately 150 entries. Entry fee $5/short story. Rules for SASE. Deadline: July 30. Unpublished submissions: not currently submitted elsewhere; entries must have received no prior awards. No limit on number of entries. Any person except Simi Valley Pen Women, interns, and their immediate families are eligible. Any genre. Word length: 2,000 words maximum. "Entries must follow rules exactly." Winners announced November 1. Winners notified by mail.

THE JACK DANIEL'S FAUX FAULKNER CONTEST, (I), Jack Daniel Distillery, *Faulkner Newsletter* of Yoknapatawpha Press and University of Mississippi, P.O. Box 248, Oxford MS 38655. (601)234-0909. E-mail: boozernhb@aol.com. Website: http://www.watervalley.net/yoknapatawphapress/index.htm. Award "to honor William Faulkner by imitating his style, themes and subject matter in a short parody." Annual competition for a 500-word (2-pages) parody. Award: 2 round-trip tickets to Memphis, plus complimentary registration and lodging for the annual Faulkner and Yoknapatawpha Conference at the University of Mississippi. Competition receives approximately 750-1,000 submissions. Judges: George Plimpton, Tom Wicker, John Berendt and Arthur Schlesinger, Jr. (judges rotate every year or so—well-known authors). Guidelines for SASE. Deadline: February 1. Previously unpublished submissions. Winner announced August 1, at Faulkner's home in Oxford MS. Winner notified April 1. Contestants grant publication rights and the right to release entries to other media and to the sponsors.

MARGUERITE DE ANGELI PRIZE, (I), Bantam Doubleday Dell Books for Young Readers, 1540 Broadway, New York NY 10036. (212)782-8633. Fax: (212)782-9452. "To encourage the writing of fiction for middle grade readers (either contemporary or historical) in the same spirit as the works of Marguerite de Angeli." Open to US and Candian writers. Annual competition for first novels for middle-grade readers (ages 7-10). Award: One BDD hardcover and paperback book contract, with $1,500 cash prize and $3,500 advance against royalties. Competition receives 300 submissions. Judges: Editors of BDD Books for Young Readers. Guidelines for SASE. Inquiries by fax OK. Deadline: Submissions must be postmarked between April 1 and June 30. Previously unpublished (middle-grade) fiction. Length: 40-144 pages. Winners announced October. Winners notified by phone and letter. List of winners available for SASE.

☑ **DEAD METAPHOR PRESS CHAPBOOK CONTEST**, Dead Metaphor Press, P.O. Box 2076, Boulder CO 80306-2076. (303)417-9398. Contact: Richard Wilmarth. Award to "promote quality writing." Annual competition for short stories. Award: 10% of the press run. Competition receives 100 submissions. Judge: Richard Wilmarth. Entry fee $10. Guidelines available in October for SASE. Deadline: October 31. Word length: 24 page limit. Winners announced at end of February.

☑ **DELACORTE PRESS ANNUAL PRIZE FOR A FIRST YOUNG ADULT NOVEL, (I)**, Delacorte Press, Department BFYR, 1540 Broadway, New York NY 10036. (212)782-9062. Fax: (212)782-9402. Contact: Wendy Lamb, executive editor. Estab. 1983. Annual award "to encourage the writing of contemporary young adult fiction." Award: Contract for publication of book; $1,500 cash prize and a $6,000 advance against royalties. Competition receives 500 submissions. Judges are the editors of Delacorte Press Books for Young Readers. Contest rules for SASE. Inquiries by fax OK. Unpublished submissions; fiction with a contemporary setting that will be suitable for ages 12-18. Deadline: December 30 (no submissions accepted prior to October 1). Writers may be previously published, but cannot have published a young adult novel before. Winners announced April. Winners notified by phone and letter. List of winners available for SASE.

✓ **DOBIE/PAISANO FELLOWSHIPS**, Texas Institute of Letters, P.O. Box 298300, Fort Worth TX 76129. (817)257-7822. E-mail: j.alter@tcu.edu. Website: http://www.prs.tcu.edu/prs/til/. Secretary: Judy Alter. Award to "honor the achievement and promise of two writers." Annual competition for fiction, poetry or nonfiction. Award: $1,200/month for six months and rent-free stay at Paisano ranch southwest of Austin, TX. Judges: committee from Texas Institute of Letters and the University of Texas. Guidelines available for SASE. Inquiries by e-mail OK. Deadline: January 4. "To be eligible, a writer must have been born in Texas or have lived in the state for at least two consecutive years at some point. The winners usually have notable publishing credits behind them in addition to promising work that is under way." Winners announced in April. List of winners available for SASE.

✓ **DOG WRITERS OF AMERICA WRITING COMPETITION**, Dog Writers of America, 3809 Plaza Dr., No. 107-309, Oceanside CA 92056. Attn: Liz Palika. Competition Co-chair: Betsy Sikora Siino. Award to "reward excellence and professionalism in dog writing." Annual competition for short stories, novels and story collections. Award: Maxwell Medallion and corporate-sponsored cash awards. Judges: A panel of specially selected judges. Entry fee $12 for each story submitted. Guidelines available for SASE. Deadline: September. Published submissions.

N **JACK DYER FICTION PRIZE, (I)**, *Crab Orchard Review*, English Dept., Southern Illinois University at Carbondale, Carbondale IL 62901-4503. (618)453-6833. Website: http://www.siu.edu/~crborchd. Award to "reward and publish exceptional fiction." Annual competition for short stories. Award: $500 and publication. Competition receives approximately 100 submissions. Judges: pre-screened by *Crab Orchard* staff; winner chosen by outside judge. Entry fee $10; year's subscription included. Guidelines available after January 1999 for SASE. Deadline March 10, 1999. Previously unpublished submissions. Word length: 6,000. "Please note that no stories will be returned." Winners announced by June 1, 1999. Winners notified by phone. List of winners available for SASE.

EATON LITERARY ASSOCIATES' LITERARY AWARDS PROGRAM, (I), Eaton Literary Associates, P.O. Box 49795, Sarasota FL 34230. (941)366-6589. Fax: (941)365-4679. E-mail: eatonlit@aol.com. Contact: Richard Lawrence, vice president. Biannual award for short stories and novels. Award: $2,500 for best book-length ms, $500 for best short story. Competition receives approx. 2,000 submissions annually. Judges are 2 staff members in conjunction with an independent agency. Entry forms or rules for SASE. Inquiries by fax and e-mail OK. Deadline: March 31 for short stories; August 31 for book-length mss. Winners announced April and September. Winners notified by mail.

ELF, ANNUAL SHORT FICTION COMPETITION, (I), *ELF: Eclectic Literary Forum*, P.O. Box 392, Tonawanda NY 14150. Phone/fax: (716)693-7006. E-mail: neubauer@buffnet.net. Website: http://www.pce.net/elf. Award for "fine writing and to encourage emerging authors." Annual competition for short stories. Editor's Awards: $500; 2 honorable mentions at $50 each. Competition receives 200 stories. Judges: editorial staff (all professors of English and published authors). Entry fee $9/story; free to subscribers. Guidelines for SASE or on website. Inquiries by fax and e-mail OK. Deadline: August 31. Unpublished submissions. Word length: 3,500 words. Winners announced in September. Winners notified by mail. List of winners available in September for SASE.

ARTHUR ELLIS AWARDS, (II, IV), Crime Writers of Canada, Box 113, 3007 Kingston Rd., Scarborough, Ontario M1M 1P1 Canada. (416)466-9826. E-mail: ap113@torfree.net.on.ca. Contact: Secretary-Treasurer. "To recognize excellence in all aspects of crime-writing." Annual competition for short stories and novels. Award: statuette (plus *maybe* cash or goods). Judges: panels of members and experts. Guidelines for SASE. Inquiries by mail or fax OK. Deadline: January 31, 1999 for published submissions that appeared in print between January 1 and December 31 of previous year. Open to Canadian residents (any citizenship) or Canadian citizens living abroad. Four complete copies of each work must be submitted. Every entry must state category entered. Categories include Best Novel, Best First Novel, Best Short Story, Best Nonfiction, Best Play and Best Juvenile. Winners announced May 1999. Winners notified by phone, mail or fax. List of winners available by phone, mail or fax after May.

N **EMERGING LESBIAN WRITERS FUND AWARDS, (II)**, Astraea National Lesbian Action Foundation, 116 E. 16th St., 7th Floor, New York NY 10003. (212)529-8021. Fax: (212)982-3321. E-mail: anlaf@aol.com. Website: http://www.astraea.org. Executive Director: Katherine Acey. Award to "recognize and encourage new/emerging writers and poets." Annual competition for fiction and poetry. Award: $10,000 (one time only grantees). Competition receives 600 submissions. Judges: Established writers/poets (2 each category). Entry fee $5. Guidelines for SASE (application form required). Deadline: March 8. Previously published submissions. U.S. residents only. Write for guidelines. "Must have at least one published work. No submissions accepted without application form." Winners announced in July. Winners notified in June by mail and phone.

☑ **EVERGREEN CHRONICLES NOVELLA CONTEST**, Evergreen Chronicles, P.O. Box 8939, Minneapolis MN 55408-0939. (612)823-6638. E-mail: evergchron@aol.com. Managing Editor: Cynthia Fogard. Award to "promote work on novellas of gay, lesbian, bisexual or transgender (GLBT) themes/content/experience." Annual competition for novellas. Award: $500/1st Prize, $100/2nd Prize. Competition receives 50 submissions per category. Judges: nationally acclaimed GLBT writers. Guidelines for SASE. Inquiries by e-mail OK. Deadline: September 30. Previously unpublished submissions. Word length: novellas with GLBT themes between 15,000-30,000 words. Winners announced in May. Winners notified by phone or mail in January. List of winners available for SASE.

EYSTER PRIZES, (II), *The New Delta Review*, LSU/Dept. of English, Baton Rouge LA 70803-5001. (504)388-4079. Contact: Editors. Award "to honor author and teacher Warren Eyster, who served as advisor to *New Delta Review* predecessors *Manchac* and *Delta*." Semiannual awards for best short story and best poem in each issue. Award: $50 and 2 free copies of publication. Competition receives 400 submissions/issue. Judges are published authors such as Jill McCorkle, Michael Martone and Robert Olen Butler. Guidelines for SASE. Deadline: September 15 for fall, February 15 for spring. Winners announced upon acceptance. Winners notified by mail. List of winners available for SASE.

N **FAMILY CIRCLE MARY HIGGINS CLARK MYSTERY/SUSPENSE SHORT-STORY CONTEST, (I)**, *Family Circle Mary Higgins Clark Mystery Magazines*, P.O. Box 4948, Grand Central Station, New York NY 10163. Award to "recognize and reward mastery of the short-story form by writers whose fiction has never appeared in a major publication." Annual competition for short stories. Award: $1,000 and publication (1st Prize); $500 (2nd Prize). Judges: panel of consulting editors appointed by *Family Circle*; winner chosen by Mary Higgins Clark. Guidelines published in the Fall issue of *Mary Higgins Clark Mystery Magazine*. Previously published submissions. Limited to mystery/suspense stories. Word length: 3,500 or less. Winners announced by July. Winners notified by phone.

VIRGINIA FAULKNER AWARD FOR EXCELLENCE IN WRITING, (II), Prairie Schooner, 201 Andrews Hall, University of Nebraska, Lincoln NE 68588-0334. (402)472-0911. Fax: (402)472-9771. E-mail: lrandolp@unlinfo.unl.edu. Website: http://www.unl.edu/schooner/psmaun.htm. Contact: Hilda Raz, editor. "An award for writing published in *Prairie Schooner* in the previous year." Annual competition for short stories, novel excerpts and translations. Award: $1,000. Judges: Editorial Board. Guidelines for SASE. Inquiries by fax and e-mail OK. "We only read mss from September through May." Work must have been published in *Prairie Schooner* in the previous year. Winners will be notified by mail. List of winners will be published in spring *Prairie Schooner*.

☑ **WILLIAM FAULKNER COMPETITION IN FICTION, (I)**, The Pirate's Alley Faulkner Society Inc., 632 Pirate's Alley, New Orleans LA 70116-3254. (504)586-1612. Fax: (504)522-9725. Contest Director: R. James. "To encourage publisher interest in writers with potential." Annual competition for short stories, novels, novellas, personal essays and poetry. Award: $7,500 for novel, $2,500 for novella, $1,500 for short story, $1,000 personal essay, $750 poetry and gold medals, plus trip to New Orleans for presentation. Competition receives 200-300 submissions per category. Judges: professional writers, academics. Entry fee $25 for each poem, essay, short story; $30 for novella; $35 for novel. Guidelines for SASE. Inquiries by fax OK but guidelines won't be faxed. Deadline: April 15. Unpublished submissions. Word length: for novels, over 50,000; for novellas, under 50,000; for short stories, under 20,000. All entries must be accompanied by official entry form which is provided with guidelines. Winners announced in September. Winners notified by telephone. List of winners available in October for SASE.

☑ **FEMINIST WRITERS GUILD LITERARY ANTHOLOGY/CONTEST, (I)**, Outrider Press, 937 Patricia Lane, Crete IL 60417. (708)672-6630. Contact: Whitney Scott, Senior Editor. Competition to collect diverse writings by feminists of all ages, genders and orientations on the theme of "Animal Stories: Feathers, Fins & Fur." Open to poetry, short stories and creative nonfiction. Award: publication in anthology; free copy to all published contributors. $150 to the best in each category; $25 for the best submission by an FWG member. Competition receives 250-275 submissions. Judges: independent panel. Entry fee $16; $12 for members. Guidelines and entry form available for SASE. Inquiries by e-mail OK. Deadline: December 31. Unpublished and published submissions. Word length: 1,750 words or less. Maximum 2 entries per person. Include SASE. Winners announced in April. List of winners available for SASE.

DOROTHY CANFIELD FISHER AWARD, (III), Vermont Dept. of Libraries, 109 State St., Montpelier VT 05609-0601. (802)828-3261. Fax: (802)828-2199. E-mail: ggreene@dol.state.vt.us. Website: http://www.dol.state.vt.us. Contact: Grace Greene, Children's Services Consultant. Estab. 1957. Annual award. "To encourage Vermont schoolchildren to become enthusiastic and discriminating readers and to honor the memory of one of Vermont's most distinguished and beloved literary figures." Award: Illuminated scroll. Publishers send the committee review copies of books to consider. Only books of the current publishing year can be considered for next year's award. Master list of titles is drawn up in March each year. Children vote each year in the spring and the award is given before the school year ends. Submissions must be "written by living American authors, be suitable for children in grades 4-8, and have literary merit. Can be nonfiction also." Inquiries by e-mail OK. Deadline: December 31. Winners announced in March. Call, write or e-mail for list of winners.

THE FLORIDA REVIEW EDITORS' AWARDS, (I), *The Florida Review*, Department of English, UCF, Orlando FL 32816. (407)823-2038. Fax: (407)823-6582. Editor: Russell Kesler. Annual competition for short stories, essays, creative nonfiction, poetry. Awards: $500 for each category and publication in summer issue. Competition receives more than 350 submissions. Judges: *The Florida Review* editorial staff. Entry fee $10 for each entry. Guidelines for SASE after January 1, 1998. Deadline: entries are accepted January through March only. Unpublished submissions. Word length: 7,500 words/prose; grouping of 3-5 poems up to 25 lines maximum. "All submissions must contain a SASE if the contest entrant wants to know the outcome of the Editors' Awards."

FLORIDA STATE WRITING COMPETITION, (I), Florida Freelance Writers Association, P.O. Box A, North Stratford NH 03590-0167. (603)922-8338. Fax: (603)922-8339. E-mail: danakcnw@moose.ncia.net. Executive Director: Dana K. Cassell. "To offer additional opportunities for writers to earn income and recognition from their writing efforts." Annual competition for short stories and novels. Award: varies from $75-125. Competition receives approximately 100 short stories; 50 novels. Judges: authors, editors and teachers. Entry fee from $5-20. Guidelines for SASE. Deadline: March 15. Unpublished submissions. Categories include literary, genre, short short and novel chapter. "Guidelines are revised each year and subject to change. New guidelines are available in fall of each year." Inquiries by fax and e-mail OK. Winners announced May 31. Winners notified by mail. List of winners available for SASE marked Winners.

FOUNDATION FOR THE ADVANCEMENT OF CANADIAN LETTERS CANADIAN LETTERS AWARD, (II, IV), In conjunction with Periodical Marketers of Canada (PMC), South Tower, 175 Bloor St., E., Suite 1007, Toronto, Ontario M4W 3R8 Canada. (416)968-7218. Fax: (416)968-6182. E-mail: pwna@periodical.org. Website: http://www.periodical.org. Award Coordinator: Janette Hatcher. "To recognize a Canadian individual who has made an outstanding contribution to writing, publishing, teaching or literary administration." Award: a statuette and a $5,000 donation to the charitable literary organization or educational institution of the winner's choice. Recipient is selected from an independent panel of judges. There is no call for entries. Inquiries by e-mail OK. Winners announced in November. List of winners available for SASE.

H.E. FRANCIS SHORT STORY AWARD, (I), Ruth Hindman Foundation, 2007 Gallatin St., Huntsville AL 35801. (256)533-6892. Fax: (256)533-6893. E-mail: maryh71997@aol.com. Chairperson: Patricia Sammon. Annual short story competition to honor H.E. Francis, retired professor of English at the University of Alabama in Huntsville. Award: $1,000. Competition receives approximately 500 submissions. Judges: distinguished writers. Entry fee. Guidelines for SASE. Deadline: December 31. Unpublished submissions. Winners announced March. Winners notified by telephone. List of winners available for SASE.

THE JOSETTE FRANK AWARD, (III, IV), (formerly Children's Book Committee Award), Children's Book Committee at Bank St. College, 610 W. 112th St., New York NY 10025. (212)875-4540. Fax: (212)875-4759. Website: http://www.bnkst.edu/bookcommittee/booklist.html. Contact: Alice B. Belgray, committee chair. Annual award. "To honor a book for children or young people which deals realistically with problems in their world. It may concern social, individual and ethical problems." Only books sent by publishers for review are considered. Books must have been published within current calendar year. Award: Certificate and cash prize. Competition receives approximately 2,000 submissions. Inquiries by e-mail and fax OK. Winners announced in March. Winners notified through their publishers and by mail.

SOUERETTE DIEHL FRASER AWARD, (II, IV), The Texas Institute of Letters, TCU Box 298300, Fort Worth TX 76129. (817)257-7822. Fax: (817)257-5075. E-mail: j.alter@tcu.edu. Website: http://www.prs.tcu.edu/prs/til/. Secretary: Judy Alter. "To recognize the best literary translation of a book into English, the translation published between January 1 and December 30 of the year prior to the award's announcement in the spring." Annual competition for translations. Award: $1,000. Judges: committee of three. Guidelines available in July for SASE mailed to Box 39800, Fort Worth TX 76129. Deadline: January 4. "Award available to translators who were born in Texas or who have lived in the state at some time for two consecutive years." Winners announced in April. Winners notified by phone or mail.

FRENCH BREAD AWARDS, *Pacific Coast Journal*, P.O. Box 23868, San Jose CA 95153. Contact: Stillson Graham, editor. Award with the goal of "finding the best fiction and poetry out there." Annual competition for short stories and poetry. Award: $50 (1st Prize), $25 (2nd Prize). Competition receives approximately 50 submissions. Judges: Editorial staff of *Pacific Coast Journal*. Entry fee $6. Guidelines for SASE. Deadline: August 1. Unpublished submissions. Length: 4,000 words. "Manuscripts will not be returned. Send SASE for winners' list. All entrants will receive issue in which first place winners are published."

✓ ***GEORGETOWN REVIEW* SHORT STORY AND POETRY CONTEST, (I)**, Georgetown Review, P.O. Box 6309 SS, Hattiesburg MS 39406-6309. (601)528-8677. E-mail: gr@georgetownreview.com. Website: http://www.georgetownreview.com. Managing Editor: Steve Conti. Award "to reward excellent fiction." Annual competition for short stories. Award: $1000 to the winning story. Runner-up stories receive publication and authors receive free subscription. Competition receives approximately 450 submissions. Judges: *GR* editors. Entry fee $10/story. Guidelines for SASE after October 15. Send SASE for info about Poetry Prize. Deadline: October 1. Unpublished submissions. Word length: 6,500 words. "Must include SASE for return of work." Winners announced in January. Winners notified by telephone. List of winners available for SASE.

N **GEORGIA STATEWIDE WRITING COMPETITIONS, (I)**, Humpus Bumpus, P.O. Box 1303, Roswell GA 30077-1303. Fax: (770)781-4676. E-mail: paulcossman@mindspring.com. Website: http://www.humpusbumpus.com. Contact: Paul A. Cossman. Award to "identify and publish new Georgia writers for the first time in order to help them launch their writing careers." Annual competitions for adults and students (K-12th grade). Award: cash and publication in trade paperback book sold at Humpus Bumpus Books and Atlanta area Barnes & Noble stores. Entry fee: $10. Guidelines available on website.

***GLIMMER TRAIN*'S FALL SHORT-STORY AWARD FOR NEW WRITERS, (I)**, Glimmer Train Press, Inc., 710 SW Madison St., Suite 504, Portland OR 97205-2900. (503)221-0836. Fax: (503)221-0837. Contest Director: Linda Burmeister Davies. Contest offered for any writer whose fiction hasn't appeared in a nationally-distributed publication with a circulation over 5,000. "Send original, unpublished short (1,200-8,000 words) story with $12 reading fee for each story entered. Guidelines available for SASE. Inquiries by fax OK. Must be postmarked between August 1 and September 30. Title page must include name, address, phone and Short Story Award for New Writers must be written on outside of envelope. No need for SASE as materials will not be returned. Notification on January 2. Winner receives $1,200 and publication in *Glimmer Train Stories*. First/second runners-up receive $500/$300, respectively, and consideration for publication. All applicants receive a copy of the issue in which winning entry is published and runners-up announced."

N ***GLIMMER TRAIN*'S FICTION OPEN, (I)**, Glimmer Train Press, Inc., 710 SW Madison St., Suite 504, Portland OR 97205-2900. (503)221-0836. Fax: (503)221-0837. Website: http://www.glimmertrain.com. Contest Director: Linda Burmeister Davies. Contest for short story, open to all writers. Award: First place $2,000, publication in *Glimmer Train Stories* (circ. 13,000) and 20 copies of that issue. First/second runners-up receive $1,000/$600 respectively and consideration for publication. Reading fee $15. Guidelines for SASE. Must be postmarked between May 1 and June 30. Unpublished submissions. No theme or word-count limitations. Winners will be called by October 15. List of winners available for SASE with story.

***GLIMMER TRAIN*'S SPRING SHORT-STORY AWARD FOR NEW WRITERS, (I)**, Glimmer Train Press, Inc., 710 SW Madison St., Suite 504, Portland OR 97205-2900. (503)221-0836. Fax: (503)221-0837. Contest Director: Linda Burmeister Davies. Contest offered for any writer whose fiction hasn't appeared in a nationally-distributed publication with a circulation over 5,000. "Send original, unpublished short (1,200-8,000 words) story with $12 reading fee for each story entered. Guidelines available for SASE. Inquiries by fax OK. Must be postmarked between February 1 and March 31. Title page must include name, address, phone and Short Story Award for New Writers must be written on outside of envelope. No need for SASE as materials will not be returned. Notification on July 1. Winner receives $1,200 and publication in *Glimmer Train Stories*. First/second runners-up receive $500/$300, respectively, and consideration for publication. All applicants receive a copy of the issue in which winning entry is published and runners-up announced."

N **GOVERNMENT OF NEWFOUNDLAND AND LABRADOR ARTS AND LETTERS COMPETITION (I, IV)**, Government of Newfoundland and Labrador Dept. of Tourism and Culture, P.O. Box 1854, St. John's, Newfoundland A1C 5P9 Canada. (709)729-5253. Fax: (709)729-5952. Secretary: Regina Best. Award "to encourage the creative talent of people of the Province of Newfoundland and Labrador." Annual competition for arts and letters. Award: $600 (1st Prize), $300 (2nd Prize), $150 (3rd Prize). Competition receives approx. 1,000 submissions. Judges: Blind judging by outside people who are professionals in their field. Guidelines for SASE. Unpublished submissions. Competition is only open to residents of this province. "There are two divisions in this competition: Junior (12-18 years) and Senior (19-on). Each entry receives a written adjudication. There are prizes in several categories; fiction; nonfiction; poetry; dramatic script; painting and 3-D art; drawing and print-making; photography; musical composition. Applications and rules and regulations for entering are available at the above address."

N **GREAT LAKES BOOK AWARDS, (III, IV)**, Great Lakes Booksellers Awards, 509 Lafayette St., Grand Haven MI 49417. (616)847-2460. Fax: (616)842-0051. Award to "recognize and reward excellence in the writing

INSIDER REPORT

Glimmer Train: looking for stories "worth finding a home for"

Susan Burmeister-Brown & Linda Burmeister Davies

The publishing background of Linda Burmeister Davies and Susan Burmeister-Brown, co-editors of *Glimmer Train Stories*, is not what you'd expect. "We didn't come to *Glimmer Train* from the publishing world at all," says Davies. "We were just avid readers with a lot of fondness for people who write." So what prompted the creation? "We're a couple of sisters who wanted to create a short story magazine that we would personally love to find in our mailbox every quarter," says Davies. In 1990 *Glimmer Train* was born.

Davies believes this atypical approach probably helped shape *Glimmer Train* into such a unique publication. She points out, "Although we publish great short fiction, we also really spotlight and honor the writer." Each 160-page issue features two interviews with writers and six short stories. Each piece is prefaced by an author profile and childhood photograph, which demonstrate of *Glimmer Train*'s dedication to the authors themselves.

This dedication prompted *Glimmer Train* to expand in new directions. Although the magazine is not heavily staffed—Davies and Brown have a very small office and can just squeeze in with their desks—these dedicated partners manage not only the magazine but also three contests. The Short-Story Award for New Writers became part of the *Glimmer Train* family in 1994. This contest, held in the spring and fall, is open to writers whose work has not appeared in a nationally distributed publication with a circulation over 5,000. The Very Short Fiction Award, established in 1997, is held in the winter and summer and welcomes submissions from both published and unpublished writers. A new contest, the Fiction Open, was added just this year and is open to all writers and all story lengths. "The contests really seem to encourage people to write and submit their work," says Davies. "The New Writer Award in particular nudges people who have been wanting to share their stories but who have hesitated to do so." She also stresses that contest deadlines give writers the extra motivation they might need to take those necessary steps toward publication.

Each contest receives an average of 600 entries from writers hoping their hard work will be rewarded. First prize for the Short-Story Award for New Writers and the Very Short Fiction Award is $1,200 and publication in *Glimmer Train*; second and third prizes are $500 and $300. The Fiction Open boasts a first prize of $2,000 and publication, and second and third prizes of $1,000 and $600.

But money is not the only reason writers should enter contests. "Once you send your work out into the world, you make room for new stories to emerge," says Davies. This creative uncluttering is fortunate since most of *Glimmer Train*'s contest winners go on to publish in other journals. "There's nothing quite like being published in a high quality,

INSIDER REPORT, *Davies*

high profile journal to boost a writer's confidence in terms of both writing and submitting their work, and also to give writers the exposure they need," Davies says. "Agents read *Glimmer Train*, big novel publishers read it, and even the people who turn good stories into movies read it."

Glimmer Train's standards for fiction are high, and the selection process begins with a small handful of people who eliminate a third of the stories in the first cut. Some standard flaws that cause a story to be passed over include clichés, stereotypes, unbelievable dialogue, endless details that don't forward the story, and the sense that "the writer feels like they've done a clever thing." Davies also warns, "Writers should be careful not to use a bunch of 'precious words.' We very much appreciate people who have a powerful use of the language, but sometimes you know somebody's been saving up a special set of words for a long time, but those words do not forward the story. I think it was Hemingway who said, 'You must kill your darlings.' "

Technicalities also make a difference. Davies points out that one of the most common mistakes writers make is forgetting to update their address on all parts of the submission—the envelope, entry fee and story. Little things do matter, and a correctly assembled submission makes a good first impression.

The slush pile can be daunting to editors, but there are some elements, such as complexity and depth, that make any good story rise above the rest. "After reading a couple of paragraphs, we should not be able to predict a character's every response," says Davies. The editors look for material that is tightly written, clear and not "fluffy." They look for characters with whom they can sympathize and empathize, material that is emotionally moving, and an important change that "needn't be loud."

"The best short stories are the ones that stick with us, that affect our consciousness and life in some way," explains Davies. "Many strong stories are about how people choose to cope with conflict, loss and adversity. If I'm able to identify with something or someone I could not previously identify with, I may become more tolerant, I may see something more clearly, I may recognize the complexity of something I thought was simple, and I might even acquire a new coping skill. I want to read material that will give me opportunities to become a bigger person."

Christine Byl, a winner of *Glimmer Train*'s New Writer Award in 1998, found the perfect combination of these elements in her story "Bloom." "She had so much character insight," says Burmeister-Brown. "She had really a glowing use of language." (See the Insider Report with Byl also in this section).

Since even the best short story is not suitable for every literary magazine, Davies advises that the best thing for writers to do is spend some time in a library or bookstore, study all the publications there, and see where their story would be most at home. "More people who are aspiring to be published writers are realizing that they really must read, and they're making the time to do that," she says. "That in turn supports literary publications, and the more publications that survive, the more places there are to send your work. Writers and publishers need each other."

This optimism, as well as the opportunities offered by *Glimmer Train*'s contests, should be encouraging to new and established writers alike. "If there was one message we could give to writers, it would be to keep on sending their work out," says Burmeister-Brown. "It helps keep the stories coming. It takes a lot of persistence, but [fine] stories are worth finding a home for."

—Margo Orlando

INSIDER REPORT

What Christine Byl can't *not* do

Christine Byl

"Don't write unless you can't *not* write," scholar Elie Wiesel once instructed writers. Christine Byl, winner of *Glimmer Train*'s Short-Story Award for New Writers in 1998, has no problem with that. "Everybody has something they can't *not* do, and you should figure out what it is," Byl says. "If it's not writing, that's fine; if it is writing, that's great. It may be opera, or carpentry, or baseball. But whatever it is that you can't not do, do it honestly."

Byl has been writing honestly since high school, where she first began paying attention to the details of craft. But unlike many young writers, Byl's writing training did not take place primarily in the classroom. She majored in English and philosophy at Calvin College in Grand Rapids, Michigan, and although she had many teachers who encouraged her "scribbling," she took no writing classes. However, the best version of "Bloom," Byl's winning story, came from a class she took with writer Bill Kittredge two years ago.

"It was a horrible first draft," says Byl of the story. "It was totally ridiculous. It was the wrong tense, it was the wrong tone, the narrator was nauseatingly clever. There was a lot of good material, but it was a very bad draft." After two years of occasionally revisiting the story, Byl found the problem—"The key was definitely getting the first-person narration right." Then, eventually, she got the courage to send "Bloom" into the world.

Byl, who admits there was "always an easy excuse" for not submitting her work, hadn't intended to enter the contest. She was beginning to submit to journals for the first time, following a friend's suggestion to choose 50 journals, tier them in groups of 10, and submit 10 manuscripts at a time until she'd gotten through all 50. "I decided I would burn the story if it was rejected from all 50 places," Byl says.

She didn't have to worry. *Glimmer Train* was included in the top group of journals, and Byl sent the story as a regular submission. When she realized that "Bloom" fit the contest's guidelines, she sent in her entry fee. "It was such a strange feeling," Byl says of winning. "Really bizarre. I still feel a little bit like the emperor with the new clothes, like I'm really a fraud but no one's noticed yet." But she also says winning has made her feel validated and more confident, tempering some of the insecurity that had made her reluctant to submit her stories.

Though she may have been reluctant to submit her work, Byl has never been reluctant to write. Interviews, nonfiction and personal essay are among her writing interests, and although several of her nonfiction pieces have been published, fiction is Byl's first love. "Fiction can contain both nonfiction and poetry," she says. "I think fiction's a lot of fun; I love making stuff up and still having it be true." Her story ideas come from a variety of sources. "I really operate phonetically a lot of the time," she says. "A phrase—and

INSIDER REPORT, *Byl*

this is the poetry part of fiction for me—just occurs to me, or a way of articulating something I have experienced. A lot of times a story will begin from that kind of experience, just a flash, not even an image. It may be just a group of words that sound great together."

Although she is dedicated to her craft, Byl does not have a fixed writing schedule. In fact, much of her writing takes place away from the computer, partly because she spends her summers working trails in the back country of Glacier National Park in northern Montana. She explains: "I think about plots when I'm hiking, I talk dialogue out loud when I'm alone, I watch people all the time, and a lot of that I consider my prewriting. By the time I sit down, I've done drafts and drafts and drafts in my head." There are some months, however, when she writes every day if time allows, and freewriting in her journal always plays a role in a project's development.

However, when Kittredge cautioned his students not to write too much, Byl listened. "Do other stuff," she says. "Climb trees, talk to kids, run a marathon, plant a garden. If writing is your whole life, your life will be boring, and your writing will be boring, too. Don't get so bogged down in being a writer that all you're doing is writing." Byl admits she reads "almost addictively, everything from Cheerios boxes to old *Time* magazines to the Russian masters," and her favorite writers include Wendell Berry, James Galvin, Wallace Stegner and Flannery O'Connor. When she's not reading, Byl enjoys rock climbing, live music and being outdoors.

Winning the *Glimmer Train* award has made Byl optimistic but practical about her next steps. "It's great to be able to say something in my cover letter besides 'I've never been published before,' " she says, and she defines herself as a writer when people ask her what she does away from the trails. Her current projects include a novel ("But it's probably working on me more than I'm working on it," she says) and several short stories, as well as ideas for a family memoir. "All those things are percolating," she says. "We'll have to see what comes of them."

Byl's success has not led her to treat writing casually, and she still struggles to balance the love/hate relationship that accompanies any art form. "A good part of the time writing is fun—it makes me feel alive and vibrating," she says. "But sometimes I hate it; I wish I didn't have to write, I wish these crazy characters would leave me alone. Then I feel wired and trapped and kind of nuts. You have to get past the intense highs and lows to just keep on doing it." But Byl knows firsthand that the rewards of writing are definitely within reach and worth the effort.

—Margo Orlando

and publishing of books that capture the spirit and enhance awareness of the region." Annual competition for fiction, children's and nonfiction. Award: $500 plus bookstore promotion. Competition receives approximately 40 submissions. Five judges each category. No entry fee. Guidelines available. Deadline June 30, 1999. Writer must be nominated by members of the GLBA. Winners announced September 1999.

☑ **GREAT LAKES COLLEGES ASSOCIATION NEW WRITERS AWARD**, Great Lakes Colleges Association Inc., 535 W. William, Suite 301, Ann Arbor MI 48103. (734)761-4833. Fax: (734)761-3939. E-mail: clark@philactr.edu. Director of New Writers Award: Mark Andrew Clark. Annual award. Winners are invited to tour the GLCA colleges. An honorarium of at least $300 will be guaranteed the author by each of the GLCA colleges they visit. Receives 30-40 entries in each category annually. Judges: Professors from member colleges. No entry fee. Guidelines available after August 1. Inquiries by fax and e-mail OK. Deadline: February 28. Unpublished submissions. First publication in fiction or poetry. Writer must be nominated by publisher. Four copies of the book should be sent to: Mark Andrew Clark, Director, New Writers Award, Philadelphia Center, North American Bldg., 121 South Broad St., Seventh Floor, Philadelphia PA 19107. Winners announced in May. Letters go to publishers who have submitted.

GREAT PLAINS STORYTELLING & POETRY READING CONTEST, (I,II), P.O. Box 438, Walnut IA 51577. (712)784-3001. Director: Robert Everhart. Estab. 1976. Annual award "to provide an outlet for writers to present not only their works but also to provide a large audience for their presentation *live* by the writer. Attendance at the event, which takes place annually in Avoca, Iowa, is *required*." Award: 1st Prize $75; 2nd Prize $50; 3rd Prize $25; 4th Prize $15; and 5th Prize $10. Entry fee: $5. Entry forms available at contest only. Deadline is day of contest, which takes place over Labor Day Weekend. Previously published or unpublished submissions.

✓ **GREEN RIVER WRITERS CONTEST, (I, II)**, Green River Writers, % Sandra Brue, P.O. Box 336, Van Buren MO 63965. (573)323-4259. E-mail: sandy-brue@nps.gov. Contact: Sandra Brue, contest director. Annual competition for short stories and novels. Award: for short stories up to 2,000 words, $150; 2,000-3,000 words $150, first chapter of novel, $50. Competition receives 400 submissions. Judges are appointed by sponsors. Entry fee $5 each, $25 total. Guidelines available after March 1 for SASE. Inquiries by e-mail OK. Deadline: October 31. Unpublished submissions. Word length: up to 3,000 words, depends on category. Winners announced in January. Winners notified by mail. List of winners available January for SASE.

✓ ***THE GREENSBORO REVIEW* LITERARY AWARDS, (I)**, English Dept., 134 McIver Bldg, UNC-Greensboro, P.O. Box 26170, Greensboro NC 27402-6170. (336)334-5459. E-mail: clarkj@fagan.uncg.edu. Website: http://www.uncg.edu/eng/mfa. Editor: Jim Clark. Annual award. Award: $250. Competition receives 1,000 submissions. Guidelines for SASE. Inquiries by fax or e-mail OK. Deadline: September 15. Unpublished submissions. "All manuscripts meeting literary award guidelines will be considered for cash award as well as for publication in *The Greensboro Review*." Winners announced in December. Winners notified by mail by December. List of winners published in the Winter issue of *The Greensboro Review*.

✓ **HACKNEY LITERARY AWARDS, (I)**, Box 549003, Birmingham Southern College, Birmingham AL 35254. (205)226-4921. Fax: (205)226-4931. E-mail: dwilson@bsc.edu. Website: http://www.bsc.edu. Contact: Dr. Myra Crawford, Hackney award chairman. Annual award for previously unpublished short stories, poetry and novels. Award: $5,000 (novel); $5,000 (poetry and short stories; 6 prizes). Competition receives approx. 500 submissions. Award chairman appoints judges and supervises the competition. Entry fee: $25 novel; $10 poetry and short story. Rules/entry form for SASE. Inquiries by fax and e-mail OK. Novel submissions must be postmarked on or before September 30. Short stories and poetry submissions must be postmarked on or before December 31. Winners announced at Writing Today Writers' Conference March 13, 1999. List of winners available by phone or for SASE, March 22.

N **THE HEARTLAND PRIZES, (III)**, *The Chicago Tribune*, 435 N. Michigan Ave., Chicago IL 60611-4041. "The Heartland Prizes are for nonfiction and the novel. To honor a novel and a book of nonfiction embodying the spirit of the nation's Heartland." Annual award for novels. Award: $5,000. Winners are notified in August. Submissions by publishers.

✓ **LORIAN HEMINGWAY SHORT STORY COMPETITION, (I)**, P.O. Box 993, Key West FL 33041-0993. (305)294-0320. Fax: (305)292-3653. E-mail: calico2419@aol.com. Website: http://www.hemingwaydays.com. Contact: Carol Shaughnessy, co-director. Award to "encourage literary excellence and the efforts of writers who have not yet had major-market success." Annual competition for short stories. Awards: $1,000 1st Prize; $500 2nd Prize; $500 3rd Prize; up to 10 honorable mentions. Competition receives 850 submissions. Judges: A panel of writers, editors and literary scholars selected by novelist Lorian Hemingway. Entry fee $10 for each story postmarked by June 1, 1999; $15 for each story postmarked between June 1 and June 15, 1999. Guidelines for SASE after February 1. Inquiries by fax and e-mail OK. Deadline: June 1, 1999 and June 15, 1999. Unpublished submissions. "Open to all writers whose fiction has not appeared in a nationally distributed publication with a circulation of 5,000 or more." Word length: 3,000 words maximum. "We look for excellence, pure and simple—no genre restrictions, no theme restrictions—we seek a writer's voice that cannot be ignored." Winners announced before August 1. Winners notified by phone. "All entrants will receive a letter from Lorian Hemingway and a list of winners by October 1."

✓ ***HIGHLIGHTS FOR CHILDREN*, (I, IV)**, 803 Church St., Honesdale PA 18431. (717)253-1080. Manuscript Coordinator: Beth Troop. Award "to honor quality stories (previously unpublished) for young readers." Three $1,000 awards. Competition receives 2,000 submissions. Judges: *Highlights* editors. Stories: up to 500 words for beginning readers (to age 8) and 900 words for more advanced readers (ages 9 to 12). No minimum word length. No entry form necessary. Guidelines for SASE. To be submitted between January 1 and February 28 to "Fiction Contest" at address above. "No violence, crime or derogatory humor. Obtain a copy of the guidelines, since the theme changes each year." Nonwinning entries returned in June if SASE is included with ms. Winners announced in June. Winners notified by phone or letter. List of winners will be sent with returned mss.

THEODORE CHRISTIAN HOEPFNER AWARD, (I), *Southern Humanities Review*, 9088 Haley Center, Auburn University AL 36849. Co-editors: Dan R. Latimer or Virginia M. Kouidis. Annual award "to award the authors of the best essay, the best short story and the best poem published in *SHR* each year." Award: $100 for the best short story. Judges: Editorial staff. Only published work in the current volume (4 issues) will be judged.

N **ZORA NEALE HURSTON/RICHARD WRIGHT AWARD, (I, IV)**, Zora Neale Hurston/Richard Wright Foundation, English Dept., Virginia Commonwealth University, Richmond VA 23284-8005. (804)225-4729. Fax: (804)828-2171. E-mail: rdunn@vcu.edu. Website: http://www.has.vcu.edu/eng/znh. Workshop Director: Robin Dunn. "Awards best fiction written by African-American college students enrolled full-time in a U.S. college or university." Annual award for short stories and novels. Award: $1,000 (1st Place); $500 (2nd Place); $250 (3rd Place); $250 (4th Place). Competition receives 50-75 submissions. Judges: published writers. Guidelines available in September for SASE. Deadline December 7. Unpublished submissions. Word length: 25 pages maximum. Winners announced in March. Winners notified by mail. List of winners available in February.

N **INDIANA REVIEW FICTION PRIZE, (I)**, *Indiana Review*, Ballantine Hall 465, Indiana University, Bloomington IN 47405. Website: http://www.indiana.edu/~inreview. Annual contest for fiction in any style and on any subject. Award: $300, publication in Spring issue of *Indiana Review* and contributor's copies (1st Place); publication (one honorable mention). Each entrant will receive a 1-year subscription to *Indiana Review*. Final judging by editorial staff of *Indiana Review*. Guidelines for SASE. No previously published works, or works forthcoming elsewhere, are eligible. Simultaneous submissions acceptable, but in event of entrant withdraw, contest fee will not be refunded. Length: 25 pages maximum, double spaced. List of winners for SASE.

INDIVIDUAL ARTIST FELLOWSHIP, Nebraska Arts Council, 3838 Davenport, Omaha NE 68131-2329. (402)421-3627. Program Manager: Suzanne Wise. Award to "recognize outstanding achievement by Nebraska writers." Competition every third year for short stories and novels. Award: $5,000 Distinguished Achievement; $1,000-2,000 Merit Awards. Competition receives 70-80 submissions per category. Judges: panel of 3. Deadline: November 15, 2000. Published or previously unpublished submissions. Nebraska residents only. Word length: 50 pages.

✓ **INDIVIDUAL ARTIST FELLOWSHIPS**, Maine Arts Commission, 25 State Horse Station, Augusta ME 04333-0025. (207)287-2750. Fax: (207)287-2335. E-mail: kathy.jones@state.me.us. Website: http://www.mainearts.com. Associate for Contemporary Arts: Kathy Ann Jones. Unrestricted funds ($3,000) awarded for artistic excellence. Biannual competition for short stories, novels and poetry. Award: $3,000. Competition receives 80-100 submissions per category. Judges: a jury of experts is selected each time. Guidelines available September 1. Inquiries by fax and e-mail OK. Deadline: February 2, 1999 and every other year. Published or previously unpublished submissions. Artists must be Maine residents. Word length: fiction or creative nonfiction (maximum 20 pages of prose). Winners announced in June. Winners notified by phone, followed by mail. List of winners available in June for SASE.

✓ **IOWA SCHOOL OF LETTERS AWARD FOR SHORT FICTION, THE JOHN SIMMONS SHORT FICTION AWARD, (I)**, Iowa Writers' Workshop, 102 Dey House, 507 N. Clinton St., Iowa City IA 52242-1000. Annual awards for short story collections. To encourage writers of short fiction. Award: publication of winning collections by University of Iowa Press the following fall. Entries must be at least 150 pages, typewritten, and submitted between August 1 and September 30. Stamped, self-addressed return packaging must accompany manuscript. Rules for SASE. Iowa Writer's Workshop does initial screening of entries; finalists (about 6) sent to outside judge for final selection. "A different well-known writer is chosen each year as judge. Any writer who has not previously published a volume of prose fiction is eligible to enter the competition for these prizes. Revised manuscripts which have been previously entered may be resubmitted."

JOSEPH HENRY JACKSON AWARD, (I, IV), Intersection for the Arts/The San Francisco Foundation, 446 Valencia St., San Francisco CA 94103. (415)626-2787. Fax: (415)626-1636. E-mail: intrsect@wenet.net. Website: http://www.wenet.net/~intrsect. Literary Program Director: Charles Wilmoth. Award "to encourage young, unpublished writers." Annual award for short stories, novels and story collections. Award: $2,000. Competition receives approximately 100 submissions. Entry form and rules available in mid-October for SASE. Inquiries by fax OK. Deadline: January 31. Unpublished submissions only. Applicant must be resident of northern California or Nevada for 3 consecutive years immediately prior to the deadline date. Age of applicant must be 20 through

35. Work cannot exceed 100 double-spaced, typed pages. "Submit a serious, ambitious portion of a book-length manuscript." Winners announced June 15. Winners notified by mail. "Winners will be announced in letter mailed to all applicants."

☑ **JAMES FELLOWSHIP FOR THE NOVEL IN PROGRESS, (I)**, The Heekin Group Foundation, P.O. Box 1534, Sisters OR 97759. Phone/fax: (541)548-4147. E-mail: hgfh1@aol.com. Fiction Director: Sarah Heekin Redfield. Award to "support unpublished writers in their writing projects." Two annual awards for novels in progress. Awards: $3,000. Receives approximately 500 applications. Judges: Invitation of publisher: past judges, Graywolf Press, SOHO Press, Dalkey Archive Press, The Ecco Press, Milkweed Editions. Upcoming judge: Four Walls Eight Windows. Application fee $25. Guidelines for SASE. Deadline: December 1. Unpublished submissions. Word length: Submit first 50-75 pages only.

JAPAN FOUNDATION ARTISTS FELLOWSHIP PROGRAM, (IV), 152 W. 57th St., 39th Floor, New York NY 10019. (212)489-0299. Fax: (212)489-0409. E-mail: chris_watanabe@jfny.org. Website: http://www.jfny.org. Program Assistant: Chris Watanabe. "This program provides artists and specialists in the arts with the opportunity to pursue creative projects in Japan and to meet and consult with their Japanese counterparts." Annual competition. Several artists fellowships from two to six months' duration during the 1998 Japanese fiscal year (April 1-March 31) are available to artists, such as writers, musicians, painters, sculptors, stage artists, movie directors, etc.; and specialists in the arts, such as scenario writers, curators, etc. Benefits include transportation to and from Japan; settling-in, research, activities and other allowances and a monthly stipend. See brochure for more details. Competition receives approximately 30-40 submissions. Judges: Foundation staff in Japan. Guidelines available after August. Inquiries by fax and e-mail OK. Deadline: December 1. "Work should be related to Japan. Applicants must be accredited artists or specialists. Affiliation with a Japanese artist or institution is required. Three letters of reference, including one from the Japanese affiliate must accompany all applications. Winners announced April 1999. Winners notified by mail. List of winners available by phone.

☑ ***JAPANOPHILE* SHORT STORY CONTEST, (I, II, IV)**, *Japanophile*, P.O. Box 7977, Ann Arbor MI 48107-7977. (734)930-1553. Fax: (734)930-9968. E-mail: jpnhand@japanophile.com. Website: http://www.japanophile.com. Editor: Susan Aitken Lapp. Estab. 1974. Annual award "to encourage quality writing on Japan-America understanding." Award: $100 plus possible publication. Competition receives 200 submissions. Entry fee: $5. Send $4 for sample copy of magazine. Guidelines available by August for SASE, e-mail or on website. Inquiries by fax and e-mail OK. Deadline: December 31. Prefers unpublished submissions. Stories should involve Japanese and non-Japanese characters, maximum 5,000 words. Winners notified in March. Winners notified by mail. List of winners available in March for SASE.

N **JEFFERSON CUP, (III, IV)**, Virginia Library Association, P.O. Box 8277, Norfolk VA 23503-0277. (757)583-0041. Fax: (757)583-5041. Annual competition for U.S. history, historical fiction or biography for young people. Award: cup and $500. Judges: Jefferson Cup Committee. Previously published one year prior to selection. Writer must be nominated by publisher.

☑ **JESSE JONES AWARD FOR FICTION (BOOK), (II, IV)**, The Texas Institute of Letters, % TCU Press, TCU Box 298300, Fort Worth TX 76129. (817)257-7822. Awards Coordinator: Judy Alter. "To honor the writer of the best novel or collection of short fiction published during the calendar year before the award is given." Annual award for novels or story collections. Award: $6,000. Competition receives 30-40 entries per year. Judges: Panel selected by TIL Council. Guidelines available in July for SASE mailed to Box 39800, Fort Worth TX 76129. Deadline: January 4. Previously published fiction, which must have appeared in print between January 1 and December 31 of the prior year. "Award available to writers who, at some time, have lived in Texas at least two years consecutively or whose work has a significant Texas theme." Winners announced in April. Winners notified by phone or mail.

☑ **JAMES JONES FIRST NOVEL FELLOWSHIP, (I)**, James Jones Society, Wilkes University, Wilkes-Barre PA 18766. (717)408-4530. E-mail: shaffer@wilkesl.wilkes.edu. Website: http://wilkes.edu/~english/jones.html. Chair, English Department: Patricia B. Heaman. Award to "honor the spirit of unblinking honesty, determination, and insight into modern culture exemplified by the late James Jones by encouraging the work of an American writer who has not published a book-length work of fiction." Annual award for unpublished novel, novella, or collection of related short stories in progress. Award: $3,000. Receives approximately 500 applications. Application fee: $15. Guidelines for SASE. Inquiries by e-mail and fax OK. Deadline: March 1. Unpublished submissions. "Award is open to American writers." Word length: 50 opening pages and a two-page thematic outline. "Name, address, telephone number on title page only." Winners announced September 1. Winners notified by phone. List of winners available October 1 for SASE. "For more information, visit us on the Web."

N **KATHA: INDIAN AMERICAN FICTION CONTEST**, *India Currents* Magazine, P.O. Box 21285, San Jose CA 95151. (408)274-6966. Fax: (408)274-2733. Managing Editor: Vandana Kumar. Award "to encourage creative writing which has as its focus India, Indian culture, Indian-Americans and America's views of India." Annual competition for short stories. Awards: $100 (1st Prize), $75 (2nd Prize), $50 (3rd Prize), 2 honorable mentions. All entrants receive a 1-year subscription to *India Currents*. Competition received 60 submissions last year. Judges: "A distinguished panel of Indian-American authors. Reading fee $10. Guidelines for SASE. Deadline: December 31. Unpublished submissions. Length: 3,000 words maximum.

ROBERT F. KENNEDY BOOK AWARDS, (II, IV), 1367 Connecticut Ave. NW, Suite 200, Washington DC 20036. (202)463-7575. Fax: (202)463-6606. E-mail: hdunn@rfkmemorial.org. Website: http://www.rfkmemorial.org. Director of the Book Award: Holly Dunn. Endowed by Arthur Schlesinger, Jr., from proceeds of his biography, *Robert Kennedy and His Times*. Annual. "To award the author of a book which most faithfully and forcefully reflects Robert Kennedy's purposes." For books published during the calendar year. Award: $2,500 cash prize awarded in the spring. Guidelines available after Summer 1998. Inquiries by fax and e-mail OK. Deadline: January 2. Looking for "a work of literary merit in fact or fiction that shows compassion for the poor or powerless or those suffering from injustice." Four copies of each book submitted should be sent, along with a $25 entry fee. Winners announced Spring 1999. Winners notified by phone. List of winners available by phone, fax or e-mail.

N KILLER FROG CONTEST, (I, II, IV), *Scavenger's Newsletter*, 519 Ellinwood, Osage City KS 66523. (785)528-3538. E-mail: foxscav1@jc.net. Website: http://www.cza.com/scav/index.html. Contact: Janet Fox. Competition "to see who can write the funniest/most overdone horror story, or poem, or produce the most outrageous artwork on a horror theme." Annual award for short stories, poems and art. Award: $25 for each of 4 categories and "coveted froggie statuette. Four runners-up in each category will receive a year's free *Scavenger* subscription." Winners also receive complimentary copies of *The Killer Frog* Anthology. Judge: Editor of *Scavenger*, Janet Fox. Guidelines available January 1 for SASE. Guidelines will also run in February or March issue of *Scavenger's Newsletter*. Submissions must be postmarked between April 1 and July 1. Published or previously unpublished submissions. Limited to horror/humor. Length: up to 4,000 words. "Write badly, throw good taste out the window, have fun!" Winners will be announced in the September issue of *Scavenger*. List of winners available for SASE.

KOREAN LITERATURE TRANSLATION AWARD, (IV), The Korean Culture and Arts Foundation, 1-130 Dongsoong-Dong, Chongro-Ku, Seoul South Korea 110-510. Phone: 82-(0)2-760-4583. Fax: 82-(0)2-760-4588. E-mail: sgkang@caibs.kcaf.or.kr. Website: http://www.kcaf.or.kr. Contact: Kang Ssang-Gu. Biannual competition for translations (of Korean Literature). Award: $50,000 (grand prize), two work-of-merit prizes of $10,000. (If it is decided that there is no work of sufficient merit for the grand prize, the finest entry will be awarded $30,000.) Competition receives 35 submissions. Judges: Translators. Guidelines available in March or April by fax or mail. Inquiries by fax and e-mail OK. Unpublished submissions. Only translations in Korean Literature previously published. (Translators or publishers may submit their works in book.) Winners announced in August. Winners notified by telephone, fax or mail. List of winners available in August.

N LAGNIAPPE FOR LITERACY, (I), Southern Louisiana Romance Writers (a chapter of Romance Writers of America), P.O. Box 1743, Metairie LA 70004-1743. (504)283-1711. Fax: (504)282-4898. E-mail: laurajohrowland@compuserve.com. Contest Coordinator: Laura Joh Rowland. Award "to offer unpublished authors feedback from published authors; to offer unpublished authors help getting published; to raise money for YMCA Educational Services' literacy training programs." Annual award for novels. Award: Entire winning ms read by an editor attending The New Orleans Popular Fiction Conference (1st Prize); 3 chapters and synopsis of winning ms read by an attending literary agent (2nd Prize). Competition receives approximately 100 submissions. Judges: First round by 3 published authors; finalists judged by editors and agents. Entry fee $15. Guidelines for SASE. Inquiries by fax and e-mail OK. Unpublished submissions. Award available to writers 18 years of age and older from any region; any genre except short stories or children's literature. Novels only. Length: Send first 5 pages of novel. Winners announced at conference and/or by mail. List of winners available for SASE.

LAWRENCE FOUNDATION PRIZE, (I), *Michigan Quarterly Review*, 3032 Rackham Bldg., Ann Arbor MI 48109-1070. (313)764-9265. Contact: Laurence Goldstein, editor. "An annual cash prize awarded to the author of the best short story published in *Michigan Quarterly Review* each year." Annual competition for short stories. Award: $1,000. "Stories must already be published in *MQR*; this is not a competition in which manuscripts are read outside of the normal submission process."

STEPHEN LEACOCK MEDAL FOR HUMOUR, (II, IV), Stephen Leacock Associates, P.O. Box 854, Orillia, Ontario L3V 6K8 Canada. (705)325-6546. Chairman, Award Committee: Jean Dickson. Award "to encourage writing of humour by Canadians." Annual competition for short stories, novels and story collections. Award: Stephen Leacock (silver) medal for humour and Laurentian Bank of Canada cash award of $5,000 (Canadian). Competition receives 50 submissions. Five judges selected across Canada. Entry fee $25 (Canadian). Guidelines for SASE. Deadline: December 30. Submissions should have been published in book form in the previous year. Open to Canadian citizens or landed immigrants only. Winners announced by April 1. Winners notified via publisher. List of winners available May 15 by mail or phone.

***LIBIDO* SHORT FICTION CONTEST**, Libido: The Journal of Sex & Sensibility, P.O. Box 146721, Chicago IL 60614. (773)275-0842. Fax: (773)275-0752. E-mail: rune@mcs.com. Co-editors: Jack Hafferkamp and Marianna Beck. Award to "find and reward exceptional short erotic fiction." Annual competition for short stories. Award: $1,000 1st Prize; $200 2nd Prize. Competition receives 400-500 submissions. Judges: *Libido* editors. Entry fee $15 for each story submitted. Guidelines available in January for SASE. Inquiries by e-mail and fax are OK. Deadline: September 1. Previously unpublished submissions. Word length: 1,000-4,000 words. "Winning stories will be well-written, insightful, humorous and arousing. Contest is open to all orientations and tastes, but the winners will fit *Libido*'s general tone and style. Humor helps." Winners will be announced in the Winter 2000 issue of *Libido*. Winners will be notified by mail or phone.

LIFETIME ACHIEVEMENT AWARD, Native Writers' Circle of the Americas, English Department, University of Oklahoma, Norman OK 73019-0240. (405)325-6231. Fax: (405)325-0831. E-mail: gearyhobson@ou.edu. Project Historian: Geary Hobson. Award to "honor the most respected of our Native American writers. Our award is the only one given to Native American authors by Native American authors." Annual competition. Author's lifetime work as a writer. Award: $1,000. Writers are voted on for the award by fellow American Indian writers. Writer must be nominated.

✓ ***LINES IN THE SAND* SHORT FICTION CONTEST**, Le Sand Publications, 1252 Terra Nova Blvd., Pacifica CA 94044-4340. (650)355-9069. Contact: Barbara J. Less, associate editor. "To encourage the writing of good short fiction, any genre." Annual competition for short stories. Award: $50, $25, or $10 and publication in *Lines in the Sand*. January/February awards edition. Honorable mentions will be published as space allows. Competition receives approximately 100 submissions. Judges: the editors. Entry fee $5. Guidelines available December 1998 for SASE. Deadline: November 30, 1999. Previously published or unpublished submissions. Word length: 2,000 words maximum. Winners announced January 2000. Winners notified by mail December 1999. List of winners available for SASE.

***LITERAL LATTÉ* FICTION AWARD**, *Literal Latté*, 61 E. 8th St., Suite 240, New York NY 10003. (212)260-5532. E-mail: litlatte@aol.com. Contact: Jenine Gordon Bockman, editor/publisher. Award to "provide talented writers with three essential tools for continued success: money, publication and recognition." Annual competition for short stories. Award: $500 1st Prize; $200 2nd Prize; $100 3rd Prize; up to 7 honorable mentions. Competition receives 300 submissions. Judges: the editors. Entry fee $10 ($15 includes subscription) for each story submitted. Guidelines available for SASE. Inquiries by e-mail OK. Deadline: January 18. Previously unpublished submissions. Open to new and established writers worldwide. Word length: 6,000 words maximum. "The First Prize Story in the First Annual Literal Latté Fiction Awards has been honored with a Pushcart Prize." Winners notified by phone. List of winners available in late April.

LONG FICTION CONTEST, (I), White Eagle Coffee Store Press, P.O. Box 383, Fox River Grove IL 60021-0383. (847)639-9200. E-mail: wecspress@aol.com. Website: http://members.aol.com/wecspress. Contact: Publisher. To promote and support the long fiction form. Annual award for short stories. Winning story receives A.E. Coppard Award—publication as chapbook plus $500, 25 contributor's copies; 40 additional copies sent to book publishers/agents and 10 press kits. Entry fee $15, ($5 for second story in same envelope). Guidelines available in April. Inquiries by fax and e-mail OK. SASE for results. Deadline: December 15. Accepts previously unpublished submissions, but previous publication of small parts with acknowledgements is OK. Simultaneous submissions OK. No limits on style or subject matter. Length: 8,000-14,000 words (30-50 pages double spaced) single story; may have multiparts or be a self-contained novel segment. Send cover with title, name, address, phone; second title page with title only. Submissions are not returned; they are recycled. "Previous winners include Adria Bernard, Doug Hornig, Christy Sheffield Sanford, Eleanor Swanson, Gregory J. Wolos. SASE for most current information." Winners announced March 30, 2000. Winners notified by phone. List of winners available March 30 for SASE.

✓ ***LOS ANGELES TIMES* BOOK PRIZES, (III)**, *L.A. Times*, ℅ Public Affairs Dept. Times Mirror Square, Los Angeles CA 90053. (213)237-5775. Fax: (213)237-4609. E-mail: tom.crouch@latimes.com. Contact: Tom Crouch, administrative coordinator. Annual award. For books published between January 1 and December 31. Award: $1,000 cash prize in each of the following categories: fiction, first fiction (the Art Seidenbaum Award) and young adult fiction. In addition, the Robert Kirsch Award recognizes the body of work by a writer living in or writing on the American West. Entry is by nomination of juries—no external nominations or submissions are accepted. Juries appointed by the *L.A. Times*. No entry fee. "Works must be published during the calendar year." Writers must be nominated by committee members. "The Times provides air fare and lodging for two nights in

Los Angeles for the winning authors, their guests and the Kirsch Award winner's principal publisher to attend the awards ceremony held in April on the eve of the *Los Angeles Times Festival of Books*."

LSU/*SOUTHERN REVIEW* SHORT FICTION AWARD (I), *The Southern Review*, 43 Allen Hall, LSU, Baton Rouge LA 70803-5005. (504)388-5108. Fax: (504)388-5098. E-mail: bmacon@unix1.sncc.lsu.edu. Contact: Michael Griffith. Award "to recognize the best first collection of short stories published in the U.S. in the past year." Annual competition. Award: $500, possible reading. Competition receives approx. 35-40 submissions. Judges: A committee of editors and faculty members. Guidelines for SASE. Deadline: January 31. Submissions must have been published between January 1 and December 31 of previous year. Only books published in the US.

MALICE DOMESTIC GRANT, (I, IV), % Bookstore, 27 W. Washington St., Hagerstown MD 21740. (301)797-8896. Fax: (301)797-9453. Grants Chair: Pam Reed. Given "to encourage unpublished writers in their pursuit—grant may be used to offset registration, travel or other expenses relating to attending writers' conferences, etc., within one year of award." Annual competition for novels and nonfiction. Award: $500. Competition receives 8-25 submissions. Judges: the Malice Domestic Board. Guidelines for SASE. Unpublished submissions. "Our genre is loosely translated as mystery stories of the Agatha Christie type, that is 'mysteries of manners.' These works usually feature amateur detective characters who know each other. No excessive gore or violence." Submit plot synopsis and 3 chapters of work in progress. Include résumé, a letter of reference from someone familiar with your work, a typed letter of application explaining qualifications for the grant and the workshop/conference to be attended or the research to be funded.

N **MARIN ARTS COUNCIL INDIVIDUAL ARTIST GRANTS, (I, II, IV)**, 251 N. San Pedro Rd., San Rafael CA 94903. (415)499-8350. Fax: (415)499-8537. Grants Coordinator: Bernadette Diamic. "For Marin County residents only. Award to provide unrestricted grants starting at $2,000 to individual artists in a variety of media." Every other year competition for short stories, novels, plays, poetry. Competition receives approx. 15-90 submissions. Judges: Professionals in the field. Guidelines for SASE. Previously published submissions and unpublished submissions. Marin County residents only.

✓ **THE MARTEN BEQUEST TRAVELLING SCHOLARSHIP, (I, IV)**, Arts Management Pty. Ltd., Station House Rawson Place, 790 George St., Sydney NSW 2000 Australia. Phone: +61-2-92125066. Fax: +61-2-9211-7762. E-mail: vbraden@ozemail.com.au. Projects Administrator: Claudia Crosariol. "The Marten Bequest is intended to augment a scholar's own resources towards affording him or her a cultural education by means of a travelling scholarship, to be awarded to one or more applicants who fulfill the required conditions and who are of outstanding ability and promise in one or more categories of the arts. The scholarships shall be used for study, maintenance and travel either in Australia or overseas. One scholarship is granted in each of nine categories which rotate in two groups on an annual basis: Instrumental Music, Painting, Singing, Prose, Poetry and Acting (even years)." Award: AUS $18,000 payable in two installments of $9,000 per annum. Competition receives 60 submissions. Panel of 6 judges. Guidelines for SASE. Deadline: last Friday in October. Winners announced in March. Winners notified by phone and mail. List of winners available by phone in late March.

N **WALTER RUMSEY MARVIN GRANT, (I, IV)**, Ohioana Library Association, 65 S. Front St., Room 1105, Columbus OH 43215-4163. (614)466-3831. Contact: Linda Hengst. "To encourage young unpublished (meaning not having a book published) writers (under age 30)." Annual competition for short stories. Award: $1,000. Guidelines for SASE. Deadline: January 31, 1998. Open to unpublished authors born in Ohio or who have lived in Ohio for a minimum of five years. Must be under 30 years of age. Up to six pieces of prose may be submitted; maximum 60 pages, minimum 10 pages.

MARY MCCARTHY PRIZE IN SHORT FICTION, (I, IV), Sarabande Books, Inc., P.O. Box 4999, Louisville KY 40204. Contact: Sarah Gorham, editor-in-chief. "To award publication and $2,000 to an outstanding collection of short stories and/or novellas, up to 300 pages; or single novella, 150 pages maximum." Competition receives 1,000 submissions. Judge: nationally known writer, changes yearly. Entry fee $15. Guidelines for SASE. Unpublished submissions. US citizens. Word length: 150-300 pages. "Writers must submit a required entry form and follow contest guildelines for ms submission. Writers must include a #10 SASE with their inquiries."

✓ **THE JOHN H. MCGINNIS MEMORIAL AWARD, (I)**, *Southwest Review*, P.O. Box 750374, 307 Fondren Library West, Southern Methodist University, Dallas TX 75275-0374. (214)768-1037. Contact: Elizabeth Mills, senior editor. Annual awards (fiction and nonfiction). Stories or essays must have been published in the *Southwest Review* prior to the announcement of the award. Awards: $1,000. Pieces are not submitted directly for the award but simply for publication in the magazine.

N **JENNY MCKEAN MOORE WRITER IN WASHINGTON, (II)**, Jenny McKean Moore Fund & The George Washington University, Dept. of English, George Washington University, Washington DC 20052. (202)994-6180. Fax: (202)994-7915. Associate Professor of English: D. McAleavey. Annual award "of a teaching residency for a different genre each year." Award: $46,000 and an "attractive benefits package." Receives 200 submissions. Judges: George Washington University English faculty and members of the J.M. Moore Fund. Guidelines for SASE. Deadline: November 15. Previously published submissions. Winners announced in February. Winners notified by phone.

MCKNIGHT ARTIST FELLOWSHIPS FOR WRITERS, Administered by the Loft, (I, IV), The Loft, Pratt Community Center, 66 Malcolm Ave. SE, Minneapolis MN 55414. (612)379-8999. Website: http://www.loft.org. Program Coordinator: Deidre Pope. "To give Minnesota writers of demonstrated ability an opportunity to work for a concentrated period of time on their writing." Annual awards of $10,000; 2 in poetry and 3 in creative prose; 2 awards of distinction of $20,000. Competition receives approximately 125-175 submissions/year. Judges are from out-of-state. Entry forms or rules available in October for SASE "or see website." Deadline: November. "Applicants *must* be Minnesota residents and must send for and observe guidelines." Winners announced by May 1. Winner notified by phone or mail. List of winners available in August for SASE.

✔ **THE MENTOR AWARD, (IV)**, *Mentor & Protege Newsletter*, P.O. Box 4382, Overland Park KS 66204-0382. (913)362-7889. Editor: Maureen Waters. "The Mentor Award Track 1 is given for supporting and promoting the art and practice of mentoring, coaching and wisdom through the written word, and thereby helping to create a new sense of community." Track 2 of the Mentor Award is open to all subjects. Quarterly and annually: Grand Prize ($250) will be awarded each January to the 1 best submission from all quarterly first-prize winners in all categories from the previous year. Competition for short stories (1,000-3,000 words); essay (700-1,500 words); feature article (1,500-3,000 words); interview (1,000-3,000 words); book review (500-1,000 words); and movie review (500-1,000 words). Fee for Mentor Award varies. Send SASE for entry form and guidelines. "The Athena Award is for published (after January 1, 1993) material. Entry fee varies by category (book, article, academic dissertation, videos, etc.). All material must be mentoring related. Plaque awarded, no monetary reward." Judges: Panel of magazine writers, publishers and book authors. Guidelines for SASE. Deadlines for quarterly competitions: March 31, June 30, September 30, December 31. Previously published (prior to January 1, 1993) and unpublished submissions. Submissions must be about "a mentor or a mentoring relationship." Winners announced quarterly. Winners notified in writing. List of winners available for SASE.

N MICHIGAN AUTHOR AWARD, (II, IV), Michigan Library Association/Michigan Center for the Book, 6810 S. Cedar, Suite 6, Lansing MI 48911. (517)694-6615. Fax: (517)694-4330. E-mail: hartzelm@mlc.lib.mi.us. Executive Director: Marianne Hartzell. "Award to recognize an outstanding published body of fiction, nonfiction, poetry and/or playscript, by a Michigan author." Annual competition for short stories, novels, story collections. Award: $1,000. Competition receives 50 submissions. Judges: Panel members represent a broad spectrum of expertise in writing, publishing and book collecting. Guidelines available in February for SASE or by e-mail. Inquiries by fax and e-mail OK. Deadline: May. Previously published submissions. Eligibility: current Michigan resident; long-time resident, recently relocated; or author whose works identify with Michigan because of subject/setting. Nominee must have 3 published works. "Only nominations are accepted, not applications." Winners announced in July. Winners notified by phone.

MID-LIST PRESS FIRST SERIES AWARD FOR SHORT FICTION, (I, II), Mid-List Press, 4324-12th Ave. South, Minneapolis MN 55407-3218. (612)822-3733. Fax: (612)823-8387. E-mail: guide@midlist.org. Website: http://www.midlist.org. Contact: Lane Stiles, senior editor. To encourage and nurture short fiction writers who have never published a collection of fiction. Annual competition for fiction collections. Award: $1,000 advance and publication. Judges: manuscript readers and the editors of Mid-List Press. Entry fee $15. Deadline: July 1. Previously published or unpublished submissions. Word length: 50,000 words minimum. "Application forms and guidelines are available for a #10 SASE, or visit our website." Winners announced in December. Winners notified by phone and mail in December.

MID-LIST PRESS FIRST SERIES AWARD FOR THE NOVEL, (I), Mid-List Press, 4324-12th Ave. South, Minneapolis MN 55407-3218. (612)822-3733. Fax: (612)823-8387. E-mail: guide@midlist.org. Website: http://www.midlist.org. Contact: Lane Stiles, senior editor. To encourage and nurture first-time novelists. Annual competition for novels. Award: $1,000 advance and publication. Competition receives approximately 500 submissions. Judges: manuscript readers and the editors of Mid-List Press. Entry fee $15. Deadline: February 1. Unpublished submissions. Word length: minimum 50,000 words. "Application forms and guidelines are available for a #10 SASE, or visit our website." Winners announced in July. Winners notified by phone and mail. Winners' list published in *Poets & Writers* and *AWP Chronicle*.

N MILKWEED EDITIONS NATIONAL FICTION PRIZE, (II), Milkweed Editions, 430 First Ave. N., Suite 400, Minneapolis MN 55401-1743. (612)332-3192. Fax: (612)332-6248. Publisher: Emilie Buchwald. Annual award for a novel, a short story collection, one or more novellas, or a combination of short stories and novellas. The Prize will be awarded to the best work of fiction that Milkweed accepts for publication during each calendar year by a writer not previously published by Milkweed Editions. The winner will receive $2,000 cash over and above any payment agreed upon at the time of acceptance. Must request guidelines; send SASE. There is no deadline. Judged by Milkweed Editions. "Please look at previous winners: *The Empress of One*, by Faith Sullivan; *Confidence of the Heart*, by David Schweidel; *Montana 1948*, by Larry Watson; and *Aquaboogie*, by Susan Straight—this is the caliber of fiction we are searching for. Catalog available for $1.50 postage, if people need a sense of our list."

N **MILKWEED EDITIONS PRIZE FOR CHILDREN'S LITERATURE, (II)**, Milkweed Editions, 430 First Ave. N., Suite 400, Minneapolis MN 55401. (612)332-3192. Fax: (612)332-6248. Website: http://www.milkweededitions.org. Publisher: Emilie Buchwald. "Our goal is to encourage writers to create books for the important age range of middle readers." Annual award for novels and biographies for children ages 8 to 12. The prize will be awarded to the best work for children ages 8 to 12 that Milkweed accepts for publication during each calendar year by a writer not previously published by Milkweed. The winner will receive $2,000 cash over and above any advances, royalties, or other payment agreed upon at the time of acceptance. There is no deadline. Judges: Milkweed Editions. Guidelines for SASE. Unpublished in book form. Page length: 110-350 pages. "Send for guidelines for children's literature and check our website to review previous winners. Winners notified upon acceptance for publication."

***MISSISSIPPI REVIEW* PRIZE**, University of Southern Mississippi/Mississippi Review, P.O. Box 5144 USM, Hattiesburg MS 39406-5144. (601)266-4321. Fax: (601)266-5757. E-mail: fb@netdoor.com. Contact: Rie Fortenberry, managing editor. Award to "reward excellence in new fiction and poetry and to find new writers who are just beginning their careers." Annual competition for short stories. Award: $750 plus publication for the winning story and poem; publication for all runners-up. Competition receives 800-1,100 submissions. Judge: guest editor/judge. Entry fee $10/story; limit 2 stories. $5/poem, limit 4 poems. Guidelines available for SASE. Deadline: May 31. Previously unpublished submissions. Word length: 6,500 words.

MODEST CONTEST, (I), *New Stone Circle*, 1185 E. 1900 North Rd., White Heath IL 61884. Fiction Editor: Mary Hays. Award "to encourage good writing." Annual competition for short stories. Awards: $100 1st Prize. Competition receives approximately 100 submissions. Judge: Mary Hays. Entry fee $10. Guidelines for SASE. Deadline: May 1. Unpublished submissions. Winners announced in July. Winners notified by mail.

✔ **MONEY FOR WOMEN**, Money for Woman/Barbara Deming Memorial Fund, Inc., Box 630125, Bronx NY 10463. Administrator: Susan Pliner. "Small grants to individual feminists in the arts." Biannual competition. Award: $200-1,000. Competition receives approximately 30 submissions. Judges: Board of Directors. Guidelines for SASE. Deadline: December 31, June 30. Limited to US and Canadian citizens. Word length: 6-25 pages. May submit own fiction. "Only for feminists in the arts. Fund includes two additional awards: the Gerty, Gerty, Gerty in the Arts, Arts Arts award for works by lesbians and The Fanny Lou Hamer Award for work which combats racism and celebrates women of color." Winners announced five months after deadline. Winners notified by mail.

N **MONTANA ARTS COUNCIL INDIVIDUAL ARTIST FELLOWSHIP, (IV)**, 316 N. Park Ave., Room 252, Helena MT 59620. (406)444-6430. Executive Director: Arlynn Fishbaugh. Annual award of $2,000. Competition receives about 80-200 submissions/year. Panelists are professional artists. Contest requirements available for SASE or e-mail at mtarts@initco.net. Deadline each year. Restricted to residents of Montana; not open to degree-seeking students.

MYSTERY MAYHEM CONTEST, (I), *Mystery Time*/Hutton Publications, P.O. Box 2907, Decatur IL 62524. Contact: Linda Hutton, editor. Award "to encourage writers to have fun writing a mystery spoof." Annual competition for short stories. Award: $10 cash and publication in *Mystery Time*. Competition receives approximately 100 submissions. Judge: Linda Hutton, editor of *Mystery Time*. Guidelines for SASE. Deadline: September 15 annually. Unpublished submissions. Word length: Must be one sentence of any length. "One entry per person, of one sentence which can be any length, which is the opening of a mystery spoof. Must include SASE. Entry form not required. All material must be typed. Flyer of previous years' winners available for $1 plus #10 SASE." Winners announced in October in Mystery Time Anthology Autumn issue.

THE NATIONAL CHAPTER OF CANADA IODE VIOLET DOWNEY BOOK AWARD, (I, IV), The National Chapter of Canada IODE, 254-40 Orchard View Blvd., Toronto, Ontario M4R 1B9 Canada. (416)487-4416. Fax: (416)487-4417. Chairman, Book Award Committee: Marty Dalton. "The award is given to a Canadian author for an English language book suitable for children 13 years of age and under, published in Canada during the previous calendar year. Fairy tales, anthologies and books adapted from another source are not eligible." Annual competition for novels, children's literature. Award: $3,000. Competition receives approx.

MARKET CATEGORIES: (I) Unpublished entries; **(II)** Published entries nominated by the author; **(III)** Published entries nominated by the editor, publisher or nominating body; **(IV)** Specialized entries.

80-100 submissions. Judges: A six-member panel of judges including four National IODE officers and two nonmembers who are recognized specialists in the field of children's literature. Guidelines for SASE. Deadline: January 31, 1999. Previously published January 1, 1998 and December 31, 1998. "The book must have been written by a Canadian citizen and must have been published in Canada during the calendar year." Word length: Must have at least 500 words of text preferably with Canadian content.

NATIONAL FEDERATION OF THE BLIND WRITER'S DIVISION FICTION CONTEST, (I), National Federation of the Blind Writer's Division, 2704 Beach Dr., Merrick NY 11566. (516)868-8718. Fax: (516)868-9076. First Vice President, Writer's Division: Lori Stayer. "To promote good writing for blind writers and Division members, blind or sighted." Annual competition for short stories. Award: $50, $40, $25, $15. Competitions receives 20 submissions. Entry fee $5/story. Guidelines for SASE. Inquiries by fax OK. Deadline: May 1, 1999 (contest opens 9/1/98). Unpublished submissions. "You don't have to be blind, but it helps. Story must be in English, and typed. SASE necessary." Critique on request, $5. Word length: 2,000 max. Winners announced July 31. Winners notified by mail. List of winners available for SASE.

NATIONAL WRITERS ASSOCIATION ANNUAL NOVEL WRITING CONTEST, (I), National Writers Association, 1450 S. Havana, Suite 424, Aurora CO 80012. (303)751-7844. Contact: Sandy Whelchel, director. Annual award to "recognize and reward outstanding ability and to increase the opportunity for publication." Award: $500 (1st Prize); $300 (2nd Prize); $100 (3rd Prize). Award judged by successful writers. Entry fee: $35. Judges' evaluation sheets sent to each entry. Contest rules and entry forms available with SASE. Opens December 1. Deadline: April 1. Unpublished submissions, any genre or category. Length: 20,000-100,000 words.

☑ **NATIONAL WRITERS ASSOCIATION ANNUAL SHORT STORY CONTEST, (I)**, National Writers Association, 1450 S. Havana, Suite 424, Aurora CO 80012-4032. (303)751-7844. Fax: (303)751-8593. E-mail: sandywrter@aol.com. Website: http://www.nationalwriters.com. Executive Director: Sandy Whelchel. Annual award to encourage and recognize writing by freelancers in the short story field. Award: $200 (1st Prize); $100 (2nd Prize); $50 (3rd Prize). Opens April 1. Entry fee $15. Guidelines available in January for SASE. All entries must be postmarked by July 1. Inquiries by fax and e-mail OK. Evaluation sheets sent to each entrant if SASE provided. Unpublished submissions. Length: No more than 5,000 words. Winners announced at the NWA Summer Conference in June. Winners notified by phone or mail. List of winners published in *Authorship*.

THE NATIONAL WRITTEN & ILLUSTRATED BY . . . AWARDS CONTEST FOR STUDENTS, (I, IV), Landmark Editions, Inc., P.O. Box 270169, Kansas City MO 64127-2135. (816)241-4919. Fax: (816)483-3755. Website: http://www.LandmarkEditions.com. Contact: Nan Thatch. "Contest initiated to encourage students to write and illustrate original books and to inspire them to become published authors and illustrators." Annual competition. "Each student whose book is selected for publication will be offered a complete publishing contract. To ensure that students benefit from the proceeds, royalties from the sale of their books will be placed in an individual trust fund, set up for each student by his or her parents or legal guardians, at a bank of their choice. Funds may be withdrawn when a student becomes of age, or withdrawn earlier (either in whole or in part) for educational purposes or in case of proof of specific needs due to unusual hardship. Reports of book sales and royalties will be sent to the student and the parents or guardians annually." Winners also receive an all-expense-paid trip to Kansas City to oversee final reproduction phases of their books. Books by students may be entered in one of three age categories: A—6 to 9 years old; B—10 to 13 years old; C—14 to 19 years old. Each book submitted must be both written and illustrated by the same student. "Any books that are written by one student and illustrated by another will be automatically disqualified." Book entries must be submitted by a teacher or librarian. Entry fee $2. For rules and guidelines, send a #10 SAE with 64¢ postage. Inquiries by fax OK. Deadline: May 1 of each year. Winners announced October. Winners notified by phone.

☑ **NCWN FICTION COMPETITION, (IV)**, North Carolina Writers' Network, 3501 Hwy. 54 W., Studio C, Chapel Hill NC 27516. (919)967-9540. Fax: (919)929-0535. E-mail: ncwn@sunsite.unc.edu. Website: http://www.sunsite.unc.edu/ncwriters. Program Coordinator: Frances Dowell. Award to "encourage and recognize the work of emerging and established North Carolina writers." Annual competition for short stories. Awards: $150 1st Place, $100 2nd Place, $50 3rd Place. Competition receives 100-150 submissions. Judges change annually. Entry fee $4 for NCWN members; $6 for nonmembers. Guidelines for SASE. Deadline: February 27. Unpublished submissions. "The award is available only to legal residents of North Carolina or out-of-state NCWN members." Word length: 6 double-spaced pages (1,500 words maximum). Winners announced in May. Winners notified by phone and letter. List of winners available for SASE.

***THE NEBRASKA REVIEW* AWARD IN FICTION**, The Nebraska Review, University of Nebraska at Omaha, Omaha NE 68182-0324. (402)554-3159. Managing Editor: James Reed. Award to "recognize short fiction of the highest possible quality." Annual competition for short stories. Award: publication plus $500. Competition receives 400-500 submissions. Judges: staff. Entry fee $10 for each story submitted. Guidelines for SASE. Deadline: November 30. Previously unpublished submissions. Word length: 5,000 words. Winners announced March 15. Winners notified by phone and/or mail in February.

☑ **NEUSTADT INTERNATIONAL PRIZE FOR LITERATURE, (III)**, *World Literature Today*, 110 Monnet Hall, University of Oklahoma, Norman OK 73019-4033. Contact: William Riggan, director. Biennial award to recognize distinguished and continuing achievement in fiction, poetry or drama. Awards: $40,000, an eagle feather cast in silver, an award certificate and a special issue of *WLT* devoted to the laureate. "We are looking for outstanding accomplishment in world literature. The Neustadt Prize is not open to application. Nominations are made only by members of the international jury, which changes for each award. Jury meetings are held in February or March of even-numbered years. Unsolicited manuscripts, whether published or unpublished, cannot be considered."

NEVADA ARTS COUNCIL ARTISTS' FELLOWSHIPS, (I, IV), 602 N. Curry St., Carson City NV 89703. (702)687-6680. Fax: (702)687-6688. E-mail: sarosse@clan.lib.nv.us. Artists' Services Program: Sharon Rosse, coordinator. Award "to honor individual artists and their artistic achievements to support artists' efforts in advancing their careers." Annual competition for fiction, nonfiction, poetry, playwriting. Award: $5,000 ($4,500 immediately, $500 after public service component completed). Competition receives approximately 25 submissions. Judges: Peer panels of professional artists. Guidelines available March 1999, no SASE required. Deadline: April 19, 1999. "Only available to Nevada writers." Word length: 25 pages prose and plays, 10 pages poetry. Winners announced June. Winners notified by mail. Entrants receive list of winners.

☑ ***THE NEW ERA* WRITING, ART, PHOTOGRAPHY AND MUSIC CONTEST, (I, IV)**, *New Era Magazine* (LDS Church), 50 E. North Temple, Salt Lake City UT 84150. (801)240-2951. Contact: Larry A. Hiller, managing editor. "To encourage young Mormon writers and artists." Annual competition for short stories. Award: partial scholarship to Brigham Young University or Ricks College or cash awards. Competition receives approximately 300 submissions. Judges: *New Era* editors. Guidelines for SASE. October 1998 issue will have ruler and entry form. Deadline: January 4, 1999. Unpublished submissions. Contest open only to 12-23-year-old members of the Church of Jesus Christ of Latter-Day Saints. Winners announced by April 15, 1999. Winners notified by letter. List of winners in the September 1999 issue.

N **NEW HAMPSHIRE STATE COUNCIL ON THE ARTS INDIVIDUAL ARTIST FELLOWSHIP, (I, II, IV)**, 40 N. Main St., Concord NH 03301-4974. (603)271-2789. Artist Services Coordinator: Audrey V. Sylvester. Fellowship "recognizes artistic excellence and professional commitment of professional artists in literature who are legal/permanent residents of the state of New Hampshire." Award: Up to $2,500. Competition gives awards in four disciplines. Judges: Panels of in-state and out-of-state experts review work samples. Guidelines for SASE. Postmark deadline July 1, 1999. Submissions may be either previously published or unpublished. Applicants must be over 18 years of age; not enrolled as fulltime students; permanent, legal residents of New Hampshire 1 year prior to application. Application form required.

N **NEW JERSEY STATE COUNCIL ON THE ARTS PROSE FELLOWSHIP, (I, IV)**, CN 306, Trenton NJ 08625. (609)292-6130. Annual grants for writers of short stories, novels, story collections. Past awards have ranged from $5,000-12,000. 1998 awards averaged $5,500. Judges: Peer panel. Guidelines for SASE. Deadline: mid-July. For either previously published or unpublished submissions. "Previously published work must be submitted as a manuscript." Applicants must be New Jersey residents. Submit several copies of short fiction, short stories or prose not exceeding 15 pages and no less than 10 pages. For novels in progress, a synopsis and sample chapter should be submitted.

☑ **NEW MILLENNIUM WRITING AWARDS**, Room S, P.O. Box 2463, Knoxville TN 37901-2463. (423)428-0389. E-mail: donwill@aol.com. Website: http://www.mach2.com/books. Contact: Don Williams, editor. Award "to promote literary excellence in contemporary fiction." Semiannual competition for short stories. Award: $1,000 plus publication in *New Millennium Writings*. Competition receives approximately 1,000 submissions. Judges: Novelists and short story writers. Entry fee: $10. Guidelines for SASE available after January 2. Inquiries by e-mail OK. Deadlines: June 15 and November 15, 1999. Unpublished submissions. No required word length. "Provide a bold, yet organic opening line, sustain the voice and mood throughout, tell an entertaining and vital story with a strong ending." Winners announced August and February 2000. Winners notified by mail and phone. All entrants will receive a list of winners, plus a copy of the journal. Send letter-sized SASE with entry for list.

NEW WRITING AWARD, (I), *New Writing Magazine*, PO Box 1812, Amherst NY 14226-7812. (716)834-1067. E-mail: newwriting@aol.com. Director: Sam Meade. "We wish to reward *new* writing. Looking for originality in form and content." New and beginning writers encouraged. Annual open competition for prose (novel, novel excerpt, scripts, short story, essay, humor, other) and poetry. Deadline: May 31 and December 31. Award: up to $3,000 for best entry. Additional awards for finalists. Possible publication. Competition receives 500 submissions. Judges: Panel of editors. Entry fee $10, $5 for each additional plus 10¢/page. Guidelines for SASE. Inquiries by e-mail OK. No application form required—simply send submission with reading fee, SASE for manuscript return or notification, and 3×5 card for each entry, including: story name, author and address. Winners announced in July and February.

NFB WRITERS' FICTION CONTEST, (I), The Writers' Division of the National Federation of the Blind, 1203 S. Fairview Rd., Columbia MO 65203-0809. (573)445-6091. President of Division: Tom Stevens. Award to "encourage members and other blind writers to write fiction." Annual competition for short stories. Award: four prizes of $50, $35, $20, $10, plus honorable mentions and possible publication in *Slate & Style*. Competition receives 20 submissions. Entry fee $5 per story. Guidelines available August 1 for SASE. Deadline: May 1. Unpublished submissions. Word length: 2,000 words (maximum). "Send a 150-word bio with each entry. Please, no erotica." Winners announced May 1. Winners notified by letter. List of winners available in July for SASE.

96 INC'S BRUCE P. ROSSLEY LITERARY AWARDS, (I, II, III, IV), 96 Inc., P.O. Box 15559, Boston MA 02215-0010. (617)267-0543. Fax: (617)262-3568. Director: Vera Gold. Award "to increase the attention for writers of merit who have received little recognition." Biennial award for short stories, novels and story collections. Award: $1,000 for the literary award and $100 for Bruce P. Rossley New Voice Award. Competition receives 400 submissions. Judges: Professionals in the fields of writing, journalism and publishing. Entry fee $10. Guidelines available after July 1999 for SASE. Deadline: September 30, 2000. Published or unpublished submissions. "In addition to writing, the writer's accomplishments in the fields of teaching and community service will also be considered." Open to writers from New England. Work must be nominated by "someone familiar with the writer's work." Winners announced November 2000. Winners notified by mail early November. Winners are honored at a reception near the end of the year. List of winners available in November.

NORTH CAROLINA ARTS COUNCIL WRITERS' RESIDENCIES, (IV), 221 E. Lane St., Raleigh NC 27601-2807. (919)733-2111, ext. 22. Fax: (919)733-4834. E-mail: dmcgill@ncacmail.dcr.state.nc.us. Website: http://www.ncarts.org. Literature Director: Deborah McGill. Award "to recognize and encourage North Carolina's finest creative writers. Every year we offer a two-month residency for one writer at the LaNapoule Art Foundation in southern France, a three-month residency for one writer at Headlands Center for the Arts (California), and a one-month residency for one writer at Vermont Studio Center." Judges: Panels of writers and editors convened by the residency centers. Guidelines available after March 1 by phone or mail. Inquiries by fax and e-mail OK. Deadline: early June. Writers must be over 18 years old, not currently enrolled in degree-granting program on undergraduate or graduate level and *must have been a resident of North Carolina for 1 full year prior to applying*. Winners announced in the Fall. Winners notified by phone. List of winners available by phone, mail or on website.

NORWEGIAN LITERATURE ABROAD GRANT (NORLA), (I), Bygdoy Allè 21, 0262 Oslo Norway. (47)22 43 48 70. Fax: (47) 22 44 52 42. E-mail: firmapost@norla.no. Manager: Kristin Brudevoll. Award to "help Norwegian fiction to be published outside Scandinavia and ensure that the tranlator will be paid for his/her work." Annual compensation for translations, 50-60% of the translation's cost. Competition receives 40-50 submissions. Judges: an advisory (literary) board of 5 persons. Guidelines for SASE. Deadline: December 15. Previously published submissions. "Application form can be obtained from NORLA. Foreign (non-Scandanavian) publishers may apply for the award."

HOWARD O'HAGAN AWARD FOR SHORT FICTION, (II, IV), Writers Guild of Alberta, 3rd Floor, Percy Page Centre, 11759 Groat Rd., Edmonton, Alberta T5M 3K6 Canada. (403)422-8174. Fax: (403)422-2663. Assistant Director: Darlene Diver. "To recognize outstanding books published by Alberta authors each year." Annual competition for short stories. Award: $500 (Canadian) cash and leather bound book. Competition receives 20-30 submissions. Judges: selected published writers across Canada. Guidelines for SASE. Deadline: December 31. Previously published submissions published between January and December 31. Open to Alberta authors only.

OHIO STATE UNIVERSITY PRESS, (II), 1070 Carmack Rd., Columbus OH 43210-1002. (614)292-6930. Fax: (614)292-2065. E-mail: ohiostatepress@osu.edu. Website: http://www.ohio-state.edu/osu-press/. Contact: Jeanette Rivard. Estab. 1957. "Small-sized university press." Publishes "scholarly and trade books." Member of Association of American University Presses (AAUP), International Association of Scholarly Publishers (IASP) and Association of American Publishers (AAP). Publishes one annual winner of poetry contest and of short fiction prize. Guidelines available September 1. Inquiries by e-mail and fax OK. Competition receives 400-500 submissions. Deadline: January 31. Winners announced in May. Winners notified by postcard.

OHIOANA AWARD FOR CHILDREN'S LITERATURE, ALICE WOOD MEMORIAL, (IV), Ohioana Library Association, 65 S. Front St., Room 1105, Columbus OH 43215-4163. (614)466-3831. Fax: (614)728-6974. E-mail: ohioana@winslo.state.oh.us. Director: Linda Hengst. Competition "to honor an individual whose body of work has made, and continues to make, a significant contribution to literature for children or young adults." Annual award of $1,000. Guidelines for SASE. Inquiries by fax and e-mail OK. Deadline: December 31 prior to year award is given. "Open to authors born in Ohio or who have lived in Ohio for a minimum of five years." Winners announced Summer 1998. Winners notified by letter. Entrants can call, e-mail or check website for winner.

☑ **OHIOANA BOOK AWARDS, (II, IV)**, Ohioana Library Association, 65 S. Front St., Room 1105, Columbus OH 43215-4163. (614)466-3831. Fax: (614)728-6974. E-mail: ohioana@winslo.state.oh.us. Contact: Linda R. Hengst, director. Annual awards granted (only if the judges believe a book of sufficiently high quality has been submitted) to bring recognition to outstanding books by Ohioans or about Ohio. Five categories: Fiction, Nonfiction, Juvenile, Poetry and About Ohio or an Ohioan. Criteria: Books written or edited by a native Ohioan or resident of the state for at least 5 years; two copies of the book MUST be received by the Ohioana Library by December 31 prior to the year the award is given; literary quality of the book must be outstanding. Awards: Certificate and glass sculpture (up to 6 awards given annually). Each spring a jury considers all books received since the previous jury. Award judged by a jury selected from librarians, book reviewers, writers and other knowledgeable people. No entry forms are needed, but they are available. "We will be glad to answer letters asking specific questions."

N **OMMATION PRESS BOOK AWARD, (I, II)**, Ommation Press, 5548 N. Sawyer, Chicago IL 60625. (312)539-5745. Annual competition for short stories, novels, story collections and poetry. Award: Book publication, 100 copies of book. Competition receives approx. 50-75 submissions. Judge: Effie Mihopoulos, editor. Entry fee $15, includes copy of former award-winning book. Guidelines for SASE. Deadline: December 31. Either previously published or unpublished submissions. Submit no more than 50 pages.

OPUS MAGNUM DISCOVERY AWARDS, (I), C.C.S. Entertainment Group, 433 N. Camden Dr., #600, Beverly Hills CA 90210. (310)288-1881. Fax: (310)288-0257. E-mail: awards@screenwriters.com. President: Carlos Abreu. Award "to discover new unpublished manuscripts." Annual competition for novels. Award: Film rights options up to $10,000. Judges: Industry professionals. Entry fee $75. Deadline: August 1 of each year. Unpublished submissions.

ORANGE BLOSSOM FICTION CONTEST, (I), *The Oak*, 1530 Seventh St., Rock Island IL 61201. (309)788-3980. Contact: Betty Mowery, editor. "To build up circulation of publication and give new authors a chance for competition and publication along with seasoned writers." Award: Subscription to *The Oak*. Competition receives approximately 75 submissions. Judges: Various editors from other publications, some published authors and previous contest winners. Entry fee six 32¢ stamps. Guidelines available after January for SASE. Word length: 500 words maximum. "May be on any subject, but avoid gore and killing of humans or animals." Deadline: July 1. Winners announced mid-July. Winners notified by letter.

OREGON INDIVIDUAL ARTIST FELLOWSHIP, (I, IV), Oregon Arts Commission, 775 Summer St. N.E., Salem OR 97310. (503)986-0082. E-mail: oregon.artscomm@state.or.us. Website: http://art.econ.state.or.us. Assistant Director: Vincent Dunn. "Award enables professional artists to undertake projects to assist their professional development." Biennial competition for short stories, novels, poetry and story collections. Award: $3,000. (Please note: ten $3,000 awards are spread over 5 disciplines—literature, music/opera, media arts, dance and theatre awarded in even-numbered years.) Competition receives 150 submissions. Guidelines available after March for SASE. Judges: Professional advisors from outside the state. Deadline: September 1. Competition limited to Oregon residents. Winners announced December. Winners notified by mail. List of winners can be requested from Oregon Arts Commission.

N **DOBIE PAISANO FELLOWSHIPS, (IV)**, Dobie House, 702 E. Dean Keeton St., Austin TX 78705. (512)471-8542. Fax: (512)471-9997. E-mail: aslate@mail.utexas.edu. Director: Audrey N. Slate. Annual fellowships for creative writing (includes short stories, novels and story collections). Award: 6 months residence at ranch; $1,200 monthly living stipend. Competition receives approximately 100 submissions. Judges: faculty of University of Texas and members of Texas Institute of Letters. Entry fee: $10. Application and guidelines available in October on request by letter, fax or e-mail. "Open to writers with a Texas connection—native Texans, people who have lived in Texas at least two years, or writers with published work on Texas and Southwest." Deadline: January 22, 1999. Winners announced in May. Winners notified by telephone followed by mail. List of winners available by mail in late May.

KENNETH PATCHEN COMPETITION, (I, II), Pig Iron Press, P.O. Box 237, Youngstown OH 44501. (330)747-6932. Contact: Jim Villani. Biannual. Awards works of fiction and poetry in alternating years. Award: publication; $500. Judge with national visibility selected annually. Entry fee $10. Competition receives 300 submissions. Guidelines available for SASE. Reading period: January 1 to December 31. Award for fiction: 1999, 2001, 2003; fiction award for novel or short story collection, either form eligible. Previous publication of individual stories, poems or parts of novel OK. Ms should not exceed 500 typed pages. Winners announced June. Winners notified by mail. List of winners available for SASE.

THE PATERSON FICTION PRIZE, The Poetry Center at Passaic County Community College, One College Boulevard, Paterson NJ 07505-1179. (973)684-6555. Fax: (973)684-5843. E-mail: m.gillan@pccc.cc.nj.us. Director: Maria Mazziotti Gillan. Award to "encourage good literature." Annual competition for short stories and novels. Award: $500. Competition receives 400 submissions. Judge: A different one every year. Guidelines available for SASE. Deadline: April 1, 1999.

***PEARL* SHORT STORY CONTEST, (I)**, *Pearl* Magazine, 3030 E. Second St., Long Beach CA 90803-5163. (562)434-4523. Contact: Marilyn Johnson, editor. Award to "provide a larger forum and help widen publishing opportunities for fiction writers in the small press; and to help support the continuing publication of *Pearl*." Annual competition for short stories. Award: $100, publication in *Pearl* and 10 copies. Competition receives approximately 150 submissions. Judges: Editors of *Pearl* (Marilyn Johnson, Joan Jobe Smith, Barbara Hauk). Entry fee $10 per story. Includes copy of magazine featuring winning story. Guidelines for SASE. Deadline: December 1-March 15. Unpublished submissions. Length: 4,000 words maximum. Include a brief biographical note and SASE for reply or return of manuscript. Accepts simultaneous submissions, but asks to be notified if story is accepted elsewhere. All submissions are considered for publication in *Pearl*. "Although we are open to all types of fiction, we look most favorably upon coherent, well-crafted narratives, containing interesting, believable characters and meaningful situations." Winners notified by mail June 1998. List of winners available for SASE.

☑ **PEN CENTER USA WEST LITERARY AWARD IN FICTION, (II, IV)**, PEN Center USA West, 672 S. LaFayette Park Place, #41, Los Angeles CA 90057. (213)365-8500. Fax: (213)365-9616. E-mail: rit2writ@ix.netcom.com. Executive Director: Sherrill Britton. To recognize fiction writers who live in the western United States. Annual competition for published novels and story collections. Award: $1,000, plaque, and honored at a ceremony in Los Angeles. Competition receives approximately 100-125 submissions. Judges: panel of writers, booksellers, editors. Entry fee $20 for each story submitted. Guidelines available in July for SASE. Inquiries by fax and e-mail OK. Deadline: December 31. Previously published submissions published between January 1, 1998 and December 31, 1998. Open only to writers living west of the Mississippi. All entries must include 4 non-returnable copies of each submission and a completed entry form. Winners announced May 1999. Winners notified by phone and mail. Call or send SASE to request press release of winners.

PEN/BOOK-OF-THE-MONTH CLUB TRANSLATION PRIZE, (II, IV), PEN American Center, 568 Broadway, New York NY 10012. (212)334-1660. Awards Coordinator: John Morrone. Award "to recognize the art of the literary translator." Annual competition for translations. Award: $3,000. Deadline: December 15. Previously published submissions within the calendar year. "Translators may be of any nationality, but book must have been published in the US and must be a book-length literary translation." Books may be submitted by publishers, agents or translators. No application form. Send three copies. "Early submissions are strongly recommended."

THE PEN/FAULKNER AWARD FOR FICTION, (II, III, IV), c/o The Folger Shakespeare Library, 201 E. Capitol St. SE, Washington DC 20003. (202)675-0345. Fax: (202)608-1719. E-mail: delaney@folger.edu. Website: http://www.folger.edu. Contact: Janice Delaney, PEN/Faulkner Foundation Executive Director. Annual award. "To award the most distinguished book-length work of fiction published by an American writer." Award: $15,000 for winner; $5,000 for nominees. Judges: Three writers chosen by the Trustees of the Award. Deadline: October 31. Published submissions only. Writers and publishers submit four copies of eligible titles published the current year. No juvenile. Authors must be American citizens.

PEN/NORMA KLEIN AWARD, (III), PEN American Center, 568 Broadway, New York NY 10012. (212)334-1660. Award Director: John Morrone. "Established in 1990 in memory of the late PEN member and distinguished children's book author, the biennial prize recognizes an emerging voice of literary merit among American writers of children's fiction. Candidates for the award are new authors whose books (for elementary school to young adult readers) demonstrate the adventuresome and innovative spirit that characterizes the best children's literature and Norma Klein's own work (but need not resemble her novels stylistically)." Award: $3,000. Judges: a panel of three distinguished children's authors. Guidelines for SASE. Previously published submissions. Writer must be nominated by other authors or editors of children's books. Next award: 1999.

☑ **JAMES D. PHELAN AWARD, (I, IV)**, Intersection for the Arts/The San Francisco Foundation, 446 Valencia St., San Francisco CA 94103-3415. (415)626-2787. Fax: (415)626-1636. E-mail: intrsect@wenet.net. Website: http://www.wenet.net/~intrsect. Literary Program Director: Charles Wilmoth. Annual award "to author of an unpublished work-in-progress of fiction (novel or short story), nonfictional prose, poetry or drama." Award: $2,000 and certificate. Competition receives 80 submissions. All submissions are read by three initial readers (change from year to year) who forward ten submissions each onto three judges (change from year to year). Judges are established Bay Area writers with extensive publishing and teaching histories. Rules and entry forms available after October 15 for SASE. Deadline: January 31. Unpublished submissions. Applicant must have been born in the state of California, but need not be a current resident, and be 20-35 years old. Winners announced June 15. Winners notified by letter.

● **A BULLET INTRODUCES COMMENTS** by the editor of *Novel & Short Story Writer's Market* indicating special information about the listing.

☑ ***PHOEBE* FICTION PRIZE**, *Phoebe*, MSN 2D6 George Mason University, 4400 University Dr., Fairfax VA 22030-4444. (703)993-2915. E-mail: phoebe@gmu.edu. Fiction Editor: Renee Sagiv, fiction editor. Award to "find and publish new and exciting fiction." Annual competition for short stories. Award: $500 and publication. Competition receives 200 submissions. Judges: known fiction writers. Entry fee $10 for each story submitted. Guidelines available after July for SASE. Deadline: December 15. Previously unpublished submissions. Word length: maximum of 25 pages. "Guidelines only (no submissions) may be requested by e-mail." Winners announced March. Winners notified by mail. List of winners available for SASE.

***PLAYBOY* COLLEGE FICTION CONTEST, (I, IV)**, *Playboy* Magazine, 680 N. Lake Shore Dr., Chicago IL 60611. (312)751-8000. Website: http://www.playboy.com. Award "to foster young writing talent." Annual competition for short stories. Award: $3,000 plus publication in the magazine. Competition receives 1,000 submissions. Judges: Staff. Guidelines available for SASE or on website. Deadline: January 1. Submissions should be unpublished. No age limit; college affiliation required. Stories should be 25 pages or fewer. "Manuscripts are not returned. Results of the contest will be sent via SASE." Winners announced in February or March. Winners notified by letter in February or March. List of winners available in February or March for SASE or on website.

***POCKETS* FICTION WRITING CONTEST, (I)**, *Pockets Magazine*, Upper Room Publications, P.O. Box 189, Nashville TN 37202-0189. (615)340-7333. Fax: (615)340-7006. (Do not send submissions via fax.) E-mail: pockets@upperroom.org. Website: http://www.upperroom.org/pockets. Associate Editor: Lynn W. Gilliam. To "find new freelance writers for the magazine." Annual competition for short stories. Award: $1,000 and publication. Competition receives 600 submissions. Judged by *Pockets* editors and editors of other Upper Room publications. Guidelines available after February 1 for SASE or on website. Inquiries by e-mail and fax OK. Deadline: August 15. Former winners may not enter. Unpublished submissions. Word length: 1,000-1,600 words. "No historical fiction or fantasy." Winners announced November 1. Winners notified by mail or phone. List of winners available for SASE.

POTOMAC REVIEW THIRD ANNUAL SHORT STORY CONTEST, P.O. Box 354, Port Tobacco MD 20677. (301)934-1412. Fax: (301)753-1648. E-mail: elilv@juno.com. Website: http://www.meral.com/potomac. Contact: Eli Flam, editor. Award to "prime the pump for top submissions, spread the word about our 'big little quarterly' and come up with winning entries to publish." Annual competition for short stories. Award: $250 and publication in the fall 1999 issue. Competition receives more than 50 submissions. Judge: A top writer or writers with no connection to the magazine. Entry fee $15; year's subscription included. Guidelines will be in the winter 1998-1999 issue, or send SASE for guidelines or order sample copy ($5 ppd). Deadline: January-March 31. Previously unpublished submissions. There are no limitations of style or provenance. Word length: up to 3,000 words. "We may publish the first runner-up as well." Winners announced by June. Winners notified via SASE if provided, otherwise in Fall 1999 issue. List of winners available for SASE.

***PRAIRIE SCHOONER* THE LAWRENCE FOUNDATION AWARD, (II)**, 201 Andrews Hall, University of Nebraska, Lincoln NE 68588-0334. (402)472-0911. Fax: (402)472-9771. E-mail: lrandolp@unlinfo.unl.edu. Website: http://www.unl.edu/schooner/psmain.htm. Contact: Hilda Raz, editor. Annual award "given to the author of the best short story published in *Prairie Schooner* during the preceding year." Award: $1,000. Inquiries by fax and e-mail OK. "Only short fiction published in *Prairie Schooner* is eligible for consideration. Manuscripts are read September-May."

THE PRESIDIO LA BAHIA AWARD, (II, IV), The Sons of the Republic of Texas, 1717 8th St., Bay City TX 77414. Phone/fax: (409)245-6644. E-mail: srttexas@tgn.net. Website: http://www.tgn.net/~srttexas. Contact: Melinda Williams. "To promote suitable preservation of relics, appropriate dissemination of data, and research into our Texas heritage, with particular attention to the Spanish Colonial period." Annual competition for novels. Award: "A total of $2,000 is available annually for winning participants, with a minimum first place prize of $1,200 for the best published book. At its discretion, the SRT may award a second place book prize or a prize for the best published paper, article published in a periodical or project of a nonliterary nature." Judges: recognized authorities on Texas history. Guidelines available in June for SASE. Inquiries by mail, fax and e-mail OK. Entries will be accepted from June 1 to September 30. Previously published submissions and completed projects. Competition is open to any person interested in the Spanish Colonial influence on Texas culture. Winners announced December. Winners notified by phone and mail. List of winners available for SASE.

🍁 ☑ ***PRISM INTERNATIONAL* SHORT FICTION CONTEST, (I)**, *Prism International*, Dept. of Creative Writing, University of British Columbia, E462-1866 Main Mall, Vancouver, British Columbia V6T 1Z1 Canada. (604)822-2514. Fax: (604)822-3616. E-mail: prism@unixg.ubc.ca. Website: http://www.arts.ubc.ca. Contest Manager: Bob Wakulich. Award: $2,000 (1st Prize); five $200 consolation prizes. Competition receives 600 submissions. Deadline: December 15 of each year. Entry fee $15 plus $5 reading fee for each story; years subscription included. Guidelines for SASE. Inquiries by fax and e-mail OK. Winners announced in June. Winners notified by mail or e-mail. List of winners available in June for SASE, e-mail or on website.

✔ **PULITZER PRIZE IN FICTION, (III, IV)**, Columbia University, 709 Journalism Bldg., Mail Code 3865, New York NY 10027. (212)854-3841. E-mail: pulitzer-feedback@pulitzer.org. Website: http://www.pulitzer.org. Administrator: Seymour Topping. Annual award for distinguished short stories, novels and story collections *first* published in America in book form during the year by an American author, preferably dealing with American life. Award: $5,000 and certificate. Competition receives 185 submissions. Guidelines available for SASE or request by phone or e-mail. Inquiries by e-mail OK. Deadline: Books published between January 1 and June 30 must be submitted by July 1. Books published between July 1 and December 31 must be submitted by November 1; books published between November 1 and December 31 must be submitted in galleys or page proofs by November 1. Submit 4 copies of the book, entry form, biography and photo of author and $50 handling fee. Open to American authors. Winners announced in April. Winners notified by telegram.

✔ **QSPELL BOOK AWARDS/HUGH MACLENNAN FICTION AWARD, (II, IV)**, Quebec Society for the Promotion of English Language Literature, 1200 Atwater, Montreal, Quebec H3Z 1X4 Canada. Phone/fax: (514)933-0878. E-mail: qspell@total.net. Website: http://www.qspell.org. QSpell Coordinator: Diana McNeil. Award "to honor excellence in writing in English in Quebec." Annual competition for short stories, novels, poetry, nonfiction, first book and translation. Award: $2,000 (Canadian) in each category; $500 for first book. Competition receives 15-20 submissions. Judges: panel of 3 jurors, different each year. Entry fee $10 (Canadian) per title. Guidelines for SASE. Inquiries by fax and e-mail OK. Deadlines: May 31 and September 30. Submissions published in previous year from May 16 to May 15. "Writer must have resided in Quebec for three of the past five years." Books may be published anywhere. Page length: more than 48 pages. Winners announced in December. Winners notified at an awards gala in December. List of winners available for SASE.

***QUARTERLY WEST* NOVELLA COMPETITION, (I)**, University of Utah, 200 S. Central Campus Dr., Room 317, Salt Lake City UT 84112-9109. (801)581-3938. Biennial award for novellas. Award: 2 prizes of $500 and publication in *Quarterly West*. Competition receives 300 submissions. Send SASE for contest rules available in June 1998. Deadline: Postmarked by December 31, 1998. Winners announced in May or June. Winners notified by phone. List of winners available for SASE.

N **QUINCY WRITERS GUILD ANNUAL CREATIVE WRITING CONTEST, (I)**, P.O. Box 433, Quincy IL 62306-0433. (217)223-7682. Vice President: Vicky Mitchell. "Award to promote writing." Annual competition for short stories, nonfiction, poetry. Awards: cash for 1st, 2nd, 3rd Place entries; certificates for honorable mention. Competition receives 30-40 submissions. Judges: Independent panel of writing professionals not affiliated with Quincy Writers Guild. Entry fee $4 (fiction and nonfiction, each entry); $2 (poetry each entry). Guidelines for SASE. Deadline: April 1, 1999. Unpublished submissions. Word length: Fiction: 3,500 words; Nonfiction: 2,000 words. Poetry: any length, any style. "Guidelines are very important and available for SASE. No entry form is required. Entries accepted after January 1." Winners announced July 1999. Winners notified by mail in June. List of winners available after July 1999 for SASE.

SIR WALTER RALEIGH AWARD, (II, IV), North Carolina Literary and Historical Association, 109 E. Jones St., Raleigh NC 27601-2807. (919)733-9375. Awards Coordinator: Jerry C. Cashion. "To promote among the people of North Carolina an interest in their own literature." Annual award for novels. Award: Statue of Sir Walter Raleigh. Competition receives 8-12 submissions. Judges: University English and history professors. Guidelines available in August for SASE. Inquiries by fax OK. Book must be an original work published during the 12 months ending June 30 of the year for which the award is given. Writer must be a legal or physical resident of North Carolina for the three years preceding the close of the contest period. Authors or publishers may submit 3 copies of their book to the above address. Winners announced November. Winners notified by mail. List of winners available for SASE.

THE REA AWARD FOR THE SHORT STORY, (IV), Dungannon Foundation, 53 W. Church Hill Rd., Washington CT 06794. (860)868-9455. Contact: Elizabeth Rea, president. Annual award for "a writer who has made a significant contribution to the short story form." Award: $30,000. Judges: 3 jurors. Work must be nominated by the jury. Award announced in spring annually. Winners notified by phone. List of winners available in Spring.

REGINA MEDAL AWARD, (III), Catholic Library Association, 100 North St., Suite 224, Pittsfield MA 01201-5109. E-mail: cla@vgernet.com. Website: http://www.cathla.org. Contact: Jean R. Bostley, SSJ executive director. Annual award. To honor continued distinguished lifetime contribution to children's literature. Award: silver medal. Award given during Easter week. Selection by a special committee; nominees are suggested by the Catholic Library Association Membership.

✔ **RHODE ISLAND STATE COUNCIL ON THE ARTS, (I, IV)**, Individual Artist's Fellowship in Literature, 95 Cedar St., Suite 103, Providence RI 02903-1062. (401)222-3880. Fax: (401)521-1351. Website: http://www.modcult.brown.edu/RISCA/. Executive Director: Randall Rosenbaum. Biennial fellowship. Award: $5,000; runner-up $1,000. Competition receives approximately 50 submissions. In-state panel makes recommendations to an out-of-state judge, who recommends finalist to the council. Entry forms and guidelines for SASE. Inquiries

"WE WANT TO PUBLISH YOUR WORK."

You would give anything to hear an editor speak those 6 magic words. So you work hard for weeks, months, even years to make that happen. You create a brilliant piece of work and a knock-out presentation, but there's still one vital step to ensure publication. You still need to submit your work to the right buyers. With rapid changes in the publishing industry it's not always easy to know who those buyers are. That's why each year thousands of writers, just like you, turn to the most current edition of this indispensable market guide.

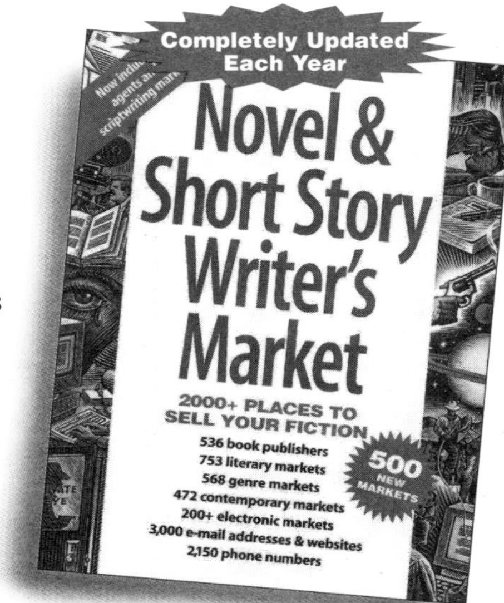

2000 Novel & Short Story Writer's Market will be published and ready for shipment in January 2000.

Keep ahead of the changes by ordering *2000 Novel & Short Story Writer's Market* today! You'll save the frustration of getting manuscripts returned in the mail stamped MOVED: ADDRESS UNKNOWN. And of NOT submitting your work to new listings because you don't know they exist. All you have to do to order the upcoming 2000 edition is complete the attached order card and return it with your payment. Order now and you'll get the 2000 edition at the 1999 price—just $22.99—no matter how much the regular price may increase!

Turn Over for More Great Books to Help Get Your Fiction Published!

☐ **Yes!** I want the most current edition of *Novel & Short Story Writer's Market*. Please send me the 2000 edition at the 1999 price – $22.99. (NOTE: *2000 Novel & Short Story Writer's Market* will be ready for shipment in January 2000.) #10625

Additional books from the back of this card:

Book	Price
#	$
#	$
#	$
#	$
Subtotal	$

*Add $3.50 postage and handling for one book; $1.50 for each additional book.

Postage & Handling	$

Payment must accompany order. Ohioans add 6% sales tax. Canadians add 7% GST.

Total	$

VISA/MasterCard orders call TOLL FREE 1-800-289-0963
8:30 to 5:00 Mon.-Fri. Eastern Time
or FAX 1-888-590-4082

☐ Payment enclosed $__________ (or)

Charge my: ☐ Visa ☐ MasterCard Exp.______

Account #______________________________

Signature______________________________

Name______________________________

Address______________________________

City______________________________

State/Prov.______________ Zip/PC ______________

30-Day Money Back Guarantee on every book you buy!

6500

Mail to: Writer's Digest Books • 1507 Dana Avenue • Cincinnati, OH 45207

by e-mail and fax OK. Deadline: April 1. Artists must be Rhode Island residents and not undergraduate or graduate students. "Program guidelines may change. Prospective applicants should contact RISCA prior to deadline." Winners announced in July. Winners notified by mail.

HAROLD U. RIBALOW PRIZE, (II, IV), *Hadassah Magazine*, 50 W. 58th St., New York NY 10019. (212)688-0227. Fax: (212)446-9521. E-mail: hadamag@aol.com. Contact: Alan M. Tigay, executive editor. Estab. 1983. Annual award "for a book of fiction on a Jewish theme. Harold U. Ribalow was a noted writer and editor who devoted his time to the discovery and encouragement of young Jewish writers." Book should have been published the year preceding the award. Award: $1,000 and excerpt of book in *Hadassah Magazine*. Deadline is April of the year following publication.

RITE OF SPRING FICTION CONTEST, (I), *Oak*, 1530 Seventh St., Rock Island IL 61201. (309)788-3980. Contact: Betty Mowery, editor. "To build up circulation of publication and provide new authors a home for work along with seasoned authors." Competition for short stories. Award: 1 year subscription to *Oak*. Competition receives 25 submissions. Judges: various editors. Entry fee six 32¢ stamps. Guidelines available in January for SASE. Deadline: September 30. "Writers must submit their own fiction of no more than 500 words. We are looking for fiction of quiet horror or fantasy." Winners announced October 1. Winners notified by letter.

SUMMERFIELD G. ROBERTS AWARD, (I, II, IV), The Sons of the Republic of Texas, 1717 8th St., Bay City TX 77414. Phone/fax: (409)245-6644. E-mail: srttexas@tgn.net. Website: http://www.tgn.net/~srttexas. Executive Secretary: Melinda Williams. "Given for the best book or manuscript of biography, essay, fiction, nonfiction, novel, poetry or short story that describes or represents the Republic of Texas, 1836-1846." Annual award of $2,500. Competition receives 10-20 submissions. Competition is judged by a panel comprised of winners of the last three years' competitions. Guidelines available after June for SASE. Inquiries by fax and e-mail OK. Deadline January 15. "The manuscripts must be written or published during the calendar year for which the award is given. Entries are to be submitted in quintuplicate and will not be returned." Winners announced March. Winners notified by mail or phone. List of winners available for SASE.

ROTTEN ROMANCE, Hutton Publications, P.O. Box 2907, Decatur IL 62524. Contact: Linda Hutton, editor. Award to "have fun writing a spoof of genre fiction." Annual competition for short stories. Award: $10 and publication. Competition receives 100 submissions. Judge: Linda Hutton, editor. Guidelines available for SASE. Inquiries by fax OK. Deadline: Valentine's Day annually. Previously unpublished submissions. Open to anyone. Word length: no more than 1 sentence, any length. "An entry form is available, but not required. Handwritten envelopes and/or entries will be discarded; all material must be typed. SASE required with entry. Tickle your sense of humor and ally it with your best writing. Study paperback romances to get a feel for the genre." Winners announced March 1. Winners notified by mail.

PLEASANT T. ROWLAND PRIZE FOR FICTION FOR GIRLS, (IV), Pleasant Company Publications, 8400 Fairway Place, Middleton WI 53562. (608)836-4848. Fax: (608)836-1999. Contact: Submissions Editor. Award to "encourage writers to turn their talents to the creation of high-quality fiction for girls and to reward talented authors of novels that successfully capture the spirit of contemporary American girls and illuminate the ways in which their lives may be personally touched by events and concerns shaping the United States today." Sponsored by Pleasant Company, publisher of The American Girls Collection series of historical fiction, American Girl Library advice and activity books, and *American Girl* magazine. Annual competition for novels appealing to girls ages 8-12. Award: $10,000. Winning author will be offered a standard contract with an advance and royalty payments for publication of the book under Pleasant Company's forthcoming contemporary fiction imprint. All entries considered for possible publication by Pleasant Company. Judges: editors of Pleasant Company Publications. No entry fee; 1 entry/person. Guidelines for SASE. Deadline: September 1. Unpublished submissions. No simultaneous submissions. US residents only. Authors whose work is now being published by Pleasant Company not eligible. Employees, their immediate family and suppliers of materials or services to Pleasant Company not eligible. Void where prohibited by law. Word length: 100-200 pages, double spaced. Submissions by authors or agents. "Stories should feature female protagonists between the ages of 8 and 12. We welcome characters of varying cultural backgrounds and family situations." Winner announced shortly after December 31. Include self-addressed stamped postcard with entry for list of winners.

THE IAN ST. JAMES AWARDS, P.O. Box 60, Cranbrook, Kent TN17 2ZR United Kingdom. 01580 212626. Fax: 01580 212041. Director: Merric Davidson. Award to "provide a better way for a writer to take a first step towards a literary career." Annual competition for short stories. Award: £2,000 top prize. Competition receives 2,500-3,000 submissions. Judges: Writers, publishers. Entry fee £6 per story. Guidelines available after January 1999 for SASE. Deadline: April 30. Previously unpublished submissions. Winners announced in July. Winners notified by mail. List of winners available September 1999 for SAE.

SCIENCE FICTION WRITERS OF EARTH (SFWoE) SHORT STORY CONTEST, (I, IV), Science Fiction Writers of Earth, P.O. Box 121293, Fort Worth TX 76121-1293. (817)451-8674. E-mail: sfwoe@flash.net.

Website: http://www.flash.net/~sfwoe. SFWoE Administrator: Gilbert Gordon Reis. Purpose "to promote the art of science fiction/fantasy short story writing." Annual award for short stories. Award: $200 (1st Prize); $100 (2nd Prize); $50 (3rd Prize). First place story is published by *Altair—Magazine of Speculative Fiction*. *Altair* also pays 3¢/word to the author of the winning story on publication. Competition receives approximately 180 submissions/year. Judge: Author Edward Bryant. Entry fee $5 for first entry; $2 for additional entries. Guidelines available in November for SASE (or print from website). Inquiries by e-mail OK. Deadline: October 30. Submissions must be unpublished. Stories should be science fiction or fantasy, 2,000-7,500 words. "Although many of our past winners are now published authors, there is still room for improvement. The odds are good for a well-written story. Contestants enjoy international competition." Winners announced January 31. Winners notified by phone. "Each contestant is mailed the contest results, judge's report, and a listing of contestant's entries."

***SE LA VIE WRITER'S JOURNAL* CONTEST, (I, IV)**, Rio Grande Press, P.O. Box 71745, Las Vegas NV 89170. Contact: Rosalie Avara, editor. Competition offered quarterly for short short stories with surprise ending. Award: Publication in the *Se La Vie Writer's Journal* plus up to $10 and contributor's copy. Judge: Editor. Entry fee $4 for each or $7 for two (payable to Rosalie Avara). Guidelines for SASE. Deadlines: March 31, June 30, September 30, December 31. Unpublished submissions. Themes: slice-of-life, mystery, adventure, social. Length: 500 words maximum, 200 words minimum.

SEATTLE ARTISTS PROGRAM, (IV), Seattle Arts Commission, 312 First Ave. N., Suite 200, Seattle WA 98109. (206)684-7310. Fax: (206)684-7172. Website: http://www.ci.seattle.wa.us/seattle/sac/home.htm. Project Manager: Irene Gómez. "Award to support development of new works by Seattle individual, generative literary artists." Biannual competition for poetry, prose/fiction, scriptwriting, screenwriting, critical writing and creative nonfiction. Award: $2,000 or $7,500. Competition receives approx. 150 submissions. Judges: peer review panels. Guidelines/application available in May for 8½×11 SASE. Deadline: July 2000. Previously published submissions or unpublished submissions. Only Seattle residents or individuals with a Seattle studio or office may apply. Word length: Word-length requirements vary; the guidelines must be read. Winners announced in October 2000. Winners notified by mail.

☑ **7 HILLS SHORT FICTION CONTEST, (V)**, Tallahassee Writers Association, P.O. Box 6996, Tallahassee FL 32314. (850)222-8731. E-mail: verna325@talweb.com. Website: http://www.twaonline.org. Fiction Chair: Verna Safran. Competition to "stimulate good writing, to use proceeds for book donations to library and for a college scholarship, to produce a literary magazine." Annual competition for short stories. Awards: $100 1st Prize, $75 2nd, $50 3rd, plus honorable mentions and publication. Judges: different each year. Entry fee $10. Guidelines available in April for SASE. Deadline: August 15. Unpublished submissions and not submitted elsewhere. "We want literary fiction, not genre fiction." Word length: 1,500-2,000. Winners announced in October. Winners notified at Writer's Workshop and by mail.

***SEVENTEEN MAGAZINE* FICTION CONTEST, (I, IV)**, *Seventeen Magazine*, 850 Third Ave., New York NY 10022-6258. Fiction Editor: Ben Schrank. To honor best short fiction by a young writer. Competition receives 5,000 submissions. Guidelines for SASE. Rules published in the November issue. Contest for 13-21 year olds. Deadline: April 30. Submissions judged by a panel of outside readers, former winners and *Seventeen*'s editors. Cash awarded to winners. First-place story published in the December or January issue. Winners announced in late 1999. Winners notified by phone or mail. List of winners available in an early issue in year 2000.

☑ **FRANCES SHAW FELLOWSHIP FOR OLDER WOMEN WRITERS**, The Ragdale Foundation, 1260 N. Green Bay Rd., Lake Forest IL 60045-1106. (847)234-1063. Fax: (847)234-1075. E-mail: ragdale1@aol.com. Website: http://nsn.ns/silus.org/lfkhome/ragdale. Director of Programming and Marketing: Sylvia Brown. Award to "nurture and support older women writers who are just beginning to write seriously." Annual competition for short stories, novels and poetry. Award: 2 months free residency at Ragdale, plus domestic travel. Competition receives 150 submissions. Judges: a panel of four anonymous women writers. Guidelines for SASE. Inquiries by fax or e-mail OK. Deadline: February 1. Previously unpublished submissions. Females over 55. Word length: 20 pages/12 short poems. "Make your letter of application interesting, covering your desire to write and the reasons you have been thwarted to this point." Winners announced April 30, 1999. Winners notified by phone.

FOR EXPLANATIONS OF THESE SYMBOLS,
SEE THE INSIDE FRONT AND BACK COVERS OF THIS BOOK.

☑ **SHORT, SHORT FICTION CONTEST, (I)**, New England Writers, P.O. Box 483, Windsor VT 05089-0483. (802)674-2315. E-mail: newvtpoets@juno.com. Editor: Frank Anthony. Competition for publication in annual *Anthology of New England Writers*. Annual competition for short stories. Award: $300. Competition receives 150 submissions. Judge: TBA, 1999. Entry fee $5. Guidelines available January 1999 for SASE. Inquires by e-mail OK. Deadline: June 15, 1999. Unpublished submissions. Word length: 1,000 words maximum. "We want well-crafted stories written for an audience with high standards." Winners announced at annual N.E.W. conference in July. List of winners available for SASE.

☑ **SHORT/SHORT FICTION PRIZE, (I)**, *Salt Hill Journal*, English Department, Syracuse University, Syracuse NY 13244-1170. (315)425-9371. E-mail: cbkoplik@syr.edu. Website: http://www-hl.syr.edu/cwp. Fiction Editor: Caryn Koplik. Annual competition to "publish the best short/short fiction being written today." Awards: $500 (1st Prize), $250 (2nd Prize), $100 (3rd Prize), all plus publication; 10 honorable mentions. Judges: final judging by nationally known writer. Entry fee $9/story. Guidelines available Fall/Winter for SASE. Inquiries by e-mail OK. Deadline: September 15, 1999. Unpublished submissions. Word length: up to 1,500 words/story. Name, address, phone number and word count on first page. Enclose SASE for results; stories not returned. Address submission to Fiction Contest. Winners announced Spring 2000. Winners notified by phone. List of winners available for SASE.

***SIDE SHOW* 8TH SHORT STORY CONTEST, (II)**, Somersault Press, P.O. Box 1428, El Cerrito CA 94530-1428. E-mail: jison@crl.com. Editor: Shelley Anderson. Award "to attract quality writers for our 300-odd page paperback fiction anthology." Awards: $200 (1st Prize); $100 (2nd Prize); $75 (3rd Prize); $5/printed page paid to all accepted writers (on publication). Competition receives 1,000 submissions. Judges: The editors of *Side Show*. Entry fee $10; year's subscription included. Leaflet available but no guidelines or restrictions on length, subject or style. Inquiries by e-mail OK. Sample copy for $10 plus $2 postage. Multiple submissions (in same mailing envelope) encouraged (only one entry fee required for each writer). No deadline. Book published when we accept 20-25 stories. "A story from *Side Show* was selected for inclusion in *Pushcart Prize XVIII: Best of the Small Presses*."

BERNICE SLOTE AWARD, (II), *Prairie Schooner*, 201 Andrews Hall, University of Nebraska, Lincoln NE 68588-0334. (402)472-0911. Contact: Hilda Raz, editor. "An award for the best work by a beginning writer published in *Prairie Schooner* during the previous year." Annual award for short stories, novel excerpts and translations. Award: $500. Judges: Editorial board. Guidelines for SASE. Unpublished submissions. Must be beginning writers (not have a book published). "We only read mss September through May." The work must have been published in the magazine to be considered for the annual prizes.

☑ **KAY SNOW CONTEST, (I, IV)**, Willamette Writers, 9045 SW Barbur Blvd., Suite 5-A, Portland OR 97219-4027. (503)452-1592. Fax: (503)452-0372. E-mail: wilwrite@teleport.com. Website: http://www.teleport.com/~wilwrite/. Contact: Bill Johnson, office manager. Award "to create a showcase for writers of all fields of literature." Annual competition for short stories; also poetry (structured and nonstructured), nonfiction, juvenile and student writers. Award: $200 1st Prize in each category, second and third prizes, honorable mentions. Competition receives approximately 500 submissions. Judges: nationally recognized writers and teachers. Entry fee $15, nonmembers; $10, members; $5, students. Guidelines for #10 SASE. Inquiries by fax and e-mail OK. Deadline: May 15 postmark. Unpublished submissions. Maximum 5 double-spaced pages or up to 3 poems per entry fee with maximum 5 double-spaced pages. Winners announced August. Winners notified by mail and phone. List of winners available for SASE. Prize winners will be honored at the two-day August Willamette Writers Conference. Press releases will be sent to local and national media announcing the winners, and excerpts from winning entries may appear in our newsletter.

☑ **SOCIETY OF CHILDREN'S BOOK WRITERS AND ILLUSTRATORS GOLDEN KITE AWARDS, (II, IV)**, Society of Children's Book Writers and Illustrators, 345 N. Maple Dr., #296, Beverly Hills CA 90210. (310)859-9887. Contact: Sue Alexander, chairperson. Annual award. "To recognize outstanding works of fiction, nonfiction and picture illustration for children by members of the Society of Children's Book Writers and Illustrators and published in the award year." Published submissions should be submitted from January to December of publication year. Deadline: December 15. Rules for SASE. Award: Statuette and plaque. Looking for quality material for children. Individual "must be member of the SCBWI to submit books."

☑ **SOCIETY OF CHILDREN'S BOOK WRITERS AND ILLUSTRATORS WORK-IN-PROGRESS GRANTS, (I, IV)**, 345 N. Maple Dr., #296, Beverly Hills CA 90210. (310)859-9887. Contact: SCBWI. Annual grant for any genre or contemporary novel for young people; also nonfiction research grant and grant for work whose author has never been published. Award: First-$1,000, second-$500 (work-in-progress). Competition receives approximately 180 submissions. Judges: Members of children's book field—editors, authors, etc. Guidelines for SASE. Deadline: February 1-May 1. Unpublished submissions. Applicants must be SCBWI members.

***SONORA REVIEW* SHORT STORY CONTEST, (I, II)**, Dept. of English, University of Arizona, Tucson AZ 85721-0067. (520)626-2555. Contact: Fiction Editor. Annual contest to encourage and support quality short fiction. $150 1st Prize plus publication in *Sonora Review*. All entrants receive copy of the magazine. Entry fee $10. Competition receives 200 submissions. Send SASE for contest rules and deadlines.

☑ **SOUTH CAROLINA ARTS COMMISSION AND *THE POST AND COURIER* NEWSPAPER (CHARLESTON, SC) SOUTH CAROLINA FICTION PROJECT, (I, IV)**, 1800 Gervais St., Columbia SC 29201. (803)734-8696. Director, Literary Arts Program: Sara June Goldstein. Award "to get money to fiction writers and to get their work published and read." Annual award for short stories. Award: $500 and publication in *The Post and Courier*. Competition receives between 200 and 400 submissions for 12 awards (up to 12 stories chosen). Judges: a panel of professional writers and Assistant Features Editor for *The Post and Courier*. Deadline: January 15. *South Carolina residents only*. Stories must not be over 2,500 words. Query for guidelines.

☑ **SOUTH CAROLINA ARTS COMMISSION LITERATURE FELLOWSHIPS AND LITERATURE GRANTS, (I, IV)**, 1800 Gervais St., Columbia SC 29201. (803)734-8696. Director, Literary Arts Program: Sara June Goldstein. "The purpose of the fellowships is to give a cash award to a deserving writer (one year in poetry, one year in creative prose) whose works are of the highest caliber." Award: $7,500 fellowship. Matching project grants up to $5,000. Judges: out-of-state panel of professional writers and editors for fellowships, and panels and SCAC staff for grants. Query for entry forms or rules. Fellowship deadline February 15. Grants deadlines April 1 and September 1. *South Carolina residents only*. "The next deadline is for creative prose."

N **SOUTH DAKOTA ARTS COUNCIL, (IV)**, 800 Governors Dr., Pierre SD 57501-2294. (605)773-3131. "Individual artist's project grants—ranging from $500 to $3,000—are planned for the fiscal year 1998 through 2000." Guidelines for SASE. Deadline: March 1. Grants are open only to residents of South Dakota.

☑ ***THE SOUTHERN REVIEW*/LOUISIANA STATE UNIVERSITY ANNUAL SHORT FICTION AWARD, (II)**, *The Southern Review*, 43 Allen Hall, Louisiana State University, Baton Rouge LA 70803-5005. (504)388-5108. Fax: (504)388-5098. E-mail: bmacon@unix1.sncc.lsu.edu. Website: http://www.lsu.edu/guests/wwwtsm. Associate Editor: Michael Griffith. Annual award "to encourage publication of good fiction." For a first collection of short stories by an American writer published in the United States appearing during calendar year. Award: $500. Possible campus reading. Competition receives 100 submissions. Guidelines available for SASE. Inquiries by fax and e-mail OK. Deadline: January 31. Two copies to be submitted by publisher or author. Looking for "style, sense of craft, plot, in-depth characters." Winners announced Summer. Winners notified by mail or phone.

SPRING FANTASY FICTION CONTEST, Women In The Arts, P.O. Box 2907, Decatur IL 62524. (217)872-0811. Contact: Vice President. Award to "encourage new writers, whether published or not." Annual competition for short stories. Award: At least $30. Competition receives 25-30 submissions. Judges: WITA members who are professional writers. Entry fee $2 for each story submitted. Guidelines available for SASE. Deadline: November 15 annually. Published or previously unpublished submissions. Open to anyone not a member of WITA. Word length: 1,500 words maximum. "Entrants must send for our contest rules and follow the specific format requirements."

SPRING FANTASY JUVENILE-FICTION CONTEST, Women In The Arts, P.O. Box 2907, Decatur IL 62524. (217)872-0811. Contact: Vice President. Award to "encourage writers of children's literature, whether published or not." Annual competition for short stories. Award: At least $30. Competition receives 10-15 submissions. Judges: WITA members who are professional writers. Entry fee $2 for each story submitted. Guidelines available for SASE. Deadline: November 15 annually. Published or previously unpublished submissions. Open to anyone not a member of WITA. Word length: 1,500 words maximum. "Entrants must send for our contest rules and follow the specific format requirements."

☑ **WALLACE E. STEGNER FELLOWSHIP, (I, IV)**, Creative Writing Program, Stanford University, Stanford CA 94305-2087. (650)723-2637. Fax: (650)723-3679. E-mail: gay-pierce@forsythe.stanford.edu. Program Administrator: Gay Pierce. Annual award for short stories, novels, poetry and story collections. Five fellowships in fiction ($15,000 stipend plus required tuition of $5,500 annually). Competition receives 650 submissions. Entry fee $40. Guidelines available in June for SASE. Inquiries by fax and e-mail OK. Deadline: December 1. For unpublished or previously published fiction writers. Residency required. Word length: 9,000 words or 40 pages. Winners announced April. Winners notified by telephone. All applicants receive notification of winners.

STONY BROOK $1,000 SHORT FICTION PRIZE, (IV), State University of New York, Department of English, Humanities Bldg., Stony Brook NY 11794-5350. (516)751-5226. E-mail: cmcgrath@notes.cc.sunysb.edu. Website: http://notes.cc.sunysb.edu/doit.nsf/webform2/literary. Director: Carolyn McGrath. Award "to recognize excellent undergraduate fiction." Annual competition for short stories. Award: $1,000. Competition receives 250-300 submissions. Judges: Faculty of the Department of English & Creative Writing Program. No entry fee. Guidelines for SASE or on website. Inquiries by e-mail OK. Deadline: March 1, 1999. Unpublished submissions. "Only undergraduates enrolled full time in American or Canadian colleges and universities for the academic year 1998-99 are eligible. Students with an Asian background are particularly encouraged to participate." Word length: 5,000 words or less. Winners announced by June 1999. Winners notified by phone. List of winners available on website or by e-mail or writing to Carolyn McGrath.

✓ ***STORY'S* SHORT SHORT STORY COMPETITION**, STORY Magazine, 1507 Dana Ave., Cincinnati OH 45207-1000. (513)531-2222, ext. 328. Fax: (513)531-1843. E-mail: competitions@fwpubs.com. Website: http://www.writersdigest.com. Editor: Lois Rosenthal. Contact: Terri Boes, promotions associate. Award to "encourage the form of the short short and to find stories for possible publication in the magazine." Contest begins June 1 and closes October 31. Award: $1,500 (1st Prize); $750 (2nd Prize); $500 (3rd Prize); $100 (4th through 10th Prizes); $50 gift certificate for Story Press books (11th through 25th Prizes). Competition receives 7,000 submissions. Judges: STORY editors. Entry fee $10. Guidelines are published in the magazine (summer and autumn issues), or available after June by e-mail, fax or SASE. Inquiries by fax and e-mail OK (not for entries). Word length: 1,500 words or less. Winners announced in spring issue 1999. Winners notified by phone or mail by January 31, 1999.

SUB-TERRAIN ANNUAL SHORT STORY CONTEST, (I), *sub-TERRAIN Magazine*, P.O. Box 1575, Bentall Center, Vancouver, British Columbia V6C 2P7 Canada. (604)876-8710. Fax: (604)879-2667. E-mail: subter@pinc.com. Contact: Brian Kaufman. Award "to inspire writers to get down to it and struggle with a form that is condensed and difficult. To encourage clean, powerful writing." Annual award for short stories. Award: $250 and publication. Runners-up also receive publication. Competition receives 150-200 submissions. Judges: An editorial collective. Entry fee $15 for one story, $5 extra for each additional story (includes 4-issue subscription). Guidelines available in November for SASE. "Contest kicks off in November." Deadline: May 15. Unpublished submissions. Length: 2,000 words maximum. Winners announced in July issue. Winners notified by phone call and press release. "We are looking for fiction that has MOTION, that goes the distance in fewer words."

✓ **THE RICHARD SULLIVAN PRIZE IN SHORT FICTION**, Creative Writing Program, Department of English and University of Notre Dame Press, Department of English, University of Notre Dame, Notre Dame IN 46556-0368. (219)631-7526. Fax: (219)631-8209. E-mail: english.righter1@nd.edu. Website: http://www.nd.edu. Director of Creative Writing: William O'Rourke. Award to "publish the second (or later) volume of short stories by an author of demonstrated excellence." Biannual competition for short stories and story collections. Award: $1,000 ($500 award, $500 advance) and publication by University of Notre Dame Press. Competition receives 150 submissions. Judges: Faculty of the Creative Writing Program. Guidelines available for SASE. Inquiries by fax and e-mail OK. Deadline: May 1-August 31, 2000. Open to any writer who has published at least one previous volume of short stories. Winners announced January 2001. Winners notified by phone and mail. List of winners available end of January 2001 for SASE.

SURREY WRITERS' CONFERENCE WRITING CONTEST, (I), Surrey School District, 12870 72nd Ave., Surrey British Columbia V3W 2M9 Canada. (604)594-2000. Fax: (604)590-2506. E-mail: ed_griffin@compuserve.com. Website: http://www.vcn.bc.ca/swc/. Coordinator: Ed Griffin. Award to "encourage beginning writers." Annual competition for short stories, poetry and nonfiction. Award: $75-$250 in each category. Competition receives 200 submissions/category. Judges: appointed by school principal. Entry fee $10; $5 for youth. Guidelines for SASE. Inquiries by e-mail OK. Deadline: September 25. Unpublished submissions. Word length: 1,000 words. Winners announced at conference on October 23. Winners not present will be notified by mail. List of winners available for SASE.

TARA FELLOWSHIP FOR SHORT FICTION, (I), The Heekin Group Foundation, P.O. Box 1534, Sisters OR 97759. (503)548-4147. E-mail: h8fhl@aol.com. Contact: Sarah Heekin Redfield, fiction director. "To support unpublished, beginning career writers in their writing projects." Two annual awards for completed short stories. Award: $1,500. Receives approximately 600 applications. Judges: Invitation of Publisher judge. Past judges: Graywolf Press, SOHO Press, Dalkey Archive Press, The Ecco Press and the *Threepenny Review*. This year's judge: *Prairie Schooner*. Application fee $25. Guidelines for SASE. Deadline: December 1. Unpublished submissions. Word length: 2,500-10,000 words.

SYDNEY TAYLOR MANUSCRIPT COMPETITION, Association of Jewish Libraries, 1327 Wyntercreek Lane, Dunwoody GA 30338. (770)394-2060. Fax: (770)671-8380. E-mail: m-psand@mindspring.com. Coordinator: Paula Sandfelder. Award to "deepen the understanding of Judaism for all children by helping to launch new writers of children's Jewish fiction." Annual competition for novels. Award: $1,000. Competition receives 25 submissions. Judges: 5 children's library. Guidelines for #10 SASE. Inquiries by fax and e-mail OK. Deadline: January 15. Previously unpublished submissions. "Children's fiction for readers 8-11 years with universal appeal and Jewish content. Writer must not have a previously published book." Word length: 64 page minimum-200 page maximum, double-spaced. Winners announced May 15, 1999. Winners notified by phone or mail. List of winners available by contacting the coordinator.

TENNESSEE ARTS COMMISSION LITERARY FELLOWSHIP, (I, II, IV), 401 Charlotte Ave., Nashville TN 37243-0780. (615)741-1701. Fax: (615)741-8559. E-mail: aswanson@mail.state.tn.us. Director of Literary Arts: Alice Swanson. Award to "honor promising writers." Annual award for fiction or poetry. Award: $2,000.

Competition receives approximately 30 submissions. Judges are out-of-state jurors. Previously published and unpublished submissions. Writers must be residents of Tennessee. Word length: 20 ms pages. Write for guidelines. Inquiries by fax and e-mail OK. This year's award is for prose.

☑ **TEXAS-WIDE WRITERS CONTEST, (I, IV)**, Byliners, P.O. Box 6218, Corpus Christi TX 78466-6218. E-mail: otter@newton.tamuk.edu. Contact: Carla Susan, president. "Contest to fund a scholarship in journalism or creative writing." Annual contest for adult and children's short stories, novels and poems. Award: Novels—1st $75, 2nd $55, 3rd $30; short stories—1st $55, 2nd $40, 3rd $20. Competition receives approximately 30 novel, 60 short story and 45 children's story submissions. Judges: Varies each year. Entry fee $5/story, $10/novel. Guidelines available for SASE. Deadline: February 28 (date remains same each year). Unpublished submissions. Limited to Texas residents and winter Texans. Length: Children's story limit 2,000 words; short story limit 3,000 words; novel 3-page synopsis plus chapter one. "Contest also has nostalgia, article and nonfiction book categories." Winners announced May 16. Winners notified by mail. List of winners available for SASE.

THURBER HOUSE RESIDENCIES, (II), The Thurber House, 77 Jefferson Ave., Columbus OH 43215. (614)464-1032. Contact: Michael J. Rosen, literary director. "Four writers/year are chosen as writers-in-residence, one for each quarter." Award for writers of novels and story collections. $5,000 stipend and housing for a quarter in the furnished third-floor apartment of James Thurber's boyhood home. Judges: Advisory panel. To apply, send letter of interest and curriculum vitae. Deadline: December 15. "The James Thurber Writer-in-Residence will teach a class in the Creative Writing Program at The Ohio State University in either fiction or poetry and will offer one public reading and a short workshop for writers in the community. Significant time outside of teaching is reserved for the writer's own work-in-progress. Candidates should have published at least one book with a major publisher, in any area of fiction, nonfiction, or poetry and should possess some experience in teaching."

THE THURBER PRIZE FOR AMERICAN HUMOR, (III), The Thurber House, 77 Jefferson Ave., Columbus OH 43215. (614)464-1032. Fax: (614)228-7445. Literary Director: Michael J. Rosen. Award "to give the nation's highest recognition of the art of humor writing." Biannual competition for novels and story collections. Awards: $5,000, Thurber statuette. Up to 3 Honor Awards may also be conferred. Judges: well-known members of the national arts community. Entry fee $25/title. Guidelines for SASE. Published submissions or accepted for publication in US for first time. No reprints or paperback editions of previously published books. Word length: no requirement. Primarily pictorial works such as cartoon collections are not considered. Work must be nominated by publisher.

TICKLED BY THUNDER ANNUAL FICTION CONTEST, Tickled By Thunder, 7385-129 St., Surrey, British Columbia V3W 7B8 Canada. (604)591-6095. E-mail: thunder@istar.ca. Website: http://home.istar.ca/~thunder. Contact: Larry Lindner, editor. "To encourage new writers." Annual competition for short stories. Award: 50% of all fees, $100 minimum (Canadian), 1 year's (4-issue) subscription plus publication. Competition receives approximately 25 submissions. Judges: The editor and other writers. Entry fee $10 (Canadian) per entry (free for subscribers but more than one story requires $5 per entry). Guidelines available for SASE. Inquiries by e-mail OK. Deadline: February 15. Unpublished submissions. Word length: 2,000 words or less. Winners announced in May. Winners notified by mail. List of winners available for SASE.

☑ **LON TINKLE AWARD**, Texas Institute of Letters, P.O. Box 298300, Fort Worth TX 76129. (817)257-7822. E-mail: j.alter@tcu.edu. Website: http://www.prs.tcu.edu/prs/til/. Secretary: Judy Alter. Award to "honor a Texas writer for excellence sustained throughout a career." Annual competition for lifetime achievement. Award: $1,500. Competition receives 40 submissions. Judges: TIL Council. Guidelines available in July for SASE sent to P.O. Box 39800, Fort Worth TX 76129. Inquiries by e-mail OK. Deadline: January 4. To be eligible, the writer must have a notable association with Texas. Writer must be nominated by a member of TIL Council. "The TIL Council chooses the winner. Applications for the award are not made, through one might suggest possible candidates to an officer or member of the Council." Winners announced in April. Winners notified by mail or phone.

☑ **TOWSON UNIVERSITY PRIZE FOR LITERATURE, (II, IV)**, Towson University Foundation, Towson University, Towson MD 21252-0001. (410)830-2128. Fax: (410)830-6392. E-mail: djones@towson.edu. Dean, College of Liberal Arts: Dan L. Jones. Annual award for novels or short story collections, previously published. Award: $1,000. Competition receives 5-10 submissions. Requirements: Writer must not be over 40; must be a Maryland resident. Guidelines available spring 1999 for SASE. Inquiries by fax and e-mail OK. Deadline: May 15, 1999. Winners announced December 1999. Winners notified by letter. List of winners available by calling or writing Dan Jones or Sue Ann Nordhoff-Klaus.

☑ **STEVEN TURNER AWARD, (II, IV)**, The Texas Institute of Letters, TCU Box 298300, Fort Worth TX 76129. (817)257-7822. Fax: (817)257-5075. E-mail: j.alter@tcu.edu. Website: http://www.prs.tcu.edu/prs/til/. Secretary: Judy Alter. "To honor the best first book of fiction published by a writer who was born in Texas or who has lived in the state for two years at some time, or whose work concerns the state." Annual award for novels and story collections. Award: $1,000. Judges: committee. Guidelines available in July for SASE sent to

P.O. Box 39800, Fort Worth TX 76129. Inquiries by e-mail OK. Deadline: January 4. Previously published submissions appearing in print between January 1 and December 31. Winners announced in April. Winners notified by mail or phone.

☑ **MARK TWAIN AWARD, (III, IV)**, Missouri Association of School Librarians, 1552 Rue Riviera, Bonne Terre MO 63628-9349. Phone/fax: (573)358-1053. E-mail: masloffice@aol.com. Estab. 1970. Annual award to introduce children to the best of current literature for children and to stimulate reading. Award: A bronze bust of Mark Twain, created by Barbara Shanklin, a Missouri sculptor. A committee selects pre-list of the books nominated for the award; statewide reader/selectors review and rate the books, and then children throughout the state vote to choose a winner from the final list. Books must be published two years prior to nomination for the award list. Publishers may send books they wish to nominate for the list to the committee members. 1) Books should be of interest to children in grades 4 through 8; 2) written by an author living in the US; 3) of literary value which may enrich children's personal lives. Inquiries by fax and e-mail OK. Winners announced in May.

N **THE MARK TWAIN AWARD FOR SHORT FICTION, (I)**, *Red Rock Review*, English Dept., J2A, 3200 E. Cheyenne Ave., N. Las Vegas NV 89030-4296. (702)651-4005. Fax: (702)651-4639. E-mail: logsdon@ccsn.nevada.edu. Website: http://www.ccsn.nevada.edu/academics/departments/English/redrock.htm. Website includes contest guidelines and general submissions guidelines. Award to "find and publish the best available works of short fiction." Annual competition for short stories. Awards: $1,000 and publication. Competition receives 230 entries. Judges: pre-judging by magazine staff and readers; winner selected by guest judge (guest judge for 1997 contest was Ron Carlson). Entry fee: $10. Guidelines available Spring 1999 for SASE. Deadline: October 31, 1999. Previously unpublished submissions. Word length: 3,500 words or less. "Author's name should not appear anywhere on manuscript. Submissions should include cover page with author's name, address and phone. No simultaneous submissions. Writing should grab the reader's attention early and show a freshness of language and voice." Winners announced Spring 2000. Winners notified by phone. List of winners available for SASE.

☑ **UPC SCIENCE FICTION AWARD, (I, IV)**, Universitat Politècnica de Catalunya Board of Trustees, gran capità 2-4, Edifici NEXUS, 08034 Barcelona, Spain. Phone: 34 93 4016343. Fax: 34 93 4017766. E-mail: cscana@rectorat.upc.es. Website: http://www.upc.es. "The award is based on the desire for integral education at UPC. The literary genre of science fiction is undoubtedly the most suitable for a university such as UPC, since it unifies the concepts of science and literature." Annual award for short stories; 1,000,000 pesetas (about $10,000 US). Competition receives 130 submissions. Judges: Professors of the university and science fiction writers. Guidelines available in February by mail, e-mail, fax or phone. Inquiries by fax and e-mail OK. Deadline: September 15, 1999. Previously unpublished entries. Length: 70-115 pages, double-spaced, 30 lines/page, 70 characters/line. Submissions may be made in Spanish, English, Catalan or French. The author must sign his work with a pseudonym and enclose a sealed envelope with full name, a personal ID number, address and phone. The pseudonym and title of work must appear on the envelope. Winners announced December 1999.

VERY SHORT FICTION SUMMER AWARD, *Glimmer Train Stories*, 710 SW Madison St., Suite 504, Portland OR 97205. (503)221-0836. Fax: (503)221-0837. Website: http://www.glimmertrain.com. Contact: Linda Burmeister Davies, editor. Annual award offered to encourage the art of the very short story. Contest opens May 1 and ends July 31; entry must be postmarked between these dates. Awards: $1,200 and publication in *Glimmer Train Stories* (1st Place), $500 (2nd Place), $300 (3rd Place). Competition receives 1,500 submissions. Entry fee: $10 per story. Guidelines available for SASE or check website. Inquiries by fax OK. Word length: 2,000 words maximum. First page of story should include name, address, phone number and word count. "VSF AWARD" must be written on outside of envelope. Materials will not be returned. Include SASE for list of winning entries. Notification on November 1.

VERY SHORT FICTION WINTER AWARD, *Glimmer Train Stories*, 710 SW Madison St., Suite 504, Portland OR 97205. (503)221-0836. Fax: (503)221-0837. Website: http://www.glimmertrain.com. Contact: Linda Burmeister Davies, editor. Award offered to encourage the art of the very short story. Contest opens November 1 and ends January 31; entry must be postmarked between these dates. Awards: $1,200 and publication in *Glimmer Train Stories* (1st Place), $500 (2nd Place), $300 (3rd Place). Entry fee: $10 per story. Guidelines available for SASE or check website. Inquiries by fax OK. Word length: 2,000 words maximum. First page of story should include name, address, phone number and word count. "VSF AWARD" must be written on outside of envelope. Materials will not be returned. Include SASE for list of winners. Notification on May 1.

MARKET CATEGORIES: (I) Unpublished entries; **(II)** Published entries nominated by the author; **(III)** Published entries nominated by the editor, publisher or nominating body; **(IV)** Specialized entries.

✓ **VIOLET CROWN BOOK AWARD, (I, IV)**, Austin Writers' League, 1501 W. Fifth St., Suite E-2, Austin TX 78703. (512)499-8914. Fax: (512)499-0441. Executive Director: Jim Bob McMillan. Award "to recognize the best books published by Austin Writers' League members over the period July 1 to June 30 in fiction, nonfiction and literary (poetry, short story collections, etc.) categories." Award: Three $1,000 cash awards and trophies. Competition receives approximately 100 submissions. Judges: A panel of judges who are not affiliated with the Austin Writers' League or Barnes & Noble. Entry fee $10. Guidelines for SASE. Deadline: August 31. Previously published submissions between July 1 and June 30. "Entrants must be Austin Writers' League members. League members reside all over the U.S. and some foreign countries. Persons may join the League when they send in entries." Publisher may also submit entry in writer's name. "Awards are co-sponsored by Barnes & Noble Booksellers. Special citations are presented to finalists."

VOGELSTEIN FOUNDATION GRANTS, (II), The Ludwig Vogelstein Foundation, Inc., P.O. Box 277, Hancock ME 04640-0277. Executive Director: Frances Pishny. "A small foundation awarding grants to individuals in the arts and humanities. Criteria are merit and need. No student aid given." Send SASE for complete information after January 1, before June 1.

N **WALDEN FELLOWSHIP, (I, IV)**, Coordinated by: Extended Campus Programs, Southern Oregon University, 1250 Siskiyou Blvd., Ashland OR 97520-5038. (503)552-6901. Fax: (541)552-6047. E-mail: friendly@sou.edu. Arts Coordinator: Brooke Friendly. Award "to give Oregon writers the opportunity to pursue their work at a quiet, beautiful farm in southern Oregon." Annual competition for all types of writing. Award: 3-6 week residencies. Competition receives approx. 30 submissions. Judges: committee judges selected by the sponsor. Guidelines for SASE. Inquiries by fax and e-mail OK. Deadline: end of November. Oregon writers only. Word length: maximum 30 pages prose, 8-10 poems. Winners announced in January. Winners notified by mail. List of winners available for SASE.

EDWARD LEWIS WALLANT MEMORIAL BOOK AWARD, (II, IV), 3 Brighton Rd., West Hartford CT 06117. Sponsored by Dr. and Mrs. Irving Waltman. Contact: Mrs. Irving Waltman. Annual award. Memorial to Edward Lewis Wallant offering incentive and encouragement to beginning writers, for books published the year before the award is conferred in the spring. Award: $500 plus award certificate. Books may be submitted for consideration to Dr. Sanford Pinsker, Department of English, Franklin & Marshall College, P.O. Box 3003, Lancaster PA 17604-3003. Deadline: December 31. "Looking for creative work of fiction by an American which has significance for the American Jew. The novel (or collection of short stories) should preferably bear a kinship to the writing of Wallant. The award will seek out the writer who has not yet achieved literary prominence." Winners announced January-February. Winners notified by phone.

WESTERN HERITAGE AWARDS, (II, IV), National Cowboy Hall of Fame, 1700 NE 63rd St., Oklahoma City OK 73111. (405)478-2250. Fax: (405)478-4714. Contact: M.J. Van Deuenter, director of publications. Annual award "to honor outstanding quality in fiction, nonfiction and art literature." Submissions are to have been published during the previous calendar year. Award: The Wrangler, a replica of a C.M. Russell Bronze. Competition receives 350 submissions. Entry fee $35. Entry forms and rules available October 1 for SASE. Inquiries by fax OK. Deadline: November 30. Looking for "stories that best capture the spirit of the West. Submit five actual copies of the work." Winners announced April. Winners notified by letter.

N **WHITING WRITERS' AWARDS, (III)**, Mrs. Giles Whiting Foundation, 1133 Avenue of the Americas, New York NY 10036-6710. Director, Writer's Program: Barbara K. Bristol. Annual award for writers of fiction, poetry, nonfiction and plays with an emphasis on emerging writers. Award: $30,000 (10 awards). Candidates are submitted by appointed nominators and chosen for awards by an appointed selection committee. Direct applications and informal nominations not accepted by the foundation. List of winners available October 30 by request.

***WIND* MAGAZINE SHORT STORY COMPETITION, (I)**, P.O. Box 24548, Lexington KY 40524. Editors: Charlie G. Hughes and Leatha F. Kendrick. Annual competition for short stories. Award: $500 and publication (1st Prize); finalists receive a 1-year subscription. Entry fee $10/story. Deadline: April 30. Word length: 5,000 words or less. List of winners available for SASE.

✓ **WISCONSIN ARTS BOARD INDIVIDUAL ARTIST PROGRAM, (II, IV)**, 101 E. Wilson St., First Floor, Madison WI 53702. (608)264-8191. Fax: (608)267-0380. E-mail: mfraire@arts.state.wi.us. Contact: Mark J. Fraire. Biennial awards for short stories, poetry, novels, novellas, drama, essay/criticism. Awards: 5 awards of $8,000. Competition receives approximately 200 submissions. Entry forms or rules available in August upon request. Inquiries by fax and e-mail OK. Deadline: September 15 of even-numbered years (1998, 2000 etc.). Wisconsin residents only. Students are ineligible. Winners announced in late December. Winner notified by mail.

WISCONSIN INSTITUTE FOR CREATIVE WRITING FELLOWSHIP, (I, II, IV), University of Wisconsin—Creative Writing, English Department, 600 N. Park St., Madison WI 53706. Director: Jesse Lee Kercheval. Competition "to provide time, space and an intellectual community for writers working on first books." Three annual awards for short stories, novels and story collections. Awards: $22,000/9-month appointment.

Competition receives 400 submissions. Judges: English Department faculty. Guidelines available for SASE; write to Ron Kuka. Deadline: month of February. Published or unpublished submissions. Applicants must have received an M.F.A. or comparable graduate degree in creative writing and not yet published a book. Limit 1 story up to 30 pages in length. Two letters of recommendation required.

☑ **THOMAS WOLFE FICTION PRIZE, (I)**, North Carolina Writers' Network, 3501 Hwy. 54 W., Studio C, Chapel Hill NC 27510. (919)967-9540. Fax: (919)929-0535. E-mail: ncwn@sunsite.unc.edu. Website: http://sunsite.unc.edu/ncwriters. Program Coordinator: Frances Dovell. "Our international literary prizes seek to recognize the best in today's writing." Annual award for fiction. Award: $500 and winning entry will be considered for publication in *Carolina Quarterly*. Competition receives 800-900 submissions. Entry fee $7. Guidelines available in spring for SASE. Inquiries by e-mail OK. Deadline: August 31. Unpublished submissions. Length: 12 double-spaced pages maximum. Winners announced December 1998. Winners notified by phone in December. List of winners available for SASE.

TOBIAS WOLFF AWARD FOR FICTION, (I), Mail Stop 9053, Western Washington University, Bellingham WA 98225. Annual competition for novels and short stories. Award: $1,000 (1st Prize); $250 (2nd Prize); $100 (3rd Prize). Judge: to be announced. Entry fee $10 for the first entry, $5/story or chapter thereafter. Guidelines for SASE. Deadline: March 1. Unpublished submissions. Length: 10,000 words or less per story or chapter. Winner announced July 1998. List of winners available for SASE.

☑ **WORLD FANTASY AWARDS**, World Fantasy Awards Association, P.O. Box 1666, Lynnwood WA 98046-1666. E-mail: sfexessec@aol.com. Contact: Peter Dennis Pautz, president. Award to "recognize excellence in fantasy literature worldwide." Annual competition for short stories, novels, story collections, anthologies, novellas and life achievement. Award: bust of HP Lovecraft. Judge: Panel. Guidelines available for SASE. Inquiries by e-mail and fax are OK. Deadline: June 30. Published submissions from previous calendar year. Word length: 10,000-40,000 novella, 10,000 short story. "All fantasy is eligible, from supernatural horror to Tolkienesque to sword and sorcery to the occult, and beyond." Winners announced November 1. List of winners available November 1.

***WRITER'S DIGEST* ANNUAL WRITING COMPETITION, (Short Story Division), (I)**, *Writer's Digest*, 1507 Dana Ave., Cincinnati OH 45207. (513)531-2690, ext. 580. E-mail: competitions@fwpubs.com. Website: http://www.writersdigest.com. Contact: Contest Director. Grand Prize is an expenses-paid trip to New York City with arrangements to meet editors/agents in winning writer's field. Other awards include cash, reference books and certificates of recognition. Names of grand prize winner and top 100 winners are announced in the November issue of *Writer's Digest*. Top entries published in booklet ($5.75). Send SASE to *WD* Writing Competition for rules and entry form, or see January through May issues of *Writer's Digest*. Deadline: May 31. Entry fee $10 per manuscript. All entries must be original, unpublished and not previously submitted to a *Writer's Digest* contest. Length: 4,000 words maximum. No acknowledgment will be made of receipt of mss nor will mss be returned. Three of the ten writing categories target short fiction: mainstream/literary, genre and children's fiction.

***WRITER'S DIGEST* NATIONAL SELF-PUBLISHED BOOK AWARDS**, *Writer's Digest*, 1507 Dana Ave., Cincinnati OH 45207. (513)531-2690, ext. 580. E-mail: competitions@fwpubs.com. Website: http://www.writersdigest.com. Contact: Contest Director. Award to "recognize and promote excellence in self-published books." Annual competition with six categories: Fiction (novel or short story collection), nonfiction, cookbooks, poetry, children's and young adult and life stories. Award: $1,000 plus an ad in *Publishers Weekly* and promotion in *Writer's Digest*. Category winners receive $300. Judges: WD staff. Entry fee $95 for each book submitted. Guidelines available for SASE. Deadline: December 15. Published submissions. Author must pay full cost and book must have been published in year of contest.

☑ **WRITERS' INTL FORUM WRITING COMPETITION, (I)**, *Writers' Intl Forum*, P.O. Box 516, Tracyton WA 98393-0516. Website: http://www.bristolservicesintl.com. Editor: Sandra E. Haven. Award "to encourage strong storyline in a tight package." Four or more competitions per year for short stories. Awards: Cash prizes and certificates (amounts vary per competition). Competition receives 200 entries. Judges: *Writers' Intl Forum* staff. Entry fees vary per competition. Guidelines available in September for SASE or on website. Previously unpublished submissions. "Length, theme, prizes, deadline, fee and other requirements vary for each competition. Entries are judged on creativity, technique, mechanics and appeal." List of winners available one month after closing. Automatically mailed with entrant's return SASE for manuscript.

***WRITERS' JOURNAL* ANNUAL FICTION CONTEST, (I)**, Val-Tech Publishing, Inc., P.O. Box 25376, St. Paul MN 55125-0376. (612)730-4280. Fax: (612)730-4356. E-mail: vhockert@aol.com. Website: http://www.sowashco.com/writersjournal. Contact: Valerie Hockert, publisher/managing editor. Annual award for short stories. Award: 1st Place, $50; 2nd Place, $25; 3rd Place, $15. Also gives honorable mentions. Competition receives approximately 500 submissions/year. Judges are Valerie Hockert and others. Entry fee $5 each. Maximum of 3 entries/person. Entry forms or rules available in May for SASE. Deadline: December 31. Maximum length is

2,000 words. Two copies of each entry are required—one *without* name or address of writer. Winners announced in January. Winners notified by mail.

***WRITERS' JOURNAL* ROMANCE CONTEST, (I)**, *Writers' Journal*, Val-Tech Publishing, Inc., P.O. Box 25376, St. Paul MN 55125-0376. (612)730-4280. Fax: (612)730-4356. E-mail: vhockert@aol.com. Website: http://www.sowashco.com/writersjournal. Competition for short stories. Award: $50 (1st Prize), $25 (2nd Prize), $15 (3rd Prize), plus honorable mentions. Competition receives 200 submissions. Entry fee $5/entry. Guidelines available in April for SASE (4 entries/person). Deadline: August 1. Unpublished submissions. Word length: 2,000 words maximum. Winners announced in September. Winners notified by mail. "Enclose #10 SASE for winner's list."

THE WRITERS' WORKSHOP INTERNATIONAL FICTION CONTEST, (I), The Writers' Workshop, 387 Beaucatcher Rd., Asheville NC 28805. (704)254-8111. Fax: (704)251-2118. Executive Director: Karen Tager. Annual awards for fiction. Awards: $500 (1st Prize), $250 (2nd Prize), $100 (3rd Prize). Competition receives approximately 350 submissions. Past judges have been Peter Matthiessen, Kurt Vonnegut, E.L. Doctorow. Entry fee $18/$15 members. Guidelines for SASE. Deadline: February 25. Unpublished submissions. Length: 4,000 words typed, double-spaced pages per story. Multiple submissions are accepted.

SENDING TO A COUNTRY other than your own? Be sure to send International Reply Coupons instead of stamps for replies or return of your manuscript.

Resources

Resources

Conferences & Workshops

Why are conferences so popular? Writers and conference directors alike tell us it's because writing can be such a lonely business otherwise—that at conferences writers have the opportunity to meet (and commiserate) with fellow writers, as well as meet and network with publishers, editors and agents. Conferences and workshops provide some of the best opportunities for writers to make publishing contacts and pick up valuable information on the business, as well as the craft, of writing.

The bulk of the listings in this section are for conferences. Most conferences last from one day to one week and offer a combination of workshop-type writing sessions, panel discussions, and a variety of guest speakers. Topics may include all aspects of writing from fiction to poetry to scriptwriting, or they may focus on a specific area such as those sponsored by the Romance Writers of America for writers specializing in romance or the SCBWI conferences on writing for children's books.

Workshops, however, tend to run longer—usually one to two weeks. Designed to operate like writing classes, most require writers to be prepared to work on and discuss their work-in-progress while attending. An important benefit of workshops is the opportunity they provide writers for an intensive critique of their work, often by professional writing teachers and established writers.

Each of the listings here includes information on the specific focus of an event as well as planned panels, guest speakers and workshop topics. It is important to note, however, some conference directors were still in the planning stages for 1999 when we contacted them. If it was not possible to include 1999 dates, fees or topics, we have provided information from 1998 so you can get an idea of what to expect. For the most current information, it's best to send a self-addressed, stamped envelope to the director in question about three months before the date(s) listed.

FINDING A CONFERENCE

Many writers try to make it to at least one conference a year, but cost and location count as much as subject matter or other considerations, when determining which conference to attend. There are conferences in almost every state and province and even some in Europe open to North Americans.

To make it easier for you to find a conference close to home—or to find one in an exotic locale to fit into your vacation plans—we've divided this section into geographic regions. The conferences appear in alphabetical order under the appropriate regional heading.

Note that conferences appear under the regional heading according to where they will be held, which is sometimes different than the address given as the place to register or send for information. The regions are as follows:

Northeast (pages 580-584): Connecticut, Maine, Massachusetts, New Hampshire, New York, Rhode Island, Vermont

Midatlantic (pages 584-585): Washington DC, Delaware, Maryland, New Jersey, Pennsylvania

LEARNING AND NETWORKING

Besides learning from workshop leaders and panelists in formal sessions, writers at conferences also benefit from conversations with other attendees. Writers on all levels enjoy sharing insights. Often, a conversation over lunch can reveal a new market for your work or let you know which editors are most receptive to the work of new writers. You can find out about recent editor changes and about specific agents. A casual chat could lead to a new contact or resource in your area.

Many editors and agents make visiting conferences a part of their regular search for new writers. A cover letter or query that starts with "I met you at the National Writers Association Conference," or "I found your talk on your company's new romance line at the Moonlight and Magnolias most interesting . . . " may give you a small leg up on the competition.

While a few writers have been successful in selling their manuscripts at a conference, the availability of editors and agents does not usually mean these folks will have the time there to read your novel or six best short stories (unless, of course, you've scheduled an individual meeting with them ahead of time). While editors and agents are glad to meet writers and discuss work in general terms, usually they don't have the time (or energy) to give an extensive critique during a conference. In other words, use the conference as a way to make a first, brief contact.

SELECTING A CONFERENCE

Besides the obvious considerations of time, place and cost, choose your conference based on your writing goals. If, for example, your goal is to improve the quality of your writing, it will be more helpful to you to choose a hands-on craft workshop rather than a conference offering a series of panels on marketing and promotion. If, on the other hand, you are a science fiction novelist who would like to meet your fans, try one of the many science fiction conferences or "cons" held throughout the country and the world.

Look for panelists and workshop instructors whose work you admire and who seem to be writing in your general area. Check for specific panels or discussions of topics relevant to what you are writing now. Think about the size—would you feel more comfortable with a small workshop of eight people or a large group of 100 or more attendees?

If your funds are limited, start by looking for conferences close to home, but you may want to explore those that offer contests with cash prizes—and a chance to recoup your expenses. A few conferences and workshops also offer scholarships, but the competition is stiff and writers interested in these should find out the requirements early. Finally, students may want to look for conferences and workshops that offer college credit. You will find these options included in the listings here. Again, send a self-addressed, stamped envelope for the most current details.

The science fiction field in particular offers hundreds of conventions each year for writers, illustrators and fans. To find additional listings for these, see *Locus* (P.O. Box 13305, Oakland

CA 94661). For more information on conferences and even more conferences from which to choose, check the May issue of *Writer's Digest*. *The Guide to Writers Conferences* (ShawGuides, 10 W. 66th St., Suite 30H, New York NY 10023) is another helpful resource now available on their website at http://www.shawguides.com.

Northeast (CT, MA, ME, NH, NY, RI, VT)

BECOME A MORE PRODUCTIVE WRITER, P.O. Box 1310, Boston MA 02117-1310. (617)266-1613. E-mail: marcia@yudkin.com. Director: Marcia Yudkin. Estab. 1991. Workshop held approximately 3 times/year. Workshop held on one Saturday in April, September, February. Average attendance 15. "Creativity workshop for fiction writers and others. Based on latest discoveries about the creative process, participants learn to access their unconscious wisdom, find their own voice, utilize kinesthetic, visual and auditory methods of writing, and bypass longstanding blocks and obstacles. Held at a hotel in central Boston."
Costs: $119.
Accommodations: List of area hotels and bed & breakfasts provided.
Additional Information: Conference brochures/guidelines are available for SASE after August. Inquiries by mail, phone or e-mail OK. "Audiotapes of seminar information also available."

☑ **BREAD LOAF WRITERS' CONFERENCE**, Middlebury College, Middlebury VT 05753. (802)443-5286. E-mail: blwc@mail.middlebury.edu. Administrative Coordinator: Carol Knauss. Estab. 1926. Annual. Conference held in late August. Conference duration: 11 days. Average attendance: 230. For fiction, nonfiction and poetry. Held at the summer campus in Ripton, Vermont (belongs to Middlebury College).
Costs: $1,690 (includes room/board) (1998).
Accommodations: Accommodations are at Ripton. Onsite accommodations $590 (1998).
Additional Information: Inquiries by fax and e-mail OK.

[N] **DOWNEAST MAINE WRITER'S WORKSHOPS**, P.O. Box 446, Stockton Springs ME 04981. (207)567-4317. Fax: (207)567-3023. E-mail: redbaron@ime.net. Website: http://www.agate.net/~herrick/writers/. Director: Janet J. Barron. Estab. 1994. Annual. Tentative dates 1999: August 6, 7, 8. Writing workshops geared towards aspiring writers. "We hold 3-day workshops during the summer each year. In intense, experimental hands-on workshops, we address, in-depth, the subject of "How to Get Your Writing Published" via expert, individual, personalized, practical guidance and inside-the-industry info from a 30-year professional writer and acquisition editor of several well-known publishing houses. Upon registration, students receive a questionnaire requesting responses re: their writing level, writing interests, and expectations from the conference. From this information, we build the workshop which is entirely geared around participants information and needs."
Costs: Tuition (includes lunch): 3-day, $295 + $19.95 for 300-page textbook ("we accept Visa and MC"). Reasonable local accommodations and meals additional (except lunch during conference).
Accommodations: Upon registration, participants receive a list of local B&Bs and Inns, most of which include large, full breakfasts in their reasonable rates. They also receive a list of area activities and events.
Additional Information: Upon registration, students receive a comprehensive, confidential questionnaire. DEMWW workshops are completely constructed around participant's answers to questionnaires. Also offers a writer's clinic for writing feedback if participants seek this type of assistance. No requirements prior to registration. For more details and free brochures, contact DEMWW at any of the numbers listed. Conference brochures available April 1999.

☑ **EASTERN WRITERS' CONFERENCE**, English Dept., Salem State College, Salem MA 01970-5353. (978)542-6330. E-mail: rod.kessler@salem.mass.edu. Conference Directors: Rod Kessler and J.D. Scrimgeour. Estab. 1977. Annual. Conference held late June. Average attendance: 60. Conference to "provide a sense of community and support for area poets and prose writers. We try to present speakers and programs of interest, changing our format from time to time. Conference-goers have an opportunity to read to an audience or have manuscripts professionally critiqued. We tend to draw regionally." Previous speakers have included Nancy Mairs, Susanna Kaysen, Tim O'Brien, Linda Weltner.
Costs: "Under $100."
Accommodations: Available on campus.
Additional Information: Conference brochure/guidelines are available April 30. Inquiries by e-mail OK. "Optional manuscript critiques are available for an additional fee."

☑ **FEMINIST WOMEN'S WRITING WORKSHOPS, INC.**, P.O. Box 6583, Ithaca NY 14851. Directors: Kit Wainer and Margo Gumosky. Estab. 1975. Workshop held every summer. Workshop duration: 8 days. Average attendance: 30-45 women writers. "Workshops provide a women-centered community for writers of all levels and genres. Workshops are held on the campuses of Hobart/William Smith Colleges in Geneva, NY. Geneva is approximately mid-way between Rochester and Syracuse. Each writer has a private room and 3 meals daily.

College facilities such as pool, tennis courts and weight room are available. FWWW invites all interests. Past speakers include Dorothy Allison, National Book Award Finalist for *Bastard Out of Carolina*, and Ruth Stone, author of *Second-Hand Coat*, *Who Is The Widow's Muse?* and *Simplicity*.
Costs: $545 for tuition, room, board.
Accommodations: Shuttle service from airports available for a fee.
Additional Information: "Writers may submit manuscripts 4-10 pages with application." Brochures/guidelines available for SASE.

✔ **THE FOUNDATIONS OF CREATIVITY® WRITING WORKSHOP**, The Elizabeth Ayres Center for Creative Writing, 155 E. 31st St., Suite 4-R, New York NY 10016-6830. (212)689-4692. Owner/Director: Elizabeth Ayres. Estab. 1990. Conference held 10 times/year. Workshops begin every 7 weeks, 1 time/week for 6 weeks. Average attendance: 10. "The purpose of the workshop is to help fledgling writers conquer their fear of the blank page; develop imaginative tools; capitalize on the strengths of their natural voice and style; develop confidence; and interact with other writers in a stimulating, supportive atmosphere." Writers' Retreats also offered 3-5 times/year in weekend and week-long formats. Average attendance: 15. "Retreats provide an opportunity for extended writing time in a tranquil setting with like-minded companions."
Costs: $245 (1998); retreats vary from $350-700 depending on duration.
Additional Information: Workshop brochures and guidelines free. Inquiries by mail or phone.

✔ **HOFSTRA UNIVERSITY SUMMER WRITERS' CONFERENCE**, 250 Hofstra University, UCCE, Hempstead NY 11549. (516)463-5016. Fax: (516)463-4833. E-mail: dcelcs@hofstra.edu. Associate Dean: Lewis Shena. Estab. 1972. Annual (every summer, starting week after July 4). Conference to be held July 12 to July 23, 1998. Average attendance: 50. Conference offers workshops in fiction, nonfiction, poetry, juvenile fiction, stage/screenwriting and, on occasion, one other genre such as detective fiction or science fiction. Site is the university campus, a suburban setting, 25 miles from NYC. Guest speakers are not yet known. "We have had the likes of Oscar Hijuelos, Robert Olen Butler, Hilma and Meg Wolitzer, Budd Schulberg and Cynthia Ozick."
Costs: Non-credit (no meals, no room): approximately $375 per workshop. Credit: Approximately $1,000/workshop (2 credits) undergraduate and $1,750 (2 credits) graduate.
Accommodations: Free bus operates between Hempstead Train Station and campus for those commuting from NYC. Dormitory rooms are available for approximately $350. Those who request area hotels will receive a list. Hotels are approximately $75 and above/night.
Additional Information: "All workshops include critiquing. Each participant is given one-on-one time of ½ hour with workshop leader. Only credit students must submit manuscripts when registering. We submit work to the Shaw Guides Contest and other Writer's Conferences and Retreats contests when appropriate." Inquiries by fax and e-mail OK.

IWWG MEET THE AGENTS AND EDITORS: THE BIG APPLE WORKSHOPS, ℅ International Women's Writing Guild, P.O. Box 810, Gracie Station, New York NY 10028-0082. (212)737-7536. Fax: (212)737-9469. E-mail: iwwg@iwwg.com. Website: http://www.iwwg.com. Executive Director: Hannelore Hahn. Estab. 1980. Biannual. Workshops typically held in April and October. Average attendance: 200. Workshops to promote creative writing and professional success. Site: Private meeting space of the City Athletic Club, midtown New York City. Sunday afternoon openhouse with agents, independent presses, published authors and editors.
Costs: $100 for the weekend.
Accommodations: Information on transportation arrangements and overnight accommodations made available.
Additional Information: Workshop brochures/guidelines are available for SASE. Inquires by fax and e-mail OK.

IWWG SUMMER CONFERENCE, ℅ International Women's Writing Guild, P.O. Box 810, Gracie Station, New York NY 10028-0082. (212)737-7536. Fax: (212)737-9469. E-mail: iwwg@iwwg.com. Website: http://www.iwwg.com. Executive Director: Hannelore Hahn. Estab. 1977. Annual. Conference usually held in August. Average attendance: 450, including international attendees. Conference to promote writing in all genres, personal growth and professional success. Conference is held "on the tranquil campus of Skidmore College in Saratoga Springs, NY, where the serene Hudson Valley meets the North Country of the Adirondacks." Sixty-five different workshops are offered everyday. Overall theme: "Writing Towards Personal and Professional Growth."
Costs: $700 for week-long program, plus room and board.
Accommodations: Transportation by air to Albany, New York, or Amtrak train available from New York City. Conference attendees stay on campus.

CAN'T FIND A CONFERENCE? Conferences are listed by region. Check the introduction to this section for a list of regional categories.

Additional Information: Conference brochures/guidelines available for SASE. Inquires by fax and e-mail OK.

☑ **MANHATTANVILLE COLLEGE WRITERS' WEEK**, 2900 Purchase St., Purchase NY 10577-2103. (914)694-3425. Fax: (914)694-3488. E-mail: rdowd@mville. Website: http://www.manhattanville.edu. Dean of Adult and Special Programs: Ruth Dowd, R.S.C.J. Estab. 1982. Annual. Conference held last week of June 1999. Average attendance: 90. Workshops include children's literature, journal writing, creative nonfiction, personal essay, poetry, fiction, travel writing and short fiction. "The Conference is designed not only for writers but for teachers of writing. Each workshop is attended by a Master teacher who works with the writers/teachers in the afternoon to help them to translate their writing skills for classroom use." Students do intensive work in the genre of their choice. Manhattanville is a suburban campus 30 miles from New York City. The campus centers around Reid Castle, the administration building, the former home of Whitelaw Reid. Workshops are conducted in Reid Castle. We feature a major author as guest lecturer during the Conference. Past speakers have included such authors as Toni Morrison, Mary Gordon, Gail Godwin, Pete Hamill and poet Mark Doty.
Costs: Conference cost was $560 in 1998 plus $30 fee.
Accommodations: Students may rent rooms in the college residence halls. More luxurious accommodations are available at neighboring hotels. In the summer of 1998 the cost of renting a room in the residence halls was $25 per night.
Additional Information: Conference brochures/guidelines are available for SASE in March. Inquiries by fax OK.

NEW ENGLAND WRITERS' WORKSHOP AT SIMMONS COLLEGE, 300 The Fenway, Boston MA 02115-5820. (617)521-2090. Fax: (617)521-3199. Conference Administrator: Cynthia Grady. Estab. 1977. Annually in summer. Workshop held 1st week of June. Workshop lasts one week. Average attendance: 45. "Adult fiction: novel, short story. Boston and its literary heritage provide a stimulating environment for a workshop of writers. Simmons College is located in the Fenway area near the Museum of Fine Arts, Symphony Hall, the Isabella Stewart Gardner Museum, and many other places of educational, cultural and social interest. Our theme is usually fiction (novel or short story) with the workshops in the morning and then the afternoon speakers either talk about their own work or talk about the 'business' of publishing." Past speakers and workshop leaders have included John Updike, Anne Beattie and Jill McCorkle as well as editors from *The New Yorker*, *The Atlantic* and Houghton Mifflin.
Costs: $550 (includes full week of workshops and speakers, individual consultations, refreshments and 2 receptions).
Accommodations: Cost is $200 for Sunday to Saturday on-campus housing. A list of local hotels is also available.
Additional Information: "Up to 30 pages of manuscript may be sent in prior to workshop to be reviewed privately with workshop leader during the week." Conference brochures/guidelines are abailable for SASE in March. Inquiries by fax OK.

☑ **ODYSSEY**, 20 Levesque Lane, Mont Vernon NH 03057. Phone/fax: (603)673-6234. E-mail: jcavelos@empire.net. Website: http://www.nhc.edu/odyssey/. Director: Jeanne Cavelos. Estab. 1995. Annual. Workshop to be held June 14 to July 23. Attendance limited to 20. "A workshop for fantasy, science fiction and horror writers that combines an intensive learning and writing experience with in-depth feedback on students' manuscripts. The only workshop to combine the overall guidance and in-depth feedback of a single instructor with the varied perspectives of guest lectures." Conference held at New Hampshire College in Manchester, New Hampshire. Previous guest lecturers included: Harlan Ellison, Jane Yolen, Elizabeth Hand, Ellen Kushner, Craig Shaw Gardner, Melissa Scott, Patricia McKillis and John Crowley.
Costs: In 1998: $1,040 tuition, $337 housing (double room), $20 application fee, $525 food (approximate), $55 processing fee to receive college credit.
Accommodations: "Workshop students stay at a New Hampshire College townhouses and eat at college."
Additional Information: Students must apply and include a writing sample. Students' works are critiqued throughout the 6 weeks. Workshop brochures and guidelines available for SASE after August. Inquiries by fax and e-mail OK.

ROBERT QUACKENBUSH'S CHILDREN'S BOOK WRITING & ILLUSTRATING WORKSHOPS, 460 E. 79th St., New York NY 10021-1443. (212)744-3822. Fax: (212)861-2761. E-mail: rqstudios@aol.com. Website: http://www.rquackenbush.com. Instructor: Robert Quackenbush. Estab. 1982. Annual. Workshop held July 12-16, 1999. Average attendance: limited to 10. Workshops to promote writing and illustrating books for children. Held at the Manhattan studio of Robert Quackenbush, author and illustrator of over 170 books for young readers. "Focus is generally on picture books, easy-to-read and early chapter books. All classes led by Robert Quackenbush."
Costs: $650 tuition covers all costs of the workshop, but does not include housing and meals. A $100 nonrefundable deposit is required with the $550 balance due two weeks prior to attendance.
Accommodations: A list of recommended hotels and restaurants is sent upon receipt of deposit.
Additional Information: Class is for beginners and professionals. Critiques during workshop. Private consultations also available at an hourly rate. "Programs suited to your needs; individualized schedules can be designed.

Write or phone to discuss your goals and you will receive a prompt reply." Conference brochures are available for SASE. Inquiries by fax and e-mail OK, but please include mailing address with inquiries.

☑ **SCBWI CONFERENCE IN CHILDREN'S LITERATURE, NYC**, P.O. Box 20233, Park West Finance Station, New York NY 10025. Co-Chairman: Frieda Gates. Estab. 1975. Annual. Conference held 1st (or 2nd) Saturday in November. Average attendance: 350. Conference is to promote writing for children: picture books; fiction; nonfiction; middle grade and young adult; meet an editor; meet an agent; financial planning for writers; marketing your book; children's multimedia; etc. Held at P.S. 166 on West 89th Street between Amsterdam and Columbus Avenues.
Costs: $65, members; $70 nonmembers; $15 additional on day of conference.
Accommodations: Write for information; hotel names will be supplied.
Additional Information: Conference brochures/guidelines are available for SASE. For information, call (718)937-6810 or (914)356-7273.

STATE OF MAINE WRITERS' CONFERENCE, P.O. Box 7146, Ocean Park ME 04063-7146. (207)934-9806 June-August; (413)596-6734 September-May. Fax: (413)796-2121. E-mail: rburns0@keaken.rmvnet or wnec.edu (September-May only). Chairman: Richard F. Burns. Estab. 1941. Annual. Conference held August 18-21, 1998. Conference duration: 4 days. Average attendance: 50. "We try to present a balanced as well as eclectic conference. There is quite a bit of time and attention given to poetry but we also have children's literature, mystery writing, travel, novels/fiction and lots of items and issues of interest to writers such as speakers who are: publishers, editors, illustrators and the like. Our concentration is, by intention, a general view of writing to publish. We are located in Ocean Park, a small seashore village 14 miles south of Portland. Ours is a summer assembly center with many buildings from the Victorian Age. The conference meets in Porter Hall, one of the assembly buildings which is listed on the National Register of Historic Places. Within recent years our guest list has included Lewis Turco, Amy MacDonald, William Noble, David McCord, Dorothy Clarke Wilson, John N. Cole, Betsy Sholl, John Tagliabue, Christopher Keane and many others. We usually have about 10 guest presenters a year."
Costs: $85 includes the conference banquet. There is a reduced fee, $40, for students ages 21 and under. The fee does not include housing or meals which must be arranged separately by the conferees.
Accommodations: An accommodations list is available. "We are in a summer resort area and motels, guest houses and restaurants abound."
Additional Information: "We have a list of about 12 contests on various genres that accompanies the program announcement. The prizes, all modest, are awarded at the end of the conference and only to those who are registered." Send SASE for program guide available in May. Inquiries by fax and e-mail OK.

☑ **VASSAR COLLEGE INSTITUTE OF PUBLISHING AND WRITING: CHILDREN'S BOOKS IN THE MARKETPLACE**, Vassar College, Box 300, Poughkeepsie NY 12604-0077. (914)437-5903. Fax: (914)437-7209. E-mail: mabruno@vassar.edu. Website: http://www.vassar.edu. Associate Director of College Relations: Maryann Bruno. Estab. 1983. Annual. Conference held mid to late June. Conference duration: 1 week. Average attendance: 30. Writing and publishing children's literature. "We offer the nuts and bolts of how to get your work published plus critiques of participants' writings." The conference is held at Vassar College, a 1,000-acre campus located in the mid-Hudson valley. The campus is self-contained, with residence halls, dining facilities, and classroom and meeting facilities. Vassar is located 90 miles north of New York City, and is accessible by car, train and air. Participants have use of Vassar's athletic facilities, including swimming, squash, tennis and jogging. Vassar is known for the beauty of its campus. "The Institute is directed by author/editor Jean Margollo and features top working professionals from the field of publishing."
Costs: $800, includes full tuition, room and three meals a day.
Accommodations: Special conference attendee accommodations are in campus residence halls.
Additional Information: Writers may submit a 10-page sample of their writing for critique, which occurs during the week of the conference. Artists' portfolios are reviewed individually. Conference brochures/guidelines are available March 1 or earlier upon request. Inquiries by fax and e-mail OK.

WESLEYAN WRITERS CONFERENCE, Wesleyan University, Middletown CT 06459. (860)685-3604. Fax: (860)347-3996. E-mail: agreene@wesleyan.edu. Website: http://www.wesleyan.edu/writing/conferer.html. Director: Anne Greene. Estab. 1956. Annual. Conference held the last week in June. Average attendance: 100. For fiction techniques, novel, short story, poetry, screenwriting, nonfiction, literary journalism, memoir. The conference is held on the campus of Wesleyan University, in the hills overlooking the Connecticut River. Meals and lodging are provided on campus. Features readings of new fiction, guest lectures on a range of topics including publishing and daily seminars. "Both new and experienced writers are welcome."
Costs: In 1998, day rate $660 (including meals); boarding students' rate $775 (including meals and room for 5 nights).
Accommodations: "Participants can fly to Hartford or take Amtrak to Meriden, CT. We are happy to help participants make travel arrangements." Overnight participants stay on campus.
Additional Information: Manuscript critiques are available as part of the program but are not required. Participants may attend seminars in several different genres. Scholarships and teaching fellowships are available, includ-

ing the Jakobson awards for new writers and the Jon Davidoff Scholarships for journalists. Inquiries by e-mail and fax OK.

N **WRITING BY DEGREES, Creative Writing Conference**, P.O. Box 574, Endicott NY 13761-0574. E-mail: bg21166@binghamton.edu. Annual conference sponsored by the Creative Writing Council at Binghamton University, SUNY. Conference held in March. Conference duration: 3 days. "The conference is designed to foster discussion in the areas of pedagogy, publication, creativity and career development. The evenings are reserved for creative readings by conference participants."
Costs: Attendance fee $10.
Additional Information: "Send SASE for conference dates, additional information and/or the official call for papers. We consider paper proposals on all aspects of creative writing, via mail or e-mail, between October 1 and December 1."

Midatlantic (DC, DE, MD, NJ, PA)

THE COLLEGE OF NEW JERSEY WRITERS' CONFERENCE, English Dept., The College of New Jersey, P.O. Box 7718, Ewing NJ 08628-0718. (609)771-3254. Fax: (609)771-3345. Director: Jean Hollander. Estab. 1980. Annual. Conference held in April. Conference duration: 9 a.m. to 10:30 p.m. Average attendance: 600-1,000. "Conference concentrates on fiction (the largest number of participants), poetry, children's literature, play and screenwriting, magazine and newspaper journalism, overcoming writer's block, nonfiction books. Conference is held at the student center at the college in two auditoriums and workshop rooms; also Kendall Theatre on campus." The focus is on various genres: romance, detective, mystery, TV writing, etc. Topics have included "How to Get Happily Published," "How to Get an Agent" and "Earning a Living as a Writer." The conference usually presents twenty or so authors, plus two featured speakers, who have included Arthur Miller, Saul Bellow, Toni Morrison, Joyce Carol Oates, Erica Jong and Alice Walker.
Costs: General registration $45, plus $10 for each workshop. Lower rates for students.
Additional Information: Brochures/guidelines available.

MONTROSE CHRISTIAN WRITER'S CONFERENCE, 5 Locust St., Montrose Bible Conference, Montrose PA 18801-1112. (717)278-1001. (800)598-5030. Fax: (717)278-3061. E-mail: mbc@epix.net. Bible Conference Director: Jim Fahringer. Estab. 1990. Annual. Conference held July. Average attendance: 75. "We try to meet a cross-section of writing needs, for beginners and advanced, covering fiction, poetry and writing for children. We meet in the beautiful village of Montrose, Pennsylvania, situated in the mountains. The Bible Conference provides motel-like accommodations and good food. The main sessions are held in the chapel with rooms available for other classes. Fiction writing has been taught each year."
Costs: In 1998 registration was $100.
Accommodations: Will meet planes in Binghamton NY and Scranton PA; will meet bus in Great Bend PA. Information on overnight accommodations is available. On-site accommodations: room and board $225-$342/week; $38-$57/day including food.
Additional Information: "Writers can send work ahead and have it critiqued for $20." Brochures/guidelines are available by e-mail and fax in March. "The attendees are usually church related. The writing has a Christian emphasis."

✓ **ST. DAVIDS CHRISTIAN WRITERS CONFERENCE**, 87 Pines Rd. E., Hadley PA 16130-1019. E-mail: audstall@nauticom.net. Registrar: Audrey Stallsmith. Estab. 1957. Annual. Conference will be held June 20-25, 1999. "Located at picturesque Geneva College, Beaver Falls PA, north of Pittsburgh." Attendance: 100. "We have a 41 year history, and are known for our family-like atmosphere and quality programs." Conference will train writers in religious and general writing through workshops in fiction, nonfiction, beginning and advanced writing, poetry, children's writing, devotional/inspirational writing. Optional tutorials and market consultations. Recent workshop leaders have included Les Stobbe, Penelope Stokes and Bob Hostetler.
Cost: Tuition is $225; room and board is $200. Optional programs are extra.
Accommodations: College dormitory rooms with linens provided, excellent food in college cafeteria. "We provide transportation from the Pittsburgh airport if prior arrangements are made."
Additional Information: Small informal critique groups do not require pre-conference manuscript submission. Sponsors annual contest for registered conferees. Categories are humorous poetry, serious poetry, fiction (short story), op-ed, children's lit, character sketch, personal experience, humorous prose. Judges are faculty members, editors or agents. Conference brochure available in March for SASE or request by e-mail.

✓ **WASHINGTON INDEPENDENT WRITERS (WIW) SPRING WRITERS CONFERENCE**, #220, 733 15th St. NW, Suite 220, Washington DC 20005-2112. (202)347-4973. Fax:: (202)628-0298. E-mail: washwriter@aol.com. Website: http://www.washwriter.org. Executive Director: Isolde Chapin. Estab. 1975. Annual. Conference held May 14-15, 1999. Conference duration: Friday evening and Saturday. Average attendance: 250. "Gives participants a chance to hear from and talk with dozens of experts on book and magazine publishing

as well as on the craft, tools and business of writing." National Press Club as conference site. Past keynote speakers include Erica Jong, Haynes Johnson, Diane Rehm and Kitty Kelley.
Costs: $125 members; $150 nonmembers; $185 membership and conference.
Additional Information: Brochures/guidelines available for SASE in February. Inquiries by fax and e-mail OK.

Midsouth (NC, SC, TN, VA, WV)

AMERICAN CHRISTIAN WRITERS CONFERENCES, P.O. Box 110390, Nashville TN 37222. (800)21-WRITE. Website: http://www.ECPA.ORG/ACW (includes schedule). Director: Reg Forder. Estab. 1981. Annual. Conference duration: 2 days. Average attendance: 100. To promote all forms of Christian writing. Conferences held throughout the year in 2 dozen cities. Usually located at a major hotel chain like Holiday Inn.
Costs: Approximately $149 plus meals and accommodation.
Accommodations: Special rates available at host hotel.
Additional Information: Conference brochures/guidelines are available for SASE.

N ✓ **DUKE UNIVERSITY WRITERS' WORKSHOP**, Box 90703, Durham NC 27708. (919)684-5375. Director: Georgann Eubanks. Estab. 1978. Annual. Workshop held in June. Average attendance: 50. To promote "creative writing: beginning, intermediate and advanced fiction; short story; scriptwriting; children's writing; poetry; creative nonfiction." Workshop held at "at a beautiful retreat center on the North Carolina coast. Nationally recognized for its academic excellence, Duke sponsors this workshop annually for creative writers of various genres."
Costs: $695 (meals and room included).
Accommodations: Single and double rooms available.
Additional Information: Critiques available. "Works-in-progress requested 3 weeks before workshop. Each participant gets *private* consult plus small-group in-class critiques." Brochures/guidelines are available. "No 'big' names, no mammoth lectures; simply *excellent*, concentrated instruction plus time to work. No glitz. Hard work. Great results."

✓ **HIGHLAND SUMMER CONFERENCE**, Box 7014, Radford University, Radford VA 24142-7014. (540)831-5366. Fax: (540)831-5004. E-mail: jasbury@runet.edu. Website: http://www.runet.edu/~arsc. Chair, Appalachian Studies Program: Dr. Grace Toney Edwards. Contact: Jo Ann Asbury, assistant to director. Estab. 1978. Annual. Conference held last 2 weeks of June 1999. Conference duration: 12 days. Average attendance: 25. "The HSC features one (two weeks) or two (one week each) guest leaders each year. As a rule, our leaders are well-known writers who have connections, either thematic, or personal, or both, to the Appalachian region. The genre(s) of emphasis depends upon the workshop leader(s). In the past we have had as guest lecturers Nikki Giovanni, Sharyn McCrumb, Gurney Norman, Denise Giardinia and George Ella Lyon. The Highland Summer Conference is held at Radford University, a school of about 9,000 students. Radford is in the Blue Ridge Mountains of southwest Virginia about 45 miles south of Roanoke, VA."
Costs: "The cost is based on current Radford tuition for 3 credit hours plus an additional conference fee. On-campus meals and housing are available at additional cost. In 1998 conference tuition was $421 for instate undergraduates, $451 for graduate students."
Accommodations: "We do not have special rate arrangements with local hotels. We do offer accommodations on the Radford University Campus in a recently refurbished residence hall. (In 1998 cost was $19-28 per night.)"
Additional Information: "Conference leaders do typically critique work done during the two-week conference, but do not ask to have any writing submitted prior to the conference beginning." Conference brochures/guidelines are available after February, 1999 for SASE. Inquiries by e-mail and fax OK.

✓ **NORTH CAROLINA WRITERS' NETWORK FALL CONFERENCE**, P.O. Box 954, Carrboro NC 27510-0954. (919)967-9540. Fax: (919)929-0535. E-mail: ncwn@sunsite.unc.edu. Website: http://sunsite.unc.edu/ncwriters. Executive Director: Linda G. Hobson. Contact: Bobbie Collins-Perry, program and services director. Estab. 1985. Annual. "1999 Conference will be held in Asheville, NC, November 19-21." Average attendance: 450. "The conference is a weekend full of workshops, panels, readings and discussion groups. It endeavors

N $

FOR EXPLANATIONS OF THESE SYMBOLS,
SEE THE INSIDE FRONT AND BACK COVERS OF THIS BOOK.

to serve writers of all levels of skill from beginning, to emerging, to established. We try to have *all* genres represented. In the past we have had novelists, poets, journalists, editors, children's writers, young adult writers, storytellers, playwrights, screenwriters, etc. We take the conference to a different location in North Carolina each year in order to best serve our entire state. We hold the conference at a conference center with hotel rooms available."

Costs: "Conference cost is approximately $130-145 and includes three to four meals."

Accommodations: "Special conference hotel rates are obtained, but the individual makes his/her own reservations. If requested, we will help the individual find a roommate."

Additional Information: Conference brochures/guidelines are available in late August for 2 first-class stamps. Inquiries by fax or e-mail OK, or look for details on website.

☑ **SEWANEE WRITERS' CONFERENCE**, 310 St. Luke's Hall, Sewanee TN 37383-1000. (931)598-1141. Fax: (931)598-1145. E-mail: cpeters@sewanee.edu. Website: http://www.sewanee.edu/writers_conference/home.html. Conference Coordinator: Cheri B. Peters. Estab. 1990. Annual. Conference held July 20-August 1, 1999. Conference duration: 12 days. Average attendance: 110. "We offer genre-based workshops in fiction, poetry, and playwriting. The Sewanee Writers' Conference uses the facilities of the University of the South. Physically, the University is a collection of ivy-covered Gothic-style buildings, located on the Cumberland Plateau in mid-Tennessee. We allow invited editors, publishers, and agents to structure their own presentations, but there is always opportunity for questions from the audience." The 1998 faculty included Pinkney Benedict, John Casey, Laura Maria Censabella, Andrew Hudgins, Margot Livesey, Alice McDermott, Brent Spencer and Mark Strand.

Costs: Full conference fee (tuition, board, and basic room) is $1,200; a single room costs an additional $50.

Accommodations: Complimentary chartered bus service is available, on a limited basis, on the first and last days of the conference. Participants are housed in University dormitory rooms. Motel or B&B housing is available but not abundantly so. Dormitory housing costs are included in the full conference fee.

Additional Information: "We offer each participant (excluding auditors) the opportunity for a private manuscript conference with a member of the faculty. These manuscripts are due one month before the conference begins." Conference brochures/guidelines are available after February, "but no SASE is necessary. The conference has available a limited number of fellowships and scholarships; these are awarded on a competitive basis." Inquiries by e-mail OK.

N ☑ **THE WRITERS' WORKSHOP**, 387 Beaucatcher Rd., Asheville NC 28805. (704)254-8111. Executive Director: Karen Tager. Estab. 1984. Held throughout the year. Conference duration: varies from 1 day to 20 weeks. Sites are throughout the South, especially North Carolina. Past guest speakers include John Le Carré, Peter Matthiessen and Eudora Welty.

Costs: Vary. Financial assistance available to low-income writers. Information on overnight accommodations is made available.

Southeast (AL, AR, FL, GA, LA, MS, PR [Puerto Rico])

ARKANSAS WRITERS' CONFERENCE, 6817 Gingerbread, Little Rock AR 72204. (501)565-8889. Counselor: Peggy Vining. Estab. 1944. Annual. Conference held first weekend in June. Average attendence: 225. "We have a variety of subjects related to writing—we have some general sessions, some more specific, but try to vary each year's subjects."

Costs: Registration: $10; luncheon: $15; banquet: $17.50, contest entry $5.

Accommodations: "We meet at a Holiday Inn—rooms available at reasonable rate." Holiday Inn has a bus to bring anyone from airport. Rooms average $64.

Additional Information: "We have 36 contest categories. Some are open only to Arkansans, most are open to all writers. Our judges are not announced before conference but are qualified, many from out of state." Conference brochures are available for SASE after February 1. "We have had 226 attending from 12 states—over 3,000 contest entries from 43 states and New Zealand, Mexico and Canada. We have a get acquainted party Thursday evening for early arrivers."

FLORIDA CHRISTIAN WRITERS CONFERENCE, 2600 Park Ave., Titusville FL 32780. (407)269-6702, ext. 202. Conference Director: Billie Wilson. Estab. 1988. Annual. Conference is held in late January. Conference duration: 5 days. Average attendance: 200. To promote "all areas of writing." Conference held at Park Avenue Retreat Center, a conference complex at a large church near Kennedy Space Center. Editors will represent over 30 publications and publishing houses.

Costs: Tuition $360, included tuition, room and board (double occupancy).

Accommodations: "We provide shuttle from the airport and from the hotel to retreat center. We make reservations at major hotel chain."

Additional Information: Critiques available. "Each writer may submit two works for critique. We have specialists in every area of writing to critique." Conference brochures/guidelines are available for SASE.

✓ **FLORIDA FIRST COAST WRITERS' FESTIVAL**, 101 W. State St., FCCJ Downtown Campus, Box 109, Jacksonville FL 32205. (904)633-8327. Fax: (904)633-8435. E-mail: kclower@fccj.org. Website: http://astro.fccj.org/WF/. Budget administrator: Kathy Clower. Estab. 1985. Annual. 1999 Festival: May 13-15. Average attendance: 150-250. All areas: mainstream plus genre. Held at Sea Turtle Inn on Atlantic Beach.
Costs: Maximum of $75 for 2 days, plus $28 for banquet tickets.
Accommodations: Sea Turtle Inn, (904)249-7402, has a special festival rate.
Additional Information: Conference brochures/guidelines are available for SASE. Inquiries by e-mail and fax OK. Sponsors contests for short fiction, poetry and novels. Novel judges are David Poyer and Elisabeth Graves. Entry fees: $30, novels; $10, short fiction; $5, poetry. Deadline: November 1 for novels and January 1 for short fiction, poems.

FLORIDA SUNCOAST WRITERS' CONFERENCE, University of South Florida, Division of Lifelong Learning, 4202 E. Fowler Ave., MGZ144, Tampa FL 33620-6610. (813)974-2403. Fax: (813)974-5732. E-mail: rubin@chuma.cas.usf.edu. Directors: Steve Rubin, Ed Hirshberg and Lagretta Lenker. Estab. 1970. Annual. Held in February. Conference duration: 3 days. Average attendance: 350-400. Conference covers poetry, short story, novel and nonfiction, including science fiction, detective, travel writing, drama, TV scripts, photojournalism and juvenile. "We do not focus on any one particular aspect of the writing profession but instead offer a variety of writing related topics including marketing. The conference is held on the picturesque university campus fronting the bay in St. Petersburg, Florida." Features panels with agents and editors. Guest speakers have included Lady P.D. James, Carolyn Forche, Marge Piercy, William Styron, David Guterson, John Updike and Joyce Carol Oates.
Costs: Call for verification.
Accommodations: Special rates available at area hotels. "All information is contained in our brochure."
Additional Information: Participants may submit work for critiquing. Extra fee charged for this service. Conference brochures/guidelines are available in October for SASE. Inquiries by e-mail and fax OK.

HEMINGWAY DAYS WRITER'S WORKSHOP AND CONFERENCE, P.O. Box 4045, Key West FL 33041-4045. (305)294-4440. Fax: (305)292-3653. E-mail: calico2419@aol.com. Director of Workshop: Dr. James Plath. Festival Director: Carol Shaughnessy. Estab. 1989. Annual. Conference held July. Conference duration: 3½ days. Average attendance: 60-100. "We deliberately keep it small so that there is a greater opportunity for participants to interact with presenting writers. The Hemingway Days Writer's Workshop and Conference focuses on fiction, poetry and Ernest Hemingway and his work. The workshop and conference is but one event in a week-long festival which honors Ernest Hemingway. The first evening features a reception and presentation of the Conch Republic Prize for Literature to a writer whose life's work epitomizes the creative spirit of Key West. Then, one day focuses on the writing of fiction, one day on the writing of poetry, and one day on Ernest Hemingway's life and work. We are offering more hands-on directed writing sessions than ever before, and combine them with our traditionally-offered presentations and after-sunset readings by critically-acclaimed writers. Most years, we also offer the opportunity for participants to have their own work critiqued. Traditionally, the Workshop & Conference is held at a resort in Key West's historic Old Town section. Directed writing exercises take place at a variety of locations in the Old Town area such as gardens and historic sites, while after-sunset readings will take place at an open-air atrium or restaurant."
Costs: $120 (1998); included all panels, directed writing exercises, attendance at all literary receptions and after-sunset readings.
Accommodations: Material available upon request.
Additional Information: Brochures/guidelines are available for SASE. "The conference/workshop is unique in that it combines studies in craft with studies in literature, and serious literary-minded events to celebrate Hemingway the writer with a week-long festival celebrating 'papa' the myth."

MOONLIGHT AND MAGNOLIAS WRITER'S CONFERENCE, 4378 Karls Gate Dr., Marietta GA 30068. Phone/fax: (770)513-1754. E-mail: WendyEth@aol.com. Estab. 1982. President, Georgia Romance Writers: Carol Springston. 1998 Conference Chair: Wendy Etherington, 2615 Suwanee Lakes Trail, Suwanee GA 30174-3164. Annual. Conference held 3rd weekend in September. Average attendance: 300. "Conference focuses on writing of women's fiction with emphasis on romance. Includes agents and editors from major publishing houses. Workshops have included: beginning writer track, general interest topics, and professional issues for the published author, plus sessions for writing for children, young adult, inspirational, multicultural and Regency. Speakers have included experts in law enforcement, screenwriting and research. Literacy raffle and advertised speaker and GRW member autographing open to the public. Published authors make up 25-30% of attendees. Brochure available for SASE in June. Send requests with SASE to Wendy Etherington.
Costs: Hotel $74/day, single, double, triple, quad (1997). Conference: non GRW members $135 (early registration).
Additional Information: Maggie Awards for excellence are presented to unpublished writers. The Maggie Award for published writers is limited to Region 3 members of Romance Writers of America. Proposals per guidelines must be submitted in early June. Please check with president for new dates. Published authors judge first round, category editors judge finals. Guidelines available for SASE in spring.

N **OZARK CREATIVE WRITERS, INC.**, 511 Perry Rd., Springdale AR 72764. (501)751-7246. President: Dusty Richards. Estab. 1973. Annual. Conference always held 2nd weekend in October. Conference duration: 2½ days. Average attendance: 250. "All types of writing. Main speaker for workshop in morning sessions—usually a novelist. Satellite speakers—afternoon—various types, including a Poetry Seminar. Conference site is the convention center. Very nice for a small group setting. Reserve early prior to September 1 to insure place."
Costs: $50 plus approximately $30 for 2 banquets. Rooms are approximately $65/night; meals extra. Registration fee allows you to enter the writing contests.
Accommodations: Chamber of Commerce will send list; 60 rooms are blocked off for OCW prior to August 15th. Accommodations vary at hotels. Many campsites also available. "Eureka Springs is a resort town near Branson, Missouri, the foothills of the beautiful Ozark Mountains."
Additional Information: We have approximately 20 various categories of writing contests. Selling writers are our judges. Entry fee required to enter. Brochures are available for SASE after May 1. "OCWI Conference is 30 years old."

SCBWI/FLORIDA ANNUAL FALL CONFERENCE, 2158 Portland Ave., Wellington FL 33414. (561)798-4824. E-mail: barcafer@aol.com. Florida Regional Advisor: Barbara Casey. Estab. 1985. Annual. Conference held in September. Conference duration: one-half day. Average attendance: 70. Conference to promote "all aspects of writing and illustrating for children. The facilities include the meeting rooms of the Library and Town Hall of Palm Springs FL (near West Palm Beach)."
Costs: $50 for SCBWI members, $55 for non-SCBWI members. Ms and art evaluations, $30.
Accommodations: Special conference rates at Airport Hilton, West Palm Beach, Florida.
Additional Information: Conference brochures/guidelines are available in July for SASE. Inquiries by e-mail OK.

WRITE FOR SUCCESS WORKSHOP: CHILDREN'S BOOKS, 3748 Harbor Heights Dr., Largo FL 33774-1207. (813)581-2484. Speaker/Coordinator: Theo Carroll. Estab. 1990. Held 3 separate evenings the last 3 weeks in March. Average attendance: 60-110. Focus is on writing and marketing for the children's book market. Site is the Clearwater, Florida Community Center. "Teaching assignments and classroom/personal critique sessions cover characterization, plotting, the importance of setting, dialogue and more. Assignments given on writing the picture book."
Costs: $85 includes materials. Limo available from Tampa airport. Information on special conference attendee accommodations available.

✓ **WRITING STRATEGIES FOR THE CHRISTIAN MARKET**, 2712 S. Peninsula Dr., Daytona Beach FL 32118-5706. (904)322-1111. Fax: (904)322-1111*9. E-mail: romy14@juno.com. Instructor: Rosemary Upton. Contact: Ms. Chris Lundy, assistant. Estab. 1991. Seminars given approximately 4 times a year. Conference duration: 3 hours. Average attendance: 10-20. Seminars include Basics I, Marketing II, Business III, Building the novel. Held in a conference room: 3-4 persons seated at each table; instructor teaches from a podium. Question and answer session provided. Critique shop included once a month, except summer (July and August). Instructors include Rosemary Upton, novelist; Kistler London, editor.
Costs: $30 for each 3-hour seminar.
Additional Information: "Designed for correspondence students as well as the classroom experience, the courses are economical and include all materials, as well as the evaluation of assignments." Those who have taken Writing Strategies instruction are able to attend an on-going monthly critiqueshop where their peers critique their work. Manual provided with each seminar. Conference brochures/guidelines are available for SASE. Inquiries by fax and e-mail OK. Independent study by mail also available.

WRITING TODAY—BIRMINGHAM-SOUTHERN COLLEGE, Box 549003, Birmingham AL 35254. (205)226-4921. Fax: (205)226-3072. E-mail: cwilson@bsc.edu. Website: http://www.bsc.edu. Director of Special Events: Martha Andrews. Estab. 1978. Annual. Conference held March 12-13, 1999. Average attendance: 400-500. "This is a two-day conference with approximately 18 workshops, lectures and readings. We try to offer workshops in short fiction, novels, poetry, children's literature, magazine writing, and general information of concern to aspiring writers such as publishing, agents, markets and research. The conference is sponsored by Birmingham-Southern College and is held on the campus in classrooms and lecture halls." The 1998 conference featured Horton Foote, Rick Brags, Lewis Nordon, Manette Ansay and Janet Burroway.
Costs: $100 for both days. This includes lunches, reception and morning coffee and rolls.
Accommodations: Attendees must arrange own transportation. Local hotels and motels offer special rates, but participants must make their own reservations.
Additional Information: "We usually offer a critique for interested writers. We have had poetry and short story critiques. There is an additional charge for these critiques." Sponsors the Hackney Literary Competition Awards for poetry, short story and novels. Guidelines available for SASE.

Midwest (IL, IN, KY, MI, OH)

ANTIOCH WRITERS' WORKSHOP, P.O. Box 494, Yellow Springs OH 45387. Director: Gilah Rittenhouse. Estab. 1984. Annual. Average attendance: 80. Workshop concentration: poetry, nonfiction and fiction. Workshop located on Antioch College campus in the Village of Yellow Springs. Speakers have included Sue Grafton, Imogene Bolls, George Ella Lyon, Herbert Martin, John Jakes and Virginia Hamilton.
Costs: Tuition is $475—lower for local and repeat—plus meals.
Accommodations: "We pick up attendees free at the airport." Accommodations made at dorms and area hotels. Cost is $16-26/night (for dorms).
Additional Information: Offers mss critique sessions. Conference brochures/guidelines are available after March 1998 for SASE.

THE COLUMBUS WRITERS CONFERENCE, P.O. Box 20548, Columbus OH 43220. (614)451-3075. Fax: (614)451-0174. E-mail: AngelaPL28@aol.com. Director: Angela Palazzolo. Estab. 1993. Annual. Conference held in September. Average attendance: 200. "The conference covers a wide variety of fiction and nonfiction topics. Writing topics have included novel, short story, children's, young adult, poetry, historical fiction, science fiction, fantasy, humor, mystery, playwriting, screenwriting, travel, humor, cookbook, technical, queries, book proposals and freelance writing. Other topics have included finding and working with an agent, targeting markets, time management, obtaining grants, sparking creativity and networking." Speakers have included Lee K. Abbott, Lore Segal, Jack Matthews, Mike Harden, Oscar Collier, Maureen F. McHugh, Ralph Keyes, Stephanie S. Tolan, J. Patrick Lewis, Tracey E. Dils, Dennis L. McKiernan, Karen Harper, Melvin Helitzer, Tracey E. Dils, J. Patrick Lewis and many other professionals in the writing field.
Costs: Early registration fee is $129 for the full conference (Friday afternoon sessions, dinner, and Saturday program); otherwise fee is $145. Early registration for the Saturday program (includes continental breakfast, lunch, and afternoon refreshments) is $89; otherwise fee is $105.
Additional Information: Call, write, e-mail or send fax to obtain a conference brochure, available mid-summer.

✓ **GREEN RIVER WRITERS NOVELS-IN-PROGRESS WORKSHOP**, 11906 Locust Rd., Middletown KY 40243-1413. (502)245-4902. E-mail: mary-odell@ntr.net. Director: Mary E. O'Dell. Estab. 1991. Annual. Conference held March 14-21, 1999. Conference duration: 1 week. Average attendance: 40. Open to persons, college age and above, who have approximately 3 chapters (60 pages) or more of a novel. Mainstream and genre novels handled by individual instructors. Short fiction collections welcome. "Each novelist instructor works with a small group (5-7 people) for five days; then agents/editors are there for panels and appointments on the weekend." Site is The University of Louisville's Shelby Campus, suburban setting, graduate dorm housing (private rooms available with shared bath for each 2 rooms). "Meetings and classes held in nearby classroom building. Grounds available for walking, etc. Lovely setting, restaurants and shopping available nearby. Participants carpool to restaurants, etc. This year we are covering mystery, fantasy, mainstream/literary, suspense, historical."
Costs: Tuition—$350, housing $20 per night private, $16 shared. Does not include meals.
Accommodations: "We do meet participants' planes and see that participants without cars have transportation to meals, etc. If participants would rather stay in hotel, we will make that information available."
Additional Information: Participants send 60 pages/3 chapters with synopsis and $25 reading fee which applies to tuition. Deadline will be in late January. Conference brochures/guidelines are available after January 1 for SASE. Inquiries by e-mail OK.

✓ **THE HEIGHTS WRITER'S CONFERENCE**, 35 N. Chillicothe Rd., Suite D, Aurora OH 44202-8741. Fax: (330)562-1217. E-mail: writersword@juno.com. Director: Lavern Hall. Estab. 1992. Annual. Conference held first Saturday in May. Average attendance: 125. "Fiction, nonfiction, science fiction, poetry, children's, marketing, etc." The conference is sponsored by Writer's World Press and held at the Cleveland Marriott East, Beachwood OH. Offers seminars on the craft, business and legal aspects of writing plus 2 teaching, hands-on workshops. "No theme; published authors and experts in their field sharing their secrets and networking for success."
Additional Information: Conference brochure available March 1 for SASE. Inquiries by e-mail and fax OK.

N **IMAGINATION**, Cleveland State University, Division of Continuing Education, 2344 Euclid Ave., Cleveland OH 44115. (216)687-4522. Contact: Neal Chandler. Estab. 1990. Annual. Conference lasts 5 days and is held in mid-July. Average attendance: 60. "Conference concentrates on fiction and poetry. Held at Mather Mansion, a restored 19th Century. Mansion on the campus of Cleveland State University." Past themes have included Writing Beyond Realism and Business of Writing. For more information send for brochure.

INDIANA UNIVERSITY WRITERS' CONFERENCE, 464 Ballantine Hall, Bloomington IN 47405. (812)855-1877. Fax: (812)855-9535. Director: Patrick Godbey. Estab. 1940. Annual. Conference/workshops held from June 21-26. Average attendance: 100. "Conference to promote poetry, fiction and nonfiction (emphasis on poetry and fiction)." Located on the campus of Indiana University, Bloomington. "We do not have themes,

although we do have panels that discuss issues such as how to publish. We also have classes that tackle just about every subject of writing. Ralph Burns, Amy Gerstler, Pinckney Benedict and Sharon Solwit spoke and taught workshops at the 1998 conference.
Costs: Approximately $300; does not include food or housing. This price does *not* reflect the cost of taking the conference for credit. "We supply conferees with options for overnight accommodations. We offer special conference rates for both the hotel and dorm facilities on site.
Additional Information: "In order to be accepted in a workshop, the writer must submit the work they would like critiqued. Work is evaluated before accepting applicant. Scholarships are available determined by an outside reader/writer, based on the quality of the manuscript." Conference brochures/guidelines available for SASE in February. "We are the second oldest writer's conference in the country. We are in our 59th year."

THE MID AMERICA MYSTERY CONFERENCE, Magna cum Murder, The E.B. Ball Center, Ball State University, Muncie IN 47306. (765)285-8975. Fax: (765)747-9566. E-mail: kkenniso@wp.bsu.edu. Estab. 1994. Annual. Conference held from October 30 to November 1. Average attendance: 400. Conference for crime and detective fiction held in the Horizon Convention Center and Historic Radisson Hotel Roberts. 1997 speakers included Lawrence Block, James Crumley, HRF Keating, Sarah Caudwell, Patricia Moyes, Harlan Coben and James Hess.
Costs: $145, which includes continental breakfasts, boxed lunches, a reception and a banquet (1997).
Additional Information: Sponsors a radio mystery script contest. Brochures or guidelines available for SASE. Inquiries by fax and e-mail OK.

N **MISSISSIPPI VALLEY WRITERS CONFERENCE**, 3403 45th St., Moline IL 61265. (309)762-8985. Conference Founder/Director: David R. Collins. Estab. 1973. Annual. Conference held June 6-11, 1999. Average attendance: 80. "Conference for all areas of writing for publication." Conference held at Augustana College, a liberal arts school along the Mississippi River. 1999 guest speakers will be bj elsner, Mel Boring, Max Collins, H.E. Francis, David McFarland, Karl Largent, Roald Tweet, Rich Johnson.
Costs: $25 for registration; $50 for 1 workshop; $90 for two; plus $40 for each additional workshops; $25 to audit.
Accommodations: On-campus facitilites available. Accommodations are available at Erickson Hall on the Augustana College campus. Cost for 6 nights is $100; cost for 15 meals is $100.
Additional Information: Conferees may submit mss to workshop leaders for personal conferences during the week. Cash awards are given at the end of the conference week by workshop leaders based on mss submitted. Conference brochures/guidelines are available for SASE. "Conference is open to the beginner as well as the polished professional—all are welcome."

✓ **OAKLAND UNIVERSITY WRITERS' CONFERENCE**, 231 Varner Hall, Rochester MI 48309-4401. (248)370-4386. Fax: (248)370-4280. E-mail: gjboddy@oakland.edu. Program Director: Gloria J. Boddy. Estab. 1961. Annual. Conference held in October. Average attendance: 400. Held at Oakland University: Oakland Center: Vandenburg Hall and O'Dowd Hall. Each annual conference covers all aspects and types of writing in 36 concurrent workshops on Saturday. Major writers from various genres are speakers for the Saturday conference and luncheon program. Individual critiques and hands-on writing workshops are conducted Friday. Areas: poetry, articles, fiction, short stories, playwriting, nonfiction, young adult, children's literature. Keynote speaker in 1998: Thomas Lynch, poet and nominee for the National Book Award.
Costs: 1998: Conference registration: $75; lunch, $12; individual ms, $48; writing workshop, $38.
Accommodations: List is available.
Additional Information: Conference brochure/guidelines available after September 1999 for SASE. Inquiries by e-mail and fax OK.

OF DARK & STORMY NIGHTS, Mystery Writers of America—Midwest Chapter, P.O. Box 1944, Muncie IN 47308-1944. (765)288-7402. E-mail: spurgeonmwa@juno.com. Workshop Director: W.W. Spurgeon. Estab. 1982. Annual. Workshop held June. Workshop duration: 1 day. Average attendance: 200. Dedicated to "writing *mystery* fiction and crime-related nonfiction. Workshops and panels presented on techniques of mystery writing from ideas to revision, marketing, investigative techniques and more, by published writers, law enforcement experts and publishing professionals." Site is Holiday Inn, Rolling Meadows IL (suburban Chicago).
Costs: $110 for MWA members; $135 for non-members; $40 extra for ms critique.
Accommodations: Easily accessible by car or train (from Chicago) Holiday Inn, Rolling Meadows $89 per night plus tax; free airport bus (Chicago O'Hare) and previously arranged rides from train.
Additional Information: "We accept manuscripts for critique (first 30 pages maximum); $40 cost. Writers meet with critics during workshop for one-on-one discussions." Brochures available for SASE after February 1.

N **OHIO WRITERS' HOLIDAY**, COFW P.O. Box 292106, Columbus OH 43229. E-mail: laurey@infinet.com. Conference Director: Rosemary Laurey. Estab. 1990. Annual. Conference held April 30-May 1. Average attendance: 120. "Womens' fiction, particularly romance fiction." Held at the Best Western North, Columbus, Ohio. Guest speakers: Paula Detmer Riggs and an editor and/or agent. Includes a meet-the-authors bookfair.
Costs: $25 Friday and $40 Saturday.

Additional Information: Conference brochures for SASE.

☑ **GARY PROVOST'S WRITERS RETREAT WORKSHOP**, % Write It/Sell It, P.O. Box 139, South Lancaster MA 01561-0139. Phone/fax: (978)368-0287 or (918)298-4866. E-mail: wrwwisi@aol.com. Website: http://www.channel1.com/wisi Director: Gail Provost Stockwell. Assistant Director: Lance Stockwell; Workshop Leader: Carol Dougherty. Estab. 1987. May 1999 workshop held at Marydale Retreat Center in Erlanger, KY (just south of Cincinnati, OH). Workshop duration: 10 days. Average attendance: 30. Focus on fiction and narrative nonfiction books in progress. All genres. "The Writers Retreat Workshop is an intensive learning experience for small groups of serious-minded writers. Founded by the late Gary Provost, one of the country's leading writing instructors and his wife Gail, an award-winning author, the WRW is a challenging and enriching adventure. The goal of the WRW staff is for students to leave with a new understanding of the marketplace and the craft of writing a novel. In the heart of a supportive and spirited community of fellow writers, students are able to make remarkable creative leaps over the course of the 10-day workshop."
Costs: Costs (discount for past participants) $1,620 for 10 days which includes all food and lodging. The Marydale Retreat Center is 5 miles from the Cincinnati airport and offers shuttle services.
Additional Information: Participants are selected based upon the appropriateness of this program for the applicant's specific writing project. Participants are asked to submit a brief overview and synopsis before the workshop and are given assignments and feedback during the 10-day workshop. Brochures/guidelines are available after November by calling 1-800-642-2494. Inquiries by fax and e-mail OK.

ROPEWALK WRITERS' RETREAT, 8600 University Blvd., Evansville IN 47712. (812)464-1863. E-mail: lcleek.ucs@smtp.usi.edu. Conference Coordinator: Linda Cleek. Estab. 1989. Annual. Conference held in June. "Celebrating 10 Years in Utopia!" Average attendance: 42. "The week-long RopeWalk Writers' Retreat gives participants an opportunity to attend workshops and to confer privately with one of four or five prominent writers. Historic New Harmony, Indiana, site of two nineteenth century utopian experiments, provides an ideal setting for this event with its retreat-like atmosphere and its history of creative and intellectual achievement. At RopeWalk you will be encouraged to write—not simply listen to others talks about writing. Each workshop will be limited to twelve participants. The New Harmony Inn and Conference Center will be headquarters for the RopeWalk Writers' Retreat. Please note that reservations at the Inn should be confirmed by May 1." 1998 faculty Pam Houston, Bob Shacochis, Ellen Bryant Voigt, Heather McHugh, Stephen Dobyns and Richard Powers.
Costs: $425 (1998), includes breakfasts and lunches.
Accommodations: Information on overnight accommodations is made available. "Room-sharing assistance; some low-cost accommodations."
Additional Information: For critiques submit mss approx. 6 weeks ahead. Brochures are available after January 15.

SELF PUBLISHING YOUR OWN BOOK, 34200 Ridge Rd., #110, Willoughby OH 44094-2954. (440)943-3047 or (800)653-4261. E-mail address: fa837@cleveland.freenet.edu. Teacher: Lea Leever Oldham. Estab. 1989. Quarterly. Conferences usually held in February, April, August and October. Conference duration: 2½ hours. Average attendance: up to 25. Conference covers copyrighting, marketing, pricing, ISBN number, Library of Congress catalog number, reaching the right customers and picking a printer. Held at Lakeland Community College, Kirtland, OH (east of Cleveland off I-90) and other locations. Classrooms are wheelchair accessible.
Additional Information: Conference guidelines are available for SASE. Inquiries by e-mail OK.

WESTERN RESERVE WRITERS & FREELANCE CONFERENCE, 34200 Ridge Rd., #110, Willoughby OH 44094. (440)943-3047 or (800)653-4261. E-mail address: fa837@cleveland.freenet.edu. Coordinator: Lea Leever Oldham. Estab. 1984. Annual. Conference held every September. Conference duration: 1 day. Average attendance: 150. "Fiction, nonfiction, inspirational, children's, poetry, humor, scifi, copyright and tax information, etc." Held "at Lakeland Community College, Kirtland, OH. Classrooms wheelchair accessible. Accessible from I-90, east of Cleveland." Panels include "no themes, simply published authors and other experts sharing their secrets."
Costs: $59 including lunch.
Additional Information: Conference brochures/guidelines are available after July 1999 for SASE. Inquiries by e-mail OK.

WESTERN RESERVE WRITERS MINI CONFERENCE, 34200 Ridge Rd., #110, Willoughby OH 44094. (440)943-3047 or (800)653-4261. E-mail address: fa837@cleveland.freenet.edu. Coordinator: Lea Leever Old-

ham. Estab. 1991. Annual. Conference held in late March. Conference duration: ½ day. Average attendance: 175. Conference to promote "fiction, nonfiction, children's, poetry, science fiction, etc." Held at Lakeland Community College, Kirtland, OH (east of Cleveland off I-90). Classrooms are wheelchair accessible. "Conference is for beginners, intermediate and advanced writers." Past speakers have included Mary Grimm, Nick Bade, James Martin and Mary Ryan.
Costs: $39.
Additional Information: Conference brochures/guidelines are available after January 1999 for SASE. Inquiries by e-mail OK.

WRITING FOR MONEY WORKSHOP, 34200 Ridge Rd., #110, Willoughby OH 44094. (440)943-3047 or (800)653-4261. E-mail: fa837@cleveland.freenet.edu. Contact: Lea Leever Oldham. Conference held several times during the year. 1999 dates and locations available by e-mail and phone. Conference duration: one day. "Covers query letters, characterization for fiction, editing grammar, manuscript preparation and marketing saleable manuscripts." Held at Lakeland Community College, Kirtland, OH. Right off I-90 and in Mayfield, OH, east of Cleveland.
Costs: $39/day.
Additional Information: Workshop brochure/guidelines are available a month prior to class. Inquiries by e-mail OK.

North Central (IA, MN, NE, ND, SD, WI)

N **BLACK HILLS WRITERS GROUP WORKSHOP**, P.O. Box 1539, Rapid City SD 55709-1539. (605)343-8661. E-mail: ra17748251@aol.com. Workshop Chair: R.T. Lawton. One-day conference held every odd-numbered year; next conference Spring 1999. Average attendance: 100. Conference concentrates on "elements of successful writing, leading to publication. All genres are covered." Held in a motel/hotel with individual rooms for seminars and large room for main speaking event. Themes planned for next conference include "What do editors want?": various fiction elements, article writing, beginners' tips, various poetry types and book-length fiction. "Seminars and panels have featured published authors from several genres."
Costs: $100 includes lunch.
Accommodations: "For those traveling a long distance to attend our workshop, the host motel/hotel offers a special conference rate."
Additional Information: "In even-numbered years, we offer the Laura Bower Van Nuys Writing Contest." Contest brochures/guidelines are available for SASE.

N **COPYRIGHT WORKSHOP**, 610 Langdon St., Madison WI 53703. (608)262-3447. Director: Christine DeSmet. Offered 2 times/year. Average attendance: 50. "Copyright law for writers, publishers, teachers, designers." Conference held at Wisconsin Center, University of Wisconsin—Madison.
Costs: $195.
Additional Information: Conference brochures/guidelines are available.

✔ **PETER DAVIDSON'S WRITER'S SEMINAR**, 982 S. Emerald Hills Dr., P.O. Box 497, Arnolds Park IA 51331-0497. (712)362-7968. Fax: (712)362-8363. Seminar Presenter: Peter Davidson. Estab. 1985. Seminars held about 30 times annually, in various sites. Offered year round. Seminars last 1 day, usually 9 a.m.-4 p.m. Average attendance: 35. "All writing areas including books of fiction and nonfiction, children's works, short stories, magazine articles, poetry, songs, scripts, religious works, personal experiences and romance fiction. All seminars are sponsored by community colleges or colleges across the U.S. Covers many topics including developing your idea, writing the manuscript, copyrighting, and marketing your work. The information is very practical—participants will be able to put into practice the principles discussed."
Costs: Each sponsoring college sets own fees, ranging from $39-59, depending on location, etc.
Accommodations: "Participants make their own arrangements. Usually, no special arrangements are available."
Additional Information: "Participants are encouraged to bring their ideas and/or manuscripts for a short, informal evaluation by seminar presenter, Peter Davidson." Conference brochures/guidelines are available for SASE. "On even-numbered years, usually present seminars in Colorado, Wyoming, Nebraska, Kansas, Iowa, Minnesota and South Dakota. On odd-numbered years, usually present seminars in Illinois, Iowa, Minnesota, Arkansas, Missouri, South Dakota and Nebraska."

GREAT LAKES WRITER'S WORKSHOP, Alverno College, 3401 S. 39 St., P.O. Box 343922, Milwaukee WI 53234-3922. (414)382-6176. Fax: (414)382-6332. Assistant Director: Cindy Jackson, Professional and Community Education. Estab. 1985. Annual. Workshop held during second week in July (Friday through Thursday). Average attendance: 250. "Workshop focuses on a variety of subjects including fiction, writing for magazines, freelance writing, writing for children, poetry, marketing, etc. Participants may select individual workshops or

opt to attend the entire week-long session. Classes are held during evenings and weekends. The workshop is held in Milwaukee, WI at Alverno College."
Costs: In 1997, cost was $99 for entire workshop. "Individual classes are priced as posted in the brochure with the majority costing $20 each."
Accommodations: Attendees must make their own travel arrangments. Accommodations are available on campus; rooms are in residence halls and are not air-conditioned. Cost in 1997 was $25 for single, $20 per person for double. There are also hotels in the surrounding area. Call (414)382-6040 for information regarding overnight accommodations.
Additional Information: "Some workshop instructors may provide critiques, but this changes depending upon the workshop and speaker. This would be indicated in the workshop brochure." Brochures are available for SASE after March. Inquiries by fax OK.

IOWA SUMMER WRITING FESTIVAL, 116 International Center, University of Iowa, Iowa City IA 52242-1802. (319)335-2534. E-mail: peggy-houston@uiowa.edu; amy-margolis@uiowa.edu. Website: http://www.edu/~iswfest. Director: Peggy Houston. Assistant Director: Amy Margolis. Estab. 1987. Annual. Festival held in June and July. Workshops are one week or a weekend. Average attendance: limited to 12/class—over 1,300 participants throughout the summer. "We offer courses in most areas of writing: novel, short story, essay, poetry, playwriting, screenwriting, humor, travel, writing for children, memoir, women's writing, romance and mystery." Site is the University of Iowa campus. Guest speakers are undetermined at this time. Readers and instructors have included Lee K. Abbott, Susan Power, Joy Harjo, Gish Jen, Abraham Verghese, Robert Olen Butler, Ethan Canin, Clark Blaise, Gerald Stern, Donald Justice, Michael Dennis Browne, Marvin Bell, Hope Edelman.
Costs: $400/week; $150, weekend workshop (1997 rates). Discounts available for early registration. Housing and meals are separate.
Accommodations: "We offer participants a choice of accommodations: dormitory, $27/night; Iowa House, $56/night; Holiday Inn, $60/night (rates subject to changes)."
Additional Information: Brochure/guidelines are available in February. Inquiries by fax and e-mail OK.

☑ **REDBIRD WRITING STUDIOS**, 3195 S. Superior St., Milwaukee WI 53207-3074. (414)481-3029. E-mail: blankda@execpc.com. Website: http://www.execpc.com/redbirdstudios. Founder/Director: Judy Bridges. Estab. 1993. Average attendance: 6-25. "Seminars and roundtable groups for writers of all ages, all levels. Sessions led by published writers who like to teach. Studios located in former convent school, overlooking Lake Michigan. Workshops planned for the next year include poetry, novels, short stories, nonfiction, creative nonfiction, travel, suspense, playwriting, writing for the children's market, getting published and business basics. Special programs for school groups and teachers." Past speakers have included Elaine Bergstrom, Kurt Chandler, Anne Landre, John Lehman and Sharon Hart Addy.
Costs: $55-$125.
Additional Information: Brochure available for SASE. Inquiries by fax and e-mail OK.

☑ **SCBWI/MINNESOTA CHAPTER CONFERENCES**, 7060 Valley Creek Rd., Suite 115215, Woodbury MN 55125. (612)739-0119. E-mail: kidlit@isd.net. "Although schedule may vary as space is available, conferences are usually held one day in spring and one day in fall. The smaller conference features local authors and editors only. The larger conference features children's book editors from New York publishing houses and well-known authors." Average attendance: 100. Speakers have included editors from Houghton Mifflin, authors Phyllis Root and Kathryn O. Galbraith and illustrator Beth Peck.
Costs: Varies: around $20 for local conference or $85 for larger conference with discounts given for SCBWI members and early registration.
Accommodations: Not included in conference cost.
Additional Information: For conference brochure, send SASE no more than 6 weeks in advance. Inquiries by e-mail OK. Ms critiques and portfolio reviews available at larger conference for an additional fee.

[N] ☑ **SPLIT ROCK ARTS PROGRAM**, University of Minnesota, 335 Nolte Center, 315 Pillsbury Dr., SE, Minneapolis MN 55455. (612)624-6800. Fax: (612)624-5891. E-mail: srap@mail.cee.umn.edu. Estab. 1982. Annual. Workshops held in July and August. Over 45 one-week intensive residential workshops held. "The Split Rock Arts Program is offered through the University of Minnesota on its Duluth campus. Over 45 one-week intensive residential workshops in writing, visual arts, fine crafts and creativity enhancement are held for 5 weeks in July and August. This unique arts community provides a nurturing environment in a beautiful setting overlooking Lake Superior and the summer port city of Duluth. Courses, which can be taken for credit, are offered in long and short fiction, nonfiction, poetry and children's literature." Instructors in 1998 included Paulette Bates Alden, Judith Barrington and Carol Bly.
Costs: $440, tuition (may vary with options). Moderately priced housing available for additional cost.
Accommodations: Campus apartments and dormitory available.
Additional Information: A limited number of scholarships are available based on qualification and need. Call for catalog.

N **UNIVERSITY OF WISCONSIN AT MADISON WRITERS INSTITUTE**, 610 Langdon St., Madison WI 53703. (608)262-3447. Director: Christine DeSmet. Estab. 1990. Annual. Conference held in July. Average attendance: 175. Conference held at University of Wisconsin at Madison. Fiction and nonfiction workshops. Guest speakers are published authors, editors and agents.
Costs: $185 for 2 days; critique fees.
Accommodations: Info on accommodations sent with registration confirmation. Critiques available. Conference brochures/guidelines are available for SASE.

WRITING TO SELL, Minneapolis Writers Conference, Box 24356, Minneapolis MN 55424. Contact: Herb Montgomery, board member. Estab. 1985. Annual conference held in August for 1 day. Average attendance: 100. Conference about writing to sell. Held in Minneapolis hotel. 1998 speakers included agent Jonathon Lazear.
Costs: $75 (1999).
Additional Information: Brochure available in May for SASE.

N ✓ **WRITING WORKSHOP**, P.O. Box 65, Ellison Bay WI 54210. (920)854-4088. E-mail: clearing@mail.wiscnet.net. Resident Manager: Don Buchholz. Estab. 1935. Annual. Conference held in June. Average attendance: 16. "General writing journal, poetry as well as fiction and nonfiction." Held in a "quiet, residential setting in deep woods on the shore of Green Bay." Past guest speakers include Lowell B. Komie (short story), T.V. Olsen (novelist) and Barbara Vroman (novelist).
Costs: In 1998, cost was $570 (twin bed) or $530 (dormitory).
Accommodations: "Two to a room with private bath in rustic log and stone buildings. Great hall type of classroom for the conference."
Additional Information: Catalog (8½×11) available upon request.

South Central (CO, KS, MO, NM, OK, TX)

ASPEN WRITERS' CONFERENCE, Box 7726, Aspen CO 81612. (800)925-2526. Fax (970)920-5700. E-mail: aspenwrite@aol.com. Executive Director: Jeanne McGovern Small. Estab. 1975. Annual. Conference held for 1 week during summer at The Aspen Institute, Aspen Meadows campus. Average attendance: 75. Conference for fiction, poetry, nonfiction and children's literature. Includes general fiction workshops; talks with agents, editor and publisher on fiction. 1997 conference featured George Nicholson, agent, Sterling Lord Litenstic; Carol Honck Smith, editor, W.W. Norton; Tom Auer, publisher, *The Bloomsbury Review*; and special guests Andrea Barrett and Rudolfo Anaya.
Costs: $495/full tuition; $125/audit only (1997)
Accommodations Free shuttle to/from airport and around town. Information on overnight accommodations available. On-campus housing; (800) number for reservations. Rates for 1997: on-campus $60/night double; $85/night single; off-campus rates vary.
Additional Information: Manuscripts to be submitted for review by faculty prior to conference. Conference brochures are available for SASE.

AUSTIN WRITERS' LEAGUE WORKSHOPS/CONFERENCES/CLASSES, E-2, 1501 W. Fifth, Austin TX 78703. (512)499-8914. Fax: (512)499-0441. Executive Director: Jim Bob McMillan. Estab. 1982. Programs ongoing through the year. Duration: varies according to program. Average attendance from 15 to 200. To promote "all genres, fiction and nonfiction, poetry, writing for children, screenwriting, playwriting, legal and tax information for writers, also writing workshops for children and youth." Programs held at AWL Resource Center/Library, other sites in Austin and Texas. Topics include: finding and working with agents and publishers; writing and marketing short fiction; dialogue; characterization; voice; research; basic and advanced fiction writing/focus on the novel; business of writing; also workshops for genres. Past speakers have included Dwight Swain, Natalie Goldberg, David Lindsey, Shelby Hearon, Gabriele Rico, Benjamin Saenz, Rosellen Brown, Sandra Scofield, Reginald Gibbons, Anne Lamott, Sterling Lord and Sue Grafton.
Costs: Varies from free to $185, depending on program. Most classes, $20-50; workshops $35-75; conferences: $125-185.
Accommodations: Special rates given at some hotels for program participants.
Additional Information: Critique sessions offered at some programs. Individual presenters determine critique requirements. Those requirements are then made available through Austin Writers' League office and in workshop promotion. Contests and awards programs are offered separately. Brochures/guidelines are available on request.

GOLDEN TRIANGLE WRITERS GUILD, 4245 Calder, Beaumont TX 77706. (409)898-4894. Administrative Assistant: Becky Blanchard. Estab. 1984. Annual. Conference held during third weekend in October. Attendance limited to 450. Held at the Holiday Inn on Walden Road in Beaumont, Texas.
Costs: $195 before September 20th; $220 after September 20th. Cost covers conference only; room not included.
Accommodations: Special conference rates available at Holiday Inn (Beaumont).
Additional Information: Sponsors a contest. Attendance required. Preliminary judging done by published

authors and/or specialists in each specific genre. Final judging done by editors and/or agents specializing in each specific area.

☑ **HEART OF AMERICA WRITERS' CONFERENCE**, Johnson County Community College, 12345 College Blvd., Overland Park KS 66210. (913)469-3838. Fax: (913)469-2586. E-mail: jchoice@johnco.cc.ks.us. Program Director: Judith Choice. Estab. 1984. Annual. Conference held in April. Average attendance: 110-160. "The conference features a choice of 16 plus sections focusing on nonfiction, children's market, fiction, journaling, essay, poetry and genre writing." Conference held in state-of-the-art conference center in suburban Kansas City. Individual sessions with agents and editors are available. Ms critiques are offered for $40. Past keynote speakers have included Natalie Goldberg, Ellen Gilchrist, Linda Hogan, David Ray, Stanley Elkin, David Shields, Luisa Valenzuela and Amy Bloom.
Costs: $100 includes lunch, reception, breaks.
Accommodations: Conference brochures/guidelines are available after December. Inquiries by mail, phone, fax or e-mail OK. "We provide lists of area hotels."

N ☑ **MAPLE WOODS COMMUNITY COLLEGE WRITERS' CONFERENCE**, 2601 NE Barry Rd., Kansas City MO 64156-1299. (816)437-3050. Fax: (816)437-3049. E-mail: schumacp@maplewoods.cc.mo.us. Website: http://www.kcmetro.cc.mo.us. Director, Community Education: Paula Schumacher. Conference held September 18, 1999. Conference duration: 1 day. Average attendance: 200-250. Nonfiction, fiction, science fiction, mystery, romance, short story, literary agents. Conference site: American Heartland Theatre, Westin Crown Center, Kansas City MO.
Costs: $79 conference and theatre ticket. Continental breakfast and break-time soft drinks included.
Additional Information: Conference information available after April 25. Request information through e-mail, fax or in writing.

NATIONAL WRITERS ASSOCIATION CONFERENCE, 1450 S. Havana, Suite 424, Aurora CO 80012. (303)751-7844. Fax: (303)751-8593. E-mail address: sandywriter@aol.com. Executive Director: Sandy Whelchel. Estab. 1926. Annual. Conference usually held in June in Denver, CO. Conference duration: 3 days. Average attendance: 200-300. General writing and marketing.
Costs: $300 (approx.).
Additional Information: Awards for previous contests will be presented at the conference. Conference brochures/guidelines are available for SASE.

THE NEW LETTERS WEEKEND WRITERS CONFERENCE, University of Missouri-Kansas City, College of Arts and Sciences Continuing Ed. Division, 215 SSB, 5100 Rockhill Rd., Kansas City MO 64110-2499. (816)235-2736. Fax: (816)235-5279. E-mail: mckinleym@umkc.edu. Estab. in the mid-70s as The Longboat Key Writers Conference. Annual. Runs during June. Conference duration is 3 days. Average attendance: 75. "The New Letters Weekend Writers Conference brings together talented writers in many genres for lectures, seminars, readings, workshops and individual conferences. The emphasis is on craft and the creative process in poetry, fiction, screenwriting, playwriting and journalism; but the program also deals with matters of psychology, publications and marketing. The conference is appropriate for both advanced and beginning writers. The conference meets at the beautiful Diastole conference center of The University of Missouri-Kansas City."
Costs: Several options are available. Participants may choose to attend as a non-credit student or they may attend for 1-3 hours of college credit from the University of Missouri-Kansas City. Conference registration includes continental breakfasts, Saturday dinner and Sunday lunch. For complete information, contact the University of Missouri-Kansas City.
Accommodations: Registrants are responsible for their own transportation, but information on area accommodations is made available.
Additional Information: Those registering for college credit are required to submit a ms in advance. Ms reading and critique is included in the credit fee. Those attending the conference for non-credit also have the option of having their ms critiqued for an additional fee. Conference brochures/guidelines are available for SASE after March. Inquiries by e-mail and fax OK.

☑ **NORTHWEST OKLAHOMA WRITER'S WORKSHOP**, P.O. Box 5994, Enid OK 73702-5994. Phone/fax: (580)237-2744. E-mail: enidwriters@hotmail.com. Website: http://www.freeyellow.com/members2/enidwritersclub/index.html. Workshop coordinator: Bev Walton-Porter. Estab. 1991. Annual. Conference held in March. Conference duration: 6 hours. Average attendance: 20-30. "Usually fiction is the concentration area. The purpose is to help writers learn more about the craft of writing and encourage writers 'to step out in faith' and

CAN'T FIND A CONFERENCE? Conferences are listed by region. Check the introduction to this section for a list of regional categories.

submit." Held in Cherokee Strip Conference Center. Past speakers have been Norma Jean Lutz, inspirational and magazine writing; Deborah Bouziden, fiction and magazine writing; Anna Meyers, children's writing; Sondra Soli, poetry; Marcia Preston, magazines, Mary Lynn, manuscript preparation and submission protocol; Jean Hager, writing mysteries.
Costs: $40; includes catered lunch.
Additional Information: Conference guidelines are available for SASE. Inquiries by e-mail and fax OK.

☑ **ROCKY MOUNTAIN BOOK FESTIVAL**, 2123 Downing St., Denver CO 80205. (303)839-8323. Fax: (303)839-8319. E-mail: ccftb_mm@compuserve.com. Website: http://www.aclin.org/code/ceftb. Program Director: Megan Maguire. Estab. 1991. Annual. Festival held first weekend in November. Average attendance: 25,000. Festival promotes published work from all genres. Held at Denver Merchandise Mart. Offers a wide variety of panels. Approximately 300 authors are scheduled to speak at the next festival including Ridley Pearson, Alice Walker, Dixie Carter, Dave Barry and Jill Kerr Conway.
Costs: $4 (adult); $1 (child).
Accommodations: Information on overnight accommodations is available.
Additional Information: Brochures/guidelines available for SASE. Inquiries by e-mail and fax OK.

☑ **ROCKY MOUNTAIN CHILDREN'S BOOK FESTIVAL**, 2123 Downing St., Denver CO 80205-5210. (303)839-8323. Fax: (303)839-8319. E-mail: ccftb_mm@compuserve.com. Program Director: Megan Maguire. Estab. 1996. Annual festival held in April. Festival duration: 2 days. Average attendance: 30,000. Festival promotes published work for and about children/families. It is solely for children's authors and illustrators—open to the public. Held at Denver Merchandise Mart. Approximately 100 authors speak annually. Past authors include Ann M. Martin, Sharon Creech, Nikki Grimes, T.A. Barron, Laura Numeroff, Jean Craighead George and Robert Munsch.
Costs: None.
Accommodations: "Information on accommodations available."
Additional Information: Send SASE for brochure/guidelines, available in December. Inquiries by fax and e-mail OK.

ROMANCE WRITERS OF AMERICA NATIONAL CONFERENCE, 3703 FM 1960 West, Suite 555, Houston TX 77068. (281)440-6885, ext. 27. Fax: (281)440-7510. Website: http://www.rwanation.com. Executive Manager: Allison Kelley. Estab. 1981. Annual. Conference held in late July or early August. Average attendance: 1,500. Over 100 workshops on writing, researching and the business side of being a working writer. Publishing professionals attend and accept appointments. Keynote speaker is renowned romance writer. Conference will be held in Anaheim, California, in 1998 and Chicago, Illinois, in 1999.
Costs: $300.
Additional Information: Annual RITA awards are presented for romance authors. Annual Golden Heart awards are presented for unpublished writers. Conference brochures/guidelines are available for SASE.

SOUTHWEST WRITERS WORKSHOP CONFERENCE, 1338 Wyoming NE, Suite B, Albuquerque NM 87112-5067. (505)293-0303. Fax: (505)237-2665. E-mail: swriters@aol.com. Website: http://www.us1.net//SWW. Estab. 1983. Annual. Conference held in August. Average attendance: about 400. "Conference concentrates on all areas of writing." Workshops and speakers include writers and editors of all genres for all levels from beginners to advanced. The 1998 keynote speaker will be David Guterson, author of *Snow Falling On Cedars*.
Costs: $265 (members) and $320 (nonmembers); includes conference sessions, 2 luncheons, 2 banquets and 2 breakfasts.
Accommodations: Usually have official airline and discount rates. Special conference rates are available at hotel. A list of other area hotels and motels is available.
Additional Information: Sponsors a contest judged by authors, editors and agents from New York, Los Angeles, etc., and from major publishing houses. Eighteen categories. Deadline: May 1. Entry fee is $24 (members) or $34 (nonmembers). Brochures/guidelines available for SASE. Inquiries by e-mail and fax OK. "An appointment (10 minutes, one-on-one) may be set up at the conference with editor or agent of your choice on a first-registered/first-served basis."

☑ **STEAMBOAT SPRINGS WRITERS GROUP**, P.O. Box 774284, Steamboat Springs CO 80477. (970)879-8079. E-mail: freiberger@compuserve.com. Director: Harriet Freiberger. Estab. 1982. Annual. Conference held July 24, 1999. Conference duration: 1 day. Average attendance: 30. "Our conference emphasizes instruction within the seminar format. Novices and polished professionals benefit from the individual attention and the camaraderie which can be established within small groups. A pleasurable and memorable learning experience is guaranteed by the relaxed and friendly atmosphere of the old train depot. Registration is limited." Steamboat Arts Council sponsors the group at the restored Train Depot.
Costs: $35 before June 15, $45 after. Fee covers all conference activities, including lunch. Lodging available at Steamboat Resorts; 10% discount for participants."
Additional Information: Available April 15. Inquiries by e-mail, phone or mail OK.

TAOS SCHOOL OF WRITING, P.O. Box 20496, Albuquerque NM 87154-0496. (505)294-4601. E-mail: spletzer@swcp.com. Website: http://www.us1.net/zollinger. Administrator: Suzanne Spletzer. Estab. 1993 by Norman Zollinger. Annual. Conference held in mid-July. Conference duration: 1 week. Average attendance: 60. "All fiction and nonfiction. No poetry or screenwriting. Purpose—to promote good writing skills. We meet at the Thunderbird Lodge in the Taos Ski Valley, NM. (We are the only ones there.) No telephones or televisions in rooms. No elevator. Slightly rustic landscape. Quiet mountain setting at 9,000 feet." Conference focuses on writing fiction and nonfiction and publishing. Previous speakers include David Morrell, Suzy McKee Charnas, Stephen R. Donaldson, Norman Zollinger, Denise Chavez, Richard S. Wheeler, Max Evans and Tony Hillerman, plus editors amd agents.
Costs: $1,200; includes tuition, room and board.
Accommodations: "Travel agent arranges rental cars or shuttle rides to Ski Valley from Albuquerque Sunport."
Additional Information: "Acceptance to school is determined by evaluation of submitted manuscript. Manuscripts are critiqued by faculty and students in the class sessions." Conference brochures/guidelines are available after January. Visit website for most current information and registration form, or e-mail, call or send SASE.

☑ **WRITERS WORKSHOP IN SCIENCE FICTION**, English Department/University of Kansas, Lawrence KS 66045-2115. (785)864-3380. Fax: (785)864-4298. E-mail: jgunn@falcon.cc.ukans.edu. Website: http://www.falcon.cc.ukans.edu/~sfcenter/. Professor: James Gunn. Estab. 1985. Annual. Conference held June 27-July 11, 1999. Average attendance: 15. Conference for writing and marketing science fiction. "Housing is provided and classes meet in university housing on the University of Kansas campus. Workshop sessions operate informally in a lounge." 1998 guest writers: Frederik Pohl, SF writer and former editor and agent; John Ordover, writer and editor.
Costs: Tuition: $400. Housing and meals are additional.
Accommodations: Several airport shuttle services offer reasonable transportation from the Kansas City International Airport to Lawrence. During past conferences, students were housed in a student dormitory at $12/day double, $22/day single.
Additional Information: "Admission to the workshop is by submission of an acceptable story. Two additional stories should be submitted by the end of June. These three stories are copied and distributed to other participants for critiquing and are the basis for the first week of the workshop; one story is rewritten for the second week." Brochures/guidelines are available after December 15 for SASE. Inquiries by phone, fax or e-mail OK. "The Writers Workshop in Science Fiction is intended for writers who have just started to sell their work or need that extra bit of understanding or skill to become a published writer."

West (AZ, CA, HI, NV, UT)

BE THE WRITER YOU WANT TO BE MANUSCRIPT CLINIC, 23350 Sereno Court, Villa 30, Cupertino CA 95014. (415)691-0300. Contact: Louise Purwin Zobel. Estab. 1969. Workshop held irregularly—usually semiannually at several locations. Workshop duration: 1-2 days. Average attendance: 20-30. "This manuscript clinic enables writers of any type of material to turn in their work-in-progress—at any stage of development—to receive help with structure and style, as well as marketing advice." It is held on about 40 campuses at different times, including University of California and other university and college campuses throughout the west.
Costs: Usually $45-65/day, "depending on campus."
Additional Information: Brochures/guidelines available for SASE.

CALIFORNIA WRITER'S CLUB CONFERENCE AT ASILOMAR, 3975 Kim Court, Sebastopol CA 95472. (707)823-8128. E-mail: GPMansergh@aol.com. Contact: Gil Mansergh, director. Estab. 1941. Annual. Held in June. Conference duration: Friday afternoon through Sunday lunch. Average attendance: 350. Conference offers opportunity to learn from and network with successful writers, agents and editors in Asilomar's beautiful and historic beach side setting on the shores of Monterey Bay. Presentations, panels, hands-on workshops and agent/editor appointments focus on writing and marketing short stories, novels, articles, books, poetry and screenplays for children and adults.
Costs: $435 includes all conference privileges, shared lodging and 6 meals. There is a $90 surcharge for a single room.
Accommodations: Part of the California State Park system, Asilomar is rustic and beautiful. Julia Morgan designed redwood and stone buildings share 105 acres of dunes and pine forests with modern AIA and National Academy of Design winning lodges. Monterey airport is a 15 minute taxi drive away.
Additional Information: First prize winners in all 7 categories of the *California Writers' Club* writing competitions receive free registration to next conference. $10 entry fee. Contest deadline is May 1, 1998. Brochure and contest submission rules will be available in late February.

☑ **DESERT WRITERS WORKSHOP/CANYONLANDS FIELD INSTITUTE**, P.O. Box 68, Moab UT 84532. (435)259-7750 or (800)860-5262. Fax: (435)259-2335. E-mail: cfiinfo@canyonlandsfieldinst.org. Website: http:canyonlandsfieldinst.org/. Executive Director and Conference Coordinator: Karla Vanderzanden. Estab.

1984. Annual. Held first weekend in November. Conference duration: 3 days. Average attendance: 30. Concentrations include fiction, nonfiction, poetry. Site is the Pack Creek Ranch, Moab, Utah. "Theme is oriented towards understanding the vital connection between the natural world and human communities." Faculty panel has included in past years Mary Sojourner, Pam Houston, Linda Hogan, Christopher Merrill, Terry Tempest Williams and Richard Shelton.
Costs: $440 (members of CFI, $425); $150 deposit, which includes meals Friday-Sunday, instruction, field trip, lodging.
Accommodations: At Pack Creek Ranch, included in cost.
Additional Information: Brochures are available for SASE. Inquiries by phone, fax or e-mail OK. "Participants may submit work in advance, but it is not required. Student readings, evaluations and consultations with guest instructors/faculty are part of the workshop. Desert Writers Workshop is supported in part by grants from the Utah Arts Council and National Endowment for the Arts. A scholarship is available. College credit is also available for an additional fee."

I'VE ALWAYS WANTED TO WRITE BUT . . ., 23350 Sereno Court, Villa 30, Cupertino CA 95014. (415)691-0300. Contact: Louise Purwin Zobel. Estab. 1969. Workshop held irregularly, several times a year at different locations. Workshop duration: 1-2 days. Average attendance: 30-50. Workshop "encourages real beginners to get started on a lifelong dream. Focuses on the basics of writing." Workshops held at about 40 college and university campuses in the West, including University of California.
Costs: Usually $45-65/day "depending on college or university."
Additional Information: Brochures/guidelines are available for SASE after August.

IWWG EARLY SPRING IN CALIFORNIA CONFERENCE, International Women's Writing Guild, P.O. Box 810, Gracie Station, New York NY 10028-0082. (212)737-7536. Fax: (212)737-9469. E-mail: iwwg@iwwg.com. Website: http://www.IWWG.com. Executive Director: Hannelore Hahn. Estab. 1982. Annual. Conference held March 12-14. Average attendance: 80. Conference to promote "creative writing, personal growth and empowerment." Site is a redwood forest mountain retreat in Santa Cruz, California.
Costs: $275 for weekend program, plus room and board; $65 per day for commuters, $125 for Saturday and Sunday only.
Accommodations: Accommodations are all at conference site.
Additional Information: Conference brochures/guidelines are available for SASE after August. Inquiries by e-mail and fax OK.

JACK LONDON WRITERS' CONFERENCE, 135 Clark Dr., San Mateo CA 94402-1002. (415)615-8331. Fax: (415)342-9155. Coordinator: Marlo Faulkner. Estab. 1987. Annual. Conference held in March. Average attendance: 200. "Our purpose is to provide access to professional writers. Workshops have covered genre fiction, nonfiction, marketing, agents, poetry and children's." Held at the San Francisco Airport Holiday Inn.
Costs: $95; includes continental breakfast, lunch and all sessions.
Additional Information: "Special rates on accommodations available at Holiday Inn." Sponsors a cash prize writing contest judged by the Peninsula branch of the California Writers Club (requirements in brochure). Brochures/guidelines available for SASE after November. Inquiries by fax OK. The Jack London Conference has had over 80 professional writers speak and 800 participants. It's sponsored by the Peninsula Branch of the California Writers' Club.

☑ **MOUNT HERMON CHRISTIAN WRITERS CONFERENCE**, P.O. Box 413, Mount Hermon CA 95041-0413. (831)430-1238. Fax: (831)335-9218. E-mail: mhsherry@aol.com. Website: http://www.mounthermon.org. Director of Specialized Programs: David R. Talbott. Estab. 1970. Annual. Conference held Friday-Tuesday over Palm Sunday weekend, March 26-30, 1999. Average attendance: 200. "We are a broad-ranging conference for all areas of Christian writing, including fiction, children's, poetry, nonfiction, magazines, books, educational curriculum and radio and TV scriptwriting. This is a working, how-to conference, with many workshops within the conference involving on-site writing assignments. The conference is sponsored by and held at the 440-acre Mount Hermon Christian Conference Center near San Jose, California, in the heart of the coastal redwoods. Registrants stay in hotel-style accommodations, and full board is provided as part of conference fees. Meals are taken family style, with faculty joining registrants. The faculty/student ratio is about 1:6 or 7. The bulk of our faculty are editors and publisher representatives from major Christian publishing houses nationwide." 1998 keynote speaker: John Fischer, songwriting, author, columnist.
Costs: Registration fees include tuition, conference sessions, resource notebook, refreshment breaks, room and board and vary from $500 (economy) to $700 (deluxe), double occupancy (1998 fees).
Accommodations: Airport shuttles are available from the San Jose International Airport. Housing is not required of registrants, but about 95% of our registrants use Mount Hermon's own housing facilities (hotel-style double-occupancy rooms). Meals with the conference are required and are included in all fees.
Additional Information: Registrants may submit 2 works for critique in advance of the conference, then have personal interviews with critiquers during the conference. No advance work is required however. Conference brochures/guidelines are available in December for SASE or by calling (888)MH-CAMPS. Inquiries by e-mail and fax OK. "The residential nature of our conference makes this a unique setting for one-on-one interaction

with faculty/staff. There is also a decided inspirational flavor to the conference, and general sessions with well-known speakers are a highlight."

N **PALM SPRINGS WRITERS CONFERENCE**, 2700 N. Cahuenga Blvd., Suite 4204, Los Angeles CA 90068. (213)874-5158. Fax: (213)874-5767. E-mail: valtrain@aol.com. Website: http://home.earthlink.net/~pswriterconf/. Contact: Mary Valentine. Estab. 1992. Annual. Conference held April 8-11, 1999. Average attendance: 230. Conference concentration is on the teaching and marketing of publishable fiction and nonfiction. "Conference is held at Marquis Hotel Resort, a first-class resort in the heart of Palm Springs. Classes on all aspects of fiction, short and long; stresses commercial, saleable fiction." Featured speakers/panelists include Catherine Coulter, Ray Bradbury, Tami Hoag, Harlan Ellison, Gerald Petievich, V.C. Andrews (Andrew Neiderman), Dianne Pugh, Arthur Lyons.
Costs: $345-395.
Accommodations: Complimentary hotel shuttle service from Palm Springs Regional Airport. Special hotel rates for Marquis Hotel.
Additional Information: "We offer critiques (half hour) for manuscripts by qualified professional writers (there is a charge), as well as free ten-minute one-on-one with agents and editors." Guidelines available for SASE. Inquiries by fax and e-mail OK.

N **PASADENA WRITERS' FORUM**, P.C.C. Extended Learning Dept., 1570 E. Colorado Blvd., Pasadena CA 91106-2003. (626)585-7608. Coordinator: Meredith Brucker. Estab. 1954. Annual. Conference held March 20. Average attendance: 200. "For the novice as well as the professional writer in any field of interest: fiction or nonfiction, including scripts, children's, humor and poetry." Conference held on the campus of Pasadena City College. A panel discussion by agents, editors or authors is featured at the end of the day.
Costs: $100, including box lunch and coffee hour.
Additional Information: Brochure upon request, no SASE necessary. "Pasadena City College also periodically offers an eight-week class 'Writing for Publication'."

✓ **SAN DIEGO STATE UNIVERSITY WRITERS' CONFERENCE**, SDSU College of Extended Studies, 5250 Campanile Drive, San Diego State University, San Diego CA 92182-1920. (619)594-2517. E-mail address: ealcaraz@mail.sdsu.edu. Website: http://www.ces.sdsu.edu. Assistant to Director of Extension and Conference Facilitator: Erin Grady Alcaraz. Estab. 1984. Annual. Conference held on 3rd weekend in January. Conference duration: 2 days. Average attendance: approximately 400. "This conference is held in San Diego, California, at the Mission Valley Doubletree. Each year the SDSU Writers Conference offers a variety of workshops for the beginner and the advanced writer. This conference allows the individual writer to choose which workshop best suits his/her needs. In addition to the workshops, editor/agent appointments and office hours are provided so attendees may meet with speakers, editors and agents in small, personal groups to discuss specific questions. A reception is offered Saturday immediately following the workshops where attendees may socialize with the faculty in a relaxed atmosphere. Keynote speaker is to be determined."
Costs: Approximately $225. This includes all conference workshops and office hours, coffee and pastries in the morning, lunch and reception Saturday evening.
Accommodations: Doubletree Mission Valley, (619)297-5466. Conference rate available for SDSU Writers Conference attendees. Attendees must make their own travel arrangements.
Additional Information: Editor/Agent sessions are private, one-on-one opportunities to meet with editors and agents to discuss your submission. To receive a brochure, e-mail, call or send a postcard to above address. No SASE required.

✓ **SCBWI/NATIONAL CONFERENCE ON WRITING & ILLUSTRATING FOR CHILDREN**, 345 N. Maple Dr., #296, Beverly Hills CA 90210-3869. (310)859-9887. Executive Director: Lin Oliver. Estab. 1972. Annual. Conference held in August. Conference duration: 4 days. Average attendance: 350. Writing and illustrating for children. Site: Century Plaza Hotel in Los Angeles. Theme: "The Business of Writing."
Costs: $295 (members); $320 (late registration, members); $340 (nonmembers). Cost does not include hotel room.
Accommodations: Information on overnight accommodations made available. Conference rates at the hotel about $125/night.
Additional Information: Ms and illustration critiques are available. Conference brochures/guidelines are available (after June) for SASE.

SCBWI/RETREAT AT ASILOMAR, 1316 Rebecca Dr., Suisun CA 94585-3603. (707)426-6776. Contact: Bobi Martin Downey, Regional Advisor. Estab. 1984. Annual. Conference held during last weekend in February. Attendance limited to 65. "The retreat is designed to refresh and encourage writers and illustrators for children. Speakers are published writers, illustrators and editors. Topics vary year to year and have included writing techniques, understanding marketing, plotting, pacing, etc. The retreat is held at the Asilomar conference grounds in Monterey. There is time for walking on the beach or strolling through the woods. Rooms have private baths and 2 beds. Meals are served semi-cafeteria style and the group eats together. Vegetarian meals also available.
Costs: $225 for SCBWI members; $250 for nonmembers.

Accommodations: "All accommodations are on-site and are included in the cost. All rooms are double occupancy. Disabled access rooms are available." Attendees must make their own transportation arrangements.
Additional Information: Scholarships available to SCBWI members. "Applicants for scholarships should write a letter explaining their financial need and describing how attending the retreat will help further their career. All applications are kept fully confidential." Brochures available for SASE. "Registration begins in October of previous year and fills quickly, but a waiting list is always formed and late applicants frequently do get in."

N WORLD HORROR CONVENTION, P.O. Box 61565, Phoenix AZ 85082-1565. (602)945-6890. Fax: (602)946-3480. E-mail: whc98@otsp.com. Website: http://www.otsp.com/otsp/whc98. Estab. 1991. Annual. Conference held in different cities. Conference duration: 4 days. Average attendance: 500. Concentration on horror-related fiction. Includes readings, panels, presentations, autographings, art show, dealers room, video/animation room, hospitality suite, etc. Featured speakers/panelists have included authors Brian Lumley and John Steakley; artist Bernie Wrightson; publisher Tom Doherty (Forge/Tor Books).
Costs: Supporting membership $30; attending membership $100.
Accommodations: Special hotel rates are available.
Additional Information: Guidelines available for SASE. Inquiries by fax and e-mail OK. "Professionals wishing to participate in our program must obtain an Attending Membership."

✓ WRANGLING WITH WRITING, Society of Southwestern Authors, P.O. Box 30355, Tucson AZ 85751. (520)296-5299. President: Penny Porter. Estab. 1971. Annual. Conference held 3 days in January. Attendance: limited to 350. Conference "to assist writers in whatever ways we can. We cover all areas." Held at the Inn Suites Hotel with hotel rooms available. Author Barbara Kingsolver; Philip Osborne, assistant managing editor (*Reader's Digest*); Gene Perret, Bob Hope's gag writer; and G. Gordon Liddy, author, radio commentator are among the featured speakers for the 1999 conference. Plus 32 workshops for all genres of writing.
Costs: $175; includes 4 meals.
Accommodations: Inn Suites Hotel in Tucson. Information included in brochure available for SASE.
Additional Information: Critiques given if ms sent ahead. Sponsors short story contest (2,500 words or less) separate from the conference. Deadline May 31. Awards given September 21. Brochures/guidelines available for SASE.

WRITE YOUR LIFE STORY FOR PAY, 23350 Sereno Court, Villa 30, Cupertino CA 95014. (415)691-0300. Contact: Louise Purwin Zobel. Estab. 1969. Workshop held irregularly, usually semiannually at several locations. Workshop duration: 1-2 days. Average attendance: 30-50. "Because every adult has a story worth telling, this conference helps participants to write fiction and nonfiction in books and short forms, using their own life stories as a base." This workshop is held on about 40 campuses at different times, inluding University of California and other university and college campuses in the West.
Costs: Usually $45-65/day, "depending on campus."
Additional Information: Brochures/guidelines available for SASE.

WRITERS CONNECTION SELLING TO HOLLYWOOD, P.O. Box 24770, San Jose CA 95154-4770. (408)445-3600. Fax: (408)445-3609. E-mail: info@sellingtohollywood.com. Website: http://www.sellingtohollywood.com. Directors: Steve and Meera Lester. Estab. 1988. Annual. Conference held in August in LA area. Conference duration: 3 days; August 7-9, 1998. Average attendance: 275. "Conference targets scriptwriters and fiction writers, whose short stories, books, or scripts have strong cinematic potential, and who want to make valuable contacts in the film industry. Full conference registrants receive a private consultation with the film industry producer or professional of his/her choice who make up the faculty. Panels, workshops, 'Ask a Pro' discussion groups and networking sessions include over 50 agents, professional film and TV scriptwriters, producers, attorneys, studio executives and consultants."
Costs: In 1998: full conference by July 15, $500, $525 after July 15. Includes some meals.
Accommodations: $90/night (in LA) for private room; $50/shared room. Discount with designated conference airline.
Additional Information: "This is the premier screenwriting conference of its kind in the country, unique in its offering of an industry-wide perspective from pros working in all echelons of the film industry. Great for making contacts." Conference brochure/guidelines available March 1, 1999; phone, e-mail, fax or send written request.

FOR EXPLANATIONS OF THESE SYMBOLS,
SEE THE INSIDE FRONT AND BACK COVERS OF THIS BOOK.

Northwest (AK, ID, MT, OR, WA, WY)

☑ **CLARION WEST WRITERS' WORKSHOP**, 340 15th Ave. E., Suite 350, Seattle WA 98112. (206)322-9083. E-mail: leijona@nwrain.com. Website: http://www.sff.net.clarionwest/. Administrator: Leslie Howle. Estab. 1983. Annual. Workshop held June 20-July 30. Workshop duration 6 weeks. Average attendance: 20. "Conference to prepare students for professional careers in science fiction and fantasy writing. Held at Seattle Central Community College on Seattle's Capitol Hill, an urban site close to restaurants and cafes, not too far from downtown." Deadline for applications: April 1.
Costs: Workshop: $1,400 ($100 discount if application received by March 1). Dormitory housing: $800, meals not included.
Accommodations: Students are strongly encouraged to stay on-site, in dormitory housing at Seattle University. Cost: $800, meals not included, for 6-week stay.
Additional Information: "This is a critique-based workshop. Students are encouraged to write a story a week; the critique of student material produced at the workshop forms the principal activity of the workshop. Students and instructors critique manuscripts as a group." Conference guidelines available for SASE. Inquiries by e-mail OK. Limited scholarships are available, based on financial need. Students must submit 20-30 pages of ms with $25 application fee to qualify for admission. Dormitory and classrooms are handicapped accessible.

FLIGHT OF THE MIND—SUMMER WRITING WORKSHOP FOR WOMEN, 622 SE 29th Ave., Portland OR 97214. (503)236-9862. Fax: (503)233-0774. E-mail: soapston@teleport.com. Website: http://www.teleport.com/~soapston/FLIGHT/. Director: Judith Barrington. Estab. 1984. Annual. Workshops held June 18-25 and June 27-July 4. Conference duration: each workshop lasts 1 week. Average attendance: 70. "Conference held at an old retreat center on the Mackenzie River in the foothills of the Oregon Cascades. Right on the river—hiking trails, hot springs nearby. Most students accommodated in single dorm rooms; a few private cabins available. We have our own cooks and provide spectacular food." Five classes—topics vary year to year; 1998 included fiction with Ursula K. LeGuin and poetry by Toi Derricotte.
Costs: Approximately $780 for tuition, board and single dorm room. Extra for private cabin; bunk room cheaper alternative.
Accommodations: Special arrangements for transportation: "We charter a bus to pick up participants in Eugene, OR, at airport, train station and bus station." Accommodations and meals are included in cost.
Additional Information: "Critiquing is part of most classes; no individual critiques. We require manuscript submissions for acceptance into workshop. (Receive about twice as many applications as spaces.)" Workshop brochures/guidelines are available after January for 1 first-class stamp (no envelope) plus name and address. Inquiries by e-mail OK. "This is a feminist-oriented workshop with a focus on work generated at the workshop. High level of seriousness by all participants."

HAYSTACK WRITING PROGRAM, PSU School of Extended Studies, P.O. Box 1491, Portland OR 97207-1491. (503)725-4186. Fax: (503)725-4840. E-mail: herringtonm@ses.pdx.edu. Website: http://extended.portals.org/haystack.htm. Contact: Maggie Herrington. Estab. 1968. Annual. Program runs from last week of June through first week of August. Workshop duration varies; one-week and weekend workshops are available throughout the six-week program. Average attendance: 10-15/workshop; total program: 325. "The program features a broad range of writing courses for writers at all skill levels. Classes are held in Cannon Beach, Oregon." Past instructors have included William Stafford, Ursula K. LeGuin, Craig Lesley, Molly Gloss, Mark Medoff, Tom Spanbauer, Sallie Tisdale.
Costs: Approximately $320/course weeklong; $150 (weekend). Does not include room and board.
Accommodations: Attendees make their own transportation arrangements. Various accommodations available including: B&B, motel, hotel, private rooms, camping, etc. A list of specific accommodations is provided.
Additional Information: Free brochure available after March. Inquiries by e-mail and fax OK. University credit (graduate or undergraduate) is available.

PACIFIC NORTHWEST WRITERS SUMMER CONFERENCE, 2033 6th Ave., #804, Seattle WA 98121. (206)443-3807. E-mail address: pnwritersconf@halcyon.com. Website: http://www.reporters.net/pnwc. Contact: Office. Estab. 1955. Annual. Conference held last weekend in July. Average attendance: 700. Conference focuses on "fiction, nonfiction, poetry, film, drama, self-publishing, the creative process, critiques, core groups, advice from pros and networking." Site is Hyatt Regency, Bellevue WA. "Editors and agents come from both coasts. They bring lore from the world of publishing. The PNWC provides opportunities for writers to get to know editors and agents. The literary contest provides feedback from professionals and possible fame for the winners."
Costs: $135-165/day. Meals and lodging are available at hotel.
Additional Information: On-site critiques are available in small groups. Literary contest in these categories: adult article/essay, adult genre novel, adult mainstream novel, adult genre short story, adult mainstream short story, juvenile article or short story, juvenile novel, nonfiction book, picture books for children, playwriting and poetry. Deadline: February 15. Up to $7,000 awarded in prizes. Send SASE for guidelines.

☑ **PORT TOWNSEND WRITERS' CONFERENCE**, Centrum, Box 1158, Port Townsend WA 98368. (360)385-3102. Director: Sam Hamill. Estab. 1974. Annual. Conference held mid-July. Average attendance: 180. Conference to promote poetry, fiction, creative nonfiction. The conference is held at a 700-acre state park on the strait of Juan de Fuca. "The site is a Victorian-era military fort with miles of beaches, wooded trails and recreation facilities. The park is within the limits of Port Townsend, a historic seaport and arts community, approximately 80 miles northwest of Seattle, on the Olympic Peninsula." There will be 5 guest speakers in addition to 10 fulltime faculty.
Costs: Approximately $400 tuition and $200 room and board. Less expensive option available.
Accommodations: "Modest room and board facilities on site." Also list of hotels/motels/inns/bed & breakfasts/ private rentals available.
Additional Information: "Admission to workshops is selective, based on manuscript submissions." Brochures/ guidelines available for SASE. "The conference focus is on the craft of writing and the writing life, not on marketing."

☑ **WILLAMETTE WRITERS CONFERENCE**, 9045 SW Barbur, Suite 5-A, Portland OR 97219-4027. (503)452-1592. Fax: (503)452-0372. E-mail: wilwrite@teleport.com. Website: http://www.tele.com/~wilwrite/. Contact: Bill Johnson, office manager. Estab. 1968. Annual. Conference held in August. Average attendance: 220. "Willamette Writers is open to all writers, and we plan our conference accordingly. We offer workshops on all aspects of fiction, nonfiction, marketing, the creative process, etc. Also we invite top notch inspirational speakers for key note addresses. Most often the conference is held on a local college campus which offers a scholarly atmosphere and allows us to keep conference prices down. Recent theme was 'Making It Work.' We always include at least one agent or editor panel and offer a variety of topics of interest to both fiction and nonfiction writers." Past editors and agents in attendance have included: Marc Aronson, senior editor, Henry Holt & Co.; Tom Colgan, senior editor, Avon Books; Charles Spicer, Senior Editor, St. Martin's Press; Sheree Bykofsky, Sheree Bykofsky Associates; Laurie Harper, Sebastian Agency; F. Joseph Spieler, The Spieler Agency; Robert Tabian and Ruth Nathan.
Costs: Cost for full conference including meals is $195 members; $250 nonmembers.
Accomodations: If necessary, these can be made on an individual basis. Some years special rates are available.
Additional Information: Conference brochures/guidelines are available in May for catalog-size SASE. Inquiries by fax and e-mail OK.

WRITE ON THE SOUND WRITERS' CONFERENCE, 700 Main St., Edmonds WA 98020. (425)771-0228. Fax: (425)771-0253. E-mail: wots@ci.edmonds.wa.us. Sponsored by Edmonds Arts Commission. Estab. 1986. Annual. Conference held first weekend in October. Conference duration: 2 days. Average attendance: 160. "Workshops and lectures are offered for a variety of writing interests and levels of expertise. It is high quality, affordable conference with limited registration."
Costs: $80 for 2 days, $45 for 1 day (1998); includes registration, morning refreshments and 1 ticket to keynote lecture.
Additional Information: Brochures available in August for SASE. Inquiries by e-mail and fax OK.

Canada

THE FESTIVAL OF THE WRITTEN ARTS, Box 2299, Sechelt, British Columbia V0N 3A0 Canada. (800)565-9631 or (604)885-9631. Fax: (604)885-3967. E-mail: written_arts@sunshine.net. Website: http://www.sunshine.net/rockwood. Festival Producer: Gail Bull. Estab. 1983. Annual. Festival held: August 12-15, 1999. Average attendance: 3,500. To promote "all writing genres." Festival held at the Rockwood Centre. "The Centre overlooks the town of Sechelt on the Sunshine Coast. The lodge around which the Centre was organized was built in 1937 as a destination for holidayers arriving on the old Union Steamship Line; it has been preserved very much as it was in its heyday. A new twelve-bedroom annex was added in 1982, and in 1989 the Festival of the Written Arts constructed a Pavilion for outdoor performances next to the annex. The festival does not have a theme. Instead, it showcases 20 or more Canadian writers in a wide variety of genres each year—the only all Canadian writer's festival."
Costs: $12 per event or $150 for a four-day pass (Canadian funds).
Accommodations: Lists of hotels and bed/breakfast available.
Additional Information: The festival runs contests during the 3½ days of the event. Prizes are books donated by publishers. Brochures/guidelines are available after April 15. Inquiries by e-mail and fax OK.

MARITIME WRITERS' WORKSHOP, Extension & Summer Session, UNB Box 4400, Fredericton, New Brunswick E3B 5A3 Canada. (506)453-4646. Fax: (506)453-3572. E-mail: coned@unb.ca. Website: http://www.unb.ca/web/coned/writers/marritrs.html. Coordinator: Glenda Turner. Estab. 1976. Annual. Conference held July 4-10, 1999. Average attendance: 50. "We offer small groups of ten, practical manuscript focus. Notice writers welcome. Workshops in four areas: fiction, poetry, nonfiction, writing for children." Site is University of New Brunswick, Fredericton campus.
Costs: $350, tuition; $135 meals; $125/double room; $145/single room (Canadian funds).
Accommodations: On-campus accommodations and meals.
Additional Information: "Participants must submit 10-20 manuscript pages which form a focus for workshop discussions." Brochures are available after March. No SASE necessary. Inquiries by e-mail and fax OK.

SAGE HILL WRITING EXPERIENCE, Box 1731, Saskatoon, Saskatchewan S7K 3S1 Canada. Phone/fax: (306)652-7395. E-mail: sage.hill@sk.sympatico.ca. Website: http://www.lights.com/sagehill. Executive Director: Steven Ross Smith. Annual. Workshops held in August and October. Workshop duration 10-21 days. Attendance: limited to 36-40. "Sage Hill Writing Experience offers a special working and learning opportunity to writers at different stages of development. Top quality instruction, low instructor-student ratio and the beautiful Sage Hill setting offer conditions ideal for the pursuit of excellence in the arts of fiction, poetry and playwriting." The Sage Hill location features "individual accommodation, in-room writing area, lounges, meeting rooms, healthy meals, walking woods and vistas in several directions." Seven classes are held: Introduction to Writing Fiction & Poetry; Fiction Workshop; Writing Young Adult Fiction Workshop; Poetry Workshop; Poetry Colloquium; Fiction Colloquium; Playwriting Lab. 1998 faculty included Sandra Birdsell, Don McKay, Elizabeth Philips, Lee Gowan, Dennis Cooley, Myrna Kostash, Dianne Warren.
Costs: $595 (Canadian) includes instruction, accommodation, meals and all facilities. Fall Poetry Colloquium: $875.
Accommodations: On-site individual accommodations located at Lumsden 45 kilometers outside Regina. Fall Colloquium is at Muenster, Saskatchewan, 150 kilometers east of Saskatchewan.
Additional Information: For Introduction to Creative Writing: A five-page sample of your writing or a statement of your interest in creative writing; list of courses taken required. For intermediate and colloquium program: A resume of your writing career and a 12-page sample of your work plus 5 pages of published work required. Application deadline is May 1. Guidelines are available after January for SASE. Inquiries by e-mail and fax OK. Scholarships and bursaries are available.

✓ **THE VICTORIA SCHOOL OF WRITING**, Box 8152, Victoria, British Columbia V8W 3R8 Canada. (250)598-5300. Fax: (250)598-0066. E-mail: writeawy@islandnet.com. Website: http://www.islandnet.com/vicwrite. Contact: Margaret Dyment. Conference held from July 20-23. "Four-day intensive workshop on beautiful Vancouver Island with outstanding author-instructors in fiction, poetry, historical fiction and writing for children."
Cost: $445 (Canadian).
Accommodations: Special hotel rates available.
Additional Information: Workshop brochures available. Inquiries by e-mail and fax OK.

A WRITER'S W*O*R*L*D, Surrey Writers' Conference, 12870 72nd Ave., Surrey, British Columbia V4P 1G1 Canada. (640)594-2000. Fax: (604)590-2506. E-mail: phoenixmcf@aol.com. Principal: Rollie Koop. Estab. 1992. Annual. Conference held in fall. Conference duration: 3 days. Average attendance: 350. Conference for fiction (romance/science fiction/fantasy/mystery—changes focus depending upon speakers and publishers scheduled), nonfiction and poetry. "For everyone from beginner to professional." Conference held at Sheraton Guildford. Guest lecturers included authors Diana Gabaldon, Don McQuinn and Daniel Wood; agents and editors.
Accommodations: On request will provide information on hotels and B&Bs. Conference rate, $90. Attendee must make own arrangements for hotel and transportation.
Additional Information: "A drawing takes place and ten people's manuscripts are critiqued by a bestselling author." Writer's contest entries must be submitted about 1 month early. Length: 1,000 words fiction, nonfiction, poetry, young writers (19 or less). 1st Prize $250, 2nd Prize $125, 3rd Prize $75. Contest is judged by a qualified panel of writers and educators. Write, call or e-mail for additional information.

International

N **THE AEGEAN CENTER FOR THE FINE ARTS WORKSHOPS**, Paros 84400, Cyclades, Greece. Phone/fax: (30)284-23287. E-mail: studyart@aegeancenter.org. Website: http://www.aegeancenter.org. Director: John A. Pack. Held 7 times/year. Workshop held May, June, July, September, October and November. Workshop duration: Spring—4-13 weeks; Summer sessions: 2-3 weeks; Fall—4-15 weeks. Average attendance: 15. "Creative writing in all its aspects." Spring workshop held at the Aegean Center "in a neoclassical 16th century townhouse in the village of Parikia with a gallery/lecture hall, well-equipped darkroom, modest library, rooms for studio space and classrooms." Location is on Paros, an island about 100 miles southeast of Athens. Fall

workshop held in Italy starting in Pistoia in 16th century Villa Rospigliosi and includes travel to Pisa, Lucca, Prato, Siena, Venice, Florence and Rome in Italy as well as Athens and, finally, Paros.
Costs: For 13-week Spring workshop, tuition is $6,000 in 1997 or $2,500/monthly session (housing included). Summer session tuition is $2,500 (includes housing). For 15-week Fall workshop, tuition is $7,500 in 1997, or $2,500 for monthly session ($2,500 Italy session only). Includes housing (villa accommodation and hotels in Italy); half board in Villa accommodation; travel while in Italy; museum entrance fees.
Accommodations: In Paros, accommodations (single occupancy apartment). All apartments have small equipped kitchen areas and private bathroom. Italy, villa accommodation and hotels.
Additional Information: College credit is available. Workshop brochures/guidelines are available for SASE or via website. Inquiries by e-mail and fax OK.

ART WORKSHOPS IN LA ANTIGUA GUATEMALA, 4758 Lyndale Ave. S, Minneapolis MN 55409-2304. (612)825-0747. Fax: (612)825-6637. E-mail: info@artguat.org. Website: http://www.artguat.org. Estab. 1995. Annual. Conference held February 19-28. Maximum class size: 10 students per class. The conference is held in either a private home or beautiful hotels. Workshop titles include: Creative Writing—the Short Story with Merna Summers (March 28-April 6, 1998).
Costs: $1,675 (includes tuition, air fare to Guatemala, lodging and ground transportation).
Accommodations: All transportation included.
Additional Information: Conference brochures/guidelines are available. Inquiries by e-mail and fax are OK.

N **THE ARVON FOUNDATION LTD. WORKSHOPS**, Totleigh Barton Sheepwash, Beaworthy, Devon EX21 5NS United Kingdom. Phone: 00 44 14 09231338. National Director: David Pease. Estab. 1968 (workshops). Workshops held April through November at 3 centers. Workshops last 4½ days. Average attendence: 16/workshop. Workshops cover all types of fiction writing. "Totleigh Barton in Devon was the first Arvon centre. Next came Lumb Bank (Hebden Bridge, West Yorkshire HX7 6DF) and now, 12 courses at Moniack Mhor (Moniack, Kirkhill, Inverness IV 5 7PQ)." Totleigh Barton is a thatched manor house. Lumb Bank is an 18th century mill owner's home and Moniack Mhor is a traditional croft house. All are in peaceful, rural settings. In the three houses there are living rooms, reading rooms, rooms for private study, dining rooms and well equipped kitchens."
Costs: In 1999 course fee will be £305 which includes food, tuition and accommodation. For those in need, a limited number of grants and bursaries are available from the Arvon Foundation.
Accommodations: There is sleeping accommodation for up to 16 course members, but only limited single room accommodation (there are 8 bedrooms at Lumb Bank, 12 bedrooms at Moniack Mhor and 13 bedrooms at Totleigh Barton). The adjacent barns at Lumb Bank and Totleigh Barton have been converted into workshop/studio space and there are writing huts in the garden.
Additional Information: Sometimes writers are required to submit work. Check for details. Conference brochure/guidelines available for SASE.

✓ **EDINBURGH UNIVERSITY CENTRE FOR CONTINUING EDUCATION CREATIVE WRITING WORKSHOPS**, 11 Buccleuch Place, Edinburgh Scotland EH8 9LW. (131)650-4400. Fax: (131)667-6097. E-mail: cce@ed.ac.uk. Website: http://www.cce.ed.ac.uk. Administrative Director of International Summer Schools: Bridget M. Stevens. Contact: Ursula Michels. Estab. 1990. Introductory course July 3-9; short story course July 10-16; playwriting course July 17-30. Average attendance: 15. Courses cover "basic techniques of creative writing, the short story and playwriting. The University of Edinburgh Centre for Continuing Education occupies traditional 18th century premises near the George Square Campus. Located nearby are libraries, banks and recreational facilities. Free use of word-processing facilities."
Costs: In 1998 cost was £195 per one-week course (tuition only).
Accommodations: Information on overnight accommodations is available. Accommodations include student dormitories, self-catering apartment and local homes.
Additional Information: Conference brochures/guidelines available after January for SASE. Inquiries by e-mail and fax OK.

✓ **PARIS WRITERS' WORKSHOP/WICE**, 20, Bd du Montparnasse, Paris, France 75015. (33-1)45.66.75.50. Fax: (33-1)40.65.96.53. E-mail: wice@wfi.fr. Website: http://www.wice.org. Director: Ellen Hinsey. Estab. 1987. Annual. Conference held first week in July. Average attendance: 40-50. "Conference concentrates on fiction (2 sections), nonfiction and poetry. Visiting lecturers speak on a variety of issues important to beginning and advanced writers. Located in the heart of Paris on the Bd. du Montparnasse, the stomping grounds of such famous American writers as Ernest Hemingway, Henry Miller and F. Scott Fitzgerald. The site consists of 4 classrooms, a resource center/library, computer room and private terrace."

Costs: $380—tuition only.

Additional Information: "Students submit 2 copies of complete ms or work-in-progress. One copy is sent in advance to writer in residence. Each student has a one-on-one consultation with writer in residence concerning ms that was submitted." Conference brochure/guidelines are available after February. Inquiries by e-mail and fax OK. "Workshop attracts many expatriate Americans and other English language students from all over Europe and North America. We can assist with finding a range of hotels, from budget to more luxurious accommodations. We are an intimate workshop with an exciting mix of more experienced, published writers and enthusiastic beginners. Past writers include CK Williams, Carolyn Kizer, Grace Paley, Jayne Anne Phillips and Marilyn Hacker."

SUMMER IN FRANCE WRITING WORKSHOPS, HCOI, Box 102, Plainview TX 79072. Phone/fax: (806)889-3533. E-mail: bettye@plainview.com. Website: http://www.o-c-s.com/educate/paar.htm. Director: Bettye Givens. Annual. Conference: 27 days in July. Average attendance: 10-15. For fiction, poetry. The classrooms are in the Val de Grace 277 Rue St. Jacques in the heart of the Latin Quarter near Luxeumbourg Park in Paris. Guest speakers include Paris poets, professors and editors (lectures in English).

Costs: Costs vary. Costs includes literature classes, art history and the writing workshop and shared apartments.

Accommodations: Some accommodations with a French family.

Additional Information: Conference brochures/guidelines are available for SASE. Inquiries by e-mail and fax OK. "Enroll early. Side trips out of Paris are planned as are poetry readings at the Paris American Academy and at Shakespeare & Co."

TŶ NEWYDD WRITER'S CENTRE, Llanystumdwy, Cricieth Gwynedd LL52 OLW, United Kingdom. Phone: 01766-522811. Fax: 01766 523095. Administrator: Sally Baker. Estab. 1990. Regular courses held throughout the year. Every course held Monday-Saturday. Average attendance: 14. "To give people the opportunity to work side by side with professional writers, in an informal atmosphere." Site is Tŷ Newydd. Large manor house. Last home of the prime minister, David Lloyd George. Situated in North Wales, Great Britain-between mountains and sea." Past featured tutors include novelists Beryl Bainbridge and Bernice Rubens.

Costs: £275 for Monday-Saturday (includes full board, tuition).

Accommodations: Transportation from railway stations arranged. Accommodation in Tŷ Newydd (onsite).

Additional Information: Brochures/guidelines are available by mail, phone or fax after January. Inquiries by fax OK. "We have had several people from U.S. on courses here in the past three years. More and more people come to us from the U.S. often combining a writing course with a tour of Wales."

THE WRITERS' SUMMER SCHOOL, SWANWICK, The New Vicarage, Woodford Halse, Daventry, NN11 3RE England. Phone/fax: 07050-630949. E-mail: bcourtie@aol.com. Website: http://dspace.dial.pipex.com/roydev/. Secretary: Brenda Courtie. Estab. 1949. Annual. Conference held August 14-20, 1999. Average attendance: 300 plus. "Conference concentrates on all fields of writing." In 1998 courses included beginners, biography, children's picture books, commercial writing, drama, novel writing, poetry, sci-fi and fantasy. Speakers in 1998 included Gyles Brandretn, Michael Tolkien and Fred Nolan.

Costs: 1998: £192-£300 per person inclusive.

Accommodations: Buses from main line station to conference centre provided.

Additional Information: Conference brochures/guidelines are available after February. Inquiries by mail, e-mail and fax OK. "The Writers' Summer School is a nonprofit-making organization."

Organizations

When you write, you write alone. It's just you and the typewriter or computer screen. Yet the writing life does not need to be a lonely one. Joining a writing group or organization can be an important step in your writing career. By meeting other writers, discussing your common problems and sharing ideas, you can enrich your writing and increase your understanding of this sometimes difficult, but rewarding life.

The variety of writers' organizations seems endless—encompassing every type of writing and writer—from small, informal groups that gather regularly at a local coffee house for critique sessions to regional groups that hold annual conferences to share technique and marketing tips. National organizations and unions fight for writers' rights and higher payment for freelancers, and international groups monitor the treatment of writers around the world.

In this section you will find state-, province- and regional-based groups. You'll also find national organizations including the National Writers Association. The Mystery Writers of America and the Western Writers of America are examples of groups devoted to a particular type of writing. Whatever your needs or goals, you're likely to find a group listed here to interest you.

SELECTING A WRITERS' ORGANIZATION

To help you make an informed decision, we've provided information on the scope, membership and goals of the organizations listed on these pages. We asked groups to outline the types of memberships available and the benefits members can expect. Most groups will provide additional information for a self-addressed, stamped envelope, and you may be able to get a sample copy of their newsletter for a modest fee.

Keep in mind joining a writers' organization is a two-way street. When you join an organization, you become a part of it and, in addition to membership fees, most groups need and want your help. If you want to get involved, opportunities can include everything from chairing a committee to writing for the newsletter to helping set up an annual conference. The level of your involvement is up to you, and almost all organizations welcome contributions of time and effort.

Selecting a group to join depends on a number of factors. As a first step, you must determine what you want from membership in a writers' organization. Then send away for more information on the groups that seem to fit your needs. Start, however, by asking yourself:

- Would I like to meet writers in my city? Am I more interested in making contacts with other writers across the country or around the world?
- Am I interested in a group that will critique and give me feedback on work-in-progress?
- Do I want marketing information and tips on dealing with editors?
- Would I like to meet other writers who write the same type of work I do or am I interested in meeting writers from a variety of fields?
- How much time can I devote to meetings and are regular meetings important to me? How much can I afford to pay in dues?
- Would I like to get involved in running the group, working on the group's newsletters, planning a conference?
- Am I interested in a group devoted to writers' rights and treatment or would I rather concentrate on the business of writing?

FOR MORE INFORMATION

Because they do not usually have the resources or inclination to promote themselves widely, finding a local writers' group is usually a word-of-mouth process. If you would like to start a writers group in your area, read The How-Tos of Money & Meetings for Writers' Groups on page 613. Also ask your local libraries and bookstores if they sponsor writers' groups in conjunction with Writer's Digest Books. If they are not already, you or a representative of the library or bookstore may call (800)289-0963, ext. 424 for a free packet of information on starting a writers' group.

If you have a computer and would like to meet with writers in other areas of the country, you will find many commercial online services, such as GEnie and America Online, have writers' sections and "clubs" online. Many free online services available through Internet also have writers' "boards."

For more information on writers' organizations, check *The Writer's Essential Desk Reference: A Companion to Writer's Market*, 2nd edition (Writer's Digest Books, 1507 Dana Ave., Cincinnati OH 45207). Other directories listing organizations for writers include the *Literary Market Place* or *International Literary Market Place* (R.R. Bowker, 121 Chanlon Rd., New Providence NJ 07974). The National Writers Association also maintains a list of writers' organizations.

✓ **ASSOCIATED WRITING PROGRAMS**, Tallwood House, Mail Stop 1E3, George Mason University, Fairfax VA 22030-9736. (703)993-4301. Fax: (703)993-4302. E-mail: awp@gmu.edu. Website: http://www.gmu.edu/departments/awp (includes FAQ, membership information/ordering, award series guidelines, links to institutional members, AWP news). Contact: Membership Services. Estab. 1967. Number of Members: 5,000 individuals and 290 institutions. Types of Membership: Institutional (universities); graduate students; individual writers; and *Chronicle* subscribers. Open to any person interested in writing; most members are students or faculty of university writing programs (worldwide). Benefits include information on creative writing programs; grants, awards and publishing opportunities for writers; job list for academe and writing-related fields; a job placement service for writers in academe and beyond. AWP holds an Annual Conference in a different US city every spring; also conducts an annual Award Series in poetry, short story collections, novel and creative nonfiction, in which winner receives $2,000 honorarium and publication by a participating press. AWP acts as agent for finalists in Award Series and tries to place their manuscript with publishers throughout the year. Manuscripts accepted January 1-February 28 only. Novel competition is for writers 32 years of age or younger; winner receives publication by St. Martin's Press and $10,000 in royalties. Send SASE for new guidelines. Publishes *The Writer's Chronicle* 6 times/year; 3 times/academic semester. Available to members for free. Nonmembers may order a subscription for $20/year; $25/year Canada; $35/year overseas. Also publishes the *AWP Official Guide to Writing Programs* which lists about 330 creative writing programs in universities across the country and in Canada. *Guide* is updated every 2 years; cost is $19.95 plus $5 for first-class mail. Dues: $57 for individuals; $37 students (must send copy of ID); additional $62 for full placement service. AWP keeps dossiers on file and sends them to school or organization of person's request. Holds two meetings per year for the Board of Directors. Send SASE for information. Inquiries by fax and e-mail OK.

✓ **AUSTIN WRITERS' LEAGUE**, Austin Writers' League, 1501 W. Fifth, E-2, Austin TX 78703. (512)499-8914. Fax: (512)499-0441. Executive Director: Jim Bob McMillan. Estab. 1981. Number of Members: 1,600. Types of Memberships: Regular, student/senior citizen, family. Monthly meetings and use of resource center/library is open to the public. "Membership includes both aspiring and professional writers, all ages and all ethnic groups." Job bank is also open to the public. Public also has access to technical assistance. Partial and full scholarships offered for some programs. Of 1,600 members, 800 reside in Austin. Remaining 800 live all over the US and in other countries. Benefits include monthly newsletter, monthly meetings, study groups, resource center/library-checkout privileges, discounts on workshops, seminars, classes, job bank, discounts on books and tapes, participation in awards programs, technical/marketing assistance, copyright forms and information, Writers Helping Writers (mentoring program). Center has 5 rooms plus 2 offices and storage area. Public space includes reception and job bank area; conference/classroom; library; and copy/mail room. Library includes 1,000 titles. Sponsors fall and spring workshops, weekend seminars, informal classes, sponsorships for special events such as readings, production of original plays, media conferences, creative writing programs for children and youth; Violet Crown Book Awards, newsletter writing awards, Young Texas Writers awards, contests for various anthologies. Publishes *Austin Writer* (monthly newsletter), sponsors with Texas Commission on the Arts Texas Literary Touring Program. Administers literature subgranting program for Texas Commission on the Arts. Membership/subscription: $40, $35-students, senior citizens, $60 family membership. Monthly meetings. Study groups set their own regular meeting schedules. Send SASE for information.

THE AUTHORS GUILD, 330 W. 42nd St., 29th Floor, New York NY 10036-6902. (212)563-5904. Fax: (212)564-8363. E-mail: staff@authorsguild.org. Website: http://www.authorsguild.org (includes publishing industry news, business, legal and membership information). Executive Director: Paul Aiken. Contact: Jack Gonzalez, membership coordinator. Inquiries by fax and e-mail OK. Purpose of organization: membership organization of 7,200 members offers services and information materials intended to help published authors with the business and legal aspects of their work, including contract problems, copyright matters, freedom of expression and taxation. Maintains staff of attorneys and legal interns to assist members. Group health insurance available. Qualifications for membership: book author published by an established American publisher within 7 years or any author who has had 3 works, fiction or nonfiction, published by a magazine or magazines of general circulation in the last 18 months. Associate membership also available. Annual dues: $90. Different levels of membership include: associate membership with all rights except voting available to an author who has a firm contract offer from an American publisher. Workshops/conferences: "The Guild and the Authors Guild Foundation conduct several symposia each year at which experts provide information, offer advice, and answer questions on subjects of concern to authors. Typical subjects have been the rights of privacy and publicity, libel, wills and estates, taxation, copyright, editors and editing, the art of interviewing, standards of criticism and book reviewing. Transcripts of these symposia are published and circulated to members." "The *Authors Guild Bulletin*, a quarterly journal, contains articles on matters of interest to published writers, reports of Guild activities, contract surveys, advice on problem clauses in contracts, transcripts of Guild and League symposia, and information on a variety of professional topics. Subscription included in the cost of the annual dues."

THE BRITISH FANTASY SOCIETY, 2 Harwood St., Stockport SK4 1JJ United Kingdom. E-mail: syrinx.2112@btinternet.com. Website: http://www.geocities.com/SoHo/6859/ (includes membership details, news, books for sale, fantasy conference details). Secretary: Robert Parkinson. Estab. 1971. Open to: "Anyone interested in fantasy. The British Fantasy Society was formed to provide coverage of the fantasy, science fiction and horror fields. To achieve this, the Society publishes its *Newsletter*, packed with information and reviews of new books and films, plus a number of other booklets of fiction and articles: *Winter Chills*, *Mystique*, *Masters of Fantasy* and *Dark Horizons*. The BFS also organises an annual Fantasy Conference at which the British Fantasy Awards are presented for categories such as Best Novel, Best Short Story and Best Film." Dues and subscription fees are £17 (UK); £25 (Europe), £30 (elsewhere). Payment in sterling only. Send SASE or IRC for information. Inquiries by e-mail OK.

BURNABY WRITERS' SOCIETY, 6584 Deer Lake Ave., Burnaby, British Columbia V5G 3T7 Canada. (604)435-6500. Corresponding Secretary: Eileen Kernaghan. Estab. 1967. Number of members: 300. "Membership is regional, but open to anyone interested in writing." Benefits include monthly market newsletter; workshops/critiques; guest speakers; information on contests, events, reading venues, etc.; opportunity to participate in public reading series. Sponsors annual competition open to all British Columbia residents; Canada Council sponsored readings; workshops. Publishes *Burnaby Writers Newsletter* monthly (except July/August), available to anyone for $30/year subscription. Dues: $30/year (includes newsletter subscription). Meets second Thursday of each month. Send SASE for information.

CALIFORNIA WRITERS' CLUB, P.O. Box 1281, Berkeley CA 94701. Website: http://www/calwriters.ndti.net. Estab. 1909. Ten branches. Number of Members: 900. Type of Memberships: Associate and active. Open to all writers. "Includes published authors, those actively pursuing a career in writing and those associated with the field of writing." Benefits include: CWC sponsors annual conference with writing contest. Publishes a monthly newsletter at state level and at branch level. Available to members only. Dues: $35/year. Send SASE for information. Inquiries by e-mail (through website OK).

CANADIAN SOCIETY OF CHILDREN'S AUTHORS, ILLUSTRATORS AND PERFORMERS (CANSCAIP), 35 Spadina Rd., Toronto, Ontario M5R 2S9 Canada. (416)515-1559. Fax: (416)515-7022. E-mail: canscaip@interlog.com. Website: http://www.interlog.com/~canscaip (includes children's authors, seminar information, art collection—samples [traveling]). Executive Secretary: Nancy Prasad. Estab. 1977. Number of Members: 1,100. Types of membership: Full professional member and friend (associate member). Open to professional active writers, illustrators and performers in the field of children's culture (full members); beginners and all other interested persons and institutions (friends). International scope, but emphasis on Canada. Benefits include quarterly newsletter, marketing opportunities, publicity via our membership directory and our "members available" list, jobs (school visits, readings, workshops, residencies, etc.) through our "members available" list, mutual support through monthly meetings. Sponsors annual workshop, "Packaging Your Imagination," held every October for beginners. Publishes *CANSCAIP News*, quarterly, available to all (free with membership, otherwise $25 Canadian). Dues: professional fees: $60 Canadian/year; friend fees: $25/year; institutional $30/year. "Professionals must have written, illustrated or performed work for children commercially, sufficient to satisfy the membership committee (more details on request)." CANSCAIP National has open meetings from September to June, monthly in Toronto. CANSCAIP West holds bimonthly meetings in Vancouver. Send SASE for information. Inquiries by fax and e-mail OK.

CINCINNATI WRITER'S PROJECT, 2592 Ferguson Rd., #9, Cincinnati OH 45238. (513)451-0410. E-mail: carolmarie_stock@mail.msj.edu. Contact: Carolmarie Stock. Estab. 1988. Organization of Cincinnati area writers. Members receive *Rough Draft*, the CWP monthly newsletter; general membership meeting held the third Thursday of each month. Members also participate in regularly scheduled workshops, critique sessions and readings in fiction, nonfiction, poetry and script/screenwriting. Members' books are offered through the CWP book catalog and at other local writers' events. Dues for one year: $25, individual; $35 family. Send SASE for information. (See the interview with Dallas Wiebe, president and cofounder of CWP, in this section.)

FEDERATION OF BRITISH COLUMBIA WRITERS, MPO Box 2206, Vancouver, British Columbia V6P 6G5 Canada. (604)267-7087. Fax: (604)267-7086. E-mail: fedbcwrt@pinc.com. Website: http://www.swifty.com/bcwa. Coordinator of Administration and Member Services: Ana Torres. Executive Director: Corey Van't Haaff. Estab. 1982. Number of Members: 800. Types of Membership: regular. "Open to established and emerging writers in any genre, province-wide." Benefits include newsletter, liaison with funding bodies, publications, workshops, readings, literary contests, various retail and educational discounts. Sponsors readings and workshops. Publishes a newsletter 4 times/year, included in membership. Dues: $60 regular. Send SASE for information. Inquiries by fax and e-mail OK.

FEMINIST WRITERS GUILD, % Outrider Press, 937 Patricia Lane, Crete IL 60417. (708)672-6630. Fax: (708)672-5820. E-mail: outriderpr@aol.com. President: Whitney Scott. Estab. 1977. Founded by outstanding writers including Adrienne Rich, Marge Piercy, Tillie Olsen and Valerie Miner. Number of members: 150. Open to: all who write seriously regardless of age, gender, orientation. Benefits include formal readings, newsletters, monthly open mikes, two themed readings annually, publications, leadership opportunities and workshops in affiliation with Outrider Press, Inc. Sponsors an annual anthology contest with cash prizes and publication. 1999 theme is animal stories: "Feathers, Fins and Fur." Send SASE for guidelines. Inquiries by e-mail OK. Dues: $25.

HORROR WRITERS ASSOCIATION (HWA), P.O. Box 50577, Palo Alto CA 94303. E-mail: hwa@horror.org. Website: http://www.horror.org. President: S.P. Somtow. Estab. 1983. Number of Members: 850. Type of Memberships: Active—writers who have one published novel or three professional stories. Associate—non-writing professionals including editors, artists, agents and booksellers. Affiliate—beginning writers and others interested in the horror genre. Sponsors the "Bram Stoker Award" for excellence in horror writing. Publishes membership directory, handbook, and bimonthly newsletter with market reports. Dues: $55/year (US); $65/year (overseas); $75/year family membership; $100/year corporate membership. Meets once a year. Send SASE for information or visit website.

MYSTERY WRITERS OF AMERICA (MWA), 17 E. 47th St., 6th Floor, New York NY 10017. (212)888-8171. Fax: (212)888-8107. Website: http://www.mysterywriters.org (includes information about the newsletter, awards and membership). Estab. 1945. Number of Members: 2,600. Type of memberships: Active (professional, published writers of fiction or nonfiction crime/mystery/suspense); associate (professionals in allied fields, i.e., editor, publisher, critic, news reporter, publicist, librarian, bookseller, etc.); corresponding (writers qualified for active membership who live outside the US). Unpublished writers may petition for Affiliate member status. Benefits include promotion and protection of writers' rights and interests, including counsel and advice on contracts, MWA courses and workshops, a national office, an annual conference featuring the Edgar Allan Poe Awards, the *MWA Anthology*, a national newsletter, regional conferences, insurance, marketing tools, meetings and research publications. Newsletter, *The Third Degree*, is published 10 times/year for members. Annual dues: $65 for US members; $32.50 for Corresponding members.

THE NATIONAL LEAGUE OF AMERICAN PEN WOMEN, INC., Headquarters: The Pen Arts Building, 1300 17th St., NW, Washington DC 20036-1973. (202)785-1997. Fax: (202)452-6868. E-mail: twbaring@umd5.umd.edu. Website: http://members.aol.com/penwomen/pen.htm. Contact: National President. Estab. 1897. Number of Members: 5,000. Types of Membership: Three classifications: Art, Letters, Music. Open to: Professional women. "Professional to us means our membership is only open to women who sell their art, writings, or music compositions. We have over 175 branches in the mainland US plus Hawaii and the Republic of Panama. Some branches have as many as 100 members, some as few as 10 or 12. It is necessary to have 5 members to form a new branch." Benefits include a bimonthly magazine and local and national competitions. Our facility is The Pen Arts Building. It is a 20-room Victorian mansion. One distinguished resident was President Abraham Lincoln's son, Robert Todd Lincoln, the former Secretary of War and Minister of Great Britain. It has a few rooms available for Pen Women visiting the D.C. area, and for Board members in session 3 times a year.

INSIDER REPORT

Dallas Wiebe: continuing a literary journey

Dallas Wiebe

Dallas Wiebe continues what has been a long and fruitful literary journey as author, teacher and mentor.

Wiebe recently reached a major milestone when he won the 1998 Ohio Governor's Award for the Arts. The award honored Wiebe for his contributions to artistic life in Ohio through outreach, teaching, and his own fiction and poetry. The citation noted Wiebe's three published collections of stories, his two novels, his community work as cofounder and president of the Cincinnati Writers' Project, and his longtime teaching career at the University of Cincinnati.

It was somehow appropriate that the award for Wiebe's life work came when it did, shortly following the publication of his novel, *Our Asian Journey* (MLR Editions Canada, 1997)—a book that is the culmination of decades of work. It was 1975, when Wiebe first began researching the novel—a sprawling, 400-page narrative of the pilgrimage to Central Asia by a group of Mennonites in the 1880s.

"I had thought the book would be done by 1980," Wiebe says with a laugh. However, the research and other writing projects prevented him from beginning serious drafting until 1981. Wiebe wrote intensively for three years before setting the manuscript aside to cool for a while. By 1987, the manuscript was complete—but the book's path to publication had just begun.

The novel circulated through numerous publishers, all of whom rejected the book as not being sufficiently commercial. This is not necessarily surprising, because Wiebe's narrative technique can be categorized as "postmodern" avant-garde—a literary style that emphasizes the artificial nature of fiction and constantly reminds the reader that the story is not real. This "metafiction" functions in contrast to traditional realistic writing, which holds a window up to the world. The narrator of *Our Asian Journey* frequently steps outside of the action to comment on the characters, the story and even the genre of fiction itself. In *Our Asian Journey*, this technique usually maintains a serious tone, but in Wiebe's short stories it is frequently used for satire, parody and irony.

Wiebe finally found a Canadian editor, Paul Tiessen of MLR Editions, who was interested in publishing *Our Asian Journey.* "When I got this chance, I decided it was the only way the book would see print," Wiebe says. MLR is a small literary press, the type that has historically supported experimental writing—including Wiebe's other work. His books of short stories—*Skyblue's Essays* (1995), *Going to the Mountain* (1988) and *The Transparent Eye-Ball* (1982) were published by Burning Deck, a small press in Rhode Island.

Why has Wiebe gravitated to an experimental style of fiction? "I find that other stuff tiresome and boring," he says, laughing. "I've always been more interested in trying to

INSIDER REPORT, *Wiebe*

write humor. I find it very hard to do serious work; I'm parodying something else." Then, turning serious, he adds: "We live in an age of extraordinary and endemic mediocrity. I like to have something in a story that reflects the contemporary literary scene. You can do that with postmodernist techniques. You can do social criticism. I try to keep in mind and recall to the reader the context in which the story exists."

Wiebe imparts his insights on the art of fiction to developing writers in the community workshops he occasionally leads for the Cincinnati Writers' Project. He cofounded the organization in 1988, and currently serves as its president. The Governor's Award for the Arts made special mention of the community outreach work he does through the Cincinnati Writers' Project.

Wiebe is a strong advocate of the value of community writing groups. The Cincinnati Writers' Project was founded to provide support to writers of all genres, not only fiction, in the Cincinnati region. The organization holds monthly meetings and workshops, and charges an annual membership fee.

"People are so dispersed that there needs to be some kind of central organization where they can meet other writers, find out about publication, and things like that," Wiebe says. "We talk in various ways about trying to find a little more coherence for literary activity in the area."

For fiction writers, having a supportive community can help develop their writing. "It helps form a community of writers, so that writers in the city can know each other and support each other," Wiebe says. "I think that's terribly important."

In forming a writers' group, Wiebe emphasizes the importance of finding a common focus to offer value for the membership. "They should have a group of people who are compatible," Wiebe says. The members should make an effort to get along personally, and recognize the common purpose: community and support as much as criticism.

This does not mean that writers should not critique each others' work, but that they should have "a common goal they're working toward," says Wiebe. It makes no sense for a poet, a romance writer and a journalist to form a group if they cannot agree on a common objective, because no member will get what they are looking for.

For many writers, a writer's group is a prime source of support not just for their own writing, but also a source of information about outlets for readings and publications, new ideas and methods to try in their work, and exposure to other genres. "That's valuable information that comes from knowing other people who are involved in the same things as you are," Wiebe says.

Although Wiebe is a strong advocate of the support a community writing group can provide, he has two cautions for fledgling fiction writers: they must be voracious readers, and should not be in rush to publish their work.

Regardless of the narrative style a writer chooses—experimental or traditional—it is critical that a writer have a deep understanding of how that style has been used by great writers in the past. They must be avid readers. Many, though, are not—a common problem among not only developing writers, but writers with established reputations, he says.

"So many people today know how to get published, but they don't know how to write. They have to know their literary history. You don't write in a vacuum," Wiebe says. "When you write a short story, you've got the whole history of the short story as a context. You have to know that history."

Some writers—especially fledgling ones—fear that immersing themselves in the work of other writers might stifle their own original development. Instead, Wiebe says, such

INSIDER REPORT, *continued*

reading is the key to originality. "You have to be different—otherwise you're just repeating," he says. And how can one be different and add something new to a tradition without knowing what has been done before? "Every sentence you put down is in that context," Wiebe says.

The relative ease of publication today (literary journals continue to proliferate) makes it tempting for writers with some skill to rush their work into print. They should not give in to such temptation, Wiebe says. "The editorial process starts with the writer. You have to decide if it's worth publishing. The writer is the first editor. A lot of writers think they have to publish everything they write. I've made some mistakes—things that I wish had never been published."

As a guard against sending out bad work, Wiebe advises writers to wait a certain period of time after they decide something is finished and ready. His own waiting period is six months. Given the success of Wiebe's own continuing literary journey, it's good advice to follow.

—*Kevin Walzer*

There are Branch and State Association competitions, as well as Biennial Convention competitions. Offers a research library of books by our members and histories of our organization. Sponsors awards biennially to Pen Women in each classification: Art, Letters, Music, and $1,000 award biennially in even-numbered year to non-Pen Women in each classification for women age 35 and over who wish to pursue special work in art, music or letters field. *The Pen Woman* is the membership magazine, published 6 times a year, free to members, $18 a year for nonmember subscribers. Dues: $40/year for national organization, from $5-10/year for branch membership and from $1-5 for state association dues. Branches hold regular meetings each month, September through May except in northern states which meet usually March through September (for travel convenience). Send SASE for information. Inquiries via e-mail OK, but prefers SASE.

NATIONAL WRITERS ASSOCIATION, 1450 S. Havana, Suite 424, Aurora CO 80012. (303)751-7844. Executive Director: Sandy Whelchel. Estab. 1937. Number of Members: 4,000. Types of Memberships: Regular membership for those without published credits; professional membership for those with published credits. Open to: Any interested writer. National/International plus we have 16 chapters in various states. Benefits include critiques, marketing advice, editing, literary agency, complaint service, chapbook publishing service, research reports on various aspects of writing, 4 contests, National Writers Press—self-publishing operation, computer bulletin board service, regular newsletter with updates on marketing, bimonthly magazine on writing related subjects, discounts on supplies, magazines and some services. Sponsors periodic conferences and workshops: short story contest opens April, closes July 1; novel contest opens December, closes April 1. Publishes *Flash Market News* (monthly publication for professional members only); *Authorship Magazine* (bimonthly publication available by subscription $20 to nonmembers). Dues: $65 regular; $85 professional. For professional membership requirement is equivalent of 3 articles or stories in a national or regional magazine; a book published by a royalty publisher, a play, TV script or movie produced. Send SASE for information. Chapters hold meetings on a monthly basis.

NEW HAMPSHIRE WRITERS' PROJECT, P.O. Box 2693, Concord NH 03302-2693. (603)226-6649. Fax: (603)226-0035. E-mail: nhwp@nh.ultranet.com. Executive Director: Patricia Scholz-Cohen. Estab. 1988. Number of Members: 750. Type of Memberships: Senior/student; individual; business. Open to anyone interested in the literary arts—writers (fiction, nonfiction, journalists, poets, scriptwriters, etc.), teachers, librarians, publishers and readers. Statewide scope. Benefits include a bimonthly publication featuring articles about NH writers and publishers; leads for writers, new books listings; and NH literary news. Also discounts on workshops, readings, conferences. Dues: $35 for individuals; $20 for seniors and full-time students; $50 for businesses. Send SASE for information. Inquiries by fax and e-mail OK.

☑ **OZARKS WRITERS LEAGUE**, P.O. Box 1433, Branson MO 65615-2612. E-mail: fred_pfister@compuserve.com. Membership Chair: Fred Pfister. Estab. 1983. Number of Members: 250. Open to: Anyone interested in writing, photography and art. Regional Scope: Missouri, Arkansas, Oklahoma, Kansas—"Greater Ozarks"

THE HOW-TOS OF MONEY & MEETINGS FOR WRITERS' GROUPS

So you've spent a lot of time longing for the company of a supportive group of fellow writers. And you've mustered the ambition—and courage—to start a writing group in your area. Now, the easy part's over. Once a person makes up his mind to begin a writers' group, a host of organizational questions follow. Below are a few of the most pressing questions.

•Where do we meet?

The specifics of where a group meets depends on the group's size, its mission, the frequency of meetings, and other factors. During its ten-year history, the Cincinnati Writers' Project has met in a variety of locations, including a used bookstore, a church community center, and its current location at a regional arts center. The group holds monthly meetings open to the public, and also conducts its business meetings in these sites.

Because writers' groups—especially new ones—have budgets ranging in size from tiny to non-existent, finding a meeting place that does not charge an access fee is beneficial. Many non-profit organizations, such as churches or community centers, provide free access to community groups. If a group is small, and its members know each other well, meeting in group members' homes is another option.

•What kind of meetings should we have?

The answer to this question depends largely on the group's mission. The Cincinnati Writers' Project (CWP) has monthly meetings open to the public because it focuses on writing in all genres. "We wanted to include everything," says co-founder Dallas Wiebe. At these meetings, professional writers in various genres discuss their craft. Speakers include journalists, poets, fiction writers, editors, and specialists in other genres. One or two meetings per year are also devoted to reading members' work.

The critique groups function as smaller, more focused groups within the larger group. For a person interested in starting a group focused on a single genre, such as poetry, monthly public meetings may not be necessary. Weekly, biweekly or monthly workshops may be more appropriate.

•What kind of budget should we have?

The size of an organization's budget depends on the size of its membership and what it hopes to accomplish. For a small organization with few expenses beyond postage and related materials, annual dues from its membership may be sufficient—especially if the organization is able to negotiate free access for things such as meeting space. CWP's poetry critique group currently meets at a local church with a private conference room and even gets free parking. "It's just wonderful," says Carol Laque, who leads the poetry group.

If a writers' group has more ambitious plans, program grants may be available from foundations and state agencies—but that may require the writers' group to legally incorporate as a nonprofit, tax-exempt organization, a process that consumes both time and money. Many granting agencies also require a nonprofit organization to fund a certain percentage of a project budget so they are not entirely dependent on grant funds.

•After the questions, the answer

There are many logistical hurdles to establishing a writers' group, but most who have founded such groups would agree: once your group is operating smoothly, leaping those hurdles is worth it.

(For more on writing groups, read *Writing Together: How to Transform Your Writing in a Writing Group*, published in 1997 by Perigee. Also, to locate an existing writers' group in your area, see the listings in this section.)

—Kevin Walzer

area. Benefits include mutual inspiration and support; information exchange. Sponsors quarterly seminars/workshops, two annual writing competitions, one annual photography competition, special conferences. Publishes quarterly newsletter, the *Owls Hoot*. Dues: $15/year. Meets quarterly—February, May, August, November. Send SASE for information. Inquiries by e-mail OK.

N **THE PRIVATE EYE WRITERS OF AMERICA (PWA)**, 407 W. 3rd St., Morestown NJ 10017. Contact: Membership Chair. Estab. 1981. The original purpose of PWA was to elevate the private story from a sub-genre of mystery to a genre all its own and to foster support and respect for the P.I. genre.

✔ **SCIENCE-FICTION AND FANTASY WRITERS OF AMERICA, INC.**, P.O. Box 171, Unity ME 04988-0171. E-mail: execdir@sfwa.org. Website: http://www.sfwa.org. Executive Director: Sharon Lee. Estab. 1965. Number of Members: 1,200. Type of Memberships: Active, associate, affiliate, institutional, estate. Open to: "Professional writers, editors, anthologists, artists in the science fiction/fantasy genres and allied professional individuals and institutions. Our membership is international; we currently have members throughout Europe, Australia, Central and South America, Canada and some in Asia." We produce a variety of journals for our members, annual membership directory and provide a grievance committee, publicity committee, circulating book plan and access to medical/life/disability insurance. We award the SFWA Nebula Awards each year for outstanding achievement in the genre at novel, novella, novelet and short story lengths." Quarterly *SFWA Bulletin* to members; nonmembers may subscribe at $15/4 issues within US/Canada; $18.50 overseas. Bimonthly *SFWA Forum* for active and associate members only. Annual *SFWA Membership Directory* for members; available to professional organizations for $60. Active membership requires professional sale in the US of at least 3 short stories or 1 full-length book. Affiliate or associate membership require at least 1 professional sale in the US or other professional sale in the US or other professional involvement in the field respectively. Dues are pro-rated quarterly; info available upon request. Business meetings are held during Annual Nebula Awards weekend and usually during the annual World SF Convention. Send SASE for information.

✔ **SCIENCE FICTION WRITERS OF EARTH**, P.O. Box 121293, Fort Worth TX 76121-1293. (817)451-8674. E-mail: sfwoe@flash.net. Website: http://www.flash.net/~sfwoe (includes contest rules, entry form, judge's report, contest results, list of writers who entered our contest, interviews with the winners, reviews of the top three stories, newsletter of interesting articles to our contestants and writers in general). Administrator: Gilbert Gordon Reis. Estab. 1980. Number of Members: 100-150. Open to: Unpublished writers of science fiction and fantasy short stories. "We have writers in Europe, Canada, Australia and several other countries, but the majority are from the US. Writers compete in our annual contest. This allows the writer to find out where he/she stands in writing ability. Winners often receive requests for their story from publishers. Many winners have told us that they believe that placing in the top ten of our contest gives them recognition and has assisted in getting their first story published." Dues: One must submit a science fiction or fantasy short story to our annual contest to be a member. Cost is $5 for membership and first story. $2 for each additional ms. The nominating committee meets several times a year to select the top ten stories of the annual contest. Author Edward Bryant selects the winners from the top ten stories. Contest deadline is October 30 and the cash awards and results are mailed out on January 31 of the following year. The first place story is published by *Altair*, magazine of speculative fiction. Information about the organization is available for SASE, by e-mail (no contest submissions) or from the Internet.

✔ **SEATTLE WRITERS ASSOCIATION**, P.O. Box 33265, Seattle WA 98133. (206)860-5207. Fax: (206)483-3519 (contact phone). President: Dick Gibbons. Estab. 1986. Number of members: approximately 130. "Open to all writers from the Pacific Northwest, published and unpublished, dedicated to writing professionally and for publication." Benefits include monthly meetings, networking, market advice, critique groups/mss review. Sponsors Winter Workshop and Writers in Performance (contest and performance). Publishes newsletter for members and available upon request. "Writers in Performance" anthology in progress. Dues: $30/year, includes newsletter. Meets first Thursday of month, 7-10 p.m., September through May. Send SASE for information.

N **SISTERS IN CRIME**, Box 442124, Lawrence KS 66044-8933. Contact: Executive Secretary. Estab. 1986. Number of Members: Over 2,000. The original purpose of this organization was to combat discrimination against women in the mystery field. Memberships are open to men as well as women, as long as they are committed to the organization and its goals. Offers membership assistance in networking and publicity.

✔ **WESTERN WRITERS OF AMERICA**, Office of the Secretary Treasurer, 1012 Fair St., Franklin TN 37064-2718. Phone/fax: (615)791-1444. E-mail: tncrutch@aol.com. Website: http://www.imt.net/~gedison/wwahome.html. Secretary Treasurer: James A. Crutchfield. Estab. 1953. Number of Members: 600. Type of Membership: Active, associate, patron. Open to: Professional, published writers who have multiple publications of fiction or nonfiction (usually at least three) about the West. Associate membership open to those with one book, a lesser number of short stories or publications or participation in the field such as editors, agents, reviewers, librarians, television producers, directors (dealing with the West). Patron memberships open to corporations, organizations and individuals with an interest in the West. Scope is international. Benefits: "By way of publications and conventions, members are kept abreast of developments in the field of Western literature and the publishing field, marketing requirements, income tax problems, copyright law, research facilities and techniques, and new publications. At conventions members have the opportunity for one-on-one conferences with editors, publishers and agents." Sponsors an annual four-day conference during fourth week of June featuring panels, lectures and seminars on publishing, writing and research. Includes the Spur Awards to honor authors of the best Western literature of the previous year. Publishes *Roundup Magazine* (6 times/year) for members. Available to nonmembers for $30. Publishes membership directory. Dues: $75 for active membership, $75 for associate membership, $250 for patron. For information on Spur Awards, send SASE. Inquiries by fax and e-mail OK.

WILLAMETTE WRITERS, 9045 SW Barbur Blvd., Suite 5A, Portland OR 97219. (503)452-1592. Fax: (503)452-0372. E-mail: wilwrite@teleport.com. Website: http://www.teleport.com/~wilwrite/. Office Manager: Bill Johnson. Estab. 1965. Number of members: 700. "Willamette Writers is a nonprofit, tax exempt corporation staffed by volunteers. Membership is open to both published and aspiring writers. WW provides support, encouragement and interaction for all genres of writers." Open to national membership, but serves primarily the Pacific Northwest. Benefits include a writers' referral service, critique groups, membership discounts, youth programs (4th-12th grades), monthly meetings with guest authors, intern program, annual writing contest, community projects, library and research services, as well as networking with other writing groups, office with writing reference and screenplay library. Sponsors annual conference held the second weekend in August; quarterly workshops; annual Kay Snow Writing Contest; and the Distinguished Northwest Writer Award. Publishes *The Willamette Writer* monthly: a 12-page newsletter for members and complimentary subscriptions. Information consists of features, how-to's, mechanics of writing, profile of featured monthly speaker, markets, workshops, conferences and benefits available to writers. Dues: $36/year; includes subscription to newsletter. Meets first Tuesday of each month; board meeting held last Tuesday of each month. Send SASE for information. Inquiries by fax and e-mail OK.

THE WRITER'S CENTER, 4508 Walsh St., Bethesda MD 20815. (301)654-8664. Website: http://www.writer.org. E-mail: postmaster@writer.org. Executive Director: Jane Fox. Estab. 1977. Number of Members: 2,200. Open to: Anyone interested in writing. Scope is regional DC, Maryland, Virginia, West Virginia, Pennsylvania. Benefits include newsletter, discounts in bookstore, workshops, public events, subscriptions to *Poet Lore*, use of equipment and annual small press book fair. Center offers workshops, reading series, equipment, newsletter and limited workspace. Sponsors workshops, conferences, award for narrative poem. Publishes *Writer's Carousel*, bimonthly. Nonmembers can pick it up at the Center. Dues: $30/year. Fees vary with service, see publications. Brochures are available for SASE. Inquiries by e-mail OK.

WRITERS' FEDERATION OF NEW BRUNSWICK, P.O. Box 37, Station A, Fredericton, New Brunswick E3B 4Y2 Canada. Phone/fax: (506)459-7228. E-mail: aa821@fan.nb.ca. Website: http://www.sjfn.nb.ca/community_hall/W/Writers_Federation_NB/index.htm. Project Coordinator: Anna Mae Snider. Estab. 1983. Number of Members: 230. Membership is open to anyone interested in writing. "This a provincial organization. Benefits include promotion of members' works through newsletter announcements and readings and launchings held at fall festival and annual general meeting. Services provided by WFNB include a Writers-in-Schools Program and manuscript reading. The WFNB sponsors a fall festival and an annual general meeting which feature workshops, readings and book launchings." There is also an annual literary competition, open to residents of New Brunswick only, which has prizes of $200, $100 and $30 in four categories: Fiction, nonfiction, children's literature and poetry; two $400 prizes for the best manuscript of poems (48 pgs.); the best short novel or collection of short stories and a category for young writers (14-18 years of age) which offers $150 (1st prize), $100 (2nd prize), $50 (3rd prize). Publishes a quarterly newsletter. Dues: $30/year; $20/year for students. Board of Directors meets approximately 5 times a year. Annual General Meeting is held in the spring of each year. Send SASE for information. Inquiries by e-mail and fax OK.

WRITERS' FEDERATION OF NOVA SCOTIA, Suite 901, 1809 Barrington St., Halifax, Nova Scotia B3J 3K8 Canada. Executive Director: Jane Buss. Estab. 1976. Number of Members: 500. Type of Memberships: General membership, student membership, Nova Scotia Writers' Council membership (professional), Honorary Life Membership. Open to anyone who writes. Provincial scope, with a few members living elsewhere in the country or the world. Benefits include advocacy of all kinds for writers, plus such regular programs as workshops and regular publications, including directories and a newsletter. Sponsors workshops, 2 annual conferences (one for general membership, the other for the professional wing), 3 book awards, one annual competition for unpublished manuscripts in various categories; a writers in the schools program, a manuscript reading service, reduced

FOR EXPLANATIONS OF THESE SYMBOLS,
SEE THE INSIDE FRONT AND BACK COVERS OF THIS BOOK.

photocopying rates. Publishes *Eastword*, 6 issues annually, available by subscription for $35 (Canadian) to nonmembers. Dues: $35/year (Canadian). Holds an annual general meeting, an annual meeting of the Nova Scotia Writers' Council, several board meetings annually. Send 5×7 SASE for information.

WRITERS GUILD OF ALBERTA, Percy Page Centre, 11759 Groat Rd., 3rd Floor, Edmonton, Alberta T5M 3K6 Canada. (403)422-8174. Fax: (403)422-2663. E-mail: writers@compusmart.ab.ca. Website: http://www.writersguildofalberta.ca. Executive Director: Miki Andrejevic. Estab. 1980. Number of Members: 700. Membership open to current and past residents of Alberta. Regional (provincial) scope. Benefits include discounts on programs offered; manuscript evaluation service available; bimonthly newsletter; contacts; info on workshops, retreats, readings, etc. Sponsors workshops 2 times/year, retreats 3 times/year, annual conference, annual book awards program (Alberta writers only). Publishes *WestWord* 6 times/year; available for $55/year (Canadian) to nonmembers. Dues: $60/year for regular membership; $20/year senior/students/limited income; $100/year donating membership—charitable receipt issued (Canadian funds). Organized monthly meetings. Send SASE for information.

N **WRITERS INFORMATION NETWORK**, P.O. Box 11337, Bainbridge Island WA 98110. (206)842-9103. Fax: (206)842-0536. E-mail: WritersInfoNetwork@juno.com or WritersInfoNetwork@mci2000.com. Websites: http://www.bluejaypub.com/win or http://www.ecpa.org/win. Director: Elaine Wright Colvin. Estab. 1980. Number of members: 1,000. Open to: All interested in writing for religious publications/publishers. Scope is national and several foreign countries. Benefits include bimonthly magazine, *The Win Informer*, market news, advocacy/grievance procedures, professional advice, writers conferences, press cards, author referral, free consultation. Sponsors workshops, conferences throughout the country each year—mailing list and advertised in *The Win Informer* magazine. Dues: $30 US; $35 foreign/year. Holds quarterly meetings in Seattle, WA. Brochures are available for SASE. Inquiries by fax and e-mail OK.

THE WRITERS ROOM, INC., 10 Astor Place, 6th Floor, New York NY 10003. (212)254-6995. Fax: (212)533-6059. Website: http://www.writersroom@writersroom.org. Executive Director: Donna Brodie. Contact: Mariana Carreño, assistant to executive director. Estab. 1978. Number of Members: 200 fulltime and 40 part-time. Open to: Any writer who shows a serious commitment to writing. "We serve a diverse population of writers, but most of our residents live in or around the NYC area. We encourage writers from around the country (and world!) to apply for residency if they plan to visit NYC for a while." Benefits include 24-hour access to the facility. "We provide desk space, storage areas for computers, typewriters, etc., a kitchen where coffee and tea are always available, bathrooms and a lounge. We also offer in-house workshops on topics of practical importance to writers and monthly readings of work-in-progress." Dues: $175 per quarter year. Send SASE for application and background information. Inquiries by fax OK.

THE WRITERS' WORKSHOP, 387 Beaucatcher Rd., Asheville NC 28805. (704)254-8111. Executive Director: Karen Ackerson. Estab. 1984. Number of Members: 1,250. Types of Memberships: Student/low income $25; family/organization $65; individual $35. Open to all writers. Scope is national and international. Benefits include discounts on workshops, quarterly newsletter, admission to Annual Celebration every summer, critiquing services through the mail. Center offers reading room, assistance with editing your work. Publishes a newsletter; also available to nonmembers ($20). Offers workshops year-round in NC and the South; 6 retreats a year, 4 readings with nationally awarded authors. Contests and classes for children and teens as well. Advisory board includes Kurt Vonnegut, E.L. Doctorow, Peter Matthiessen, Reynolds Price, John Le Carre and Eudora Welty. Also sponsors international contests in fiction, poetry and creative nonfiction. Brochures are available for SASE.

Publications of Interest to Fiction Writers

This section features listings for magazines and newsletters that focus on writing or the publishing industry. While many of these are not markets for fiction, they do offer articles, marketing advice or other information valuable to the fiction writer. Several magazines in this section offer actual market listings while others feature reviews of books in the field and news on the industry.

The timeliness factor is a primary reason most writers read periodicals. Changes in publishing happen very quickly and magazines can help you keep up with the latest news. Some magazines listed here, including *Writer's Digest* and *Fiction Writer*, cover the entire field of writing, while others such as *The Mystery Review*, *Locus* (science fiction) and *Factsheet Five* (zines) focus on a particular type of writing. We've also added publications which focus on a particular segment of the publishing industry.

Information on some publications for writers can be found in the introductions to other sections in this book. In addition, many of the literary and commercial magazines for writers listed in the markets sections are helpful to the fiction writer. Keep an eye on the newsstand and library shelves for others and let us know if you've found a publication particularly useful.

ABOUT CREATIVE TIME SPACES, ACT I Creativity Center, P.O. Box 30854, Palm Beach Gardens FL 33420. Editor: Charlotte Plotsky, M.S. International sourcebook of information, photos and other materials on retreats, colonies, communities, residencies and other programs for artists of all disciplines, including writers. Send SASE for details.

N **THE ARMCHAIR DETECTIVE**, Box 929, Bound Brook NJ 08805-0929. Contact: Editor-in-Chief. Estab. 1967. Quarterly. Includes interviews with mystery writers, essays, film reviews, industry news, new bookstores, overseas reports, convention listings and market listings.

FACTSHEET FIVE, P.O. Box 170099, San Francisco CA 94117-0099. Biannually. "The definitive guide to the 'zine revolution. *Factsheet Five* reviews over 2,000 small press publications each issue. Send in your independent magazine for review." Sample copy: $6. Subscriptions: $20 for individuals and $40 for institutions.

N **FICTION WRITER**, F&W Publications, 1507 Dana Ave., Cincinnati OH 45207. (513)531-2690. Fax: (513)531-1843. E-mail: dawnr@fwpubs.com. Website: http://www.writersdigest.com. Editor: Peter Blocksom. Quarterly. "*Fiction Writer* inspires beginning, intermediate and advanced writers through lively instruction on all aspects of fiction writing, combining within its pages the best qualities of a stimulating workshop, a challenging class and a supportive writing group. Through three key components—how-to features, essays on the craft of writing, and coverage of marketing trends—it supplies the tools every fiction writer needs. The magazine's writers include published authors and accomplished writing teachers, all of whom show readers the path to success— whether success be simply the pleasures of creation or the thrill of publication." Lists fiction markets. Sample copies available for $5.25. Subscriptions: (800)289-0963. Note: As with other listings in this section, this is not a market. Do not send mss.

FICTION WRITER'S GUIDELINE, P.O. Box 4065, Deerfield Beach, FL 33442. Editor: Blythe Camenson. Bimonthly. Our publication is "an eight page newsletter with agent/editor/author interviews, how-to articles on writing fiction and getting it published, fiction markets, conference listings, Q&A column, success stories and more." Sample copies available for $3.50. Subscriptions: $21/year; free to members of Fiction Writer's Connection. "Membership in FWC is $64/year; includes a free newsletter, free critiquing, and a toll-free hotline for questions and free advice. Send SASE for information."

GILA QUEEN'S GUIDE TO MARKETS, P.O. Box 97, Newton NJ 07860-0097. (973)579-1537. Fax: (973)579-6441. E-mail: gilaqueen@aol.com or gilaqueen@worldnet.att.net. Website: http://www.geocities.com/Athens/Aegean/7844/gila/index.html. Editor: Kathryn Ptacek. "Includes complete guidelines for fiction (different genres), poetry, nonfiction, greeting cards, etc. Also includes 'theme section' each issue—science fiction/fantasy/

horror, mystery/suspense, romance, western, Canadian, regional, women's markets, religious, etc. and 'mini-markets.' Regular departments include new address listings, dead/suspended markets, moving editors, anthologies, markets to be wary of, publishing news, etc. Every issue contains updates (of stuff listed in previous issues), new markets, conferences, contests. Publishes articles on writing topics, self-promotion, reviews of software and books of interest to writers, etc." Sample copy: $6. Subscriptions: $34/year (US); $38/year (Canada); $50/year (overseas).

GOTHIC JOURNAL, P.O. Box 6340, Elko NV 89802-6340. (702)738-3520. Fax: (702)738-3524. E-mail: kglass@gothicjournal.com. Website: http://GothicJournal.com/romance/. Publisher: Kristi Lyn Glass. Bimonthly. "*Gothic Journal* is a news and review magazine for readers, writers and publishers of romantic suspense, romantic mysteries, and supernatural, gothic, and woman-in-jeopardy romance novels. It contains articles, reviews, letters, author profiles, market news, book lists and more." Lists fiction markets. Reviews novels and short story collections. Sample copies available for $4 plus $2 postage and handling. Subscriptions: $24/year (6 issues); $30/year (Canada); $36/year (foreign). Note: *As with other listings in this section, this is not a "market," do not send mss.*

LAMBDA BOOK REPORT, P.O. Box 73910, Washington DC 20056. (202)462-7924. Editor: Kanani Kauka. Monthly. "This review journal of contemporary gay and lesbian literature appeals to both readers and writers. Fiction queries published regularly." Lists fiction markets. Reviews novels, short story collections, poetry and nonfiction. Send review copies to Attn: Book Review Editor. Single copy price is $4.95/US. Subscriptions: $34.95/year (US); international rate: $58.95 (US $); Canada/Mexico: $46.95/year (US $).

LOCUS, The Newspaper of the Science Fiction Field, P.O. Box 13305, Oakland CA 94661. Editor: Charles N. Brown. Monthly. "Professional newsletter of science fiction, fantasy and horror; has news, interviews of authors, book reviews, column on electronic publishing, forthcoming books listings, monthly books-received listings, etc." Lists markets for fiction. Reviews novels or short story collections. Sample copies available. Single copy price: $4.50. Subscription price: $43/year, (2nd class mail) for US, $48 (US)/year, (2nd class) for Canada; $48 (US)/year (2nd class) for overseas.

MYSTERY READERS JOURNAL, P.O. Box 8116, Berkeley CA 94707. Contact: Editor. Estab. 1984. Includes interviews, essays, mystery news, new bookstores, overseas reports and convention listings.

THE MYSTERY REVIEW, A Quarterly Publication for Mystery & Suspense Readers, P.O. Box 233, Colborne, Ontario K0K 1S0 Canada. (613)475-4440. Editor: Barbara Davey. Quarterly. "Book reviews, information on new releases, interviews with authors and other people involved in mystery, 'real life' mysteries, out-of-print mysteries, mystery/suspense films, word games and puzzles with a mystery theme." Reviews mystery/suspense novels and short story collections. Send review copies to editor. Single copy price is $5.95 CDN in Canada/$5.95 US in the United States. Subscriptions: $21.50 CDN (includes GST) in Canada; $20 US in the US and $28 US elsewhere.

MYSTERY SCENE, P.O. Box 669, Cedar Rapids IA 52406-0669. Contact: Editors. Estab. 1985. Bimonthly. Includes interviews with authors, essays, book reviews, film reviews, new bookstores, software reviews, overseas reports, convention listings and market listings.

NEW WRITER'S MAGAZINE, P.O. Box 5976, Sarasota FL 34277. (941)953-7903. E-mail: newriters@aol.com. Editor: George J. Haborak. Bimonthly. "*New Writer's Magazine* is a publication for aspiring writers. It features 'how-to' articles, news and interviews with published and recently published authors. Will use fiction that has a tie-in with the world of the writer." Lists markets for fiction. Reviews novels and short story collections. Send review copies to Editor. Send #10 SASE for guidelines. Sample copies available; single copy price is $3. Subscriptions: $15/year, $25/2 years. Canadian $20 (US funds). International $35/year (US funds).

OHIO WRITER, P.O. Box 91801, Cleveland OH 44101. (216)932-8444. Editor: Ron Antonucci. Bimonthly. "Interviews with Ohio writers of fiction and nonfiction; current fiction markets in Ohio." Lists fiction markets. Reviews novels and short story collections. Sample copies available for $2.50. Subscriptions: $15/year; $40/3 years; $20/institutional rate.

FOR EXPLANATIONS OF THESE SYMBOLS, SEE THE INSIDE FRONT AND BACK COVERS OF THIS BOOK.

THE REGENCY PLUME, 711 D. St. N.W., Ardmore OK 73401. Editor: Marilyn Clay. Bimonthly. "The newsletter focus is on providing accurate historical facts relating to the Regency period: customs, clothes, entertainment, the wars, historical figures, etc. I stay in touch with New York editors who acquire Regency romance novels. Current market info appears regularly in newsletter—see Bits & Scraps." Current Regency romances are "Previewed." Sample copy available for $4; single copy price is $4, $5 outside States. Subscriptions: $18/year for 6 issues; $22 Canada; $26 foreign. ("Check must be drawn on a US bank. Postal money order okay.") Back issues available. Send SASE for subscription information, article guidelines or list of research and writing aids available, such as audiotapes, historical maps, books on Regency period furniture, Regency romance writing contest, etc.

N **ROMANTIC TIMES MAGAZINE**, 55 Bergen St., Brooklyn NY 11201. (718)237-1097. Monthly. Features reviews, news and interviews of interest to the romance reader. Each issue also has special features such as photo tours of authors' houses, interviews with male cover models and articles on romantic pursuits (teas, salons, etc.). Subscriptions: $42/year in U.S.; $66/year in Canada.

N **ROMANCE WRITERS REPORT**, Romance Writers of America, 13700 Veterans Memorial, Suite 315, Houston TX 77014. (281)440-6885. Fax: (281)440-7510. E-mail: infobox@rwanational.com. Editor: Charis McEachern. Monthly publication of Romance Writers of America, Inc. Subscriptions included as part of RWA membership. Includes articles, essays and tips written by established writers, contest and conference information and articles by romance editors.

SCAVENGER'S NEWSLETTER, 519 Ellinwood, Osage City KS 66523. (913)528-3538. Editor: Janet Fox. Monthly. "A market newsletter for SF/fantasy/horror/mystery writers with an interest in the small press. Articles about SF/fantasy/horror/mystery writing/marketing. Now using Flash fiction to 1,200 words, genres as above. No writing-related material for fiction. Payment for articles and fiction is $4 on acceptance." Lists markets for fiction. Sample copies available. Single copy price: $2.50. Subscription price: $17/year, $8.50/6 months. Canada: $20, $10 overseas $26, $13 (US funds only).

SCIENCE FICTION CHRONICLE, P.O. Box 022730, Brooklyn NY 11202-0056. (718)643-9011. Editor: Andrew I. Porter. Monthly. Publishes nonfiction, nothing about UFOs. "Monthly newsmagazine for professional writers, editors, readers of SF, fantasy, horror." Lists markets for fiction "updated every 4 months." Reviews novels, small press publications, audiotapes and short story collections. Send review copies to SFC and also to Don D'Ammassa, 323 Dodge St., E. Providence RI 02914. Sample copies available with 9×12 SAE with $1.24 postage; single copy price is $3.50 (US) or £3.50 (UK). Subscriptions: $42 first class US and Canada; $49 overseas. *Note: As with other listings in this section, this is not a "market"—Do not send mss or artwork.*

THE SMALL PRESS BOOK REVIEW, P.O. Box 176, Southport CT 06490. (203)332-7629. Editor: Henry Berry. Quarterly. "Brief reviews of all sorts of books from small presses/independent publishers." Addresses of publishers are given in reviews. Reviews novels and short story collections. Send review copies to editor. Published electronically via the Internet.

SMALL PRESS REVIEW/SMALL MAGAZINE REVIEW, P.O. Box 100, Paradise CA 95967. (916)877-6110. Editor: Len Fulton. Bimonthly. "Publishes news and reviews about small publishers, books and magazines." Lists markets for fiction and poetry. Reviews novels, short story and poetry collections. Sample copies available. Subscription price: $25/year.

SPECULATIONS, 1111 W. El Camino Real, Suite 109-400, Sunnyvale CA 94087-1057. E-mail: denise@speculations.com. Website: http://www.speculations.com. Editor: Denise Lee. Bimonthly. "Magazine for writers who wish to break into or increase their presence within the science fiction, fantasy, horror or 'other' speculative fiction genres. We publish instruction, advice, editorials, columns, genre-specific articles, questions and answers with the experts, resource guides, interviews with editors, publishers and agents, and—of course—the best market information available anywhere." Sample copies free. Subscriptions: $25/year in US; $30/year in Canada; $40/year overseas.

A VIEW FROM THE LOFT, 66 Malcolm Ave. SE, Minneapolis MN 55414. (612)379-8999, ext. 13. Editor: Ellen Hawley. Monthly. "Publishes articles on writing and list of markets for fiction, poetry and creative nonfiction." Sample copies available; single copy price is $4 US. Subscriptions: $40 in Twin Cities metro area; $25 elsewhere in US; $35 international, $20 low income/student. (Subscription available only as part of Loft membership; rates are membership rates.)

N **THE WRITER**, 120 Boylston St., Boston MA 02116-4615. Editor: Sylvia K. Burack. Monthly. Contains articles on improving writing techniques and getting published. Includes market lists of magazine and book publishers. Subscription price: $28/year, $52/2 years. Canadian and foreign at additional $10/year surface, $30/year airmail. Also publishes *The Writer's Handbook*, an annual book on all fields of writing plus market lists of magazine and book publishers.

N ✓ **WRITER'S CAROUSEL**, The Writer's Center, 4508 Walsh St., Bethesda MD 20815-6006. (301)654-8664. Editor: Allan Lefcowitz. Bimonthly. "*Writer's Carousel* publishes book reviews and articles about writing and the writing scene." Lists fiction markets. Reviews novels and short story collections. Sample copies available. Subscriptions: $30 Writer's Center Membership.

THE WRITER'S CHRONICLE, (formerly *AWP Chronicle*), Associated Writing Programs, George Mason University, Tallwood House, Mail Stop 1E3, Fairfax VA 22030. (703)993-4301. E-mail: awp@gmu.edu. Website: http://web.gmu.edu/departments/awp/. Editor: D.W. Fenza. 6 times/year. Essays on contemporary literature and articles on the teaching of creative writing only. Does *not* publish fiction. Lists fiction markets (back pages for "Submit"). Sample copies available; single copy price $5 (includes postage). Subscription: $20/year; $25/year Canada; $35/year overseas.

✓ **WRITER'S DIGEST**, 1507 Dana Ave., Cincinnati OH 45207. (513)531-2690. Associate Editor: Dawn Ramirez. Monthly. "*Writer's Digest* is a magazine of techniques and markets. We *inspire* the writer to write, *instruct* him or her on how to improve that work, and *direct* him or her toward appropriate markets." Lists markets for fiction, nonfiction, poetry. Single copy price: $3.50. Subscription price: $27.

WRITER'S DIGEST BOOKS–MARKET BOOKS, 1507 Dana Ave., Cincinnati OH 45207. (513)531-2690. Annual. In addition to *Novel & Short Story Writer's Market*, Writer's Digest Books also publishes *Writer's Market*, *Poet's Market*, *Children's Writer's and Illustrator's Market* and the *Guide to Literary Agents*. All include articles and listings of interest to writers. All are available at bookstores, libraries or through the publisher. (Request catalog.)

N **THE WRITER'S GAZETTE**, HCR 1 Box 309, Leeds NY 12451. (518)943-1440. Fax: (518)943-0702. Editor: Kelly O'Donnell. Quarterly newsletter for writers. "We publish articles and poetry that deal with the art of writing." Includes self-help, how-to articles and first-person experiences on writing; also book reviews. Sample copy available for $2, 6×9 SAE and 4 first-class stamps or 2 IRCs.

WRITERS' JOURNAL, Val-Tech Publishing, Inc., P.O. Box 25376, St. Paul MN 55125-0376. Managing Editor: Valerie Hockert. Bimonthly. "Provides a creative outlet for writers of fiction." Sample copies available. Single copy price: $3.99; $5.75 (Canadian). Subscription price: $19.97; $23.97 Canada.

✓ **WRITER'S YEARBOOK**, 1507 Dana Ave., Cincinnati OH 45207. (513)531-2690. Associate Editor: Dawn Ramirez. Annual. "A collection of the best writing *about* writing, with an exclusive survey of the year's 100 top markets for article-length nonfiction." Single copy price: $4.99.

Websites of Interest

BY MEGAN LANE

More and more these days, I find myself wondering how I ever lived without the Internet and the World Wide Web. I'm sure I got out more in those ancient times, but I never felt as powerful or as confident about being able to find the answer to any question my inquisitive brain might pose. Even if you refuse to use the Internet, it's virtually impossible to ignore it. Web addresses are popping up in the corners of TV screens, in print ads and even on the packaging of food we eat. But despite all the naying of the naysayers, there is useful information to be found in the vast network of cyberspace. So, enough with the excuses. Even if you don't own a computer, your local library does and now that you can easily access the Internet through your television, you'll have to find some more difficult bit of technology to shun. And even though my eyes are bloodshot from surfing for the past several hours (or is it days?), I've managed to compile a tiny and woefully incomplete listing of websites that fiction writers shouldn't miss.

WRITER'S DIGEST WEBSITE

http://www.writersdigest.com
This site includes daily markets, articles, interviews and information about writing books and magazines from *Writer's Digest*. It also has a huge, searchable database of writer's guidelines from thousands of publishers.

LITERARY FICTION

The English Server Fiction Collection: http://english-server.hss.cmu.edu/fiction/. "This site offers works of and about fiction collected from our members, contributing authors worldwide, and texts in the public domain." Includes: short fiction, novels, magazines of and about contemporary fiction and criticism, Internet sites publishing fiction, literary criticism, organizations which present awards for excellent fiction, plays, screenplays and dramatic criticism, epic and short verse, and poetic criticism.

Zuzu's Petals Literary Resources: http://www.zuzu.com. "With 700+ organized links to helpful resources for writers, artists, performers, and researchers, it is our goal to unearth and present some of the best links and information for the online creative community." Includes links to magazines, readings, conferences, workshops and more.

GENRE FICTION

Children's Literature Web Guide: http://www.ucalgary.ca/~dkbrown/index.html. "The Children's Literature Web Guide is an attempt to gather together and categorize the growing number of Internet resources related to books for children and young adults. Much of the information you can find through these pages is provided by others: fans, schools, libraries, and commercial enterprises involved in the book world." This comprehensive site for children's book writers and illustrators includes links to authors, publishers, booksellers, conferences and events, as well as other sites of interest.

Con-Tour: http://www.con-tour.com. "Con-Tour is a magazine for people who enjoy the fantasy, sci-fi, comic, gaming, and related conventions that are held all over the world. ConTour features listings of upcoming conventions, with highlights and reviews. We also have interviews with guests, fans, artists; and writers; pictures of fans, and nude pictorials of the women (and men) of fandom." The web version includes a list of conventions with hot links to their own websites. The website and magazine are not for the faint of heart, but true fanatics will have fun with what the zany editors throw at them.

The Market List: http://www.marketlist.com. Web magazine of genre fiction marketing information. "Each version includes over 100 current markets for genre fiction, with info on response times, genres accepted, payment rates and more."

The Mystery Writers' Forum: http://www.zott.com/mysforum/default.html. "This is a threaded bulletin board system geared specifically for writers and aspiring writers interested in gaining information about the publishing industry, writing advice and business information about the mystery genre." Discussions are separated into categories including agents, bookstores, contests, critique corner, death details and industry news.

Romance Central: http://romance-central.com. "Workshops are the heart of Romance Central. When we share knowlege and exchange ideas, we enhance our work and ourselves. Writers should view their peers as brothers and sisters, not competition. And by peers, I mean anyone who feels compelled to put words on paper." Great place for giving and receiving advice about romance writing.

Roundup Online Magazine: http://www.imt.net/~gedison/wwa.html. Official magazine of the Western Writers of America. Includes contest information, reviews of westerns and essays about the genre.

MAGAZINES

Electronic Newsstand: http://enews.com. Massive index of commercial magazines, searchable by title. Provides links to the magazine's website, description of current issue, subscription information and recommendations for similar magazines. A magazine in itself, this site also offers news about the magazine publishing industry and updates on the goings on at individual magazines.

John Hewitt's Writer's Resource Center: http://www.azstarnet.com/~poewar/writer/writer.html. Comprehensive writing site that includes links to consumer, trade and literary magazines. Also catalogs articles by Hewitt covering topics from overcoming writer's isolation to a directory of writers' colonies, associations and organizations of interest to writers.

BOOK PUBLISHERS

A-list Ingram Top Demand: http://www.ingrambook.com/Surf/product_info/category_info/fiction.htm. Lists by category of top 50 books requested from the book distributor Ingram. Includes links to descriptions of the books, complete with publisher names and ISBNs. Great way to see who's publishing the best in each genre. Includes adult, espionage/thriller, fantasy, general fiction, men's adventure, historical, religious, mystery/detective, horror, psychological suspense, romance, science fiction and western.

AcqWeb's Directory of Publisher and Vendors: http://www.library.vanderbilt.edu/law/acqs/pubr.html. Gigantic catalog of links to publishers. Subject headings include: general and multiple subject publishers, associations and institutes, electronic publications including online & CD-ROM, reprints, university presses, literature and fiction, children's literature, poetry, science fiction and fantasy.

Arachnoid Writer's Alliance: http://www.vena.com/arachnoid. This site "presents a collection of books for sale by independent and self-published authors." Gives you an idea of what struggling writers are up to. Includes author bios, contact information and short excerpts from books.

Books A to Z: http://www.booksatoz.com. "This site is intended to be a working tool to enable anyone to produce, distribute or find books. We will also list large numbers of resources for research in books and libraries. All of these areas are neglected and often overlooked in the commercial world. We will not attempt to make a gigantic site listing everything, but we will attempt to provide access to at least some resources in every area of book production, sales and research." Includes links to professional and creative services, production and technical info, bookmaking materials for sale, organizations and groups, events and news, book and music publishers, bookstores and searchers, marketing and distribution, academic and research tools.

Publishers' Catalogs: http://www.lights.com/publisher. This massive site includes a specific geographic index, which lists countries like Albania, Luxembourg, Thailand and Uruguay, as well as the US and UK. The alphabetical lists of publishers link with their websites. But what sets this site apart is its webhosting service for publishers. If a company doesn't have its catalog online, Northern Lights Internet Solutions can do it for them.

ORGANIZATIONS

Canadian Authors Association: http://www.islandnet.com/~caa/national.html. "The Association was founded to promote recognition of Canadian writers and their works, and to foster and develop a climate favorable to the creative arts. Its objectives:
To work for the encouragement and protection of writers.
To speak for writers before government and other inquires.
To sponsor awards and otherwise encourage work of literary and artistic merit.
To publish *Canadian Author, The Canadian Writer's Guide* and other publications designed to improve the professionalism of Canadian writers."

Horror Writers Association: http://www.horror.org. "The Horror Writers Association (HWA) was formed in the 1980s to bring together writers and others professionally interested in horror and dark fantasy, and to foster a greater appreciation of dark fiction among the general public. To this end, among other benefits, the organization issues a regular newsletter, presents the Bram Stoker Awards, and provides members with the latest news on paying markets. We have sponsored a series of successful members-only anthologies. Members also gain access to the private HWA areas on various online services, including Genie's Science Fiction Roundtables (especially SFRT4), Compuserve's SFLitForum 2, SFF-Net, and Dueling Modems, and can, if they choose, receive informational bulletins by e-mail."

National Writers Union: http://www.nwu.org/. "The National Writers Union (NWU) is the trade union for freelance writers of all genres. We are committed to improving the economic and working conditions of freelance writers through the collective strength of our members. We are a modern, innovative union offering grievance-resolution, industry campaigns, contract advice, health and dental plans, member education, job banks, networking, social events and much more. The NWU is affiliated with the United Automobile Workers (UAW) and through them with the AFL-CIO. Founded in 1983, the NWU has local and organizing committees throughout the country. Our 4,500 members include journalists, book authors, poets, copywriters, academic authors, cartoonists, and technical and business writers. The NWU has a Supporters Circle open to individuals or organizations who are not writers but wish to support the union."

PEN American Center: http://www.pen.org. "PEN American Center, the largest of nearly130 Centers worldwide that compose International PEN, is a membership association of prominent literary writers and editors. As a major voice of the literary community, the organization seeks to defend the freedom of expression wherever it may be threatened, and to promote and encourage the recognition and reading of contemporary literature."

Romance Writers of America: http://www.rwanational.com. "RWA is a non-profit professional/educational association of 8,200 romance writers and other industry professionals. We are 'The Voice of Romance.' "

Society of Children's Book Writers and Illustrators: http://www.scbwi.org. "The only professional organization dedicated to serving the people who write, illustrate, or share a vital interest in children's literature. Whether you are a professional writer, a famous illustrator, a beginner with a good idea, or somewhere in between, SCBWI is here to serve you. Our website has a dual purpose: It exists as a service to our members as well as offering information about the children's publishing industry and our organization to non-members."

The Writers Guild of America: http://www.wga.org. "Home of the 8,500 professional writers who, since 1933, have created your favorite movies, television shows, and now, many of your favorite interactive games. All of these visions started with a script and a writer. In the beginning was the word. And the word was funny, dramatic, romantic, terrifying and dozens of other things that have entertained, moved and educated you. Here at our website, we hope to make film, television, interactive and other mass media writing—and writers—more familiar and accessible. Whether you are a writer, an aspiring writer, an entertainment professional or purely a member of the viewing public, we are happy to have you visit with us."

INSPIRATION

Creating a Celebration of Women Writers: http://www.cs.cmu.edu/afs/cs.cmu.edu/user/mmbt/www/women/celebration.html. "While a number of original sources are already available on the World Wide Web, there are many gaps in the available material. We therefore hope to encourage many people to contribute texts and supporting information about women writers. We propose to make the construction of the exhibit a public process, providing a shared resource for information about the materials in preparation. An initial list of women writers and available online works is provided. We hope that people will commit to scanning or typing in specific works. People are welcome to suggest further additions to the list. We are looking for complete works (not excerpts or single chapters) that are either in the public domain, or authorized by the copyright holder. (Details about copyright restrictions and instructions for submitting works are provided.) As people agree to scan in resources, their names and the works they have agreed to enter will be annotated to the list." This site is an amazing resource of links to the works and biographies of women writers throughout history as well as other resources for and about women writers.

The Unpublished Writer: http://www.unpub.com. "Only writing that has been rejected by other publications, accompanied by that rejection letter, is eligible for publication on this site. With nothing more than the support of friends and simmering anger about having some of my poetry rejected, I started this site for others like myself. Before I knew it, misery found company and the site started becoming populated with other such authors posting some stellar work."

WRITING RULES

Elements of Style by William Strunk, Jr.: http://www.columbia.edu/acis/bartleby/strunk. The full text of the English language's most used guide to grammar.

Grammar Girl's Guide to the English Language: http://www.geocities.com/Athens/Parthenon/1489. If Strunk is too dry for you, try Grammar Girl—a supereditor with an attitude. She's compiled a mass of rules and pet peeves to steer any wayward writer back onto the good grammar track.

The Inkspot: http://www.inkspot.com. "Inkspot is a resource for writers. The Internet is a rich resource of information useful to writers but changes so quickly each day that it is often difficult to keep up with new developments. I started Inkspot for my own personal use but realized that other writers might benefit from it as well." Offers many, many links to writing resources on the Web. Definitely a good place to start looking for answers to any writing-related question.

William Safire's Rules for Writers: http://www.chem.gla.ac.uk/protein/pert/safire.rules.html. File this under great things to tape next to your computer—a tongue-in-cheek look at some important grammar rules.

RESEARCH RESOURCES

The Crime Writer: http://www.svn.net/mikekell/crimewriter.html. "If you are an author in the areas of true crime or criminology, published or not, this is your site. We hope to provide a meeting place and resources for authors in this genre who use the Internet as a primary source of information gathering, researching and networking." Includes links to resources that provide information on crime, current crime news and the criminal justice system, as well as general writing and news resources.

ViVa: A Current Bibliography of Women's History in Historical and Women's Studies Journals: http://www.iisg.nl/~womhist/. "ViVa is short for 'Vrouwengeschiedenis in het Vaktijdschrift', which is Dutch for 'Women's history in scholarly periodicals'. Articles in English, French, German and Dutch are selected for ViVa from more than 60 European and American periodicals." Great place to find details about the daily lives of women throughout history. Sample citation: "Anderson, Olive, 'Emigration and marriage break up in mid-Victorian England', Economic History Review 50 (1997) 1, 104-109."

Dr. Jim Weinrich's AIDS and Sexology Page: http://math.ucsd.edu/~weinrich. Don't snicker. This page of information and links is invaluable to any writer of contemporary fiction. The prime rule of fiction—write what you know—should really be write what you can learn a lot about. This site allows you to safely learn the how's and why's of human sexuality as well as its devastating modern consequences.

The best way to find information about specific research topics is through a search engine like Yahoo (http://www.yahoo.com) or Infoseek (http://www.infoseek.com). I did an exact phrase search on Yahoo for "life in" and came up with 478 matches. The websites covered everything from life in concentration camps to life in early Wisconsin to retired life in a motor home to life in ancient Egypt.

It still amazes me how much information waits at our fingertips. Certainly a vast portion of the Internet is taken up by commercial sites and time wasters, but the rest is filled with invaluable resources that are only a deep breath and a few mouse clicks away. If you lack experience with computers or the Internet, the library may be the best place to start. They can offer you friendly advice and a guiding hand. Otherwise, hop on board and start surfing. Your fiction will shine with the details you glean from cyberspace and every little touch can put you that much closer to your ultimate goal—publication.

Canadian Writers Take Note

While much of the information contained in this section applies to all writers, here are some specifics of interest to Canadian writers:

Postage: When sending an SASE from Canada, you will need an International Reply Coupon. Also be aware, a GST tax is required on postage in Canada and for mail with postage under $5 going to destinations outside the country. Since Canadian postage rates are voted on in January of each year (after we go to press), contact a Canada Post Corporation Customer Service Division, located in most cities in Canada, for the most current rates.

Copyright: For information on copyrighting your work and to obtain forms, write Copyright and Industrial Design, Phase One, Place du Portage, 50 Victoria St., Hull, Quebec K1A 0C9 or call (819)997-1936.

The public lending right: The Public Lending Right Commission has established that eligible Canadian authors are entitled to payments when a book is available through a library. Payments are determined by a sampling of the holdings of a representative number of libraries. To find out more about the program and to learn if you are eligible, write to the Public Lending Right Commission at 350 Albert St., P.O. Box 1047, Ottawa, Ontario K1P 5V8 or call (613)566-4378 for information. The Commission, which is part of The Canada Council, produces a helpful pamphlet, *How the PLR System Works,* on the program.

Grants available to Canadian writers: Most province art councils or departments of culture provide grants to resident writers. Some of these, as well as contests for Canadian writers, are listed in our Contests and Awards section. For national programs, contact The Canada Council, Writing and Publishing Section, P.O. Box 1047, Ottawa, Ontario K1P 5V8 or call (613)566-4338 for information. Fax: (613)566-4390. Website: http://www.canadacouncil.ca.

For more information: More details on much of the information listed above and additional information on writing and publishing in Canada are included in the *Writer's Essential Desk Reference: A Companion to Writer's Market*, 2nd edition, published by Writer's Digest Books. In addition to information on a wide range of topics useful to all writers, the book features a detailed chapter for Canadians, Writing and Selling in Canada, by Fred Kerner.

See the Organizations and Resources section of *Novel & Short Story Writer's Market* for listings of writers' organizations in Canada. Also contact The Writer's Union of Canada, 24 Ryerson Ave., Toronto, Ontario M5T 2P3; call them at (416)703-8982 or fax them at (416)703-0826. E-mail: twuc@the-wire.com. Website: http://www.swifty.com/twuc. This organization provides a wealth of information (as well as strong support) for Canadian writers, including specialized publications on publishing contracts; contract negotiations; the author/editor relationship; author awards, competitions and grants; agents; taxes for writers, libel issues and access to archives in Canada.

Printing and Production Terms Defined

In most of the magazine listings in this book you will find a brief physical description of each publication. This material usually includes the number of pages, type of paper, type of binding and whether or not the magazine uses photographs or illustrations.

Although it is important to look at a copy of the magazine to which you are submitting, these descriptions can give you a general idea of what the publication looks like. This material can provide you with a feel for the magazine's financial resources and prestige. Do not, however, rule out small, simply produced publications as these may be the most receptive to new writers. Watch for publications that have increased their page count or improved their production from year to year. This is a sign the publication is doing well and may be accepting more fiction.

You will notice a wide variety of printing terms used within these descriptions. We explain here some of the more common terms used in our listing descriptions. We do not include explanations of terms such as Mohawk and Karma which are brand names and refer to the paper manufacturer. *Getting it Printed*, by Mark Beach (Writer's Digest Books), is an excellent publication for those interested in learning more about printing and production.

PAPER

acid-free: Paper that has a low or no acid content. This type of paper resists deterioration from exposure to the elements. More expensive than many other types of paper, publications done on acid-free paper can last a long time.

bond: Bond paper is often used for stationery and is more transparent than text paper. It can be made of either sulphite (wood) or cotton fiber. Some bonds have a mixture of both wood and cotton (such as "25 percent cotton" paper). This is the type of paper most often used in photocopying or as standard typing paper.

coated/uncoated stock: Coated and uncoated are terms usually used when referring to book or text paper. More opaque than bond, it is the paper most used for offset printing. As the name implies, uncoated paper has no coating. Coated paper is coated with a layer of clay, varnish or other chemicals. It comes in various sheens and surfaces depending on the type of coating, but the most common are dull, matte and gloss.

cover stock: Cover stock is heavier book or text paper used to cover a publication. It comes in a variety of colors and textures and can be coated on one or both sides.

CS1/CS2: Most often used when referring to cover stock, CS1 means paper that is coated only on one side; CS2 is paper coated on both sides.

newsprint: Inexpensive absorbent pulp wood paper often used in newspapers and tabloids.

text: Text paper is similar to book paper (a smooth paper used in offset printing), but it has been given some texture by using rollers or other methods to apply a pattern to the paper.

vellum: Vellum is a text paper that is fairly porous and soft.

Some notes about paper weight and thickness: Often you will see paper thickness described in terms of pounds such as 80 lb. or 60 lb. paper. The weight is determined by figuring how many pounds in a ream of a particular paper (a ream is 500 sheets). This can be confusing, however, because this figure is based on a standard sheet size and standard sheet sizes vary depending on the type of paper used. This information is most helpful when comparing papers of the same type. For example, 80 lb. book paper versus 60 lb. book paper. Since the size of the paper is the same it would follow that 80 lb. paper is the thicker, heavier paper.

Some paper, especially cover stock, is described by the actual thickness of the paper. This is expressed in a system of points. Typical paper thicknesses range from 8 points to 14 points thick.

PRINTING

letterpress: Letterpress printing is printing that uses a raised surface such as type. The type is inked and then pressed against the paper. Unlike offset printing, only a limited number of impressions can be made, as the surface of the type can wear down.

offset: Offset is a printing method in which ink is transferred from an image-bearing plate to a "blanket" and from the blanket to the paper.

sheet-fed offset: Offset printing in which the paper is fed one piece at a time.

web offset: Offset printing in which a roll of paper is printed and then cut apart to make individual sheets.

There are many other printing methods but these are the ones most commonly referred to in our listings.

BINDING

case binding: In case binding, signatures (groups of pages) are stitched together with thread rather than glued together. The stitched pages are then trimmed on three sides and glued into a hardcover or board "case" or cover. Most hardcover books and thicker magazines are done this way.

comb binding: A comb is a plastic spine used to hold pages together with bent tabs that are fed through punched holes in the edge of the paper.

perfect binding: Used for paperback books and heavier magazines, perfect binding involves gathering signatures (groups of pages) into a stack, trimming off the folds so the edge is flat and gluing a cover to that edge.

saddle stitched: Publications in which the pages are stitched together using metal staples. This fairly inexpensive type of binding is usually used with books or magazines that are under 80 pages.

Smythe-sewn: Binding in which the pages are sewn together with thread. Smythe is the name of the most common machine used for this purpose.

spiral binding: A wire spiral that is wound through holes punched in pages is a spiral bind. This is the binding used in spiral notebooks.

Glossary

Advance. Payment by a publisher to an author prior to the publication of a book, to be deducted from the author's future royalties.

All rights. The rights contracted to a publisher permitting a manuscript's use anywhere and in any form, including movie and book club sales, without additional payment to the writer.

Anthology. A collection of selected writings by various authors.

Auction. Publishers sometimes bid against each other for the acquisition of a manuscript that has excellent sales prospects.

Backlist. A publisher's books not published during the current season but still in print.

Book producer/packager. An organization that may develop a book for a publisher based upon the publisher's idea or may plan all elements of a book, from its initial concept to writing and marketing strategies, and then sell the package to a book publisher and/or movie producer.

Cliffhanger. Fictional event in which the reader is left in suspense at the end of a chapter or episode, so that interest in the story's outcome will be sustained.

Clip. Sample, usually from a newspaper or magazine, of a writer's published work.

Cloak-and-dagger. A melodramatic, romantic type of fiction dealing with espionage and intrigue.

Commercial. Publishers whose concern is salability, profit and success with a large readership.

Contemporary. Material dealing with popular current trends, themes or topics.

Contributor's copy. Copy of an issue of a magazine or published book sent to an author whose work is included.

Copublishing. An arrangement in which the author and publisher share costs and profits.

Copyediting. Editing a manuscript for writing style, grammar, punctuation and factual accuracy.

Copyright. The legal right to exclusive publication, sale or distribution of a literary work.

Cover letter. A brief letter sent with a complete manuscript submitted to an editor.

"Cozy" (or "teacup") mystery. Mystery usually set in a small British town, in a bygone era, featuring a somewhat genteel, intellectual protagonist.

Cyberpunk. Type of science fiction, usually concerned with computer networks and human-computer combinations, involving young, sophisticated protagonists.

E-mail. Mail that has been sent electronically using a computer and modem.

Experimental fiction. Fiction that is innovative in subject matter and style; avant-garde, non-formulaic, usually literary material.

Exposition. The portion of the storyline, usually the beginning, where background information about character and setting is related.

Fair use. A provision in the copyright law that says short passages from copyrighted material may be used without infringing on the owner's rights.

Fanzine. A noncommercial, small-circulation magazine usually dealing with fantasy, horror or science-fiction literature and art.

First North American serial rights. The right to publish material in a periodical before it appears in book form, for the first time, in the United States or Canada.

Galleys. The first typeset version of a manuscript that has not yet been divided into pages.

Genre. A formulaic type of fiction such as romance, western or horror.

Gothic. A genre in which the central character is usually a beautiful young woman and the setting an old mansion or castle, involving a handsome hero and real danger, either natural or supernatural.

Graphic novel. An adaptation of a novel into a long comic strip or heavily illustrated story of 40 pages or more, produced in paperback.

Hard-boiled detective novel. Mystery novel featuring a private eye or police detective as the protagonist; usually involves a murder. The emphasis is on the details of the crime.

Horror. A genre stressing fear, death and other aspects of the macabre.

Imprint. Name applied to a publisher's specific line (e.g. Owl, an imprint of Henry Holt).

Interactive fiction. Fiction in book or computer-software format where the reader determines the path the story will take by choosing from several alternatives at the end of each chapter or episode.

International Reply Coupon (IRC). A form purchased at a post office and enclosed with a letter or manuscript to a international publisher, to cover return postage costs.

Juvenile. Fiction intended for children 2-12.
Libel. Written or printed words that defame, malign or damagingly misrepresent a living person.
Literary. The general category of serious, non-formulaic, intelligent fiction, sometimes experimental, that most frequently appears in little magazines.
Literary agent. A person who acts for an author in finding a publisher or arranging contract terms on a literary project.
Mainstream. Traditionally written fiction on subjects or trends that transcend experimental or genre fiction categories.
Malice domestic novel. A traditional mystery novel that is not hard-boiled; emphasis is on the solution. Suspects and victims know one another.
Manuscript. The author's unpublished copy of a work, usually typewritten, used as the basis for typesetting.
Mass market paperback. Softcover book on a popular subject, usually around 4×7, directed to a general audience and sold in drugstores and groceries as well as in bookstores.
Ms(s). Abbreviation for manuscript(s).
Multiple submission. Submission of more than one short story at a time to the same editor. Do not make a multiple submission unless requested.
Narration. The account of events in a story's plot as related by the speaker or the voice of the author.
Narrator. The person who tells the story, either someone involved in the action or the voice of the writer.
New Age. A term including categories such as astrology, psychic phenomena, spiritual healing, UFOs, mysticism and other aspects of the occult.
Nom de plume. French for "pen name"; a pseudonym.
Novella (also novelette). A short novel or long story, approximately 7,000-15,000 words.
#10 envelope. 4×9½ envelope, used for queries and other business letters.
Offprint. Copy of a story taken from a magazine before it is bound.
One-time rights. Permission to publish a story in periodical or book form one time only.
Outline. A summary of a book's contents, often in the form of chapter headings with a few sentences outlining the action of the story under each one; sometimes part of a book proposal.
Payment on acceptance. Payment from the magazine or publishing house as soon as the decision to print a manuscript is made.
Payment on publication. Payment from the publisher after a manuscript is printed.
Pen name. A pseudonym used to conceal a writer's real name.
Periodical. A magazine or journal published at regular intervals.
Plot. The carefully devised series of events through which the characters progress in a work of fiction.
Proofreading. Close reading and correction of a manuscript's typographical errors.
Proofs. A typeset version of a manuscript used for correcting errors and making changes, often a photocopy of the galleys.
Proposal. An offer to write a specific work, usually consisting of an outline of the work and one or two completed chapters.
Protagonist. The principal or leading character in a literary work.
Public domain. Material that either was never copyrighted or whose copyright term has expired.
Pulp magazine. A periodical printed on inexpensive paper, usually containing lurid, sensational stories or articles.
Query. A letter written to an editor to elicit interest in a story the writer wants to submit.
Reader. A person hired by a publisher to read unsolicited manuscripts.
Reading fee. An arbitrary amount of money charged by some agents and publishers to read a submitted manuscript.
Regency romance. A genre romance, usually set in England between 1811-1820.
Remainders. Leftover copies of an out-of-print book, sold by the publisher at a reduced price.
Reporting time. The number of weeks or months it takes an editor to report back on an author's query or manuscript.
Reprint rights. Permission to print an already published work whose rights have been sold to another magazine or book publisher.
Roman à clef. French "novel with a key." A novel that represents actual living or historical characters and events in fictionalized form.
Romance. The genre relating accounts of passionate love and fictional heroic achievements.
Royalties. A percentage of the retail price paid to an author for each copy of the book that is sold.
SAE. Self-addressed envelope.

No Matter What Your Writing Interest,
Writer's Digest School Can Help You Get Published

Novel Writing Workshop: You'll iron out your plot, create your main characters, develop a dramatic background, and complete the opening scenes and summary of your novel's complete story. Plus, you'll pinpoint potential publishers for your type of book.

NEW! **Getting Started in Writing:** Whether you're a beginning writer or ready to explore "new to you" genres, this sampler workshop will guide you through various types of writing. From short fiction and novels to articles and nonfiction books, we'll help you discover where your natural writing talents lie.

Writing & Selling Short Stories: Learn how to create believable characters, write vivid, true-to-life dialogue, fill your scenes with conflict, and keep your readers on the edge of their seats. Plus, discover a simple method for plotting any short story.

Writing & Selling Nonfiction Articles: Master the components for effective article writing and selling. You'll learn how to choose attention-grabbing topics, conduct stirring interviews, write compelling query letters, and slant a single article for a variety of publications.

Writing Your Life Stories: Learn how to weave the important events of your personal or family's history into a heartfelt story. You'll plan a writing strategy, complete a dateline of events, and discover how to combine factual events with narrative flow.

Writer's Digest Criticism Service: Have an experienced, published writer review your manuscripts before you submit them for pay. Whether you write books, articles, short stories or poetry, you'll get professional, objective feedback on what's working well, what needs strengthening, and which markets you should pursue.

The Elements of Effective Writing: Discover how to conquer the pesky grammar and usage problems that hold so many writers back. You'll refresh your basic English composition skills through step-by-step lessons and writing exercises designed to help keep your manuscripts out of the rejection pile.

SASE. Self-addressed stamped envelope.
Science fiction. Genre in which scientific facts and hypotheses form the basis of actions and events.
Second serial (reprint) rights. Permission for the reprinting of a work in another periodical after its first publication in book or magazine form.
Self-publishing. In this arrangement, the author keeps all income derived from the book, but he pays for its manufacturing, production and marketing.
Sequel. A literary work that continues the narrative of a previous, related story or novel.
Serial rights. The rights given by an author to a publisher to print a piece in one or more periodicals.
Serialized novel. A book-length work of fiction published in sequential issues of a periodical.
Setting. The environment and time period during which the action of a story takes place.
Short short story. A condensed piece of fiction, usually under 700 words.
Simultaneous submission. The practice of sending copies of the same manuscript to several editors or publishers at the same time. Some people refuse to consider such submissions.
Slant. A story's particular approach or style, designed to appeal to the readers of a specific magazine.
Slice of life. A presentation of characters in a seemingly mundane situation which offers the reader a flash of illumination about the characters or their situation.
Slush pile. A stack of unsolicited manuscripts in the editorial offices of a publisher.
Social Fiction. Fiction written with the purpose of bringing about positive changes in society.
Speculation (or Spec). An editor's agreement to look at an author's manuscript with no promise to purchase.
Speculative Fiction (SpecFic). The all-inclusive term for science fiction, fantasy and horror.
Splatterpunk. Type of horror fiction known for its very violent and graphic content.
Subsidiary. An incorporated branch of a company or conglomerate (e.g. Alfred Knopf, Inc., a subsidiary of Random House, Inc.).
Subsidiary rights. All rights other than book publishing rights included in a book contract, such as paperback, book club and movie rights.
Subsidy publisher. A book publisher who charges the author for the cost of typesetting, printing and promoting a book. Also Vanity publisher.
Subterficial fiction. Innovative, challenging, nonconventional fiction in which what seems to be happening is the result of things not so easily perceived.
Suspense. A genre of fiction where the plot's primary function is to build a feeling of anticipation and fear in the reader over its possible outcome.
Synopsis. A brief summary of a story, novel or play. As part of a book proposal, it is a comprehensive summary condensed in a page or page and a half.
Tabloid. Publication printed on paper about half the size of a regular newspaper page (e.g. *The National Enquirer*).
Tearsheet. Page from a magazine containing a published story.
Theme. The dominant or central idea in a literary work; its message, moral or main thread.
Trade paperback. A softbound volume, usually around 5×8, published and designed for the general public, available mainly in bookstores.
Unsolicited manuscript. A story or novel manuscript that an editor did not specifically ask to see.
Vanity publisher. See Subsidy publisher.
Viewpoint. The position or attitude of the first- or third-person narrator or multiple narrators, which determines how a story's action is seen and evaluated.
Western. Genre with a setting in the West, usually between 1860-1890, with a formula plot about cowboys or other aspects of frontier life.
Whodunit. Genre dealing with murder, suspense and the detection of criminals.
Work-for-hire. Work that another party commissions you to do, generally for a flat fee. The creator does not own the copyright and therefore cannot sell any rights.
Young adult. The general classification of books written for readers 12-18.

Category Index

Our Category Index makes it easy for you to identify publishers who are looking for a specific type of fiction. The index is divided into types of fiction, including a section of electronic magazines. Under each fiction category are magazines and book publishers looking for that kind of fiction. Publishers who are not listed under a fiction category either accept all types of fiction or have not indicated specific subject preferences. Also not appearing here are listings that need very specific types of fiction, e.g., "fiction about fly fishing only." To use this index to find a book publisher for your mainstream novel, for instance, go to the Mainstream/Contemporary section and look under Book Publishers. Finally, read individual listings *carefully* to determine the publishers best suited to your work.

For a listing of agents and the types of fiction they represent, see the Literary Agents Category Index beginning on page 159.

ADVENTURE

Magazines

Book Publishers

ALL CATEGORIES OF FICTION

Magazines

Book Publishers

CHILDRENS/ JUVENILE

Magazines

Book Publishers

COMICS/GRAPHIC NOVELS

Magazines

Book Publishers

CONDENSED NOVEL

Magazines

ELECTRONIC MAGAZINES

Magazines

EROTICA

Magazines

Book Publishers

ETHNIC/ MULTICULTURAL

Magazines

Book Publishers

EXPERIMENTAL

Magazines

Book Publishers

FAMILY SAGA

Book Publishers

FANTASY

Magazines

Book Publishers

FEMINIST

Magazines

Book Publishers

GAY

Magazines

Book Publishers

GLITZ

Magazines

Book Publishers

HISTORICAL

Magazines

Book Publishers

HORROR

Magazines

Book Publishers

HUMOR/SATIRE

Magazines

Book Publishers

Book Publishers

MAINSTREAM/ CONTEMPORARY

Magazines

Book Publishers

MILITARY/WAR

Book Publishers

MYSTERY/ SUSPENSE

Magazines

REGIONAL

Magazines

Book Publishers

RELIGIOUS/ INSPIRATIONAL

Magazines

Book Publishers

ROMANCE

Magazines

Book Publishers

SCIENCE FICTION

Magazines

Book Publishers

SENIOR CITIZEN/ RETIREMENT

Magazines

Book Publishers

SERIALIZED/ EXCERPTED NOVEL

Magazines

SHORT STORY COLLECTIONS

Magazines

Book Publishers

SPORTS

Magazines

Book Publishers

THRILLER/ ESPIONAGE

Book Publishers

TRANSLATIONS

Magazines

Book Publishers

WESTERN

Magazines

Book Publishers

YOUNG ADULT/ TEEN

Magazines

Book Publishers

General Index

Markets that appeared in the 1998 edition of *Novel & Short Story Writer's Market* but are not included in this edition are identified by a two-letter code explaining why the market was omitted: **(ED)**—Editorial Decision, **(NS)**—Not Accepting Submissions, **(NR)**—No (or late) Response to Listing Request, **(OB)**—Out of Business, **(RR)**—Removed by Market's Request, **(UC)**—Unable to Contact, **(UF)**—Uncertain Future.

A

B

C

Companies that appeared in the 1998 edition of *Novel & Short Story Writer's Market*, but do not appear this year, are listed in this General Index with the following codes explaining why these markets were omitted: (ED)—Editorial Decision, (NS)—Not Accepting Submissions, (NR)—No (or late) Response to Listing Request, (OB)—Out of Business, (RR)—Removed by Market's Request, (UC)—Unable to Contact, (UF)—Uncertain Future.

D

E

F

Companies that appeared in the 1998 edition of *Novel & Short Story Writer's Market*, but do not appear this year, are listed in this General Index with the following codes explaining why these markets were omitted: (ED)—Editorial Decision, (NS)—Not Accepting Submissions, (NR)—No (or late) Response to Listing Request, (OB)—Out of Business, (RR)—Removed by Market's Request, (UC)—Unable to Contact, (UF)—Uncertain Future.

G

H

I

Companies that appeared in the 1998 edition of *Novel & Short Story Writer's Market*, but do not appear this year, are listed in this General Index with the following codes explaining why these markets were omitted: (ED)—Editorial Decision, (NS)—Not Accepting Submissions, (NR)—No (or late) Response to Listing Request, (OB)—Out of Business, (RR)—Removed by Market's Request, (UC)—Unable to Contact, (UF)—Uncertain Future.

M

Companies that appeared in the 1998 edition of *Novel & Short Story Writer's Market*, but do not appear this year, are listed in this General Index with the following codes explaining why these markets were omitted: (ED)—Editorial Decision, (NS)—Not Accepting Submissions, (NR)—No (or late) Response to Listing Request, (OB)—Out of Business, (RR)—Removed by Market's Request, (UC)—Unable to Contact, (UF)—Uncertain Future.

N

Companies that appeared in the 1998 edition of *Novel & Short Story Writer's Market*, but do not appear this year, are listed in this General Index with the following codes explaining why these markets were omitted: (ED)—Editorial Decision, (NS)—Not Accepting Submissions, (NR)—No (or late) Response to Listing Request, (OB)—Out of Business, (RR)—Removed by Market's Request, (UC)—Unable to Contact, (UF)—Uncertain Future.

Companies that appeared in the 1998 edition of *Novel & Short Story Writer's Market*, but do not appear this year, are listed in this General Index with the following codes explaining why these markets were omitted: (ED)—Editorial Decision, (NS)—Not Accepting Submissions, (NR)—No (or late) Response to Listing Request, (OB)—Out of Business, (RR)—Removed by Market's Request, (UC)—Unable to Contact, (UF)—Uncertain Future.

S

T

Companies that appeared in the 1998 edition of *Novel & Short Story Writer's Market*, but do not appear this year, are listed in this General Index with the following codes explaining why these markets were omitted: (ED)—Editorial Decision, (NS)—Not Accepting Submissions, (NR)—No (or late) Response to Listing Request, (OB)—Out of Business, (RR)—Removed by Market's Request, (UC)—Unable to Contact, (UF)—Uncertain Future.

GENERAL INDEX

U

V

W

Companies that appeared in the 1998 edition of *Novel & Short Story Writer's Market*, but do not appear this year, are listed in this General Index with the following codes explaining why these markets were omitted: (ED)—Editorial Decision, (NS)—Not Accepting Submissions, (NR)—No (or late) Response to Listing Request, (OB)—Out of Business, (RR)—Removed by Market's Request, (UC)—Unable to Contact, (UF)—Uncertain Future.